THE DAVIS EDITION

פירוש בעל הטורים על התורה

BAAL HATURIM CHUMASH

The ArtScroll Series®

Rabbi Nosson Scherman / Rabbi Meir Zlotowitz

General Editors

FIRST EDITION
First Impression . . . May 2004
SECOND EDITION
First Impression . . . November 2007
Second Impression . . . September 2011

Published and Distributed by
MESORAH PUBLICATIONS, Ltd.
4401 Second Avenue
Brooklyn, New York 11232

Distributed in Europe by
LEHMANNS
Unit E, Viking Business Park
Rolling Mill Road
Jarrow, Tyne & Wear NE32 3DP
England

Distributed in Australia & New Zealand by
GOLDS WORLD OF JUDAICA
3-13 William Street
Balaclava, Melbourne 3183
Victoria Australia

Distributed in Israel by
SIFRIATI / A. GITLER — BOOKS
6 Hayarkon Street
Bnei Brak 51127

Distributed in South Africa by
KOLLEL BOOKSHOP
Ivy Common 105 William Road
Norwood 2192, Johannesburg, South Africa

ARTSCROLL SERIES® / THE DAVIS EDITION
BAAL HATURIM CHUMASH
VOL. 5 — DEVARIM / DEUTERONOMY

4401 Second Avenue / Brooklyn, N.Y. 11232 / (718) 921-9000 / www.artscroll.com

---

ISBN 10: 1-57819-132-7 / ISBN 13: 978-1-57819-132-1

Typography by CompuScribe at ArtScroll Studios, Ltd.
Custom Bound by **Sefercraft, Inc.,** Brooklyn, N.Y.

A PROJECT OF THE

Mesorah Heritage Foundation

פירוש בעל הטורים
על התורה

chumash

ספר דברים
DEVARIM/DEUTERONOMY

The ArtScroll Series®

Published by

ARTSCROLL®
Mesorah Publications, ltd.

THE DAVIS EDITION

BAAL HATURIM

THE TORAH: WITH THE BAAL HATURIM'S CLASSIC COMMENTARY TRANSLATED, ANNOTATED, AND ELUCIDATED

Hebrew text of the *Baal HaTurim* based on Rabbi Yaakov Koppel Reinitz' manuscript edition

Translation of the *Baal HaTurim* by Rabbi Eliyahu Touger

Edited, elucidated and annotated by **Rabbi Avie Gold**

Designed by Rabbi Sheah Brander

The Davis Edition of the Baal HaTurim
is dedicated to the memory of
our beloved son and brother

Simcha ז״ל

שמחה אליעזר דוד ז״ל ב״ר יוסף חיים שיחי׳

נקטף באבי ימיו, א׳ דר״ח תמוז תשס״ד

His name was Simcha and he brought simcha to everyone
around him.
Young in years but with the wisdom and sensitivity of a mature man,
he radiated warmth and understanding.

When his chaverim needed encouragement, they turned to him.
When someone was in trouble, he sensed it and came forward to help.
When his yeshiva needed someone to care, to arrange, to organize,
it was always Simcha who took the initiative.

He was taken from us so suddenly at the too-young age of sixteen!
Who can imagine the extent of the loss, to his family and Klal Yisrael?
We can only nurse his glowing legacy of goodness and pray
that Hashem Yisbarach will fill the gaping void and comfort
all who loved him and cannot forget him.

תנצב״ה

Yosef and Edie Davis

Moshe and Chevie   Yehoshua and Elana
Ahuva and Shaul Weinreb   Eli and Chasi
Shoni and Shimmy Braun   Nesanel and Perl,
Yisroel Mordechai and Elky
and families

This volume of
The Davis Edition of the Baal HaTurim
is dedicated in memory of our beloved grandparents

Rabbi Shrage Moshe
and Zise Reche Silver ז״ל

הרב שרגא משה בן ר׳ יוסף ז״ל
נפטר ט׳ טבת תשכ״ו
זיסא רעכע בת ר׳ יהודה לייב ע״ה
נפטרה ח׳ סיון תשכ״ט

They came to America in the early '30's and brought the Torah world of Lithuania with them. They settled in Chicago where he was a shochet and baal korei par excellence. Our grandfather remained a talmid of Slobodka all his life. It was said of him that the way he davened was a living lesson of total concentration.

Together our grandparents built a home and family whose goal is to live up to Klal Yisrael's timeless devotion to Torah and Yiras Shamayim.

We pray that, with Hashem's help, we can fulfill their aspirations and be worthy of their mesiras nefesh.

Yosef and Edie Davis

**Moshe and Chevie   Yehoshua and Elana
Ahuva and Shaul Weinreb   Eli and Chasi
Shoni and Shimmy Braun   Nesanel and Perl,
and families**

Yisroel Mordechai and Simcha Eliezer Dovid

Table of Contents

לזכר נשמת זקני אבי אבי

ר' אברהם יצחק ב"ר נחום ז"ל גאלד

נולד בערך שנת תרמ"ג בדאבעטסק שבגאליציא

ונפטר בשם טוב תשעה באב תרצ"א

ולזכר נשמת זקנתי אם אבי

האשה החשובה רחל בת ר' יצחק (זיסוויין) ע"ה

נולדה בערך תרמ"ד בבאליגראד שבגאליציא

ונפטרה בשם טוב שבת קודש ז' סיון יום ב' דשבועות תשט"ו

ומ"כ בעיר נו יארק תנצב"ה

פרשת דברים

Parashas Devarim

א/א א אֵלֶּה הַדְּבָרִים אֲשֶׁר דִּבֶּר מֹשֶׁה אֶל־כָּל־יִשְׂרָאֵל

בעל הטורים

א (א) אֵלֶּה הַדְּבָרִים. {״דְּבָרִים״, ״הַדְּבָרִים״, ״אֵלֶּה הַדְּבָרִים״} רֶמֶז ג׳ פְּעָמִים – נֶאֶמְרוּ בְסִינַי, וְנִשְׁנוּ בְּאֹהֶל מוֹעֵד, וְנִשְׁתַּלְּשׁוּ בְּעַרְבוֹת מוֹאָב. וְעַל כָּל מִצְוָה וּמִצְוָה נִכְרְתוּ י״ו בְּרִיתוֹת בְּסִינַי, וְי״ו בְּאֹהֶל מוֹעֵד, וְי״ו בְּעַרְבוֹת מוֹאָב, שֶׁהֵן מ״ח. וּכְנֶגְדָּן הִזְהִיר מ״ח פְּעָמִים בַּתּוֹרָה עַל עֲבוֹדָה זָרָה; וְהִזְהִיר מ״ח פְּעָמִים בַּתּוֹרָה עַל הַגֵּר שֶׁבָּא לִדָּבֵק בַּתּוֹרָה, שֶׁנִּכְרְתוּ עָלֶיהָ מ״ח בְּרִיתוֹת:

❑ בְּרֵאשִׁי״ת וְאֵלֶּ״ה וַיִּקְרָ״א וַיְדַבֵּ״ר אֵלֶּ״ה – סוֹפֵי תֵבוֹת בְּגִימַטְרִיָּא יִרְאַת, זֶהוּ ״רֵאשִׁית

BAAL HATURIM ELUCIDATED

I.

1. אֵלֶּה הַדְּבָרִים — THESE ARE THE WORDS. {[The three elements of this phrase] — דְּבָרִים, *words;* הַדְּבָרִים, *the words;* אֵלֶּה הַדְּבָרִים, *these are the words* — are[1]}[1a] an allusion to [the] three times [that Moses spoke these words]: They were [first] said at [Mount] Sinai;[1b] they were said a second time at the Tent of Meeting;[1c] and a third time[2] on the plains of Moab.[2a] Concerning each and every *mitzvah*:[3]

---

1. The passage enclosed in braces is not found in most printed editions, but does appear in the first printed edition (Constantinople, 1514) and in the manuscripts used by *Shoham Yakar.* According to this reading, the Baal HaTurim explains why the Torah uses the wordy phrase, אֵלֶּה הַדְּבָרִים אֲשֶׁר דִּבֶּר מֹשֶׁה, *these are the words that Moses spoke,* instead of the more concise, וַיְדַבֵּר מֹשֶׁה דְּבָרִים אֵלֶּה, *Moses spoke these words.* Note that although we have translated both דְּבָרִים and הַדְּבָרִים as *the words,* there is a difference. In Hebrew syntax, the definite article prefix ־הַ often indicates that the noun to which it is affixed refers to an object or concept with which the listener or reader is already acquainted. Thus, the prefix ־ה of the term הַדְּבָרִים indicates that these words have been spoken on a previous occasion. Finally, the demonstrative pronoun אֵלֶּה, *these,* implies yet another repetition of these words. Accordingly, the phrase אֵלֶּה הַדְּבָרִים, *these are the words,* implies that Moses uttered them no less than three times (*VeChur LaZahav;* similarly, *Shoham Yakar*).

1a. *Ittur Bikkurim* writes that the Basel (1536?) edition of *Mikraos Gedolos,* which he generally used for the Baal HaTurim text, was missing all of the Baal HaTurim's comments to verses 1-7. He proceeds by transcribing those comments from the Venice (1544) edition of the Baal HaTurim. However, that edition does not include the passage presented here in braces. Consequently, *Ittur Bikkurim* explains the Baal HaTurim's allusion with a slightly different twist, with the entire allusion coming from the term הַדְּבָרִים, *the words.* Thus: The singular form דָּבָר, *word,* refers to one; the plural form דְּבָרִים, *words,* adds one more; and the definite article prefix ־הַ, *the,* adds a third. Accordingly, Moses spoke these words three times. *Ittur Bikkurim's* interpretation has its roots in a Talmudic passage regarding the number of categories of labor that are forbidden on the Sabbath. Based on the phrase אֵלֶּה הַדְּבָרִים [which can also mean *these are the matters*] (*Exodus* 35:1), used regarding the Sabbath, the Talmud sets that number at thirty-nine: דָּבָר, *matter,* is one; דְּבָרִים, in the plural, refers to at least two matters; the prefix ־הַ adds a third; and the *gematria* of אֵלֶּה is thirty-six, yielding a total of thirty-nine. Thus, the number of matters (i.e., labors) forbidden on the Sabbath is thirty-nine (*Shabbos* 70a, 97b).

1b. See *Exodus,* Ch. 20.

1c. See *Leviticus* 1:1.

2. Although almost all editions of the Baal HaTurim read וְנִשְׁלְשׁוּ, *they were tripled,* the text follows the few editions that read וְנִשְׁתַּלְּשׁוּ, literally, *they presented themselves a third time,* for that is the term found in the Talmudic sources (*Chagigah* 6b; *Sotah* 37b; *Zevachim* 115b).

2a. See v. 5 below; see also *Rashi* to *Sotah* 37b, s.v., ונשתלשו בערבות מואב.

3. Unlike *Rashi,* who understands the phrase אֵלֶּה הַדְּבָרִים, *these are the words,* as a reference to Moses' words of rebuke, *Ramban* explains it as referring to the *mitzvos* that appear throughout the Book of *Deuteronomy,* beginning with the

1 *These are the words that Moses spoke to all Israel,*

BAAL HATURIM ELUCIDATED

sixteen covenants[4] were established [between God and Israel] at [Mount] Sinai; sixteen at the Tent of Meeting; sixteen on the plains of Moab — a total of forty-eight.[5] Corresponding to these, there are forty-eight instances in the Torah in which [God] admonished [Israel] regarding idol worship;[6] and forty-eight instances in the Torah where He admonished [them] regarding the convert[6a] who has come to cling to the Torah over which forty-eight covenants had been executed.[7]

❑ [The first words of each of the Five Books of the Torah, respectively, are] בְּרֵאשִׁית (*Genesis*), וְאֵלֶּה (*Exodus*), וַיִּקְרָא (*Leviticus*), וַיְדַבֵּר (*Numbers*) and אֵלֶּה (*Deuteronomy*). The *gematria* of the final letters [ת ה א ר ה] (611) is equal to that of יִרְאַת, *fear of,* and thus [it is written], רֵאשִׁית חָכְמָה יִרְאַת ה׳, *The beginning of wisdom*[8]

Ten Commandments (5:6-18 below). The Baal HaTurim's comment follows *Ramban.*

4. The text follows *Shoham Yakar's* manuscript edition and most of the later printed editions which read בְּרִיתוֹת, *covenants.* In place of בְּרִיתוֹת, the early printed editions use the word כְּרִיתוֹת, but, with the same meaning. This latter form is based on the Torah's terminology for the finalization and formalization of a compact between two parties, כְּרִיתַת בְּרִית, literally, *execution of a covenant* (see e.g., 4:23 and 5:2 below). Thus, we find another noun — כְּרִיתָה (plural, כְּרִיתוֹת), from the verb כרת, *to execute* — used by the Sages of the Talmud as a synonym for בְּרִית, *covenant.* Indeed, the passage adduced by the Baal HaTurim in this comment appears in two forms: The Talmud uses בְּרִיתוֹת, while the *Tosefta* (*Sotah* 8:7) uses כְּרִיתוֹת. (For further discussion, see the Baal HaTurim to *Numbers* 14:16, with note 56, and to *Leviticus* 16:14.)

5. *Sotah* 37a-b — The Rabbis taught: The term בָּרוּךְ, *Blessed,* [was stated] regarding [all the *mitzvos*] in general, and *Blessed* [was stated] regarding [each *mitzvah*] in particular; the term אָרוּר, *Cursed,* [was stated] regarding [the desecration of all *mitzvos*] in general, and *Cursed* [was stated] regarding [each *mitzvah*] in particular (see *Sotah,* 37b, cited by *Rashi* to Deuteronomy 11:29). [Now the fulfillment of *mitzvos* entails a variety of aspects:] לִלְמֹד וּלְלַמֵּד לִשְׁמֹר וְלַעֲשׂוֹת, *to learn, to teach, to observe* and *to do,* thus there are four [aspects of each *mitzvah* for which "Blessed" was stated as a generalization and four for which "Blessed" referred to a particular]. Four and four make eight ["Blessed's"; similarly there are eight "Cursed's"]. Eight and eight make sixteen [covenants between God and Israel]. Likewise at Sinai [there were sixteen covenants] and likewise at the Plains of Moab . . . Hence, there were forty-eight covenants sealed regarding each and every *mitzvah* (interpretation based on *Minchas Bikkurim* to *Tosefta Sotah* 8:7).

6. *Midrash Tanchuma, Vayikra* 2; *Yalkut Shimoni* II, 601. Neither of these Midrashim identifies the forty-eight verses.

6a. See note 6. However, the Talmud states: Why does the Torah admonish [Israel] regarding a convert in thirty-six — some say forty-six — places? (*Bava Metzia* 59b; see *Tosafos* to *Kiddushin* 70b, s.v., קָשִׁים, which has the reading בכ״ד מְקוֹמוֹת, *in twenty-four places*).

7. *Tanchuma, Vayikra* 2. The Midrash states that the Torah admonished forty-eight times regarding the convert who renounced idolatry about which the Torah admonished Israel forty-eight times. The Baal HaTurim adds: . . .and who accepted the Torah regarding which Israel executed forty-eight covenants. Presumably, this refers to the forty-eight covenants executed regarding each and every *mitzvah* of the Torah, as the Baal HaTurim mentioned at the beginning of this comment.

8. In the context of the psalm, this verse teaches the proper way for a person to use wisdom. All wisdom comes from the Master of Wisdom, God. Each person is endowed with a measure of wisdom, which can be used to draw the person closer to God and to the fulfillment of God's will regarding that particular person. Or, it can be used in a perverse manner that will run counter to life's purpose and will separate the person from the source of wisdom. Therefore, the psalmist teaches that a person must restrain his

בְּעֵבֶר הַיַּרְדֵּן בַּמִּדְבָּר בָּעֲרָבָה מוֹל סוּף בֵּין־פָּארָן
ב וּבֵין־תֹּפֶל וְלָבָן וַחֲצֵרֹת וְדִי זָהָב׃ אַחַד עָשָׂר
יוֹם מֵחֹרֵב דֶּרֶךְ הַר־שֵׂעִיר עַד קָדֵשׁ בַּרְנֵעַ׃
ג וַיְהִי בְּאַרְבָּעִים שָׁנָה בְּעַשְׁתֵּי־עָשָׂר חֹדֶשׁ בְּאֶחָד

בעל הטורים

חָכְמָה יִרְאַת ה׳ ״. וּבְגִימַטְרִיָּא תּוֹרָה:

❑ רָאשֵׁי תֵבוֹת שֶׁל חֲמִשָּׁה חֻמְשֵׁי תוֹרָה ב׳ ו׳ ו׳ א׳ בְּגִימַטְרִיָּא אֶהְיֶה; וְסוֹף הָאוֹתִיּוֹת שֶׁל חֲמִשָּׁה חֻמְשֵׁי תוֹרָה מ׳ מ׳ י׳ ו׳ ל׳ בְּגִימַטְרִיָּא הוּא אֱלֹהֵינוּ זֶה. וְזֶהוּ ״וְאֶת אַחֲרֹנִים אֲנִי הוּא״:

❑ **מוֹל.** ב׳ בַּמָּסוֹרֶת – ״מוֹל סוּף״; וְאִידָךְ ״מֹל אֶת בְּנֵי יִשְׂרָאֵל שֵׁנִית״. חֲמִשָּׁה דְבָרִים נֶאֶמְרוּ בְקָנֶה – אֵין מוֹהֲלִין בּוֹ, וְאֵין חוֹתְכִין בּוֹ בָּשָׂר, וְאֵין שׁוֹחֲטִין בּוֹ, וְאֵין מְקַנְּחִין בּוֹ, כִּדְאִיתָא בְּמַסֶּכֶת חֻלִּין. וְזֶהוּ שֶׁאָמַר לוֹ הַקָּדוֹשׁ בָּרוּךְ הוּא לִיהוֹשֻׁעַ, ״עֲשֵׂה לְךָ חַרְבוֹת צֻרִים״ וְאַל תָּמוּל בְּקָנֶה הַגָּדֵל בַּסּוּף, פֵּרוּשׁ בַּאֲגַם. וְזֶהוּ ״מוֹל סוּף״, ״מֹל אֶת בְּנֵי יִשְׂרָאֵל״:

(ג) **בְּאַרְבָּעִים.** ב׳ בַּמָּסוֹרֶת – ״וַיְהִי בְּאַרְבָּעִים״; {״מָגֵן אִם יֵרָאֶה וָרֹמַח} בְּאַרְבָּעִים

BAAL HATURIM ELUCIDATED

is fear of HASHEM (*Psalms* 111:10). This is also the *gematria* of the word תּוֹרָה, *Torah.*[9]

❑ The initial letters of the Five Books of the Torah — ב ו ו ו א[10] — have a combined *gematria* (21) equal to that of the Divine Name אֶהְיֶה (*Exodus* 3:14).[10a] And the final letters of the Five Books of the Torah — מ מ י ו ל[11] — have a combined *gematria* (126) equal to that of the phrase הוּא אֱלֹהֵינוּ זֶה, literally, *He, our God, This.*[12] And that is [the meaning of the verse], וְאֶת אַחֲרֹנִים אֲנִי הוּא, *And the last, I am He* (*Isaiah* 41:4).[13]

---

wisdom from severing itself from its source, thus leading itself on a path of self-destruction. And that restraint is fear of God. Thus, רֵאשִׁית חָכְמָה, *the beginning* [i.e., the prime rule] *of wisdom* [is that it be restrained by] יִרְאַת ה׳, *fear of* HASHEM (based on *Malbim*).

In the realm of רֶמֶז, *allusion,* the Baal HaTurim interprets that verse: רֵאשִׁית חָכְמָה, [The words at] *the beginning of* [the Five Books of Divine] *Wisdom* [guide a person to] יִרְאַת ה׳, *fear of* HASHEM.

9. Thus, the concept of יִרְאַת ה׳, *fear of* HASHEM, is equated with Torah study (see *Radak* to *Psalms* 111:10).

One Mishnah states: Anyone who places his fear of sin before his wisdom, that person's wisdom will remain . . . (*Avos* 3:9). Another Mishnah states: If there is no fear [of God], there cannot be any wisdom . . . (*Avos* 3:17). The Vilna Gaon cites the verse from *Psalms* as the source of both these teachings (A.S.).

10. See the Baal HaTurim's previous comment.

10a. See the Baal HaTurim's comment there.

11. The respective last words are: *Genesis,* בְּמִצְרָיִם; *Exodus,* מַסְעֵיהֶם; *Leviticus,* סִינָי; *Numbers,* יְרֵחוֹ; and *Deuteronomy,* יִשְׂרָאֵל.

12. The Baal HaTurim's source for the phrase הוּא אֱלֹהֵינוּ זֶה is unknown. Although its literal meaning is *He, our God, This,* it seems obvious that the phrase has a much deeper kabbalistic meaning. Indeed, we find that אֱלֹהֵינוּ is not the only reference to God in this phrase, for both הוּא, *He,* and זֶה, *This,* are interpreted elsewhere as Divine Names (see *Succah* 45a, with *Tosafos,* s.v., אני והו; and *Menachos* 53b). Accordingly, the phrase הוּא אֱלֹהֵינוּ זֶה comprises three references to God (*Ittur Bikkurim*).

13. Although the Baal HaTurim adduces only the last stich of the verse from *Isaiah* to intimate that

on the other side of the Jordan, concerning the wilderness, concerning the Arabah, opposite the swampland, between Paran and Tophel, and Laban, and Hazeroth, and Di-zahab; 2 *eleven days from Horeb, by way of Mount Seir to Kadesh-barnea.*
3 *It was in the fortieth year, in the eleventh month, on the first*

BAAL HATURIM ELUCIDATED

❑ **מול** — OPPOSITE. The masoretic note, ב׳, means that this word appears twice in the *Tanach*:[13a] (i) here, מוֹל סוּף, *opposite the swampland*[14]; and (ii) מֹל אֶת בְּנֵי יִשְׂרָאֵל שֵׁנִית, *Circumcise the Children of Israel a second time* (*Joshua* 5:2).[14a] [The similarity of expression alludes to a Talmudic dictum:] Five matters were stated regarding a קָנֶה, *reed*:[15] We do not circumcise with it; we do not cut meat with it, we do not slaughter with it, we do not wipe with it . . . as is stated in tractate *Chullin.*[16]

Accordingly, this is what God said to Joshua, *"Make sharp knives for yourself"* (*Joshua* 5:2), but do not circumcise with [sharpened] reeds that grow in the סוּף, i.e., *the swampland.* Thus, [the connection between] מוֹל סוּף, *opposite*[17] [*the reeds of*] *the swampland,* מֹל אֶת בְּנֵי יִשְׂרָאֵל, *circumcise the Children of Israel.*[18]

3. בְּאַרְבָּעִים — IN THE FORTIETH. The masoretic note, ב׳, means that this word appears twice in the *Tanach*: (i) here, וַיְהִי בְּאַרְבָּעִים, *It was in the fortieth;* and (ii){מָגֵן} אִם יֵרָאֶה וָרֹמַח} בְּאַרְבָּעִים אֶלֶף בְּיִשְׂרָאֵל}, {*Was* [*even*] *a shield or spear seen*} *among forty*

the respective last letters of the Five Books allude to God's Name, the stich preceding that one may also be adduced, for it intimates that another Divine Name — אֶהְיֶה — is alluded to by the initial letters of the Five Books. That stich reads, אֲנִי ה׳ רִאשׁוֹן, which may be understood, *I am Hashem, at the beginning* (*VeChur LaZahav*).

13a. The full masoretic note reads: ב׳ בִּתְרֵי לִישָּׁנֵי חַד חָסֵר וְחַד מָלֵא, *Twice, with two meanings; one spelled defectively* (מֹל, without a ו); *and one spelled in full* (מוֹל, with a ו).

In our verse, the word is a preposition; it is spelled in full — מוֹל; and has the same meaning as מוּל, *opposite.* The pronunciation מוֹל appears only twice in the *Tanach,* here and in *Nehemiah* 12:38 where it is spelled מוֹאל. The pronunciation מוּל appears thirty-four times (e.g., 2:19 and 3:29 below). In the verse adduced from *Joshua,* the word is an imperative form of the verb מוּל, *to circumcise;* and is spelled defectively, מֹל, without a ו.

14. Translation of סוּף as *swampland* follows the Baal HaTurim at the end of this comment, and is in accordance with one opinion in the Talmud (*Sotah* 12b). According to the other opinion, it refers to the יַם סוּף, *Sea of Reeds* (see *Rashi* here, s.v., מוֹל סוּף, and at *Exodus* 2:3, s.v., ותשם בסוף).

14a. The full verse reads: *At that time* HASHEM *said to Joshua, "Make for yourself sharp knives and, once more, circumcise the Children of Israel a second time."*

15. Each of these matters is either a halachic or a practical precaution against potential damage due to the splintering of the reed.

16. *Chullin* 16b. Although the Baal HaTurim writes, חֲמִשָּׁה דְבָרִים, *five matters,* he lists only four. This is probably the result of a typographical error, for extant versions of the Talmud read: ה׳ דְּבָרִים נֶאֶמְרוּ בְקְרוּמִית שֶׁל קָנֶה, *Five matters were stated regarding the stem of a reed:* אֵין שׁוֹחֲטִין בָּהּ, *We do not slaughter with it;* וְאֵין מָלִין בָּהּ, *and we do not circumcise with it;* וְאֵין מְחַתְּכִין בָּהּ בָּשָׂר, *and we do not cut meat with it;* וְאֵין מְחַצְּצִין בָּהּ שִׁנַּיִם, *and we do not pick* [*one's*] *teeth with it;* וְאֵין מְקַנְּחִים בָּהּ, *and we do not wipe* [*a wound*] *with it.*

17. That is, with something other than.

18. *Maharam MiRothenburg.*

לַחֹ֖דֶשׁ דִּבֶּ֤ר מֹשֶׁה֙ אֶל־בְּנֵ֣י יִשְׂרָאֵ֔ל כְּכֹ֗ל אֲשֶׁ֨ר צִוָּ֧ה
ד יְהוָ֛ה אֹת֖וֹ אֲלֵהֶֽם׃ אַחֲרֵ֣י הַכֹּת֗וֹ אֵ֚ת סִיחֹן֙ מֶ֣לֶךְ
הָֽאֱמֹרִ֔י אֲשֶׁ֥ר יוֹשֵׁ֖ב בְּחֶשְׁבּ֑וֹן וְאֵ֗ת ע֚וֹג מֶ֣לֶךְ הַבָּשָׁ֔ן
ה אֲשֶׁר־יוֹשֵׁ֥ב בְּעַשְׁתָּרֹ֖ת בְּאֶדְרֶֽעִי׃ בְּעֵ֥בֶר הַיַּרְדֵּ֖ן
בְּאֶ֣רֶץ מוֹאָ֑ב הוֹאִ֣יל מֹשֶׁ֔ה בֵּאֵ֛ר אֶת־הַתּוֹרָ֥ה הַזֹּ֖את
ו לֵאמֹֽר׃ יְהוָ֧ה אֱלֹהֵ֛ינוּ דִּבֶּ֥ר אֵלֵ֖ינוּ בְּחֹרֵ֣ב לֵאמֹ֑ר

בעל הטורים

אֶלֶף בְּיִשְׂרָאֵל״. לוֹמַר אִם יִהְיֶה ת״ח אֶחָד בֵּין אַרְבָּעִים אֶלֶף, אֵין צְרִיכִים לֹא מָגֵן וְלֹא רֹמַח, כִּי ת״ח מֵגֵן עֲלֵיהֶם מֵאוֹיְבֵיהֶם. דְּאַיְרֵי הָתָם בְּת״ח, שֶׁנֶּאֱמַר ״לִבִּי לְחוֹקְקֵי יִשְׂרָאֵל״, וְהָכָא נַמִּי כְּתִיב בַּתְרֵיהּ עִנְיַן הַתּוֹרָה, שֶׁנֶּאֱמַר ״הוֹאִיל מֹשֶׁה בֵּאֵר אֶת הַתּוֹרָה״:

(ה) **הוֹאִיל.** ג׳ בַּמָּסוֹרֶת – ״הוֹאִיל מֹשֶׁה״; וְאִידָךְ ״כִּי הוֹאִיל ה׳ לַעֲשׂוֹת {אֶתְכֶם לוֹ לְעָם}״; ״הוֹאִיל הָלַךְ אַחֲרֵי צָו״. הַיְנוּ דְּאָמְרִינַן, בֵּין כָּךְ וּבֵין כָּךְ קְרוּיִין בָּנָיו שֶׁל מָקוֹם, בֵּין עוֹשִׂין רְצוֹנוֹ שֶׁל מָקוֹם שֶׁמְּקַיְּמִין אֶת הַתּוֹרָה, דְּהַיְנוּ ״הוֹאִיל מֹשֶׁה״, וּבֵין עוֹבְדִין עֲבוֹדָה זָרָה, דְּהַיְנוּ ״הוֹאִיל הָלַךְ אַחֲרֵי צָו״, ״הוֹאִיל ה׳ לַעֲשׂוֹת אֶתְכֶם לוֹ לְעָם״:

❑ **אֶת הַתּוֹרָה הַזֹּאת לֵאמֹר.** וּסְמִיךְ לֵהּ ״ה׳ אֱלֹהֵינוּ״, כְּלוֹמַר, הִזְהִירָם עַל יִחוּד הַשֵּׁם:

(ו) **בְּחֹרֵב לֵאמֹר.** כְּתִיב חָסֵר {״בַּחֹרֶב״}. שֶׁאִם לֹא תְקַיְּמוּ אֶת הַתּוֹרָה, ״וְהֵבֵאתִי עֲלֵיכֶם חֶרֶב״:

BAAL HATURIM ELUCIDATED

thousand in Israel? (*Judges* 5:8). This latter verse implies that if there would be one Torah scholar[19] among forty thousand [Israelites], there would be need of neither shield nor spear [for protection], for the Torah scholar[19] would protect [all forty thousand of] them from their enemies.[20] And the verse [from *Judges*] refers to Torah scholars, as is stated there (v. 9), לִבִּי לְחוֹקְקֵי יִשְׂרָאֵל, *My heart is with the lawgivers*[21]

19. Unlike the style used throughout this work, in this comment the text has left the abbreviations that appear in the early printed editions. Now, the abbreviation ת״ח is used for both the singular תַּלְמִיד חָכָם, *Torah scholar,* and the plural תַּלְמִידֵי חֲכָמִים, *Torah scholars.* In the Baal HaTurim's comment, the singular form is indicated by the use of the singular adjective אֶחָד, *one,* and the singular verb מֵגֵן, *he protects* (from the root גנן, *to shield, to protect*).

However, both *Tanna DeVei Eliyahu,* the Midrash upon which the Baal HaTurim's allusion presumably is based (see note 20 below), and *Maharam MiRothenburg,* the source of the allusion, speak of two Torah scholars: The Midrash reads, זוּג אֶחָד תַּלְמִידֵי חֲכָמִים, *one pair of Torah scholars*; while *Maharam MiRothenburg* reads, שְׁנֵי תַּלְמִידֵי חֲכָמִים, *two Torah scholars*. Accordingly, *Shoham Yakar* suggests that the abbreviation be read in the plural, תַּלְמִידֵי חֲכָמִים and be translated [*a pair of*] *Torah scholars,* so that the singular verbs would refer to the singular noun "pair." Indeed, one Baal HaTurim manuscript cryptically reads, תַּלְמִידֵי חֲכָמִים אֶחָד, literally, *one Torah scholars.*

20. *Tanna DeVei Eliyahu* 10 — So said the Holy One, Blessed is He, "My son, build for Me a Torah study hall and the great reward that is stored in My treasurehouse will be yours; and I will rescue Israel [from their enemies] for your sake," as it is written, *When it* [*Israel*] *chose new gods, war came to its gates. Was* [*even*] *a shield or a spear seen among forty thousand in Israel?* (*Judges* 5:8). From this verse the Sages expounded: Should forty thousand [warriors] of Israel gather and go forth to battle, then, if there is one pair of Torah scholars among them, it is the same as if they held shield and buckler and a two-edged sword in their hands. That is the implication of the verse, *Was* [*even*] *a shield or spear seen among forty thousand in Israel.*

21. *Rashi* (based on *Sanhedrin* 5a) interprets, לִבִּי

of the month, when Moses spoke to the Children of Israel, according to everything that HASHEM commanded him to them, [4] *after he had smitten Sihon, king of the Amorite, who dwelt in Heshbon, and Og, king of Bashan, who dwelt in Ashtaroth, in Edrei.* [5] *On the other side of the Jordan in the land of Moab, Moses desired to explain this Torah, saying:*

[6] *HASHEM, our God, spoke to us in Horeb, saying: It*

BAAL HATURIM ELUCIDATED

of Israel.[22] Similarly, our passage is followed by the topic of Torah [scholarship], for the narrative continues, *Moses began explaining this Torah* (v. 5).[23]

5. הוֹאִיל — DESIRED.[24] The masoretic note, ג׳, means that this word appears three times in the *Tanach*: (i) here, הוֹאִיל מֹשֶׁה, *Moses desired;* (ii) כִּי הוֹאִיל ה׳ לַעֲשׂוֹת {אֶתְכֶם לוֹ לְעָם}, *For HASHEM has desired to make {you for a people unto Him}* (*I Samuel* 12:22); and (iii) הוֹאִיל הָלַךְ אַחֲרֵי צָו, *he has desired to follow after filth*[25] (*Hosea* 5:11). This is reminiscent of what [the Sages] have stated: In either case, [you] are called children of the Omnipresent,[26] [in other words,] whether they do the will of the Omnipresent, i.e., they fulfill [the *mitzvos* of] the Torah, as in our verse, *Moses desired* [*to explain this Torah*], and [even if] they worship idols, i.e., *he has desired to follow after filth,* [in either case] *HASHEM has desired to make you for a people unto Him.*

❑ **אֶת הַתּוֹרָה הַזֹּאת לֵאמֹר — THIS TORAH, SAYING.** Juxtaposed to this is the phrase ה׳ אֱלֹהֵינוּ, *HASHEM, our God,* as if to say, [Moses] admonished them with regard to the unique oneness of HASHEM.

6. בְּחֹרֵב לֵאמֹר — IN HOREB, SAYING. [The word בְּחֹרֵב is] spelled defectively, without a ו[27] {[as if it were vowelized] בַּחֶרֶב, *with a sword*}. [Thus, God was saying,] "If you do not observe the Torah, *I will bring a sword upon you* (*Leviticus* 26:25)."[28]

לְחוֹקְקֵי יִשְׂרָאֵל, *My heart is with the lawgivers of Israel,* as a declaration of love for the scholars of Israel (see also *Radak's* alternative explanation of this clause).

22. The Midrash states that a pair of Torah scholars can serve to protect Israel from its enemies but does not adduce a proof verse. The Baal HaTurim shows that the Midrash is based on the verse following the one it cites.

23. *Maharam MiRothenburg.*

24. The translation of הוֹאִיל as *he desired* follows Ibn Ezra's interpretation of our verse in his comments to *Genesis* 18:27. According to most commentaries it means *he began* (*Targum Onkelos*; *Targum Yonasan ben Uziel*; *Rashi*; *Ibn Ezra* here).

25. A euphemism for idolatry.

26. *Kiddushin* 36a — The verse states, *You are children to HASHEM, your God* (*Deuteronomy* 14:1), [which, according to one opinion means,] at a time when you act in the manner of children, you are called "children [of HASHEM]"; but when you do not act in the manner of children, you are not called children [of HASHEM] . . . A second opinion differs: In either case, you are called "children of HASHEM," as it is stated, *They are foolish children* (*Jeremiah* 4:22), and, *children in whom there is no loyalty* (*Deuteronomy* 32:20).

27. It is not clear why the Baal HaTurim chose to explain the missing ו in this particular verse. The name חוֹרֵב, *Horeb,* an alternate name for Mount Sinai, appears seventeen times in the *Tanach,* twelve of those times in the Torah. Only once is it spelled חוֹרֵב, in full, with a ו — in *Exodus* 33:6, where a masoretic note reads, לֵית מָלֵא בְּתוֹרָה, *There is no other* [verse in which this word is] *spelled in full in the Torah.* Nevertheless, only at this verse does the Baal HaTurim comment on the spelling of the word.

28. *Peirush HaRokeach;* see *Sifrei* to 11:12; *Vayikra Rabbah* 35:5.

ז רַב־לָכֶם שֶׁבֶת בָּהָר הַזֶּה: פְּנוּ | וּסְעוּ לָכֶם וּבֹאוּ הַר
הָאֱמֹרִי וְאֶל־כָּל־שְׁכֵנָיו בָּעֲרָבָה בָהָר וּבַשְּׁפֵלָה
וּבַנֶּגֶב וּבְחוֹף הַיָּם אֶרֶץ הַכְּנַעֲנִי וְהַלְּבָנוֹן עַד־הַנָּהָר
ח הַגָּדֹל נְהַר־פְּרָת: רְאֵה נָתַתִּי לִפְנֵיכֶם אֶת־הָאָרֶץ
בֹּאוּ וּרְשׁוּ אֶת־הָאָרֶץ אֲשֶׁר נִשְׁבַּע יְהוָה לַאֲבֹתֵיכֶם
לְאַבְרָהָם לְיִצְחָק וּלְיַעֲקֹב לָתֵת לָהֶם וּלְזַרְעָם
ט אַחֲרֵיהֶם: וָאֹמַר אֲלֵכֶם בָּעֵת הַהִוא לֵאמֹר לֹא־אוּכַל

בעל הטורים

(ז) **פְּנוּ.** פֵּ״א כְּפוּלָה – יֵשׁ לָכֶם לִפְנוֹת מִכָּל מַעֲשִׂים רָעִים. אִי נַמִּי, בְּכָל מָקוֹם שֶׁאַתֶּם פּוֹנִים הָעֲנָנִים עִמָּכֶם:

(ח) **רְאֵה נָתַתִּי לִפְנֵיכֶם.** הַקָּדוֹשׁ בָּרוּךְ הוּא אָמַר כָּךְ לְמֹשֶׁה לֵאמֹר לְיִשְׂרָאֵל. אִי נַמִּי, ״רְאֵה״ חוֹזֵר עַל כָּל אֶחָד וְאֶחָד:

(ט) **וָאֹמַר אֲלֵכֶם.** חָסֵר יוּ״ד, כִּי עֶשֶׂר פְּעָמִים הוֹכִיחָם; וְעֶשֶׂר פְּעָמִים כְּתִיב מִיתַת מֹשֶׁה בַּתּוֹרָה:

BAAL HATURIM ELUCIDATED

7. פְּנוּ — TURN. [According to a scribal tradition,] the פ of this word is written [in Torah scrolls] in the enhanced form known as פ׳ כְּפוּלָה, *doubled* פ.[29] [As if to say,] You should turn away from all manner of evil.[30] Alternatively: [It implies,]

29. Among the unusual forms used for specific letters in the Torah is the פ׳ כְּפוּלָה, *doubled* פ, which is also known as פ׳ לְפוּפָה (or, פ׳ מְלֻפָּף), *rolled* פ. Unlike the usual פ which is drawn as a י suspended from the roof of a כ, this unusual פ has a miniature פ in place of a י. Thus, the פ of פְּנוּ is described in *Sefer Tagin* as one of "191 in the Torah whose mouths are on the inside." See illustration.

The Baal HaTurim also comments on the פ׳

Usual פ (a). Doubled פ according to *Kiryas Sefer* (b); *Machzor Vitry* (c); *Badei HaAron* (d); and the Gaster ms. (e).

כְּפוּלָה at *Exodus* 31:17, *Numbers* 20:10, 23:3, and *Deuteronomy* 5:4, 6:25, 7:12, 7:20, 9:7, 13:6, 15:8, 16:16, 17:6 and 17:8.

30. The doubled פ indicates that the word פְּנוּ, *turn around,* should be understood as if it were written twice, to emphasize how careful one must be to avoid evil (*VeChur LaZahav*).

However, it is not clear how the verse alludes to evil matters. Perhaps the Baal HaTurim refers to the following Midrash: רַב לָכֶם שֶׁבֶת, *It is enough for you, dwelling* [*by this mountain*], [i.e.,] רַע הוּא לָכֶם יְשִׁיבַתְכֶם בָּהָר הַזֶּה, *Your dwelling by this mountain is bad for you.* פְּנוּ וּסְעוּ לָכֶם וּבֹאוּ, *Turn around and let yourselves journey, and come . . .* [because,] רַע הוּא הַבַּטָּלָה, *idleness is bad* (*Sifrei* to vv. 6-7, not found in all editions; see also *Yalkut Shimoni*).

Alternatively: The Baal HaTurim's comment is based on *Targum Yonasan ben Uzziel's* rendering of רַב (v. 6) as בִּישׁ, the Aramaic equivalent of רַע, *bad* (A. S.)

It is noteworthy that in the letter-exchange system known as אַח״ס בְּטַ״ע [in which the alphabet is divided into three parts — (i) the first seven letters; (ii) the next seven letters; and (iii) the final eight

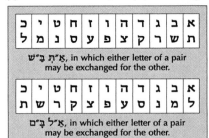

כ	י	ט	ח	ז	ו	ה	ד	ג	ב	א
ל	מ	נ	ס	ע	פ	צ	ק	ר	ש	ת

אַ״ת בַּ״שׁ, in which either letter of a pair may be exchanged for the other.

כ	י	ט	ח	ז	ו	ה	ד	ג	ב	א
ת	ש	ר	ק	צ	פ	ע	ס	נ	מ	ל

אַ״ל בַּ״ם, in which either letter of a pair may be exchanged for the other.

is enough for you, dwelling by this mountain. [7] *Turn around and let yourselves journey, and come to the Amorite mountain and all its neighbors, in the Arabah, on the mountain, and in the lowland, and in the south, and at the seacoast; the land of the Canaanite and the Lebanon, until the great river, the Euphrates River.* [8] *See! I have placed before you the land; come and possess the land that* HASHEM *swore to your forefathers, to Abraham, to Isaac, and to Jacob, to give them and their children after them.*

[9] *I said to you at that time, saying, "I cannot carry*

--------------------------- BAAL HATURIM ELUCIDATED ---------------------------

wherever you turn, the Clouds [of Glory] will accompany you.[31]

8. רְאֵה נָתַתִּי לִפְנֵיכֶם — SEE![32] I HAVE PLACED BEFORE YOU. The Holy One, Blessed is He, told this to Moses[33] to tell to the people.[34]

Alternatively: [The singular form] רְאֵה, *see,* refers to each and every individual [Israelite].[35]

9. וָאֹמַר אֲלֵכֶם — I SAID TO YOU. [The term אֲלֵכֶם, *to you,* is] spelled defectively,[36] without a י (= 10), for [Moses] rebuked them ten times;[37] and his death is

letters — with the first letters of each part forming the set אח"ס; the second letters forming the set בט"ע, and so on (see illustration), the letters ב and ע may be exchanged for one another, thus רָב may be understood as רָע (*VeChur LaZahav*).

31. The Baal HaTurim does not explain the connection between our verse and the Clouds of Glory.

32. The imperative verb רְאֵה, *See!*, is in the singular, seemingly speaking to the nation as a unit [thus the singular רְאֵה, rather than the plural form רְאוּ]. However, that understanding is difficult, for almost every reference to the Israelite nation in this passage (1:6—2:1) is couched in the plural. There are three exceptions: the word רְאֵה in our verse, which is the subject of the Baal HaTurim's present comment; all five verbs and four pronouns in verse 21, although the Baal HaTurim does not mention that verse in his comment, his second interpretation here may be applied to that verse (see note 35 below); and the first half of verse 31, explained in the Baal HaTurim's comment there.

33. That is, unlike the plural verbs in this passage, which have the Israelites as their subject, the subject of the singular verb רְאֵה is Moses. God told Moses, "See [to your responsibility to tell Israel in My Name], 'I have placed before [all of] you the land …' "

34. *Peirush HaRokeach.*

35. Sometimes the Torah addresses Israel in the plural, addressing the entire nation as a group, as if to say, "all of you together"; at other times the Torah uses the singular, as if to say, "each of you individually."

The Baal HaTurim makes a similar comment at 11:26 below.

36. The word אֲלֵיכֶם, *to you,* appears twenty-seven times in the Torah and an additional forty-three times in the rest of *Tanach.* In only six of those appearances is it spelled defectively, אֲלֵכֶם, without a י. The Baal HaTurim comments on the omitted י both here and at verse 20 below, but not on the other four verses (*Genesis* 42:14; *Exodus* 7:4 and 9; and verse 29 below).

In his comments to our verse, the Baal HaTurim writes that the omitted י in the phrase וָאֹמַר אֲלֵכֶם alludes to the ten admonitions, while in his comments to verse 20 below, the Baal HaTurim writes that the omitted י of the identical phrase in that verse alludes to the ten spies. This is because in our verse, the phrase introduces verses of general admonition (vv. 9-12). Thus, the Baal HaTurim relates the omitted י to the ten admonitions. In verse 20, however, the phrase introduces Moses' admonition that specifically addressed the incident of the spies. Thus, the Baal HaTurim relates the omitted י of that verse to the ten spies (*VeChur LaZahav*).

37. *Peirush HaRokeach.*

י לְבַדִּי שְׂאֵת אֶתְכֶם: יְהוָה אֱלֹהֵיכֶם הִרְבָּה אֶתְכֶם
שני יא וְהִנְּכֶם הַיּוֹם כְּכוֹכְבֵי הַשָּׁמַיִם לָרֹב: יְהוָה אֱלֹהֵי
אֲבוֹתֵכֶם יֹסֵף עֲלֵיכֶם כָּכֶם אֶלֶף פְּעָמִים וִיבָרֵךְ
יב אֶתְכֶם כַּאֲשֶׁר דִּבֶּר לָכֶם: אֵיכָה אֶשָּׂא לְבַדִּי טָרְחֲכֶם
יג וּמַשַּׂאֲכֶם וְרִיבְכֶם: הָבוּ לָכֶם אֲנָשִׁים חֲכָמִים
וּנְבֹנִים וִידֻעִים לְשִׁבְטֵיכֶם וַאֲשִׂימֵם בְּרָאשֵׁיכֶם:

בעל הטורים

(י) וְהִנְּכֶם. ב׳ בַּמָּסוֹרֶת — ״וְהִנְּכֶם הַיּוֹם כְּכוֹכְבֵי הַשָּׁמַיִם״; וְאִידָךְ ״וְהִנְּכֶם הֹלְכִים אִישׁ אַחֲרֵי שְׁרִרוּת לִבּוֹ״. פֵּרוּשׁ, אַף עַל פִּי שֶׁהֲלַכְתֶּם אַחֲרֵי שְׁרִירוּת לִבְּכֶם, ״הִנְּכֶם הַיּוֹם כְּכוֹכְבֵי הַשָּׁמַיִם לָרֹב״:

(יא) וִיבָרֵךְ. ב׳ בַּמָּסוֹרֶת — ״וִיבָרֵךְ אֶתְכֶם כַּאֲשֶׁר דִּבֶּר לָכֶם״; וְאִידָךְ ״וִיבָרֵךְ כָּל בָּשָׂר שֵׁם קָדְשׁוֹ״. כֵּיוָן שֶׁיְּבָרֵךְ אֶתְכֶם, יְבָרֵךְ כָּל בָּשָׂר שֵׁם קָדְשׁוֹ, שֶׁיֹּאמְרוּ בָּרוּךְ שֶׁקִּיֵּם הַבְטָחָתוֹ:

(יג) וַאֲשִׂמֵם בְּרָאשֵׁיכֶם. ״וַאֲשִׂמֵם״ כְּתִיב חָסֵר יוּ״ד. לוֹמַר לְךָ כִּי עֶשֶׂר פְּעָמִים הֻזְהֲרוּ עַל הַדַּיָּנִין בַּתּוֹרָה:

BAAL HATURIM ELUCIDATED

recorded ten times in the Torah.[38]

10. וְהִנְּכֶם — AND BEHOLD! YOU ARE . . . The masoretic note, ב׳, means that this word appears twice in the *Tanach*: (i) here, וְהִנְּכֶם הַיּוֹם כְּכוֹכְבֵי הַשָּׁמַיִם, *and behold! you are today like the stars of the heavens;* and (ii) וְהִנְּכֶם הֹלְכִים אִישׁ אַחֲרֵי שְׁרִרוּת לִבּוֹ, *and behold, you are proceeding, each man after the conception of his* [*evil*] *heart* (*Jeremiah* 16:12). The explanation [of the similarity of expression] is that [Moses is telling the people,] "Although you have been proceeding after the conception of your hearts, nevertheless, *behold! you are today like the stars of the heavens in abundance.*[39]

11. וִיבָרֵךְ — AND HE WILL BLESS. The masoretic note, ב׳, means that this word

38. *Peirush HaRokeach* — There the comment reads: . . . corresponding to the ten times that Moses' death [is mentioned] in the Torah. But *Peirush HaRokeach* does not explain the connection between the ten admonitions and the death of Moses.

Ten Scriptural verses (enumerated below) contain words of the root מות, *to die,* with regard to Moses. The death of Moses is mentioned in other verses (e.g., *Numbers* 27:13 and 31:2, see the Baal HaTurim's comment there), but verbs of the root מות do not appear in those verses. Although the Baal HaTurim writes בַּתּוֹרָה, *in the Torah,* two of the ten verses are found in the Book of *Joshua.*

The Midrash enumerates the ten verses regarding Moses' death [in an apparently haphazard order (*Maharzu*)]. The first eight verses are in *Deuteronomy*: (i) הֵן קָרְבוּ יָמֶיךָ לָמוּת — 31:14; (ii) וּמֻת בָּהָר — 32:50; (iii) כִּי אָנֹכִי מֵת — 4:22; (iv) כִּי יָדַעְתִּי אַחֲרֵי מוֹתִי — 31:29; (v) וְאַף כִּי אַחֲרֵי מוֹתִי — 31:27; (vi) לִפְנֵי מוֹתוֹ — 33:1; (vii) וּמֹשֶׁה בֶּן מֵאָה וְעֶשְׂרִים שָׁנָה בְּמֹתוֹ — 34:7; (viii) וַיָּמָת שָׁם מֹשֶׁה עֶבֶד ה׳ — 34:5; and two more in the Book of *Joshua,* (ix) וַיְהִי אַחֲרֵי מוֹת מֹשֶׁה — 1:1; and (x) מֹשֶׁה עַבְדִּי מֵת — 1:2 (*Pesikta DeRav Kahana; Devarim Rabbah* 11:10). *Devarim Rabbah* continues: This teaches that the decree that Moses not enter into the Land of Israel was handed down on ten occasions, but was not sealed until [the tenth time, i.e., the ten verses allude to the ten occasions, but the verses are not the actual ten occasions, for the last three verses were written after his passing].

39. See the Baal HaTurim to v. 5 above, s.v., הוֹאִיל.

you alone. [10] HASHEM, *your God, has multiplied you and behold! you are today like the stars of the heavens in abundance.* [11] HASHEM, *the God of your forefathers, will add to you a thousand times yourselves, and He will bless you as He has spoken of you.* [12] *How can I alone carry your contentiousness, your burdens, and your quarrels?* [13] *Provide for yourselves distinguished men, who are wise, understanding, and well known to your tribes, and I shall appoint them as your heads."*

─────────── BAAL HATURIM ELUCIDATED ───────────

appears twice in the *Tanach:* (i) here, וִיבָרֶךְ אֶתְכֶם כַּאֲשֶׁר דִּבֶּר לָכֶם, *and He will bless you as He has spoken of you;* and (ii) וִיבָרֵךְ כָּל בָּשָׂר שֵׁם קָדְשׁוֹ, *and may all flesh bless His Holy Name (Psalms* 145:21). [The similarity of expression implies that] as soon as He will bless You, all flesh will bless His Holy name. They will say, "Blessed [is He] Who has fulfilled His promise."

❑ {The Baal HaTurim's other comment on this verse appears at 33:1 below, s.v. מֹשֶׁה.}

13. וַאֲשִׂמֵם בְּרָאשֵׁיכֶם — AND I SHALL PLACE THEM AS YOUR HEADS. The word וַאֲשִׂמֵם, *and I shall place,* is spelled defectively,[40] without a י (= 10). This indicates to you that the Torah admonished ten times regarding judges.[41]

40. *Rashi* (in many editions), *R' Yehudah Ha-Chassid, Rabbeinu Shimshon,* the Baal HaTurim, and others state that the word is spelled וַאֲשִׂמֵם, without a י. Other *Rishonim,* including the *Rama* and *Meiri,* testify that it is spelled וַאֲשִׂימֵם, with a י. The word does not recur in the *Tanach,* but does appear once, without the וְ prefix, in *I Kings* 5:23. In both places, the masoretic note reads simply לֵית, *There is no* [other]. Much has been written regarding the proper spelling of this word: See *Teshuvos HaRashba Hameyuchasos LaRamban* 272; *Teshuvos Chelkas Yaakov, Yoreh Deah* 153; *Or Torah (R' Menachem di Lonzano); Minchas Shai;* and the supercommentaries to *Rashi.*

41. *Peirush HaRokeach.* In his notes to *Peirush HaRokeach,* Rabbi Chaim Kanievsky שליט"א refers this to *Otzar HaMidrashim,* p. 140. The *Midrash Hashkeim* there reads: Come and see how beloved the judges are before the Omnipresent, Blessed is He, for He has balanced them on the scale with the Ten Commandments. For each of the Ten Commandments is a *mitzvah* unto itself, and, in truth, ten positive *mitzvos* and ten negative *mitzvos* are stated regarding the judges. The negative *mitzvos* are: (i-ii) לֹא תַכִּירוּ פָנִים בַּמִּשְׁפָּט, *You shall not show favoritism in judgment . . .* לֹא תָגוּרוּ מִפְּנֵי אִישׁ, *you*

shall not tremble before any man (Deuteronomy 1:17); (iii-v) לֹא תַעֲשׂוּ עָוֶל בַּמִּשְׁפָּט, *You shall not commit perversion in judgment,* לֹא תִשָּׂא פְנֵי דָל, *you shall not favor the impoverished,* וְלֹא תֶהְדַּר פְּנֵי גָדוֹל, *and you shall not honor the great (Leviticus* 19:15); (vi) לֹא תַטֶּה מִשְׁפַּט אֶבְיֹנְךָ, *You shall not pervert the judgment of your destitute (Exodus* 23:6); (vii) לֹא תַטֶּה מִשְׁפַּט גֵּר יָתוֹם, *You shall not pervert the judgment of a convert* [or] *an orphan (Deuteronomy* 24:17); (viii-x) לֹא תַטֶּה מִשְׁפָּט, *You shall not pervert judgment,* לֹא תַכִּיר פָּנִים, *you shall not show favoritism,* וְלֹא תִקַּח שֹׁחַד, *and you shall not accept a bribe (Deuteronomy* 16:19). Thus you have learned that the judges are as beloved to God as the Ten Commandments.

It is not clear why that *Midrash* lists those ten *mitzvos* in this particular order, jumping from *Deuteronomy* to *Leviticus* to *Exodus,* then back to *Deuteronomy.* But it is noteworthy that with regard to the first three *mitzvos,* the Torah uses the plural form for *you shall not,* while the next seven are couched in the singular. It is likewise not clear why that *Midrash* does not enumerate the ten positive *mitzvos* to which it refers. Similarly, it is not clear why certain *mitzvos* are included in that number, while other *mitzvos* that are certainly addressed to judges are omitted.

יד וַתַּעֲנוּ אֹתִי וַתֹּאמְרוּ טוֹב־הַדָּבָר אֲשֶׁר־דִּבַּרְתָּ
טו לַעֲשׂוֹת: וָאֶקַּח אֶת־רָאשֵׁי שִׁבְטֵיכֶם אֲנָשִׁים
חֲכָמִים וִידֻעִים וָאֶתֵּן אוֹתָם רָאשִׁים עֲלֵיכֶם שָׂרֵי
אֲלָפִים וְשָׂרֵי מֵאוֹת וְשָׂרֵי חֲמִשִּׁים וְשָׂרֵי עֲשָׂרֹת

בעל הטורים

דָּבָר אַחֵר – "וַאֲשִׁמֵם" חָסֵר, לוֹמַר לְךָ כִּי הָאָשָׁם הוּא בָרָאשִׁים, בִּשְׁבִיל שֶׁיֵּשׁ בְּיָדָם לִמְחוֹת וְאֵינָם מוֹחִין:

(טו) וָאֶתֵּן אוֹתָם רָאשִׁים. "אוֹתָם" מָלֵא וָי"ו. לוֹמַר לְךָ שֶׁהָיָה בָהֶם שֵׁשׁ מִדּוֹת שְׁמוּנָה בְּפֶרֶק הַנֶּחְנָקִין – אֵיזֶהוּ בֶּן הָעוֹלָם הַבָּא? כָּל מִי שֶׁהוּא שְׁפַל בֶּרֶךְ, עִנְוְתָן, שַׁיִיף וְעָיֵיל, שָׁיֵיף וְנָפִיק, גָּרִיס בְּאוֹרַיְתָא תְּדִירָא, וְלָא מַחֲזִיק טִיבוּתָא לְנַפְשֵׁהּ:

❑ **שָׂרֵי אֲלָפִים וְשָׂרֵי מֵאוֹת וְשָׂרֵי חֲמִשִּׁים וְשָׂרֵי עֲשָׂרֹת.** אַרְבַּע פְּעָמִים "שָׂרֵי" כְּנֶגֶד אַרְבָּעָה דְגָלִים:

BAAL HATURIM ELUCIDATED

Alternatively: וַאֲשִׁמֵם is spelled defectively to indicate to you that the [41a]אָשָׁם, *guilt,* lies with the head leaders,[42] for it is within their power to protest, yet they do not protest.[43]

15. וָאֶתֵּן אוֹתָם רָאשִׁים — AND I APPOINTED THEM AS HEADS. The word אוֹתָם, *them,* is spelled in full, with a ו (= 6). This is to indicate that the judges possessed the six positive qualities enumerated in chapter *HaNechnakin:*[44] Who is destined for a

41a. Although the verse reads וַאֲשִׁמֵם, with a שׁ, the Baal HaTurim's comment treats it as if it were spelled with a שׁ, hence אָשָׁם, *guilt.*

42. *Sifrei,* cited by *Rashi.* That is, the phrase וַאֲשִׁמֵם בְּרָאשֵׁיכֶם is understood as if it were vowelized וַאֲשָׁמָם בְּרָאשֵׁיכֶם, *and their guilt is upon your head leaders,* meaning that the guilt of the sinful members of the nation is upon the leaders who should have rebuked them, but did not.

43. *Rashi.*

The Mishnah states: A cow may not go out [on the Sabbath] . . . with a strap between her horns. The cow of Rabbi Elazar ben Azariah would go out with a strap between her horns, against the will of the Sages (*Shabbos* 5:4 [54b]). The *gemara* questions this Mishnah: Did [Rabbi Elazar ben Azariah] have but one cow? . . . Why, he would give twelve thousand calves as his annual tithe [i.e., his cows bore 120,000 calves each year, so that his tithe came to 12,000 calves]! . . . [In truth,] It was not his cow [that went out with a strap], but that of the woman who lived next door to him. However, because he did not protest to her, it was considered as his.

The Talmud then cites three related teachings: Whoever has the ability to [successfully] protest against [the misdeeds of] members of his household, but does not protest, is caught up in [i.e., will be punished for the misdeeds of] the members of his household; . . . against the people of his city, [but does not,] is caught up in the people of his city; . . . against the entire world, [but does not,] is caught up in the entire world (*Shabbos* 54b).

44. The tenth chapter of tractate *Sanhedrin,* also called *Eilu Hein HaNechnakin.* The adduced Talmudic passage appears there on page 88b. Although that passage does not speak of judges in particular, nevertheless, it appears immediately after a discussion regarding the criteria to be used in selecting judges.

The Talmud there states: Anyone who is wise and humble and whom the people find pleasing shall be [appointed] a judge in his city. And from there [i.e., the municipal courts] they promote [judges of proven ability to the national court that sits at the entrance] to the Temple Mount; from there [to the court that sits at the entrance] to the Temple Courtyard; and from there to [the Sanhedrin (Supreme Court) that sits in] the

[14] *You answered me and said, "The thing that you have proposed to do is good."*

[15] *So I took the heads of your tribes, distinguished men, who were wise and well known, and I appointed them as heads over you, leaders of thousands, leaders of hundreds, leaders of fifties, and leaders of tens, and*

BAAL HATURIM ELUCIDATED

share in the World to Come? Anyone who (i) is humble;[45] (ii) is modest;[46] (iii) bends upon entering;[47] (iv) bends upon leaving;[48] (v) studies Torah constantly; and (vi) does not insist on receiving recognition [for his accomplishments].[49]

❑ **שָׂרֵי אֲלָפִים וְשָׂרֵי מֵאוֹת וְשָׂרֵי חֲמִשִּׁים וְשָׂרֵי עֲשָׂרֹת — LEADERS OF THOUSANDS, LEADERS OF HUNDREDS, LEADERS OF FIFTIES, AND LEADERS OF TENS.** The word שָׂרֵי, *leaders of,* appears four times, corresponding to the four *degalim* (divisions)[49a] [of the Israelite camp].[50]

Chamber of Hewn Stone.

The Talmudic discussion continues with the passage adduced by the Baal HaTurim. Thus, it may be understood as a group of additional qualifications for a judicial candidate. Moreover, this understanding of the Talmudic sequence is bolstered by a Midrashic teaching: Anyone who decides a case with absolute loyalty to the truth attains for himself life in the World to Come, as it is stated (*Isaiah* 56:1), *Thus said HASHEM, "Observe justice and perform righteous deeds . . ."* [the prophet goes on to enumerate certain other *mitzvos* and to describe the eternal life awaiting those who fulfill them] (*Midrash Tanchuma, Shofetim* 8). Accordingly, in order to be able to judge with absolute loyalty to the truth, one must possess the six qualities enumerated in the Talmud (*VeChur LaZahav*).

45. Literally, *of lowered knee,* i.e., willing to bend.

46. The first two qualities are apparently the same, except that the first speaks of external humility that one shows to others, while the second refers to internal humility that one feels within his essential being (*Ben Yehoyada*).

47. Before entering another person's home, he bends, i.e., he lowers his head and eyes, so that he not become covetous of the host's possessions, but he need not act in this manner in his own home, for whatever is there is his (*Ben Yehoyada*).

48. That is, he lowers his head and eyes when he leaves his own home for the public thoroughfares and marketplaces (see note 47).

49. *Sanhedrin* 88b; *Peirush HaRokeach.*

49a. Unlike those who understand דֶּגֶל as *flag* or *banner* (e.g., *Targum Yonasan ben Uzziel* to *Numbers* 2:3; *Metzudas Tzion* to *Song of Songs* 2:4), *Rashi* understands the noun דֶּגֶל, *degel,* and its verb form דגל as referring to "a division; a disposition of forces or hosts, such as a military formation." Thus, *Rashi* (*Numbers* 2:2) writes, כָּל דֶּגֶל יִהְיֶה לוֹ אוֹת מַפָּה צְבוּעָה תְּלוּיָה בוֹ, *Each "degel" shall have for itself a sign, namely, a colored sheet of cloth hanging in its midst.* Clearly, *degel* cannot mean "flag" in that sentence. Rather, it means "division." See also *Rashi's* comments to *Psalms* 20:6; *Song of Songs* 2:4; and, especially, *Isaiah* 5:26, s.v., נֵס לַגּוֹיִם, where he describes a flag in detail, yet never once uses the word דֶּגֶל. From the Baal HaTurim's comments to *Numbers* 2:2 and in *Peirush HaTur HaAroch* there, it is apparent that the Baal HaTurim agrees with *Rashi's* understanding of the word.

50. The connection between the four appearances of שָׂרֵי and the four Israelite camps (see *Numbers,* Ch. 2) is not clear.

Both here and at *Exodus* 18:21, *Peirush HaRokeach,* the Baal HaTurim's apparent source for this comment, has a much longer version. Here he writes: *Leaders of thousands, leaders of hundreds, leaders of fifties, and leaders of tens*; thus [we have] four categories, corresponding to the four *degalim* who were the descendants of four Matriarchs (see next paragraph) . . . [*Peirush HaRokeach* continues with an additional seven groups of four].

The arrangement of each *degel* (see *Numbers,* Ch. 2) placed the children of the same mother

טו וְשֹׁטְרִים לְשִׁבְטֵיכֶם: וָאֲצַוֶּה אֶת־שֹׁפְטֵיכֶם בָּעֵת
הַהִוא לֵאמֹר שָׁמֹעַ בֵּין־אֲחֵיכֶם וּשְׁפַטְתֶּם צֶדֶק בֵּין־
יז אִישׁ וּבֵין־אָחִיו וּבֵין גֵּרוֹ: לֹא־תַכִּירוּ פָנִים בַּמִּשְׁפָּט

בעל הטורים

❏ **וְשֹׁטְרִים לְשִׁבְטֵיכֶם. וָאֲצַוֶּה.** רֶמֶז לְמַקֵּל וּרְצוּעָה שֶׁצִּוָּה אוֹתָם שֶׁיִּסְבְּלוּ מִן הַשּׁוֹטְרִים שֶׁיִּרְדּוּ אוֹתָם בְּמַקֵּל וּרְצוּעָה:

(טז) **וָאֲצַוֶּה אֶת שֹׁפְטֵיכֶם בָּעֵת הַהִוא.** כָּל דַּיָּן וְדַיָּן בְּדוֹרוֹ, כְּמֹשֶׁה בְדוֹרוֹ. וְזֶהוּ "אֶת שֹׁפְטֵיכֶם בָּעֵת הַהִוא" שֶׁיִּהְיֶה בוֹ:

❏ **וָאֲצַוֶּה אֶת שֹׁפְטֵיכֶם בָּעֵת.** רָאשֵׁי תֵבוֹת וָאֵשֵׁב. לוֹמַר לְךָ שֶׁצָּרִיךְ שֶׁיֵּשֵׁב הַדַּיָּן:

❏ **וָאֲצַוֶּה אֶת שֹׁפְטֵיכֶם בָּעֵת הַהִוא לֵאמֹר.** סוֹפֵי תֵבוֹת בְּגִימַטְרִיָּא תַּמְתִּין בְּכָל דִּינֶיךָ, שֶׁצָּרִיךְ שֶׁיִּהְיוּ מְתוּנִים בַּדִּין:

(יז) **לֹא תַכִּירוּ פָנִים בַּמִּשְׁפָּט.** תָּגִין עַל פֵּ"א – לוֹמַר "פְּתַח פִּיךָ לְאִלֵּם":

BAAL HATURIM ELUCIDATED

❏ וְשֹׁטְרִים לְשִׁבְטֵיכֶם וָאֲצַוֶּה — AND OFFICERS FOR YOUR TRIBES. AND I COMMANDED. This is an allusion to the rod and the whip[51] that he commanded the people to endure [the punishments meted out] by the officers who would prod them with rod and whip.[52]

16. וָאֲצַוֶּה אֶת שֹׁפְטֵיכֶם בָּעֵת הַהִוא — AND I COMMANDED YOUR JUDGES AT THAT TIME. Each and every judge in relation to his generation is considered as Moses in relation to his generation.[53] And that is the implication of אֶת שֹׁפְטֵיכֶם בָּעֵת הַהִוא, *your judges at that time,* in which they will be [sitting as judges].[53a]

---

together whenever possible. Thus, Reuben, Simeon and Levi, the three oldest sons of Leah, should have been together. However, since Levi had been assigned a special, higher status among the tribes it was not included among the *degalim;* rather, Gad, the older son of Leah's maidservant Zilpah, replaced Levi in the *degel* of Reuben's camp. The *degel* of Judah's camp included Judah, Issachar and Zebulun, three of Leah's sons; the *degel* of Ephraim's camp consisted of the tribes descended from the offspring of Rachel — Ephraim, Manasseh and Benjamin; the fourth *degel* was made up of Dan, Asher and Naphtali, sons of Zilpah and Bilhah — Dan headed that *degel* because he was the oldest among them.

51. According to the Midrash, the שׁוֹטְרִים, *officers,* were assigned to carrying out sentences of corporal punishment such as *makkos* (lashes with a whip), meted out by the judges when appropriate (*Sifrei,* cited by *Rashi*).

According to the Talmud, the verse *and I commanded your judges* implies that Moses admonished them not to spare the rod or whip when it is the appropriate sentence (*Sanhedrin* 7b).

52. The noun שֵׁבֶט can mean either *tribe* or *rod,* and the form שִׁבְטֵיכֶם can mean either *your tribes* or *your rods.* The Baal HaTurim interprets לְשִׁבְטֵיכֶם of our verse as if it appears twice: וְשֹׁטְרִים לְשִׁבְטֵיכֶם, *and officers of your rods,* לְשִׁבְטֵיכֶם וָאֲצַוֶּה, *to your tribes have I commanded,* i.e., I have commanded your officers to wield the rod and I have commanded your tribes to bear up under them (*VeChur LaZahav,* based on *Shoham Yakar*). The verse also alludes to the רְצוּעָה, *whip,* for the *gematria* of שִׁבְטֵכֶם (spelled defectively, without the י) is 371, equal to that of רְצוּעָה (A.S.).

53. *Rosh Hashanah* 25b, cited in *Rashi* to 17:9 and 19:17 below.

53a. That is, the time frame referred to by the phrase בָּעֵת הַהִוא, *at that time,* is not the era in which Moses is speaking to Israel; rather, it is the particular generation during which any subsequent judge will be serving on the court.

officers for your tribes. [16] *And I commanded your judges at that time, saying, "Listen between your brethren and judge them with righteousness, between a man and his brother or his litigant.* [17] *You shall not show favoritism in judgment,*

BAAL HATURIM ELUCIDATED

❑ וָאֲצַוֶּה אֶת שֹׁפְטֵיכֶם בָּעֵת — AND I COMMANDED YOUR JUDGES AT [THAT] TIME. The initial letters of these words spell the word וָאֵשֵׁב, *and I sat,* to indicate to you that the judge must sit.[54]

❑ וָאֲצַוֶּה אֶת שֹׁפְטֵיכֶם בָּעֵת הַהִוא לֵאמֹר — AND I COMMANDED YOUR JUDGES AT THAT TIME, SAYING. The *gematria* of the final letters of these words (1046) is equal to that of the phrase תַּמְתִּין בְּכָל דִּינֶיךָ, *Be deliberate in all your judgments.* For it is incumbent upon [judges] to be deliberate in judgment.[55]

17. לֹא תַכִּירוּ פָנִים בַּמִּשְׁפָּט — YOU SHALL NOT SHOW FAVORITISM IN JUDGMENT. [According to a scribal tradition,] the פ [of פָּנִים] is written with *tagin* [crownlets].[56] This indicates [that the judge must heed the verse], פְּתַח פִּיךָ לְאִלֵּם, *open your mouth*[57] *on behalf of the mute* (*Proverbs* 31:8).[58]

54. *Peirush HaRokeach.* The Talmud states that the judges are required to remain seated [during a trial (see *Shulchan Aruch, Choshen Mishpat* 28:6) and especially while handing down a verdict at the conclusion of the trial (*Shevuos* 30b).

55. See *Avos* 1:1; *Sifrei,* cited by *Rashi.*

56. According to the kabbalistic work *Peri Eitz Chaim* (*Shaar Kerias Shema* 1), in the regular Torah script, seven of the twenty-two letters of the *alef-beis,* identified by the mnemonic שַׁעַטְנֵ״ז גֵּ״ץ, are adorned with three *tagin,* i.e., crownlets or titles; six letters, בְּדֶ״ק חַיָּ״ה, are adorned with one crownlet; and the remaining nine, מְלָאכֶ״ת סוֹפֵ״ר, have no *tagin.* However, certain specific letters are written with more than the usual number of *tagin,* and those extra *tagin* indicate that there is an allusion hidden in the word or phrase in which they occur. See illustration.

(a)

(a) Usual פ; (b) פ with three *tagin, Machzor Vitry*; (c) פ with five *tagin, Badei HaAron.*

Sefer Tagin enumerates eighty-three words in the Torah in which the letter פ is written with *tagin* — three *tagin,* according to the Paris edition and *Badei HaAron*; five, according to the *Machzor Vitry* edition. See illustration. The words פָּנִים and הַמִּשְׁפָּט (see the Baal HaTurim, s.v., כִּי הַמִּשְׁפָּט, below) of our verse appear on that list, but the word בַּמִּשְׁפָּט does not. However, the manuscript of *Peirush HaRokeach* shows *tagin* on the letters פ of פָּנִים and בַּמִּשְׁפָּט, implying that the scribe who wrote that manuscript may have had access to a variant version of *Sefer Tagin,* one that is no longer extant.

57. The name of the letter פ can be spelled in three different ways: פֵּ״א פֵּ״ה פֵּ״י. The spelling פֵּ״ה is reminiscent of the word פֶּה, *mouth,* while the spelling פֵּ״י recalls the word פִּי, *mouth of* (see note 58).

58. *Peirush HaRokeach*; see *Kesubos* 36a. In *Peirush HaRokeach,* the full verse from *Proverbs* is adduced: פְּתַח פִּיךָ לְאִלֵּם אֶל דִּין כָּל בְּנֵי חֲלוֹף, *Open your mouth on behalf of the mute for justice — [on behalf of] all orphaned children. Peirush HaRokeach* states that the two letters פ of our verse (see second paragraph of note 56 above) are written with *tagin* to allude to that verse, which begins with a פ and ends with a פ. If that

Letters with three *tagin*
Letters with one *tag*
Letters with no *tagin*

א/יז כַּקָּטֹן כַּגָּדֹל תִּשְׁמָעוּן לֹא תָגוּרוּ מִפְּנֵי־אִישׁ כִּי הַמִּשְׁפָּט לֵאלֹהִים הוּא וְהַדָּבָר אֲשֶׁר יִקְשֶׁה מִכֶּם

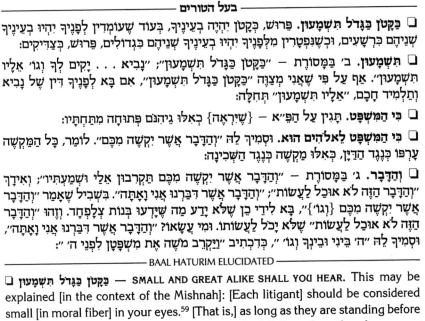

בעל הטורים

❑ **כַּקָּטֹן כַּגָּדֹל תִּשְׁמָעוּן.** פֵּרוּשׁ, כְּקָטָן יִהְיֶה בְעֵינֶיךָ, בְּעוֹד שֶׁעוֹמְדִין לְפָנֶיךָ יִהְיוּ בְעֵינֶיךָ שְׁנֵיהֶם כִּרְשָׁעִים, וּכְשֶׁנִּפְטָרִין מִלְּפָנֶיךָ יִהְיוּ בְעֵינֶיךָ שְׁנֵיהֶם כִּגְדוֹלִים, פֵּרוּשׁ, כְּצַדִּיקִים:

❑ **תִּשְׁמָעוּן.** ב׳ בַּמָּסוֹרֶת – ״כַּקָּטֹן כַּגָּדֹל תִּשְׁמָעוּן״; ״נָבִיא . . . יָקִים לְךָ וְגוֹ׳ אֵלָיו תִּשְׁמָעוּן״. אַף עַל פִּי שֶׁאֲנִי מְצַוֶּה ״כַּקָּטֹן כַּגָּדֹל תִּשְׁמָעוּן״, אִם בָּא לְפָנֶיךָ דִּין שֶׁל נָבִיא וְתַלְמִיד חָכָם, ״אֵלָיו תִּשְׁמָעוּן״ תְּחִלָּה:

❑ **כִּי הַמִּשְׁפָּט.** תָּגִין עַל הַפֵּ״א – {שֶׁיִּרְאֶה} כְּאִלּוּ גֵיהִנֹּם פְּתוּחָה מִתַּחְתָּיו:

❑ **כִּי הַמִּשְׁפָּט לֵאלֹהִים הוּא.** וּסְמִיךְ לֵהּ ״וְהַדָּבָר אֲשֶׁר יִקְשֶׁה מִכֶּם״. לוֹמַר, כָּל הַמַּקְשֶׁה עָרְפּוֹ כְּנֶגֶד הַדַּיָּן, כְּאִלּוּ מַקְשֶׁה כְּנֶגֶד הַשְּׁכִינָה:

❑ **וְהַדָּבָר.** ג׳ בַּמָּסוֹרֶת – ״וְהַדָּבָר אֲשֶׁר יִקְשֶׁה מִכֶּם תַּקְרִבוּן אֵלַי וּשְׁמַעְתִּיו״; וְאִידָךְ ״וְהַדָּבָר הַזֶּה לֹא אוּכַל לַעֲשׂוֹת״; ״וְהַדָּבָר אֲשֶׁר דִּבַּרְנוּ אֲנִי וָאַתָּה״. בִּשְׁבִיל שֶׁאָמַר ״וְהַדָּבָר אֲשֶׁר יִקְשֶׁה מִכֶּם {וְגוֹ׳}״, בָּא לִידֵי כֵן שֶׁלֹּא יָדַע מַה שֶּׁיָּדְעוּ בְּנוֹת צְלָפְחָד. וְזֶהוּ ״וְהַדָּבָר הַזֶּה לֹא אוּכַל לַעֲשׂוֹת״ שֶׁלֹּא יָכֹל לַעֲשׂוֹתוֹ. וּמִי עֲשָׂאוֹ? ״וְהַדָּבָר אֲשֶׁר דִּבַּרְנוּ אֲנִי וָאַתָּה״, וּסְמִיךְ לֵהּ ״ה׳ בֵּינִי וּבֵינְךָ וְגוֹ׳ ״, כִּדְכְתִיב ״וַיַּקְרֵב מֹשֶׁה אֶת מִשְׁפָּטָן לִפְנֵי ה׳ ״:

BAAL HATURIM ELUCIDATED

❑ **כַּקָּטֹן כַּגָּדֹל תִּשְׁמָעוּן** — SMALL AND GREAT ALIKE SHALL YOU HEAR. This may be explained [in the context of the Mishnah]: [Each litigant] should be considered small [in moral fiber] in your eyes.[59] [That is,] as long as they are standing before you, they should both be considered as wicked.[60] But when they leave your presence, they should both be considered as great [of stature], i.e., as righteous people.[61]

❑ **תִּשְׁמָעוּן** — SHALL YOU HEAR. The masoretic note, ב׳, means that this word appears twice in the *Tanach*: (i) here, כַּקָּטֹן כַּגָּדֹל תִּשְׁמָעוּן, *small and great alike shall you hear;* and (ii) נָבִיא . . . יָקִים לְךָ . . . אֵלָיו תִּשְׁמָעוּן, *A prophet . . . [HASHEM] shall establish for you — to him shall you hearken* (*Deuteronomy* 18:15). [The similarity of expression can be interpreted as if God is alluding to a Talmudic passage:] "Although I am commanding, *small and great alike shall you hear,* if a case involving a prophet or a Torah sage comes before you, *to him shall you hearken* first[62] [i.e., you should try the case in which he is a party before any other cases].[63]

---

were the Baal HaTurim's intention, however, he would have adduced the verse in its entirety. Additionally, it is clear from his comment to הַמִּשְׁפָּט that he did not have the reading בַּמִּשְׁפָּט in the manuscript of the *Sefer Tagin* before him. Perhaps, the Baal HaTurim interprets the *tagin* as indicating that the פ should be understood as if it were doubled, thus alluding to the doubled פ of פְּתַח פִּיךָ (*VeChur LaZahav*).

59. *Avos* 1:8.

60. In other words, do not be awed by a litigant's exalted political, economic, social, etc., status (*Rabbeinu Ovadiah*).

61. *Peirush HaRokeach.*

62. *Shevuos* 30a.

63. According to *Tosafos* the priority treatment is only given when the two cases arrive before

small and great alike shall you hear; you shall not tremble before any man, for the judgment is God's; but the matter that will be too difficult for you, you shall

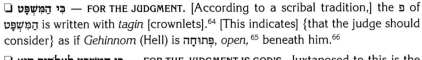

BAAL HATURIM ELUCIDATED

❑ כִּי הַמִּשְׁפָּט — FOR THE JUDGMENT. [According to a scribal tradition,] the פ of הַמִּשְׁפָּט is written with *tagin* [crownlets].[64] [This indicates] {that the judge should consider} as if *Gehinnom* (Hell) is פְּתוּחָה, *open,*[65] beneath him.[66]

❑ כִּי הַמִּשְׁפָּט לֵאלֹהִים הוּא — FOR THE JUDGMENT IS GOD'S. Juxtaposed to this is the phrase, וְהַדָּבָר אֲשֶׁר יִקְשֶׁה מִכֶּם, *but the matter that will be too difficult*[67] *for you.* This indicates that anyone who acts with stiff-necked stubbornness against a judge is considered as acting stubbornly against God.[68]

❑ וְהַדָּבָר — BUT THE MATTER. The masoretic note, ג׳, means that this word appears three times in the *Tanach*: (i) here, וְהַדָּבָר אֲשֶׁר יִקְשֶׁה מִכֶּם תַּקְרִבוּן אֵלַי וּשְׁמַעְתִּיו, *but the matter that will be too difficult for you, you shall bring to me and I shall hear it;* (ii) וְהַדָּבָר הַזֶּה לֹא אוּכַל לַעֲשׂוֹת, *but this matter I shall not be able to do* (*I Kings* 20:9); and (iii) וְהַדָּבָר אֲשֶׁר דִּבַּרְנוּ אֲנִי וָאָתָּה, *but the matter of which we have spoken, I and you* (*I Samuel* 20:23). [The similarity of expression may be explained according to the Midrash:] Because [Moses] said [here], *"But the matter that is too difficult for you, [you shall bring to me],"* [therefore] he came into a situation in which he did not know that which the daughters of Zelophehad knew. Thus [Moses said], *"But this matter I shall not be able to do,* i.e., he is not able to do it." [If so,] who will do it? [The answer is in the verse:] *But the matter of which we have spoken, I and you,* juxtaposed to which is, . . . ה׳ בֵּינִי וּבֵינְךָ, *HASHEM [will be the witness] between me and you [forever]*; as it is written, *And Moses brought their claim before HASHEM* (*Numbers* 27:5).[69]

---

the judge at the same time. When one arrives before the other, the earlier one takes precedence. The Baal HaTurim, however, writes: The judge must give precedence to the case that comes before him first, as it is stated, *small and great alike shall you hear.* Nevertheless, he must hear the case of a Torah sage first, even if that case came later, for that is a display of honor for his Torah [knowledge] (*Tur, Choshen Mishpat* 15:1).

64. See note 56 above.

65. That is, the unusual פ stands for פְּתוּחָה, *open.*
It is noteworthy that the word תָּג may be interpreted as the abbreviation of תַּחְתָּיו גֵּיהִנֹּם. Thus, תָּג פ׳ may be understood as *beneath him, Gehinnom is open* (*VeChur LaZahav*).

66. *Sanhedrin* 7a.

67. The verb root קשה can refer to hardness, difficulty or stubbornness. In the context of our verse it means *it will be difficult,* but the Baal HaTurim's allusion interprets it as *he will be stubborn.*

68. *Sanhedrin* 110a — Whoever challenges his Torah teacher['s authority] is like one who challenges God . . .; whoever picks a quarrel with his teacher is like one who picks a quarrel with God . . .; whoever complains about his teacher is like one who complains about God.

69. *Sifrei* (also *Sanhedrin* 8a; cited by *Rashi*) — [Moses' statement is viewed as antithetical to his usual demeanor as the humblest of men. Therefore] God said to Moses, "Will you decide the difficult case? By your life, I will show you that you will not [be able to] judge the difficult case. I will send a [relatively simple] case before you, [one] that your student's student will be able to decide, yet you will be incapable of trying that case." To what does this refer? To the case of the daughters of Zelophehad (see *Numbers* 27:1-11).

יח תַּקְרִבוּן אֵלַי וּשְׁמַעְתִּיו: וָאֲצַוֶּה אֶתְכֶם בָּעֵת הַהִוא
יט אֵת כָּל־הַדְּבָרִים אֲשֶׁר תַּעֲשׂוּן: וַנִּסַּע מֵחֹרֵב וַנֵּלֶךְ
אֵת כָּל־הַמִּדְבָּר הַגָּדוֹל וְהַנּוֹרָא הַהוּא אֲשֶׁר
רְאִיתֶם דֶּרֶךְ הַר הָאֱמֹרִי כַּאֲשֶׁר צִוָּה יהוה אֱלֹהֵינוּ
כ אֹתָנוּ וַנָּבֹא עַד קָדֵשׁ בַּרְנֵעַ: וָאֹמַר אֲלֵכֶם בָּאתֶם
כא עַד־הַר הָאֱמֹרִי אֲשֶׁר־יהוה אֱלֹהֵינוּ נֹתֵן לָנוּ: רְאֵה
נָתַן יהוה אֱלֹהֶיךָ לְפָנֶיךָ אֶת־הָאָרֶץ עֲלֵה רֵשׁ
כַּאֲשֶׁר דִּבֶּר יהוה אֱלֹהֵי אֲבֹתֶיךָ לָךְ אַל־תִּירָא
שלישי כב וְאַל־תֵּחָת: וַתִּקְרְבוּן אֵלַי כֻּלְּכֶם וַתֹּאמְרוּ נִשְׁלְחָה
אֲנָשִׁים לְפָנֵינוּ וְיַחְפְּרוּ־לָנוּ אֶת־הָאָרֶץ וְיָשִׁבוּ
אֹתָנוּ דָּבָר אֶת־הַדֶּרֶךְ אֲשֶׁר נַעֲלֶה־בָּהּ וְאֵת
כג הֶעָרִים אֲשֶׁר נָבֹא אֲלֵיהֶן: וַיִּיטַב בְּעֵינַי הַדָּבָר
וָאֶקַּח מִכֶּם שְׁנֵים עָשָׂר אֲנָשִׁים אִישׁ אֶחָד
כד לַשָּׁבֶט: וַיִּפְנוּ וַיַּעֲלוּ הָהָרָה וַיָּבֹאוּ עַד־נַחַל אֶשְׁכֹּל

בעל הטורים

(יז־יח) וּשְׁמַעְתִּיו. וָאֲצַוֶּה אֶתְכֶם. אַזְהָרָה לְצִבּוּר, שֶׁתְּהֵא אֵימַת הַדַּיָּן עֲלֵיהֶם:

(יט) הַמִּדְבָּר הַגָּדוֹל. מָלֵא וָי״ו – נָחָשׁ, שָׂרָף, {וְ}עַקְרָב, {וְ}צִמָּאוֹן; צִיָּה, {וְ}צַלְמָוֶת:

❑ **וַנָּבֹא.** חָסֵר וָי״ו – לוֹמַר, חֲסַרְתֶּם ו׳ אֶלֶף רַגְלִי:

(כ) וָאֹמַר אֲלֵכֶם. חָסֵר יוּ״ד – נִתְחַסַּרְתֶּם עַל יְדֵי עֲשָׂרָה מְרַגְּלִים:

BAAL HATURIM ELUCIDATED

17-18. וּשְׁמַעְתִּיו וָאֲצַוֶּה אֶתְכֶם — AND I SHALL HEAR IT. AND I COMMANDED YOU. This is an admonition to the community that they should regard a judge with reverence.[70]

19. הַמִּדְבָּר הַגָּדוֹל — THAT GREAT WILDERNESS. [The word הַגָּדוֹל, literally, *the great,* is] spelled in full,[71] with a ו (= 6). [This is an allusion to the six factors that made the wilderness daunting:] snake, fiery-serpent {and} scorpion {and} thirst; desolation {and} the shadow of death.[72]

70. *Sanhedrin* 8a.

71. The word הַגָּדוֹל appears twenty-six times in the Torah; eighteen of those times it is spelled defectively, הַגָּדֹל, without a ו; the remaining eight times it is spelled in full, הַגָּדוֹל, with a ו. The Baal HaTurim explains the implication of the full spelling in our verse, but not in any of the other seven.

72. The six factors enumerated by the Baal HaTurim are gleaned from two verses: *He leads you through the great and awesome wilderness* — נָחָשׁ שָׂרָף וְעַקְרָב וְצִמָּאוֹן, *of snake, fiery serpent and scorpion and thirst* (8:15 below); and, *He has lead us in the wilderness . . .* בְּאֶרֶץ צִיָּה וְצַלְמָוֶת, *in a land of desolation and the shadow of death* (*Jeremiah* 2:6). The conjunctive prefixes

bring to me and I shall hear it." [18] *I commanded you at that time all the things that you should do.*

[19] *We journeyed from Horeb and we went through the entire great wilderness — that awesome one — that you saw, by way of the Amorite mountain, as* HASHEM, *our God, commanded us, and we came until Kadesh-barnea.*

[20] *Then I said to you, "You have come until the Amorite mountain that* HASHEM, *our God, gives us.* [21] *See —* HASHEM, *your God, has placed the land before you; go up and possess, as* HASHEM, *God of your forefathers, has spoken to you. Do not fear and do not lose resolve."*

[22] *All of you approached me and said, "Let us send men ahead of us and let them spy out the land, and bring word back to us: the road on which we should ascend and the cities to which we should come."*

[23] *The idea was good in my eyes, so I took from you twelve men, one man for each tribe.* [24] *They turned and ascended the mountain and came until the Valley of Eshcol,*

BAAL HATURIM ELUCIDATED

❑ **וַנָּבֹא** — AND WE CAME. [This word is spelled] defectively,[73] without a ו (= 6). This indicates [that Moses told them,] "You are missing six thousand[74] people."

20. וָאֹמַר אֲלֵכֶם — THEN I SAID TO YOU. [The word אֲלֵכֶם is spelled] defectively,[75] without a י (= 10). [This indicates that Moses told them further:[76]] "You have become diminished because of ten [of the] spies."[77]

-וְ, *and,* that appear in the text in braces are based on the exact wording of their respective verses and appear in some editions of the Baal HaTurim. Most editions, however, including the early printed editions and *Shoham Yakar's* manuscript edition, omit those prefixes.

73. A masoretic note reads: ג׳ חֲסֵרִים בְּלִישָׁנָא, *The term* [נָבוֹא, with and without a prefix] *is spelled defectively* [without a ו] *three times* [in the *Tanach*]. The three are: (i) וַנָּבֹא in our verse; (ii-iii) נָבֹא in verse 22 below and in *II Kings* 7:12. The term appears spelled in full — נָבוֹא — in eleven other verses.

74. The Baal HaTurim gives no indication regarding the identity of the six thousand men to whom he refers. The phrase ו׳ אֶלֶף רַגְלִי, literally, *six thousand on foot,* recalls the verse כְּשֵׁשׁ מֵאוֹת אֶלֶף רַגְלִי הַגְּבָרִים, *about six hundred thousand men on foot* (*Exodus* 12:37), the number of men aged twenty to sixty who left Egypt at the exodus. *Shoham Yakar* suggests that the word מֵאוֹת was inadvertently omitted from the manuscripts and from there to the printed editions. Accordingly, the number refers to the count of those who died as a consequence of the spies' evil report (see *Numbers* 14:11-35; see the Baal HaTurim's next comment).

75. See note 36 above.

76. See the Baal HaTurim's previous comment with note 74.

77. Verses 19-21 are Moses' introductory words regarding the incident of the spies, about which he intends to admonish the people. The omitted י (= 10) indicates that only ten of the spies were responsible for the dire consequences.

כה וַיֵּרְגְּל֖וּ אֹתָ֑הּ וַיִּקְח֤וּ בְיָדָם֙ מִפְּרִ֣י הָאָ֔רֶץ וַיּוֹרִ֖דוּ
אֵלֵ֑ינוּ וַיָּשִׁ֤בוּ אֹתָ֙נוּ֙ דָבָ֔ר וַיֹּ֣אמְר֔וּ טוֹבָ֣ה הָאָ֔רֶץ
כו אֲשֶׁר־יְהוָֹ֥ה אֱלֹהֵ֖ינוּ נֹתֵ֣ן לָ֑נוּ וְלֹ֣א אֲבִיתֶ֔ם לַעֲלֹ֑ת
כז וַתַּמְר֕וּ אֶת־פִּ֖י יְהוָֹ֣ה אֱלֹהֵיכֶ֑ם וַתֵּרָגְנ֣וּ בְאָהֳלֵיכֶ֔ם
וַתֹּ֣אמְר֔וּ בְּשִׂנְאַ֤ת יְהוָֹה֙ אֹתָ֔נוּ הוֹצִיאָ֖נוּ מֵאֶ֣רֶץ
כח מִצְרָ֑יִם לָתֵ֥ת אֹתָ֛נוּ בְּיַ֥ד הָאֱמֹרִ֖י לְהַשְׁמִידֵֽנוּ: אָנָ֣ה ׀
אֲנַ֣חְנוּ עֹלִ֗ים אַחֵ֠ינוּ הֵמַ֨סּוּ אֶת־לְבָבֵ֜נוּ לֵאמֹ֗ר עַ֣ם
גָּד֤וֹל וָרָם֙ מִמֶּ֔נּוּ עָרִ֛ים גְּדֹלֹ֥ת וּבְצֻרֹ֖ת בַּשָּׁמָ֑יִם
כט וְגַם־בְּנֵ֥י עֲנָקִ֖ים רָאִ֥ינוּ שָֽׁם: וָאֹמַ֖ר אֲלֵכֶ֑ם לֹא־
ל תַעַרְצ֥וּן וְלֹֽא־תִֽירְא֖וּן מֵהֶֽם: יְהוָֹ֤ה אֱלֹהֵיכֶם֙
הַהֹלֵ֣ךְ לִפְנֵיכֶ֔ם ה֖וּא יִלָּחֵ֣ם לָכֶ֑ם כְּכֹ֤ל אֲשֶׁ֨ר עָשָׂ֤ה
לא אִתְּכֶם֙ בְּמִצְרַ֔יִם לְעֵינֵיכֶֽם: וּבַמִּדְבָּר֙ אֲשֶׁ֣ר רָאִ֔יתָ

— בעל הטורים —

(כח) הֵמַסּוּ. וּבִיהוֹשֻׁעַ אוֹמֵר "הִמְסִיו". עַל יְדֵי עֲשָׂרָה מְרַגְּלִים:

❑ לְבָבֵנוּ. ד' בַּמָּסוֹרֶת – "הֵמַסּוּ אֶת לְבָבֵנוּ"; "נַּשְׁמַע וַיִּמַּס לְבָבֵנוּ"; "לְהַטּוֹת לְבָבֵנוּ"; "נְשָׂא לְבָבֵנוּ אֶל כַּפָּיִם". אֲחֵרִים נָמַס לְבָבָם מִפְּנֵיכֶם, כְּדִכְתִיב "נַּשְׁמַע וַיִּמַּס לְבָבֵנוּ", עַל כֵּן הָיָה לָכֶם לְהַטּוֹת לְבַבְכֶם אֵלָיו. וְלֹא עֲשִׂיתֶם כֵּן, אֶלָּא אֲמַרְתֶּם "הֵמַסּוּ אֶת לְבָבֵנוּ", עַל כֵּן "נְשָׂא לְבָבֵנוּ אֶל כַּפָּיִם", וּסְמִיךְ לֵהּ "סַכּוֹתָה בָאַף וַתִּרְדְּפֵנוּ", כְּדִכְתִיב "וַיִּרְדְּפוּ אֶתְכֶם כַּאֲשֶׁר תַּעֲשֶׂינָה הַדְּבֹרִים":

(לא) וּבַמִּדְבָּר אֲשֶׁר רָאִיתָ. לְשׁוֹן יָחִיד. "בְּכָל הַדֶּרֶךְ אֲשֶׁר הֲלַכְתֶּם", לְשׁוֹן רַבִּים. שֶׁלֹּא הָיָה

— BAAL HATURIM ELUCIDATED —

28. הֵמַסּוּ — **THEY HAVE MELTED.** In *Joshua* (14:8), [the parallel term] הִמְסִיו [which has an additional י (= 10)] is used [for *they have melted*]. This indicates that it was because of ten [of the] spies.[78]

❑ לְבָבֵנוּ — **OUR HEARTS.** The masoretic note, ד, means that this word appears four times in the *Tanach*: (i) here, הֵמַסּוּ אֶת לְבָבֵנוּ, [*our brothers*] *have melted our hearts*; (ii) וַנִּשְׁמַע וַיִּמַּס לְבָבֵנוּ, *We heard and our hearts melted*[79] (*Joshua* 2:11); (iii) לְהַטּוֹת

---

78. Caleb was recalling to Joshua the time that he and Joshua were sent, together with ten other spies, each representing his respective tribe, to spy out the Land of Canaan. He said, *"You are aware of the matter that* HASHEM *told Moses . . . Moses the servant of* HASHEM *sent me . . . to spy out the land and I brought back a [favorable] report as was in my heart. My brethren who went up with me [*הִמְסִיו*], have melted the heart of the people . . ."* (*Joshua* 14:6-8). Whereas Caleb did

not specify that "my brethren" numbered ten, Scripture records his word as הִמְסִיו (with a superfluous י), rather than הֵמַסּוּ (which Moses used), to allude to the number of spies involved in the misdeed.

79. Before leading Israel into the Land of Canaan, Joshua sent two spies [Caleb and Phinehas (*Tanchuma, Shelach* 1)] to spy out Jericho. They took lodging at the home of Rahab the innkeeper. She saw through their

and spied it out. [25] *They took in their hands from the fruit of the land and brought it down to us; they brought back word to us and said, "Good is the land that* HASHEM, *our God, gives us!"*
[26] *But you did not wish to ascend, and you rebelled against the word of* HASHEM, *your God.* [27] *You slandered in your tents and said, "Because of* HASHEM*'s hatred for us did He take us out of the land of Egypt, to deliver us into the hand of the Amorite to destroy us.* [28] *To where shall we ascend? Our brothers have melted our hearts, saying, 'A people greater and taller than we, cities great and fortified to the heavens, and even children of giants have we seen there!'"*
[29] *Then I said to you, "Do not be broken and do not fear them!* [30] HASHEM, *your God, Who goes before you — He shall make war for you, like everything He did for you in Egypt, before your eyes.* [31] *And in the wilderness, as you have seen,*

BAAL HATURIM ELUCIDATED

לְבָבֵנוּ, *to turn our hearts*[80] (*I Kings* 8:58); and (iv) נִשָּׂא לְבָבֵנוּ אֶל כַּפָּיִם, *Let us raise our hearts toward the clouds* (*Lamentations* 3:41).[81] [The similarity of expression may be understood as an admonition to the people:] "The hearts of other nations melted before you, as it is written, '*We* [*Canaanites*] *heard and our hearts melted.*' Therefore it would have been appropriate for you to turn your hearts to Him.[82] But you did not act in that manner; rather, you said, '[*Our brothers*] *have melted our hearts.*' Therefore it was necessary to *raise our hearts toward the clouds.*"[83] For juxtaposed to that is, סַכּוֹתָה בָאַף וַתִּרְדְּפֵנוּ, *You have covered Yourself with anger and pursued us* (*Lamentations* 3:43). And thus is written (v. 44 below), וַיִּרְדְּפוּ אֶתְכֶם כַּאֲשֶׁר תַּעֲשֶׂינָה הַדְּבֹרִים, [*The Amorite . . .*] *pursued you as the bees would do.*

❑ {The Baal HaTurim's comment to עָרִים גְּדֹלֹת וּבְצוּרֹת בַּשָּׁמָיִם appears at 3:5 below.}

29. {The Baal HaTurim's comment to לֹא תַעַרְצוּן וְלֹא תִירְאוּן appears at *Exodus* 9:30.}

31. וּבַמִּדְבָּר אֲשֶׁר רָאִיתָ — AND IN THE WILDERNESS, AS YOU HAVE SEEN. [The word רָאִיתָ, *you have seen,* is] a singular verb. [But the latter half of the verse states,] בְּכָל הַדֶּרֶךְ אֲשֶׁר הֲלַכְתֶּם, *on the entire way that you traveled* [using the form הֲלַכְתֶּם, *you traveled*], a plural verb.[83a] [This indicates] that the path was not

disguises and confided to them that the Canaanites were afraid of Joshua and the Israelites who were coming to conquer their land. She told them, *"We have heard how* HASHEM *dried up the waters of the Sea of Reeds . . . and what you did to the two kings of the Amorites . . . Sihon and Og . . . We heard and our hearts melted . . ."* (*Joshua* 2:10-11).

80. At the dedication of the *Beis HaMikdash,* King Solomon blessed the nation, *"May* HASHEM, *our God, be with us . . . to turn our hearts to Him, to walk in His ways . . ."* (*I Kings* 8:57-58).

81. The full verse reads: *Let us raise our hearts toward the clouds, to God in the heavens.*

82. As implied by the verse from *Kings.*

83. In prayer to God in the heavens above.

83a. The Baal HaTurim addresses a similar question in his comments to verse 8 above (see note 32 there).

אֲשֶׁר נְשָׂאֲךָ֙ יְהוָ֣ה אֱלֹהֶ֔יךָ כַּאֲשֶׁ֥ר יִשָּׂא־אִ֖ישׁ
אֶת־בְּנ֑וֹ בְּכָל־הַדֶּ֙רֶךְ֙ אֲשֶׁ֣ר הֲלַכְתֶּ֔ם עַד־בֹּאֲכֶ֖ם
לב עַד־הַמָּק֥וֹם הַזֶּֽה: וּבַדָּבָ֖ר הַזֶּ֑ה אֵֽינְכֶם֙ מַאֲמִינִ֔ם
לג בַּֽיהוָ֖ה אֱלֹהֵיכֶֽם: הַהֹלֵ֣ךְ לִפְנֵיכֶ֣ם בַּדֶּ֗רֶךְ לָת֥וּר לָכֶ֛ם
מָק֖וֹם לַֽחֲנֹֽתְכֶ֑ם בָּאֵ֣שׁ ׀ לַ֗יְלָה לַרְאֹֽתְכֶם֙ בַּדֶּ֙רֶךְ֙ אֲשֶׁ֣ר
לד תֵּֽלְכוּ־בָ֔הּ וּבֶֽעָנָ֖ן יוֹמָֽם: וַיִּשְׁמַ֥ע יְהוָ֖ה אֶת־ק֣וֹל
לה דִּבְרֵיכֶ֑ם וַיִּקְצֹ֖ף וַיִּשָּׁבַ֥ע לֵאמֹֽר: אִם־יִרְאֶ֥ה אִישׁ֙
בָּֽאֲנָשִׁ֣ים הָאֵ֔לֶּה הַדּ֥וֹר הָרָ֖ע הַזֶּ֑ה אֵ֚ת הָאָ֣רֶץ הַטּוֹבָ֔ה

— בעל הטורים —

הַדֶּרֶךְ לְכֻלָּם בְּשָׁוֶה. אֶלָּא לְכָל אֶחָד {וְאֶחָד} לְפִי מַה שֶׁהָיָה צָרִיךְ הָיָה הֶעָנָן נוֹשֵׂא אוֹתוֹ, יֵשׁ בִּגְבוֹהַּ וְיֵשׁ בְּנָמוּךְ:

(לב) אֵֽינְכֶם מַאֲמִינִם. חָסֵר יוּ"ד – שֶׁעֶשֶׂר פְּעָמִים נִסִּיתֶם אוֹתוֹ:

(לה) אִישׁ בָּֽאֲנָשִׁים הָאֵלֶּה. סוֹפֵי תֵבוֹת "מֹשֶׁה" – שֶׁגַּם הוּא בִּכְלַל הַשְּׁבוּעָה:

☐ בָּֽאֲנָשִׁים. ג' בַּמָּסוֹרֶת – "אִם יִרְאֶה אִישׁ בָּֽאֲנָשִׁים"; "וַיֵּחָלוּ בָֽאֲנָשִׁים הַזְּקֵנִים"; "זָקֵן בָּא בָֽאֲנָשִׁים". מְלַמֵּד שֶׁהָיְתָה הַגְּזֵרָה אַף עַל מֹשֶׁה וְאַהֲרֹן. דִּכְתִיב "בָּֽאֲנָשִׁים הַזְּקֵנִים" וּכְתִיב "זָקֵן בָּא בָֽאֲנָשִׁים", הַיְנוּ מֹשֶׁה וְאַהֲרֹן, שֶׁהָיוּ בָּאִים בְּאוּכְלוּסָא וְיוֹצְאִין בְּאוּכְלוּסָא:

— BAAL HATURIM ELUCIDATED —

the same for each of them. Rather, the cloud would provide for each {and every} individual according to his needs — some at the heights and some at the depths.[84,85]

32. אֵֽינְכֶם מַאֲמִינִם — YOU DO NOT BELIEVE. [The word מַאֲמִינִם is spelled] defectively, without a [second] י (= 10). [This is an admonition reminding the people] that on ten occasions you tested[85a] [God's patience].[86]

---

84. The clouds that accompanied the Israelites during their sojourn in the wilderness were seven in number: four on their four sides, one above them, one beneath their feet, and one in front of them to guide them. These clouds would lower the heights and raise the depths [so that the road would be level]; they would sweep away snakes and scorpions and anything else that stood in their path . . . (Sifrei, Bamidbar 1:34).

When the clouds leveled the road for the Israelites, it did so to a different degree for each individual: For the infirm it made the road smoother; for the more vigorous it left some elevations and depressions. This explains how all of the nation — the young and vigorous, the elderly and infirm — were able to cover the same distance, keeping pace with one another throughout their journey (VeChur LaZahav).

85. Peirush HaRokeach; see also the Baal Ha-Turim to Exodus 15:13, s.v., נָחִיתָ.

85a. See Numbers 14:22.

86. Peirush HaRokeach; Arachin 15a-b. The ten are: (i) At the Sea of Reeds, where the Israelites complained, "Were there no graves in Egypt, that you took us to die in the wilderness" (Exodus 14:11); (ii) after crossing the sea, the Israelites complained, "Just as we are coming out of the sea over here, so are the Egyptians coming out at another point, on the other side, and now they will renew their pursuit," as alluded to in the verse, They rebelled about the sea at the Sea of Reeds (Psalms 106:7); (iii-iv) when the manna first fell, the Israelites were commanded to eat it all and not to leave any over until the next morning, nevertheless some of them left over

that HASHEM, *your God, bore you, as a man carries his son, on the entire way that you traveled, until you arrived at this place.* [32] *Yet in this matter you do not believe in* HASHEM, *your God,* [33] *Who goes before you on the way to seek out for you a place for you to encamp, with fire by night to show you the road that you should travel and with a cloud by day!"*

[34] HASHEM *heard the sound of your words, and He was incensed and He swore, saying,* [35] *"If [even] a man among these men, this evil generation, shall see the good land*

BAAL HATURIM ELUCIDATED

35. אִישׁ בָּאֲנָשִׁים הָאֵלֶּה — A MAN AMONG THESE MEN. The final letters of these three words [may be rearranged to] spell the name מֹשֶׁה, *Moses.* For he was also included in the oath.[87]

❑ **בָּאֲנָשִׁים** — AMONG [THESE] MEN. The masoretic note, ג׳, means that this word appears three times in the *Tanach*:[88] (i) here, אִם יִרְאֶה אִישׁ בָּאֲנָשִׁים, *if* [*even*] *a man among the*[*se*] *men;* (ii) וַיָּחֵלּוּ בָּאֲנָשִׁים הַזְּקֵנִים, *they began among the men, the elders* (*Ezekiel* 9:6); זָקֵן בָּא בַאֲנָשִׁים, *an elder who comes among men* (*I Samuel* 17:12).[89] This [similarity of expression] teaches that the decree [of death in the desert] also included Moses and Aaron, as it is written, *among the men, the elders,*[90] and it is [also] written, *he is an elder, who comes among men,*[91] [verses] that refer to Moses and Aaron, for they would come with a multitude and leave with a multitude.

(see *Exodus* 16:19-20) and they were told not to gather manna on the Sabbath, yet some of them did go out in an attempt to gather manna (see *Exodus* 16:27); (v-vi) twice the nation improperly demanded meat (see *Exodus* 16:3 and *Numbers* 11:4); (vii-viii) twice the nation complained about a lack of water (see *Exodus* 15:24 and 17:2); (ix) the incident with the golden calf (*Exodus,* Ch. 32); and (x) the incident of the spies (*Numbers,* Chs. 13-14).

87. The verse could have stated tersely, אִם יִרְאוּ הָאֲנָשִׁים הָאֵלֶּה, *if these men will see,* rather than the more wordy, אִם יִרְאֶה אִישׁ בָּאֲנָשִׁים הָאֵלֶּה, *if a man among these men will see.* The Midrash (*Tanchuma, Vayeishev* 4) explains that the extraneous word אִישׁ, *a man,* is used to include Moses, who is elsewhere referred to with the phrase, וְהָאִישׁ מֹשֶׁה, *and the man Moses* (*Numbers* 12:3). The Baal HaTurim finds a second allusion to Moses in the final letters of אִישׁ בָּאֲנָשִׁים הָאֵלֶּה. Interestingly, *Peirush HaRokeach* finds that same allusion in the final letters of יִרְאֶה אִישׁ בָּאֲנָשִׁים.

88. The full note reads: ג׳ב׳קָמְצִין וְא׳פַּתָּח, *Three, two vowelized with a kamatz and one with a patach.* The different vowelizations indicate a subtle difference in meaning: אֲנָשִׁים means *men;* הָאֲנָשִׁים, with the definite article prefix -הָ, means *the men.* When the prepositional prefix -בְּ, *in* or *among,* is added to a word that begins with a *chataf* vowel, such as the א of אֲנָשִׁים, the vowel under the -ב changes to that of the *chataf,* thus אֲנָשִׁים, *men,* becomes בַּאֲנָשִׁים, *among men.* However, when the -בְּ prefix is added to a word that begins with the definite article prefix -ה, the ה is dropped, and its vowel is adopted by the -ב, thus הָאֲנָשִׁים, *the men,* becomes בָּאֲנָשִׁים, *among the men.* [The fact that the prefix sometimes appears as a -בּ and sometimes as a -ב is a function of its relationship to the word that precedes it. The meaning is the same, with or without the *dagesh.*]

89. An idiomatic description of Jesse, father of David, as one of the elders of the nation. Whenever he would leave or enter, he was always *among men,* i.e., accompanied by multitudes of people (*Berachos* 58a).

90. That is, the elders are counted among the men.

91. That is, the term זָקֵן, *elder,* as used here, refers to one who is always accompanied by multitudes (see note 89 above).

לו אֲשֶׁר נִשְׁבַּעְתִּי לָתֵת לַאֲבֹתֵיכֶם: זוּלָתִי כָּלֵב
בֶּן־יְפֻנֶּה הוּא יִרְאֶנָּה וְלוֹ־אֶתֵּן אֶת־הָאָרֶץ אֲשֶׁר
לז דָּרַךְ־בָּהּ וּלְבָנָיו יַעַן אֲשֶׁר מִלֵּא אַחֲרֵי יהוה: גַּם־בִּי
הִתְאַנַּף יהוה בִּגְלַלְכֶם לֵאמֹר גַּם־אַתָּה לֹא־תָבֹא
לח שָׁם: יְהוֹשֻׁעַ בִּן־נוּן הָעֹמֵד לְפָנֶיךָ הוּא יָבֹא שָׁמָּה
רביעי לט אֹתוֹ חַזֵּק כִּי־הוּא יַנְחִלֶנָּה אֶת־יִשְׂרָאֵל: וְטַפְּכֶם
אֲשֶׁר אֲמַרְתֶּם לָבַז יִהְיֶה וּבְנֵיכֶם אֲשֶׁר לֹא־יָדְעוּ
הַיּוֹם טוֹב וָרָע הֵמָּה יָבֹאוּ שָׁמָּה וְלָהֶם אֶתְּנֶנָּה וְהֵם
מ יִירָשׁוּהָ: וְאַתֶּם פְּנוּ לָכֶם וּסְעוּ הַמִּדְבָּרָה דֶּרֶךְ
מא יַם־סוּף: וַתַּעֲנוּ ׀ וַתֹּאמְרוּ אֵלַי חָטָאנוּ לַיהוה
אֲנַחְנוּ נַעֲלֶה וְנִלְחַמְנוּ כְּכֹל אֲשֶׁר־צִוָּנוּ יהוה
אֱלֹהֵינוּ וַתַּחְגְּרוּ אִישׁ אֶת־כְּלֵי מִלְחַמְתּוֹ וַתָּהִינוּ
מב לַעֲלֹת הָהָרָה: וַיֹּאמֶר יהוה אֵלַי אֱמֹר לָהֶם לֹא
תַעֲלוּ וְלֹא־תִלָּחֲמוּ כִּי אֵינֶנִּי בְּקִרְבְּכֶם וְלֹא תִּנָּגְפוּ
מג לִפְנֵי אֹיְבֵיכֶם: וָאֲדַבֵּר אֲלֵיכֶם וְלֹא שְׁמַעְתֶּם
מד וַתַּמְרוּ אֶת־פִּי יהוה וַתָּזִדוּ וַתַּעֲלוּ הָהָרָה: וַיֵּצֵא
הָאֱמֹרִי הַיֹּשֵׁב בָּהָר הַהוּא לִקְרַאתְכֶם וַיִּרְדְּפוּ
אֶתְכֶם כַּאֲשֶׁר תַּעֲשֶׂינָה הַדְּבֹרִים וַיַּכְּתוּ אֶתְכֶם
מה בְּשֵׂעִיר עַד־חָרְמָה: וַתָּשֻׁבוּ וַתִּבְכּוּ לִפְנֵי יהוה
וְלֹא־שָׁמַע יהוה בְּקֹלְכֶם וְלֹא הֶאֱזִין אֲלֵיכֶם:

בעל הטורים

(**לח**) **יְהוֹשֻׁעַ בִּן נוּן הָעֹמֵד לְפָנֶיךָ.** שֶׁגָּדוֹל שִׁמּוּשָׁהּ יוֹתֵר מִלִּמּוּדָהּ:

(**לט**) **יִירָשׁוּהָ.** ב׳ בַּמָּסֹרֶת – ״וְהֵם יִירָשׁוּהָ״; ״עַד עוֹלָם יִירָשׁוּהָ״. שֶׁנִּתְּנָה לָהֶם הָאָרֶץ יְרֻשַּׁת עוֹלָם. וּלְעוֹלָם לֹא הָיוּ גוֹלִין מִמֶּנָּה אִם לֹא שֶׁחָטְאוּ:

BAAL HATURIM ELUCIDATED

38. יְהוֹשֻׁעַ בִּן נוּן הָעֹמֵד לְפָנֶיךָ — JOSHUA SON OF NUN, WHO STANDS BEFORE YOU.[92] [Joshua shall lead the people] because serving [one who teaches Torah] surpasses [merely] studying Torah[93] [under his tutelage].[93a]

92. That is, who stands before you, attending to your needs.

93. This is derived from the Torah's use of הָעֹמֵד, *who stands,* rather than הַלֹּמֵד, *who studies* (*Ittur Bikkurim*). It is noteworthy that in the letter exchange known as אַ״ט בַּ״ח (see the Baal HaTurim to *Beha'alosecha* with note 103), the letters ל and ע are interchangeable. Accordingly, לֹמֵד may be understood as עֹמֵד, and עֹמֵד may be understood as לֹמֵד (*VeChur LaZahav*).

that I swore to give to your forefathers. ³⁶ Except for Caleb son of Jephunneh: He shall see it, and to him shall I give the land on which he walked, and to his children, because he followed HASHEM wholeheartedly."

³⁷ With me, as well, HASHEM became angry because of you, saying: You, too, shall not come there. ³⁸ Joshua son of Nun, who stands before you, he shall come there; strengthen him, for he shall cause Israel to inherit it. ³⁹ And as for your youngsters, of whom you said, "They will be taken captive," and your children who did not know good from evil this day — they will come there; to them shall I give it and they shall possess it. ⁴⁰ And as for you, turn yourselves around and journey to the wilderness, by way of the Sea of Reeds.

⁴¹ Then you spoke up and said to me, "We have sinned to HASHEM! We shall go up and do battle according to everything that HASHEM, our God, has commanded us!" Every man of you girded his weapons of war, and you were ready to ascend the mountain!

⁴² HASHEM said to me: Tell them, "Do not ascend and do not do battle, for I am not among you; so that you not be struck down before your enemies."

⁴³ So I spoke to you, but you did not listen. You rebelled against the word of HASHEM, and you were willful and climbed the mountain. ⁴⁴ The Amorite who dwell on that mountain went out against you and pursued you as the bees would do; they struck you in Seir until Hormah. ⁴⁵ Then you retreated and wept before HASHEM, but HASHEM did not listen to your voice and He did not hearken to you.

— BAAL HATURIM ELUCIDATED —

39. יִירָשׁוּהָ — [AND THEY] SHALL POSSESS IT. The masoretic note, ב׳, means that this word appears twice in the *Tanach*: (i) here, וְהֵם יִירָשׁוּהָ, *and they shall possess it;* and (ii) עַד עוֹלָם יִירָשׁוּהָ, *they shall possess it until eternity* (Isaiah 34:17). [The similarity of expression indicates] that the land was given to them as an eternal inheritance. And they would never have been exiled from it, if they had not sinned [when they were in the land].

44. {The Baal HaTurim's comment to this verse appears at verse 28 above.}

93a. *Pesikta Zutresa [Midrash Lekach Tov]; Berachos* 7b; *Ralbag* to *Joshua* 1:1.

מו וַתֵּשְׁבוּ בְקָדֵשׁ יָמִים רַבִּים כַּיָּמִים אֲשֶׁר יְשַׁבְתֶּם׃
ב א וַנֵּפֶן וַנִּסַּע הַמִּדְבָּרָה דֶּרֶךְ יַם־סוּף כַּאֲשֶׁר
דִּבֶּר יהוה אֵלָי וַנָּסָב אֶת־הַר־שֵׂעִיר יָמִים
חמישי ב־ג רַבִּים׃ וַיֹּאמֶר יהוה אֵלַי לֵאמֹר׃ רַב־לָכֶם סֹב

בעל הטורים

(מו) **כַּיָּמִים.** ד׳ בַּמָּסוֹרֶת — ״כַּיָּמִים אֲשֶׁר יְשַׁבְתֶּם״; ״כַּיָּמִים הָרִאשֹׁנִים״; ״כַּיָּמִים אֲשֶׁר נָחוּ בָהֶם הַיְּהוּדִים״; ״וְעַתָּה לֹא כַיָּמִים הָרִאשֹׁנִים״, בִּזְכַרְיָה בִּנְבוּאַת בַּיִת שֵׁנִי. וְזֶהוּ שֶׁפֵּרַשׁ רַשִׁ״י, שֶׁיָּשְׁבוּ בְקָדֵשׁ י״ט שָׁנָה, כְּמוֹ שֶׁיָּשְׁבוּ בִּשְׁאָר הַמַּסָּעוֹת. כְּמוֹ הָתָם ״כַּיָּמִים הָרִאשֹׁנִים״, שֶׁהָיוּ יָמִים אַחֲרוֹנִים כָּרִאשֹׁנִים, גַּם בְּכָאן הָיוּ יָמִים אֵלּוּ כַּיָּמִים הָאֲחֵרִים. וְהָתָם כִּי לֹא כַיָּמִים הָרִאשׁוֹנִים, דִּכְתִיב בְּהוּ ״וְלַיּוֹצֵא וְלַבָּא אֵין שָׁלוֹם״, אֶלָּא ״כַּיָּמִים אֲשֶׁר נָחוּ״, דִּכְתִיב ״כִּי זֶרַע הַשָּׁלוֹם הַגֶּפֶן תִּתֵּן פִּרְיָהּ וְגוֹ׳ ״ עַד ״וִהְיִיתֶם בְּרָכָה אַל תִּירָאוּ״:

ב (ג) **רַב לָכֶם סֹב.** תָּגִין עַל הַסָּמֶ״ךְ — לְפִי שֶׁכִּבֵּד אֶת אָבִיו שֶׁהָיָה בֶן שִׁשִּׁים בְּלִדְתּוֹ אוֹתָם. וּלְכָךְ עָתִיד לְהַחֲרִיב הַבַּיִת שֶׁהוּא שִׁשִּׁים אַמָּה:

BAAL HATURIM ELUCIDATED

46. **כַּיָּמִים** — AS THE DAYS. The masoretic note, ד׳, means that this word appears four times in the *Tanach*: (i) here, כַּיָּמִים אֲשֶׁר יְשַׁבְתֶּם, *as the days that you dwelt;* (ii) כַּיָּמִים הָרִאשֹׁנִים, *as the first days*[94] (*Deuteronomy* 10:10); (iii) כַּיָּמִים אֲשֶׁר נָחוּ בָהֶם הַיְּהוּדִים, *as the days during which the Jews rested* (*Esther* 9:22); and (iv) וְעַתָּה לֹא כַיָּמִים הָרִאשֹׁנִים, *but now, not as the earlier days,* in [the Book of] *Zechariah* (8:11), in the prophecy regarding the Second Temple.[94a] This [similarity of expression] is in accordance with *Rashi's* commentary, which explains that the nation spent nineteen years in Kadesh, the same amount of time they spent in all the other journeys collectively. Thus, just as there [at Mount Sinai the verse states], *as the first days,* for the last days were like the first,[95] so, too, here, these days [at Kadesh] were like the other days.[95a] Conversely, there [the later days, i.e., the

94. That verse teaches that Moses spent the same number of days on Mount Sinai — forty — the second time he ascended as he did the first time he ascended.

94a. That passage reads: *Thus said* HASHEM, *Master of Legions: Let your hands be strong, you who hear these days these words from the mouths of the prophets, which [were spoken] on the day that the foundation was laid for the Temple of* HASHEM, *Master of Legions — the Sanctuary — to be built. For before those days, people had no earnings, nor were there earnings from animals; those who travel back and forth had no peace because of the enemy; and I set everyone, man against his neighbor. But now, not as the earlier days am I toward the remnant of this people — the word of* HASHEM, *Master of Legions. For [then shall be] the seed of peace: The vine shall give her fruit, the land gives forth its produce, and the heavens give forth their dew. I have bestowed all these upon the remnant of this people. And it will happen that just as you, O House of Judah and the House of Israel, had been a curse for the nations, so will I save you and you shall be a blessing. Do not fear, and let your hands be strong* (Zechariah 8:9-13).

95. That is, both instances of Moses' remaining on the mountain were of equal duration — forty days.

95a. Although Israel actually spent forty years in the journey from Egypt to the Land of Israel, the first year was spent at Mount Sinai and the last year in the Plains of Moab on the border of Canaan. Thus, the journey itself took thirty-eight years. Nineteen of those years were spent while the nation encamped in Kadesh. The other

46 *You dwelt in Kadesh for many days, as the days that you dwelt.*

2

1 *We turned and journeyed to the Wilderness toward the Sea of Reeds, as HASHEM spoke to me, and we circled Mount Seir for many days.*

2 *HASHEM said to me, saying:* 3 *It is enough for you, circling*

BAAL HATURIM ELUCIDATED

days of the Second Temple] will be *not as the earlier days* about which it is written, וְלַיּוֹצֵא וְלַבָּא אֵין שָׁלוֹם, *and for the one who goes out and for the one who comes in there is no peace* (*Zechariah* 8:10). Rather, they will be as *the days during which* [*the Jews*] *rested,* and so it is written, כִּי זֶרַע הַשָּׁלוֹם הַגֶּפֶן תִּתֵּן פִּרְיָהּ . . . וִהְיִיתֶם בְּרָכָה אַל תִּירָאוּ, *For* [*then shall be*] *the seed of peace: The vine shall give her fruit . . . and you shall be a blessing; do not fear* (*Zechariah* 8:12-13).

II.

3. רַב לָכֶם סֹב — IT IS ENOUGH FOR YOU, CIRCLING. [According to a scribal tradition,] the letter ס (= 60) of the word סֹב, *circling,* is written with *tagin* [crownlets].[96] [They were not to provoke the children of Esau[97]] because he honored his father [Isaac][98] who was sixty years old when he begot him.[99] For this same reason, [Esau] was destined to destroy the Temple[100] that measured sixty cubits.[101]

nineteeen were divided among the other journeys and encampments (*Rashi* to *Numbers* 33:1).

96. See first paragraph of note 56 above.

The Paris edition of *Sefer Tagin* states that there are sixty words in which the letter ס is written with four *tagin* (see illustration). However, the list in that source enumerates only fifty-two of those instances, but סב is not included. The *Machzor Vitry* version of *Sefer Tagin* states that there are sixty-seven letters ס written with *tagin,* enumerating less than sixty; and סב does appear on that list.

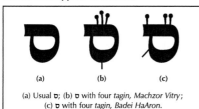

(a) (b) (c)

(a) Usual ס; (b) ס with four *tagin, Machzor Vitry;* (c) ס with four *tagin, Badei HaAron.*

97. In our passage (vv. 1-8), the Israelites are prohibited from provoking the children of Esau when they pass through their land.

98. See the Baal HaTurim to v. 5 below, s.v., יְרֻשָּׁה לְעֵשָׂו, with note 110.

99. *Peirush HaRokeach; Rimzei Rabbeinu Yoel;* see *Genesis* 25:26.

100. See *Devarim Rabbah* 1:17.

101. *Peirush HaRokeach.* This refers to the interior of the *Beis HaMikdash* which measured sixty *amos* [cubits] from east to west [i.e., front to back] and twenty *amos* from north to south (see *Middos* 4:7).

Alternatively: The Baal HaTurim refers to the height of the *Beis HaMikdash.* For the Temple destroyed by Esau's Roman descendants was the Second Temple, which had originally been built in the time of Ezra and Nehemiah and subsequently redesigned and rebuilt by Herod during the latter half of the Second Temple era. According to the Mishnah, that Temple stood one hundred *amos* tall (*Middos* 4:6). Nevertheless, when that Temple was originally built, it stood only sixty *amos* high (see *Ezra* 6:3). Thus, the Baal HaTurim's "sixty *amos*" refers to its size when it was first built (*VeChur LaZahav*).

Alternatively: There are three different measurements that are called אַמָּה, *cubit*: one comprises five *tefachim* (handbreadths); another, six *tefachim,* and the third, ten *tefachim* (commentary on *Bereishis Rabbah* ascribed to *Rashi,* 31:10, s.v., ולמה קורין; see also *Teshuvos Rama*

ד אֶת־הָהָר הַזֶּה פְּנוּ לָכֶם צָפֹנָה: וְאֶת־הָעָם צַו
לֵאמֹר אַתֶּם עֹבְרִים בִּגְבוּל אֲחֵיכֶם בְּנֵי־עֵשָׂו
הַיֹּשְׁבִים בְּשֵׂעִיר וְיִירְאוּ מִכֶּם וְנִשְׁמַרְתֶּם מְאֹד:
ה אַל־תִּתְגָּרוּ בָם כִּי לֹא־אֶתֵּן לָכֶם מֵאַרְצָם עַד
מִדְרַךְ כַּף־רָגֶל כִּי־יְרֻשָּׁה לְעֵשָׂו נָתַתִּי אֶת־הַר
ו שֵׂעִיר: אֹכֶל תִּשְׁבְּרוּ מֵאִתָּם בַּכֶּסֶף וַאֲכַלְתֶּם
ז וְגַם־מַיִם תִּכְרוּ מֵאִתָּם בַּכֶּסֶף וּשְׁתִיתֶם: כִּי יהוה
אֱלֹהֶיךָ בֵּרַכְךָ בְּכֹל מַעֲשֵׂה יָדֶךָ יָדַע לֶכְתְּךָ
אֶת־הַמִּדְבָּר הַגָּדֹל הַזֶּה זֶה | אַרְבָּעִים שָׁנָה יהוה
ח אֱלֹהֶיךָ עִמָּךְ לֹא חָסַרְתָּ דָּבָר: וַנַּעֲבֹר מֵאֵת אַחֵינוּ
בְנֵי־עֵשָׂו הַיֹּשְׁבִים בְּשֵׂעִיר מִדֶּרֶךְ הָעֲרָבָה מֵאֵילַת
*פסקא באמצע פסוק וּמֵעֶצְיֹן גָּבֶר * וַנֵּפֶן וַנַּעֲבֹר דֶּרֶךְ מִדְבַּר מוֹאָב:

בעל הטורים

(ד) **וְיִירְאוּ מִכֶּם.** כָּתוּב בִּשְׁנֵי יוּדִ״ן – בִּשְׁבִיל עֶשֶׂר בְּרָכוֹת שֶׁנִּתְבָּרֵךְ יַעֲקֹב:

(ה) **עַד מִדְרַךְ כַּף רָגֶל.** עַד ״דָּרַךְ כּוֹכָב מִיַּעֲקֹב״. עַד שֶׁיָּבוֹא זְמַן שֶׁנֶּאֱמַר ״פּוּרָה דָּרַכְתִּי לְבַדִּי״:

❑ **כַּף רָגֶל.** ״לְעֵת תָּמוּט רַגְלָם״. עַד שֶׁיַּגִּיעַ ״תִּרְמְסֶנָּה רָגֶל רַגְלֵי עָנִי וְגוֹ׳״:

❑ **יְרֻשָּׁה לְעֵשָׂו.** בְּגִימַטְרִיָּא בִּשְׁבִיל מִצְוַת כִּבּוּד:

BAAL HATURIM ELUCIDATED

4. וְיִירְאוּ מִכֶּם — THEY WILL FEAR YOU. [102]וְיִירְאוּ is spelled with a double י (= 10), an allusion to the ten blessings with which Jacob was blessed[103] [by Isaac].[104]

MiPano 3). According to some opinions (cited by *Radak* to *Ezekiel* 41:8), the *amah* used by Ezekiel to measure the height of the Temple was larger than the standard *amah*. It is possible, then, that the Temple walls were measured with a ten-*tefach amah*. If so, the sixty *amos* mentioned in *Ezra* were each ten *tefachim* long, for a total height of six hundred *tefachim*, while the hundred *amos* of the Mishnah were six-*tefach amos*, for a total of six hundred *tefachim*. Accordingly, the verse and the Midrash refer to the same height, but use different systems of measurements (Rabbi N. Piontak, *HaMaayan*, *Teves* 5747). Thus, the Baal HaTurim's sixty *amos* refers to the same height — six hundred *tefachim* — as the Mishnah's one hundred *amos*.

102. The word יִירְאוּ (or, וְיִירְאוּ), *they will fear*, appears six times in the *Tanach*, always beginning with a doubled י; the second י is part of the verb root ירא, *to fear*, while the first י is a prefix which, together with the suffix ־וּ, indicates the third person plural in the future tense. The word appears another four times in the Torah with the conjunctive prefix ־וְ, *and*. Three of those times (*Deuteronomy* 17:13, 19:20 and 21:21) it is spelled וְיִרְאוּ, with only one י. Only in our verse does it retain the second י. The Baal HaTurim explains the implication of that second י.

103. The ten blessings are: *And may God give you (i) of the dew of the heavens and (ii) of the fatness of the earth, and (iii) abundant grain and (iv) wine. (v) Peoples will serve you, and (vi) regimes will prostate themselves to you; (vii) be a lord to your kinsmen, and (viii) your mother's sons will prostrate themselves to you; (ix) cursed be the ones who curse you, and (x) blessed be the ones who bless you* (*Genesis* 27:28-29; see the Baal HaTurim there).

104. That is, Esau's descendants will fear Ja-

this mountain; turn yourselves northward. [4] *You shall command the people, saying, "You are passing through the boundary of your brothers the children of Esau, who dwell in Seir; they will fear you, but you should be very careful.* [5] *You shall not provoke them, for I shall not give you of their land even a tread of a foot-sole, for an inheritance to Esau have I given Mount Seir.* [6] *You shall purchase food from them for money so that you may eat; also water shall you buy from them for money so that you may drink.* [7] *For HASHEM, your God, has blessed you in all your handiwork; He knew your way in this great wilderness; this forty-year period HASHEM, your God, was with you; you did not lack a thing."* [8] *So we passed from our brothers, the children of Esau who dwell in Seir, from the way of the Arabah, from Elath and from Ezion-geber and we turned and passed on the way of the Moabite desert.*

BAAL HATURIM ELUCIDATED

5. עַד מִדְרַךְ כַּף רָגֶל — EVEN (LITERALLY, UNTIL) A TREAD OF A FOOT-SOLE. [This means,] until [the fulfillment of the verse], דָּרַךְ כּוֹכָב מִיַּעֲקֹב, *A star has treaded forth from Jacob* (*Numbers* 24:17).[105] [God is saying, *"I shall not give you their land*] until the time arrives when פּוּרָה דָּרַכְתִּי לְבַדִּי, *I will have treaded on a winepress on My own account"*[106] (*Isaiah* 63:3).[106a]

❑ **כַּף רָגֶל** — A FOOT-SOLE. [This refers,] לְעֵת תָּמוּט רַגְלָם, *to the time their foot will falter*[107] (32:35 below). Until the time arrives when תִּרְמְסֶנָּה רָגֶל רַגְלֵי עָנִי, *A foot will trample it, the feet of a humble man*[108] . . . (*Isaiah* 26:6).

❑ **יְרֻשָּׁה לְעֵשָׂו** — AN INHERITANCE TO ESAU. The *gematria* of this phrase (921) is equivalent[109] to that of בִּשְׁבִיל מִצְוַת כִּיבּוּד, *because of the mitzvah of honoring* [his father].[110]

cob's descendants because Isaac chose to bless Jacob rather than Esau, and Isaac's "blessing" actually comprised ten blessings (see note 103).

105. In *Peirush HaTur HaAroch* to that verse, the Baal HaTurim explains it as a reference to *Mashiach* (see *Yerushalmi, Taanis* 4:5 and *Nedarim* 3:8), who will gather all of Israel from one end of the world to the other, just as a star "treads" across the heavens, from one end of the sky to the other.

106. The prophet compares the descendants of Esau in Messianic times to grapes in a winepress waiting to be crushed. Even if Israel will not be found worthy at that time, God will, nevertheless, crush "the grapes" on His own account (*Radak*).

106a. See *Rashi*.

107. That is, when they will be in exile (see *Targum Onkelos* to that verse).

108. A reference to *Mashiach* who is described as עָנִי, *a humble man* (*Zechariah* 9:9; translation of עָנִי as *a humble man* follows *Rashi* to that verse).

109. The spelling of כִּיבּוּד with a י follows *Peirush HaRokeach*, the Baal HaTurim's apparent source. The principle of *im hakollel* allows 921 to be considered equivalent to 922, the *gematria* of the Baal HaTurim's phrase.

110. *Targum Yonasan ben Uzziel; Devarim Rabbah* 1:15; see the Baal HaTurim to *Genesis* 37:1.

ט וַיֹּ֨אמֶר יְהֹוָ֜ה אֵלַ֗י אַל־תָּ֙צַר֙ אֶת־מוֹאָ֔ב וְאַל־תִּתְגָּ֥ר
בָּ֖ם מִלְחָמָ֑ה כִּ֠י לֹֽא־אֶתֵּ֨ן לְךָ֤ מֵֽאַרְצוֹ֙ יְרֻשָּׁ֔ה כִּ֣י

י לִבְנֵי־ל֔וֹט נָתַ֥תִּי אֶת־עָ֖ר יְרֻשָּֽׁה: הָאֵמִ֥ים לְפָנִ֖ים
יֽ יָ֣שְׁבוּ בָ֑הּ עַ֣ם גָּד֥וֹל וְרַ֛ב וָרָ֖ם כָּעֲנָקִֽים: רְפָאִ֛ים יֵחָשְׁב֥וּ
אַף־הֵ֖ם כָּעֲנָקִ֑ים וְהַמֹּ֣אָבִ֔ים יִקְרְא֥וּ לָהֶ֖ם אֵמִֽים:

יֽב וּבְשֵׂעִ֞יר יָשְׁב֣וּ הַחֹרִים֮ לְפָנִים֒ וּבְנֵ֤י עֵשָׂו֙ יִֽירָשׁ֔וּם
וַיַּשְׁמִידוּם֙ מִפְּנֵיהֶ֔ם וַיֵּשְׁב֖וּ תַּחְתָּ֑ם כַּאֲשֶׁ֧ר עָשָׂ֣ה

יֽג יִשְׂרָאֵ֗ל לְאֶ֙רֶץ֙ יְרֻשָּׁת֔וֹ אֲשֶׁר־נָתַ֥ן יְהֹוָ֖ה לָהֶֽם: עַתָּ֗ה
קֻ֚מוּ וְעִבְר֣וּ לָכֶ֔ם אֶת־נַ֖חַל זָ֑רֶד וַֽנַּעֲבֹ֖ר אֶת־נַ֥חַל זָֽרֶד:

יֽד וְהַיָּמִ֞ים אֲשֶׁר־הָלַ֣כְנוּ ׀ מִקָּדֵ֣שׁ בַּרְנֵ֗עַ עַ֤ד אֲשֶׁר־
עָבַ֙רְנוּ֙ אֶת־נַ֣חַל זֶ֔רֶד שְׁלֹשִׁ֥ים וּשְׁמֹנֶ֖ה שָׁנָ֑ה עַד־תֹּ֨ם
כָּל־הַדּ֜וֹר אַנְשֵׁ֤י הַמִּלְחָמָה֙ מִקֶּ֣רֶב הַמַּֽחֲנֶ֔ה כַּאֲשֶׁ֛ר

טֽו נִשְׁבַּ֥ע יְהֹוָ֖ה לָהֶֽם: וְגַ֤ם יַד־יְהֹוָה֙ הָ֣יְתָה בָּ֔ם לְהֻמָּ֖ם
טֽז מִקֶּ֣רֶב הַֽמַּחֲנֶ֑ה עַ֖ד תֻּמָּֽם: וַיְהִ֨י כַאֲשֶׁר־תַּ֜מּוּ כָּל־
יֽז אַנְשֵׁ֧י הַמִּלְחָמָ֛ה לָמ֖וּת מִקֶּ֥רֶב הָעָֽם:
וַיְדַבֵּ֧ר

יֽח יְהֹוָ֛ה אֵלַ֖י לֵאמֹֽר: אַתָּ֨ה עֹבֵ֤ר הַיּוֹם֙ אֶת־גְּב֣וּל מוֹאָ֔ב
יֽט אֶת־עָֽר: וְקָרַבְתָּ֗ מ֚וּל בְּנֵ֣י עַמּ֔וֹן אַל־תְּצֻרֵ֖ם וְאַל־
תִּתְגָּ֣ר בָּ֑ם כִּ֣י לֹֽא־אֶ֠תֵּ֠ן מֵאֶ֙רֶץ֙ בְּנֵֽי־עַמּוֹן֙ לְךָ֣ יְרֻשָּׁ֔ה

כֽ כִּ֥י לִבְנֵי־ל֖וֹט נְתַתִּ֥יהָ יְרֻשָּֽׁה: אֶֽרֶץ־רְפָאִ֞ים תֵּחָשֵׁ֤ב
אַף־הִוא֙ רְפָאִ֤ים יָֽשְׁבוּ־בָהּ֙ לְפָנִ֔ים וְהָ֣עַמֹּנִ֔ים יִקְרְא֥וּ

כֽא לָהֶ֖ם זַמְזֻמִּֽים: עַ֣ם גָּד֥וֹל וְרַ֛ב וָרָ֖ם כָּעֲנָקִ֑ים וַיַּשְׁמִידֵ֤ם
יְהֹוָה֙ מִפְּנֵיהֶ֔ם וַיִּֽירָשֻׁ֖ם וַיֵּֽשְׁב֥וּ תַחְתָּֽם: כַּאֲשֶׁ֤ר עָשָׂה֙

כֽב לִבְנֵ֣י עֵשָׂ֔ו הַיֹּֽשְׁבִ֖ים בְּשֵׂעִ֑יר אֲשֶׁ֨ר הִשְׁמִ֤יד אֶת־
הַֽחֹרִי֙ מִפְּנֵיהֶ֔ם וַיִּֽירָשֻׁם֙ וַיֵּֽשְׁב֣וּ תַחְתָּ֔ם עַ֖ד הַיּ֥וֹם הַזֶּֽה:

כֽג וְהָֽעַוִּ֛ים הַיֹּֽשְׁבִ֥ים בַּֽחֲצֵרִ֖ים עַד־עַזָּ֑ה כַּפְתֹּרִ֗ים
כֽד הַיֹּֽצְאִ֣ים מִכַּפְתֹּ֔ר הִשְׁמִידֻ֖ם וַיֵּֽשְׁב֥וּ תַחְתָּֽם: ק֣וּמוּ סְּע֗וּ
וְעִבְרוּ֘ אֶת־נַ֣חַל אַרְנֹן֒ רְאֵ֣ה נָתַ֣תִּי בְיָדְךָ֗ אֶת־סִיחֹ֣ן

═══════════ בעל הטורים ═══════════

(כד) רְאֵה נָתַתִּי בְיָדְךָ אֶת סִיחֹן. מְלַמֵּד שֶׁהֶרְאָהוּ שָׂרוֹ שֶׁל סִיחוֹן וְיָדוֹ כְּפוּתָה:

─────────── BAAL HATURIM ELUCIDATED ───────────

9. {The Baal HaTurim's comment to אַל תָּצַר אֶת מוֹאָב appears at *Genesis* 13:11-12.}

⁹ *HASHEM said to me: You shall not distress Moab and you shall not provoke war with them, for I shall not give you an inheritance from their land, for to the children of Lot have I given Ar as an inheritance.* ¹⁰ *The Emim dwelled there previously, a great and populous people, and tall as the giants.* ¹¹ *They, too, were considered Rephaim, like the giants; and the Moabites called them Emim.* ¹² *And in Seir the Horites dwelled previously, and the children of Esau drove them away from before themselves and dwelled in their place, as Israel did to the land of its inheritance, which HASHEM gave them.* ¹³ *Now, rise up and get yourselves across Zered Brook — so we crossed Zered Brook.*

¹⁴ *The days that we traveled from Kadesh-barnea until we crossed Zered Brook were thirty-eight years, until the end of the entire generation, the men of war, from the midst of the camp, as HASHEM swore to them.* ¹⁵ *Even the hand of HASHEM was on them to confound them from the midst of the camp, until their end.* ¹⁶ *So it was that the men of war finished dying from amidst the people . . .*

¹⁷ *HASHEM spoke to me, saying:* ¹⁸ *This day you shall cross the border of Moab, at Ar,* ¹⁹ *and you shall approach opposite the children of Ammon; you shall not distress them and you shall not provoke them, for I shall not give any of the land of the children of Ammon to you as an inheritance, for to the children of Lot have I given it as an inheritance.* ²⁰ *It, too, is considered the land of the Rephaim; the Rephaim dwelled in it previously, and the Ammonites called them Zamzumim.* ²¹ *A great and populous people, and tall as giants, and HASHEM destroyed them before them, and they drove them out and dwelled in their place,* ²² *just as he did for the children of Esau who dwell in Seir, who destroyed the Horite before them; they drove them out and dwelled in their place until this day.* ²³ *As for the Avvim who dwell in open cities until Gaza, the Caphtorim who went out of Caphtor destroyed them, and dwelled in their place.* ²⁴ *Rise up and cross Arnon Brook; see! into your hand I have delivered Sihon*

───────────── BAAL HATURIM ELUCIDATED ─────────────

24. רְאֵה נָתַתִּי בְיָדְךָ אֶת סִיחֹן — **SEE! INTO YOUR HAND I HAVE DELIVERED SIHON.** This teaches that [God] showed [Moses] Sihon's [guardian] angel with its hand tied.[111]

───────────────────────────────────────

111. *Peirush HaRokeach;* see also *Tanchuma 4, Devarim Rabbah* 1:22-23, and *Rashi* to v. 31 below.

The Baal HaTurim's comment answers two questions: The time about which Moses was speaking was prior to the war with Sihon. If so,

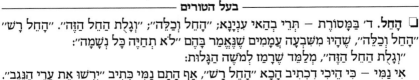

מֶ֣לֶךְ־חֶשְׁבּ֧וֹן הָאֱמֹרִ֛י וְאֶת־אַרְצ֖וֹ הָחֵ֣ל רָ֑שׁ וְהִתְגָּ֥ר
כה בּ֖וֹ מִלְחָמָֽה׃ הַיּ֣וֹם הַזֶּ֗ה אָחֵל֙ תֵּ֤ת פַּחְדְּךָ֙ וְיִרְאָ֣תְךָ֔

בעל הטורים

❑ **הָחֵל.** ד׳ בַּמָּסוֹרֶת – תְּרֵי בְּהַאי עִנְיָנָא; ״הָחֵל וְכַלֵּה״; ״וְגָלֻת הַחֵל הַזֶּה״. ״הָחֵל רָשׁ״ ״הָחֵל וְכַלֵּה״, שֶׁהָיוּ מִשִּׁבְעָה עֲמָמִים שֶׁנֶּאֱמַר בָּהֶם ״לֹא תְחַיֶּה כָּל נְשָׁמָה״:

״וְגָלֻת הַחֵל הַזֶּה״, מְלַמֵּד שֶׁרָמַז לְמֹשֶׁה הַגָּלוּת:

אִי נַמִּי – כִּי הֵיכִי דִּכְתִיב הָכָא ״הָחֵל רָשׁ״, אַף הָתָם נַמִּי כְּתִיב ״יָרְשׁוּ אֵת עָרֵי הַנֶּגֶב״. וְכִדְאִיתָא בְּתַנְחוּמָא, כָּל הַנִּסִּים שֶׁעָשָׂה הַקָּדוֹשׁ בָּרוּךְ הוּא בַּמִּדְבָּר עָתִיד לַעֲשׂוֹת לְיִשְׂרָאֵל בְּצִיּוֹן:

(כה) הַיּוֹם הַזֶּה. רָמַז שֶׁיַּעֲמוֹד לוֹ הַשֶּׁמֶשׁ, שֶׁהַשֶּׁמֶשׁ נִקְרָא יוֹם. ״הַזֶּה אָחֵל״ בְּגִימַטְרִיָּא בַּחַמָּה:

❑ **אָחֵל.** ג׳ בַּמָּסוֹרֶת – ״אָחֵל תֵּת פַּחְדְּךָ״; ״אָחֵל גַּדֶּלְךָ״; ״וְלֹא אַחֵל אֶת שֵׁם קָדְשִׁי עוֹד״. זֶהוּ שֶׁדָּרְשׁוּ שֶׁעָמְדָה חַמָּה לְמֹשֶׁה כְּמוֹ שֶׁעָמְדָה לִיהוֹשֻׁעַ. וּמְנָלָן דְּאַיְרֵי בַּעֲמִידַת חַמָּה? דִּכְתִיב ״וְאֶת שֵׁם קָדְשִׁי אוֹדִיעַ . . . וְלֹא אַחֵל אֶת שֵׁם קָדְשִׁי עוֹד״, וּבַעֲמִידַת הַחַמָּה נוֹדַע שֵׁם קָדְשׁוֹ בְּכָל הָאָרֶץ:

BAAL HATURIM ELUCIDATED

❑ הָחֵל — BEGIN. The masoretic note, ד׳, means that this word appears four times in the *Tanach*:[112] (i-ii) [הָחֵל רָשׁ, *begin to drive out*] twice in this passage (here and v. 31); (iii) הָחֵל וְכַלֵּה, [literally,] *begin and bring to a conclusion* (*I Samuel* 3:12); and (iv) וְגָלֻת הַחֵל הַזֶּה, *and this exile* [*that is*] *beginning*[113] (*Obadiah* 1:20). [The similarity of expression may be explained as follows: Moses' words here refer to the Amorites. He commands regarding them,] *"Begin to drive out; begin and bring to a conclusion,"* for they are of the seven [Canaanite] nations of whom it is stated, לֹא תְחַיֶּה כָּל נְשָׁמָה, *You shall not allow any person to live* (20:16 below).

The phrase, וְגָלֻת הַחֵל הַזֶּה, *and this exile* [*that is*] *beginning,* teaches that God intimated to Moses the [eventual] exile.[113a]

Alternatively: Just as Scripture writes here הָחֵל רָשׁ, *begin to drive out* [which may also be understood as *begin to take possession*], so, too, does that same verse [from *Obadiah*] state, יָרְשׁוּ אֵת עָרֵי הַנֶּגֶב, *Take possession of the cities of the south.* As the *Midrash Tanchuma* relates: All the miracles that the Holy One, Blessed is He, performed [for the Israelites] in the wilderness, He will again

---

why did he use the past tense term נָתַתִּי, *I have delivered,* instead of אֶתֵּן, *I will deliver*? Moreover, why was Moses told רְאֵה, *See!* when there was nothing to see, for Sihon had not yet been defeated? (A.S.).

112. The full note reads: ד׳ ג׳ קָמְצִין וא׳ פַּתָּח, *Four, three vowelized* הָחֵל, *with a kamatz, and one* הַחֵל, *with a patach.*

113. Although most commentaries and translations follow *Targum Yonasan ben Uzziel* in which הַחֵל הַזֶּה is rendered עַמָּא הָדֵין, *this nation,* as if it were spelled הַחַיִל (or הַחַיִל). Our translation follows *Ibn Ezra's* first interpretation which understands הַחֵל as if it were vowelized הָחֵל. This view seems to be validated by the masoretic note, which does not state בִּתְרֵי לִישְׁנֵי, *with two meanings,* as do the masoretic notes that discuss synonymous words with diverse meanings.

113a. Perhaps Moses said, הָחֵל רָשׁ, *begin to drive out,* as an allusion to the fact that their entry into the Land of Israel would be only the beginning. Their possession of the land would eventually be disrupted by exile. But ultimately they would return to conclude their act of possessing it (Y.S.).

114. *Tanchuma* 1 — The Midrash there adduces five expressions that are used regarding both

king of Heshbon, the Amorite, and his land; begin to drive [him] out, and provoke war with him. 25 *This day I will begin to place dread of you and fear of you on the*

BAAL HATURIM ELUCIDATED

perform for Israel in Zion.[114]

25. הַיּוֹם הַזֶּה — THIS DAY. [God] intimidated [to Moses] that the sun would stand still for him,[115] for the sun is called יוֹם, *day.*[116] Indeed, the *gematria* of הַזֶּה אָחֵל, *this* [*day*] *I shall begin* (56), is equivalent[117] to that of בַּחַמָּה, *with the sun.*[118]

❑ **אָחֵל — I WILL BEGIN.** The masoretic note,[119] ג׳, means that this word appears three times in the *Tanach*: (i) here, אָחֵל תֵּת פַּחְדְּךָ, *I will begin to place dread of you;* (ii) אָחֵל גַּדֶּלְךָ, *I will begin to exalt you* (*Joshua* 3:7); and (iii) [with a different meaning in,] וְלֹא אַחֵל אֶת שֵׁם קָדְשִׁי עוֹד, *and I will not desecrate My holy Name any longer* (*Ezekiel* 39:7).[120] This [similarity of expression] is [the basis of] that which the Sages expounded: The sun stood still for Moses, just as it stood still for Joshua.[121] But how do we know that it refers to the sun's standing still? It is written: *I will make My holy Name known . . . and I will not desecrate My holy Name any longer.* And it was through [the miracle of] the sun standing still that God's holy Name became known throughout the world.[122]

Israel in the wilderness and Israel in Zion after its ultimate return from exile. For example, regarding the wilderness we find the phrase אֵלֶּה הַדְּבָרִים (1:1 above), and that same phrase is used regarding Israel in Zion (*Isaiah* 42:16); regarding the wilderness, וַה׳ הֹלֵךְ לִפְנֵיהֶם יוֹמָם, *HASHEM is going before them by day* (*Exodus* 13:21), and regarding Zion, כִּי הֹלֵךְ לִפְנֵיכֶם ה׳, *for HASHEM is going before them* (*Isaiah* 52:12). However, the verses adduced by the Baal HaTurim do not appear in that passage of the Midrash.

115. See the Baal HaTurim's next comment.

116. The Baal HaTurim makes this same point in his comments to *Exodus* 29:38 and *Numbers* 28:3. See also the Baal HaTurim to 4:4 below, s.v., כֻּלְּכֶם הַיּוֹם; and *Rashi* to *Genesis* 3:8, s.v., לְרוּחַ הַיּוֹם, and 18:1, s.v., כְּחֹם הַיּוֹם; *Numbers* 28:3; *Malachi* 3:19; *Song of Songs* 4:6; and *Avodah Zarah* 4a, s.v., היום הבא.

117. The principle of *im hakollel* allows 55, the *gematria* of the Baal HaTurim's term, to be considered equivalent to 56.

118. *Peirush HaRokeach.* Thus, it is due to the sun's standing still that they will fear you.

119. The full note reads: ג׳ ב׳ קָמְצִין וְא׳ פַּתָּח, *Three, two spelled* [אָחֵל] *with a kamatz, and one spelled* [אַחֵל] *with a patach.*

Note that, in the causative active *hifil* conjugation, words of the verb root חלל can mean either *to begin* or *to desecrate.* Accordingly, in our verse and in *Joshua,* the word אָחֵל means *I will begin;* whereas, in the verse from *Ezekiel,* אַחֵל means *I will desecrate.* And, by extension, when it refers to desecration, it is spelled with a *patach,* and when it refers to beginning, it is spelled with a *kamatz* [thus, לֹא יַחֵל, *he shall not desecrate* (*Numbers* 30:3), with a *patach* under the י; but, יָחֵל, *he will begin* (*Judges* 10:18 and 13:5), with a *kamatz* under the י].

120. That verse reads in full: וְאֶת שֵׁם קָדְשִׁי אוֹדִיעַ בְּתוֹךְ עַמִּי יִשְׂרָאֵל, *I will make My holy Name known among My people Israel,* וְלֹא אַחֵל אֶת שֵׁם קָדְשִׁי עוֹד, *and I will not desecrate My holy Name any longer,* וְיָדְעוּ הַגּוֹיִם כִּי אֲנִי ה׳ קָדוֹשׁ בְּיִשְׂרָאֵל, *then the nations will know that I am HASHEM, the Holy One in Israel.*

121. *Taanis* 20a; *Avodah Zarah* 25a — There were three people on whose behalf the sun remained in the east [i.e., the sun stood still in the heavens, delaying sunset for a period of time]. They were Moses, Joshua and Nakdimon ben Gurion [whose story is told in the Talmud there]. And regarding Joshua, Scripture states, *The sun stood still . . .* (*Joshua* 10:13). But how do we know that the sun stood still for Moses? Rabbi Elazar said: It is derived from the similarity of expression, regarding Moses is written, אָחֵל תֵּת פַּחְדְּךָ, and regarding Joshua is written, אָחֵל גַּדֶּלְךָ.

122. *Avodah Zarah* 25a. When a general wins a

עַל־פְּנֵי הָעַמִּים תַּחַת כָּל־הַשָּׁמָיִם אֲשֶׁר יִשְׁמְעוּן
כו שִׁמְעֲךָ וְרָגְזוּ וְחָלוּ מִפָּנֶיךָ: וָאֶשְׁלַח מַלְאָכִים
מִמִּדְבַּר קְדֵמוֹת אֶל־סִיחוֹן מֶלֶךְ חֶשְׁבּוֹן דִּבְרֵי
כז שָׁלוֹם לֵאמֹר: אֶעְבְּרָה בְאַרְצֶךָ בַּדֶּרֶךְ בַּדֶּרֶךְ אֵלֵךְ
כח לֹא אָסוּר יָמִין וּשְׂמֹאול: אֹכֶל בַּכֶּסֶף תַּשְׁבִּרֵנִי
וְאָכַלְתִּי וּמַיִם בַּכֶּסֶף תִּתֶּן־לִי וְשָׁתִיתִי רַק אֶעְבְּרָה
כט בְרַגְלָי: כַּאֲשֶׁר עָשׂוּ־לִי בְּנֵי עֵשָׂו הַיֹּשְׁבִים בְּשֵׂעִיר
וְהַמּוֹאָבִים הַיֹּשְׁבִים בְּעָר עַד אֲשֶׁר־אֶעֱבֹר אֶת־
הַיַּרְדֵּן אֶל־הָאָרֶץ אֲשֶׁר־יְהוָה אֱלֹהֵינוּ נֹתֵן לָנוּ:
ל וְלֹא אָבָה סִיחֹן מֶלֶךְ חֶשְׁבּוֹן הַעֲבִרֵנוּ בּוֹ כִּי־
הִקְשָׁה יְהוָה אֱלֹהֶיךָ אֶת־רוּחוֹ וְאִמֵּץ אֶת־לְבָבוֹ
ששי לא לְמַעַן תִּתּוֹ בְיָדְךָ כַּיּוֹם הַזֶּה: וַיֹּאמֶר יְהוָה אֵלַי
רְאֵה הַחִלֹּתִי תֵּת לְפָנֶיךָ אֶת־סִיחֹן וְאֶת־אַרְצוֹ
לב הָחֵל רָשׁ לָרֶשֶׁת אֶת־אַרְצוֹ: וַיֵּצֵא סִיחֹן לִקְרָאתֵנוּ
לג הוּא וְכָל־עַמּוֹ לַמִּלְחָמָה יָהְצָה: וַיִּתְּנֵהוּ יְהוָה
אֱלֹהֵינוּ לְפָנֵינוּ וַנַּךְ אֹתוֹ וְאֶת־בָּנָו וְאֶת־כָּל־עַמּוֹ:
לד וַנִּלְכֹּד אֶת־כָּל־עָרָיו בָּעֵת הַהִוא וַנַּחֲרֵם אֶת־כָּל־
לה עִיר מְתִם וְהַנָּשִׁים וְהַטָּף לֹא הִשְׁאַרְנוּ שָׂרִיד: רַק
הַבְּהֵמָה בָּזַזְנוּ לָנוּ וּשְׁלַל הֶעָרִים אֲשֶׁר לָכָדְנוּ:
לו מֵעֲרֹעֵר אֲשֶׁר עַל־שְׂפַת־נַחַל אַרְנֹן וְהָעִיר אֲשֶׁר־
בַּנַּחַל וְעַד־הַגִּלְעָד לֹא הָיְתָה קִרְיָה אֲשֶׁר שָׂגְבָה
לז מִמֶּנּוּ אֶת־הַכֹּל נָתַן יְהוָה אֱלֹהֵינוּ לְפָנֵינוּ: רַק
אֶל־אֶרֶץ בְּנֵי־עַמּוֹן לֹא קָרָבְתָּ כָּל־יַד נַחַל יַבֹּק

בעל הטורים

(לה) **רַק הַבְּהֵמָה.** "רַק" מִעוּטָא הוּא. רַק הַכְּחוּשִׁים, אֲבָל הַשְּׁמֵנִים רֵאשִׁית הַחֵרֶם הִקְרַבְנוּ לַה':

BAAL HATURIM ELUCIDATED

29. {The Baal HaTurim's comment to כַּאֲשֶׁר עָשׂוּ לִי בְּנֵי עֵשָׂו appears at 23:8 below.}

local battle, people in a distant land know nothing about his victory. But when the sun stood still for Joshua, the entire world was able to see [the miracle] and they were in awe of him *peoples under the entire heaven, when they hear of your reputation, and they will tremble and be anxious before you."*

26 I sent messengers from the Wilderness of Kedemoth to Sihon king of Heshbon, words of peace, saying, 27 "Let me pass through your land; only on the road shall I go; I will not stray right or left. 28 Food you will sell to me for money, and I shall eat; and you will give me water for money, and I shall drink — only let me pass through on foot; 29 as the children of Esau who dwell in Seir did for me, and the Moabites who dwell in Ar — until I cross the Jordan to the land that HASHEM, our God, gives us." 30 But Sihon king of Heshbon was not willing to let us pass through it, for HASHEM, your God, hardened his spirit and made his heart stubborn, in order to give him into your hand, like this very day.

31 HASHEM said to me: See, I have begun to deliver before you Sihon and his land; begin to drive out, to possess his land.

32 Sihon went out toward us — he and his entire people — for battle, to Jahaz. 33 HASHEM, our God, gave him before us, and we smote him and his sons and his entire people. 34 We captured all his cities at that time, and we destroyed every populated city, with the women and the youngsters; we did not leave a survivor. 35 Only the animals did we loot for ourselves, and the booty of the cities that we captured: 36 from Aroer, which is by the shore of Arnon Brook, and the city that is by the brook, and until Gilead — there was no city that was too strong for us; HASHEM, our God, gave everything before us. 37 Only to the land of the children of Ammon did you not draw near, everywhere near Jabbok Brook

---
──────────── BAAL HATURIM ELUCIDATED ────────────

35. רַק הַבְּהֵמָה — ONLY THE ANIMALS. The term רַק, *only,* implies an exclusion.[123] [This implies that they said, "We took as spoils] only the weak [animals]; while the healthy [animals], the prime among those to be segregated,[124] we offered to HASHEM."[125]

❏ {The Baal HaTurim's other comments to this verse appear at *Numbers* 21:14 and at 3:7 below.}

(*Rashi,* there, s.v., והיכא רמיזא).

123. As used in Scriptures, the terms אַךְ and רַק imply exclusions; the terms אֶת and גַּם imply inclusions.

124. The Baal HaTurim borrows this phrase from *I Samuel* 15:21, see *Rashi* there. The translation follows *Rashi* to *Numbers* 21:2-3.

125. See the Baal HaTurim to 26:2 below.

א וְעָרֵי הָהָר וְכֹל אֲשֶׁר־צִוָּה יהוה אֱלֹהֵינוּ: וַנֵּפֶן וַנַּעַל
דֶּרֶךְ הַבָּשָׁן וַיֵּצֵא עוֹג מֶלֶךְ־הַבָּשָׁן לִקְרָאתֵנוּ הוּא
ב וְכָל־עַמּוֹ לַמִּלְחָמָה אֶדְרֶעִי: וַיֹּאמֶר יהוה אֵלַי
אַל־תִּירָא אֹתוֹ כִּי בְיָדְךָ נָתַתִּי אֹתוֹ וְאֶת־כָּל־
עַמּוֹ וְאֶת־אַרְצוֹ וְעָשִׂיתָ לּוֹ כַּאֲשֶׁר עָשִׂיתָ לְסִיחֹן
ג מֶלֶךְ הָאֱמֹרִי אֲשֶׁר יוֹשֵׁב בְּחֶשְׁבּוֹן: וַיִּתֵּן יהוה
אֱלֹהֵינוּ בְּיָדֵנוּ גַּם אֶת־עוֹג מֶלֶךְ־הַבָּשָׁן וְאֶת־
כָּל־עַמּוֹ וַנַּכֵּהוּ עַד־בִּלְתִּי הִשְׁאִיר־לוֹ שָׂרִיד:
ד וַנִּלְכֹּד אֶת־כָּל־עָרָיו בָּעֵת הַהִוא לֹא הָיְתָה
קִרְיָה אֲשֶׁר לֹא־לָקַחְנוּ מֵאִתָּם שִׁשִּׁים עִיר כָּל־
ה חֶבֶל אַרְגֹּב מַמְלֶכֶת עוֹג בַּבָּשָׁן: כָּל־אֵלֶּה עָרִים
בְּצֻרֹת חוֹמָה גְבֹהָה דְּלָתַיִם וּבְרִיחַ לְבַד מֵעָרֵי
ו הַפְּרָזִי הַרְבֵּה מְאֹד: וַנַּחֲרֵם אוֹתָם כַּאֲשֶׁר עָשִׂינוּ
לְסִיחֹן מֶלֶךְ חֶשְׁבּוֹן הַחֲרֵם כָּל־עִיר מְתִם הַנָּשִׁים
ז וְהַטָּף: וְכָל־הַבְּהֵמָה וּשְׁלַל הֶעָרִים בַּזּוֹנוּ לָנוּ:

בעל הטורים

ג (א) **דֶּרֶךְ הַבָּשָׁן.** עַל שֵׁם שֵׁן שֶׁגָּדַל לוֹ, כִּדְאִיתָא בְּהָרוֹאֶה:

(ה) גְּבֹהָה דְּלָתַיִם וּבְרִיחַ. סוֹפֵי תֵבוֹת ״חֵמָה״. דִּכְתִיב ״עָרִים גְּדֹלֹת וּבְצוּרֹת בַּשָּׁמָיִם״:

(ז) בַּזּוֹנוּ לָנוּ. תְּחִלָּה אָמַר ״בָּזַזְנוּ לָנוּ״. שֶׁמִּתְּחִלָּה הָיְתָה הַבִּזָּה חֲבִיבָה בְּעֵינֵיהֶם. וּלְבַסּוֹף הָיְתָה כָּל כָּךְ עַד שֶׁהָיְתָה בְזוּיָה בְּעֵינֵיהֶם, וְזֶהוּ ״בַּזּוֹנוּ לָנוּ״:

BAAL HATURIM ELUCIDATED

III.

1. דֶּרֶךְ הַבָּשָׁן — BY WAY OF THE BASHAN. [The region was given the name Bashan[126]] because of the unique tooth that he grew, as related in Chapter *HaRoeh.*[127]

126. The term בָּשָׁן alludes to בָּא שֵׁן, *a tooth came* (*Ittur Bikkurim*). Whereas שֵׁן is usually identified as a feminine noun [e.g., שְׁלֹשׁ הַשִּׁנַּיִם, *with three teeth* (*I Samuel* 2:13), using the feminine form שְׁלֹשׁ for *three*] we would expect the Baal HaTurim's allusion to read בָּאָה שֵׁן, in the feminine! Nevertheless, the word שֵׁן is also found as a masculine noun [e.g., הַשֵּׁן הָאֶחָד מָצוּק, *one tooth jutted out* (*I Samuel* 14:5), which has the masculine forms הָאֶחָד, *one,* and מָצוּק, literally, *he jutted out*]. Thus, the allusion is grammatically sound (*VeChur LaZahav*).

127. The ninth chapter of tractate *Berachos* is called *HaRoeh.* The Talmud there (54b) speaks of the proper blessing to be recited by a person who sees a place where a miracle occurred to our ancestors. One of the miracle sites is referred to as "the stone that Og, king of Bashan, attempted to throw upon the Israelites." The Talmud cites a tradition regarding that stone: Og thought, "How big is the Israelite camp? Three *parsaos* [opinions regarding the modern-day equivalent range from 7.1 to 8.6 miles] by three *parsaos.* I shall uproot a mountain that is three *parsaos* square, throw it upon them, and kill them." He uprooted

and the cities of the mountain, and everywhere that
HASHEM, our God, commanded us.

3 1 *We turned and ascended by way of the Bashan, and Og*
king of Bashan went out toward us, he and his entire
people, for war at Edrei. 2 *HASHEM said to me: Do not fear*
him, for in your hand have I given him and his entire people
and his land, and you shall do to him as you did to Sihon
king of the Amorite, who dwells in Heshbon. 3 *HASHEM, our*
God, gave into our hand also Og king of the Bashan and his
entire people, and we smote him until no survivor was left of
him. 4 *We captured all his cities at that time; there was no*
city that we did not take from them — sixty cities, the entire
region of Argob — the kingdom of Og in the Bashan. 5 *All*
these were fortified cities, with a high wall, doors and bar,
aside from open cities, very many. 6 *We destroyed them, as*
we did to Sihon king of Heshbon, destroying every popu-
lated city, the women and the youngsters. 7 *And all the*
animals and the booty of the cities we looted for ourselves.

BAAL HATURIM ELUCIDATED

5. גְּבֹהָה דְּלָתַיִם וּבְרִיחַ — HIGH [WALL], DOORS AND BAR. The final letters of these words [taken in reverse order] spell חַמָּה, *sun*; and so it is written, עָרִים גְּדֹלֹת וּבְצוּרֹת בַּשָּׁמָיִם, *cities great and fortified to the heavens* (1:28 above; 9:1 below).[128]

7. בַּזּוֹנוּ לָנוּ — WE LOOTED FOR OURSELVES. At first, the Torah used the form, בָּזַזְנוּ לָנוּ, *we looted for ourselves* (2:35 above), for, at first, the loot was precious in their eyes. But, at the end, there was so much of it that it became worthless in their eyes. Thus, בַּזּוֹנוּ לָנוּ, [which may be understood as בָּזִינוּ לָנוּ,] *we scorned it.*[129]

---

such a mountain and carried it over his head. God then sent ants that bored into the mountain, causing it to fall on Og's head. When Og tried to shake it off, the teeth on either side of his mouth grew long, extending into the mountain so that he could not extricate himself from it.

The *Rashba* interprets this Talmudic passage allegorically (see note 17 to 54b in the Schottenstein edition of tractate *Berachos*).

128. Our verse reads, *fortified cities with a high wall, door and bar,* while the other two verses describe *cities great and fortified to the heavens.* The Baal HaTurim shows that they refer to the same thing: בַּשָּׁמָיִם, *to the heavens,* refers to the sun; and גְּבֹהָה דְּלָתַיִם וּבְרִיחַ, *high* [*wall*], *doors and bar,* also alludes to the sun.

The Baal HaTurim's comment also explains why the verse uses the singular בְּרִיחַ, *bar,* in conjunction with the plural דְּלָתַיִם, *doors.* We would expect the plural בְּרִיחִים. The Torah uses the singular, which ends in a ח, to allude to the sun.

129. *Rashi* to 2:35 above.

Both בָּזַזְנוּ and בַּזּוֹנוּ mean *we looted.* They are two forms of the root בזז, *to loot.* Roots in which the second and third letters are the same, such as בזז, are called כְּפוּלִים, *doubled.* Such verbs are sometimes conjugated like regular verbs; thus, בָּזַזְנוּ has the same form as, e.g., לָקַחְנוּ, *we took* (3:4). At other times, doubled verbs are conjugated as irregular verbs. In that case, one of the doubled letters is dropped and the other takes a *dagesh,* thus בַּזּוֹנוּ.

But why does the Torah change forms here? The Midrash (*Sifrei*) explains that בַּזּוֹנוּ may be understood as if it read בָּזִינוּ, *we scorned* (see *Malachi* 1:6), of the root בזה, *to scorn.* For when

ח וַנִּקַּח בָּעֵת הַהִוא֙ אֶת־הָאָ֔רֶץ מִיַּ֗ד שְׁנֵי֙ מַלְכֵ֣י הָאֱמֹרִ֔י אֲשֶׁ֖ר בְּעֵ֣בֶר הַיַּרְדֵּ֑ן מִנַּ֥חַל אַרְנֹ֖ן עַד־הַ֥ר חֶרְמֽוֹן: ט צִידֹנִ֛ים יִקְרְא֥וּ לְחֶרְמ֖וֹן שִׂרְיֹ֑ן וְהָ֣אֱמֹרִ֔י י יִקְרְאוּ־לֹ֖ו שְׂנִֽיר: כֹּ֣ל ׀ עָרֵ֣י הַמִּישֹׁ֗ר וְכָל־הַגִּלְעָד֙ וְכָל־הַבָּשָׁ֜ן עַד־סַלְכָ֣ה וְאֶדְרֶ֔עִי עָרֵ֖י מַמְלֶ֥כֶת ע֖וֹג יא בַּבָּשָֽׁן: כִּ֣י רַק־ע֞וֹג מֶ֣לֶךְ הַבָּשָׁן֮ נִשְׁאַר֮ מִיֶּ֣תֶר הָֽרְפָאִים֒ הִנֵּ֤ה עַרְשׂוֹ֙ עֶ֣רֶשׂ בַּרְזֶ֔ל הֲלֹ֣ה הִ֔וא בְּרַבַּ֖ת בְּנֵ֣י עַמּ֑וֹן תֵּ֧שַׁע אַמּ֣וֹת אָרְכָּ֗הּ וְאַרְבַּ֥ע אַמּ֛וֹת רָחְבָּ֖הּ יב בְּאַמַּת־אִֽישׁ: וְאֶת־הָאָ֧רֶץ הַזֹּ֛את יָרַ֖שְׁנוּ בָּעֵ֣ת הַהִ֑וא מֵעֲרֹעֵ֞ר אֲשֶׁר־עַל־נַ֣חַל אַרְנֹ֗ן וַחֲצִ֤י הַֽר־ יג הַגִּלְעָד֙ וְעָרָ֔יו נָתַ֕תִּי לָרֽאוּבֵנִ֖י וְלַגָּדִֽי: וְיֶ֨תֶר הַגִּלְעָ֜ד וְכָל־הַבָּשָׁן֙ מַמְלֶ֣כֶת ע֔וֹג נָתַ֕תִּי לַחֲצִ֖י שֵׁ֣בֶט הַֽמְנַשֶּׁ֑ה כֹּ֣ל חֶ֤בֶל הָֽאַרְגֹּב֙ לְכָל־הַבָּשָׁ֔ן הַה֥וּא יִקָּרֵ֖א אֶ֥רֶץ יד רְפָאִֽים: יָאִ֣יר בֶּן־מְנַשֶּׁ֗ה לָקַח֙ אֶת־כָּל־חֶ֣בֶל אַרְגֹּ֔ב עַד־גְּב֥וּל הַגְּשׁוּרִ֖י וְהַמַּֽעֲכָתִ֑י וַיִּקְרָא֩ אֹתָ֨ם עַל־שְׁמ֜וֹ טו אֶת־הַבָּשָׁ֗ן חַוֹּ֤ת יָאִיר֙ עַ֣ד הַיּ֣וֹם הַזֶּֽה: וּלְמָכִ֖יר נָתַ֥תִּי טז אֶת־הַגִּלְעָֽד: וְלָרֽאוּבֵנִ֣י וְלַגָּדִ֗י נָתַ֕תִּי מִן־הַגִּלְעָד֙

בעל הטורים

(יא) **הֲלֹה הוא.** כְּתִיב בְּהֵ"א — יָבוֹא מִי שֶׁמָּלַךְ הל"ה שָׁנִים, וְהוּא דוֹר חֲמִישִׁי — שַׁלְמוֹן, בֹּעַז, עוֹבֵד, יִשַׁי, דָּוִד — וְיִקַּח הֶעָרִים הָאֵלֶּה:

דָּבָר אַחֵר — מֹשֶׁה, שֶׁהָיָה הֵ"א הֵ"א אַמָּה, וְדִלֵּג י' אַמָּה, וּכְלֵי מִלְחַמְתּוֹ י' אַמָּה, וְהִכָּהוּ בְּקַרְסֻלּוֹ שֶׁהָיָה י' אַמָּה:

BAAL HATURIM ELUCIDATED

11. הֲלֹה הוא — BEHOLD! IT IS. The word הֲלֹה is spelled[130] with a final ה (= 5). [As if to say,] let [David] who reigned for forty[131] years and who was of the fifth generation[131a]

the Israelites defeated Sihon, each man [בזו] looted for himself whatever he could take — jewelry, clothing, utensils, animals. But by the time they defeated Og, they had already taken so much loot that they [בזה] scorned everything except gold and silver (*Rashi*).

130. *Rimzei Rabbeinu Yoel;* cf. *Peirush Ha-Rokeach.* The word הֲלוֹא (or הֲלֹא), *is it not* or *behold,* appears in the *Tanach,* with or without a ו, more than two hundred times. In every instance, it is spelled with an א, except in our verse where

the א is replaced by a ה. The *gematria* of הֲלֹה is 40, thus the Baal HaTurim's two allusions.

131. See *I Kings* 2:11.

131a. The ה (= 5) which is used in place of the א here can refer to the fifth generation after the nation entered the Land of Canaan; and that was the generation of David. For the Midrash (*Seder Olam* 12) states that David's great-great-grandfather, Salmah son of Nahshon, entered the land with Joshua. Taken together, the word הֲלֹה is a prophetic hint that, five generations from the

[8] *At that time we took the land from the hand of the two kings of the Amorite that were on the other side of the Jordan, from Arnon Brook to Mount Hermon —* [9] *Sidonians would refer to Hermon as Sirion, and the Amorites would call it Senir —* [10] *all the cities of the plain, the entire Gilead, and the entire Bashan until Salcah and Edrei, the cities of the kingdom of Og in the Bashan.* [11] *For only Og king of the Bashan was left of the remaining Rephaim — behold! his bed was an iron bed, in Rabbah of the children of Ammon — nine cubits was its length and four cubits its width, by the cubit of that man.*

[12] *And we possessed that land at that time; from Aroer, which is by Arnon Brook, and half of the mountain of Gilead and its cities did I give to the Reubenite and the Gadite.* [13] *The rest of the Gilead and the entire Bashan, the kingdom of Og, did I give to half the tribe of Manasseh, the entire region of the Argov of the entire Bashan, that is called the land of Rephaim.* [14] *Jair son of Manasseh took the entire region of Argov until the border of the Geshurite and the Maacathite, and he named them, the Bashan, after himself, "Havvoth-jair," until this day.* [15] *To Machir I gave the Gilead.* [16] *To the Reubenite and the Gadite I gave from the Gilead*

─────────────── BAAL HATURIM ELUCIDATED ───────────────

— Salmon,[132] Boaz, Obed, Jesse, David (*Ruth* 4:21-22) — conquer these cities.

Alternatively: [The unusual spelling alludes to] Moses, who stood twice five cubits tall, and jumped ten cubits with his ten-cubit-long weapon, and he struck Og on his ankle which measured ten cubits.[133]

time Moses was speaking, King David would conquer the city of Rabbah of the Children of Ammon (see *II Samuel* 12:29) where he would see Og's bed, which will still be on display there at that time (*Peirush HaRokeach*).

132. This name appears with three spellings: שַׂלְמָא (*I Chronicles* 2:11,51,54); שַׂלְמָה (*Ruth* 4:20); and שַׂלְמוֹן (*Ruth* 4:21). According to the Midrash, he entered the Land of Canaan with Joshua and outlived him (*Seder Olam Rabbah* 12). If so, he was already alive when Moses spoke our passage. Thus, Moses began the count from his own generation to that of David with Salmah/Salmon (*VeChur LaZahav*).

Interestingly, the *gematria* of שַׂלְמָא, the first

name of the five generations, is 371, which [by the principle of *im hakollel*] is considered equivalent to 372, the *gematria* of בֶּן יִשַׁי, *son of Jesse*, i.e., David, the representative of the fifth generation (*VeChur LaZahav*).

133. *Berachos* 54b — The Talmud there describes how Moses killed Og. Moses was ten *amos* tall (see *Shabbos* 92a). He took a ten-*amah*-long axe, jumped ten *amos* up, struck Og on his ankle and killed him. The source fo Baal Ha-Turim's statement that Og's ankle measured ten cubits is unknown.

The *Rashba* interprets this Talmudic passage allegorically (see note 17 to 54b in the Schottenstein edition of tractate *Berachos*).

וְעַד־נַחַל אַרְנֹן תּוֹךְ הַנַּחַל וּגְבֻל וְעַד יַבֹּק הַנַּחַל
יז גְּבוּל בְּנֵי עַמּוֹן׃ וְהָעֲרָבָה וְהַיַּרְדֵּן וּגְבֻל מִכִּנֶּרֶת וְעַד
יָם הָעֲרָבָה יָם הַמֶּלַח תַּחַת אַשְׁדֹּת הַפִּסְגָּה
יח מִזְרָחָה׃ וָאֲצַו אֶתְכֶם בָּעֵת הַהִוא לֵאמֹר יהוָה
אֱלֹהֵיכֶם נָתַן לָכֶם אֶת־הָאָרֶץ הַזֹּאת לְרִשְׁתָּהּ
חֲלוּצִים תַּעַבְרוּ לִפְנֵי אֲחֵיכֶם בְּנֵי־יִשְׂרָאֵל כָּל־
יט בְּנֵי־חָיִל׃ רַק נְשֵׁיכֶם וְטַפְּכֶם וּמִקְנֵכֶם יָדַעְתִּי
כִּי־מִקְנֶה רַב לָכֶם יֵשְׁבוּ בְּעָרֵיכֶם אֲשֶׁר נָתַתִּי לָכֶם׃
מפטיר כ עַד אֲשֶׁר־יָנִיחַ יהוָה ׀ לַאֲחֵיכֶם כָּכֶם וְיָרְשׁוּ
גַם־הֵם אֶת־הָאָרֶץ אֲשֶׁר יהוָה אֱלֹהֵיכֶם נֹתֵן לָהֶם
בְּעֵבֶר הַיַּרְדֵּן וְשַׁבְתֶּם אִישׁ לִירֻשָּׁתוֹ אֲשֶׁר נָתַתִּי
כא לָכֶם׃ וְאֶת־יְהוֹשׁוּעַ צִוֵּיתִי בָּעֵת הַהִוא לֵאמֹר עֵינֶיךָ
הָרֹאֹת אֵת כָּל־אֲשֶׁר עָשָׂה יהוָה אֱלֹהֵיכֶם לִשְׁנֵי
הַמְּלָכִים הָאֵלֶּה כֵּן־יַעֲשֶׂה יהוָה לְכָל־הַמַּמְלָכוֹת
כב אֲשֶׁר אַתָּה עֹבֵר שָׁמָּה׃ לֹא תִּירָאוּם כִּי יהוָה
אֱלֹהֵיכֶם הוּא הַנִּלְחָם לָכֶם׃ ססס

ק״ה פסוקים. מלכי״ה סימן.

BAAL HATURIM ELUCIDATED

22. {The Baal HaTurim's comment to לֹא תִּירָאוּם appears at 3:23 below.}

until Arnon Brook, the midst of the brook and the border, until Jabbok Brook, the border of the children of Ammon, ¹⁷ and the Arabah and the Jordan and its border, from Kinnereth to the Arabah Sea, the Salt Sea, below the waterfalls from the mountaintop, eastward.

¹⁸ I commanded you at that time, saying, "HASHEM, your God, gave you this land for a possession, armed shall you cross over before your brethren, the Children of Israel, all the men of accomplishment. ¹⁹ Only your wives, young-sters, and your livestock — I know that you have abundant livestock — shall dwell in your cities that I have given you. ²⁰ Until HASHEM shall give rest to your brethren like yourselves, and they, too, shall possess the land that HASHEM, your God, gives them on the other side of the Jordan; then you shall return, every man to his inheritance that I have given you."

²¹ I commanded Joshua at that time, saying, "Your eyes that have seen everything that HASHEM, your God, has done to these two kings; so will HASHEM do to all the kings there where you cross over. ²² You shall not fear them, for HASHEM, your God — it is He Who shall wage war for you."

פרשת ואתחנן

Parashas Va'eschanan

ג/כג־כד כג־כד **וָאֶתְחַנַּן אֶל־יהוה בָּעֵת הַהִוא לֵאמֹר: אֲדֹנָי**
יֱהוִה אַתָּה הַחִלּוֹתָ לְהַרְאוֹת אֶת־עַבְדְּךָ אֶת־

בעל הטורים

ג (כג) **וָאֶתְחַנַּן.** לְעֵיל כְּתִיב "לֹא תִּירָאוּם", חִזַּקְתִּי אֶת יִשְׂרָאֵל, אוּלַי יְרַחֵם עָלָי:

❑ **וָאֶתְחַנַּן.** בְּגִימַטְרִיָּא "שִׁירָה", שֶׁאָמַר לְפָנָיו שִׁירָה כְּדֵי שֶׁיִּשְׁמַע תְּפִלָּתוֹ:

❑ סָמַךְ "ה' אֱלֹהֵיכֶם" לְ"וָאֶתְחַנַּן". לוֹמַר "שִׁוִּיתִי ה' לְנֶגְדִּי תָמִיד":

(כד) **הַחִלּוֹתָ.** ב' בַּמָּסוֹרֶת – "אַתָּה הַחִלּוֹתָ"; "אֲשֶׁר הַחִלּוֹתָ לִנְפֹּל לְפָנָיו". "אַתָּה הַחִלּוֹתָ לְהַרְאוֹת" בְּמַה שֶּׁכָּבַשְׁתָּ לְפָנַי סִיחוֹן וְעוֹג. וְזֶהוּ "הַחִלּוֹתָ לְהַרְאוֹת", בְּמַה שֶׁ"הַחִלּוֹתָ לִנְפֹּל לְפָנָיו":

❑ "תַּחֲנוּנִים יְדַבֶּר רָשׁ, וְעָשִׁיר יַעֲנֶה עַזּוֹת", רָמוּז "מֹשֶׁה". וּמַתְחִיל הַפָּסוּק בְּתָ' וּמְסַיֵּם בְּתָ', לְפִי שֶׁלֹּא זָכָה לִכָּנֵס בָּאָרֶץ, שֶׁהִיא ת' פַּרְסָה עַל ת' פַּרְסָה. {וְכֵן שְׁנֵי רֵישִׁי"ן שֶׁל "יְדַבֶּר" "וְעָשִׁיר" שֶׁבֵּין אוֹתִיּוֹת שֶׁל מֹשֶׁה עוֹלֶה ת' – שֶׁהִתְפַּלֵּל לִכָּנֵס לָאָרֶץ שֶׁהִיא ת' פַּרְסָה}:

BAAL HATURIM ELUCIDATED

III.

23. וָאֶתְחַנַּן — I PRAYED.[1] Written [in the verse just] before [this one] is [Moses' exhortation to Israel], לֹא תִּירָאוּם, *You shall not fear them* (3:22). [Moses thought,] "I encouraged Israel. Perhaps He will have mercy upon me."[2]

❑ **וָאֶתְחַנַּן — I PRAYED.** The *gematria* of this word is equal to that of שִׁירָה, *song.* Moses recited songs [of praise] before God, so that He would accept his prayer.[3]

❑ The phrase ה' אֱלֹהֵיכֶם, *HASHEM, your God* (3:22 above), is juxtaposed with וָאֶתְחַנַּן, *I prayed,* to indicate [that Moses meant], שִׁוִּיתִי ה' לְנֶגְדִּי תָמִיד, *I have set HASHEM in front of me always* (*Psalms* 16:8).[4]

1. Moses' statement, "*I prayed to HASHEM at that time,*" is an indication that Moses picked that particular time for it was an auspicious moment for prayer. The Baal HaTurim explains why Moses thought so.

2. The Baal HaTurim's intent is unclear. Various approaches have been suggested to explain the comment. According to *Atros Addar*, Moses thought, "Perhaps in the merit of the masses, within whose hearts I have implanted the concept of fearing nobody and nothing except for God Himself — perhaps, in their merit — God will accept my entreaties."

Alternatively: The wording of the last two verses of the previous *sidra* requires explanation. Moses said, "*I commanded Joshua at that time, saying,* 'עֵינֶיךָ הָרֹאֹת, *your* (singular) *eyes that have seen* ... אֲשֶׁר אַתָּה עֹבֵר שָׁמָּה, *there where you* (singular) *are crossing over,* לֹא תִּירָאוּם, *you* (plural) *shall not fear them,* כִּי... הוּא הַנִּלְחָם לָכֶם, *for ... it is He Who shall wage war for you* (plural)' " (3:21-22). Why did Moses shift from second person singular to second person plural, especially when he seemingly addressed both verses to Joshua? The Baal HaTurim explains that after speaking the first verse to Joshua, Moses turned to the entire nation and encouraged them to be staunch in their faith in God, "*For HASHEM, your God, it is He Who shall wage war for you.* And then, וָאֶתְחַנַּן אֶל ה', *I shall have prayed to HASHEM,* to allow me to enter the Land of Canaan; perhaps He will have mercy upon me in the merit of my prayers on your behalf" (*Yad Aharon*).

3. The Baal HaTurim's comment may be understood in accordance with a parallel comment in *Paaneach Raza*: The *gematria* of וָאֶתְחַנַּן (515) is equal to that of תְּפִלָּה, *prayer,* and to that of שִׁירָה, *song,* for prayer requires sweet-sounding melody.

4. Elsewhere, with regard to the laws of prayer [i.e., *Shemoneh Esrei*], the Baal HaTurim writes: A *baraisa* states: One who prays must direct his heart, as it is stated (*Psalms* 10:17), *Direct their*

[23] I prayed to HASHEM at that time, saying, [24] "My Lord, HASHEM/ELOHIM, You have begun to show Your servant

BAAL HATURIM ELUCIDATED

24. הַחִלּוֹתָ — YOU HAVE BEGUN. The masoretic note, ב׳, means that this word appears twice in the *Tanach*: (i) here, אַתָּה הַחִלּוֹתָ, *You have begun;* and (ii) אֲשֶׁר הַחִלּוֹתָ לִנְפֹּל לְפָנָיו, *whom you have begun to fall before* (*Esther* 6:13). [The similarity of expression indicates that Moses said to God,] "Whereas You have conquered Sihon and Og before me, *You have begun to show* [me . . .]."[5] Thus the verses mean: *You have begun to show,* by the fact that *You have begun* [to cause him, i.e., Sihon and Og] *to fall before him* [i.e., Moses].[6]

❑ The verse, תַּחֲנוּנִים יְדַבֶּר רָשׁ וְעָשִׁיר יַעֲנֶה עַזּוֹת, *A poor man will speak supplications, and a rich man will respond with sharp words* (*Proverbs* 18:23), alludes to Moses.[7] Furthermore, that verse begins with the letter ת (= 400) [of תַּחֲנוּנִים] and ends with the letter ת [of עַזּוֹת], alluding to the fact that Moses was not successful [in his bid] to enter the Land of Israel, a land that measures four hundred *parsah* by four hundred *parsah.*[8] {Additionally: The two [final] letters ר (= 200) of יְדַבֵּר and וְעָשִׁיר that are between the [final] letters מֹשֶׁה[9] have a *gematria* of four hundred — referring to the fact that Moses prayed to enter the land which measures four hundred *parsah.*}[10]

heart; let Your ear be attentive (*Berachos* 31a). This means that one must concentrate on the meaning of the words that he utters with his lips, and must consider himself as if the *Shechinah* (God's Immanent Presence) is before him, as it is stated, שִׁוִּיתִי ה׳ לְנֶגְדִּי תָמִיד, *I have set HASHEM in front of me always* (*Tur, Orach Chaim* 98). Thus, in order to direct his heart and to concentrate on his prayer, Moses set God's Name, ה׳ אֱלֹהִיכֶם, in the verse before his prayer (*Vechur LaZahav*).

5. That is, now that You have conquered Sihon and Og during my lifetime and incorporated their lands with the Land of Canaan as the area that would become the Land of Israel, You have indicated to me that it is appropriate for me to pray that You rescind Your decree forbidding me to enter the Land of Canaan (*VeChur LaZahav;* based upon *Sifrei* to עֵת הַהִוא, cited by *Rashi* here; see also *Rashi* to *Numbers* 27:12).

6. The text is based on *Ittur Bikkurim's* suggested emendation. The early printed editions, as well as *Shoham Yakar's* manuscript edition, read: וְזֶהוּ ״הַחִלּוֹתָ לִנְפֹּל לְפָנָיו״ בְּמָה שֶׁהִתְחַלְתָּ לִנְפֹּל, *Thus: "You have begun to fall before him," by the fact that you have begun to fall.*

7. The Midrash identifies the poor man of that verse and his supplications as Moses praying that he be permitted to enter the Land of Israel; while the rich man and his sharp response refers to the Holy One, Blessed is He, Who replied (v. 26 below), *"Do not continue to speak to Me further about this matter"* (*Devarim Rabbah* 2:4; *Yalkut Shimoni,* II, 959).

Moreover, we find Moses' name hidden in the verse from *Proverbs,* for the final letters of the first, third and fifth words of the verse, תַּחֲנוּנִי״ם יְדַבֶּר רָ״שׁ וְעָשִׁיר יַעֲנֶ״ה עַזּוֹת, combine to spell the name מֹשֶׁה (*Peirush HaRokeach*). Further on in this comment, the Baal HaTurim explains the allusion of the final letters of the remaining three words.

8. *Zohar,* III, 84a; see *Rashi* to *Numbers* 13:25. Opinions regarding the modern-day equivalent of the *parsah* range between 2.3 and 2.9 miles. Thus, the area of the Biblical *Eretz Yisrael* was somewhere between 846,400 square miles (about the size of present-day Iran, Iraq and Jordan) and 1,345,600 square miles (larger than the combined area of present-day Iran, Turkey, Iraq, Syria, Jordan, Lebanon and Israel).

9. See second paragraph of note 7 above.

10. *Peirush HaRokeach.* The passage enclosed in braces is not found in the printed editions but does appear in *Shoham Yakar's* edition and in *Peirush HaRokeach,* the Baal HaTurim's source for this comment.

ג/כה גָּדְלְךָ וְאֶת־יָדְךָ הַחֲזָקָה אֲשֶׁר מִי־אֵל בַּשָּׁמַיִם
וּבָאָרֶץ אֲשֶׁר־יַעֲשֶׂה כְמַעֲשֶׂיךָ וְכִגְבוּרֹתֶךָ:
כה אֶעְבְּרָה־נָּא וְאֶרְאֶה אֶת־הָאָרֶץ הַטּוֹבָה אֲשֶׁר

בעל הטורים

❑ **לְהַרְאוֹת.** תָּג עַל הָרֵי״שׁ, הִרְאִיתַנִי אַף מַה שֶּׁלֹּא בִקַּשְׁתִּיךָ:

❑ **לְהַרְאוֹת.** ג׳ בַּמָּסוֹרֶת – ״לְהַרְאוֹת אֶת עַבְדְּךָ״; וְאִידָךְ ״לְהַרְאוֹת הָעַמִּים וְהַשָּׂרִים אֶת יָפְיָהּ״; ״אֲשֶׁר נִתַּן בְּשׁוּשָׁן לְהַשְׁמִידָם נָתַן לוֹ לְהַרְאוֹת אֶת אֶסְתֵּר״. זֶהוּ שֶׁדָּרְשׁוּ, שֶׁהֶרְאָה לוֹ הַקָּדוֹשׁ בָּרוּךְ הוּא לְמשֶׁה כָּל מַה שֶּׁאֵרַע לְיִשְׂרָאֵל, הֵיאַךְ יֵשְׁבוּ בְשַׁלְוָתָן, וְכָל הַמְּצִיקִין שֶׁעֲתִידִין לְהָצִיק לָהֶן. וְזֶהוּ ״לְהַרְאוֹת הָעַמִּים וְהַשָּׂרִים אֶת יָפְיָהּ״, הֵיאַךְ הֵם בְּיָפְיָם וּבְשַׁלְוָתָם. ״לְהַשְׁמִידָם נָתַן לוֹ לְהַרְאוֹת״, שֶׁהֶרְאָהוּ הַמְּצִיקִין לָהֶן:

❑ **אֶת עַבְדְּךָ.** שֶׁאָמַרְתָּ ״לֹא כֵן עַבְדִּי משֶׁה״.

❑ הַפָּסוּק מַתְחִיל בְּא׳ וּמְסַיֵּם בְּכ׳, וְיֵשׁ בּוֹ כ״א תֵּבוֹת, כְּנֶגֶד ״אַךְ טוֹב לְיִשְׂרָאֵל״; וּכְנֶגֶד ״אֶהְיֶה״:

(כה) **אֶעְבְּרָה נָּא.** הַיַּרְדֵּן נ׳ אַמָּה. לֹא אֶעֱבֹר אֶלָּא אַמָּה אֶחָת:

BAAL HATURIM ELUCIDATED

❑ **לְהַרְאוֹת** — TO SHOW. [According to a scribal tradition,] the ר of this word is written with a *tag* [crownlet].[11] [This indicates that Moses said,] "You have shown me even what I have not requested of You."[12]

11. Regarding *tagin,* see note 56 to *parashas Devarim* above.

Sefer Tagin disagrees with *Peri Eitz Chayim* regarding the absence of *tagin* on the letter ר (see illustration), for it enumerates one hundred fifty words in the Torah in which the letter ר is written with two *tagin* [including לְהַרְאוֹת of our verse]; and ends that list with the statement, "The others have [only] one *tag.*" Accordingly, the Baal HaTurim writes תָּג, in the singular, rather than תָּגִין, in the plural, for he is referring to the extra *tag* on this particular ר (cf. the Baal HaTurim to *Numbers* 12:13).

12. *Shoham Yakar* explains the Baal HaTurim's comment in light of *Sifrei* to *Numbers* 27:12 (see the Baal HaTurim there). That Midrash states:

ר with two *tagin*
Usual ר according to *SeferTagin*
Usual ר according to *Peri Eitz Chaim*

The Omnipresent showed Moses the distant [parts of the land as clearly] as the near; the hidden [as clearly] as the revealed; everything that is called the Land of Israel . . . The Omnipresent showed Moses all the chambers of the Land of Israel as if it were a set table, as it is written (*Deuteronomy* 34:1), *HASHEM showed him the entire land.*

However, *Shoham Yakar* does not explain how the *tagin* on the letter ר allude to God showing Moses more land than Moses had requested. Perhaps, the two *tagin* are viewed as an indication that the ר (=200) should be considered twice. If so, it represents the number 400 and alludes to the entire Land of Israel, which has an area of four hundred *parsah* by four hundred *parsah* (*VeChur LaZahav;* see the Baal HaTurim's preceding comment with note 8).

It is not clear, however, how Moses can be saying, "You have shown me even more of the land . . .," at this point (v. 24), for God has merely consented to show Moses the land (v. 27) in response to Moses' request to enter into it (v. 25).

Accordingly, it is suggested that the Baal HaTurim is not referring to God showing him the Land of Israel. Rather, he refers to the periods of

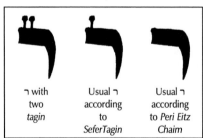

*Your greatness and Your strong hand, for what power is
there in the heavens or on the earth that can perform
according to Your deeds and according to Your mighty
acts?* ²⁵ *Let me now cross over and see the good land that is*

--- BAAL HATURIM ELUCIDATED ---

❑ לְהַרְאוֹת — **TO SHOW.** The masoretic note, 'ג, means that this word appears three times in the *Tanach*: (i) here, לְהַרְאוֹת אֶת עַבְדְּךָ, *to show Your servant;* (ii) לְהַרְאוֹת הָעַמִּים וְהַשָּׂרִים אֶת יָפְיָהּ, *to show the peoples and the princes her beauty* (*Esther* 1:11); and (iii) אֲשֶׁר נִתַּן בְּשׁוּשָׁן לְהַשְׁמִידָם נָתַן לוֹ לְהַרְאוֹת אֶת אֶסְתֵּר, *that was distributed in Shushan to destroy them, he gave to him to show to Esther* (*Esther* 4:8). This [similarity of expression] is [an allusion to] what our Sages have expounded: The Holy One, Blessed is He, showed Moses all that would happen to Israel — how they would dwell in their tranquil times, as well as all the oppressors who were destined to oppress them.[13] Thus, the verse, *to show the peoples and the princes her beauty,* i.e., how they would be in their beauty and in their tranquility; and the verse, *to destroy them, he gave to him to show,* i.e., he showed him those who would oppress them.[14]

❑ אֶת עַבְדְּךָ — **YOUR SERVANT.** [Moses described himself in this manner, recalling how God said about him,] לֹא כֵן עַבְדִּי מֹשֶׁה, *Not so is My servant Moses* (*Numbers* 12:7).[15]

❑ This verse begins with an א (= 1) and ends with a כ (= 20),[15a] and contains twenty-one words, corresponding to [the word אַךְ, *only,* in the verse,] אַךְ טוֹב לְיִשְׂרָאֵל, *Only goodness for Israel* (*Psalms* 73:1), and corresponding to [God's Name] אֶהְיֶה, *I Shall Be* (*Exodus* 3:14).[15b]

25. אֶעְבְּרָה נָּא — **LET ME NOW CROSS OVER.** [With the word נָּא, Moses was intimating:] The Jordan is נ (= 50) cubits wide.[16] I do not intend to cross it more than א (= 1) cubit.[17]

---

prosperity and tranquility and to the vicissitudes that the nation would undergo in the future, as described in the Baal HaTurim's next comment. Accordingly, the allusion of the two *tagin* on the letter ר indicates that the word לְהַרְאוֹת, *to show* (from the root ראה, which begins with a ר), stands for two visions that God showed Moses, Israel in tranquil times and Israel in oppressive times (*VeChur LaZahav*).

13. *Sifrei* to 34:1 below, cited in *Rashi* to that verse.

14. See the Baal HaTurim to *Numbers* 21:4.

15. *Tanchuma* 4. *Rashi* explains that the terms גְּדְלְךָ, *Your greatness,* and יָדְךָ הַחֲזָקָה, *Your strong hand,* both refer to the Attributes of Divine Mercy and Beneficence. Thus, the verse represents *only goodness for Israel* (Y.S.).

15a. Although this phenomenon appears thirty times in the Torah and another 105 times in the rest of the *Tanach*, the Baal HaTurim comments on it only twice, here and at 4:34 below, where he explains the connection between אַךְ and אֶהְיֶה. See also the Baal HaTurim's comment to *Exodus* 20:14, s.v., עֲשֶׂרֶת הַדִּבְּרוֹת.

15b. See the Baal HaTurim to *Exodus* 3:14, where he explains the significance of this Name.

16. *Sifrei* to v. 26; see also the Baal HaTurim to *Numbers* 10:35-36 and 32:32.

17. *Peirush HaRokeach.* Although the Baal HaTurim seems to mean that Moses asked permission to cross one cubit into the Jordan, the *Peirush HaRokeach* reads, [Moses said,] "Permit me to traverse one cubit of the Land [of Israel]."

ג/כו כו בְּעֵ֣בֶר הַיַּרְדֵּ֑ן הָהָ֥ר הַטּ֛וֹב הַזֶּ֖ה וְהַלְּבָנֹֽן׃ וַיִּתְעַבֵּ֨ר יהוָ֥ה בִּי֙ לְמַ֣עַנְכֶ֔ם וְלֹ֥א שָׁמַ֖ע אֵלָ֑י וַיֹּ֨אמֶר יהוָ֤ה אֵלַי֙ רַב־לָ֔ךְ

בעל הטורים

❑ **וְהַלְּבָנֹן.** חָסֵר וָי״ו – עַל שֵׁם ו׳ דְּבָרִים שֶׁבְּ״זֹאת הַתּוֹרָה לָעֹלָה לַמִּנְחָה וְלַחַטָּאת וְלָאָשָׁם וְלַמִּלּוּאִים וּלְזֶבַח הַשְּׁלָמִים״.

❑ מִן ״וָאֶתְחַנַּן״ עַד ״וְהַלְּבָנֹן״ אַרְבָּעִים תֵּבוֹת, לוֹמַר, זְכֹר לִי אַרְבָּעִים יוֹם שֶׁעָמַדְתִּי לְפָנֶיךָ בָּהָר.

❑ לְעוֹלָם יְסַדֵּר אָדָם שִׁבְחוֹ שֶׁל מָקוֹם וְאַחַר כָּךְ יִתְפַּלֵּל. מְנָא לָן? מִמֹּשֶׁה – ״אֶת גָּדְלְךָ״ זֶה הָאֵל הַגָּדוֹל; ״וְאֶת יָדְךָ הַחֲזָקָה״ זֶה אַתָּה גִבּוֹר; ״אֲשֶׁר מִי אֵל בַּשָּׁמַיִם״, כְּנֶגֶד ״אַתָּה קָדוֹשׁ״. ״אֶעְבְּרָה נָּא״, {מִכָּאן שֶׁ}אַל יִשְׁאַל אָדָם צְרָכָיו בְּג׳ רִאשׁוֹנוֹת:

(כו) **רַב לָךְ.** פֵּרוּשׁ, אַתָּה הִתְחַלְתָּ לְסַפֵּר בְּשִׁבְחִי. רַב הוּא אֶצְלְךָ וְגָדוֹל מִמְּךָ מִלְּסַפֵּר בּוֹ:
דָּבָר אַחֵר – הָרַב שֶׁלְּךָ וְגָדוֹל מִמְּךָ, וְהוּא אָדָם הָרִאשׁוֹן, עַל יָדוֹ נִקְנְסָה מִיתָה לַכֹּל, וְאִי אֶפְשָׁר לְךָ לְהִנָּצֵל מִמֶּנָּה:
דָּבָר אַחֵר – ״רַב לָךְ״ הַרְבֵּה פְּעָמִים עָשִׂיתָ כְּנֶגְדִּי – אָמַרְתָּ ״שְׁלַח נָא בְּיַד תִּשְׁלָח״, וְ״לָמָה הֲרֵעֹתָה״, ״הֲצֹאן וּבָקָר״, וְ״הַסֶּלַע.״ אִי אֶפְשָׁר לִי לִסְבֹּל לְךָ יוֹתֵר:

BAAL HATURIM ELUCIDATED

❑ וְהַלְּבָנֹן — **AND THE LEBANON.** This word is spelled defectively,[18] without a ו (= 6). This is an allusion to the six offerings mentioned in the verse, זֹאת הַתּוֹרָה לָעֹלָה לַמִּנְחָה וְלַחַטָּאת וְלָאָשָׁם וְלַמִּלּוּאִים וּלְזֶבַח הַשְּׁלָמִים, *This is the law of* (i) *the burnt-offering, of* (ii) *the meal-offering, and of* (iii) *the sin-offering, and of* (iv) *the guilt-offering; and of* (v) *the inauguration-offerings, and of* (vi) *the peace-offering sacrifice* (*Leviticus* 7:37).[19]

❑ There are forty words from וָאֶתְחַנַּן until וְהַלְּבָנֹן,[20] as if Moses was saying, "Remember on my behalf, the forty days that I stood before You on Mount [Sinai]."[21]

❑ [The Talmud states:] A person should always set forth praise of the Omnipresent and then pray. How do we know this? From [the prayer of] Moses.[22] [His

18. The word לְבָנוֹן, with and without a prefix or suffix, appears seventy-one times in the *Tanach* — three of those appearances are in the Torah (*Deuteronomy* 1:7, 3:5 and 11:24) — each time spelled in full, לְבָנוֹן, with a ו, except in our verse.

19. *Targum Onkelos* renders וְהַלְּבָנֹן as וּבֵית מַקְדְּשָׁא, *and the Beis HaMikdash* (see also *Gittin* 56a). The Talmud explains that it is called לְבָנוֹן, literally, *whitener,* because it whitens, i.e., cleanses Israel of sin (*Yoma* 39b). The Midrash explains that when Moses prayed to see the לְבָנוֹן, he meant the *Beis HaMikdash* (*Sifrei* to *Bamidbar* 27:12, cited by *Rashi* here).

The Baal HaTurim adds that Moses did not pray that he be permitted merely to see the *Beis HaMikdash.* He wished to bring offerings and to observe the *Kohanim* performing the Altar services. Thus, the word לְבָנֹן, without the ו, implies that Moses said, "If I am denied permission to see the לְבָנוֹן, then I cannot participate in the six types of offerings" (*VeChur LaZahav*).

20. That is, וְהַלְּבָנֹן is the fortieth word in this *sidra.*

21. See *Devarim Rabbah* 11:9.

22. *Berachos* 32a — A person should always set forth praise of the Holy One, Blessed is He, and then pray. How do we know this? From Moses, for it is written, *"I prayed to HASHEM at that time."* And it is written further [i.e., Moses goes on to describe his prayer], *"My Lord, HASHEM/ELOHIM, You have begun to show Your servant Your greatness and Your strong hand, for what power is there in the heavens or on the earth that can perform anything like Your deeds or like Your mighty acts?"* [i.e., Moses set forth praise of

on the other side of the Jordan, this good mountain and the Lebanon."

[26] *But* HASHEM *became angry with me because of you, and He did not listen to me;* HASHEM *said to me, "It is enough for you!*

BAAL HATURIM ELUCIDATED

use of the term] אֶת גָּדְלְךָ, *Your greatness,* refers to [the first blessing[23] of *Shemoneh Esrei* which praises Him as] הָאֵל הַגָּדוֹל, *the great God.* [Moses'] וְאֶת יָדְךָ הַחֲזָקָה, *and Your strong hand,* refers to [the second blessing which begins] אַתָּה גִּבּוֹר, *You are mighty.* [And the phrase] אֲשֶׁר מִי אֵל בַּשָּׁמַיִם, *for what power is there in the heaven,* refers to [the third blessing]: אַתָּה קָדוֹשׁ, *You are holy.*[24] [Only then did Moses make his request,] *Let me now cross over.* {We derive from this, that} a person should not ask for his needs in the first three [blessings].

26. רַב לָךְ — IT IS ENOUGH[25] FOR YOU! This means: [God replied to Moses,] "You began to relate My praise. *It is too much for you* and greater than your capacity to relate."[26]

Alternatively: [God was telling Moses,] "*Your master,*[25] who was greater than you, i.e., Adam, the first man, caused through his deed that death was decreed on all human beings, and it is impossible for you to be saved from it."[27]

Alternatively: רַב לָךְ [means, God told Moses,] "*Many times,*[25] *you* have acted against Me: You said, 'שְׁלַח נָא בְּיַד תִּשְׁלָח, *Send through whomever You will send!*' (*Exodus* 4:13); and 'לָמָה הֲרֵעֹתָה, *Why have You done evil?*' (*Exodus* 5:22); and 'הֲצֹאן וּבָקָר, *Can sheep and cattle* [*be slaughtered?*]' (*Numbers* 11:22); and 'הַסֶּלַע, [*Shall we bring forth water for you from*] *this rock?*' (*Numbers* 20:10). I cannot forbear you any longer."[28]

God]. [Only] after that it is written, *"Let me now cross over and see the good land . . ."* [i.e., only after setting forth praise, he prayed that he be permitted to enter the Land of Israel].

23. The custom of beginning *Shemoneh Esrei* — the basic purpose of which is to pray that God provide all of our needs — with three blessings of praise is based on the Talmudic teaching cited in note 22 above. The Baal HaTurim shows how those three blessings are implicit in Moses' words. For further study of this theme, see *Rashba* to *Berachos* 32a (cited in note 59 in the Schottenstein Edition of the Talmud).

24. For the conclusion of that blessing refers to God as הָאֵל הַקָּדוֹשׁ, *the holy God.*

25. Literally, [*too*] *much* or [*too*] *many.* The word רַב can also mean *rabbi* or *master.* In his alternative explanations, the Baal HaTurim uses each of these translations.

26. The Talmud relates that a man once served as *chazzan* in Rabbi Chanina's synagogue. After the words הָאֵל הַגָּדוֹל הַגִּבּוֹר וְהַנּוֹרָא, *The great, the mighty and the awesome God,* the *chazzan* added, הָאַדִּיר וְהֶחָזָק וְהָאַמִּיץ, *the glorious and the strong and the powerful.* After the prayer service, Rabbi Chanina asked him, "And did you complete all the praises of your Master? [You should know that even] regarding the three praises, 'the great, the mighty and the awesome,' that are included in the standard blessing, the only reason we are permitted to recite them is because Moses wrote them in the Torah (*Deuteronomy* 10:17) and the Men of the Great Assembly recited them in prayer (see *Nehemiah* 9:32). Had they not done so, we would not be permitted to mention even those three praises. Yet you add others! Your praises are comparable to one who wished to describe a fabulously wealthy man, one who owned millions of gold coins, yet he extolled him as possessing silver coins. Is that not a debasement of the rich man?" (*Megillah* 25a).

27. *Tanchuma* 4.

28. See *Tanchuma* 6.

כז אַל־תּוֹסֶף דַּבֵּר אֵלַי עוֹד בַּדָּבָר הַזֶּה׃ עֲלֵה ׀ רֹאשׁ הַפִּסְגָּה וְשָׂא עֵינֶיךָ יָמָּה וְצָפֹנָה וְתֵימָנָה וּמִזְרָחָה

בעל הטורים

דָּבָר אַחֵר – אֲפִלּוּ בַּדָּבָר הַמּוּעָט שֶׁאַתָּה עוֹשֶׂה שֶׁלֹּא כְּהֹגֶן, הוּא "רַב לָךְ" לְפִי חָכְמָתֶךָ׃

דָּבָר אַחֵר – בָּזֶה יִוָּדַע שֶׁ"רַב לָךְ", כִּי אֲנִי רַבְּךָ. כִּי כַּמָּה פְּעָמִים נִצַּחְתַּנִי, וְעַתָּה לֹא תוּכַל לְנַצְּחֵנִי׃

דָּבָר אַחֵר – "רַב לָךְ", אַתָּה יֵשׁ לְךָ רַב {וְיָכוֹל לְהַתִּיר נִדְרְךָ}. אֲבָל אֲנִי אֵין לִי רַב שֶׁיַּתִּיר שְׁבוּעָתִי {שֶׁנִּשְׁבַּעְתִּי} "לָכֵן לֹא תָבִיאוּ"׃

דָּבָר אַחֵר – הִגִּיעָה הַשָּׁעָה שֶׁיֵּשׁ לְךָ רַב, כִּי כְּבָר הִגִּיעַ זְמַנּוֹ שֶׁל יְהוֹשֻׁעַ, וְאֵין רַבָּנוּתוֹ נִכָּר בְּעוֹדְךָ חָי׃

דָּבָר אַחֵר – אַל תִּירָא מִמַּלְאַךְ הַמָּוֶת, כִּי הָרַב שֶׁלְּךָ יַעֲסֹק בְּךָ׃

דָּבָר אַחֵר – "רַב לָךְ", הַרְבֵּה טוֹבוֹת מְתֻקָּנִים לְךָ, "מָה רַב טוּבְךָ אֲשֶׁר צָפַנְתָּ לִּירֵאֶיךָ"׃

BAAL HATURIM ELUCIDATED

Alternatively: [It is as if God told Moses,] "Even if you commit a minor infraction, it is considered as *too much for you,*[28a] in proportion to your [superior] wisdom."[29]

Alternatively: [God was telling Moses,] "Through this, you will see that *you have a Master,*[29a] for I am your Master. Although on several occasions you have prevailed over Me,[30] but this time you will not be able to prevail over Me."

Alternatively, [God told Moses,] "רַב לָךְ, *you have a rabbi*[30a] {who will be able to annul your vow.[31]}[32] I have no *rabbi* who can annul My oath[33] {that I swore},

28a. See note 25 above.

29. See *Bava Kamma* 50a — The Holy One, Blessed is He, is strict with those who surround Him [i.e., those who are close to Him], even regarding [a deviation as slight as] a hairsbreadth.

29a. See note 25 above.

30. For example, after the incident of the golden calf: *Hashem said to Moses, "I have seen this people . . . desist from Me; let My anger flare up against them and I shall consume them . . ." And Moses entreated before Hashem . . . "Why, Hashem, should Your anger flare up against Your people? . . . Remember for the sake of Abraham, Isaac and Israel, Your servants, to whom You swore . . . 'I shall increase your offspring like the stars of the heavens . . . '." And Hashem reconsidered regarding the evil that He declared He would do to His people* (*Exodus* 32:9-14). Similarly, after the incident of the spies (see *Numbers* 14:11-20) and after the rebellion of Korah (see *Numbers* 16:20-24).

30a. See note 25 above.

31. The Torah provides a mechanism for the annulment of vows, oaths and the like. One who has made a vow or taken an oath may come before a single sage [the exact qualifications are a matter of dispute, nevertheless, in post-Talmudic times no individual is considered knowledgeable enough to be recognized as a "sage" with respect to annulling vows (see *Shulchan Aruch, Yoreh Deah* 228:1 and 334:42, with commentaries)] or a panel of at least three learned men and request that they nullify his or her vow. If the sage or panel determines that there is sufficient halachic basis for such annulment, they may annul it.

32. The phrases enclosed in braces appear in *Shoham Yakar's* manuscript edition but not in the printed editions.

33. This comment is difficult, for the Talmud relates that Rabbah bar bar Chanah was once traveling through the wilderness and came to Mount Sinai. There he heard a Heavenly voice saying, "Woe is to Me, for I have sworn [to send Israel into exile] and now that I have sworn, who

Do not continue to speak to Me further about this matter. 27 *Ascend to the top of the cliff and raise your eyes westward, northward, southward, and eastward, and*

BAAL HATURIM ELUCIDATED

'לָכֵן לֹא תָבִיאָה, *Therefore*[34] *you will not bring* [*this congregation into the land that I have given them*]' " (*Numbers* 20:12).

Alternatively: [God said,] "The time has come for *you* to *have a master,* i.e., for the time of Joshua's leadership has already arrived, but his leadership is not recognizable while you are yet alive."[35]

Alternatively: [God was telling Moses,] "Do not fear the angel of death, for *your Master,* [i.e., I Myself,] will tend to you[r burial]."[36]

Alternatively: [God said to Moses,] "רַב לָךְ, *There is much* [*good prepared*] *for you,* [as it is stated,] מָה רַב טוּבְךָ אֲשֶׁר צָפַנְתָּ לִּירֵאֶיךָ, *How abundant is Your goodness that You have stored away for those who fear You!*" (*Psalms* 31:20).[37]

❑ {The Baal HaTurim's comment to אַל תּוֹסֶף appears at *Exodus* 10:28.}

27. {The Baal HaTurim's comment to וְשָׂא appears at *Numbers* 3:40.}

---

can annul [My oath] for Me?" When Rabbah bar bar Chanah returned and related the incident to the Rabbis, they said, ". . . You should have said [to God], 'It is annulled for You . . .' " (*Bava Basra* 74a; see *Tosafos,* s.v., ועבשיו). The implication of this passage is that had Rabbah bar bar Chanah said, "It is annulled for You," God's oath would have been annulled.

Moreover, according to one opinion in the Talmud, when Moses entreated God to spare the nation after the incident of the golden calf (see note 30 above), God had actually taken an oath to destroy them, yet Moses was able to annul God's oath (*Berachos* 32a). Accordingly, in our situation, Moses should have been able to respond to God, "It is annulled for You," as he had done on the earlier occasion.

Perhaps the answer lies in two other Talmudic passages. The Torah states, *If a man takes a vow or swears an oath . . . he shall not desecrate his word* (*Numbers* 30:3). One passage infers from that verse, *"he" shall not desecrate "his" word,* but someone else may, i.e., a sage may annul the vow or oath for him (*Chagigah* 10a). A second passage adds that *"he" shall not desecrate "his" word* implies that even a sage may not annul his own vows (*Nedarim* 81b). Moreover, it does not matter whether he took the vow himself or someone else pronounced a vow against him (e.g., someone made an oath that prohibited this particular sage from entering the vower's home), in either case, this sage cannot become the agent to annul any vow that concerns him (*Ritva*; based on *Yerushalmi, Nedarim* 5:4). Accordingly, although we find that Moses was able to annul God's oath regarding destroying the nation after the incident of the golden calf, nevertheless, he could not annul God's oath regarding Moses' entering the Land of Israel. For, with regard to the first oath, God specifically excluded Moses from the consequences — *And now, desist from Me. Let My anger flare up against them and I shall consume them; and I shall make you a great nation* (*Exodus* 30:10). Therefore, Moses could annul that oath. But Moses was not able to annul the second oath, for he was the prohibited object of that oath (*VeChur LaZahav*).

In this matter, the Baal HaTurim seems to be at odds with the kabbalistic concept (based on *Isaiah* 14:27) that God can annul His own vows (*Tikkunei Zohar* 143a, s.v., קָם רַבִּי שִׁמְעוֹן, included in the Yom Kippur *Machzor* just before כָּל נִדְרֵי).

34. The word לָכֵן, *therefore,* implies an oath, as it is stated (*I Samuel* 3:14), וְלָכֵן נִשְׁבַּעְתִּי לְבֵית עֵלִי, *therefore I have sworn concerning the house of Eli* (*Tanchuma, Va'eira* 2 and *Shofetim* 1, cited by *Rashi* to *Numbers* 20:12).

35. *Sotah* 13b; see *Rashi* there, s.v., רב יש לך; see also *Rashi* to 31:2 below, s.v., לֹא אוּכַל.

36. See *Sotah* 14a, cited in *Rashi* to 34:6 below.

37. *Sifrei,* cited by *Rashi.* The word רַב in our verse alludes to the word רַב in that verse.

כח וּרְאֵ֣ה בְעֵינֶ֔יךָ כִּי־לֹ֥א תַעֲבֹ֖ר אֶת־הַיַּרְדֵּ֣ן הַזֶּ֑ה׃ וְצַ֣ו אֶת־יְהוֹשֻׁ֗עַ וְחַזְּקֵ֣הוּ וְאַמְּצֵ֔הוּ כִּי־ה֣וּא יַעֲבֹ֗ר לִפְנֵי֙ הָעָ֣ם הַזֶּ֔ה וְהוּא֙ יַנְחִ֣יל אוֹתָ֔ם אֶת־הָאָ֖רֶץ אֲשֶׁ֥ר תִּרְאֶֽה׃ כט וַנֵּ֣שֶׁב בַּגָּ֔יְא מ֖וּל בֵּ֥ית פְּעֽוֹר׃

ד א וְעַתָּ֣ה יִשְׂרָאֵ֗ל שְׁמַ֤ע אֶל־הַֽחֻקִּים֙ וְאֶל־הַמִּשְׁפָּטִ֔ים אֲשֶׁ֧ר אָֽנֹכִ֛י מְלַמֵּ֥ד אֶתְכֶ֖ם לַֽעֲשׂ֑וֹת לְמַ֣עַן תִּֽחְי֗וּ וּבָאתֶם֙ וִֽירִשְׁתֶּ֣ם אֶת־הָאָ֔רֶץ אֲשֶׁ֧ר יְהֹוָ֛ה אֱלֹהֵ֥י אֲבֹֽתֵיכֶ֖ם נֹתֵ֥ן לָכֶֽם׃ ב לֹ֣א תֹסִ֗פוּ עַל־הַדָּבָר֙ אֲשֶׁ֤ר אָֽנֹכִי֙ מְצַוֶּ֣ה אֶתְכֶ֔ם וְלֹ֥א תִגְרְע֖וּ מִמֶּ֑נּוּ לִשְׁמֹ֗ר אֶת־מִצְוֺת֙ יְהֹוָ֣ה אֱלֹֽהֵיכֶ֔ם אֲשֶׁ֥ר אָֽנֹכִ֖י מְצַוֶּ֥ה אֶתְכֶֽם׃

בעל הטורים

(כח) וְחַזְּקֵהוּ. ב' בַּמָּסוֹרֶת. "וְצַו אֶת יְהוֹשֻׁעַ וְחַזְּקֵהוּ"; "הַחֲזֵק מִלְחַמְתְּךָ אֶל הָעִיר וְהָרְסָהּ וְחַזְּקֵהוּ" בְּיוֹאָב. כְּמוֹ שֶׁיּוֹאָב הָיָה שַׂר הַצָּבָא, כָּךְ הָיָה יְהוֹשֻׁעַ שַׂר צָבָא אַף בְּחַיֵּי מֹשֶׁה כְּדֵי לְהַחֲזִיקוֹ. כְּמוֹ שֶׁמְפֹרָשׁ בְּמִלְחֶמֶת עֲמָלֵק:

ד (א) מְלַמֵּד אֶתְכֶם לַעֲשׂוֹת. שֶׁהַתַּלְמוּד מֵבִיא לִידֵי מַעֲשֶׂה:

(ב) וְלֹא תִגְרְעוּ מִמֶּנּוּ לִשְׁמֹר אֶת. סוֹפֵי תֵּבוֹת תרי"ג:

▯ אֲשֶׁר אָנֹכִי מְצַוֶּה אֶתְכֶם. וּסְמִיךְ לֵהּ "עֵינֵיכֶם הָרֹאוֹת", שֶׁאֵין לַדַּיָּן אֶלָּא מַה שֶׁעֵינָיו רוֹאוֹת:

BAAL HATURIM ELUCIDATED

28. וְחַזְּקֵהוּ — AND ENCOURAGE HIM. The masoretic note, ב׳, means that this word appears twice in the *Tanach*: (i) here, וְצַו אֶת יְהוֹשֻׁעַ וְחַזְּקֵהוּ, *You shall command Joshua and encourage him;* and (ii) הַחֲזֵק מִלְחַמְתְּךָ אֶל הָעִיר וְהָרְסָהּ וְחַזְּקֵהוּ, *Strengthen your battle against the city and destroy it; and encourage him* (II Samuel 11:25), regarding Joab. [This indicates that] just as Joab was the commander of the army, so too, was Joshua commander of the army even in Moses' lifetime, in order to strengthen [Joshua], as is related in the narrative about the war against Amalek.[38]

IV.

1. {The Baal HaTurim's comment to וְעַתָּה יִשְׂרָאֵל appears at 10:12 below.}

▯ מְלַמֵּד אֶתְכֶם לַעֲשׂוֹת — TEACH YOU TO DO. [This phrase alludes to the concept] that study leads to deed.[39]

2. וְלֹא תִגְרְעוּ מִמֶּנּוּ לִשְׁמֹר אֶת — AND YOU SHALL NOT SUBTRACT FROM IT, TO OBSERVE

---

38. See *Exodus* 17:9-13; see also *Sifrei* to *Numbers* 27:18, cited by *Rashi* there, s.v., וְסָמַכְתָּ.
39. *Peirush HaRokeach*; see *Ibn Ezra*. The Talmud states: Study is great because it leads to deed (*Megillah* 27a; *Kiddushin* 40b; *Bava Kamma* 17a). However, no verses are adduced there to lend Scriptural support to this concept. The Baal HaTurim finds such support in our verse.

see with your eyes, for you shall not cross this Jordan. [28] You shall command Joshua, and encourage him and give him resolve, for he shall cross before this people and he shall cause them to inherit the land that you will see."

[29] So we remained in the valley, opposite Beth-peor.

4

[1] And now, O Israel, listen to the decrees and to the ordinances that I teach you to do, so that you may live, and you will come and possess the land that HASHEM, the God of your forefathers, gives you. [2] You shall not add to the word that I command you, and you shall not subtract from it, to observe the commandments of HASHEM, your God, that I command you.

BAAL HATURIM ELUCIDATED

THE. The [*gematria* of the] final letters of these words is 613 [the number of *mitzvos*[40] commanded in the Torah].[41]

❑ **אֲשֶׁר אָנֹכִי מְצַוֶּה אֶתְכֶם** — **THAT I COMMAND YOU.** Juxtaposed to this is the phrase עֵינֵיכֶם הָרֹאוֹת, *Your eyes, they see* (v. 3). [This teaches] that a judge is required to render judgment based only on what his eyes perceive [i.e., the evidence before his eyes].[42]

40. The Talmud expounds on the number of *mitzvos* commanded to Israel in the Torah: Six hundred and thirteen *mitzvos* were told to Moses — 365 negative [i.e., you shall not do] commandments, corresponding to the number of days in the solar year; and 248 positive [i.e., you shall do] commandments, corresponding to the number of *eivarim* [i.e., body parts that contain bone, flesh and sinews] of the human body . . . Which verse teaches this number? תּוֹרָה צִוָּה לָנוּ מֹשֶׁה מוֹרָשָׁה, [which may be understood,] *Moses commanded us* תּוֹרָה *as a heritage* (33:4 below), and the *gematria* of תּוֹרָה is 611. [Add to that total two more, for the first two of the Ten Commandments,] *I am HASHEM, your God* and *You shall have no other gods,* [we did not hear from Moses, rather,] we heard directly from the Almighty.

41. *Peirush HaRokeach; Paaneach Raza.* In *Paaneach Raza,* the comment continues: For the number of *mitzvos* may not be decreased from six hundred thirteen.

Why does the allusion to 613 appear in the phrase regarding subtracting from the *mitzvos,* rather than in the phrase regarding adding to them? Because, based upon supporting verses in the Torah, the Rabbis [from Kings David and Solomon through the Second Temple era] added seven *mitzvos,* such as Chanukah and Purim (*Peirush HaRokeach*).

42. *Sanhedrin* 6b — Judges should know Whom they are judging [i.e., who will be affected by their decision, namely, God, for He will have to rectify the consequences of any miscarriage of justice (*Rashi*)]; and in Whose presence they are judging [i.e., God, see below]; and Who will exact punishment [if they render a false decision], as it is stated, *God stands in the Divine assembly, He shall judge among the judges* (*Psalms* 82:1). And so is it stated regarding King Jehoshaphat, *He* [*Jehoshaphat*] *said to the judges, "Scrutinize what you are doing* [i.e., examine the evidence in a case carefully], *for you are not judging* [*only*] *man, rather* [*you are judging*] *HASHEM" and He is with you in the matter of judgment* (*II Chronicles* 19:6). Now, perhaps a judge will say, "Why do I need this trouble? [i.e., if I make an error, I will be punished (*Rashi*)]." Therefore the verse states, *and He is with you in the matter of judgment,* which implies that a judge is required to render judgment based only on what his eyes perceive [i.e., he must try the case with the intention of rendering his decision righteously and truthfully, and then he will not be subject to punishment (*Rashi*)].

Although the Talmud adduces a verse from *Chronicles,* the Baal HaTurim finds an allusion to this teaching in the Torah.

[1855] **DEVARIM** / VA'ESCHANAN

ד/ג-ה ג עֵינֵיכֶם֙ הָרֹא֔וֹת אֵ֥ת אֲשֶׁר־עָשָׂ֥ה יהו֖ה בְּבַ֣עַל פְּע֑וֹר
כִּ֣י כָל־הָאִ֗ישׁ אֲשֶׁ֤ר הָלַךְ֙ אַחֲרֵ֣י בַֽעַל־פְּע֔וֹר הִשְׁמִיד֛וֹ
ד יהו֥ה אֱלֹהֶ֖יךָ מִקִּרְבֶּֽךָ׃ וְאַתֶּם֙ הַדְּבֵקִ֔ים בַּֽיהו֖ה
שני ה אֱלֹהֵיכֶ֑ם חַיִּ֥ים כֻּלְּכֶ֖ם הַיּֽוֹם׃ רְאֵ֣ה ׀ לִמַּ֣דְתִּי אֶתְכֶ֗ם
חֻקִּים֙ וּמִשְׁפָּטִ֔ים כַּאֲשֶׁ֥ר צִוַּ֖נִי יהו֣ה אֱלֹהָ֑י לַעֲשׂ֣וֹת כֵּ֔ן

בעל הטורים

(ד) **וְאַתֶּם הַדְּבֵקִים.** תָּגִין עַל הַקוּ״ף – רֶמֶז לְמֵאָה בְרָכוֹת שֶׁצָּרִיךְ לְבָרֵךְ בְּכָל יוֹם:

❑ **כֻּלְּכֶם הַיּוֹם.** וּסְמִיךְ לֵהּ ״לִמַּדְתִּי אֶתְכֶם״, דִּשְׁמַעְתָּא בָעֲיָא צְלוּתָא כַשֶּׁמֶשׁ, וְזֶהוּ ״הַיּוֹם . . . לִמַּדְתִּי״:

וְעוֹד ״כֻּלְּכֶם הַיּוֹם {. . . לִמַּדְתִּי}״ שֶׁזְּכוּת הָרַבִּים מְסַיַּעַת:

(ה) **לִמַּדְתִּי אֶתְכֶם.** בְּחִנָּם. {״צִוַּנִי ה׳.״ בְּגִימַטְרִיָּא בְּלִמּוּד בְּחִנָּם:}

BAAL HATURIM ELUCIDATED

4. **וְאַתֶּם הַדְּבֵקִים** — BUT YOU, THOSE WHO CLING. [According to a scribal tradition,] the ק (= 100) of this phrase is written with [three] *tagin*[43] [crownlets]. This is an allusion to the hundred blessings that each person is obligated to recite every day.[44]

❑ **כֻּלְּכֶם הַיּוֹם** — YOU ARE ALL... THIS DAY.[45] Juxtaposed to this is, לִמַּדְתִּי אֶתְכֶם, *I have taught you.* [This is an allusion to the Talmudic statement:] Because a halachic discussion requires clarity of mind like [the clarity of] the sun['s light].[46] Thus,

43. Regarding *tagin,* see first paragraph of note 56 to *parashas Devarim* above.

ק with one *tag*
ק with three *tagin*

Although the letter ק is usually crowned with only one *tag,* according to the ancient *Sefer Tagin,* the ק of הַדְּבֵקִים is one of 185 (one version lists only 181) in the Torah that are uncharacteristically crowned with three *tagin* (see illustration).

44. The Talmud states: A person is obligated to recite [a minimum of] one hundred blessings every day, as it is said (10:12 below), וְעַתָּה יִשְׂרָאֵל מָה ה׳ אֱלֹהֶיךָ שֹׁאֵל מֵעִמָּךְ, *and now, O Israel, what does* HASHEM, *your God, ask of you?* (*Menachos* 43b). That is, read the word מָה, *what,* as if it were spelled מֵאָה, *one hundred* (*Rashi*). The verse then means: *And now, O Israel, one hundred* [*blessings*] HASHEM, *your God, asks of you.* The Baal HaTurim's comment teaches how one brings himself to cling to God the entire day — namely, by reciting one hundred blessings every day (*Shoham Yakar*).

For a listing of more than one hundred blessings routinely recited every weekday and for how to compensate for the twenty-nine fewer blessings in the *Amidah* prayers of *Shabbos* and *yom tov,* see *Mishnah Berurah* 46:14. Interestingly, the Baal HaTurim writes elsewhere that the *Anshei Kenesses HaGedolah* instituted so many morning blessings in order to enable people to recite one hundred blessings every day (*Tur, Orach Chaim* 46).

The Baal HaTurim speaks about the concept of a hundred blessings each day in his comments to *Genesis* 14:19; *Exodus* 38:27; *Deuteronomy* 5:7, 10:12, 31:16 and 33:1.

45. The term הַיּוֹם, *today,* can also be understood as a reference to the sun (see *Rashi, Genesis* 3:8, s.v. **לְרוּחַ הַיּוֹם**, and 18:1, s.v., **כְּחֹם הַיּוֹם**, *Numbers* 28:3; *Malachi* 3:19, s.v., **כִּי הִנֵּה**; *Song of Songs* 4:6; and *Avodah Zarah* 4a, s.v., **היום בא**), and that is how the Baal HaTurim's first interpretation renders it. See also the Baal HaTurim to *Exodus* 29:38, s.v., **שָׁנָה שְׁנַיִם**; *Numbers* 28:3, s.v., **לַיּוֹם**; and 2:25 above, s.v., **הַיּוֹם הַזֶּה**.

46. Printed editions of the Talmud read: **דִּשְׁמַעְתָּא בְּעָא צִילוּתָא כְּיוֹמָא דְאַסְתָּנָא**, *Because a halachic discussion requires clarity* [of mind (*Rashi*)] *like* [*the clarity of*] *a day of the north wind* [for the north wind brings sunny weather (*Rashi* to *Eruvin* 65a)] (*Megillah* 28b). Two questions arise: Whereas the

[3] *Your eyes, they see what* HASHEM *has done with Baal-peor, for every man that followed Baal-peor —* HASHEM, *your God, destroyed him from your midst.* [4] *But you — those who cling to* HASHEM, *your God — you are all alive this day.*

[5] *See, I have taught you decrees and ordinances, as* HASHEM, *my God, has commanded me, to do so in the*

BAAL HATURIM ELUCIDATED

[the juxtaposition of] *this day* [i.e., *this sun*] . . . *I have taught you.*

Alternatively: [The juxtaposition of] *You are all . . . today* {with *I have taught*}[47] [is an allusion to the Mishnaic[48] teaching] that the merit of the many assists.[49]

5. לִמַּדְתִּי אֶתְכֶם — **I HAVE TAUGHT** without charge[50] {[as alluded to in] the *gematria* of the phrase צִוַּנִי ה׳, *HASHEM has commanded me* (182) [which] is equal to that of בְּלִמּוּד בְּחִנָּם, by teaching without charge[51]}.[52]

Baal HaTurim's comment is based on the Scriptural term הַיּוֹם (see note 45), and whereas the Talmud uses the term כְּיוֹמָא, why does the Baal HaTurim use the term כַּשֶּׁמֶשׁ, *like the sun,* rather than כְּיוֹמָא, as in the Talmudic version? Additionally, whereas the Talmudic phrase is in Aramaic, why did the Baal HaTurim use the Hebrew term כַּשֶּׁמֶשׁ, rather than the Aramaic term כְּשִׁמְשָׁא?

In truth, the Munich manuscript of the Talmud has a shorter version of the Talmudic statement. It says simply, דִּשְׁמַעְתָּא בָּעֲיָא צִילוּתָא, *Because a halachic discussion requires clarity* [*of mind*], and that is the version cited by the *Rif* and the *Rosh* (father of the Baal HaTurim). Presumably, the Baal HaTurim had that version in his copy of the Talmud. Accordingly, the Baal HaTurim's comment should be read: [. . . an allusion to the Talmudic statement:] "דִּשְׁמַעְתָּא עֲיָא צִילוּתָא, *Because a halachic discussion requires clarity* [*of mind*]," [i.e., the mind must be clear] כַּשֶּׁמֶשׁ, *like the sun* [*'s light*] (*VeChur LaZahav*).

47. The words enclosed in braces are not found in the printed edition, but do appear in *Shoham Yakar's* manuscript edition.

48. One mishnah states: All who occupy themselves with the affairs of the community should do so for the sake of Heaven, for then, the merit of their [i.e., the community's] forebears will assist them, for their righteousness stands forever (*Avos* 2:2).

Another mishnah states: If one is instrumental in bringing merit for the masses [by teaching them Torah and encouraging them to fulfill its *mitzvos*], no sin will ever result from his actions . . . Moses brought merit for himself and merit for the masses, therefore the merit of the masses is credited to him, as it is stated [regarding Moses] (*Deuteronomy* 33:21), *He carried out the righteous ways of* HASHEM *and His ordinances with Israel* (*Avos* 5:18).

49. A fuller version of this comment appears in *Peirush HaRokeach,* presumably the Baal HaTurim's source: Moses said [to God], "Is it possible that I strived for naught at the head of Your children — whom I kept alive with my prayers (see note 30 above) — when I taught them Your Torah?" God replied, "The Torah shall be called by your name." [And so the prophet wrote], זִכְרוּ תּוֹרַת מֹשֶׁה עַבְדִּי, *Remember the Torah of Moses, My servant* (*Malachi* 3:22). Therefore the Torah juxtaposed *you are all . . . today* with *See, I have taught you.* [As if Moses were saying,] "The merit of the masses [i.e., כֻּלְּכֶם, *all of you*] stands you [plural] in good stead."

50. See *Nedarim* 37a, cited in note 52 below.

51. The passage enclosed in braces is not found in the printed editions, but does appear in *Shoham Yakar's* manuscript edition. However, that edition contains a typographical error, and reads, אֶלְמוּד בְּחִנָּם.

52. The Talmud states that one may not charge a fee for teaching Torah [i.e., for teaching per se; however, a teacher may get paid for peripheral services, such as minding the pupils or teaching them the *trop* (cantillation notes)].

This law is derived from our passage, as the Talmud continues: For it is written, [Moses said,] "HASHEM *commanded me at that time to teach you* [*decrees and ordinances*]" (v. 14 below); and it is also written, [Moses said,] *"See, I have taught*

ד/ו בְּקֶרֶב הָאָרֶץ אֲשֶׁר אַתֶּם בָּאִים שָׁמָּה לְרִשְׁתָּהּ:
ו וּשְׁמַרְתֶּם וַעֲשִׂיתֶם כִּי הִוא חָכְמַתְכֶם וּבִינַתְכֶם
לְעֵינֵי הָעַמִּים אֲשֶׁר יִשְׁמְעוּן אֵת כָּל־הַחֻקִּים
הָאֵלֶּה וְאָמְרוּ רַק עַם־חָכָם וְנָבוֹן הַגּוֹי הַגָּדוֹל הַזֶּה:

בעל הטורים

❑ ט״ו פְּעָמִים לְמִידוֹת בְּמִשְׁנֵה תוֹרָה. רֶמֶז, בֶּן ט״ו לַמִּשְׁנָה:

❑ **בָּאִים שָׁמָּה לְרִשְׁתָּהּ. וּשְׁמַרְתֶּם.** כְּדִכְתִיב ״וַיִּתֵּן לָהֶם אַרְצוֹת גּוֹיִם . . . בַּעֲבוּר יִשְׁמְרוּ חֻקָּיו:

(ו) **הָאֵלֶּה וְאָמְרוּ רַק עַם.** סוֹפֵי תֵבוֹת ״מִקְוֶה״ וְרָאשֵׁי תֵבוֹת ״עֶרְוָה״. לָמָּה עֶרְוַת אָחוֹת אֲסוּרָה וְעֶרְוַת בַּת אָחִיו מֻתֶּרֶת? וְלָמָּה מִקְוֶה אַרְבָּעִים סְאָה מְטַהֵר, וְאִם חָסֵר קֻרְטוֹב אֵינוֹ מְטַהֵר? ״רַק״ מִיעוּטָא הוּא, שֶׁאֵינָם יוֹדְעִים טַעַם כִּלְאַיִם וּפָרָה וְכַיּוֹצֵא בָּהֶם:

BAAL HATURIM ELUCIDATED

❑ Fifteen verbs of the root למד, *to learn* or *to teach,* appear in *Deuteronomy.*[53] This is an allusion that בֶּן ט״ו לַמִּשְׁנָה, *A fifteen-year-old is for Mishnah.*[54]

---

you decrees and ordinances, as HASHEM, my God, has commanded me. [That is,] just as I taught you Torah without charge, so too, shall you teach Torah to others without charge" (*Nedarim* 37a).

53. That is, fifteen verbs that refer to learning or teaching Torah and *mitzvos.* They appear in verses 4:1, 4:5, 4:10 twice, 4:14, 5:1, 5:28, 6:1, 11:19, 14:23, 17:19, 31:12, 31:13, 31:19 and 31:22. Two other words of the root למד appear in 18:9 and 20:18, but they do not refer to teaching or learning Torah and *mitzvos* (*VeChur LaZahav*).

54. *Avos* 5:21 reads: בֶּן חָמֵשׁ שָׁנִים לַמִּקְרָא, *A five-year-old is for Scripture;* בֶּן עֶשֶׂר לַמִּשְׁנָה, *a ten-year-old is for Mishnah;* בֶּן שְׁלֹשׁ עֶשְׂרֵה לַמִּצְוֹת, *a thirteen-year old is for mitzvos;* בֶּן חָמֵשׁ עֶשְׂרֵה לַגְּמָרָא, *a fifteen-year-old is for Gemara* [i.e., Talmud]. Accordingly, we would expect the Baal HaTurim to have written either בֶּן ט״ו לַתַּלְמוּד or בֶּן ט״ו לַגְּמָרָא, and indeed, that is how this comment reads in *Peirush HaRokeach* (see also *R' Chaim Paltiel*). However, *Shoham Yakar's* manuscript edition, as well as the early printed editions, reads לַמִּשְׁנָה, which many later editions have emended to לַגְּמָרָא.

Nevertheless, it is possible to explain the Baal HaTurim's comment without any changes. *Rashi* explains the above-mentioned Mishnah in two ways: It may mean that until a boy is five years old, he is not ready for Scripture; before his tenth birthday, he is not ready for Mishnah; and before his fifteenth, he is not ready for *Gemara.* But the Mishnah makes no mention of when he should be proficient in each particular area of study. Or, it may mean that by the time one is five years old, he should already be able to read and understand the simple meaning of Scriptural verses; within the next five years he should complete the entirety of the *Tanach.* At age ten, he should be able to read and understand the simple meaning of the Mishnah; within the next five years he should complete all of the Mishnah. At age fifteen, he should be able to begin delving deeply into the study of *gemara.* According to this interpretation, the age of ten is relevant to both Scripture and Mishnah; while the age of fifteen is relevant to both Mishnah and *gemara.*

Now, it seems impossible to reconcile the Baal HaTurim's comment with *Rashi's* first interpretation of the Mishnah, for each age bracket relates to only one area of study. But according to *Rashi's* second interpretation, the Mishnah says בֶּן חָמֵשׁ עֶשְׂרֵה לַגְּמָרָא, meaning that at age fifteen a boy should have already mastered the Mishnah and be ready to start the study of *Gemara.* Thus, the Mishnah speaks of the fifteen-year-old with regard to *Gemara*: He should be ready to study it. The Baal HaTurim, on the other hand, speaks of the fifteen-year-old with regard to Mishnah: He should be proficient in it already. Accordingly, the Baal HaTurim is not quoting the words of the Mishnah, and that is why he writes merely, רֶמֶז, *an allusion,* rather than, רֶמֶז לְמַאֲמָרָם, *an allusion to their statement,* as he often does (*VeChur LaZahav*).

midst of the land, there to where you are coming, to take possession of it. 6 *You shall safeguard and perform [them], for that is your wisdom and your understanding in the eyes of the peoples, who shall hear all these decrees and who shall say, "Surely a wise and discerning people is this great nation!"*

BAAL HATURIM ELUCIDATED

❑ בָּאִים שָׁמָּה לְרִשְׁתָּהּ. וּשְׁמַרְתֶּם — TO WHERE YOU ARE COMING, TO TAKE POSSESSION OF IT. YOU SHALL SAFEGUARD . . . [THEM].[54a] [This] is in accordance with that which is written, וַיִּתֵּן לָהֶם אַרְצוֹת גּוֹיִם . . . בַּעֲבוּר יִשְׁמְרוּ חֻקָּיו, *And He gave them the lands of nations . . . so that they might safeguard His decrees* (*Psalms* 105:44-45).[55]

6. הָאֵלֶּה וְאָמְרוּ רַק עַם — THESE . . . AND WHO SHALL SAY, "SURELY A . . . PEOPLE." The final letters of these words [in reverse order] spell the word מִקְוֶה, *mikveh.* And their initial letters [in reverse order] spell the word עֶרְוָה, *nakedness.*[56] [They might ask:][57] "Why are relations with one's sister forbidden, while relations with one's brother's daughter are permitted?"[57a] Or, "Why does a *mikveh* containing forty *se'ah*[58] of water convey purity, yet if a mere *kurtov*[59] is missing it does not convey purity? [Nevertheless,][60] the term רַק implies an exclusion,[61] for they do not understand[62] the rationale for the *mitzvos* of forbidden mixtures (*Leviticus* 19:19), the [red] cow (*Numbers* Ch. 19), and similar matters.[63]

54a. That is, וּשְׁמַרְתֶּם, *you shall safeguard,* of verse 6 refers to the חֻקִּים וּמִשְׁפָּטִים, *decrees and ordinances,* of verse 5.

55. Thus, וּשְׁמַרְתֶּם should be understood as, *if you will safeguard.* See *Tanchuma, Re'eh* 8. This concept — the nation of Israel inherited the Land of Israel in the merit of their observing the *mitzvos* of the Torah — also appears in the Baal HaTurim's comments to *Exodus* 6:8 and 13:11, and *Deuteronomy* 26:15, s.v., אֶרֶץ זָבַת חָלָב.

56. A euphemism for incest or other forbidden relations.

57. Unlike verses 1,5,8 and 14, which speak of חֻקִּים וּמִשְׁפָּטִים, *decrees and ordinances,* our verse mentions only הַחֻקִּים, *the decrees.* The Talmud defines מִשְׁפָּטִים as those laws, such as murder or theft, that, had they not been included in the *mitzvos,* would nevertheless have been introduced by governmental decree. While חֻקִּים are *mitzvos,* such as *sha'atnez* (see *Leviticus* 19:19) and the purification of a *metzora* (see *Leviticus* Chs. 13-14), that [had they not been written in the Torah, would never have entered the human mind; indeed,] the Satan and the non-Jewish nations question their validity (*Yoma* 67b). Whereas our verse speaks only of חֻקִּים, the Baal HaTurim finds an allusion to two such matters that those adversaries may ask (*Shoham Yakar*).

57a. That is: Why is a man prohibited from marrying his father's daughter (his sister), yet permitted to marry his father's granddaughter (his brother's daughter)?

58. A *se'ah* is a measure of volume. Opinions regarding its modern-day equivalent range between 2.25 and 4 gallons. The minimum volume for a *mikveh* is forty *se'ah.*

59. A *kurtov* is a measure of volume equal to 1/64 of a *log* or 1/1536 of a *se'ah,* i.e., sixteen-millionths of a kosher *mikveh.*

60. That is, even though *mitzvah* observance *is your wisdom and understanding in the eyes of the peoples,* nevertheless . . .

61. As used in the Torah, the terms אַךְ and רַק imply exclusions; the terms אֶת and גַּם imply inclusions (*Yerushalmi Berachos* 9:5; see also *Rosh Hashanah* 17b).

62. That is, they do not accept the validity of certain *mitzvos* because they do not understand the rationale behind them.

63. *Peirush HaRokeach;* from *Tanchuma, Chukas* 8, cited in *Rashi* to *Numbers* 19:2; see also *Yoma* 67b, with *Rashi,* s.v. חוק.

ז כִּי מִי־גוֹי גָּדוֹל אֲשֶׁר־לוֹ אֱלֹהִים קְרֹבִים אֵלָיו
ח כַּיהוָה אֱלֹהֵינוּ בְּכָל־קָרְאֵנוּ אֵלָיו: וּמִי גּוֹי גָּדוֹל
אֲשֶׁר־לוֹ חֻקִּים וּמִשְׁפָּטִים צַדִּיקִם כְּכֹל הַתּוֹרָה
ט הַזֹּאת אֲשֶׁר אָנֹכִי נֹתֵן לִפְנֵיכֶם הַיּוֹם: רַק הִשָּׁמֶר
לְךָ וּשְׁמֹר נַפְשְׁךָ מְאֹד פֶּן־תִּשְׁכַּח אֶת־הַדְּבָרִים
אֲשֶׁר־רָאוּ עֵינֶיךָ וּפֶן־יָסוּרוּ מִלְּבָבְךָ כֹּל יְמֵי חַיֶּיךָ
י וְהוֹדַעְתָּם לְבָנֶיךָ וְלִבְנֵי בָנֶיךָ: יוֹם אֲשֶׁר עָמַדְתָּ
לִפְנֵי יהוָה אֱלֹהֶיךָ בְּחֹרֵב בֶּאֱמֹר יהוָה אֵלַי
הַקְהֶל־לִי אֶת־הָעָם וְאַשְׁמִעֵם אֶת־דְּבָרָי אֲשֶׁר
יִלְמְדוּן לְיִרְאָה אֹתִי כָּל־הַיָּמִים אֲשֶׁר הֵם חַיִּים
יא עַל־הָאֲדָמָה וְאֶת־בְּנֵיהֶם יְלַמֵּדוּן: וַתִּקְרְבוּן
וַתַּעַמְדוּן תַּחַת הָהָר וְהָהָר בֹּעֵר בָּאֵשׁ עַד־לֵב
יב הַשָּׁמַיִם חֹשֶׁךְ עָנָן וַעֲרָפֶל: וַיְדַבֵּר יהוָה אֲלֵיכֶם
מִתּוֹךְ הָאֵשׁ קוֹל דְּבָרִים אַתֶּם שֹׁמְעִים וּתְמוּנָה
יג אֵינְכֶם רֹאִים זוּלָתִי קוֹל: וַיַּגֵּד לָכֶם אֶת־
בְּרִיתוֹ אֲשֶׁר צִוָּה אֶתְכֶם לַעֲשׂוֹת עֲשֶׂרֶת הַדְּבָרִים

בעל הטורים

(ט) **וּשְׁמֹר נַפְשְׁךָ.** ״נֵר ה׳ נִשְׁמַת אָדָם״. נֵרְךָ בְּיָדִי וְנֵרִי בְּיָדְךָ, אִם תִּשְׁמֹר נֵרִי אֶשְׁמֹר נֵרְךָ:

❑ **וְהוֹדַעְתָּם לְבָנֶיךָ וְלִבְנֵי בָנֶיךָ.** ג׳ נוּנִי״ן הֲפוּכִין. לוֹמַר שֶׁכָּל מִי שֶׁהוּא וּבְנוֹ וּבֶן בְּנוֹ תַּלְמִידֵי חֲכָמִים, שׁוּב אֵין הַתּוֹרָה פּוֹסֶקֶת מִזַּרְעוֹ:

BAAL HATURIM ELUCIDATED

9. וּשְׁמֹר נַפְשְׁךָ — AND GUARD YOUR SOUL. [The juxtaposition of this phrase with the remembrance of the revelation at Sinai later in this verse, can be understood on the basis of the verse,] נֵר ה׳ נִשְׁמַת אָדָם, *The lamp of HASHEM is a man's soul* (*Proverbs* 20:27). [God tells Israel,] "Your lamp[64] is in My hand, while My lamp[65] is in your hand. If you will safeguard My lamp, I will safeguard your lamp."[66]

❑ **וְהוֹדַעְתָּם לְבָנֶיךָ וְלִבְנֵי בָנֶיךָ** — AND MAKE THEM KNOWN TO YOUR CHILDREN AND TO YOUR CHILDREN'S CHILDREN. [According to a scribal tradition,] the three letters נ in this phrase are written in reverse.[67] This is to indicate that whoever is himself [a

64. That is, your soul.

65. That is, the Torah and *mitzvos* as it is stated, כִּי נֵר מִצְוָה וְתוֹרָה אוֹר, *for a mitzvah is a lamp and Torah is light* (*Proverbs* 6:23).

66. *Devarim Rabbah* 4:4; see the Baal HaTurim to 8:5 below.

67. According to the *Sefer Tagin* (ed. *Machzor Vitry*), נ׳ דַּעֲקִים בְּזַנְבֵיהּ נ׳ בְּאוֹרַיְתָא, *The letter* נ *with its tail bent* [*appears*] *fifty times in the Torah.* The three letters נ of this passage — לְבָנֶיךָ וְלִבְנֵי בָנֶיךָ — are included in that listing. Others (*Meiri* in *Kiryas Sefer*) refer to these three letters as

[7] *For which is a great nation that has a God Who is close to it, as is* HASHEM, *our God, whenever we call to Him?* [8] *And which is a great nation that has righteous decrees and ordinances, such as this entire Torah that I place before you this day?* [9] *Only guard yourself and guard your soul very much, lest you forget the things that your eyes have beheld and lest you remove them from your heart all the days of your life, and make them known to your children and to your children's children —* [10] *the day that you stood before* HASHEM, *your God, at Horeb, when* HASHEM *said to me, "Gather the people to Me and I shall let them hear My words, so that they shall learn to fear Me all the days that they live on the earth, and they shall teach their children."*

[11] *So you approached and stood at the foot of the mountain, and the mountain was burning with fire up to the heart of heaven, darkness, cloud, and thick cloud.*

[12] HASHEM *spoke to you from the midst of the fire; you were hearing the sound of words, but you were not seeing a likeness, only a sound.* [13] *He told you of His covenant that He commanded you to observe — the Ten Statements —*

BAAL HATURIM ELUCIDATED

Torah scholar] and whose son and grandson are Torah scholars, then the Torah will never depart from his descendants.[68]

מְעֻגָּלוֹת לְמַעְלָה וּלְמַטָּה, *rounded on top and on bottom* (see illustration). *Peirush HaRokeach* refers to them as הָפַךְ נ׳ רַגְלֶיהָ לַאֲחוֹרֶיהָ, *He reversed the* נ, *its foot behind it,* which can be used to describe the versions of the נ found in *Machzor Vitry* and *Badei HaAron.*

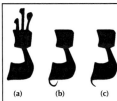

(a)
(b)
(c)

Usual נ (a). Bent נ, according to *Machzor Vitry* (b), *Badei HaAron* (c).

The Baal HaTurim's description of these letters נ as הֲפוּכִין, *in reverse,* does not seem to agree with any of the forms of נ in the illustration. Perhaps he means that they are drawn like the נוּנִי״ן הֲפוּכִין that precede and follow *Numbers* 10:35-36 (see *Shabbos* 115b), but that is unlikely, for there the reversed letters are used as signs to set the passage apart from its neighbors, while here they are letters of words.

For further discussion about the נ׳ הֲפוּכָה, see *Minchas Shai* and *Tikkun Soferim* (Dubna) to the last word in *parashas Noach* and the sources cited by them.

68. *Peirush HaRokeach;* see *Bava Metzia* 85a. Neither *Peirush HaRokeach* nor the Baal HaTurim explain the connection between the unusual letters נ and the three generations. Perhaps *Peirush HaRokeach's* caveat at the end of his comment addresses that issue. He writes: However, if a son of one of these Torah scholars marries the daughter of a man who is himself unlearned in Torah [and who has not educated his sons in Torah], then [as the Talmud (*Bava Basra* 110a) teaches,] most sons follow in the ways of their mother's brothers and the chain will be broken . . .

It is possible, then, that the reversed letters indicate that the generations are guaranteed to continue in Torah scholarship only if they constantly look back to the example of their forebears (*VeChur LaZahav*).

יד וַיִּכְתְּבֵ֔ם עַל־שְׁנֵ֖י לֻח֥וֹת אֲבָנִֽים׃ וְאֹתִ֞י צִוָּ֤ה יְהוָה֙
בָּעֵ֣ת הַהִ֔וא לְלַמֵּ֣ד אֶתְכֶ֔ם חֻקִּ֖ים וּמִשְׁפָּטִ֑ים
לַעֲשֹׂתְכֶ֣ם אֹתָ֔ם בָּאָ֕רֶץ אֲשֶׁ֥ר אַתֶּ֛ם עֹבְרִ֥ים שָׁ֖מָּה
טו לְרִשְׁתָּֽהּ׃ וְנִשְׁמַרְתֶּ֥ם מְאֹ֖ד לְנַפְשֹׁתֵיכֶ֑ם כִּ֣י לֹ֤א
רְאִיתֶם֙ כָּל־תְּמוּנָ֔ה בְּי֗וֹם דִּבֶּ֨ר יְהוָ֧ה אֲלֵיכֶ֛ם בְּחֹרֵ֖ב
טז מִתּ֥וֹךְ הָאֵֽשׁ׃ פֶּ֨ן־תַּשְׁחִת֔וּן וַעֲשִׂיתֶ֥ם לָכֶ֛ם פֶּ֖סֶל
יז תְּמוּנַ֣ת כָּל־סָ֑מֶל תַּבְנִ֥ית זָכָ֖ר א֥וֹ נְקֵבָֽה׃ תַּבְנִ֕ית
כָּל־בְּהֵמָ֖ה אֲשֶׁ֣ר בָּאָ֑רֶץ תַּבְנִית֙ כָּל־צִפּ֣וֹר כָּנָ֔ף
יח אֲשֶׁ֥ר תָּע֖וּף בַּשָּׁמָֽיִם׃ תַּבְנִ֕ית כָּל־רֹמֵ֖שׂ בָּאֲדָמָ֑ה
תַּבְנִ֛ית כָּל־דָּגָ֥ה אֲשֶׁר־בַּמַּ֖יִם מִתַּ֥חַת לָאָֽרֶץ׃
יט וּפֶן־תִּשָּׂ֨א עֵינֶ֜יךָ הַשָּׁמַ֗יְמָה וְֽרָאִ֨יתָ אֶת־הַשֶּׁ֜מֶשׁ
וְאֶת־הַיָּרֵ֗חַ וְאֶת־הַכּֽוֹכָבִים֙ כֹּ֚ל צְבָ֣א הַשָּׁמַ֔יִם
וְנִדַּחְתָּ֛ וְהִשְׁתַּחֲוִ֥יתָ לָהֶ֖ם וַעֲבַדְתָּ֑ם אֲשֶׁ֨ר חָלַ֜ק יְהוָ֤ה
אֱלֹהֶ֙יךָ֙ אֹתָ֔ם לְכֹל֙ הָֽעַמִּ֔ים תַּ֖חַת כָּל־הַשָּׁמָֽיִם׃
כ וְאֶתְכֶם֙ לָקַ֣ח יְהוָ֔ה וַיּוֹצִ֥א אֶתְכֶ֛ם מִכּ֥וּר הַבַּרְזֶ֖ל
מִמִּצְרָ֑יִם לִהְי֥וֹת ל֛וֹ לְעַ֥ם נַחֲלָ֖ה כַּיּ֥וֹם הַזֶּֽה׃

בעל הטורים

(כ) וַיּוֹצִא. ד׳ בַּמָּסֹרֶת — "וַיּוֹצִא אֶתְכֶם מִכּוּר הַבַּרְזֶל"; "וַיּוֹצִא עַמּוֹ בְשָׂשׂוֹן"; "וַיּוֹצִא נוֹזְלִים מִסָּלַע"; "וַיּוֹצִא אֶת בֶּן הַמֶּלֶךְ". "וַיּוֹצִא אֶתְכֶם מִכּוּר הַבַּרְזֶל" "וַיּוֹצִא עַמּוֹ בְשָׂשׂוֹן", שֶׁנֶּאֱמַר "וּבְנֵי יִשְׂרָאֵל יֹצְאִים בְּיָד רָמָה". וְהוֹצִיא לָהֶם "נוֹזְלִים מִסָּלַע", וְהֶעֱמִידוּ מֶלֶךְ, שֶׁנֶּאֱמַר "וַיְהִי בִישֻׁרוּן מֶלֶךְ":

BAAL HATURIM ELUCIDATED

16. {The Baal HaTurim's comment to פֶּסֶל appears at *Exodus* 32:19.}

16-18. {The Baal HaTurim's comment to תַּבְנִית appears at 5:8 below.}

20. וַיּוֹצִא — AND HE BROUGHT [YOU] OUT. The masoretic note, ד׳, means that this word appears four times in the *Tanach*: (i) here, וַיּוֹצִא אֶתְכֶם מִכּוּר הַבַּרְזֶל, *and He brought you out of the iron crucible;* (ii) וַיּוֹצִא עַמּוֹ בְשָׂשׂוֹן, *and He brought out His nation with joy* (*Psalms* 105:43); (iii) וַיּוֹצִא נוֹזְלִים מִסָּלַע, *and He brought forth flowing waters from the rock* (*Psalms* 78:16); and (iv) וַיּוֹצִא אֶת בֶּן הַמֶּלֶךְ, *and he brought out the son of the king*[68a] (*II Kings* 11:12). [The similarity of expression can be explained as follows:] *He brought you out of the iron crucible, and He brought His nation out in joy,* as it is said, וּבְנֵי יִשְׂרָאֵל יֹצְאִים בְּיָד רָמָה, *and the Children of Israel were going out with an*

68a. That verse continues: *and placed upon him the crown and the Testimony . . .* (see note 72 below).

4/14-20 and He inscribed them on two stone tablets. [14] HASHEM commanded me at that time to teach you decrees and ordinances, that you shall perform them in the land to which you cross, to possess it. [15] But you shall greatly beware for your souls, for you did not see any likeness on the day HASHEM spoke to you at Horeb, from the midst of the fire, [16] lest you act corruptly and make yourselves a carved image, a likeness of any shape; a form of a male or a female; [17] a form of any animal that is on the earth; a form of any winged bird that flies in the heaven; [18] a form of anything that creeps on the ground; a form of any fish that is in the water under the earth; [19] and lest you raise your eyes to the heaven and you see the sun, and the moon, and the stars — the entire legion of heaven — and you be drawn astray and bow to them and worship them, which HASHEM, your God, has apportioned to all the peoples under the entire heaven! [20] But HASHEM has taken you, and He brought you out of the iron crucible, of Egypt, to be a nation of heritage for Him, as this very day.

──────────── BAAL HATURIM ELUCIDATED ────────────

upraised arm[68b] (*Exodus* 14:8). And then, He brought forth for them *flowing waters from the rock.* And they established [Him][69] as [their] King,[70] as it is written, וַיְהִי בִישֻׁרוּן מֶלֶךְ, *He became King*[71] *over Jeshurun* (*Deuteronomy* 33:5).[72]

68b. That is, while the Egyptians were pursuing the Israelites with all kinds of curses and blasphemies on their lips, the Israelites were exalting and extolling God with joyous songs of praise and glory (*Mechilta*).

69. That is, they accepted God as their King. Alternatively: The word should be vowelized וְהֶעֱמִידוּ, *He established him*, i.e., God established Moses as king over Israel. See notes 71, 72 and 73 below.

70. Thus, the connection to the verse that mentions *the son of the king.*

71. In *Peirush HaTur HaAroch* to that verse, the Baal HaTurim cites three interpretations all based on the juxtaposition of that verse with the verse, תּוֹרָה צִוָּה לָנוּ מֹשֶׁה, *Moses commanded us regarding the Torah* (33:4): (i) by uniting together in mind and deed to follow the Torah, Israel established God as its King (*Rashi; Ramban*); (ii) having been taught the Torah by Moses, Israel appointed him as their king (*Ibn Ezra*); (iii) the

Torah became the metaphoric king over Israel (*Ibn Ezra,* citing *R' Yehudah HaLevi*). The Baal HaTurim's intention in the present comment may be understood in light of either of the first two of these interpretations (see note 69 above; see note 72 below for a third understanding of this comment).

72. *R' Yehudah HaChassid,* in a parallel comment to the masoretic note, writes: And when He brought them out He gave them the Torah and a crown of splendor. This is comparable to a king who [had been captured and subsequently] was ransomed from prison. His redeemer gave the king royal raiment and a crown. Similarly with Israel, *He brought out the son of the king and placed upon him the crown and the Testimony* [i.e., a Torah scroll, which the Torah (*Deuteronomy* 17:18-19) requires a king of Israel to have with him at all times (*Rashi* to *Kings* 11:12)].

According to that version, the king refers to Israel attaining the status of royalty. Perhaps, that is also the Baal HaTurim's intention.

כא וַיהוָה הִתְאַנַּף־בִּי עַל־דִּבְרֵיכֶם וַיִּשָּׁבַע לְבִלְתִּי
עָבְרִי אֶת־הַיַּרְדֵּן וּלְבִלְתִּי־בֹא אֶל־הָאָרֶץ הַטּוֹבָה
כב אֲשֶׁר יהוה אֱלֹהֶיךָ נֹתֵן לְךָ נַחֲלָה׃ כִּי אָנֹכִי מֵת
בָּאָרֶץ הַזֹּאת אֵינֶנִּי עֹבֵר אֶת־הַיַּרְדֵּן וְאַתֶּם עֹבְרִים
כג וִירִשְׁתֶּם אֶת־הָאָרֶץ הַטּוֹבָה הַזֹּאת׃ הִשָּׁמְרוּ לָכֶם
פֶּן־תִּשְׁכְּחוּ אֶת־בְּרִית יהוה אֱלֹהֵיכֶם אֲשֶׁר כָּרַת
עִמָּכֶם וַעֲשִׂיתֶם לָכֶם פֶּסֶל תְּמוּנַת כֹּל אֲשֶׁר צִוְּךָ
כד יהוה אֱלֹהֶיךָ׃ כִּי יהוה אֱלֹהֶיךָ אֵשׁ אֹכְלָה הוּא אֵל
קַנָּא׃
כה כִּי־תוֹלִיד בָּנִים וּבְנֵי בָנִים וְנוֹשַׁנְתֶּם בָּאָרֶץ
וְהִשְׁחַתֶּם וַעֲשִׂיתֶם פֶּסֶל תְּמוּנַת כֹּל וַעֲשִׂיתֶם הָרַע
כו בְּעֵינֵי יהוה־אֱלֹהֶיךָ לְהַכְעִיסוֹ׃ הַעִידֹתִי בָכֶם הַיּוֹם
אֶת־הַשָּׁמַיִם וְאֶת־הָאָרֶץ כִּי־אָבֹד תֹּאבֵדוּן מַהֵר

בעל הטורים

(כד) כִּי ה' אֱלֹהֶיךָ אֵשׁ אֹכְלָה הוּא, אֵל קַנָּא. כִּי תוֹלִיד. רֶמֶז, לְאַחַר כ"י שָׁנָה אַחֲרֵי מוֹתוֹ יַעַבְדוּ עֲבוֹדָה זָרָה, פֶּסֶל מִיכָה׃

(כו) הַעִידֹתִי. מָלֵא יו"ד, אִיתֵי בֵהּ י' לְפַרְסוּמֵי לְמִלְּתָא׃

BAAL HATURIM ELUCIDATED

22. {The Baal HaTurim's comment to אָנֹכִי מֵת appears at *Genesis* 50:5.}

23. {The Baal HaTurim's comment to פֶּסֶל appears at *Exodus* 32:19.}

24-25. **כִּי ה' אֱלֹהֶיךָ אֵשׁ אֹכְלָה הוּא אֵל קַנָּא. כִּי תוֹלִיד [. . .]** — FOR HASHEM, YOUR GOD — HE IS A CONSUMING FIRE, A ZEALOUS GOD. WHEN YOU BEGET [. . .][73] [The juxtaposition of these two verses are] an allusion [to the fact] that when כִּי (= 30) years[74] will have passed after the death of Moses, they [Israel] would worship a false deity, Micah's idol.[75]

73. An ellipsis has been inserted, for it seems obvious that the Baal HaTurim's comment is based in part upon the phrase וַעֲשִׂיתֶם פֶּסֶל, *and you will make a graven idol,* that appears later in the verse.

74. See the Baal HaTurim to 31:27 below.

75. The narrative of Micah and his temple of idolatry appears in *Judges* 17 and 18. According to some sources, he was the same Micah who had made an idol in Egypt and had carried it with him at the splitting of the Sea of Reeds. [Although the narrative of Micah's idol appears at the end of the Book of *Judges,* the incident is not recorded in proper chronological sequence for it occurred during the time of the first Judge, Othniel son of Kenaz, and the Aramean king Cushan (*Rashi* and *Radak* to *Judges* 17:1).]

The Midrash relates: Pharaoh had decreed that, if the Israelite slaves would not meet their quota of bricks, their children would be cemented into the walls to complete the structures. When Moses voiced a grievance to God over this, God told him that those who were being killed in this way would have been wicked

²¹ *HASHEM became angry with me because of your deeds, and He swore that I would not cross the Jordan and not come to the good Land that HASHEM, your God, gives you as a heritage.* ²² *For I am dying in this land; I am not crossing the Jordan — but you are crossing and you shall possess this good land.* ²³ *Beware for yourselves lest you forget the covenant of HASHEM, your God, that He has sealed with you, and you make yourselves a carved image, a likeness of anything, as HASHEM, your God, has commanded you.* ²⁴ *For HASHEM, your God — He is a consuming fire, a zealous God.*

²⁵ *When you beget children and grandchildren and will have been long in the land, you will grow corrupt and make a graven idol, a likeness of anything, and you will do evil in the eyes of HASHEM, your God, to anger Him.* ²⁶ *I set witnesses against you this day — the heavens and the earth — that you will surely perish quickly*

———— BAAL HATURIM ELUCIDATED ————

❑ {The Baal HaTurim's comment to פֶּסֶל appears at *Exodus* 32:19.}

26. הַעִידֹתִי — **I SET WITNESSES.** This word is spelled in full, with a י (= 10) [after the ע],[76] [as if Moses said,] "I will bring ten to publicize[77] the matter."[78]

---

had they been permitted to live. God then gave Moses permission to save one of those children, so that he might see the truth of God's words. The child that Moses saved was Micah (*Tanchuma, Ki Sisa* 19; see also *Sanhedrin* 101b, with *Rashi* s.v., נתמכמך בבנין). According to one opinion in *Midrash Tanchuma*, it was this Micah who was responsible for the manufacture of the golden calf.

For other aspects of Micah and his idol see the Baal HaTurim's comments to *Exodus* 2:16, 5:7, 12:11, 14:8, 14:29 and 18:3; *Numbers* 2:31 and 10:25.

76. This verb form appears five times in the *Tanach*: twice spelled הַעִידֹתִי, with the first י (here and *Jeremiah* 42:19); three times spelled הַעִדֹתִי, without that י (8:19 and 30:19 below, and *Jeremiah* 11:7).

77. According to the Talmud, certain *mitzvos* require the presence of ten people in order that the matter become public knowledge (see *Kesubos* 7b). Here, Moses called upon two witnesses, heaven and earth; however, in order to publicize the matter, he needed ten.

78. Whereas Moses was speaking to the entire nation at this time, a lot more than ten people, why was it necessary for him to assemble ten people? Some commentaries explain that when Moses appointed heaven and earth as witnesses, he meant those who dwell in heaven, the angels, and those who dwell on earth, people (*Ibn Ezra*). Now, regarding the heavenly beings, *Rambam* (*Hilchos Yesodei HaTorah* 2:7) states that there are precisely ten categories of angels. Moses alluded to those ten by inserting the י (= 10) in הַעִידֹתִי. But to which people was Moses referring? He could not have been asking the Israelites to be witnesses against themselves. Nor could he have requested nations living far from *Eretz Yisrael* to keep tabs on them. Rather, he must have meant the ten nations whose lands were to become the Land of Israel: the seven Canaanite nations, along with Edom, Ammon and Moab (see *Rashi* to *Genesis* 15:19). With the extra י in הַעִידֹתִי, Moses alluded not only to the ten categories of angels, but to those ten nations as well (*VeChur LaZahav*).

מֵעַל הָאָרֶץ אֲשֶׁר אַתֶּם עֹבְרִים אֶת־הַיַּרְדֵּן שָׁמָּה
לְרִשְׁתָּהּ לֹא־תַאֲרִיכֻן יָמִים עָלֶיהָ כִּי הִשָּׁמֵד
כז תִּשָּׁמֵדוּן: וְהֵפִיץ יְהוָה אֶתְכֶם בָּעַמִּים וְנִשְׁאַרְתֶּם
מְתֵי מִסְפָּר בַּגּוֹיִם אֲשֶׁר יְנַהֵג יְהוָה אֶתְכֶם שָׁמָּה:
כח וַעֲבַדְתֶּם־שָׁם אֱלֹהִים מַעֲשֵׂה יְדֵי אָדָם עֵץ וָאֶבֶן
אֲשֶׁר לֹא־יִרְאוּן וְלֹא יִשְׁמְעוּן וְלֹא יֹאכְלוּן וְלֹא
כט יְרִיחֻן: וּבִקַּשְׁתֶּם מִשָּׁם אֶת־יְהוָה אֱלֹהֶיךָ וּמָצָאתָ
ל כִּי תִדְרְשֶׁנּוּ בְּכָל־לְבָבְךָ וּבְכָל־נַפְשֶׁךָ: בַּצַּר לְךָ
וּמְצָאוּךָ כֹּל הַדְּבָרִים הָאֵלֶּה בְּאַחֲרִית הַיָּמִים
לא וְשַׁבְתָּ עַד־יְהוָה אֱלֹהֶיךָ וְשָׁמַעְתָּ בְּקֹלוֹ: כִּי אֵל
רַחוּם יְהוָה אֱלֹהֶיךָ לֹא יַרְפְּךָ וְלֹא יַשְׁחִיתֶךָ וְלֹא

בעל הטורים

(כז) בָּעַמִּים. בְּגִימַטְרִיָּא בֵּין הַבַּבְלִיִּים; ״בַּגּוֹיִם״ בְּגִימַטְרִיָּא בְּהַמָּדִי; ״יְנַהֵג״ בְּגִימַטְרִיָּא בְּיָוָן; ״שָׁמָּה״ בְּגִימַטְרִיָּא מֵרוֹמִיִּים. הֲרֵי רְמוּזִים כָּאן אַרְבַּע גָּלֻיּוֹת:

(כח) וַעֲבַדְתֶּם שָׁם אֱלֹהִים. וְאֵינוֹ אוֹמֵר ״אֱלֹהִים אֲחֵרִים״ כְּמוֹ שֶׁאוֹמֵר בְּכָל מָקוֹם. רֶמֶז לְמַה שֶּׁאָמְרוּ, יִשְׂרָאֵל שֶׁבְּחוּצָה לָאָרֶץ, עוֹבְדֵי עֲבוֹדָה זָרָה בְּטָהֳרָה הֵם:

BAAL HATURIM ELUCIDATED

27. בָּעַמִּים — AMONG THE PEOPLES. The *gematria* of this word (162) is equivalent[79] to that of בֵּין הַבַּבְלִיִּים, *among the Babylonians*; the *gematria* of בַּגּוֹיִם, *among the nations* (61), is equal to that of [80]בְּהַמָּדִי, *among the Medes*; the *gematria* of יְנַהֵג, *will lead* (68), is equal to that of בְּיָוָן, *in Greece*; and the *gematria* of שָׁמָּה, *there* (345), is equivalent[81] to that of מֵרוֹמִיִּים, *from the Romans.*[82] Thus all four exiles are alluded to in this verse.[83]

79. The *gematria* of the Baal HaTurim's term is 161, which the principle of *im hakollel* allows to be considered equivalent to 162.

80. The text follows *Shoham Yakar's* manuscript edition. Most other editions read וּבְמָדַי, *and in Media,* which has a *gematria* of 62. The principle of *im hakollel* then allows 61 to be considered equivalent to 62.

81. The principle of *im hakollel* allows 345 to be considered equivalent to 346, the *gematria* of the Baal HaTurim's term.

82. The Roman Empire is referred to as Edom about whom the prophet states, וְהָיְתָה אֱדוֹם לְשַׁמָּה, *Edom will become a wasteland* (*Jeremiah* 49:17). Thus, שָׁמָּה, which is spelled with the same letters as שַׁמָּה, is an apt allusion to Edom/Rome. Moreover, by the principle of *im hakollel,* the *gematria* of בְּאֶרֶץ אֱדוֹם, *in the land of Edom* (344), may be considered equivalent to 345, the *gematria* of שָׁמָּה (*Matzreif LaKesef*).

83. Throughout the Talmud and Midrash, and based on the Book of *Daniel* (Ch. 8), Israel's long series of exiles and persecutions are always treated as four main periods of subjugation to foreign oppressors — either in the Land of Israel or in the Diaspora. These periods are known collectively as אַרְבַּע מַלְכֻיּוֹת, *the Four Kingdoms* (*Daniel* 8:22), and each is called by the name of the empire dominant in the world at that particular time. The first, called גָּלוּת בָּבֶל, *the Babylonian Exile,* began when Nebuchadnezzar king of Babylon conquered the Land of Israel

from the land to which you are crossing the Jordan to possess; you shall not have lengthy days upon it, for you will be destroyed. [27] *HASHEM will scatter you among the peoples, and you will be left a limited number of people among the nations, there where HASHEM will lead you.* [28] *There you will serve gods, the handiwork of man, of wood and stone, which do not see, and do not hear, and do not eat, and do not smell.*

[29] *From there you will seek HASHEM, your God, and you will find Him, if you search for Him with all your heart and all your soul.* [30] *When you are in distress and all these things have befallen you, at the end of days, you will return unto HASHEM, your God, and hearken to His voice.* [31] *For HASHEM, your God, is a merciful God, He will not abandon you nor destroy you, and He will not*

———— BAAL HATURIM ELUCIDATED ————

28. וַעֲבַדְתֶּם שָׁם אֱלֹהִים — **THERE YOU WILL SERVE GODS.** This verse does not say אֱלֹהִים אֲחֵרִים, [which can be understood as] *the gods of others,* as it usually does.[84] This alludes to our Sages' statement: The Israelites who are in the Diaspora serve alien deities in purity[85] [i.e., unintentionally[86]].[87]

29. {The Baal HaTurim's comment to וּבִקַּשְׁתֶּם appears at *Numbers* 16:10.}

---

and destroyed the First Temple. The second, called גָּלוּת מָדַי וּפָרַס, *the Median-Persian Exile* (*Daniel* 8:20), began when that empire succeeded the Babylonians as the leading world power. Although the Medes permitted the Jewish return to the Land of Israel and the building of the Second Temple, the early years of that *Beis HaMikdash* were still considered a part of the exile, because Israel was not sovereign in its land. Paradoxically, during the entire third period, גָּלוּת יָוָן, *the Greek Exile* (*Daniel* 8:21), Israel lived in its land and the Temple stood. Nevertheless, it was a very turbulent era marked with civil strife, foreign domination, vicious anti-religious campaigns, and the rejection of Torah values by a large number of Jews who adopted Greek culture with all its abominations. The downfall of the Greek Empire and the rise of Rome marked the beginning of גָּלוּת אֱדוֹם, *the Edomite* or *Roman Exile.* And we are still in the grip of that millennia-long exile today.

84. Twenty times in the Torah (*Exodus* 20:3 and 23:13; *Deuteronomy* 5:7, 6:14, 7:4, 8:19, 11:16 and 28, 13:3,7 and 14, 17:3, 18:20, 28:14,36

and 64, 29:25, 30:17, 31:18 and 20) and more than forty times in the rest of the *Tanach.* In his commentary to *Exodus* 20:3, *Rashi* explains אֱלֹהִים אֲחֵרִים as אֱלֹהִים שֶׁל אֲחֵרִים, *the gods of others,* i.e., things that are not gods, yet some people consider them to be gods. Although the Baal HaTurim usually explains that term as *other gods,* here he seems to be following *Rashi's* opinion.

85. *Avodah Zarah* 8a. In a lengthy analysis of the differences between the Land of Israel and all other lands, the *Ramban* explains that while God takes a direct hand in sustaining the Land of Israel, the other lands receive their sustenance from God through the hand of intermediary angelic princes. As a consequence, those people living in the other lands tend to loosen their connections to God, and attach themselves, to some degree, to those angelic princes — a form of unintentional idolatry (see *Ramban* to *Leviticus* 18:25, cited in *Peirush HaAroch* there).

86. *Rashi.*

87. *Peirush HaRokeach.*

לב יִשְׁכַּח אֶת־בְּרִית אֲבֹתֶיךָ אֲשֶׁר נִשְׁבַּע לָהֶם: כִּי
שְׁאַל־נָא לְיָמִים רִאשֹׁנִים אֲשֶׁר־הָיוּ לְפָנֶיךָ לְמִן־
הַיּוֹם אֲשֶׁר בָּרָא אֱלֹהִים ׀ אָדָם עַל־הָאָרֶץ
וּלְמִקְצֵה הַשָּׁמַיִם וְעַד־קְצֵה הַשָּׁמָיִם הֲנִהְיָה כַּדָּבָר
לג הַגָּדוֹל הַזֶּה אוֹ הֲנִשְׁמַע כָּמֹהוּ: הֲשָׁמַע עָם קוֹל
אֱלֹהִים מְדַבֵּר מִתּוֹךְ־הָאֵשׁ כַּאֲשֶׁר־שָׁמַעְתָּ אַתָּה
לד וַיֶּחִי: אוֹ ׀ הֲנִסָּה אֱלֹהִים לָבוֹא לָקַחַת לוֹ גוֹי
מִקֶּרֶב גּוֹי בְּמַסֹּת בְּאֹתֹת וּבְמוֹפְתִים וּבְמִלְחָמָה
וּבְיָד חֲזָקָה וּבִזְרוֹעַ נְטוּיָה וּבְמוֹרָאִים גְּדֹלִים

בעל הטורים

(לד) או הֲנִסָּה. כָּל אַלְפָא בֵּיתָא בְּזֶה הַפָּסוּק. שֶׁרָצָה הַקָּדוֹשׁ בָּרוּךְ הוּא לִתֵּן לְיִשְׂרָאֵל הַתּוֹרָה בְּמִצְרַיִם, אֶלָּא שֶׁאָמְרָה מִדַּת הַדִּין, נַסֵּה אוֹתָם תְּחִלָּה {קֹדֶם שֶׁתַּשְׁמִיעֵם דְּבָרֶיךָ}. לְכָךְ ״הֲנִסָּה״ ב׳ בַּמָּסוֹרֶת – הָכָא, וְאִידָךְ ״הֲנִסָּה דָבָר אֵלֶיךָ תִּלְאֶה״, שֶׁאָמְרָה מִדַּת הַדִּין, נַסֵּה אוֹתָם קֹדֶם שֶׁתַּשְׁמִיעֵם דְּבָרֶיךָ:

❑ וְהַפָּסוּק מַתְחִיל בְּאָלֶ״ף וּמְסַיֵּם בְּכַ״ף, ״אַךְ טוֹב לְיִשְׂרָאֵל״. וְהוּא עוֹלֶה כְּשֵׁם אֶהְיֶה אֲשֶׁר נִגְלָה בּוֹ לְמֹשֶׁה לְהוֹצִיאָם מִמִּצְרַיִם, וּבוֹ מַכֶּה לָאֻמּוֹת, ״וְאַךְ אוֹתְךָ״. שִׁבְעָה דְבָרִים מֻזְכָּרִים כָּאן – בְּמַסֹּת, בְּאֹתֹת, בְּמוֹפְתִים, בְּמִלְחָמָה, בְּיָד חֲזָקָה, בִּזְרוֹעַ נְטוּיָה, וּבְמוֹרָאִים גְּדֹלִים – כְּנֶגֶד שִׁבְעָה יָמִים שֶׁשִּׁמְּשָׁה כָּל מַכָּה וּמַכָּה, וּכְנֶגְדָּן שִׁבְעָה יָמִים שֶׁל פֶּסַח:

BAAL HATURIM ELUCIDATED

32. {The Baal HaTurim's comment to בָּרָא אֱלֹהִים appears at *Genesis* 1:1.}

❑ {The Baal HaTurim's comment to עַל הָאָרֶץ appears at 11:21 below.}

34. אוֹ הֲנִסָּה — OR HAS [GOD][87a] EVER ADMINISTERED A TEST. This verse contains every letter in the *alef-beis.*[88] The Holy One, Blessed is He, desired to give the Torah to Israel while they were yet in Egypt, but the Attribute of Strict Justice said, "Test them first {before You make Your words known to them[88a]}."[89]

87a. According to *Rashi* the term אֱלֹהִים of our verse is secular and refers to the gods of idolatrous nations. However, the Baal HaTurim follows *Targum Onkelos* and *Ibn Ezra* who interpret it as the Name of God.

88. There are twenty-six verses in the *Tanach* that contain all twenty-two letters of the *aleph-beis;* the Baal HaTurim comments on the two that are in the Torah.

The twenty-six verses are: (i) *Exodus* 16:16; (ii) *Deuteronomy* 4:34; (iii) *Joshua* 23:13; (iv-vi) *II Kings* 4:39, 6:32, 7:8; (vii-viii) *Isaiah* 5:25, 66:17; (ix-x) *Jeremiah* 22:3, 32:29; (xi-xii) *Ezekiel* 17:9, 38:12; (xiii-xiv) *Hosea* 10:8, 13:2; (xv) *Amos* 9:13; (xvi) *Zephaniah* 3:8; (xvii) *Zechariah* 6:11; (xviii) *Ecclesiastes* 4:8; (xix) *Esther* 3:13; (xx-xxiii) *Daniel* 2:45, 3:22, 4:20, 7:19; (xxiv) *Ezra* 7:28; (xxv) *Nehemiah* 3:7; and (xxvi) *II Chronicles* 26:11.

Ezekiel 38:12 contains all five final forms ך ם ן ף ץ, but does not have the regular forms of כ פ צ. Only the verse from *Zephaniah* contains all twenty-two letters as well as the five final forms.

88a. The phrase enclosed in braces is not found in the printed editions, but does appear in the manuscripts used by *Shoham Yakar.*

89. *Peirush HaRokeach*; see *Yalkut Shimoni*, *Beshalach* 273.

forget the covenant of your forefathers that He swore to them. 32 *For inquire now regarding the early days that preceded you, from the day when God created man on the earth, and from one end of heaven to the other end of heaven: Has there ever been anything like this great thing or has anything like it been heard?* 33 *Has a people ever heard the voice of God speaking from the midst of the fire as you have heard, and survived?* 34 *Or has God ever administered a test [whether] to come to take for himself a nation from amidst a nation, with challenges, with signs, and with wonders, and with war, and with a strong hand, and with an outstretched arm, and with greatly awesome deeds,*

BAAL HATURIM ELUCIDATED

Thus, also, the masoretic note ב׳, which means that this word appears twice in the *Tanach:* (i) here; and (ii) הֲנִסָּה דָבָר אֵלֶיךָ תִּלְאֶה, *If He tests you with a matter, will you become wearied?* (*Job* 4:2). [This indicates] that the Attribute of Strict Justice said, "Test them before You make Your words known to them."

❑ The verse begins with an א and ends with a ב,[89a] [alluding to the verse] אַךְ טוֹב לְיִשְׂרָאֵל, *Only goodness for Israel* (*Psalms* 73:1). Moreover, the *gematria* of אַךְ (21) is equal to that of the Divine Name אֶהְיֶה, *I Will Be* (*Exodus* 3:14),[90] by which God revealed Himself to Moses in order to take the Jews out of Egypt. And with that Name He smites the nations [as indicated by the verse,] וָאַךְ אוֹתְךָ, *and I have smitten*[91] *you* (*Exodus* 9:15).[92] [Thus,] the verse enumerates seven[92a] ways [in which God smote Egypt]: (i) with challenges; (ii) with signs, (iii) with wonders, (iv) with war, (v) with a strong hand, (vi) with an outstretched arm, and (vii) with greatly awesome deeds, corresponding to the seven days that each plague lasted,[93] and, corresponding to them, there are[94] seven days of Pesach.[95]

89a. Although this phenomenon occurs thirty times in the Torah and another 105 times in the rest of the *Tanach,* the Baal HaTurim comments on it only twice, here and at 3:24 above (see the Baal HaTurim there, with notes 15a and 15b).

90. See the Baal HaTurim to that verse.

91. The word וָאַךְ is composed of the future form אַךְ, *I will smite,* with the conversive וָ־ prefix which changes it to the past — וָאַךְ, *I have smitten.* And the *gematria* of אַךְ is twenty-one.

92. *Peirush HaRokeach.*

92a. The word וָאַךְ alludes to both 21 (see note 91) and 7. For the word is pronounced as if it were spelled וָא־אַךְ, in which the *gematria* of the first syllable is 7, and that of the second is 21 (A.S.).

93. See *Tanchuma, Va'eira* 13, cited in *Rashi* to *Exodus* 7:25.

94. The reading וּכְנֶגְדָּן שִׁבְעָה יָמִים ..., *and, corresponding to them, there are seven days . . .* follows *Peirush HaRokeach,* the Baal HaTurim's apparent source for this comment, and *Shoham Yakar's* manuscript edition. The printed editions read, וּכְנֶגֶד שִׁבְעָה יָמִים..., *and corresponding to the seven days . . .*

95. *Peirush HaRokeach.*

כְּכֹל אֲשֶׁר־עָשָׂה לָכֶם יהוָה אֱלֹהֵיכֶם בְּמִצְרַיִם
לה לְעֵינֶיךָ: אַתָּה הָרְאֵתָ לָדַעַת כִּי יהוָה הוּא הָאֱלֹהִים
לו אֵין עוֹד מִלְּבַדּוֹ: מִן־הַשָּׁמַיִם הִשְׁמִיעֲךָ אֶת־קֹלוֹ
לְיַסְּרֶךָּ וְעַל־הָאָרֶץ הֶרְאֲךָ אֶת־אִשּׁוֹ הַגְּדוֹלָה
לז וּדְבָרָיו שָׁמַעְתָּ מִתּוֹךְ הָאֵשׁ: וְתַחַת כִּי אָהַב
אֶת־אֲבֹתֶיךָ וַיִּבְחַר בְּזַרְעוֹ אַחֲרָיו וַיּוֹצִאֲךָ בְּפָנָיו
לח בְּכֹחוֹ הַגָּדֹל מִמִּצְרָיִם: לְהוֹרִישׁ גּוֹיִם גְּדֹלִים

בעל הטורים

☐ **בְּמִצְרַיִם לְעֵינֶיךָ.** וּסְמִיךְ לֵהּ "אַתָּה הָרְאֵתָ". כְּשֶׁעָשִׂיתִי שְׁפָטִים בְּמִצְרַיִם וּבֵאלֹהֵיהֶם, יְדַעְתֶּם כִּי אֲנִי ה׳:

(לה) **הָרְאֵתָ.** ב׳ בַּמָּסוֹרֶת – "אַתָּה הָרְאֵתָ לָדַעַת"; "אֲשֶׁר הָרְאֵיתָ בָּהָר". {מֵהֵיכָן הָרְאֵתָ לָדַעַת? בָּהָר.} שֶׁהֶרְאָה לָהֶם שָׁמַיִם וּשְׁמֵי הַשָּׁמַיִם, וְרָאוּ שֶׁאֵין אֶלָּא רָשׁוּת אֶחָד:

(לו) **הֶרְאֲךָ אֶת אִשּׁוֹ הַגְּדוֹלָה.** וּסְמִיךְ לֵהּ "וְתַחַת כִּי אָהַב אֶת אֲבֹתֶיךָ". לוֹמַר, כָּל מַה שֶׁהֶרְאָה לְמֹשֶׁה הֶרְאָהוּ בִּזְכוּת הָאָבוֹת:

(לז) **וְתַחַת.** ב׳ בַּמָּסוֹרֶת – "וְתַחַת כִּי אָהַב אֶת אֲבֹתֶיךָ"; "וְתַחַת הָרָקִיעַ". וְזֶהוּ שֶׁאָמְרוּ, הָאָבוֹת הֵן הֵן הַמֶּרְכָּבָה. וְזֶהוּ גַם כֵּן "מִתּוֹךְ הָאֵשׁ. וְתַחַת כִּי אָהַב", לוֹמַר שֶׁהֵם תּוֹךְ הָאֵשׁ שֶׁל שְׁכִינָה:

BAAL HATURIM ELUCIDATED

☐ **בְּמִצְרַיִם לְעֵינֶיךָ** — IN EGYPT BEFORE YOUR EYES. Juxtaposed to this is the verse: אַתָּה הָרְאֵתָ, *You have been shown . . .*[96] As if God were saying, "When I enacted harsh measures against the Egyptians and against their gods, you became aware that I am God."[97]

35. הָרְאֵתָ — YOU HAVE BEEN SHOWN. The masoretic note,[98] ב׳, means that this word appears twice in the *Tanach*: (i) here, אַתָּה הָרְאֵתָ לָדַעַת, *you have been shown in order to know;* and (ii) אֲשֶׁר הָרְאֵיתָ בָּהָר, *as you have been shown on the mountain* (*Exodus* 26:30).[99] {[This indicates that Moses said,] "Where were *you shown in order to know*? [You were shown] *on the mountain.*"}[100] For [there] He showed

---

96. An ellipsis has been inserted, for it seems obvious the Baal HaTurim's comment is based on the full verse: *You have been shown in order to know that HASHEM, He is the God; there is no other besides Him.*

97. *Mechilta* to *Shemos* 14:4 — God told Moses, *"I will be glorified through Pharaoh and his entire army, then Egypt will know that I am HASHEM"* (*Exodus* 14:4). This verse tells us that when the Omnipresent exacts punishment from the wicked nations, His Name becomes exalted in the world . . .

Thus, just as there, *Israel saw the great hand that Hashem inflicted upon Egypt and the people revered Hashem* (*Exodus* 14:31), similarly here, when Israel saw God's strong hand inflict the plagues upon Egypt, they revered Hashem (Y. S.).

98. The full note reads, ב׳ חַד חָסֵר וְחַד מָלֵא, *Two, one spelled defectively* (הָרְאֵתָ) *and one spelled in full* (הָרְאֵיתָ).

99. The Baal HaTurim to that verse makes a similar comment.

100. The passage enclosed in braces is not found in the printed editions, but does appear in *Shoham Yakar's* manuscript edition.

such as everything that HASHEM, your God, did for you in Egypt before your eyes? [35] *You have been shown in order to know that HASHEM, He is the God! There is no other besides Him!*

[36] *From heaven He caused you to hear His voice in order to teach you, and on earth He showed you His great fire, and you heard His words from the midst of the fire;* [37] *and, because He loved your forefathers, He chose his offspring after him, and took you out before Himself with His great strength from Egypt;* [38] *to drive away from before you nations that are greater*

───────────── BAAL HATURIM ELUCIDATED ─────────────

them heaven and the celestial heights, and they saw that there is only one Authority.[101]

❑ {The Baal HaTurim's comment to אֵין עוֹד appears at v. 39 below.}

36. הֶרְאֲךָ אֶת אִשּׁוֹ הַגְּדוֹלָה — HE SHOWED YOU HIS GREAT FIRE. Juxtaposed to this is the phrase: וְתַחַת כִּי אָהַב אֶת אֲבֹתֶיךָ, *and because He loved your forefathers.* This is to indicate that whatever He showed to Moses He showed him in the merit of the forefathers.[102]

37. וְתַחַת — AND BECAUSE. The masoretic note,[103] ב׳, means that this word appears twice in the *Tanach*: (i) here, וְתַחַת כִּי אָהַב אֶת אֲבֹתֶיךָ, *and because He loved your forefathers;* and (ii) וְתַחַת הָרָקִיעַ, *and beneath the expanse (Ezekiel* 1:23) [in the passage describing the Divine Chariot, i.e., the Throne of Glory]. This reflects the [Sages'] statement: The Patriarchs, they are the Divine Chariot.[104] This also reflects the juxtaposition of the phrase, *from the midst of the fire,* with *because He loved [your forefathers],* i.e., they are in the midst of the fire of the Divine Presence.

---

101. *Pesikta Rabbasi* 20, cited by Rashi; see also the Baal HaTurim to *Exodus* 20:2, s.v., אָנֹכִי and 26:30, and to *Deuteronomy* 9:4.

102. See *Shemos Rabbah* 28:1 — The Holy One, Blessed is He, said to Moses, "The Torah was given to you only in the merit of Abraham ..."
Shoham Yakar raises a question regarding the Baal HaTurim's intent in this comment: The Midrash cited above expounds on the verse, *You have ascended on high ... (Psalms* 68:19), which, the Midrash explains, refers to Moses of whom it is said, *Moses ascended to God ... (Exodus* 19:3). Accordingly, God was speaking to Moses. However, in our verse, Moses was speaking to Israel. If so, shouldn't the allusion be to Moses' telling the nation, "Whatever God showed to you, He showed you in the merit of your forefathers"?

103. The full note reads: ב׳ ר׳׳פ, which means, ב׳ רֵישׁ פָּסוּק, *Twice at the beginning of a verse.* The word appears, with a variety of meanings, a total of thirty times in the *Tanach,* only three of them in the Torah. Besides our verse, it appears in וְתַחַת רַגְלָיו כְּמַעֲשֵׂה לִבְנַת הַסַּפִּיר, *and under His feet was something made of white sapphire (Exodus* 24:10), which, like the verse from *Ezekiel,* refers to the Throne of Glory, and as a result, some editions of the Baal HaTurim cite that verse in lieu of the one from *Ezekiel;* although the Baal HaTurim's allusion works just as well with that verse, the masoretic note cannot refer to that verse, for the phrase וְתַחַת רַגְלָיו does not appear at the beginning of its verse. The other Torah verse is וְתַחַת כָּל עֵץ רַעֲנָן, *and under every leafy tree* (12:2 below).

104. *Bereishis Rabbah* 47:6, 82:6; *Zohar* III, 28b, 217a.

וַעֲצֻמִים מִמְּךָ מִפָּנֶיךָ לַהֲבִיאֲךָ לָתֶת־לְךָ אֶת־
לט אַרְצָם נַחֲלָה כַּיּוֹם הַזֶּה: וְיָדַעְתָּ הַיּוֹם וַהֲשֵׁבֹתָ
אֶל־לְבָבֶךָ כִּי יהוה הוּא הָאֱלֹהִים בַּשָּׁמַיִם מִמַּעַל
מ וְעַל־הָאָרֶץ מִתָּחַת אֵין עוֹד: וְשָׁמַרְתָּ אֶת־חֻקָּיו
וְאֶת־מִצְוֹתָיו אֲשֶׁר אָנֹכִי מְצַוְּךָ הַיּוֹם אֲשֶׁר יִיטַב
לְךָ וּלְבָנֶיךָ אַחֲרֶיךָ וּלְמַעַן תַּאֲרִיךְ יָמִים עַל־
הָאֲדָמָה אֲשֶׁר יהוה אֱלֹהֶיךָ נֹתֵן לְךָ כָּל־הַיָּמִים:
שלישי מא אָז יַבְדִּיל מֹשֶׁה שָׁלֹשׁ עָרִים בְּעֵבֶר הַיַּרְדֵּן מִזְרְחָה
מב שָׁמֶשׁ: לָנֻס שָׁמָּה רוֹצֵחַ אֲשֶׁר יִרְצַח אֶת־רֵעֵהוּ
בִּבְלִי־דַעַת וְהוּא לֹא־שֹׂנֵא לוֹ מִתְּמֹל שִׁלְשֹׁם וְנָס
מג אֶל־אַחַת מִן־הֶעָרִים הָאֵל וָחָי: אֶת־בֶּצֶר בַּמִּדְבָּר
בְּאֶרֶץ הַמִּישֹׁר לָראוּבֵנִי וְאֶת־רָאמֹת בַּגִּלְעָד לַגָּדִי

בעל הטורים

(לט) אֵין עוֹד. וּשְׁאָר קְרִיָּה ״וְאֵין עוֹד״ וָי״ו יְתֵרָה. וְהֵם ו׳ פְּעָמִים בִּקְרִיָּה, ו׳ פְּעָמִים ״אֲדוֹן כָּל הָאָרֶץ״, כְּנֶגֶד ו׳ קְצָוֹת – מַעְלָה וּמַטָּה וְאַרְבַּע רוּחוֹת:

(מ) סָמַךְ ״וְשָׁמַרְתָּ אֶת חֻקָּיו וְאֶת מִצְוֹתָיו״ לְ״אָז יַבְדִּיל״. לוֹמַר, שֶׁתּוֹרָה וּמִצְוֹת קוֹלְטוֹת:

(מב) רוֹצֵחַ. מָלֵא וָי״ו. שֶׁרָצַח הָאָדָם שֶׁנִּבְרָא בַּשִּׁשִּׁי, וְעָבַר עַל ״לֹא תִרְצָח״ שֶׁהוּא דִבּוּר שִׁשִּׁי:

BAAL HATURIM ELUCIDATED

39. אֵין עוֹד — THERE IS NO OTHER. Elsewhere in Scripture, [we find the expression] וְאֵין עוֹד, *and there is no other,* with the added conjunctive prefix ־וְ, *and.* But [regarding the appearances of אֵין עוֹד,] they are found six times in Scripture.[105] [Similarly,] the phrase אֲדוֹן כָּל הָאָרֶץ, *Lord of the entire earth,* appears six times.[106] [There you have three allusions[107] to the number 6,] corresponding to the six directions: up, down, and the four sides [i.e., north, south, east, west].[108]

105. They are: (i-ii) *Deuteronomy* 4:35, 39; (iii) *I Kings* 8:60; (iv) *II Kings* 4:6; (v) *Jeremiah* 48:2; and (vi) *Psalms* 74:9.

The early printed editions, as well as *Shoham Yakar's* manuscript edition, read, וְכֵן ו׳ פְּעָמִים וְאֵין עוֹד״ קְרִיָּה, כְּתִיבֵי״ *Similarly, the expression* וְאֵין עוֹד *is written six times in the Tanach.* However, that version is difficult, because the expression וְאֵין עוֹד actually appears nine times: (i-vii) *Isaiah* 45:5, 6, 14, 18, 21, 22 and 46:9; (viii) *Joel* 2:27; and (ix) *Ecclesiastes* 9:5.

106. They are: (i-ii) *Joshua* 3:11 and 13; (iii) *Micah* 4:13, with the prepositional prefix ־לְ; (iv-v) *Zechariah* 4:14 and 6:4; and (vi) *Psalms* 97:5.

107. They are: (i) The six appearances of אֵין עוֹד; (ii) the prefix ־וְ (= 6) affixed to all other appearances of אֵין עוֹד; and (iii) the six verses that refer to God as אֲדוֹן כָּל הָאָרֶץ.

108. *Peirush HaRokeach.*

The concept of six directions is found in *halachah:* When reciting the first verse of the *Shema,* a person should concentrate upon the fact that God is One, there is no other, in the *and mightier than you, to bring you, to give you their land as an inheritance, as this very day.* [39] *You shall know this day and take to your heart that HASHEM, He is the God — in heaven above and on the earth below — there is none other.* [40] *You shall observe His decrees and His commandments that I command you this day, so that He will do good to you and to your children after you, and so that you will prolong your days on the land that HASHEM, your God, gives you, for all the days.*

[41] *Then Moses set aside three cities on the bank of the Jordan, toward the rising sun,* [42] *for a killer to flee there, who will have killed his fellow without knowledge, but who was not an enemy of his from yesterday and before yesterday — then he shall flee to one of these cities and live:* [43] *Bezer in the wilderness, in the land of the plain, of the Reubenite; Ramoth in the Gilead, of the Gadite;*

BAAL HATURIM ELUCIDATED

40. The Torah has juxtaposed the verse, וְשָׁמַרְתָּ אֶת חֻקָּיו וְאֶת מִצְוֹתָיו, *You shall observe His decrees and His commandments,* with the verse: אָז יַבְדִּיל [מֹשֶׁה], *Then [Moses] set aside* [cities of refuge]. This indicates that the Torah and its *mitzvos* offer refuge.[109,110]

42. רוֹצֵחַ — A KILLER. This word is spelled in full,[111] with a ו (= 6). [This alludes to the fact] that he has killed a man who was created on the sixth day, and has thus violated לֹא תִרְצָח, *You shall not kill* (*Exodus* 20:13), the sixth of the Ten Commandments.

heavens, on the earth, in all four directions of the heavens (*Berachos* 13b); the *lulav*-bundle is waved in these six directions (*Succah* 37b); and the meal-offerings are waved in this manner (*Menachos* 62a).

109. The text follows all printed editions. *Shoham Yakar* records a manuscript version that continues: בִּפְנֵי הַפֻּרְעָנוּת, *in the face of retribution.*

Although the Baal HaTurim writes that both Torah [i.e., Torah study] and *mitzvah* [performance] provide refuge, they do not do so equally. The Talmud records a dispute concerning that difference: According to one opinion, at the moment that a person is engaged in the performance of a *mitzvah,* that *mitzvah* both protects [against retribution (*Rashi*)] and rescues [from the machinations of the evil inclination (*Rashi*)]; however, when he is no longer engaged in performing that *mitzvah* [i.e., he has completed its performance], it protects, but does not rescue. Torah, on the other hand, both protects and saves, while one is engaged in its study and when he has concluded that study [session].

According to a second opinion, at the moment that a person is engaged in Torah study, it both protects and rescues him; however, once he has concluded that study session, it protects him but does not rescue him. A *mitzvah,* on the other hand, whether while one is still engaged in its performance or has concluded it, protects but does not rescue (*Sotah* 21a).

110. *Peirush HaRokeach;* see *Makkos* 10a.

111. The word רוֹצֵחַ appears twenty-two times in the Torah. In each case, it is spelled defectively, רֹצֵחַ, without a ו, except in our verse where it is spelled in full (see *Minchas Shai*).

ד/מד־ה/א

מד וְאֶת־גּוֹלָן בַּבָּשָׁן לַמְנַשִּׁי: וְזֹאת הַתּוֹרָה אֲשֶׁר־שָׂם
מה מֹשֶׁה לִפְנֵי בְּנֵי יִשְׂרָאֵל: אֵלֶּה הָעֵדֹת וְהַחֻקִּים
וְהַמִּשְׁפָּטִים אֲשֶׁר דִּבֶּר מֹשֶׁה אֶל־בְּנֵי יִשְׂרָאֵל
מו בְּצֵאתָם מִמִּצְרָיִם: בְּעֵבֶר הַיַּרְדֵּן בַּגַּיְא מוּל בֵּית פְּעוֹר
בְּאֶרֶץ סִיחֹן מֶלֶךְ הָאֱמֹרִי אֲשֶׁר יוֹשֵׁב בְּחֶשְׁבּוֹן אֲשֶׁר
מז הִכָּה מֹשֶׁה וּבְנֵי יִשְׂרָאֵל בְּצֵאתָם מִמִּצְרָיִם: וַיִּירְשׁוּ
אֶת־אַרְצוֹ וְאֶת־אֶרֶץ | עוֹג מֶלֶךְ־הַבָּשָׁן שְׁנֵי מַלְכֵי
מח הָאֱמֹרִי אֲשֶׁר בְּעֵבֶר הַיַּרְדֵּן מִזְרַח שָׁמֶשׁ: מֵעֲרֹעֵר
אֲשֶׁר עַל־שְׂפַת־נַחַל אַרְנֹן וְעַד־הַר שִׂיאֹן הוּא
מט חֶרְמוֹן: וְכָל־הָעֲרָבָה עֵבֶר הַיַּרְדֵּן מִזְרָחָה וְעַד יָם
הָעֲרָבָה תַּחַת אַשְׁדֹּת הַפִּסְגָּה:

ה רביעי א וַיִּקְרָא מֹשֶׁה אֶל־כָּל־יִשְׂרָאֵל וַיֹּאמֶר אֲלֵהֶם שְׁמַע
יִשְׂרָאֵל אֶת־הַחֻקִּים וְאֶת־הַמִּשְׁפָּטִים אֲשֶׁר אָנֹכִי דֹּבֵר

בעל הטורים

(מג) **וְאֶת גּוֹלָן בַּבָּשָׁן.** וּסְמִיךְ לֵיהּ ״וְזֹאת הַתּוֹרָה״. רֶמֶז, הֱוֵי גוֹלֶה לִמְקוֹם תּוֹרָה:

☐ **גֹּלָן.** חָסֵר וָי״ו. שֶׁשִּׁשָּׁה אֵינָן גּוֹלִין, כְּגוֹן אָב הַמַּכֶּה לִבְנוֹ וְהָרַב לְתַלְמִידוֹ, כִּדְאִיתָא בְּמַסֶּכֶת מַכּוֹת:

(מה) **אֵלֶּה הָעֵדֹת.** {הָעֵדֹת} בְּגִימַטְרִיָּא תַּלְמוּד:

BAAL HATURIM ELUCIDATED

43. וְאֶת גּוֹלָן בַּבָּשָׁן — AND GOLAN IN THE BASHAN. Juxtaposed with this is the phrase וְזֹאת הַתּוֹרָה, [literally,] *This is the Torah.* An allusion to [the Mishnah]: הֱוֵי גוֹלֶה, *Exile yourself,* [111a] to a place of Torah.[112]

☐ **גֹּלָן** — GOLAN. This word is spelled defectively,[113] without a ו (= 6). For there are six [unintentional killers] who are not exiled: A father who smites his son; a teacher who chastises his student; . . . as recorded in tractate *Makkos.* [114]

111a. A play on the similarity between גוֹלָן and גּוֹלֶה.

112. *Avos* 4:14.

113. The Baal HaTurim's statement is difficult, for the name גּוֹלָן appears four times in the *Tanach.* Two of those times, it is spelled in full, גּוֹלָן, with a ו (here, and in *I Chronicles* 6:56). The other two times, it appears as a קְרִי וּכְתִיב, *keri uchesiv,* i.e., it is spelled גָּלוֹן, but is pronounced גּוֹלָן (*Joshua* 20:8 and 21:27). Indeed, those two occurrences appear on a list entitled ס״ב מִלִּין דִּכְתִבָן מְקַדֵּם מְאַחַר, *Sixty-two words that are spelled with the earlier* [*letter appearing*] *later,* in the compilation of masoretic notes known as *Achlah VeAchlah* (list 91 in the Frensdorff edition; list 73 in the Madrid edition). Additionally, the *Rama* (who predated the Baal HaTurim by a century) writes: גּוֹלָן is spelled in full, with a ו, and a masoretic note states, כֻּלְּהוֹן מְלֵאִים, *They are all spelled in full,* i.e., every occurrence of the term גּוֹלָן uses the full spelling.

114. *Peirush HaRokeach* — The six cases in which the killer is exempt from exile are found in the first and second *mishnayos* of the second

and Golan in the Bashan, of the Manassite.

⁴⁴ This is the Torah that Moses placed before the Children of Israel. ⁴⁵ These are the testimonies, the decrees, and the ordinances that Moses spoke to the Children of Israel, when they left Egypt, ⁴⁶ on the bank of the Jordan, in the valley, opposite Beth-peor, in the land of Sihon, king of the Amorite, who dwells in Heshbon, whom Moses and the Children of Israel smote when they went out of Egypt. ⁴⁷ They possessed his land and the land of Og the king of Bashan, two kings of the Amorite, which are on the bank of the Jordan, where the sun rises; ⁴⁸ from Aroer that is by the shore of Arnon Brook until Mount Sion, which is Hermon, ⁴⁹ and the entire Arabah, the eastern bank of the Jordan until the Sea of the Arabah, under the waterfalls of the cliffs.

5

¹ Moses called all of Israel and said to them: Hear, O Israel, the decrees and the ordinances that I speak in your

─────────── BAAL HATURIM ELUCIDATED ───────────

45. אֵלֶּה הָעֵדֹת — **THE TESTIMONIES.** The *gematria* of הָעֵדֹת (479) is equivalent[115] to that of תַּלְמוּד, *Talmud.*[116]

chapter of tractate *Makkos.* Each of those *mishnayos* gives three examples of a general rule:

The first *mishnah* states that an unintentional killer is liable to exile only if the killing occurred in the course of descent. But if the killing did not occur in the course of descent, he is not exiled. The examples given are: (i) If one was smoothing tar on a sloped roof and the roller fell upon and killed another person, then if the killing occurred in the course of pushing the roller downwards, the killer is exiled, but if the roller was being pulled upwards, the killer is exempt from exile; (ii) similarly, if one was raising or lowering a cask by rope, if the rope snapped while the cask was being lowered, the killer is exiled, but if, while the cask was being raised, the killer is exempt; and (iii) similarly, if a person fell off a ladder onto a passerby.

The second *mishnah* states that one who kills unintentionally as a result of doing an optional act, such as the example found in the Torah, chopping wood (see *Deuteronomy* 19:5), is exiled; but one who killed while performing a *mitzvah* is exempt. The *mishnah* gives three

examples: (i) A father hitting his child to discipline him; (ii) a teacher chastising his pupil; and (iii) an agent of the court administering corporal punishment.

115. The principle of *im hakollel* allows 479 to be considered equivalent to 480, the *gematria* of the Baal HaTurim's term.

116. That is, תּוֹרָה שֶׁבְּעַל פֶּה, *the Oral Torah,* the explanations of תּוֹרָה שֶׁבִּכְתָב, *the Written Torah,* that were originally transmitted orally by Moses at Mount Sinai and from generation to generation — father to son; teacher to student — until they were compiled and canonized as the Talmud.

Apparently, the Baal HaTurim wishes to explain why 4:44 speaks of הַתּוֹרָה אֲשֶׁר שָׂם מֹשֶׁה, *the Torah that Moses placed,* while 4:45 mentions, הָעֵדֹת . . . אֲשֶׁר דִּבֶּר מֹשֶׁה, *the testimonies that Moses spoke.* He explains that הַתּוֹרָה refers to the Written Torah, which Moses wrote on a scroll that he placed before the nation; while הָעֵדֹת refers to the Oral Torah, which Moses spoke, i.e., transmitted orally, but did not commit to writing (*VeChur LeZahav*). The Baal HaTurim finds a similar allusion in the term עַל פִּי (*Exodus* 34:27).

בְּאָזְנֵיכֶם הַיּוֹם וּלְמַדְתֶּם אֹתָם וּשְׁמַרְתֶּם לַעֲשֹׂתָם׃
ב־ג יְהוָה אֱלֹהֵינוּ כָּרַת עִמָּנוּ בְּרִית בְּחֹרֵב׃ לֹא
אֶת־אֲבֹתֵינוּ כָּרַת יְהוָה אֶת־הַבְּרִית הַזֹּאת כִּי
אִתָּנוּ אֲנַחְנוּ אֵלֶּה פֹה הַיּוֹם כֻּלָּנוּ חַיִּים׃
ד פָּנִים ׀ בְּפָנִים דִּבֶּר יְהוָה עִמָּכֶם בָּהָר מִתּוֹךְ הָאֵשׁ׃
ה אָנֹכִי עֹמֵד בֵּין־יְהוָה וּבֵינֵיכֶם בָּעֵת הַהִוא לְהַגִּיד
לָכֶם אֶת־דְּבַר יְהוָה כִּי יְרֵאתֶם מִפְּנֵי הָאֵשׁ
ו וְלֹא־עֲלִיתֶם בָּהָר לֵאמֹר׃ *אָנֹכִי יְהוָה
אֱלֹהֶיךָ אֲשֶׁר הוֹצֵאתִיךָ מֵאֶרֶץ מִצְרַיִם מִבֵּית
ז עֲבָדִים׃ לֹא־יִהְיֶה לְךָ אֱלֹהִים אֲחֵרִים עַל־פָּנָי׃
ח לֹא־תַעֲשֶׂה לְךָ פֶסֶל כָּל־תְּמוּנָה אֲשֶׁר בַּשָּׁמַיִם
מִמַּעַל וַאֲשֶׁר בָּאָרֶץ מִתָּחַת וַאֲשֶׁר בַּמַּיִם מִתַּחַת
ט לָאָרֶץ׃ לֹא־תִשְׁתַּחֲוֶה לָהֶם וְלֹא תָעָבְדֵם כִּי אָנֹכִי
יְהוָה אֱלֹהֶיךָ אֵל קַנָּא פֹּקֵד עֲוֺן אָבוֹת עַל־
י בָּנִים וְעַל־שִׁלֵּשִׁים וְעַל־רִבֵּעִים לְשֹׂנְאָי׃ וְעֹשֶׂה
יא חֶסֶד לַאֲלָפִים לְאֹהֲבַי וּלְשֹׁמְרֵי °מצותו׃ לֹא [°מִצְוֺתָי ק׳]

בעל הטורים

ה (ד) פָּנִים בְּפָנִים. פֵּ״א כְּפוּלָה. לוֹמַר, בְּפָנִים מְאִירוֹת, בְּפָנִים מַסְבִּירוֹת:

(ח) פֶּסֶל כָּל תְּמוּנָה. וּבַדִּבְּרוֹת הָרִאשׁוֹנוֹת כְּתִיב ״וְכָל תְּמוּנָה״, וָי״ו יְתֵרָה כְּנֶגֶד שִׁשָּׁה דְבָרִים — ״תַּבְנִית זָכָר אוֹ נְקֵבָה תַּבְנִית כָּל בְּהֵמָה... תַּבְנִית כָּל צִפּוֹר... תַּבְנִית כָּל רֹמֵשׂ... תַּבְנִית כָּל דָּגָה״:

(ט) סָמַךְ ״אֵל קַנָּא״ לְ״לֹא תִשָּׂא״, שֶׁכָּל הַנִּשְׁבָּע לַשֶּׁקֶר, כְּאִלּוּ עוֹבֵד עֲבוֹדָה זָרָה:

(י־יא) סָמַךְ ״וּלְשֹׁמְרֵי מִצְוֺתָי״ לְ״לֹא תִשָּׂא״. שֶׁאֲפִילּוּ בִשְׁמִירַת מִצְוָה יֵשׁ מִשּׁוּם ״לֹא תִשָּׂא״.

BAAL HATURIM ELUCIDATED

V.

4. פָּנִים בְּפָנִים — FACE TO FACE. [According to a scribal tradition, each פ in this phrase is written in the enhanced form known as] פ׳ כְּפוּלָה, doubled פ.[117] This is to indicate [that God spoke to Israel] with a radiant countenance, with a welcoming countenance.[118]

6-18. {The reader is advised to see the Baal HaTurim's other comments to the Ten Commandments at *Exodus* 20:2-14.}

117. See note 29 to *parashas Devarim* and the illustration there. *Sefer Tagin* includes the two letters פ of our phrase among the "191 in the Torah whose mouths are on the inside."

118. *Peirush HaRokeach;* see also *Maseches Soferim* 16:2.

ears today; learn them, and be careful to perform them.
[2] *HASHEM, our God, sealed a covenant with us at Horeb.* [3] *Not*
with our forefathers did HASHEM seal this covenant, but with
us — we who are here, all of us alive today. [4] *Face to face did*
HASHEM speak with you on the mountain, from amid the fire.
[5] *I was standing between HASHEM and you at that time, to*
relate the word of HASHEM to you — for you were afraid of the
fire and you did not ascend the mountain — saying:
[6] *I am HASHEM, your God, Who has taken you out of the*
land of Egypt, from the house of slavery. [7] *You shall not*
have other gods in My Presence. [8] *You shall not make*
yourself a carved image of any likeness of that which is in
the heavens above or on the earth below or in the water
beneath the earth. [9] *You shall not prostrate yourself to them*
nor worship them, for I am HASHEM, your God — a zealous
God, Who visits the sin of fathers upon children to the third
and fourth generations, for My enemies; [10] *but Who shows*
kindness for thousands [of generations], to those who love
Me and to those who observe My commandments.

BAAL HATURIM ELUCIDATED

8. פֶּסֶל כָּל תְּמוּנָה — A CARVED IMAGE OF ANY LIKENESS. In the first version of the Ten Commandments, this reads [פֶּסֶל] וְכָל תְּמוּנָה, *a carved image or any likeness* (*Exodus* 20:4), with an extra ו (= 6), corresponding to the six forbidden forms [mentioned earlier]: תַּבְנִית זָכָר אוֹ נְקֵבָה תַּבְנִית כָּל בְּהֵמָה ... תַּבְנִית כָּל צִפּוֹר ... תַּבְנִית כָּל רֹמֵשׂ ... תַּבְנִית כָּל דָּגָה, *a form of* (i) *a male or* (ii) *a female*; (iii) *a form of any animal* . . .; (iv) *a form of any* [*winged*] *bird* . . .; (v) *a form of anything that creeps* . . .; (vi) *a form of any fish* (4:16-18 above).

❑ {The Baal HaTurim's comment to פֶּסֶל appears at *Exodus* 32:19.}

9. Scripture juxtaposed [the commandment that describes God as] אֵל קַנָּא, *a zealous God,* with [the commandment regarding false oaths, that begins], לֹא תִשָּׂא, *You shall not take* . . . (v. ii), for anyone who swears falsely is considered as a worshiper of idols.[119]

❑ {The Baal HaTurim's comment to וְעַל שִׁלֵּשִׁים וְעַל רִבֵּעִים appears at *Numbers* 16:29, s.v., וּפְקֻדַּת כָּל אָדָם.}

10. Scripture juxtaposed the phrase וּלְשֹׁמְרֵי מִצְוֹתָי, *and to those who observe My commandments,* with לֹא תִשָּׂא, *You shall not take* [*the Name of HASHEM* . . . *in vain*],

119. *Tanna DeVei Eliyahu Rabbah* 26.

THE TEN COMMANDMENTS ARE READ WITH TWO DIFFERENT SETS OF *TROP* (CANTILLATION NOTES). THE VERSION PRESENTED IN THE TEXT IS USED BY THE INDIVIDUAL WHO IS REVIEWING THE WEEKLY *SIDRAH*. THE VERSION USED BY THE READER FOR THE PUBLIC TORAH READING ON THE SABBATH APPEARS IN A BOX ON PAGE 1902.

תִשָּׂא אֶת־שֵׁם־יְהוָה אֱלֹהֶיךָ לַשָּׁוְא כִּי לֹא יְנַקֶּה
יב יְהוָה אֵת אֲשֶׁר־יִשָּׂא אֶת־שְׁמוֹ לַשָּׁוְא: שָׁמוֹר
אֶת־יוֹם הַשַּׁבָּת לְקַדְּשׁוֹ כַּאֲשֶׁר צִוְּךָ יְהוָה אֱלֹהֶיךָ:
יג-יד שֵׁשֶׁת יָמִים תַּעֲבֹד וְעָשִׂיתָ כָּל־מְלַאכְתֶּךָ: וְיוֹם
הַשְּׁבִיעִי שַׁבָּת לַיהוָה אֱלֹהֶיךָ לֹא־תַעֲשֶׂה כָל־
מְלָאכָה אַתָּה | וּבִנְךָ־וּבִתֶּךָ וְעַבְדְּךָ־וַאֲמָתֶךָ וְשׁוֹרְךָ
וַחֲמֹרְךָ וְכָל־בְּהֶמְתֶּךָ וְגֵרְךָ אֲשֶׁר בִּשְׁעָרֶיךָ לְמַעַן
טו יָנוּחַ עַבְדְּךָ וַאֲמָתְךָ כָּמוֹךָ: וְזָכַרְתָּ כִּי עֶבֶד הָיִיתָ
בְּאֶרֶץ מִצְרַיִם וַיֹּצִאֲךָ יְהוָה אֱלֹהֶיךָ מִשָּׁם בְּיָד חֲזָקָה
וּבִזְרֹעַ נְטוּיָה עַל־כֵּן צִוְּךָ יְהוָה אֱלֹהֶיךָ לַעֲשׂוֹת אֶת־
טז יוֹם הַשַּׁבָּת: כַּבֵּד אֶת־אָבִיךָ וְאֶת־אִמֶּךָ כַּאֲשֶׁר

בעל הטורים

שֶׁהָעוֹשֶׂה מִצְוָה שֶׁלֹּא לְשֵׁם שָׁמַיִם, כְּאִלּוּ נוֹשֵׂא שֵׁם שָׁמַיִם לְבַטָּלָה:

אִי נַמִּי – שֶׁמַּזְהִיר שֶׁלֹּא תַעֲבֹר עַל "לֹא תִשָּׂא" בְּעִנְיַן שְׁמִירַת מִצְוָה, שֶׁהֲרֵי נִשְׁבָּעִין לְקַיֵּם הַמִּצְוָה:

(יב) סָמַךְ שַׁבָּת לְ"לֹא תִשָּׂא", שֶׁבִּשְׁנֵיהֶם נֶאֱמַר חִלּוּל – "וְלֹא תִשָּׁבְעוּ בִשְׁמִי לַשָּׁקֶר וְחִלַּלְתָּ", "מְחַלְלֶיהָ מוֹת יוּמָת":

❑ **שָׁמוֹר אֶת יוֹם הַשַּׁבָּת.** רָאשֵׁי תֵבוֹת **שְׁאִיָּה**, וְסוֹפֵי תֵבוֹת **רֹתֶם**. לוֹמַר לְךָ, הַנִּדּוֹנִין בִּשְׁאִיָּה וְגַחֲלֵי רֹתֶם, נוֹחִין בְּשַׁבָּת:

(טז) סָמַךְ "כַּבֵּד אֶת אָבִיךָ" לְשַׁבָּת. שֶׁגַּם בְּשַׁבָּת כְּתִיב "וְכִבַּדְתּוֹ", וְצָרִיךְ לְכַבְּדוֹ בְּמַאֲכָל וּכְסוּת:

BAAL HATURIM ELUCIDATED

for even in the observance of a *mitzvah,* one can be guilty of taking God's Name in vain. One who fulfills a *mitzvah* for a purpose other than for the sake of Heaven is considered as having taken God's Name in vain.[120]

Alternatively: The verse is cautioning that one should not transgress the commandment against taking false oaths with regard to the observance of the commandments, for the Talmud[121] states that oaths may be taken to encourage the observance of the commandments.[122]

12. Scripture juxtaposed the commandment regarding the Sabbath with the commandment of **לֹא תִשָּׂא**, *You shall not take . . .,* for the concept of desecration is stated concerning each of them.[122a] [With regard to swearing falsely,] וְלֹא תִשָּׁבְעוּ בִשְׁמִי לַשָּׁקֶר וְחִלַּלְתָּ, *You shall not swear falsely by My Name, thereby desecrating . . .* (*Leviticus* 19:12); [and with regard to the Sabbath,] מְחַלְלֶיהָ מוֹת

120. *Pesikta Rabbasi* 22:5.

121. *Nedarim* 8a.

122. Even when one takes an oath as a form of self-encouragement to fulfill *mitzvos,* that oath must be fulfilled (see *Yoreh De'ah* 203:6).

122a. See *Shabbos* 33a.

11 *You shall not take the Name of* HASHEM, *your God, in vain, for* HASHEM *will not absolve anyone who takes His Name in vain.*

12 *Safeguard the Sabbath day to sanctify it, as* HASHEM, *your God, has commanded you.* 13 *Six days shall you labor and accomplish all your work;* 14 *but the seventh day is Sabbath to* HASHEM, *your God; you shall not do any work — you, your son, your daughter, your slave, your maidservant, your ox, your donkey, and your every animal, and your convert within your gates, in order that your slave and your maidservant may rest like you.* 15 *And you shall remember that you were a slave in the land of Egypt, and* HASHEM, *your God, has taken you out from there with a strong hand and an outstretched arm; therefore* HASHEM, *your God, has commanded you to make the Sabbath day.*

16 *Honor your father and your mother, as* HASHEM,

──────── BAAL HATURIM ELUCIDATED ────────

יוּמָת, *its desecrators shall be put to death (Exodus 31:14).*

❑ שָׁמוֹר אֶת יוֹם הַשַּׁבָּת — SAFEGUARD THE SABBATH DAY. The initial letters of these words spell the word שְׁאִיָּה, *ruin.* [123] The last letters of [שָׁמוֹר אֶת יוֹם] spell the word רֹתֶם, *rotem.* [124] Even those who are sentenced to ruin and *rotem* coals [in *Gehinnom*] are given respite on the Sabbath. [125]

❑ {The Baal HaTurim's further comment on this verse appears at *Leviticus* 26:2.}

16. Scripture juxtaposed [the commandment of] כַּבֵּד אֶת אָבִיךָ, *honor your father,* with [the commandment about] the Sabbath, for also regarding the Sabbath is written, וְכִבַּדְתּוֹ, *and you shall honor it (Isaiah 58:13).* That is, one must honor [the Sabbath] with food [126] and clothing. [127]

---

123. A reference to *Gehinnom,* the place of ultimate ruin.

124. The *rotem* is a wilderness shrub/tree that *Rashi* (*I Kings* 19:4) renders *juniper.* According to the Midrash, *rotem*-wood coals differ from those of other woods. Whereas the embers of other woods cool off on the inside as well as on the outside, *rotem* coals, even when they cool on the outside, remain very hot on the inside for a long period (*Bereishis Rabbah* 98:19; cited in *Rashi* to *Psalms* 120:4). According to the Talmud the term גַּחֲלֵי רְתָמִים, *rotem coals,* is a reference to *Gehinnom* (*Arachin* 15:2).

125. *Zohar, Vayakhel* 203b — When the *Shabbos* arrives, all manner of harsh fires are hidden and covered over. This includes even the fires of *Gehinnom,* so that the sinful ones being punished there also find rest.

The Baal HaTurim discusses this concept further in his comments to *Exodus* 31:17, s.v., וַיִּנָּפַשׁ, see note 54 there; and *Exodus* 35:3, s.v., לֹא תְבַעֲרוּ אֵשׁ.

126. *Shabbos* 118b.

127. *Shabbos* 113a.

Similarly, honor of one's father and mother involves food and clothing (*Kiddushin* 31b; see also the Baal HaTurim to *Exodus* 20:12, s.v., כַּבֵּד, with note 96).

ה/טז צִוְּךָ יהוה אֱלֹהֶיךָ לְמַעַן | יַאֲרִיכֻן יָמֶיךָ וּלְמַעַן יִיטַב לָךְ

בעל הטורים

❏ **כַּאֲשֶׁר צִוְּךָ ה׳ אֱלֹהֶיךָ.** סוֹפֵי תֵבוֹת בְּגִימַטְרִיָּא מָרָה:

❏ **וּלְמַעַן יִיטַב לָךְ.** תָּגִין עַל הַטֵּי״ת. שֶׁעִבְּרַתּוּ אִמּוֹ תִּשְׁעָה חֳדָשִׁים, וְאָבִיו וְאִמּוֹ נִזְהֲרוּ מִתֵּשַׁע מִדּוֹת הָאֲמוּרוֹת בִּנְדָרִים, וְזֶה סִימָנָם, אסנ״ת משגע״ח. נוֹטָרִיקוֹן – בְּנֵי אֲנוּסָה, בְּנֵי שְׂנוּאָה, בְּנֵי נִדָּה, בְּנֵי תְמוּרָה, בְּנֵי מְרִיבָה, בְּנֵי שִׁכְרוּת, בְּנֵי גְרוּשַׁת הַלֵּב, בְּנֵי עִרְבּוּבְיָא, בְּנֵי חֲצוּפָה:

פֵּרוּשׁ בְּנֵי אֲנוּסָה – אֵין צָרִיךְ לוֹמַר שֶׁאִם אָנַס אִשָּׁה וְהוֹלִיד מִמֶּנָּה בֵּן, אֶלָּא אֲפִלּוּ הִיא אִשְׁתּוֹ וַאֲנָסָהּ לְתַשְׁמִישׁ. וְכֵן שָׁנִינוּ בְּמַסֶּכֶת כַּלָּה, מִפְּנֵי מָה הַוְיָן לֵהּ לְאָדָם בָּנִים בַּעֲלֵי מוּמִין? מִפְּנֵי שֶׁתּוֹבְעָהּ, וְאִשְׁתּוֹ אֵינָהּ נִתְבַּעַת לוֹ, פֵּרוּשׁ, אֵינָהּ מִתְרַצָּה לוֹ. וְרַבִּי יְהוּדָה אוֹמֵר, מִפְּנֵי שֶׁאוֹמֶרֶת לוֹ בִּשְׁעַת תַּשְׁמִישׁ אֲנוּסָה אֲנִי. וְאִיכָּא בֵּינַיְהוּ, רוֹצָה וְאֵינָהּ רוֹצָה:

וְכֵן אִיתָא בְּעֵרוּבִין, כָּל הַכּוֹפֶה אִשְׁתּוֹ לִדְבַר מִצְוָה נִקְרָא חוֹטֵא, שֶׁנֶּאֱמַר "גַּם בְּלֹא דַעַת נֶפֶשׁ לֹא טוֹב". נִמְצָא כִּי הָאֹנֶס אָסוּר אַף בְּאִשְׁתּוֹ, אֶלָּא אִם הוּא צָרִיךְ לְאוֹתוֹ מַעֲשֶׂה, יְפַיֵּס וְאַחַר כָּךְ יִבְעֹל:

בְּנֵי שְׂנוּאָה – כְּמַשְׁמָעָהּ. וְהוּא שֶׁשְּׂנוּאָה בִּשְׁעַת תַּשְׁמִישׁ. {אֲבָל אִם הִיא רְצוּיָה בִּשְׁעַת תַּשְׁמִישׁ,} אַף עַל פִּי שֶׁהִיא שְׂנוּאָה, שָׁרֵי:

BAAL HATURIM ELUCIDATED

❏ **כַּאֲשֶׁר צִוְּךָ ה׳ אֱלֹהֶיךָ** — AS HASHEM, YOUR GOD, COMMANDED YOU. The *gematria* of the final letters of these words (245) is equal to that of מָרָה, *Marah.*[128]

❏ {Regarding the spelling of יַאֲרִיכֻן, see the Baal HaTurim to *Exodus* 20:13.}[129]

❏ {Regarding the order of the phrases לְמַעַן יַאֲרִיכֻן יָמֶיךָ and וּלְמַעַן יִיטַב לָךְ, see the Baal HaTurim to 22:7 below.}

❏ **וּלְמַעַן יִיטַב לָךְ** — AND SO THAT IT WILL BE GOOD FOR YOU. According to a scribal tradition, the ט (= 9) of יִיטַב is written with [extra] *tagin.*[130] [This underscores to a person] that his mother carried him for nine months, and that his father and mother were careful with regard to the nine [undesirable] attributes mentioned in tractate *Nedarim,* that are referred to collectively by the mnemonic אסנ״ת משגע״ח,[131] an acronym for: (i) בְּנֵי אֲנוּסָה, *children of a forced*

128. The Talmud teaches that laws referred to in the verse, שָׁם שָׂם לוֹ חֹק וּמִשְׁפָּט, *There [in Marah] He established a decree and an ordinance* (*Exodus* 15:25), include the commandment — *Honor your father and mother.* Thus, *as* HASHEM, *your God, commanded you,* means "as He commanded you previously in Marah" (*Sanhedrin* 56b, cited by *Rashi*). It is noteworthy that the Talmud there explains our verse as a reference to both observing the Sabbath and honoring one's parents. This is an additional explanation of the juxtaposition of these two commandments (Y. S.).

129. See notes 97 and 98 there.

130. See first paragraph of note 56 to *parashas Devarim.*

According to *Sefer Tagin,* the ט of יִיטַב is one of 67 in the Torah that are drawn with four *tagin* instead of the usual three (see illustration).

Usual ט with three *tagin*
ט with four *tagin*
ט with five *tagin*

Although *Sefer Tagin* assigns four *tagin* to this ט, it is not clear that the Baal HaTurim agrees with that count, for in his comments to *Exodus* 2:2, he speaks of a two-*tagin* [or, perhaps, a five-*tagin*] ט (see notes 37 and 38 there).

131. The Baal HaTurim will first enumerate the nine attributes referred to by this abbreviation. Then he will proceed to discuss and explain each

your God, commanded you, so that your days will be lengthened and so that it will be good for you, upon the

─────────── BAAL HATURIM ELUCIDATED ───────────

woman; [132] (ii) בְּנֵי שְׂנוּאָה, *children of a despised wife;* (iii) בְּנֵי נִדָּה, *children of a niddah (an unpurified menstruant);* [133] (iv) בְּנֵי תְמוּרָה, *children of an exchanged woman;* (v) בְּנֵי מְרִיבָה, *children of strife;* [134] (vi) בְּנֵי שִׁכְרוּת, *children of drunkenness;* (vii) בְּנֵי גְרוּשַׁת הַלֵּב, *children of a woman whose husband has decided to divorce her;* [134a] (viii) בְּנֵי עִרְבּוּבְיָא, *children of mingling;* and (ix) בְּנֵי חֲצוּפָה, *children of a brazen woman.* [135,136]

To explain these terms:

(i) בְּנֵי אֲנוּסָה, *children of a forced woman* — It need not be stated regarding a man who forced a woman to whom he was not married, and begot a child through her; rather, it refers to even an instance when a man forces himself upon his wife. And thus have we learned in tractate *Kallah*: Why is it that a man begets sons with physical blemishes? Because he makes demands of his wife, but she is not won over, i.e., she does not consent. Rabbi Yehudah says: Because she tells him at the time of marital relations, "I am being forced." The difference between the two opinions is a woman who is wavering — she consents, yet does not consent. [137]

Similarly, the Talmud states in tractate *Eruvin*: Whoever forces his wife [to perform] the *mitzvah* [of procreation] is called a sinner, as it is said (*Proverbs 19:2*), גַּם בְּלֹא דַעַת נֶפֶשׁ לֹא טוֹב, *Also, for without the knowledge of the soul, it is not good.* [137a]

Thus we find that the use of force is forbidden even with regard to one's own wife. Rather, if a man feels a need for relations, he should appease [his wife], and then cohabit.

(ii) בְּנֵי שְׂנוּאָה, *children of a despised wife* — This means precisely what it says, but refers only to the time of relations. {If, however, she is desired at the time of relations}, [137b] although she is generally despised, it is permitted.

of the nine. According to the Talmud, children conceived under any of these nine circumstances are apt to be degenerate.

132. The Talmudic source reads, בְּנֵי אֵימָה בְּנֵי אֲנוּסָה, *children of fear, children of a forced woman,* as the first undesirable attribute.

133. The Talmudic source reads, בְּנֵי נִדּוּי, *children of one who is under a ban.* The Baal HaTurim cites that version in *Tur, Orach Chaim* 240.

Another version reads בְּנֵי אָמָה, *children of a slave girl* (see *Peirush HaRosh*).

134. Alternatively: בְּנֵי מוֹרֶדֶת, *children of a rebellious wife* (cited below and in *Tur*).

134a. Literally, *children of one divorced by the heart.*

135. *Kallah Rabbasi* 1; *Nedarim* 20b.

136. The remainder of this comment (until וְנִקְרָא פּוֹשֵׁעַ, *and he is called a sinner*) appears in virtually all the printed editions. However, *Shoham Yakar* reports that it is not found in the extant manuscripts. Whether the Baal HaTurim included it in his original commentary cannot be determined with certainty. However, the fact that he first presents the list without any variant readings, and then proceeds to explain each term using a different text as the primary reading and that which he presents here as a variant, tends to indicate that the remainder of the comment is a later addition. In any case, the passage is based on the Talmud (*Nedarim* 20b) and the Baal HaTurim does include it in *Tur, Orach Chaim* 240.

137. That is, she acquiesces, but does not really want to participate.

137a. *Eruvin* 100b.

137b. The passage enclosed in braces is absent in the early printed edition. It was included in the later printed editions at the suggestion of *Ittur Bikkurim.*

בְּנֵי נִדָּה – אַף עַל פִּי שֶׁאֵינוֹ מַמְזֵר מִן הַתּוֹרָה. וְיֵשׁ מְפָרְשִׁים, שֶׁהִיא אָז בְּנִדּוּי, שֶׁאֲסוּרִין בְּתַשְׁמִישׁ הַמִּטָּה. וְהוּא הַדִּין נַמִּי אִם אֶחָד מֵהֶם אָבֵל:

בְּנֵי תְמוּרָה – שֶׁהָיָה מְכַוֵּן לְעֶרְוָה וְנִזְדַּמְּנָה לוֹ אִשְׁתּוֹ. וְיֵשׁ מְפָרְשִׁים, אֲפִילוּ שְׁתֵּי נָשָׁיו, שֶׁנִּתְכַּוֵּן לָזוֹ וְנִזְדַּמְּנָה לוֹ הָאַחֶרֶת:

בְּנֵי מוֹרֶדֶת – דְּאָמְרָה לֵהּ, לָא בָעֵינָא לָךְ, וְאַף עַל פִּי כֵן הוּא מְשַׁמֵּשׁ עִמָּהּ, וַהֲרֵי הִיא אֶצְלוֹ כְּזוֹנָה, וַאֲפִלּוּ אִם הוּא מִדַּעְתָּהּ. וּלְנֻסְחָא אַחֲרִינָא, בְּנֵי מְרִיבָה, שֶׁהֵם מִתְקוֹטְטִים בְּיַחַד בְּכָל פַּעַם. דְּהָוְיָא בִיאָה זוֹ כְּמוֹ זְנוּת, כֵּיוָן שֶׁאֵינָהּ מִתּוֹךְ אַהֲבָה:

בְּנֵי שִׁכְרוּת – שֶׁהוּא אוֹ הִיא שִׁכּוֹרִים:

בְּנֵי גְרוּשַׁת הַלֵּב – שֶׁבְּלִבּוֹ לְגָרְשָׁהּ אֲפִלּוּ אֵין בְּלִבּוֹ שִׂנְאָה, כְּגוֹן מֵאוֹתָן שֶׁכּוֹפִין לְהוֹצִיא, וְגָמַר בְּלִבּוֹ לְגָרְשָׁהּ וְאַחַר כָּךְ בָּא עָלֶיהָ:

בְּנֵי עִרְבּוּבְיָא – שֶׁמְּשַׁמֵּשׁ עִם אִשְׁתּוֹ וְנָתַן דַּעְתּוֹ עַל אַחֶרֶת, אֲפִלּוּ שְׁתֵּיהֶן נָשָׁיו:

בְּנֵי חֲצוּפָה – שֶׁתּוֹבַעְתּוֹ בְּפֶה, וַהֲרֵי הִיא כְּזוֹנָה וְאָסוּר לְקַיְּמָהּ. אֲבָל מִי שֶׁאִשְׁתּוֹ מְרַצָּה אוֹתוֹ בִדְבָרִים שֶׁל רִצּוּי וּמְקַשֶּׁטֶת עַצְמָהּ לְפָנָיו כְּדֵי שֶׁיִּתֵּן דַּעְתּוֹ עָלֶיהָ, עַל זוֹ אָמְרוּ רַבּוֹתֵינוּ ז״ל, שֶׁיּוֹצְאִים מִמֶּנָּה בָּנִים חֲכָמִים וּנְבוֹנִים, כְּלֵאָה שֶׁיָּצָא מִמֶּנָּה יִשָּׂשכָר:

וְכָל אֵלוּ תֵּשַׁע הַמִּדּוֹת, אֲפִלּוּ לִפְרִיָּה וּרְבִיָּה, כְּגוֹן שֶׁאֵינָהּ מְעֻבֶּרֶת, אֲפִלּוּ הָכֵי בְּכָל אֵלּוּ הַמִּדּוֹת פּוֹגֵם הַוָּלָד, וְנִקְרָא פּוֹשֵׁעַ:

❑ וְצָרִיךְ לְכַבְּדָם בְּתִשְׁעָה דְבָרִים, מַאֲכִיל וּמַלְבִּישׁ וְכוּ׳, כִּדְאִיתָא בְּפֶרֶק קַמָּא דְקִדּוּשִׁין:

❑ שֶׁבַע עֶשְׂרֵה תֵבוֹת יְתֵרוֹת דִּבְּרוֹת אַחֲרוֹנוֹת עַל הָרִאשׁוֹנוֹת, כְּמִנְיַן טוֹב. וְזֶהוּ

BAAL HATURIM ELUCIDATED

(iii) בְּנֵי נִדָּה, *children of a niddah* — Even though the Torah does not consider the children of such a forbidden relationship as *mamzeirim* (bastards).[137c] There are some who interpret this term as meaning the children of a mother who is under a ban, for such people are prohibited from cohabitation.[137d] This law also applies if one of the marital partners is in mourning [i.e., the week of *shivah*].

(iv) בְּנֵי תְמוּרָה, *children of an exchange* — A man intended to engage in relations with a woman forbidden to him, but happened upon his own wife. Others interpret this as referring even to a man who is married to two women, and intended to have relations with the one, but happened upon the other.

(v) בְּנֵי מוֹרֶדֶת, *children of a rebellious wife*[137e] — If she says to him, "I do not want you," and he nevertheless cohabits with her, she is considered as a harlot regarding him, even if — at the time — she consents.[137f]

According to the alternative version — בְּנֵי מְרִיבָה, *children of strife* — this refers to a couple who are constantly quarreling. Accordingly, relations between them is tantamount to harlotry, because the act is not motivated by love.

137c. Although the Torah prohibits any cohabitation involving a *niddah* who has not purified himself in a *mikveh,* nevertheless, children conceived of such a union are not considered *mamzeirim* (*Yevamos* 49a).

137d. See note 133 above.

137e. Earlier, the Baal HaTurim refers to this as בְּנֵי מְרִיבָה, *children of strife* (see note 134 above); here he gives the alternative reading first.

137f. That is, she says, "I do not want to remain married to you," yet consents to cohabitation. Their union is not an act of marital conjugation; rather it is tantamount to harlotry (see *Orach Chayim* 240:3; with *Magen Avraham* 10 and *Mishnah Berurah* 17).

(vi) בְּנֵי שִׁכְרוּת, *children of drunkenness* — This applies whether he or she is drunk [at the time of relations].

(vii) בְּנֵי גְרוּשַׁת הַלֵּב, *children of a woman whose husband has decided to divorce her* — that is, in his heart, he has decided to divorce her, even if there is no hate in his heart — e.g., an instance where the Sages compel a couple to divorce — and he made up his mind to divorce her, but then cohabited with her.

(viii) בְּנֵי עַרְבּוּבְיָא, *children of mingling* — This refers to an instance in which a husband engages in relations with his wife while thinking of another woman, even if they are both his wives.

(ix) בְּנֵי חֲצוּפָה, *children born of a brazen woman* — A woman who verbally demands of her husband [to engage in relations with her] is considered like a prostitute and he is forbidden to remain married to her. However, one whose wife appeases him with words of enticement and preens herself before him so that he should take notice of her, regarding such a woman our Rabbis, of blessed memory have said that she will bear wise and knowledgeable sons, just as did [the Matriarch] Leah who bore Issachar.

Regarding each of these nine [aforementioned undesirable] attributes, even if they cohabited with the intention of [fulfilling the *mitzvah* of] "be fruitful and multiply," for example, if she is not pregnant at the time, still and all, when any of these attributes are present, the baby is considered tainted and he [i.e., the parent][137g] is called a sinner.

[Alternatively: The unusual ט indicates that] one must honor one's parents in nine ways: with food, with clothing, etc., as is stated in the first chapter of tractate *Kiddushin*.[138]

❑ There are seventeen more words in this latter version of the Ten Commandments than in the first version (*Exodus* 20:2-14),[138a] equal to the *gematria* of טוֹב,

---

137g. The interpolated phrase seems to reflect the Baal HaTurim's understanding of the Talmud. According to the *Rambam* (*Issurei Bi'ah* 21:12), the reference is to the baby, who will have tendencies toward wickedness and sin.

138. The Baal HaTurim apparently refers to *Kiddushin* 31b; however, only six examples of honor are enumerated there: מַאֲכִיל וּמַשְׁקֶה מַלְבִּישׁ וּמְכַסֶּה מַכְנִיס וּמוֹצִיא, *provide* [*them with*] *food and provide drink, clothing and cover, escort in and escort out.*

A parallel statement in the Jerusalem Talmud adds a seventh example, adding וּמַנְעִיל, *and provide shoes,* after וּמְכַסֶּה, *and cover* (*Yerushalmi Kiddushin* 1:7). A third listing, this one with eight examples, is found in the Midrash: מַאֲכִיל וּמַשְׁקֶה מַרְבִּיץ מַרְחִיץ סָךְ וּמַנְעִיל וּמַכְנִיס וּמוֹצִיא, *provide food and provide drink, provide resting place, bathe, anoint, and provide shoes and escort in and escort out* (*Pesikta Rabbasi* 24:2). Were we to combine the lists, we would add two more — מַלְבִּישׁ וּמְכַסֶּה — to the eight of the Midrash, for a total of ten. If so, how does the Baal HaTurim arrive at the number nine?

Perhaps, the Baal HaTurim's version of the Talmud included all the examples of the combined lists. Notice, however, that even though each of the sources begins with מַאֲכִיל וּמַשְׁקֶה, the Baal HaTurim omits the term וּמַשְׁקֶה. Apparently, he reckons providing food and providing drink as one act. Thus, the combined list enumerates nine ways in which one is obligated to honor one's parents (*VeChur LaZahav*; for an alternative understanding, see *Shoham Yakar*).

138a. The first version contains 172 words; the second 189. Three of the commandments have more words in the second version than in the first: The fourth (*Shabbos*) has nine more; the fifth (honoring parents), four; and the tenth (not to covet), one.

יז עַל הָאֲדָמָה אֲשֶׁר־יהוָה אֱלֹהֶיךָ נֹתֵן לָךְ׃ לֹא
תִּרְצַח וְלֹא תִּנְאָף וְלֹא תִּגְנֹב וְלֹא־
יח תַעֲנֶה בְרֵעֲךָ עֵד שָׁוְא׃ וְלֹא תַחְמֹד

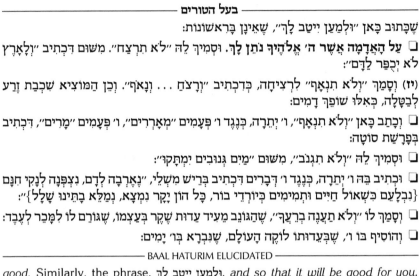

בעל הטורים

שֶׁכָּתוּב כָּאן "וּלְמַעַן יִיטַב לָךְ", שֶׁאֵינָן בָּרִאשׁוֹנוֹת:

❑ **עַל הָאֲדָמָה אֲשֶׁר ה' אֱלֹהֶיךָ נֹתֵן לָךְ.** וּסְמִיךְ לֵהּ "לֹא תִרְצַח". מִשּׁוּם דִּכְתִיב "וְלָאָרֶץ לֹא יְכֻפַּר לַדָּם":

(יז) וְסָמַךְ "וְלֹא תִנְאָף" לִרְצִיחָה, כְּדִכְתִיב "וְרָצֹחַ . . . וְנָאֹף". וְכֵן הַמּוֹצִיא שִׁכְבַת זֶרַע לְבַטָּלָה, כְּאִלּוּ שׁוֹפֵךְ דָּמִים:

❑ וְכָתַב כָּאן "וְלֹא תִנְאָף", ו' יְתֵרָה, כְּנֶגֶד ו' פְּעָמִים "מְאָרְרִים", ו' פְּעָמִים "מָרִים", דִּכְתִיב בְּפָרָשַׁת סוֹטָה:

❑ וּסְמִיךְ לֵהּ "וְלֹא תִגְנֹב", מִשּׁוּם "מַיִם גְּנוּבִים יִמְתָּקוּ":

❑ וּכְתִיב בֵּהּ ו' יְתֵרָה, כְּנֶגֶד ו' דְּבָרִים דִּכְתִיב בְּרֵישׁ מִשְׁלֵי, "נֶאֶרְבָה לְדָם, נִצְפְּנָה לְנָקִי חִנָּם {נִבְלָעֵם כִּשְׁאוֹל חַיִּים וּתְמִימִים כְּיוֹרְדֵי בוֹר, כָּל הוֹן יָקָר נִמְצָא, נְמַלֵּא בָתֵּינוּ שָׁלָל}":

❑ וְסָמַךְ לוֹ "וְלֹא תַעֲנֶה בְרֵעֲךָ", שֶׁהַגּוֹנֵב מֵעִיד עֵדוּת שֶׁקֶר בְּעַצְמוֹ, שֶׁגּוֹרֵם לוֹ לִמָּכֵר לְעֶבֶד:

❑ וְהוֹסִיף בּוֹ ו', שֶׁבְּעֵדוּתוֹ לוֹקֶה הָעוֹלָם, שֶׁנִּבְרָא בְּו' יָמִים:

BAAL HATURIM ELUCIDATED

good. Similarly, the phrase, וּלְמַעַן יִיטַב לָךְ, *and so that it will be good for you,* appears here but is not included in the first version.[139]

❑ {The Baal HaTurim's comment to כַּאֲשֶׁר צִוְּךָ ה' אֱלֹהֶיךָ, is found at this point in most editions, appears above as the second comment to this verse.}

❑ **עַל הָאֲדָמָה אֲשֶׁר ה' אֱלֹהֶיךָ נֹתֵן לָךְ** — UPON THE LAND THAT HASHEM, YOUR GOD, GIVES YOU. Juxtaposed to this is [the prohibition], לֹא תִרְצַח, *You shall not kill.* [This can be explained] in accordance with the verse, וְלָאָרֶץ לֹא יְכֻפַּר לַדָּם, *the land will not be atoned for regarding the blood* [*that was spilled in it*] (*Numbers* 35:33).[139a]

17. Scripture juxtaposed וְלֹא תִנְאָף, *you shall not commit adultery,* with the prohibition against killing, in accordance with the verse, רָצֹחַ וְנָאֹף, *killing and committing adultery* (*Jeremiah* 7:9).[140] And similarly, [our Sages teach that] a person who releases seed in vain is considered as if he shed blood.[141]

❑ [The prohibition against adultery is] written here, וְלֹא[142] תִנְאָף, with an extra ו (= 6), corresponding to the six appearances of the word מְאָרְרִים, *that cause curse,*

139. The absence of this phrase from the original version and its inclusion in the second version is the subject of a Talmudic discussion (*Bava Kamma* 54b).

139a. That is, the Land of Israel cannot abide injustice or sinfulness.

140. The text follows the early printed editions. Some later editions cite a different verse: וְרָצֹחַ וְגָנֹב וְנָאֹף, *and killing and stealing and committing adultery* (*Hosea* 4:2). However, in that verse *stealing* is interposed between *killing* and *adultery,* whereas our verse places stealing after adultery.

141. *Niddah* 13a.

142. The corresponding verse in the first version (*Exodus* 20:13) reads לֹא תִנְאָף, without the conjunctive prefix -וְ, *and.*

land that HASHEM, your God, gives you.

17 *You shall not kill; and you shall not commit adultery; and you shall not steal; and you shall not bear vain witness against your fellow.*

BAAL HATURIM ELUCIDATED

and the six appearances of the word מָרִים, *bitter,* in the passage concerning a *sotah*[143] [a woman suspected of adultery].[143a]

❑ Juxtaposed to this [prohibition against adultery] is וְלֹא תִגְנֹב, *and you shall not steal,* reflecting [the simile used to describe adultery], מַיִם גְּנוּבִים יִמְתָּקוּ, *Stolen waters are sweet* (*Proverbs* 9:17).[144]

❑ [The prohibition against stealing] is written here [וְלֹא תִגְנֹב[144a]] with an extra ו (= 6), corresponding to the six evils mentioned at the beginning of *Proverbs* (1:11-13):[145] [*If they say, "Come with us;*] (i) נֶאֶרְבָה לְדָם, *We will lie in ambush for bloodshed;* (ii) נִצְפְּנָה לְנָקִי חִנָּם, *we will lurk for the innocent, without cause;* {(iii) נִבְלָעֵם כִּשְׁאוֹל חַיִּים, *we will swallow them as does the grave — alive;* (iv) וּתְמִימִים כְּיוֹרְדֵי בוֹר, *and whole — as those who descend into the pit;* (v) כָּל הוֹן יָקָר נִמְצָא, *we will find all* [*their*] *precious treasure;* (vi) נְמַלֵּא בָתֵּינוּ שָׁלָל, *we will fill our houses with spoil*}.[146]

❑ Juxtaposed to this [prohibition against stealing] is וְלֹא תַעֲנֶה בְרֵעֲךָ, *you shall not bear* [*vain*] *witness against your fellow.* For a person who steals gives false testimony against himself, for he causes himself to be sold as a slave (see *Exodus* 22:1-2).[147]

❑ Scripture has added a ו (= 6), וְלֹא[148] תַעֲנֶה, for [as the Talmud[149] teaches,] his testimony causes the world, which was created in six days, to be stricken.[150]

143. *Numbers* 5:11-31. The word הַמְאָרְרִים appears there six times (vv. 18, 19, 22, 24 [twice] and 27); the word מָרִים appears six times — four times with the prefix הַ־, (vv. 18, 19, 23 and 24), and twice with the prefix לְ־ (vv. 24 and 27).

143a. *Peirush HaRokeach* to *Exodus* 20:13.

144. See *Nedarim* 91b.

144a. The corresponding verse in the first version (*Exodus* 20:13) reads לֹא תִגְנֹב, without the prefix וְ־.

145. Verse 10 there reads: *My son, if sinners seduce you, do not be enticed.* The passage continues with the six forms of enticement cited by the Baal HaTurim.

146. *Peirush HaRokeach* to *Exodus* 20:13.

The text follows *Shoham Yakar's* manuscript edition which adduces all six evils mentioned in *Proverbs.* Most other editions quote the first two, then add וְכָלְהוּ, *etc.*

147. The Baal HaTurim does not explain why stealing and thus causing oneself to be sold as a slave is tantamount to bearing false witness. It has been suggested that a crook who is ignorant of Torah law might falsely testify that he has no money with which to compensate his victim, thinking that the court will allow him off scot-free. However, as a result of that false testimony he will be sold as a slave (*VeChur LaZahav*).

148. The corresponding verse in the first version (*Exodus* 20:13) reads לֹא תַעֲנֶה, without the prefix וְ־.

149. *Succah* 29a — On account of four matters [i.e., four types of undesirable behavior] the sun is stricken ... And on account of four [other] matters the luminaries [i.e., the other heavenly bodies] are stricken: (i) on account of forgers of documents; (ii) bearers of false testimony ...

150. *Peirush HaRokeach* to *Exodus* 20:13.

אֵ֖שֶׁת רֵעֶ֑ךָ וְלֹ֨א תִתְאַוֶּ֜ה בֵּ֣ית רֵעֶ֗ךָ
שָׂדֵ֜הוּ וְעַבְדּ֣וֹ וַאֲמָת֗וֹ שׁוֹר֣וֹ וַחֲמֹר֔וֹ וְכֹ֖ל אֲשֶׁ֥ר
חמישי יט לְרֵעֶֽךָ׃ אֶת־הַדְּבָרִ֣ים הָאֵ֡לֶּה דִּבֶּ֨ר יְהוָ֜ה
אֶל־כָּל־קְהַלְכֶ֗ם בָּהָר֙ מִתּ֣וֹךְ הָאֵ֔שׁ הֶעָנָ֖ן וְהָעֲרָפֶ֑ל
ק֥וֹל גָּד֖וֹל וְלֹ֣א יָסָ֑ף וַֽיִּכְתְּבֵ֗ם עַל־שְׁנֵי֙ לֻחֹ֣ת אֲבָנִ֔ים
כ וַֽיִּתְּנֵ֖ם אֵלָֽי׃ וַיְהִ֗י כְּשָׁמְעֲכֶ֤ם אֶת־הַקּוֹל֙ מִתּ֣וֹךְ
הַחֹ֔שֶׁךְ וְהָהָ֖ר בֹּעֵ֣ר בָּאֵ֑שׁ וַתִּקְרְב֣וּן אֵלַ֔י כָּל־רָאשֵׁ֥י
כא שִׁבְטֵיכֶ֖ם וְזִקְנֵיכֶֽם׃ וַתֹּאמְר֗וּ הֵ֣ן הֶרְאָ֜נוּ יְהוָ֤ה
אֱלֹהֵ֙ינוּ֙ אֶת־כְּבֹד֣וֹ וְאֶת־גָּדְל֔וֹ וְאֶת־קֹל֥וֹ שָׁמַ֖עְנוּ
מִתּ֣וֹךְ הָאֵ֑שׁ הַיּ֤וֹם הַזֶּה֙ רָאִ֔ינוּ כִּֽי־יְדַבֵּ֧ר אֱלֹהִ֛ים
כב אֶת־הָאָדָ֖ם וָחָֽי׃ וְעַתָּה֙ לָ֣מָּה נָמ֔וּת כִּ֣י תֹֽאכְלֵ֔נוּ
הָאֵ֥שׁ הַגְּדֹלָ֖ה הַזֹּ֑את אִם־יֹסְפִ֣ים ׀ אֲנַ֗חְנוּ לִ֠שְׁמֹעַ
כג אֶת־ק֨וֹל יְהוָ֧ה אֱלֹהֵ֛ינוּ ע֖וֹד וָמָֽתְנוּ׃ כִּ֣י מִ֣י כָל־בָּשָׂ֡ר
אֲשֶׁ֣ר שָׁמַ֣ע קוֹל֩ אֱלֹהִ֨ים חַיִּ֜ים מְדַבֵּ֧ר מִתּוֹךְ־הָאֵ֛שׁ
כד כָּמֹ֖נוּ וַיֶּֽחִי׃ קְרַ֤ב אַתָּה֙ וּֽשְׁמָ֔ע אֵ֛ת כָּל־אֲשֶׁ֥ר יֹאמַ֖ר
יְהוָ֣ה אֱלֹהֵ֑ינוּ וְאַ֣תְּ ׀ תְּדַבֵּ֣ר אֵלֵ֗ינוּ אֵת֩ כָּל־אֲשֶׁ֨ר

בעל הטורים

❑ וְסָמַךְ לוֹ "וְלֹא תַחְמֹד", שֶׁלֹּא יַחְמֹד אֵשֶׁת חֲבֵרוֹ וְיָעִיד בּוֹ עֵדוּת שֶׁקֶר לוֹמַר שֶׁמֵּת, כְּדֵי שֶׁיִּשָּׂאֶנָּה:

(יח) שָׂדֵהוּ. הוֹסִיף כָּאן, שֶׁכְּבָר הִגִּיעוּ קָרוֹב לָאָרֶץ וְהָיָה לָהֶם שָׂדוֹת:

(כד) וְאַתְּ תְּדַבֵּר. בְּקוֹל נָמוּךְ כְּאִשָּׁה, בְּעִנְיָן שֶׁנּוּכַל לִסְבֹּל:

❑ **וְאַתְּ תְּדַבֵּר.** בְּגִימַטְרִיָּא שְׁמוֹנֶה דִּבְּרוֹת:

BAAL HATURIM ELUCIDATED

❑ Juxtaposed to this [prohibition against false witness] is וְלֹא תַחְמֹד, *you shall not covet,* i.e., a man should not covet his fellow's wife, [for that could lead him] to testify falsely that he [the other man] has died, all in order to enable himself to marry her.

18. שָׂדֵהוּ — HIS FIELD. [This term] is added here, for they were already close to the Land [of Canaan] and they had fields.[151]

151. *Peirush HaRokeach* to *Exodus* 20:13 — All the assets listed in the first version of the *Aseres HaDibros* appear in the second version as well; however, the second version adds שָׂדֵהוּ, *his field*. This is because, in the fortieth year, they [i.e., Reuben, Gad and half of Manasseh] were already living in the lands of Sihon and Og. [Thus, some of the nation already had their own fields.]

A question may be asked: The second version of the *Aseres HaDibros* was given to Moses a

¹⁸ *And you shall not covet your fellow's wife, you shall not desire your fellow's house, his field, his slave, his maidservant, his ox, his donkey, or anything that belongs to your fellow.*

¹⁹ *These words HASHEM spoke to your entire congregation on the mountain, from the midst of the fire, the cloud, and the thick cloud — a great voice, never to be repeated — and He inscribed them on two stone tablets and gave them to me.* ²⁰ *It happened that when you heard the voice from the midst of the darkness and the mountain was burning in fire, that you — all the heads of your tribes and your elders — approached me.*

²¹ *They said, "Behold! HASHEM, our God, has shown us His glory and His greatness, and we have heard His voice from the midst of the fire; this day we saw that HASHEM will speak to a person and he can live.* ²² *But now, why should we die when this great fire consumes us? If we continue to hear the voice of HASHEM, our God, any longer, we will die!* ²³ *For is there any human that has heard the voice of the Living God speaking from the midst of the fire, as we have, and lived?* ²⁴ *You should approach and hear whatever HASHEM, our God, will say, and you should speak to us whatever*

─────────────── BAAL HATURIM ELUCIDATED ───────────────

24. וְאַתְּ תְּדַבֵּר — **AND YOU**[152] **SHOULD SPEAK,** softly, like a woman, so that we will be able to endure.[153]

❑ וְאַתְּ תְּדַבֵּר — **AND YOU SHOULD SPEAK.** The *gematria* of this phrase (1013) is equal to that of שְׁמוֹנֶה דִּבְּרוֹת, *eight commandments.*[154]

mere eighty days after he had broken the first version. But at that time they were no closer to the Land of Canaan than they had been when God gave Moses the first version!

The comment does not refer to the chronological history of the two versions. Rather, it refers to the respective positions of the two versions: The first version appears in *Exodus*, the Book that describes the Egyptian slavery, the redemption and exodus, and the nation's first year in the wilderness. But the second version appears in *Deuteronomy*, whose events took place during the fortieth year, when the nation was about to enter the land (*VeChur LaZahav*).

152. The word אַתָּה occurs in the *Tanach* more than 700 times (five of those times it appears as a קְרִי וּכְתִיב, i.e., it is spelled את, but is pronounced אַתָּה — *I Samuel* 24:18; *Psalms* 6:4; *Job* 1:10; *Ecclesiastes* 7:22; and *Nehemiah* 9:6). In every instance, it is the masculine, singular,

second-person pronoun *you.* The parallel feminine form אַתְּ appears 57 times. However, in three instances אַתְּ is used for the masculine: (i) in *Numbers* 11:15 it refers to God; (ii) in our verse it refers to Moses; and (iii) *Ezekiel* 28:14 uses אַתְּ for the king of Tyre.

In our verse both forms are used with reference to Moses. The Baal HaTurim explains this unexpected use of the feminine form (*VeChur LaZahav*).

153. *Zohar, III,* 261a — The people were so frightened by the powerful voice of God that they requested Moses to be an intermediary and relay God's word to them.

154. *Rabbeinu Ephraim* (*MiKesivah Ashkenazis*); *Rimzei Rabbeinu Yoel;* see *Makkos* 24a — Moses taught the nation 611 *mitzvos*, the other two, i.e., the first two of the Ten Commandments were heard directly from God. [Thus, eight commandments were heard from Moses.]

כה יְדַבֵּ֨ר יְהוָ֤ה אֱלֹהֵ֙ינוּ֙ אֵלֶ֔יךָ וְשָׁמַ֖עְנוּ וְעָשִׂ֑ינוּ וַיִּשְׁמַ֣ע
יְהוָ֗ה אֶת־ק֤וֹל דִּבְרֵיכֶם֙ בְּדַבֶּרְכֶ֣ם אֵלָ֔י וַיֹּ֤אמֶר יְהוָה֙
אֵלַ֔י שָׁמַ֗עְתִּי אֶת־ק֛וֹל דִּבְרֵ֥י הָעָ֥ם הַזֶּ֖ה אֲשֶׁ֣ר דִּבְּר֣וּ
כו אֵלֶ֑יךָ הֵיטִ֖יבוּ כָּל־אֲשֶׁ֥ר דִּבֵּֽרוּ: מִֽי־יִתֵּ֡ן וְהָיָה֩ לְבָבָ֨ם
זֶ֜ה לָהֶ֗ם לְיִרְאָ֥ה אֹתִ֛י וְלִשְׁמֹ֥ר אֶת־כָּל־מִצְוֺתַ֖י
כז כָּל־הַיָּמִ֑ים לְמַ֨עַן יִיטַ֥ב לָהֶ֛ם וְלִבְנֵיהֶ֖ם לְעֹלָֽם: לֵ֖ךְ
אֱמֹ֣ר לָהֶ֑ם שׁ֥וּבוּ לָכֶ֖ם לְאָהֳלֵיכֶֽם: וְאַתָּ֗ה פֹּה֙ עֲמֹ֣ד
כח עִמָּדִ֔י וַאֲדַבְּרָ֣ה אֵלֶ֗יךָ אֵ֧ת כָּל־הַמִּצְוָ֛ה וְהַחֻקִּ֥ים
וְהַמִּשְׁפָּטִ֖ים אֲשֶׁ֣ר תְּלַמְּדֵ֑ם וְעָשׂ֣וּ בָאָ֔רֶץ אֲשֶׁ֧ר
כט אָנֹכִ֛י נֹתֵ֥ן לָהֶ֖ם לְרִשְׁתָּֽהּ: וּשְׁמַרְתֶּ֣ם לַעֲשׂ֔וֹת כַּאֲשֶׁ֥ר
צִוָּ֛ה יְהוָ֥ה אֱלֹהֵיכֶ֖ם אֶתְכֶ֑ם לֹ֣א תָסֻ֔רוּ יָמִ֖ין וּשְׂמֹֽאל:

בעל הטורים

(כח) וְאַתָּה פֹּה. תָּגִין עַל הַפֵּ"א. רָמַז לוֹ שֶׁיַּעֲמֹד בִּפְרִישׁוּת וּבְטָהֳרָה:
דָּבָר אַחֵר – וְאַתָּה בֶן פ' שָׁנִים, וְתִחְיֶה כְּמִנְיַן עֲמוֹד שָׁנִים:

▫ עֲמָדִי. יוּ"ד כְּפוּפָה, שֶׁתַּעֲמֹד בְּאֵימָה לְפָנַי, כָּפוּף:
דָּבָר אַחֵר – בִּשְׁבִילְךָ יָרַדְתִּי י' יְרִידוֹת, וְנָתַתִּי לְךָ י' דִּבְּרוֹת:

BAAL HATURIM ELUCIDATED

28. וְאַתָּה פֹּה — **BUT AS FOR YOU, HERE.** [According to a scribal tradition,] the פ of this phrase is written with *tagin*. [155] [God] alluded to [Moses] that he should stand [before Him] in abstinence[156] and purity.[157]

Alternatively: [The unusual פ (= 80) indicates that, at Mount Sinai,[158] God said to Moses,] "You are now eighty years old,[159] and you will live until you reach 120 years,[160] the *gematria* of עֲמוֹד."[161,162]

---

155. See note 56 to *parashas Devarim*. Our phrase also appears on the list in *Sefer Tagin*.

155a. See *Targum Yonasan ben Uzziel*.

156. *Shabbos* 87a — Moses permanently abstained from cohabiting with his wife. [Their period of separation began either from the time of the Revelation at Sinai when all of Israel was commanded to abstain for three days (*Rashi*); or from the time God first spoke to him from the burning bush (*Tosafos*). At that time, either Moses erected a separate tent for his wife or they were divorced (*Tosafos* to *Yevamos* 62a, s.v., רכתיב).] Moses did this of his own volition. Nevertheless, our verse teaches that God viewed Moses' act favorably.

157. That is, the *tagin* on the letter פ indicates

פְּרִישׁוּת, *abstinence*, which leads to purity (A. S.).

158. Here, Moses is quoting what God told him at Sinai.

159. See *Exodus* 7:7.

160. See 34:7 below.

161. Although the verse uses the defective spelling, עֲמֹד, without a ו, the Baal HaTurim adds the ו for the sake of the allusion. This is a common practice in the realm of *remez* (allusion).

162. This comment appears in *Rimzei Rabbeinu Yoel* with a little more elaboration: Now you are eighty years old. You will live to the age of עֲמוֹד (120), then you will עֲמוֹד עִמָּדִי, *stand with Me*, i.e., stand with Me in Heaven and perform My service. And thus the Midrash (*Sifrei* to 34:5) expounds: Moses did not die; rather, he stands

HASHEM, our God, will speak to you — then we shall hear and we shall do."

²⁵ *HASHEM heard the sound of your words when you spoke to me, and HASHEM said to me, "I heard the sound of the words of this people, that they have spoken to you; they did well in all that they spoke.* ²⁶ *Who can assure that this heart should remain theirs, to fear Me and observe all My commandments all the days, so that it should be good for them and for their children forever?* ²⁷ *Go say to them, 'Return to your tents.'* ²⁸ *But as for you, stand here with Me and I shall speak to you the entire commandment, and the decrees, and the ordinances that you shall teach them and they shall perform in the land that I give them, to possess it."*

²⁹ *You shall be careful to act as HASHEM, your God, commanded you, you shall not stray to the right or left.*

——————————— BAAL HATURIM ELUCIDATED ———————————

❏ עִמָּדִי — **WITH ME.** [According to a scribal tradition,] the י (= 10) of this word is to be written in a bent form.[163] [As if God were telling Moses,] "You shall stand in awe before Me, bent over."[164]

Alternatively: [God intimated to Moses,] "I descended ten descents for your sake[165] and I gave you the Ten Commandments."[166]

and serves above.

163. According to *Sefer Tagin*, the י of עִמָּדִי is one of eighty-three that are written in the Torah scrolls in the embellished shape known as יי כְּפוּפָה, *bent yud* (see illustration). The Baal HaTurim expounds on two other appearances of the "bent י," in his comments to *Genesis* 32:11 and 37:1.

The usual form of the letter י in Torah scrolls.	Variations of the embellished י according to: (a) Badei HaAron; (b) Machzor Vitri; (c) Parma ms.; and (d) Gaster's ms.
	a b c d

164. That is, the unusual shape of the י indicates that the word עִמָּדִי may be interpreted as two words, עֲמֹד י, *You shall stand in the shape of a bent י*. That is, Moses, who is *exceedingly humble, more than any person on the face of the earth* (*Numbers* 12:3), is alluded to by the י, the smallest of all the letters; moreover, not to an

ordinary י, but to one that is bent over in humble reverence before God (*VeChur LaZahav*).

165. The Baal HaTurim's intent here is unclear. Some suggest that he is referring to the ten descents enumerated in the following Midrash. The Holy One, Blessed is He, descended ten descents to the earth . . . they are : (i) Once to the Garden of Eden; (ii) once regarding the generation of the Tower of Babel; (iii) once to Sodom; (iv) once at the [burning bush]; (v) once at Sinai; (vi-vii) twice at the cleft in the rock; (viii-ix) twice at the Tabernacle; and (x) once in the Time to Come (*Pirkei DeRabbi Eliezer* 14). However, it is difficult to interpret the first three and the tenth of those descents as being "for your [Moses'] sake."

Perhaps the Baal HaTurim refers to ten verses that speak of God descending for Moses' sake, even though two or more may refer to the same incident. If so, the following ten verses are suggested: Six from *Exodus* — 3:8, 19:11, 19:18, 19:20, 33:9 (see *Rashi* to v. 10) and 34:5; three from *Numbers* 11:17, 11:25 and 12:5; and one from *Nehemiah* — 9:13 (*VeChur LaZahav*).

166. *Peirush HaRokeach.*

ה/ל-ו/ד

ל בְּכָל־הַדֶּרֶךְ אֲשֶׁר צִוָּה יהוה אֱלֹהֵיכֶם אֶתְכֶם תֵּלֵכוּ
לְמַעַן תִּחְיוּן וְטוֹב לָכֶם וְהַאֲרַכְתֶּם יָמִים בָּאָרֶץ
ו א אֲשֶׁר תִּירָשׁוּן: וְזֹאת הַמִּצְוָה הַחֻקִּים וְהַמִּשְׁפָּטִים
אֲשֶׁר צִוָּה יהוה אֱלֹהֵיכֶם לְלַמֵּד אֶתְכֶם לַעֲשׂוֹת
ב בָּאָרֶץ אֲשֶׁר אַתֶּם עֹבְרִים שָׁמָּה לְרִשְׁתָּהּ: לְמַעַן
תִּירָא אֶת־יהוה אֱלֹהֶיךָ לִשְׁמֹר אֶת־כָּל־חֻקֹּתָיו
וּמִצְוֹתָיו אֲשֶׁר אָנֹכִי מְצַוֶּךָּ אַתָּה וּבִנְךָ וּבֶן־בִּנְךָ כֹּל
ג יְמֵי חַיֶּיךָ וּלְמַעַן יַאֲרִכֻן יָמֶיךָ: וְשָׁמַעְתָּ יִשְׂרָאֵל
וְשָׁמַרְתָּ לַעֲשׂוֹת אֲשֶׁר יִיטַב לְךָ וַאֲשֶׁר תִּרְבּוּן מְאֹד
כַּאֲשֶׁר דִּבֶּר יהוה אֱלֹהֵי אֲבֹתֶיךָ לָךְ אֶרֶץ זָבַת
חָלָב וּדְבָשׁ:

ע׳ רבתי ד׳ רבתי
ששי ד **שְׁמַע** יִשְׂרָאֵל יהוה אֱלֹהֵינוּ יהוה ׀ אֶחָ**ד**:

בעל הטורים

ו (ג) **כַּאֲשֶׁר דִּבֶּר ה׳ אֱלֹהֵי אֲבֹתֶיךָ לָךְ.** וּסְמִיךְ לֵהּ ״שְׁמַע יִשְׂרָאֵל״. שֶׁהִזְכִּיר אֵלּוּ הַשֵּׁמוֹת, כְּנֶגֶד הָאָבוֹת – ״ה׳ ״ כְּנֶגֶד אַבְרָהָם, דִּכְתִיב בֵּהּ ״אֲנִי ה׳ אֲשֶׁר הוֹצֵאתִיךָ וְגוֹ׳ ״; ״אֱלֹהֵינוּ״ כְּנֶגֶד יִצְחָק, דִּכְתִיב בֵּהּ ״אָנֹכִי אֱלֹהֵי אַבְרָהָם אָבִיךָ״; ״ה׳ אֶחָד״ כְּנֶגֶד יַעֲקֹב, שֶׁנֶּאֱמַר בּוֹ ״אֲנִי ה׳ ״:

❑ {**אֶרֶץ זָבַת חָלָב וּדְבָשׁ.**} י״ו פְּעָמִים כְּתִיב ״זָבַת חָלָב וּדְבַשׁ״ בַּתּוֹרָה, כְּנֶגֶד לְדִידִי חֲזַאי חָלָב וּדְבַשׁ דְּכָל יִשְׂרָאֵל, וְהָוֵי י״ו פַּרְסָאוֹת:

(ד) עַיִ״ן דָּ״שְׁמַע״ גְּדוֹלָה. שֶׁשִּׁבְעִים שֵׁמוֹת יֵשׁ לְיִשְׂרָאֵל. וְנָתַן לָהֶם תּוֹרָה שֶׁיֵּשׁ לָהּ שִׁבְעִים

BAAL HATURIM ELUCIDATED

VI.

3. **כַּאֲשֶׁר דִּבֶּר ה׳ אֱלֹהֵי אֲבֹתֶיךָ לָךְ** — AS HASHEM, THE GOD OF YOUR FOREFATHERS, SPOKE FOR YOU. Juxtaposed to this [verse, which refers to God as both ה׳, *HASHEM,* and אֱלֹהֵי אֲבֹתֶיךָ] is the verse שְׁמַע יִשְׂרָאֵל, *Hear, O Israel* [which refers to God as ה׳, *HASHEM,* אֱלֹהֵינוּ, *our God,* ה׳ אֶחָד, *HASHEM is One*]. These particular Names are used corresponding to the Patriarchs:[166a] The Name ה׳, *HASHEM,* corresponds to Abraham, about whom is written, [God said,] "אֲנִי ה׳ אֲשֶׁר הוֹצֵאתִיךָ, *I am HASHEM Who brought you out. . .*" (*Genesis* 15:7); the Name אֱלֹהֵינוּ, *our God,* to Isaac, about whom is written, [God said,] "אָנֹכִי אֱלֹהֵי אַבְרָהָם אָבִיךָ, *I am the God of your father Abraham*" (*Genesis* 26:24); and the Name ה׳ אֶחָד, *HASHEM is One,* to Jacob, about whom is stated, [God said,] "אֲנִי ה׳, *I am HASHEM*" (*Genesis* 28:13).

❑ {אֶרֶץ זָבַת חָלָב וּדְבָשׁ — A LAND FLOWING WITH MILK AND HONEY.}[167] The Torah states זָבַת חָלָב וּדְבַשׁ, *flowing with milk and honey,* sixteen times,[167a] corresponding to

166a. See the Baal HaTurim's comment to verse 5 below.

167. The rubric is absent from virtually all printed editions. It is found, however, in *Shoham Yakar's* manuscript edition.

167a. It is not clear to which sixteen verses the

30 *On the entire way that HASHEM, your God, commanded you shall you go, so that you shall live and it will be good for you, and you shall prolong your days in the land that you shall possess.*

6 1 *This is the commandment, and the decrees, and the ordinances that HASHEM, your God, commanded to teach you, to perform in the land to which you are crossing, to possess it,* 2 *so that you will fear HASHEM, your God, to observe all His decrees and commandments that I command you — you, your child, and your grandchild — all the days of your life, so that your days will be lengthened.* 3 *You shall hearken, O Israel, and beware to perform, so that it will be good for you, and so that you will increase very much, as HASHEM, the God of your forefathers, spoke for you — a land flowing with milk and honey.*

4 *Hear, O Israel: HASHEM is our God, HASHEM is the One and*

BAAL HATURIM ELUCIDATED

the statement, "I have seen the [flow of] milk and honey of the entire [Land of] Israel, and it measured sixteen *parsah.*"[167b]

4. [According to the masoretic tradition,] the ע (=70) of the word שְׁמַע, *hear,* is written larger than usual,[168] corresponding to the seventy names of Israel.[169] And He gave them the Torah which has seventy names,[170] and which

Baal HaTurim refers. For the expression זָבַת חָלָב וּדְבָשׁ appears only fifteen times in the Torah (*Exodus* 3:8, 3:17, 13:5, 33:3; *Leviticus* 20:24; *Numbers* 13:27, 14:8, 16:13 [where it refers to Egypt], 16:14; *Deuteronomy* 6:3, 11:9, 26:9, 26:15, 27:3 and 31:20) and five more times in the rest of the *Tanach* (*Joshua* 5:6; *Jeremiah* 11:5, 32:22; *Ezekiel* 20:6 and 20:15).

167b. Two statements regarding the volume of the flow of milk and honey are recorded in the Talmud: (i) *Reish Lakish* said, "I have seen the flow of milk and honey of Sepphoris (a city within the Land of Israel) and it measured sixteen *mil* [a *mil* equals 2000 *amos*], by sixteen *mil* . . ." [Opinions regarding the modern-day equivalent of a *mil* range between .595 and .715 mile. Thus, the area described was between 90.6 and 130.9 square miles.] (ii) Rabbah bar bar Chanah quoted Rabbi Yochanan as having said, "I have seen the flow of milk and honey of the entire Land of Israel and it measured . . . twenty-two *parsah* [a *parsah* equals 4 *mil*] in length and six *parsah* in breadth [between 748 and 1080 square miles] (*Megillah* 6a). Accordingly, the Baal HaTurim's source for this comment cannot be the Talmud, for he speaks of the entire Land of Israel, while using the dimensions of only one city within the land. Rather, it is probably found in a Midrash that is no longer extant (*VeChur LaZahav*).

168. Traditionally, certain particular letters are written in the Torah scroll larger than usual. That form indicates that a special lesson is to be learned from that letter. The ע of שְׁמַע and ד of אֶחָד are two such letters. In these comments, the Baal HaTurim will explain the implication of these unusual forms here. Other verses at which the Baal HaTurim expounds on larger than usual letters are: *Genesis* 27:46; *Leviticus* 13:33; *Numbers* 14:17; *Deuteronomy* 18:13, 29:27, and 32:6.

169. The word שְׁמַע may be read as two words — שֵׁם, *name,* and ע׳, *seventy* (*Peirush HaRokeach*). The Baal HaTurim enumerates the seventy names of Israel in his comments to *Numbers* 11:16.

170. Various Midrashim enumerate the seventy names by which Scripture refers to the Torah. See *Midrash Shir HaShirim Zuta; Midrash HaGadol, Bereishis* 46:8; and *Peirush Lekach Tov, Shir HaShirim, hakdamah.*

ה וְאָהַבְתָּ אֵת יהוה אֱלֹהֶיךָ בְּכָל־לְבָבְךָ וּבְכָל־נַפְשְׁךָ

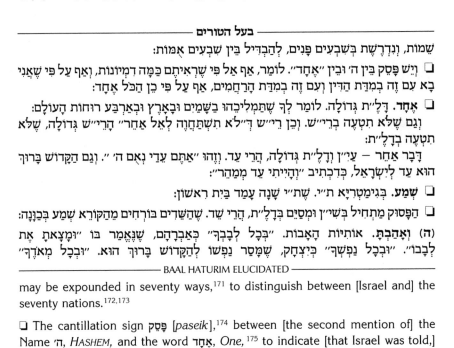

בעל הטורים

שֵׁמוֹת, וְנִדְרֶשֶׁת בְּשִׁבְעִים פָּנִים, לְהַבְדִּיל בֵּין שִׁבְעִים אֻמּוֹת:

❑ וְיֵשׁ פָּסֵק בֵּין ה׳ וּבֵין ״אֶחָד״. לוֹמַר, אַף אַל פִּי שֶׁרְאִיתֶם כַּמָּה דִמְיוֹנוֹת, וְאַף עַל פִּי שֶׁאֲנִי בָא עִם זֶה בְּמִדַּת הַדִּין וְעִם זֶה בְּמִדַּת הָרַחֲמִים, אַף עַל פִּי כֵן הַכֹּל אֶחָד:

❑ **אֶחָד.** דָּלֶ״ת גְּדוֹלָה. לוֹמַר לְךָ שֶׁתַּמְלִיכֵהוּ בַּשָּׁמַיִם וּבָאָרֶץ וּבְאַרְבַּע רוּחוֹת הָעוֹלָם: וְגַם שֶׁלֹּא תִטְעֶה בְּרֵי״שׁ. וְכֵן רֵי״שׁ דְּ״לֹא תִשְׁתַּחֲוֶה לְאֵל אַחֵר״ הָרֵי״שׁ גְּדוֹלָה, שֶׁלֹּא תִטְעֶה בְּדָלֶ״ת:

דָּבָר אַחֵר — עַיִ״ן וְדָלֶ״ת גְּדוֹלָה, הֲרֵי עֵד. וְזֶהוּ ״אַתֶּם עֵדַי נְאֻם ה׳ ״. וְגַם הַקָּדוֹשׁ בָּרוּךְ הוּא עֵד לְיִשְׂרָאֵל, כִּדְכְתִיב ״וְהָיִיתִי עֵד מְמַהֵר״:

❑ **שְׁמַע.** בְּגִימַטְרִיָּא ת״י. שֶׁת״י שָׁנָה עָמַד בַּיִת רִאשׁוֹן:

❑ הַפָּסוּק מַתְחִיל בְּשִׁי״ן וּמְסַיֵּם בְּדָלֶ״ת, הֲרֵי שֵׁד. שֶׁהַשֵּׁדִים בּוֹרְחִים מֵהַקּוֹרֵא שְׁמַע בְּכַוָּנָה:

(ה) **וְאָהַבְתָּ.** אוֹתִיּוֹת הָאָבוֹת. ״בְּכָל לְבָבְךָ״ כְּאַבְרָהָם, שֶׁנֶּאֱמַר בּוֹ ״וּמָצָאתָ אֶת לְבָבוֹ״. ״וּבְכָל נַפְשְׁךָ״ כְּיִצְחָק, שֶׁמָּסַר נַפְשׁוֹ לְהַקָּדוֹשׁ בָּרוּךְ הוּא. ״וּבְכָל מְאֹדֶךָ״

BAAL HATURIM ELUCIDATED

may be expounded in seventy ways,[171] to distinguish between [Israel and] the seventy nations.[172,173]

❑ The cantillation sign פָּסֵק [*paseik*],[174] between [the second mention of] the Name ה׳, *HASHEM,* and the word אֶחָד, *One,*[175] to indicate [that Israel was told,] "Although you saw several different manifestations, even though I manifest Myself with the Attribute of Judgment to one person, and with the Attribute of Mercy to another person, nevertheless, all are one."[176]

❑ אֶחָד — ONE. [According to the masoretic tradition,] the ד (= 4) of this word is written in the Torah scrolls larger than usual.[176a] This indicates to you that you

171. *Zohar* I, 47b; *Bereishis Rabbah* 13:16.

172. This refers to the seventy offspring of Noah whose names appear in *Genesis,* Ch. 10 (*Bereishis Rabbah* 14:12; see also the Baal HaTurim's comments at *Genesis* 25:25, with note 25).

173. *Peirush HaRokeach.*

174. Also called פְּסִיק, *pesik.* This *taam* (cantillation sign; plural, *te'amim*) appears as a vertical line in the space between two words. It is used to indicate a pause after a *taam* whose usual function is to draw the reading forward. For example, the *te'amim* מֵרְכָא, *meircha,* and מֻנַּח, *munach,* indicate that the reader should not pause after that word, but should include the following word(s) in the same phrase. The note אֶתְנַחְתָּא, *esnachta,* on the other hand, indicates a pause, like a semicolon. Occasionally, a *pesik* follows a *munach* or a *meircha* to indicate that in that particular verse, the *taam* takes on the role of a pause, like a comma.

The Baal HaTurim explains more about the פָּסֵק in his comments to *Genesis* 22:14; *Exodus* 15:18; *Leviticus* 10:6; *Numbers* 3:2, 3:38, 5:22 and 9:10.

175. The text follows virtually all the later printed editions, and is in accord with the cantillation found in extant *Chumashim.* However, the early printed editions, as well as *Shoham Yakar's* manuscript edition, read, בֵּין ה׳ לֶאֱלֹהֵינוּ, *between [the first mention of] the Name HASHEM and the Name Eloheinu.* But that reading is contradicted by virtually every extant printed and manuscript *Chumash.* Moreover, the last two words of the Baal HaTurim's comment — הַכֹּל אֶחָד, *all are one* — indicate that the proper reading is אֶחָד.

176. See *Rashi* to *Exodus* 20:2.

176a. See note 168 above.

Only. [5] *You shall love* HASHEM, *your God, with all your heart, with all your soul, and with all your resources.*

BAAL HATURIM ELUCIDATED

[i.e., Israel] are to recognize God's Kingship in the heavens and on the earth, and in the four directions of the world.[177]

Additionally: [The ד is written larger than usual] so that it not be read as a ר.[178] Similarly, in the verse, לֹא תִשְׁתַּחֲוֶה לְאֵל אַחֵר, *You shall not prostrate yourself to an alien god* (*Exodus* 34:14), the ר is written larger than usual, so that it not be mistaken for a ד.[179]

Alternatively: The ע and ד of this verse are written larger than usual, spelling the word עֵד, *witness,* recalling the verse, אַתֶּם עֵדַי נְאֻם ה׳, *You are My witnesses — the word of* HASHEM (*Isaiah* 43:10). And the Holy One, Blessed is He, is a witness for Israel, as it is written, וְהָיִיתִי עֵד מְמַהֵר, *and I will be a swift witness* (*Malachi* 3:5).[180]

❑ שְׁמַע — HEAR. The *gematria* of this word is 410, alluding to the four hundred ten years that the First Temple stood.[181]

❑ The verse begins with a ש and ends with a ד,[181a] spelling the word שֵׁד, *destructive spirit.* [This indicates] that destructive spirits flee from a person who recites the *Shema* with the proper intent.[182]

5. וְאָהַבְתָּ — YOU SHALL LOVE. The letters of this word are the same as those of הָאָבוֹת, *the Patriarchs.* [The phrase,] בְּכָל לְבָבְךָ, *with all your heart,* refers to Abraham, of whom it is said, וּמָצָאתָ אֶת לְבָבוֹ [נֶאֱמָן], *You found his heart* [*faithful*] (*Nehemiah* 9:8); וּבְכָל נַפְשְׁךָ, *with all your soul,* refers to Isaac, who offered to sacrifice his soul for the Holy One, Blessed is He; and וּבְכָל מְאֹדֶךָ, *and with all your resources,*

---

177. *Peirush HaRokeach*; see note 108 above.

The comment is difficult because the heavens, the earth and the four directions are six entities, while the letter ד alludes to only four! Indeed, *Peirush HaRokeach,* the Baal HaTurim's source for this comment, does not include the words בַּשָּׁמַיִם וּבָאָרֶץ, *in the heavens and on the earth.* Indeed, in recording the laws of the *Shema,* the Baal HaTurim writes: One should extend the enunciation of the letter ח long enough to think in his heart that God is One in the heavens and on the earth; and, while enunciating the ד, a person should think about God being One in all four directions (*Tur, Orach Chaim* 61). Perhaps the words בַּשָּׁמַיִם וּבָאָרֶץ were not in the original comment, but were added by a later copyist (*VeChur LaZahav*).

178. ה׳ אֶחָד means HASHEM *is One;* but if the ד were read as a ר, the word אֶחָד would be read אַחֵר, *other,* or *alien,* giving a heretical twist to the verse. Conversely, as the Baal HaTurim continues, the ר of אַחֵר is enlarged so that it not be confused with a ד, and read incorrectly as אֶחָד.

179. *Peirush HaRokeach*; see also *Tur, Orach Chaim* 61:7.

180. *Zohar* II, 236b.

181. In a similar comment, *Peirush HaRokeach* writes that the juxtaposition of אֶרֶץ זָבַת חָלָב וּדְבָשׁ, *a land flowing with milk and honey,* with the word שְׁמַע (=40), alludes to the 410 years during which Israel enjoyed the land of milk and honey in the merit of the First Temple.

For further allusions to this number, see the Baal HaTurim to *Genesis* 1:2, 25:27; *Exodus* 6:4, 25:8, 27:20, 29:40, 38:21; *Leviticus* 16:3, 25:10 and 19, 26:9.

181a. This phenomenon does not occur in any other verse in the Torah, although it does occur nine other times in the rest of the *Tanach.*

182. *Berachos* 5a; see also *Tosafos, Berachos* 2a, s.v., מאימתי.

ו/ו־יא

ו וּבְכָל־מְאֹדֶךָ׃ וְהָיוּ הַדְּבָרִים הָאֵלֶּה אֲשֶׁר אָנֹכִי מְצַוְּךָ
ז הַיּוֹם עַל־לְבָבֶךָ׃ וְשִׁנַּנְתָּם לְבָנֶיךָ וְדִבַּרְתָּ בָּם בְּשִׁבְתְּךָ
ח בְּבֵיתֶךָ וּבְלֶכְתְּךָ בַדֶּרֶךְ וּבְשָׁכְבְּךָ וּבְקוּמֶךָ׃ וּקְשַׁרְתָּם
ט לְאוֹת עַל־יָדֶךָ וְהָיוּ לְטֹטָפֹת בֵּין עֵינֶיךָ׃ וּכְתַבְתָּם
י עַל־מְזֻזוֹת בֵּיתֶךָ וּבִשְׁעָרֶיךָ׃ וְהָיָה כִּי־יְבִיאֲךָ ׀
יְהוָה אֱלֹהֶיךָ אֶל־הָאָרֶץ אֲשֶׁר נִשְׁבַּע לַאֲבֹתֶיךָ
לְאַבְרָהָם לְיִצְחָק וּלְיַעֲקֹב לָתֶת לָךְ עָרִים גְּדֹלֹת
יא וְטֹבֹת אֲשֶׁר לֹא־בָנִיתָ׃ וּבָתִּים מְלֵאִים כָּל־טוּב
אֲשֶׁר לֹא־מִלֵּאתָ וּבֹרֹת חֲצוּבִים אֲשֶׁר לֹא־חָצַבְתָּ
כְּרָמִים וְזֵיתִים אֲשֶׁר לֹא־נָטָעְתָּ וְאָכַלְתָּ וְשָׂבָעְתָּ׃

בעל הטורים

כְּיַעֲקֹב, דִּכְתִיב בֵּהּ "וְכֹל אֲשֶׁר תִּתֶּן לִי עַשֵּׂר אֲעַשְּׂרֶנּוּ לָךְ":

(ז) וּבְקוּמֶךָ. תָּגִין עַל הַקּוּ"ף. לוֹמַר, כְּשֶׁיַּעֲמֹד בַּבֹּקֶר יִתְפַּלֵּל מֵאָה בְרָכוֹת. וְיִנָּצֵל מִצ"ח קְלָלוֹת וְעוֹד שְׁתַּיִם, "גַּם כָּל חֳלִי וְכָל מַכָּה":

(ח) יָדֶךָ. בְּגִימַטְרִיָּא גּוֹבַהּ הַיָּד:

❑ **לְטֹטָפֹת.** ט' תָּגִין. כְּנֶגֶד תִּשְׁעָה אֵבָרִים שֶׁבָּרֹאשׁ:

(י) סָמַךְ "וְהָיָה כִּי יְבִיאֲךָ" לְפָרָשַׁת "שְׁמַע", לוֹמַר לְךָ שֶׁבִּזְכוּת תּוֹרָה תְּפִלִּין וּמְזוּזָה יִכָּנְסוּ לָאָרֶץ:

BAAL HATURIM ELUCIDATED

refers to Jacob, of whom it is written, [he said,] וְכֹל אֲשֶׁר תִּתֶּן לִי עַשֵּׂר אֲעַשְּׂרֶנּוּ לָךְ, *Whatever You will give me, I shall repeatedly tithe to You* (*Genesis* 28:22).[183]

❑ {The Baal HaTurim's comment to בְּכָל לְבָבְךָ וּבְכָל נַפְשְׁךָ appears at 26:16 below.}

7. וּבְקוּמֶךָ — AND WHEN YOU ARISE. [According to a scribal tradition,] the ק (= 100) of this word is written with *tagin*.[184] This indicates that from the time one arises in the morning [and through the rest of the day] one should recite [at least] one hundred blessings.[184a] Thus he will be preserved from the ninety-eight curses,[185] and two more, גַּם כָּל חֳלִי וְכָל מַכָּה, *even any illness and any blow* (28:61 below).[186]

8. יָדֶךָ — YOUR ARM. The *gematria* of this word (34) is equivalent[187] to that of the

183. *Peirush HaRokeach.*

184. See note 43 above. The word וּבְקוּמֶךָ also appears on the list in *Sefer Tagin.*

184a. See note 44 above.

185. This refers to the ninety-eight curses that appear in the verses of admonition in *parashas Ki Savo* (28:15-68 below). The Baal HaTurim's other comments regarding the ninety-eight curses appear at *Leviticus* 27:3; *Deuteronomy* 7:15 and 28:61.

186. These two are not included in the count of ninety-eight for, as that verse states, they are *not written in this . . . Torah.*

187. The principle of *im hakollel* allows 34 to be considered equivalent to 35, the *gematria* of the Baal HaTurim's phrase.

⁶ *And these matters that I command you today shall be upon your heart.* ⁷ *You shall teach them thoroughly to your children and you shall speak of them while you sit in your home, while you walk on the way, when you retire and when you arise.* ⁸ *Bind them as a sign upon your arm and let them be ornaments between your eyes.* ⁹ *And write them on the doorposts of your house and upon your gates.*

¹⁰ *It shall be that when* HASHEM, *your God, brings you to the land that* HASHEM *swore to your forefathers, to Abraham, to Isaac, and to Jacob, to give you — great and good cities that you did not build,* ¹¹ *houses filled with every good thing that you did not fill, chiseled cisterns that you did not chisel, orchards and olive trees that you did not plant — and you shall eat and be satisfied —*

─────────────── BAAL HATURIM ELUCIDATED ───────────────

phrase גּוֹבַהּ הַיָּד, *the high portion of the arm.* ¹⁸⁸

❑ לְטֹטָפֹת — ORNAMENTS. [According to a scribal tradition,] this word is written with nine *tagin*, ¹⁸⁹ corresponding to the nine *eivarim* (organs)¹⁹⁰ of the head.

10. The Torah juxtaposed the passage beginning . . . [וְהָיָה כִּי יְבִיאֲךָ [ה׳, *It shall be that when [*HASHEM *your God] brings you* . . . to the passage of *Shema*, to indicate to you that in the merit of Torah study, *tefillin*, and *mezuzah*, ¹⁹¹ the Jews will enter *Eretz Yisrael*. ¹⁹²

11. {The Baal HaTurim's comment to וּבָתִּים appears at 8:12 below.}

188. The Talmud interprets another verse that speaks of the *tefillin* of the arm, לְךָ לְאוֹת עַל יָדְךָ, *for you a sign on your arm* (Exodus 13:9), as referring to "the high portion of the arm," i.e., the biceps, as the proper place for the *tefillin* (Menachos 37b). The *gemara* there cites three opinions regarding how — in the realm of *peshat* (the simple meaning of the verse) — the verse implies the biceps. In this comment, the Baal HaTurim finds a fourth implication, this one in the realm of *remez* (allusion).

189. Regarding *tagin*, see note 56 to *parashas Devarim*.

We would expect the word לְטֹטָפֹת to have six *tagin* — three on each ט; but none on any of the other three letters. However, *Sefer Tagin* contains a listing of 83 words in which the פ is crowned with

tagin — three according to the Paris edition; five according to the *Machzor Vitry* edition — including the word לְטֹטָפֹת. Thus, according to one version of the *Sefer Tagin*, the word לְטֹטָפֹת is written with nine *tagin*, three each on the three letters טטפ (see illustration).

190. An אֵבֶר, *eiver*, is a body part containing bone, flesh and sinew (Chullin 102b; see Bartenura to Ohalos 1:7). The Mishnah (Ohalos 1:8) enumerates two hundred and forty-eight *eivarim* of the human body. According to that Mishnah, there are nine *eivarim* in the head.

191. These three *mitzvos* are mentioned in the last three verses (7-9) of the passage of *Shema*.

192. The second passage of the daily recitation of the *Shema* (11:13-21 below) mentions these same three *mitzvos* — *tefillin* (v. 18), Torah study (v. 19), *mezuzah* (v. 20) — followed by, In order to prolong your days and the days of your children upon the ground that Hashem has sworn to your forefathers . . . (v. 21).

יב הִשָּׁמֶר לְךָ פֶּן־תִּשְׁכַּח אֶת־יהוה אֲשֶׁר הוֹצִיאֲךָ
יג מֵאֶרֶץ מִצְרַיִם מִבֵּית עֲבָדִים: אֶת־יהוה אֱלֹהֶיךָ
יד תִּירָא וְאֹתוֹ תַעֲבֹד וּבִשְׁמוֹ תִּשָּׁבֵעַ: לֹא תֵלְכוּן
אַחֲרֵי אֱלֹהִים אֲחֵרִים מֵאֱלֹהֵי הָעַמִּים אֲשֶׁר
טו סְבִיבוֹתֵיכֶם: כִּי אֵל קַנָּא יהוה אֱלֹהֶיךָ בְּקִרְבֶּךָ
פֶּן־יֶחֱרֶה אַף־יהוה אֱלֹהֶיךָ בָּךְ וְהִשְׁמִידְךָ מֵעַל פְּנֵי
טז הָאֲדָמָה: לֹא תְנַסּוּ אֶת־יהוה אֱלֹהֵיכֶם
יז כַּאֲשֶׁר נִסִּיתֶם בַּמַּסָּה: שָׁמוֹר תִּשְׁמְרוּן אֶת־מִצְוֹת
יח יהוה אֱלֹהֵיכֶם וְעֵדֹתָיו וְחֻקָּיו אֲשֶׁר צִוָּךְ: וְעָשִׂיתָ
הַיָּשָׁר וְהַטּוֹב בְּעֵינֵי יהוה לְמַעַן יִיטַב לָךְ וּבָאתָ
וְיָרַשְׁתָּ אֶת־הָאָרֶץ הַטֹּבָה אֲשֶׁר־נִשְׁבַּע יהוה
יט לַאֲבֹתֶיךָ: לַהֲדֹף אֶת־כָּל־אֹיְבֶיךָ מִפָּנֶיךָ כַּאֲשֶׁר
כ דִּבֶּר יהוה: כִּי־יִשְׁאָלְךָ בִנְךָ מָחָר לֵאמֹר
מָה הָעֵדֹת וְהַחֻקִּים וְהַמִּשְׁפָּטִים אֲשֶׁר צִוָּה
כא יהוה אֱלֹהֵינוּ אֶתְכֶם: וְאָמַרְתָּ לְבִנְךָ עֲבָדִים
הָיִינוּ לְפַרְעֹה בְּמִצְרָיִם וַיֹּצִיאֵנוּ יהוה מִמִּצְרַיִם
כב בְּיָד חֲזָקָה: וַיִּתֵּן יהוה אוֹתֹת וּמֹפְתִים גְּדֹלִים
וְרָעִים | בְּמִצְרַיִם בְּפַרְעֹה וּבְכָל־בֵּיתוֹ לְעֵינֵינוּ:
כג וְאוֹתָנוּ הוֹצִיא מִשָּׁם לְמַעַן הָבִיא אֹתָנוּ לָתֶת לָנוּ
כד אֶת־הָאָרֶץ אֲשֶׁר נִשְׁבַּע לַאֲבֹתֵינוּ: וַיְצַוֵּנוּ יהוה
לַעֲשׂוֹת אֶת־כָּל־הַחֻקִּים הָאֵלֶּה לְיִרְאָה אֶת־יהוה
אֱלֹהֵינוּ לְטוֹב לָנוּ כָּל־הַיָּמִים לְחַיֹּתֵנוּ כְּהַיּוֹם הַזֶּה:

בעל הטורים

(יג) תִּירָא. בְּגִימַטְרִיָּא תַּלְמִידֵי חֲכָמִים:

(יט) לַהֲדֹף. חָסֵר וָי״ו. כִּי הַגִּרְגָּשִׁי עָמַד וּפָנָה:

BAAL HATURIM ELUCIDATED

13. תִּירָא — YOU SHALL FEAR. The *gematria* of this word, 611, is equivalent[193] to that of the phrase תַּלְמִידֵי חֲכָמִים, *Torah scholars.*[194]

193. The principle of *im hakollel* allows 611 to be considered equivalent to 612, the *gematria* of the Baal HaTurim's phrase.

194. *Peirush HaRokeach*; see *Bava Kamma* 41b — The Talmud there expounds on the superfluous word אֶת that begins this verse: It extends the

¹² *beware for yourself lest you forget HASHEM Who took you out of the land of Egypt, from the house of slavery.* ¹³ *HASHEM, your God, you shall fear, Him you shall serve, and in His Name you shall swear.* ¹⁴ *You shall not follow after other gods, the gods of the peoples that are around you.* ¹⁵ *For a zealous God is HASHEM, your God, among you — lest the wrath of HASHEM, your God, will flare against you and He destroy you from upon the face of the earth.*

¹⁶ *You shall not test HASHEM, your God, as you tested Him at Massah.* ¹⁷ *You shall surely observe the commandments of HASHEM, your God, and His testimonies and His decrees that He commanded you.* ¹⁸ *You shall do what is fair and good in the eyes of HASHEM, so that it will be good for you, and you shall come and possess the good land that HASHEM swore to your forefathers,* ¹⁹ *to push away all your enemies from before you, as HASHEM spoke.*

²⁰ *If your child asks you tomorrow, saying, "What are the testimonies and the decrees and the ordinances that HASHEM, our God, commanded you?"*

²¹ *You shall say to your child, "We were slaves to Pharaoh in Egypt, and HASHEM took us out of Egypt with a strong hand.* ²² *HASHEM placed signs and wonders, great and harmful, against Egypt, against Pharaoh and against his entire household, before our eyes.* ²³ *And He took us out of there in order to bring us, to give us the land that He swore to our forefathers.* ²⁴ *HASHEM commanded us to perform all these decrees, to fear HASHEM, our God, for our good, all the days, to give us life, as this very day.*

────────────── BAAL HATURIM ELUCIDATED ──────────────

19. לַהֲדֹף — **TO PUSH AWAY.** This word is spelled defectively,[195] without a ו (= 6), for the Girgashites fled on their own accord.[196]

---

concept of awe of God to include awe and reverence for Torah scholars. The Baal HaTurim finds a further allusion to this concept in the *gematria* of תִּירָא.

195. The *mekor* (gerundive infinitive) of a verb can be vowelized with or without the vowel letter ו. The Baal HaTurim explains why the form without the ו is used in our verse (*VeChur LaZahav*).

196. *Peirush HaRokeach.* Israel was commanded to destroy the seven Canaanite nations that lived

in *Eretz Yisrael* before Israel conquered it: (i) *the Hittite;* (ii) *and the Girgashite;* (iii) *and the Amorite;* (iv) *and the Canaanite;* (v) *and the Perizzite;* (vi) *and the Hivvite;* (viii) *and the Jebusite* (7:1 below). Yet elsewhere (e.g., *Exodus* 33:2; 20:17 below) only six nations are listed. According to the Talmud (*Yerushalmi, Sheviis* 6:1) and Midrash (*Vayikra Rabbah* 17:6), the Girgashites fled on their own (see note 30 to *parashas Eikev*), offering no resistance at all (cited in *Rashi* to *Exodus* 33:2).

כה וּצְדָקָ֖ה תִּֽהְיֶה־לָּ֑נוּ כִּֽי־נִשְׁמֹ֨ר לַעֲשׂ֜וֹת אֶת־
כָּל־הַמִּצְוָ֣ה הַזֹּ֗את לִפְנֵ֛י יְהוָ֥ה אֱלֹהֵ֖ינוּ כַּאֲשֶׁ֥ר
צִוָּֽנוּ: ז א כִּ֤י יְבִֽיאֲךָ֙ יְהוָ֣ה אֱלֹהֶ֔יךָ אֶל־הָאָ֕רֶץ
אֲשֶׁר־אַתָּ֥ה בָא־שָׁ֖מָּה לְרִשְׁתָּ֑הּ וְנָשַׁ֣ל גּֽוֹיִם־רַבִּ֣ים ׀
מִפָּנֶ֡יךָ הַֽחִתִּי֩ וְהַגִּרְגָּשִׁ֨י וְהָאֱמֹרִ֜י וְהַכְּנַעֲנִ֣י וְהַפְּרִזִּ֗י
וְהַֽחִוִּי֙ וְהַיְבוּסִ֔י שִׁבְעָ֣ה גוֹיִ֔ם רַבִּ֥ים וַעֲצוּמִ֖ים
ב מִמֶּֽךָּ: וּנְתָנָ֞ם יְהוָ֧ה אֱלֹהֶ֛יךָ לְפָנֶ֖יךָ וְהִכִּיתָ֑ם
הַחֲרֵ֤ם תַּחֲרִים֙ אֹתָ֔ם לֹֽא־תִכְרֹ֥ת לָהֶ֛ם בְּרִ֖ית
ג וְלֹ֥א תְחָנֵּֽם: וְלֹ֥א תִתְחַתֵּ֖ן בָּ֑ם בִּתְּךָ֙ לֹֽא־תִתֵּ֣ן
ד לִבְנ֔וֹ וּבִתּ֖וֹ לֹֽא־תִקַּ֥ח לִבְנֶֽךָ: כִּֽי־יָסִ֤יר אֶת־בִּנְךָ֙
מֵֽאַחֲרַ֔י וְעָבְד֖וּ אֱלֹהִ֣ים אֲחֵרִ֑ים וְחָרָ֤ה אַף־יְהוָה֙
ה בָּכֶ֔ם וְהִשְׁמִֽידְךָ֖ מַהֵֽר: כִּ֣י־אִם־כֹּ֤ה תַעֲשׂוּ֙ לָהֶ֔ם
מִזְבְּחֹתֵיהֶ֣ם תִּתֹּ֔צוּ וּמַצֵּבֹתָ֖ם תְּשַׁבֵּ֑רוּ וַאֲשֵֽׁירֵהֶם֙
ו תְּגַדֵּע֔וּן וּפְסִֽילֵיהֶ֖ם תִּשְׂרְפ֣וּן בָּאֵֽשׁ: כִּ֣י עַ֤ם קָדוֹשׁ֙
אַתָּ֔ה לַיהוָ֣ה אֱלֹהֶ֑יךָ בְּךָ֣ בָּחַ֣ר ׀ יְהוָ֣ה אֱלֹהֶ֗יךָ לִֽהְי֥וֹת
ל֣וֹ לְעַ֣ם סְגֻלָּ֔ה מִכֹּל֙ הָֽעַמִּ֔ים אֲשֶׁ֖ר עַל־פְּנֵ֥י הָאֲדָמָֽה:

──────── בעל הטורים ────────

(כה) **הַמִּצְוָה הַזֹּאת לִפְנֵי ה' אֱלֹהֵינוּ.** מְלַמֵּד שֶׁהַמִּצְוֹת בָּאוֹת וּמְעִידוֹת לִפְנֵי ה'. וּפֵ"א
דְּ"לִפְנֵי" כְּפוּלָה. לוֹמַר שֶׁנִּכְנָסוֹת לִפְנַי וְלִפְנִים:

❑ **כַּאֲשֶׁר צִוָּנוּ. כִּי יְבִיאֲךָ.** בִּשְׂכַר הַמִּצְוֹת:

ז (א) וְנָשַׁל. ג' בַּמָּסוֹרֶת – "וְנָשַׁל גּוֹיִם רַבִּים"; "וְנָשַׁל ה' אֱלֹהֶיךָ אֶת הַגּוֹיִם הָאֵל מִפָּנֶיךָ";
"וְנָשַׁל הַבַּרְזֶל מִן הָעֵץ". אֶלְמָלֵא שֶׁחָטְאוּ יִשְׂרָאֵל לֹא הָיוּ צְרִיכִין לִכְלֵי זַיִן. וְזֶהוּ "וְנָשַׁל
גּוֹיִם", "וְנָשַׁל הַבַּרְזֶל":

──────── BAAL HATURIM ELUCIDATED ────────

25. הַמִּצְוָה הַזֹּאת לִפְנֵי ה' אֱלֹהֵינוּ — THIS [ENTIRE] COMMANDMENT BEFORE HASHEM, OUR
GOD. This teaches that the *mitzvos* come and testify before God.[197] [Moreover,
according to a scribal tradition,] the פ in the word לִפְנֵי, *before,* is written in the
enhanced form known as פ כְּפוּלָה, *doubled* פ.[198] This is to indicate that [the
mitzvos] enter לִפְנַי וְלִפְנִים, [God's] *innermost places.* [199]

❑ כַּאֲשֶׁר צִוָּנוּ. כִּי יְבִיאֲךָ — AS HE COMMANDED US. When [HASHEM, your God,] will

───────────────────────────

197. See *Avodah Zarah* 2a — Every *mitzvah*
that Israel performs in this world comes to
testify for them in the World to Come (see also

Avodah Zarah 5a).
198. See note 29 to *parashas Devarim.*
199. *Peirush HaRokeach.*

דברים / ואתחנן

[25] *And it will be a merit for us if we are careful to perform this entire commandment before HASHEM, our God, as He commanded us.*

7

[1] *When HASHEM, your God, will bring you to the land to which you come to possess it, and He will thrust away many nations from before you — the Hittite, the Girgashite, the Amorite, the Canaanite, the Perizzite, the Hivvite, and the Jebusite — seven nations greater and mightier than you,* [2] *and HASHEM, your God, will deliver them before you, and you will smite them — you shall utterly destroy them; you shall not seal a covenant with them nor shall you show them favor.* [3] *You shall not intermarry with them; you shall not give your daughter to his son, and you shall not take his daughter for your son,* [4] *for he will cause your child to turn away from after Me and they will worship other gods; then HASHEM's wrath will burn against you, and He will destroy you quickly.* [5] *Rather, so shall you do to them: Their altars shall you demolish; their pillars shall you break; their sacred trees shall you cut down; and their carved images shall you burn in fire.*

[6] *For you are a holy people to HASHEM, your God; HASHEM, your God, has chosen you to be for Him a treasured people above all the peoples that are on the face of the earth.*

BAAL HATURIM ELUCIDATED

bring you. [The juxtaposition of these two phrases indicates] that [Israel's entry into the land will come] as a reward for [fulfilling] the *mitzvos.*[200]

VII.

1. וְנָשַׁל — HE WILL THRUST AWAY. The masoretic note ג׳ means that this term appears three times in the *Tanach*: (i) here, וְנָשַׁל גּוֹיִם רַבִּים, *He will thrust away many nations*; (ii) וְנָשַׁל ה׳ אֱלֹהֶיךָ אֶת הַגּוֹיִם הָאֵל מִפָּנֶיךָ, *HASHEM, your God, will thrust these nations from before you* (7:22 below); and (iii) וְנָשַׁל הַבַּרְזֶל מִן הָעֵץ, *and the iron will slip away from the wood* (19:5 below). [The similarity of expression indicates that] had Israel not sinned, they would have no need for [iron] weapons.[201] [Rather, God] *will thrust away the nations,* and *the iron* [weapons] *will slip away* also.

5. {The Baal HaTurim's comment to וּפְסִילֵיהֶם appears at *Exodus* 32:19.}

200. *Peirush HaRokeach*; see *Kiddushin* 37b.

201. *Sifrei* to 1:8 above; see also the Baal HaTurim to 1:3 above.

ז לֹא מֵרֻבְּכֶם מִכָּל־הָעַמִּים חָשַׁק יהוה בָּכֶם וַיִּבְחַר
ח בָּכֶם כִּי־אַתֶּם הַמְעַט מִכָּל־הָעַמִּים: כִּי מֵאַהֲבַת
יהוה אֶתְכֶם וּמִשָּׁמְרוֹ אֶת־הַשְּׁבֻעָה אֲשֶׁר נִשְׁבַּע
לַאֲבֹתֵיכֶם הוֹצִיא יהוה אֶתְכֶם בְּיָד חֲזָקָה וַיִּפְדְּךָ
מפטיר ט מִבֵּית עֲבָדִים מִיַּד פַּרְעֹה מֶלֶךְ־מִצְרָיִם: וְיָדַעְתָּ
כִּי־יהוה אֱלֹהֶיךָ הוּא הָאֱלֹהִים הָאֵל הַנֶּאֱמָן שֹׁמֵר
הַבְּרִית וְהַחֶסֶד לְאֹהֲבָיו וּלְשֹׁמְרֵי מִצְוֹתָו לְאֶלֶף
י דּוֹר: וּמְשַׁלֵּם לְשֹׂנְאָיו אֶל־פָּנָיו לְהַאֲבִידוֹ לֹא
יא יְאַחֵר לְשֹׂנְאוֹ אֶל־פָּנָיו יְשַׁלֶּם־לוֹ: וְשָׁמַרְתָּ אֶת־
הַמִּצְוָה וְאֶת־הַחֻקִּים וְאֶת־הַמִּשְׁפָּטִים אֲשֶׁר אָנֹכִי
מְצַוְּךָ הַיּוֹם לַעֲשׂוֹתָם: פפפ קי״ח פסוקים. עזיא״ל סימן.

בעל הטורים

(ז) לֹא מֵרֻבְּכֶם. כְּתִיב חָסֵר וָי״ו. לוֹמַר, לֹא מֵרַבָּנוּת שֶׁבָּכֶם, שֶׁאַתֶּם מַמְעִיטִים עַצְמְכֶם:

❑ **כִּי אַתֶּם הַמְעַט.** ה׳ מְעַט — נ״ז מִשְׁפָּחוֹת בְּפָרָשַׁת פִּינְחָס וְח׳ בַּלְוִיִּם הֲרֵי ס״ה. וּכְשֶׁתִּצְטָרֵף עִמָּהֶם חָמֵשׁ בְּנוֹת צְלָפְחָד יִהְיוּ ע׳:

BAAL HATURIM ELUCIDATED

7. לֹא מֵרֻבְּכֶם — NOT BECAUSE YOU ARE MORE NUMEROUS. The word מֵרֻבְּכֶם is spelled defectively,[202] without a ו.[203] This indicates [that the phrase can be

202. Three words of the root רבב, *to be numerous,* appear in the *Tanach* with the ֻ vowelization — מֵרֻבְּכֶם (here); כְּרֻבָּם (*Hosea* 4:7); and מְרֻבָּבוֹת (*Psalms* 144:13) — the vowelization רוּ does not appear in *Tanach.*

203. The text follows *Shoham Yakar's* manuscript edition. The other printed editions read כְּתִיב חָסֵר לוֹמַר מֵרַבָּנוּת שֶׁלָּכֶם, *It is spelled defectively. This indicates that . . . because of your self-aggrandizement.* But that reading is in accordance with neither the Talmudic source (*Chullin* 89a) nor the remainder of the comment, שֶׁאַתֶּם מַמְעִיטִים עַצְמְכֶם, *for you make yourselves small.*

[7] *Not because you are more numerous than all the peoples did* HASHEM *desire you and choose you, for you are the fewest of all the peoples.* [8] *Rather, because of* HASHEM*'s love for you and because He observes the oath that He swore to your forefathers did He take you out with a strong hand and redeem you from the house of slavery, from the hand of Pharaoh, king of Egypt.* [9] *You must know that* HASHEM*, your God — He is the God, the faithful God, Who safeguards the covenant and the kindness for those who love Him and for those who observe His commandments, for a thousand generations.* [10] *And He repays His enemies in his lifetime to make him perish; He shall not delay for His enemy — in his lifetime He shall repay him.* [11] *You shall observe the commandment, and the decrees and the ordinances that I command you today, to perform them.*

BAAL HATURIM ELUCIDATED

interpreted as if Moses were saying,] "לֹא מֵרֻבְּנוּת שֶׁלָּכֶם, *Not because of your self-aggrandizement,* for you make yourself small [i.e., you are humble]."[204]

❑ כִּי אַתֶּם הַמְעַט — **FOR YOU ARE THE FEWEST.** [The word הַמְעַט, *the fewest,* can be understood as if it were two words, ה׳ מְעַט, *five less.* There are fifty-seven [Israelite] families enumerated in *parashas Pinchas* (*Numbers* 26:1-51) and eight Levite families (26:57-62), for a total of sixty-five.[205] Nevertheless, when the [families of the] five daughters of Zelophehad are added, the total is seventy.[206]

11. {The Baal HaTurim's comment to הַיּוֹם לַעֲשׂוֹתָם appears at 7:12 below.

204. *Chullin* 89a, cited by *Rashi.*

205. Five less than the seventy nations of the world (*Rashi* to *Numbers* 26:36).

206. *Peirush HaRokeach.*

THE TEN COMMANDMENTS WITH THE *TROP* (CANTILLATION NOTES) USED BY THE READER FOR THE PUBLIC TORAH READING ON THE SABBATH (see page 1876).

אָנֹכִי יְהוָה אֱלֹהֶיךָ אֲשֶׁר הוֹצֵאתִיךָ מֵאֶרֶץ מִצְרַיִם מִבֵּית
עֲבָדִים לֹא יִהְיֶה לְךָ אֱלֹהִים אֲחֵרִים עַל־פָּנַי לֹא תַעֲשֶׂה־לְךָ
פֶסֶל ׀ כׇּל־תְּמוּנָה אֲשֶׁר בַּשָּׁמַיִם ׀ מִמַּעַל וַאֲשֶׁר בָּאָרֶץ מִתַּחַת
וַאֲשֶׁר בַּמַּיִם ׀ מִתַּחַת לָאָרֶץ לֹא־תִשְׁתַּחֲוֶה לָהֶם וְלֹא
תָעׇבְדֵם כִּי אָנֹכִי יְהוָה אֱלֹהֶיךָ אֵל קַנָּא פֹּקֵד עֲוֺן אָבוֹת
עַל־בָּנִים וְעַל־שִׁלֵּשִׁים וְעַל־רִבֵּעִים לְשֹׂנְאָי וְעֹשֶׂה חֶסֶד
לַאֲלָפִים לְאֹהֲבַי וּלְשֹׁמְרֵי מִצְוֺתָי׃   לֹא תִשָּׂא
אֶת־שֵׁם־יְהוָה אֱלֹהֶיךָ לַשָּׁוְא כִּי לֹא יְנַקֶּה יְהוָה אֵת אֲשֶׁר־
יִשָּׂא אֶת־שְׁמוֹ לַשָּׁוְא׃   שָׁמוֹר אֶת־יוֹם הַשַּׁבָּת
לְקַדְּשׁוֹ כַּאֲשֶׁר צִוְּךָ ׀ יְהוָה אֱלֹהֶיךָ שֵׁשֶׁת יָמִים תַּעֲבֹד וְעָשִׂיתָ
כׇּל־מְלַאכְתֶּךָ וְיוֹם הַשְּׁבִיעִי שַׁבָּת ׀ לַיהוָה אֱלֹהֶיךָ לֹא תַעֲשֶׂה
כׇל־מְלָאכָה אַתָּה וּבִנְךָ־וּבִתֶּךָ וְעַבְדְּךָ־וַאֲמָתֶךָ וְשׁוֹרְךָ וַחֲמֹרְךָ
וְכׇל־בְּהֶמְתֶּךָ וְגֵרְךָ אֲשֶׁר בִּשְׁעָרֶיךָ לְמַעַן יָנוּחַ עַבְדְּךָ וַאֲמָתְךָ
כָּמוֹךָ וְזָכַרְתָּ כִּי־עֶבֶד הָיִיתָ ׀ בְּאֶרֶץ מִצְרַיִם וַיֹּצִאֲךָ יְהוָה
אֱלֹהֶיךָ מִשָּׁם בְּיָד חֲזָקָה וּבִזְרֹעַ נְטוּיָה עַל־כֵּן צִוְּךָ יְהוָה
אֱלֹהֶיךָ לַעֲשׂוֹת אֶת־יוֹם הַשַּׁבָּת׃   כַּבֵּד אֶת־
אָבִיךָ וְאֶת־אִמֶּךָ כַּאֲשֶׁר צִוְּךָ יְהוָה אֱלֹהֶיךָ לְמַעַן ׀ יַאֲרִיכֻן
יָמֶיךָ וּלְמַעַן יִיטַב לָךְ עַל הָאֲדָמָה אֲשֶׁר־יְהוָה אֱלֹהֶיךָ נֹתֵן
לָךְ׃   לֹא תִרְצָח׃   וְלֹא תִנְאָף׃   וְלֹא
תִגְנֹב׃   וְלֹא־תַעֲנֶה בְרֵעֲךָ עֵד שָׁוְא׃   וְלֹא
תַחְמֹד אֵשֶׁת רֵעֶךָ   וְלֹא תִתְאַוֶּה בֵּית רֵעֶךָ שָׂדֵהוּ
וְעַבְדּוֹ וַאֲמָתוֹ שׁוֹרוֹ וַחֲמֹרוֹ וְכֹל אֲשֶׁר לְרֵעֶךָ׃

פרשת עקב

Parashas Eikev

יב וְהָיָ֣ה ׀ עֵ֣קֶב תִּשְׁמְע֗וּן אֵ֤ת הַמִּשְׁפָּטִים֙ הָאֵ֔לֶּה וּשְׁמַרְתֶּ֥ם וַעֲשִׂיתֶ֖ם אֹתָ֑ם וְשָׁמַר֩ יהוֹה אֱלֹהֶ֨יךָ לְךָ֜

─────────── בעל הטורים ───────────

ז (יב) וְהָיָה עֵקֶב. לְעֵיל מִנֵּהּ כְּתִיב "הַיּוֹם לַעֲשׂוֹתָם", וּסְמִיךְ לֵהּ "עֵקֶב". כְּלוֹמַר, "הַיּוֹם לַעֲשׂוֹתָם", אֲבָל שְׂכָרָם בְּ"עֵקֶב", פֵּרוּשׁ, בַּסּוֹף:

❑ עֵקֶ"ב תֵּבוֹת יֵשׁ בַּעֲשֶׂר דִּבְּרוֹת. וְזֶהוּ "בְּשָׁמְרָם עֵקֶב רָב" – אִם תִּשְׁמֹר עק"ב, תִּזְכֶּה לְ"מָה רַב טוּבְךָ אֲשֶׁר צָפַנְתָּ לִירֵאֶיךָ":

❑ עֵקֶב. עֲשֵׂה תּוֹרָתְךָ קֶבַע:

❑ עֵקֶב. עֲנָוָה לְמַד מִן הֶעָקֵב הַזֶּה שֶׁהוֹלֵךְ אַחַר הָרֶגֶל דֶּרֶךְ עֲנָוָה. וּלְפִיכָךְ אֵינוֹ נִגָּף כְּמוֹ אֶצְבְּעוֹת הָרַגְלַיִם:

❑ הַמִּשְׁפָּטִים. פֵּ"א כְּפוּלָה – שֶׁיֵּשׁ לְפַשְׁפֵּשׁ וְלַחְקֹר אַחַר עֹמֶק הַדִּין:

❑ תִּשְׁמְעוּן . . . וּשְׁמַרְתֶּם וַעֲשִׂיתֶם. ג' – כְּנֶגֶד מִקְרָא מִשְׁנָה תַּלְמוּד:

❑ וְשָׁמַר ה' אֱלֹהֶיךָ לְךָ. אִם "עֵקֶב תִּשְׁמְעוּן", יִשְׁמֹר לְךָ הַבְּרִית שֶׁנֶּאֱמַר בְּאַבְרָהָם,

─────────── BAAL HATURIM ELUCIDATED ───────────

12. וְהָיָה עֵקֶב — THE END WILL BE.[1] Just before this [i.e., at the end of the previous *parashah*] the Torah stated, הַיּוֹם לַעֲשׂוֹתָם, *today, to perform them* (7:11), and juxtaposed to that is עֵקֶב, as if to say, "*Today, to perform them,* but their reward will come at the end [i.e., in the World to Come]."[2]

❑ The *gematria* of עֵקֶב (172) is equal to the number of words in the Ten Commandments.[3] And that is the intent of the verse, בְּשָׁמְרָם עֵקֶב רָב, *for observing them, there is abundance in the end* (Psalms 19:12). [That verse implies:] If you will observe עֵקֶב, *the 172* [words of the Ten Commandments], you will merit [רָב, the *abundance* spoken of in the verse], מָה רַב טוּבְךָ אֲשֶׁר צָפַנְתָּ לִירֵאֶיךָ, *How abundant is Your goodness that You have hidden away for those who fear You* (Psalms 31:20).[4]

❑ עֵקֶב — THE END. [The letters of this word can be rearranged to spell קֶבַע, *permanent, fixed.* Thus, our verse alludes to the Mishnah's injunction:] Make your Torah[5]

─────────────────────────────────

1. In *Peirush HaTur HaAroch,* the Baal HaTurim cites three interpretations for the term עֵקֶב [which usually means *because, as a consequence of*] in our verse. Two of them interpret עֵקֶב as a variant form of עָקֵב, *heel,* and explain the word as a metaphor [e.g., *Rashi* interprets עֵקֶב as "the *mitzvos* that a person considers as inconsequential, trampling them under his *heel*"]. Another opinion (that of anonymous commentaries quoted by the *Ramban*) states that just as the term רֹאשׁ, *head,* is used as a metaphor for the beginning [e.g., רֹאשׁ הַשָּׁנָה, *the beginning of the year*], so is the term עָקֵב, *heel,* used as a metaphor for the end. Both the translation of the verse and the Baal HaTurim's first comment follow this last interpretation. In his fourth comment to this

verse, the Baal HaTurim interprets עֵקֶב as *heel.*

2. *Devarim Rabbah* 3:3; see also *Eruvin* 22a, cited in *Rashi* to 7:11 above.

3. *Peirush HaRokeach;* see also the Baal Ha-Turim to *Genesis* 26:5. There are one hundred and seventy-two words in the first version of the Ten Commandments (*Exodus* 20:2-14, see the Baal HaTurim's last three comments to verse 13 there); the second version (5:6-18 above) has seventeen words more (see the Baal HaTurim to verse 16 there, s.v., שֶׁבַע עֶשְׂרֵה).

4. *Peirush HaRokeach;* see also *Midrash Tanchuma* 1.

5. This refers to establishing a fixed daily period for Torah study (*Bartenura*). Although the

^{12} The end will be [that] you will hearken to these ordinances, you will observe and you will perform them; and [then] HASHEM, your God, will safeguard for you

———————————— BAAL HATURIM ELUCIDATED ————————————

a fixed point [in your life].[6]

❑ עֵקֶב — THE HEEL.[7] Learn humility from this heel that walks behind the foot, in a humble way, and therefore is not stubbed as are the toes.

❑ הַמִּשְׁפָּטִים — ORDINANCES. [According to a scribal tradition,] the פ of this word is written [in the Torah scrolls] in the enhanced form known as פ' כְּפוּלָה, doubled פ.[8] [This indicates] that it is necessary [for the judge] to probe[9] and to investigate [in order to arrive at] the depths of the law.[10]

❑ תִּשְׁמְעוּן . . . וּשְׁמַרְתֶּם וַעֲשִׂיתֶם — YOU WILL HEARKEN . . . YOU WILL OBSERVE AND YOU WILL PERFORM THEM. [The verse uses] three [verbs],[11] corresponding to Scripture,[12] Mishnah[13] and Talmud.[14]

❑ וְשָׁמַר ה' אֱלֹהֶיךָ לְךָ — AND [THEN] HASHEM, YOUR GOD, WILL SAFEGUARD FOR YOU. If you will hearken to עֵקֶב [i.e., to the 172 words of the Ten Commandments][14a] then He will safeguard for you the covenant that is stated regarding Abraham,[14b]

verse speaks of *mitzvah* observance in general, making no specific reference to Torah study, the Baal HaTurim interprets the three words תִּשְׁמְעוּן . . . וּשְׁמַרְתֶּם וַעֲשִׂיתֶם as references to Torah study (see s.v., תִּשְׁמְעוּן, below, with notes 12-14).

6. *Avos* 1:15.

7. See note 1 above. The Baal HaTurim is playing on King Solomon's statement, עֵקֶב עֲנָוָה יִרְאַת ה', *The end of humility is reverence for HASHEM* (Proverbs 22:4). Explained in a novel manner, the phrase עֵקֶב עֲנָוָה means, *the heel is [the paradigm of] humility.*

8. See note 29 to *parashas Devarim* and the accompanying illustration. *Sefer Tagin* includes the פ of הַמִּשְׁפָּטִים of our verse on the list of "191 in the Torah whose mouths are on the inside."

9. The doubled פ alludes to the two letters פ of the word לְפַשְׁפֵּשׁ, *to probe* (Shoham Yakar).

10. See the Baal HaTurim's first comment to *parashas Mishpatim.*

11. The Torah uses three, seemingly redundant, verbs. It could have stated simply, תִּשְׁמְעוּן, *you will hearken,* or תִּשְׁמְרוּן, *you will observe,* or תַּעֲשׂוּן, *you will perform.* The Baal HaTurim explains the implication of the three verbs.

12. That is, תִּשְׁמְעוּן refers to Scripture, וּשְׁמַרְתֶּם to Mishnah, and וַעֲשִׂיתֶם to Talmud (see notes 13 and 14).

13. On the verse, וּשְׁמַרְתֶּם לַעֲשׂוֹת אֵת כָּל הַחֻקִּים, *You shall observe, to perform all the decrees . . .* (11:32 below), the *Sifrei* (cited in Rashi to 4:6 above) expounds: וּשְׁמַרְתֶּם זוֹ מִשְׁנָה, *The word* וּשְׁמַרְתֶּם *refers to the Mishnah.*

14. (See note 13.) The *Sifrei* continues, וַעֲשִׂיתֶם זוֹ מַעֲשֶׂה, *the word* וַעֲשִׂיתֶם *refers to* performance. [Now, it appears strange that the *Sifrei,* while expounding on the verse וּשְׁמַרְתֶּם לַעֲשׂוֹת, *you shall observe, to perform,* should quote the phrase from our verse וּשְׁמַרְתֶּם וַעֲשִׂיתֶם, *and you will observe and you will perform!* Although we do not know whether the "misquote" was intentional or a copyist's error, we can say with more than a modicum of conviction that both לַעֲשׂוֹת and וַעֲשִׂיתֶם refer to performance (VeChur LaZahav).] Moreover, the Talmud states: The following question was placed before the elders: What is more important, תַּלְמוּד, *Talmud* [literally, (Torah) study], or מַעֲשֶׂה, *performance* [of *mitzvos*]? . . . They all agreed that Talmud is more important for it leads to the performance of *mitzvos* (Kiddushin 40b). Thus, וַעֲשִׂיתֶם of our verse refers to Talmud, which leads to performance (Shoham Yakar).

14a. See the Baal HaTurim's second comment to this *sidra,* with note 3.

14b. As our verse states, אֲשֶׁר נִשְׁבַּע לַאֲבֹתֶיךָ, *that He swore to your forefathers,* i.e., to Abraham (A.S.).

אֶת־הַבְּרִית וְאֶת־הַחֶסֶד אֲשֶׁר נִשְׁבַּע לַאֲבֹתֶיךָ:
יג וַאֲהֵבְךָ וּבֵרַכְךָ וְהִרְבֶּךָ וּבֵרַךְ פְּרִי־בִטְנְךָ וּפְרִי־
אַדְמָתֶךָ דְּגָנְךָ וְתִירֹשְׁךָ וְיִצְהָרֶךָ שְׁגַר־אֲלָפֶיךָ
וְעַשְׁתְּרֹת צֹאנֶךָ עַל הָאֲדָמָה אֲשֶׁר־נִשְׁבַּע לַאֲבֹתֶיךָ
יד לָתֶת לָךְ: בָּרוּךְ תִּהְיֶה מִכָּל־הָעַמִּים לֹא־יִהְיֶה בְךָ
טו עָקָר וַעֲקָרָה וּבִבְהֶמְתֶּךָ: וְהֵסִיר יהוה מִמְּךָ כָּל־חֹלִי

בעל הטורים

"עֵקֶב אֲשֶׁר שָׁמַע אַבְרָהָם בְּקֹלִי וַיִּשְׁמֹר":

❑ **וְשָׁמַר.** בְּגִימַטְרִיָּא לֶעָתִיד לָבֹא:

(יג) וַאֲהֵבְךָ. בִּזְכוּת אַבְרָהָם, שֶׁנֶּאֱמַר בּוֹ "זֶרַע אַבְרָהָם אֹהֲבִי":

❑ **וּבֵרַכְךָ.** בִּזְכוּת יִצְחָק, שֶׁנֶּאֱמַר בּוֹ "וַיְבָרֶךְ אֱלֹהִים אֶת יִצְחָק":

❑ **וְהִרְבֶּךָ.** בִּזְכוּת יַעֲקֹב, שֶׁנֶּאֱמַר בּוֹ "פְּרֵה וּרְבֵה":

❑ **וּבֵרַךְ.** ג' – הָכָא חַד, וּתְרֵי. בְּפָרָשַׁת מִשְׁפָּטִים:

❑ הַפָּסוּק מַתְחִיל בְּוָי"ו וּמְסַיֵּם בְּכָ"ף – וְכֵן "וְיִתֶּן לְךָ הָאֱלֹהִים מִטַּל הַשָּׁמַיִם", הַבְּרָכוֹת שֶׁבֵּרַךְ יִצְחָק לְיַעֲקֹב, מַתְחִילִין בְּוָי"ו וּמְסַיְּמִין בְּכָ"ף, שֶׁיִּהְיוּ לְךָ כָּל אוֹתָן הַבְּרָכוֹת:

(יד) בָּרוּךְ תִּהְיֶה מִכָּל הָעַמִּים. הַפָּסוּק מַתְחִיל בְּבֵי"ת וּמְסַיֵּם בְּכָ"ף – לוֹמַר, שֶׁבִּזְכוּת הַתּוֹרָה שֶׁיֵּשׁ בָּהּ כ"ב אוֹתִיּוֹת:

❑ **לֹא יִהְיֶה בְךָ עָקָר וַעֲקָרָה.** בְּגִימַטְרִיָּא בְּדִבְרֵי הַתּוֹרָה:

(טו) כָּל חֹלִי. עוֹלֶה צ"ח. שֶׁיָּסִיר מִמְּךָ צ"ח קְלָלוֹת:

BAAL HATURIM ELUCIDATED

עֵקֶב אֲשֶׁר שָׁמַע אַבְרָהָם בְּקֹלִי וַיִּשְׁמֹר, *because*[14c] *Abraham hearkened to My voice, and observed . . .*" (*Genesis* 26:5).

❑ **וְשָׁמַר — WILL SAFEGUARD.** The *gematria* of this word (546) is equivalent[15] to that of לֶעָתִיד לָבֹא, *for the Time to Come* [i.e., in the future].[16]

13. וַאֲהֵבְךָ — HE WILL LOVE YOU.[17] In the merit of Abraham, regarding whom it is said, זֶרַע אַבְרָהָם אֹהֲבִי, *the seed of Abraham, who loves Me* (*Isaiah* 41:8).

❑ **וּבֵרַכְךָ — AND HE WILL BLESS YOU.**[17] In the merit of Isaac, regarding whom it is said, וַיְבָרֶךְ אֱלֹהִים אֶת יִצְחָק, *God blessed Isaac* (*Genesis* 25:11).

❑ **וְהִרְבֶּךָ — AND HE WILL MULTIPLY YOU.**[17] In the merit of Jacob, regarding whom it is said, פְּרֵה וּרְבֵה, *Be fruitful and multiply* (*Genesis* 35:11).[18]

14c. See note 1 above.

15. The principle of *im hakollel* allows 546 to be considered equivalent to 547, the *gematria* of the Baal HaTurim's phrase.

16. *Peirush HaRokeach.* The Midrash states: The blessings with which the Patriarchs blessed Israel is preserved for them לֶעָתִיד לָבֹא, *for the Time to Come,* as is stated, וְשָׁמַר ה' אֱלֹהֶיךָ, *and then* HASHEM, *your God, will safeguard . . . that He swore to your forefathers* (*Devarim Rabbah* 3:4; see also the Baal HaTurim's first comment to this verse).

17. These three comments (s.v., וַאֲהֵבְךָ; s.v., וּבֵרַכְךָ, and s.v., וְהִרְבֶּךָ) should be read as one.

18. *Pesikta Zutresa* [*Midrash Lekach Tov*], who cites *Genesis* 48:4 — הִנְנִי מַפְרְךָ וְהִרְבִּיתִךָ, *Behold! I will make you fruitful and I will multiply you* — in

the covenant and the kindness that He swore to your forefathers. 13 *He will love you, and He will bless you and He will multiply you, and He will bless the fruit of your womb and the fruit of your Land; your grain, your wine, and your oil; the offspring of your cattle and the flocks of your sheep and goats; on the Land that He swore to your forefathers to give you.* 14 *You will be the most blessed of all the peoples; there will be no infertile male or infertile female among you or among your animals.* 15 *HASHEM will remove from you every illness;*

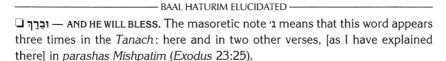

BAAL HATURIM ELUCIDATED

❑ וּבֵרַךְ — AND HE WILL BLESS. The masoretic note ג׳ means that this word appears three times in the *Tanach*: here and in two other verses, [as I have explained there] in *parashas Mishpatim* (*Exodus* 23:25).

❑ This verse begins with a ו and ends with a ך.[19] Similarly, the blessings with which Isaac blessed Jacob — וְיִתֶּן לְךָ הָאֱלֹהִים מִטַּל הַשָּׁמַיִם, *and may God give you of the dew of the heaven . . .* [וּמְבָרְכֶיךָ בָּרוּךְ, *and those who bless you are blessed*] (*Genesis* 27:28-29) — begin with a ו and end with a ך. [This indicates] that [Moses was saying,] "You will receive all the blessings of those verses."

14. בָּרוּךְ תִּהְיֶה מִכָּל הָעַמִּים — YOU WILL BE THE MOST BLESSED OF ALL THE PEOPLES. This verse begins with a ב (= 2) and ends with a ך (= 20).[20] This indicates that [the blessings will come to Israel] in the merit of the Torah which employs [the] twenty-two letters [of the *aleph-beis*].[21]

❑ לֹא יִהְיֶה בְךָ עָקָר וַעֲקָרָה — THERE WILL BE NO INFERTILE MALE OR INFERTILE FEMALE AMONG YOU. The *gematria* of this phrase (834) is equal to that of בְּדִבְרֵי הַתּוֹרָה, *in the words of the Torah.*[22]

15. כָּל חֹלִי — EVERY ILLNESS. The *gematria* of this phrase is 98. [Moses was saying, "If you fulfill the conditions of verse 12, then] God will remove from you the ninety-eight curses [enumerated in the Admonition (28:15-68 below)[23]]."[24]

place of *Genesis* 35:11.

19. Although this phenomenon appears in 206 verses in the Torah (including four of the first five verses of this *sidra,* plus another ten scattered throughout the *sidra*) and another 420 in the rest of *Tanach,* this is the only one about which the Baal HaTurim comments.

20. Although this phenomenon appears nine times in the Torah and another fifty-four in the rest of *Tanach,* this is the only one about which the Baal HaTurim comments. The other instances of this phenomenon in the Torah are *Genesis* 40:19; *Leviticus* 25:15; *Numbers* 18:10; *Deuteronomy* 28:4, 28:5, 28:6, 28:32 and 33:25.

21. *R' Ephraim*; see also the Baal HaTurim to 26:11 below, s.v., הַטּוֹב.

22. According to one view in the Talmud, the term עָקָר of our verse refers to the Torah teacher who is not successful in producing proficient students; while the term עֲקָרָה refers to one whose prayers do not bear fruit (*Bechoros* 44b). The Baal HaTurim finds an allusion to the first part of the Talmudic statement in the *gematria* of the verse (*Shoham Yakar*).

Alternatively: The Talmud states: Scripture considers a person who teaches someone else's child Torah as if that teacher had borne the child (*Sanhedrin* 19b). Thus, one who acquires Torah knowledge but does not share it with others is considered infertile, childless (*Yad Aharon*).

23. See the Baal HaTurim to v. 61 there, and to 6:7 above.

24. *R' Yehudah HaChassid; Peirush HaRokeach.*

וְכָל־מַדְוֵי מִצְרַ֫יִם הָרָעִים אֲשֶׁ֣ר יָדַ֔עְתָּ לֹ֥א יְשִׂימָ֖ם
בָּ֑ךְ וּנְתָנָ֖ם בְּכָל־שֹׂנְאֶֽיךָ: וְאָכַלְתָּ֣ אֶת־כָּל־הָ֣עַמִּ֗ים
אֲשֶׁ֨ר יְהוָ֤ה אֱלֹהֶ֙יךָ֙ נֹתֵ֣ן לָ֔ךְ לֹא־תָח֥וֹס עֵֽינְךָ֖ עֲלֵיהֶ֑ם
וְלֹ֤א תַֽעֲבֹד֙ אֶת־אֱלֹ֣הֵיהֶ֔ם כִּֽי־מוֹקֵ֥שׁ ה֖וּא לָֽךְ:   כִּ֣י
תֹאמַ֣ר בִּלְבָֽבְךָ֔ רַבִּ֛ים הַגּוֹיִ֥ם הָאֵ֖לֶּה מִמֶּ֑נִּי אֵיכָ֥ה
אוּכַ֖ל לְהֽוֹרִישָֽׁם: לֹ֥א תִירָ֖א מֵהֶ֑ם זָכֹ֣ר תִּזְכֹּ֗ר אֵ֤ת
אֲשֶׁר־עָשָׂה֙ יְהוָ֣ה אֱלֹהֶ֔יךָ לְפַרְעֹ֖ה וּלְכָל־מִצְרָֽיִם:
הַמַּסֹּ֨ת הַגְּדֹלֹ֜ת אֲשֶׁר־רָא֣וּ עֵינֶ֗יךָ וְהָֽאֹתֹ֤ת וְהַמֹּֽפְתִים֙
וְהַיָּ֤ד הַֽחֲזָקָה֙ וְהַזְּרֹ֣עַ הַנְּטוּיָ֔ה אֲשֶׁ֥ר הוֹצִֽאֲךָ֖ יְהוָ֣ה
אֱלֹהֶ֑יךָ כֵּֽן־יַֽעֲשֶׂ֞ה יְהוָ֤ה אֱלֹהֶ֙יךָ֙ לְכָל־הָ֣עַמִּ֔ים אֲשֶׁר־
אַתָּ֥ה יָרֵ֖א מִפְּנֵיהֶֽם: וְגַם֙ אֶת־הַצִּרְעָ֔ה יְשַׁלַּ֛ח יְהוָ֥ה
אֱלֹהֶ֖יךָ בָּ֑ם עַד־אֲבֹ֗ד הַנִּשְׁאָרִ֛ים וְהַנִּסְתָּרִ֖ים מִפָּנֶֽיךָ:

טו

טז

יז

יח

יט

כ

--- בעל הטורים ---

(יח) זָכֹר תִּזְכֹּר. חָסֵר וָי״ו. לוֹמַר, שֶׁתִּזְכֹּר מַה שֶּׁעָשָׂה לְ״שֵׁשׁ מֵאוֹת רֶכֶב בָּחוּר״:

(יט) הַמַּסֹּת הַגְּדֹלֹת. כָּל הָאַלְפָא בֵּיתָא בְּזֶה הַפָּסוּק, חוּץ מִבֵּי״ת. רֶמֶז, כִּי עוֹד יַעֲשֶׂה פַּעַם שֵׁנִית נִפְלָאוֹת ״כִּימֵי צֵאתְךָ מֵאֶרֶץ מִצְרָיִם״:

(כ) אֶת הַצִּרְעָה. בְּגִימַטְרִיָּא שְׁתַּיִם הָיוּ:

❑ **עַד אֲבֹד.** חָסֵר וָי״ו, וְעוֹלֶה ז׳. שֶׁיֵּאָבֵד ז׳ אֻמּוֹת:

❑ **מִפָּנֶיךָ.** פֵּ״א כְּפוּלָה – לוֹמַר, מִפָּנֶיךָ וּמִפְּנֵי שְׁלוּחֶיךָ:

--- BAAL HATURIM ELUCIDATED ---

18. זָכֹר תִּזְכֹּר — YOU SHALL REMEMBER. This term[25] is spelled defectively, without a ו (= 6), to indicate [that Moses was telling them,] "Remember what God did to [Pharaoh's] שֵׁשׁ מֵאוֹת רֶכֶב בָּחוּר, *six hundred elite chariots (Exodus 14:7)*."[25a]

19. הַמַּסֹּת הַגְּדֹלֹת — THE GREAT TESTS. This verse contains every letter of the *aleph-beis* except a ב (= 2). The allusion is that these miracles will be repeated a second time, [with the coming of *Mashiach*, as it is written,] כִּימֵי צֵאתְךָ מֵאֶרֶץ מִצְרָיִם, *As in the days of your going forth from the land of Egypt [I will show them wonders]* (Micah 7:15).[26]

---

25. Both זָכֹר and תִּזְכֹּר are spelled defectively, but the comment does not specify which word the Baal HaTurim is discussing. However, the word תִּזְכֹּר appears eight times in the *Tanach*: six times spelled without a ו (here; 16:3 below; *II Samuel* 19:20; *Isaiah* 64:8; *Psalms* 25:7; and *Job* 11:16), and twice spelled תִּזְכּוֹר, with a ו (*Habakkuk* 3:2 and *Lamentations* 3:20). The word זָכֹר also appears eight times in the *Tanach*: twice spelled defectively (here and in *Jeremiah* 31:19),

and six times spelled in full (*Exodus* 13:3 and 20:8; *Deuteronomy* 24:9 and 25:17; *Joshua* 1:13; and *Lamentations* 3:20). Accordingly, the Baal HaTurim's comment refers to the absent ו of זָכֹר. Moreover, the masoretic note at this word reads ב׳ חַסֵרִים, *Two spelled defectively*, and that note is the probable basis for this comment.

25a. See the Baal HaTurim's comments at *Exodus* 14:24, s.v., וַיָּהָם, and 15:1, s.v., אָשִׁירָה.

26. *Paaneach Raza*.

and all the bad maladies of Egypt that you knew — He will
not put them upon you, but will put them upon all your foes.
16 *You will devour all the peoples that* HASHEM, *your God,*
will deliver to you; your eye shall not pity them; you shall
not worship their gods, for it is a snare for you.
17 *Perhaps you will say in your heart, "These nations are*
more numerous than I; how will I be able to drive them out?"
18 *Do not fear them! You shall remember what* HASHEM,
your God, did to Pharaoh and to all of Egypt. 19 *The great*
tests that your eyes saw, and the signs, the wonders, the
strong hand, and the outstretched arm with which HASHEM,
your God, took you out — so shall HASHEM, *your God, do*
to all the peoples before whom you fear. 20 *Also the*
hornet-swarm will HASHEM, *your God, send among them,*
until the survivors and hidden ones perish before you.

BAAL HATURIM ELUCIDATED

20. אֶת הַצִּרְעָה — THE HORNET-SWARM. The *gematria* of this phrase (771) is equal to that of שְׁתַּיִם הָיוּ, *There were two.*[27]

❑ **עַד אֲבֹד** — UNTIL . . . PERISH. The word אֲבֹד is spelled defectively, without a ו, so that its *gematria* is 7. For God will cause seven nations to perish.[28]

❑ **מִפָּנֶיךָ** — BEFORE YOU. [According to a scribal tradition,] the פ of this word is written [in the Torah scrolls] in the enhanced form known as פ׳ כְּפוּלָה, doubled פ.[29] This indicates [that those nations will perish both] *before you,* and before your agent.[30]

---

27. *Peirush HaRokeach.* The Talmud cites a *baraisa*: The hornet-swarm did not cross the Jordan with the Israelites. [A question is raised:] No? But it is written, *I shall send the hornet-swarm before you and it will drive away the Hivvite, the Canaanite and the Hittite before you* (*Exodus* 23:28) [implying that the hornet-swarm crossed into the Land of Canaan]? Rabbi Shimon ben Lakish explained: The swarm remained on the eastern bank of the Jordan and shot its venom across the river at the Canaanites on the opposite bank; the venom blinded them and made them sterile . . . Rav Papa explained: There were two independent hornet-swarms, one in the days of Moses and one in the days of Joshua; Moses' hornets did not cross the Jordan, Joshua's did (*Sotah* 36a). The Baal HaTurim finds an allusion to Rav Papa's opinion in the *gematria* of הַצִּרְעָה.

28. *Peirush HaRokeach; Paaneach Raza;* see 7:1 above. See also the Baal HaTurim to 6:19 with note 205. There is a double allusion in the Baal HaTurim's comment: The *gematria* of אֲבֹד indicates that seven nations will be driven from the land; while the missing ו (= 6) indicates that six of those seven will be destroyed. For, as the Baal HaTurim mentions above (6:19, see note 205 there), the Girgashite would flee without offering any resistance (*Shoham Yakar*).

29. See note 29 to *parashas Devarim* and the accompanying illustration. *Sefer Tagin* includes the word מִפָּנֶיךָ of our verse on the list of "191 in the Torah whose mouths are on the inside."

30. The Baal HaTurim's שְׁלוּחֲךָ, *your agent,* refers either to the hornet-swarm that יְשַׁלַּח ה׳ . . . בָּם, HASHEM *. . . will send among them,* or to the angel spoken of in the verses (*Exodus* 23:20,23), הִנֵּה אָנֹכִי שֹׁלֵחַ מַלְאָךְ לְפָנֶיךָ, *Behold! I send an angel before you . . .* כִּי יֵלֵךְ מַלְאָכִי לְפָנֶיךָ, *for My angel shall go before you,* וֶהֱבִיאֲךָ אֶל הָאֱמֹרִי וְהַחִתִּי וְהַפְּרִזִּי וְהַכְּנַעֲנִי הַחִוִּי וְהַיְבוּסִי, *and bring you to the Amorite, the Hittite, the Perizzite, the Canaanite, the Hivvite, and the Jebusite,* וְהִכְחַדְתִּיו, *and I will annihilate them* (*Shoham Yakar*).

Alternatively: שְׁלוּחֲךָ, literally, *that which you*

כא לֹא תַעֲרֹץ מִפְּנֵיהֶם כִּי־יהוה אֱלֹהֶיךָ בְּקִרְבֶּךָ אֵל
כב גָּדוֹל וְנוֹרָא: וְנָשַׁל יהוה אֱלֹהֶיךָ אֶת־הַגּוֹיִם הָאֵל
מִפָּנֶיךָ מְעַט מְעָט לֹא תוּכַל כַּלֹּתָם מַהֵר פֶּן־
כג תִּרְבֶּה עָלֶיךָ חַיַּת הַשָּׂדֶה: וּנְתָנָם יהוה אֱלֹהֶיךָ
כד לְפָנֶיךָ וְהָמָם מְהוּמָה גְדֹלָה עַד הִשָּׁמְדָם: וְנָתַן
מַלְכֵיהֶם בְּיָדֶךָ וְהַאֲבַדְתָּ אֶת־שְׁמָם מִתַּחַת
הַשָּׁמָיִם לֹא־יִתְיַצֵּב אִישׁ בְּפָנֶיךָ עַד הִשְׁמִדְךָ אֹתָם:

בעל הטורים

(כא) אֵל גָּדוֹל וְנוֹרָא. וְלֹא אָמַר "גִּבּוֹר". אֶלָּא הִזְכִּיר "גָּדוֹל" כְּנֶגֶד אַבְרָהָם, דִּכְתִיב בֵּהּ "הָאָדָם הַגָּדוֹל". "וְנוֹרָא" כְּנֶגֶד יַעֲקֹב, דִּכְתִיב בֵּהּ "מַה נּוֹרָא הַמָּקוֹם הַזֶּה". וְהִזְכִּיר אֵלּוּ, שֶׁמָּצִינוּ שֶׁנִּלְחֲמוּ – אַבְרָהָם עִם הַמְּלָכִים, וְיַעֲקֹב כְּנֶגֶד לָבָן וְעֵשָׂו. אֲבָל לֹא מָצִינוּ בְּיִצְחָק שֶׁנִּלְחַם:

(כג) וְהָמָם. ב׳ בַּמָּסוֹרֶת – "וְהָמָם מְהוּמָה גְּדֹלָה"; "וְהָמַם גִּלְגַּל עֶגְלָתוֹ וגו׳ ". מְלַמֵּד שֶׁעָשָׂה לָהֶם כְּמוֹ לְמִצְרַיִם, דִּכְתִיב בְּהוּ "וַיָּסַר אֵת אֹפַן מַרְכְּבֹתָיו":

BAAL HATURIM ELUCIDATED

21. אֵל גָּדוֹל וְנוֹרָא — GOD, GREAT AND AWESOME. This verse does not include גִּבּוֹר, *mighty.*[31] Rather, it mentions גָּדוֹל, *great,* corresponding to Abraham, of whom it is written, הָאָדָם הַגָּדוֹל, *the great man*[32] (*Joshua* 14:15); and וְנוֹרָא, corresponding to Jacob, of whom it is written, [*He said,*] מַה נּוֹרָא הַמָּקוֹם הַזֶּה, *"How awesome is this place!"* (*Genesis* 28:17).[33] The verse alludes to these [two], for we find that both were involved in battle: Abraham with the [four] kings[34] and Jacob

have sent, refers to Joshua's letter to the kings of the Canaanite nations. As the Talmud and Midrash teach: Joshua sent three missives to the Land of Israel before he entered the land. [He wrote to them,] "If any nation wishes to leave the land, let it leave. If any nation wishes to come to peace[ful terms with us], let it make peace. If any nation wishes to do battle, let it do battle." [Upon reading Joshua's letter,] the Girgashite nation believed that it was the will of God that they should leave the Land of Canaan; they did so and journeyed to Africa (*Yerushalmi, Sheviis* 6:1; *Vayikra Rabbah* 17:6). Accordingly, the Baal HaTurim's comment means: The doubled פ indicates that the verse should be read repetitively — עַד אֲבֹד, *until there will perish* [literally, *be lost*], six nations מִפָּנֶיךָ, *before you;* and, עַד אֲבֹד, *until there will be lost,* the Girgashite מִפְּנֵי שְׁלוּחֲךָ, *before your missive* (*VeChur LaZahav*).

31. Later, Moses refers to HASHEM as הָאֵל הַגָּדֹל הַגִּבֹּר וְהַנּוֹרָא, *the God, the Great, the Mighty and the Awesome* (10:17 below).

32. According to the Midrash this refers to Abraham (*Bereishis Rabbah* 14:6; see note 33 below).

33. That is, אֵל גָּדוֹל should be understood as, *God of the great one,* i.e., Abraham, who is called הָאָדָם הַגָּדוֹל, *the great man;* and אֵל . . . נוֹרָא should be understood as *God of the one who used the term* נוֹרָא, i.e., Jacob (*VeChur LaZahav*).

Alternatively: גָּדוֹל alludes to Abraham's comprehension of God, thus Abraham is called הָאָדָם הַגָּדוֹל, *the man of the Great One,* a term synonymous with אִישׁ הָאֱלֹהִים, *the man of God* (33:1 below). And נוֹרָא alludes to Jacob's comprehension of God — Who is often referred to as הַמָּקוֹם, *the Omnipresent,* literally, *the place* (see e.g., *Bereishis Rabbah* 68:9; *Yoma* 85b) — thus, Jacob's expression מַה נּוֹרָא הַמָּקוֹם הַזֶּה may be understood as, *How awesome is this Omnipresent One!* (*VeChur LaZahav*).

34. See *Genesis* 14:13-16.

[21] *You shall not be broken before them, for HASHEM, your God is among you; God, great and awesome.*

[22] *HASHEM, your God, will thrust these nations from before you little by little; you will not be able to annihilate them quickly, lest the beasts of the field increase against you.* [23] *HASHEM, your God, will deliver them before you, and He will confound them with great confusion, until their destruction.* [24] *He will deliver their kings into your hand and you shall cause their name to perish from under the heaven; no man will stand up against you until you have destroyed them.* [25] *The*

with Laban[35] and with Esau.[36] However, we do not find that Isaac engaged in battle.[37]

22. {The Baal HaTurim's comment to וְנָשַׁל appears at 7:1 above.}

23. **וְהָמָם — AND HE WILL CONFOUND THEM.** The masoretic note,[38] ב׳, means that this word appears twice in the *Tanach*: (i) here, וְהָמָם מְהוּמָה גְדֹלָה, *He will confound them with great confusion;* and (ii) וְהָמַם גִּלְגַּל עֶגְלָתוֹ וְגוֹ׳, *the wheel of his wagon will break . . .* (*Isaiah* 28:28). The similarity of expression indicates that [in the wars to conquer the Canaanite nations,] God did to them as He did to Egypt [at the Sea of Reeds], about which is written, וַיָּסַר אֵת אֹפַן מַרְכְּבֹתָיו, *He removed the wheel*[39] *of its chariots* (*Exodus* 14:25).[40]

35. Laban had accused Jacob of leading his daughters away like *captives of the sword* (*Genesis* 31:26), which *Rashi* explains as prisoners of war (see also *Rashi* to *Leviticus* 26:25, s.v., נקם ברית), implying that Jacob was engaged in a war with Laban.

36. When Jacob learned that Esau was marching toward him with a band of four hundred armed men, Jacob made three types of preparation: He prepared a tribute; he offered prayer to God; and he girded for war (*Tanchuma Yashan, Vayishlach* 6; cited by *Rashi* to *Genesis* 32:9, s.v., והיה המחנה).

37. *Peirush HaRokeach.*

38. The full note reads: ב׳ אֶחָד קָמֵץ וְאֶחָד פַּתָּח, *Twice; one* vowelized (וְהָמָם), *with a kamatz, and one* (וְהָמַם), *with a patach.* Despite their similar orthography, the two words are not grammatically or etymologically related. Just as we find קָם, *he arose* (34:10 below), from the root קום, *to arise,* so too הָם, *he confounded,* from the root הום [or הים], *to confound.* The pronominal suffix ־ם means *them,* thus, הָמָם, *he confounded them;* and the conversive prefix ־וְ changes the tense from past to future — וְהָמָם, *he will confound them.* The word וְהָמַם, on the other hand, is from the root המם, which is classified among the כְּפוּלִים [verb roots whose second and third letters are the same], and which can mean either *to confound* or *to break, to smash.* Thus, הָמַם, *it broke*; and with the conversive ־וְ prefix, וְהָמַם, *it will break* (see *Radak, Sefer HaShorashim,* הים and המם).

39. The words אוֹפָן and גַּלְגַּל both mean *wheel* (see *Rashi* to *Ezekiel* 10:2).

It is noteworthy that the *gematriaos* of these two words, when spelled בְּמִלּוּאָם, *in their fullness,* are equal. That is, when the letters of אוֹפָן are spelled out — אל״ף ו״ו פ״ה נו״ן — their *gematria* is 314; and when the letters of גַּלְגַּל are spelled out — גימ״ל למ״ד גימ״ל למ״ד — their *gematria* is also 314 (*VeChur LaZahav*).

40. See *Mechilta* 14:25.

כה פְּסִילֵי אֱלֹהֵיהֶם תִּשְׂרְפוּן בָּאֵשׁ לֹא־תַחְמֹד כֶּסֶף
וְזָהָב עֲלֵיהֶם וְלָקַחְתָּ לָךְ פֶּן תִּוָּקֵשׁ בּוֹ כִּי תוֹעֲבַת
כו יהוה אֱלֹהֶיךָ הוּא: וְלֹא־תָבִיא תוֹעֵבָה אֶל־בֵּיתֶךָ
וְהָיִיתָ חֵרֶם כָּמֹהוּ שַׁקֵּץ ׀ תְּשַׁקְּצֶנּוּ וְתַעֵב ׀ תְּתַעֲבֶנּוּ
כִּי־חֵרֶם הוּא:

ח א כָּל־הַמִּצְוָה אֲשֶׁר אָנֹכִי מְצַוְּךָ הַיּוֹם תִּשְׁמְרוּן
לַעֲשׂוֹת לְמַעַן תִּחְיוּן וּרְבִיתֶם וּבָאתֶם וִירִשְׁתֶּם
ב אֶת־הָאָרֶץ אֲשֶׁר־נִשְׁבַּע יהוה לַאֲבֹתֵיכֶם: וְזָכַרְתָּ
אֶת־כָּל־הַדֶּרֶךְ אֲשֶׁר הוֹלִיכְךָ יהוה אֱלֹהֶיךָ זֶה
אַרְבָּעִים שָׁנָה בַּמִּדְבָּר לְמַעַן עַנֹּתְךָ לְנַסֹּתְךָ לָדַעַת

בעל הטורים

(כה) **פְּסִילֵי אֱלֹהֵיהֶם תִּשְׂרְפוּן בָּאֵשׁ.** וּסְמִיךְ לֵהּ ״כִּי חֵרֶם הוּא״. וְלָכֵן דָּן יְהוֹשֻׁעַ אֶת עָכָן, שֶׁעָבַר עַל הַחֵרֶם, בִּשְׂרֵפָה:

(כו) **כִּי חֵרֶם הוּא.** וּסְמִיךְ לֵהּ ״כָּל הַמִּצְוָה״. לוֹמַר שֶׁהָעוֹבֵר עַל הַחֵרֶם כְּעוֹבֵר עַל כָּל הַמִּצְוֹת. וְ״חֵרֶם״ אוֹתִיּוֹת רמ״ח, שֶׁנִּפְרָעִין מֵרמ״ח אֵבָרָיו. וְאִם יַחְזוֹר בִּתְשׁוּבָה יִהְיֶה ״רַחֵם״, וְזֶהוּ ״בְּרֹגֶז רַחֵם תִּזְכּוֹר״:

ח (א) **לַאֲבֹתֵיכֶם.** וּסְמִיךְ לֵהּ ״וְזָכַרְתָּ אֶת כָּל הַדֶּרֶךְ״. לוֹמַר שֶׁתִּזְכֹּר דֶּרֶךְ שֶׁהָלְכוּ בוֹ אֲבוֹתֶיךָ וְתֵלֵךְ בּוֹ גַּם אַתָּה:

BAAL HATURIM ELUCIDATED

25. פְּסִילֵי אֱלֹהֵיהֶם תִּשְׂרְפוּן בָּאֵשׁ — THE CARVED IMAGES OF THEIR GODS YOU SHALL BURN IN THE FIRE. Juxtaposed to this is **כִּי חֵרֶם הוּא**, *for it is banned*[40a] (v. 26). Therefore, Joshua sentenced Achan, who violated the *cheirim* [regarding the booty from Jericho],[41] to burning.[42]

❑ {The Baal HaTurim's other comment to **פְּסִילֵי** appears at *Exodus* 32:19.}

26. כִּי חֵרֶם הוּא — FOR IT IS BANNED. Juxtaposed to this is, כָּל הַמִּצְוָה, *All the*

40a. The word חֵרֶם [*cheirem*] can refer to a ban or a consecration; in either case one may not derive any benefit from the subject of the *cheirem*.

41. See *Joshua* 6:16-19; 7:1; and 7:19-26.

42. Achan's fate is the subject of a dispute among the Sages and the commentators. The Talmud cites one opinion regarding the meaning of the verse, *All of Israel pelted him with stone, and they burned them with fire, and they stoned them with stones* (*Joshua* 7:25): The verse means that what were fit to be burned [i.e., garments and utensils (*Rabbeinu Chananel*; *Rashi*)] were burned; what were fit to be stoned [i.e., Achan and his livestock (*Rashi*)] were stoned (*Sanhedrin* 44a; cited by *Rashi* to *Joshua* 7:25).

A Midrash offers a different opinion: Achan was burned because [he transgressed against the *cheirem* when] he extended his hand to take booty from Jericho (*Tanchuma, Vayeishev* 2).

Another Midrash merges the two views cited above: Achan violated the *cheirem* on the Sabbath, carrying booty from Jericho to his tent . . . Accordingly, he was stoned for desecrating the Sabbath, then burned for transgressing against the *cheirem* (*Bamidbar Rabbah* 23:6; see also *Targum Yonasan ben Uzziel* and *Radak* to *Joshua* 7:25).

carved images of their gods you shall burn in the fire; you shall not covet and take for yourself the silver and gold that is on them, lest you be ensnared by it, for it is an abomination of H*ASHEM*, *your God.* 26 *And you shall not bring an abomination into your home and become banned like it; you shall surely loathe it and you shall surely abominate it, for it is banned.*

8

1 *All the commandments that I command you today you shall observe to perform, so that you may live and increase, and come and possess the land that* H*ASHEM swore to your forefathers.* 2 *You shall remember the entire road on which* H*ASHEM*, *your God, led you these forty years in the wilderness so as to afflict you, to test you, to know*

BAAL HATURIM ELUCIDATED

commandments . . .[42a] (8:1). This indicates that anyone who violates a *cheirem*[42b] is considered as having violated all the commandments.[43,43a]

Moreover, the letters of חֵרֶם, *cheirem,* are the same as רמ״ח, *248* [the number of *eivarim*[44] in the human body], [for if a person violates a *cheirem,*] retribution is visited upon that person's two hundred forty-eight *eivarim.* However, if that person will repent, the word [חֵרֶם] will turn to [the gerundive infinitive] רַחֵם, *being merciful,* as reflected [by the verse,] בְּרֹגֶז רַחֵם תִּזְכּוֹר, *In wrath, remember to be merciful* (*Habakkuk* 3:2).[45]

VIII.

1. לַאֲבֹתֵיכֶם — TO YOUR FOREFATHERS. Juxtaposed to this is, וְזָכַרְתָּ אֶת כָּל הַדֶּרֶךְ, *You shall remember the entire road* (v. 2). This is to indicate that you should remember the path trodden by your forefathers and you, too, should tread that path.

42a. Translation follows *Mizrachi.*

42b. See note 40a above.

43. *Tanchuma, Vayeishev* 2.

43a. See the Baal HaTurim's comment to v. 25. It is noteworthy that the *millui* of עָכָן, i.e., the concealed parts of its letters' names [the name of the letter ע is spelled עַיִ״ן, the concealed part being יִ״ן (=60); the concealed part of כָּ״ף is ף (=80); and that of נו״ן is ו״ן (=56)] has a *gematria* of 196, equal to that of כָּל הַמִּצְוָה. Thus, concealed within Achan was the ability to perform all the *mitzvos,* yet he trespassed on the *cheirem* which was tantamount to trespassing on כָּל הַמִּצְוָה (*VeChur LaZahav*).

44. An *eiver* [plural, *eivarim*] is a body part containing bone, flesh and cords [i.e., sinews, veins, nerves, etc.] (*Chullin* 102b; *Rambam,* commentary to *Zevachim* 3:4; see *Bartenura* to *Ohalos* 1:7). The Mishnah (*Ohalos* 1:8) enumerates the 248 *eivarim* of the human body. For lack of a precise English equivalent, אֵבֶר is often translated organ or limb.

45. See *Moed Katan* 17a. The Talmud there discusses שַׁמְתָּא, a form of חֵרֶם, *ban.* According to one opinion, a ban pronounced against a person is like animal fat smeared on the tiles of an oven [which, once it has been absorbed by the tile, can never be removed fully (*Rashi*)]. A second opinion disagrees: When one is placed under a ban, the ban pervades all two hundred forty-eight *eivarim,* as it is written, וְהָיְתָה הָעִיר חֵרֶם, *the city shall be under a cheirem* (*Joshua* 6:17), and the *gematria* of חֵרֶם is 248. But once the ban is removed, it departs from every one of the two hundred forty-eight *eivarim,* for it is written, בְּרֹגֶז רַחֵם תִּזְכּוֹר, *In wrath, remember to be merciful,* and the *gematria* of רַחֵם is 248.

אֶת־אֲשֶׁ֨ר בִּלְבָבְךָ֜ הֲתִשְׁמֹ֧ר מִצְוֺתָ֛ו אִם־לֹֽא:
ג וַיְעַנְּךָ֮ וַיַּרְעִבֶ֒ךָ֒ וַיַּֽאֲכִֽלְךָ֤ אֶת־הַמָּן֙ אֲשֶׁ֣ר לֹא־
יָדַ֔עְתָּ וְלֹ֥א יָֽדְע֖וּן אֲבֹתֶ֑יךָ לְמַ֣עַן הוֹדִֽיעֲךָ֗ כִּ֠י
לֹ֣א עַל־הַלֶּ֤חֶם לְבַדּוֹ֙ יִֽחְיֶ֣ה הָֽאָדָ֔ם כִּ֛י עַל־כָּל־
ד מוֹצָ֥א פִֽי־יהו֖ה יִֽחְיֶ֣ה הָֽאָדָֽם: שִׂמְלָ֨תְךָ֜ לֹ֤א בָֽלְתָה֙
מֵֽעָלֶ֔יךָ וְרַגְלְךָ֖ לֹ֣א בָצֵ֑קָה זֶ֖ה אַרְבָּעִ֥ים שָׁנָֽה:

――― בעל הטורים ―――

(ג) וַיַּֽאֲכִֽלְךָ אֶת הַמָּן . . . לְמַעַן הֽוֹדִיעֲךָ. מְלַמֵּד שֶׁבַּֽאֲכִילַת הַמָּן נִתַּן לָהֶם דֵּעָה. וְכֵן בְּעֶזְרָא
הוּא אוֹמֵר "וּמַנְּךָ נָתַתָּ לָהֶם לְהַשְׂכִּילָם". וְזֶהוּ, לֹא נִתְּנָה תוֹרָה אֶלָּא לְאֽוֹכְלֵי הַמָּן:

❏ עַל הַלֶּחֶם. ב' – דֵּין "לֹא עַל הַלֶּחֶם לְבַדּוֹ יִֽחְיֶה הָֽאָדָם"; וְאִידָךְ "וְהִקְרַבְתֶּם עַל הַלֶּחֶם".
שֶׁבִּזְכוּת הַקָּרְבָּנוֹת הָעוֹלָם נִזּוֹן:

❏ יִֽחְיֶה הָֽאָדָם. וּסְמִיךְ לֵהּ "שִׂמְלָֽתְךָ לֹא בָֽלְתָה". רֶמֶז לְמַה שֶּׁאָֽמְרוּ, שֶׁעוֹמְדִין בְּלִבוּשֵׁיהֶם,
קַל נָחֹמֶר מֵֽחִטָּה. וְזֶהוּ, כְּשֶׁ"יִֽחְיֶה הָֽאָדָם, שִׂמְלָֽתְךָ לֹא בָֽלְתָה":

(ד) אַרְבָּעִים שָׁנָה. וּסְמִיךְ לֵהּ "וְיָדַעְתָּ עִם לְבָבֶךָ". רֶמֶז, עַד מ' שָׁנָה לֹא קָם אֵֽינָשׁ אַדַּֽעְתָּא

――― BAAL HATURIM ELUCIDATED ―――

3. וַיַּֽאֲכִֽלְךָ אֶת הַמָּן . . . לְמַעַן הֽוֹדִיעֲךָ — THEN HE FED YOU THE MANNA . . . IN ORDER TO
MAKE YOU KNOW. This teaches that by eating manna, they were endowed with
wisdom. Similarly, it is stated in the Book of *Ezra*,[46] וּמַנְּךָ נָתַתָּ לָהֶם לְהַשְׂכִּילָם, *Your*
manna You gave to them in order to make them wise.[47] This is in accordance with

46. According to tradition (*Tanchuma, Ki Sisa* 16, cited by *Rashi* to *Exodus* 31:18; *Zohar* III, 293b), there are twenty-four Books in the *Tanach* (see chart). The common practice of dividing *Samuel, Kings, Ezra-Nehemiah* and *Chronicles* into two parts is of non-Jewish origin. It, as well as chapter and verse numbers, was introduced into *Tanach* by sixteenth-century Christian printers. [Because

Jews were not always permitted to own printing presses, they often had to rely on non-Jewish printers authorized by the church to publish Hebrew books.] Thus, what we incorrectly call the Book of *Nehemiah* the Baal HaTurim refers to as the Book of *Ezra*.

47. This verse fragment is presented here as it appears in all editions of the Baal HaTurim and

Torah – 5 – תורה			
(1) *Genesis*	(א) בְּרֵאשִׁית	(12) *Ezekiel*	(יב) יְחֶזְקֵאל
(2) *Exodus*	(ב) שְׁמוֹת	(13) *The Twelve Prophets*	(יג) תְּרֵי עָשָׂר
(3) *Leviticus*	(ג) וַיִּקְרָא	Writings – 11 – כתובים	
(4) *Numbers*	(ד) בַּמִּדְבָּר	(14) *Psalms*	(יד) תְּהִלִּים
(5) *Deuteronomy*	(ה) דְּבָרִים	(15) *Proverbs*	(טו) מִשְׁלֵי
Prophets – 8 – נביאים		(16) *Job*	(טז) אִיוֹב
(6) *Joshua*	(ו) יְהוֹשֻׁעַ	(17) *Song of Songs*	(יז) שִׁיר הַשִּׁירִים
(7) *Judges*	(ז) שׁוֹפְטִים	(18) *Ruth*	(יח) רוּת
(8) *Samuel (I and II)*	(ח) שְׁמוּאֵל (א' וב')	(19) *Lamentations*	(יט) אֵיכָה
(9) *Kings (I and II)*	(ט) מְלָכִים (א' וב')	(20) *Ecclesiastes*	(כ) קֹהֶלֶת
(10) *Isaiah*	(י) יְשַׁעְיָה	(21) *Esther*	(כא) אֶסְתֵּר
(11) *Jeremiah*	(יא) יִרְמְיָה	(22) *Daniel*	(כב) דָּנִיֵּאל
		(23) *Ezra (and Nechemiah)*	(כג) עֶזְרָא (נְחֶמְיָה)
		(24) *Chronicles (I and II)*	(כד) דִּבְרֵי הַיָּמִים (א' וב')

what is in your heart, whether you would observe His commandments or not. 3 *He afflicted you and let you hunger, then He fed you the manna that you did not know, nor did your forefathers know, in order to make you know that not by bread alone does man live, rather by everything that emanates from the mouth of God does man live.* 4 *Your garment did not wear out upon you and your feet did not swell, these forty years.*

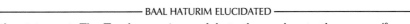

the statement: The Torah was given solely to those who ate the manna.[48]

❑ **עַל הַלֶּחֶם** — BY BREAD. The masoretic note, ב׳, means that this word appears twice in the *Tanach*: (i) here, לֹא עַל הַלֶּחֶם לְבַדּוֹ יִחְיֶה הָאָדָם, *not by bread alone does man live;* and (ii) וְהִקְרַבְתֶּם עַל הַלֶּחֶם, *you shall offer with the bread* (*Leviticus* 23:18).[49] [This indicates] that in the merit of the Altar offerings, the world is granted sustenance.[50]

❑ **יִחְיֶה הָאָדָם** — DOES MAN LIVE. Juxtaposed to this is שִׂמְלָתְךָ לֹא בָלְתָה, *Your garment did not wear out* (v. 4). This is an allusion to our Sages' statement that [the dead who will be brought back to life] are destined to arise in their garments, a concept derived logically by comparison to a kernel of wheat.[51] Thus, the juxtaposed phrases can be understood to mean: When *man comes back to life, your garment will not have been worn out.*[52]

4. {The Baal HaTurim's comment to שִׂמְלָתְךָ לֹא בָלְתָה מֵעָלֶיךָ appears at *Exodus* 3:22.}

❑ **אַרְבָּעִים שָׁנָה** — FORTY YEARS. Juxtaposed to this is וְיָדַעְתָּ עִם לְבָבֶךָ, *you should know in your heart* (v. 5). This is an allusion [to the Talmudic teaching]: A person does not comprehend his master's mind until forty years.[53]

in *Peirush HaRokeach*; however, it is not an exact quote. The actual verse reads: וְרוּחֲךָ הַטּוֹבָה נָתַתָּ לְהַשְׂכִּילָם וּמַנְךָ לֹא מָנַעְתָּ מִפִּיהֶם וּמַיִם נָתַתָּה לָהֶם לִצְמָאָם, *Your good spirit You gave [to them] in order to make them wise, and Your manna You did not withhold from their mouths, and water You gave to them for their thirst* (*Nehemiah* 9:20). It is not clear why the words of the verse are presented out of order.

48. The Midrash states that permission to expound on the Torah was granted solely to those who ate the manna. That is, they were granted the opportunity to delve deeply into the meaning of the words and could thus draw exegetical inferences. This is because those who partook of the manna were not required to labor and toil and devote their time to earning a livelihood. Thus, they were free to spend their time in study (*Mechilta* 16:4; *Tanchuma, Beshalach* 20).

The Baal HaTurim expounds further on this theme in his comments to *Exodus* 16:4 and 25:2; and *Numbers* 11:8 and 19:2.

49. In his comments to that verse, the Baal HaTurim explains the masoretic note in a different manner.

50. *Avos DeRabbi Nassan* 4:4.

51. *Kesubos* 111b; *Sanhedrin* 90b; see also *Bereishis Rabbah* 95:1. The Talmud teaches that the righteous are destined to be resurrected in their garments. We may prove this through a *kal vachomer* [i.e., an *a priori* argument] based upon wheat: If a grain of wheat that is placed naked into the ground emerges with many garments, how much more so the righteous who are buried in garments.

52. *Rimzei Rabbeinu Yoel.*

53. *Avodah Zarah* 5b.

ח/ה־ח ה וְיָדַעְתָּ עִם־לְבָבֶךָ כִּי כַּאֲשֶׁר יְיַסֵּר אִישׁ אֶת־בְּנוֹ יְהוָה
ו אֱלֹהֶיךָ מְיַסְּרֶךָּ׃ וְשָׁמַרְתָּ אֶת־מִצְוֺת יְהוָה אֱלֹהֶיךָ
ז לָלֶכֶת בִּדְרָכָיו וּלְיִרְאָה אֹתוֹ׃ כִּי יְהוָה אֱלֹהֶיךָ
מְבִיאֲךָ אֶל־אֶרֶץ טוֹבָה אֶרֶץ נַחֲלֵי מָיִם עֲיָנֹת
ח וּתְהֹמֹת יֹצְאִים בַּבִּקְעָה וּבָהָר׃ אֶרֶץ חִטָּה וּשְׂעֹרָה

בעל הטורים

דְּרַבֵּהּ. וְכֵן, בֶּן אַרְבָּעִים לַבִּינָה. "וּלְבָבוֹ יָבִין", לְבָבוֹ עוֹלֶה מ'. וְכֵן גַּם כֵּן הַלֵּב בְּאֶמְצַע הַגּוּף, כְּמוֹ הַמֵּ"ם שֶׁהִיא בְּאֶמְצַע הָאַלְפָא {בֵּיתָא}:

(ה) **מְיַסְּרֶךָּ.** תָּגִין עַל מֵ"ם. לוֹמַר שֶׁהַנְּשָׁמָה נוֹצְרָה בְּמ' יוֹם, וְהַתּוֹרָה נִתְּנָה לְמ' יוֹם. וְאִם לֹא תִשְׁמֹר הַתּוֹרָה שֶׁנִּתְּנָה לְמ' יוֹם, מְיַסֶּרְךָ וְנוֹטֵל מִמְּךָ נִשְׁמָתְךָ שֶׁנּוֹצְרָה בְּמ' יוֹם:

(ו) **לָלֶכֶת בִּדְרָכָיו.** בְּגִימַטְרִיָּא לִלְמוֹד תּוֹרָה:

❑ **וּלְיִרְאָה אֹתוֹ.** לָמָּה? "כִּי ה' אֱלֹהֶיךָ מְבִיאֲךָ אֶל אֶרֶץ טוֹבָה", וְלֹא תִהְיֶה כְּפוּי טוֹבָה:

(ח) **אֶרֶץ חִטָּה וּשְׂעֹרָה.** עֶשֶׂר תֵּבוֹת בַּפָּסוּק. לְכָךְ צָרִיךְ לִתֵּן עֶשֶׂר אֶצְבָּעוֹת בַּפַּת בִּשְׁעַת בְּרָכָה:

BAAL HATURIM ELUCIDATED

Similarly, the Mishnaic dictum: A forty-year-old acquires understanding.[54,55]

[In this context, we can also interpret the phrase,] וּלְבָבוֹ יָבִין, *and his heart will understand* (*Isaiah* 6:10): the *gematria* of לְבָבוֹ, *his heart,* is 40.[55a] [There is a] further [similarity] — The heart is in the center of the body, like the מ (= 40), which is in the center {of the alphabet[55b]}.[56]

---

54. *Avos* 5:21.

55. *Peirush HaRokeach.*

55a. Thus, וּלְבָבוֹ יָבִין may be understood as, וּלְבָבוֹ, *and* [*at age*] 40, יָבִין, *he will understand.*

55b. The words enclosed in braces are not found in the early printed editions. They were added to some of the later editions at the suggestion of *Ittur Bikkurim.*

56. A Midrash states: *Where can wisdom be found?* (*Job* 28:12). Rabbi Eliezer says: In the head [or, beginning]. Rabbi Yehoshua says: In the heart [or, center] . . .

The Midrash continues: King Solomon said, "[My father maintains that wisdom is found at the beginning, but I maintain that wisdom is found in the center, therefore,] I shall not do as my father did. My father opened [the book of] his wisdom with the beginning of the alphabet and ended with the center — he opened with the beginning אַשְׁרֵי הָאִישׁ (*Psalms* 1:1) [which begins with א]; he ended with the center [for the last verse begins] כֹּל הַנְּשָׁמָה (*Psalms* 150:6) [and the letters כ״ל are at the center of the *aleph-beis,* ten letters precede them, ten letters follow them (*Zayis Raanan*)]. But I shall not do it that way; rather, I shall open with the center of the alphabet [i.e., *Proverbs* begins with the letter מ of the word מִשְׁלֵי; the *aleph-beis* comprises twenty-two letters, five of which have two forms [e.g., כ and ך] for a total of twenty-seven letters, thirteen before the מ, thirteen after (thus: אבגדהוזחטיכךל מ םנןסעפףצץקרשת)], and I shall conclude with the end of the alphabet [the initial letters of the last twenty-two verses of *Proverbs* (31:10-31) are in the order of the *aleph-beis*; thus, the last verse begins with a ת, the last letter of the alphabet]. I shall open with the center of the alphabet, in the place of wisdom, i.e., in the heart, in the center of man's body. Thus, we find that King David embraced the view of Rabbi Eliezer, while his son King Solomon embraced the view of Rabbi Yehoshua (*Yalkut Shimoni* II, 929).

In the words of the prophet Isaiah, the Baal HaTurim finds an allusion to the view of King Solomon and Rabbi Yehoshua. Thus, וּלְבָבוֹ, *and* [*with the letter*] מ (= 40), יָבִין, *he will understand.*

5 You should know in your heart that just as a father will chastise his son, so HASHEM, your God, chastises you. 6 You shall observe the commandments of HASHEM, your God, to go in His ways and to revere Him. 7 For HASHEM, your God, is bringing you to a good land: a land with streams of water, of springs and underground water coming forth in valley and mountain; 8 a land of wheat, barley,

BAAL HATURIM ELUCIDATED

5. מְיַסְּרֶךָּ — CHASTISES YOU. [According to a scribal tradition,] the מ (= 40) of this word is written with *tagin* [crownlets].[57] This is to indicate [a connection between the soul and the Torah] for the soul is given form forty days [after conception], and the Torah was given [to Moses on Mount Sinai] in forty days. [This implies a warning:] If you do not keep the Torah which was given in forty days, [God] will chastise you and take from you your soul which was given form in forty days.[58]

6. לָלֶכֶת בִּדְרָכָיו — TO GO IN HIS WAYS. The *gematria* of this phrase (722) is equivalent[59] to that of לִלְמוֹד תּוֹרָה, *to study Torah.*[60]

❑ **וּלְיִרְאָה אֹתוֹ** — AND TO REVERE HIM. Why? ... כִּי ה׳ אֱלֹהֶיךָ מְבִיאֲךָ אֶל אֶרֶץ טוֹבָה, *For HASHEM, your God, is bringing you to a good land* ... (vv. 7-10), and you should not be ungrateful.

8. ... אֶרֶץ חִטָּה וּשְׂעֹרָה — A LAND OF WHEAT, BARLEY ... There are ten words in this verse. Therefore all ten fingers should be placed on the loaf when reciting the blessing over bread.[61]

57. Regarding *tagin,* see note 56 to *parashas Devarim.*

Sefer Tagin enumerates thirty-nine words in the Torah in which the letter מ is written with *tagin* — three, according to *Sefer Tagin* (*Paris* ms.) and *Machzor Vitry;* four, according to *Badei HaAron.* See illustration. The word מְיַסְּרֶךָּ of our verse appears on that list.

(a) (b) (c)

(a) Usual מ without *tagin*; (b) מ with three *tagin, Machzor Vitry*; (c) מ with four *tagin, Badei HaAron.*

58. *Menachos* 99b; see the Baal HaTurim to 4:9 above, s.v., וּשְׁמֹר נַפְשְׁךָ.

59. The principle of *im hakollel* allows 721, the *gematria* of the Baal HaTurim's phrase, to be considered equivalent to 722

60. Only through Torah study can one learn how *to go in His ways* (*Yad Aharon;* see also note 14 above).

61. *Peirush HaRokeach.*

The Talmud cites a dispute regarding the wording of the blessing over bread: The Rabbis say, הַמּוֹצִיא, *The One Who brings forth;* a dissenting opinion states that the proper wording is מוֹצִיא, *Who brings forth* [without the definite article prefix ־הַ] ... The *halachah* is in accordance with the Rabbis (*Berachos* 38a-b). Elsewhere, the Talmud explains that the prefix ־הַ serves to prevent the מ of מוֹצִיא from being slurred over or merged with the ם of הָעוֹלָם — thus, הָעוֹלָמוֹצִיא; the additional ־הַ forces the two letters מ to be pronounced distinctly. If so, why do we not emend the phrase לֶחֶם מִן הָאָרֶץ in order to separate the ם of לֶחֶם from the מ of מִן? (*Yerushalmi, Berachos* 6:1). That is, the blessing could have used פַּת, a synonym for לֶחֶם (A.S.). Alternatively, it could have said, הַמּוֹצִיא לֶחֶם הָאָרֶץ, *Who brings forth the earth's bread* (see *Numbers* 15:19), or הַמּוֹצִיא מִן הָאָרֶץ לֶחֶם [לַחְמָהּ], *Who brings forth from the earth [its] bread* (*VeChur LeZahav*).

In extant editions of the *Talmud Yerushalmi,* the question remains unanswered (see *Mareh Panim*). However, *Tosafos* (to *Berachos* 38b, s.v., והלכתא) cites the *Yerushalmi* and continues: The phrase לֶחֶם מִן הָאָרֶץ is taken from a Scriptural verse, מַצְמִיחַ חָצִיר לַבְּהֵמָה וְעֵשֶׂב לַעֲבֹדַת הָאָדָם לְהוֹצִיא לֶחֶם מִן הָאָרֶץ, *He causes grass to grow for the*

ט וְגֶפֶן וּתְאֵנָה וְרִמּוֹן אֶרֶץ־זֵית שֶׁמֶן וּדְבָשׁ: אֶרֶץ אֲשֶׁר
לֹא בְמִסְכֵּנֻת תֹּאכַל־בָּהּ לֶחֶם לֹא־תֶחְסַר כֹּל בָּהּ אֶרֶץ

בעל הטורים

וְעוֹד, כְּנֶגֶד עֶשֶׂר מִצְוֹת שֶׁנַּעֲשׂוּ בַּפַּת – "לֹא תַחֲרֹשׁ"; "לֹא תִזְרַע כִּלְאָיִם"; לֶקֶט; שִׁכְחָה; פֵּאָה; "לֹא תַחְסֹם"; תְּרוּמָה; וּמַעֲשֵׂר רִאשׁוֹן וְשֵׁנִי; וְחַלָּה:

(ט) תֶּחְסַר. ג' – "לֹא תֶחְסַר כֹּל בָּהּ"; "וְצַפַּחַת הַשֶּׁמֶן לֹא תֶחְסָר"; "וּבֶטֶן רְשָׁעִים תֶּחְסָר". אַף עַל פִּי שֶׁזֶּה נֶאֱמַר בָּאָרֶץ, הַצַּדִּיקִים בְּכָל מָקוֹם לֹא תֶחְסַר לָהֶם. שֶׁהֲרֵי אֵלִיָּהוּ הָלַךְ לְצָרְפַת וְשָׁם אָמַר לָהּ "לֹא תֶחְסָר". אֲבָל הָרְשָׁעִים, בְּכָל מָקוֹם תֶּחְסַר לָהֶם:

❑ לֹא תֶחְסַר. תָּגִין עַל הָרֵי"שׁ – לוֹמַר שֶׁהִיא "רֹאשׁ עַפְרוֹת תֵּבֵל":

BAAL HATURIM ELUCIDATED

Additionally: [The ten words] correspond to the ten *mitzvos* observed in the [process of making] bread: (i) . . . לֹא תַחֲרֹשׁ, *You shall not plow* [*with an ox and a donkey together*] (22:10 below); (ii) לֹא תִזְרַע . . . כִּלְאָיִם, *You shall not plant* [*your vineyard*] *with mixed seeds* (22:9 below); the laws regarding (iii) *leket* [gleanings],[62] (iv) *shich'chah* [forgotten sheaves],[63] and (v) *peah* [corner of the field];[62] (vi) לֹא . . . תַחְסֹם, *You shall not muzzle* [*an ox in its threshing*] (25:4 below); and the separation of (vii) *terumah* [the priestly portion of the crops],[64] (viii) the first tithe,[65] (ix) the second tithe,[66] and (x) *challah* [the priestly portion of the dough].[67,68]

❑ {The Baal HaTurim's comment to וְגֶפֶן וּתְאֵנָה appears at *Numbers* 20:5.}

9. תֶּחְסַר — YOU WILL [NOT] LACK. The masoretic note, ג׳, means that this word appears three times in the *Tanach*:[69] (i) here, לֹא תֶחְסַר כֹּל בָּהּ, *you will not lack*

animal, and herbage for the man to cultivate, to bring forth bread from the earth (*Psalms* 104:14). [Therefore we do not tamper with the wording by adding a prefix ־הַ.] *Tosafos* continues: And whereas that verse from *Psalms* contains ten words, it is proper to hold the bread with ten fingers when reciting the blessing.

The Baal HaTurim finds this same allusion in the ten words of our verse. A question may be raised: The verse adduced by *Tosafos* speaks of bread; accordingly, *Tosafos* infers that the count of ten words alludes to bread, thus, it is proper to hold the bread with ten fingers. But the verse adduced by the Baal HaTurim names five fruits and two grains; accordingly, we would expect the Baal HaTurim to use a more inclusive term than בַּפַּת, *in the bread,* one that would include the other species mentioned in the verse.

Elsewhere, the Baal HaTurim states that the blessing over bread contains ten words, corresponding to the ten words in each of four verses (*Psalms* 104:14 and 145:15; *Deuteronomy* 8:8; and *Genesis* 27:28) that speak of God providing food (*Tur, Orach Chaim* 167).

62. See *Leviticus* 19:9, 23:22.

63. See *Deuteronomy* 24:19.

64. See *Numbers* 18:12.

65. See *Numbers* 18:21,24; see also note 74 to 18:1 below.

66. See 14:22-26 below; see also note 74 to 18:1 below.

67. See *Numbers* 15:20.

68. *Yerushalmi, Challah* 1:6. There, *"you shall not muzzle,"* is listed before *leket, shich'chah* and *peah,* and that is how it appears in *Mishnah Berurah* 167:24. Elsewhere, however, the Baal HaTurim omits לֹא תַחְסֹם and inserts the *mitzvah* of *Bikkurim* in its place (*Tur, Orach Chaim* 167), and that is how the list is cited by *Be'er Heitev.* See also *Beis Yosef* and *Perishah.*

69. The full note reads: ג׳ ב׳ קָמָצִין וא׳ פַּתָּח, *Three, two vowelized* (תֶּחְסָר) *with a kamatz and one* (תֶּחְסַר) *with a patach.* The different vowelization does not affect the meaning of the word. Rather, it is a function of the *te'amim* (cantillation notes). In our verse, the *ta'am* under the ס is a *meircha,* a note that opens the way for the reading to flow to the next word, thus the vowel *patach* [from the root פתח, *to open*]. The *te'amim* used in the other two

grape, fig, and pomegranate; a land of oil-olives and date-honey; 9 *a land where you will eat bread without poverty — you will not lack anything in it; a land*

BAAL HATURIM ELUCIDATED

anything in it; (ii) וְצַפַּחַת הַשֶּׁמֶן לֹא תֶחְסָר, *and the flask of oil will not lack* (*I Kings* 17:14); and (iii) וּבֶטֶן רְשָׁעִים תֶּחְסָר, *but the stomach of the wicked will lack* (*Proverbs* 13:25). [This similarity of expressions indicates that] although our verse specifically speaks of "the land" [i.e., *Eretz Yisrael*], nevertheless, [if you are among] the righteous — wherever [you may be] — you will not lack [anything].[70] Thus Elijah went to Zarephath[71] (*I Kings* 17:9-10) and there he told [the widow], "[*the flask of oil*] *will not lack.*" But [if you are among] the wicked — wherever [you may be] — you will lack [everything].

❑ **לֹא תֶחְסַר** — YOU WILL NOT LACK. [According to a scribal tradition,] the ר of תֶּחְסַר is written with *tagin* [crownlets].[72] This is to indicate that [the Land of Israel] is

verses are *esnachta* and *sof passuk,* each of which indicates a pause, like a comma or period. The vowel then changes to a *kamatz* [from the root קמץ, *to close*].

The masoretic note ignores the fact that one of the three words begins with a ת, while the other two begin with a תּ. Again, the meaning of the verse is not affected. Generally, any of the six letters בג״ד כפ״ת takes a *dagesh* at the beginning of a word. Thus, תֶּחְסָר in *Proverbs.* However, when that word is connected by the *te'amim* to the word before it, and that word ends in one of the vowel letters אהו״י, the *dagesh* is dropped, thus, לֹא תֶחְסַר in our verse and in *Kings.*

70. The reading לֹא תֶחְסַר לָהֶם, *they will not lack anything,* follows *Shoham Yakar's* manuscript edition. Many printed editions read לֹא תֶחְסַר לֶחֶם, *bread will not be lacking.* That latter reading seems incorrect, because the parallel phrase regarding the wicked reads תֶּחְסַר לָהֶם in all editions (*VeChur LaZahav*).

71. The early printed editions, as well as *Shoham Yakar's* manuscript edition, read לצרפית, and that reading appears in most later editions. However, that is not the name found in *Kings.* Indeed, there is no mention in Scripture, Talmud or Midrash of a place named צרפית, with a י.

God commanded Elijah to travel צָרְפָתָה, *to* צָרְפַת (*I Kings* 17:9,10); according to *Radak* and others, that צָרְפַת was a city within the boundaries of *Eretz Yisrael.* The name צָרְפַת appears again in *Obadiah* (v. 20), where it is mentioned as one of the lands of the Diaspora, and is usually understood as a reference to France (see *Rashi, Ibn Ezra, Radak*). Now, it is clear that the Baal HaTurim disagrees with *Radak* who places Elijah's צָרְפַת within the Land of Israel, for the Baal HaTurim's comment contrasts בָּאָרֶץ, *in the land,* with הָלַךְ לְצָרְפַת, *he went to Zarephath,* i.e., out of the land. Nevertheless, the Baal HaTurim certainly does not understand Elijah's צָרְפַת as France, for Elijah was sent *to Zarephath that is at Sidon* (v. 9), and the city of Sidon was located on the boundary of *Eretz Yisrael* (see *Genesis* 10:19). If so, the Baal HaTurim and *Radak* agree regarding the general location of Zarephath; but they disagree regarding the boundary of *Eretz Yisrael.* According to *Radak,* Zarephath was south of Sidon and within the boundaries of the land. According to the Baal HaTurim, Zarephath was north of Sidon, outside the boundary (*VeChur LaZahav*).

72. Regarding *tagin,* see note 56 to *parashas Devarim.*

Sefer Tagin states that there are 150 instances in the Torah of a ר with two *tagin.* Although the word תֶּחְסַר of our verse does not appear on that list, it must be noted that that list is incomplete [containing less than 150 entries] in both the Paris edition and in the version included in *Machzor Vitry.*

ר with two *tagin* | Usual ר according to *SeferTagin* | Usual ר according to *Peri Eitz Chaim*

ח/י אֲשֶׁר אֲבָנֶיהָ בַרְזֶל וּמֵהֲרָרֶיהָ תַּחְצֹב נְחֹשֶׁת:
י וְאָכַלְתָּ וְשָׂבָעְתָּ וּבֵרַכְתָּ אֶת־יהוה אֱלֹהֶיךָ עַל־

בעל הטורים

(י) **וְאָכַלְתָּ {וְשָׂבָעְתָּ} וּבֵרַכְתָּ.** הַיְנוּ בִּרְכַּת הַמָּזוֹן. וְכֵן נַמִּי צָרִיךְ לְבָרֵךְ לְפָנָיו. פֵּרוּשׁ, "וְאָכַלְתָּ וְשָׂבָעְתָּ, וּבֵרַכְתָּ" כְּבָר. שֶׁאָסוּר {לְאָדָם} לֵהָנוֹת מִן הָעוֹלָם הַזֶּה בְּלֹא בְרָכָה, שֶׁנֶּאֱמַר, "לַה' הָאָרֶץ וּמְלוֹאָהּ". אֲבָל לְאַחַר שֶׁבֵּרַךְ הוּא אוֹכֵל מִשֶּׁלּוֹ, שֶׁנֶּאֱמַר, "וְהָאָרֶץ נָתַן לִבְנֵי אָדָם". וְזֶהוּ "אָמַרְתְּ לַה' אֲדֹנָי אָתָּה טוֹבָתִי בַּל עָלֶיךָ", שֶׁכֵּיוָן שֶׁהוֹדֵיתִי לַה' אֵין הַטּוֹבָה מִשֶּׁלְּךָ:

❑ **וְאָכַלְתָּ.** בְּגִימַטְרִיָּא זֶהוּ בִּכְזַיִת:

❑ **וְאָכַלְתָּ וְשָׂבָעְתָּ.** וּסְמִיךְ לֵהּ "פֶּן תִּשְׁכַּח". שֶׁצָּרִיךְ לְהַזְכִּיר יוֹם הַמִּיתָה בְּבִרְכַּת הַמָּזוֹן. וּלְכָךְ תִּקְּנוּ הַטּוֹב וְהַמֵּטִיב, עַל הֲרוּגֵי בֵיתָר שֶׁנִּתְּנוּ לִקְבוּרָה:

BAAL HATURIM ELUCIDATED

the subject of the verse, וְרֹאשׁ עַפְרוֹת תֵּבֵל, *and the first dusts of the world*[73] (*Proverbs* 8:26).[74]

10. וְאָכַלְתָּ {וְשָׂבָעְתָּ} וּבֵרַכְתָּ — YOU[75] WILL EAT {AND YOU WILL BE SATIATED}[76] AND YOU WILL BLESS. This refers to Grace after Meals.[77] We must also recite a blessing before eating.[78] [In that vein,] the verse can be interpreted: You will eat and you will be satisfied, and you will have already blessed. For it is forbidden {for a person} to benefit from this world without [reciting] a blessing, as indicated by the verse, לַה' הָאָרֶץ וּמְלוֹאָהּ, *The earth and its fullness belong to HASHEM* (*Psalms* 24:1). However, after one has recited a blessing, one eats of one's own, as it is stated, וְהָאָרֶץ נָתַן לִבְנֵי אָדָם, *but He has given the earth to mankind* (*Psalms* 115:16).[79] This is

73. That verse reads in full: עַד לֹא עָשָׂה אֶרֶץ וְחוּצוֹת וְרֹאשׁ עַפְרוֹת תֵּבֵל, *When He had not yet made earth and outer areas and the first dusts of the world.* The Midrash expounds on that verse: אֶרֶץ, *earth,* refers to all the other lands [i.e., other than the Land of Israel]; וְחוּצוֹת, *and outer areas,* refers to [inhospitable] wilderness areas; וְרֹאשׁ עַפְרוֹת תֵּבֵל, *and the first dusts of the [habitable] world,* refers to the Land of Israel (*Sifrei* 37 to 11:10 below).

74. The name of the letter ר is רֵישׁ, the Aramaic equivalent of the Hebrew word רֹאשׁ, *head* or *first.* Thus, the *tagin* on the ר of לֹא תֶחְסַר indicate that the phrase refers to the land described as רֵישׁ or רֹאשׁ, namely, *Eretz Yisrael,* which is called רֹאשׁ עַפְרוֹת תֵּבֵל (*VeChur LaZahav*). This is in accordance with the opinion that God created the world from a central point — the site of the *Beis HaMikdash* — from which it expanded until He said to it, "דַּי, *Enough!*" (*Yoma* 54b). Thus, *Eretz Yisrael* (specifically, the Temple Mount in Jerusalem) is literally *the first dusts of the world.*

Alternatively: רֹאשׁ עַפְרוֹת תֵּבֵל means *the highest* [from רֹאשׁ, *head,* the highest part of the human body] *dusts of the world,* another reference to *Eretz Yisrael,* which the Talmud (*Kiddushin* 69a; *Sanhedrin* 87a) describes as the highest of all lands (*VeChur LaZahav*).

75. The comment beginning וְאָכַלְתָּ וְשָׂבָעְתָּ that appears at this point in virtually all the later printed editions is presented below as the third comment to this verse. See note 82 below for the reason.

76. Inexplicably, the word וְשָׂבָעְתָּ has been omitted from virtually all editions of the Baal HaTurim. However, it does appear in *Shoham Yakar's* manuscript edition.

77. *Berachos* 48b.

78. The obligation to recite a blessing after eating to satiation is of Scriptural origin. However, the concept of reciting a blessing before eating is a Rabbinic injunction based upon Scriptural verses, as the Baal HaTurim explains further on in this comment. (See *Berachos* 35a, with *Tosafos,* s.v., לפניו לכ"ש; *Rambam, Hilchos Berachos* 1:1-2.)

79. *Berachos* 35a — *Psalms* 24:1 speaks to a person who has not yet recited a blessing, "Beware, you may not eat, because *the earth and its fullness belong to HASHEM*"; but 115:16 speaks to one who has recited the proper blessing, "You may eat, because *He has given the earth to mankind.*"

whose stones are iron and from whose mountains you will mine copper. 10 *You will eat and you will be satiated and you shall bless* H*ASHEM*, *your God, for the*

BAAL HATURIM ELUCIDATED

[also the implication of the verse], אָמַרְתְּ לַה׳ אֲדֹנָי אָתָּה טוֹבָתִי בַּל עָלֶיךָ, *You have said to* H*ASHEM*, *"You are my Lord, I have no claim to Your benefit"* (*Psalms* 16:2).[79a] Thus, once I have acknowledged [You] HASHEM [as my Lord], the benefit no longer comes from You [for You have granted it to me].[80]

❑ וְאָכַלְתָּ — YOU WILL EAT. The *gematria* of this word (457) is equal to that of זֶהוּ בִּכְזַיִת, *This refers to an olive-sized portion.*[81]

❑ וְאָכַלְתָּ וְשָׂבָעְתָּ . . . — YOU[82] WILL EAT AND YOU WILL BE SATIATED [AND YOU SHALL BLESS] Juxtaposed to this is the passage (vv. 11-20) beginning, [*Guard yourself*] פֶּן תִּשְׁכַּח, *lest you forget . . .* [The juxtaposition indicates] that it is necessary to recall the day of death within the text of Grace after Meals.[83] For this reason the Sages established the blessing . . . הַטּוֹב וְהַמֵּטִיב, *He is good and does good . . .* [the fourth blessing of Grace after Meals which was composed] to recall the martyrs of Beitar who were [ultimately] brought to burial.[84]

❑ {The Baal HaTurim's comment to וּבֵרַכְתָּ אֶת ה׳ appears at *Genesis* 14:19.}

79a. The translation of this verse follows *Rashi;* the Baal HaTurim's allusion is explained in note 80.

80. *Yerushalmi, Berachos* 6:1 — The Talmud there states that the verse, *the earth and its fullness belong to* H*ASHEM*, teaches that one who takes benefit from the world has trespassed on that which is holy, unless he has first redeemed the object from which he benefits by performing a *mitzvah* . . . and what is the nature of that redemption? It is [the recitation of] a blessing . . . As it is stated: *You have said* [*a blessing*] *to* H*ASHEM*, *"You are my Lord,"* [*and He has responded,*] *"That from which you benefit is not Mine* [*rather, it belongs to you*]." That is, if you have eaten after having recited a blessing, it is considered as if you have eaten of your own for you have purchased it with your blessing (*Peirush MiBaal Sefer Chareidim*)].

81. See *Berachos* 41a-b, where the Talmud explains the verse, *a land of wheat and barley . . . a land of oil-olives and date-honey* (v. 8 above), as a sort of table of the volume measures required for the fulfillment of positive *mitzvos* [e.g., the amount of matzah one must eat at the Pesach *seder*] or for the transgression of negative *mitzvos* [e.g., the amount one must eat before being subject to punishment for the violation of Yom Kippur]. The term אֶרֶץ זֵית שֶׁמֶן, *a land of oil-olives,* is explained there as, "a land in which the majority of its [halachic] measurements involve [the volume of] an olive." *Rashi* offers four examples, all Scripturally proscribed foods — *cheilev* [certain animal fats]; animal blood; *nosar* [sacrificial meat that has not been consumed within its specified time]; and *piggul* [an offering rendered invalid by means of an improper intent on the part of the one performing the service]. Thus, the Baal HaTurim finds an allusion in the word וְאָכַלְתָּ of our verse, that "eating" implies an olive-sized portion.

82. In the early printed editions, the Baal HaTurim's six comments to verses 9-12 appear in a seemingly haphazard order: (i-ii) וְאָכַלְתָּ . . . וּבֵרַכְתָּ and וְאָכַלְתָּ בְּגִימַטְרִיָּא — v. 10; (iii) תֶּחְסַר — v. 9; (iv) וּבָתִּים — v. 12; (v) לֹא תֶחְסַר — v. 9; and (vi) וְאָכַלְתָּ וְשָׂבָעְתָּ — v. 10. Although virtually all later editions have rearranged the order of the comments, with וְאָכַלְתָּ וְשָׂבָעְתָּ appearing as the first, we have presented it third, because its matter-of-fact reference to וּבֵרַכְתָּ as Grace after Meals indicates that it follows the comment, s.v., וְאָכַלְתָּ . . . וּבֵרַכְתָּ.

83. Those verses (11-20) speak of the sequence of dangers that are apt to follow on the heels of satiation, leading to the dire warning, כִּי אָבֹד תֹּאבֵדוּן, *for you will surely perish* (v. 19); thus, they allude to the day of death.

84. *Berachos* 48b — The fourth blessing, הַטּוֹב וְהַמֵּטִיב, was composed by the Sages in Yavneh on account of the martyrs of Beitar, on the day that their bodies were afforded burial.

This Talmudic teaching refers to the hundreds of thousands of inhabitants of Beitar — the

ח/יא־טו שני יא הָאָ֫רֶץ הַטֹּבָ֖ה אֲשֶׁ֥ר נָֽתַן־לָֽךְ׃ הִשָּׁ֣מֶר לְךָ֔ פֶּן־תִּשְׁכַּ֖ח
אֶת־יְהוָ֣ה אֱלֹהֶ֑יךָ לְבִלְתִּ֨י שְׁמֹ֤ר מִצְוֺתָיו֙ וּמִשְׁפָּטָ֣יו
יב וְחֻקֹּתָ֔יו אֲשֶׁ֛ר אָנֹכִ֥י מְצַוְּךָ֖ הַיּֽוֹם׃ פֶּן־תֹּאכַ֖ל וְשָׂבָ֑עְתָּ
יג וּבָתִּ֥ים טֹבִ֛ים תִּבְנֶ֖ה וְיָשָֽׁבְתָּ׃ וּבְקָֽרְךָ֤ וְצֹֽאנְךָ֙
יִרְבְּיֻ֔ן וְכֶ֥סֶף וְזָהָ֖ב יִרְבֶּה־לָּ֑ךְ וְכֹ֥ל אֲשֶׁר־לְךָ֖ יִרְבֶּֽה׃
יד וְרָ֖ם לְבָבֶ֑ךָ וְשָֽׁכַחְתָּ֙ אֶת־יְהוָ֣ה אֱלֹהֶ֔יךָ הַמּוֹצִֽיאֲךָ֛
טו מֵאֶ֥רֶץ מִצְרַ֖יִם מִבֵּ֥ית עֲבָדִֽים׃ הַמּוֹלִ֨יכְךָ֜ בַּמִּדְבָּ֣ר ׀
הַגָּדֹ֣ל וְהַנּוֹרָ֗א נָחָ֤שׁ ׀ שָׂרָף֙ וְעַקְרָ֔ב וְצִמָּא֖וֹן

בעל הטורים

(יב) ובתים. ד׳ בַּמָּסוֹרֶת — ״וּבָתִּים טֹבִים תִּבְנֶה״; ״וּבָתִּים מְלֵאִים כָּל טוּב״; ״וְחָמְדוּ שָׂדוֹת וְגָזָלוּ וּבָתִּים וְנָשָׂאוּ״; ״וּבָתִּים מֵאֵין אָדָם״. אִם תִּשְׁמֹר מִצְוֹתָיו, תִּמְצָא ״בָּתִּים מְלֵאִים כָּל טוּב״, ״וּבָתִּים טֹבִים תִּבְנֶה״. אֲבָל אִם רָם לְבָבְךָ וְתִגְזֹל שָׂדוֹת וּבָתִּים, אָז ״וּבָתִּים מֵאֵין אָדָם״:

(יג) ובקרך וצאנך ירבין וכסף וזהב. סָמַךְ כֶּסֶף וְזָהָב לְצֹאן, לוֹמַר לְךָ, הָרוֹצֶה שֶׁיַּעֲשִׁיר יַעֲסֹק בִּבְהֵמָה דַקָּה. וּמִכָּל מָקוֹם כְּתִיב ״יִרְבְּיֻן״ חָסֵר וָי״ו, לוֹמַר שֶׁאִם מַרְעֶה בִּשְׂדוֹת אֲחֵרִים, נְכָסָיו מִתְמוֹטְטִין:

(טו) נחש שרף ועקרב וצמאון. בְּגִימַטְרִיָּא בְּכַשְׂדִּים, בְּפָרַס, בְּמָקֵדוֹן וּבְשֵׂעִיר:

BAAL HATURIM ELUCIDATED

❑ {The Baal HaTurim's comment to עַל הָאָרֶץ appears at 11:21 below.}

12. וּבָתִּים — AND HOUSES. The masoretic note, ד׳, means that this word appears four times in the *Tanach*: (i) here, וּבָתִּים טֹבִים תִּבְנֶה, *and you will build good houses;* (ii) וּבָתִּים מְלֵאִים כָּל טוּב, *and houses filled with every good thing* (6:11 below); (iii) וְחָמְדוּ שָׂדוֹת וְגָזָלוּ וּבָתִּים וְנָשָׂאוּ, *They coveted fields* [*which*] *they seized, and houses,* [*which*] *they took away* (*Micah* 2:2); and (iv) וּבָתִּים מֵאֵין אָדָם, *and houses without a man* (*Isaiah* 6:11). [The similarity of expression implies:] If you will observe His *mitzvos,* you will find *houses filled with every good thing,*[85] and *you will build*

stronghold of the unsuccessful and ill-fated Bar Kochba revolution — who were slaughtered by Hadrian's Roman legions. For many years, the Roman conquerors would not allow their corpses to be brought to burial. Finally, Rabban Gamliel was able to bribe the Roman officials, who allowed the martyrs' remains to be buried. When the Jews came into Beitar to perform the burials, they discovered that the dead bodies had remained intact and fresh, despite the many years that had passed since they had been massacred (see *Abudraham, Hilchos Berachos*).

85. According to *Shoham Yakar,* the Baal HaTurim refers to the Midrash that describes the reaction of the inhabitants of Canaan when they realized that the Israelites would be coming into their land. To prevent Israel from taking their wealth, the Canaanites and Amorites sought hiding places where they could secrete their possessions. God said, "I have promised Israel *houses filled with every good thing.* If the Canaanites hide everything in the fields and caves, My promise will not be fulfilled." So He placed the thought into the minds of the inhabitants and they cemented their valuables into the walls of their houses. Once the Israelites had taken possession of the land, God caused *tzaraas* to appear on the walls where these treasures were hidden. That was a blessing, not an affliction, for by removing and replacing the building stones, the home owner would discover a store of hidden treasure (*Vayikra Rabbah* 14:6, cited by *Rashi* to *Leviticus* 14:34).

good land that He gave you.

[11] *Guard yourself, lest you forget* HASHEM, *your God, by not observing His commandments, His ordinances, and His decrees, which I command you today,* [12] *lest you will eat and will be satiated, and you will build good houses and settle,* [13] *and your cattle and your flocks will increase, and silver and gold will increase for you, and everything that you have will increase —* [14] *and your heart will become haughty and you will forget* HASHEM, *your God, Who took you out of the land of Egypt from the house of slavery,* [15] *Who leads you through the great and awesome wilderness — of snake, fiery serpent, and scorpion, and thirst*

BAAL HATURIM ELUCIDATED

good houses. But if your heart becomes haughty, and you will steal fields and houses, then the *houses* [*will be*] *without a man.*[85a]

13. וּבְקָרְךָ וְצֹאנְךָ יִרְבְּיֻן וְכֶסֶף וְזָהָב — AND YOUR CATTLE AND YOUR FLOCKS WILL INCREASE, AND SILVER AND GOLD. Scripture juxtaposed silver and gold with flocks[86] to indicate to you [that] a person who desires to become wealthy should raise small livestock.[87] Nevertheless, the word יִרְבְּיֻן, *they will increase,* is spelled defectively, without a ו, to imply that if a person grazes his flocks in fields belonging to others,[87a] his wealth will founder.[88]

15. נָחָשׁ שָׂרָף וְעַקְרָב וְצִמָּאוֹן — SNAKE, FIERY SERPENT, AND SCORPION, AND THIRST. The *gematria* of this phrase (1509) is equivalent[89] to that of, בְּכַשְׂדִּים בְּפָרַס בְּמַקֵּדוֹן וּבְשֵׂעִיר, *With the Chaldeans* [i.e., the Babylonians], *with Persia, with Macedonia* [i.e., Greece], *and with Seir* [Rome, i.e., Edom].[89a,90]

85a. Measure for measure: If you seize houses illegally, you will be left with nobody to dwell in them: An allusion to this concept may be found in the *gematria* of גְּזֵלָה, *stolen property* — 45, which is equal to that of אָדָם, man. Thus, if there will be גְּזֵלָה, there will not be any אָדָם *(VeChur LaZahav).*

86. The term צֹאן, *flocks,* refers to sheep and goats, which the Talmud calls בְּהֵמָה דַקָּה, *small livestock,* as opposed to בָּקָר, *cattle,* i.e., oxen, which the Talmud calls בְּהֵמָה גַסָּה, *large livestock.*

87. *Chullin* 84b.

87a. Most later editions follow the early printed editions which read, בְּשָׂדוֹת אֲחֵרוֹת, *in other fields.* However, that reading seems stilted — fields other than what or which? The text follows the few later editions that have emended the comment to בְּשָׂדוֹת אֲחֵרִים, *in the fields of others.*

88. Two passages in the Talmud seem to contradict one another. One is cited by the Baal HaTurim: A person who desires to become wealthy should raise small livestock. The other states: . . . and those who raise small livestock . . . will never see a sign of blessing (*Pesachim* 50b).

Rabbeinu Tam (cited in *Tosafos* to *Pesachim* and *Chullin*) explains that one passage refers to small livestock raised in a settled area, where the jealousy of others may bring an עַיִן הָרָע, *evil eye,* upon the flock, while the other refers to livestock raised on the range, where they do not attract attention.

The Baal HaTurim reconciles the two passages in another manner: One speaks of livestock grazed either on the owner's private fields or on public pastureland, while the other refers to flocks left to graze on the private property of others (*Shoham Yakar*).

89. The principle of *im hakollel* allows 1508, the *gematria* of the Baal HaTurim's phrase, to be considered equivalent to 1509.

89a. The Baal HaTurim refers to the four exiles (see note 83 to *parashas Va'eschanan*).

90. *Peirush HaRokeach;* see *Midrash Tehillim*

אֲשֶׁר אֵין־מָיִם הַמּוֹצִיא לְךָ מַיִם מִצּוּר הַחַלָּמִישׁ:
*ב׳ טעמים טז *הַמַּאֲכִלְךָ מָן בַּמִּדְבָּר אֲשֶׁר לֹא־יָדְעוּן אֲבֹתֶיךָ
לְמַעַן עַנֹּתְךָ וּלְמַעַן נַסֹּתֶךָ לְהֵיטִבְךָ בְּאַחֲרִיתֶךָ:
יז וְאָמַרְתָּ בִּלְבָבֶךָ כֹּחִי וְעֹצֶם יָדִי עָשָׂה לִי אֶת־הַחַיִל
יח הַזֶּה: וְזָכַרְתָּ אֶת־יהוה אֱלֹהֶיךָ כִּי הוּא הַנֹּתֵן לְךָ כֹּחַ
לַעֲשׂוֹת חָיִל לְמַעַן הָקִים אֶת־בְּרִיתוֹ אֲשֶׁר־נִשְׁבַּע
לַאֲבֹתֶיךָ כַּיּוֹם הַזֶּה:
יט וְהָיָה אִם־שָׁכֹחַ תִּשְׁכַּח אֶת־יהוה אֱלֹהֶיךָ וְהָלַכְתָּ
אַחֲרֵי אֱלֹהִים אֲחֵרִים וַעֲבַדְתָּם וְהִשְׁתַּחֲוִיתָ לָהֶם
כ הַעִדֹתִי בָכֶם הַיּוֹם כִּי אָבֹד תֹּאבֵדוּן: כַּגּוֹיִם אֲשֶׁר
יהוה מַאֲבִיד מִפְּנֵיכֶם כֵּן תֹּאבֵדוּן עֵקֶב לֹא תִשְׁמְעוּן
בְּקוֹל יהוה אֱלֹהֵיכֶם:
ט א שְׁמַע יִשְׂרָאֵל אַתָּה עֹבֵר הַיּוֹם אֶת־הַיַּרְדֵּן לָבֹא
לָרֶשֶׁת גּוֹיִם גְּדֹלִים וַעֲצֻמִים מִמֶּךָּ עָרִים גְּדֹלֹת
ב וּבְצֻרֹת בַּשָּׁמָיִם: עַם־גָּדוֹל וָרָם בְּנֵי עֲנָקִים אֲשֶׁר
אַתָּה יָדַעְתָּ וְאַתָּה שָׁמַעְתָּ מִי יִתְיַצֵּב לִפְנֵי בְּנֵי עֲנָק:
ג וְיָדַעְתָּ הַיּוֹם כִּי יהוה אֱלֹהֶיךָ הוּא־הָעֹבֵר לְפָנֶיךָ אֵשׁ
אֹכְלָה הוּא יַשְׁמִידֵם וְהוּא יַכְנִיעֵם לְפָנֶיךָ וְהוֹרַשְׁתָּם
שלישי ד וְהַאֲבַדְתָּם מַהֵר כַּאֲשֶׁר דִּבֶּר יהוה לָךְ: אַל־תֹּאמַר
בִּלְבָבְךָ בַּהֲדֹף יהוה אֱלֹהֶיךָ אֹתָם | מִלְּפָנֶיךָ לֵאמֹר

בעל הטורים

(כ) כַּגּוֹיִם. ג׳ — "כַּגּוֹיִם אֲשֶׁר ה׳ מַאֲבִיד"; "נִהְיֶה כַגּוֹיִם"; "וַיְקַטְּרוּ שָׁם {בְּכָל בָּמוֹת} כַּגּוֹיִם". מִדָּה כְּנֶגֶד מִדָּה, בִּשְׁבִיל "וַיְקַטְּרוּ שָׁם . . . כַּגּוֹיִם" וְאָמְרוּ אִם לֹא "נִהְיֶה כַגּוֹיִם", עַל כֵּן "כַּגּוֹיִם אֲשֶׁר ה׳ מַאֲבִיד מִפְּנֵיכֶם כֵּן תֹּאבֵדוּן":

BAAL HATURIM ELUCIDATED

❑ {The Baal HaTurim cites this verse in his comments to *Genesis* 37:24, s.v., רֵק.}

18. {The Baal HaTurim cites this verse in his comments to *Numbers* 27:16, s.v., יִפְקֹד.}

20. כַּגּוֹיִם — LIKE THE NATIONS. The masoretic note, ג׳, means that this word

(*Shocher Tov*) to 63:2 — נָחָשׁ refers to Babylonia; שָׂרָף to Medea [i.e., Persia and Medea]; עַקְרָב to Greece; and וְצִמָּאוֹן to Edom [i.e., Rome].

where there was no water — Who brings forth water for you from the rock of flint, ¹⁶ *Who feeds you manna in the wilderness, which your forefathers knew not, in order to afflict you and in order to test you, to do good for you in your end.* ¹⁷ *And you may say in your heart, "My strength and the might of my hand made me all this wealth!"* ¹⁸ *Then you shall remember* H*ASHEM, your God: that it is He Who gives you strength to make wealth, in order to establish His covenant that He swore to your forefathers, as this day.*

¹⁹ *It shall be that if you forget* H*ASHEM, your God, and go after other gods, and worship them and prostrate yourself to them — I testify against you today that you will surely perish,* ²⁰ *like the nations that* H*ASHEM causes to perish before you, so will you perish because you will not have hearkened to the voice of* H*ASHEM, your God.*

9

¹ *Hear, O Israel, today you cross the Jordan, to come and drive out nations that are greater and mightier than you, cities great and fortified to the heavens,* ² *a great and lofty people, children of giants, that you knew and of whom you have heard, "Who can stand up against the children of the giant?"* ³ *But you know today that* H*ASHEM, your God — He crosses before you, a consuming fire; He will destroy them and He will subjugate them before you; you will drive them out and cause them to perish quickly, as* H*ASHEM spoke to you.*

⁴ *Do not say in your heart, when* H*ASHEM pushes them away from before you, saying, "Because of my*

───────── BAAL HATURIM ELUCIDATED ─────────

appears three times in the *Tanach*: (i) here, כַּגּוֹיִם אֲשֶׁר ה' מַאֲבִיד, *like the nations that* H*ASHEM causes to perish;* (ii) נִהְיֶה כַגּוֹיִם, *we shall be like the nations* (*Ezekiel* 20:32); and (iii) וַיְקַטְּרוּ שָׁם {בְּכָל בָּמוֹת} כַּגּוֹיִם, *They burned incense there* {*at all their high places,*} *like the nations* (*II Kings* 17:11). [The similarity of expression reflects the principle of] measure for measure. Because *they burned incense there . . . like the nations,* and they said, "Is it not [proper that] *we shall be like the nations?*" Therefore [they will be subject to the threat], *like the nations that* H*ASHEM causes to perish before you, so will you perish.*

IX.

1. {The Baal HaTurim's comment to עָרִים גְּדֹלֹת וּבְצֻרֹת בַּשָּׁמָיִם appears at 3:5 above.}

בְצִדְקָתִי הֱבִיאַנִי יְהוָה לָרֶשֶׁת אֶת־הָאָרֶץ הַזֹּאת
ה וּבְרִשְׁעַת הַגּוֹיִם הָאֵלֶּה יְהוָה מוֹרִישָׁם מִפָּנֶיךָ׃ לֹא
בְצִדְקָתְךָ וּבְיֹשֶׁר לְבָבְךָ אַתָּה בָא לָרֶשֶׁת אֶת־
אַרְצָם כִּי בְּרִשְׁעַת ׀ הַגּוֹיִם הָאֵלֶּה יְהוָה אֱלֹהֶיךָ
מוֹרִישָׁם מִפָּנֶיךָ וּלְמַעַן הָקִים אֶת־הַדָּבָר אֲשֶׁר
נִשְׁבַּע יְהוָה לַאֲבֹתֶיךָ לְאַבְרָהָם לְיִצְחָק וּלְיַעֲקֹב׃
ו וְיָדַעְתָּ כִּי לֹא בְצִדְקָתְךָ יְהוָה אֱלֹהֶיךָ נֹתֵן לְךָ
אֶת־הָאָרֶץ הַטּוֹבָה הַזֹּאת לְרִשְׁתָּהּ כִּי עַם־קְשֵׁה־
ז עֹרֶף אָתָּה׃ זְכֹר אַל־תִּשְׁכַּח אֵת אֲשֶׁר־הִקְצַפְתָּ
אֶת־יְהוָה אֱלֹהֶיךָ בַּמִּדְבָּר לְמִן־הַיּוֹם אֲשֶׁר־
יָצָאתָ ׀ מֵאֶרֶץ מִצְרַיִם עַד־בֹּאֲכֶם עַד־הַמָּקוֹם הַזֶּה
ח מַמְרִים הֱיִיתֶם עִם־יְהוָה׃ וּבְחֹרֵב הִקְצַפְתֶּם אֶת־
ט יְהוָה וַיִּתְאַנַּף יְהוָה בָּכֶם לְהַשְׁמִיד אֶתְכֶם׃ בַּעֲלֹתִי
הָהָרָה לָקַחַת לוּחֹת הָאֲבָנִים לוּחֹת הַבְּרִית
אֲשֶׁר־כָּרַת יְהוָה עִמָּכֶם וָאֵשֵׁב בָּהָר אַרְבָּעִים יוֹם

בעל הטורים

ט (ד) הֱבִיאַנִי. ד׳ בַּמָּסוֹרֶת – ״הֱבִיאַנִי ה׳ לָרֶשֶׁת״; ״בְּמַרְאוֹת אֱלֹהִים הֱבִיאַנִי אֶל אֶרֶץ יִשְׂרָאֵל״; ״הֱבִיאַנִי אֶל בֵּית הַיָּיִן״; ״הֱבִיאַנִי הַמֶּלֶךְ חֲדָרָיו״. זֶהוּ שֶׁדָּרְשׁוּ חֲכָמֵינוּ ז״ל, רָאֲתָה שִׁפְחָה עַל הַיָּם מַה שֶּׁלֹּא רָאָה יְחֶזְקֵאל. וְזֶהוּ, ״בְּמַרְאוֹת אֱלֹהִים הֱבִיאַנִי״, שֶׁכֻּלָּם הָיוּ נְבִיאִים וְזָכוּ לְמַרְאֵה {אֱלֹהִים}. וְכֵן בְּמַתַּן תּוֹרָה ״הֱבִיאַנִי אֶל בֵּית הַיָּיִן״, פֵּרוּשׁ, לִפְנֵי הַר סִינַי, וְנָתַן לִי הַתּוֹרָה שֶׁנִּדְרֶשֶׁת בְּשִׁבְעִים פָּנִים, ״הֱבִיאַנִי הַמֶּלֶךְ חֲדָרָיו״ וְהֶרְאַנִי הַשָּׁמַיִם וּשְׁמֵי הַשָּׁמָיִם׃

(ז) אֵת אֲשֶׁר הִקְצַפְתָּ. פֵּ״א כְּפוּלָה. לוֹמַר, קֶצֶף אַחַר קֶצֶף׃

(ט) וָאֵשֵׁב בָּהָר. בְּגִימַטְרִיָּא לְתַלְמוּדוֹ׃

BAAL HATURIM ELUCIDATED

4. הֱבִיאַנִי — [HASHEM] BROUGHT ME. The masoretic note, ד׳, means that this word appears four times in the *Tanach*: (i) here, הֱבִיאַנִי ה׳ לָרֶשֶׁת, *HASHEM brought me to take possession;* (ii) בְּמַרְאוֹת אֱלֹהִים הֱבִיאַנִי אֶל אֶרֶץ יִשְׂרָאֵל, *in visions of God He brought me to the Land of Israel* (*Ezekiel* 40:2); (iii) הֱבִיאַנִי אֶל בֵּית הַיָּיִן, *He brought me to the house of wine* (*Song of Songs* 2:4); and (iv) הֱבִיאַנִי הַמֶּלֶךְ חֲדָרָיו, *The King brought me into His chamber* (*Song of Songs* 1:4). This [similarity of expression] is [an allusion to] what our Sages, of blessed memory, have expounded: At the Sea of Reeds, a maidservant saw [Divine revelations] that [even the prophet] Ezekiel did not see.[91] And that is [what is meant by], *in visions of God He brought*

91. *Mechilta, Beshalach* 15:2; *Shir HaShirim Rabbah* 3:9; cited by *Rashi* to *Exodus* 15:2, s.v., זֶה אֵלִי.

righteousness HASHEM brought me to take possession of this land and because of the wickedness of these nations did HASHEM drive them away from before you." [5] *Not because of your righteousness and the uprightness of your heart are you coming to possess their land, but because of the wickedness of these nations does HASHEM, your God, drive them away from before you, and in order to establish the word that HASHEM swore to your forefathers, to Abraham, to Isaac, and to Jacob.* [6] *And you should know that not because of your righteousness does HASHEM, your God, give you this good land to possess it, for you are a stiff-necked people.*

[7] *Remember, do not forget, that you provoked HASHEM, your God, in the wilderness; from the day you went forth from the land of Egypt until your arrival at this place, you have been rebels against HASHEM.* [8] *And in Horeb you provoked HASHEM, and HASHEM became angry with you to destroy you.* [9] *When I ascended the mountain to receive the tablets of stone, the Tablets of the Covenant that HASHEM sealed with you, and I sat on the mountain for forty days*

──────────────── BAAL HATURIM ELUCIDATED ────────────────

me, for they[91a] were all prophets and merited seeing *visions {of God}.* Similarly, at the Giving of the Torah, *He brought me to the house of wine,* i.e., before Mount Sinai,[92] and gave me the Torah, which can be expounded in seventy ways.[93] And [at that time], *the King brought me into His chambers,* showing me the heavens and the celestial heights.[94]

7. אֵת אֲשֶׁר הִקְצַפְתָּ — THAT YOU PROVOKED. [According to a scribal tradition,] the פ of הִקְצַפְתָּ is written [in the Torah scrolls] in the enhanced form known as פ׳ כְּפוּלָה, *doubled* פ.[95] This is to imply provocation after provocation.[96]

9. וָאֵשֵׁב בָּהָר — AND I SAT ON THE MOUNTAIN. The *gematria* of this phrase (516) is equal to that of לְתַלְמוּדוֹ, *for the sake of its study.*[97]

91a. That is, all those who left Egypt, even the maidservants.

92. *Shir HaShirim Rabbah* 2:4.

93. The *gematria* of יַיִן, *wine,* is 70; thus, יַיִן alludes to the Torah which may be expounded in seventy ways (*Bamidbar Rabbah* 15-16); and which is called by seventy names (see the Baal HaTurim to 6:4 above, s.v., עָיֵ"ן יִשְׁמַע).

94. *Pesikta Rabbasi* 20, cited by *Rashi* to 4:35 above; see also the Baal HaTurim to that verse and to *Exodus* 20:2, s.v., אָנֹכִי, and 26:30.

95. See note 29 to *parashas Devarim* and the accompanying illustration. *Sefer Tagin* includes

the פ of הִקְצַפְתָּ in our verse on the list of "191 in the Torah where mouths are on the inside."

96. That is, the doubled פ of הִקְצַפְתָּ, *you provoked,* indicates that Israel provoked God repeatedly.

97. *Peirush HaRokeach.* According to the Talmud, our verse refers to Moses studying the Torah on the mountain: One verse states, וָאֵשֵׁב בָּהָר, *and I sat on the mountain,* while another verse reads, וְאָנֹכִי עָמַדְתִּי בָהָר, *and I stood on the mountain* (10:10 below)! [The two verses are reconciled:] Moses stood while learning the Torah from God; he sat while reviewing it by himself (*Megillah* 21a).

Alternatively: The Torah was given in two

וְאַרְבָּעִים לַיְלָה לֶחֶם לֹא אָכַלְתִּי וּמַיִם לֹא שָׁתִיתִי׃
י וַיִּתֵּן יהוה אֵלַי אֶת־שְׁנֵי לוּחֹת הָאֲבָנִים כְּתֻבִים
בְּאֶצְבַּע אֱלֹהִים וַעֲלֵיהֶם כְּכָל־הַדְּבָרִים אֲשֶׁר דִּבֶּר
יא יהוה עִמָּכֶם בָּהָר מִתּוֹךְ הָאֵשׁ בְּיוֹם הַקָּהָל׃ וַיְהִי מִקֵּץ
אַרְבָּעִים יוֹם וְאַרְבָּעִים לָיְלָה נָתַן יהוה אֵלַי אֶת־שְׁנֵי
יב לֻחֹת הָאֲבָנִים לֻחוֹת הַבְּרִית׃ וַיֹּאמֶר יהוה אֵלַי קוּם
רֵד מַהֵר מִזֶּה כִּי שִׁחֵת עַמְּךָ אֲשֶׁר הוֹצֵאתָ מִמִּצְרָיִם
סָרוּ מַהֵר מִן־הַדֶּרֶךְ אֲשֶׁר צִוִּיתִם עָשׂוּ לָהֶם מַסֵּכָה׃
יג וַיֹּאמֶר יהוה אֵלַי לֵאמֹר רָאִיתִי אֶת־הָעָם הַזֶּה וְהִנֵּה
יד עַם־קְשֵׁה־עֹרֶף הוּא׃ הֶרֶף מִמֶּנִּי וְאַשְׁמִידֵם וְאֶמְחֶה
אֶת־שְׁמָם מִתַּחַת הַשָּׁמָיִם וְאֶעֱשֶׂה אוֹתְךָ לְגוֹי־
טו עָצוּם וָרָב מִמֶּנּוּ׃ וָאֵפֶן וָאֵרֵד מִן־הָהָר וְהָהָר בֹּעֵר
טז בָּאֵשׁ וּשְׁנֵי לוּחֹת הַבְּרִית עַל שְׁתֵּי יָדָי׃ וָאֵרֶא וְהִנֵּה
חֲטָאתֶם לַיהוה אֱלֹהֵיכֶם עֲשִׂיתֶם לָכֶם עֵגֶל מַסֵּכָה
סַרְתֶּם מַהֵר מִן־הַדֶּרֶךְ אֲשֶׁר־צִוָּה יהוה אֶתְכֶם׃
יז וָאֶתְפֹּשׂ בִּשְׁנֵי הַלֻּחֹת וָאַשְׁלִכֵם מֵעַל שְׁתֵּי יָדָי

בעל הטורים

(י) וַעֲלֵיהֶם כְּכָל הַדְּבָרִים. בְּגִימַטְרִיָּא זֶה תַּלְמוּד:

(יב) הוֹצֵאתָ מִמִּצְרָיִם. פֵּרוּשׁ, מֵהָעִיר צֹעַן. וּבְכָל מָקוֹם אוֹמֵר "מֵאֶרֶץ מִצְרַיִם", פֵּרוּשׁ, מִכָּל הָאָרֶץ:

(יז) וָאַשְׁלִכֵם. חָסֵר יוּ"ד — שֶׁפָּרְחוּ י' הַדִּבְּרוֹת מֵהֶם:

BAAL HATURIM ELUCIDATED

10. וַעֲלֵיהֶם כְּכָל הַדְּבָרִים — AND ON THEM WERE ALL THE WORDS. The *gematria* of this phrase (492) is equal to that of זֶה תַּלְמוּד, *This refers to the Talmud.* [98]

---

divisions: One was presented in written form and is called תּוֹרָה שֶׁבִּכְתָב, *the Written Torah,* or מִקְרָא, *Scripture;* the other is called תּוֹרָה שֶׁבְּעַל פֶּה, *the Oral Torah,* and includes the explanations, interpretations and expositions of the Written Torah that were originally transmitted only orally, but were later permitted to be committed to writing, first the Mishnah, the Tosefta, and other *baraisos,* and then the Talmud [or *Gemara,* Aramaic for Talmud]. We often find the term Talmud used as a synonym for the Oral Torah.

Accordingly, the term עָמַדְתִּי, *I stood,* would refer to the time Moses was studying Scripture, while וָאֵשֵׁב, *and I sat,* would refer to his study of Talmud (*Peirush HaRokeach*). If so, it is possible that the Baal HaTurim's לְתַלְמוּדוֹ means *for the sake of its Talmudic aspect* (*VeChur LaZahav;* see the Baal HaTurim's next comment).

98. *Peirush HaRokeach;* see note 97 above.

The Talmud expounds on this phrase: The verse could have said עֲלֵיהֶם [without the prefix ־וְ, *and*], yet it says וַעֲלֵיהֶם; it could have said כָּל, *all,* yet it says כְּכָל, [literally,] *like all;* and it could have said דְּבָרִים [without the prefix ־הַ, *the*], yet it and forty nights; bread I did not eat, and water I did not drink. ¹⁰ And HASHEM gave me the two stone tablets, inscribed with the finger of HASHEM, and on them were all the words that HASHEM spoke with you on the mountain from the midst of the fire, on the day of the congregation.

¹¹ It was at the end of forty days and forty nights that HASHEM gave me the two stone tablets, the Tablets of the Covenant. ¹² Then HASHEM said to me, "Arise, descend quickly from here, for your people that you brought forth from Egypt has become corrupt; they have strayed quickly from the way that I commanded them; they have made themselves a molten image."

¹³ HASHEM said to me, saying, "I have seen this people, and behold! it is a stiff-necked people. ¹⁴ Release Me, and I shall destroy them and erase their name from under the heavens, and I shall make you a mightier, more numerous nation than they!" ¹⁵ So I turned and descended from the mountain as the mountain was burning in fire, and the two Tablets of the Covenant were in my two hands.

¹⁶ Then I saw and behold! you had sinned to HASHEM, your God; you made yourselves a molten calf; you strayed quickly from the way that HASHEM commanded you. ¹⁷ I grasped the two tablets and threw them from my two hands,

--- BAAL HATURIM ELUCIDATED ---

12. הוֹצֵאתָ מִמִּצְרָיִם — **YOU BROUGHT FORTH FROM EGYPT.** This means from the city of Zoan.[99] Usually the Torah states, מֵאֶרֶץ מִצְרַיִם, from *"the land of"* Egypt, which refers to the entire country.[100]

17. וָאַשְׁלִכֵם — **AND I THREW THEM.** This word is spelled defectively, without a י (= 10). [This indicates that the letters inscribed into the tablets of] the Ten Commandments flew away from them [i.e., from the broken tablets].[101]

says הַדְּבָרִים. The three superfluous letters serve to include not just Scripture, but also Mishnah, Talmud [specifically, in this context, the halachic portions] and Aggadah [the homiletic portions of the Talmud] (*Yerushalmi, Megillah* 4:1). The Baal HaTurim shows how these words allude to the Talmud (*Shoham Yakar*).

99. The city of צֹעַן, Zoan, was the seat of Egyptian royalty (see *Rashi* to 11:10 below, s.v., לֹא כְאֶרֶץ מצרים הוא).

100. Verse 7 above reads, יָצָאתָ מֵאֶרֶץ מִצְרַיִם, you went forth from the land of Egypt; while our verse states, אֲשֶׁר הוֹצֵאתָ מִמִּצְרָיִם, whom you brought forth from Egypt, omitting the word אֶרֶץ, land of. Similarly, in *parashas Ki Seitzei* we find, כִּי עֶבֶד הָיִיתָ בְּמִצְרַיִם, that you were a slave in Egypt (24:18), and, four verses later, כִּי עֶבֶד הָיִיתָ בְּאֶרֶץ מִצְרָיִם, that you were a slave in the land of Egypt. The Baal HaTurim explains the implication of the different wording.

101. *Peirush HaRokeach; R' Chaim Paltiel.* The Talmud expounds on the phrase וָאֲשַׁבְּרֵם לְעֵינֵיכֶם, and I broke them before your eyes, that appears later in our verse: The Tablets were broken, but the letters flew [back up to their Heavenly source] (*Pesachim* 87b).

ט/יח-כד יח וָאֶשְׁבְּרֵם לְעֵינֵיכֶם׃ וָאֶתְנַפַּל לִפְנֵי יְהֹוָה כָּרִאשֹׁנָה
אַרְבָּעִים יוֹם וְאַרְבָּעִים לַיְלָה לֶחֶם לֹא אָכַלְתִּי וּמַיִם
לֹא שָׁתִיתִי עַל כׇּל־חַטַּאתְכֶם אֲשֶׁר חֲטָאתֶם לַעֲשׂוֹת
יט הָרַע בְּעֵינֵי יְהֹוָה לְהַכְעִיסוֹ׃ כִּי יָגֹרְתִּי מִפְּנֵי הָאַף
וְהַחֵמָה אֲשֶׁר קָצַף יְהֹוָה עֲלֵיכֶם לְהַשְׁמִיד אֶתְכֶם
כ וַיִּשְׁמַע יְהֹוָה אֵלַי גַּם בַּפַּעַם הַהִוא׃ וּבְאַהֲרֹן הִתְאַנַּף
יְהֹוָה מְאֹד לְהַשְׁמִידוֹ וָאֶתְפַּלֵּל גַּם־בְּעַד אַהֲרֹן בָּעֵת
כא הַהִוא׃ וְאֶת־חַטַּאתְכֶם אֲשֶׁר־עֲשִׂיתֶם אֶת־הָעֵגֶל
לָקַחְתִּי וָאֶשְׂרֹף אֹתוֹ ׀ בָּאֵשׁ וָאֶכֹּת אֹתוֹ טָחוֹן הֵיטֵב
עַד אֲשֶׁר־דַּק לְעָפָר וָאַשְׁלִךְ אֶת־עֲפָרוֹ אֶל־הַנַּחַל
כב הַיֹּרֵד מִן־הָהָר׃ וּבְתַבְעֵרָה וּבְמַסָּה וּבְקִבְרֹת הַתַּאֲוָה
כג מַקְצִפִים הֱיִיתֶם אֶת־יְהֹוָה׃ וּבִשְׁלֹחַ יְהֹוָה אֶתְכֶם
מִקָּדֵשׁ בַּרְנֵעַ לֵאמֹר עֲלוּ וּרְשׁוּ אֶת־הָאָרֶץ אֲשֶׁר
נָתַתִּי לָכֶם וַתַּמְרוּ אֶת־פִּי יְהֹוָה אֱלֹהֵיכֶם וְלֹא
כד הֶאֱמַנְתֶּם לוֹ וְלֹא שְׁמַעְתֶּם בְּקֹלוֹ׃ מַמְרִים הֱיִיתֶם

בעל הטורים

(יט) יָגֹרְתִּי. ד׳ — ״כִּי יָגֹרְתִּי מִפְּנֵי הָאַף וְהַחֵמָה״; ״הַעֲבֵר חֶרְפָּתִי אֲשֶׁר יָגֹרְתִּי״; ״וַאֲשֶׁר יָגֹרְתִּי יָבֹא לִי״; ״יָגֹרְתִּי כָל עַצְּבֹתָי יָדַעְתִּי כִּי לֹא תְנַקֵּנִי״. ״יָגֹרְתִּי מִפְּנֵי הָאַף וְהַחֵמָה״ וְהִתְפַּלַּלְתִּי שֶׁתַּעֲבִיר חֶרְפָּתִי, ״פֶּן יֹאמְרוּ הָאָרֶץ וְגוֹ׳״. ״וַאֲשֶׁר יָגֹרְתִּי יָבֹא לִי״, פֵּרוּשׁ, לִי לְבַדִּי, כִּי אַף עַל פִּי שֶׁשָּׁמַעְתָּ תְּפִלָּתִי עַל יִשְׂרָאֵל, ״לֹא תְנַקֵּנִי״ וּתְמִיתֵנִי בַּמִּדְבָּר וְלֹא אֶכָּנֵס לָאָרֶץ:

(כא) לְעָפָר. ג׳ בַּמָּסוֹרֶת — ״אֲשֶׁר דַּק לְעָפָר״; ״וַיָּדֶק לְעָפָר״; ״הֵדַק לְעָפָר״ בְּיֹאשִׁיָּהוּ כְּשֶׁבִּעֵר הָעֲבוֹדָה זָרָה. וְהַיְנוּ דְּאָמְרִינַן בַּעֲבוֹדָה זָרָה, מְפָרֵר וְזוֹרֶה לָרוּחַ.

(כד) מַמְרִים הֱיִיתֶם. הַפָּסוּק מַתְחִיל בְּמ״ם וּמְסַיֵּם בְּמ״ם — לוֹמַר לְךָ שֶׁבְּכׇל מ׳ שָׁנָה שֶׁהֱיִיתֶם בַּמִּדְבָּר הֱיִיתֶם מַמְרִים:

BAAL HATURIM ELUCIDATED

19. יָגֹרְתִּי — I WAS FEARFUL. The masoretic note, ד׳, means that this word appears four times in the *Tanach*: (i) here, כִּי יָגֹרְתִּי מִפְּנֵי הָאַף וְהַחֵמָה, *for I was fearful because of the wrath and the blazing anger;*[101a] (ii) הַעֲבֵר חֶרְפָּתִי אֲשֶׁר יָגֹרְתִּי, *Remove my disgrace, which I feared* (*Psalms* 119:39); (iii) וַאֲשֶׁר יָגֹרְתִּי יָבֹא לִי, *and that which I feared, it shall come upon me* (*Job* 3:24); and (iv) יָגֹרְתִּי כָל עַצְּבֹתָי יָדַעְתִּי כִּי לֹא תְנַקֵּנִי, *I feared all my sorrows; I knew that You would not acquit me* (*Job* 9:28). [The similarity of expression can be explained as follows: Moses said,] *"I was fearful because of the wrath and blazing anger,* and I prayed that my disgrace[102] be

101a. See the Baal HaTurim's comments to *Exodus* 4:24 and 33:5 (with note 114); and to *Numbers* 25:11.

102. That is, the disgrace that would come if God

and I broke them before your eyes. [18] *Then I threw myself down before* HASHEM *as the first time — forty days and forty nights — bread I did not eat and water I did not drink, because of your entire sin that you committed, to do that which is evil in the eyes of* HASHEM, *to anger Him,* [19] *for I was fearful because of the wrath and the blazing anger that* HASHEM *provoked against you to destroy you; and* HASHEM *hearkened to me that time, as well.* [20] HASHEM *became very angry with Aaron to destroy him, so I prayed also for Aaron at that time.* [21] *And your sin, for you made the calf, I took it and burned it in fire, and I pounded it — grinding it well, until it was fine — into dust, and I threw its dust into the brook that descended from the mountain.*

[22] *And in Taberah, in Massah, and in Kibroth-hattaavah you were provoking* HASHEM, [23] *and when* HASHEM *sent you from Kadesh-barnea, saying, "Go up and possess the land that I gave you" — then you rebelled against the word of* HASHEM, *your God; you did not believe Him and you did not hearken to His voice.* [24] *You have been rebels against*

BAAL HATURIM ELUCIDATED

removed,[103] *lest the land* [*from which You brought us out*] *will say* . . . (v. 28 below). [Yet,] *that which I feared, it shall come upon me,* i.e., upon me alone. [Then Moses said to God,] "Even though You fulfilled my prayer on behalf of Israel, nevertheless, *You will not acquit me,* [103a] rather, You will cause me to die in the wilderness and I will not enter the Land [of Israel]."

21. לְעָפָר — INTO DUST. The masoretic note, ג׳, means that this word appears three times in the *Tanach*: (i) here, אֲשֶׁר דַּק לְעָפָר, [*and I pounded it — grinding it well, until*] *it was fine — into dust;* and (ii-iii) וַיָּדֶק לְעָפָר, *and he ground* [*it*] *into dust* (*II Kings* 23:6), and הֵדַק לְעָפָר, *he ground it into dust* (*II Kings* 23:15), regarding King Josiah when he purged [every vestige of] idolatry [from the Temple]. This alludes to what the Sages have said in tractate *Avodah Zarah*: Grind [them] and scatter [them] to the wind.[104]

24. מַמְרִים הֱיִיתֶם — YOU HAVE BEEN REBELS. This verse begins with a מ (= 40) and ends with a ם (= 40).[104a] This is to indicate to you [that Moses meant to say,] "For the entire forty-year period[105] that you have been in the wilderness, you have been rebels."[105a]

---

would not answer my prayer that Israel be spared.

103. Thus, the connection to the verse from *Psalms.*

103a. See 1:37 above; see also the Baal HaTurim's two comments at 1:35 above.

104. *Avodah Zarah* 43b.

104a. This phenomenon appears fourteen times in the Torah and eighty-five other times in the rest of *Tanach.* The Baal HaTurim comments about it four times: here; *Leviticus* 24:3; *Numbers* 15:21; and *Deuteronomy* 10:7.

105. That is, from the beginning of the forty years, as alluded to by the letter מ at the beginning of the verse, until the end of the forty years, as alluded to by the ם at the end of the verse.

105a. *Peirush HaRokeach.*

כה עִם־יְהוָה מִיּוֹם דַּעְתִּי אֶתְכֶם: וָאֶתְנַפַּל לִפְנֵי יְהוָה
אֵת אַרְבָּעִים הַיּוֹם וְאֶת־אַרְבָּעִים הַלַּיְלָה אֲשֶׁר
הִתְנַפָּלְתִּי כִּי־אָמַר יְהוָה לְהַשְׁמִיד אֶתְכֶם:
כו וָאֶתְפַּלֵּל אֶל־יְהוָה וָאֹמַר אֲדֹנָי יֱהֹוִה אַל־תַּשְׁחֵת
עַמְּךָ וְנַחֲלָתְךָ אֲשֶׁר פָּדִיתָ בְּגָדְלֶךָ אֲשֶׁר־הוֹצֵאתָ
כז מִמִּצְרַיִם בְּיָד חֲזָקָה: זְכֹר לַעֲבָדֶיךָ לְאַבְרָהָם
לְיִצְחָק וּלְיַעֲקֹב אַל־תֵּפֶן אֶל־קְשִׁי הָעָם הַזֶּה
כח וְאֶל־רִשְׁעוֹ וְאֶל־חַטָּאתוֹ: פֶּן־יֹאמְרוּ הָאָרֶץ אֲשֶׁר
הוֹצֵאתָנוּ מִשָּׁם מִבְּלִי יְכֹלֶת יְהוָה לַהֲבִיאָם אֶל־
הָאָרֶץ אֲשֶׁר־דִּבֶּר לָהֶם וּמִשִּׂנְאָתוֹ אוֹתָם הוֹצִיאָם
כט לַהֲמִתָם בַּמִּדְבָּר: וְהֵם עַמְּךָ וְנַחֲלָתֶךָ אֲשֶׁר הוֹצֵאתָ
בְּכֹחֲךָ הַגָּדֹל וּבִזְרֹעֲךָ הַנְּטוּיָה:
י רביעי א בָּעֵת הַהִוא אָמַר יְהוָה אֵלַי פְּסָל־לְךָ שְׁנֵי־לוּחֹת
אֲבָנִים כָּרִאשֹׁנִים וַעֲלֵה אֵלַי הָהָרָה וְעָשִׂיתָ לְּךָ
ב אֲרוֹן עֵץ: וְאֶכְתֹּב עַל־הַלֻּחֹת אֶת־הַדְּבָרִים אֲשֶׁר
הָיוּ עַל־הַלֻּחֹת הָרִאשֹׁנִים אֲשֶׁר שִׁבַּרְתָּ וְשַׂמְתָּם
ג בָּאָרוֹן: וָאַעַשׂ אֲרוֹן עֲצֵי שִׁטִּים וָאֶפְסֹל שְׁנֵי־לֻחֹת
אֲבָנִים כָּרִאשֹׁנִים וָאַעַל הָהָרָה וּשְׁנֵי הַלֻּחֹת בְּיָדִי:
ד וַיִּכְתֹּב עַל־הַלֻּחֹת כַּמִּכְתָּב הָרִאשׁוֹן אֵת עֲשֶׂרֶת
הַדְּבָרִים אֲשֶׁר דִּבֶּר יְהוָה אֲלֵיכֶם בָּהָר מִתּוֹךְ

בעל הטורים

(כו) אֲדֹנָי ה׳ אַל תַּשְׁחֵת. מֵ״אֲדֹנָי״ עַד ״וּבִזְרֹעֲךָ הַנְּטוּיָה״, שֶׁהוּא סוֹף הַתְּפִלָּה, נ״ח תֵּבוֹת — שֶׁמָּצָא חֵן לְפָנָיו וְשָׁמַע תְּפִלָּתוֹ. וְזֶהוּ ״בּוֹרֵא נִיב שְׂפָתָיִם״ — נוב כְּתִיב:

BAAL HATURIM ELUCIDATED

26. אֲדֹנָי ה׳ אַל תַּשְׁחֵת — MY LORD, HASHEM/ELOHIM, DO NOT DESTROY. From [the first word of Moses' prayer,] אֲדֹנָי, *My Lord,* until וּבִזְרֹעֲךָ הַנְּטוּיָה, *and with Your outstretched arm* (9:29), which is the conclusion of that prayer, there are fifty-eight words. For [Moses] found חֵן[106], *favor,* before God and He accepted his prayer. This is [also the implication of] בּוֹרֵא נִיב שְׂפָתָיִם, *I create the fruit of the lips*[107]

106. The *gematria* of חֵן is 58.

107. The translation of נִיב as *fruit* [related to תְּנוּבָה (*Isaiah* 27:6)] is based on the Talmud (*Yerushalmi, Berachos* 5:5), and that is how *Ibn Ezra* (*Isaiah* 57:19; *Proverbs* 10:31) explains it. Another Talmudic passage (*Berachos* 34b; also *Vayikra Rabbah* 16:9) understands נִיב as *fluency of speech* [related to נִבֵּיתָ (*Jeremiah* 26:9)], and

HASHEM from the day that I knew you!
25 I threw myself down before HASHEM for the forty days
and the forty nights that I threw myself down, for HASHEM
had intended to destroy you. 26 I prayed to HASHEM and
said, "My Lord, HASHEM/ELOHIM, do not destroy Your
people and Your heritage that You redeemed in Your
greatness, that You took out of Egypt with a strong hand.
27 Remember for the sake of Your servants, for Abraham,
for Isaac, and for Jacob; do not turn to the stubbornness of
this people, and to its wickedness and to its sin, 28 lest the
land from which You brought us out will say, 'For lack of
HASHEM's ability to bring them to the land of which He
spoke to them, and because of His hatred of them did He
take them out to let them die in the wilderness.' 29 Yet they
are Your people and Your heritage, whom You took out with
Your great strength and with Your outstretched arm."

10
1 At that time HASHEM said to me, "Carve for yourself two
stone tablets like the first ones, and ascend to Me to the
mountain, and make a wooden Ark for yourself. 2 And I
shall inscribe on the tablets the words that were on the first
tablets that you smashed, and you shall place them in the
Ark."
3 So I made an Ark of cedarwood and I carved out two
stone tablets like the first ones; then I ascended the moun-
tain with the two tablets in my hand. 4 He inscribed on the
tablets according to the first script, the Ten Statements that
HASHEM spoke to you on the mountain from the midst of the

BAAL HATURIM ELUCIDATED

(*Isaiah* 57:19), [for the word נִיב of that verse] is spelled נוב[108] (= 58).

27. {The Baal HaTurim's comments to this verse appear at *Exodus* 32:13, *Leviticus* 26:42 and *Numbers* 16:15.}

X.

2. {The Baal HaTurim's comment to וְשַׂמְתָּם בָּאָרוֹן appears at *Genesis* 47:6.}

that is how *Targum* and *Radak* translate it. [This disagreement between the commentators extends to the phrase פִּי צַדִּיק יָנוּב חָכְמָה (*Proverbs* 10:31). According to *Ibn Ezra,* that phrase means, *The mouth of the righteous person will make itself fruitful with wisdom;* according to *Targum, Rashi* and *Radak* it means, *The mouth of the righteous person will speak wisdom.*] According to the Talmudic and Midrashic sources cited above, the expression is a metaphor for prayer.

108. The word נִיב is an example of a קְרִי וּכְתִיב, *keri uchesiv,* a word spelled one way in Scripture [in this case, נוב], but pronounced differently [in this case, נִיב].

ה הָאֵשׁ בְּיוֹם הַקָּהָל וַיִּתְּנֵם יהוה אֵלָי: וָאֵפֶן וָאֵרֵד
מִן־הָהָר וָאָשִׂם אֶת־הַלֻּחֹת בָּאָרוֹן אֲשֶׁר עָשִׂיתִי
ו וַיִּהְיוּ שָׁם כַּאֲשֶׁר צִוַּנִי יהוה: וּבְנֵי יִשְׂרָאֵל נָסְעוּ
מִבְּאֵרֹת בְּנֵי־יַעֲקָן מוֹסֵרָה שָׁם מֵת אַהֲרֹן וַיִּקָּבֵר
ז שָׁם וַיְכַהֵן אֶלְעָזָר בְּנוֹ תַּחְתָּיו: מִשָּׁם נָסְעוּ הַגֻּדְגֹּדָה
ח וּמִן־הַגֻּדְגֹּדָה יָטְבָתָה אֶרֶץ נַחֲלֵי מָיִם: בָּעֵת הַהִוא
הִבְדִּיל יהוה אֶת־שֵׁבֶט הַלֵּוִי לָשֵׂאת אֶת־אֲרוֹן

בעל הטורים

י (ו) וּבְנֵי יִשְׂרָאֵל נָסְעוּ מִבְּאֵרֹת בְּנֵי יַעֲקָן מוֹסֵרָה שָׁם מֵת אַהֲרֹן. סָמַךְ מִיתַת אַהֲרֹן לִשְׁבִירַת הַלּוּחוֹת. לוֹמַר לְךָ, קָשָׁה מִיתַת הַצַּדִּיקִים כִּשְׁבִירַת הַלּוּחוֹת. וְגַם, תַּלְמִיד חָכָם שֶׁמֵּת הַכֹּל נַעֲשִׂין קְרוֹבָיו, וּצְרִיכִין לִקְרֹעַ עָלָיו כְּמוֹ עַל סֵפֶר תּוֹרָה שֶׁנִּשְׂרַף.

וְעוֹד – סָמַךְ "וָאָשִׂם אֶת הַלֻּחֹת בָּאָרוֹן" אֵצֶל מִיתַת אַהֲרֹן, לוֹמַר, סֵפֶר תּוֹרָה שֶׁבָּלָה קוֹבְרִין אוֹתוֹ אֵצֶל תַּלְמִיד חָכָם. וְעוֹד, לוֹמַר, קִיֵּם זֶה מַה שֶּׁכָּתוּב בָּזֶה:

❑ **וַיִּקָּבֵר . . . וַיְכַהֵן.** מִיתַת צַדִּיקִים מְכַפֶּרֶת כְּבִגְדֵי כְהֻנָּה:

(ז) מִשָּׁם נָסְעוּ הַגֻּדְגֹּדָה. הַפָּסוּק מַתְחִיל בְּמֵ"ם וּמְסַיֵּם בְּמֵ"ם – לוֹמַר שֶׁכָּל מ' שָׁנָה הָיָה הַבְּאֵר עִמָּהֶם:

(ח) בָּעֵת הַהִוא הִבְדִּיל ה' אֶת שֵׁבֶט הַלֵּוִי. סָמַךְ כָּאן, לוֹמַר שֶׁהַלְוִיִּם הֶחֱזִירוּ אֶת יִשְׂרָאֵל:

❑ סָמַךְ "מָיִם" לְ"לָשֵׂאת אֶת אֲרוֹן . . . וּלְבָרֵךְ", לוֹמַר שֶׁצָּרִיךְ לִטֹּל יָדָיו כְּדֵי לִשָּׂא כַּפָּיו:

BAAL HATURIM ELUCIDATED

6. וּבְנֵי יִשְׂרָאֵל נָסְעוּ מִבְּאֵרֹת בְּנֵי יַעֲקָן מוֹסֵרָה שָׁם מֵת אַהֲרֹן — THE CHILDREN OF ISRAEL JOURNEYED FROM BEEROTH-BENE-JAAKAN TO MOSERAH; THERE AARON DIED. Scripture juxtaposed Aaron's death with the breaking of the tablets (vv. 1-5), to indicate to you that the death of righteous men is as distressing as the destruction of the tablets.[109] And [it also implies that] when a Torah sage dies, all people become his relatives and are required to rend their garments,[110] just as they must do for a Torah scroll that has been burnt.[110]

Additionally: The verse juxtaposed *I placed the tablets in the Ark* (v. 5) with the death of Aaron, to indicate that a Torah scroll that has become worn out[111] should be buried next to a Torah sage.[112] Also, it is to imply: This one [the Torah sage] fulfilled what is written in that one [the Torah scroll].[113]

❑ **וַיִּקָּבֵר . . . וַיְכַהֵן — AND HE [AARON] WAS BURIED . . . AND [ELAZAR HIS SON] MINISTERED.** [This teaches that] the death of the righteous generates atonement

109. *Yerushalmi, Yoma* 1:1; *Vayikra Rabbah* 20:12; cited by *Rashi* to v. 7.

110. *Tosefta, Moed Katan* 2:9; *Moed Katan* 25a; see *Rashi* and the Baal HaTurim to *Leviticus* 10:6, s.v., וַאֲחֵיכֶם.

111. That is, that has become worn out to the point that it can no longer be used for the public Torah reading.

112. See *Megillah* 26b.

113. See *Bava Kamma* 17a.

fire, on the day of the congregation, and HASHEM gave them
to me. 5 *I turned and descended from the mountain, and I*
placed the tablets in the Ark that I had made, and they
remained there as HASHEM had commanded me.
6 *The Children of Israel journeyed from Beeroth-bene-*
jaakan to Moserah; there Aaron died and he was buried
there, and Elazar his son ministered in his place. 7 *From*
there they journeyed to Gudgod, and from Gudgod to
Jotbathah, a land of brooks of water. 8 *At that time,*
HASHEM set apart the tribe of Levi to carry the Ark of the

BAAL HATURIM ELUCIDATED

just as the priestly garments[114] do.[115]

7. מִשָּׁם נָסְעוּ הַגֻּדְגֹּדָה — FROM THERE THEY JOURNEYED TO GUDGOD. This verse begins with a מ (= 40) and ends with a מ,[116] to indicate that for the entire forty years [that Israel was in the wilderness] the well was with them.[117]

8. בָּעֵת הַהִוא הִבְדִּיל ה׳ אֶת שֵׁבֶט הַלֵּוִי — AT THAT TIME, HASHEM SET APART THE TRIBE OF LEVI. Scripture juxtaposed [this verse regarding the Levites] here [with the verses regarding the death of Aaron,] to indicate that [when Aaron died and the Israelites retreated back toward Egypt] the Levites compelled the Israelites to return [to their journey toward the Land of Canaan].[118]

❑ Scripture juxtaposed מָיִם, *water* (v. 7), to לָשֵׂאת אֶת אֲרוֹן . . . וּלְבָרֵךְ, *to carry the Ark . . . and to bless,* to indicate that [a Kohen] must wash his hands in order to raise them[119] [while reciting the priestly blessing].[120]

114. The Talmud (*Zevachim* 88b; *Arachin* 16a) expounds upon the nature of the sins for which each priestly garment atones.

115. *Moed Katan* 28a.

116. See note 104a above.

117. See *Taanis* 9a. The connection between the places mentioned in this verse and the well is not clear, especially since the verse states that *Jotbathah was a land of brooks of water,* implying that the well was not needed in that area. Perhaps that itself is the Baal HaTurim's intention: Lest one think that the well which supplied Israel with water in the wilderness did so only when there was no other water to be had, the verse begins and ends with the letter מ — whose name מ״ם is related to מַיִם, *water,* and whose *gematria* is forty — to teach us that the well's waters were with the Israelites for the entire forty years, even when other sources of water were available (*VeChur LaZahav*).

118. *Yerushalmi, Yoma* 1:1 and *Sotah* 1:10; cited by *Rashi* to v. 6 and to *Numbers* 26:13.

119. *Sotah* 39a.

120. *Peirush HaRokeach.* It is not clear why the Baal HaTurim included the phrase לָשֵׂאת אֶת אֲרוֹן, *to carry the Ark,* in this comment (*Shoham Yakar*). However, in *Peirush HaRokeach,* the comment appears in an expanded version: Scripture juxtaposed מָיִם, *water,* to לָשֵׂאת אֶת אֲרוֹן, *to carry the Ark,* for they would wash their hands [before carrying it]; [and it juxtaposed] מָיִם to לְשָׁרְתוֹ, *to serve Him,* for the Torah states, [*When they come to the Tent of Meeting,*] *they shall wash with water and not die* [*or when they approach the Altar to serve* . . . (*Exodus* 30:20); [and it juxtaposed] מָיִם to וּלְבָרֵךְ בִּשְׁמוֹ, *and to bless in His Name,* because [as the Talmud (*Sotah* 39a) states:] A Kohen who has not washed his hands may not raise his hands [in blessing]. Perhaps the Baal HaTurim's comment originally appeared in a similar expanded version but was inadvertently shortened due to a scribal error (*VeChur LaZahav*).

Alternatively: In the absence of the *Beis HaMikdash,* it is customary for the Kohanim to stand

בְּרִית־יְהוָה לַעֲמֹד לִפְנֵי יְהוָה לְשָׁרְתוֹ וּלְבָרֵךְ בִּשְׁמוֹ
ט עַד הַיּוֹם הַזֶּה: עַל־כֵּן לֹא־הָיָה לְלֵוִי חֵלֶק וְנַחֲלָה
עִם־אֶחָיו יְהוָה הוּא נַחֲלָתוֹ כַּאֲשֶׁר דִּבֶּר יְהוָה
י אֱלֹהֶיךָ לוֹ: וְאָנֹכִי עָמַדְתִּי בָהָר כַּיָּמִים הָרִאשֹׁנִים
אַרְבָּעִים יוֹם וְאַרְבָּעִים לָיְלָה וַיִּשְׁמַע יְהוָה אֵלַי גַּם
יא בַּפַּעַם הַהִוא לֹא־אָבָה יְהוָה הַשְׁחִיתֶךָ: וַיֹּאמֶר יְהוָה
אֵלַי קוּם לֵךְ לְמַסַּע לִפְנֵי הָעָם וְיָבֹאוּ וְיִירְשׁוּ
אֶת־הָאָרֶץ אֲשֶׁר־נִשְׁבַּעְתִּי לַאֲבֹתָם לָתֵת לָהֶם:
חמישי יב וְעַתָּה יִשְׂרָאֵל מָה יְהוָה אֱלֹהֶיךָ שֹׁאֵל מֵעִמָּךְ

בעל הטורים

(י) **לֹא אָבָה.** ג׳ — ״לֹא אָבָה ה׳ הַשְׁחִיתֶךָ״; ״וְיִשְׂרָאֵל לֹא אָבָה לִי״; ״לֹא אָבָה יַבְּמִי״. {אַף עַל פִּי שֶׁ״יִשְׂרָאֵל לֹא אָבָה לִי״, ״לֹא אָבָה ה׳ הַשְׁחִיתֶךָ״. ״לֹא אָבָה יַבְּמִי״,} קְרִי בֵהּ לֹא אָבָה אֶלָּא יַבְּמִי, כִּדְכְתִיב ״כִּי לֹא אַלְמָן יִשְׂרָאֵל וִיהוּדָה מֵאֱלֹהָיו״:

(יא) **קוּם לֵךְ לְמַסַּע.** שְׁלֹשָׁה תָגִין עַל הַקּוּ״ף — שֶׁאֶזְכֹּר לָהֶם זְכוּת אַבְרָהָם, שֶׁאָמַרְתִּי לוֹ ״קוּם הִתְהַלֵּךְ בָּאָרֶץ לְאָרְכָּהּ וּלְרָחְבָּהּ כִּי לְךָ אֶתְּנֶנָּה״:

❑ **אֲשֶׁר נִשְׁבַּעְתִּי לַאֲבֹתָם לָתֵת לָהֶם.** וּסְמִיךְ לֵהּ ״וְעַתָּה יִשְׂרָאֵל מָה ה׳ אֱלֹהֶיךָ שֹׁאֵל מֵעִמָּךְ כִּי אִם לְיִרְאָה״, לוֹמַר לְךָ שֶׁהָאָבוֹת הָיוּ יִרְאֵי הַשֵּׁם:

(יב) **מָה ה׳ אֱלֹהֶיךָ שֹׁאֵל מֵעִמָּךְ.** ״מָה״ בְּאַ״תְ בַּ״שׁ י״צ, שֶׁשּׁוֹאֵל מִמְּךָ מֵאָה בְרָכוֹת

BAAL HATURIM ELUCIDATED

10. {The Baal HaTurim's comment to כַּיָּמִים appears at 1:46 above.}

❑ **לֹא אָבָה — [HASHEM] DID NOT DESIRE.** The masoretic note, ג׳, means that this phrase appears three times in the *Tanach*:[121] (i) here, לֹא אָבָה ה׳ הַשְׁחִיתֶךָ, *HASHEM did not desire to destroy you;* (ii) וְיִשְׂרָאֵל לֹא אָבָה לִי, *Israel did not desire Me* (*Psalms* 81:12); and (iii) לֹא אָבָה יַבְּמִי, *He did not desire to take me in levirate marriage* (*Deuteronomy* 25:7). {[The similarity of expression indicates that Moses said,] "Even though [God said,] *'Israel did not desire Me,'* nevertheless, *HASHEM did not desire to destroy you.*" [To which Israel replied,] ״לֹא אָבָה יַבְּמִי״,}[121a] which may be read as, "לֹא אָבָה, *He did not desire* [anything else] but, יַבְּמִי, *to take me in levirate marriage.*"[122] As is written,

before the *Aron HaKodesh* [holy ark] at the front of the synagogue while pronouncing the priestly blessing (see *Shulchan Aruch, Orach Chayim* 128:10). Accordingly, the verse may be interpreted in the following manner: מָיִם, [he must wash his hands with] *water,* [in order] לָשֵׂאת, *to raise* [them], אֶת אֲרוֹן, *next to the ark,* וּלְבָרֵךְ, *and to bless* (*VeChur LaZahav*).

121. The word אָבָה appears twenty-eight times in the *Tanach,* twenty-five times preceded by the word וְלֹא, *and not,* the other three times, by the word לֹא, without the conjunctive prefix (see *Tosafos, Yevamos* 106b, s.v., מודה).

121a. The passage enclosed in braces is not found in most printed editions. It does appear in *Shoham Yakav's* manuscript edition.

122. The Baal HaTurim's repunctuation of that verse is based on the טְעָמִים, *cantillation notes* (*trop*). The *meircha* under the ל of לֹא indicates that that word is connected to the next one; the

covenant of HASHEM, to stand before HASHEM to serve Him and to bless in His Name until this day. 9 *Therefore, Levi did not have a share and a heritage with his brethren; HASHEM is his heritage, as HASHEM, your God, had spoken of him.*

10 *I stood on the mountain as the first days — forty days and forty nights — and HASHEM listened to me this time, as well, and HASHEM did not desire to destroy you.* 11 *HASHEM said to me, "Arise, go on the journey before the people; let them come and possess the land that I swore to their forefathers to give to them."*

12 *And now, O Israel, what does HASHEM, your God, ask of*

BAAL HATURIM ELUCIDATED

כִּי לֹא אַלְמָן יִשְׂרָאֵל וִיהוּדָה מֵאֱלֹהָיו, *For neither Israel nor Judah is widowed from his God* (*Jeremiah* 51:5).

11. קוּם לֵךְ לְמַסַּע — ARISE, GO ON THE JOURNEY. [According to a scribal tradition,] the ק of קוּם is written [in the Torah scrolls] with three *tagin* (crownlets).[123] [This indicates] that [God said], "I will remember for their sake the merit of Abraham, to whom I said, קוּם[124] הִתְהַלֵּךְ בָּאָרֶץ לְאָרְכָּהּ וּלְרָחְבָּהּ כִּי לְךָ אֶתְּנֶנָּה, *Arise, walk about the land through its length and breadth! For to you will I give it* (*Genesis* 13:17).

❑ **אֲשֶׁר נִשְׁבַּעְתִּי לַאֲבֹתָם לָתֵת לָהֶם** — THAT I SWORE TO THEIR FOREFATHERS TO GIVE TO THEM. Juxtaposed to this is, וְעַתָּה יִשְׂרָאֵל מָה ה׳ אֱלֹהֶיךָ שֹׁאֵל מֵעִמָּךְ כִּי אִם לְיִרְאָה, *Now, O Israel, what does HASHEM, your God, ask of you? Only to fear* (v. 12). This is to indicate to you that the Patriarchs were God-fearing people.[125]

12. מָה ה׳ אֱלֹהֶיךָ שֹׁאֵל מֵעִמָּךְ — WHAT DOES HASHEM, YOUR GOD, ASK OF YOU. In the letter-exchange system known as אַ״תְּ בַּ״שׁ[126], the letters מ and ה are exchanged for י (= 10) and צ (= 90) respectively, [alluding to the Talmudic teaching] that God asks one

tipcha under the ב of אָבָה indicates a slight pause after that word. Thus the three-word phrase לֹא אָבָה יַבְּמִי may be understood as two phrases: לֹא אָבָה and יַבְּמִי (*VeChur LaZahav*).

usual ק with one *tag* — ק with three *tagin*

123. Regarding *tagin,* see note 56 to *parashas Devarim.*

According to *Sefer Tagin,* קוּם of our verse is one of "181 [(Paris ed.) or 185 (*Machzor Vitry*)] words in the Torah in which the ק is written with three *tagin.*"

124. That is, the *tagin* on the ק of קוּם refer us to another verse in which God said קוּם (A.S.).

125. The Torah describes four people as God fearing: Abraham, about whom an angel testified, *"Now I know that you are a God-fearing man . . ."* (*Genesis* 22:12); Joseph, who said of himself, *"I fear God"* (*Genesis* 42:18); and Jochebed and Miriam [Shifrah and Puah], about whom the Torah states, *But the midwives feared God* (*Exodus* 1:17, see also v. 21 there). However, we do not find any explicit statement regarding Isaac or Jacob with respect to fear of God. Lest one think, Heaven forbid, that they were lacking in that trait, the Baal HaTurim finds an allusion in our verse that teaches us about their fear of God (*VeChur LaZahav*).

126. אַ״תְּ בַּ״שׁ is a system of letter exchange in

כ	י	ט	ח	ז	ו	ה	ד	ג	ב	א
ל	מ	נ	ס	ע	פ	צ	ק	ר	ש	ת

אַ״תְּ בַּ״שׁ, in which either letter of a pair may be exchanged for the other.

כִּי אִם־לְיִרְאָה אֶת־יְהוָה אֱלֹהֶיךָ לָלֶכֶת בְּכָל־דְּרָכָיו
וּלְאַהֲבָה אֹתוֹ וְלַעֲבֹד אֶת־יְהוָה אֱלֹהֶיךָ בְּכָל־לְבָבְךָ
יג וּבְכָל־נַפְשֶׁךָ׃ לִשְׁמֹר אֶת־מִצְוֺת יְהוָה וְאֶת־חֻקֹּתָיו
יד אֲשֶׁר אָנֹכִי מְצַוְּךָ הַיּוֹם לְטוֹב לָךְ׃ הֵן לַיהוָה אֱלֹהֶיךָ
הַשָּׁמַיִם וּשְׁמֵי הַשָּׁמָיִם הָאָרֶץ וְכָל־אֲשֶׁר־בָּהּ׃

בעל הטורים

בְּכָל יוֹם. וְכֵן יֵשׁ בַּפָּסוּק מֵאָה אוֹתִיּוֹת. וְכֵן ״מִמְּךָ״ עוֹלֶה מֵאָה:

❑ **וְעַתָּה יִשְׂרָאֵל.** ב׳ דִּסְמִיכֵי — הָכָא; וְאִידָךְ ״וְעַתָּה יִשְׂרָאֵל שְׁמַע אֶל הַחֻקִּים״. כְּנֶגֶד שְׁתֵּי תוֹרוֹת, תּוֹרָה שֶׁבִּכְתָב וְתוֹרָה שֶׁבְּעַל פֶּה:

(יד) **הֵן לַה׳ אֱלֹהֶיךָ.** הַפָּסוּק מַתְחִיל וּמְסַיֵּם בְּהֵ״א — לוֹמַר שֶׁבְּהֵ״א נִבְרָא הָעוֹלָם. וּכְנֶגֶד חֲמִשָּׁה חֻמְשֵׁי תוֹרָה:

❑ וְעֶשֶׂר תֵּבוֹת בַּפָּסוּק, לוֹמַר לֹא יָרְדָה שְׁכִינָה לְמַטָּה מֵעֲשָׂרָה:

❑ **הָאָרֶץ וְכָל אֲשֶׁר בָּהּ.** וּסְמִיךְ לֵהּ ״רַק בַּאֲבֹתֶיךָ״. לוֹמַר שֶׁהָאָרֶץ וְכָל אֲשֶׁר בָּהּ לֹא נִבְרֵאת אֶלָּא בִּזְכוּת הָאָבוֹת:

BAAL HATURIM ELUCIDATED

hundred blessings[127] of you every day.[128] And for this same reason, there are one hundred letters in our verse.[129] Similarly, the *gematria* of מִמְּךָ, *of you,* [130] is 100.

❑ **וְעַתָּה יִשְׂרָאֵל — AND NOW, O ISRAEL.**[130a] The masoretic note, ב׳ דִּסְמִיכֵי, means that this phrase appears twice in the *Tanach*: (i) here; and (ii) וְעַתָּה יִשְׂרָאֵל שְׁמַע אֶל הַחֻקִּים, *And now, O Israel, listen to the decrees* (4:1 above). This corresponds to

which א, the first letter of the alphabet, may be exchanged with ת, the last letter; ב, the second letter, may be exchanged with ש, the second to last; and so on (see illustration). Thus, the name אַ״תְּ בַּ״שׁ, after the first two pairs of letter exchanges.

127. The *gematria* of ו״ץ is 100.

128. *Peirush HaRokeach;* see *Menachos* 43b; see the Baal HaTurim to 4:4 above, with note 44.

129. In our Torah scrolls, this verse contains exactly ninety-nine letters. However, there are two conflicting masoretic traditions regarding the spelling of the word שׁאַל/שׁוֹאֵל in our verse. The defective spelling שֹׁאֵל is used in our Torah scrolls, in accordance with a masoretic note adduced by the *Ramah* (*Masores Seyag LaTorah*) and by *Rabbeinu Bachya* (*Kad HaKemach,* s.v., ברכה). However, *Rabbeinu Tam* records a masoretic note reading, פָּסוּק זֶה כּוּלֵּהּ בַּר מְאָה אָתְיָן וְשׁוֹאֵל מָלֵא, *This verse contains one hundred letters in its entirety and* שׁוֹאֵל *is spelled in full* (*Sefer HaManhig*). The later kabbalistic work *Heichal HaBerachah* writes: שֹׁאֵל is to be spelled defectively; however, if it has been spelled in full in a particular Torah scroll, that scroll may be used, but only if no other scroll is available.

In each of the other six appearances of שֹׁאֵל (*II Samuel* 3:13 and 14:18; *I Kings* 2:16; *Jeremiah* 38:14; *Micah* 7:3; and [with the prefix וְ־] *Deuteronomy* 18:11) it is spelled defectively, without a ו.

For more opinions regarding the "hundred" letters of this verse, see *Tosafos* to *Menachos* 43b, s.v., שׁוֹאֵל; and *Minchas Shai* to our verse.

130. Our verse uses the word מֵעִמָּךְ for *of you.* The Baal HaTurim is referring to the word מִמְּךָ that appears in a parallel verse: וּמָה ה׳ דּוֹרֵשׁ מִמְּךָ, *And what does* HASHEM *require of you?* (*Micah* 6:8). And that verse is adduced by the *Abudraham* as an allusion to the hundred blessings (*Shoham Yakar*).

130a. In the verse, this phrase precedes the phrase used as the rubric of the comment before this one. It is not clear why the Baal HaTurim presents the two comments out of the order of the verse.

you? Only to fear HASHEM, *your God, to go in all His ways and to love Him, and to serve* HASHEM, *your God, with all your heart and with all your soul,* [13] *to observe the commandments of* HASHEM *and His decrees, which I command you today, for your benefit.* [14] *Behold! To* HASHEM, *your God, are the heavens and highest heavens, the earth and everything that is in it.*

BAAL HATURIM ELUCIDATED

the two divisions of the Torah: תּוֹרָה שֶׁבִּכְתָב, *the Written Torah,* and תּוֹרָה שֶׁבְּעַל פֶּה, *the Oral Torah.*[131]

14. הֵן לַה׳ אֱלֹהֶיךָ — BEHOLD! TO HASHEM, YOUR GOD. This verse begins with a ה (= 5) and ends with a ה.[132] This alludes to the fact that the world was created with the letter ה.[133] It also corresponds to the five Books of the Torah.[134]

❑ There are ten words in the verse, to indicate that the Divine Presence never descended lower than ten handbreadths [above the earth].[135]

❑ {The Baal HaTurim's other comment to הֵן appears at 31:14 below.}

❑ **הָאָרֶץ וְכָל אֲשֶׁר בָּהּ — THE EARTH AND EVERYTHING THAT IS IN IT.** Juxtaposed to this is the phrase, רַק בַּאֲבֹתֶיךָ, *only regarding your forefathers,* to indicate that the earth, along with everything within it, was created only in the merit of the Patriarchs.[136]

---

131. See note 97 above. It is noteworthy that the combined *gematria* of בִּכְתָב (= 424) and בְּעַל פֶּה (= 187) is 611, equal to that of תּוֹרָה (*VeChur LaZahav*).

132. This phenomenon occurs in twenty-six verses in the Torah and another hundred and eighty in the rest of *Tanach.* The Baal HaTurim comments on four of those verses: *Genesis* 19:23; *Numbers* 23:24; here; and 11:30 below.

133. Traditionally, certain letters are written in the Torah scroll smaller than others. That form indicates that a special lesson is to be learned from that letter. The ה of בְּהִבָּרְאָם, *when they were created,* of the verse, *These are the products of the heavens and the earth when they were created . . .* (*Genesis* 2:4), is such a letter. The small ה indicates that the word may be read as two words — בְּה׳ בְּרָאָם, *He created them with [the letter]* ה — that is, God took the letter ה from His Name and with it He created the heavens and the earth of this world.

The Talmud explains that, like the letter ה, this world is closed on three sides and open on one. The opening gives the person who desires to wander on the pathways of evil the chance to do so. Nevertheless, there is another small opening through which the repentant sinner may return. The World to Come, on the other hand, was created with the letter י, because the י is the smallest of the letters and the righteous who will be worthy of the World to Come will be a small percentage of the world's population (*Menachos* 29b).

The Baal HaTurim thus explains that our verse, which speaks of the heavens and earth as belonging to God, begins and ends with the letter ה׳, as an allusion to the basis of God's ownership: He created the world — with the letter ה — and therefore it is His (*VeChur LaZahav*).

134. The world was created for the sake of the Torah (*Shoham Yakar;* see the Baal HaTurim to *Genesis* 1:1, s.v., בְּרֵאשִׁית בָּרָא).

135. *Succah* 4b-5a — The Ark was nine *tefachim* [handbreadths] high and its cover was one *tefach* thick, for a total of ten. And it is written, *. . . and I shall speak to you from atop the cover* (*Exodus* 25:22). It was taught in a *baraisa* . . . The *Shechinah* [Immanent Divine Presence] has never descended below [onto the earth] and neither Moses nor Elijah ever ascended on high [into the heavens], as it is written, *As for the heavens — the heavens are unto* HASHEM; *but as for the earth — He gave it to mankind* (*Psalms* 115:16). [But we have just shown that the *Shechinah* descended to the top of the Ark, ten *tefachim* off the ground. Therefore, the *baraisa* must mean that the *Shechinah* never descended closer than ten *tefachim* to the earth.]

136. *Peirush HaRokeach;* see *Vayikra Rabbah* 36:5. In four other places the Baal HaTurim

טו רַק בַּאֲבֹתֶיךָ חָשַׁק יְהוָה לְאַהֲבָה אוֹתָם וַיִּבְחַר
בְּזַרְעָם אַחֲרֵיהֶם בָּכֶם מִכָּל־הָעַמִּים כַּיּוֹם הַזֶּה׃
טז וּמַלְתֶּם אֵת עָרְלַת לְבַבְכֶם וְעָרְפְּכֶם לֹא תַקְשׁוּ
יז עוֹד׃ כִּי יְהוָה אֱלֹהֵיכֶם הוּא אֱלֹהֵי הָאֱלֹהִים וַאֲדֹנֵי
הָאֲדֹנִים הָאֵל הַגָּדֹל הַגִּבֹּר וְהַנּוֹרָא אֲשֶׁר לֹא־יִשָּׂא
יח פָנִים וְלֹא יִקַּח שֹׁחַד׃ עֹשֶׂה מִשְׁפַּט יָתוֹם וְאַלְמָנָה
יט וְאֹהֵב גֵּר לָתֶת לוֹ לֶחֶם וְשִׂמְלָה׃ וַאֲהַבְתֶּם אֶת־הַגֵּר
כ כִּי־גֵרִים הֱיִיתֶם בְּאֶרֶץ מִצְרָיִם׃ אֶת־יְהוָה אֱלֹהֶיךָ
כא תִּירָא אֹתוֹ תַעֲבֹד וּבוֹ תִדְבָּק וּבִשְׁמוֹ תִּשָּׁבֵעַ׃ הוּא
תְהִלָּתְךָ וְהוּא אֱלֹהֶיךָ אֲשֶׁר־עָשָׂה אִתְּךָ אֶת־
הַגְּדֹלֹת וְאֶת־הַנּוֹרָאֹת הָאֵלֶּה אֲשֶׁר רָאוּ עֵינֶיךָ׃

בעל הטורים

(טו) רַק בַּאֲבֹתֶיךָ. מִעוּט הוּא, שֶׁגַּם עֲלֵיהֶם יֵשׁ דִּין – אַבְרָהָם ״בַּמָּה אֵדַע״; יִצְחָק אָהַב אֶת עֵשָׂו; יַעֲקֹב אָמַר ״נִסְתְּרָה דַרְכִּי מֵה׳ ״:

❑ סָמַךְ לְ״רַק בַּאֲבֹתֶיךָ״ ״וּמַלְתֶּם״, לוֹמַר שֶׁתָּמוּלוּ עָרְלַת הַלֵּב, כְּמוֹ שֶׁעָשׂוּ הָאָבוֹת:

(יח) וְאֹהֵב. ב׳ – ״וְאֹהֵב גֵּר״; ״וְרָשָׁע וְאֹהֵב חָמָס שָׂנְאָה נַפְשׁוֹ״. אוֹהֵב אֶת הַגֵּר, אֲבָל הָאוֹהֵב חָמָס, ״שָׂנְאָה נַפְשׁוֹ״:

(כ) אֶת ה׳ אֱלֹהֶיךָ תִּירָא. ״תִּירָא״ בְּגִימַטְרִיָּא תּוֹרָה:

BAAL HATURIM ELUCIDATED

15. רַק בַּאֲבֹתֶיךָ — ONLY REGARDING YOUR FOREFATHERS. The word רַק, *only,* is considered an exclusion,[137] for we find judgment directed even against the Patriarchs: Regarding Abraham — [He was judged for saying,] *"Whereby shall I know? . . ."* (*Genesis* 15:8); Isaac, [because] he loved Esau; and Jacob [because he] said, "נִסְתְּרָה דַרְכִּי מֵה׳, *My way is hidden from HASHEM*"[138] (*Isaiah* 40:27).[139]

---

states that the world was created in the merit of Abraham — *Genesis* 1:1, 2:4, 12:1 and 21:29. Only here does he include the other Patriarchs.

According to this comment, the juxtaposed phrases are translated: הַשָּׁמַיִם וּשְׁמֵי הַשָּׁמַיִם הָאָרֶץ וְכָל אֲשֶׁר בָּהּ רַק בַּאֲבֹתֶיךָ, *The heavens and the highest heavens, the earth and everything that is in it, are only for the sake of your forefathers* (*Shoham Yakar*).

137. *Bereishis Rabbah* 22:2 — As used in Scriptures, the terms אַךְ and רַק imply exclusions; the terms אֶת and גַּם imply inclusions.

138. The full verse reads: *Why do you say, O Jacob, and declare, O Israel, "My way is hidden from HASHEM, and from my God has my judgment passed?"* In context, Jacob and Israel are references to the nation, i.e., the Children of Israel, the House of Jacob. Midrashically, both names refer to the Patriarch Jacob/Israel, specifically, when he said to his sons, *"Why did you treat me so ill by telling the man that you had another brother?"* (*Genesis* 43:6). At that point God said, "I am engaged in setting his son as a king over Egypt, and he says [to his sons], *'Why did you treat me so ill?'* [as if they were the masters of his fate (*Maharzu*)]." That is the impact of the verse, *My way is hidden from HASHEM . . .* [as if, Heaven forbid, Jacob were denying God's role in bringing about Jacob's present situation] (*Bereishis Rabbah* 91:10).

139. *Shir HaShirim Rabbah* to 1:4; see also *Arachin* 17a.

¹⁵ *Only regarding your forefathers did HASHEM cherish to love them, and He chose their offspring after them — you — from among all the peoples, as this day.* ¹⁶ *You shall circumcise the foreskin of your heart and no longer stiffen your neck.* ¹⁷ *For HASHEM, your God — He is the God of the powers and the Lord of the lords; the God, the Great, the Mighty and the Awesome, Who does not show favor and Who does not accept a bribe.* ¹⁸ *He carries out the judgment of orphan and widow, and He loves the convert to give him bread and garment.* ¹⁹ *You shall love the convert for you were strangers in the land of Egypt.*

²⁰ *HASHEM, your God, shall you fear, Him shall you serve, to Him shall you cleave, and in His Name shall you swear.* ²¹ *He is your praise and He is your God, Who did for you these great and awesome things that your eyes saw.*

————————————— BAAL HATURIM ELUCIDATED ——————————————

❑ Juxtaposed to [the verse beginning] רַק בַּאֲבֹתֶיךָ, *only your forefathers,* is the command וּמַלְתֶּם, *You shall circumcise* [*the foreskin of your heart*], to indicate that you should circumcise the foreskin of the heart, just as the forefathers did.[140]

18. וְאֹהֵב — **AND HE LOVES.** The masoretic note, ב׳, means that this word appears twice in the *Tanach*: (i) here, וְאֹהֵב גֵּר, *and He loves the convert;* and (ii) וְרָשָׁע וְאֹהֵב חָמָס שָׂנְאָה נַפְשׁוֹ, *but a wicked person and one who loves violence, His soul despises* (*Psalms* 11:5). [Although] He loves the convert, nevertheless, [a convert] who loves violence, *His soul despises.*[140a]

20. אֶת ה׳ אֱלֹהֶיךָ תִּירָא — **HASHEM, YOUR GOD, SHALL YOU FEAR.** The *gematria* of תִּירָא, *you shall fear* (611), is equal to that of תּוֹרָה, *Torah.*[140b]

---

140. This comment and the one that precedes it should be read together. A person may think, "Of course God loved the Patriarchs. They were perfect people, totally free of any trace of sin. But how can I think that God loves me when I am so blemished with sin. I cannot even begin to be like the Patriarchs." Such thoughts could lead a person away from repentance. Therefore, God said, "See, even the Patriarchs had to be brought to judgment, yet they repented and atoned and I forgave them. You can do the same thing by cutting

away the barrier in your heart and returning to Me" (A.S.)

140a. The words interpolated in brackets are suggested by *Shoham Yakar,* based on *Midrash Shocher Tov* 146:9.

140b. According to the Midrash, it was Jochebed's fear of God (see note 125 above) that afforded her the merit to have a son through whom the Torah would be given to Israel. Thus, we see that the reward for fear of God is Torah (*Shemos Rabbah* 40:1).

כב בְּשִׁבְעִים נֶפֶשׁ יָרְדוּ אֲבֹתֶיךָ מִצְרָיְמָה וְעַתָּה שָׂמְךָ

יא א יְהוָה אֱלֹהֶיךָ כְּכוֹכְבֵי הַשָּׁמַיִם לָרֹב: וְאָהַבְתָּ אֵת
יְהוָה אֱלֹהֶיךָ וְשָׁמַרְתָּ מִשְׁמַרְתּוֹ וְחֻקֹּתָיו וּמִשְׁפָּטָיו

ב וּמִצְוֺתָיו כָּל־הַיָּמִים: וִידַעְתֶּם הַיּוֹם כִּי | לֹא
אֶת־בְּנֵיכֶם אֲשֶׁר לֹא־יָדְעוּ וַאֲשֶׁר לֹא־רָאוּ אֶת־
מוּסַר יְהוָה אֱלֹהֵיכֶם אֶת־גָּדְלוֹ אֶת־יָדוֹ הַחֲזָקָה

ג וּזְרֹעוֹ הַנְּטוּיָה: וְאֶת־אֹתֹתָיו וְאֶת־מַעֲשָׂיו אֲשֶׁר
עָשָׂה בְּתוֹךְ מִצְרָיִם לְפַרְעֹה מֶלֶךְ־מִצְרַיִם וּלְכָל־

ד אַרְצוֹ: וַאֲשֶׁר עָשָׂה לְחֵיל מִצְרַיִם לְסוּסָיו וּלְרִכְבּוֹ
אֲשֶׁר הֵצִיף אֶת־מֵי יַם־סוּף עַל־פְּנֵיהֶם בְּרָדְפָם

ה אַחֲרֵיכֶם וַיְאַבְּדֵם יְהוָֹה עַד הַיּוֹם הַזֶּה: וַאֲשֶׁר עָשָׂה

ו לָכֶם בַּמִּדְבָּר עַד־בֹּאֲכֶם עַד־הַמָּקוֹם הַזֶּה: וַאֲשֶׁר
עָשָׂה לְדָתָן וְלַאֲבִירָם בְּנֵי אֱלִיאָב בֶּן־רְאוּבֵן אֲשֶׁר
פָּצְתָה הָאָרֶץ אֶת־פִּיהָ וַתִּבְלָעֵם וְאֶת־בָּתֵּיהֶם
וְאֶת־אָהֳלֵיהֶם וְאֵת כָּל־הַיְקוּם אֲשֶׁר בְּרַגְלֵיהֶם

ז בְּקֶרֶב כָּל־יִשְׂרָאֵל: כִּי עֵינֵיכֶם הָרֹאֹת אֶת כָּל־

בעל הטורים

(כב) **בְּשִׁבְעִים נֶפֶשׁ.** הַפָּסוּק מַתְחִיל וּמְסַיֵּם בְּבֵי"ת – לוֹמַר שֶׁיַּעֲקֹב הִזְהִירָם שֶׁיִּדְבְּקוּ אִישׁ
בְּבֵיתוֹ, וְלֹא יִתְעָרְבוּ בַּמִּצְרִים. וּלְכָךְ נִקְרְאוּ "בֵּית יַעֲקֹב":

יא (ד) וַיְאַבְּדֵם. ב' – "וַיְאַבְּדֵם ה'"; "מַשְׂגִּיא לַגּוֹיִם וַיְאַבְּדֵם". זֶהוּ שֶׁיֵּשׁ בַּמִּדְרָשׁ שֶׁנִּדְמָה
לְפַרְעֹה כְּסוּסְיָא נְקֵבָה כְּדֵי לְמָשְׁכוֹ בַיָּם לְאַבְּדוֹ, וְזֶהוּ "מַשְׂגִּיא לַגּוֹיִם וַיְאַבְּדֵם":

--- BAAL HATURIM ELUCIDATED ---

22. בְּשִׁבְעִים נֶפֶשׁ — WITH SEVENTY SOULS. This verse begins with the letter ב
(בֵּי"ת)[141] and ends with a ב.[142] This indicates that Jacob warned [each of his
seventy descendants] to cling to his own household and not to intermarry with
the Egyptians. For that reason, [the women of Israel] are described as בֵּית יַעֲקֹב,
the House of Jacob. [143]

❏ {The Baal HaTurim's comment to שָׂמְךָ appears at *Exodus* 2:14.}

---

141. The word בַּיִת, the name of the letter ב,
means *house of* or *household of* and is often used
as a metaphor for *wife* (e.g., see first Mishnah in
Yoma), which is how the Baal HaTurim uses it
here.

142. This phenomenon occurs four times in the

Torah (*Genesis* 3:19; *Exodus* 12:18; *Leviticus*
7:2; and here) and fifteen more times in the rest
of *Tanach*. The Baal HaTurim does not comment
on the other occurrences.

143. *Peirush HaRokeach.*

22 *With seventy souls did your ancestors descend to Egypt, and now HASHEM, your God, has made you like the stars of heaven for abundance.*

11 1 *You shall love HASHEM, your God, and you shall safeguard His charge, His decrees, His ordinances, and His commandments, all the days.* 2 *You should know today that it is not your children who did not know and who did not see the chastisement of HASHEM, your God, His greatness, His strong hand, and His outstretched arm;* 3 *His signs and His deeds that He performed in the midst of Egypt, to Pharaoh, king of Egypt, and to all his land;* 4 *and what He did to the army of Egypt, to its horses and its riders, over whom He swept the waters of the Sea of Reeds when they pursued you, and HASHEM destroyed them until this day;* 5 *and what He did for you in the wilderness, until you came to this place;* 6 *and what He did to Dathan and Abiram the sons of Eliab son of Reuben, when the earth opened its mouth wide and swallowed them, and their households, and their tents, and all the fortunes at their feet, in the midst of all Israel.* 7 *Rather it is your own eyes that see all*

BAAL HATURIM ELUCIDATED

XI.

4. וַיְאַבְּדֵם — AND [HASHEM] DESTROYED THEM. The masoretic note, ב׳, means that this word appears twice in the *Tanach*: (i) here, וַיְאַבְּדֵם ה׳, *and HASHEM destroyed them;* and (ii) מַשְׂגִּיא[144] לַגּוֹיִם וַיְאַבְּדֵם, *He increases*[144] *nations and destroys them* (*Job* 12:23). Thus the Midrash states that [God set] an image before Pharaoh that appeared to him as a she-horse to draw him into the sea, to destroy him.[145] Thus, מַשְׂגִּיא לַגּוֹיִם וַיְאַבְּדֵם [is to be understood as if it read מַשְׁגִּיא instead of מַשְׂגִּיא], *He leads nations astray and destroys them.*

6. {The Baal HaTurim's comment to וְאֵת כָּל הַיְקוּם אֲשֶׁר בְּרַגְלֵיהֶם appears at *Genesis* 7:4.}

---

144. The word משגיא of that verse is traditionally vowelized מַשְׂגִּיא, from the root שגא, *to increase,* and refers to bringing about an increase in population and in sovereignty (*Rashi*). However, various Midrashim (e.g., *Mechilta* to *Exodus* 14:2, cited by *Rashi* there, s.v., לפני בעל צפן; *Shemos Rabbah* 15:10) interpret the word as if it were vowelized מַשְׁגִּיא, from the root שגה, *to lead to error;* accordingly, the verse means that God leads nations astray as part of the process of destroying them. The Baal HaTurim's comment follows this second understanding of the word. See *Minchas Shai* (*Job* 12:23) for a fuller discussion of this word.

145. God saw that Pharaoh hesitated, afraid to enter the sea. What did He do? He rode, so to speak, on a thin cloud, giving it the image of a she-horse. Then, He paraded the horse image before Pharaoh's cavalry until the male war horses were aroused and began to pursue the she-horse. God then rode his cloud/horse down into the sea, and Pharaoh's frenzied steeds followed (*Tanchuma, Shofetim* 14).

יא/ח־יד ח מַעֲשֵׂה יהוה הַגָּדֹל אֲשֶׁר עָשָׂה: וּשְׁמַרְתֶּם אֶת־כָּל־
הַמִּצְוָה אֲשֶׁר אָנֹכִי מְצַוְּךָ הַיּוֹם לְמַעַן תֶּחֶזְקוּ וּבָאתֶם
וִירִשְׁתֶּם אֶת־הָאָרֶץ אֲשֶׁר אַתֶּם עֹבְרִים שָׁמָּה
ט לְרִשְׁתָּהּ: וּלְמַעַן תַּאֲרִיכוּ יָמִים עַל־הָאֲדָמָה אֲשֶׁר
נִשְׁבַּע יהוה לַאֲבֹתֵיכֶם לָתֵת לָהֶם וּלְזַרְעָם אֶרֶץ זָבַת
ששי י חָלָב וּדְבָשׁ: כִּי הָאָרֶץ אֲשֶׁר אַתָּה בָא־שָׁמָּה
לְרִשְׁתָּהּ לֹא כְאֶרֶץ מִצְרַיִם הִוא אֲשֶׁר יְצָאתֶם מִשָּׁם
אֲשֶׁר תִּזְרַע אֶת־זַרְעֲךָ וְהִשְׁקִיתָ בְרַגְלְךָ כְּגַן הַיָּרָק:
יא וְהָאָרֶץ אֲשֶׁר אַתֶּם עֹבְרִים שָׁמָּה לְרִשְׁתָּהּ אֶרֶץ הָרִים
יב וּבְקָעֹת לִמְטַר הַשָּׁמַיִם תִּשְׁתֶּה־מָּיִם: אֶרֶץ אֲשֶׁר־
יהוה אֱלֹהֶיךָ דֹּרֵשׁ אֹתָהּ תָּמִיד עֵינֵי יהוה אֱלֹהֶיךָ בָּהּ
יג מֵרֵשִׁית הַשָּׁנָה וְעַד אַחֲרִית שָׁנָה: וְהָיָה
אִם־שָׁמֹעַ תִּשְׁמְעוּ אֶל־מִצְוֹתַי אֲשֶׁר אָנֹכִי מְצַוֶּה
אֶתְכֶם הַיּוֹם לְאַהֲבָה אֶת־יהוה אֱלֹהֵיכֶם וּלְעָבְדוֹ
יד בְּכָל־לְבַבְכֶם וּבְכָל־נַפְשְׁכֶם: וְנָתַתִּי מְטַר־אַרְצְכֶם

בעל הטורים

(יב־יג) מֵרֵשִׁית הַשָּׁנָה. אוֹתִיּוֹת מִתִּשְׁרֵי:

❑ סָמַךְ "עֵינֵי ה' אֱלֹהֶיךָ בָּהּ" לְ"וְהָיָה". לוֹמַר, אִם שָׁמֹעַ תִּשְׁמַע, "עֵינֵי ה' אֱלֹהֶיךָ בָּהּ", כִּי "כַּמַּיִם הַפָּנִים לַפָּנִים":

❑ **וְעַד אַחֲרִית שָׁנָה. וְהָיָה אִם שָׁמֹעַ.** לוֹמַר, אִם תִּשְׁמְעוּ עַד אַחֲרִית הַשָּׁנָה, יִתֵּן הַגְּשָׁמִים בִּזְמַנָּם וּבְמָקוֹם הַצָּרִיךְ לָהֶם. וְאִם הָיוּ צַדִּיקִים בִּתְחִלַּת הַשָּׁנָה, וְהַקָּדוֹשׁ בָּרוּךְ הוּא גָּזַר עֲלֵיהֶם גְּשָׁמִים, וְסָרְחוּ, מוֹרִידָן בַּיַּמִּים וּבַמִּדְבָּרוֹת:

(יג־יד) בְּכָל לְבַבְכֶם וּבְכָל נַפְשְׁכֶם. וְנָתַתִּי מְטַר. לוֹמַר שֶׁאֵין נַעֲנִים עַל הַמָּטָר אֶלָּא אִם כֵּן

BAAL HATURIM ELUCIDATED

12-13. מֵרֵשִׁית הַשָּׁנָה — FROM THE BEGINNING OF THE YEAR. The word מֵרֵשִׁית, *from the beginning,* is spelled[146] with the same letters as מִתִּשְׁרֵי, *from Tishrei.*[147]

146. The א of the word רֵאשִׁית, *first,* like the א of ראש, *head* or *beginning,* is not vowelized and not pronounced. Rather, the word is pronounced as if it were spelled רֵשִׁית. Nevertheless, the word appears more than 50 times in the *Tanach,* each time spelled with an א, only in our verse does Scripture omit the א.

147. *Peirush HaRokeach.* The Talmud records a dispute regarding the month in which God created the world. According to one opinion, the world was created in Tishrei. According to the second opinion, the world was created in Nissan (*Rosh Hashanah* 10b-11a). *Halachah* (Torah law) integrates both views. Thus, Nissan is called *the first of the months of the year* (*Exodus* 12:2), yet in the prayers of Rosh Hashanah, on the first day of Tishrei, we recite הַיּוֹם הֲרַת עוֹלָם, *On this day the world was born.* In the defective spelling of

the great work of HASHEM, which He did.

^{8} *So you shall observe the entire commandment that I command you today, so that you will be strong, and you will come and possess the land to which you are crossing, to possess it,* ^{9} *and so that you will prolong your days on the land that HASHEM swore to your forefathers to give them and to their offspring — a land flowing with milk and honey.*

^{10} *For the land to which you come, to possess it — it is not like the land of Egypt that you left, where you would plant your seed and water it on foot like a vegetable garden.* ^{11} *But the land to which you cross over to possess it is a land of mountains and valleys; from the rain of heaven it drinks water;* ^{12} *a land that HASHEM, your God, seeks out; constantly, the eyes of HASHEM, your God, are upon it, from the beginning of the year to year's end.*

^{13} *It will be that if you listen to My commandments that I command you today, to love HASHEM, your God, and to serve Him with all your heart and with all your soul,* ^{14} *then I shall provide the rain of your land in its*

――――――――――――― BAAL HATURIM ELUCIDATED ―――――――――――――

❑ Scripture juxtaposed עֵינֵי ה׳ אֱלֹהֶיךָ בָּהּ, *the eyes of Hashem, your God, are . . . upon it,* [147a] with וְהָיָה [אִם שָׁמֹעַ תִּשְׁמְעוּ], *It will be that [if you listen. . .],* to indicate that if you are [constantly] listening [to His *mitzvos*], then *the eyes of HASHEM, your God, are upon it* [147a] [in accordance with the verse], כַּמַּיִם הַפָּנִים לַפָּנִים, *as water reflects a face back to a face* (Proverbs 27:19).

❑ וְעַד אַחֲרִית שָׁנָה. וְהָיָה אִם שָׁמֹעַ — **TO YEAR'S END. IT WILL BE THAT IF YOU LISTEN.** This [juxtaposition] indicates that [Moses was saying,] "If you will [continue] obeying [God's commandments] until the year's end, then God will bring rains at their proper time and at the place that needs them." But if they will have been righteous at the beginning of the year, so that God decreed rain for them, and they then reverted to evil ways, the rains will descend in the seas and in the wildernesses.[148]

❑ **13-14.** בְּכָל לְבַבְכֶם וּבְכָל נַפְשְׁכֶם. וְנָתַתִּי מְטַר — **WITH ALL YOUR HEART AND WITH ALL YOUR SOUL, THEN I SHALL PROVIDE THE RAIN OF.** This [juxtaposition of phrases] indicates that their prayers for rain will not be answered unless they set

מֵרֵשִׁית, the Baal HaTurim finds an allusion to the opinion that the world was created in Tishrei (see the Baal HaTurim to *Genesis* 1:1, s.v., בְּרֵאשִׁית, and s.v., בְּרֵאשִׁית בָּרָא).

147a. Unlike *Rashi*, who interprets עֵינֵי ה׳ אֱלֹהֶיךָ בָּהּ as עִתִּים לְטוֹבָה וְעִתִּים לְרָעָה , *sometimes for good, sometimes for bad,* the Baal HaTurim under-

stands the phrase to refer only to the good. Thus, he states "If you are [constantly] listening [to His *mitzvos*], then *the eyes of HASHEM . . . are upon it* (VeChur LaZahav).

148. *Rosh Hashanah* 17b — God will not rescind His decree for a year of abundant rainfall. Rather, He will move the rain away from areas of

בְּעִתּוֹ יוֹרֶה וּמַלְקוֹשׁ וְאָסַפְתָּ דְגָנֶךָ וְתִירֹשְׁךָ וְיִצְהָרֶךָ׃
טו וְנָתַתִּי עֵשֶׂב בְּשָׂדְךָ לִבְהֶמְתֶּךָ וְאָכַלְתָּ וְשָׂבָעְתָּ׃
טז הִשָּׁמְרוּ לָכֶם פֶּן־יִפְתֶּה לְבַבְכֶם וְסַרְתֶּם וַעֲבַדְתֶּם
יז אֱלֹהִים אֲחֵרִים וְהִשְׁתַּחֲוִיתֶם לָהֶם׃ וְחָרָה אַף־יהוה
בָּכֶם וְעָצַר אֶת־הַשָּׁמַיִם וְלֹא־יִהְיֶה מָטָר וְהָאֲדָמָה
לֹא תִתֵּן אֶת־יְבוּלָהּ וַאֲבַדְתֶּם מְהֵרָה מֵעַל הָאָרֶץ
יח הַטֹּבָה אֲשֶׁר יהוה נֹתֵן לָכֶם׃ וְשַׂמְתֶּם אֶת־דְּבָרַי אֵלֶּה
עַל־לְבַבְכֶם וְעַל־נַפְשְׁכֶם וּקְשַׁרְתֶּם אֹתָם לְאוֹת
יט עַל־יֶדְכֶם וְהָיוּ לְטוֹטָפֹת בֵּין עֵינֵיכֶם׃ וְלִמַּדְתֶּם אֹתָם
אֶת־בְּנֵיכֶם לְדַבֵּר בָּם בְּשִׁבְתְּךָ בְּבֵיתֶךָ וּבְלֶכְתְּךָ
כ בַדֶּרֶךְ וּבְשָׁכְבְּךָ וּבְקוּמֶךָ׃ וּכְתַבְתָּם עַל־מְזוּזוֹת בֵּיתֶךָ

בעל הטורים

יְכַוְּנוּ לְהִתְפַּלֵּל בְּכָל לֵב׃

❑ **בְּעִתּוֹ.** בְּגִימַטְרִיָּא בַּלֵּילוֹת׃

(טז) לְבַבְכֶם וְסַרְתֶּם וַעֲבַדְתֶּם אֱלֹהִים אֲחֵרִים וְהִשְׁתַּחֲוִיתֶם לָהֶם. שִׁבְעָה מֵמִי״ן בְּסוֹפֵי תֵבוֹת. וּכְנֶגְדָּן ״פִּתְחִי לִי אֲחֹתִי רַעְיָתִי יוֹנָתִי תַמָּתִי שֶׁרֹּאשִׁי״, שִׁבְעָה יוּדִי״ן בְּסוֹפֵי תֵבוֹת. לוֹמַר, כָּל הַמּוֹדֶה בַּעֲבֹדָה זָרָה, כְּכוֹפֵר בְּי׳ הַדִּבְּרוֹת שֶׁנִּתְּנוּ לְמ׳ יוֹם׃

וְכֵן – שִׁבְעָה מֵמִי״ן, כִּי שִׁבְעָה מוּמִין כְּתוּבִים בַּעֲבֹדָה זָרָה, ״פֶּה לָהֶם וְלֹא יְדַבֵּרוּ, עֵינַיִם לָהֶם וְלֹא יִרְאוּ. . .״׃

(כ) וּכְתַבְתָּם עַל מְזוּזוֹת בֵּיתֶךָ. וְסָמִיךְ לֵהּ ״לְמַעַן יִרְבּוּ״. שֶׁעַל יְדֵי הַמְּזוּזָה לֹא יָבוֹא הַמַּשְׁחִית

BAAL HATURIM ELUCIDATED

[their intentions] to pray wholeheartedly.[149]

❑ **בְּעִתּוֹ** — IN ITS PROPER TIME. The *gematria* of this word (478) is equal to that of בַּלֵּילוֹת, *during the nights.*[150]

16. לְבַבְכֶם וְסַרְתֶּם וַעֲבַדְתֶּם אֱלֹהִים אֲחֵרִים וְהִשְׁתַּחֲוִיתֶם לָהֶם — YOUR HEART . . . AND YOU TURN ASTRAY AND SERVE OTHER GODS[151] AND PROSTRATE YOURSELVES TO THEM. [Here are] seven words [in a row] that all conclude with the letter ם (= 40).[152] Corresponding

---

human settlement so that it will not produce any beneficial results for the wicked.

149. See the Baal HaTurim to *Genesis* 2:6.

150. *Rabbeinu Ephraim* (*MiKesivah Ashkenazis*); see *Toras Kohanim, Bechukosai* 1:1, cited by *Rashi* here.

151. That is, things, other than the One true God, which in the mind of their worshipers are gods.

152. The phenomenon of at least seven consecutive words within the same verse ending with the letter ם occurs four times in the Torah. In two of those verses, every word ends with a ם: *Genesis* 32:15 contains eight such words and *Numbers* 29:33 contains seven. In his comments to *Genesis* 32:15, the Baal HaTurim comments on both those verses. The other two occurrences are in verse fragments that contain seven consecutive words ending in ם: here; and *Exodus* 12:11, where the Baal HaTurim does not comment.

proper time, the early and the late rains, that you may gather in your grain, your wine, and your oil. [15] *I shall provide grass in your field for your cattle and you will eat and you will be satisfied.* [16] *Beware for yourselves, lest your heart be seduced and you turn astray and serve other gods and prostrate yourselves to them.* [17] *Then the wrath of HASHEM will blaze against you; He will restrain the heaven so there will be no rain, and the ground will not yield its produce; and you will be swiftly banished from the goodly land that HASHEM gives you.* [18] *You shall place these words of Mine upon your heart and upon your soul; you shall bind them for a sign upon your arm and let them be an ornament between your eyes.* [19] *You shall teach them to your children to discuss them, while you sit in your home, while you walk on the way, when you retire and when you arise.* [20] *And you shall write them on the doorposts of your house*

BAAL HATURIM ELUCIDATED

to them [are God's words to Israel], פִּתְחִי לִי אֲחֹתִי רַעְיָתִי יוֹנָתִי תַמָּתִי שֶׁרֹּאשִׁי, *Open to Me, My sister, My companion, My dove, My perfect one; for My head . . .* (*Song of Songs* 5:2), seven words that conclude with the letter י (= 10). This indicates that anyone who acknowledges a false deity is considered as denying the Ten Commandments[152a] that were given to Moses after [he was on the mountain for] forty days.[153]

Additionally: The seven letters ם allude to the seven מוּמִין, *blemishes,* [154] that are written regarding false deities: . . . פֶּה לָהֶם וְלֹא יְדַבֵּרוּ עֵינַיִם לָהֶם וְלֹא יִרְאוּ, *They have a mouth, but cannot speak; they have eyes, but cannot see . . .* [155] (*Psalms* 115:5-7).

20. וּכְתַבְתָּם עַל מְזוּזוֹת בֵּיתֶךָ — AND YOU SHALL WRITE THEM ON THE DOORPOSTS OF YOUR HOUSE. Juxtaposed to this is לְמַעַן יִרְבּוּ [יְמֵיכֶם], *in order to prolong [your days]* (v. 21). [This indicates] that because of the *mezuzah,* a destructive force will not enter your homes.[156]

152a. See *Nedarim* 25a.

153. The seven words of our verse that end in ם speak explicitly about idolatry. However, the seven words from *Song of Songs* neither end in ם nor speak of idolatry. *Peirush HaRokeach,* the Baal HaTurim's source for this comment, adds a short sentence that sheds light on the allusion: אַ״תְ בַּ״שׁ י׳ הִיא מ׳, *In the* אַ״תְ בַּ״שׁ *letter exchange* (see note 126 above), י *corresponds* to מ. Thus, the seven letters י of *Song of Songs* correspond to the seven letters ם of our verse.

154. The Baal HaTurim is playing on the similarity between מֵ״ם, the name of the letter, and the word מוּם, *blemish.*

155. King David described seven flaws found in idols, each ending with the letter ם. The seven are: פֶּה לָהֶם, *They have a mouth, but cannot speak;* עֵינַיִם לָהֶם, *they have eyes, but cannot see;* אָזְנַיִם לָהֶם, *they have ears, but cannot hear;* אַף לָהֶם, *they have a nose, but cannot smell;* יְדֵיהֶם, *their hands cannot feel;* רַגְלֵיהֶם, *their feet cannot walk; they cannot utter a sound* בִּגְרוֹנָם, *from their throat* (*Psalms* 115:5-7, recited as part of *Hallel* on the festivals). The seven letters ם in our verse allude to the seven flaws described by King David.

156. *Mechilta* to 12:23.

See *Shabbos* 32b. According to one opinion there, the juxtaposition of these two verses

יא/כא־כה כא וּבִשְׁעָרֶיךָ: לְמַעַן יִרְבּוּ יְמֵיכֶם וִימֵי בְנֵיכֶם עַל
הָאֲדָמָה אֲשֶׁר נִשְׁבַּע יהוה לַאֲבֹתֵיכֶם לָתֵת לָהֶם
שביעי ומפטיר כב כִּימֵי הַשָּׁמַיִם עַל־הָאָרֶץ: כִּי אִם־שָׁמֹר
תִּשְׁמְרוּן אֶת־כָּל־הַמִּצְוָה הַזֹּאת אֲשֶׁר אָנֹכִי מְצַוֶּה
אֶתְכֶם לַעֲשֹׂתָהּ לְאַהֲבָה אֶת־יהוה אֱלֹהֵיכֶם לָלֶכֶת
כג בְּכָל־דְּרָכָיו וּלְדָבְקָה־בוֹ: וְהוֹרִישׁ יהוה אֶת־כָּל־
הַגּוֹיִם הָאֵלֶּה מִלִּפְנֵיכֶם וִירִשְׁתֶּם גּוֹיִם גְּדֹלִים
כד וַעֲצֻמִים מִכֶּם: כָּל־הַמָּקוֹם אֲשֶׁר תִּדְרֹךְ כַּף־רַגְלְכֶם
בּוֹ לָכֶם יִהְיֶה מִן־הַמִּדְבָּר וְהַלְּבָנוֹן מִן־הַנָּהָר נְהַר־
כה פְּרָת וְעַד הַיָּם הָאַחֲרוֹן יִהְיֶה גְּבֻלְכֶם: לֹא־יִתְיַצֵּב
אִישׁ בִּפְנֵיכֶם פַּחְדְּכֶם וּמוֹרַאֲכֶם יִתֵּן | יהוה אֱלֹהֵיכֶם

בעל הטורים

אֶל בָּתֵּיכֶם. וּסְמִיךְ לֵהּ "אִם שָׁמֹר תִּשְׁמְרוּן", עַל שֵׁם "ה' שֹׁמְרֶךָ ה' צִלְּךָ עַל יַד יְמִינֶךָ":

(כא) **עַל הָאָרֶץ.** תֵּשַׁע פְּעָמִים "עַל הָאָרֶץ" בְּזֶה הַסֵּפֶר, כְּנֶגֶד תִּשְׁעָה שְׁבָטִים שֶׁנָּטְלוּ חֵלֶק מֵעֵבֶר לַיַּרְדֵּן:

(כב) **כִּי אִם שָׁמֹר.** בְּגִימַטְרִיָּא תּוֹרָה:

(כד) **כָּל הַמָּקוֹם אֲשֶׁר תִּדְרֹךְ.** וּבִיהוֹשֻׁעַ כְּתִיב "כָּל מָקוֹם" חָסֵר הֵ"א – שֶׁה' שְׁבָטִים לֹא הוֹרִישׁ יְהוֹשֻׁעַ:

(כה) **וּמוֹרַאֲכֶם.** ב' – "פַּחְדְּכֶם וּמוֹרַאֲכֶם יִתֵּן ה' אֱלֹהֵיכֶם"; "וּמוֹרַאֲכֶם וְחִתְּכֶם יִהְיֶה עַל כָּל

BAAL HATURIM ELUCIDATED

And juxtaposed [to those two verses] is אִם שָׁמֹר תִּשְׁמְרוּן, *if you will observe* (v. 22),[157] alluding to the promise, ה' שֹׁמְרֶךָ ה' צִלְּךָ עַל יַד יְמִינֶךָ, *HASHEM is your Guardian; HASHEM is your [protective] Shade at your right hand*[157a] (*Psalms* 121:5).[158]

21. **עַל הָאָרֶץ** — UPON THE LAND.[159] This phrase appears nine times in this Book of *Deuteronomy*,[160] corresponding to the nine tribes that received [their entire] portion on the [western] side of the Jordan.

teaches that the underlying spiritual cause for the death of young children is their parents' negligence regarding the *mitzvah* of affixing a *mezuzah* to their doorpost. Thus, the Baal HaTurim states, when the *mezuzah* is in place, the destructive force [i.e., the angel of death] does not enter the house [to snatch the young ones].

157. The root שמר can mean *to observe/obey* or *to (safe)guard.*

157a. According to the Talmud (*Menachos* 33b), the phrase *at your right hand* alludes to the *mezuzah,* which is placed on the right doorpost.

158. *Peirush HaRokeach.*

159. The translation of this verse follows *Ibn Ezra.* The verse should be understood: *In order to prolong your days . . .* [*then*] *as long as the days of the heavens are,* [*so shall be your days*] *upon the land.*

160. They are: (i) 4:32; (ii) 8:10; (iii) 11:21; (iv-v) 12:16 and 24; (vi) 15:23; (vii) 22:6; (viii) 23:21; and (ix) 28:56.

and upon your gates. [21] In order to prolong your days and the days of your children upon the ground that HASHEM has sworn to your forefathers to give them — like the days of the heavens — upon the land.

[22] For if you will observe this entire commandment that I command you, to perform it, to love HASHEM, your God, to walk in all His ways and to cleave to Him, [23] HASHEM will drive out all these nations from before you, and you will drive out greater and mightier nations than yourselves. [24] The entire place where the sole of your foot will tread shall be yours— from the wilderness and the Lebanon, from the river, the Euphrates River, until the Western Sea shall be your boundary. [25] No man will stand up against you; HASHEM, your God, will set the dread of you and the fear of you

BAAL HATURIM ELUCIDATED

❑ {The Baal HaTurim cites this verse in his comment to *Numbers* 11:12.}

22. כִּי אִם שָׁמֹר — **FOR IF YOU WILL OBSERVE.** The *gematria* of this phrase (611) is equal to that of תּוֹרָה, *Torah.*[161]

24. כָּל הַמָּקוֹם אֲשֶׁר תִּדְרֹךְ — **THE ENTIRE PLACE WHERE [THE SOLE OF YOUR FOOT] WILL TREAD.** [In the parallel verse] in the Book of *Joshua* (1:3), this reads, כָּל מָקוֹם, *every place,*[162] without the prefix ־הַ (=5). [This alludes to the fact that] there were five tribes [from whose apportioned territories] Joshua did not drive out[162a] [the native inhabitants].[163]

25. וּמוֹרַאֲכֶם — **AND THE FEAR OF YOU.** The masoretic note, ב׳, means that this word appears twice in the *Tanach*: (i) here, וּמוֹרַאֲכֶם יִתֵּן ה׳ אֱלֹהֵיכֶם, *HASHEM, your God, will set the dread of you and the fear of you;* and (ii) פַּחְדְּכֶם וּמוֹרַאֲכֶם וְחִתְּכֶם יִהְיֶה עַל כָּל חַיַּת הָאָרֶץ, *The fear of you and the dread of you shall be upon every beast of the*

161. *Peirush HaRokeach;* see also *Rashi.* The *Sifrei* states that the phrase כִּי אִם שָׁמֹר, *for if you will observe* [alternatively: *for if you will guard*], teaches that just as a person must guard his money that it not be lost, so must one guard the Torah learning that he has acquired, lest it be lost.

162. The phrase כָּל הַמָּקוֹם, literally, *the entire place,* with the definite article prefix ־הַ on the second word and no prefix on the first word, appears twice in the *Tanach,* both times in the Torah — here and *Genesis* 20:13. While the phrase כָּל מָקוֹם, literally, *every place* or *each place,* with no prefix on either word, appears twice in *Tanach,* both times in the *Neviim* (Prophets) — *Joshua* 1:3 and *Isaiah* 7:23.

The first eight words of our verse and the first eight words of the verse from *Joshua* are almost identical, except that our verse reads הַמָּקוֹם, with the prefix ־הַ, while the word from *Joshua* omits that prefix.

162a. That is, he died before he had completed the conquest of the Land of Canaan.

163. *Peirush HaRokeach,* who adds the words, בְּרֹאשׁ שֹׁפְטִים, *at the beginning of the Book of Judges.* This refers to the first chapter of *Judges,* where we find the expression (וְ)לֹא הוֹרִישׁ, *(and) he did not drive out,* five times: (i) וְלֹא הוֹרִישׁ מְנַשֶּׁה, *Manasseh did not drive out* — v. 27; (ii) וְאֶפְרַיִם לֹא הוֹרִישׁ — v. 29; (iii) זְבוּלֻן לֹא הוֹרִישׁ — v. 30; (iv) אָשֵׁר לֹא הוֹרִישׁ — v. 31; and (v) נַפְתָּלִי לֹא הוֹרִישׁ — v. 33.

יא/כה עַל־פְּנֵי כָל־הָאָרֶץ אֲשֶׁר תִּדְרְכוּ־בָהּ כַּאֲשֶׁר דִּבֶּר
לָכֶם: ססס קי״א פסוקים. אי״ק סימן. יעל״א סימן.

בעל הטורים

חַיַּת הָאָרֶץ״. מְלַמֵּד שֶׁכְּשֶׁנִּכְנְסוּ יִשְׂרָאֵל הָיָה מוֹרָאָם אַף ״עַל כָּל חַיַּת הָאָרֶץ״, כִּדְכְתִיב ״וְהִשְׁבַּתִּי חַיָּה רָעָה מִן הָאָרֶץ״, וּכְעִנְיָן שֶׁנֶּאֱמַר לִימוֹת הַמָּשִׁיחַ ״וְנַעַר קָטֹן נֹהֵג בָּם״:

BAAL HATURIM ELUCIDATED

earth (*Genesis* 9:2). This [similarity of expression] teaches that when the Israelites entered [Canaan], fear of them fell even upon the beasts of the land, as it is written, וְהִשְׁבַּתִּי חַיָּה רָעָה מִן הָאָרֶץ, *I will cause the wildness of beasts to cease from the land* (*Leviticus* 26:6).[164] This is in accordance with what is stated

164. See the Baal HaTurim to that verse.

11/25   on the entire face of the earth where you will tread, as He has spoken to you.

regarding the era of *Mashiach,* וְנַעַר קָטֹן נֹהֵג בָּם, *and a young boy will lead them* (*Isaiah* 11:6).[165]

❑ {The Baal HaTurim's comment to לָכֶם appears at 11:26 below, s.v., דָּבָר אַחֵר לְעֵיל.}

───────────────────────────

165. The full verse reads: *The wolf will dwell with the sheep and the leopard will lie with the young goat; a calf, a lion cub and a fatling [will be] together and a young boy will lead them.* Thus, the awe of the King *Mashiach* will fall upon the beasts, just as the awe of Israel fell upon them when the Israelites entered the Land of Canaan.

פרשת ראה ⸉

Parashas Re'eh

כו רְאֵה אָנֹכִי נֹתֵן לִפְנֵיכֶם הַיּוֹם בְּרָכָה וּקְלָלָה:

בעל הטורים

(כו) רְאֵה אָנֹכִי. אָמַר בִּלְשׁוֹן יָחִיד, וּפֵרוּשׁוֹ, "רְאֵה" אָמַר לְכָל אֶחָד וְאֶחָד:
וְיֵשׁ מְפָרְשִׁים — לִיהוֹשֻׁעַ אָמַר "רְאֵה אָנֹכִי", וְהִזְהִירוֹ לְבָרֵךְ אֶת יִשְׂרָאֵל כְּשֶׁיַּעַבְרוּ אֶת הַיַּרְדֵּן:
וְיֵשׁ מְפָרְשִׁים — לְפִי שֶׁקְּלָלוֹת וּבְרָכוֹת שֶׁבְּמִשְׁנֵה תוֹרָה כֻּלָּם נֶאֶמְרוּ בִּלְשׁוֹן יָחִיד:
דָּבָר אַחֵר — "רְאֵה אָנֹכִי", רְאֵה עֲשֶׂרֶת הַדִּבְּרוֹת שֶׁפָּתַח בְּ"אָנֹכִי" וּתְקַיֵּם אוֹתָם, כִּי כָל הַמִּצְוֹת כְּלוּלוֹת בָּהֶם:
דָּבָר אַחֵר — "רְאֵה אָנֹכִי", פֵּרוּשׁ, מִמֶּנִּי תִרְאוּ וְכֵן תַּעֲשׂוּ:
דָּבָר אַחֵר — "רְאֵה" לְשׁוֹן יָחִיד, "לִפְנֵיכֶם" לְשׁוֹן רַבִּים. וְהַיְנוּ דְּאָמְרִינַן, כֵּיצַד סֵדֶר הַמִּשְׁנָה? מֹשֶׁה שׁוֹנֶה לְאַהֲרֹן פִּרְקוֹ, וְאַחַר כָּךְ נִכְנְסוּ בָנָיו וְכוּ׳, כִּדְאִיתָא בְּעֵרוּבִין:
דָּבָר אַחֵר — לְעֵיל כְּתִיב "לָכֶם" וּסְמִיךְ לֵהּ "רְאֵה אָנֹכִי נֹתֵן לִפְנֵיכֶם הַיּוֹם בְּרָכָה". כְּלוֹמַר, לָכֶם אֲנִי אוֹמֵר שֶׁתִּתְבַּחֲרוּ בְרָכָה:
דָּבָר אַחֵר — "רְאֵה", כִּי הַמַּפִּיל גּוֹרָל עִם חֲבֵרוֹ מְכַסֶּה הַגּוֹרָלוֹת וְהַחֲלָקִים, שֶׁלֹּא יְבָרֵר חֲבֵרוֹ חֵלֶק הַיָּפֶה. אֲבָל אַתָּה, רְאֵה הַגּוֹרָלוֹת וּרְאֵה הַחֲלָקִים "וּבָחַרְתָּ בַּחַיִּים". וְזֶהוּ "אַתָּה

BAAL HATURIM ELUCIDATED

26. רְאֵה אָנֹכִי — SEE, I. [Moses[1]] used the singular verb [רְאֵה, *see*[2]], meaning that the command "רְאֵה, *See!*" was said to each person individually.[3]

[Alternatively:] There are those who explain that [Moses] said רְאֵה אָנֹכִי, *See, I* . . ., to Joshua. He bid him to bless the Israelites[3a] after they crossed the Jordan.[4]

[Alternatively:] There are those who explain that [the verb is in the singular, because] the curses and the blessings in the Book of *Deuteronomy*[5] are stated in the singular.[6]

---

1. *Targum Yonasan ben Uzziel.*

2. The imperative רְאֵה is masculine singular and means *Look*! or *See*! But the rest of the passage is couched in the plural: לִפְנֵיכֶם, *before you* (plural) — v. 26; תִּשְׁמְעוּ, *you* (pl.) *shall listen* — v. 27; etc. Thus, we would expect the passage to begin with the plural form רְאוּ, rather than רְאֵה. Additionally: Whereas the passage speaks of the incorporeal concepts of blessing and curse, what were the people to see? Each of the Baal HaTurim's eight comments to this verse addresses one or both of these questions. The Baal HaTurim includes the first three and the last of these comments in *Peirush HaTur HaAroch* also.

3. *Ibn Ezra;* see also the Baal HaTurim to 1:8 above.

Atros Addar suggests that this comment is to be understood in accordance with the Midrash: When God uttered the Ten Commandments, He modulated His voice to accommodate each person according to his ability to hear and assimilate God's words (*Pesikta DeRav Kahana* 12, *BaChodesh HaShlishi; Shemos Rabbah* 5:9, 29:1, 34:1; cited by *Rashi* to *Psalms* 29:4). If *Atros Addar* is correct, this first comment and the fourth comment to this verse should be read together, for one is a continuation of the other (*VeChur LaZahav*).

3a. That is, Moses said, "*See* [singular, i.e., you Joshua shall see] that *I present before you* [plural, i.e., Joshua and the rest of the nation] *today, a blessing.* Similarly, you [Joshua] shall present a blessing to the nation after they have crossed the Jordan" (*VeChur LaZahav*).

4. Cf. *Peirush HaRokeach.*

5. See 27:15-28:68 below.

6. See *Megillah* 31b, where the Talmud notes that the blessings and curses of *Leviticus* (26:3-45) are couched in the plural, while those of *Deuteronomy* are in the singular.

The Baal HaTurim explains that whereas the blessings and curses in *Deuteronomy* are addressed to each individual Israelite, Moses used the singular form when he began to speak of them in our passage.

26 See, I present before you today a blessing and a curse.

BAAL HATURIM ELUCIDATED

Alternatively: The phrase רְאֵה אָנֹכִי means, [Moses said,] "See the Ten Commandments,[7] which begin with the word אָנֹכִי, *I* (*Exodus* 20:2; *Deuteronomy* 5:6), and fulfill them, for all the *mitzvos* are included within them."[8]

Alternatively: [Moses said,] "רְאֵה אָנֹכִי, *See me,* i.e., observe me and emulate my example."[9]

Alternatively: רְאֵה, *see,* is in the singular, while לִפְנֵיכֶם, *before You,* is in the plural. This is in accordance with a Talmudic passage: What was the order in which the Oral Torah was taught? Moses would teach Aaron his portion. Then Aaron's sons entered, and so on . . . as related in tractate *Eruvin.*[10]

Alternatively: The previous *parashah* concludes with [כַּאֲשֶׁר דִּבֶּר] לָכֶם, [*as He has spoken*][11] *to you,* and juxtaposed to that is, רְאֵה אָנֹכִי נֹתֵן לִפְנֵיכֶם הַיּוֹם בְּרָכָה, *see, I present before you today a blessing.* As if to say, [God said to Israel,] "I say לָכֶם, *to you,* that you should choose blessing."[12]

Alternatively: רְאֵה, *see* [refers to the drawing of lots]. Generally, when two people draw lots, the person holding the lots covers them so that the other one should not be able to pick out the more desirable portion directly. Here, however, [God says,] "רְאֵה, *See,* the lots, see the portions, and you shall choose life."[13] And that is the meaning of the verse, אַתָּה תּוֹמִיךְ גּוֹרָלִי, *You guide my*

7. *Rosh; Daas Zekeinim MiBaalei HaTosafos.*

8. See the Baal HaTurim to *Exodus* 20:13, s.v., וְיֵשׁ בָּהֶם תרי״ב אוֹתִיּוֹת.

Rav Saadiah Gaon composed *Azharos,* in which he enumerates the 613 *mitzvos,* categorizing them according to the Ten Commandments (see *Ibn Ezra* toward the end of his comments at *Exodus* 20:1).

9. *Tanchuma* 4.

10. *Eruvin* 54b. The full passage reads: What was the order in which the Oral Torah was taught? Moses learned from the mouth of the Almighty. [Then] Aaron entered [into Moses' presence] and Moses taught him his portion, after which Aaron moved aside [from in front of Moses] and sat at Moses' left. [Then] Aaron's sons entered and Moses taught them their portion [which he had just taught to Aaron], after which his sons moved aside, Elazar sat at Moses' right and Ithamar sat at Aaron's left . . . [Then] the elders entered and Moses taught them their portion [again, the same portion he had taught Aaron and his sons], after which the elders moved aside. [Then] all the nation entered and Moses taught them their [i.e., that same] portion. Thus we find that [each portion was heard from Moses] by Aaron four times; by his sons three times; by the elders twice; and by all the people once. [Then] Moses left and Aaron taught his portion to everyone else; Aaron left and his sons taught their portion to everyone else; his sons left and the elders taught their portion to everyone else. Thus we find that each person heard [that portion] four times.

The Baal HaTurim's comment explains that whereas Moses initially taught each portion to Aaron only, he would couch his second person pronoun in the singular. But once the audience grew to include others besides Aaron, Moses would switch to the plural, for he was addressing a group. To allude to Moses' method of teaching, our passage begins in the singular, then switches to the plural.

11. The interpolation of two more words — כַּאֲשֶׁר דִּבֶּר, *as He has spoken* — from the last verse of the previous *parashah* is suggested by *Shoham Yakar.*

12. The juxtaposed phrases are read as if they were one verse: *As He has spoken to you, "See, I present before you today a blessing."*

13. We would expect the Baal HaTurim to write וּבָחַרְתָּ בַּבְּרָכָה, *and you shall choose blessing.* His use of בַּחַיִּים, *life,* in place of blessing, is a borrowing from another verse, one that equates blessing with life, and curse with death: *Life and*

כז אֶת־הַבְּרָכָה אֲשֶׁר תִּשְׁמְעוּ אֶל־מִצְוֺת יהוה אֱלֹהֵיכֶם
כח אֲשֶׁר אָנֹכִי מְצַוֶּה אֶתְכֶם הַיּוֹם: וְהַקְּלָלָה אִם־לֹא
תִשְׁמְעוּ אֶל־מִצְוֺת יהוה אֱלֹהֵיכֶם וְסַרְתֶּם מִן־הַדֶּרֶךְ
אֲשֶׁר אָנֹכִי מְצַוֶּה אֶתְכֶם הַיּוֹם לָלֶכֶת אַחֲרֵי אֱלֹהִים
כט אֲחֵרִים אֲשֶׁר לֹא־יְדַעְתֶּם: וְהָיָה כִּי יְבִיאֲךָ יהוה
אֱלֹהֶיךָ אֶל־הָאָרֶץ אֲשֶׁר־אַתָּה בָא־שָׁמָּה לְרִשְׁתָּהּ

בעל הטורים

תּוֹמִיךְ גּוֹרָלִי״, שֶׁאַתָּה תוֹמֵךְ בְּיָדִי לִתְּנָהּ עַל הַגּוֹרָל הַטּוֹב וְלִבְרֹר אוֹתוֹ:

(כז) אֶת הַבְּרָכָה. בִּבְרָכָה אָמַר ״אֶת״, לְשׁוֹן רִבּוּי, כִּי ״לֹא נָפַל דָּבָר אֶחָד מִכֹּל דְּבָרוֹ הַטּוֹב״. וּבִקְלָלָה לֹא אָמַר ״אֶת״ אֶלָּא ״וְהַקְּלָלָה״:

דָּבָר אַחֵר – ״אֶת הַבְּרָכָה״ מֵאָלֶ״ף עַד תָּי״ו, מֵ״אִם בְּחֻקֹּתַי״ עַד ״קוֹמְמִיּוּת״. ״וְהַקְּלָלָה״ מִוָּא״ו עַד הֵ״א, מִ״וְאִם לֹא תִשְׁמְעוּ״ עַד ״בְּיַד מֹשֶׁה״ {וּלְכָךְ אָמַר ״וְהַקְּלָלָה״}:

❏ בִּקְלָלָה אָמַר ״אִם לֹא תִשְׁמְעוּ״. וּבִבְרָכָה אָמַר ״אֲשֶׁר תִּשְׁמְעוּ״, וְלֹא אָמַר ״אִם״ בִּלְשׁוֹן סָפֵק. וְאָמַר ״אֲשֶׁר״ מִלְּשׁוֹן ״אַשְׁרֵי״, שֶׁנֶּאֱמַר ״אַשְׁרֵי אָדָם שֹׁמֵעַ לִי״:

❏ **אֶת הַבְּרָכָה אֲשֶׁר תִּשְׁמְעוּ.** סוֹפֵי תֵבוֹת תּוֹרָה. שֶׁבִּזְכוּת הַתּוֹרָה יָבֹאוּ הַבְּרָכוֹת:

BAAL HATURIM ELUCIDATED

lot (*Psalms* 16:5), for You [God] guide my hand, placing it on the good lot, and [cause me] to pick it.[14]

27. אֶת הַבְּרָכָה — THE BLESSING. With regard to the blessings, he said, אֶת,[15] an inclusionary term,[16] for not an item has fallen away from the entirety[17] of His good word.[18] With regard to the curse, by contrast, he did not say אֶת, merely וְהַקְּלָלָה.[19]

Alternatively: אֶת הַבְּרָכָה [may be interpreted, the entire gamut of] blessing from א to ת,[20] i.e., from [the א of] אִם בְּחֻקֹּתַי, *If* [*You will follow*] *My decrees . . .,*

death have I placed before you, blessing and curse; וּבָחַרְתָּ בַּחַיִּים, *and you shall choose life* (30:19 below).

14. *Sifrei;* cited by *Rashi* in his comments to 30:19 below and to *Psalms* 16:5.

15. From a grammatical standpoint, the word אֶת adds nothing to the translation; the phrase means *the blessing,* whether אֶת is present or omitted. Indeed, in speaking of the curse, Moses did not use the word אֶת, rather he said simply, וְהַקְּלָלָה, *and the curse* (v. 28). The Baal HaTurim now offers two explanations for the word אֶת in our verse.

16. According to the first principle in the *baraisa* known as "The Thirty-two *Middos* [Principles] of R' Eliezer son of R' Yose HaGelili" (which appears after tractate *Berachos* in most editions of the Talmud), certain terms used by Scripture are inclusionary. The Talmud identifies אֶת as such a word (*Yerushalmi Berachos* 9:5).

17. Had the verse omitted the form אֶת, we would be able to interpret הַבְּרָכָה, *the blessing,* as referring to even a part of the blessing. Therefore, the verse begins with אֶת, to imply the blessing in its entirety.

18. *Midrash Tanchuma* 4 — God said to them, "If you will fulfill My will, then even though I wrote a small number of blessings for you, I will increase them for you; moreover, I will not bring the curses upon you . . . as it is stated: *Not an item has fallen away from the entirety of His good word that He has spoken through the hand of Moses, His servant* (*I Kings* 8:56).

19. The Baal HaTurim repeats this comment in *Peirush HaTur HaAroch.*

20. This expression usually refers to the first and last letters of the *alef-beis* and means "from

[27] *The blessing: that you shall listen to the commandments of* HASHEM, *your God, that I command you today.* [28] *And the curse: if you do not listen to the commandments of* HASHEM, *your God, and you stray from the path that I command you today, to follow other gods that you did not know.*

[29] *It shall be that when* HASHEM, *your God, brings you to the land to which you come, to possess it, then you*

BAAL HATURIM ELUCIDATED

until [the ת of] קוֹמְמִיּוּת, *erect* (*Leviticus* 26:3-13).

But the term וְהַקְּלָלָה[20a] [may be interpreted as limiting the curse to the small area] from ו to ה, from [the ו of] וְאִם לֹא תִשְׁמְעוּ, *But if you will not listen,* until [the ה of] בְּיַד מֹשֶׁה, *through the hand of Moses* (*Leviticus* 26:14-46).[21] {Therefore our verse states וְהַקְּלָלָה.[22]}[22a]

❑ With regard to the curse, he said, אִם לֹא תִשְׁמְעוּ, *If you will not listen,* [making the matter conditional,] while with regard to the blessing he said, אֲשֶׁר תִּשְׁמְעוּ, *that you shall listen,* but he did not say אִם, *if,* an expression of doubt.[23] Rather, he said, אֲשֶׁר, which is related to the word אַשְׁרֵי, *praiseworthy,*[24] alluding to the verse, אַשְׁרֵי אָדָם שֹׁמֵעַ לִי, *Praiseworthy is the person who hearkens unto Me* (*Proverbs* 8:34).

❑ אֶת הַבְּרָכָה אֲשֶׁר תִּשְׁמְעוּ — **THE BLESSING: THAT YOU SHALL LISTEN.** The final letters of these words can be rearranged to spell תּוֹרָה, *Torah.*[24a] [This indicates] that the blessings will come in the merit of the Torah.[25]

beginning to end" [like the English phrase, "from A to Z"]. See, for example, *Avodah Zarah* 4a; the Baal HaTurim to 18:13 and 33:20 below. And that is how the Midrash (*Tanna DeVei Eliyahu Rabbah* 18) explains the אֶת of our verse. However, in our case it has a double meaning: It means the entire gamut and it also means literally from the letter א to the letter ת, i.e., the word אֶת refers to a passage that begins with the letter א and ends with the letter ת.

20a. Virtually all editions of the Baal HaTurim read וּבַקְּלָלָה, *with regard to the curse,* a word that appears in the previous comment where it is used in apposition to בַּבְּרָכָה, *with regard to the blessing.* However, in the present comment, it is used in apposition to the wording of the verse אֶת הַבְּרָכָה and, as such, has been emended to וְהַקְּלָלָה (see also note 22 below; *VeChur LaZahav*).

21. That is, וְהַקְּלָלָה is understood as ו״ה קְלָלָה, which means both *the curse that is [as narrow as the distance] from* ו *to* ה and *the curse that begins with* ו *and ends with* ה.

22. The phrase enclosed in brackets does not appear in the early printed editions. Another indication that the proper reading earlier in this comment is וְהַקְּלָלָה (see note 20a above), which obviates the need for this phrase (A.S.)

22a. *Midrash Tanchuma* 4a; see *Bava Basra* 88b-89a.

23. That is, אִם, *if,* implies a condition, and we cannot be sure at the onset whether the condition will ever be fulfilled.

24. See *Rashi* to *Leviticus* 4:22.

24a. Although this phenomenon occurs one hundred twenty-seven times in the Torah, within a given verse [and many more times where the four words span two verses], the Baal HaTurim comments about only six of those appearances (*Genesis* 18:19; *Leviticus* 6:1; *Numbers* 28:1; *Deuteronomy* 11:27, 21:16; and [in his comment to 33:3] 29:14).

25. *Peirush HaRokeach;* see *Bereishis Rabbah* 41:9.

[1957] **DEVARIM** / RE'EH

וְנָתַתָּה אֶת־הַבְּרָכָה עַל־הַר גְּרִזִּים וְאֶת־הַקְּלָלָה
ל עַל־הַר עֵיבָל: הֲלֹא־הֵמָּה בְּעֵבֶר הַיַּרְדֵּן אַחֲרֵי
דֶּרֶךְ מְבוֹא הַשֶּׁמֶשׁ בְּאֶרֶץ הַכְּנַעֲנִי הַיֹּשֵׁב בָּעֲרָבָה
לא מוּל הַגִּלְגָּל אֵצֶל אֵלוֹנֵי מֹרֶה: כִּי אַתֶּם עֹבְרִים
אֶת־הַיַּרְדֵּן לָבֹא לָרֶשֶׁת אֶת־הָאָרֶץ אֲשֶׁר־יְהוָה
אֱלֹהֵיכֶם נֹתֵן לָכֶם וִירִשְׁתֶּם אֹתָהּ וִישַׁבְתֶּם־בָּהּ:
לב וּשְׁמַרְתֶּם לַעֲשׂוֹת אֵת כָּל־הַחֻקִּים וְאֶת־הַמִּשְׁפָּטִים
יב א אֲשֶׁר אָנֹכִי נֹתֵן לִפְנֵיכֶם הַיּוֹם: אֵלֶּה הַחֻקִּים
וְהַמִּשְׁפָּטִים אֲשֶׁר תִּשְׁמְרוּן לַעֲשׂוֹת בָּאָרֶץ אֲשֶׁר
נָתַן יְהוָה אֱלֹהֵי אֲבֹתֶיךָ לְךָ לְרִשְׁתָּהּ כָּל־הַיָּמִים
ב אֲשֶׁר־אַתֶּם חַיִּים עַל־הָאֲדָמָה: אַבֵּד תְּאַבְּדוּן אֶת־
כָּל־הַמְּקֹמוֹת אֲשֶׁר עָבְדוּ־שָׁם הַגּוֹיִם אֲשֶׁר אַתֶּם
יֹרְשִׁים אֹתָם אֶת־אֱלֹהֵיהֶם עַל־הֶהָרִים הָרָמִים
ג וְעַל־הַגְּבָעוֹת וְתַחַת כָּל־עֵץ רַעֲנָן: וְנִתַּצְתֶּם
אֶת־מִזְבְּחֹתָם וְשִׁבַּרְתֶּם אֶת־מַצֵּבֹתָם וַאֲשֵׁרֵיהֶם

בעל הטורים

(ל) **הֲלֹא הֵמָּה בְּעֵבֶר הַיַּרְדֵּן.** סוֹפֵי תֵבוֹת "אַהֲרֹן". לְפִי שֶׁעַד עַתָּה הָיוּ הָעֲנָנִים עַל יָדוֹ, שֶׁהָיוּ מַרְאִים לָהֶם הַדֶּרֶךְ, וְעַתָּה פָּסְקוּ הָעֲנָנִים. לְכָךְ צָרִיךְ לִתֵּן לָהֶם סִימָן לֵידַע הַדָּרֶךְ:

❑ הַפָּסוּק מַתְחִיל וּמְסַיֵּם בְּהֵ"א, שֶׁצִּוָּה לָהֶם לַעֲשׂוֹת ה' דְבָרִים, "וְנִתַּצְתֶּם . . . וְשִׁבַּרְתֶּם . . . תִּשְׂרְפוּן . . . תְּגַדֵּעוּן, וְאִבַּדְתֶּם." וְכֵן אָמַר לָהֶם ה' דְּבָרִים לְסִימָן", מְבוֹא הַשֶּׁמֶשׁ, בְּאֶרֶץ הַכְּנַעֲנִי, הַיֹּשֵׁב בָּעֲרָבָה, מוּל הַגִּלְגָּל, אֵצֶל אֵלוֹנֵי מֹרֶה":

BAAL HATURIM ELUCIDATED

30. הֲלֹא הֵמָּה בְּעֵבֶר הַיַּרְדֵּן — ARE THEY NOT ON THE OTHER SIDE OF THE JORDAN. The final letters of these words spell אַהֲרֹן, *Aaron.*[25a] For until this time, the clouds of glory that showed [the Israelites] the way had come in his merit,[26] but now, the clouds ceased.[27] Thus it was necessary to provide them with landmarks, that they may know the way.[28]

❑ The verse begins with a ה (= 5) and ends with a ה,[29] for Moses commanded

25a. Although this phenomenon occurs four other times in the Torah (*Genesis* 4:5; *Exodus* 2:14; *Leviticus* 13:10; *Deuteronomy* 22:26), this is the only appearance about which the Baal HaTurim comments.

26. See the Baal HaTurim to *Exodus* 16:10.

27. See *Rosh Hashanah* 3a, cited by *Rashi* to *Numbers* 21:1; see the Baal HaTurim to *Numbers* 20:29 with note 84.

28. See *Sotah* 33b, with *Rashi*, s.v., כדרך שהראה להם.

29. This phenomenon occurs in twenty-six

11/30-**12**/3 *shall deliver the blessing on Mount Gerizim and the curse on Mount Ebal.* 30 *Are they not on the other side of the Jordan, far, in the direction of the sunset, in the land of the Canaanite, that dwells in the plain, far from Gilgal, near the plains of Moreh?* 31 *For you are crossing the Jordan to come and possess the land that HASHEM, your God, gives you; you shall possess it and you shall settle in it.* 32 *You shall observe to perform all the decrees and the ordinances that I present before you today.*

12 1 *These are the decrees and the ordinances that you shall observe to perform in the land that HASHEM, the God of your forefathers, has given you, to possess it, all the days that you live on the land.* 2 *You shall utterly destroy all the places where the nations that you are driving away worshiped their gods: on the high mountains and on the hills, and under every leafy tree.* 3 *You shall demolish their altars; you shall break their pillars; and their sacred trees*

BAAL HATURIM ELUCIDATED

them to take five actions [against idolatry]: (i) וְנִתַּצְתֶּם, *You shall demolish;* (ii) וְשִׁבַּרְתֶּם, *you shall break;* (iii) תִּשְׂרְפוּן, *you shall burn;* (iv) תְּגַדֵּעוּן, *you shall cut down;* and (v) וְאִבַּדְתֶּם, *and you shall obliterate* (12:3 below).[30] Additionally, Moses described five landmarks[30a] [in this verse]: (i) *in the direction of the sunset*; (ii) *in the land of the Canaanite*; (iii) *that dwells in the plain*; (iv) *far from Gilgal*; and (v) *near the plain of Moreh.*[31]

---

verses in the Torah and another hundred and eighty in the rest of *Tanach.* The Baal HaTurim comments on four of those verses: *Genesis* 19:23; *Numbers* 23:24; 10:14 above; and here.

30. *Peirush HaRokeach.* The connection between the five actions against idols and our verse that describes the geographical landmarks of Mount Gerizim and Mount Ebal is not explained by either *Peirush HaRokeach* or the Baal HaTurim. Perhaps the connection is based on a Talmudic passage regarding the religious status of the כּוּתִים, *Cutheans* (see *II Kings* 17:6,24-41): The Sages found a Cuthean dove-idol at the top of Mount Gerizim (*Chullin* 6a). Thus, the Baal HaTurim associates Mount Gerizim with idolatry (*VeChur LaZahav*).

30a. There is a sixth phrase instructing Israel to rid its land of idols, a phrase that precedes the other five: אַבֵּד תְּאַבְּדוּן, *You shall utterly destroy* (12:2). Presumably, the Baal HaTurim understands that statement as a general command, while the five actions of verse 3 are considered as five ways by which that command is to be carried out (*VeChur LaZahav*).

31. *Peirush HaRokeach.* The significance of five landmarks is not explained by either *Peirush HaRokeach* or the Baal HaTurim.

Once again, there is a sixth phrase at the beginning of the verse — בְּעֵבֶר הַיַּרְדֵּן אַחֲרֵי, *on the other side of the Jordan, far* — that may be considered a landmark. Presumably, the Baal HaTurim understands that phrase as a general location that covers a very large area, as if it were the name of a country, while the other five are considered as detailed landmarks that pinpoint the exact location of Mounts Gerizim and Ebal (*VeChur LaZahav*).

תִּשְׂרְפוּן בָּאֵשׁ וּפְסִילֵי אֱלֹהֵיהֶם תְּגַדֵּעוּן וְאִבַּדְתֶּם
ד אֶת־שְׁמָם מִן־הַמָּקוֹם הַהוּא: לֹא־תַעֲשׂוּן כֵּן
ה לַיהוָה אֱלֹהֵיכֶם: כִּי אִם־אֶל־הַמָּקוֹם אֲשֶׁר־
יִבְחַר יהוָה אֱלֹהֵיכֶם מִכָּל־שִׁבְטֵיכֶם לָשׂוּם אֶת־
ו שְׁמוֹ שָׁם לְשִׁכְנוֹ תִדְרְשׁוּ וּבָאתָ שָׁמָּה: וַהֲבֵאתֶם

בעל הטורים

יב (ג) **תִּשְׂרְפוּן.** ג׳ בַּמָּסוֹרֶת – בְּהַאי עִנְיָנָא. וְהַיְנוּ דִתְנַן שָׁלשׁ אֲשֵׁרוֹת הֵן, וְזֶהוּ ״וַאֲשֵׁירֵיהֶם תִּשְׂרְפוּן״ ג׳:

(ג-ד) **וְאִבַּדְתֶּם אֶת שְׁמָם . . . לֹא תַעֲשׂוּן כֵּן.** אַזְהָרָה לְמוֹחֵק הַשֵּׁם. ״לֹא תַעֲשׂוּן״ בְּגִימַטְרִיָּא אַזְהָרָה עַל כָּל מֹחֵק שֵׁם:

(ה) **אֶל הַמָּקוֹם.** בְּאַ״תְ בַּ״שׁ, ת״ך צידפ״י, בְּגִימַטְרִיָּא זֶהוּ יְרוּשָׁלַיִם. מָקוֹם בְּגִימַטְרִיָּא לְצִיּוֹן:

❑ **וּבָאתָ שָׁמָּה.** ב׳ בַּמָּסוֹרֶת – ״לְשִׁכְנוֹ תִדְרְשׁוּ וּבָאתָ שָׁמָּה״; ״וּבָאתָ שָׁמָּה וּרְאֵה שָׁם יֵהוּא״, בְּעִנְיַן אֱלִישָׁע שֶׁצִּוָּה לִמְשֹׁחַ יֵהוּא לְמֶלֶךְ. מַה מֶּלֶךְ בִּמְשִׁיחָה, אַף כָּל עִנְיַן הַקָּרְבָּנוֹת בִּמְשִׁיחָה – הַכֵּלִים אֵין מִתְקַדְּשִׁים אֶלָּא בִּמְשִׁיחָה, וְכֹהֵן גָּדוֹל בִּמְשִׁיחָה:

BAAL HATURIM ELUCIDATED

XII.

3. תִּשְׂרְפוּן — YOU SHALL BURN. The masoretic note, ג׳, means that this word appears three times in the *Tanach* (here; and 7:5 and in 7:25 above), all referring to the same subject [the obliteration of idols]. This alludes to the teaching of the Mishnah: There are three types of *Asheirah* trees.[32] Thus [the masoretic note], *you shall burn their sacred trees,* three.[33]

3-4. וְאִבַּדְתֶּם אֶת שְׁמָם . . . לֹא תַעֲשׂוּן כֵּן — AND YOU SHALL OBLITERATE THEIR NAMES ... YOU SHALL NOT DO THIS. This is an admonition not to erase [God's] name.[34] Indeed, the *gematria* of לֹא תַעֲשׂוּן, *You shall not do* (857), is equivalent[35] to that of אַזְהָרָה עַל כָּל מֹחֵק שֵׁם, *a warning against all those who erase* [*God's*] *Name.*

32. *Avodah Zarah* 3:7 [48a]. That Mishnah begins by distinguishing between three types of idolatrous buildings; then three types of idolatrous stones; and lastly, three types of idolatrous trees: There are three [categories of idolatrous] sacred trees — (i) If a tree was initially planted for idolatry, it is prohibited; (ii) if [an idolater] lopped off or trimmed [the branches of a tree] for idolatry [i.e., in order to worship the new growth that will sprout], then one must remove [and destroy] the new growth; (iii) if [an idolater] set an idol under [a tree] and subsequently nullified [alternative text: removed] the idol, the tree is permitted.

33. See note 32 above. Although the Mishnah states אֲסוּרָה, *it is prohibited,* with regard to only two of the three types of *asheirah* trees, indicating that only those two are subject to burning, the Talmud goes on to explain that the term מוּתֶּרֶת, *it is permitted,* in the third case, applies only after the idol has been removed. However, as long as the idol remains under the tree, the tree is *prohibited.* Thus, the allusion to three forbidden *asheiros* (A.S.).

34. *Sifrei; Makkos* 22a; cited by *Rashi* to v. 4.

35. The principle of *im hakollel* allows 856,

you shall burn in the fire; their carved images you shall cut down; and you shall obliterate their names from that place.

4 You shall not do this to HASHEM, your God. 5 Rather, only at the place that HASHEM, your God, will choose from among all your tribes to place His Name there; you shall seek out His resting place and you shall come there. 6 And you shall bring

BAAL HATURIM ELUCIDATED

❑ {The Baal HaTurim's other comments to verse 3 appear at *Numbers* 33:52 and at 11:30 above.}

5. אֶל הַמָּקוֹם — AT THE PLACE. In the *alef-beis* exchange[36] known as אַ״תְ בַּ״שׁ, the letters of אֶל הַמָּקוֹם may be exchanged for the letters ת״ב צידפ״י, the *gematria* of which (614) is equal to that of זֶהוּ יְרוּשָׁלַיִם, *This refers to Jerusalem.* And the *gematria* of מָקוֹם, *place* (186), is equal to that of לְצִיּוֹן, *to Zion.*[37]

❑ **וּבָאתָ שָּׁמָּה** — AND YOU SHALL COME THERE. The masoretic note, ב׳, means that this word appears twice in the *Tanach*:[37a] (i) here, לְשִׁכְנוֹ תִדְרְשׁוּ וּבָאתָ שָּׁמָּה, *you shall seek out His resting place and you shall come there;* and (ii) וּבָאתָ שָׁמָּה וּרְאֵה שָׁם יֵהוּא[38], *And when you will come there, you will see Jehu*[38] *there* (*II Kings* 9:2), in the passage in which [the prophet] Elisha commanded [one of his students] to anoint Jehu as king. [The similarity of expression indicates that] just as a king is [enthroned] through anointment,[38a] so too, everything about the Altar offerings is [accomplished] through anointment: the [sacred] vessels cannot become consecrated except through anointment;[39] and the Kohen Gadol [enters his office] through anointment.[40]

---

the *gematria* of the Baal HaTurim's phrase, to be considered equivalent to 857.

36. See note 126 to *parashas Eikev.*

37. See *Sifrei.*

37a. The masoretic note reads in full: ב׳ חד סוף פסוק וחד ריש פסוק, *Two, one at the end of the verse, and one at the beginning of the verse.* For our verse ends with that phrase; while the verse in *Kings* opens with it.

38. The text follows the early printed editions. Many later editions substitute וְהוּא, *and it,* for יֵהוּא, *Jehu.* The comment then reads: "וּבָאתָ שָׁמָּה וּרְאֵה שָׁם", *And when you will come there, you will see there* (*II Kings* 9:2), . . . וְהוּא בְּעִנְיַן אֱלִישָׁע, *and it is in the passage in which* [*the prophet*] *Elisha . . .* We have rejected that reading for two reasons: First, because, in describing the context of a verse he has just adduced, the Baal HaTurim uses the term בְּעִנְיַן, *in the passage,* in at least twenty-four other comments, yet, he does not preface that word with וְהוּא, *and it is,* in any of those instances; second, the gist of the Baal HaTurim's comment depends on the fact that the second appearance of וּבָאתָ שָׁמָּה refers to anointment of a king; but the verse fragment, וּבָאתָ שָׁמָּה וּרְאֵה שָׁם, includes neither anointment nor kingship! However, with the inclusion of the name יֵהוּא, *Jehu,* the fragment refers to kingship (*VeChur LaZahav*).

38a. See *Horayos* 11b.

39. *Shavuos* 15a. The Talmud there states that the sacred vessels made by Moses were sanctified through anointment; however, any vessels produced in later generations are not anointed, rather they acquire their sanctity through actually being used in the Temple service (see also *Rambam, Hilchos Kelei HaMikdash* 1:12).

40. See *Horayos* 11b.

שָׁ֣מָּה עֹלֹֽתֵיכֶם֙ וְזִבְחֵיכֶ֔ם וְאֵת֙ מַעְשְׂרֹ֣תֵיכֶ֔ם וְאֵ֖ת
תְּרוּמַ֣ת יֶדְכֶ֑ם וְנִדְרֵיכֶם֙ וְנִדְבֹ֣תֵיכֶ֔ם וּבְכֹרֹ֥ת בְּקַרְכֶ֖ם
ז וְצֹאנְכֶֽם׃ וַאֲכַלְתֶּם־שָׁ֗ם לִפְנֵי֙ יְהוָ֣ה אֱלֹהֵיכֶ֔ם
וּשְׂמַחְתֶּ֗ם בְּכֹל֙ מִשְׁלַ֣ח יֶדְכֶ֔ם אַתֶּ֖ם וּבָתֵּיכֶ֑ם אֲשֶׁ֥ר
ח בֵּרַכְךָ֖ יְהוָ֥ה אֱלֹהֶֽיךָ׃ לֹ֣א תַעֲשׂ֔וּן כְּ֠כֹל אֲשֶׁ֨ר אֲנַ֧חְנוּ
ט עֹשִׂ֛ים פֹּ֖ה הַיּ֑וֹם אִ֖ישׁ כָּל־הַיָּשָׁ֥ר בְּעֵינָֽיו׃ כִּ֥י
לֹא־בָאתֶ֖ם עַד־עָ֑תָּה אֶל־הַמְּנוּחָה֙ וְאֶל־הַֽנַּחֲלָ֔ה
י אֲשֶׁר־יְהוָ֥ה אֱלֹהֶ֖יךָ נֹתֵ֥ן לָֽךְ׃ וַעֲבַרְתֶּם֮ אֶת־הַיַּרְדֵּן֒
וִֽישַׁבְתֶּ֣ם בָּאָ֔רֶץ אֲשֶׁר־יְהוָ֥ה אֱלֹהֵיכֶ֖ם מַנְחִ֣יל
אֶתְכֶ֑ם וְהֵנִ֨יחַ לָכֶ֧ם מִכָּל־אֹיְבֵיכֶ֛ם מִסָּבִ֖יב
שני יא וִֽישַׁבְתֶּם־בֶּֽטַח׃ וְהָיָ֣ה הַמָּק֗וֹם אֲשֶׁר־יִבְחַ֨ר יְהוָ֜ה
אֱלֹהֵיכֶ֥ם בּוֹ֙ לְשַׁכֵּ֤ן שְׁמוֹ֙ שָׁ֔ם שָׁ֣מָּה תָבִ֔יאוּ אֵ֖ת

בעל הטורים

(ו) עֹלֹתֵיכֶם וְזִבְחֵיכֶם. ח׳ דְּבָרִים מֻזְכָּרִים כָּאן, כְּנֶגֶד ח׳ פְּעָמִים ״פני ה׳ ״ דִּכְתִיבֵי בָּרֶגֶל:

(ח) אֲנַחְנוּ עֹשִׂים פֹּה הַיּוֹם. סוֹפֵי תֵבוֹת בְּגִימַטְרִיָּא הַלְוִיִּם. כִּי עַתָּה הַלְוִיִּם נוֹשְׂאִים {הָאָרוֹן}. וּכְשֶׁתַּעַבְרוּ הַיַּרְדֵּן לֹא יִשְׂאוּ אוֹתוֹ:

(יא) לְשַׁכֵּן שְׁמוֹ שָׁם שָׁמָּה. רֶמֶז לִשְׁתֵּי מְחִיצוֹת, אַחַת לְקָדְשֵׁי קָדָשִׁים וְאַחַת לְקָדָשִׁים קַלִּים:

BAAL HATURIM ELUCIDATED

6. עֹלֹתֵיכֶם וְזִבְחֵיכֶם — YOUR BURNT-OFFERINGS AND YOUR SLAUGHTERINGS. Eight items[41] are mentioned in this verse, corresponding to the eight times the phrase פני ה׳[42] is written with regard to the festivals.[43]

---

41. *Peirush HaRokeach.* Although a cursory reading of the verse reveals only seven items — (i) עֹלֹתֵיכֶם, *your burnt-offerings,* (ii) וְזִבְחֵיכֶם, *and your [peace offerings] slaughterings,* (iii) וְאֵת מַעְשְׂרֹתֵיכֶם, *and your tithes,* (iv) וְאֵת תְּרוּמַת יֶדְכֶם, *and what is set aside by your hand* [i.e., *bikkurim (Rashi)*], (v) וְנִדְרֵיכֶם, *and your vow offerings,* (vi) וְנִדְבֹתֵיכֶם, *and your free-will offerings,* (vii) וּבְכֹרֹת בְּקַרְכֶם וְצֹאנְכֶם, *and the firstborn of your cattle and your flock* — the Midrash (*Sifrei,* cited by *Rashi*) teaches that the word מַעְשְׂרֹתֵיכֶם, *your tithes,* includes two different elements — מַעֲשֵׂר בְּהֵמָה, *the animal tithe,* and מַעֲשֵׂר שֵׁנִי, *the second tithe* — both of which are to be brought to Jerusalem. Thus, the verse lists eight items (*VeChur LaZahav*).

42. The reason that this phrase has been left without vowelization is explained in note 43.

43. *Peirush HaRokeach.* At first glance, the Baal HaTurim's wording פני ה׳ refers to the phrase פְּנֵי ה׳, *before HASHEM,* as in 16:16 below. However, that phrase appears only seven times, the first three of which are not related to the festivals: *Genesis* 19:13 and 27; *Exodus* 32:11 and 34:24; *Deuteronomy* 16:16 (twice) and 31:11 (*Ittur Bikkurim*).

The parallel comment in *Peirush HaRokeach,* the Baal HaTurim's source, reads: וח׳ לא יראו פני פני ה׳ פני אדון ברגלים, *and eight* [*appearances of the phrases*] [וְ]לֹא יֵרָאוּ פָנַי (*Exodus* 23:15 and 34:20), פְּנֵי ה׳ (*Exodus* 34:24; *Deuteronomy* 16:16 [twice] and 31:11), and פְּנֵי הָאָדֹן (*Exodus* 23:17 and 34:23), *with regard to the festivals.*

Thus, the Baal HaTurim's wording פני ה׳ means: *the word* פני [regardless of its vowelization] *with reference to HASHEM,* i.e., פָּנָי, *before Me,* or פְּנֵי ה׳, *before HASHEM,* or פְּנֵי הָאָדֹן, *before the Lord.* Accordingly, the phrase פני ה׳ has not been vowelized in the text.

there your burnt-offerings and your [peace-offerings] slaughterings, and your tithes and what is set aside by your hand, your vow offerings and your free-will offerings, and the firstborn of your cattle and your flocks. [7] You shall eat there before HASHEM, your God, and you shall rejoice with your every undertaking, you and your households, as HASHEM, your God, has blessed you.

[8] You shall not do like everything that we do here today — [rather,] every man what is proper in his eyes — [9] for you will not yet have come to the resting place or to the heritage that HASHEM, your God, gives you.

[10] You shall cross the Jordan and settle in the land that HASHEM, your God, causes you to inherit, and He will give you rest from all your enemies all around, and you will dwell securely.

[11] It shall be that the place that HASHEM, your God, will choose it to rest His Name there, to there shall you bring

BAAL HATURIM ELUCIDATED

8. אֲנַחְנוּ עֹשִׂים פֹּה הַיּוֹם — WE DO HERE TODAY. The *gematria* of the final letters of these words (91) is equal to that of הַלְוִיִּם, *the Levites.* For [Moses said,] "At the present time, the Levites are carrying {the Ark[44]}, but when you cross the Jordan, they will not carry it."[45]

11. לְשַׁכֵּן שְׁמוֹ שָׁם שָׁמָּה — TO REST HIS NAME THERE, THERE. [The repetitive שָׁם, *there,* שָׁמָּה, *to there,* is] an allusion to two partitions: one for the most holy offerings; and one for the offerings of lesser sanctity.[46]

44. The reading follows the emendation found in some later printed editions of the Baal HaTurim. At least one manuscript used by *Shoham Yakar* reads, הַמִּשְׁכָּן, *the Tabernacle;* but the source for that version is unknown. For we find that when the nation crossed the Jordan, *Joshua then spoke to the Kohanim . . . "Carry the Ark . . ." so they carried the Ark . . . HASHEM said to Joshua, ". . . and you shall command the Kohanim, bearers of the Ark . . ."* (*Joshua* 3:6-8). And the verses that follow (Chs. 3-4) identify the *Kohanim* as "bearers of the Ark" at least seven more times. However, we do not find a single verse anywhere in the *Tanach* that refers to the Kohanim carrying the *Mishkan* (Tabernacle). Indeed, the first three *parashiyos* of *Sefer Bamidbar (Numbers)* consistently mentions the Levites as the bearers of the *Mishkan* (see, e.g., *Numbers* 1:50-51; 2:17; 4:15; 24-27; etc.). The early printed editions, as well as many later ones, read כִּי עַתָּה הַלְוִיִּם נוֹשְׂאִים וּכְשֶׁתַּעַבְרוּ, *At the present time, the Levites are carrying, but when you cross the . . .,* without specifying what the Levites are carrying. As noted above, some later editions emend the comment by adding הָאָרוֹן, *the Ark.*

45. *Peirush HaRokeach;* see *Sotah* 33b.

46. *Sifrei* (in some editions).

The offerings classified as קָדְשֵׁי קָדָשִׁים, *most holy* (literally, *holies of holies*), must be eaten within, and may not be removed from, the Tabernacle [or Temple] Courtyard. Thus, their partition [i.e., the delineator of the area to which they are confined] was the curtains surrounding the Courtyard of the Tabernacle [or the wall surrounding the Temple Courtyard]. The offerings classified as קָדָשִׁים קַלִּים, *of lesser sanctity* (literally, *light holies*), must be eaten within, and may not be removed from the Israelite encampment [or within the city walls of Jerusalem] (see *Mishnah Zevachim,* Ch. 5).

כָּל־אֲשֶׁר אָנֹכִי מְצַוֶּה אֶתְכֶם עוֹלֹתֵיכֶם וְזִבְחֵיכֶם
מַעְשְׂרֹתֵיכֶם וּתְרֻמַת יֶדְכֶם וְכֹל מִבְחַר נִדְרֵיכֶם
יב אֲשֶׁר תִּדְּרוּ לַיהוָה: וּשְׂמַחְתֶּם לִפְנֵי יְהוָה אֱלֹהֵיכֶם
אַתֶּם וּבְנֵיכֶם וּבְנֹתֵיכֶם וְעַבְדֵיכֶם וְאַמְהֹתֵיכֶם
וְהַלֵּוִי אֲשֶׁר בְּשַׁעֲרֵיכֶם כִּי אֵין לוֹ חֵלֶק וְנַחֲלָה
יג אִתְּכֶם: הִשָּׁמֶר לְךָ פֶּן־תַּעֲלֶה עֹלֹתֶיךָ בְּכָל־
יד מָקוֹם אֲשֶׁר תִּרְאֶה: כִּי אִם־בַּמָּקוֹם אֲשֶׁר־יִבְחַר
יְהוָה בְּאַחַד שְׁבָטֶיךָ שָׁם תַּעֲלֶה עֹלֹתֶיךָ וְשָׁם
טו תַּעֲשֶׂה כֹּל אֲשֶׁר אָנֹכִי מְצַוֶּךָּ: רַק בְּכָל־אַוַּת נַפְשְׁךָ
תִּזְבַּח ׀ וְאָכַלְתָּ בָשָׂר כְּבִרְכַּת יְהוָה אֱלֹהֶיךָ

בעל הטורים

(יג) **עֹלֹתֶיךָ בְּכָל מָקוֹם אֲשֶׁר תִּרְאֶה.** סוֹפֵי תֵבוֹת הַכַּרְמֶל. "בְּכָל" בְּגִימַטְרִיָּא אֵלִיָּהוּ. רֶמֶז לְאֵלִיָּהוּ, שֶׁיַּעֲלֶה עוֹלוֹת בְּהַר הַכַּרְמֶל:

(יד) **שְׁבָטֶיךָ.** בְּגִימַטְרִיָּא שֵׁבֶט יְהוּדָה:

❑ **שָׁם תַּעֲלֶה עֹלֹתֶיךָ.** רָאשֵׁי תֵבוֹת תֵּשַׁע. ט׳ דְּבָרִים אַתָּה מַעֲלֶה עַל הַמִּזְבֵּחַ – עוֹלָה, חַטָּאת, אָשָׁם, שְׁלָמִים, מִנְחָה, שֶׁמֶן, לְבוֹנָה, יַיִן, מָיִם:

(טו) **כְּבִרְכַּת.** ב׳ בַּמָּסוֹרֶת – "תִּזְבַּח וְאָכַלְתָּ בָשָׂר כְּבִרְכַּת ה׳ "; "כְּבִרְכַּת ה׳ אֱלֹהֶיךָ אֲשֶׁר נָתַן לָךְ", גַּבֵּי עוֹלַת רְאִיָּה. וְהַיְנוּ דִתְנַן, מִי שֶׁיֵּשׁ לוֹ אוֹכְלִין מְרֻבִּין {וּנְכָסִים מְרֻבִּין} מֵבִיא עוֹלוֹת מְרֻבִּים {וּשְׁלָמִים מְרֻבִּים}. וְזֶהוּ "תִּזְבַּח וְאָכַלְתָּ בָשָׂר {כְּבִרְכַּת ה׳ אֱלֹהֶיךָ}" –

BAAL HATURIM ELUCIDATED

13. עֹלֹתֶיךָ בְּכָל מָקוֹם אֲשֶׁר תִּרְאֶה — YOUR BURNT-OFFERINGS IN ANY PLACE THAT YOU SEE. The final letters of these words can be rearranged to spell הַכַּרְמֶל, [*Mount*] *Carmel.* And the *gematria* of בְּכָל, *in any* (52), is equal to that of אֵלִיָּהוּ, *Elijah.* [This is] an allusion to the fact that [the prophet] Elijah would one day bring burnt-offerings on Mount Carmel[46a] [in his confrontation with the prophets of the Baal].[47]

14. שְׁבָטֶיךָ — YOUR TRIBES. The *gematria* of this word (341) is equal to that of שֵׁבֶט יְהוּדָה, *the tribe of Judah.*[48]

46a. An act which under normal circumstances would be prohibited, but which Elijah, a prophet whose credentials were proven on previous occasions, permitted on an *ad hoc* basis.

47. *Peirush HaRokeach;* see *I Kings* 18:19-39; see also *Sifrei, Yevamos* 90b, *Sanhedrin* 89b, cited by *Rashi.*

Additional allusions to the incident at Mount Carmel may be found in our verse: The final letters of אֲשֶׁר תִּרְאֶה spell הַר, *Mount,* while the *gematria* of the final letters of הִשָּׁמֶר לְךָ פֶּן תַּעֲלֶה עֹלֹתֶיךָ (295) is equal to that of הַכַּרְמֶל, *Carmel.* Moreover, the remaining words בְּכָל מָקוֹם alludes to the prophet and his adversaries on that occasion, for the *gematria* of בְּכָל מָקוֹם (238) is equal to that of אֵלִיָּהוּ וּנְבִיאֵי הַבַּעַל, *Elijah and the prophets of the Baal idol* (*VeChur LaZahav*).

48. *Peirush HaRokeach.* The city of Jerusalem and the Temple lie in the territory of Judah. *Rashi* (both here and at 33:12 below) cites the *Sifrei* which explains the phrase בְּאַחַד שְׁבָטֶיךָ, *among one of your tribes,* as a reference to Benjamin, in whose portion the *Beis HaMikdash* was built. *Ittur Bikkurim* explains that the two opinions are not in

everything that I command you: your burnt-offerings and your [peace-offerings] slaughterings, your tithes and what you set aside by your hand, and the choicest of your vow offerings that you will vow to HASHEM. ¹² *You shall rejoice before HASHEM, your God — you, your sons and your daughters, your slaves and your maidservants, and the Levite who is in your cities, for he has no share and inheritance with you.* ¹³ *Beware for yourself lest you bring up your burnt-offerings in any place that you see.* ¹⁴ *Rather, only in the place that HASHEM will choose, among one of your tribes, there shall you bring up your burnt-offerings, and there shall you do all that I command you.*
¹⁵ *However, in your soul's desire you may slaughter and you may eat meat, according to the blessing of HASHEM, your God,*

────────────────── BAAL HATURIM ELUCIDATED ──────────────────

❑ שָׁם תַּעֲלֶה עֹלֹתֶיךָ — **THERE SHALL YOU BRING UP YOUR BURNT-OFFERINGS.** The first letters of these words can be rearranged to spell תֵּשַׁע, *nine.* Nine things are offered on the Altar: (i) the burnt-offering; (ii) the sin-offering; (iii) the guilt-offering; (iv) the peace-offering;[48a] (v) the meal-offering; (vi) oil; (vii) frankincense; (viii) wine; and (ix) water.[49]

15. כְּבִרְכַּת — **ACCORDING TO THE BLESSING.** The masoretic note, ב׳, means that this word appears twice in the *Tanach*: (i) here, תִּזְבַּח וְאָכַלְתָּ בָשָׂר כְּבִרְכַּת ה׳, *and you may slaughter and you may eat meat, according to the blessing of HASHEM;* and (ii) כְּבִרְכַּת ה׳ אֱלֹהֶיךָ אֲשֶׁר נָתַן לָךְ, *according to the blessing that HASHEM, your God, has given you* (16:17 below) with reference to the burnt-offering of the pilgrimage festival. This [similarity of expression] is in accordance with what is taught in the Mishnah: One who has many eaters[50] {and many assets[51]} should bring many burnt-offerings {and many peace-offerings[51]}.[52] This is how our verse, ⁵¹{כְּבִרְכַּת ה׳ אֱלֹהֶיךָ} תִּזְבַּח וְאָכַלְתָּ בָשָׂר, may be rendered:

────────────────────────────

disagreement, for the Talmud cites a *baraisa*: Which parts of the Temple compound were within Judah's portion? The Temple Mount, the chambers and the Courtyards. And which parts were in Benjamin's portion? The *Ulam* [entrance hall], the Sanctuary and the Holy of Holies. There was a strip extending from Judah's portion into Benjamin's portion; the Altar was built upon that strip (*Yoma* 12a). Thus, the Altar can be said to stand in either Judah's portion or Benjamin's.

48a. Included in this category are the תּוֹדָה, *thanksgiving-offering;* בְּכוֹר, *firstborn offering;* מַעֲשֵׂר, *animal-tithe offering;* and פֶּסַח, *pesach offering* (see the *Baal HaTurim* to *Numbers* 28:3, with note 86).

49. *Peirush HaRokeach.*

50. That is, many people with whom to share the meat of the offering.

51. The words in braces do not appear in most editions of the Baal HaTurim. They do appear, however, in *Shoham Yakar's* manuscript edition.

52. *Chagigah* 1:5 (8b). The full Mishnah reads: One who has many eaters but few assets should bring many peace-offerings and few burnt-offerings. One who has many assets but few eaters should bring many burnt-offerings and few peace-offerings. One who has few of both [eaters and assets], of him it is said, "[He should bring a burnt-offering worth] one silver coin and [a peace-offering worth] two silver coins." One who has many of both [eaters and

אֲשֶׁר נָתַן־לְךָ בְּכָל־שְׁעָרֶיךָ הַטָּמֵא וְהַטָּהוֹר יֹאכְלֶנּוּ
טז כַּצְּבִי וְכָאַיָּל: רַק הַדָּם לֹא תֹאכֵלוּ עַל־הָאָרֶץ
יז תִּשְׁפְּכֶנּוּ כַּמָּיִם: לֹא־תוּכַל לֶאֱכֹל בִּשְׁעָרֶיךָ מַעְשַׂר
דְּגָנְךָ וְתִירֹשְׁךָ וְיִצְהָרֶךָ וּבְכֹרֹת בְּקָרְךָ וְצֹאנֶךָ וְכָל־
יח נְדָרֶיךָ אֲשֶׁר תִּדֹּר וְנִדְבֹתֶיךָ וּתְרוּמַת יָדֶךָ: כִּי אִם־
לִפְנֵי יהוה אֱלֹהֶיךָ תֹּאכְלֶנּוּ בַּמָּקוֹם אֲשֶׁר יִבְחַר יהוה
אֱלֹהֶיךָ בּוֹ אַתָּה וּבִנְךָ וּבִתֶּךָ וְעַבְדְּךָ וַאֲמָתֶךָ וְהַלֵּוִי
אֲשֶׁר בִּשְׁעָרֶיךָ וְשָׂמַחְתָּ לִפְנֵי יהוה אֱלֹהֶיךָ בְּכֹל
יט מִשְׁלַח יָדֶךָ: הִשָּׁמֶר לְךָ פֶּן־תַּעֲזֹב אֶת־הַלֵּוִי כָּל־יָמֶיךָ
כ עַל־אַדְמָתֶךָ: כִּי־יַרְחִיב יהוה אֱלֹהֶיךָ אֶת־גְּבֻלְךָ
כַּאֲשֶׁר דִּבֶּר־לָךְ וְאָמַרְתָּ אֹכְלָה בָשָׂר כִּי־תְאַוֶּה
נַפְשְׁךָ לֶאֱכֹל בָּשָׂר בְּכָל־אַוַּת נַפְשְׁךָ תֹּאכַל בָּשָׂר:

בעל הטורים

"תִּזְבַּח" דְּהַיְנוּ עוֹלוֹת, "וְאָכַלְתָּ בָשָׂר" דְּהַיְנוּ שְׁלָמִים – הַכֹּל תַּרְבֶּה לְפִי "בִּרְכַּת ה' אֱלֹהֶיךָ אֲשֶׁר נָתַן לָךְ":

(יז) **וּתְרוּמַת יָדֶךָ.** וּסְמִיךְ לֵהּ "לִפְנֵי ה' ", {רֶמֶז לְבִכּוּרִים שֶׁצְּרִיכִין הֲנָחָה לִפְנֵי ה',} כִּי "תְרוּמַת יָדֶךָ" הַיְנוּ בִּכּוּרִים:

(יט) **פֶּן תַּעֲזֹב אֶת הַלֵּוִי.** וּסְמִיךְ לֵהּ "כִּי יַרְחִיב". לוֹמַר לְךָ "מַתָּן אָדָם יַרְחִיב לוֹ":

(כ) **תֹּאכַל בָּשָׂר.** וּסְמִיךְ לֵהּ "כִּי יִרְחַק". לוֹמַר שֶׁיִּתְרַחֵק אָדָם מִלֶּאֱכֹל בָּשָׂר, כִּדְאִיתָא בְּפֶרֶק כִּסּוּי הַדָּם:

BAAL HATURIM ELUCIDATED

תִּזְבַּח, *you may slaughter,* i.e., burnt-offerings;[53] וְאָכַלְתָּ בָשָׂר, *and you may eat meat,* i.e., peace-offerings — and everything should be done generously according to בִּרְכַּת ה' אֱלֹהֶיךָ אֲשֶׁר נָתַן לָךְ, *the blessing that HASHEM, your God, has given you.*[54]

assets], of him it is said, *Each man according to what his hand can give, according to the blessing that HASHEM, your God, has given you* (*Deuteronomy* 16:17).

The Baal HaTurim's citation is a paraphrase of the fourth case in the Mishnah.

53. The verb תִּזְבַּח, here translated *you may slaughter,* is in the future tense, literally, *you will slaughter,* while the verb וְאָכַלְתָּ, which is also rendered in the future, *and you may eat,* is actually the past tense form אָכַלְתָּ, *you have eaten,* with the conversive prefix וְ־, changing it from past to future. In truth, we would expect the Torah to use parallel construction — either תִּזְבַּח וְתֹאכַל or וְזָבַחְתָּ וְאָכַלְתָּ (as in 27:7 below). The Baal HaTurim explains that the switch of language is an allusion to the adduced Mishnah. The burnt-offering is slaughtered and the peace-offering is slaughtered. But, unlike the burnt-offering that is placed in its entirety upon the Altar's fire, parts of the peace-offering are eaten by its owner and his family and guests. Thus, to indicate that the verb תִּזְבַּח, *you may slaughter,* refers to both the burnt-offering and the peace-offering, while וְאָכַלְתָּ, *and you may eat,* refers to the peace-offering only, the Torah used different verb forms (*VeChur LaZahav*).

54. See *Rashi* to 16:17 below.

12/16-20 *that He has given you in all your cities; the contaminated one and the pure one may eat it, like the deer and the gazelle. ¹⁶ However, you shall not eat the blood; you shall spill it onto the earth, like water.*

¹⁷ In your [outlying] cities, you may not eat: the tithe of your grain, and your wine, and your oil; the firstborn of your cattle and your flocks; all your vow offerings that you vow and your free-will offerings; and what is set aside by your hand. ¹⁸ Rather you shall eat them before HASHEM, your God, in the place that HASHEM, your God, will choose — you, your son, your daughter, your slave, your maidservant, and the Levite who is in your cities — and you shall rejoice before HASHEM, your God, in your every undertaking. ¹⁹ Beware for yourself lest you forsake the Levite, all your days on your land.

²⁰ When HASHEM, your God, will broaden your boundary as He spoke to you, and you say, "I would eat meat," for you will have a desire to eat meat, to your heart's entire desire you may eat meat.

─────────── BAAL HATURIM ELUCIDATED ───────────

16. {The Baal HaTurim's comment to עַל הָאָרֶץ appears at 11:21 above.}

17. וּתְרוּמַת יָדֶךָ — **AND WHAT IS SET ASIDE BY YOUR HAND.** Juxtaposed to this is the phrase, לִפְנֵי ה׳, *before HASHEM* (v. 18). {This is an allusion to the law that *bikkurim* (the first-fruits-offering) must be placed *before HASHEM* [i.e., before the Altar in the Temple Courtyard],[55]}[56] for the phrase וּתְרוּמַת יָדֶךָ, *and what is set aside by your hand,* refers to *bikkurim.*[57]

19. פֶּן תַּעֲזֹב אֶת הַלֵּוִי — **LEST YOU FORSAKE THE LEVITE.**[58] Juxtaposed to this is, כִּי יַרְחִיב, *for*[59] [*then HASHEM, your God,*] *will broaden* [*your boundary*][60] (v. 20). This indicates to you that מַתָּן אָדָם יַרְחִיב לוֹ, *A man's gift broadens for him* (Proverbs 18:16).[61]

20. תֹּאכַל בָּשָׂר — **YOU MAY EAT MEAT.** Juxtaposed to this is כִּי יִרְחַק, *if it will be far.* This indicates that a person should distance himself from eating meat,[62] as is taught in Chapter *Kisui HaDam.*[63]

───────────────────────────

55. See 26:4 below.

56. The words in braces do not appear in most editions of the Baal HaTurim. They do appear, however, in *Shoham Yakar's* manuscript edition.

57. *Makkos* 17a, cited by *Rashi* here and at v. 6 above.

58. The word פֶּן, *lest,* implies a negative ("you shall not") commandment (*Sifrei*). Thus, the verse means, *You shall not forsake the Levite.*

59. In the context of the passage, כִּי means *when;* however, for purposes of the allusion, the Baal HaTurim renders it *for* or *because.*

60. That is, He will increase your possessions.

61. *Devarim Rabbah* 4:8,10; see also *Rashi* to *Proverbs* 18:16.

62. The juxtaposed phrases then read: תֹּאכַל בָּשָׂר כִּי יִרְחַק, *You may eat meat, but it should be at a distance,* i.e., only once in a while. According to the Talmud (see note 63 below), this means only on the Sabbath.

63. Chapter *Kisui HaDam* is the sixth chapter of tractate *Chullin.* The Talmud there offers food regimens that are in accordance with a person's financial status. The very indigent should eat

יב/כא־כד כא כִּֽי־יִרְחַ֨ק מִמְּךָ֜ הַמָּק֗וֹם אֲשֶׁ֨ר יִבְחַ֜ר יהוה אֱלֹהֶ֗יךָ
לָשׂ֣וּם שְׁמוֹ֮ שָׁם֒ וְזָבַחְתָּ֞ מִבְּקָרְךָ֣ וּמִצֹּֽאנְךָ֗ אֲשֶׁ֨ר נָתַ֤ן
יהוה֙ לְךָ֔ כַּאֲשֶׁ֖ר צִוִּיתִ֑ךָ וְאָֽכַלְתָּ֙ בִּשְׁעָרֶ֔יךָ בְּכֹ֖ל אַוַּ֥ת
כב נַפְשֶֽׁךָ׃ אַ֗ךְ כַּאֲשֶׁ֨ר יֵאָכֵ֤ל אֶֽת־הַצְּבִי֙ וְאֶת־הָ֣אַיָּ֔ל כֵּ֖ן
כג תֹּֽאכְלֶ֑נּוּ הַטָּמֵא֙ וְהַטָּה֔וֹר יַחְדָּ֖ו יֹאכְלֶֽנּוּ׃ רַ֣ק חֲזַ֗ק
לְבִלְתִּי֙ אֲכֹ֣ל הַדָּ֔ם כִּ֥י הַדָּ֖ם ה֣וּא הַנָּ֑פֶשׁ וְלֹא־תֹאכַ֥ל
כד הַנֶּ֖פֶשׁ עִם־הַבָּשָֽׂר׃ לֹ֖א תֹּאכְלֶ֑נּוּ עַל־הָאָ֥רֶץ תִּשְׁפְּכֶ֖נּוּ

בעל הטורים

(כא) **כִּי יִרְחַק.** הַפָּסוּק מַתְחִיל וּמְסַיֵּם בְּכָ״ף. לוֹמַר, אַף עַל פִּי שֶׁשָּׁחַט, צָרִיךְ לְהַכְנִיס בּוֹ כַּף יָדוֹ וְלִבְדֹּק הָרֵאָה:

❑ **כַּאֲשֶׁר צִוִּיתִךָ.** בְּגִימַטְרִיָּא רוֹב אֶחָד בְּעוֹף וְרוֹב שְׁנַיִם בִּבְהֵמָה:

❑ **כַּאֲשֶׁר.** נוֹטָרִיקוֹן רֻבּוֹ שֶׁל אֶחָד כְּכֻלּוֹ:

(כב) **אַךְ כַּאֲשֶׁר יֵאָכֵל אֶת הַצְּבִי וְאֶת הָאַיָּל.** "אַךְ" מִעוּטָא הוּא, שֶׁאֵינוֹ חַיָּב בְּמַתָּנוֹת:

(כג) **עִם הַבָּשָׂר.** בְּגִימַטְרִיָּא בְּבָשָׂר מִן הֶחָי:

(כד) **תִּשְׁפְּכֶנּוּ.** בְּגִימַטְרִיָּא פָּטוּר מִלְּכַסּוֹתוֹ:

BAAL HATURIM ELUCIDATED

21. **כִּי יִרְחַק** — IF IT WILL BE FAR. This verse begins and ends with the letter כ.[64] This indicates that although a person has slaughtered [properly], he still must insert his hand[65] [into the carcass] to check the lungs.[66]

---

vegetables; those with some means may eat fish; those of ample means may eat meat; and the wealthy may fill their pots with meat every day of the week. But, on the Sabbath, everyone may eat meat (*Chullin* 84a, as explained by *Maharsha;* see also *Rambam, Hilchos Dei'os* 5:10).

64. This phenomenon occurs twenty-six times in the Torah and another eighty-seven times in the rest of the *Tanach.* Indeed, nine such verses appear in *parashas Re'eh*: 12:9,14,18, 21; 13:7,19; 15:11,12,19. However, the Baal HaTurim does not comment on any other verse that begins and ends with a כ, except ours.

65. The name of the letter — כַּף — is related to the word כַּף, which may refer to *a spoon* (see *Numbers* 7:14), *the sole of the foot* (11:24 above), *the hipbone* (*Genesis* 32:25), *the palm of the hand* (*Leviticus* 14:15), or *the full hand* (*Genesis* 31:42). In this comment, the Baal HaTurim interprets the letter כ as an allusion to a person's hand.

66. Despite the general rule that an apparently healthy living animal is considered to be free of *treifos* (physical conditions that usually would not allow the animal to live another year) and that it is therefore not necessary to inspect a carcass for such things, the lungs are an exception, for it is not uncommon to find an otherwise healthy animal with diseased lungs. Hence, the Rabbis decreed that after an animal is slaughtered, its lungs must be checked (see *Rashi* to *Chullin* 12a, s.v. פסח; see also *Tur* and *Shulchan Aruch, Yoreh Deah* 37:1).

The second Bobover Rebbe gave this comment a novel twist. The *Rema* discusses the status of an incomplete lung: The custom is to render kosher a defect that has the shape of the letter ך; but if the defect is shaped like the letter כ, it is a *treifah* (*Yoreh Deah* 36:8). This is all alluded to by our verse: The phrase כִּי יִרְחַק, with which it begins, may be understood as, כִּי, *If the defect is in the shape of a* כ [as in the word כִּי] then, יִרְחַק, *it will be distant,* i.e., it is not kosher; while the end of the verse, וְאָכַלְתָּ בִּשְׁעָרֶיךָ בְּכֹל אַוַּת נַפְשֶׁךָ, may be understood, *but you may eat it in your cities according to your heart's desire when the defect is in the shape of a* ך [as in the word נַפְשֶׁךָ] (*Kedushas Tzion*).

12/21-24 [21] *If it will be far from you — the place that HASHEM, your God, will choose to place His Name there — you may slaughter from your cattle and your flocks that HASHEM has given you, as I have commanded you, and you may eat in your cities according to your heart's entire desire.* [22] *Even as the deer and the gazelle are eaten, so you may eat it, the contaminated one and the pure one may eat it together.* [23] *Only be strong not to eat the blood — for the blood, it is the life — and you shall not eat the life with the meat.* [24] *You shall not eat it, you shall pour it onto the ground*

─────────────── BAAL HATURIM ELUCIDATED ───────────────

❑ כַּאֲשֶׁר צִוִּיתִךְ — **AS I HAVE COMMANDED YOU.** The *gematria* of this phrase (1047) is equal to that of, רוֹב אֶחָד בְּעוֹף וְרוֹב שְׁנַיִם בִּבְהֵמָה, *the greater part of one for a bird, and the greater part of two for an animal.* [67]

❑ כַּאֲשֶׁר — **AS.** When reversed, the letters of this word form the acronym of the phrase, רֻבּוֹ שֶׁל אֶחָד כְּכֻלּוֹ, [*severing*] *the greater part of one is equivalent to* [*severing it in*] *its entirety.* [68]

22. אַךְ כַּאֲשֶׁר יֵאָכֵל אֶת הַצְּבִי וְאֶת הָאַיָּל — **EVEN AS THE DEER AND THE HART ARE EATEN.** The word אַךְ, *even,* implies an exclusion, [69] [in this case indicating] that they are not obligated regarding the [priestly] gifts. [70]

23. עִם הַבָּשָׂר — **WITH THE MEAT.** The *gematria* of this phrase (617) is equal to that of בְּבָשָׂר מִן הַחַי, *with meat taken from a live animal.* [71]

24. {The Baal HaTurim's comment to עַל הָאָרֶץ appears at 11:21 above.}

❑ תִּשְׁפְּכֶנּוּ — **YOU SHALL POUR IT.** The *gematria* of this word (856) is equivalent [72] to

---

67. *Rosh, Paaneach Raza, Daas Zekeinim MiBaalei HaTosafos,* citing the Tosafist Rabbi Yaakov of Corbeil; see also *Tosafos* to *Chullin* 28a, s.v., וְעַל.

The Talmud (*Chullin* 28a) cites a *baraisa* that infers from our verse that God taught Moses the laws of *shechitah* (ritual slaughter): [Shechitah] concerns [severing] the esophagus (food pipe) and the trachea (wind pipe); and it concerns [severing] the greater part of one [of those two pipes] for a bird, and the greater part of both [pipes] for an animal.

68. *Tosafos* to *Chullin* 28a, s.v., וְעַל; see note 67 above.

69. According to the second principle in the *baraisa* known as "The Thirty-two *Middos* [Principles] of R' Eliezer son of R' Yose HaGelili" (which appears after tractate *Berachos* in most editions of the Talmud), certain terms used

by Scripture are exclusionary. The Talmud identifies אַךְ as such a word (*Rosh Hashanah* 17b; *Sanhedrin* 49a; *Yerushalmi Berachos* 9:5).

70. See Rashi to v. 15 above, s.v., כצבי וכאיל.

71. *Peirush HaRokeach.* According to one opinion in the Talmud, our verse prohibits eating from אֵבָר מִן הַחַי, *an eiver that has been severed from a live animal* (see the Baal HaTurim to *Genesis* 13:13, with note 42) while the prohibition against eating בָּשָׂר מִן הַחַי, *meat from a live animal,* is derived from another verse (*Exodus* 22:30). According to a second opinion there, both prohibitions are derived from our verse (*Chullin* 102b).

72. The principle of *im hakollel* allows 856 to be considered equivalent to 857, the *gematria* of the Baal HaTurim's phrase.

כה כַּמָּיִם: לֹא תֹּאכְלֶנּוּ לְמַעַן יִיטַב לְךָ וּלְבָנֶיךָ
כו אַחֲרֶיךָ כִּי־תַעֲשֶׂה הַיָּשָׁר בְּעֵינֵי יהוה: רַק
קָדָשֶׁיךָ אֲשֶׁר־יִהְיוּ לְךָ וּנְדָרֶיךָ תִּשָּׂא וּבָאתָ
כז אֶל־הַמָּקוֹם אֲשֶׁר־יִבְחַר יהוה: וְעָשִׂיתָ עֹלֹתֶיךָ
הַבָּשָׂר וְהַדָּם עַל־מִזְבַּח יהוה אֱלֹהֶיךָ וְדַם־זְבָחֶיךָ
יִשָּׁפֵךְ עַל־מִזְבַּח יהוה אֱלֹהֶיךָ וְהַבָּשָׂר תֹּאכֵל:

בעל הטורים

(כו) **וּנְדָרֶיךָ.** ב׳ בַּמָּסוֹרֶת – ״וּנְדָרֶיךָ תִּשָּׂא וּבָאתָ״; ״וּנְדָרֶיךָ תְשַׁלֵּם״. וְהַיְנוּ דִתְנַן, דִּנְדָרִים אִם מֵתוּ אוֹ נִגְנְבוּ חַיָּב בְּאַחֲרָיוּתָן. וְזֶהוּ ״וּנְדָרֶיךָ תְשַׁלֵּם״. הֵיאַךְ? ״וּנְדָרֶיךָ תִּשָּׂא״, שֶׁאַתָּה חַיָּב בְּאַחֲרָיוּתָן עַד שֶׁתְּבִיאֵם, כִּדְאָמְרִינַן, כֵּיוָן דַּאֲמַר עָלַי, כְּמַאן דְּטָעִין לֵהּ אַכַּתְפֵּהּ דָּמֵי:

(כז) **וְהַבָּשָׂר תֹּאכֵל.** וּסְמִיךְ לֵהּ ״שְׁמֹר וְשָׁמַעְתָּ״. לוֹמַר, עַם הָאָרֶץ אָסוּר לֶאֱכֹל בָּשָׂר, כִּדְאִיתָא בִּפְסָחִים:

BAAL HATURIM ELUCIDATED

that of פָּטוּר מִלְּכַסּוֹתוֹ, *exempt from covering*[73] *it.*[73a,74]

73. See *Leviticus* 17:13. That verse states the *mitzvah* of כִּסּוּי הַדָּם, *covering the blood,* which obligates one to cover the blood spilled by the ritual slaughter of a kosher חַיָּה, *beast* [i.e., any of the seven listed in 14:5 below], or kosher עוֹף, *bird.* The Mishnah (*Chullin* 6:1 [83b]) teaches that kosher domesticated animals [i.e., oxen, sheep, and goats, see 14:4 below] are excluded from this obligation. The *gemara* assumes that the exclusion is based upon the fact that the verse mentions חַיָּה, *beast,* and עוֹף, *bird,* but omits בְּהֵמָה, *domesticated animal.* Accordingly, the question is raised: Elsewhere we have learned that the category of בְּהֵמָה is included in the term חַיָּה [i.e., חַיָּה (literally, *living* being) includes both wild beasts and domesticated animals]; if so, why are they excluded from the law of covering the blood? The Talmud answers: There is another verse that exempts them — עַל הָאָרֶץ תִּשְׁפְּכֶנּוּ כַּמָּיִם, *you shall spill it onto the ground like water* (see note 74 below regarding that verse), which compares the blood of a בְּהֵמָה to water. Now, just as water need not be covered, so, too, such blood need not be covered (*Chullin* 84a).

73a. *Peirush HaRokeach.*

74. The phrase, עַל הָאָרֶץ תִּשְׁפְּכֶנּוּ כַּמָּיִם, appears three times in the *Tanach,* all three times in our *parashah*: (i) Verses 15-16 above speak of animals that had been consecrated and then, before being slaughtered, acquired a disqualifying blemish; such animals may be redeemed, slaughtered, and eaten as unconsecrated meat, רַק הַדָּם לֹא תֹאכֵלוּ, *however, you shall not eat the blood,* עַל הָאָרֶץ תִּשְׁפְּכֶנּוּ כַּמָּיִם; (ii) our verse speaks of the blood spilled by the slaughter of animals that have never been consecrated, לֹא תֹּאכְלֶנּוּ, *you shall not eat it,* עַל הָאָרֶץ תִּשְׁפְּכֶנּוּ כַּמָּיִם; and (iii) regarding the blood of a blemished *bechor* (first-born male animal), we are commanded, רַק אֶת דָּמוֹ לֹא תֹאכֵל, *however, you shall not eat its blood,* עַל הָאָרֶץ תִּשְׁפְּכֶנּוּ כַּמָּיִם (15:23 below).

But, whereas the same phrase appears in three verses, how are we to know to which of the three the Talmudic passage adduced in note 73 refers? And, *Shoham Yakar* asks, if the same teaching can be derived from any of the three verses, why did the Baal HaTurim choose to present it at verse 24, when he could have presented it at verse 16 the first time it appears, and where *Rashi* cites it?

In truth, the text of the printed editions of the Talmud may be incomplete, for in the Munich manuscript of 5103 [1343, the most complete Talmud manuscript that has been preserved], as well as in *Yalkut Shimoni* (*Parashas Shemini* 542), the passage contains two more words, לֹא תֹאכְלֶנּוּ, thus citing our verse in its entirety. If so, the Baal HaTurim's source is the Talmud itself. However, we may assume that those two words did not appear in the manuscript Talmud used by *Rashi,* and so he ascribed the teaching to v. 16, the first verse that contains the phrase (*VeChur LaZahav*).

like water. ²⁵ You shall not eat it, in order that it be well with you and your children after you, when you do what is right in the eyes of HASHEM.

²⁶ But, your sanctities that you will have and your vow offerings — you shall carry [them], and you shall come to the place that HASHEM will choose. ²⁷ You shall perform your burnt-offerings, the flesh and the blood, upon the Altar of HASHEM, your God; and the blood of your [peace-offerings] slaughterings shall be poured upon the Altar of HASHEM, your God, and you shall eat the meat.

─────────── BAAL HATURIM ELUCIDATED ───────────

26. וּנְדָרֶיךָ — AND YOUR VOW OFFERINGS. The masoretic note, ב׳, means that this word appears twice in the *Tanach*: (i) here, וּנְדָרֶיךָ תִּשָּׂא וּבָאתָ, *your vow offerings, you shall carry [them] and you shall come;* and (ii) וּנְדָרֶיךָ תְשַׁלֵּם, *and you should pay your vows* (*Job* 22:27). This [similarity of expression] can be interpreted in accordance with what has been taught in the Mishnah: With regard to *nedarim* (vow offerings),[75] if [the designated animal] died or was stolen, one bears the responsibility [of replacing it]. Thus, *you should pay your vows* [regardless of what has happened to them]. And how [does this apply]? *Your vow offerings you shall carry,* i.e., you shall bear the responsibility for them until you bring them [as you have vowed]. As the Talmud states: Since he has said, "I am obligated," it is as if [he said that the burden of responsibility is to be] borne on his shoulders.[76]

27. וְהַבָּשָׂר תֹּאכֵל — AND YOU SHALL EAT THE MEAT. Juxtaposed to this is the phrase, שְׁמֹר וְשָׁמַעְתָּ, *Safeguard and hearken.* This [juxtaposition] indicates [that] an unlearned person is prohibited from eating meat,[77] as is taught in tractate *Pesachim.* [78]

75. The Mishnah states: What is a *neder* [vow offering] and what is a *nedavah* [free-will offering]? [That is, how do they differ with regard to the manner of their sanctification?] With regard to a *neder,* one says [for example], "I am obligated to bring a burnt-offering" [subsequently designating a specific animal or bird with which he will fulfill his vow]. With regard to a *nedavah,* one says [for example], "This [animal or bird] is hereby [sanctified as] a burnt-offering." And what is the [halachic] difference between a *neder* and a *nedavah*? If a *neder*-animal died or was stolen or lost, the vower bears the responsibility [of replacing it]; but if a *nedavah* animal died or was stolen or lost, he does not bear the responsibility [of replacing it] (*Kinnim* 1:1; cited in *Megillah* 8a).

76. *Megillah* 8a.

77. That is, the combined phrases may be interpreted: וְהַבָּשָׂר תֹּאכֵל, *you may eat the meat,*

[but only under the following conditions,] שְׁמֹר, *you shall observe* [the commandments], וְשָׁמַעְתָּ, *and you shall hear* [i.e., understand (see the Baal HaTurim's next comment)]. Thus, one who is unlearned is prohibited from eating meat (see note 78 below).

78. *Peirush HaRokeach;* see *Pesachim* 49b, where the Talmud derives this law from *Leviticus* 11:46. The commentaries differ in the interpretation of the Talmudic passage. According to one view, it refers to the unlearned boor [or anyone else, for that matter] eating meat that was slaughtered or prepared by him without the supervision of someone learned in the relevant *halachos* regarding kosher meat. This prohibition is then based on his ignorance of the pertinent *halachos* (*Ritva; Ran;* for alternative, literal interpretations of the Talmudic passage, see *She'eilos Useshuvos Radbaz* II, 796; and *Maharal, Nesivos Olam, Nesiv HaTorah* 15).

שָׁמֹ֣ר וְשָׁמַעְתָּ֗ אֵ֚ת כָּל־הַדְּבָרִ֣ים הָאֵ֔לֶּה אֲשֶׁ֥ר אָנֹכִ֖י
מְצַוֶּ֑ךָּ לְמַ֩עַן֩ יִיטַ֨ב לְךָ֜ וּלְבָנֶ֤יךָ אַֽחֲרֶ֙יךָ֙ עַד־עוֹלָ֔ם כִּ֤י

שלישי
כט תַֽעֲשֶׂה֙ הַטּ֣וֹב וְהַיָּשָׁ֔ר בְּעֵינֵ֖י יְהוָ֥ה אֱלֹהֶֽיךָ: כִּֽי־
יַכְרִ֨ית יְהוָ֤ה אֱלֹהֶ֙יךָ֙ אֶת־הַגּוֹיִ֔ם אֲשֶׁ֨ר אַתָּ֥ה בָֽא־
שָׁ֛מָּה לָרֶ֥שֶׁת אוֹתָ֖ם מִפָּנֶ֑יךָ וְיָֽרַשְׁתָּ֣ אֹתָ֔ם וְיָֽשַׁבְתָּ֖
ל בְּאַרְצָֽם: הִשָּׁ֣מֶר לְךָ֗ פֶּן־תִּנָּקֵשׁ֙ אַֽחֲרֵיהֶ֔ם אַֽחֲרֵ֖י
הִשָּֽׁמְדָ֣ם מִפָּנֶ֑יךָ וּפֶן־תִּדְרֹ֤שׁ לֵֽאלֹֽהֵיהֶם֙ לֵאמֹ֔ר
אֵיכָ֠ה יַֽעַבְד֞וּ הַגּוֹיִ֤ם הָאֵ֙לֶּה֙ אֶת־אֱלֹ֣הֵיהֶ֔ם וְאֶֽעֱשֶׂה־
לא כֵּ֖ן גַּם־אָֽנִי: לֹֽא־תַֽעֲשֶׂ֣ה כֵ֔ן לַֽיהוָ֖ה אֱלֹהֶ֑יךָ כִּי֩
כָל־תּֽוֹעֲבַ֨ת יְהוָ֜ה אֲשֶׁ֣ר שָׂנֵ֗א עָשׂוּ֙ לֵֽאלֹ֣הֵיהֶ֔ם כִּ֣י
גַ֤ם אֶת־בְּנֵיהֶם֙ וְאֶת־בְּנֹ֣תֵיהֶ֔ם יִשְׂרְפ֥וּ בָאֵ֖שׁ

יג
א לֵֽאלֹֽהֵיהֶֽם: אֵ֣ת כָּל־הַדָּבָ֗ר אֲשֶׁ֤ר אָֽנֹכִי֙ מְצַוֶּ֤ה
אֶתְכֶ֔ם אֹת֥וֹ תִשְׁמְר֖וּ לַֽעֲשׂ֑וֹת לֹֽא־תֹסֵ֣ף עָלָ֔יו וְלֹ֥א
תִגְרַ֖ע מִמֶּֽנּוּ:
ב כִּֽי־יָק֤וּם בְּקִרְבְּךָ֙ נָבִ֔יא א֖וֹ חֹלֵ֣ם חֲל֑וֹם וְנָתַ֤ן אֵלֶ֙יךָ֙

בעל הטורים

(כח) **שָׁמֹר וְשָׁמַעְתָּ.** אֵין בּוּר יְרֵא חֵטְא וְלֹא עַם הָאָרֶץ חָסִיד:

☐ **כִּי תַעֲשֶׂה הַטּוֹב וְהַיָּשָׁר בְּעֵינֵי ה'.** וּסְמִיךְ לֵהּ "כִּי יַכְרִית". לוֹמַר, שֶׁאֵין יוֹצְאִין לַמִּלְחָמָה
אֶלָּא צַדִּיקִים שֶׁעוֹשִׂים הַטּוֹב וְהַיָּשָׁר:

(כט) **לָרֶשֶׁת אוֹתָם.** וְלֹא לָמַס:

☐ **אֹתָם.** וְלֹא שְׁאָר הָאֻמּוֹת:

יג (ב) **כִּי יָקוּם בְּקִרְבְּךָ.** "בְּקִרְבְּךָ" בְּגִימַטְרִיָּא זוֹ הָאִשָּׁה:

--- BAAL HATURIM ELUCIDATED ---

28. שָׁמֹר וְשָׁמַעְתָּ — SAFEGUARD AND HEARKEN. [This is to be understood in accordance with the Mishnah:[78a]] A boor cannot fear sin, and an unlearned person cannot be pious.[79]

☐ כִּי תַעֲשֶׂה הַטּוֹב וְהַיָּשָׁר בְּעֵינֵי ה' — WHEN YOU DO WHAT IS GOOD AND WHAT IS UPRIGHT IN THE EYES OF HASHEM. Juxtaposed to this is כִּי יַכְרִית, When [HASHEM, your God] will cut down [the Canaanites with whom you will battle]. This is to indicate that none may go out to war [on behalf of Israel] except righteous people who do

---

78a. Avos 2:5.
79. Pesikta Zutresa [Midrash Lekach Tov]. As Rashi teaches: The term שָׁמֹר, safeguard, refers

to Torah study — you are required to "safeguard it in your innards" (see Proverbs 22:18), so that it not be forgotten.

12/28-13/2   28 *Safeguard and hearken to all these words that I command you, in order that it be well with you and your children after you forever, when you do that which is good and upright in the eyes of HASHEM, your God.*

29 When HASHEM, your God, will cut down the nations, to which you come to drive them away from before you, and you will take possession from them and settle in their land, 30 beware for yourself lest you be attracted after them after they have been destroyed before you, and lest you seek out their gods, saying, "How did these nations worship their gods, and even I will do the same." 31 You shall not do so to HASHEM, your God, for everything that is an abomination of HASHEM, that He hates, have they done to their gods; for even their sons and their daughters have they burned in the fire for their gods.

13   *1 The entire word that I command you, that shall you observe to do; you shall not add to it and you shall not subtract from it.*

2 If there should arise in your midst a prophet or a dreamer of a dream, and he will produce to you a

———————————— BAAL HATURIM ELUCIDATED ————————————

what is good and what is upright [in the eyes of HASHEM].[80]

29. לָרֶשֶׁת אוֹתָם — TO DRIVE THEM AWAY,[81] and not to press [them] into [your] service.[82]

אֹתָם — THEM.[83] [This implies that you must drive away only "them," i.e., the inhabitants of Canaan,] but not the other nations.

XIII.

2. כִּי יָקוּם בְּקִרְבְּךָ — IF THERE SHOULD ARISE IN YOUR MIDST. The *gematria* of בְּקִרְבְּךָ, *in your midst* (324 {387}), is equal to that of זוֹ הָאִשָּׁה, *This refers to the woman.*[84]

---

80. See *Sotah* 44a; see also the Baal HaTurim to *Numbers* 31:4.

81. The translation follows one version of *Targum Onkelos;* an alternative version renders, *to take possession from them.*

82. See *Rambam, Raavad,* and *Kesef Mishneh* to *Hil. Melachim* 6:4.

83. The word אוֹתָם appears twice in our verse, once spelled אוֹתָם in full, with a ו; the second time spelled defectively, אֹתָם, without a ו. In his first comment, the Baal HaTurim explains the first אוֹתָם; in his second comment, he explains

the second (*Ittur Bikkurim*). Accordingly, the absence of the ו (= 6) in the second אֹתָם may be seen as an allusion to the six nations that Israel had to drive away [for, as the Baal HaTurim explained earlier (6:19, see note 205 there), the Girgashites fled on their own] (*VeChur LaZahav*).

84. The text follows *Peirush HaRokeach, Rimzei Rabbeinu Yoel* and *Shoham Yakar's* manuscript edition. According to the *Sifrei,* the term בְּקִרְבְּךָ, *in your midst,* teaches that this law applies equally to everyone *in your midst,* a woman as well as a man.

ג אֹ֖ות אֹ֣ו מֹופֵ֑ת וּבָ֤א הָאֹות֙ וְהַמֹּופֵ֔ת אֲשֶׁר־דִּבֶּ֥ר
אֵלֶ֖יךָ לֵאמֹ֑ר נֵלְכָ֞ה אַחֲרֵ֨י אֱלֹהִ֧ים אֲחֵרִ֛ים אֲשֶׁ֥ר
ד לֹֽא־יְדַעְתָּ֖ם וְנָֽעָבְדֵֽם׃ לֹ֣א תִשְׁמַ֗ע אֶל־דִּבְרֵי֙ הַנָּבִ֣יא
הַה֗וּא אֹ֛ו אֶל־חֹולֵ֥ם הַחֲלֹ֖ום הַה֑וּא כִּ֣י מְנַסֶּ֞ה יְהֹוָ֤ה
אֱלֹֽהֵיכֶם֙ אֶתְכֶ֔ם לָדַ֗עַת הֲיִשְׁכֶ֤ם אֹֽהֲבִים֙ אֶת־יְהֹוָ֣ה
ה אֱלֹהֵיכֶ֔ם בְּכׇל־לְבַבְכֶ֖ם וּבְכׇל־נַפְשְׁכֶֽם׃ אַחֲרֵ֨י יְהֹוָ֧ה
אֱלֹהֵיכֶ֛ם תֵּלֵ֖כוּ וְאֹתֹ֣ו תִירָ֑אוּ וְאֶת־מִצְוֺתָ֣יו תִּשְׁמֹ֗רוּ
ו וּבְקֹלֹ֤ו תִשְׁמָ֙עוּ֙ וְאֹתֹ֣ו תַֽעֲבֹ֔דוּ וּבֹ֖ו תִדְבָּקֽוּן׃ וְהַנָּבִ֣יא
הַה֡וּא אֹ֣ו חֹלֵם֩ הַחֲלֹ֨ום הַה֜וּא יוּמָ֗ת כִּ֣י דִבֶּר־סָרָ֣ה
עַל־יְהֹוָ֣ה אֱלֹֽהֵיכֶ֡ם הַמֹּוצִ֣יא אֶתְכֶם֩ ׀ מֵאֶ֨רֶץ
מִצְרַ֜יִם וְהַפֹּֽדְךָ֙ מִבֵּ֣ית עֲבָדִ֔ים לְהַדִּֽיחֲךָ֙ מִן־הַדֶּ֔רֶךְ
אֲשֶׁ֧ר צִוְּךָ֛ יְהֹוָ֥ה אֱלֹהֶ֖יךָ לָלֶ֣כֶת בָּ֑הּ וּבִֽעַרְתָּ֥ הָרָ֖ע
ז מִקִּרְבֶּֽךָ׃ כִּ֣י יְסִֽיתְךָ֡ אָחִ֣יךָ בֶן־אִ֠מֶּ֠ךָ אֹֽו־בִנְךָ֨ אֹֽו־
בִתְּךָ֜ אֹ֣ו ׀ אֵ֣שֶׁת חֵיקֶ֗ךָ אֹ֧ו רֵֽעֲךָ֛ אֲשֶׁ֥ר כְּנַפְשְׁךָ֖ בַּסֵּ֑תֶר

─── בעל הטורים ───

(ו) וְהַפֹּֽדְךָ. פֵּ"א כְּפוּלָה. פְּדִיָּה אַחַר פְּדִיָּה:

❑ וּבִֽעַרְתָּ הָרָע מִקִּרְבֶּךָ. וּסְמִיךְ לֵהּ "כִּי יְסִיתְךָ". שֶׁאֵין טוֹעֲנִין לַמֵּסִית:

(ז) כִּי יְסִיתְךָ. רָאשֵׁי תֵּבוֹת בְּגִימַטְרִיָּא בְּיָחוּד. רֶמֶז לְיִחוּד מִן הַתּוֹרָה:

❑ כְּנַפְשְׁךָ. ב' בַּמָּסֹרֶת – "אֲשֶׁר כְּנַפְשְׁךָ"; "כְּנַפְשְׁךָ שָׂבְעֶךָ". הַיְנוּ דְאִיתָא בְחֻלִּין, אֵין
הֲסָתָה בִּדְבָרִים. וְהָא כְּתִיב "כִּי יְסִיתְךָ"? הַהוּא נַמֵּי בַּאֲכִילָה וּשְׁתִיָּה. וְהַיְנוּ "כְּנַפְשְׁךָ" כְּמוֹ
"כְּנַפְשְׁךָ שָׂבְעֶךָ" דְּהַיְנוּ אֲכִילָה:

─── BAAL HATURIM ELUCIDATED ───

6. וְהַפֹּֽדְךָ — **AND HE WHO REDEEMS YOU.** [According to a scribal tradition,] the פ of this word is written [in the Torah scrolls] in the enhanced form known as פ' כְּפוּלָה, *doubled* פ.[85] [This implies] redemption after redemption.[86]

❑ וּבִֽעַרְתָּ הָרָע מִקִּרְבֶּךָ — **AND YOU SHALL DESTROY THE EVIL FROM YOUR MIDST.** Juxtaposed to this is כִּי יְסִיתְךָ, *If your brother will entice you.* [The juxtaposition teaches] that we do not offer defenses on behalf of the enticer.[87]

7. כִּי יְסִיתְךָ — **IF YOUR BROTHER WILL ENTICE YOU.** The *gematria* of the initial letters of these words (30) is equal to that of בְּיָחוּד, *in seclusion.* This is an allusion to

---

85. See note 29 to *parashas Devarim* and the accompanying illustration. *Sefer Tagin* includes the פ of וְהַפֹּֽדְךָ of our verse on the list of "191 in the Torah whose mouths are on the inside."

86. The doubled פ is understood to imply that פּוֹדֶה, *He redeems,* [and] פּוֹדֶה, *He redeems [again]*, i.e., time after time.
87. *Sanhedrin* 29a; see the Baal HaTurim's first comment to verse 9 below.

sign or a wonder, 3 *and the sign or the wonder comes about,*
of which he spoke to you, saying, "Let us follow other gods,
those that you did not know and we shall worship them!" —
4 *do not hearken to the words of that prophet or to that*
dreamer of a dream, for HASHEM, your God, is testing you to
know whether you love HASHEM, your God, with all your
heart and with all your soul. 5 *HASHEM, your God, shall you*
follow and Him shall you fear; His commandments shall you
observe and to His voice shall you hearken; Him shall you
serve and to Him shall you cleave. 6 *And that prophet and*
that dreamer of a dream shall be put to death, for he had
spoken perversion against HASHEM, your God — He Who
takes you out of the land of Egypt, and He Who redeems
you from the house of slavery — to make you stray from the
path on which HASHEM, your God, has commanded you to
go; and you shall destroy the evil from your midst.
7 *If your brother, the son of your mother, or your son*
or your daughter, or the wife of your bosom, or your
friend who is like your own soul will entice you secretly,

BAAL HATURIM ELUCIDATED

[the Biblical origin of the prohibition against] seclusion.[88]

❑ כְּנַפְשְׁךָ — LIKE YOUR OWN SOUL. The masoretic note, ב׳, means that this word appears twice in the *Tanach*: (i) here, אֲשֶׁר כְּנַפְשְׁךָ, *who is like your own soul;* and (ii) כְּנַפְשְׁךָ שָׂבְעֶךָ, *as is* [*the desire of*] *your soul, to your fill*[88a] (*Deuteronomy* 23:25). This juxtaposition is in accordance with what is stated in tractate *Chullin*: There is no enticement with words [alone].[89] [The question is raised:] But the Torah states, *If* [*one*] *will entice you*? That also refers to food and drink.[90] Thus, כְּנַפְשְׁךָ of our verse is to be understood in the same way as כְּנַפְשְׁךָ שָׂבְעֶךָ, *as is* [*the desire of*] *your soul, to your fill,* which speaks of eating.[91]

88. The Talmud (*Kiddushin* 80b) explains that our verse refers specifically to *your brother, the son of your mother,* but does not mention one's paternal brother, in order to teach us that a man is permitted to be in a secluded place with his mother (as well as, a father and daughter, a grandparent with his or her grandchild, and a brother and sister). [For the logic through which this is educed from our verse, see note 20 in the Schottenstein edition of *Kiddushin.*] Implicit in this exposition is the fact that a man may not seclude himself with any other woman forbidden to him in marriage, for if such seclusion was permitted, we would not need a verse to permit the seclusion of a mother with her son. Thus, the Talmud sees our verse as the Scriptural source that prohibits a man and woman from secluding themselves together. Nevertheless, our verse says nothing explicit regarding seclusion. Therefore the Baal HaTurim seeks an allusion in the initial letters of our phrase (*VeChur LaZahav*).

88a. That verse permits a hired hand to eat his fill of the grapes that he is harvesting.

89. That is, enticement to idolatry is best effected through dining and wining the target victim, rather than through reasoning and logic (*Rashi*).

90. *Chullin* 4a.

91. *Maharam MiRothenburg.*

לֵאמֹר נֵלְכָה וְנַעַבְדָה אֱלֹהִים אֲחֵרִים אֲשֶׁר לֹא
ח יָדַעְתָּ אַתָּה וַאֲבֹתֶיךָ: מֵאֱלֹהֵי הָעַמִּים אֲשֶׁר
סְבִיבֹתֵיכֶם הַקְּרֹבִים אֵלֶיךָ אוֹ הָרְחֹקִים מִמֶּךָּ
ט מִקְצֵה הָאָרֶץ וְעַד־קְצֵה הָאָרֶץ: לֹא־תֹאבֶה לוֹ
וְלֹא תִשְׁמַע אֵלָיו וְלֹא־תָחוֹס עֵינְךָ עָלָיו וְלֹא־
י תַחְמֹל וְלֹא־תְכַסֶּה עָלָיו: כִּי הָרֹג תַּהַרְגֶנּוּ
יָדְךָ תִּהְיֶה־בּוֹ בָרִאשׁוֹנָה לַהֲמִיתוֹ וְיַד כָּל־הָעָם
יא בָּאַחֲרֹנָה: וּסְקַלְתּוֹ בָאֲבָנִים וָמֵת כִּי בִקֵּשׁ לְהַדִּיחֲךָ

בעל הטורים

❑ **אֲשֶׁר לֹא יָדַעְתָּ אַתָּה וַאֲבֹתֶיךָ.** כְּתִיב בְּמֵסִית, לְפִי שֶׁ״רֵעֲךָ ... כְּנַפְשְׁךָ״, דְּהַיְנוּ אָבִיו, מֵסִית אוֹתוֹ לֵאמֹר, לֹא תִלְמַד לַעֲשׂוֹת מֵאֲבֹתֶיךָ שֶׁהוּא אֲבִי אָבִיךָ, אֶלָּא תִּלְמַד מֵאָבִיךָ:

(ט) **וְלֹא תָחוֹס עֵינְךָ עָלָיו.** בְּגִימַטְרִיָּא אֵין טוֹעֲנִין לְמֵסִית:

❑ **וְלֹא תְכַסֶּה.** ב׳ בַּמָּסוֹרֶת — ״וְלֹא תְכַסֶּה עָלָיו״; ״וְלֹא תְכַסֶּה עוֹד עַל הֲרוּגֶיהָ״. זֶהוּ שֶׁדָּרְשׁוּ בְּמֵסִית, שֶׁאִם יָצָא מִבֵּית דִּין חַיָּב אֵין מַחֲזִירִין אוֹתוֹ לִזְכוּת. וְזֶהוּ ״וְלֹא תְכַסֶּה עוֹד עַל הֲרוּגֶיהָ״, פֵּרוּשׁ, עַל מִי שֶׁיָּצָא לֵהָרֵג:

BAAL HATURIM ELUCIDATED

❑ **אֲשֶׁר לֹא יָדַעְתָּ אַתָּה וַאֲבֹתֶיךָ — THAT YOU DID NOT KNOW — YOU OR YOUR FOREFATHERS.** [*Or your forefathers*] is stated with regard to the enticer,[92] because the phrase, *your friend . . . like your own soul,* refers to the person's own father[93] who seeks to entice him [to serve other gods] by saying, "Do not learn what to do[93a] from your forefathers,[94] i.e., your father's father, rather learn from your father."[95]

92. Three passages in a row mention אֱלֹהִים אֲחֵרִים, *other gods,* i.e., creatures or things other than the true God, which in the mind of their worshipers are gods. In verse 3, that phrase is followed by, אֲשֶׁר לֹא יְדַעְתָּם, literally, *that you* [singular] *did not know them,* and in verse 14 by, אֲשֶׁר לֹא יְדַעְתֶּם, *that you* [plural] *did not know.* While in our verse, it is followed by אֲשֶׁר לֹא יָדַעְתָּ אַתָּה וַאֲבֹתֶיךָ, *that you* [singular] *did not know — you or your forefathers.* The Baal HaTurim explains why *your forefathers* is added in our verse (*Shoham Yakar*).

93. *Sifrei,* cited by *Rashi.*

93a. The phrase לֹא תִלְמַד לַעֲשׂוֹת, *do not learn what to do,* is borrowed from 18:9 below.

94. That is, despite the fact that the Torah uses the plural form אֲבֹתֶיךָ, literally, *your fathers,* the term does not include "your father," only "your forefathers," for your father is the very enticer about whom the verse is speaking.

95. This comment appears in at least three versions: (i) The version that appears in the text here follows *Ittur Bikkurim* [see (iii) below] and *Shoham Yakar* [see (ii) below]; in this version the term לֵאמֹר is not a quote from the verse, rather it serves to introduce the father's words of enticement; (ii) the version that appears in the manuscript upon which *Shoham Yakar* based the major part of his edition — כְּתִיב בְּמֵסִית, [*or your forefathers*] *is stated with regard to the enticer,* לְפִי שֶׁ״רֵעֲךָ ... כְּנַפְשְׁךָ״ דְּהַיְנוּ אָבִיו, *because the phrase "your friend . . . like your own soul" refers to the person's own father,* מֵסִית אוֹתוֹ, *who seeks to entice him,* "... לֵאמֹר," *"by saying,* ['Let us go and . . .']." [If this happens,] תִּלְמַד לַעֲשׂוֹת מֵאֲבֹתֶיךָ, *learn what to do from your forefathers,* וְלֹא תִלְמַד מֵאָבִיךָ, *but do not learn from your father* [*Shoham Yakar* reports that a marginal gloss in that manuscript emends it to the version presented in the text here]; in this second version, the term לֵאמֹר is a quote from the verse and stands in for the remainder of the verse,

saying, "Let us go and worship other gods," that you did not know — you or your forefathers, [8] from the gods of the peoples that are all around you, those near to you or those far from you, from one end of the earth to the other end of the earth — [9] you shall not accede to him and not hearken to him; your eye shall not take pity on him, you shall not be compassionate and you shall not cover for him. [10] Rather, you shall surely kill him; your hand shall be the first against him to kill him, and the hand of the entire people afterwards. [11] You shall pelt him with stones and he shall die, for he sought to make you stray

BAAL HATURIM ELUCIDATED

9. וְלֹא תָחוֹס עֵינְךָ עָלָיו — YOUR EYE SHALL NOT TAKE PITY ON HIM. The *gematria* of this phrase (777) is equivalent[96] to that of אֵין טוֹעֲנִין לְמֵסִית, *we do not offer defenses on behalf of the enticer.*[97]

❑ **וְלֹא תְכַסֶּה — AND YOU SHALL NOT COVER.** The masoretic note, ב׳, means that this phrase appears twice in the *Tanach*:[98] (i) here, וְלֹא תְכַסֶּה עָלָיו, *and you shall not cover for him;* and (ii) וְלֹא תְכַסֶּה עוֹד עַל הֲרוּגֶיהָ, *and she shall no longer cover her slain* (*Isaiah* 26:21). This [similarity of expression] is [an allusion to] what the Sages expounded regarding an enticer: If he has been condemned by the court, we do not return him [to the court to probe] for a merit [that might exonerate him].[99] Thus the verse, *she shall no longer cover her slain,* "her slain" meaning one condemned to be executed.

---

while what follows it is a new thought; and (iii) the version that appears in the early printed editions reads like the text presented here, except for the last three words, which read וְלֹא תִלְמַד מֵאָבִיךָ, as does the manuscript version, rather than אֶלָּא תִלְמַד מֵאָבִיךָ, like the text presented here; but since these last three words contradict the father's words of enticement, *Ittur Bikkurim* emends וְלֹא to אֶלָּא; and that is how the comment appears in most later printed editions.

Despite the marginal gloss to the manuscript and *Ittur Bikkurim's* emendation of the early printed editions, the two of which are identical, and the adoption of that version by most later printed editions, version (iii) appears to be able to stand without emendation, thus דְּהַיְנוּ אָבִיו, *this refers to his own father,* מֵסִית אוֹתוֹ לֵאמֹר, *who seeks to entice him by saying,* לֹא תִלְמַד לַעֲשׂוֹת מֵאֲבֹתֶיךָ, *"Do not learn what to do from your fathers,"* שֶׁהוּא אֲבִי אָבִיךָ, *i.e., your father's father."* וְלֹא תִלְמַד מֵאָבִיךָ, *But [in such a case] you should not learn from your father* (*VeChur LaZahav*).

96. The *gematria* of the Baal HaTurim's phrase is 796, nineteen more than that of the Scriptural phrase. Accordingly, many later printed editions begin the comment with the parenthesized addition, עִם הָאוֹתִיּוֹת וְהַתֵּבוֹת, *including the letters and the words,* i.e., the principle of *im ha'osios* allows us to add 15 and the principle of *im hateivos* allows another 4, for a total of 796.

Alternatively: The Baal HaTurim's phrase should be emended to וְאֵין לִטְעוֹן לְהַמֵּסִית, *and it is not [proper] to offer defenses for the enticer,* which has a *gematria* of 777 (*Matzreif LaKesef*).

97. *Sanhedrin* 29a; see the Baal HaTurim's second comment to v. 6 above. The Talmud derives this rule from the words וְלֹא תַחְמֹל וְלֹא תְכַסֶּה עָלָיו, *you shall not be compassionate and you shall not cover for him,* that appear at the end of our verse.

98. The form תְּכַסֶּה is a singular future tense verb that can be either second person masculine, *you shall cover,* or third person feminine, *she shall cover.* In our verse it is masculine, in the verse from *Isaiah* its antecedent is the feminine noun הָאָרֶץ, *the land.*

99. *Sanhedrin* 33b; see also *Rambam, Hilchos Sanhedrin* 11:5; *Chazon Ish, Sanhedrin* 21.

מֵעַל יהוה אֱלֹהֶיךָ הַמּוֹצִיאֲךָ מֵאֶרֶץ מִצְרַיִם מִבֵּית
יב עֲבָדִים: וְכָל־יִשְׂרָאֵל יִשְׁמְעוּ וְיִרָאוּן וְלֹא־יוֹסִפוּ
יג לַעֲשׂוֹת כַּדָּבָר הָרָע הַזֶּה בְּקִרְבֶּךָ: כִּי־תִשְׁמַע
בְּאַחַת עָרֶיךָ אֲשֶׁר יהוה אֱלֹהֶיךָ נֹתֵן לְךָ לָשֶׁבֶת
יד שָׁם לֵאמֹר: יָצְאוּ אֲנָשִׁים בְּנֵי־בְלִיַּעַל מִקִּרְבֶּךָ
וַיַּדִּיחוּ אֶת־יֹשְׁבֵי עִירָם לֵאמֹר נֵלְכָה וְנַעַבְדָה
טו אֱלֹהִים אֲחֵרִים אֲשֶׁר לֹא־יְדַעְתֶּם: וְדָרַשְׁתָּ
וְחָקַרְתָּ וְשָׁאַלְתָּ הֵיטֵב וְהִנֵּה אֱמֶת נָכוֹן הַדָּבָר
טז נֶעֶשְׂתָה הַתּוֹעֵבָה הַזֹּאת בְּקִרְבֶּךָ: הַכֵּה תַכֶּה
אֶת־יֹשְׁבֵי הָעִיר הַהִוא לְפִי־חָרֶב הַחֲרֵם אֹתָהּ
וְאֶת־כָּל־אֲשֶׁר־בָּהּ וְאֶת־בְּהֶמְתָּהּ לְפִי־חָרֶב:
יז וְאֶת־כָּל־שְׁלָלָהּ תִּקְבֹּץ אֶל־תּוֹךְ רְחֹבָהּ וְשָׂרַפְתָּ
בָאֵשׁ אֶת־הָעִיר וְאֶת־כָּל־שְׁלָלָהּ כָּלִיל לַיהוה
יח אֱלֹהֶיךָ וְהָיְתָה תֵּל עוֹלָם לֹא תִבָּנֶה עוֹד: וְלֹא־
יִדְבַּק בְּיָדְךָ מְאוּמָה מִן־הַחֵרֶם לְמַעַן יָשׁוּב יהוה
מֵחֲרוֹן אַפּוֹ וְנָתַן־לְךָ רַחֲמִים וְרִחַמְךָ וְהִרְבֶּךָ
יט כַּאֲשֶׁר נִשְׁבַּע לַאֲבֹתֶיךָ: כִּי תִשְׁמַע בְּקוֹל יהוה
אֱלֹהֶיךָ לִשְׁמֹר אֶת־כָּל־מִצְוֹתָיו אֲשֶׁר אָנֹכִי מְצַוְּךָ

בעל הטורים

(טו) **וְדָרַשְׁתָּ וְחָקַרְתָּ וְשָׁאַלְתָּ הֵיטֵב.** לְפִי שֶׁנֶּאֱמַר "כִּי תִשְׁמַע בְּאַחַת עָרֶיךָ", בִּשְׁמִיעָה בְּעָלְמָא. לְכָךְ מַזְהִיר אוֹתְךָ שֶׁתִּדְרֹשׁ וְתַחְקֹר הֵיטֵב:

(יח) **וְרִחַמְךָ וְהִרְבֶּךָ.** שֶׁלֹּא תִדְאַג לוֹמַר, הֶחֱרַבְתִּי עִיר וְיוֹשְׁבֶיהָ. לְכָךְ מְבַשֶּׂרְךָ לוֹמַר שֶׁלֹּא תִדְאַג, וַיַּפְרְךָ וְיַרְבֶּךָ:

❑ **וְנָתַן לְךָ רַחֲמִים וְרִחַמְךָ.** וּסְמִיךְ לֵהּ "בָּנִים אַתֶּם". לוֹמַר לְךָ שֶׁכָּל מִי שֶׁיֵּשׁ לוֹ רַחֲמִים וּמְרַחֵם עַל הַבְּרִיּוֹת, הַקָּדוֹשׁ בָּרוּךְ הוּא מְרַחֵם עָלָיו כְּאָב עַל הַבֵּן:

BAAL HATURIM ELUCIDATED

15. **וְדָרַשְׁתָּ וְחָקַרְתָּ וְשָׁאַלְתָּ הֵיטֵב** — YOU SHALL SEEK OUT AND YOU SHALL INVESTIGATE AND YOU SHALL INQUIRE — WELL. Whereas the Torah has stated, כִּי תִשְׁמַע בְּאַחַת עָרֶיךָ, *If you will hear in one of your cities* (v. 13) [you might think that] mere hearsay [is sufficient to punish the accused]. Therefore the verse admonishes you that you should seek out and investigate well.[100]

100. *R' Yehudah HaChassid; Ramban.*

from near HASHEM, your God, Who takes you out of Egypt, from the house of slavery. [12] *All Israel shall hear and fear, and they shall not again do such an evil thing in your midst.*

[13] *If you will hear — in one of your cities that HASHEM, your God, gives you in which to dwell — [a report], saying,* [14] *"Lawless men have emerged from your midst, and they have caused the dwellers of their city to go astray, saying, 'Let us go and worship other gods, that you did not know' " —* [15] *you shall seek out and you shall investigate and you shall inquire — well, and behold! it is true, the word is correct, this abomination was committed in your midst.* [16] *You shall surely smite the inhabitants of that city with the edge of the sword; lay it waste and everything that is in it, and its animals, with the edge of the sword.* [17] *You shall gather together all its booty to the midst of its open square, and you shall burn in fire completely the city and all its booty to HASHEM, your God, and it shall be an eternal heap, it shall not be rebuilt.* [18] *No part of the banned property may adhere to your hand, so that HASHEM will turn back from His burning wrath; and He will give you mercy and He will be merciful to you and He will multiply you, as He swore to your forefathers,* [19] *when you hearken to the voice of HASHEM, your God, to observe all His commandments that I command you*

BAAL HATURIM ELUCIDATED

18. וְרִחַמְךָ וְהִרְבֶּךָ — AND HE WILL BE MERCIFUL TO YOU AND HE WILL MULTIPLY YOU. [This is stated] so that you not become dismayed, saying, "I have destroyed a city and its inhabitants." Therefore, the Torah informs you that you need not be dismayed,[101] for He will make you fruitful and He will make you numerous.[102]

❑ **וְנָתַן לְךָ רַחֲמִים וְרִחַמְךָ — AND HE WILL GIVE YOU MERCY AND HE WILL BE MERCIFUL TO YOU.** Juxtaposed to that is, בָּנִים אַתֶּם, *You are children* (14:1), to indicate to you that any person who has mercy and who is merciful to others, God will be merciful to him,[103] like a father to his son.[104]

101. *Tosefta, Sanhedrin* 14:1 — Do not become apprehensive that the relatives of the inhabitants of the wayward city whom you have put to death will turn against you to avenge their relatives' death. For God will put His love into their hearts and they will acknowledge that you have judged and punished justly.

102. The text follows the early printed editions and *Shoham Yakar's* manuscript edition. Some later editions follow *Ittur Bikkurim's* suggested emendation that substitutes the verse's phrase וְרִחַמְךָ וְהִרְבֶּךָ, *and He will be merciful to you and He will multiply you,* for the Baal HaTurim's phrase, וְיַפְרְךָ וְיַרְבֶּךָ, *He will make you fruitful and He will make you numerous,* a phrase borrowed from *Genesis* 28:3.

103. *Shabbos* 151b.

104. *See Psalms* 103:13.

יד/א־ה רביעי א הַיּוֹם לַעֲשׂוֹת הַיָּשָׁר בְּעֵינֵי יהוה אֱלֹהֶיךָ׃ בָּנִים
אַתֶּם לַיהוה אֱלֹהֵיכֶם לֹא תִתְגֹּדְדוּ וְלֹא־תָשִׂימוּ
ב קָרְחָה בֵּין עֵינֵיכֶם לָמֵת׃ כִּי עַם קָדוֹשׁ אַתָּה לַיהוה
אֱלֹהֶיךָ וּבְךָ בָּחַר יהוה לִהְיוֹת לוֹ לְעַם סְגֻלָּה
ג מִכֹּל הָעַמִּים אֲשֶׁר עַל־פְּנֵי הָאֲדָמָה׃ לֹא
ד תֹאכַל כָּל־תּוֹעֵבָה׃ זֹאת הַבְּהֵמָה אֲשֶׁר תֹּאכֵלוּ
ה שׁוֹר שֵׂה כְשָׂבִים וְשֵׂה עִזִּים׃ אַיָּל וּצְבִי

בעל הטורים

(יט) **לַעֲשׂוֹת הַיָּשָׁר בְּעֵינֵי ה׳.** וּסְמִיךְ לֵהּ "בָּנִים אַתֶּם". דִּבִזְמַן שֶׁעוֹשִׂין רְצוֹנוֹ שֶׁל מָקוֹם, קְרוּיִם בָּנִים:

יד (**א**) סָמַךְ מֵת לְעִיר הַנִּדַּחַת. לוֹמַר לְךָ שֶׁעֲבוֹדָה זָרָה חֲשׁוּבָה כְּמֵת. וְגַם שֶׁהָיוּ מִתְגּוֹדְדִים לִפְנֵי עֲבוֹדָה זָרָה כְּמוֹ עַל מֵת:

❑ **בָּנִים אַתֶּם.** בַּפָּסוּק הַזֶּה יֵשׁ שְׁנֵים עָשָׂר תֵּבוֹת, כְּנֶגֶד שְׁנֵים עָשָׂר שְׁבָטִים, שֶׁנִּקְרְאוּ בָּנִים לַה׳:

(**ב**) **מִכֹּל הָעַמִּים אֲשֶׁר עַל פְּנֵי הָאֲדָמָה.** וּסְמִיךְ לֵהּ "לֹא תֹאכַל כָּל תּוֹעֵבָה". לוֹמַר לְךָ שֶׁלֹּא יִתְעָרְבוּ בָּאֻמּוֹת. וְהָאֻמּוֹת נִמְשְׁלוּ לִבְהֵמוֹת:

❑ בַּבְּהֵמוֹת הִתִּיר שָׁלֹשׁ בְּהֵמוֹת וְשֶׁבַע חַיּוֹת כְּנֶגֶד עֲשֶׂרֶת הַדִּבְּרוֹת:

(**ד**) **עִזִּים.** וּסְמִיךְ לֵהּ "אַיָּל". רֶמֶז לְהָא דְּאִיתָא בְּחֻלִּין, עִזָּא דְּכַרְכּוּז מִין חַיָּה הוּא:

BAAL HATURIM ELUCIDATED

19. **לַעֲשׂוֹת הַיָּשָׁר בְּעֵינֵי ה׳** — TO DO WHAT IS RIGHT IN THE EYES OF HASHEM. Juxtaposed to this is, בָּנִים אַתֶּם, *You are children.* [This indicates] that when they [Israel] carry out the will of the Omnipresent, they are called [His] children.[105]

XIV.

1. Scripture has juxtaposed [this law regarding] a dead person to the passage concerning a wayward [idolatrous] city (13:13-19), to indicate to you that an idol is considered like a corpse.[106] Also, the idolaters would cut themselves before false deities,[107] just as they would for a dead person.

❑ **בָּנִים אַתֶּם** — YOU ARE CHILDREN. There are twelve words in this verse, corresponding to the twelve tribes that are all called children of HASHEM.[108]

2. **מִכֹּל הָעַמִּים אֲשֶׁר עַל פְּנֵי הָאֲדָמָה** — FROM AMONG ALL THE PEOPLES THAT ARE ON THE FACE OF THE EARTH. Juxtaposed to this is, לֹא תֹאכַל כָּל תּוֹעֵבָה, *You shall not eat any abomination* [i.e., non-kosher creatures]. This [juxtaposition] teaches you not to intermingle [i.e., intermarry][108a] with the nations, for the [various] nations are

105. *Peirush HaRokeach;* see the Baal HaTurim to 1:5 above, with note 26.

106. *Chullin* 13b — the Talmud compares an idol to a corpse with regard to the minimum size that generates *tumah* (contamination).

107. This practice is described in *I Kings* 18:28.

108. *Rimzei Rabbeinu Yoel.*

108a. The Torah often uses bread as a euphe-

today, to do what is right in the eyes of HASHEM, *your God.*

1 *You are children to* HASHEM, *your God — you shall not cut yourselves and you shall not make a bald spot between your eyes for a dead person.* 2 *For you are a holy people to* HASHEM, *your God, and* HASHEM *has chosen you for Himself to be a treasured people, from among all the peoples that are on the face of the earth.*

3 *You shall not eat any abomination.* 4 *These are the animals that you may eat: oxen, sheep, and goats;* 5 *ayal, tzvi,*

BAAL HATURIM ELUCIDATED

allegorized by [various species of] animals.[109]

❑ Among the animals, Scripture has permitted three species of domestic animals (v. 4 below) and seven species of wild beasts (v. 5 below), corresponding to the Ten Commandments.[110]

4. {אֲשֶׁר תֹּאכֵלוּ may be understood in light of the Baal HaTurim's comment to *Leviticus* 11:2, s.v., אֲשֶׁר תֹּאכְלוּ.}

❑ **עִזִּים** — GOATS. Juxtaposed to this is אַיָּל, *ayal,*[111] an allusion to that which is stated in tractate *Chullin*: The goat of Karkuz[111a] is a species of wild beast.[112]

mism for marital intimacy (see *Rashi* and Baal HaTurim to *Genesis* 39:6 and *Rashi* to *Exodus* 2:20; A.S.).

109. That is, Scripture often employs an animal species as a metaphor for a particular nation, e.g., *Ezekiel* 23:20; *Psalms* 22:13; *Daniel* 8:20-21 (see *Rashi* to *Genesis* 15:10).

110. *Midrash Tadshei.* — And because Israel accepted the Torah, therefore He permitted ten species to them: *oxen, sheep, goat . . .*

111. The names of two animals are spelled the same, but are pronounced differently: The אַיִל [accent on the אַ] (e.g., *Numbers* 7:15; *Deuteronomy* 32:14) is a male sheep after its first year [after its thirteenth month, with regard to Altar offerings], and is classified as a בְּהֵמָה, *domestic animal;* while the אַיָּל [accent on the יָּ] (e.g., 12:15 above; *Song of Songs* 2:9) is usually identified as a member of the deer or the antelope family, and is classified as a חַיָּה, *wild beast.* The halachic ramifications of these classifications are discussed in the second paragraph of note 112 below.

111a. Extant editions of the Talmud read עִזָּא כַּרְכּוּז, without a prefix on the second word, and that is what *Rashi* calls this species. Since the meaning of כַּרְכּוּז is unknown from any other source, it is not clear whether it is a place name [i.e., Karkuzian goat] or descriptive term. Therefore the term has been transliterated in lowercase letters in the Talmudic passage adduced in note 112. The Baal HaTurim, on the other hand, adds the prefix דְּ־, *of,* indicating that כַּרְכּוּז is a place name [interestingly, both readings appear in *Tosafos,* s.v., והרי עז דחרוקות]; thus, in the Baal HaTurim's comment it has been rendered *goat of Karkuz* (*VeChur LaZahav*).

112. *Chullin* 59b — The Talmud discusses the halachic status of the עִזָּא כַּרְכּוּז, *the karkuz-goat.* [The name indicates that this creature is a species of goat and should be classified as a domestic animal; on the other hand, the composition of its horns identifies it as a wild beast (*Rashi*).] The Talmud concludes that it is a wild beast.

This classification is more than academic, for it has halachic ramifications: The חֵלֶב, *cheilev,* i.e., the suet and certain other fats of domestic animals, may not be eaten (see *Leviticus* 7:23), while the *cheilev* of wild beasts is permitted; the blood of the slaughter of wild beasts must be covered with earth or the like, while that of domestic beasts need not be covered (see the Baal HaTurim to 12:24 above, with note 73).

By ending the list of domestic animals with עִזִּים, *goats,* and juxtaposing it with the list of wild beasts, the Torah alludes to the goat of

ו וַיַּחְמוּר וְאַקּוֹ וְדִישֹׁן וּתְאוֹ וָזָמֶר: וְכָל־בְּהֵמָה
מַפְרֶסֶת פַּרְסָה וְשֹׁסַעַת שֶׁסַע שְׁתֵּי פְרָסוֹת מַעֲלַת
ז גֵּרָה בַּבְּהֵמָה אֹתָהּ תֹּאכֵלוּ: אַךְ אֶת־זֶה לֹא
תֹאכְלוּ מִמַּעֲלֵי הַגֵּרָה וּמִמַּפְרִיסֵי הַפַּרְסָה
הַשְּׁסוּעָה אֶת־הַגָּמָל וְאֶת־הָאַרְנֶבֶת וְאֶת־הַשָּׁפָן
כִּי־מַעֲלֵה גֵרָה הֵמָּה וּפַרְסָה לֹא הִפְרִיסוּ טְמֵאִים
ח הֵם לָכֶם: וְאֶת־הַחֲזִיר כִּי־מַפְרִיס פַּרְסָה הוּא
וְלֹא גֵרָה טָמֵא הוּא לָכֶם מִבְּשָׂרָם לֹא תֹאכֵלוּ

בעל הטורים

(ז) **טְמֵאִים הֵם לָכֶם.** וּסְמִיךְ לֵהּ "וְאֶת הַחֲזִיר". לוֹמַר לְךָ שֶׁאָסוּר לְגַדֵּל חֲזִירִים:

(ח) וְסָמַךְ "מִבְּשָׂרָם לֹא תֹאכֵלוּ" לְ"אֶת זֶה תֹּאכְלוּ מִכֹּל אֲשֶׁר בַּמָּיִם". כְּלוֹמַר, אַף עַל פִּי שֶׁאָסַרְתִּי לֶאֱכֹל מִבְּשָׂרָם, אֲשֶׁר מֵהֶם בַּמַּיִם תֹּאכֵלוּ, דְּחַמְרָא דְיַמָּא שְׁרֵי:

דָּבָר אַחֵר – "לֹא תֹאכֵלוּ . . . אֶת זֶה תֹּאכְלוּ". לוֹמַר, שֶׁקִּרְבֵי דָגִים אֵין לוֹקְחִים אֶלָּא מִן הַמֻּמְחֶה. דִּקְרֵי בֵהּ "לֹא תֹאכֵלוּ", אֶלָּא אִם כֵּן יֹאמַר "אֶת זֶה" הוּא שֶׁלָּקַחְתִּי מִפְּלוֹנִי צַיָּד וְכָשֵׁר הוּא:

BAAL HATURIM ELUCIDATED

6. {The Baal HaTurim's comment to this verse appears at *Exodus* 22:9.}

7. {The Baal HaTurim's comment to מִמַּעֲלֵי הַגֵּרָה appears at *Leviticus* 11:4.}

❑ **טְמֵאִים הֵם לָכֶם** — THEY ARE UNCLEAN TO YOU. Juxtaposed to this is וְאֶת הַחֲזִיר, *and the pig,* to indicate to you that it is forbidden to raise pigs.[113]

Karkuz. Accordingly, the Baal HaTurim's statement, "Juxtaposed to this is אַיָּל," does not refer to אַיָּל per se, rather he uses the term that heads the list of wild beasts to stand in for the entire list (*VeChur LaZahav*).

113. According to one Mishnah, it is forbidden to deal in foodstuffs that are halachically forbidden to be eaten (*Sheviis* 7:3). Thus, it is forbidden to raise swine for human consumption. However, the Torah's injunction against eating pork does not prohibit the use of porcine by-products for non-food uses, e.g., lubricating hides with pig fat (*Tosafos* to *Bava Kamma* 82b, s.v., לא יגדל אדם).

Another Mishnah, however, states: We may not raise swine anywhere (*Bava Kamma* 7:7 [79b]). The Talmud explains that this second prohibition was enacted in response to an event that occurred during the internal strife of the Hasmonean dynasty: The brothers Hyrkanus and Aristobolus were vying for the Hasmonean throne. One brother was quartered in Jerusalem [which he controlled], while the other was [encamped with Pompey's Roman legions that he had enlisted to help him oust his brother] outside the city. Each day, those in the city would lower a basket of coins [from the Temple treasury] over the city wall and those outside [who, despite their political differences with those inside, did not want to interfere with the Temple service] would [purchase and] send up [lambs for] the daily *tamid*-offerings. There was an old man who was familiar with "Greek wisdom" [a cryptic language used by royalty, but unintelligible to the commoners (*Rashi* to 83a)] who said to [the besieging brother, in this cryptic language,] "As long as they engage in the Temple service, they will not be delivered into your hands." The next day, when those inside lowered the coins, those outside sent up a pig. When it was halfway up the wall, it dug its hooves into the wall and the entire Land of Israel

yachmur, akko, dishon, teo, and zamer. 6 *And every animal*
that has a split hoof, which is completely separated in two
hooves, that brings up its cud among animals — it may
you eat. 7 *But this shall you not eat from among those*
that bring up their cud or have a completely separated split
hoof: the camel, the hare, and the hyrax, for they bring up
their cud, but their hoof is not split — they are unclean
to you; 8 *and the pig, for it has a split hoof, but not the*
cud — it is unclean to you; from their meat you shall not eat

BAAL HATURIM ELUCIDATED

8. Scripture has juxtaposed, מִבְּשָׂרָם לֹא תֹאכֵלוּ, *from their meat you shall not eat,* with אֶת זֶה תֹּאכְלוּ מִכֹּל אֲשֶׁר בַּמָּיִם, *this you may eat of everything that is in the water,* as if to say, "Although I have prohibited you from eating their meat, you may nevertheless eat the water animal that resembles them,"[114] for [as the Talmud teaches]: The sea donkey is permitted.[115]

Alternatively: [The juxtaposition of] לֹא תֹאכֵלוּ, *you shall not eat,* [with] אֶת זֶה תֹּאכְלוּ, *this you may eat,* is to indicate that the fatty innards of fish [that have been removed from the fish] should not be purchased except from an expert.[116] For we may read these phrases as, לֹא תֹאכֵלוּ, *you shall not eat,* unless that person says, "*This* [*you may eat*] because I purchased it from So-and-So the fisherman, and it is kosher."[117]

— an area of four hundred *parsah* by four hundred *parsah* — trembled. At that time, the Rabbis proclaimed: Cursed is the man who raises pigs; and cursed is the person who teaches his son "Greek wisdom" (*Bava Kamma* 82b).

114. The Talmud states that every animal found on land has its counterpart in the sea except for the חֻלְדָּה [usually rendered *weasel* (see *Rashi* to *Leviticus* 11:29, s.v., הַחֹלֶד)] (*Yerushalmi, Shabbos* 14:1: *Chullin* 127a).

115. *Avodah Zarah* 39a — חֲמָרָא דְיַמָּא שְׁרֵי תּוֹרָא דְיַמָּא אֲסִיר, *The "donkey of the sea" is permitted; the "ox of the sea" is forbidden*; וְסִימָנָיךְ, *and your mnemonic is,* טָמֵא טָהוֹר טָהוֹר טָמֵא, *the impure one is pure; the pure one is impure,* i.e., the sea animal that corresponds to the impure (non-kosher) land donkey is pure (kosher); but the sea animal that corresponds to the kosher land ox is non-kosher. [The Baal HaTurim also discusses this concept in his comments to *Leviticus* 11:2 and 8.]

It should be noted that, although Modern Hebrew uses חֲמוֹר הַיָּם (literally, *donkey of the sea*) for the kosher *codfish* and פָּרַת יָם (literally, *sea cow*) for the non-kosher *manatee* (also called sea cow in English), we have no way of knowing whether those are the species to which the Talmud refers. It is possible that the Talmud's correspondence of sea animal to land animal is based on their essential character, rather than to their external appearance.

116. *Avodah Zarah* 40a. The term מֻמְחֶה, *expert,* as used here refers to one who is proficient regarding the identification of kosher fish (*Rashi,* as cited by *Ramban* and *Ran*), or who is known to be scrupulous regarding *kashrus* (*Re'ah; Ritva*).

117. The translation follows the first opinion in note 116 above. According to the second opinion there, the comment is translated: ". . . I purchased it from So-and-So the fisherman, who is [known to be] *kosher* [i.e., trustworthy]." Alternatively: [The seller says,] ". . . I purchased it from So-and-So the fisherman." And that fisherman is [known to be] *kosher* [i.e., trustworthy] (*VeChur LaZahav*).

ט וּבְנִבְלָתָם לֹא תִגָּעוּ׃ אֶת־זֶה֙ תֹּֽאכְל֔וּ מִכֹּ֖ל
אֲשֶׁ֣ר בַּמָּ֑יִם כֹּ֣ל אֲשֶׁר־ל֞וֹ סְנַפִּ֧יר וְקַשְׂקֶ֛שֶׂת תֹּאכֵֽלוּ׃
י וְכֹ֨ל אֲשֶׁ֤ר אֵין־לוֹ֙ סְנַפִּ֣יר וְקַשְׂקֶ֔שֶׂת לֹ֖א תֹאכֵ֑לוּ
יא טָמֵ֥א ה֖וּא לָכֶֽם׃ כָּל־צִפּ֥וֹר טְהֹרָ֖ה תֹּאכֵֽלוּ׃
יב וְזֶ֕ה אֲשֶׁ֥ר לֹא־תֹאכְל֖וּ מֵהֶ֑ם הַנֶּ֥שֶׁר וְהַפֶּ֖רֶס
יג וְהָעָזְנִיָּֽה׃ וְהָרָאָה֙ וְאֶת־הָ֣אַיָּ֔ה וְהַדַּיָּ֖ה לְמִינָֽהּ׃
יד־טו וְאֵ֥ת כָּל־עֹרֵ֖ב לְמִינֽוֹ׃ וְאֵת֙ בַּ֣ת הַֽיַּעֲנָ֔ה וְאֶת־

בעל הטורים

❏ **וּבְנִבְלָתָם לֹא תִגָּעוּ.** וּסְמִיךְ לֵהּ ״אֶת זֶה תֹּאכְלוּ״. לוֹמַר שֶׁיֵּשׁ נְבֵלָה שֶׁתֹּאכַל מִמֶּנָּה, כְּגוֹן נְבֵלָה מֻסְרַחַת שֶׁאֵינָהּ רְאוּיָה לְגֵר:

❏ **לֹא תִגָּעוּ.** בְּגִימַטְרִיָּא חַיָּיב לְטַהֵר בָּרֶגֶל:

(ט) **תֹּאכֵלוּ.** וּסְמִיךְ ״וְכֹל אֲשֶׁר אֵין לוֹ״. לְהַתִּיר דָּג טָהוֹר שֶׁנִּמְצָא בְּתוֹךְ דָּג טָמֵא:

(י) **טָמֵא הוּא לָכֶם.** וּסְמִיךְ לֵהּ ״כָּל צִפּוֹר״. לְרַבּוֹת צִפּוֹר מְשֻׁלַּחַת שֶׁל מְצֹרָע:

(יב) **הַנֶּשֶׁר.** הִתְחִיל בַּנֶּשֶׁר מִפְּנֵי שֶׁהוּא מֶלֶךְ בָּעוֹפוֹת, שֶׁנֶּאֱמַר, ״אִם עַל פִּיךָ יַגְבִּיהַּ נָשֶׁר״. ״אִם עַל פִּיךָ״ סוֹפֵי תֵבוֹת מֶלֶךְ:

(טו) יַעֲנָה, שֶׁמְּעַנָּה אֶת בָּנֶיהָ וְאֵינָהּ מְרַחֶמֶת עֲלֵיהֶם. וְכֵן הָעֹרֵב אַכְזָרִי עַל בָּנָיו, לְכָךְ סְמָכוֹ לָהּ:

BAAL HATURIM ELUCIDATED

❏ וּבְנִבְלָתָם לֹא תִגָּעוּ — AND YOU SHALL NOT TOUCH THEIR CARCASSES. Juxtaposed to this is אֶת זֶה תֹּאכְלוּ, *this you may eat,* to indicate that there is a *neveilah*[118] from which you may eat, e.g., a rotting carcass that is not fit (as food) for a convert.[119]

❏ לֹא תִגָּעוּ — YOU SHALL NOT TOUCH. The *gematria* of this phrase (510) is equivalent[120] to that of חַיָּיב לְטַהֵר בָּרֶגֶל, *One must purify oneself* [in preparation] *for the festival.*[121]

9. תֹּאכֵלוּ — YOU MAY EAT. Juxtaposed is וְכֹל אֲשֶׁר אֵין לוֹ, *and anything that does not*

---

118. That is, the carcass of an animal that died or was killed by any means other than *shechitah* (ritual slaughtering).

119. *Peirush HaRokeach.* Verse 21 below teaches that although *neveilah* (see note 118) may not be eaten by a Jew, it may be given or sold to a non-Jew, for he is permitted to eat it. The Talmud interprets that verse as limiting the prohibition against eating *neveilah* to that which is considered edible by one who is not bound by the kosher laws of the Torah (*Avodah Zarah* 67b).

In this case, the Torah's use of the term גֵּר does not refer to a גֵּר צֶדֶק, *righteous convert,* i.e., a non-Jew who has accepted all of the Torah's *mitzvos* and has undergone formal conversion through circumcision [in the case of a male] and immersion in a *mikveh.* Rather, it refers to a גֵּר תּוֹשָׁב, literally, *resident convert,* i.e., a non-Jew who has rejected his gentile ways and has accepted upon himself the seven Noachide commandments. Whereas he has repudiated idolatry, and accepted the obligation of living in accordance with the seven *mitzvos,* albeit as a gentile, he is permitted to make his residence in the Land of Israel (see *Rashi* to v. 21 below, s.v., לגר).

120. The principle of *im hakollel* allows 509, the *gematria* of the Baal HaTurim's phrase, to be considered equivalent to 510.

121. *Peirush HaRokeach;* see *Rosh Hashanah* 16b, cited by *Rashi;* see also the Baal HaTurim to *Leviticus* 22:32, s.v., מְקַדִּשְׁכֶם.

and you shall not touch their carcasses.
9 *This you may eat of everything that is in the water:*
anything that has fins and scales you may eat. 10 *And*
anything that does not have fins or scales you shall not eat;
it is unclean to you.
11 *Every clean bird, you may eat.* 12 *This is what you shall*
not eat from among them: the nesher, the peres, the ozniah;
13 *the raah, the ayah, and the dayah according to its kind;*
14 *and every oreiv according to its kind;* 15 *the bas haya'anah,*

BAAL HATURIM ELUCIDATED

have. This is to permit [eating] a kosher fish that is found within a non-kosher fish.[122]

❑ {The Baal HaTurim's other comment regarding kosher fish appears at *Leviticus* 11:9-12, s.v., לֹא הִזְכִּיר.}

10. טָמֵא הוּא לָכֶם — IT IS UNCLEAN TO YOU. Juxtaposed to this is כָּל צִפּוֹר, *every bird* (v. 11). This is to include the *metzora's* set-free bird.[123]

12. הַנֶּשֶׁר — THE NESHER. The verse lists the נֶשֶׁר, *eagle,*[124] first, because it is the king of the birds.[125] As it is stated, אִם עַל פִּיךָ יַגְבִּיהַּ נָשֶׁר, *Does the eagle mount up at your command?* (*Job* 39:27). The final letters of אִם עַל פִּיךָ spell the word מֶלֶךְ, *king.*[126]

14. {The Baal HaTurim's comment to עֹרֵב לְמִינוֹ appears at *Leviticus* 11:15.}

15. [This species is called] יַעֲנָה, *yaanah,*[127] because it oppresses its young, and is not compassionate to them. The עֹרֵב, *oreiv,*[128] is also cruel to its young;[129] therefore, it is juxtaposed with [the *bas hayaanah*].[130]

122. See *Bechoros* 7b.

123. The cleansing or purification of a *metzora* involves two birds, one of which is slaughtered, the other set free (see *Leviticus* 14:1-7). The Talmud explains that the verse, *Every clean bird, you may eat* (v. 11), includes the *metzora's* set-free bird (*Kiddushin* 57a, cited by *Rashi* to v. 11). Accordingly, the Baal HaTurim's comment, which seemingly contradicts the Talmud, requires explanation. In truth, the Talmud (there) states that the set-free bird is forbidden, but only until its release. Once it has been set free, it may be recaptured, slaughtered and eaten, as it is stated, *every clean bird you may eat.* Thus, we may say that both the Talmud and the Baal HaTurim understand the expression כָּל צִפּוֹר, *every bird,* as a reference to the *metzora's* non-slaughtered bird. The Talmud links that phrase to what comes after it, thus, כָּל צִפּוֹר טְהֹרָה תֹּאכֵלוּ, *you may eat the metzora's bird,* after it has been set free; while the Baal HaTurim connects it to the preceding verse, thus, טָמֵא הוּא לָכֶם כָּל צִפּוֹר, *the metzora's bird is unclean to you,* before it has been set free.

124. The נֶשֶׁר, *nesher,* is commonly identified as the eagle. However, based on the Talmud's description of the *nesher* (*Chullin* 61a), some question that identification (see *Peirush HaRosh* and *Daas Zekeinim MiBaalei HaTosafos*).

125. The Talmud (*Chagigah* 13b) states: The king of beasts is the lion; the king of the domestic animals is the ox; the king of the birds is the *nesher;* and man exalts himself upon them, and the Holy One, Blessed is He, exalts Himself upon all of them and upon the whole world in its entirety.

126. *Peirush HaRokeach;* see also the Baal HaTurim to *Leviticus* 11:13.

127. From the root ענה, *to oppress.*

128. Although עֹרֵב, *oreiv,* is usually rendered *raven,* many question that identification (*Peirush HaRosh; Daas Zekeinim MiBaalei HaTosafos;* see the Baal HaTurim to *Leviticus* 11:15 with note 86).

129. *Eruvin* 22a.

130. *Peirush HaRokeach.*

טז הַתַּחְמָס וְאֶת־הַשָּׁחַף וְאֶת־הַנֵּץ לְמִינֵהוּ: אֶת־
יז הַכּוֹס וְאֶת־הַיַּנְשׁוּף וְהַתִּנְשָׁמֶת: וְהַקָּאָת וְאֶת־
יח הָרָחָמָה וְאֶת־הַשָּׁלָךְ: וְהַחֲסִידָה וְהָאֲנָפָה לְמִינָהּ
יט וְהַדּוּכִיפַת וְהָעֲטַלֵּף: וְכֹל שֶׁרֶץ הָעוֹף טָמֵא הוּא
כ־כא לָכֶם לֹא יֵאָכֵלוּ: כָּל־עוֹף טָהוֹר תֹּאכֵלוּ: לֹא
תֹאכְלוּ כָל־נְבֵלָה לַגֵּר אֲשֶׁר־בִּשְׁעָרֶיךָ תִּתְּנֶנָּה
וַאֲכָלָהּ אוֹ מָכֹר לְנָכְרִי כִּי עַם קָדוֹשׁ אַתָּה לַיהוָה
אֱלֹהֶיךָ לֹא־תְבַשֵּׁל גְּדִי בַּחֲלֵב אִמּוֹ:
חמישי כב עַשֵּׂר תְּעַשֵּׂר אֵת כָּל־תְּבוּאַת זַרְעֶךָ הַיֹּצֵא הַשָּׂדֶה
כג שָׁנָה שָׁנָה: וְאָכַלְתָּ לִפְנֵי | יהוָה אֱלֹהֶיךָ בַּמָּקוֹם

בעל הטורים

(כא) **לֹא תְבַשֵּׁל.** בְּגִימַטְרִיָּא, אִיסּוּר אֲכִילָה וּבִישּׁוּל וַהֲנָאָה:

(כב) סָמַךְ "עַשֵּׂר תְּעַשֵּׂר וְגוֹ' הַיֹּצֵא הַשָּׂדֶה שָׁנָה" לְבָשָׂר בְּחָלָב. לוֹמַר, כְּשֵׁם שֶׁתַּעֲרֹבֶת שֶׁל בָּשָׂר בְּחָלָב אָסוּר, כֵּן גַּם כֵּן אָסוּר הַתַּעֲרוּבוֹת שֶׁל כִּלְאַיִם בַּשָּׂדֶה. וְאִם תִּשְׁמֹר מֵהַתַּעֲרֹבֶת, אָז אֲבַשֵּׁל פֵּרוֹתֶיךָ בִּזְמַנָּן וְתִתְעַשֵּׁר:

❑ וְסָמַךְ "בַּחֲלֵב אִמּוֹ" לְ"שָׁנָה שָׁנָה", לוֹמַר שֶׁמֵּינֶקֶת חֲבֵרוֹ לֹא תִנָּשֵׂא בְּתוֹךְ שְׁנָתַיִם. וִיהִי הַוָּלָד בַּחֲלֵב אִמּוֹ שְׁתֵּי שָׁנִים:

BAAL HATURIM ELUCIDATED

15-17. {In his comments to *Leviticus* 11:16-18, the Baal HaTurim explains many of the bird names of these verses.}

21. [131]**לֹא תְבַשֵּׁל** — YOU SHALL NOT COOK. The *gematria* of this phrase (763) is equivalent[132] to that of [131]אִיסּוּר אֲכִילָה וּבִישּׁוּל וַהֲנָאָה, *a prohibition against eating, cooking, and deriving benefit.* [133]

22. Scripture juxtaposed עַשֵּׂר תְּעַשֵּׂר ... הַיֹּצֵא הַשָּׂדֶה שָׁנָה שָׁנָה, *you shall surely*

131. The text follows *Shoham Yakar's* manuscript edition and that is how the comment reads in *Peirush HaRokeach,* the Baal HaTurim's apparent source. The principle of *im hakollel* allows 763 to be considered equivalent to 764, the *gematria* of the Baal HaTurim's phrase.

132. See note 131. In the early printed editions, the word גְּדִי is added to the rubric, bringing its *gematria* to 780, and וּבִשּׁוּל is spelled without a י, reducing the *gematria* of the Baal HaTurim's phrase to 754, a difference of 26. To reconcile the numbers, *Ittur Bikkurim,* who had neither Baal HaTurim manuscripts nor *Peirush HaRokeach* before him, suggests emending the Baal HaTurim's phrase to, זֶה אִיסּוּר הָאֲכִילָה וּבִישּׁוּל וַהֲנָאָה, *This refers to a prohibition against . . .,* adding זֶה (= 12), ־הָ (= 5), and י (= 10) to וּבִישּׁוּל, which brings the *gematria* to 781; the principle of *im hakollel* then allows 780 to be considered equivalent to 781. Some later editions emend the Baal HaTurim's phrase to, [הִיא] אִיסּוּר אֲכִילָה וּבִישּׁוּל וַהֲנָאָה, [*It is*] *a prohibition against . . .,* which has a *gematria* of 780, equal to that of לֹא תְבַשֵּׁל גְּדִי.

133. *Peirush HaRokeach.* The Talmud states: The verse, לֹא תְבַשֵּׁל גְּדִי בַּחֲלֵב אִמּוֹ, *you shall not cook a kid in its mother's milk,* [appears] three times [in the Torah] (*Exodus* 23:19 and 34:26; *Deuteronomy* 14:21) — once to prohibit eating, once to prohibit deriving benefit, and once to

the tachmos, the shachaf, and the netz, according to its kind; 16 *the kos, the yanshuf, and the tinshemes;* 17 *the ka'as, the rachamah, and the shalach;* 18 *the chasidah, and the anafah according to its kind, the duchifas and the atalef.* 19 *And every flying swarming creature is unclean to you; they shall not be eaten.* 20 *Every clean bird may you eat.* 21 *You shall not eat any carcass; to the stranger who is in your cities shall you give it that he may eat it, or sell it to a gentile, for you are a holy people to HASHEM, your God; you shall not cook a kid in its mother's milk.*

22 *You shall surely tithe the entire crop of your planting, the produce of the field, year by year.* 23 *And you shall eat before HASHEM, your God, in the place that He*

BAAL HATURIM ELUCIDATED

tithe . . . the produce of your field, year by year, with [the prohibition against] meat and milk to indicate that just like a mixture of meat and milk [that has been cooked together] is forbidden, so too, *kilayim* [a mixture of species[134] that have been cooked, i.e., ripened,[135] together] in the field is forbidden. "But," [God says,] "if you will observe the prohibition against *kilayim,* then I will cook [i.e., ripen] your produce in its season, and you will prosper."[136]

❑ Scripture juxtaposed בַּחֲלֵב אִמּוֹ, *in its mother's milk,* with שָׁנָה שָׁנָה, *year by year,*[137] to indicate that a [widowed or divorced] nursing mother should not remarry within two years [of her nursling's birth] so that the baby will be [nurtured] with its mother's milk for two years.[138]

prohibit cooking (*Chullin* 115b).

134. See *Leviticus* 19:19. The Talmud states that just as meat by itself is permitted and milk by itself is permitted, yet their mixture is forbidden, so, too, regarding *kilayim,* each species by itself is permitted, but their mixture is forbidden (*Pesachim* 44b).

135. The basic meaning of the root בשל is *to cook.* It is also used in the borrowed sense of *to ripen* (e.g., *Genesis* 40:10).

136. *Peirush HaRokeach.* The term עַשֵּׂר תְּעַשֵּׂר, literally, *tithing you shall tithe,* is understood as, עַשֵּׂר בִּשְׁבִיל שֶׁתִּתְעַשֵּׁר, *tithe in order that you shall prosper* [reading תְּעַשֵּׂר as if it were spelled with a שׁ instead of a שׂ] (*Shabbos* 119a; see the Baal HaTurim to 26:11 below).

137. For *year by year* or *year after year,* Scripture usually uses either שָׁנָה בְשָׁנָה (*Leviticus* 25:53; 15:20 below; and ten more times in the *Tanach*) or בְּכָל שָׁנָה וְשָׁנָה (*Esther* 9:21 and 27). Only in our verse do we find שָׁנָה שָׁנָה, with no prefix on the second word. The Baal HaTurim's comment finds an allusion that takes the phrase out of the context of this passage and explains the truncated phrase as an allusion to an unrelated Rabbinical enactment (*VeChur LaZahav*).

138. See *Kesubos* 60b (see also *Rambam, Hilchos Geirushin* 11:25-26) — After a discussion that includes a number of opinions regarding how long an unmarried nursing mother [e.g., a divorcee] must wait before she is permitted to be remarried [to any man other than the baby's father], the Talmud establishes the *halachah* at twenty-four months, excluding the baby's day of birth and the day of the mother's remarriage. However, the Talmud does not adduce Scriptural support for its decision. The Baal HaTurim finds an allusion in our verse.

אֲשֶׁר־יִבְחַר לְשַׁכֵּן שְׁמוֹ שָׁם מַעְשַׂר דְּגָנְךָ תִּירֹשְׁךָ
וְיִצְהָרֶךָ וּבְכֹרֹת בְּקָרְךָ וְצֹאנֶךָ לְמַעַן תִּלְמַד לְיִרְאָה
כד אֶת־יְהוָה אֱלֹהֶיךָ כָּל־הַיָּמִים׃ וְכִי־יִרְבֶּה מִמְּךָ
הַדֶּרֶךְ כִּי לֹא תוּכַל שְׂאֵתוֹ כִּי־יִרְחַק מִמְּךָ הַמָּקוֹם
אֲשֶׁר יִבְחַר יְהוָה אֱלֹהֶיךָ לָשׂוּם שְׁמוֹ שָׁם כִּי
כה יְבָרֶכְךָ יְהוָה אֱלֹהֶיךָ׃ וְנָתַתָּה בַּכָּסֶף וְצַרְתָּ הַכֶּסֶף
בְּיָדְךָ וְהָלַכְתָּ אֶל־הַמָּקוֹם אֲשֶׁר יִבְחַר יְהוָה
כו אֱלֹהֶיךָ בּוֹ׃ וְנָתַתָּה הַכֶּסֶף בְּכֹל אֲשֶׁר־תְּאַוֶּה נַפְשְׁךָ
בַּבָּקָר וּבַצֹּאן וּבַיַּיִן וּבַשֵּׁכָר וּבְכֹל אֲשֶׁר תִּשְׁאָלְךָ
נַפְשֶׁךָ וְאָכַלְתָּ שָּׁם לִפְנֵי יְהוָה אֱלֹהֶיךָ וְשָׂמַחְתָּ
כז אַתָּה וּבֵיתֶךָ׃ וְהַלֵּוִי אֲשֶׁר־בִּשְׁעָרֶיךָ לֹא תַעַזְבֶנּוּ
כח כִּי אֵין לוֹ חֵלֶק וְנַחֲלָה עִמָּךְ׃ מִקְצֵה ׀ שָׁלֹשׁ
שָׁנִים תּוֹצִיא אֶת־כָּל־מַעְשַׂר תְּבוּאָתְךָ בַּשָּׁנָה
כט הַהִוא וְהִנַּחְתָּ בִּשְׁעָרֶיךָ׃ וּבָא הַלֵּוִי כִּי אֵין־לוֹ
חֵלֶק וְנַחֲלָה עִמָּךְ וְהַגֵּר וְהַיָּתוֹם וְהָאַלְמָנָה
אֲשֶׁר בִּשְׁעָרֶיךָ וְאָכְלוּ וְשָׂבֵעוּ לְמַעַן יְבָרֶכְךָ יְהוָה
טו ששי א אֱלֹהֶיךָ בְּכָל־מַעֲשֵׂה יָדְךָ אֲשֶׁר תַּעֲשֶׂה׃ מִקֵּץ

בעל הטורים

(כה) וְצַרְתָּ. ב׳ בַּמָּסוֹרֶת — ״וְצַרְתָּ הַכֶּסֶף בְּיָדְךָ״; ״וְצַרְתָּ אוֹתָם בִּכְנָפֶיךָ״. וְהַיְנוּ דִתְנַן, הַמַּפְקִיד מָעוֹת אֵצֶל חֲבֵרוֹ וּצְרָרָן וְהִפְשִׁילָן לַאֲחוֹרָיו, חַיָּב. וּמְפָרֵשׁ טַעְמָא, אָמַר קְרָא ״וְצַרְתָּ הַכֶּסֶף בְּיָדְךָ״, אַף עַל פִּי שֶׁצְּרוּרִין, יִהְיוּ בְיָדְךָ. וְזֶהוּ אַף עַל פִּי שֶׁצַּרְתָּ אוֹתָם בִּכְנָפֶיךָ יִהְיוּ בְיָדֶךָ:

(כט) יְבָרֶכְךָ ה׳ אֱלֹהֶיךָ בְּכָל מַעֲשֵׂה יָדְךָ. וּסְמִיךְ לֵהּ ״וְזֶה דְּבַר הַשְּׁמִטָּה שָׁמוֹט״. {וְזֶהוּ דִכְתִיב ״וְצִוִּיתִי אֶת בִּרְכָתִי וְגוֹ׳ וְעָשָׂת אֶת הַתְּבוּאָה לִשְׁלֹשׁ הַשָּׁנִים״:

BAAL HATURIM ELUCIDATED

25. **וְצַרְתָּ** — YOU SHALL BIND. The masoretic note, ב׳, means that this word appears twice in the *Tanach*: (i) here, וְצַרְתָּ הַכֶּסֶף בְּיָדְךָ, *you shall bind the money in your hand;* and (ii) וְצַרְתָּ אוֹתָם בִּכְנָפֶיךָ, *and bind them into your skirts* (*Ezekiel* 5:3). This [similarity of expression] alludes to a Mishnah: If a person deposits money with another for safekeeping, and the trustee binds them [in a cloth] and slings them over his shoulder, the trustee is liable [if the money is lost or stolen].[139] The Talmud explains that this law is based on our verse, *you shall bind the money in your hand,* i.e., even if the money is bound, it should still be in your hand.[140]

139. *Bava Metzia* 3:10 [42a].
140. *Bava Metzia* 42a.

*will choose to rest His Name there — the tithe of your grain,
your wine, and your oil, and the firstborn of your cattle and
your flocks, so that you will learn to fear* HASHEM, *your God,
all the days.* [24] *If the road will be too long for you, so that
you cannot carry it, because the place that* HASHEM, *your
God, will choose to place His Name there is far from
you, for* HASHEM, *your God, will have blessed you —* [25] *then
you may exchange it for money; you shall bind the money
in your hand, and go to the place that* HASHEM, *your God,
will choose.* [26] *You may spend the money for whatever
your soul desires — for cattle, for flocks, for wine, or for
alcoholic beverage, or anything that your soul wishes; you
shall eat it there before* HASHEM, *your God, and rejoice —
you and your household.* [27] *You shall not forsake the Levite
who is in your cities, for he has no portion or inheritance
with you.*

[28] *At the end of three years you shall take out every tithe
of your crop in that year and set it down within your cities.*
[29] *Then the Levite can come — for he has no portion or
inheritance with you — and the proselyte, the orphan, and
the widow who are in your cities, so they may eat and be
satisfied, in order that* HASHEM, *your God, will bless you in
all your handiwork that you may undertake.*

BAAL HATURIM ELUCIDATED

Similarly, even if you have bound them in your skirts, they should still be in your hand.

29. יְבָרֶכְךָ ה׳ אֱלֹהֶיךָ בְּכָל מַעֲשֵׂה יָדְךָ — HASHEM, YOUR GOD, WILL BLESS YOU IN ALL YOUR HANDIWORK. Juxtaposed to this is, וְזֶה דְּבַר הַשְּׁמִטָּה שָׁמוֹט, *This is the matter of the release, release.*[141] {This [juxtaposition] is in accordance with the verse, וְצִוִּיתִי אֶת בִּרְכָתִי . . . וְעָשָׂת אֶת הַתְּבוּאָה לִשְׁלֹשׁ הַשָּׁנִים, *I will ordain My blessing . . . and it will yield a crop sufficient for the three-year period* (*Leviticus* 25:21).[141a]

141. The passage enclosed in braces that spans this comment and the next is absent from virtually all printed editions. However, it does appear in the manuscripts used by *Shoham Yakar.* Because of the omission, these two comments are treated as one, and the commentaries are hard put to explain the Baal HaTurim's intention. As is often the case, the copyist's or typesetter's omission can be attributed to the fact that a word or phrase appears two times in close proximity. In our case, the verse fragment, וְזֶה דְּבַר הַשְּׁמִטָּה שָׁמוֹט, appears in both comments, as part of the text of the comment to 14:29, and as the rubric of the comment to 15:2 (*VeChur LaZahav*).

141a. That is, just as that verse promises blessing for the one who upholds the laws of the Sabbatical year with regard to crops, so does the juxtaposition of 14:29 with 15:1-2 indicate a blessing for the one who upholds the laws regarding the release of debts in that year. Neither of them will suffer any loss as a result of observing the *mitzvah* (A.S.)

ב שֶׁבַע־שָׁנִים תַּעֲשֶׂה שְׁמִטָּה: וְזֶה דְּבַר הַשְּׁמִטָּה
שָׁמוֹט כָּל־בַּעַל מַשֵּׁה יָדוֹ אֲשֶׁר יַשֶּׁה בְּרֵעֵהוּ
לֹא־יִגֹּשׂ אֶת־רֵעֵהוּ וְאֶת־אָחִיו כִּי־קָרָא שְׁמִטָּה
ג לַיהוָה: אֶת־הַנָּכְרִי תִּגֹּשׂ וַאֲשֶׁר יִהְיֶה לְךָ אֶת־
ד אָחִיךָ תַּשְׁמֵט יָדֶךָ: אֶפֶס כִּי לֹא יִהְיֶה־בְּךָ
אֶבְיוֹן כִּי־בָרֵךְ יְבָרֶכְךָ יהוָה בָּאָרֶץ אֲשֶׁר יהוָה
ה אֱלֹהֶיךָ נֹתֵן־לְךָ נַחֲלָה לְרִשְׁתָּהּ: רַק אִם־שָׁמוֹעַ
תִּשְׁמַע בְּקוֹל יהוָה אֱלֹהֶיךָ לִשְׁמֹר לַעֲשׂוֹת אֶת־
כָּל־הַמִּצְוָה הַזֹּאת אֲשֶׁר אָנֹכִי מְצַוְּךָ הַיּוֹם:
ו כִּי־יהוָה אֱלֹהֶיךָ בֵּרַכְךָ כַּאֲשֶׁר דִּבֶּר־לָךְ וְהַעֲבַטְתָּ
גּוֹיִם רַבִּים וְאַתָּה לֹא תַעֲבֹט וּמָשַׁלְתָּ בְּגוֹיִם
ז רַבִּים וּבְךָ לֹא יִמְשֹׁלוּ: כִּי־יִהְיֶה בְךָ
אֶבְיוֹן מֵאַחַד אַחֶיךָ בְּאַחַד שְׁעָרֶיךָ בְּאַרְצְךָ
אֲשֶׁר־יהוָה אֱלֹהֶיךָ נֹתֵן לָךְ לֹא תְאַמֵּץ אֶת־
לְבָבְךָ וְלֹא תִקְפֹּץ אֶת־יָדְךָ מֵאָחִיךָ הָאֶבְיוֹן:

בעל הטורים

טו (ב) וְזֶה דְּבַר הַשְּׁמִטָּה שָׁמוֹט.} שֶׁצָּרִיךְ לוֹמַר לוֹ מְשַׁמֵּט אָנִי:

❑ **יַשֶּׁה.** ב׳ בַּמָּסוֹרֶת – ״אֲשֶׁר יַשֶּׁה בְּרֵעֵהוּ״; ״כִּי יַשֶּׁה לְךָ אֱלוֹהַּ מֵעֲוֹנֶךָ״. שֶׁאִם תְּשַׁמֵּט, יַשֶּׁה לְךָ מֵעֲוֹנֶךָ:

(ג־ד) תַּשְׁמֵט יָדֶךָ. אֶפֶס. פֵּרוּשׁ, מִעוּטָא הוּא, שֶׁאִם יֵשׁ מַשְׁכּוֹן בְּיָדְךָ אֵינוֹ מְשַׁמֵּט:

❑ **אֶבְיוֹן כִּי בָרֵךְ יְבָרֶכְךָ.** וְהַיְנוּ דִּכְתִיב ״כִּי יַעֲמֹד לִימִין אֶבְיוֹן״:

BAAL HATURIM ELUCIDATED

XV.

2. וְזֶה דְּבַר הַשְּׁמִטָּה שָׁמוֹט — THIS IS THE WORD[142] **OF THE RELEASE, RELEASE.**}[143] [As the Mishnah teaches: If a debtor wishes to repay a debt from which the *shemittah* year has released him,] the creditor must explicitly say to him, "I am releasing . . ."[144]

❑ **יַשֶּׁה — HE WOULD CLAIM DUE.** The masoretic note, ב׳, means that this word appears twice in the *Tanach*:[145] (i) here, אֲשֶׁר יַשֶּׁה בְּרֵעֵהוּ, *what he would claim due*

142. The term דָּבָר [construct form, דְּבַר] can mean *matter* (e.g., 17:8 below), *thing* (2:7 above) or *word* (18:20 below). Although, in the context of this verse, דְּבַר means *matter of,* in the Baal HaTurim's allusion it is used to mean *word of.*

143. See note 141 above.

144. *Sheviis* 10:8. Thus, our verse may be interpreted: *This is the word* [*to be spoken*] regarding the release, "[*I am*] *releasing.*"

145. The verb of the root יַשֶּׁה is נשה, which can

[1]*At the end of seven years you shall institute a release.* [2] *This is the matter of the release: Every creditor shall release his hold over what he would claim due from his fellow; he shall not press his fellow or his brother, for He has proclaimed a release for HASHEM.* [3] *You may press the gentile; but over what you have with your brother, you shall release your hold.* [4] *However, there shall not be among you a destitute person; for, HASHEM will surely bless you in the land that HASHEM, your God, will give you as an inheritance, to possess it,* [5] *only if you will hearken to the voice of HASHEM, your God, to observe, to perform this entire commandment that I command you today.* [6] *For HASHEM, your God, has blessed you as He has told you; you will lend to many nations, but you will not borrow; and you will dominate many nations, but they will not dominate you.*

[7] *If there shall be a destitute person among you, any of your brethren in any of your cities, in your land that HASHEM, your God, gives you, you shall not harden your heart or close your hand against your destitute brother.*

BAAL HATURIM ELUCIDATED

from his fellow and (ii) כִּי יַשֶּׁה לְךָ אֱלוֹהַּ מֵעֲוֺנֶךָ, *that God forget for your sake some of your iniquities* (*Job* 11:6). [The similarity indicates] that if you will release [debts as commanded], then, for your sake, God will "forget" your iniquities.

3-4. תַּשְׁמֵט יָדֶךָ. אֶפֶס — YOU SHALL RELEASE YOUR HOLD. HOWEVER. [The term אֶפֶס, *however,*] is an exclusionary word. [It implies] that if you hold collateral [against a debt], [the *shemittah* year] does not release [that debt].[146]

❑ **אֶבְיוֹן כִּי בָרֵךְ יְבָרֶכְךָ** — A DESTITUTE PERSON, FOR [HASHEM] WILL SURELY BLESS YOU. This is [what is meant by] the verse, כִּי יַעֲמֹד לִימִין אֶבְיוֹן, *For He will stand at the right of a destitute person* (*Psalms* 109:31).[147]

mean *to dun, to claim one's due* (e.g., in our verse) or *to forget, to cause to forget* (e.g., *Genesis* 41:51). According to *Rashi,* the term יַשֶּׁה in *Job* means *He will dun,* and refers to retribution for sins; according to *Ibn Ezra,* that word means *He will forget* or *He will cause to be forgotten,* and refers to forgiveness. The Baal HaTurim's comment follows *Ibn Ezra* (*VeChur LaZahav*).

146. *Sheviis* 10:2.

The Midrash derives from our verse that *shemittah,* the Sabbatical year, releases only those debts that have not yet been collected, for the verse states אֶת אָחִיךָ, *with your brother,* i.e., that which is in his hand, thus, excluding שֶׁל אָחִיךָ, *of your brother,* i.e., something of your brother's that is in your hand (*Sifrei*). When a loan is secured by collateral held by the lender, it is not considered a loan that has not yet been collected, for the creditor has certain rights to the collateral as long as the debt has not yet been repaid (*Rambam, Peirush HaMishnayos*). The Baal HaTurim derives this law from the juxtaposition of אֶפֶס with יָדֶךָ, as if to say, *unless [the debt is already secured by what is] in your hand.*

147. *Peirush HaRokeach.*

בעל הטורים

(ח) פָּתֹחַ. פֵּ״א כְּפוּלָה — לוֹמַר, פְּתַח לוֹ יָדְךָ וְגַם פִּיךָ לְשַׁדְּלוֹ בִּדְבָרִים:

דָּבָר אַחֵר — הָרָאוּי לְפַת, תֵּן לוֹ פַּת, הָרָאוּי לְמַעֲדַנִּים, תֵּן לוֹ מַעֲדַנִּים, וְתַפֵּק לוֹ בְּכָל מִינֵי פְּתִיחָה:

דָּבָר אַחֵר — ״פָּתֹחַ תִּפְתַּח״, אִם הוּא מִתְבַּיֵּשׁ, תְּבִיאֵם לוֹ לְפִתְחוֹ:

דָּבָר אַחֵר — ״פָּתֹחַ תִּפְתַּח״, כְּפֹל הַדָּבָר. וְכֵן ״נָתוֹן תִּתֵּן לוֹ״, ״הַעֲנֵיק תַּעֲנִיק לוֹ״. לוֹמַר שֶׁאֵין שִׁעוּר לְהַעֲנָקָה, אֶלָּא תִּתֵּן וְתַחְזוֹר וְתִתֵּן:

❑ פָּתֹחַ. חָסֵר וָי״ו — מִצְוָה בְּיוֹם ו׳ לִתֵּן פַּת לָעֲנִיִּים, תַּקָּנַת עֶזְרָא:

❑ פָּתֹחַ. ג׳ בַּמָּסוֹרֶת — ב׳ בְּהַאי עִנְיָנָא; וְאִידָךְ ״פָּתוֹחַ נִפְתְּחוּ שַׁעֲרֵי אַרְצֵךְ״. לוֹמַר שֶׁאִם תִּפְתַּח לוֹ יָדְךָ, יִפָּתְחוּ לְךָ שַׁעֲרֵי שָׁמַיִם כְּדֵי לְקַבֵּל תְּפִלָּתְךָ. וְאִם לָאו, לֹא

BAAL HATURIM ELUCIDATED

8. פָּתֹחַ — OPEN. [According to a scribal tradition,] the פ of this word is written [in the Torah scrolls] in the enhanced form known as פ׳ כְּפוּלָה, *doubled* פ.[148] This indicates that you [who are giving the loan] should open, not only your hand, but also your mouth,[148a] and speak reassuring words to him [the recipient].[149]

Alternatively: [The doubled פ of the gerundive verb פָּתֹחַ, literally, *opening,* indicates two openings of the hand.] One for whom bread is appropriate, [open your hand to] give him bread; one for whom delicacies are appropriate, [open your hand to] give him delicacies.[150] Thus, you should satisfy him by [opening your hand] with a variety of openings.[151]

Alternatively: פָּתֹחַ תִּפְתַּח, literally, *opening, you shall open.* [This indicates that] if the pauper is embarrassed [to accept grants], bring them to his door.[152]

Alternatively: [The double verb form] פָּתֹחַ תִּפְתַּח, literally, *opening, you shall open,* [indicates] that you shall open double.[152a] Similarly, נָתוֹן תִּתֵּן לוֹ, *giving you*

148. See note 29 to *parashas Devarim* and the accompanying illustration. *Sefer Tagin* includes the phrase פתח תפתח on the list of "191 letters פ in the Torah whose mouths are on the inside." The version of that *sefer* found in *Machzor Vitry* does not specify whether it refers to the phrase in verse 8 or the one in verse 11. But, the version found in the Paris (1866) edition states בַּתְרָא, *the latter.* Nevertheless, three other sources testify to the unusual letters פ in our verse: (i) the *Meiri (Kiryas Sefer);* (ii) an ancient Torah scroll in Amsterdam (see Rabbi Yitzchak Ratzabi's article in Volume 29 of *Torah Sheleimah,* p. 224, note 10); and (iii) the Gaster manuscript Chumash known as the Tittled Bible. The first two sources have the unusual letters פ in verse 8; the third has them in both verse 8 and verse 11.

148a. The name of the letter may be spelled פֵּ״ה and is related to the word פֶּה, *mouth.*

149. See the Baal HaTurim to verse 10 below, with note 160.

150. *Sifrei* (see also the Baal HaTurim to v. 10 below, with note 161). The term מַעֲדַנִּים, *delicacies,* refers to rich meat, aged wine, and fattened fowl.

151. The reading בְּכָל מִינֵי פְּתִיחָה, *in a variety of openings,* follows *Shoham Yakar's* manuscript edition and is appropriate in a comment to the word פָּתֹחַ. Most editions, however, read בְּכָל מִינֵי מְתִיקָה, *with a variety of sweets.*

152. The verb פָּתֹחַ is related to, and spelled the same way as, the noun פֶּתַח, *opening* or *doorway.* Thus, פָּתֹחַ תִּפְתַּח may be understood as if it were vowelized פֶּתַח תִּפְתַּח, [*at his*] *doorway, you shall open* [*your hand*].

152a. The reading כְּפֹל, *You shall double,* in the imperative follows the early printed editions. Many later editions, including that of *Shoham*

[8] *Rather, you shall surely open your hand to him; you shall lend*

shall give him (v. 10); הַעֲנֵיק תַּעֲנִיק לוֹ, *granting you shall grant him* (v. 14). This indicates that there is no maximum to the extent of these grants, rather you should give and give again.[153]

❑ פָּתֹחַ — OPEN. This word is spelled defectively,[153a] without a ו (= 6). [This indicates that] there is a *mitzvah* to give bread to the poor on [Friday,] the sixth day of the week — an enactment of Ezra.[154]

❑ פָּתֹחַ — OPEN. The masoretic note, ג׳, means that this word appears three times in the *Tanach*:[154a] (i-ii) twice in this passage (here and in v. 11); and (iii) פָּתוֹחַ נִפְתְּחוּ שַׁעֲרֵי אַרְצֵךְ, *opened wide are the gates of your land*[155] (*Nahum* 3:13). This [similarity of expression] indicates that if you open your hand [to the poor], the gates of Heaven[156] will be opened for you, in order to receive your prayers. But if [you do] not, they will

Yakar, read כָּפֵל, *[The verse] used a double verb form . . .*

153. *Sifrei,* cited by *Rashi* to our verse and to v. 10.

153a. The form פָּתֹחַ is a *makor,* i.e., a gerundive infinitive, that indicates ongoing action, *opening.* As such, it may be spelled with or without a ו (see note 154a below).

154. The Talmud lists ten laws enacted by Ezra. One of these enactments is that bread should be baked on every *erev Shabbos* [eve of the Sabbath] so that loaves would be available for the poor (*Yerushalmi, Megillah* 4:1). A parallel passage in *Talmud Bavli* reads: A woman should arise early and bake so that bread would be available for the poor (*Bava Kamma* 82a). The second passage does not mention *erev Shabbos.* However, the *Shittah Mekubetzes* cites three interpretations: According to the *Meiri,* it refers to whatever day a particular woman is wont to bake; according to *Rabbeinu Yehonasan* there are two possible interpretations — either it means every day of the week a woman should arise early and bake, or it refers to *erev Shabbos,* so that just as the *lechem hapanim* of the *Beis HaMikdash* was baked on Friday and lasted for a whole week, so should bread be baked for the poor every Friday so that they should have what to eat the following week.

154a. The note appears at *Nahum* 3:13 and reads: ג׳ ב׳ חָסֵר וְא׳ מָלֵא, *Three, two of them spelled defectively* [פָּתֹחַ, without a ו] and one spelled in full [פָּתוֹחַ, with a ו].

155. In the context of the prophet's words, this verse bodes destruction: *For your enemies' sake, opened wide are the gates of your land.* Nevertheless, the Baal HaTurim takes the phrase out of context and finds a beneficent message in it.

The early printed editions incorrectly have שַׁעֲרֵי שָׁמַיִם, *the gates of heaven.* See second paragraph of note 156 below.

156. Some ask: How can the Baal HaTurim interpret שַׁעֲרֵי אַרְצֵךְ, literally, *the gates of your earth,* as "the gates of Heaven"? Two possibilities present themselves: The place of Heavenly reward for those who are righteous in this world is referred to as the World to Come (see *Rambam, Hilchos Teshuvah* 8:1-2). And the Mishnah states: All of Israel has a portion in the World to Come, as it is stated (*Isaiah* 60:21), *Your people are all righteous, they shall forever inherit* אָרֶץ, *the land* (*Sanhedrin* 10:1 [90a]). Thus, we find אָרֶץ used with reference to Heaven (*VeChur LaZahav*).

A second possibility is that the Baal HaTurim's original comment did not include the word אַרְצֵךְ; rather, he adduced only פָּתוֹחַ נִפְתְּחוּ שַׁעֲרֵי, *opened wide are the gates of . . .,* for in the realm of *remez* (allusion) grammatical rules are often bent, just as phrases are interpreted out of their Scriptural context. However, a copyist who was not familiar with that verse realized that, grammatically, the word שַׁעֲרֵי, *the gates of,* cannot stand on its own, so, based on the rest of the comment, he added what he incorrectly assumed to be the next word of the verse — שָׁמַיִם, *Heaven.* And, as noted above in note 155, that is the reading found in the early printed editions. Later editions corrected the wording of the verse, without realizing that the Baal HaTurim's intention was to stop at שַׁעֲרֵי (*VeChur LaZahav*).

ט דֵּי מַחְסֹרוֹ אֲשֶׁר יֶחְסַר לוֹ: הִשָּׁמֶר לְךָ פֶּן־יִהְיֶה
דָבָר עִם־לְבָבְךָ בְלִיַּעַל לֵאמֹר קָרְבָה שְׁנַת־הַשֶּׁבַע
שְׁנַת הַשְּׁמִטָּה וְרָעָה עֵינְךָ בְּאָחִיךָ הָאֶבְיוֹן וְלֹא
י תִתֵּן לוֹ וְקָרָא עָלֶיךָ אֶל־יהוה וְהָיָה בְךָ חֵטְא: נָתוֹן
תִּתֵּן לוֹ וְלֹא־יֵרַע לְבָבְךָ בְּתִתְּךָ לוֹ כִּי בִּגְלַל ׀
הַדָּבָר הַזֶּה יְבָרֶכְךָ יהוה אֱלֹהֶיךָ בְּכָל־מַעֲשֶׂךָ וּבְכֹל
יא מִשְׁלַח יָדֶךָ: כִּי לֹא־יֶחְדַּל אֶבְיוֹן מִקֶּרֶב הָאָרֶץ
עַל־כֵּן אָנֹכִי מְצַוְּךָ לֵאמֹר פָּתֹחַ תִּפְתַּח אֶת־יָדְךָ
יב לְאָחִיךָ לַעֲנִיֶּךָ וּלְאֶבְיֹנְךָ בְּאַרְצֶךָ: כִּי־יִמָּכֵר
לְךָ אָחִיךָ הָעִבְרִי אוֹ הָעִבְרִיָּה וַעֲבָדְךָ שֵׁשׁ
שָׁנִים וּבַשָּׁנָה הַשְּׁבִיעִת תְּשַׁלְּחֶנּוּ חָפְשִׁי מֵעִמָּךְ:

בעל הטורים

יִפָּתְחוּ לְךָ, שֶׁנֶּאֱמַר ״אֹטֵם אָזְנוֹ מִזַּעֲקַת דָּל {גַּם הוּא יִקְרָא וְלֹא יֵעָנֶה}״:

☐ **דֵּי מַחְסֹרוֹ אֲשֶׁר יֶחְסַר.** רָאשֵׁי תֵבוֹת דְּמַאי. שֶׁמַּאֲכִילִין אֶת הָעֲנִיִּים דְּמַאי:

(י) **נָתוֹן.** מָלֵא וָי״ו. שֶׁזּוֹכֶה לו׳ בְּרָכוֹת, כִּדְאִיתָא בְּפֶרֶק קַמָּא דְבָבָא בַּתְרָא:

☐ **בְּתִתְּךָ לוֹ.** ב׳ בַּמָּסוֹרֶת – הָכָא; וְאִידָךְ ״בְּתִתְּךָ לוֹ לֶחֶם וְחֶרֶב״ גַּבֵּי דָוִד. לוֹמַר שֶׁצָּרִיךְ לִתֵּן לְכָל אֶחָד לְפִי מַה שֶּׁהוּא צָרִיךְ, כְּמוֹ שֶׁנָּתַן לְדָוִד לֶחֶם וְגַם חָרֶב:

(יב־יג) **תְּשַׁלְּחֶנּוּ . . . וְכִי תְשַׁלְּחֶנּוּ . . . לֹא תְשַׁלְּחֶנּוּ.** ג׳ פְּעָמִים – לְיוֹצֵא בְּתוֹךְ שֵׁשׁ,

BAAL HATURIM ELUCIDATED

not be opened for you, as it is stated, {אֹטֵם אָזְנוֹ מִזַּעֲקַת דָּל {גַּם הוּא יִקְרָא וְלֹא יֵעָנֶה, *One who stops up his ear from* [*hearing*] *the cry of the pauper* {*he too will call out, but he will not be answered*}[156a] (*Proverbs* 21:13).[156b]

☐ **דֵּי מַחְסֹרוֹ אֲשֶׁר יֶחְסַר** — ENOUGH FOR HIS LACK THAT IS LACKING. The initial letters of these words form the word דְּמַאי, *demai.*[157] [This alludes to the law] that *demai*

156a. Most printed editions adduce only the first half of the verse, followed by וְגוֹ׳, *etc.* However, *Shoham Yakar's* manuscript edition cites the verse in its entirety. Unfortunately, the later editions that cite the full verse have not deleted וְגוֹ׳, thus making it appear as if part of the verse has been omitted. In truth, however, the verse is complete.

156b. See *Shabbos* 55a; see also *Shulchan Aruch, Yoreh Deah* 247:3 and 249:14.

157. Crops grown in the Land of Israel must be tithed. Before their tithes have been set aside, they are called טֶבֶל, *tevel* [a contraction of the Aramaic phrase, טָב לָא, *not good* (*Kaftor VaFerach* 2; *Bartenura* to *Berachos* 7:1)], and may not be eaten. Therefore a learned farmer would not sell his crops until they were tithed, lest the buyer eat without tithing. A minority of unlearned people, although they may have been careful not to eat *tevel,* were not particular about passing *tevel* on to others. Accordingly, the Rabbis enacted the requirement to tithe any produce obtained from an unlearned person. Such produce is called דְּמַאי, *demai,* a contraction of the Aramaic דָּא מַאי, *What is this? Demai* must be properly tithed before it may be eaten or sold, lest the unlearned seller did not tithe his

him his requirement, enough for his lack that is lacking to him. ⁹ *Beware lest there be a lawless thought in your heart, saying, "The seventh year approaches, the release year," and you will look malevolently upon your destitute brother and refuse to give him — then he may appeal against you to HASHEM, and it will be a sin upon you.* ¹⁰ *You shall surely give him, and let your heart not feel bad in your giving to him, for in return for this matter, HASHEM, your God, will bless you in all your deeds and in your every undertaking.* ¹¹ *For destitute people will not cease to exist within the land; therefore I command you, saying, "You shall surely open your hand to your brother, to your poor, and to your destitute in your land."*

¹² *If your brother, a Hebrew man or a Hebrew woman, will be sold to you, he shall serve you for six years, and in the seventh year you shall send him out — free — from you.*

───────────── BAAL HATURIM ELUCIDATED ─────────────

may be given to the poor.[158]

10. נָתוֹן — GIVE. This word is spelled in full,[159] with a ו (= 6). For [the giver] merits six blessings, as taught in the first chapter of tractate *Bava Basra.*[160]

❑ בְּתִתְּךָ לוֹ — IN YOUR GIVING TO HIM. The masoretic note, ב׳, means that this word appears twice in the *Tanach* : (i) here; and (ii) בְּתִתְּךָ לוֹ לֶחֶם וְחֶרֶב, *in your giving to him bread and a sword* (*I Samuel* 22:13), with regard to [Ahimelech's gift to] David. This indicates that one must give to each [indigent] person according to what he requires,[161] just as [Ahimelech] gave David [what he needed, namely,] bread, and even a sword.[162]

12-13. תְּשַׁלְּחֶנּוּ . . . וְכִי תְשַׁלְּחֶנּוּ . . . לֹא תְשַׁלְּחֶנּוּ — YOU SHALL SEND HIM OUT . . . WHEN YOU SEND HIM OUT . . . YOU SHALL NOT SEND HIM OUT. [The verb תְּשַׁלְּחֶנּוּ is stated] three times [in these two verses, corresponding to three possible times when a Hebrew servant is sent to his freedom]: (i) To the one sent out in the midst of his six-year

---

produce. Nevertheless, since the majority of unlearned people were scrupulous regarding tithing their crops, the Rabbis relaxed their enactment in certain cases, including donating *demai* to a pauper (see *Demai* 3:1).

158. *Paaneach Raza.*

159. The term נָתוֹן is a *makor* and, as such, may be spelled with or without a ו (see note 153a above). The expression נָתוֹן תִּתֵּן appears three times in the Torah: (i) here, where it is spelled in full; (ii-iii) in *Numbers* 21:2 and 27:7, where it is spelled defectively, נָתֹן תִּתֵּן, without a ו. The word also appears, with a prefix, in *Genesis* 41:43, where it is spelled

in full, וְנָתוֹן, with a ו after the ת.

160. *Bava Basra* 9b — One who gives even a small coin to a pauper will be blessed with six blessings . . . but one who comforts him with words will be blessed with eleven blessings.

161. *Kesubos* 67b (see also the Baal HaTurim to v. 8 with note 150) — This includes even a horse to ride and a servant to run before him, if that is what he is accustomed to.

162. The Baal HaTurim's comment interprets the phrase as בְּתִתְּךָ, *In your giving,* לוֹ, [see that it is appropriate] *to him,* i.e., to his needs (*VeChur LaZahav*).

יג וְכִי־תְשַׁלְּחֶ֥נּוּ חָפְשִׁ֖י מֵעִמָּ֑ךְ לֹ֥א תְשַׁלְּחֶ֖נּוּ רֵיקָֽם:

יד הַעֲנֵ֤יק תַּעֲנִיק֙ ל֔וֹ מִצֹּ֣אנְךָ֔ וּמִֽגׇּרְנְךָ֖ וּמִיִּקְבֶ֑ךָ אֲשֶׁ֧ר בֵּרַכְךָ֛ יהוה אֱלֹהֶ֖יךָ תִּתֶּן־לֽוֹ: טו וְזָכַרְתָּ֗ כִּ֣י עֶ֤בֶד הָיִ֙יתָ֙ בְּאֶ֣רֶץ מִצְרַ֔יִם וַֽיִּפְדְּךָ֖ יהוה אֱלֹהֶ֑יךָ עַל־כֵּ֞ן אָֽנֹכִ֧י מְצַוְּךָ֛ אֶת־הַדָּבָ֥ר הַזֶּ֖ה הַיּֽוֹם: טז וְהָיָה֙ כִּֽי־יֹאמַ֣ר אֵלֶ֔יךָ לֹ֥א אֵצֵ֖א מֵֽעִמָּ֑ךְ כִּ֤י אֲהֵֽבְךָ֙ וְאֶת־בֵּיתֶ֔ךָ כִּי־ט֥וֹב ל֖וֹ עִמָּֽךְ: יז וְלָקַחְתָּ֣ אֶת־הַמַּרְצֵ֗עַ וְנָתַתָּ֤ה בְאׇזְנוֹ֙ וּבַדֶּ֔לֶת וְהָיָ֥ה לְךָ֖ עֶ֣בֶד עוֹלָ֑ם וְאַ֥ף לַאֲמָתְךָ֖ תַּעֲשֶׂה־כֵּֽן: יח לֹֽא־יִקְשֶׁ֣ה בְעֵינֶ֗ךָ בְּשַׁלֵּֽחֲךָ֙ אֹת֤וֹ חׇפְשִׁי֙ מֵֽעִמָּ֔ךְ כִּ֗י מִשְׁנֶה֙ שְׂכַ֣ר שָׂכִ֔יר עֲבָֽדְךָ֖ שֵׁ֣שׁ שָׁנִ֑ים וּבֵֽרַכְךָ֙ יהוה אֱלֹהֶ֔יךָ בְּכֹ֖ל אֲשֶׁ֥ר תַּעֲשֶֽׂה:

יט כׇּל־הַבְּכ֡וֹר אֲשֶׁר֩ יִוָּלֵ֨ד בִּבְקָרְךָ֤ וּבְצֹֽאנְךָ֙ הַזָּכָ֔ר

בעל הטורים

וּבְסוֹף שֵׁשׁ, וְיוֹצֵא בַּיּוֹבֵל:

(**יד**) **הַעֲנֵיק. מָלֵא י'** — כִּי בְּי' מַכּוֹת הֶעֱנַקְתִּיךָ מִשְּׁלֹשָׁה דְבָרִים, "כְּלֵי כֶסֶף וּכְלֵי זָהָב וּשְׂמָלֹת". לָכֵן הַעֲנִיקֵהוּ שְׁלֹשָׁה דְבָרִים, "מִצֹּאנְךָ וּמִגׇּרְנְךָ וּמִיִּקְבֶךָ". וְהַיְנוּ דִכְתִיב "וְזָכַרְתָּ כִּי עֶבֶד הָיִיתָ {בְּאֶרֶץ מִצְרַיִם}":

(**טו**) **הַיּוֹם.** וּסְמִיךְ לֵהּ "וְהָיָה כִּי יֹאמַר אֵלֶיךָ". לוֹמַר שֶׁרְצִיעָה בַּיּוֹם וְלֹא בַּלַּיְלָה:

(**יט**) סָמַךְ "כׇּל הַבְּכוֹר" לְפָרָשַׁת עֶבֶד. לוֹמַר כְּשֵׁם שֶׁאֲנִי אוֹסֵר לְךָ לַעֲבֹד בִּבְכוֹר, כָּךְ

BAAL HATURIM ELUCIDATED

term;[163] (ii) at the end of the six-year term;[164] (iii) and the one sent out in the Jubilee[165] year.[166]

14. הַעֲנֵיק — EXTEND [A GRANT]. This term is spelled in full,[167] with a י (= 10). [It is as if God is saying,] "Because I extended three types of grants to you following the ten plagues — כְּלֵי כֶסֶף וּכְלֵי זָהָב וּשְׂמָלֹת, *silver vessels, gold vessels, and garments* (Exodus 3:22 and 12:35) — therefore you shall extend three types of grants to him — מִצֹּאנְךָ וּמִגׇּרְנְךָ וּמִיִּקְבֶךָ, *from your flocks, from your threshing floor, and from your wine cellar.* And that is why the [next] verse states, וְזָכַרְתָּ כִּי עֶבֶד הָיִיתָ

---

163. That is, if he redeems himself by buying back his freedom; if his master dies during his term of servitude; or, in the case of a maidservant, when she comes of age.

164. See verse 12 here and *Exodus* 21:2.

165. See *Leviticus* 25:40; see also *Rashi* to *Exodus* 21:6, s.v., ועבדו לעולם.

166. See *Kiddushin* 16b — The commandment

to extend a grant (v. 14) includes all Hebrew servants sent out to their freedom at one of these three times.

167. The term הַעֲנֵיק does not appear elsewhere in the *Tanach*. It is a *makor* (gerundive infinitive) in the *hifil* (causative active conjugation) and such forms are usually spelled defectively, without a י (e.g., הַחֲרֵם, 20:17 below; הַחֲרֵשׁ, *Numbers* 30:15).

[13] *But when you send him out — free — from you, you shall not send him out empty handed.* [14] *Extend [a grant] to him generously from your flocks, from your threshing floor, and from your wine cellar; as HASHEM, your God, has blessed you, so shall you give him.* [15] *You shall remember that you were a slave in the land of Egypt, and HASHEM, your God, redeemed you; therefore, I command you regarding this matter today.* [16] *In the event he will say to you, "I will not leave you," for he loves you and your household, for it is good for him with you,* [17] *then you shall take the awl and put it through his ear and the door, and he shall be for you an eternal slave; even to your maidservant shall you do the same.* [18] *It shall not be difficult in your eyes when you send him away free from you, for twice the wage of a hired hand — six years — has he served you; and HASHEM, your God, will bless you in all that you do.*

[19] *Every firstborn male that is born in your cattle and in your*

BAAL HATURIM ELUCIDATED

{בְּאֶרֶץ מִצְרָיִם}, *You shall remember that you were a slave {in the land of Egypt}* (v. 15).[167a]

15. הַיּוֹם — TODAY. Juxtaposed to this is, וְהָיָה כִּי יֹאמַר אֵלֶיךָ, *And [if] it will be that he will say to you . . .* This indicates that the matter of boring is [to take place] by day, not at night.[168]

18. {The Baal HaTurim's comment to this verse appears at 30:16 below.}

19. Scripture juxtaposed כָּל הַבְּכוֹר, *every firstborn,* with the passage concerning the Hebrew servant (vv. 12-18 above). This indicates that [God said], "Just as I have prohibited you from performing work with a *bechor* (first-born male animal),

167a. *Peirush HaRokeach.* The Scriptural phrase enclosed in braces is not found in any editions of the Baal HaTurim. It does appear, however, in *Peirush HaRokeach.*

168. *Sifrei — Therefore, I command you regarding this matter* הַיּוֹם, *today* [literally, *the day*]. This teaches that we do the boring during *the day,* but we do not do the boring at night.

Rabbi David Pardo questions what connection our verse has to the bored ear, for in truth it is part of the passage about extending grants to the freed servant (*Peirush Sifrei DeVei Rav*). The *Malbim* explains that the *Sifrei* does not refer to the act of boring; indeed, no such law appears in the codes. Rather, it refers to the servant's statement which leads to the boring, i.e., the topic of the next verse. That statement is only effective if it is made before the end of the last day of his servitude. Should that day pass, the servant's statement is disregarded and he is set free (*HaTorah VeHaMitzvah*).

Indeed, the *Rambam* does not rule regarding boring the servant's ear at night, but he does state: The servant must make his statement during his term of servitude, but if he says it after his six years have ended, his ear is not bored . . . thus, for example, there must still remain at least one *perutah's* worth of time on the last day of his term . . . (*Hilchos Avadim* 3:10). The *Kesef Mishneh* cites *Sifrei* as the source for the *Rambam's* ruling.

טו/כ־טז/ו תַּקְדִּישׁ לַיהוָה אֱלֹהֶיךָ לֹא תַעֲבֹד בִּבְכֹר שׁוֹרֶךָ
כ וְלֹא תָגֹז בְּכוֹר צֹאנֶךָ: לִפְנֵי יהוה אֱלֹהֶיךָ תֹאכְלֶנּוּ
שָׁנָה בְשָׁנָה בַּמָּקוֹם אֲשֶׁר־יִבְחַר יהוה אַתָּה
כא וּבֵיתֶךָ: וְכִי־יִהְיֶה בוֹ מוּם פִּסֵּחַ אוֹ עִוֵּר כֹּל מוּם רָע
כב לֹא תִזְבָּחֶנּוּ לַיהוָה אֱלֹהֶיךָ: בִּשְׁעָרֶיךָ תֹּאכְלֶנּוּ
כג הַטָּמֵא וְהַטָּהוֹר יַחְדָּו כַּצְּבִי וְכָאַיָּל: רַק אֶת־דָּמוֹ
לֹא תֹאכֵל עַל־הָאָרֶץ תִּשְׁפְּכֶנּוּ כַּמָּיִם:

טז א שָׁמוֹר אֶת־חֹדֶשׁ הָאָבִיב וְעָשִׂיתָ פֶּסַח לַיהוָה
אֱלֹהֶיךָ כִּי בְּחֹדֶשׁ הָאָבִיב הוֹצִיאֲךָ יהוה אֱלֹהֶיךָ
ב מִמִּצְרַיִם לָיְלָה: וְזָבַחְתָּ פֶּסַח לַיהוָה אֱלֹהֶיךָ צֹאן
וּבָקָר בַּמָּקוֹם אֲשֶׁר יִבְחַר יהוה לְשַׁכֵּן שְׁמוֹ שָׁם:
ג לֹא־תֹאכַל עָלָיו חָמֵץ שִׁבְעַת יָמִים תֹּאכַל־עָלָיו
מַצּוֹת לֶחֶם עֹנִי כִּי בְחִפָּזוֹן יָצָאתָ מֵאֶרֶץ מִצְרַיִם
לְמַעַן תִּזְכֹּר אֶת־יוֹם צֵאתְךָ מֵאֶרֶץ מִצְרַיִם כֹּל יְמֵי
ד חַיֶּיךָ: וְלֹא־יֵרָאֶה לְךָ שְׂאֹר בְּכָל־גְּבֻלְךָ שִׁבְעַת
יָמִים וְלֹא־יָלִין מִן־הַבָּשָׂר אֲשֶׁר תִּזְבַּח בָּעֶרֶב בַּיּוֹם
ה הָרִאשׁוֹן לַבֹּקֶר: לֹא תוּכַל לִזְבֹּחַ אֶת־הַפָּסַח
ו בְּאַחַד שְׁעָרֶיךָ אֲשֶׁר־יהוה אֱלֹהֶיךָ נֹתֵן לָךְ: כִּי
אִם־אֶל־הַמָּקוֹם אֲשֶׁר־יִבְחַר יהוה אֱלֹהֶיךָ לְשַׁכֵּן
שְׁמוֹ שָׁם תִּזְבַּח אֶת־הַפֶּסַח בָּעֶרֶב כְּבוֹא הַשֶּׁמֶשׁ

בעל הטורים

לֹא תַעֲבֹד בְּעֶבֶד עִבְרִי עֲבֹדַת עֶבֶד. וּכְשֵׁם שֶׁהַמּוּם פּוֹסֵל בִּבְכוֹר, כָּךְ הַמּוּם פּוֹסֵל בִּרְצִיעָה:

טז (ב) וְזָבַחְתָּ פֶּסַח. וּסְמִיךְ לֵהּ "לֹא תֹאכַל עָלָיו חָמֵץ". לוֹמַר לְךָ שֶׁאֵין שׁוֹחֲטִין הַפֶּסַח עַל הֶחָמֵץ:

BAAL HATURIM ELUCIDATED

so too, you shall not perform slave labor with a Hebrew servant.[169] And, just as a blemish disqualifies a firstborn [from the Altar], so too, a blemish disqualifies with regard to boring [the servant's ear]."[170]

169. *Peirush HaRokeach;* see *Leviticus* 25:39.

170. The Baal HaTurim's intent here is unclear. Perhaps he refers to the Talmudic passage that excludes a Hebrew servant who is a *Kohen* from the law of boring, for such boring would inflict a disqualifying blemish and he would no longer be permitted to serve in the Temple (see *Kiddushin* 21b).

15/20-16/6 *flock, you shall sanctify to HASHEM, your God; you shall not work with the firstborn of your ox nor shall you shear the firstborn of your flock.* ²⁰ *Before HASHEM, your God, shall you eat it, year by year, in the place that HASHEM will choose, you and your household.* ²¹ *If it shall have a blemish — lameness or blindness or any serious blemish — you shall not slaughter it to HASHEM, your God.* ²² *In your cities shall you eat it, the contaminated one and the pure one alike, like the deer and the gazelle.* ²³ *However you shall not eat its blood; you shall spill it onto the ground like water.*

16 ¹ *You shall observe the month of springtime and perform the pesach-offering for HASHEM, your God, for in the month of springtime HASHEM, your God, took you out of Egypt at night.* ² *You shall slaughter the pesach-offering to HASHEM, your God, from the flock, and [also offer] cattle, in the place where HASHEM will choose to rest His Name.* ³ *You shall not eat leavened bread with it, for seven days you shall eat matzos because of it, bread of affliction, for you departed from the land of Egypt in haste — so that you will remember the day of your departure from the land of Egypt all the days of your life.*

⁴ *No leaven of yours shall be seen throughout your boundary for seven days, nor shall any of the flesh that you slaughter on the afternoon before the first day remain overnight until morning.* ⁵ *You may not slaughter the pesach-offering in one of your cities that HASHEM, your God, gives you;* ⁶ *except at the place that HASHEM, your God, will choose to rest His Name, there shall you slaughter the pesach-offering in the afternoon, when the sun descends,*

──────────── BAAL HATURIM ELUCIDATED ────────────

23. {The Baal HaTurim's comment to עַל הָאָרֶץ appears at 11:21 above.}

XVI.

2. וְזָבַחְתָּ פֶּסַח — YOU SHALL SLAUGHTER THE PESACH-OFFERING. Juxtaposed to this is, לֹא־תֹאכַל עָלָיו חָמֵץ, *You shall not eat leavened bread with it.* This [juxtaposition] is to indicate to you that we do not slaughter the *pesach*-offering over *chametz*. [171]

3. {The Baal HaTurim's comment to בְּחִפָּזוֹן appears at *Exodus* 12:11.}

───

171. That is, as long as we still have *chametz* in our possession (see *Exodus* 23:18; 34:25).

ז מוֹעֵד צֵאתְךָ מִמִּצְרָיִם: וּבִשַּׁלְתָּ וְאָכַלְתָּ בַּמָּקוֹם אֲשֶׁר
יִבְחַר יהוה אֱלֹהֶיךָ בּוֹ וּפָנִיתָ בַבֹּקֶר וְהָלַכְתָּ לְאֹהָלֶיךָ:
ח שֵׁשֶׁת יָמִים תֹּאכַל מַצּוֹת וּבַיּוֹם הַשְּׁבִיעִי עֲצֶרֶת
ט לַיהוה אֱלֹהֶיךָ לֹא תַעֲשֶׂה מְלָאכָה: שִׁבְעָה
שָׁבֻעֹת תִּסְפָּר־לָךְ מֵהָחֵל חֶרְמֵשׁ בַּקָּמָה תָּחֵל לִסְפֹּר
י שִׁבְעָה שָׁבֻעוֹת: וְעָשִׂיתָ חַג שָׁבֻעוֹת לַיהוה אֱלֹהֶיךָ
מִסַּת נִדְבַת יָדְךָ אֲשֶׁר תִּתֵּן כַּאֲשֶׁר יְבָרֶכְךָ יהוה
יא אֱלֹהֶיךָ: וְשָׂמַחְתָּ לִפְנֵי ׀ יהוה אֱלֹהֶיךָ אַתָּה וּבִנְךָ
וּבִתֶּךָ וְעַבְדְּךָ וַאֲמָתֶךָ וְהַלֵּוִי אֲשֶׁר בִּשְׁעָרֶיךָ וְהַגֵּר
וְהַיָּתוֹם וְהָאַלְמָנָה אֲשֶׁר בְּקִרְבֶּךָ בַּמָּקוֹם אֲשֶׁר יִבְחַר
יב יהוה אֱלֹהֶיךָ לְשַׁכֵּן שְׁמוֹ שָׁם: וְזָכַרְתָּ כִּי־עֶבֶד הָיִיתָ
בְּמִצְרָיִם וְשָׁמַרְתָּ וְעָשִׂיתָ אֶת־הַחֻקִּים הָאֵלֶּה:

בעל הטורים

(ט) שִׁבְעָה שָׁבֻעֹת תִּסְפָּר לָךְ. שְׁתֵּי סְפִירוֹת בַּפָּסוּק. לוֹמַר לְךָ דְּמִצְוָה לְמִמְנֵי יוֹמֵי וּמִצְוָה לְמִמְנֵי שָׁבוּעֵי:

❑ **מֵהָחֵל.** ב׳ בַּמָּסוֹרֶת – ״מֵהָחֵל חֶרְמֵשׁ״; וְאִידָךְ ״מֵהָחֵל הַתְּרוּמָה״. {פֵּרוּשׁ, אֵי זֶה חֶרְמֵשׁ? ״מֵהָחֵל הַתְּרוּמָה״} דְּהַיְנוּ עֹמֶר שֶׁהוּא רֵאשִׁית לַמְּנָחוֹת, כִּתְרוּמָה שֶׁהִיא רֵאשִׁית:

❑ **בַּקָּמָה תָּחֵל לִסְפֹּר.** קְרֵי בֵהּ בְּקִמָּה. שֶׁצָּרִיךְ לְבָרֵךְ {עַל} הָעֹמֶר מְעֻמָּד:

(יא) וְשָׂמַחְתָּ. לֹא נֶאֶמְרָה שִׂמְחָה בְּפֶסַח, שֶׁהַתְּבוּאָה עֲדַיִן בַּשָּׂדֶה. וּבַעֲצֶרֶת, שֶׁהַתְּבוּאָה כְּבָר נִקְצֶרֶת וַעֲדַיִן הַיַּיִן בַּגְּפָנִים, נֶאֶמְרָה שִׂמְחָה אַחַת. וּבְסֻכּוֹת, שֶׁהַכֹּל בַּבַּיִת, נֶאֶמְרוּ בוֹ שְׁתֵּי שְׂמָחוֹת:

(יב) הַחֻקִּים הָאֵלֶּה. כְּתִיב בַּעֲצֶרֶת, לְפִי שֶׁנִּתְּנָה בוֹ הַתּוֹרָה:

BAAL HATURIM ELUCIDATED

9. שִׁבְעָה שָׁבֻעֹת תִּסְפָּר לָךְ — YOU SHALL COUNT SEVEN WEEKS FOR YOURSELF. The verse contains two verbs of the root ספר, *to count.*[172] This is to indicate to you that there is a *mitzvah* to count the days and [another] *mitzvah* to count the weeks.[173]

❑ **מֵהָחֵל — FROM THE BEGINNING OF.** The masoretic note, ב׳, means that this word appears twice in the *Tanach*: (i) here, מֵהָחֵל חֶרְמֵשׁ, *from when the sickle begins;* and (ii) מֵהָחֵל הַתְּרוּמָה, *from the beginning [of the bringing] of the terumah* (*II*

172. תִּסְפָּר, *you shall count,* and לִסְפֹּר, *to count.*

173. *Chagigah* 17b — The Talmud explains that the verse, תִּסְפְּרוּ חֲמִשִּׁים יוֹם, *you shall count fifty days* (*Leviticus* 23:16), teaches that it is a *mitzvah* to count the days; and the verse, שִׁבְעָה שָׁבֻעֹת תִּסְפָּר לָךְ, *you shall count seven weeks for yourself* (here), teaches that it is a *mitzvah* to count the weeks.

Although the wording of the Talmud seems to imply two *mitzvos,* the *Rambam* codifies them as one: And it is a *mitzvah* to count the days with the weeks (*Hilchos Temidin Umusafin* 7:22). Accordingly, the Baal HaTurim finds an allusion to the two countings in the same verse, in order to show that, in reality, they are two parts of the same *mitzvah* (*Shoham Yakar*).

16/7-12 *the appointed time of your departure from Egypt.* 7 *You shall roast it and eat it in the place that* HASHEM, *your God, will choose, and in the morning you may turn back and go to your tents.* 8 *For a six-day period you shall eat matzos and on the seventh day shall be an assembly to* HASHEM, *your God; you shall not perform labor.*

9 *You shall count seven weeks for yourself; from the beginning of the sickle at the standing crop, you shall begin to count seven weeks.* 10 *Then you shall observe the Festival of Shavuos for* HASHEM, *your God; the voluntary offerings that you give should be commensurate with how much* HASHEM, *your God, will have blessed you.* 11 *You shall rejoice before* HASHEM, *your God — you, your son, your daughter, your slave, your maidservant, the Levite who is in your cities, the proselyte, the orphan, and the widow who are among you — in the place that* HASHEM, *your God, will choose to rest His Name.* 12 *You shall remember that you were a slave in Egypt, and you shall observe and perform these decrees.*

BAAL HATURIM ELUCIDATED

Chronicles 31:10). {This may be explained: Which sickle? *From the beginning of the terumah,*[174]} i.e., the *omer* which is the first of the meal-offerings,[175] just as *terumah* is called *the first [of your grain]* (18:4 below).

❑ **בְּקָמָה תָּחֵל לִסְפֹּר** — AT THE STANDING CROP, YOU SHALL BEGIN TO COUNT. Read this as if it were vowelized בְּקֹמָה, *when one rises,* [indicating] that one should recite the blessing over the counting of the *omer* while standing.[176]

11. וְשָׂמַחְתָּ — YOU SHALL REJOICE. שִׂמְחָה, *joy,* is not mentioned with regard to Pesach, for the grain is still in the field.[177] With regard to Shavuos, when the grain has been harvested, but the wine is still in [the grapes on] the vine, שִׂמְחָה, *joy,* is mentioned once.[178] But with regard to Succos, when everything has been brought in, שִׂמְחָה, *joy,* is mentioned twice.[179,180]

12. הַחֻקִּים הָאֵלֶּה — THESE DECREES. [The concept of חֻקִּים, *decrees,*] is mentioned with regard to Shavuos,[181] for the Torah was given[181a] on it.[182]

174. The words enclosed in braces are not found in the printed editions. However, they do appear in *Shoham Yakar's* manuscript editions.

175. *Menachos* 68b and 84b.

176. See *Tur, Orach Chaim* 585; *Rosh,* end of *Pesachim* with *Hagahos HaGriv; R' Yehudah HaChassid.*

See also *Shulchan Aruch, Orach Chaim* 8:1, with *Magen Avraham, Peri Megadim,* et al., regarding the requirement to stand while reciting any blessing over a *mitzvah.*

177. And the farmer is not yet ready to celebrate his joy over the new crop.

178. וְשָׂמַחְתָּ, *you shall rejoice* (v. 11).

179. וְשָׂמַחְתָּ, *you shall rejoice* (v. 14), and וְהָיִיתָ אַךְ שָׂמֵחַ, *and you shall be only joyous* (v. 15).

180. *Peirush HaRokeach.*

181. But not with regard to Pesach or Succos.

181a. *Pesachim* 68b.

182. *Peirush HaRokeach.* In *Peirush HaTur Ha-*

טז/יג־יז מפטיר יג חַג הַסֻּכֹּת תַּעֲשֶׂה לְךָ שִׁבְעַת יָמִים בְּאָסְפְּךָ
יד מִגָּרְנְךָ וּמִיִּקְבֶךָ: וְשָׂמַחְתָּ בְּחַגֶּךָ אַתָּה וּבִנְךָ וּבִתֶּךָ
וְעַבְדְּךָ וַאֲמָתֶךָ וְהַלֵּוִי וְהַגֵּר וְהַיָּתוֹם וְהָאַלְמָנָה
טו אֲשֶׁר בִּשְׁעָרֶיךָ: שִׁבְעַת יָמִים תָּחֹג לַיהוָה אֱלֹהֶיךָ
בַּמָּקוֹם אֲשֶׁר־יִבְחַר יהוָה כִּי יְבָרֶכְךָ יהוָה אֱלֹהֶיךָ
בְּכֹל תְּבוּאָתְךָ וּבְכֹל מַעֲשֵׂה יָדֶיךָ וְהָיִיתָ אַךְ שָׂמֵחַ:
טז שָׁלוֹשׁ פְּעָמִים | בַּשָּׁנָה יֵרָאֶה כָל־זְכוּרְךָ אֶת־פְּנֵי |
יהוָה אֱלֹהֶיךָ בַּמָּקוֹם אֲשֶׁר יִבְחָר בְּחַג הַמַּצּוֹת
וּבְחַג הַשָּׁבֻעוֹת וּבְחַג הַסֻּכּוֹת וְלֹא יֵרָאֶה אֶת־פְּנֵי
יז יהוָה רֵיקָם: אִישׁ כְּמַתְּנַת יָדוֹ כְּבִרְכַּת יהוָה אֱלֹהֶיךָ
אֲשֶׁר נָתַן־לָךְ: ססס קכ״ו פסוקים. פליא״ה סימן.

בעל הטורים

(יג) הַסֻּכֹּת תַּעֲשֶׂה לְךָ וְגוֹ׳ בְּאָסְפְּךָ מִגָּרְנְךָ. רֶמֶז לְנוֹיֵי סֻכָּה, לְעַטְּרָהּ בְּשִׁבֳּלִים:

(טז) כָּל זְכוּרְךָ. בְּגִימַטְרִיָּא גְּדֹלִים וּקְטַנִּים:

❑ אֶת פְּנֵי. פֵּ״א כְּפוּלָה — לוֹמַר פָּנִים בְּפָנִים. וּכְשֵׁם שֶׁבָּא לִרְאוֹת כָּךְ בָּא לֵרָאוֹת:

BAAL HATURIM ELUCIDATED

13. הַסֻּכֹּת תַּעֲשֶׂה לְךָ . . . בְּאָסְפְּךָ מִגָּרְנְךָ — YOU SHALL MAKE THE SUCCOS . . . WITH WHAT[183] YOU GATHER IN FROM YOUR THRESHING FLOOR. This is an allusion to the adornments of the succah; to decorate it with stalks of grain.[184]

Aroch, the Baal HaTurim gives two reasons for the Torah's use of the term חֻקִּים with regard to Shavuos: First, citing *Rambam,* because [the term חֹק, *decree,* refers to a *mitzvah* whose rationale is not within the realm of human logic and] the Torah does not explain the meaning of [alternatively: the reason for] the count of seven weeks and the count of fifty days; second, because it is the day on which the Torah was given.

183. The Baal HaTurim's comment takes these words out of the context of the verse. The translation of the rubric is literal and follows the comment.

184. *Succah* 10a — In describing the halachic status of the items used to decorate the succah, the Talmud mentions: colored cloths and embroidered linens; nuts, almonds, peaches, and pomegranates; clusters of grapes and wreaths of grain; wine, oil, and flour.

13 *You shall make the Festival of Succos for a seven-day period, when you gather in from your threshing floor and from your wine cellar.* **14** *You shall rejoice on your festival — you, your son, your daughter, your slave, your maidservant, the Levite, the proselyte, the orphan, and the widow who are in your cities.* **15** *A seven-day period shall you celebrate to* HASHEM, *your God, in the place that* HASHEM, *your God, will choose, for* HASHEM *will have blessed you in all your crop and in all your handiwork, and you will be only joyous.*

16 *Three times a year all your males should appear before* HASHEM, *your God, in the place that He will choose: on the Festival of Matzos, the Festival of Shavuos, and the Festival of Succos; and he shall not appear before* HASHEM *empty handed,* **17** *each man according to what his hand can give, according to the blessing of* HASHEM, *your God, that He has given to you.*

─────────────── BAAL HATURIM ELUCIDATED ───────────────

16. כָּל זְכוּרְךָ — ALL YOUR MALES. The *gematria* of this phrase (303) is equivalent[184a] to that of גְּדֹלִים וּקְטַנִּים, *adults and minors.* [185]

❏ אֶת פְּנֵי — BEFORE. [According to a scribal tradition,] the פ of this word is written in the enhanced form known as פ' כְּפוּלָה, *doubled* פ.[186] This implies that on the pilgrimage festivals, the Israelites would come "face to face" with God [as it were]. Just as God would come [to the Temple] to see [the pilgrims], so too, would He come to be seen [by them].[187]

❏ {The Baal HaTurim's other comments to this verse appear at 16:18 below.}

17. {The Baal HaTurim's comments to this verse appear at 12:15 above and 16:18 below.}

───────────────────────────────

184a. The principle of *im hakollel* allows 302, the *gematria* of the Baal HaTurim's phrase, to be considered equivalent to 303.

185. *Chagigah* 2a.

186. See note 29 to *parashas Devarim* and the accompanying illustration. The word פְּנֵי of our verse does not appear on the list in *Sefer Tagin*.

187. *Chagigah* 4b.

פרשת שופטים &

Parashas Shofetim

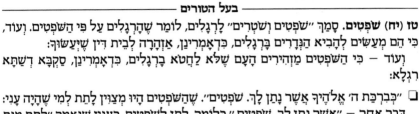

יח שֹׁפְטִ֣ים וְשֹֽׁטְרִ֗ים תִּֽתֶּן־לְךָ֙ בְּכָל־שְׁעָרֶ֔יךָ אֲשֶׁ֨ר

בעל הטורים

טז (יח) שֹׁפְטִים. סָמַךְ "שֹׁפְטִים וְשֹׁטְרִים" לָרְגָלִים, לוֹמַר שֶׁהָרְגָלִים עַל פִּי הַשֹּׁפְטִים. וְעוֹד, כִּי הֵם מְעַשִּׂים לְהָבִיא הַנְּדָרִים בָּרְגָלִים, כִּדְאָמְרִינַן, אַזְהָרָה לְבֵית דִּין שֶׁיְּעַשּׂוּךָ:

וְעוֹד – כִּי הַשֹּׁפְטִים מַזְהִירִים הָעָם שֶׁלֹּא לַחֲטֹא בָרְגָלִים, כִּדְאָמְרִינַן, סַקְבָּא דְשַׁתָּא רִגְלָא:

❑ "כְּבִרְכַּת ה' אֱלֹהֶיךָ אֲשֶׁר נָתַן לָךְ. שֹׁפְטִים". שֶׁהַשֹּׁפְטִים הָיוּ מְצֻוִּין לָתֵת לְמִי שֶׁהָיָה עָנִי:

דָּבָר אַחֵר – "אֲשֶׁר נָתַן לָךְ, שֹׁפְטִים." כְּלוֹמַר, לִתֵּן לַשֹּׁפְטִים, כְּעִנְיָן שֶׁנֶּאֱמַר "לָתֵת מְנָת הַכֹּהֲנִים וְהַלְוִיִּם לְמַעַן יֶחֶזְקוּ בְּתוֹרַת ה' ":

❑ "אִישׁ כְּמַתְּנַת יָדוֹ . . . שֹׁפְטִים". רֶמֶז שֶׁמְּמַשְׁכְּנִין עַל הַצְּדָקָה:

BAAL HATURIM ELUCIDATED

18. שֹׁפְטִים — JUDGES. Scripture juxtaposed the passage that begins שֹׁפְטִים וְשֹׁטְרִים, *judges and officers,* [1] with the passage concerning the festivals (16:1-17), to indicate that the festivals are [determined] by the judges;[2] and also that they compel the people to bring their vow offerings during the festivals,[3] as [the Talmudic Sages] state: [This[4] is] an admonition to [the justices of] the court that they should compel[5] you.[6,7]

1. The term שופטים refers to the *judges,* those who pass judgment, while the term שטרים refers to the *officers* of the court who are appointed to carry out the decisions and verdicts of the judges (*Tanchuma* 2, cited by *Rashi*). The Baal HaTurim's comment will explain why each of these terms has been juxtaposed with the passage regarding the festivals (see note 7 below).

2. *Peirush HaRokeach.* The new month was proclaimed by the judges of the *Sanhedrin,* based upon the sighting of the emerging moon after its nonvisible stage. And that proclamation would fix the festivals; e.g., if the *Sanhedrin* proclaimed Sunday to be the first day of Nissan, then the festival of Pesach would begin two Sundays later, on the fifteenth of Nissan; if Monday were declared the first of Tishrei, then Yom Kippur, the tenth of that month, would fall on Wednesday of the following week (see *Rosh Hashanah* 25a; *Chagigah* 18a).

3. One who has obligated himself to bring a vow offering must do so before the next pilgrimage festival has passed. Thus, the Talmud (*Rosh Hashanah* 6a) states: When one festival has passed him [and he has not fulfilled his vow], he has transgressed on a positive commandment; as it is written (*Deuteronomy* 12:5-6), וּבָאתָ שָׁמָּה, וַהֲבֵאתֶם שָׁמָּה . . . וְנִדְרֵיכֶם, *and you shall come there; and you shall bring there . . . and your vow offerings . . .* (*Rosh Hashanah* 4b, cited by *Rashi* to 6a). That is, at the time you come [to the *Beis HaMikdash*] to celebrate [the pilgrimage festival], you shall bring everything for which you have become obligated (*Rambam, Hilchos Ma'asei HaKorbanos* 14:13).

4. *Rosh Hashanah* 6a — The Talmud there refers to the verse: מוֹצָא שְׂפָתֶיךָ תִּשְׁמֹר וְעָשִׂיתָ, *The issuance of your lips, you shall observe and you shall do* (*Deuteronomy* 23:24). That verse is interpreted as containing three commandments: (a) The phrase מוֹצָא שְׂפָתֶיךָ, *the issuance of your lips,* is a positive commandment [to fulfill your vow]; (b) the term תִּשְׁמֹר, *you shall observe,* is a negative commandment, i.e., do not neglect to fulfill your vow [as the Talmud teaches elsewhere: As used in the Torah, forms of the verb שמר indicate a negative commandment (*Eruvin* 96a; *Makkos* 13b)]; and (c) the term וְעָשִׂיתָ, *and you shall do,* is an admonition to [the justices of] the court that they should compel you [to fulfill your vow].

5. The translation of שֶׁיְּעַשּׂוּךָ as *they shall compel you* follows *Rashi* to *Kesubos* 77a, s.v., אין מעשין; *Tosafos Rid* to *Gittin* 88b, s.v., פי' גט מעושה.

6. *Rosh Hashanah* 6a; see note 4 above; see also the Baal HaTurim to *Numbers* 30:2, and 26:19 below, s.v., וְלִהְיוֹתְךָ.

7. *Peirush HaRokeach.* See note 1 above. Ac-

18 Judges and officers you shall appoint for yourself in all your

BAAL HATURIM ELUCIDATED

Additionally, the judges are wont to admonish the people not to sin during the festivals, for, as [the Sages] state: סַקְבָּא דְשַׁתָּא רִגְלָא, *The sore spot of the year* [with regard to immorality] *is the festival.*[8]

❑[8a] [The previous *parashah* ended,] כְּבִרְכַּת ה׳ אֱלֹהֶיךָ אֲשֶׁר נָתַן לָךְ, *according to the blessing of* HASHEM*, your God, that He has given to you* (16:17), [and our *parashah* begins,] שֹׁפְטִים, *judges.* [This juxtaposition implies] that the judges command[8b] [the people] to provide [charity funds[9]] for the poor.[10]

Alternatively: [The juxtaposition of the verses,] אֲשֶׁר נָתַן לָךְ, שֹׁפְטִים, *that He has given to you; judges,* means [*that He has given to you*] to give to the *judges;*[10a] as it is stated, לָתֵת מְנָת הַכֹּהֲנִים וְהַלְוִיִּם לְמַעַן יֶחֶזְקוּ בְּתוֹרַת ה׳, *to give the portion of the Kohanim and the Levites, so that they could strengthen themselves in the Torah of* HASHEM (*II Chronicles* 31:4).[11]

❑[8a] [The sequence] אִישׁ כְּמַתְּנַת יָדוֹ . . . שֹׁפְטִים, *each man according to what his hand can give . . . judges,* alludes [to the law] that [court-appointed charity collectors] are authorized to seize property as a pledge for [an unpaid] charity[12] [obligation].[13]

---

cordingly, the term שֹׁפְטִים, *judges,* is juxtaposed to the festivals, for it is the judges who fix the dates of the festivals; and the term שֹׁטְרִים, *officers,* is juxtaposed to the festivals, for it is the officers who, at the bidding of the judges, compel the people to fulfill their vows that are due on the festivals (*VeChur LaZahav*).

8. *Peirush HaRokeach.*

Kiddushin 81a; see also the Baal HaTurim to *Leviticus* 19:29. On the festivals, people dress in attractive clothing, celebrate with an excess of food and drink and have more idle time. Consequently, they are more likely to be tempted into sin on *Yom Tov* than during the rest of the year (*Aruch* cited by *Ittur Bikkurim*). Moreover, the festivals are usually a time for public lectures attended by both men and women. This leads to the mingling of men and women after the lecture, and that could conceivably lead to transgression of the laws of seclusion or worse (*Rashi*). It is to atone for relaxing one's guard during the festivals that it has become customary to fast [on the first Monday, Thursday, Monday of the months] following Pesach and Succos (*Tosafos*).

8a. In some editions, these four comments [s.v., כְּבִרְכַּת . . . אִישׁ . . . שָׁלוֹשׁ . . . יֵרָאֶה] appear at the end of *parashas Re'eh.*

8b. The reading מצווין (i.e., מְצַוִּין), *are commanded,* follows the later printed editions, and is also found in *Shoham Yakar's* manuscript edition. The early printed editions, however, read מצויין (i.e., מְצוּיִן), *are found* or *are available.*

9. *Shoham Yakar.*

10. That is, the court may compel people of means to donate charity for the sake of the needy (see *Bava Basra* 8b, with *Tosafos,* s.v., אכפיה; see also the Baal HaTurim's comment, s.v., אִישׁ כְּמַתְּנַת, below).

10a. That is, to those who study Torah and thus are capable of judging properly.

11. The Talmud states: Whoever does not provide for Torah scholars with his property will never see a sign of blessing (*Sanhedrin* 92a). And: All [the good] that the prophets prophesy is for . . . one who engages in business on behalf of the Torah scholars (*Sanhedrin* 97a).

12. *Bava Basra* 8b; see note 10 above.

13. *Rabbeinu Ephraim* (*MiKesivah Ashkenazis*).

❑ "שָׁלוֹשׁ פְּעָמִים" וּסְמִיךְ "שֹׁפְטִים". שֶׁבִּשְׁלֹשָׁה מְקוֹמוֹת סַנְהֶדְרִין יוֹשְׁבִים – בְּהַר הַבַּיִת וּבָעֲזָרָה וּבְלִשְׁכַּת הַגָּזִית. וְכֵן שָׁלֹשׁ שׁוּרוֹת שֶׁל תַּלְמִידִים יוֹשְׁבִין לִפְנֵי הַסַּנְהֶדְרִין:

❑ "יֵרָאֶה כָל זְכוּרְךָ" וּסְמִיךְ לֵהּ "שֹׁפְטִים". שֶׁחַיָּב אָדָם לְהַקְבִּיל פְּנֵי רַבּוֹ בָּרֶגֶל:

❑ **שֹׁפְטִים.** בְּגִימַטְרִיָּא ע' סַנְהֶדְרִים:

❑ **שֹׁפְטִים.** בְּגִימַטְרִיָּא מְכַשֵּׁף. שֶׁמַּעֲמִידִין מְכַשֵּׁף בַּעֲלֵי כְשָׁפִים, שֶׁיּוֹדְעִים לְבַטֵּל הַכְּשָׁפִים:

❑ **שֹׁפְטִים.** תָּגִין לְמַעְלָה וּלְמַטָּה – יִרְאֶה הַדַּיָּן כְּאִלּוּ חֶרֶב מִלְמַעְלָה, וְגֵיהִנֹּם פְּתוּחָה מִלְּמַטָּה:

❑ **תִּתֶּן לְךָ.** וְלֹא לַגּוֹיִם – "מַגִּיד דְּבָרָיו לְיַעֲקֹב, חֻקָּיו וּמִשְׁפָּטָיו לְיִשְׂרָאֵל". "חֻקָּיו וּמִשְׁפָּטָיו" בְּגִימַטְרִיָּא דִּיּוּקֵי מִשְׁפָּטָיו:

❑ **בְּכָל שְׁעָרֶיךָ.** בְּכָל מַה שֶּׁאַתָּה מְשַׂעֵר מָמוֹן חֲבֵרְךָ, הֵן לְמִסִּים הֵן לְהָטִיל צְדָקָה:

BAAL HATURIM ELUCIDATED

❑ [The previous *parashah* states,] שָׁלוֹשׁ פְּעָמִים, *three times* (16:16), and juxtaposed to that is שֹׁפְטִים, *judges,* [alluding to the fact] that a *Sanhedrin* sat in [each of] three places:[13a] on the Temple Mount; in the Courtyard; and in the Chamber of Hewn Stone.[14] Additionally: [It alludes to the] three rows of students [that] sat before the *Sanhedrin.*[15]

❑ [The previous *parashah* states,] יֵרָאֶה כָל זְכוּרְךָ, *all your males should appear* (16:16), and juxtaposed to that is שֹׁפְטִים, *judges.* [This indicates] that a person is obligated to visit his Torah master[16] during the festivals.[16a]

❑ **שֹׁפְטִים** — JUDGES. The *gematria* of this word (439) is equal to that of ע' סַנְהֶדְרִים[17] *70, Sanhedrim.*[18]

13a. The three were all called *Sanhedrin,* but they were not all the same; two comprised twenty-three judges each, while the third, the one in the Chamber of Hewn Stone, had seventy-one members (*Rambam, Hilchos Sanhedrin* 1:3).

14. *Peirush HaRokeach;* see *Sanhedrin* 86b.

15. *Peirush HaRokeach;* see *Sanhedrin* 37a. The three rows of twenty-three students sat before each twenty-three member court. When necessary, under certain specified conditions, individual or pairs of these students would be asked to join the panel of justices.

16. Whereas the major criteria for judgeship was knowledge of all facets of Torah law, the judges were the most qualified teachers in the nation.

16a. *Peirush HaRokeach;* see *Rosh Hashanah* 16b.

17. The reading סַנְהֶדְרִים, *Sanhedrim,* is found in *Paaneach Raza, Rimzei Rabbeinu Yoel* and in *Shoham Yakar's* manuscript edition. Most editions incorrectly read סַנְהֶדְרִין, *Sanhedrin;* but the *gematria* of the Baal HaTurim's phrase is then 449, ten more than that of שׁפטים. The misspelling may be traced to the early printed editions of the Baal HaTurim, the earliest of which (Constantinople, 1514) reads סנהדרי׳. Presumably, the typesetter was unable to determine the validity of the manuscript spelling סנהדרים, so he abbreviated the word. A later edition (Venice, 1544) "improved" the text by spelling out the word סנהדרין (*VeChur LaZahav*).

Although the high court of Torah law is usually referred to as the סַנְהֶדְרִין, *Sanhedrin,* the variant form סַנְהֶדְרִים, *Sanhedrim,* is occasionally used by the Midrash (e.g., *Sifrei* to *Numbers* 11:16, שִׁבְעִים אִישׁ, שֶׁתְּהֵא סַנְהֶדְרִים שֶׁל שִׁבְעִים [*HASHEM said to Moses, "Gather to Me*] *seventy men," so that there shall be a Sanhedrim of seventy*) and by the *Rishonim* (e.g., *Machzor Vitry* p. 357; *Kuzari* 2:64 and 3:39; *Ralbach, teshuvah* 147).

18. *Paaneach Raza; Rimzei Rabbeinu Yoel.* This refers to the seventy members of the *Sanhedrin.* Even though, in reality, the *Sanhedrin* comprised seventy-one justices, the Torah speaks of seventy (*Numbers* 11:16); Moses, who stood at their head, was the seventy-first (*Sanhedrin* 2a). Thus, the Baal HaTurim states, ע' סַנְהֶדְרִים, *70* [members of the] *Sanhedrin* (*VeChur LaZahav*).

❏ שֹׁפְטִים — JUDGES. The *gematria* of this word (439) is equivalent[19] to that of מְכַשֵּׁף, *sorcerer*. For they would appoint a sorcerer, i.e., masters of sorcery[20] who know how to negate sorcery.[21]

❏ שֹׁפְטִים — JUDGES. [According to a scribal tradition,] there are *tagin*[22] [crownlets] above and below [the letter פ of this word].[23] [This indicates that] a judge should feel as if a sword were hanging above [him], and *Gehinnom* were open beneath [him].[24]

❏ תִּתֶּן לְךָ — YOU SHALL APPOINT FOR YOURSELF, but not for gentiles.[25] [Thus the verse,] מַגִּיד דְּבָרָיו לְיַעֲקֹב, *He relates His words to Jacob,* חֻקָּיו וּמִשְׁפָּטָיו לְיִשְׂרָאֵל, *His statutes and His judgments to Israel (Psalms 147:19).*[26] The *gematria* of the phrase חֻקָּיו וּמִשְׁפָּטָיו, *His statutes and His judgments,* (575) is equal to that of דִּיּוּקֵי מִשְׁפָּטָיו, *the fine points of His judgments.*

❏ בְּכָל שְׁעָרֶיךָ — IN ALL YOUR CITIES.[27] [This phrase can be understood as] in accord with whatever you [i.e., the judge] assess your fellow's financial worth — with regard to both taxes and obligations to charity.

───────────────────────

19. The principle of *im hakollel* allows 439 to be considered equivalent to 440, the *gematria* of the Baal HaTurim's term.

20. *Sanhedrin* 17a. The term "masters of sorcery" does not apply to sorcerers *per se*; rather it refers to Torah scholars who had studied the black arts in order to understand and to instruct, i.e., to teach what is permitted and what is forbidden (*Sifrei,* cited in *Rashi* to 18:9 below). For the prohibition against sorcery includes practicing and using sorcery; it does not include studying the field in order to know how to determine whether a particular act incurs capital punishment (*Tosafos* to *Menachos* 65a, s.v., בעלי כשפים).

21. Members of the *Sanhedrin* had to be "masters of sorcery" in order to be able to carry out the death sentence against sorcerers who might otherwise have been able to use their sorcery to protect themselves from capital punishment. Also, with their knowledge of the black arts the "masters" could reveal the truth about those who were using sorcery to mislead the people (*Rashi* to *Sanhedrin* 17a and *Menachos* 65a, s.v., ובעלי כשפים).

22. See note 56 to *parashas Devarim.* The פ of the word שֹׁפְטִים of our verse appears on the list in the Paris edition of *Sefer Tagin* [incorrectly spelled with a prefix ה-]. Although it is absent from the list in *Machzor Vitry,* that list contains only eight-one of the eighty-three words that contain such a פ.

23. By describing the *tagin* as appearing both above and below the letter, the Baal HaTurim apparently refers to the version found in *Machzor Vitry* (see illustration at note 56 to *parashas Devarim*).

24. *Yevamos* 109b; *Sanhedrin* 7a; see also the Baal HaTurim to 1:17 above, s.v., כִּי הַמִּשְׁפָּט.

25. *Tanchuma* 5.

The Talmud cites a *baraisa*: Just as the Israelites have been commanded to set up courts of law in each and every province and in each and every city, so have the Noahites [בְּנֵי נֹחַ, literally, *children of Noah,* a generic term for non-Jews] been commanded to set up courts of law in each and every province and in each and every city (*Sanhedrin* 56b). The Baal HaTurim's comment explains that Israel is not responsible for the establishment of the Noahite courts (see *Ramban* to *Bereishis* 34:13).

26. That passage continues: *He did not do so for any other nation; and as for [His] judgments, they do not know them . . . (Psalms 147:20).*

27. In context, the term שְׁעָרֶיךָ is the noun שְׁעָרִים, literally, *gateways,* but often translated by *Targum Onkelos* as cities; the ם is dropped and the *chirik* under the ר is changed to a *segol* when the possessive suffix ךָ-, *your,* is added — thus, שְׁעָרֶיךָ, *your cities.* But the noun שַׁעַר can also be used as a variant form of שִׁעוּר, *calculation* or *measure* (e.g., *Genesis* 26:12, מֵאָה שְׁעָרִים, literally, *a hundred measures*). Accordingly, שְׁעָרֶיךָ can be understood as *your calculations* or *your assessments,* and that is how the Baal HaTurim's comment interprets the word.

טז/יט־יז/א יהוה אֱלֹהֶיךָ נֹתֵן לְךָ לִשְׁבָטֶיךָ וְשָׁפְטוּ אֶת־הָעָם
יט מִשְׁפַּט־צֶדֶק: לֹא־תַטֶּה מִשְׁפָּט לֹא תַכִּיר פָּנִים
וְלֹא־תִקַּח שֹׁחַד כִּי הַשֹּׁחַד יְעַוֵּר עֵינֵי חֲכָמִים
כ וִיסַלֵּף דִּבְרֵי צַדִּיקִם: צֶדֶק צֶדֶק תִּרְדֹּף לְמַעַן
תִּחְיֶה וְיָרַשְׁתָּ אֶת־הָאָרֶץ אֲשֶׁר־יהוה אֱלֹהֶיךָ
כא נֹתֵן לָךְ: לֹא־תִטַּע לְךָ אֲשֵׁרָה כָּל־עֵץ אֵצֶל
כב מִזְבַּח יהוה אֱלֹהֶיךָ אֲשֶׁר תַּעֲשֶׂה־לָּךְ: וְלֹא־תָקִים
יז א לְךָ מַצֵּבָה אֲשֶׁר שָׂנֵא יהוה אֱלֹהֶיךָ: לֹא־

בעל הטורים

❑ **לִשְׁבָטֶיךָ וְשָׁפְטוּ.** לוֹמַר, שֶׁמִּצְוָה לַשֵּׁבֶט לִשְׁפֹּט שִׁבְטוֹ:

❑ **וְשָׁפְטוּ.** אוֹתִיּוֹת וּפָשׁוּט. יְהִי חָבִיב עָלֶיךָ דִּין שֶׁל פָּשׁוּט לְדַקְדֵּק בּוֹ כְּדִין שֶׁל מֵאָה מָנֶה:

❑ **שֹׁפְטִים . . . וְשָׁפְטוּ . . . מִשְׁפַּט.** הֲרֵי שְׁלֹשָׁה, שֶׁדִּינֵי מָמוֹנוֹת בִּשְׁלֹשָׁה:

(כא) **אֲשֵׁרָה.** בְּגִימַטְרִיָּא דַּיָּן שֶׁאֵינוֹ הָגוּן. שֶׁכָּל הַמַּעֲמִיד דַּיָּן שֶׁאֵינוֹ הָגוּן, כְּאִלּוּ נוֹטֵעַ אֲשֵׁרָה אֵצֶל הַמִּזְבֵּחַ:

❑ **אֲשֵׁרָה כָּל עֵץ אֵצֶל מִזְבַּח.** בְּגִימַטְרִיָּא רָשָׁע אֵצֶל צַדִּיק:

(כב) **אֲשֶׁר שָׂנֵא ה' אֱלֹהֶיךָ.** וּסְמִיךְ לֵהּ "לֹא תִזְבַּח" – לְרַבּוֹת רוֹבֵעַ וְנִרְבָּע, מֻקְצֶה וְנֶעֱבָד:

BAAL HATURIM ELUCIDATED

❑ **לִשְׁבָטֶיךָ וְשָׁפְטוּ** — ACCORDING TO YOUR TRIBES; AND THEY SHALL JUDGE. [The juxtaposition of these phrases] indicates that it is a *mitzvah* for a tribe to judge [the members of] its tribe.[28]

❑ **וְשָׁפְטוּ** — AND THEY SHALL JUDGE. The letters of this term can be rearranged to spell וּפָשׁוּט, *and a penny.* It shall be as precious to you to scrutinize the details of a case involving a penny as those of a case involving a hundred *maneh.*[29]

❑ **שֹׁפְטִים . . . וְשָׁפְטוּ . . . מִשְׁפַּט** — JUDGES . . . AND THEY SHALL JUDGE . . . JUDGMENT. Thus there are three [words of the root שפט, *to judge,* in this verse], for cases involving financial matters require three [judges].[30]

21. אֲשֵׁרָה — AN ASHEIRAH-TREE. The *gematria* of this word (506) is equivalent[30a] to that of דַּיָּן שֶׁאֵינוֹ הָגוּן, *a judge who is not fit.* [This alludes to the Talmudic teaching] that whoever appoints an unqualified judge is considered as if he has planted an *asheirah*-tree next to the Altar.[31]

28. *Sanhedrin* 16b.

29. *Sanhedrin* 8a. Although the Talmud there uses the term פְּרוּטָה for *penny,* the Baal HaTurim uses פָּשׁוּט [literally, *simple,* i.e., the simplest of coin; alternatively, a corruption of the Talmudic term פְּשִׁיטָא, a synonym for פְּרוּטָה], a term commonly used during the Middle Ages to refer to the coin of the smallest denomination in circulation at any given time in any given land.

30. *Peirush HaRokeach;* see *Sanhedrin* 2a.

30a. The principle of *im hakollel* allows 505, the *gematria* of the Baal HaTurim's phrase, to be considered equivalent to 506.

31. *Sanhedrin* 7b. The Talmud there states:

cities that HASHEM, your God, gives to you — according to your tribes; and they shall judge the people with righteous judgment. 19 *You shall not pervert judgment, you shall not show favoritism, and you shall not accept a bribe, for the bribe will blind the eyes of the wise and make just words crooked.* 20 *Righteousness, righteousness shall you pursue, so that you will live and possess the land that HASHEM, your God, gives you.*

21 *You shall not plant for yourselves an asheirah — any tree — next to the Altar of HASHEM, your God, that you shall make for yourself.* 22 *And you shall not erect for yourselves a pillar, which HASHEM, your God, hates.*

BAAL HATURIM ELUCIDATED

❑ אֲשֵׁרָה כָּל עֵץ אֵצֶל מִזְבַּח — **AN ASHEIRAH-TREE — ANY TREE — NEXT TO THE ALTAR.** The *gematria* of this phrase (894) is equivalent[32] to that of רָשָׁע אֵצֶל צַדִּיק, *a wicked person next to a righteous person.*[33]

22. אֲשֶׁר שָׂנֵא ה׳ אֱלֹהֶיךָ — **WHICH HASHEM, YOUR GOD, HATES.** Juxtaposed to this is לֹא תִזְבַּח, *you shall not slaughter.*[34] This is to include [in the prohibition] any animal that has been used for bestiality or has been set aside for idolatry or has actually been worshiped.[35]

Whoever appoints an unqualified judge is considered as having planted an *asheirah-tree* [i.e., a tree used for idolatry] in Israel . . . and if [one appoints such a judge] in a place where scholars dwell, he is considered to have planted [an *asheirah*-tree] next to the Altar . . . [the Talmud then adduces our verses].

The Baal HaTurim's comment combines the two statements of the Talmud (see note 33 below).

32. The principle of *im hakollel* allows 894 to be considered equivalent to 895, the *gematria* of the Baal HaTurim's phrase.

33. *Peirush HaRokeach.* Presumably, the allusion of the *gematria* is a continuation of the preceding comment regarding the appointment of an unqualified judge despite the availability of a Torah scholar to assume that position.

The Baal HaTurim refers to a person who accepts an appointment to the bench, despite the fact that he is unqualified for that position, as רָשָׁע, *a wicked person;* and to the qualified judge as צַדִּיק, *a righteous person.*

Indeed, *Targum Yonasan ben Uzziel* paraphrases our verse: Just as you are not permitted to set an *asheirah*-tree at the side of the Altar of HASHEM, similarly you are not permitted to couple an ignorant man with wise judges to teach you what you are to do. *Ketores HaSammim* explains that the *Targum* combines two Talmudic statements [adduced in note 31 above]: Just as it is forbidden to set an idolatrous *asheirah*-tree next to the Altar, because the Altar functions to bring atonement, while the *asheirah*-tree brings destruction to the world, so it is forbidden to set an unqualified judge next to a Torah scholar, because the Torah scholar implants the law, while the other uproots the law.

Alternatively: The Baal HaTurim refers to the practice of not burying a רָשָׁע, *wicked person,* next to a צַדִּיק, *righteous person* (*Sanhedrin* 47a). Although the Talmud infers this rule from a different Scriptural source, our verse can be seen as an allusion to it, for the Talmud considers the wicked person like an *asheirah*-tree and the righteous person like the Altar, and the Torah prohibits one to be in proximity to the other (*Yad Aharon*).

34. The two phrases can be read together: *That which HASHEM, your God, hates, you shall not slaughter [for HASHEM, your God].*

35. *Sifrei* derives the inclusion of such animals from the phrase כִּי תוֹעֲבַת ה׳ אֱלֹהֶיךָ הוּא, *because that is an abomination unto HASHEM, your God.*

תִּזְבַּח֩ לַיהוָ֨ה אֱלֹהֶ֜יךָ שׁ֣וֹר וָשֶׂ֗ה אֲשֶׁ֨ר יִהְיֶ֥ה בוֹ֙ מ֔וּם כֹּ֖ל דָּבָ֣ר רָ֑ע כִּ֧י תוֹעֲבַ֛ת יהוָ֥ה אֱלֹהֶ֖יךָ ה֥וּא: ב כִּֽי-יִמָּצֵ֣א בְקִרְבְּךָ֗ בְּאַחַ֣ד שְׁעָרֶ֔יךָ אֲשֶׁר-יהוָ֥ה אֱלֹהֶ֖יךָ נֹתֵ֣ן לָ֑ךְ אִ֣ישׁ אוֹ-אִשָּׁ֗ה אֲשֶׁ֨ר יַעֲשֶׂ֜ה אֶת-הָרַ֨ע בְּעֵינֵ֧י יהוָֽה-אֱלֹהֶ֛יךָ לַעֲבֹ֥ר בְּרִיתֽוֹ: ג וַיֵּ֗לֶךְ וַיַּֽעֲבֹד֙ אֱלֹהִ֣ים אֲחֵרִ֔ים וַיִּשְׁתַּ֖חוּ לָהֶ֑ם וְלַשֶּׁ֣מֶשׁ ׀ א֣וֹ לַיָּרֵ֗חַ א֛וֹ לְכָל-צְבָ֥א הַשָּׁמַ֖יִם אֲשֶׁ֥ר לֹא-צִוִּֽיתִי: ד וְהֻגַּד-לְךָ֖ וְשָׁמָ֑עְתָּ וְדָרַשְׁתָּ֣ הֵיטֵ֔ב וְהִנֵּ֤ה אֱמֶת֙ נָכ֣וֹן הַדָּבָ֔ר נֶעֶשְׂתָ֛ה הַתּוֹעֵבָ֥ה הַזֹּ֖את בְּיִשְׂרָאֵֽל: ה וְהֽוֹצֵאתָ֣ אֶת-הָאִ֣ישׁ הַה֡וּא א֣וֹ אֶת-הָאִשָּׁ֣ה הַהִ֡וא אֲשֶׁ֣ר עָשׂ֣וּ אֶת-הַדָּבָ֣ר הָרָ֣ע הַזֶּ֣ה אֶל-שְׁעָרֶ֔יךָ אֶת-הָאִ֖ישׁ א֣וֹ אֶת-הָאִשָּׁ֑ה וּסְקַלְתָּ֥ם בָּאֲבָנִ֖ים וָמֵֽתוּ: ו עַל-פִּ֣י ׀ שְׁנַ֣יִם עֵדִ֗ים א֛וֹ שְׁלֹשָׁ֥ה עֵדִ֖ים יוּמַ֣ת הַמֵּ֑ת

בעל הטורים

יז (א) כֹּל דָּבָר רָע כִּי תוֹעֲבַת. לוֹמַר לְךָ, כָּל הַמְנַבֵּל אֶת פִּיו נִקְרָא תוֹעֵבָה וְשָׂנָאוּי:

☐ **כֹּל דָּבָר רָע.** וּכְתִיב בַּתְרֵהּ "אִישׁ אוֹ אִשָּׁה אֲשֶׁר יַעֲשֶׂה אֶת הָרַע ... וַיֵּלֶךְ וַיַּעֲבֹד אֱלֹהִים אֲחֵרִים". לוֹמַר שֶׁהַדִּבּוּר וְהַמַּחֲשָׁבָה בַּעֲבוֹדָה זָרָה מִצְטָרְפִין לְמַעֲשֶׂה:

(ו) עַל פִּי שְׁנַיִם עֵדִים. פֵּ"א כְּפוּלָה — לוֹמַר, דַּוְקָא מִפִּיהֶם וְלֹא מִפִּי כְתָבָם:

☐ **יוּמַת הַמֵּת.** הָרְשָׁעִים בְּחַיֵּיהֶם נִקְרָאִים מֵתִים:

BAAL HATURIM ELUCIDATED

XVII.

1. כֹּל דָּבָר רָע כִּי תוֹעֲבַת — ANY BAD THING,[36] BECAUSE [THAT IS] AN ABOMINATION. This indicates to you [that] anyone who profanes his mouth [with foul language] is called "abomination,"[37] and "hateful"[38] [unto God].

☐ **כֹּל דָּבָר רָע** — ANY BAD THING. Following this [verse] is written, אִישׁ אוֹ אִשָּׁה אֲשֶׁר יַעֲשֶׂה אֶת הָרַע ... וַיֵּלֶךְ וַיַּעֲבֹד אֱלֹהִים אֲחֵרִים, *a man or woman who will do that which is evil . . .*

The Baal HaTurim finds an additional allusion to those animals in the juxtaposition of the verses (see also *Rambam, Hilchos Issurei HaMizbe'ach* 3:6-7).

It is noteworthy that the *gematria* of אֲשֶׁר שָׁנָא הוּי"ה אֱלֹהֶיךָ לֹא, is 975, equal to that of רוֹבֵעַ אוֹ נִרְבָּע, מֻקְצֶה אוֹ נֶעֱבָד (*VeChur LaZahav*).

36. The verb root דבר means *to speak*. Its related noun דָּבָר (plural, דְּבָרִים) thus means *a word,* and, by extension, is used for *a thing* or *a matter.* In

the context of our verse, the phrase כֹּל דָּבָר רָע means *any bad thing;* nevertheless, the Baal HaTurim's comment interprets it as *any bad word* (see also *Rashi,* here; and the Baal Ha-Turim to 23:10 below, s.v., מִכֹּל דָּבָר רָע, and 24:5 below, s.v., לְכָל דָּבָר נָקִי).

37. In our verse, תוֹעֲבַת ה', *an abomination unto* HASHEM.

38. In the preceding verse (16:22), אֲשֶׁר שָׂנֵא ה', *which* HASHEM *hates.*

[1] *You shall not slaughter for* Hashem, *your God, an ox or a lamb or kid in which there will be a blemish, any bad thing, because that is an abomination unto* Hashem, *your God.*

[2] *If there will be found among you — in one of your cities that* Hashem, *your God, gives you — a man or woman who will do what is evil in the eyes of* Hashem, *your God, violating His covenant,* [3] *and he went and served other gods and prostrated himself to them, or to the sun or to the moon or to any host of the heavens, regarding which I have not commanded,* [4] *and it will be told to you [the judges] and you will hear; then you shall investigate well, and behold! it is true, the testimony is correct — this abomination was done in Israel —* [5] *then you shall remove that man or that woman who did this evil thing, to [whichever of] your cities [in which the sin was committed] — the man or the woman — and you shall pelt them with stones, so that they will die.* [6] *By the testimony of two witnesses or three witnesses, the condemned person shall be put to death;*

BAAL HATURIM ELUCIDATED

and he will go and serve other gods[39] (vv. 2-3). This indicates that, with regard to idolatry, speech[40] and thought[41] are reckoned as part of the actual deed.[42,43]

3. {The Baal HaTurim's comment to אֲשֶׁר לֹא צִוִּיתִי appears at *Leviticus* 10:1.}

6. עַל פִּי שְׁנַיִם עֵדִים — BY THE TESTIMONY[43a] OF TWO WITNESSES. [According to a scribal tradition] the פ [of the word פִּי] is written in the [enhanced] form called פ׳ כְּפוּלָה, *doubled* פ.[44] This is to indicate [that the testimony of witnesses is acceptable only] from their mouths,[45] but not from their writings.[46]

❏ {The Baal HaTurim's comment to the phrase עַל פִּי appears at *Genesis* 43:7.}

❏ **יוּמַת הַמֵּת** — THE CONDEMNED PERSON[47] SHALL BE PUT TO DEATH. [This teaches that] even while the wicked are alive, they are considered as dead.[48]

39. That is, things — other than the true God — that in the mind of their worshipers are gods.

40. As is stated, כֹּל דָּבָר רָע, *any bad word* (see note 36 above), whether actually spoken or merely thought.

41. That is, even those intentions [to sin] that one thought in his mind, but did not speak with his mouth.

42. As דָּבָר, *word,* is juxtaposed to אֲשֶׁר יַעֲשֶׂה, *who will do,* i.e., deed.

43. *Kiddushin* 40a — A thought to do good is reckoned as part of the actual deed . . . but God does not reckon a thought to do bad as part of the actual deed . . . If so, what does the prophet mean by, *to take hold of the House of Israel in their heart* (*Ezekiel* 14:5)? . . . That verse refers to idol worship . . .

43a. Literally, *by the mouth of.*

44. See note 29 to *parashas Devarim.* The word פִּי of our verse appears on the list in *Sefer Tagin.*

45. The name of the letter, פֵּ״ה, is reminiscent of the word פֶּה, *mouth.* The "doubled פ" then is interpreted as if פֶּה, *mouth,* or פִּי, *mouth of,* were written twice, thereby emphasizing "by the mouth of," but not by any other means, for a written message sent to the court by the witnesses is not acceptable.

46. *Peirush HaRokeach;* see *Gittin* 71a.

47. Literally, *the dead person.*

48. *Berachos* 18b.

ז לֹא יוּמַת עַל־פִּי עֵד אֶחָד: יַד הָעֵדִים תִּהְיֶה־בּוֹ
בָרִאשֹׁנָה לַהֲמִיתוֹ וְיַד כָּל־הָעָם בָּאַחֲרֹנָה וּבִעַרְתָּ
הָרָע מִקִּרְבֶּךָ:
ח כִּי יִפָּלֵא מִמְּךָ דָבָר לַמִּשְׁפָּט בֵּין־דָּם | לְדָם בֵּין־דִּין
לְדִין וּבֵין נֶגַע לָנֶגַע דִּבְרֵי רִיבֹת בִּשְׁעָרֶיךָ וְקַמְתָּ
וְעָלִיתָ אֶל־הַמָּקוֹם אֲשֶׁר יִבְחַר יהוה אֱלֹהֶיךָ בּוֹ:
ט וּבָאתָ אֶל־הַכֹּהֲנִים הַלְוִיִּם וְאֶל־הַשֹּׁפֵט אֲשֶׁר יִהְיֶה
בַּיָּמִים הָהֵם וְדָרַשְׁתָּ וְהִגִּידוּ לְךָ אֵת דְּבַר הַמִּשְׁפָּט:* (* חצי הספר בפסוקים)
י וְעָשִׂיתָ עַל־פִּי הַדָּבָר אֲשֶׁר יַגִּידוּ לְךָ מִן־הַמָּקוֹם
הַהוּא אֲשֶׁר יִבְחַר יהוה וְשָׁמַרְתָּ לַעֲשׂוֹת כְּכֹל אֲשֶׁר
יא יוֹרוּךָ: עַל־פִּי הַתּוֹרָה אֲשֶׁר יוֹרוּךָ וְעַל־הַמִּשְׁפָּט
אֲשֶׁר־יֹאמְרוּ לְךָ תַּעֲשֶׂה לֹא תָסוּר מִן־הַדָּבָר אֲשֶׁר־
יב יַגִּידוּ לְךָ יָמִין וּשְׂמֹאל: וְהָאִישׁ אֲשֶׁר־יַעֲשֶׂה בְזָדוֹן
לְבִלְתִּי שְׁמֹעַ אֶל־הַכֹּהֵן הָעֹמֵד לְשָׁרֶת שָׁם אֶת־יהוה
אֱלֹהֶיךָ אוֹ אֶל־הַשֹּׁפֵט וּמֵת הָאִישׁ הַהוּא וּבִעַרְתָּ
יג הָרָע מִיִּשְׂרָאֵל: וְכָל־הָעָם יִשְׁמְעוּ וְיִרָאוּ וְלֹא יְזִידוּן

בעל הטורים

(ח) כִּי יִפָּלֵא. פֵּ"א כְּפוּלָה עֲקוּמָה – לוֹמַר, בְּמֻפְלָא שֶׁבְּבֵית דִּין, וְאֵינוֹ חַיָּב כִּי אִם בְּתוֹרָה שֶׁבְּעַל פֶּה:

(ט,יב) ב׳ פְּעָמִים "הַשּׁוֹפֵט" בַּפָּרָשָׁה, שֶׁהֵם בְּגִימַטְרִיָּא שִׁבְעִים סַנְהֶדְרִין, שֶׁצָּרִיךְ שֶׁיַּמְרֶה עַל בֵּית דִּין הַגָּדוֹל:

(יג) וְכָל הָעָם יִשְׁמְעוּ וְיִרָאוּ. וּסְמִיךְ לֵהּ "אָשִׂימָה עָלַי מֶלֶךְ". שֶׁכֵּן כְּתִיב בַּמֶּלֶךְ "כָּל אִישׁ אֲשֶׁר יַמְרֶה אֶת פִּיךָ":

❑ **וְלֹא יְזִידוּן עוֹד.** וּסְמִיךְ לֵהּ "אָשִׂימָה עָלַי מֶלֶךְ". שֶׁכֵּן אָמַר דָּוִד, "לְהַכְרִית מֵעִיר ה׳ כָּל פֹּעֲלֵי אָוֶן":

BAAL HATURIM ELUCIDATED

8. כִּי יִפָּלֵא — IF . . . IS HIDDEN. [According to a scribal tradition,] the פ [of יִפָּלֵא] is written in the [enhanced] form called פ׳ כְּפוּלָה עֲקוּמָה, *doubled,*[49] *bent* פ.[50] This is to indicate [that the verse] refers to the primary judge;[51] and that it applies only to points of תּוֹרָה שֶׁבְּעַל פֶּה,[52] *the Oral Law.*[52]

49. See note 29 to *parashas Devarim.* The word יִפָּלֵא of our verse appears on the list in *Sefer Tagin.*

50. Although the Baal HaTurim comments on the פ׳ כְּפוּלָה more than a dozen times, only here does he use the term פ׳ כְּפוּלָה עֲקוּמָה, a usage that does not appear in any other known source.

51. *Sanhedrin* 87a. It is noteworthy that the *gematria* of כִּי יִפָּלֵא is 15, equal to that of מֻפְלָא, *primary judge* (A.S.)

52. As noted in note 45 above, the name of the letter, פֵּ״ה, is reminiscent of the word פֶּה, *mouth.* Thus, it refers to תּוֹרָה שֶׁבְּעַל פֶּה, *the Oral Law,*

he shall not be put to death by the testimony of one witness. [7] *The hand of the witnesses shall be upon him first to put him to death, and the hand of the entire people afterward; and you shall destroy the evil from your midst.*

[8] *If a matter of judgment is hidden from you, between blood and blood, between verdict and verdict, between plague and plague, matters of dispute in your cities — you shall rise up and ascend to the place that* HASHEM, *your God, will choose.* [9] *You shall come to the Kohanim, the Levites, and to the judge who will be in those days; you shall inquire and they will tell you the word of judgment.* [10] *You shall do according to the word that they will tell you, from that place that* HASHEM *will choose, and you shall be careful to do according to everything that they will teach you.* [11] *According to the teaching that they will teach you and according to the judgment that they will say to you, shall you do; you shall not deviate from the word that they will tell you, right or left.* [12] *And the man that will act with willfulness, not listening to the Kohen who stands there to serve* HASHEM, *your God, or to the judge, that man shall die, and you shall destroy the evil from among Israel.* [13] *The entire nation shall listen and fear, and they shall not act willfully any more.*

─────────── BAAL HATURIM ELUCIDATED ───────────

9,12. The term [52a]הַשּׁוֹפֵט, *the judge,* appears twice in this passage, and their combined *gematria* (800) is equivalent[53] to that of שִׁבְעִים סַנְהֶדְרִין, *seventy [judges of the] Sanhedrin,* [54] teaching that to be held liable, he [i.e., the rebellious elder] must rebel against the decision of the highest court.[55]

13. וְכָל הָעָם יִשְׁמְעוּ וְיִרָאוּ — THE ENTIRE NATION SHALL LISTEN AND FEAR. Juxtaposed to this is אָשִׂימָה עָלַי מֶלֶךְ, *I will set a king over myself.* For thus is written regarding the king,[56] כָּל אִישׁ אֲשֶׁר יַמְרֶה אֶת פִּיךָ, *Any man who will rebel against your utterance . . . [will be put to death]* (Joshua 1:18).

❏ וְלֹא יְזִידוּן עוֹד — AND THEY SHALL NOT ACT WILLFULLY ANY MORE. Juxtaposed to this is אָשִׂימָה עָלַי מֶלֶךְ, *I will set a king over myself.* For thus said [King] David [describing his duty as king], לְהַכְרִית מֵעִיר ה׳ כָּל פֹּעֲלֵי אָוֶן, *to excise from the city of* HASHEM *all doers of evil* (Psalms 101:8).[57]

───────────────────────────────

literally, *the Torah that is on the mouth.*

52a. Although the Torah uses the defective spelling הַשֹּׁפֵט, without a ו, for purposes of the allusion the Baal HaTurim uses the full spelling הַשּׁוֹפֵט, with a ו.

53. The principle of *im hakollel* allows 800 to be considered equivalent to 801, the *gematria* of the Baal HaTurim's phrase.

54. Alternatively: סַנְהֶדְרִין שִׁבְעִים, *the Sanhedrin of seventy.*

55. *Sanhedrin* 16a; see also *Sanhedrin* 86b.

56. The adduced verse refers to Joshua, whom the Talmud refers to as a king (see *Yoma* 73b; see also *Rambam, Hilchos Melachim* 1:3 and 3:8).

57. See *Rambam, Hilchos Melachim* 4:10; see

עֽוֹד׃ יד כִּֽי־תָבֹ֣א אֶל־הָאָ֗רֶץ אֲשֶׁ֨ר יְהוָ֤ה אֱלֹהֶ֙יךָ֙
נֹתֵ֣ן לָ֔ךְ וִֽירִשְׁתָּ֖הּ וְיָשַׁ֣בְתָּה בָּ֑הּ וְאָֽמַרְתָּ֗ אָשִׂ֤ימָה עָלַי֙
מֶ֔לֶךְ כְּכָל־הַגּוֹיִ֖ם אֲשֶׁ֥ר סְבִיבֹתָֽי׃ טו שׂ֣וֹם תָּשִׂ֤ים עָלֶ֙יךָ֙

בעל הטורים

(יד) **כִּי תָבוֹא.** בְּגִימַטְרִיָּא בִּימֵי שְׁמוּאֵל:

❏ **וְיָשַׁבְתָּה.** מָלֵא הֵ״א – לְאַחַר ה׳ דוֹרוֹת שֶׁאָלוּ מֶלֶךְ:

❏ **כְּכָל הַגּוֹיִם אֲשֶׁר סְבִיבֹתָי.** וּלְכָךְ שָׁאֲלוּ מֶלֶךְ בִּימֵי שְׁמוּאֵל. כִּי עַד עַתָּה לֹא הָיָה לַפְּלִשְׁתִּים מֶלֶךְ אֶלָּא סְרָנִים:

❏ וְאַחַר פָּרָשַׁת עֲבֹדָה זָרָה וַאֲשֵׁרָה כְּתִיב פָּרָשַׁת מֶלֶךְ. לוֹמַר שֶׁהַמֶּלֶךְ מְצֻוֶּה לְהָסִיר הָאֲשֵׁרוֹת וּלְבַעֵר עֲבֹדָה זָרָה:

(טו) **שׂוֹם תָּשִׂים עָלֶיךָ.** בְּגִימַטְרִיָּא שְׁלֹשִׁים מַעֲלוֹת. לוֹמַר שֶׁהַמַּלְכוּת נִקְנֵית בִּשְׁלֹשִׁים מַעֲלוֹת:

BAAL HATURIM ELUCIDATED

14. [58]**כִּי תָבוֹא** — WHEN YOU COME. The *gematria* of this phrase[58a] (439) is equal to that of בִּימֵי שְׁמוּאֵל, *in the days of Samuel.*[59]

❏ [58]**וְיָשַׁבְתָּה** — AND YOU SETTLE. This term is spelled in full,[60] with a ה (= 5). It was after five generations that the Jews asked for a king.[61]

also the Baal HaTurim's last comment to verse 14 below.

58. The three comments, s.v., כִּי תָבוֹא, וְיָשַׁבְתָּה, כְּכָל הַגּוֹיִם, should be read together as if they were one.

58a. Although the verse uses the defective spelling תָבֹא, without a ו, for purposes of the allusion the Baal HaTurim's comment spells the word in full, תָבוֹא, with a ו.

59. It was in the days of the prophet Samuel that Israel asked for a king (see *I Samuel,* Ch. 8; see also the Baal HaTurim's comment below, s.v., כְּכָל הַגּוֹיִם אֲשֶׁר סְבִיבֹתָי).

60. Whereas Moses' words to Israel that are recorded in the Book of *Deuteronomy* were spoken shortly before the nation was to enter the Holy Land, it is not surprising to find words of the roots ירש, *to take possession,* and ישב, *to settle,* recurring throughout the Book. Indeed, in five verses the two roots appear together (11:31 and 12:29 above; here; 19:1 and 26:1 below). In our verse, each of the two verbs ends in the letter ה, but those letters serve different purposes. In וִירִשְׁתָּהּ, it is a ה מַפִּיק, *mapik* [pronounced] ה, as indicated by the dot, and means *her* or *it.* Thus, וִירִשְׁתָּהּ is composed of וְיָרַשְׁתָּ, *you will take possession* (see 12:29 and 16:20 above), and the *mapik* ה suffix which adds *of it.* The change of vowels is the result of the lengthening of the word by adding the *mapik* ה.

However, that is not the meaning of the ה of וְיָשַׁבְתָּה. In fact, from a grammatical point of view, the ה serves no function in that word. Rather, the word is an alternative form of וְיָשַׁבְתָּ, which is how it is spelled the other four times that it appears in *Deuteronomy* (8:12, vowelized וְיָשָׁבְתָּ because it is at the end of its verse; 12:29; 19:1; and 26:1) and elsewhere in the *Tanach.* Thus, this superfluous ה must be explained as a *remez* [allusion].

61. Scripture states: *and Salmon begot Boaz; and Boaz begot Obed; and Obed begot Jesse; and Jesse begot David* (*Ruth* 4:21-22). Accordingly, there will be five generations [Salmon, Boaz, Obed, Jesse, David], from the time mentioned at the beginning of our verse, *when you come into the land,* until the time mentioned later, when *you will say, "I will set a king over myself . . ."* The superfluous ה alludes to those generations. Thus, the word וְיָשַׁבְתָּה may be understood as two words וְיָשַׁבְתָּ ה׳, *and you will settle for five* [*generations*], and the five generations are those of (i) Salmon, who entered the Land of Canaan with Joshua, whom he outlived (*Seder Olam Rabbah* 12); (ii) Boaz; (iii) Obed; (iv) Jesse; and (v) Saul, who was

[14] *When you come to the land that* HASHEM, *your God, gives you, and you take possession of it, and you settle in it, and you will say, "I will set a king over myself, like all the nations that are around me."* [15] *You shall surely set over yourself*

BAAL HATURIM ELUCIDATED

❑ בְּכָל הַגּוֹיִם אֲשֶׁר סְבִיבֹתָי[58] — LIKE ALL THE NATIONS THAT ARE AROUND ME. And for this reason [the Israelites first] asked for a king during the days of Samuel. For until that time, the Philistines[62] did not have a king, only governors.

❑ Following the passages concerning pagan deities (17:2-7) and *asheirah*-trees (16:21-22), the Torah writes the passage concerning a king. This is to indicate that the king is commanded to remove the *asheirah*-trees and destroy idolatry.[63]

15. שׂוּם תָּשִׂים עָלֶיךָ — YOU SHALL SURELY SET OVER YOURSELF. The *gematria* of this phrase (1226) is equal to that of שְׁלֹשִׁים מַעֲלוֹת, *thirty prerogatives,* to indicate that kingship is acquired along with thirty prerogatives.[64]

---

contemporaneous with David (*R' Chaim Paltiel*; see the Baal HaTurim to 3:11 above).

62. The other primary power in the region.

63. See *Rambam, Hilchos Melachim* 4:10; *Radak* to *II Kings* 23:29; see also the Baal HaTurim to verse 13 above, s.v., וְלֹא יְזִידוּן עוֹד.

64. *Peirush HaRokeach.* The *Baraisa* states: Torah [study] is greater than *kehunah* (priesthood) or kingship, for kingship is acquired along with thirty prerogatives, and priesthood is acquired along with twenty-four; but Torah [study] is acquired in forty-eight ways [all of which edify, enlighten and uplift a person's moral and spiritual character] (*Avos* 6:5).

The *Vilna Gaon* (*Beiurei HaGra*) enumerates thirty prerogatives of kingship that are mentioned in Scripture and another thirty that appear in the Mishnah. The thirty Scriptural prerogatives are listed in *I Samuel* (8:11-17): (i) אֶת אֲשֶׁר יִמְלֹךְ עֲלֵיכֶם, *he will reign over you;* (ii) בְּנֵיכֶם יִקָּח, *he will take your sons;* (iii) וְשָׂם לוֹ בְּמֶרְכַּבְתּוֹ, *and place [them] in his chariot brigade;* (iv) וּבְפָרָשָׁיו, *and in his cavalry;* (v) וְרָצוּ לִפְנֵי מֶרְכַּבְתּוֹ, *and they will run before his chariot;* (vi) וְלָשׂוּם לוֹ שָׂרֵי אֲלָפִים, *he will appoint for himself captains of thousands;* (vii) וְשָׂרֵי חֲמִשִּׁים, *and captains of fifty;* (viii) וְלַחֲרֹשׁ חֲרִישׁוֹ, *to plow his furrow;* (ix) וְלִקְצֹר קְצִירוֹ, *and to reap his harvest;* (x) וְלַעֲשׂוֹת כְּלֵי מִלְחַמְתּוֹ, *and to produce his implements of war;* (xi) וּכְלֵי רִכְבּוֹ, *and the furnishings of his chariot;* (xii) וְאֶת בְּנוֹתֵיכֶם יִקָּח, *he will take your daughters;* (xiii-xv) לְרַקָּחוֹת וּלְטַבָּחוֹת וּלְאֹפוֹת, *as perfumers, cooks, and bakers;* (xvi-xviii) וְאֶת שְׂדוֹתֵיכֶם וְאֶת כַּרְמֵיכֶם וְזֵיתֵיכֶם הַטּוֹבִים יִקָּח, *he will take the best of your fields, your vineyards, and your olive trees;* (xix) וְנָתַן לַעֲבָדָיו, *and he will present them to his servants;* (xx-xxi) וְזַרְעֵיכֶם וְכַרְמֵיכֶם יַעְשֹׂר, *he will take a tenth of your grains and your vines;* (xxii-xxiii) וְנָתַן לְסָרִיסָיו וְלַעֲבָדָיו, *and he will present them to his officers and to his servants;* (xxiv-xxvii) וְאֶת עַבְדֵיכֶם וְאֶת שִׁפְחוֹתֵיכֶם וְאֶת בַּחוּרֵיכֶם הַטּוֹבִים וְאֶת חֲמוֹרֵיכֶם יִקָּח, *he will take your servants and your maidservants and your best young men and your donkeys;* (xxviii) וְעָשָׂה לִמְלַאכְתּוֹ, *and press them into his service;* (xxix) צֹאנְכֶם יַעְשֹׂר, *he will take a tenth of your sheep;* (xxx) וְאַתֶּם תִּהְיוּ לוֹ לַעֲבָדִים; *and you will be slaves unto him.*

Thirty prerogatives of the king are found in the Mishnah (*Sanhedrin* 2:2-5): (i-ii) הַמֶּלֶךְ לֹא דָן וְלֹא דָנִין אוֹתוֹ, *The king may not judge* [i.e., as a member of the court panel of judges] *nor be judged;* (iii-iv) לֹא מֵעִיד וְלֹא מְעִידִין אוֹתוֹ, *he may not testify nor be testified against;* (v-vi) לֹא חוֹלֵץ וְלֹא חוֹלְצִין לְאִשְׁתּוֹ, *he does not perform chalitzah, nor is chalitzah performed with his wife;* (vii-viii) לֹא מְיַבֵּם וְלֹא מְיַבְּמִין לְאִשְׁתּוֹ, *he does not perform yibum, nor is yibum performed with his wife;* (ix) וְאֵין נוֹשְׂאִין אַלְמָנָתוֹ, *no one may marry his widow;* (x) מֵת לוֹ מֵת אֵינוֹ יוֹצֵא מִפֶּתַח פַּלְטְרִין שֶׁלּוֹ, *if his close relative dies, he does not leave the entrance of his palace;* (xi) וּכְשֶׁמַּבְרִין אוֹתוֹ, כָּל הָעָם מְסֻבִּין עַל הָאָרֶץ וְהוּא מֵסֵב עַל הַדַּרְגָּשׁ, *when they serve him the mourner's meal, all the people sit on the floor and he sits on the dargash;* (xii) וּמוֹצִיא לְמִלְחֶמֶת הָרְשׁוּת עַל פִּי בֵית דִּין שֶׁל שִׁבְעִים וְאֶחָד, *he may wage a discretionary war with the consent of the court of seventy-one;* (xiii) וּפוֹרֵץ לַעֲשׂוֹת לוֹ דֶרֶךְ וְאֵין מְמַחִין בְּיָדוֹ, *he may break through to make a path for*

מֶ֫לֶךְ אֲשֶׁר יִבְחַר יהוה אֱלֹהֶיךָ בּוֹ מִקֶּרֶב אַחֶיךָ
תָּשִׂים עָלֶיךָ מֶלֶךְ לֹא תוּכַל לָתֵת עָלֶיךָ אִישׁ נָכְרִי
טז אֲשֶׁר לֹא־אָחִיךָ הוּא׃ רַק לֹא־יַרְבֶּה־לּוֹ סוּסִים
וְלֹא־יָשִׁיב אֶת־הָעָם מִצְרַיְמָה לְמַעַן הַרְבּוֹת סוּס
וַיהוה אָמַר לָכֶם לֹא תֹסִפוּן לָשׁוּב בַּדֶּרֶךְ הַזֶּה עוֹד׃
יז וְלֹא יַרְבֶּה־לּוֹ נָשִׁים וְלֹא יָסוּר לְבָבוֹ וְכֶסֶף וְזָהָב
יח לֹא יַרְבֶּה־לּוֹ מְאֹד׃ וְהָיָה כְשִׁבְתּוֹ עַל כִּסֵּא
מַמְלַכְתּוֹ וְכָתַב לוֹ אֶת־מִשְׁנֵה הַתּוֹרָה הַזֹּאת עַל־
יט סֵפֶר מִלִּפְנֵי הַכֹּהֲנִים הַלְוִיִּם׃ וְהָיְתָה עִמּוֹ וְקָרָא בוֹ
כָּל־יְמֵי חַיָּיו לְמַעַן יִלְמַד לְיִרְאָה אֶת־יהוה אֱלֹהָיו
לִשְׁמֹר אֶת־כָּל־דִּבְרֵי הַתּוֹרָה הַזֹּאת וְאֶת־הַחֻקִּים
כ הָאֵלֶּה לַעֲשֹׂתָם׃ לְבִלְתִּי רוּם־לְבָבוֹ מֵאֶחָיו וּלְבִלְתִּי
סוּר מִן־הַמִּצְוָה יָמִין וּשְׂמֹאול לְמַעַן יַאֲרִיךְ יָמִים

בעל הטורים

❑ **מִקֶּרֶב אַחֶיךָ.** בְּגִימַטְרִיָּא מִשֵּׁבֶט יְהוּדָה:

(כ) **לְבִלְתִּי רוּם לְבָבוֹ מֵאֶחָיו.** הַפָּסוּק מַתְחִיל וּמְסַיֵּם בְּלָמֶ״ד – רֶמֶז שֶׁיֵּצֵא מַלְכוּת מִיהוּדָה, שֶׁשְּׁמוֹ עוֹלֶה ל׳. וְל׳ מַעֲלוֹת בַּמַּלְכוּת. וְדָוִד ״בֶּן שְׁלֹשִׁים שָׁנָה . . . בְּמָלְכוֹ״. וּלְכָךְ אָמַר שִׁירָה שֶׁמַּתְחֶלֶת בְּלָמֶ״ד, וְהִיא ״לַמְנַצֵּחַ לְעֶבֶד ה׳ לְדָוִד״:

❑ **לְמַעַן יַאֲרִיךְ יָמִים.** מֶלֶךְ שֶׁמָּלַךְ בֶּן שְׁלֹשִׁים יַאֲרִיךְ יָמִים, וְלֹא שָׁאוּל. וּלְכָךְ סָמַךְ ״לֹא יִהְיֶה

BAAL HATURIM ELUCIDATED

❑ **מִקֶּרֶב אַחֶיךָ** — FROM AMONG YOUR BRETHREN. The *gematria* of this phrase (381) is equal to that of מִשֵּׁבֶט יְהוּדָה, *from the tribe of Judah.*[65]

16. {The Baal HaTurim's comment to לֹא תֹסִפוּן appears at *Genesis* 44:23.}

20. לְבִלְתִּי רוּם לְבָבוֹ מֵאֶחָיו — SO THAT HIS HEART DOES NOT BECOME HAUGHTY OVER HIS

himself and no one may impede him; (xiv) דֶּרֶךְ הַמֶּלֶךְ וְכָל אֵין לוֹ שִׁעוּר, *the king's path has no limits;* (xv-xvi) הָעָם בּוֹזְזִין וְנוֹתְנִין לְפָנָיו וְהוּא נוֹטֵל חֵלֶק בְּרֹאשׁ, *the people plunder and place [it] before him, and he takes the first portion;* (xvii-xix) ״לֹא יַרְבֶּה לּוֹ סוּסִים . . . וְלֹא יַרְבֶּה לּוֹ נָשִׁים . . . וְכֶסֶף וְזָהָב לֹא יַרְבֶּה לּוֹ מְאֹד״, *"he shall not have too many horses for himself . . . he shall not have too many wives for himself . . . and he shall not greatly increase silver and gold for himself"* (*Deuteronomy* 17:16-17); (xx-xxiv) וְכוֹתֵב לוֹ סֵפֶר תּוֹרָה לִשְׁמוֹ, יוֹצֵא לַמִּלְחָמָה מוֹצִיאָהּ עִמּוֹ, נִכְנָס מַכְנִיסָהּ עִמּוֹ, יוֹשֵׁב בַּדִּין הִיא עִמּוֹ, מֵסֵב הִיא כְּנֶגְדּוֹ, *he writes a Torah scroll for himself, when he goes out to war he takes it with him, when he returns he brings it back with him, when he sits in judgment it is with him, when he reclines it is before him;* (xxv-xxvii) אֵין רוֹכְבִין עַל סוּסוֹ, וְאֵין יוֹשְׁבִין עַל כִּסְאוֹ, וְאֵין מִשְׁתַּמְּשִׁין בְּשַׁרְבִיטוֹ, *one may not ride on his horse; and one may not sit on his throne; and we may not use his scepter;* (xxviii-xxx) וְאֵין רוֹאִין אוֹתוֹ כְּשֶׁהוּא מִסְתַּפֵּר, וְלֹא כְּשֶׁהוּא עָרֹם, וְלֹא בְּבֵית הַמֶּרְחָץ, *and we may not observe him when he is cutting his hair or when he is naked or in the bathhouse.*

65. *Peirush HaRokeach.* Once David will be anointed king, the kingship will not depart from his offspring (see *Rashi, Ramban* and *Peirush HaTur HaAroch* to *Genesis* 49:10; see also *Rambam, Hilchos Melachim* 1:9).

*a king whom HASHEM, your God, shall choose; from among
your brethren shall you set a king over yourself; you cannot
place over yourself a foreign man, who is not your brother.
16 But, he shall not have too many horses for himself, so that
he will not return the people to Egypt in order to increase
horses, for HASHEM has said to you, "You shall no longer
return on this road again." 17 And he shall not have too many
wives for himself, so that his heart not turn astray; and he
shall not greatly increase silver and gold for himself. 18 It shall
be that when he sits on the throne of his kingdom, he shall
write for himself two copies of this Torah in a scroll, from
before the Kohanim, the Levites. 19 It shall be with him, and he
shall read from it all the days of his life, so that he will learn to
fear HASHEM, his God, to observe all the words of this Torah
and these decrees, to perform them, 20 so that his heart does
not become haughty over his brethren and not turn from the
commandment, right or left, so that he will prolong [his] days*

BAAL HATURIM ELUCIDATED

BRETHREN. This verse begins and ends[65a] with the letter ל (= 30). This is an allusion to the fact that kingship will emerge from [the tribe of] יְהוּדָה, *Judah,* [65b] whose name has a *gematria* of 30; and to the thirty prerogatives acquired along with kingship;[66] and to David who was בֶּן שְׁלֹשִׁים שָׁנָה ... בְּמָלְכוֹ, *thirty years old when he began to reign* (*II Samuel* 5:4).[67] And thus, David recited a song of praise that begins with the letter ל, that is, לַמְנַצֵּחַ לְעֶבֶד ה׳ לְדָוִד, *For the Conductor; by the servant of HASHEM, by David* (*Psalms* 18:1).[68]

❑ לְמַעַן יַאֲרִיךְ יָמִים — **SO THAT HE WILL PROLONG [HIS] DAYS.** [In the context of the above comment, it can be said:] A king who began to reign at age thirty [i.e., David], will prolong [his] days, but not [King] Saul.[68a] For the following reason, Scripture juxtaposed [the passage beginning] לֹא יִהְיֶה לַכֹּהֲנִים, *there shall not be*

65a. This phenomenon appears nine times in the Torah and forty-one more times in the rest of the *Tanach.* The Baal HaTurim discusses it in his comments to *Leviticus* 11:47 and 21:22; *Numbers* 13:24; and here. The other five verses in the Torah are: *Leviticus* 27:33; *Numbers* 1:14 and 13:13; and *Deuteronomy* 23:18 and 24:6.

65b. See the Baal HaTurim to v. 15 above, s.v., מִקֶּרֶב אַחֶיךָ, with note 65.

66. *R' Chaim Paltiel;* see note 64 above.

67. *Peirush HaTur HaAroch.*

68. Although seventy-four psalms begin with the letter ל [fifty-five of them with the word לַמְנַצֵּחַ — two with the phrase, לַמְנַצֵּחַ לְעֶבֶד ה׳ לְדָוִד (18 and 36)], the Baal HaTurim apparently adduces psalm 18 because its concluding verse speaks of David's unending kingship — *He* [God] *magnifies the salvations of His king* [*David*], *and does kindness for His anointed one, for David and for his offspring, forever* — which is the theme of the Baal HaTurim's comment (*VeChur LaZahav*).

68a. King Saul's age is shrouded in mystery. Although the prophet states, *Saul was one year old when he reigned* (*I Samuel* 13:1), the Talmud explains that verse as a metaphor meaning that Saul was as innocent of sin as a one-year-old (*Yoma* 22b). In the realm of *peshat* (the simple meaning of the verse), that phrase is explained as, *In* [or, *after*] *the first year of Saul's reign* (see

א עַל־מַמְלַכְתּוֹ הוּא וּבָנָיו בְּקֶרֶב יִשְׂרָאֵל: לֹא־
יִהְיֶה לַכֹּהֲנִים הַלְוִיִּם כָּל־שֵׁבֶט לֵוִי חֵלֶק וְנַחֲלָה
ב עִם־יִשְׂרָאֵל אִשֵּׁי יהוה וְנַחֲלָתוֹ יֹאכֵלוּן: וְנַחֲלָה לֹא־
יִהְיֶה־לּוֹ בְּקֶרֶב אֶחָיו יהוה הוּא נַחֲלָתוֹ כַּאֲשֶׁר דִּבֶּר־

━━━━━━━━━━ בעל הטורים ━━━━━━━━━━

לַכֹּהֲנִים" וְאַחֲרָיו פָּרָשַׁת "אוֹב", דְּמִשּׁוּם מַעֲשֶׂה דְּנֹב עִיר הַכֹּהֲנִים וּמִשּׁוּם שֶׁשָּׁאַל בְּאוֹב,
נִטְרַד מִמַּלְכוּתוֹ:

יח (א) לֹא יִהְיֶה לַכֹּהֲנִים. סָמַךְ לְפָרָשַׁת מֶלֶךְ, כִּי עַל פִּי כֹּהֵן גָּדוֹל הַמֶּלֶךְ הוּא נִמְשָׁח.
וְהִקְדִּים מֶלֶךְ, שֶׁגָּדוֹל הוּא מִמֶּנּוּ:

וְעוֹד רֶמֶז – שֶׁעַל הַנָּשִׂיא יִהְיֶה הָעוֹלָה וְהַמִּנְחָה וְהַנֶּסֶךְ:

וְעוֹד – מַה כֹּהֵן וְלֵוִי נוֹטְלִין מַעֲשֵׂר, כָּךְ הַמֶּלֶךְ "צֹאנְכֶם יַעֲשֹׂר":

❑ **אִשֵּׁי ה' וְנַחֲלָתוֹ.** וּכְתִיב בַּתְרֵהּ "וְזֶה יִהְיֶה מִשְׁפַּט הַכֹּהֲנִים", דְּכֹהֲנִים מִשֻּׁלְחָן גָּבוֹהַּ קָא
זָכוּ. "הַלְוִיִּם" בְּגִימַטְרִיָּא הַשֵּׁם בַּאֲדֹנָ"י יהו"ה. וְזֶהוּ "ה' הוּא נַחֲלָתוֹ":

━━━━━━━━━━ BAAL HATURIM ELUCIDATED ━━━━━━━━━━

for the Kohanim (18:1-8), [to the passage concerning the king,] and after that the passage (18:9-22) [containing the prohibition against inquiring] of an *Ov* (v. 11), for it is because of the incident at Nob, city of the *Kohanim,* [69] and because he inquired of an *Ov* practitioner, that [Saul] was expelled from his kingship. [70]

XVIII.

1. לֹא יִהְיֶה לַכֹּהֲנִים — THERE SHALL NOT BE FOR THE KOHANIM. This passage [concerning the *Kohanim*] is juxtaposed to the passage concerning a king, for it is by the order of the *Kohen Gadol* that the king is anointed. [71] The [passage concerning the] king is [mentioned] first because he is greater than [the *Kohen Gadol*]. [72]

An additional allusion: [The juxtaposition indicates] that the responsibility for the burnt-offering and the meal-offering and the libation will be upon the king. [73]

━━━━━━━━━━━━━━━━━━━━

Rashi, Radak, et al.). Nevertheless, the Midrash (*Seder Olam* 13) seemingly states that Saul was twenty-nine [variant reading, twenty-five] when Samuel anointed him (see *Mahari Kara* to *I Samuel* 13:1, missing in some editions). Thus, the Baal HaTurim states that Saul was not yet thirty when he reigned. [According to the Vilna Gaon, however, *Seder Olam* refers to David's age at his anointment, not Saul's (see *Limchasseh Asik*).] Saul's reign lasted for three years (*Zevachim* 118b).

69. See *I Samuel,* Ch. 22.

70. See *I Samuel,* Ch. 28; see also *II Kings,* Ch. 11.

71. *Peirush HaTur HaAroch;* see *I Kings* 1:39 and

II Chronicles 23:1-11.

72. See the *Baraisa* adduced at the beginning of note 64 above. Whereas that *Baraisa* places Torah study on a higher plane than either *kehunah* (priesthood) or *malchus* (kingship) on the basis of the number of מַעֲלוֹת, prerogatives or advantages, each calling entails, it follows that the thirty prerogatives of kingship place the king on a higher plane than that of the *Kohen* who has but twenty-four prerogatives (*VeChur LaZahav*).

Alternatively: The king receives preference over the *Kohen Gadol* (*Yerushalmi, Horayos* 3:5) with regard to distribution of honors and benefits and to redemption of captives (*Shoham Yakar*).

73. The comment paraphrases *Ezekiel* 45:17,

over his kingdom, he and his sons amid Israel.

18

[1] *There shall not be for the Kohanim, the Levites — the entire tribe of Levi — a portion and an inheritance with Israel; the fire-offerings of* HASHEM *and His inheritance shall they eat.* [2] *He shall not have an inheritance among his brethren;* HASHEM *is his inheritance, as He spoke to him.*

BAAL HATURIM ELUCIDATED

Additionally: Just as the *Kohen* and the Levite take tithe [portions], so too, a king [as the prophet states], צֹאנְכֶם יַעְשֹׂר, *He will take a tenth of your sheep*[74] (*I Samuel* 8:17).

❑ **אִשֵּׁי ה׳ וְנַחֲלָתוֹ — THE FIRE-OFFERINGS OF HASHEM AND HIS INHERITANCE.** This verse is followed by the phrase, וְזֶה יִהְיֶה מִשְׁפַּט הַכֹּהֲנִים, *this shall be the due of the Kohanim* (v. 3), for the *Kohanim* receive their portion from the table of the Most High.[75] Thus, the *gematria* of הַלְוִיִּם, *the Levites,* (91) is equal to the [combined] *gematria* of God's Name [as it is pronounced] אֲדֹנָי and [as it is written] י־ה־ו־ה. This reflects the statement: ה׳ הוּא נַחֲלָתוֹ, HASHEM *is his inheritance* (v. 2).

. . . וְעַל הַנָּשִׂיא יִהְיֶה הָעוֹלוֹת וְהַמִּנְחָה וְהַנֵּסֶךְ, *and upon the king will be* [*the responsibility*] *for the burnt-offerings and the meal-offering and the libation.* In the *Book* of *Ezekiel,* the term נָשִׂיא, usually translated *leader* or *prince,* is used for *king* (see, e.g., *Targum Yonasan ben Uzziel* to *Ezekiel* 30:13; *Rashi* to *Ezekiel* 12:10; *Radak* and *Metzudos* to *Ezekiel* 7:27). Nevertheless, in the particular verse adduced by the Baal HaTurim, *Targum Yonasan ben Uzziel* renders נָשִׂיא as רַבָּא, *leader,* and *Rashi* also cites two opinions: his own, that it refers to the *Kohen Gadol,* and that of R' Menachem, who maintains that it means the king. The Baal HaTurim's comment follows the view of R' Menachem.

74. The term מַעֲשֵׂר, *tithe,* or *one-tenth,* literally refers to each of five tithes ordained by the Torah: (i) מַעֲשֵׂר רִאשׁוֹן, *maaser rishon* (the first tithe), is set aside from crops grown in *Eretz Yisrael* and given to a Levite (see *Numbers* 18:21,24); (ii) מַעֲשֵׂר מִן הַמַּעֲשֵׂר (*Numbers* 18:26) or מַעְשַׂר הַמַּעֲשֵׂר (*Nehemiah* 10:39), *a tenth of a tenth,* i.e., one-tenth of the *maaser rishon,* also called תְּרוּמַת מַעֲשֵׂר, *terumas maaser* (e.g., *Demai* 2:4; *Terumos* 3:5; *Bava Metzia* 4:8), is set aside by the Levite and given to a *Kohen* who must treat it with the sanctity of *terumah;* (iii) מַעֲשֵׂר שֵׁנִי, *maaser sheini* (the second tithe), one-tenth of that which remains after *maaser rishon* has been separated from the crop is set aside and is subsequently brought to Jerusalem where it is eaten under certain rules of ritual purity by the owner and anyone with whom he chooses to share it (see *Leviticus* 27:30-31; *Deuteronomy* 14:23-26); (iv) מַעֲשַׂר עָנִי, *maser ani* (the pauper's tithe), replaces *maaser sheini* during the third and sixth year of each seven-year *Shemittah* cycle; it is distributed to the poor and bears no particular sanctity (see *Deuteronomy* 26:12); (v) מַעֲשַׂר בְּהֵמָה, *masar beheimah* (the animal tithe), one-tenth of the calves, lambs and kids born each year, set aside to be brought as Altar offerings (see *Leviticus* 27:32-33), their meat to be eaten under certain rules of sanctity by the owner and anyone with whom he chooses to share it (see *Zevachim* 5:8 [56b]).

Accordingly, the Baal HaTurim's statement "just as the *Kohanim* and Levites are granted tithes" must refer to *maaser* of the produce of the field, for neither the *Kohen* nor the Levite receives a share of *masar beheimah.* If so, it is not clear why the Baal HaTurim adduces the phrase צֹאנְכֶם יַעְשֹׂר, *He will take a tenth of your sheep* (*I Samuel* 8:17), when the earlier phrase וְזַרְעֵיכֶם וְכַרְמֵיכֶם יַעְשֹׂר, *He will take a tenth of your grains and your vines* (8:15; the full passage [*I Samuel* 8:11-17] is adduced in note 64 above), seems more appropriate (*VeChur LaZahav*).

75. *Kiddushin* 52b. The portion of the Altar offerings that are eaten by the *Kohanim* are not considered theirs, *per se,* rather, they are like guests eating a portion from God's table.

ג לֽוֹ: וְזֶ֡ה יִהְיֶה֩ מִשְׁפַּ֨ט הַכֹּהֲנִ֜ים מֵאֵ֣ת הָעָ֗ם מֵאֵ֛ת זֹבְחֵ֥י הַזֶּ֖בַח אִם־שׁ֣וֹר אִם־שֶׂ֑ה וְנָתַן֙ לַכֹּהֵ֔ן

ד הַזְּרֹ֥עַ וְהַלְּחָיַ֖יִם וְהַקֵּבָ֑ה רֵאשִׁ֨ית דְּגָֽנְךָ֜ תִּירֹֽשְׁךָ֣

ה וְיִצְהָרֶ֗ךָ וְרֵאשִׁ֛ית גֵּ֥ז צֹֽאנְךָ֖ תִּתֶּן־לֽוֹ: כִּ֣י ב֗וֹ בָּחַ֛ר יְהֹוָ֥ה אֱלֹהֶ֖יךָ מִכׇּל־שְׁבָטֶ֑יךָ לַעֲמֹ֧ד לְשָׁרֵ֛ת בְּשֵׁם־

רביעי ו יְהֹוָ֖ה ה֥וּא וּבָנָ֖יו כׇּל־הַיָּמִֽים: וְכִֽי־יָבֹ֨א הַלֵּוִ֜י מֵאַחַ֤ד שְׁעָרֶ֨יךָ֙ מִכׇּל־יִשְׂרָאֵ֔ל אֲשֶׁר־ה֖וּא גָּ֣ר שָׁ֑ם וּבָא֙ בְּכׇל־אַוַּ֣ת נַפְשׁ֔וֹ אֶל־הַמָּק֖וֹם אֲשֶׁר־יִבְחַ֥ר

ז יְהֹוָֽה: וְשֵׁרֵ֗ת בְּשֵׁם֙ יְהֹוָ֣ה אֱלֹהָ֔יו כְּכׇל־אֶחָיו֙ הַלְוִיִּ֔ם

ח הָעֹמְדִ֥ים שָׁ֖ם לִפְנֵ֥י יְהֹוָֽה: חֵ֥לֶק כְּחֵ֖לֶק יֹאכֵ֑לוּ לְבַ֥ד

בעל הטורים

(ד) רֵאשִׁ֨ית דְּגָֽנְךָ. בְּגִימַטְרִיָּא מְשֶׁתְּמָרַח:

☐ גֵּז. ב' בַּמָּסוֹרֶת — "גֵּז צֹאנְךָ"; "כְּמָטָר עַל גֵּז". וְהַיְנוּ דְאָמְרִינַן שֶׁצָּרִיךְ לִתְּנוֹ לוֹ כְּשֶׁהוּא מְלֻבָּן. וְזֶהוּ "כְּמָטָר עַל גֵּז", שֶׁיְּהֵא מְלֻבָּן וְלֹא צוֹאִי, אָז "רֵאשִׁית גֵּז צֹאנְךָ תִּתֶּן לוֹ":

(ו) וְכִי יָבֹא הַלֵּוִי. בְּגִימַטְרִיָּא זֶה הוּא כֹהֵן:

(ח) כְּחֵלֶק. ב' בַּמָּסוֹרֶת — "חֵלֶק כְּחֵלֶק יֹאכֵלוּ"; "{כִּי כְּחֵלֶק הַיֹּרֵד בַּמִּלְחָמָה} וּכְחֵלֶק הַיֹּשֵׁב עַל הַכֵּלִים". דְּאָמְרִינַן, כֹּהֵן בַּעַל מוּם חוֹלֵק בַּקֳּדָשִׁים אַף עַל פִּי שֶׁפָּסוּל בַּעֲבֹדָה. וְהַיְנוּ לְפִי שֶׁיּוֹשֵׁב עַל הַכֵּלִים:

BAAL HATURIM ELUCIDATED
---

4. רֵאשִׁ֨ית דְּגָֽנְךָ — THE FIRST OF YOUR GRAIN. The *gematria* of this phrase (988) is equal to that of מְשֶׁתְּמָרַח, *when it has been smoothed over.* [76]

☐ {The Baal HaTurim also comments on the term רֵאשִׁית at 21:17 and 26:2 below.}

☐ גֵּז — THE SHEARING.[77] The masoretic note, ב', means that this word appears twice in the *Tanach*: (i) here, גֵּז צֹאנְךָ, *the shearing of your flock*; and (ii) כְּמָטָר עַל גֵּז, *like rain upon cut vegetation* (Psalms 72:6). This [similarity of expression] is in accordance with that which the Sages have said [regarding the first shearing]: It should be given to the *Kohen* when it is whitened.[78] Thus, the phrase, *like rain*

---

76. *Peirush HaTur HaAroch;* see *Maasros* 1:6. The obligation of tithing one's grain crops takes effect with the act of מֵרוּחַ, *meiruach* (smoothing down), which is done after the grain has been threshed and winnowed to separate the kernels from the chaff. The kernels are gathered into a heap and subjected to *meiruach*. According to the *Rambam* (*Hilchos Maaser* 3:13), *Rash* and *R' Ovadiah MiBartenura* (based on *Yerushalmi, Maasros* 1:4), *meiruach* is the smoothing over of the heap with an implement such as a pitchfork. According to

another opinion stated by the *Rambam* (*Peirush HaMishnayos, Maasros* 1:6 and *Peah* 1:6), *meiruach* consists of removing any chaff that has remained in the heaped-up grain.

77. The noun גֵּז (from גזז, to cut, shear, clip) refers to something that has been cut from where it had been growing, such as shorn wool, mown grass or hair clippings.

78. *Chullin* 138a. This refers to the five-*selaim*-minimum weight of the wool given to the *Kohen*,

[3] *This shall be the due of the Kohanim from the people, from those who perform a slaughter, whether of an ox or of the flock: he shall give the Kohen the foreleg, the jaw, and the maw.* [4] *The first of your grain, your wine, and your oil, and the first of the shearing of your flock you shall give him.* [5] *For him has HASHEM chosen from among all your tribes, to stand and to minister in the name of HASHEM, him and his sons, all the days.*

[6] *When the Levite will come from one of your cities, from all of Israel, where he sojourns, and he comes with all the desire of his soul to the place that HASHEM will choose,* [7] *[there] he shall minister in the name of HASHEM, his God, like all of his brethren, the Levites, who stand there before HASHEM.* [8] *They shall eat equal portions, except for*

BAAL HATURIM ELUCIDATED

upon cut vegetation, indicating that it should be whitened, not sullied.[78a] Only then, *the first shearing of your flock you shall give him.*[79]

6. וְכִי יָבֹא הַלֵּוִי — WHEN THE LEVITE WILL COME. The *gematria* of this phrase (100) is equivalent[80] to that of זֶה הוּא כֹּהֵן, *This refers to a Kohen.*[81]

8. כְּחֵלֶק — LIKE PORTION.[82] The masoretic note, ב׳, means that this word appears twice in the *Tanach*:[83] (i) here, חֵלֶק כְּחֵלֶק יֹאכֵלוּ, *They shall eat equal portions;* and (ii) {כִּי כְּחֵלֶק הַיֹּרֵד בַּמִּלְחָמָה} וּכְחֵלֶק הַיֹּשֵׁב עַל הַכֵּלִים, {*for like the portion of the one who goes down into the fray*}[84] *so is the portion of the one who guards the implements* [left behind] (*I Samuel* 30:24). This is [in accordance with] that which the Sages have said: A blemished *Kohen* receives a portion of the offerings, even though he is ineligible to perform the [Altar] service;[85] and that is because he guards the implements.[86]

---

i.e., the wool must weigh five *selaim* after the receiving *Kohen* will have whitened it. But the donor need not whiten it himself before giving it to the *Kohen* (see *Tur, Yoreh Deah* 333).

78a. *Chullin* 135a.

79. *Maharam MiRothenburg.*

80. The principle of *im hakollel* allows 99, the *gematria* of the Baal HaTurim's phrase, to be considered equivalent to 100.

81. *Peirush HaRokeach;* see *Sifrei,* cited by *Rashi* — [Whereas the verse uses the term הַלֵּוִי, *the Levite,*] one might think that the verse speaks of one who is merely a Levite [i.e., he has no more special calling other than Levite, as opposed to a *Kohen,* who is also a Levite, for he is from the tribe of Levi, but also has the more specialized title *Kohen,* for he is from the family of Aaron, the first *Kohen*]. The Torah teaches otherwise by stating וְשֵׁרֵת, *he shall minister* [i.e., perform the priestly Temple service] (v. 7), which implies that the passage speaks only of those who are eligible to serve, i.e., *Kohanim,* but the Levite is excluded.

82. The phrase חֵלֶק כְּחֵלֶק, literally, *portion like portion,* is an idiom meaning *equal-sized portions.*

83. The full note reads: ב׳ וא׳ וּכְחֵלֶק, [*The word* כְּחֵלֶק *appears*] *twice; and once* [*more*] וּכְחֵלֶק [*with the conjunctive prefix* -וּ].

84. The first part of the verse, which is where the other instance of כְּחֵלֶק appears, has inexplicably been omitted from both the manuscripts and the printed editions.

85. *Zevachim* 102a.

86. *Maharam MiRothenburg.*

ט מִמְּכָרָ֖יו עַל־הָֽאָבֽוֹת: כִּ֤י אַתָּה֙ בָּ֣א אֶל־
הָאָ֕רֶץ אֲשֶׁר־יְהֹוָ֥ה אֱלֹהֶ֖יךָ נֹתֵ֣ן לָ֑ךְ לֹֽא־תִלְמַ֣ד
י לַעֲשׂ֔וֹת כְּתוֹעֲבֹ֖ת הַגּוֹיִ֥ם הָהֵֽם: לֹֽא־יִמָּצֵ֣א בְךָ֔
מַעֲבִ֥יר בְּנֽוֹ־וּבִתּ֖וֹ בָּאֵ֑שׁ קֹסֵ֣ם קְסָמִ֔ים מְעוֹנֵ֥ן
יא וּמְנַחֵ֖שׁ וּמְכַשֵּֽׁף: וְחֹבֵ֖ר חָ֑בֶר וְשֹׁאֵ֥ל אוֹב֙ וְיִדְּעֹנִ֔י
יב וְדֹרֵ֖שׁ אֶל־הַמֵּתִֽים: כִּֽי־תוֹעֲבַ֥ת יְהֹוָ֖ה כָּל־עֹ֣שֵׂה
אֵ֑לֶּה וּבִגְלַ֣ל הַתּֽוֹעֵבֹ֣ת הָאֵ֔לֶּה יְהֹוָ֣ה אֱלֹהֶ֔יךָ מוֹרִ֥ישׁ
יג אוֹתָ֖ם מִפָּנֶֽיךָ: תָּמִ֣ים תִּֽהְיֶ֔ה עִ֖ם יְהֹוָ֥ה אֱלֹהֶֽיךָ:
יד כִּ֣י | הַגּוֹיִ֣ם הָאֵ֗לֶּה אֲשֶׁ֤ר אַתָּה֙ יוֹרֵ֣שׁ אוֹתָ֔ם
אֶל־מְעֹֽנְנִ֥ים וְאֶל־קֹֽסְמִ֖ים יִשְׁמָ֑עוּ וְאַתָּ֕ה לֹ֣א כֵ֔ן
טו נָ֣תַן לְךָ֔ יְהֹוָ֖ה אֱלֹהֶֽיךָ: נָבִ֙יא מִקִּרְבְּךָ֤ מֵאַחֶ֙יךָ֙ כָּמֹ֔נִי

―――――― בעל הטורים ――――――

(ט) כִּי אַתָּה בָּא. סָמַךְ כָּאן שׁוֹאֵל אוֹב, לוֹמַר שֶׁהַמֶּלֶךְ שׁוֹאֵל בָּאוּרִים וְלֹא בָּאוֹב:

(י) קֹסֵם קְסָמִים מְעוֹנֵן וּמְנַחֵשׁ. "קֶסֶם" בְּגִימַטְרִיָּא אוֹחֵז בְּמַקְלוֹ. "מְעוֹנֵן" בְּגִימַטְרִיָּא אוֹחֲזֵי
הָעֵינַיִם. "מְנַחֵשׁ" נוֹטָרִיקוֹן מִפִּי נָפְלָה חֲתִיכָה שֶׁלִּי. דָּבָר אַחֵר – מַקֵּל נָחָשׁ חֻלְדָּה שׁוּעָל:

(יג) תָּמִים. תָּי"ו גְּדוֹלָה – שֶׁאִם תֵּלֵךְ בִּתְמִימוּת, כְּאִלּוּ קִיַּמְתָּ מֵאָלֶ"ף וְעַד תָּי"ו:

(טו) נָבִיא מִקִּרְבְּךָ. הַפָּסוּק מַתְחִיל וּמְסַיֵּם בְּנוּ"ן – לוֹמַר שֶׁיֵּדַע נוּ"ן שַׁעֲרֵי בִינָה:

―――――― BAAL HATURIM ELUCIDATED ――――――

9. כִּי אַתָּה בָּא — WHEN YOU COME. Juxtaposed to this is [the prohibition against divining the future by] inquiring of an *Ov* practitioner (v. 11), to indicate that the king should inquire [about the future] through the *Urim* [*VeTummim*],[87] and not through an *Ov* practitioner.[88]

10. קֹסֵם קְסָמִים מְעוֹנֵן וּמְנַחֵשׁ — A PRACTITIONER OF DIVINATION, A MAGICIAN OR A READER OF OMENS. The *gematria* of the word קֶסֶם (200) is equal to that of אוֹחֵז בְּמַקְלוֹ, *he grasps his staff.*[89]

The *gematria* of מְעוֹנֵן, *magician*, (216) is equivalent[90] to that of אוֹחֲזֵי הָעֵינַיִם, *practitioners of legerdemain* [literally, *those who grasp the eyes*].[91]

87. A reference to the אוּרִים וְתֻמִּים, properly pronounced, *Urim VeSummim,* but popularly, *Urim VeTummim:* a writing of the Ineffable Name [i.e., the Divine Name of seventy-two letters (see the Baal HaTurim to *Exodus* 28:30)] which was placed into the fold of the *Kohen Gadol*'s breastplate and which would cause the letters engraved on the stones of the breastplate to light up in prophetic response to questions asked of God (see *Exodus* 28:30 with *Rashi; Numbers* 27:21, *I Samuel* 28:6 and *Ezra* 2:63).

88. *Peirush HaRokeach;* see *Rashi* to v. 14 below; see the Baal HaTurim to *Leviticus* 21:1, with note 7; and the Baal HaTurim's last comment to 17:20 above.

89. *Peirush HaRokeach.* The Midrash (*Sifrei;* cited by *Rashi*) uses this phrase to describe the practice of a קֹסֵם: He grasps his staff and predicts the future.

90. The principle of *im hakollel* allows 216 to be considered equivalent to 217, the *gematria* of the Baal HaTurim's phrase.

91. *Peirush HaRokeach.* The Midrash (*Sifrei*) and Talmud (*Sanhedrin* 65b; cited by *Rashi*) cite one

what was transacted by the forefathers.

⁹ *When you come to the land that* HASHEM, *your God, gives you, you shall not learn to act according to the abominations of those nations.* ¹⁰ *There shall not be found among you one who causes his son or daughter to pass through the fire, a practitioner of divination, a magician or a reader of omens or a sorcerer;* ¹¹ *or an animal charmer or an inquirer of Ov or Yid'oni or a consulter of the dead.* ¹² *For anyone who does these is an abomination of* HASHEM, *and because of these abominations* HASHEM, *your God, ban-ishes [the nations] from before you.* ¹³ *You shall be whole-hearted with* HASHEM, *your God.* ¹⁴ *For these nations that you are possessing — they hearken to astrologers and diviners; but as for you — not so has* HASHEM, *your God, given for you.*

¹⁵ *A prophet from your midst, from your brethren, like me,*

――――――――――――――― BAAL HATURIM ELUCIDATED ―――――――――――――――

The term מְנַחֵשׁ, *a reader of omens,* is the acronym of the phrase מִפִּי נָפְלָה חֲתִיכָה שֶׁלִּי, *From my mouth fell a piece of my food.* ⁹² Alternatively: [It is the acronym of:] מַקֵּל נָחָשׁ חֻלְדָּה שׁוּעָל, *staff, snake, weasel, fox.* ⁹³

13. תָּמִים — WHOLEHEARTED. [According to a scribal tradition,] the ת of this word is [to be written] oversized.⁹⁴ [This indicates] that if you will walk wholeheartedly with God, you will be considered as having fulfilled [the entire Torah] from א until ת.⁹⁵

15. נָבִיא מִקִּרְבְּךָ — A PROPHET FROM YOUR MIDST. This verse both begins and ends with the letter נ⁹⁶ (= 50). [This is] to indicate that he knew the [Torah which contains within it]⁹⁷ fifty gates of understanding.⁹⁸

---

opinion that understands the word מְעוֹנֵן to be akin to עַיִן, *eye;* a מְעוֹנֵן then is one who grasps the eyes, i.e., sleight of hand.

92. *Peirush HaRokeach.* The Midrash (*Sifrei*) and Talmud (*Sanhedrin* 65b; cited by *Rashi*) use a similar phrase to describe an example of the omens used by a מְנַחֵשׁ.

93. Among the various omens described by the Midrash (*Sifrei*) and Talmud (*Sanhedrin* 65b-66a) are: His staff fell from his hand; a snake was at his right side; a fox was at his left. The Talmud adds that the מְנַחֵשׁ divines by means of weasels, birds and fish.

94. This word appears in the masoretic compila-tion *Achlah VeAchlah* (ed. Frensdorff, list 92) and in the *Massorah Rabbasa* (list 1) on lists of twenty-seven such letters — one appearance for each of the twenty-two regular letters and the five final forms — ך ם ן ף ץ.

95. *Peirush HaRokeach.* The expression "from א to ת" is an idiom for "from beginning to end." (See the Baal HaTurim to 11:27 above, with note 20.)

96. This phenomenon also appears in *Leviticus* 13:9 (where the Baal HaTurim is silent about it) and *Numbers* 32:32 (see the Baal HaTurim's comment there) and eight more times in the rest of Scripture (*Jeremiah* 50:8; *Psalms* 46:5, 77:21, 78:12; *Proverbs* 7:17, 20:27; *Song of Songs* 4:11; and *I Chronicles* 12:2).

97. The interpolation is from *Peirush Ha-Rokeach.*

98. *Rosh Hashanah* 21b; *Nedarim* 38a — Fifty gates of understanding were created in the world, all but one were given to Moses.

The fifty gates are the subject of a lengthy discourse by the Raavad in his introduction to *Sefer Yetzirah.*

טו יָקִים לְךָ יהוה אֱלֹהֶיךָ אֵלָיו תִּשְׁמָעוּן: כְּכֹל
אֲשֶׁר־שָׁאַלְתָּ מֵעִם יהוה אֱלֹהֶיךָ בְּחֹרֵב בְּיוֹם
הַקָּהָל לֵאמֹר לֹא אֹסֵף לִשְׁמֹעַ אֶת־קוֹל יהוה אֱלֹהָי
וְאֶת־הָאֵשׁ הַגְּדֹלָה הַזֹּאת לֹא־אֶרְאֶה עוֹד וְלֹא
יז־יח אָמוּת: וַיֹּאמֶר יהוה אֵלָי הֵיטִיבוּ אֲשֶׁר דִּבֵּרוּ: נָבִיא
אָקִים לָהֶם מִקֶּרֶב אֲחֵיהֶם כָּמוֹךָ וְנָתַתִּי דְבָרַי בְּפִיו
יט וְדִבֶּר אֲלֵיהֶם אֵת כָּל־אֲשֶׁר אֲצַוֶּנּוּ: וְהָיָה הָאִישׁ
אֲשֶׁר לֹא־יִשְׁמַע אֶל־דְּבָרַי אֲשֶׁר יְדַבֵּר בִּשְׁמִי
כ אָנֹכִי אֶדְרֹשׁ מֵעִמּוֹ: אַךְ הַנָּבִיא אֲשֶׁר יָזִיד לְדַבֵּר
דָּבָר בִּשְׁמִי אֵת אֲשֶׁר לֹא־צִוִּיתִיו לְדַבֵּר וַאֲשֶׁר
יְדַבֵּר בְּשֵׁם אֱלֹהִים אֲחֵרִים וּמֵת הַנָּבִיא הַהוּא:

בעל הטורים

❑ וְיֵשׁ בּוֹ עֶשֶׂר תֵּבוֹת – לוֹמַר שֶׁתִּשְׁמַע לוֹ כְּמוֹ לַעֲשֶׂרֶת הַדִּבְּרוֹת:

❑ **תִּשְׁמָעוּן.** ב׳ בַּמָּסוֹרֶת – ״אֵלָיו תִּשְׁמָעוּן״; ״כַּקָּטֹן כַּגָּדֹל תִּשְׁמָעוּן״. לוֹמַר, אֶחָד קָטָן וְאֶחָד גָּדוֹל, שְׁמַע אֵלָיו:

❑ **כָּמֹנִי.** בְּגִימַטְרִיָּא עָנָו:

(טז) **כְּכֹל אֲשֶׁר שָׁאַלְתָּ.** ״כְּכֹל״ עוֹלֶה שִׁבְעִים. לוֹמַר, שֶׁשָּׁמַעְתִּי לִשְׁאֵלָתְךָ וְשַׂמְתִּי עֲלֵיהֶם שִׁבְעִים זְקֵנִים. וְגַם, כַּאֲשֶׁר יִשְׁאֲלוּ יִשְׂרָאֵל נְבִיאִים, יִתֵּן לָהֶם נְבִיאִים:

(יח) **נָבִיא אָקִים לָהֶם.** בְּגִימַטְרִיָּא זֶהוּ יִרְמְיָהוּ. זֶה הוֹכִיחָן וְזֶה הוֹכִיחָן וְכוּ׳, כִּדְאִיתָא בִּפְסִיקְתָּא:

BAAL HATURIM ELUCIDATED

❑ The verse contains ten words, to indicate that you must heed a prophet as [you must heed] the Ten Commandments.[99]

❑ תִּשְׁמָעוּן — **YOU SHALL HEARKEN.** The masoretic note, ב׳, means that this word appears twice in the *Tanach*: (i) here, אֵלָיו תִּשְׁמָעוּן, *to him you shall hearken;* and (ii) כַּקָּטֹן כַּגָּדֹל תִּשְׁמָעוּן, *Small and great alike you shall hear* (*Deuteronomy* 1:17).[100] This [similarity of expression] indicates that whether a prophet's stature is [relatively] small or great, you should heed him.[101]

99. The initial letters of the last two words in verse 14 and the ten words of verse 15 have a combined *gematria* of 613, to indicate that you must heed a prophet as you must heed the six hundred and thirteen *mitzvos* (*VeChur LaZahav*).

Alternatively: Just as you heard eight of the Ten Commandments from me, a prophet, so must you heed every prophet in israel (A.S.).

100. In his comments to that verse, the Baal HaTurim explains the masoretic note in a different manner.

101. *Rosh Hashanah* 25b; see *Rashi* to 17:9 above, s.v., ואל השפט, and 19:17 below, s.v., אשר יהיו. The Talmud states that relative to his generation, Jephthah the Gileadite (see *Judges* 11:1-12:7) [the least of the Judges with respect to

shall HASHEM*, your God, establish for you — to him you shall hearken.* 16 *According to all that you asked of* HASHEM*, your God, in Horeb on the day of the congregation, saying, "I can no longer hear the voice of* HASHEM*, my God, and this great fire I can no longer see, so that I shall not die."*

17 *Then* HASHEM *said to me: They have done well in what they have said.* 18 *I will establish a prophet for them from among their brethren, like you, and I will place My words in his mouth; He shall speak to them everything that I will command him.* 19 *And it shall be that the man who will not hearken to My words that he shall speak in My name, I will exact from him.* 20 *But the prophet who willfully shall speak a word in My name, that which I have not commanded him to speak, or who shall speak in the name of other gods — that prophet shall die.*

BAAL HATURIM ELUCIDATED

❑ **כָּמוֹנִי**[102] — LIKE ME. The *gematria* of this word (126) is equivalent to the term עָנָו, *a humble person.*[103]

16. בְּכֹל אֲשֶׁר שָׁאַלְתָּ — ACCORDING TO ALL THAT YOU ASKED. The *gematria* of בְּכֹל, *according to all,* is 70.[104] This is to indicate that [Moses was telling the people, "God said to me,] 'I have heeded your request, and I have appointed seventy elders over them.'" And similarly [in the future], when Israel will ask for prophets, prophets will be given to them.[105]

18. נָבִיא אָקִים לָהֶם — I WILL ESTABLISH A PROPHET FOR THEM. The *gematria* of this phrase (289) is equal to that of זֶהוּ יִרְמְיָהוּ, *This refers to Jeremiah,* for as the *Pesikta* states: This one [Moses] admonished them and that one [Jeremiah] admonished them . . .[106]

20. {The Baal HaTurim's comment to יָזִיד appears at *Exodus* 21:14.}

Torah knowledge — the Midrash refers to him as "a pauper in Torah like the twig of a date-palm" (*Tanchuma, Bechukosai* 5)] was equal to Samuel [the greatest of the Judges] in his generation.

102. Although the Torah uses the defective spelling כָּמֹנִי, without a ו, for purposes of the allusion, the Baal HaTurim spells it in full with a ו, a practice not uncommon in the realm of *remez* (allusion).

103. The verse cannot mean that a prophet must be of equal stature with Moses, for that could never be, as the Torah states: *Never again has there arisen in Israel a prophet like Moses* (34:10 below). Rather, it means that a prophet, on his own level, must possess a measure of the character trait associated with Moses, that of an עָנָו, *humble man* (see *Numbers* 12:3; see also *Nedarim* 38a).

104. Thus, the phrase may be understood: בכ״ל אֲשֶׁר שָׁאַלְתָּ, *the seventy that you requested.*

105. The text follows the later printed editions. The early printed editions, as well as *Shoham Yakar's* manuscript edition, read: וְגַם אֲנִי כַּאֲשֶׁר שָׁאֲלוּ יִשְׂרָאֵל נָאֶתֵּן לָהֶם נְבִיאִים, *And similarly, regarding Me, when Israel requested prophets, I gave them prophets.*

106. *Pesikta DeRav Kahana* 13. The Midrash there cites our verse, *I will establish a prophet for them . . . like you,* and then lists six ways in which the life of Jeremiah paralleled that of Moses, the sixth being that both Moses and Jeremiah admonished the nation.

יח/כא־יט/ז

כא וְכִי תֹאמַר בִּלְבָבֶךָ אֵיכָה נֵדַע אֶת־הַדָּבָר אֲשֶׁר
כב לֹא־דִבְּרוֹ יהוה: אֲשֶׁר יְדַבֵּר הַנָּבִיא בְּשֵׁם יהוה
וְלֹא־יִהְיֶה הַדָּבָר וְלֹא יָבֹא הוּא הַדָּבָר אֲשֶׁר
לֹא־דִבְּרוֹ יהוה בְּזָדוֹן דִּבְּרוֹ הַנָּבִיא לֹא תָגוּר
יט א מִמֶּנּוּ: כִּי־יַכְרִית יהוה אֱלֹהֶיךָ אֶת־הַגּוֹיִם
אֲשֶׁר יהוה אֱלֹהֶיךָ נֹתֵן לְךָ אֶת־אַרְצָם וִירִשְׁתָּם
ב וְיָשַׁבְתָּ בְעָרֵיהֶם וּבְבָתֵּיהֶם: שָׁלוֹשׁ עָרִים תַּבְדִּיל
לָךְ בְּתוֹךְ אַרְצְךָ אֲשֶׁר יהוה אֱלֹהֶיךָ נֹתֵן לְךָ
ג לְרִשְׁתָּהּ: תָּכִין לְךָ הַדֶּרֶךְ וְשִׁלַּשְׁתָּ אֶת־גְּבוּל אַרְצְךָ
אֲשֶׁר יַנְחִילְךָ יהוה אֱלֹהֶיךָ וְהָיָה לָנוּס שָׁמָּה
ד כָּל־רֹצֵחַ: וְזֶה דְּבַר הָרֹצֵחַ אֲשֶׁר־יָנוּס שָׁמָּה וָחָי
אֲשֶׁר יַכֶּה אֶת־רֵעֵהוּ בִּבְלִי־דַעַת וְהוּא לֹא־שֹׂנֵא
ה לוֹ מִתְּמֹל שִׁלְשֹׁם: וַאֲשֶׁר יָבֹא אֶת־רֵעֵהוּ בַיַּעַר
לַחְטֹב עֵצִים וְנִדְּחָה יָדוֹ בַגַּרְזֶן לִכְרֹת הָעֵץ וְנָשַׁל
הַבַּרְזֶל מִן־הָעֵץ וּמָצָא אֶת־רֵעֵהוּ וָמֵת הוּא יָנוּס
ו אֶל־אַחַת הֶעָרִים־הָאֵלֶּה וָחָי: פֶּן־יִרְדֹּף גֹּאֵל הַדָּם
אַחֲרֵי הָרֹצֵחַ כִּי יֵחַם לְבָבוֹ וְהִשִּׂיגוֹ כִּי־יִרְבֶּה
הַדֶּרֶךְ וְהִכָּהוּ נָפֶשׁ וְלוֹ אֵין מִשְׁפַּט־מָוֶת כִּי לֹא
ז שֹׂנֵא הוּא לוֹ מִתְּמוֹל שִׁלְשׁוֹם: עַל־כֵּן אָנֹכִי מְצַוְּךָ

בעל הטורים

יט (ג) וְשִׁלַּשְׁתָּ. ב׳ בַּמָּסוֹרֶת — ״וְשִׁלַּשְׁתָּ אֶת גְּבוּל אַרְצְךָ״; ״וְשִׁלַּשְׁתָּ תֵּרֵד מְאֹד״. רֶמֶז לְמַה שֶׁאָמְרוּ, דֶּרֶךְ יְרִידָה גּוֹלֶה, דֶּרֶךְ עֲלִיָּה אֵינוֹ גּוֹלֶה. וְזֶהוּ ״תֵּרֵד״, שֶׁהֲרָגוֹ דֶּרֶךְ יְרִידָה, אָז ״וְשִׁלַּשְׁתָּ״, שֶׁיֵּלֵךְ אֶל עָרֵי הַמִּקְלָט:

BAAL HATURIM ELUCIDATED

XIX.

3. וְשִׁלַּשְׁתָּ — YOU SHALL DIVIDE BY THREE.[106a] The masoretic note, ב׳, means that this word appears twice in the *Tanach*: (i) here, וְשִׁלַּשְׁתָּ אֶת גְּבוּל אַרְצְךָ, *and you shall divide by three* [*the territory within*] *the border of your land*; and (ii) וְשִׁלַּשְׁתָּ תֵּרֵד מְאֹד, *For three days you shall go down deep* [*in hiding*] (*I Samuel* 20:19).

106a. That is, make three east-west lines of division that will divide the land into four equal-sized portions; and set two cities of refuge upon each line, one east of the Jordan, one west of the Jordan. Accordingly, from the southern border northward until the first pair of cities will be the same distance as between the first and second pairs. And that same distance will also separate the second pair from the third and the third from the northern border (*Makkos* 9b, cited by *Rashi*).

[21] *When you say in your heart, "How can we know the*
word that HASHEM has not spoken?" [22] *If the prophet will*
speak in the Name of HASHEM and that thing will not occur
and not come about — that is the word that HASHEM has not
spoken; with willfulness has the prophet spoken it, you
should not fear him.

19 [1]*When HASHEM, your God, will cut down the nations whose*
land HASHEM, your God, gives you, and you will take
possession of them, and you will settle in their cities and in
their houses, [2] *you shall separate three cities for yourselves in*
the midst of your land, that HASHEM, your God, gives you to
take possession of it. [3] *Prepare the way for yourself; you shall*
divide by three [the territory within] the boundary of your
land that HASHEM, your God, causes you to inherit; and it
shall be for any killer to flee there. [4] *This is the matter of the*
killer who shall flee there and live: One who will strike his
fellow without knowledge, and he did not hate him from
yesterday or before yesterday; [5] *or who will come with his*
fellow into the forest to hew trees, and his hand will swing the
axe to cut the tree, and the iron will slip from the wood and
will find his fellow and he will die, he shall flee to one of these
cities and live, [6] *lest the redeemer of the blood chase after the*
killer, for his heart will be hot, and he will overtake him for the
way was long, and he will strike him mortally — and there is
no judgment of death upon him, for he did not hate him from
yesterday and before yesterday. [7] *Therefore I command you,*

BAAL HATURIM ELUCIDATED

[This similarity is] an allusion to that which the Sages have said: [If the person strikes the victim] while on the way down, he is exiled; while on the way up, he is not exiled.[107] Thus, if תֵּרֵד, *you shall go down,* i.e., he killed while on the way down, then, you shall divide by three,[107a] i.e., the killer shall flee to a city of refuge.

5. {The Baal HaTurim's comment to וַאֲשֶׁר יָבֹא appears at *Numbers* 27:17.}

107. *Makkos* 7a-b. That is, if the inadvertent killer was, for example, on the downswing of his axe when the killing occurred, then he is subject to exile to one of the cities of refuge; but if, in this example, he was on the upswing, then he is not subject to exile. Similarly, if he was coming down a ladder and fell on his victim, thereby killing him, he would be subject to exile; but if he was ascending the ladder, he would not be subject to exile.

107a. Alternatively: The Baal HaTurim is explaining וְשִׁלַּשְׁתָּ as if it read וְשִׁלְשַׁלְתָּ, *you shall lower [as if] by chain* [as the Mishnah states: הָיָה מְשַׁלְשֵׁל בֶּחָבִית, *if he was lowering a cask* (*Makkos* 7a)]. If so, the comment reads, *if . . . he killed on the way down, then, "you shall go down,"* i.e., the killer shall flee . . . *(VeChur LaZahav).*

ח לֵאמֹר שָׁלֹשׁ עָרִים תַּבְדִּיל לָךְ: וְאִם־יַרְחִיב יהוה
אֱלֹהֶיךָ אֶת־גְּבֻלְךָ כַּאֲשֶׁר נִשְׁבַּע לַאֲבֹתֶיךָ וְנָתַן לְךָ
ט אֶת־כָּל־הָאָרֶץ אֲשֶׁר דִּבֶּר לָתֵת לַאֲבֹתֶיךָ: כִּי־תִשְׁמֹר
אֶת־כָּל־הַמִּצְוָה הַזֹּאת לַעֲשֹׂתָהּ אֲשֶׁר אָנֹכִי מְצַוְּךָ
הַיּוֹם לְאַהֲבָה אֶת־יהוה אֱלֹהֶיךָ וְלָלֶכֶת בִּדְרָכָיו
כָּל־הַיָּמִים וְיָסַפְתָּ לְךָ עוֹד שָׁלֹשׁ עָרִים עַל הַשָּׁלֹשׁ
י הָאֵלֶּה: וְלֹא יִשָּׁפֵךְ דָּם נָקִי בְּקֶרֶב אַרְצְךָ אֲשֶׁר יהוה
אֱלֹהֶיךָ נֹתֵן לְךָ נַחֲלָה וְהָיָה עָלֶיךָ דָּמִים:
יא וְכִי־יִהְיֶה אִישׁ שֹׂנֵא לְרֵעֵהוּ וְאָרַב לוֹ וְקָם עָלָיו
וְהִכָּהוּ נֶפֶשׁ וָמֵת וְנָס אֶל־אַחַת הֶעָרִים הָאֵל: וְשָׁלְחוּ
יב זִקְנֵי עִירוֹ וְלָקְחוּ אֹתוֹ מִשָּׁם וְנָתְנוּ אֹתוֹ בְּיַד גֹּאֵל
יג הַדָּם וָמֵת: לֹא־תָחוֹס עֵינְךָ עָלָיו וּבִעַרְתָּ דַם־הַנָּקִי
יד מִיִּשְׂרָאֵל וְטוֹב לָךְ: לֹא תַסִּיג גְּבוּל רֵעֲךָ

ששי

בעל הטורים

(יא) הֶעָרִים {הָאֵל}. לוֹמַר שֶׁחֲזָקוֹת הָיוּ וְעָרֵי מִבְצָר, שֶׁלֹּא יָבוֹא עֲלֵיהֶם גּוֹאֵל הַדָּם בְּחָיִל:

(יג־יד) מִיִּשְׂרָאֵל וְטוֹב לָךְ. לֹא תַסִּיג. דְּבַעֲוֹן מַסִּיג גְּבוּל נֶחֱרַב הַבַּיִת. "הוֹי מַגִּיעֵי בַיִת בְּבַיִת":

❑ סָמַךְ "לֹא תַסִּיג גְּבוּל רֵעֲךָ" לְרוֹצֵחַ. שֶׁלֹּא תֹאמַר, הוֹאִיל וּמֻתָּר לַהֲרֹג הָרוֹצֵחַ, אַסִּיג גְּבוּלוֹ שֶׁלֹּא יִהְיֶה מָמוֹנוֹ חָמוּר עָלָיו מִגּוּפוֹ:

❑ **לֹא תַסִּיג גְּבוּל.** אַזְהָרָה לְבֵית דִּין, שֶׁלֹּא יַחֲלִיפוּ אַחַת מֵעָרֵי מִקְלָט בְּעִיר אַחֶרֶת:

BAAL HATURIM ELUCIDATED

7. {The comment, s.v., שָׁלֹשׁ עָרִים, that appears in many editions at this verse, is presented at verse 11 below, s.v., הֶעָרִים הָאֵל.}

11. {הָאֵל} הֶעָרִים — {THESE} CITIES.[108] [The Torah uses the variant הָאֵל, *these,* rather than the more common הָאֵלֶּה][109] to indicate that [the cities of refuge] were strategically strong and well fortified, lest the redeemer of the blood pursue the killer with a band of soldiers.[110]

---

108. The text follows *Shoham Yakar's* manuscript edition. The early printed editions omit the word הָאֵל, *this.* Some later editions lost the prefix הָ־, and read עָרִים. Even later editions added the word שָׁלֹשׁ and attached the comment to the phrase שָׁלֹשׁ עָרִים in verse 7 or 9.

109. The Hebrew word for "these" is אֵלֶּה or הָאֵלֶּה and that is how it appears hundreds of times in the Torah. However, in eight verses the final ה is omitted and the word appears as הָאֵל. Thus, we find that the phrase "these cities" appears as הֶעָרִים הָאֵלֶּה in verse 5, but as הֶעָרִים הָאֵל in verse 11. Both the Talmud (*Bava Basra* 88b) and Midrash (*Bereishis Rabbah* 50:6) explain that the word אֵל can also mean *powerful,* as in אֵילֵי מוֹאָב, *the powers of Moab* (*Exodus* 15:15; see also *Ezekiel* 17:13), and that is how the Baal HaTurim's comment interprets the phrase הֶעָרִים הָאֵל, *the strong cities.*

110. The Baal HaTurim's source for this comment is not known. With regard to the permissibility of fortifying a city of refuge, see *Mishneh LaMelech, Hilchos Rotze'ach* 8:8 and *She'eilos Useshuvos*

saying: You shall separate three cities for yourselves.

⁸ *When* HASHEM *will broaden your boundary, as He swore to your forefathers, and He will give you the entire land that He spoke to your forefathers to give,* ⁹ *when you observe this entire commandment to perform it — which I command you today — to love* HASHEM, *your God, and to walk in His ways all the years, then you shall add three more cities to these three.* ¹⁰ *Innocent blood shall not be shed in the midst of your land that* HASHEM, *your God, gives as an inheritance, for then blood will be upon you.*

¹¹ *But if there will be a man who hates his fellow, and ambushes him and rises up against him, and strikes him mortally and he dies, and he flees to one of these cities —* ¹² *then the elders of his city shall send and take him from there and place him in the hand of the redeemer of the blood, and he shall die.* ¹³ *Your eye shall not pity him; you shall remove [those who spilled] the innocent one's blood from Israel; and it shall be good for you.*

¹⁴ *You shall not usurp your fellow's property, which*

─────────── BAAL HATURIM ELUCIDATED ───────────

13-14. מִיִּשְׂרָאֵל וְטוֹב לָךְ. לֹא תַסִּיג — FROM ISRAEL AND IT SHALL BE GOOD FOR YOU. YOU SHALL NOT USURP. [The juxtaposition of these verses indicates] that it is due to those who usurp property that the *Beis HaMikdash* was destroyed, [as it is written,] הוֹי מַגִּיעֵי בַיִת בְּבַיִת, *Woe [to] those who cause house to encroach against house* [111] (*Isaiah 5:8*). [112]

❏ The verse juxtaposed, לֹא תַסִּיג גְּבוּל רֵעֲךָ, *you shall not usurp your fellow's property,* [113] with the passage concerning a killer. This is to prevent one from saying, "Whereas it is permissible to put the killer to death, I shall usurp his property, in order that his property not be regarded more seriously than his life." [114]

❏ לֹא תַסִּיג גְּבוּל — [Literally,] YOU SHALL NOT MOVE A BOUNDARY. This is an admonition to the court not to exchange one of the cities of refuge for another city. [115]

Doveiv Meisharim, I, 45, cited by Shoham Yakar in the appendix.

111. The prophet states: הוֹי מַגִּיעֵי בַיִת בְּבַיִת, *Woe to those who cause house to encroach against house,* שָׂדֶה בְשָׂדֶה יַקְרִיבוּ, *who make field approach field . . .* בָּתִּים רַבִּים לְשַׁמָּה יִהְיוּ, *prestigious houses* [see *Radak*] *will be laid waste,* גְּדֹלִים וְטוֹבִים מֵאֵין יוֹשֵׁב, *great and splendid [houses] without [their legitimate] residents* (*Isaiah 5:8-9*). Thus, the destruction of the prestigious, great and splendid *Beis HaMikdash* can be traced to the transgression of usurping property from one's

neighbor (*VeChur LaZahav*).

Alternatively: The phrase הוֹי מַגִּיעֵי בַיִת בְּבַיִת may be understood as, *Woe to those who cause* [the sin of usurping someone else's] *house to encroach against* [God's] *House* and bring about its destruction (*VeChur LaZahav*).

112. *Peirush HaRokeach.*

113. Literally, *you shall not move back your fellow's boundary marker.*

114. *Peirush HaRokeach;* see *Bava Kamma 119a.*

115. See *Sifrei Zuta, parashas Masei.*

אֲשֶׁר גָּבְלוּ רִאשֹׁנִים בְּנַחֲלָתְךָ אֲשֶׁר תִּנְחַל בָּאָרֶץ
טו אֲשֶׁר יהוה אֱלֹהֶיךָ נֹתֵן לְךָ לְרִשְׁתָּהּ: לֹא־יָקוּם
עֵד אֶחָד בְּאִישׁ לְכָל־עָוֺן וּלְכָל־חַטָּאת בְּכָל־חֵטְא
אֲשֶׁר יֶחֱטָא עַל־פִּי ׀ שְׁנֵי עֵדִים אוֹ עַל־פִּי שְׁלֹשָׁה־
טז עֵדִים יָקוּם דָּבָר: כִּי־יָקוּם עֵד־חָמָס בְּאִישׁ לַעֲנוֹת
יז בּוֹ סָרָה: וְעָמְדוּ שְׁנֵי־הָאֲנָשִׁים אֲשֶׁר־לָהֶם הָרִיב

בעל הטורים

❑ **לְרִשְׁתָּהּ.** וּסְמִיךְ לֵהּ "לֹא יָקוּם עֵד אֶחָד בְּאִישׁ". שֶׁאֵינוֹ יָכוֹל לְהָעִיד, עַד כָּאן גְּבוּל תְּחוּמְךָ, וְהַיְנוּ מָמוֹן. "לְכָל עָוֺן", הַיְנוּ נְפָשׁוֹת. "וּלְכָל חַטָּאת", הַיְנוּ קָרְבָּן:

(טו) {**שְׁנֵי עֵדִים.**} לְמַעְלָה כְּתִיב "עַל פִּי שְׁנַיִם עֵדִים". דְּהָכָא אַיְרֵי בְּמָמוֹן, וְאֵין מְאַיְּמִין עֲלֵיהֶם כָּל כָּךְ כְּמוֹ בִנְפָשׁוֹת:

(יז) **הָרִיב.** ב׳ בַּמָּסוֹרֶת – "אֲשֶׁר לָהֶם הָרִיב"; "וְלִפְנֵי הִתְגַּלַּע הָרִיב נְטוֹשׁ". זֶהוּ שֶׁאָמְרוּ, מִשֶּׁבָּא לְפָנֶיךָ הַדִּין, וְאַתָּה יוֹדֵעַ לְהֵיכָן הַדִּין נוֹטֶה, אִי אַתָּה רַשַּׁאי לִבְצֹעַ. דְּמִשֶּׁעָמְדוּ "הָאֲנָשִׁים אֲשֶׁר לָהֶם הָרִיב . . . וְדָרְשׁוּ הַשֹּׁפְטִים וְכוּ׳" שֶׁיִּשְׁפְּטוּ בֵּינֵיהֶם. אֲבָל "לִפְנֵי הִתְגַּלַּע הָרִיב נְטוֹשׁ":

BAAL HATURIM ELUCIDATED

❑ **לְרִשְׁתָּהּ** — TO POSSESS IT. Juxtaposed to this is לֹא יָקוּם עֵד אֶחָד בְּאִישׁ, *One witness shall not stand up against a man* (v. 15). [This indicates] that [one witness] may not testify, "Until this point is the boundary of your property,"[116] i.e., [cases involving] monetary law;[117] *for any iniquity,* [teaches the same with regard to] cases involving capital punishment;[118] and *for any error,* refers to [questions involving] an Altar offering.[119]

15. {**שְׁנֵי עֵדִים — [BY THE TESTIMONY OF] TWO WITNESSES.**}[120] Earlier, it is written, עַל פִּי שְׁנַיִם עֵדִים, *by the testimony of two*[121] *witnesses* (17:6 above). For our verse speaks of cases involving monetary law, and witnesses in cases of monetary law are not warned with the same degree of severity regarding telling the truth as are witnesses in capital cases.[122]

---

116. Compare *Kesubos* 28a.

117. The *Sifrei* derives monetary law from לְכָל עָוֺן, *for any iniquity* (v. 15).

118. The *Sifrei* derives capital cases from לֹא יָקוּם עֵד אֶחָד בְּאִישׁ, *one witness shall not stand up against a man* (v. 15).

119. *Sifrei*; see *Kereisos* 11b.

120. The rubric enclosed in braces is absent from virtually all printed editions; it does appear, however, in *Shoham Yakar's* manuscript edition.

121. Despite the identical translation, the Hebrew verses differ. Whereas our verse uses שְׁנֵי for *two*, the earlier verse uses שְׁנַיִם. Generally, שְׁנַיִם is used when the number is not followed by a noun [e.g., שְׁנַיִם שְׁנַיִם בָּאוּ, *They came two by two* (*Genesis* 7:9); טוֹבִים הַשְּׁנַיִם מִן הָאֶחָד, *Two are better than one* (*Ecclesiastes* 4:9)]. The shorter form שְׁנֵי, however, is in the construct state and connects the number to the noun that appears immediately after it [e.g., לִשְׁנֵי הַמְּלָכִים הָאֵלֶּה, *to these two kings* (3:21 above); וּשְׁנֵי לוּחֹת הַבְּרִית, *and the two tablets of the covenant* (9:15 above)]. Thus, the expected form in our case would be שְׁנֵי עֵדִים, as it appears in our verse, or עֵדִים שְׁנַיִם, a usage that does not appear in the *Tanach* but is found in the Talmud (*Yerushalmi, Yevamos* 15:4). Accordingly, the Baal HaTurim explains the implication of the unusual phrase שְׁנַיִם עֵדִים that is used in 17:6 above.

122. See *Sanhedrin* 29a, 37a. However, it is not

the early ones marked out, in your inheritance that you shall inherit, in the land that HASHEM, your God, gives you to possess it.

¹⁵ *One witness shall not stand up against a man for any iniquity or for any error, regarding any sin that he may commit; by the testimony of two witnesses or by the testimony of three witnesses shall a matter be confirmed.* ¹⁶ *If a false witness stands against a man to speak up spuriously against him,* ¹⁷ *then the two men [and those] who have the quarrel*

— BAAL HATURIM ELUCIDATED —

17. הָרִיב — **THE QUARREL.** The masoretic note, ב׳, means that this word appears twice in the *Tanach*: (i) here, אֲשֶׁר לָהֶם הָרִיב, *[those] who have the quarrel;* and (ii) וְלִפְנֵי הִתְגַּלַּע הָרִיב נְטוֹשׁ, *and before it is revealed, abandon the quarrel* (*Proverbs* 17:14). This [similarity of expression] is what [the Sages meant when] they said: Once a case has come before you, and you know in which direction the law is leaning, you are not permitted to suggest a compromise.[123] For from the time that they, *the men who have the quarrel,* shall stand . . . *and the judges will inquire . . .,* then it is incumbent [on the court] to judge between them. But *before it*[124] *is revealed* [to the judges], [they may] *abandon the quarrel.*[125]

---

clear how the Baal HaTurim connects this practice to the superfluous ם of שְׁנַיִם.

The following halachic analysis sheds light on Baal HaTurim's comment: In capital cases, the witnesses must constitute a pair from the time of the deed about which they testify. However, if each of the two saw the act from a different vantage point and each was unaware of the other's presence (e.g., they observed the incident from different windows), they are not considered a pair of witnesses; rather, they are two individuals, and as such, their testimony cannot condemn the accused to death. In civil cases, on the other hand, the witnesses need not constitute a pair until they stand in testimony before the *beis din* [court]. This halachic difference accounts for the terminology of the two verses. The ending ־יִם often indicates a matched pair [thus, for example, the plural of יָד, *hand,* is יָדַיִם, *a pair of hands,* but when יָד is used in a borrowed form, such as for "handle" or "share," the plural is יָדוֹת (see *Genesis* 47:24; *Exodus* 26:17)]. Therefore, to indicate that there are different criteria regarding the two types of witness, the Torah refers to the capital witnesses as שְׁנַיִם, *a matched pair,* עֵדִים *[who are] witnesses,* but changes its wording regarding witnesses in a civil lawsuit where the minimum number of witnesses is two, but they need not be an established pair, rather, it is sufficient if they are merely שְׁנֵי עֵדִים, *two wit-*

nesses (*Maharil Diskin* cited in *Shaarei Aharon*).

123. *Sanhedrin* 6b — The Talmud there records a dispute regarding the propriety of judges arbitrating a compromise rather than deciding a civil case according to the strict dictates of the law. According to the opinion which is accepted as *halachah,* such arbitration is considered a meritorious deed. This view is derived from the verse, אֱמֶת וּמִשְׁפַּט שָׁלוֹם שִׁפְטוּ, *With truth and judgment of peace shall you judge* (*Zechariah* 8:16), by the following reasoning: Where there is judgment [i.e., where the judge decides a case by the letter of the law], there is no peace [for the losing party feels that he was wronged]; and where there is peace [i.e., both sides agree], there is no judgment [i.e., they will not appear in court for judgment]. What then does the verse mean by *judgment of peace?* It must refer to compromise which is acceptable to both parties and thereby fosters peace. If so, the verse teaches that compromise is a legitimate method of settling cases of civil law. Moreover, the prophet advocates compromise.

See also *Sanhedrin* 32b, where the Talmud discusses the guidelines for arbitrating compromises. The Baal HaTurim's other comments regarding arbitration appear at *Exodus* 21:1.

124. That is, the applicable law. Alternatively, the arguments of litigants.

125. That is, suggest a compromise.

לִפְנֵ֣י יְהוָ֑ה לִפְנֵ֤י הַכֹּֽהֲנִים֙ וְהַשֹּׁ֣פְטִ֔ים אֲשֶׁ֥ר יִהְי֖וּ
יח בַּיָּמִ֥ים הָהֵֽם׃ וְדָרְשׁ֥וּ הַשֹּׁפְטִ֖ים הֵיטֵ֑ב וְהִנֵּ֤ה עֵֽד־
יט שֶׁ֙קֶר֙ הָעֵ֔ד שֶׁ֖קֶר עָנָ֥ה בְאָחִֽיו׃ וַעֲשִׂ֣יתֶם ל֔וֹ כַּאֲשֶׁ֥ר
זָמַ֖ם לַעֲשׂ֣וֹת לְאָחִ֑יו וּבִֽעַרְתָּ֥ הָרָ֖ע מִקִּרְבֶּֽךָ׃
כ וְהַנִּשְׁאָרִ֖ים יִשְׁמְע֣וּ וְיִרָ֑אוּ וְלֹֽא־יֹסִ֨פוּ לַעֲשׂ֜וֹת
כא ע֗וֹד כַּדָּבָ֥ר הָרָ֛ע הַזֶּ֖ה בְּקִרְבֶּֽךָ׃ וְלֹ֥א תָח֖וֹס עֵינֶ֑ךָ
נֶ֣פֶשׁ בְּנֶ֗פֶשׁ עַ֤יִן בְּעַ֙יִן֙ שֵׁ֣ן בְּשֵׁ֔ן יָ֥ד בְּיָ֖ד רֶ֥גֶל
כ א בְּרָֽגֶל׃ כִּֽי־תֵצֵ֨א לַמִּלְחָמָ֜ה עַל־אֹיְבֶ֗ךָ וְרָאִ֜יתָ
ס֤וּס וָרֶ֙כֶב֙ עַ֚ם רַ֣ב מִמְּךָ֔ לֹ֥א תִירָ֖א מֵהֶ֑ם כִּֽי־יְהוָ֤ה
ב אֱלֹהֶ֙יךָ֙ עִמָּ֔ךְ הַמַּֽעַלְךָ֖ מֵאֶ֥רֶץ מִצְרָֽיִם׃ וְהָיָ֕ה
כְּקָֽרָבְכֶ֖ם אֶל־הַמִּלְחָמָ֑ה וְנִגַּ֥שׁ הַכֹּהֵ֖ן וְדִבֶּ֥ר אֶל־
ג הָעָֽם׃ וְאָמַ֤ר אֲלֵהֶם֙ שְׁמַ֣ע יִשְׂרָאֵ֔ל אַתֶּ֨ם קְרֵבִ֥ים
הַיּ֛וֹם לַמִּלְחָמָ֖ה עַל־אֹיְבֵיכֶ֑ם אַל־יֵרַ֣ךְ לְבַבְכֶ֗ם אַל־
ד תִּֽירְא֧וּ וְאַל־תַּחְפְּז֛וּ וְאַל־תַּעַרְצ֖וּ מִפְּנֵיהֶֽם׃ כִּ֚י יְהוָ֣ה
אֱלֹהֵיכֶ֔ם הַהֹלֵ֖ךְ עִמָּכֶ֑ם לְהִלָּחֵ֥ם לָכֶ֛ם עִם־אֹיְבֵיכֶ֖ם
ה לְהוֹשִׁ֥יעַ אֶתְכֶֽם׃ וְדִבְּר֣וּ הַשֹּֽׁטְרִים֮ אֶל־הָעָ֣ם לֵאמֹר֒
מִֽי־הָאִ֞ישׁ אֲשֶׁ֨ר בָּנָ֤ה בַֽיִת־חָדָשׁ֙ וְלֹ֣א חֲנָכ֔וֹ יֵלֵ֖ךְ
וְיָשֹׁ֣ב לְבֵית֑וֹ פֶּן־יָמוּת֙ בַּמִּלְחָמָ֔ה וְאִ֥ישׁ אַחֵ֖ר
ו יַחְנְכֶֽנּוּ׃ וּמִֽי־הָאִ֞ישׁ אֲשֶׁ֨ר נָטַ֥ע כֶּ֙רֶם֙ וְלֹ֣א חִלְּל֔וֹ יֵלֵ֖ךְ
וְיָשֹׁ֣ב לְבֵית֑וֹ פֶּן־יָמוּת֙ בַּמִּלְחָמָ֔ה וְאִ֥ישׁ אַחֵ֖ר
ז יְחַלְּלֶֽנּוּ׃ וּמִֽי־הָאִ֞ישׁ אֲשֶׁ֨ר אֵרַ֤שׂ אִשָּׁה֙ וְלֹ֣א לְקָחָ֔הּ
יֵלֵ֖ךְ וְיָשֹׁ֣ב לְבֵית֑וֹ פֶּן־יָמוּת֙ בַּמִּלְחָמָ֔ה וְאִ֥ישׁ אַחֵ֖ר
ח יִקָּחֶֽנָּה׃ וְיָסְפ֣וּ הַשֹּׁטְרִים֮ לְדַבֵּ֣ר אֶל־הָעָם֒ וְאָמְר֔וּ

בעל הטורים

(כא) יָד בְּיָד רֶגֶל בְּרָגֶל. וּסְמִיךְ לֵהּ "כִּי תֵצֵא לַמִּלְחָמָה". לוֹמַר, מְחֻסְּרֵי אֵבֶר אֵין יוֹצְאִין לַמִּלְחָמָה:

BAAL HATURIM ELUCIDATED

21. {The Baal HaTurim's comment to עַיִן בְּעַיִן appears at *Numbers* 14:14.}

❑ **יָד בְּיָד רֶגֶל בְּרָגֶל** — HAND FOR HAND, FOOT FOR FOOT. Juxtaposed to this is כִּי תֵצֵא לַמִּלְחָמָה, *when you will go out to war* (20:1). This is to indicate that men who are

shall stand before HASHEM, *before the Kohanim and the*
judges who will be in those days. [18] *The judges shall inquire*
thoroughly, and behold! the testimony was false testimony;
he testified falsely against his fellow. [19] *You shall do to him as*
he conspired to do to his fellow, and you shall destroy the evil
from your midst. [20] *And those who remain shall hearken and*
fear; and they shall not continue again to do such an evil
thing in your midst. [21] *Your eye shall not pity; life for life, eye*
for eye, tooth for tooth, hand for hand, foot for foot.

20 [1] *When you will go forth to war against your enemy, and you*
see horse and chariot — a people more numerous than you
— you shall not fear them, for HASHEM, *your God, is with*
you, Who brought you up from the land of Egypt. [2] *It shall be*
that when you draw near to the war, the Kohen shall
approach and speak to the people.

[3] *He shall say to them, "Hear, O Israel, you are coming*
near to the battle against your enemies; let your heart not be
faint; do not be afraid, do not panic, and do not be broken
before them. [4] *For* HASHEM, *your God, is the One Who goes*
with you, to fight for you against your enemies, to save you."

[5] *Then the officers shall speak to the people, saying, "Who*
is the man who has built a new house and has not
inaugurated it? Let him go and return to his house, lest he die
in the war and another man will inaugurate it. [6] *And who is*
the man who has planted a vineyard and not redeemed it?
Let him go and return to his house, lest he die in the war and
another man will redeem it. [7] *And who is the man who has*
betrothed a woman and not married her? Let him go and
return to his house, lest he die in the war and another man
will marry her."

[8] *The officers shall continue speaking to the people and say,*

BAAL HATURIM ELUCIDATED

lacking a limb do not go forth to battle.[126]

XX.

1. {The Baal HaTurim's comment to עַל אֹיִבְךָ appears at 21:10 below; see note 9 there.}

2. {The Baal HaTurim's comment to וְנִגַּשׁ appears at *Exodus* 24:2.}

126. *Sifrei,* cited by *Rashi* to 20:1.

מִֽי־הָאִ֤ישׁ הַיָּרֵא֙ וְרַ֣ךְ הַלֵּבָ֔ב יֵלֵ֖ךְ וְיָשֹׁ֣ב לְבֵית֑וֹ כ/ט־כ
ט וְלֹ֥א יִמַּ֛ס אֶת־לְבַ֥ב אֶחָ֖יו כִּלְבָבֽוֹ׃ וְהָיָ֛ה כְּכַלֹּ֥ת
הַשֹּׁטְרִ֖ים לְדַבֵּ֣ר אֶל־הָעָ֑ם וּפָֽקְד֛וּ שָׂרֵ֥י צְבָא֖וֹת
י בְּרֹ֥אשׁ הָעָֽם׃ כִּֽי־תִקְרַ֣ב אֶל־עִ֔יר לְהִלָּחֵ֖ם שביעי
יא עָלֶ֑יהָ וְקָרָ֥אתָ אֵלֶ֖יהָ לְשָׁלֽוֹם׃ וְהָיָה֙ אִם־שָׁל֣וֹם
תַּֽעַנְךָ֔ וּפָתְחָ֖ה לָ֑ךְ וְהָיָ֞ה כָּל־הָעָ֣ם הַנִּמְצָא־בָ֗הּ יִהְי֥וּ
יב לְךָ֛ לָמַ֖ס וַעֲבָדֽוּךָ׃ וְאִם־לֹ֤א תַשְׁלִים֙ עִמָּ֔ךְ וְעָשְׂתָ֥ה
יג עִמְּךָ֖ מִלְחָמָ֑ה וְצַרְתָּ֖ עָלֶֽיהָ׃ וּנְתָנָ֛הּ יהוָ֥ה אֱלֹהֶ֖יךָ
יד בְּיָדֶ֑ךָ וְהִכִּיתָ֥ אֶת־כָּל־זְכוּרָ֖הּ לְפִי־חָֽרֶב׃ רַ֣ק הַ֠נָּשִׁים
וְהַטַּ֨ף וְהַבְּהֵמָ֜ה וְכֹל֩ אֲשֶׁ֨ר יִהְיֶ֥ה בָעִ֛יר כָּל־שְׁלָלָ֖הּ
תָּבֹ֣ז לָ֑ךְ וְאָכַלְתָּ֙ אֶת־שְׁלַ֣ל אֹיְבֶ֔יךָ אֲשֶׁ֥ר נָתַ֛ן יהוָ֥ה
טו אֱלֹהֶ֖יךָ לָֽךְ׃ כֵּ֤ן תַּעֲשֶׂה֙ לְכָל־הֶ֣עָרִ֔ים הָרְחֹקֹ֥ת מִמְּךָ֖
טז מְאֹ֑ד אֲשֶׁ֛ר לֹא־מֵעָרֵ֥י הַגּֽוֹיִם־הָאֵ֖לֶּה הֵֽנָּה׃ רַ֗ק מֵעָרֵ֤י
הָֽעַמִּים֙ הָאֵ֔לֶּה אֲשֶׁר֙ יהוָ֣ה אֱלֹהֶ֔יךָ נֹתֵ֥ן לְךָ֖ נַחֲלָ֑ה
יז לֹ֥א תְחַיֶּ֖ה כָּל־נְשָׁמָֽה׃ כִּֽי־הַחֲרֵ֣ם תַּחֲרִימֵ֗ם הַֽחִתִּ֤י
וְהָֽאֱמֹרִי֙ הַכְּנַעֲנִ֣י וְהַפְּרִזִּ֔י הַחִוִּ֖י וְהַיְבוּסִ֑י כַּאֲשֶׁ֥ר
יח צִוְּךָ֖ יהוָ֥ה אֱלֹהֶֽיךָ׃ לְמַ֗עַן אֲשֶׁ֤ר לֹֽא־יְלַמְּד֤וּ אֶתְכֶם֙
לַעֲשׂ֔וֹת כְּכֹל֙ תּֽוֹעֲבֹתָ֔ם אֲשֶׁ֥ר עָשׂ֖וּ לֵאלֹהֵיהֶ֑ם
יט וַחֲטָאתֶ֖ם לַיהוָ֥ה אֱלֹהֵיכֶֽם׃ כִּֽי־תָצ֣וּר
אֶל־עִיר֩ יָמִ֨ים רַבִּ֜ים לְהִלָּחֵ֧ם עָלֶ֣יהָ לְתָפְשָׂ֗הּ
לֹֽא־תַשְׁחִ֤ית אֶת־עֵצָהּ֙ לִנְדֹּ֤חַ עָלָיו֙ גַּרְזֶ֔ן כִּ֚י מִמֶּ֣נּוּ
תֹאכֵ֔ל וְאֹת֖וֹ לֹ֣א תִכְרֹ֑ת כִּ֤י הָֽאָדָם֙ עֵ֣ץ הַשָּׂדֶ֔ה
כ לָבֹ֥א מִפָּנֶ֖יךָ בַּמָּצֽוֹר׃ רַ֞ק עֵ֣ץ אֲשֶׁר־תֵּדַ֗ע כִּ֣י
לֹא־עֵ֤ץ מַאֲכָל֙ ה֔וּא אֹת֥וֹ תַשְׁחִ֖ית וְכָרָ֑תָּ וּבָנִ֣יתָ

בעל הטורים

כ (ח) הַיָּרֵא. ב׳ בַּמָּסוֹרֶת — ״הַיָּרֵא וְרַךְ הַלֵּבָב״; ״הַיָּרֵא אֶת דְּבַר ה׳ ״. וְזֶהוּ שֶׁאָמְרוּ, הַיָּרֵא מֵעֲבֵרוֹת שֶׁבְּיָדוֹ, כִּדְכְתִיב ״הַיָּרֵא אֶת דְּבַר ה׳ ״:

BAAL HATURIM ELUCIDATED

8. הַיָּרֵא — [THE MAN] WHO IS FEARFUL. The masoretic note, ב׳, means that this word appears twice in the *Tanach*: (i) here, הַיָּרֵא וְרַךְ הַלֵּבָב, *[the man] who is fearful or faint of heart;* and (ii) הַיָּרֵא אֶת דְּבַר ה׳, *the one who feared the word of* HASHEM (*Exodus* 9:20). This reflects what the Sages have said, [our verse refers to] the

"Who is the man who is fearful or faint of heart? Let him go and return to his house, and let him not melt the heart of his fellows, like his heart." ⁹ *When the officers have finished speaking to the people, the leaders of the legions shall take command at the head of the people.*

¹⁰ *When you draw near to a city to wage war against it, you shall call out to it for peace.* ¹¹ *It shall be that if it responds to you in peace and opens for you, then the entire people found within it shall be as tribute for you, and they shall serve you.* ¹² *But if it does not make peace with you, but makes war with you, you shall besiege it.* ¹³ HASHEM *shall deliver it into your hand, and you shall smite all its males by the blade of the sword.* ¹⁴ *Only the women, the youngsters, the animals, and everything that will be in the city — all its booty — may you plunder for yourselves; you shall eat the booty of your enemies, which* HASHEM, *your God, gave you.* ¹⁵ *So shall you do to all the cities that are very distant from you, which are not of the cities of these nations.* ¹⁶ *But from the cities of these peoples that* HASHEM, *your God, gives you as an inheritance, you shall not allow any person to live.* ¹⁷ *Rather you shall utterly destroy them: the Hittite, the Amorite, the Canaanite, the Perizzite, the Hivvite, and the Jebusite, as* HASHEM, *your God, has commanded you,* ¹⁸ *so that they will not teach you to act according to all their abominations that they performed for their gods, so that you will sin to* HASHEM, *your God.*

¹⁹ *When you besiege a city for many days to wage war against it to seize it, do not destroy its trees by swinging an axe against them, for from it you will eat, and you shall not cut it down; is the tree of the field a man that it should enter the siege before you?* ²⁰ *Only a tree that you know is not a food tree, it you may destroy and cut down, and build a*

──────── BAAL HATURIM ELUCIDATED ────────

one who is fearful because of the sins he had committed, as is written, *the one who feared the word of* HASHEM.¹²⁷

16. {The Baal HaTurim's comments to לֹא תְחַיֶּה appear at *Exodus* 22:17 and *Deuteronomy* 2:24.}

---

127. *R' Yehudah HaChassid;* see *Sotah* 44a, cited by *Rashi.* Here, the Baal HaTurim uses that verse to explain this one; there, he uses this verse to explain that one.

מָצוֹר עַל־הָעִיר אֲשֶׁר־הִוא עֹשָׂה עִמְּךָ מִלְחָמָה עַד
רִדְתָּהּ׃

כא
א כִּי־יִמָּצֵא חָלָל בָּאֲדָמָה אֲשֶׁר יְהוָה אֱלֹהֶיךָ נֹתֵן לְךָ
ב לְרִשְׁתָּהּ נֹפֵל בַּשָּׂדֶה לֹא נוֹדַע מִי הִכָּהוּ׃ וְיָצְאוּ זְקֵנֶיךָ
וְשֹׁפְטֶיךָ וּמָדְדוּ אֶל־הֶעָרִים אֲשֶׁר סְבִיבֹת הֶחָלָל׃
ג וְהָיָה הָעִיר הַקְּרֹבָה אֶל־הֶחָלָל וְלָקְחוּ זִקְנֵי הָעִיר
הַהִוא עֶגְלַת בָּקָר אֲשֶׁר לֹא־עֻבַּד בָּהּ אֲשֶׁר לֹא־
ד מָשְׁכָה בְּעֹל׃ וְהוֹרִדוּ זִקְנֵי הָעִיר הַהִוא אֶת־הָעֶגְלָה
אֶל־נַחַל אֵיתָן אֲשֶׁר לֹא־יֵעָבֵד בּוֹ וְלֹא יִזָּרֵעַ

בעל הטורים

(כ) **מִלְחָמָה עַד רִדְתָּהּ.** בְּגִימַטְרִיָּא זֶה הוּא אַף שַׁבָּת:

כא (א) **כִּי יִמָּצֵא חָלָל.** סָמַךְ לְפָרָשַׁת מִלְחָמָה. שֶׁבִּשְׁעַת מִלְחָמָה דֶּרֶךְ לִמְצֹא חֲלָלִים:

❑ **בָּאֲדָמָה.** בְּגִימַטְרִיָּא בְּגָלוּי:

(ב) **וּמָדְדוּ.** ב׳ בַּמָּסוֹרֶת – ״וּמָדְדוּ אֶל הֶעָרִים״; ״וּמָדְדוּ אֶת תָּכְנִית״. שֶׁמּוֹדְדִין מֵרֹאשׁוֹ, שֶׁהוּא עִקַּר תְּכוּנַת הָאָדָם:

❑ **אֲשֶׁר.** אוֹתִיּוֹת רֹאשׁ. שֶׁמּוֹדְדִין מֵרֹאשׁוֹ. ״אֲשֶׁר סְבִיבֹת הֶחָלָל״ בְּגִימַטְרִיָּא בְּרֹאשׁוֹ שֶׁל הָרוּג:

(ג־ד) **לֹא עֻבַּד בָּהּ . . . לֹא מָשְׁכָה בְּעֹל . . . לֹא יֵעָבֵד . . . וְלֹא יִזָּרֵעַ.** הֲרֵי אַרְבַּע מִצְוֹת, לְכַפֵּר עַל אַרְבַּע רוּחוֹת הָעוֹלָם. וְכֵן אַרְבַּע פְּעָמִים ״חָלָל״ וְאַרְבַּע פְּעָמִים ״עֶגְלָה״ בַּפָּרָשָׁה:

BAAL HATURIM ELUCIDATED

20. מִלְחָמָה עַד רִדְתָּהּ — WAR UNTIL IT IS CONQUERED. The *gematria* of this phrase (806) is equivalent[128] to that of זֶה הוּא אַף שַׁבָּת, *This [applies] even on the Sabbath.*[129]

XXI.

1. כִּי יִמָּצֵא חָלָל — IF A CORPSE WILL BE FOUND. This phrase is juxtaposed to the passage regarding war,[129a] for at a time of war, it is common to discover corpses.[130]

❑ **בָּאֲדָמָה — ON THE LAND.** The *gematria* of this word (52) is equivalent[131] to that of בְּגָלוּי, *in the open.*[132]

2. וּמָדְדוּ — AND THEY SHALL MEASURE. The masoretic note, ב׳, means that this

128. The principle of *im hakollel* allows 806 to be considered equivalent to 807, the *gematria* of the Baal HaTurim's phrase.

129. *Peirush HaRokeach;* see *Shabbos* 19a — The Talmud there derives from the phrase עַד רִדְתָּהּ, *until it is conquered,* that an army may continue its siege, even on the Sabbath. The siege need not be ended until the enemy has been totally vanquished (see the Baal HaTurim to *Exodus* 31:13).

129a. This comment seems to be an abridged version of the Baal HaTurim's comment to 21:10 below.

130. The parallel comment in *Peirush HaRokeach* reads: For at a time of war, a man meets his enemy and murders him.

131. The principle of *im hakollel* allows 51, the *gematria* of the Baal HaTurim's term, to be considered equivalent to 52.

132. *Peirush HaRokeach;* see *Sotah* 44b — The Talmud there expounds on the word בָּאֲדָמָה, *on the ground*: This means that the corpse is *on the ground,* not buried in or under a heap.

bulwark against the city that makes war with you, until it is conquered.

21 [1] *If a corpse will be found on the ground that HASHEM, your God, gives you to possess it, fallen in the field, it was not known who smote him,* [2] *your elders and judges shall go out and they shall measure to the cities that are around the corpse.* [3] *It shall be that the city nearest the corpse, the elders of that city shall take a she-calf of the cattle, one with which no work has been done, one that has not pulled with a yoke.* [4] *The elders of that city shall bring the she-calf down to a harsh valley, one that cannot be worked and cannot be sown,*

BAAL HATURIM ELUCIDATED

word appears twice in the *Tanach*: (i) here, **וּמָדְדוּ אֶל הֶעָרִים**, *and they shall measure to the cities;* and (ii) **וּמָדְדוּ אֶת תָּכְנִית**, *and let them calculate the design* (*Ezekiel* 43:10). [This alludes to the law] that we measure the distance [from the corpse to the cities] from its head, for it is the prime feature of a person.[133]

❑ **אֲשֶׁר** — THAT ARE. This word is spelled with the same letters as the word **ראש**, *head,* [another allusion] that we measure from the head.[134] Indeed, the *gematria* of the phrase **אֲשֶׁר סְבִיבֹת הֶחָלָל**, *that are around the corpse* (1048), is equivalent[135] to that of **בְּרֹאשׁוֹ שֶׁל הָרוּג**, *at the head of the slain man.*

3-4. לֹא עֻבַּד בָּהּ . . . לֹא מָשְׁכָה בְּעֹל . . . לֹא יֵעָבֵד . . . וְלֹא יִזָּרֵעַ — [ONE WITH WHICH] NO WORK HAS BEEN DONE, [ONE THAT] HAS NOT PULLED WITH A YOKE . . . [ONE THAT] CANNOT BE WORKED AND CANNOT BE SOWN. [The Torah mentions] four prohibitions, in order to bring atonement upon the four sides (i.e., directions) of the world.[136] Similarly, the word **חָלָל**, *corpse,* appears four times[137] and the term **עֶגְלָה**, *calf,* appears four times[138] in this passage.[139]

133. *Sotah* 45b — The Talmud cites two views regarding from which part of the corpse the measurement should be made: the navel or the nose. The Baal HaTurim's allusion supports the latter opinion.

134. *Peirush HaRokeach.* See note 133.

135. The *gematria* of the Baal HaTurim's phrase is 1053, five more than that of the Scriptural phrase. Although the verse uses the defective spelling סְבִיבֹת, without a ו (= 6), for the sake of the allusion, the Baal HaTurim uses the full spelling סְבִיבוֹת (as it is spelled in *Numbers* 11:31-32). The *gematria* is then 1054 and the principle of *im hakollel* allows 1053, the *gematria* of the Baal HaTurim's phrase, to be considered equivalent to 1054.

136. *Peirush HaRokeach*; see *Makkos* 11a. The connection between the four verbs and the four directions is unclear.

Nevertheless, it is noteworthy that the *gematria* of לֹא עֻבַּד בָּהּ . . . לֹא מָשְׁכָה בְּעֹל . . . לֹא יֵעָבֵד בּוֹ וְלֹא יִזָּרֵעַ is 1061, equal to that of מִזְרָח וּמַעֲרָב וְצָפוֹן וְדָרוֹם, *east and west and north and south (VeChur LaZahav).*

137. The first time, in verse 1 without any prefix; the other three times, הֶחָלָל, with the definite article prefix -הָ (vv. 2,3 and 6).

138. The first time, עֶגְלַת בָּקָר, *a she-calf of the cattle* (v. 3); the other three times, הָעֶגְלָה, with the definite article prefix -הָ (vv. 4 [twice] and 6). It is noteworthy that the *gematria* of עֶגְלַת בָּקָר (805) plus that of three times הָעֶגְלָה (113 x 3 = 339) is 1144, which is equal to the *gematria* of the Baal HaTurim's phrase עַל אַרְבַּע רוּחוֹת הָעוֹלָם, *upon the four sides of the world (VeChur LaZahav).*

In his comments at *Genesis* 45:27, the Baal HaTurim offers a different explanation for the fourfold appearance of עֶגְלָה in our passage.

139. *Peirush HaRokeach,* who adds the fourfold appearance of the word דָּם, *blood*: three times

ה וְעָרְפוּ־שָׁם אֶת־הָעֶגְלָה בַּנָּחַל: וְנִגְּשׁוּ הַכֹּהֲנִים בְּנֵי
לֵוִי כִּי בָם בָּחַר יהוה אֱלֹהֶיךָ לְשָׁרְתוֹ וּלְבָרֵךְ בְּשֵׁם
ו יהוה וְעַל־פִּיהֶם יִהְיֶה כָּל־רִיב וְכָל־נָגַע: וְכֹל זִקְנֵי
הָעִיר הַהִוא הַקְּרֹבִים אֶל־הֶחָלָל יִרְחֲצוּ אֶת־
ז יְדֵיהֶם עַל־הָעֶגְלָה הָעֲרוּפָה בַנָּחַל: וְעָנוּ וְאָמְרוּ (מפטיר)
יָדֵינוּ לֹא °שפכה אֶת־הַדָּם הַזֶּה וְעֵינֵינוּ לֹא רָאוּ: [°שָׁפְכוּ ק׳]
ח כַּפֵּר לְעַמְּךָ יִשְׂרָאֵל אֲשֶׁר־פָּדִיתָ יהוה וְאַל־תִּתֵּן
דָּם נָקִי בְּקֶרֶב עַמְּךָ יִשְׂרָאֵל וְנִכַּפֵּר לָהֶם הַדָּם:
ט וְאַתָּה תְּבַעֵר הַדָּם הַנָּקִי מִקִּרְבֶּךָ כִּי־תַעֲשֶׂה הַיָּשָׁר
בְּעֵינֵי יהוה: ססס צ״ז פסוקים. סלו״א סימן.

בעל הטורים

(ז) לֹא שָׁפְכָה. כְּתִיב בְּהֵ״א, שֶׁלֹּא נָגַעְנוּ בוֹ בְּה׳ אֶצְבְּעוֹתֵינוּ:

וְעוֹד – כִּי הַנֶּפֶשׁ יֵשׁ לָהּ ה׳ שֵׁמוֹת. וְלָכֵן נָתַן דָּוִד לְיוֹאָב ה׳ קְלָלוֹת כְּשֶׁהָרַג לְאַבְנֵר – ״זָב וּמְצֹרָע וּמַחֲזִיק בַּפֶּלֶךְ וְנֹפֵל בַּחֶרֶב וַחֲסַר לָחֶם״:

(ח) כַּפֵּר לְעַמְּךָ יִשְׂרָאֵל. מִכָּאן שֶׁכָּל יִשְׂרָאֵל עֲרֵבִין זֶה לָזֶה:

❑ **כַּפֵּר לְעַמְּךָ יִשְׂרָאֵל אֲשֶׁר פָּדִיתָ.** רָאשֵׁי תֵבוֹת בְּגִימַטְרִיָּא זֶה הַכֹּהֲנִים:

BAAL HATURIM ELUCIDATED

4. {The Baal HaTurim's comment to וְעָרְפוּ appears at 32:2 below.}

6. {The Baal HaTurim's comment to וְכֹל זִקְנֵי appears at *Genesis* 50:7.}

7. לֹא שָׁפְכָה — HAVE NOT SPILLED. This term is spelled with a [140]ה (= 5) [indicating that the elders said,] "We did not touch him with [any of] our five fingers."[141]

Additionally: [It is spelled with a ה to allude to the dead man's soul,] for the soul has five names.[142] And therefore David pronounced five curses against

---

with the definite article prefix ־הַ (vv. 7,8,9) and once without a prefix (v. 8).

140. This word is an example of a קְרִי וּכְתִיב, *keri uchesiv.* The *kesiv* (spelling) of the words is שפכה, as if it were vowelized שָׁפְכָה, *she spilled,* while the *keri* (pronunciation) is שָׁפְכוּ, *they spilled* (as in *Leviticus* 14:41).

141. *R' Yehudah HaChassid.*

142. *R' Yehudah HaChassid.* The Midrash (*Bereishis Rabbah* 14:9) lists the five names as, נֶפֶשׁ רוּחַ נְשָׁמָה יְחִידָה חַיָּה, adducing Scriptural verses that use these terms and discussing the reasons for and implications of each name. The Baal HaTurim also speaks of the five names for the soul

and they shall decapitate the calf in the valley. ⁵ The Kohanim, the offspring of Levi, shall approach, for them has HASHEM, your God, chosen to minister to Him and to bless with the Name of HASHEM, and according to their word shall be every quarrel and every plague.

⁶ All the elders of that city, who are closest to the corpse, shall wash their hands over the she-calf that was decapitated in the valley. ⁷ They shall speak up and say, "Our hands have not spilled this blood, and our eyes did not see. ⁸ Atone for Your people Israel that You have redeemed, O HASHEM: Do not place innocent blood in the midst of Your people Israel!" Then the blood shall be atoned for them.

⁹ But you shall remove [those who spilled] the innocent one's blood from your midst when you do what is upright in the eyes of HASHEM.

─────── BAAL HATURIM ELUCIDATED ───────

Joab when he murdered Abner: זָב וּמְצֹרָע וּמַחֲזִיק בַּפֶּלֶךְ וְנֹפֵל בַּחֶרֶב וַחֲסַר לָחֶם [May there never cease from Joab's house [men who can be characterized as] (i) zav, [142a] (ii) metzora, [142b] (iii) crippled, [142c] (iv) felled by the sword and (v) lacking food (II Samuel 3:29).

❏ {The Baal HaTurim's further comment to verse 7 appears at Genesis 37:14.}

8. כַּפֵּר לְעַמְּךָ יִשְׂרָאֵל — ATONE FOR YOUR PEOPLE ISRAEL. This teaches that all Israel are guarantors for one another. [143]

❏ כַּפֵּר לְעַמְּךָ יִשְׂרָאֵל אֲשֶׁר פָּדִיתָ — ATONE FOR YOUR PEOPLE ISRAEL THAT YOU HAVE REDEEMED. The gematria of the initial letters of these words (141) is equivalent [144] to that of זֶה הַכֹּהֲנִים, This [is said by] the Kohanim. [145]

in his comments to Exodus 29:40; Leviticus 16:14, s.v., וְחָמֵשׁ טְבִילוֹת; Leviticus 23:27; and Numbers 35:8.

142a. See Leviticus, 15:1-15.

142b. See Leviticus Chs. 13-14.

142c. Literally, one who clutches a crutch.

143. See the Baal HaTurim to 21:21 below, with note 57. We would expect them to have said, "Do not place innocent blood in the midst of this city." The implication of, in the midst of Your people Israel, is that all Israel are responsible for one another (Peirush HaRokeach).

144. The principle of im hakollel allows 141 to be considered equivalent to 142, the gematria of the Baal HaTurim's phrase.

145. See Sotah 46a; see also Rashi and Targum Onkelos.

פרשת כי תצא ﴾

Parashas Ki Seitzei

י כִּי־תֵצֵא לַמִּלְחָמָה עַל־אֹיְבֶיךָ וּנְתָנוֹ יהוה

—————————— בעל הטורים ——————————

כא (י) כִּי תֵצֵא. לָמָּה כְתִיב פָּרָשַׁת עֶגְלָה עֲרוּפָה בֵּין שְׁתֵּי מִלְחָמוֹת? הִקְדִּים לָהּ מִלְחָמָה, שֶׁאִם יֹאמַר הַשּׂוֹנֵא, אֶהֱרֹג כִּי עֵת מִלְחָמָה, וְיֹאמְרוּ, הָאוֹיְבִים הֲרָגוּהוּ בַּמִּלְחָמָה. וּכְתִיב מִלְחָמָה אַחֲרֶיהָ, לוֹמַר, תְּבַעֵר דָּם הַנָּקִי לַהֲרֹג אֶת הָרוֹצֵחַ, וְאַחַר כָּךְ תֵּלֵךְ בַּמִּלְחָמָה וּתְנֻצֵּחַ. וְלֹא הָיוּ מַנִּיחִים לֵילֵךְ שׂוֹנְאִים בַּמִּלְחָמָה יַחַד, שֶׁמָּא יַהַרְגוּ זֶה לָזֶה בַּמִּלְחָמָה:

❏ ״כִּי תַעֲשֶׂה הַיָּשָׁר...״ וּסְמִיךְ לֵהּ ״כִּי תֵצֵא לַמִּלְחָמָה״. שֶׁאֵין יוֹצְאִין לַמִּלְחָמָה אֶלָּא צַדִּיקִים:

❏ ״ה׳ ״. וּסְמִיךְ לֵהּ ״כִּי תֵצֵא לַמִּלְחָמָה״. לוֹמַר שֶׁהַשֵּׁם יוֹצֵא עִמְּךָ, כָּעִנְיָן שֶׁנֶּאֱמַר ״וְיָצָא ה׳ וְנִלְחַם בַּגּוֹיִם״:

❏ **כִּי תֵצֵא.** צֵא אֲלֵיהֶם, וְאַל תַּנִּיחֵם לָבוֹא עָלֶיךָ, פֶּן יַשְׁחִיתוּ הָאָרֶץ:

❏ **עַל אֹיְבֶךָ.** חָסֵר יו״ד – שֶׁבְּמִלְחֶמֶת יָחִיד הַכָּתוּב מְדַבֵּר:

—————————— BAAL HATURIM ELUCIDATED ——————————

10. כִּי תֵצֵא — IF[1] YOU WILL GO FORTH. Why is the passage concerning the decapitated calf (21:1-9 above) written between two [passages that speak of] wars (20:1-20 and 21:10-14)?[1a] [Scripture] placed [the topic of] war before that passage [as a warning] lest someone who bears hatred against another person will think, "I will slay him [now], for it is a time of war and people will say, 'The enemy [forces] slew him in the course of the battle.' "[2]

———————————————————————

1. The translation is based on the Baal Ha-Turim's fourth comment to this *parashah*. See note 7 below.

1a. In the Baal HaTurim's comments to 21:1 above, he explains why the passage of the *eglah arufah* (vv. 1-9) follows a passage that speaks of war (20:1-20). In his comments here, the Baal HaTurim explains why the passage of the decapitated calf is followed by our verse which mentions war.

2. *Peirush HaRokeach.* The potential killer will think, "I am now able to slay my personal enemy with impunity, for the legal system will attribute his death to a war party of the national enemy." However, the Baal HaTurim does not explain how the ritual of the *eglah arufah* (decapitated calf) will prevent the hater from carrying out his plan.

It has been suggested that the deterrent can be found in the Midrash cited by *Targum Yonasan ben Uzziel* at 21:8 above. After rendering that verse into Aramaic, the *Targum* adds: Immediately [upon the completion of the ritual of the *eglah arufah*], a bed of worms streams forth from the calf's navel, sets forth after the murderer and crawls all over him; the court then seizes him and brings him to justice. Accordingly, the passage of

the *eglah arufah* is a warning to the potential killer, "You will be found out and you will be tried for murder" (*Ittur Bikkurim*).

There is an underlying difficulty to the Baal HaTurim's comment: The Mishnah states that if the corpse was found near the border that separates *Eretz Yisrael* from another country or near a city in which the majority of residents are not Jewish, then the laws of the *eglah arufah* do not apply (*Sotah* 45b). This is because the phrase כִּי יִמָּצֵא, *If there be found* (21:1 above), which introduces the passage of *eglah arufah,* excludes any area in which murder is commonplace, such as a hostile border or a war zone (see *Rashi* to *Sotah* 45b); or because of the probability that the murderer was from the non-Jewish majority living in that area (*Rambam, Hilchos Rotzeach* 9:5). If so, the case presented by the Baal HaTurim — a corpse found during wartime — would not entail an *eglah arufah!*

It is possible that the Baal HaTurim is speaking of a murder that took place in an area free of hostilities in which the majority of the population was Jewish, but where (the murderer thought) the body would not be found. The murderer figured that since it was a time of war, the missing man would be assumed to have

10 If you will go forth to war against your enemies, HASHEM,

BAAL HATURIM ELUCIDATED

[Another passage concerning] war is written after it, to indicate [to the court], "You shall remove the innocent blood by putting the murderer to death; after that you may go forth to war and you will be victorious."

[To prevent an occurrence such as the one described at the beginning of this comment, the officials] would not allow [personal] enemies to go out to war together, lest one of them kill the other during the battle.[3]

❑ [The last verse of the previous *parashah* states,] *when you do what is upright . . .* and juxtaposed to that is, *if you will go forth to war . . .* [This is to indicate] that only righteous men may go out to war.[4]

❑ [The last word of the previous *parashah* is] ה׳, HASHEM, and juxtaposed to it is, *if you will go forth to war . . .* This indicates that God goes forth with you [to the battlefield],[5] as it is stated, וְיָצָא ה׳ וְנִלְחַם בַּגּוֹיִם, *HASHEM will go forth and wage war against the nations* (*Zechariah* 14:3).[6]

❑ כִּי תֵצֵא — IF[7] YOU WILL GO FORTH. [The verse implies that Moses is saying,] "Go out against them; do not allow them to come against you, lest they destroy the land."[8]

❑ אֹיְבֶךָ[9] — YOUR ENEMY. This word is spelled defectively,[9] without a י, indicating

been murdered or captured by the enemy. Nevertheless, the corpse was found and the *eglah arufah* was brought (*Nachal Eisan* 6:4).

Alternatively: The beginning of the comment must be read together with the last sentence: In truth, the laws of the *eglah arufah* would not apply and there would be no deterrent to prevent the murderer from carrying out his plan. Therefore, to prevent such an occurrence, the officials would not allow personal enemies to go out to war together *(VeChur LaZahav).*

3. *Peirush HaRokeach.*

4. *Peirush HaRokeach;* see *Sotah* 44a and *Kiddushin* 76b; see also the Baal HaTurim to 12:28 above, s.v., כִּי.

5. The Baal HaTurim's intention is unclear because his allusion merely repeats the concept that God accompanies Israel into battle against its enemies, a concept that has been stated explicitly in verses 20:1 and 4 above. [Additionally, we may ask: Why does the Baal HaTurim adduce a verse that mentions God fighting against the nations, with no mention of Israel or the Israelite army, as proof that "HASHEM goes forth with you" (*VeChur LaZahav*)?] It has been suggested that the comment should read, שֶׁהַשֵּׁם יוֹצֵא לְפָנֶיךָ, *that HASHEM goes forth before you,* rather than עִמְּךָ, *with you.* And that is the implication of the juxtaposed phrase: ה׳ כִּי תֵצֵא לַמִּלְחָמָה, HASHEM [will be there before you] *if you will go out to war* (*Atros Addar*). Indeed, *Peirush HaRokeach,* the Baal HaTurim's apparent source for this comment, adduces the verse from *Zechariah,* as well as another verse, ה׳ יָצָא לְפָנֶיךָ, *HASHEM has gone forth before you* (*Judges* 4:14).

6. *Peirush HaRokeach;* see *Midrash Tanchuma, Shofetim* 17.

7. Although this same phrase is usually translated as *when you will go forth* (e.g., 20:1 above), the implication of the Baal HaTurim's comment is that the second stich of the verse — *HASHEM . . . will deliver him into your hand* — is conditional on the first stich — *If you will go forth . . .*

8. *Sifrei* — If you will do what is stated in the passage, then *HASHEM, your God, will deliver him into your hand.*

Despite the fact that *HASHEM will go forth and wage war against the nations* [that threaten to attack you] (see the Baal HaTurim's previous comment with note 5), nevertheless, we do not rely upon miracles (*Pesachim* 64b), but must do our part, knowing that the ultimate victory comes from God (*VeChur LaZahav*).

9. The word אוֹיֵב means *enemy;* its plural form is אוֹיְבִים or אֹיְבִים, *enemies.* When the second person singular possessive pronominal suffix ךָ־,

כא/יא־יב יא אֱלֹהֶיךָ בְּיָדֶךָ וְשָׁבִיתָ שִׁבְיוֹ: וְרָאִיתָ בַּשִּׁבְיָה אֵשֶׁת
יב יְפַת־תֹּאַר וְחָשַׁקְתָּ בָהּ וְלָקַחְתָּ לְךָ לְאִשָּׁה: וַהֲבֵאתָהּ
אֶל־תּוֹךְ בֵּיתֶךָ וְגִלְּחָה אֶת־רֹאשָׁהּ וְעָשְׂתָה אֶת־

בעל הטורים

❑ **שִׁבְיוֹ.** בְּגִימַטְרִיָּא וְאִם יִהְיוּ כְנַעֲנִים:

(יא) **אֵשֶׁת.** בְּגִימַטְרִיָּא בְּשַׂר נְבֵלָה מְאוּסָה. כְּמוֹ שֶׁדָּרְשׁוּ חֲכָמִים, מוּטָב שֶׁיֹּאכְלוּ יִשְׂרָאֵל בְּשַׂר תְּמוּתוֹת שְׁחוּטוֹת וְאַל יֹאכְלוּ בְּשַׂר תְּמוּתוֹת נְבֵלוֹת:

❑ **לְךָ לְאִשָּׁה. וַהֲבֵאתָהּ אֶל תּוֹךְ בֵּיתֶךָ.** לוֹמַר, לְאַחַר שֶׁתְּגַיֵּר אוֹתָהּ וְתִהְיֶה לְךָ לְאִשָּׁה, וְלֹא בְגֵיוּתָהּ:

(יב) **וְגִלְּחָה אֶת רֹאשָׁהּ.** לְפִי שֶׁהֵטִיבָה רֹאשָׁהּ לְפַתּוֹתֶךָ:

❑ **וְעָשְׂתָה אֶת צִפָּרְנֶיהָ.** לְפִי שֶׁרָמְזָה לְךָ בָּהֶם לְפַתּוֹתֶךָ:

BAAL HATURIM ELUCIDATED

that the verse speaks of the war of an individual.[10]

❑ שִׁבְיוֹ — **HIS CAPTIVITY.**[11] The *gematria* of this phrase (318) is equal to that of וְאִם

---

your, is added, the singular form usually becomes אֹיִבְךָ (e.g., 28:55,57 below), while the plural form becomes אֹיְבֶיךָ (e.g., 20:14 above and 23:10 below). However, when the singular form appears with a *ta'am* (cantillation note) that indicates a major pause [i.e., a *sof passuk,* which acts like a period, or an *esnachta,* which acts like a semi-colon], the singular form אֹיִבְךָ changes to אֹיְבֶךָ (e.g., 28:53 below). Now, there is no difference in the pronunciation of the singular אֹיְבֶךָ, with only one י, and the plural אֹיְבֶיךָ, with a second י after the ב. Consequently, there seems to be a confusion regarding the spelling of that word in our verse. The Baal HaTurim states here that it is the singular אֹיְבֶךָ that appears in our verse; but that is not what appears in the Torah scrolls. Indeed, a masoretic note that appears at 20:1 above and again at 28:53 below states, ב׳ חֲסֵרִים, *This word appears twice with a defective spelling.* Thus, *Or Torah* cites both the *Ramah* (*Masores Siyag La-Torah*) and the *Meiri* (*Kiryas Sefer*) who agree that in our verse the word is to be spelled אֹיְבֶיךָ, in the plural.

It has been suggested that the Baal HaTurim intended that this comment appear at 20:1, but "due to the rapidness [with which he wrote]," he imprecisely wrote the comment at our verse (*Minchas Shai*). However, whereas *R' Yehudah HaChassid* (*Taamei Masores HaMikra*), the Baal HaTurim's apparent source [a work not available to the *Minchas Shai*], also places this comment at 21:10, the "rapidness" mentioned by *Minchas Shai* would be that of *R' Yehudah HaChassid,* not the Baal HaTurim.

10. See *Sifrei,* cited by *Rashi.* In his parallel comment, *R' Yehudah HaChassid* uses the term מִלְחֶמֶת רְשׁוּת, *an optional war,* i.e., a war not ordained by the Torah, as are the wars against Amalek and the seven Canaanite nations, rather than the term מִלְחֶמֶת יָחִיד, *the war of an individual,* used by the Baal HaTurim. Nevertheless, it seems clear that the Baal HaTurim's term refers to an optional war and the word יָחִיד, *individual,* refers to the king or general who took the initiative to send forth troops.

11. Three similar words appear in this passage: שִׁבְיוֹ, *his* or *its captivity* (v. 10); בַּשִּׁבְיָה, *in the captivity* (v. 11); and שִׁבְיָהּ, *her captivity* (v. 13). At first glance, the three are different forms of the same basic noun שְׁבִי, *captivity* or *captive(s).* But that cannot be, for the ־ָה ending of בַּשִּׁבְיָה would then have no meaning. In truth, there are two nouns with the same meaning: the grammatically masculine שְׁבִי and grammatically feminine שִׁבְיָה. [Note the word "grammatically," for שְׁבִי can refer to either male captives (as in *Jeremiah* 48:46) or female captives (as in *Numbers* 21:1, see *Rashi* there).] Accordingly, the ־ָה ending of בַּשִּׁבְיָה is not a suffix, but an integral part of the noun שִׁבְיָה. The other two words, שִׁבְיוֹ and שִׁבְיָהּ, are forms of the noun שְׁבִי, with the suffixes ־וֹ, *his,* and ־ָהּ, *her,* respectively. If they were forms of שִׁבְיָה, the final ה would change to a ת when the suffixes are added — שִׁבְיָתוֹ and שִׁבְיָתָהּ, respectively.

your God, will deliver him into your hand, and you will seize his [people in] captivity; 11 *and you will see in the captivity a woman who is beautiful of form, and you will desire her, you may take her to yourself for a wife.* 12 *You shall bring her into your house; she shall shave her head and let her nails*

BAAL HATURIM ELUCIDATED

יִהְיוּ כְנַעֲנִים, [*even*] *if they will be Canaanites.*[12]

11. אֵשֶׁת — A WOMAN. The *gematria* of this word (701) is equal to that of בְּשַׂר נְבֵלָה מְאוּסָה, *meat from a repugnant dying animal.*[13] For, as the Sages have expounded: It is preferable for Israelites to eat the meat of fatally ill animals that were properly slaughtered [just before they would have died of their sickness], than to eat meat from fatally ill animals that have died of their sickness.[14]

❑ **לְךָ לְאִשָּׁה. וַהֲבֵאתָהּ אֶל תּוֹךְ בֵּיתֶךָ** — [YOU MAY TAKE HER] TO YOURSELF FOR A WIFE. YOU SHALL BRING HER INTO YOUR HOUSE. [The juxtaposition of these verses is] to indicate [that] only after you will convert her[14a] and she will become your wife [may you bring her into your house], but not while she is still in her gentile status.[15]

12. וְגִלְּחָה אֶת רֹאשָׁהּ — SHE SHALL SHAVE HER HEAD, because she adorned her head in order to entice you.[16]

❑ **וְעָשְׂתָה אֶת צִפָּרְנֶיהָ** — AND LET HER NAILS GROW, because she made lewd motions with them in order to entice you.[16]

---

12. *Peirush HaRokeach.* Regarding Scripturally ordained wars, such as the war against Amalek or the wars to conquer the Land of Canaan, the Torah states, *you shall not allow any person* [*of the enemy*] *to live* (20:16 above). Thus, our verse, which speaks of captives, must refer to an optional war. Although Canaanites encountered during the Scripturally ordained war of conquest must be put to death, nevertheless, Canaanites living outside the Land of Canaan, who have been taken captive by Israel during an optional war, are allowed to live (*Sifrei* and *Sotah* 35b, cited by *Rashi* here and at 20:11 above).

13. Flesh from a sick animal that dies of its sickness may not be eaten, for it has not undergone *shechitah* (ritual slaughter). Although, from a halachic standpoint, if the sick animal had undergone *shechitah* its meat would be permitted, it is nevertheless considered repugnant. The beautiful war captive is homiletically compared to such a repugnant piece of meat (see note 14 below).

14. *Kiddushin* 21b-22a. In explaining the Torah's rationale for allowing a Jewish soldier to cohabit [albeit, under strictly regulated conditions] with a woman who would be forbidden to him under other circumstances, one opinion cited by the Talmud states: It is preferable for Israelites to eat the meat . . .

That is, just as such meat is repugnant (see note 13 above), yet may be eaten after the prescribed procedure of *shechitah* has released it from its forbidden state, despite its lingering repugnance, similarly, the act of cohabiting with this captive is repugnant, yet may be performed after the prescribed conditions [as set forth in our passage] have been met. Nevertheless, the act remains repugnant and, as a consequence, he will grow to despise her, as indicated by the juxtaposition of the passage of the beautiful captive with the passage of the despised wife (*Midrash Tanchuma* 1, cited by *Rashi*).

14a. See note 19 below.

15. See *Kiddushin* 21b-22a with *Tosafos*, s.v., שלא.

16. *Sifrei* (to v. 13, cited by *Rashi*) states this as the reason that she is not permitted to retain *the garment of her captivity*: For the daughters of the accursed nations adorn themselves in times of war in order to entice others [i.e., the invading soldiers] to sin with them. The Baal HaTurim extends this concept to her hair and her fingernails.

יג צִפָּרְנֶיהָ: וְהֵסִירָה אֶת־שִׂמְלַת שִׁבְיָהּ מֵעָלֶיהָ
וְיָשְׁבָה בְּבֵיתֶךָ וּבָכְתָה אֶת־אָבִיהָ וְאֶת־אִמָּהּ יֶרַח
יָמִים וְאַחַר כֵּן תָּבוֹא אֵלֶיהָ וּבְעַלְתָּהּ וְהָיְתָה לְךָ
יד לְאִשָּׁה: וְהָיָה אִם־לֹא חָפַצְתָּ בָּהּ וְשִׁלַּחְתָּהּ
לְנַפְשָׁהּ וּמָכֹר לֹא־תִמְכְּרֶנָּה בַּכָּסֶף לֹא־תִתְעַמֵּר
טו בָּהּ תַּחַת אֲשֶׁר עִנִּיתָהּ: כִּי־תִהְיֶיןָ לְאִישׁ
שְׁתֵּי נָשִׁים הָאַחַת אֲהוּבָה וְהָאַחַת שְׂנוּאָה

בעל הטורים

(יג) **יֶרַח יָמִים.** וְלֹא אָמַר "חֹדֶשׁ". לוֹמַר לְךָ, מָה הַיָּרֵחַ אוֹרוֹ פָּגוּם כְּנֶגֶד אוֹר הַשֶּׁמֶשׁ, אַף גּוֹיָה מְאוּסָה הִיא כְּנֶגֶד בַּת יִשְׂרָאֵל:

(יד) **וְשִׁלַּחְתָּהּ לְנַפְשָׁהּ.** בְּגִימַטְרִיָּא לְנַפְשָׁהּ לֹא בְּבֵית הָעֲבוֹדָה זָרָה:

❑ **אֲשֶׁר עִנִּיתָהּ. כִּי תִהְיֶיןָ** . לוֹמַר לְךָ שֶׁלֹּא יְעַנֶּה אוֹתָהּ בַּהֲוָיוֹת שֶׁל בִּיאָה:

(טו) **שְׁתֵּי נָשִׁים הָאַחַת אֲהוּבָה וְהָאַחַת שְׂנוּאָה.** מַרְבֶּה נָשִׁים מַרְבֶּה כְשָׁפִים. לוֹמַר לְךָ, כֵּיוָן שֶׁיֵּשׁ לוֹ שְׁתֵּי נָשִׁים, הָאַחַת עוֹשָׂה בִכְשָׁפֶיהָ כְּדֵי שֶׁיִּשְׂנָא הַשְּׁנִיָּה:

BAAL HATURIM ELUCIDATED

13. יֶרַח יָמִים — FOR A MONTH OF DAYS. Scripture did not use חֹדֶשׁ [for *month*].[17] This is to indicate to you [that] just as the light of the moon is blemished when compared to the light of the sun, so too, a gentile woman is repugnant when compared to a daughter of Israel.[18]

14. וְשִׁלַּחְתָּהּ לְנַפְשָׁהּ — THEN YOU SHOULD SEND HER OUT ON HER OWN. The *gematria* of this phrase (1214) is equal to that of לְנַפְשָׁהּ לֹא בְּבֵית הָעֲבוֹדָה זָרָה, *On her own, but not in a house of idolatry.*[19]

17. Scripture uses various nouns for *month.* In most instances (86 in the Torah; 195 in the rest of the *Tanach*), the word of choice is a form of the noun חֹדֶשׁ, literally, *renewal,* a reference to the fact that a month begins with the renewal of the moon. Twelve verses (*Exodus* 2:2; here; 33:14 below; and nine more in the rest of the *Tanach*) use forms of the term יֶרַח, related to יָרֵחַ, *moon.* [Three verses (*Isaiah* 24:23, 30:26; *Song of Songs* 6:10) use the word לְבָנָה, literally *white one.*] In his comment here, the Baal HaTurim explains why our verse uses the comparatively rare יֶרַח, instead of the more common חֹדֶשׁ. In his comments to *Exodus* 2:2, he connects the plural form יְרָחִים used in that verse with the same form in 33:14 below and in two verses in *Job.*

18. *Rashi* (based on *Sifrei* and *Yevamos* 48a) explains that all the conditions set forth in this passage are designed to make her less attractive, even repugnant, to the soldier who has taken her, "so that the daughter of Israel should be joyful, while this one is sad; the daughter of Israel should be adorning herself, while this one is growing repulsive."

19. *Peirush HaRokeach,* based on *Sifrei.* Most editions of *Sifrei* read: לְנַפְשָׁהּ וְלֹא לְבֵית אֱלֹהֶיהָ, *on her own, but not to the house of her gods.* And that is how the *Rambam* (*Hilchos Melachim* 8:5-7) records the *halachah.* For *Rambam* maintains that her initial conversion must be of her own volition; accordingly, she has become Jewish and we do not allow her to backslide into idolatry.

Ramban, in his comments to verse 12, notes that when her conversion is not of her own volition she is not required to keep all of the Torah's laws. At verse 14, however he cites a different version of the *Sifrei*: לְנַפְשָׁהּ וְלֹא לְבֵית אָבִיהָ, *on her own, but not to her father's house.* He then states that he is uncertain whether the *Sifrei* means that, despite the fact that she was grow. [13] *She shall remove the garment of her captivity from upon herself and sit in your house and she shall weep for her father and her mother for a month of days; and after that you may come to her and live with her, and she shall be a wife to you.* [14] *But it shall be that if you do not desire her, then you shall send her out on her own, but you may not sell her for money; you shall not lord it over her, because you have afflicted her.*

[15] *When two women will be [married] to one man — the one beloved and the [other] one despised — and*

──────────── BAAL HATURIM ELUCIDATED ────────────

❏ אֲשֶׁר עִנִּיתָהּ. כִּי תִהְיֶיןָ — **YOU HAVE AFFLICTED HER; WHEN [TWO WOMEN] WILL BE.**[20] This [juxtaposition of phrases] indicates to you that he may not afflict her in matters of cohabitation.[21]

15. שְׁתֵּי נָשִׁים הָאַחַת אֲהוּבָה וְהָאַחַת שְׂנוּאָה — **TWO WOMEN ... THE ONE BELOVED AND THE [OTHER] ONE DESPISED.** [The Mishnah states,] The more wives, the more witchcraft.[22] This[23] indicates to you [that] when a man has two wives,[24] each one will use her witchcraft to cause her husband to despise the other.[24a]

────────────────────────────

coerced into converting, her conversion is nevertheless valid, and we therefore consider her Jewish and do not allow her to return to her idolatrous family; or if her involuntary conversion remains valid only if she eventually accepts it willingly. In the latter instance, the *Sifrei* is telling us that she is free to be on her own — even if she wishes to return to her former ways. However, her erstwhile captor may not have a hand in sending her to her father's home, for it is forbidden to assist sinners in their sinfulness.

20. Scripture often uses a form of the verb היה, *to be,* as a euphemism for the act of consummating a marriage, e.g., וְהָיְתָה לְאִישׁ אַחֵר, *and she was [married] to another man* (24:2 below). And that is how the Baal HaTurim's allusion interprets the word תִהְיֶיןָ, literally, *she will be.*

21. That is, once he has rejected her as a wife, he is forbidden from cohabiting with her, as if she were a harlot, just as he is enjoined לֹא תִתְעַמֵּר בָּהּ, *you shall not lord it over her* [translation follows Ramban, as cited by the Baal HaTurim in *Peirush HaTur HaAroch*].

22. *Avos* 2:7.

23. That is, the Mishnah's teaching.

24. The Torah does not prohibit polygamy. As long as a man can fulfill the three basic obligations described in *Exodus* 21:10, he may take a second wife or even more. However, about one thousand years ago, *Rabbeinu Gershom Me'or HaGolah* [the Light of the Diaspora] promulgated a ban against the practice of taking more than one wife at a time, an enactment that was immediately accepted as *halachah* by Ashkenazic Jewry. The fact that Sephardic men rarely have more than one wife today is not based on Rabbeinu Gershom's ban, rather it is due to the practical consideration that, today, most Sephardim live in countries [including the State of Israel] that have secular laws forbidding bigamy.

24a. In a parallel comment in *Peirush HaTur HaAroch,* the Baal HaTurim looks at that Mishnah from a different perspective: When a man has two wives, one will certainly be more beloved, for [the Mishnah teaches], "The more wives, the more witchcraft," and each one will use her witchcraft to cause their husband to love her more.

Both versions appear in the *Avos* commentary of *Rabbeinu Yonah,* who writes: Each will use her witchcraft to cause her husband to love her. But the "despised one" [i.e., the one who has been bested by the rival wife] will redouble her witchcraft until his heart will be turned in anger against her rival. Moreover, the sin of practicing witchcraft [see *Exodus* 22:17] will be upon his head.

כא/טו וְיָֽלְדוּ־לוֹ֮ בָנִים֒ הָאֲהוּבָה֙ וְהַשְּׂנוּאָ֔ה וְהָיָ֛ה הַבֵּ֥ן הַבְּכֹ֖ר לַשְּׂנִיאָֽה׃
טז וְהָיָ֗ה בְּיוֹם֙ הַנְחִיל֣וֹ אֶת־בָּנָ֔יו

בעל הטורים

❑ **וְהָיָה הַבֵּן הַבְּכֹר לַשְּׂנִיאָה.** וְהַיְנוּ בְּנֵי הַשְּׂנוּאָה, שֶׁהוּא מִבְּנֵי תֵּשַׁע מִדּוֹת שֶׁמָּנָה בִּנְדָרִים. וּלְכָךְ סָמַךְ לוֹ בֵּן סוֹרֵר וּמוֹרֶה, שֶׁיִּהְיֶה הַבֵּן סוֹרֵר וּמוֹרֶה:

❑ **לַשְּׂנִיאָה.** אוֹתִיּוֹת לְנִשֻּׂאֶיהָ. לוֹמַר שֶׁשְּׂנוּאָה בְּנִשּׂוּאֶיהָ, שֶׁהֵם בִּפְסוּלִין:

❑ בַּמִּדְרָשׁ דּוֹרֵשׁ – ״לְאִישׁ״ זֶה הַקָּדוֹשׁ בָּרוּךְ הוּא. ״אֲהוּבָה״ אֵלּוּ הָאֻמּוֹת, שֶׁמַּרְאָה לָהֶם פָּנִים. ״שְׂנוּאָה״ אֵלּוּ יִשְׂרָאֵל, שֶׁמַּסְתִּיר מֵהֶם פָּנִים. ״בְּיוֹם הַנְחִילוֹ״ לֶעָתִיד לָבוֹא. לֹא יְבַכֵּר כִּי אִם ״בְּנִי בְכֹרִי יִשְׂרָאֵל״:

(טז) בְּיוֹם הַנְחִילוֹ אֶת בָּנָיו. סוֹפֵי תֵבוֹת מוֹתוֹ – רֶמֶז לְמַאי דְּאָמַר רַב יְהוּדָה, שְׁלֹשָׁה שֶׁנִּכְנְסוּ לְבַקֵּר אֶת הַחוֹלֶה בַּיּוֹם, רָצוּ כּוֹתְבִין רָצוּ עוֹשִׂין דִּין. בַּלַּיְלָה, כּוֹתְבִין וְאֵין עוֹשִׂין דִּין. וְזֶה מַה שֶּׁמְּצַוֶּה בִּשְׁעַת מוֹתוֹ, אִם הוּא בַּיּוֹם יֵשׁ לוֹ תוֹרַת דִּין:

BAAL HATURIM ELUCIDATED

❑ **וְהָיָה הַבֵּן הַבְּכֹר לַשְּׂנִיאָה** — AND THE FIRSTBORN SON WILL BE [BORN] TO THE DESPISED ONE. This is [what the Sages refer to as] children of a despised wife, which is included among the nine undesirable attributes mentioned in tractate *Nedarim.*[25] Therefore, the passage of the wayward and rebellious son is juxtaposed to this one, for the son [conceived in this manner] will become wayward and rebellious.[26]

❑ **לַשְּׂנִיאָה** — TO THE DESPISED ONE. The letters [of this word may be rearranged to] spell לְנִשֻּׂאֶיהָ, *regarding her marriage.*[27] This is to indicate that the hate is directed at her marriage, for it involves an unacceptable [union].[28]

25. *Nedarim* 20b; cited in the Baal HaTurim's comment to 5:16 above, s.v., וּלְמַעַן יִיטַב לָךְ, paragraph (ii).

26. *Tanchuma* 1, cited by *Rashi* to v. 11; see also *Sanhedrin* 107a.

27. The term שְׂנוּאָה, *despised one,* appears six times in the Torah (*Genesis* 29:31 and 33; and four times in our passage), as well as twice elsewhere in the *Tanach* (*Isaiah* 60:15 and *Proverbs* 30:23). Only in our verse do we find the variant form שְׂנִיאָה, which has the same meaning. The Baal HaTurim explains why the verse uses this unusual form.

In *Peirush HaRokeach,* however, this comment appears on the word שְׂנוּאָה, the letters of which may be rearranged to spell נְשׂוּאָה, *a married woman.*

28. *Kiddushin* 68a — The Talmud there records a dispute regarding the status of certain marriages between a man and woman whom the Torah prohibits from cohabiting with each other. Our passage is adduced as proof that some of those marriages are valid [i.e., even though the partners are prohibited from cohabitation, their marriage forbids either of them from marrying certain relatives of the other, even after he issues her a bill of divorce]: The Torah states, *When two women will be married to one man — the one beloved and the [other] one despised . . .* But is there one [wife] who is despised by God or one who is beloved by God? [All that had to be stated is, אֶת הַבְּכֹר יַכִּיר, *he must recognize the firstborn.* Clearly, that would apply universally, including the case of the beloved and the despised wives (*Rashi*).] Therefore the Torah must be referring to two wives, one whose marriage is beloved in God's eyes [i.e., she and her husband are permitted to each other] and the other whose marriage is despised in God's eyes [i.e., the partners are forbidden to each other]. Nevertheless, the verse confirms their marriage as valid by stating, כִּי תִהְיֶיןָ לְאִישׁ שְׁתֵּי נָשִׁים, *When two women will be [married] to one man.*

they bear him sons, the beloved one and the despised one, and the firstborn son will be [born] to the despised one; ¹⁶ *then it will be that on the day he bequeaths to his sons*

─────────── BAAL HATURIM ELUCIDATED ───────────

❏ The Midrash[29] expounds [on our verse]: לְאִישׁ, *to a man,* refers to the Holy One, Blessed is He;[30] אֲהוּבָה, *beloved,* refers to the [gentile] nations, whom He treats with favor [in this world]; שְׂנוּאָה, *despised,* refers to Israel, from whom God hides His face;[31] בְּיוֹם הַנְחִילוֹ, *on the day that he bequeaths,* [refers to] the Time to Come. [At that time,] He cannot give the right of the firstborn to any but [the one of whom it is written], בְּנִי בְכֹרִי יִשְׂרָאֵל, *My firstborn son is Israel (Exodus 4:22).*[32]

16. בְּיוֹם הַנְחִילוֹ אֶת בָּנָיו — ON THE DAY HE BEQUEATHS TO HIS SONS. The last letters of these words spell מוֹתוֹ, *his death,*[33] an allusion to the teaching of Rav Yehudah:[33a] Three people who entered to visit a sick person[34] during the day — if they desire, they may write;[35] if they desire, they may execute a judgment.[36] [But if they visit] at night — they may write,[35] but they may not execute a judgment.[37]

Now, regarding this one [i.e., the subject of our verse], whatever he instructs at the time of his death,[38] if it is daytime[39] it can have the status of a judgment.[40,40a]

───────────

29. The source Midrash for this comment is not known. An enhanced version of the comment appears in *R' Ephraim* (see note 30). Additionally, *unlike* the Baal HaTurim, who explains "the beloved wife" as a collective metaphor for all the other nations, *R' Ephraim* explains it as a metaphor for אֻמָּה הָרְשָׁעָה, *the evil nation.*

30. *R' Ephraim* adds: As it is written, ה' אִישׁ מִלְחָמָה, *HASHEM is the Master* (literally, *Man*) *of war (Exodus* 15:3). שְׁתֵּי נָשִׁים, *two wives,* the Assembly of Israel and the wicked nation.

31. *R' Ephraim* adduces *Isaiah* 60:15, in which the prophet says to Zion, "*Instead of your being* עֲזוּבָה וּשְׂנוּאָה, *forsaken and despised.*"

32. *R' Ephraim.*

33. *Rimzei Rabbeinu Yoel.* Although this phenomenon occurs eight other times in the Torah *(Genesis* 9:23 and 37:32; *Leviticus* 7:16, 19:23 and 25:50; *Numbers* 10:8 and 23:9; *Deuteronomy* 27:22), this is the only appearance about which the Baal HaTurim comments.

33a. *Bava Basra* 113b.

34. Rav Yehudah is discussing the case of a deathly ill person who wishes to bequeath certain parts of his estate to particular people [in

the form of a gift, not as an inheritance] while he is still alive, but the transfer of property should not be valid until his death, at which time it will take effect retroactively (see *Rashbam*). This type of bequeathal is subject to adjudication by a court of three judges and, as such, may be adjudicated only during the daytime, not at night.

35. That is, they may each assume the role of witness and sign a document that will later be validated by a court of three.

36. That is, they may jointly assume the role of the court and validate the bequeathal right then and there.

37. For, as stated above (note 34), such matters may be adjudicated only by day, not at night.

38. Thus, the allusion of the word מוֹתוֹ, *his death,* in the final letters.

39. Thus, the allusion of the first word of the phrase, בְּיוֹם, which can mean *by day.*

40. Thus, the allusion of the concluding phrase of the passage, לוֹ מִשְׁפַּט הַבְּכֹרָה, which can mean, *to him is the judgment of the firstborn* (v. 17).

40a. *Peirush HaRokeach.*

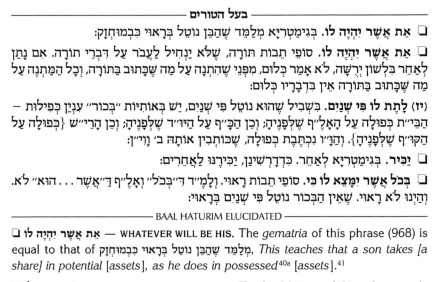

כא/יז אֶת אֲשֶׁר־יִהְיֶה לוֹ לֹא יוּכַל לְבַכֵּר אֶת־בֶּן־הָאֲהוּבָה
יז עַל־פְּנֵי בֶן־הַשְּׂנוּאָה הַבְּכֹר: כִּי אֶת־הַבְּכֹר בֶּן־
הַשְּׂנוּאָה יַכִּיר לָתֶת לוֹ פִּי שְׁנַיִם בְּכֹל אֲשֶׁר־יִמָּצֵא לוֹ

בעל הטורים

❑ **אֵת אֲשֶׁר יִהְיֶה לוֹ.** בְּגִימַטְרִיָּא מְלַמֵּד שֶׁהַבֵּן נוֹטֵל בְּרָאוּי כִּבְמוּחְזָק:

❑ **אֵת אֲשֶׁר יִהְיֶה לוֹ.** סוֹפֵי תֵבוֹת תּוֹרָה, שֶׁלֹּא יַנְחִיל לַעֲבֹר עַל דִּבְרֵי תוֹרָה. אִם נָתַן לְאַחֵר בִּלְשׁוֹן יְרֻשָּׁה, לֹא אָמַר כְּלוּם, מִפְּנֵי שֶׁהִתְנָה עַל מַה שֶּׁכָּתוּב בַּתּוֹרָה, וְכָל הַמַּתְנֶה עַל מַה שֶּׁכָּתוּב בַּתּוֹרָה אֵין בִּדְבָרָיו כְּלוּם:

(יז) **לָתֶת לוֹ פִּי שְׁנַיִם.** בִּשְׁבִיל שֶׁהוּא נוֹטֵל פִּי שְׁנַיִם, יֵשׁ בְּאוֹתִיּוֹת "בְּכוֹר" עִנְיַן כְּפִילוּת — הַבֵּי"ת כְּפוּלָה עַל הָאָלֶ"ף שֶׁלְּפָנֶיהָ; וְכֵן הַכָּ"ף עַל הַיּוּ"ד שֶׁלְּפָנֶיהָ; וְכֵן הָרֵי"שׁ {כְּפוּלָה עַל הַקּוּ"ף שֶׁלְּפָנֶיהָ}. וְהַוָּ"ו נִכְתֶּבֶת כְּפוּלָה, שֶׁכּוֹתְבִין אוֹתָהּ ב׳ וָוִי"ן:

❑ **יַכִּיר.** בְּגִימַטְרִיָּא לְאַחֵר. כִּדְדָרְשִׁינַן, יַכִּירֶנּוּ לַאֲחֵרִים:

❑ **בְּכֹל אֲשֶׁר יִמָּצֵא לוֹ כִּי.** סוֹפֵי תֵבוֹת רָאוּי. וְלָמֶ"ד דִּ"בְּכֹל" וְאָלֶ"ף דַּ"אֲשֶׁר . . . הוּא" לֹא. וְהַיְנוּ לֹא רָאוּי. שֶׁאֵין הַבְּכוֹר נוֹטֵל פִּי שְׁנַיִם בְּרָאוּי:

BAAL HATURIM ELUCIDATED

❑ **אֵת אֲשֶׁר יִהְיֶה לוֹ** — WHATEVER WILL BE HIS. The *gematria* of this phrase (968) is equal to that of מְלַמֵּד שֶׁהַבֵּן נוֹטֵל בְּרָאוּי כִּבְמוּחְזָק, *This teaches that a son takes [a share] in potential* [assets], *as he does in possessed*[40a] [*assets*].[41]

❑ **אֵת אֲשֶׁר יִהְיֶה לוֹ** — WHATEVER WILL BE HIS. The final letters of these four words can be rearranged to spell תּוֹרָה, *Torah.*[42] Implied is that he may not bequeath [his estate as an inheritance] in a manner which runs contrary to the Torah. [Thus] if he bequeathed property, using an expression that implies an inheritance[42a] [as opposed to a gift] to someone other [than his Torah-ordained heirs], his statements are of no consequence, because he made a stipulation that runs contrary to the Torah, and if anyone makes a stipulation that runs contrary to the Torah, his words have no validity.[43]

17. לָתֶת לוֹ פִּי שְׁנַיִם — TO GIVE HIM A DOUBLE PORTION. Whereas [a firstborn] receives a double portion, each of the letters of the word בְּכוֹר, *firstborn,* alludes to the concept of doubling. The [*gematria* of] ב is [2,] double [that of] the א [= 1] that precedes it; the [*gematria* of] כ is [20,] double [that of] the י [= 10] that precedes it; and similarly, the [*gematria* of] ר[43a] {is [200,] double that of the ק [= 100] that precedes it}.[43b] And

40b. See note 46 below.

41. *Rimzei Rabbeinu Yoel. Sifrei* infers this law from our phrase. The Baal HaTurim adds that the *gematriaos* are identical.

42. *Rimzei Rabbeinu Yoel.* Although this phenomenon occurs 127 times in the Torah, the Baal HaTurim comments on it only six times (*Genesis* 18:19; *Leviticus* 6:1-2; *Numbers* 28:1-2; *Deuteronomy* 11:27; 21:16; and 29:14 [comment appears at 33:3]).

42a. The text follows the early printed editions. Many later editions read בִּשְׁבִיל יְרוּשָּׁה, *as an inheritance,* in place of בִּלְשׁוֹן יְרוּשָּׁה, *an expression that implies an inheritance.*

43. *Bava Basra* 126b, 130a.

43a. *Peirush HaRokeach.*

43b. The passage presented in braces is not found in the printed editions, but does appear in *whatever will be his, he cannot give the right of the first-born to the son of the beloved one ahead of the son of the despised one, the firstborn.* 17 *Rather, he must recognize the firstborn, the son of the despised one, to give him a double portion in all that is found with him;*

BAAL HATURIM ELUCIDATED

the ו[44] [also relates to the concept of doubling, because its name] is spelled וָ״ו, with a double ו.[44a]

❑ יַכִּיר — HE MUST RECOGNIZE. The *gematria* of this word (240) is equivalent[45] to that of לְאַחֵר, *to another* [*person*]. As the Sages expound: He [the father] may identify him to others.[45a]

❑ בְּכֹל אֲשֶׁר יִמָּצֵא לוֹ כִּי — IN ALL THAT IS FOUND WITH HIM, FOR. The final letters [of אֲשֶׁר יִמָּצֵא לוֹ כִּי] spell רָאוּי, *potential* [*assets*]; and the ל of בְּכֹל together with the א of הוּא[45b] spell לֹא, *not.* Thus, [our verse alludes to the phrase,] לֹא רָאוּי, [indicating] that the firstborn does not receive a double portion of potential [assets].[46]

---

one of the manuscripts used by *Shoham Yakar.*

44. Although our verse uses the defective spelling בְּכֹר, without a ו, the Baal HaTurim includes that letter in his allusion, for the Torah sometimes (e.g., 25:6 below; interestingly, both spellings appear in *Exodus* 13:15) uses the full spelling בְּכוֹר (*Ittur Bikkurim*). And since our verse omits the letter ו, the Baal HaTurim does not explain its "doubleness" immediately after he explains that of the כ; rather, he waits until he has completed the allusion with regard to the spelling in this passage, then he continues with the allusion of the ו (*Ittur Bikkurim*). Alternatively: The Baal HaTurim first speaks of the three letters that allude to "doubleness" in the same manner, each has a *gematria* double that of the letter that precedes it in the *aleph-beis.* Then he mentions the ו, which alludes to "doubleness" in a different manner (*Ittur Bikkurim*).

44a. Note that, like the name of the letter וָ״ו, the name of the letter הֵ״ה also alludes to "doubleness." Thus, the Baal HaTurim's allusion is also applicable to the words הַבְּכֹר and הַבְּכֹרָה of our passage. Moreover, in the term הַבְּכֹרָה (v. 17) there is another allusion to the firstborn's double portion in his inheritance. For the *gematria* of יְרוּשָּׁה, *inheritance,* is 521, and double that equals 1042; which is also the *gematria* of הַבְּכֹרָה spelled with its *millui* — ה״ה בי״ת כ״ף רי״ש ה״ה. Thus, הַבְּכֹרָה alludes to a double יְרוּשָּׁה (*VeChur LaZahav*).

45. The principle of *im hakollel* allows 239, the *gematria* of the the Baal HaTurim's term, to be considered equivalent to 240.

45a. *Bava Basra* 127b — Although (a) a witness is disqualified from testifying in court in a case involving a close relative, such as his son, and (b) two witnesses are necessary to remove the presumption that until now would place the inheritance in the possession of the previously known relative, nevertheless a father may testify regarding the identity of his firstborn son. The Baal HaTurim finds an allusion to that rule in our verse.

45b. The text follows the early printed editions which read, ולמ״ד דבכל ואל״ף דאשר הוא לא, which seemingly means, *and the* ל of בְּכֹל *and the* א *of* אֲשֶׁר . . . הוּא, *which together spell* לֹא, *not.* But that translation is problematic, for the word אשר is then superfluous, and the comment should have stated ואל״ף דהוא, *and the* א *of* הוּא.

Shoham Yakar's manuscript edition omits the word הוּא. Accordingly, the Baal HaTurim's allusion to the word לֹא is found in the adjacent letters ל of בְּכֹל and א of אֲשֶׁר. But it is unusual for the Baal HaTurim to split an allusion in this fashion, taking one word from the final letters of a phrase and another word from two letters that are adjacent to each other in two words. It is therefore suggested that the Baal HaTurim meant to combine the final ל of the word בְּכֹל, that precedes the phrase that spells רָאוּי, with the final א of the word הוּא, that follows that phrase, and the entire allusion is executed in one manner. If so, the word אֲשֶׁר in the comment is due to a copyist's error (*VeChur LaZahav*).

46. *Bechoros* 51b-52a. A person's heirs share in both the assets that are in his possession at the

כא/יח-כ יח כִּֽי־הוּא֙ רֵאשִׁ֣ית אֹנ֔וֹ ל֖וֹ מִשְׁפַּ֥ט הַבְּכֹרָֽה׃ כִּֽי־
יִהְיֶ֣ה לְאִ֗ישׁ בֵּ֚ן סוֹרֵ֣ר וּמוֹרֶ֔ה אֵינֶ֣נּוּ שֹׁמֵ֔עַ בְּק֥וֹל אָבִ֖יו
יט וּבְק֣וֹל אִמּ֑וֹ וְיִסְּר֣וּ אֹת֔וֹ וְלֹ֥א יִשְׁמַ֖ע אֲלֵיהֶֽם׃ וְתָ֥פְשׂוּ ב֖וֹ
אָבִ֣יו וְאִמּ֑וֹ וְהוֹצִ֧יאוּ אֹת֛וֹ אֶל־זִקְנֵ֥י עִיר֖וֹ וְאֶל־שַׁ֥עַר
כ מְקֹמֽוֹ׃ וְאָמְר֞וּ אֶל־זִקְנֵ֣י עִיר֗וֹ בְּנֵ֤נוּ זֶה֙ סוֹרֵ֣ר וּמֹרֶ֔ה

בעל הטורים

❑ **רֵאשִׁית אֹנוֹ.** כָּל "רֵאשִׁית" הוּא מֻבְחָר – "רֵאשִׁית דְּגָנְךָ"; "קֹדֶשׁ יִשְׂרָאֵל לַה' רֵאשִׁית תְּבוּאָתֹה":

❑ **לוֹ מִשְׁפַּט הַבְּכֹרָה. כִּי יִהְיֶה לְאִישׁ.** לוֹמַר, מִשְׁפַּט בְּכֹרָה לְאִישׁ וְאֵין מִשְׁפַּט בְּכֹרָה לְאִשָּׁה:

(יח) סוֹרֵר. בְּגִימַטְרִיָּא זֶה אַבְשָׁלוֹם בֶּן דָּוִיד:

(כ) בְּנֵנוּ. חָסֵר יוּ"ד – כְּאִלּוּ עָבַר עַל עֲשֶׂרֶת הַדִּבְּרוֹת:

❑ **וּמֹרֶה.** חָסֵר וָי"ו – כִּי מָרָה יִהְיֶה לוֹ בָּאַחֲרוֹנָה:

BAAL HATURIM ELUCIDATED

❑ **רֵאשִׁית אֹנוֹ** — **FIRST OF HIS VIGOR.** The term רֵאשִׁית, [usually translated] *first,* refers to that which is prime [or choice],[47] [as reflected in,] רֵאשִׁית דְּגָנְךָ, *the first of your grain*[47a] (*Deuteronomy* 18:4), [and in,] קֹדֶשׁ יִשְׂרָאֵל לַה' רֵאשִׁית תְּבוּאָתֹה, *Israel is holy to* HASHEM, *the first of His crop* (*Jeremiah* 2:3).[48]

❑ **לוֹ מִשְׁפַּט הַבְּכֹרָה. כִּי יִהְיֶה לְאִישׁ** — **TO HIM IS THE LAW OF THE FIRSTBORN. IF THERE WILL BE UNTO A MAN.** [These phrases are juxtaposed] to indicate [that] the law of the firstborn applies to [the estate of] the father [of the firstborn], but the law of the firstborn does not apply to [the estate of] the mother [of the firstborn].[49]

18. סוֹרֵר — **WAYWARD.** The *gematria* of this word (466) is equivalent[50] to that of זֶה אַבְשָׁלוֹם בֶּן דָּוִיד[51], *This refers to Absalom the son of David.*[52]

time of his death and the assets that are potentially his, but have not yet accrued to him at the time of his death [e.g., the estate that the deceased would eventually inherit from his still-living parent or a debt that had not yet been repaid at the time of the lender's death, but subsequently was repaid]. However, the Talmud infers from the phrase, בְּכֹל אֲשֶׁר יִמָּצֵא לוֹ, *in all that is found with him,* that the double portion of the firstborn is only with regard to assets already in the deceased's possession before his death, but not to potential assets. In the latter, all the sons share equally.

47. Even the firstborn of the despised wife (*Shoham Yakar*).

47a. A reference to *terumah,* the priestly portion (see *Rashi*).

48. *Peirush HaRokeach,* who adduces the additional verses *Exodus* 23:19; *Numbers* 15:20; *Deuteronomy* 18:4; and *Proverbs* 8:22, as well as *Isaiah* 41:4 and 27; *Jeremiah* 17:12, which use ראשון in place of רֵאשִׁית.

49. *Peirush HaRokeach;* see *Bechoros* 51a-52b and *Bava Basra* 111b.

50. The principle of *im hakollel* allows 466 to be considered equivalent to 467, the *gematria* of the Baal HaTurim's phrase.

51. The early printed editions, as well as some later editions, spell דָּוִד without a י (see next paragraph), which leaves the Baal HaTurim's phrase with a *gematria* of 457, nine less than that of the Scriptural term. Other later editions follow *Ittur Bikkurim's* emendation, spelling דָּוִיד with a י, and that is the reading in *Shoham Yakar's* manuscript edition.

King David's name appears 1023 times in Scripture: 760 times spelled defectively, דָּוִד, without a י; and 263 times spelled in full, דָּוִיד, with a י. Absalom's name appears more than one *for he is the first of his vigor, to him is the law of the firstborn.*

18 *If there will be unto a man a wayward and rebellious son, who does not hearken to the voice of his father and the voice of his mother, and they discipline him, but he does not hearken to them;* 19 *then his father and mother shall grasp him and take him out to the elders of his city and the gate of his place.* 20 *They shall say to the elders of his city, "This son of ours is wayward and rebellious;*

BAAL HATURIM ELUCIDATED

20. בְּנֵנוּ — THIS SON OF OURS. This term is spelled without a י (= 10).[53] [This implies] that he is considered to have transgressed the Ten Commandments.[54]

❑ **וּמֹרֶה — AND REBELLIOUS.** This word is spelled without a ו, for the son's end will be [55]מָרָה, *bitter.*[56]

---

hundred times in Scripture, but only once is he called אַבְשָׁלוֹם בֶּן דָּוִד (*II Samuel* 13:1), and there the name דָּוִד is spelled without a י. Nevertheless, for purposes of his allusion, the Baal HaTurim uses the full spelling.

Alternatively: the Baal HaTurim's phrase should be emended to read, סוֹרֵר בְּגִימַטְרִיָּא, *The gematria of* סוֹרֵר (466) *is equivalent* to (465) *the gematria of* כְּאַבְשָׁלוֹם בֶּן דָּוִד, *such as Absalom son of David* (Rabbi Eliyahu Katz, *Or Torah,* V. 3, no. 7 *Kislev* 5731).

52. Although Absalom's rebellion did not place him in the halachic (legal) category of the בֵּן סוֹרֵר וּמוֹרֶה of our passage, the Talmud (*Sanhedrin* 107a) nevertheless compares him to that wayward and rebellious son.

53. The word בָּנֵינוּ, spelled with a י, is a plural noun meaning *our sons* or *our children.* It appears (with or without a prefix) three times in the Torah (*Genesis* 31:16; *Exodus* 10:9; and *Deuteronomy* 29:28) and eleven other times elsewhere in the *Tanach.* The related form בְּנֵנוּ, without a י, is a singular noun and means *our son,* and that is the intent in our verse (the only appearance of this word in the entire *Tanach*). Accordingly, the Baal HaTurim's statement regarding the omitted ו requires explanation.

A number of creative suggestions have been forthcoming in recent years. Almost all of them shift the word that is the basis of the Baal HaTurim's allusion from בְּנֵנוּ to some other word, either in this verse or in the Baal HaTurim's previous comment. See Rabbi A.A.Y. Blau's *Ephneh VeEshneh* (reprinted in *HaDarom,* Nisan 5739); Rabbi A.A. Katz (*Buchareste Rav* of Flatbush) in *Kerem Shlomo,* Elul 5739; and *Shoham Yakar's* appendix *Harchavas HaDas.*

Unfortunately, when those articles were written, their authors did not have access to *Peirush HaRokeach* (the volume on *Bamidbar-Devarim* was first published in 5741, almost two years after the articles appeared in print), the Baal HaTurim's apparent source. There, the comment reads:

> בְּנֵנוּ זֶה חָסֵר י׳ כְּאִילוּ עוֹבֵר עַל י׳ דִּבְּרוֹת וְרָמַז עַל אַבְשָׁלוֹם שֶׁהָיָה בֶּן יְפַת תֹּאַר שֶׁיִּהְיֶה בֵּן סוֹרֵר וּמוֹרֶה. לְאִישׁ בֶּן בְּגִימַטְרִיָּא זֶה בְּאַבְשָׁלוֹם.
>
> *The phrase* בְּנֵנוּ זֶה *is spelled defectively, without a* י׳*, as if [to imply that] he transgressed the Ten Commandments. And it alludes to Absalom, who was the son of a beautiful captive and who was to become a wayward and rebellious son, [for] the gematria of* לְאִישׁ בֶּן *is 393, equal to that of* זֶה בְּאַבְשָׁלוֹם*. This [occurred] with Absalom.*

And whereas none of the suggestions in the aforementioned articles can be applied to that version of the comment, we remain with an enigmatic comment that continues to defy explanation. May HASHEM open our eyes (*VeChur LaZahav*).

54. *Peirush HaRokeach.*

55. In verse 18, the word וּמוֹרֶה is spelled in full, with a ו after the מ. In our verse, it is spelled defectively, וּמֹרֶה, without that ו. As such, it may be understood as if it were vowelized וּמָרָה, *and bitter.*

The Baal HaTurim's wording in this comment is a paraphrase of *II Samuel* 2:26.

56. *R' Yehudah HaChassid.*

כא אֵינֶ֫נּוּ שֹׁמֵ֫עַ בְּקֹלֵ֫נוּ זוֹלֵ֫ל וְסֹבֵ֑א: וּרְגָמֻ֫הוּ כָּל־אַנְשֵׁ֨י

עִיר֤וֹ בָֽאֲבָנִים֙ וָמֵ֔ת וּבִֽעַרְתָּ֥ הָרָ֖ע מִקִּרְבֶּ֑ךָ וְכָל־

שני כב יִשְׂרָאֵ֖ל יִשְׁמְע֥וּ וְיִרָֽאוּ: וְכִֽי־יִהְיֶ֣ה בְאִ֗ישׁ

חֵ֛טְא מִשְׁפַּט־מָ֖וֶת וְהוּמָ֑ת וְתָלִ֥יתָ אֹת֖וֹ עַל־

כג עֵֽץ: לֹֽא־תָלִ֨ין נִבְלָת֜וֹ עַל־הָעֵ֗ץ כִּֽי־קָב֤וֹר תִּקְבְּרֶ֨נּוּ֙

בַּיּ֣וֹם הַה֔וּא כִּֽי־קִלְלַ֥ת אֱלֹהִ֖ים תָּל֑וּי וְלֹ֤א

תְטַמֵּא֙ אֶת־אַדְמָ֣תְךָ֔ אֲשֶׁר֙ יְהֹוָ֣ה אֱלֹהֶ֔יךָ נֹתֵ֥ן לְךָ֖

כב א נַֽחֲלָֽה: לֹֽא־תִרְאֶה֩ אֶת־שׁ֨וֹר אָחִ֜יךָ א֤וֹ אֶת־שֵׂיוֹ֙

──────── בעל הטורים ────────

(כא) וּבִֽעַרְתָּ֥ הָרָ֖ע מִקִּרְבֶּ֑ךָ וְכָל יִשְׂרָאֵל. וּסְמִיךְ לֵהּ "וְכִֽי־יִהְיֶ֣ה בְאִ֗ישׁ חֵ֛טְא". לוֹמַר לְךָ שֶׁכָּל יִשְׂרָאֵל עֲרֵבִים זֶה לָזֶה, לְבַעֵר וּלְהוֹכִיחַ הַחוֹטְאִים:

(כב) לְעֵיל כְּתִיב "וּרְגָמֻ֫הוּ" וְסָמַךְ לוֹ פָּרָשַׁת נִתְלִין. לוֹמַר שֶׁכָּל הַנִּסְקָלִין נִתְלִין:

(כג) עַל הָעֵץ. וּסְמִיךְ לֵהּ "כִּֽי קָב֤וֹר תִּקְבְּרֶ֨נּוּ֙". לוֹמַר שֶׁגַּם הָעֵץ נִקְבָּר עִמּוֹ. וְעוֹד, לִקְבֹּר בָּאָרוֹן:

☐ נֹתֵן לְךָ. וּסְמִיךְ לֵהּ "וְהִתְעַלַּמְתָּ". לוֹמַר, כָּל שֶׁבִּשֶּׁלּוֹ מַחֲזִיר, אַף בְּשֶׁל חֲבֵרוֹ מַחֲזִיר:

כב (א) לֹא תִרְאֶה אֶת שׁוֹר אָחִיךָ. סָמַךְ הַשָּׁבַת אֲבֵדָה לִקְבוּרָה. שֶׁאִם הוּא כֹהֵן וְהוּא בְּבֵית הַקְּבָרוֹת, עַל זֶה נֶאֱמַר "וְהִתְעַלַּמְתָּ":

──────── BAAL HATURIM ELUCIDATED ────────

21. וּבִֽעַרְתָּ֥ הָרָ֖ע מִקִּרְבֶּ֑ךָ וְכָל יִשְׂרָאֵל — AND YOU SHALL REMOVE THE EVIL FROM YOUR MIDST; AND ALL ISRAEL. Juxtaposed to this is, וְכִֽי־יִהְיֶה בְאִישׁ חֵטְא, *If there will be with a man a sin.* This [juxtaposition] indicates to you that all Israel are guarantors for one another,[57] [and are obligated] to destroy and to rebuke the sinners.[58]

22. The previous verse states וּרְגָמֻ֫הוּ, *they shall pelt him* [i.e., put him to death by stoning], and juxtaposed to that is the passage regarding those who are hanged. [This juxtaposition is] to indicate that [the corpses of] all who are stoned[58a] are hanged.[59]

23. עַל הָעֵץ — ON THE GALLOWS. Juxtaposed to this phrase is כִּֽי קָבוֹר תִּקְבְּרֶנּוּ, *rather you shall surely bury him.* This [juxtaposition] is to indicate that the gallows [on which the corpse had been hanged] is buried with him.[60] It also implies that

57. *Shevuos* 39a. The Talmud uses this phrase to indicate that just as the guarantor of a loan is responsible for the borrower's debt, so are all Jews liable for the sins of an individual against whom they could have protested but did not.

58. The Baal HaTurim also speaks of this concept at *Exodus* 22:21 and *Deuteronomy* 21:8.

58a. That is, all those upon whom the *beis din* carried out the sentence of death by stoning.

59. *Peirush HaRokeach.* The Talmud (*Sanhedrin* 45b) records a dispute regarding the parameters of this law. According to one opinion, it applies to every person who has been stoned to death by *beis din.* According to the other opinion, it is applicable only in regard to two of the sins punishable by stoning — blasphemy and idolatry.

60. *Peirush HaRokeach;* see *Yerushalmi, Nazir* 7:1.

he does not hearken to our voice; he is a glutton and a drunkard." 21 *All the men of his city shall pelt him with stones and he shall die; and you shall remove the evil from your midst; and all Israel shall hear and they shall fear.*

22 *If there will be with a man a sin whose judgment is death, he shall be put to death, and you shall hang him on a gallows.* 23 *His body shall not remain for the night on the gallows, rather you shall surely bury him on that day, for a hanging person is a curse of God, and you shall not contaminate your land, which HASHEM, your God, gives you as an inheritance.*

22 1 *You shall not see the ox of your brother's or his sheep or*

BAAL HATURIM ELUCIDATED

he is buried in a coffin.[61,61a]

❑ נֹתֵן לְךָ — GIVES YOU. Juxtaposed to this is וְהִתְעַלַּמְתָּ, *and you shall hide yourself* (22:1). This is to indicate [that] whatever a person would return of his own, he must also return to a colleague.[62]

XXII.

1. לֹא תִרְאֶה אֶת שׁוֹר אָחִיךָ — YOU SHALL NOT SEE THE OX OF YOUR BROTHER. The Torah juxtaposes [the laws of] returning a lost article (vv. 1-3) with [the laws concerning] burial (21:23). [This alludes to the law] that if a *Kohen* [spots] a lost article that is in a cemetery, [he may not enter the cemetery in order to retrieve it, for] regarding this is stated, וְהִתְעַלַּמְתָּ, *you shall hide yourself.*[63]

The Talmud there concludes that any implement used by the court in carrying out the sentence, such as the stone used for stoning and the scarf used for strangulation, must be buried with the body. This law applies to the gallows as well, even though it was not used in the execution itself, for the body is hanged only after death.

61. The word עֵץ can mean either *wood* or *tree* and, by extension, *a gallows.* In this comment, the Baal HaTurim interprets it as *a wooden vessel,* thus, a coffin.

61a. *Bereishis Rabbah* 19:8.

Elsewhere (*Tur, Yoreh Deah* 362), the Baal HaTurim writes: The verse כִּי קָבוֹר תִּקְבְּרֶנּוּ, *rather you shall surely bury him,* teaches that burial should be directly in the ground, not in a coffin. Therefore, one who places his deceased relative in a coffin, and does not bury him in the ground, has transgressed, for he is obligated to bury him in the ground. However, if he places him in a coffin and buries him [with the coffin] in the earth, he has not transgressed; nevertheless, it is preferable to bury directly in the earth, for such burial is a *mitzvah,* even outside of the Land of Israel. [Still in all,] each community should follow its own custom in this matter.

62. *Bava Metzia* 30b; see the Baal HaTurim to 22:4 below. When returning a found object to its owner, one is not required to do that which is considered below his dignity. Thus, an elder or a scholar, who would not lead even his own stray animal home, need not return a stray animal to its owner. For the term וְהִתְעַלַּמְתָּ teaches that there are occasions on which *you shall hide yourself,* such as the case of an elder or a scholar.

63. *Peirush HaRokeach; Sifrei.* See note 62. A *Kohen* must guard himself from contracting *tumah*-impurity through contact with the dead or with a grave (see *Leviticus* 21:1).

נִדָּחִים וְהִתְעַלַּמְתָּ מֵהֶם הָשֵׁב תְּשִׁיבֵם לְאָחִיךָ:
ב וְאִם־לֹא קָרוֹב אָחִיךָ אֵלֶיךָ וְלֹא יְדַעְתּוֹ וַאֲסַפְתּוֹ
אֶל־תּוֹךְ בֵּיתֶךָ וְהָיָה עִמְּךָ עַד דְּרֹשׁ אָחִיךָ אֹתוֹ
ג וַהֲשֵׁבֹתוֹ לוֹ: וְכֵן תַּעֲשֶׂה לַחֲמֹרוֹ וְכֵן תַּעֲשֶׂה
לְשִׂמְלָתוֹ וְכֵן תַּעֲשֶׂה לְכָל־אֲבֵדַת אָחִיךָ אֲשֶׁר־

בעל הטורים

(ב) וַאֲסַפְתּוֹ. ב׳ בַּמָּסוֹרֶת — ״וַאֲסַפְתּוֹ אֶל תּוֹךְ בֵּיתֶךָ״; ״וַאֲסַפְתּוֹ מִצָּרַעְתּוֹ״. זֶהוּ שֶׁאָמְרוּ, נְגָעִים בָּאִים עַל צָרֵי עַיִן. שֶׁאֵינוֹ רוֹצֶה לְהַשְׁאִיל כֵּלָיו וְאוֹמֵר, אֵין לִי. וּלְמָחָר נְגָעִים בָּאִים עַל בֵּיתוֹ, ״וְצִוָּה הַכֹּהֵן וּפִנּוּ אֶת הַבַּיִת״ וּמוֹצִיאִין הַכֵּלִים, וְרוֹאִין הַכֹּל שֶׁיֵּשׁ לוֹ. וְזֶהוּ ״וַאֲסַפְתּוֹ אֶל תּוֹךְ בֵּיתֶךָ״, שֶׁמְּאַסֵּף כֵּלָיו אֶל בֵּיתוֹ וְאֵינוֹ מַשְׁאִילָם, ״וַאֲסַפְתּוֹ מִצָּרַעְתּוֹ״, שֶׁצָּרַעַת בָּאָה עָלָיו:

דָּבָר אַחֵר — הַחוֹשֵׁד בִּכְשֵׁרִים לוֹקֶה בְגוּפוֹ. וּמִי שֶׁאָבְדָה לוֹ אֲבֵדָה, חוֹשֵׁד בַּכֹּל אַף בִּכְשֵׁרִים, וְלוֹקֶה בְגוּפוֹ בְּצָרַעַת. וְנִמְצָא כְּשֶׁתֶּאֱסֹף הָאֲבֵדָה לְבֵיתְךָ וְתַחֲזִירֶנָּה לוֹ, אָז לֹא יַחְשֹׁד עוֹד בַּאֲחֵרִים, וְתֶאֱסֹף אוֹתוֹ מִצָּרַעְתּוֹ:

❑ **עַד דְּרֹשׁ אָחִיךָ אֹתוֹ.** פֵּרוּשׁ, שֶׁיִּדְרֹשׁ הָאוֹת שֶׁלּוֹ, שֶׁיִּתֵּן לוֹ סִימָן בּוֹ. וְזֶהוּ שֶׁאָמְרוּ רַבּוֹתֵינוּ ז״ל, דָּרְשֵׁהוּ אִם רַמַּאי אִם לַאו. מַאי לַאו, בְּסִימָנִים כְּפֵלִים:

BAAL HATURIM ELUCIDATED

2. וַאֲסַפְתּוֹ — YOU SHALL GATHER IT. The masoretic note, ב׳, means that this word appears twice in the *Tanach*: (i) here, וַאֲסַפְתּוֹ אֶל תּוֹךְ בֵּיתֶךָ, *you shall gather it into your house;* and (ii) וַאֲסַפְתּוֹ מִצָּרַעְתּוֹ, *that you shall gather* [i.e., *heal*][64] *him from his tzaraas* (*II Kings* 5:6). This [similarity of expression] is the basis for what our Sages have stated: *Tzaraas* afflictions come upon misers. [A miser is] one who is unwilling to lend out his property, saying instead, "I do not have [that article]." At a later date, his house will become afflicted with *tzaraas,* and then, *the Kohen shall command, and they shall clear the house* (*Leviticus* 14:36), and they will take out all the utensils, and everyone will see that he does, in fact, have [that article].[65]

Thus, when *you shall gather it inside your house,* i.e., one gathers his possessions into his house and refuses to lend them [to others], then *you shall gather in from his tzaraas,* i.e., *tzaraas* will afflict his house.

Alternatively: [The Talmud teaches:] A person who suspects the innocent is punished by bodily affliction [i.e., *tzaraas*].[66] Someone who loses an article becomes suspicious of everyone, even honest people; therefore his body is afflicted with *tzaraas.* Thus, when you will "gather in" the lost object into your house and you will return it to him, the loser will no longer suspect others [of

64. In his comments to that verse, *Rashi* explains that Scripture refers to the healing of a *metzora* as אֲסִיפָה, *gathering in,* because while his affliction is still upon him, people avoid him; however, once he is healed, he is able to gather together with other people.

65. *Arachin* 16a; see also the Baal HaTurim to 24:10 below.

66. *Shabbos* 97a.

goat cast off, and hide yourself from them; rather you shall surely return them to your brother. 2 *If your brother is not near you and you do not know him, you shall gather it to your house, and it shall remain with you until your brother inquires regarding it, and you return it to him.* 3 *So shall you do for his donkey, so shall you do for his garment, and so shall you do for any lost article of your brother that*

BAAL HATURIM ELUCIDATED

theft], and you will gather him in from his *tzaraas.*

❑ **עַד דְּרֹשׁ אָחִיךָ אֹתוֹ** — UNTIL YOUR BROTHER INQUIRES REGARDING IT. This means that he will inquire regarding its sign, i.e., he will tell [the finder] of an identifying mark on [the found article].[67] And thus have our Sages, of blessed memory, stated: [This verse means,] inquire of him [to determine] if he is or is not a liar.[67a] And how [can you do this]? With double identifying marks.[68]

67. Taken simply, the term אֹתוֹ means *it.* The Baal HaTurim, however, understands it as the noun אוֹת, *sign,* with the possessive pronoun וֹ-, *his.* Thus, אֹתוֹ, *his sign,* i.e., the identifying mark that testifies to his ownership of the object.

67a. *Bava Metzia* 27b.

68. The reading בְּסִימָנִים כְּפֵלִים, *with double identifying marks,* follows the majority of manuscripts and the early printed editions. [Whereas that term is unknown from any other source, many later printed editions read בְּסִימָנִים שֶׁעָלֶיהָ, *with the identifying marks that are upon it.*]

Ittur Bikkurim attempts to explain the term בְּסִימָנִים כְּפֵלִים: He suggests that even though the Talmud states that a found article may not be returned to a claimant who is a known liar despite his knowledge of a *siman* [identifying mark], it is possible that the Baal HaTurim is of the opinion that with two *simanim* the article may be returned. But, whereas *Ittur Bikkurim's* suggestion does not appear in any of the halachic codes, he ends his comment, "However, the matter requires further reflection."

Alternatively: The *Maggid Mishneh (Hilchos Gezeilah VaAveidah* 13:3) distinguishes between three classes of *simanim.* The best he calls סִימָנִים מֻבְהָקִים בְּיוֹתֵר, *extremely clear simanim,* such as a hole adjacent to a particular letter [*Lechem Mishneh* refers to their class as מֻבְהָק מִן הַמֻּבְהָקִים, *clearest of the clear*]. Torah law requires that a found article be returned to a claimant on the basis of such a *siman.* The next class is that of סִימָנִים חֲשׁוּבִים, *worthy simanim,* such as the dimensions of the lost object. In that case the article must be returned, but the source of that law as Scriptural or Rabbinical is the topic of a Talmudic dispute. Finally, סִימָנִים גְּרוּעִין, *weak simanim,* such as, "it is long" or "it is heavy," are not acceptable proof of ownership.

Opinions differ among the codifiers and commentaries to the codes regarding the claimant known to be a liar (see *Rambam, Hilchos Gezeilah VaAveidah* 13:3, with *Raavad, Maggid Mishneh* and *Lechem Mishneh; Tur* and *Shulchan Aruch Choshen Mishpat* 267:5 and the commentaries there). What emerges from their discussions is that according to some opinions, anyone, even a liar, who identifies an article with a סִימָן מֻבְהָק מִן הַמֻּבְהָקִים must be given that article. This may be what the Baal HaTurim means by the phrase סִימָנִים כְּפֵלִים, *double identifying marks (VeChur LaZahav).*

Shoham Yakar records a variant manuscript version that reads מאי לאו בסימנים נפלים והתעלמת. According to that reading, our comment ends at the word בְּסִימָנִים, *with identifying marks.* That is, you test the claimant to determine whether he is telling the truth by asking him to provide *simanim.* The next comment then begins with the rubric, נֹפְלִים . . . וְהִתְעַלַּמְתָּ, with the word נֹפְלִים included. Unable to explain why the word נֹפְלִים is included in the rubric, *Shoham Yakar* rejects this version. Nevertheless, it is possible that the Baal HaTurim included the word נֹפְלִים to emphasize that the comment belongs at וְהִתְעַלַּמְתָּ of verse 4 and not at the same word in verse 1 (A.S.; see note 69 below).

ד תֹּאבַד מִמֶּנּוּ וּמְצָאתָהּ לֹא תוּכַל לְהִתְעַלֵּם: לֹא־
תִרְאֶה אֶת־חֲמוֹר אָחִיךָ אוֹ שׁוֹרוֹ נֹפְלִים בַּדֶּרֶךְ
ה וְהִתְעַלַּמְתָּ מֵהֶם הָקֵם תָּקִים עִמּוֹ: לֹא־יִהְיֶה
כְלִי־גֶבֶר עַל־אִשָּׁה וְלֹא־יִלְבַּשׁ גֶּבֶר שִׂמְלַת אִשָּׁה כִּי
תוֹעֲבַת יהוה אֱלֹהֶיךָ כָּל־עֹשֵׂה אֵלֶּה:
ו כִּי יִקָּרֵא קַן־צִפּוֹר ׀ לְפָנֶיךָ בַּדֶּרֶךְ בְּכָל־עֵץ ׀

בעל הטורים

(ד) **וְהִתְעַלַּמְתָּ.** לוֹמַר שֶׁפְּעָמִים שֶׁאַתָּה מִתְעַלֵּם, כְּגוֹן זָקֵן וְאֵינָהּ לְפִי כְבוֹדוֹ:

(ה) **כְּלִי גֶבֶר עַל אִשָּׁה.** בְּגִימַטְרִיָּא כְּלִי תוֹרָה. רֶמֶז שֶׁלֹּא יְלַמֵּד אָדָם לְבִתּוֹ תוֹרָה:

❑ **עַל אִשָּׁה.** ב׳ בַּמָּסוֹרֶת – ״כְלִי גֶבֶר עַל אִשָּׁה״; ״אִם נִפְתָּה לִבִּי עַל אִשָּׁה״. זֶהוּ שֶׁאָמְרוּ, שֶׁמַּיְרֵי בְּאִשָּׁה שֶׁלּוֹבֶשֶׁת כְּלִי גֶבֶר כְּדֵי לְהִתְנַכֵּר וְלִזְנוֹת, כְּדִכְתִיב ״אִם נִפְתָּה לִבִּי עַל אִשָּׁה וְעַל פֶּתַח רֵעִי אָרָבְתִּי״:

❑ **כִּי תוֹעֲבַת ה׳ . . . כִּי יִקָּרֵא קַן צִפּוֹר.** לוֹמַר שֶׁלֹּא יִסְתַּכֵּל בְּעוֹף וּבְעוֹפֶפֶת כְּשֶׁנִּזְקָקִין זֶה לָזֶה:

(ו) **יִקָּרֵא קַן.** בְּגִימַטְרִיָּא פְּרָט לִמְזוּמָּן:

BAAL HATURIM ELUCIDATED

4. **וְהִתְעַלַּמְתָּ** — AND HIDE YOURSELF. This indicates that sometimes you may hide yourself, e.g., an elder [who discovers a fallen animal,] for whom such action is beneath his dignity.[69]

5. **כְּלִי גֶבֶר עַל אִשָּׁה** — MALE GARB ON A WOMAN. The *gematria* of this phrase (671) is equal to that of כְּלִי תוֹרָה, *the garb of Torah.* [This is] an allusion [to the Talmudic opinion] that a man should not teach Torah to his daughter.[70]

❑ **עַל אִשָּׁה** — ON A WOMAN. The masoretic note, ב׳, means that this word appears twice in the *Tanach*: (i) here, כְּלִי גֶבֶר עַל אִשָּׁה, *male garb on a woman;* and (ii) אִם נִפְתָּה לִבִּי עַל אִשָּׁה, *if my heart has been enticed regarding a woman* (*Job* 31:9).[71] This [similarity of expression] is [an allusion to] what our Sages have said: The verse at hand speaks of a woman putting on man's cloth-

69. See note 62 above. Although the Talmudic passage cited there refers to the term וְהִתְעַלַּמְתָּ of verse 1 where it refers to a found animal, the Baal HaTurim extends the concept to the same term in our verse, where it speaks of raising a fallen animal (A.S.).

70. *Rimzei Rabbeinu Yoel.*

The Talmud (*Sotah* 20a) cites two conflicting opinions regarding the propriety of teaching the intricacies of Torah to one's daughter. According to one view, such knowledge will help her resist the temptation to sin. A dissenting opinion states that it will allow her to explore legal loopholes that will lead her to sin.

71. That verse continues: וְעַל פֶּתַח רֵעִי אָרָבְתִּי, *or [if] I have lurked at my neighbor's door.* In the context in which it appears, Job is saying, "If I have ever been enticed by my *yetzer hara* (evil inclination) regarding a woman or if I have ever lurked lasciviously at my neighbor's door waiting for his wife to appear, then punish me in any way that I deserve." For purposes of his allusion, the Baal HaTurim interprets the verse in a novel fashion (see note 72 below).

22/4-6 *may become lost from him and you find it; you shall not hide yourself.*

4 *You shall not see the donkey of your brother or his ox falling on the road and hide yourself from them; you shall surely stand them up, with him.*

5 *There shall not be the male garb on a woman, and a man shall not wear a woman's garment, for anyone who does so is an abomination of* HASHEM.

6 *If a bird's nest happens to be before you on the road, on any*

BAAL HATURIM ELUCIDATED

ing to disguise herself [in order to intermingle with men] and commit harlotry;[71a] as the other verse states: אִם נִפְתָּה לִבִּי עַל אִשָּׁה[72] וְעַל פֶּתַח רֵעִי אָרָבְתִּי, *if my heart has been enticed upon a woman*[72] *or I have lurked at my neighbor's door.*

❑ כִּי תוֹעֲבַת ה׳ . . . כִּי יִקָּרֵא קַן צִפּוֹר — **FOR [IT] IS AN ABOMINATION OF HASHEM . . . IF A BIRD'S NEST HAPPENS TO BE.** [The juxtaposition of these two verses is] to indicate that one should not gaze upon a male bird and female bird while they are mating.[73]

6. יִקָּרֵא קַן — **NEST HAPPENS TO BE.** The *gematria* of this phrase (461) is equivalent[74] to that of פְּרָט לִמְזוּמָּן, *excluding one that is on hand.*[75]

71a. *Nazir* 59a, cited by *Rashi.*

72. The Baal HaTurim interprets the term עַל אִשָּׁה [translated above as *regarding a woman* (see note 71 above)] in its literal sense *on a woman,* i.e., the verse means: *If my heart has been* able to become *enticed* because of the man's clothing that were *on a woman, or I* was able to *have lurked at my* female *neighbor's door.* In other words, because people saw her clothing and thought she was a man, I was able to be enticed by her and to lurk at her door without anyone accusing me of lewdness (*VeChur LaZahav*).

73. *Peirush HaRokeach; Avodah Zarah* 20a-b. The Talmud there expounds on the verse, וְנִשְׁמַרְתָּ מִכֹּל דָּבָר רָע, *you shall guard against any evil thing* [i.e., even an evil thought] (23:10 below): [That verse teaches] that a man should not gaze upon [something that might arouse lewd thoughts, such as . . .] nor upon a male and female donkey nor upon a male and female pig, וְלֹא בְעוֹפוֹת, *nor upon birds,* while they are mating . . .

Another version of the Talmudic passage reads, וְלֹא בְעוֹף וְלֹא בְעוֹפֶפֶת, *nor upon a male bird nor upon a female bird,* in place of וְלֹא בְעוֹפוֹת, *nor upon birds* (*Rosh* and *Ein Yaakov;* see also *Tosafos* to *Bava Metzia* 91a, s.v., מין במינו), and that must have been the version in the Baal HaTurim's copy of the Talmud.

The Baal HaTurim often seeks to understand juxtaposed verses as if they were one. Accordingly, he connects the phrase, כִּי תוֹעֲבַת ה׳ כָּל עֹשֵׂה אֵלֶּה, *for an abomination of* HASHEM *is anyone who does this,* with the phrase, כִּי יִקָּרֵא קַן צִפּוֹר, *If a bird's nest happens.* But, birds do not do acts that are abominable to HASHEM. Accordingly, the verse must refer to the person who sees the nest, i.e., the person should not look into the nest when the birds are mating *(VeChur LaZahav).*

74. The principle of *im hakollel* allows 461 to be considered equivalent to 462, the *gematria* of the Baal HaTurim's phrase.

75. *R' Yehudah HaChassid; Chullin* 139a — The phrase, *If a nest happens to be,* implies that the nest was encountered by happenstance; it was not מְזֻמָּן, *on hand,* literally, *prepared,* i.e., a bird kept for the keeper's use, such as for poultry.

אוֹ עַל־הָאָרֶץ אֶפְרֹחִים אוֹ בֵיצִים וְהָאֵם רֹבֶצֶת
עַל־הָאֶפְרֹחִים אוֹ עַל־הַבֵּיצִים לֹא־תִקַּח הָאֵם
ז עַל־הַבָּנִים: שַׁלֵּחַ תְּשַׁלַּח אֶת־הָאֵם וְאֶת־הַבָּנִים
שלישי ח תִּקַּח־לָךְ לְמַעַן יִיטַב לָךְ וְהַאֲרַכְתָּ יָמִים: כִּי

בעל הטורים

❑ **אֶפְרֹחִים אוֹ בֵיצִים.** בְּגִימַטְרִיָּא בִּצְרִיכִין לְאִמָּן:

❑ **עַל הַבָּנִים.** ב׳ בַּמָּסוֹרֶת – ״לֹא תִקַּח הָאֵם עַל הַבָּנִים״; וְאִידָךְ ״כִּי כֹה אָמַר ה׳ עַל הַבָּנִים וְעַל הַבָּנוֹת הַיִּלּוֹדִים בַּמָּקוֹם הַזֶּה וְגוֹ׳ מְמוֹתֵי תַחֲלֻאִים יָמֻתוּ״. אִם תְּקַיֵּם הַמִּצְוָה, יַאֲרִיכוּן יָמֶיךָ, וְאִם לַאו, ״כֹּה אָמַר ה׳ וְגוֹ׳ מְמוֹתֵי תַחֲלֻאִים יָמֻתוּ״:

(ז) **וְהַאֲרַכְתָּ יָמִים.** בְּגִימַטְרִיָּא בְּעוֹלָם שֶׁכֻּלּוֹ אָרוֹךְ:

❑ **וְהַאֲרַכְתָּ יָמִים.** וּסְמִיךְ לֵהּ ״כִּי תִבְנֶה בַּיִת חָדָשׁ״. לוֹמַר לְךָ, אִם תִּבְנֶה בַּיִת חָדָשׁ, עֲשֵׂה לוֹ מַעֲקֶה כְּדֵי שֶׁיַּאֲרִיכוּ בוֹ יָמִים וְלֹא יִפְּלוּ מִמֶּנּוּ {וְלֹא יָמוּתוּ}:

וְעוֹד – עִקַּר אֲרִיכוּת יָמִים הוּא בִּשְׁבִיל בִּנְיַן בַּיִת חָדָשׁ, שֶׁהוּא בֵּית הַמִּקְדָּשׁ. וְעַל כֵּן {אַף ד׳}בְּכִיבּוּד אָב וָאֵם הִקְדִּים ״וְהַאֲרַכְתָּ יָמִים״ לְ״לְמַעַן יִיטַב לָךְ״ {לֹא כֵן הָכָא}, כְּדֵי לְהַסְמִיךְ ״וְהַאֲרַכְתָּ יָמִים״ לְ״תִבְנֶה בַּיִת חָדָשׁ״:

BAAL HATURIM ELUCIDATED

❑ {The Baal HaTurim's comment to עַל הָאָרֶץ appears at 11:21 above.}

❑ **אֶפְרֹחִים אוֹ בֵיצִים** — YOUNG BIRDS OR EGGS. The *gematria* of this phrase (498) is equivalent[76] to that of בִּצְרִיכִין לְאִמָּן, *when they* [*still*] *need their mother.*[76a]

❑ {The Baal HaTurim's comment to רֹבֶצֶת appears at *Genesis* 49:25.}

❑ **עַל הַבָּנִים** — [WHEN SHE IS] WITH[76b] THE YOUNG. The masoretic note, ב׳, means that this word appears twice in the *Tanach*: (i) here, לֹא תִקַּח הָאֵם עַל הַבָּנִים, *you shall not take the mother [when she is] with the young;* and (ii) כִּי כֹה אָמַר ה׳ עַל הַבָּנִים וְעַל הַבָּנוֹת הַיִּלּוֹדִים בַּמָּקוֹם הַזֶּה ... מְמוֹתֵי תַחֲלֻאִים יָמֻתוּ, *For thus said* HASHEM *concerning*[76b] *the sons and concerning the daughters who are born in this place . . . "They will die as victims of diseases"* (*Jeremiah* 16:3-4). [The similarity of expression indicates

76. The *gematria* of the Baal HaTurim's phrase is 503, five more than that of the Scriptural phrase. The early printed editions read בִּצְרִיכִים לְאִמָּן, which has the same meaning, but lowers the *gematria* of the Baal HaTurim's phrase to 493, five less than that of the Scriptural phrase. To reconcile the *gematriaos*, *Ittur Bikkurim* has made two emendations to the Baal HaTurim's comment: (i) He changed בִּצְרִיכִין to בִּצְרִיכִים, bringing its phrases' *gematria* to 503, and (ii) added a ו to the Scriptural spelling (אֶפְרוֹחִים in lieu of אֶפְרֹחִים), bringing the *gematria* of that phrase to 504, and the principle of *im hakollel* allows one to be added to the *gematria* of the Baal HaTurim's phrase, so that it is considered equivalent to 504. And that is the reading found in most later editions.

Alternatively: The Scriptural phrase should be spelled without the added ו, keeping its *gematria* at 498. And the Baal HaTurim's בִּצְרִיכִים should retain its final ם, giving it a *gematria* of 493. The prefix בְּ־ should be replaced by the prefix וּ־, adding four to the *gematria* for a total of 497, which the principle of *im hakollel* allows to be considered equivalent to 498 (*VeChur LaZahav*).

76a. *Chullin* 140b.

76b. Literally, *on.*

tree or on the ground — young birds or eggs — and the mother is roosting on the young birds or on the eggs, you shall not take the mother [when she is] with the young. [7] You shall surely send away the mother and take the young for yourself, so that it will be good for you and you will have prolonged days.

──────────── BAAL HATURIM ELUCIDATED ────────────

that] if you observe this *mitzvah,* you will prolong your days,[77] but if not, *thus said* HASHEM . . . *"They will die as victims of diseases."*

❑ {The Baal HaTurim's other comment to הָאֵם עַל הַבָּנִים appears at *Genesis* 32:12.}

7. {The Baal HaTurim's comment to תְּשַׁלַּח appears at *Exodus* 15:7.}

❑ וְהַאֲרַכְתָּ יָמִים — **AND YOU WILL HAVE PROLONGED DAYS.** The *gematria* of this phrase (732) is equivalent[78] to that of בְּעוֹלָם שֶׁכֻּלּוֹ אָרוֹךְ, *in a world that is wholly prolonged* [i.e., the World to Come].[79]

❑ וְהַאֲרַכְתָּ יָמִים — **AND YOU WILL HAVE PROLONGED DAYS.** Juxtaposed to this is [the passage that begins], כִּי תִבְנֶה בַּיִת חָדָשׁ, *when you will build a new house.* This indicates to you [that] when you would build a new house, you should construct a guardrail for it in order that [the occupants] shall have prolonged days, for nobody will fall from it {and nobody will die[80]}.[81]

Additionally: The fundamental concept of prolonged days is for building a new house, namely, the Holy Temple. Therefore, {even though}[82] with regard to honoring one's father and mother, the Torah first states, [the concept described in our verse as] וְהַאֲרַכְתָּ יָמִים, *and you will have prolonged days,* [82a] and then, לְמַעַן יִיטַב לָךְ, *so that it will be good for you;* {but not so here [where the order of the phrases is reversed]}[82] in order to juxtapose *you will have prolonged days* with *you will build a new house.*

---

77. As verse 7 states, וְהַאֲרַכְתָּ יָמִים, *and you will have prolonged days.*
   The verse only states that fulfillment of this *mitzvah* will be rewarded with longevity. The Baal HaTurim adds that its transgression, i.e., taking the mother bird while it is with its young or its eggs may be punished with death, Heaven forbid (A.S.)

78. The principle of *im hakollel* allows 731, the *gematria* of the Baal HaTurim's phrase, to be considered equivalent to 732.

79. *Peirush HaRokeach.* The Talmud states that the renewal of prolonged life refers to the enhanced life of the World to Come in which there is no suffering or loss (*Chullin* 142a; see note 84 below).

80. The phrase enclosed in braces is not found in most printed editions. It does appear in one of the manuscripts used by *Shoham Yakar.* See note 77 above.

81. *Peirush HaRokeach.*

82. The words presented in braces are not found in the early printed editions or in *Shoham Yakar's* editions. However, they do appear in many later printed editions.

82a. This refers to the Ten Commandments in which is written, לְמַעַן יַאֲרִיכֻן יָמֶיךָ, *so that your days will be lengthened* (5:16 above). It is not clear why the Baal HaTurim did not adduce the wording of that verse. Perhaps the comment originally read, אֲרִיכַת יָמִים, *longevity,* which a coypist changed to וְהַאֲרַכְתָּ יָמִים (A.S.).

תִבְנֶה֙ בַּ֣יִת חָדָ֔שׁ וְעָשִׂ֥יתָ מַעֲקֶ֖ה לְגַגֶּ֑ךָ וְלֹא־תָשִׂ֤ים
ט דָּמִים֙ בְּבֵיתֶ֔ךָ כִּֽי־יִפֹּ֥ל הַנֹּפֵ֖ל מִמֶּֽנּוּ׃ לֹא־תִזְרַ֥ע כַּרְמְךָ֖
כִּלְאָ֑יִם פֶּן־תִּקְדַּ֗שׁ הַמְלֵאָ֤ה הַזֶּ֙רַע֙ אֲשֶׁ֣ר תִּזְרָ֔ע
י וּתְבוּאַ֖ת הַכָּֽרֶם׃ לֹא־תַחֲרֹ֥שׁ בְּשׁוֹר־וּבַחֲמֹ֖ר יַחְדָּֽו׃

בעל הטורים

(ח) לְעֵיל כְּתִיב "לְמַעַן יִיטַב לָךְ", וְסָמַךְ כָּאן "כִּי יִפֹּל הַנֹּפֵל מִמֶּנּוּ". רֶמֶז לְמַה שֶׁדָּרְשׁוּ, הֲרֵי שֶׁעָלָה בְּאִילָן כְּדֵי לְשַׁלֵּחַ אֶת הָאֵם וְנָפַל וּמֵת, הֵיכָן אֲרִיכוּת יָמִים שֶׁל זֶה? {וְהֵיכָן טוֹבָתוֹ שֶׁל זֶה? אֶלָּא "לְמַעַן יַאֲרִיכֻן יָמֶיךָ" לְעוֹלָם שֶׁכֻּלּוֹ אָרֹךְ, "וּלְמַעַן יִיטַב לָךְ" לְעוֹלָם שֶׁכֻּלּוֹ טוֹב}:

❑ **כִּי יִפֹּל הַנֹּפֵל.** וּסְמִיךְ לֵהּ "לֹא תִזְרַע". רֶמֶז לִדְרַבִּי יֹאשִׁיָּה דְּאָמַר, עַד שֶׁיִּזְרַע חִטָּה וּשְׂעֹרָה וְחַרְצָן בְּמַפֹּלֶת יָד:

(ט) **הַמְלֵאָה.** ב׳ בַּמָּסוֹרֶת – "פֶּן תִּקְדַּשׁ הַמְלֵאָה"; "כַּאֲשֶׁר תָּעִיק הָעֲגָלָה הַמְלֵאָה לָהּ עָמִיר". וְזֶהוּ שֶׁאָמְרוּ שֶׁצָּרִיךְ לְהַרְחִיק בְּכִלְאַיִם כִּמְלֹא צֶמֶד בָּקָר. וּשְׁנֵיהֶם רְפוּיִם – שֶׁצָּרִיךְ לִמְדֹּד בְּאַרְבַּע אַמּוֹת שׁוֹחֲקוֹת. וְאֶחָד יֵשׁ דָּגוּשׁ, "כַּעֲצָמִים בְּבֶטֶן הַמְּלֵאָה":

(י) **לֹא תַחֲרֹשׁ בְּשׁוֹר וּבַחֲמֹר.** טָמֵא וְטָהוֹר. רֶמֶז שֶׁלֹּא יִשְׁתַּתֵּף צַדִּיק עִם רָשָׁע:

BAAL HATURIM ELUCIDATED

8. Earlier is written, לְמַעַן יִיטַב לָךְ, *so that it will be good for you* (v. 7), and juxtaposed here is the verse, כִּי יִפֹּל הַנֹּפֵל מִמֶּנּוּ, *if the falling one will fall from it.* This is an allusion to what the Sages have expounded concerning a person who climbed a tree in order to send away the mother bird and fell to his death. [One might ask:] Where are this one's prolonged days? {Where is the good for this one? Rather [we must say that the verse means,] *So that . . . you will have prolonged days* in a world that is wholly prolonged. *So that it will be good for you* in the world that is wholly good.[83]}[84]

❑ **כִּי יִפֹּל הַנֹּפֵל** — IF THE FALLING ONE WILL FALL. This phrase is followed by the verse beginning, לֹא תִזְרַע, *You shall not sow.* [The juxtaposition is] an allusion to the opinion of Rabbi Yoshiah who says: [One is not liable for sowing a mixture of species] until he sows wheat, barley, and grape seeds in the same fall from his hand.[85]

---

83. The words presented in braces are not found in the printed editions. However, they do appear in the manuscripts used by *Shoham Yakar.*

84. *Chullin* 142a — Regarding the *mitzvah* of honoring parents the Torah states, *so that your days will be prolonged and so that it will be good for you* (*Deuteronomy* 5:16). Regarding the *mitzvah* of sending away the mother bird the Torah states, *so that it will be good for you and you will have prolonged days.* Yet, there was once a father who told his son, "Climb up to the tower and get me some young birds." The son climbed the tower, sent away the mother bird and took the young. On the way down, he fell and died. If so, where are his prolonged days? And where is his good life? Evidently, the Torah speaks of your days as being prolonged in the world that is entirely good, i.e., the World to Come.

85. *Peirush HaRokeach* to v. 9; *Berachos* 22a; *Kiddushin* 39a; cited by *Rashi* here. The prohibition against planting a mixture of seeds of different species in the same field appears in *Leviticus* 19:19. Here, the Torah speaks specifically about a vineyard, i.e., grapevines. Rabbi Yoshiah interprets our verse as follows: לֹא תִזְרַע, *you shall not sow,* i.e., the verse speaks of a new sowing, not of an established vineyard, כַּרְמְךָ, the seeds of *your vineyard,* together with כִּלְאָיִם, *a mixture* of other seeds.

Thus, according to Rabbi Yoshiah, our verse prohibits sowing three types of seed together: grapeseed, as implied by כַּרְמְךָ, along with at least two other species, as implied by כִּלְאָיִם. The Talmud

⁸ When you will build a new house, you shall make a fence for your roof, so that you will not place blood [guilt] in your house if the falling one will fall from it. ⁹ You shall not sow your vineyard with a mixture, lest it will prohibit the fullness of the seed that you plant and the produce of the vineyard.

¹⁰ You shall not plow with an ox and with a donkey together.

──────────── BAAL HATURIM ELUCIDATED ────────────

9. הַמְלֵאָה — THE FULLNESS. The masoretic note, ב׳, means that this word appears twice in the *Tanach*: (i) here, פֶּן תִּקְדַּשׁ הַמְלֵאָה, *lest it will prohibit the fullness;* and (ii) כַּאֲשֶׁר תָּעִיק הָעֲגָלָה הַמְלֵאָה לָהּ עָמִיר, *just as a wagon is encumbered when it is filled with sheaves* (Amos 2:13). This [similarity of expression] is [reflected in] what the Sages have said [with regard to mixed species]: It is necessary to set between the mixed species a distance equivalent to מְלֹא צֶמֶד בָּקָר, *the full width of a team of oxen.* ⁸⁶ Moreover, in both [of the two verses], the מ [of the word הַמְלֵאָה] is soft.⁸⁷ [This alludes to the fact] that the four cubits must be measured loosely.⁸⁸ The term appears once more, that time with a *dagesh,* in, כַּעֲצָמִים בְּבֶטֶן הַמְּלֵאָה, *like the bones [growing] in a full womb* (Ecclesiastes 11:5).⁸⁹

10. לֹא תַחֲרֹשׁ בְּשׁוֹר וּבַחֲמֹר — YOU SHALL NOT PLOW WITH AN OX AND WITH A DONKEY, i.e., a non-kosher animal [donkey] together with a kosher animal [ox].⁹⁰ This is an allusion [to the ethic] that a righteous man should not enter into partnership with a wicked man.⁹¹

───

uses the example of wheat, barley, and grapeseed sown בְּמַפֹּלֶת יָד, *in a fall from the hand.* The Baal HaTurim shows that the Talmudic term מַפֹּלֶת is borrowed from the phrase יִפֹּל הַנֹּפֵל, for these three words share the root נפל, *to fall* or *to throw down.*

86. A span of four *amos* (*Bava Basra* 83a; see *Bartenura* to *Sheviis* 1:5). The Baal HaTurim's comment relates the Talmud's use of מְלֹא, *full,* with the verse's הַמְלֵאָה, *the fullness.*

87. That is, the expected *dagesh* (הַמְּלֵאָה) that usually follows the definite article prefix הַ־ (e.g., *Genesis* 41:7) is absent. Grammatically, a letter without a *dagesh* is called רָפוּי, literally, *soft;* while a letter with a *dagesh* is called חָזָק, literally, *hard.* Those terms refer to the slightly stronger pronunciation indicated by the *dagesh.*

88. Literally, *smiling amos.* The *amah* is measured at six *tefachim* (fist breadths). This measurement can be done in either of two ways: אַמּוֹת שׂוֹחֲקוֹת, *smiling amos,* i.e., with the fingers held loosely together [like slightly parted smiling lips] to form a fist; or אַמּוֹת עֲצֵבוֹת, *sad amos,* i.e., with the fingers held tightly together [like the compressed lips of a sad face]. The loose [smiling] *amah* is then slightly longer than the tight [sad]

amah. With regard to *kilayim* (mixed seeds) the law takes a strict approach and the Talmud ordains that the species must be separated by four *amos* measured loosely (*Eruvin* 3b).

89. *Maharam MiRothenburg.* This last verse is really not relevant to the Baal HaTurim's allusion. He included it to show that, in truth, in the other two appearances, the מ of הַמְלֵאָה should have had a *dagesh,* as it does in *Ecclesiastes.* If so, the absence of the *dagesh* indicates that we are to derive a lesson from those words, namely, that the measurement is made in loose *amos* (*Ittur Bikkurim*).

90. The Talmud records a dispute whether the Torah's statement, *with an ox and with a donkey,* refers strictly to a kosher animal with a non-kosher animal as in the example of the verse (in which case, two kosher animals of different species would be prohibited by Rabbinic decree); or to any two species of animal regardless of the kashruth status of either one (see *Kilayim* 8:2 with commentaries). The Baal HaTurim's allusion is unaffected by that dispute.

91. In the words of the Mishnah: Distance yourself from a bad neighbor; and do not bind yourself to a wicked person (*Avos* 1:7).

כב/יא־יב יא־יב לֹ֥א תִלְבַּ֙שׁ֙ שַֽׁעַטְנֵ֔ז צֶ֥מֶר וּפִשְׁתִּ֖ים יַחְדָּֽו: גְּדִלִ֖ים
תַּֽעֲשֶׂה־לָּ֑ךְ עַל־אַרְבַּ֛ע כַּנְפ֥וֹת כְּסֽוּתְךָ֖ אֲשֶׁ֥ר תְּכַסֶּה־

בעל הטורים

❑ **תַחֲרֹשׁ.** ב׳ בַּמָּסוֹרֶת – ״לֹא תַחֲרֹשׁ בְּשׁוֹר וּבַחֲמֹר״; ״אַל תַּחֲרֹשׁ עַל רֵעֲךָ רָעָה״. וְזֶהוּ שֶׁמְּפָרֵשׁ טַעַם שֶׁלֹּא לַחֲרֹשׁ בְּשׁוֹר וּבַחֲמוֹר, לְפִי שֶׁהַשּׁוֹר מַעֲלֶה גֵרָה וְהַחֲמוֹר אֵינוֹ מַעֲלֶה גֵרָה. וּכְשֶׁיִּרְאֶה הַשּׁוֹר מַעֲלֶה גֵרָה יִהְיֶה סָבוּר שֶׁהוּא אוֹכֵל, וּמִצְטַעֵר. וְזֶהוּ ״אַל תַּחֲרֹשׁ עַל רֵעֲךָ רָעָה״, שֶׁגּוֹרֵם לַחֲמוֹר שֶׁחוֹרֵשׁ עַל רֵעֵהוּ רָעָה:

(יא) **לֹא תִלְבַּשׁ.** בְּגִימַטְרִיָּא אֲסוּרָה לֵהָנוֹת. שֶׁאֲפִלּוּ בֶּגֶד אָרֹךְ וּבוֹ כִלְאַיִם מִצַּד אֶחָד, אָסוּר לְהִתְכַּסּוֹת בָּהּ מִצַּד הַשֵּׁנִי:

(יב) **גְּדִלִים.** ב׳ בַּמָּסוֹרֶת – ״גְּדִלִים תַּעֲשֶׂה לָּךְ״; ״גְּדִלִים מַעֲשֵׂה שַׁרְשְׁרוֹת״. וְזֶהוּ שֶׁאָמְרוּ בְּפֶרֶק הַתְּכֵלֶת, גְּדִיל שְׁנַיִם. דִּתְרֵי ״גְדִלִים״ כְּתִיב, וּפָתְלֵהוּ מִתּוֹכוֹ, כְּדִכְתִיב ״מַעֲשֵׂה שַׁרְשְׁרוֹת״, כְּדֶרֶךְ שֶׁעוֹשִׂין שַׁרְשְׁרוֹת:

❑ **אֲשֶׁר תְּכַסֶּה.** בְּגִימַטְרִיָּא לְהָבִיא בִּכְסוּת סוּמָא שֶׁהוּא חַיָּב:

BAAL HATURIM ELUCIDATED

❑ **תַחֲרֹשׁ** — YOU SHALL [NOT] PLOW. The masoretic note, ב׳, means that this word appears twice in the *Tanach*:[92] (i) here, לֹא תַחֲרֹשׁ בְּשׁוֹר וּבַחֲמֹר, *You shall not plow with an ox and with a donkey;* and (ii) אַל תַּחֲרֹשׁ עַל רֵעֲךָ רָעָה, *Do not devise evil against your neighbor* (*Proverbs* 3:29). This [alludes to] an explanation given for not plowing with an ox and a donkey together: The ox chews its cud, but the donkey does not chew its cud. Thus when [the donkey] will see the ox chewing its cud, it will think that the other animal is eating and it will be distraught.[93] Thus, [the verse from *Proverbs* may be interpreted,] *Do not cause your neighbor to devise evil,* for [by plowing with an ox and a donkey,] he might cause the donkey to think negatively about its neighbor [the ox].[93]

11. לֹא תִלְבַּשׁ — YOU SHALL NOT WEAR. The *gematria* of this phrase (763) is equal to that of אֲסוּרָה לֵהָנוֹת, *It is forbidden to derive benefit.*[94] Even if a garment is long and has *shaatnez* at [only] one end, it is forbidden to cover oneself with the other end.[95]

12. גְּדִלִים — TASSELS. The masoretic note, ב׳, means that this word appears twice in the *Tanach*: (i) here, גְּדִלִים תַּעֲשֶׂה לָּךְ, *make tassels for yourself;* and (ii) גְּדִלִים מַעֲשֵׂה שַׁרְשְׁרוֹת, *and tassels of chainwork* (*I Kings* 7:17). This similarity of

92. The full note appears in *Proverbs*: ב׳ בִּתְרֵי לִישָּׁנֵי, *Twice, with two* [*different*] *meanings.* In our verse it refers to plowing; in *Proverbs* it refers to thinking. Nevertheless, *Rashi* (to *Proverbs*) explains that just as one plows a field to prepare it for the sowing season, so does the plotter of evil prepare his heart to plot and to scheme.

93. *Peirush HaRosh; Moshav Zekeinim,* citing R' Shmuel ben David Ibn Shoham, a contemporary of the Baal HaTurim's father, the *Rosh.*

94. *Peirush HaRokeach.* This refers to benefit of wearing, as the Mishnah states: *Shaatnez* is permitted in all [other] respects, and is forbidden only with respect to wearing (*Kilayim* 8:1).

95. *Yerushalmi, Kilayim* 9:1 — Even if the end that contains wool and linen is lying on the ground [and remains in place when the other end is moved], nevertheless, it is forbidden to cover oneself with such a garment.

11 *You shall not wear shaatnez [i.e., combined fibers], wool and linen together.*

12 *You shall make tassels for yourself on the four corners of your garment with which you cover yourself.*

BAAL HATURIM ELUCIDATED

expression alludes to that which is stated in the chapter *HaTecheiles*[96] [with regard to the number of strands in the *tzitzis*]. The singular form גָּדִיל implies two [doubled] strands,[97] for גְּדִלִים is written two times.[98] They are wound with each other, as implied by the phrase מַעֲשֵׂה שַׁרְשְׁרוֹת, *chainwork,* i.e., in the manner that chains are made.

❑ אֲשֶׁר תְּכַסֶּה — WITH [WHICH] YOU COVER YOURSELF. The *gematria* of this phrase (986) is equivalent[99] to that of לְהָבִיא בִּכְסוּת סוּמָא שֶׁהוּא חַיָּיב, *to include the garment of a blind person, for even he is obligated.*[100]

96. Until a few decades ago, virtually all editions of the Baal HaTurim read ב״ה, an abbreviation that usually stands for בֵּית הִלֵּל, *the Academy of Hillel.* More recently published editions, such as the one in the reader's hands at this moment, are wont to spell out abbreviated terms in the text. Thus, some newer editions read בֵּית הִלֵּל. The reference is then to a *baraisa* recorded in tractate *Menachos* (41b), in which *Beis Shammai* maintains that the fringes on each corner of the *tzitzis* should contain four doubled strands, while *Beis Hillel* requires three doubled strands. Accordingly, the Baal HaTurim's comment ascribes *Beis Shammai's* view to *Beis Hillel.* But, there is another version of that *baraisa,* cited by *Maharal* (*Chiddushei Aggados* to *Menachos* 43b), that reverses the opinions, i.e., four strands according to *Beis Hillel,* three according to *Beis Shammai,* and that may have been the reading in the Baal HaTurim's copy of the Talmud. However, that suggestion is highly unlikely because the *Rosh* (*Hilchos Tzitzis* 12), who was the father and teacher of the Baal HaTurim, adduces the first version of the *baraisa.* Moreover, the *Sifrei,* the source of the *baraisa,* reads: The halachah follows *Beis Shammai* (A.S.).

The reading, בְּפֶרֶק הַתְּכֵלֶת, is found in *Mekorei Baal HaTurim,* and means the fourth chapter of tractate *Menachos.* Although the baraisa adduced above is also found in that chapter, the Baal HaTurim's wording indicates that he is referring to the words of Rav recorded on 39b there (see *Ittur Bikkurim*).

97. The term גְּדִלִים implies that the tassels have to be braided together, and thus *Targum Onkelos* renders the phrase מַעֲשֵׂה עֲבֹת, *braidwork,* as עוֹבַד גְּדִילוּ, and the phrase שַׁרְשְׁרֹת הָעֲבֹתֹת, *the braided chain,* as תִּכַּיָּא גְּדִילָתָא (*Exodus* 28:14; see *Tosafos* to *Menachos* 41b, s.v., בית). And whereas one cannot braid less than two strands, the singular term גָּדִיל must refer to at least two doubled strands. And since the Torah uses the plural form גְּדִילִים, it must refer to at least a second גָּדִיל, for a total of four doubled strands (*Menachos* 39b, as explained by *Rashi*).

98. The Talmud (see note 97 above) reads: גָּדִיל שְׁנַיִם, *The singular form* גָּדִיל *implies two* [*doubled strands*], גְּדִלִים אַרְבָּעָה, *the plural form* גְּדִלִים *implies four.* Thus, the Baal HaTurim's statement דִּתְרֵי גְּדִלִים כְּתִיב, *for* גְּדִלִים *is written two times* — which implies that the number of strands is determined by the number of times the word גְּדִלִים appears in Scripture — differs from the Talmudic exposition. [Moreover, if such reasoning is carried to its logical conclusion, each doorway would require twenty-nine *mezuzos,* for the singular form of מְזוּזָה appears nine times in the *Tanach,* and the plural form appears ten times!] Perhaps, the Baal HaTurim's comment is the victim of a scribal error and should read, דַּהֲרֵי גְּדִלִים כְּתִיב, *for see, the verse uses the plural form* גְּדִלִים [implying two more doubled threads], rather than דִּתְרֵי גְּדִלִים כְּתִיב *(VeChur LaZahav).*

99. The principle of *im hakollel* allows 985, the *gematria* of the Baal HaTurim's phrase, to be considered equivalent to 986.

100. *Menachos* 43a — Whereas the *mitzvah* of *tzitzis* requires that וּרְאִיתֶם אֹתוֹ, *you shall see it* (*Numbers* 15:39), we could have thought to exempt a blind man's garment from *tzitzis,* for he cannot see them. Nevertheless, the verse states, אֲשֶׁר תְּכַסֶּה בָּהּ, *with which you cover yourself,* which implies any garment that a man wears.

יג בָּהּ: כִּֽי־יִקַּ֥ח אִ֖ישׁ אִשָּׁ֑ה וּבָ֥א אֵלֶ֖יהָ וּשְׂנֵאָֽהּ:
יד וְשָׂ֥ם לָהּ֙ עֲלִילֹ֣ת דְּבָרִ֔ים וְהוֹצִ֥א עָלֶ֖יהָ שֵׁ֣ם רָ֑ע
וְאָמַ֗ר אֶת־הָאִשָּׁ֤ה הַזֹּאת֙ לָקַ֔חְתִּי וָאֶקְרַ֣ב אֵלֶ֔יהָ
טו וְלֹא־מָצָ֥אתִי לָ֖הּ בְּתוּלִֽים: וְלָקַ֛ח אֲבִ֥י הַֽנַּעֲרָ֖

בעל הטורים

❑ **אֲשֶׁר תְּכַסֶּה בָּהּ. כִּי יִקַּח.** רֶמֶז לְהָא דְאִיתָא בִנְדָרִים, רַבִּי אֱלִיעֶזֶר מְגַלֶּה טֶפַח וּמְכַסֶּה טֶפַח בְּעֵת בִּיאָה:

דָּבָר אַחֵר – רֶמֶז "אֲשֶׁר תְּכַסֶּה בָּהּ, כִּי יִקַּח". רֶמֶז לְתַלְמִיד חָכָם, שֶׁמַּאֲפִיל בְּטַלִּיתוֹ:

דָּבָר אַחֵר – רֶמֶז "כִּי יִקַּח" "אֲשֶׁר תְּכַסֶּה". מְלַמֵּד שֶׁמְּכַסִּין לוֹ עַל עֲוֹנוֹתָיו:

(יג) וּבָא אֵלֶיהָ. ב' בַּמָּסוֹרֶת – "וּבָא אֵלֶיהָ וּשְׂנֵאָהּ"; "וּבָא אֵלֶיהָ מֶלֶךְ גָּדוֹל". וְדָרְשׁוּ אוֹתוֹ עַל יֵצֶר הָרָע. גַּם בְּכָאן, בִּשְׁבִיל שֶׁהָלַךְ אַחַר יִצְרוֹ הָרָע, סוֹפוֹ לְשִׂנְאתָהּ, לְהוֹצִיא עָלֶיהָ שֵׁם רָע:

(יד) וְהוֹצִא עָלֶיהָ שֵׁם רָע. חָסֵר יוּ"ד – כְּאִלּוּ עָבַר עַל עֲשֶׂרֶת הַדִּבְּרוֹת. וְכֵן, לֹא נֶחְתַּם גְּזַר דִּין עַל אֲבוֹתֵינוּ עַד שֶׁהוֹצִיאוּ עֲשָׂרָה הַמְרַגְּלִים דִּבָּה:

(טו) אֲבִי הַנַּעֲרָ. כְּתִיב חָסֵר הֵ"א – שֶׁהָלְכָה כְּנַעַר. לְכָךְ הוֹצִיא עָלֶיהָ שֵׁם רָע:

BAAL HATURIM ELUCIDATED

❑ **אֲשֶׁר תְּכַסֶּה בָּהּ. כִּי יִקַּח** — WITH WHICH YOU COVER YOURSELF. IF A [MAN] WILL TAKE [A WIFE]. This is an allusion to that which is stated in tractate *Nedarim*:[101] Rabbi Eliezer would uncover a handbreadth and cover a handbreadth during marital relations.[102]

Alternatively: [The juxtaposition of these phrases,] אֲשֶׁר תְּכַסֶּה בָּהּ, כִּי יִקַּח — *with which you cover yourself, if* [*a man*] *will take* [*a wife*], is an allusion to the teaching that a Torah scholar[103] [may engage in marital relations during the day,[104] after] using his garment to make it dark.[105]

Alternatively: [The juxtaposition of] כִּי יִקַּח, *if* [*a man*] *takes* [*a wife*], [with,] אֲשֶׁר תְּכַסֶּה, *with which you cover,* is an allusion [to the teaching that on the day of one's marriage,] they cover over his sins.[106]

13. וּבָא אֵלֶיהָ — AND HE WILL COME TO HER. The masoretic note, ב׳, means that this phrase appears twice in the *Tanach*: (i) here, וּבָא אֵלֶיהָ וּשְׂנֵאָהּ, *and he will come*[106a]

101. *Nedarim* 20b, where this statement appears as part of his wife's description of her husband's extreme modesty with regard to marital relations.

102. *Peirush HaRokeach;* see the commentaries to *Nedarim* 20b.

103. That is, one who is well versed in the modesty required by the Torah (*Rashi*).

104. A time when cohabitation, which should be reserved for the darkness of night or a windowless room, is usually forbidden.

105. *Niddah* 17a.

106. *Rabbeinu Ephraim* (*MiKesivah Ashkenazis*); see *Yerushalmi, Bikkurim* 3:3; see also *Rashi* to *Genesis* 36:3; see also the Baal HaTurim to 24:5 below, s.v., דָּבָר אַחֵר.

106a. The word בָּא is in the past tense, *he came.* The prefix ־ו may be either the conversive ו that changes the tense from past to future, thus, וּבָא, *he will come,* or the conjunctive ו that connects the verb to that which precedes it, thus וּבָא, *and he came.* In the context of our verse, וּבָא is in the future; in the context of *Ecclesiastes,* וּבָא is in the past.

[13] *If a man will take a wife, and he will come to her and will [subsequently] despise her,* [14] *and he will make wanton accusations against her, and spread a bad name about her, and say, "I took this woman, and I came near to her and I did not find signs of virginity on her."* [15] *Then the father of the girl*

BAAL HATURIM ELUCIDATED

to her and will despise her; and (ii) וּבָא אֵלֶיהָ מֶלֶךְ גָּדוֹל, *and there came*[106a] *against her a great king* (*Ecclesiastes* 9:14). The Sages interpret [the *great king*] as the evil inclination.[107] In our verse, too, because the man followed his evil inclination, he will ultimately come to despise her, [and] to spread a bad name about her.[108]

14. וְהוֹצִא עָלֶיהָ שֵׁם רָע — AND HE SPREAD A BAD NAME ABOUT HER. The word וְהוֹצִא, *and he spread,* is spelled defectively, without a י (= 10). [This indicates that he is considered] as if he had transgressed the Ten Commandments.[109]

Additionally: [The omission of the letter י (= 10) alludes to the fact that] the decree against our ancestors [that they would die in the wilderness] was not sealed until the ten spies made wanton accusations[109a] [against the Land of Israel].[110]

15. אֲבִי הַנַּעֲרָ[111] — THE FATHER OF THE GIRL. The term הַנַּעֲרָ, *the girl,* is spelled

107. *Nedarim* 32b.

108. According to *Rashi,* our verse is an example of the Mishnaic dictum, עֲבֵרָה גוֹרֶרֶת עֲבֵרָה, *Sin drags sin* [*in its wake*], i.e., as a consequence of sin, a person is faced with the opportunity to commit another sin. Thus, because the man of our verse transgressed on the prohibition, לֹא תִשְׂנָא, *You shall not hate* (*Leviticus* 19:17), he will ultimately come to transgress the prohibition against speaking evil.

The Baal HaTurim's comment, on the other hand, seemingly places both his hatred and his libel in the wake of his first sin, that of following his evil inclination, but does not specify the nature of the sin that led to his hatred. *Shoham Yakar* proposes that the Baal HaTurim is saying the same as *Rashi,* but the comment contains a scribal error that transposed two words, סוֹפוֹ, *he will ultimately,* and לְשָׂנְאוֹתָהּ, *to despise her.* If we were to reverse those words, the comment would read: Because he followed his evil inclination to despise her, he will ultimately spread a bad name about her.

109. *Peirush HaRokeach.* The Baal HaTurim often interprets an omitted י as an allusion to transgression of the Ten Commandments (e.g., 21:20 above).

109a. See *Numbers* 13:32; 14:36-37.

110. *Peirush HaRokeach;* see *Arachin* 15a.

111. Halachically, the term נַעֲרָה, *naarah,* here translated *girl,* refers to a girl who is at least twelve years old, during the first six months after reaching *na'arus* [adolescence]. Until that period, she is considered a child; after that period, she is an adult; and during that period, with regard to certain matters she is considered still a child under her father's control [e.g., he may annul her vows], while regarding others, she is an adult. However, as will be explained, the Torah does not always use the term נַעֲרָה in its halachic sense. Another point to consider is the fact that the term appears in the Torah, with or without a prefix, a total of twenty-two times (fourteen times in this passage — vv. 15 twice, 16,19,20,21,23,24,25,26 twice, 27,28 and 29; and 8 times in *Genesis* — 24:14,16,28,55,57; 34:3 twice, and 12), with all but one in the form of a *keri uchesiv* [a word spelled one way in the Torah scroll, but pronounced differently]. Thus, throughout the Torah we find the *kesiv* [spelling] נער, without the final ה. The only exception is in verse 19 below, where it is spelled הַנַּעֲרָה, with a final ה. The Talmud explains the difference: The Torah uses the full spelling in the halachic sense of a girl during her first six months of adolescence. The term then includes only a girl during her six-month period of *na'arus,* but excludes girls who are either older or younger. However, when the shortened spelling is used, it can refer to any girl whose six-month period of *na'arus* has not yet ended, and may include a girl who

כב/טו-כא וְאִמָּהּ וְהוֹצִיאוּ אֶת־בְּתוּלֵי הַנַּעֲרָ אֶל־זִקְנֵי הָעִיר
טז הַשָּׁעְרָה: וְאָמַר אֲבִי הַנַּעֲרָ אֶל־הַזְּקֵנִים אֶת־בִּתִּי
יז נָתַתִּי לָאִישׁ הַזֶּה לְאִשָּׁה וַיִּשְׂנָאֶהָ: וְהִנֵּה־הוּא שָׂם
עֲלִילֹת דְּבָרִים לֵאמֹר לֹא־מָצָאתִי לְבִתְּךָ בְּתוּלִים
וְאֵלֶּה בְּתוּלֵי בִתִּי וּפָרְשׂוּ הַשִּׂמְלָה לִפְנֵי זִקְנֵי הָעִיר:
יח וְלָקְחוּ זִקְנֵי הָעִיר־הַהִוא אֶת־הָאִישׁ וְיִסְּרוּ אֹתוֹ:
יט וְעָנְשׁוּ אֹתוֹ מֵאָה כֶסֶף וְנָתְנוּ לַאֲבִי הַנַּעֲרָה כִּי הוֹצִיא
שֵׁם רָע עַל בְּתוּלַת יִשְׂרָאֵל וְלוֹ־תִהְיֶה לְאִשָּׁה
כ לֹא־יוּכַל לְשַׁלְּחָהּ כָּל־יָמָיו: וְאִם־אֱמֶת הָיָה
כא הַדָּבָר הַזֶּה לֹא־נִמְצְאוּ בְתוּלִים לַנַּעֲרָ: וְהוֹצִיאוּ
אֶת־הַנַּעֲרָ אֶל־פֶּתַח בֵּית־אָבִיהָ וּסְקָלוּהָ אַנְשֵׁי
עִירָהּ בָּאֲבָנִים וָמֵתָה כִּי־עָשְׂתָה נְבָלָה בְּיִשְׂרָאֵל

בעל הטורים

(טז) אֶת בִּתִּי נָתַתִּי. בְּגִימַטְרִיָּא הַפֶּה שֶׁאָסַר הוּא הַפֶּה שֶׁהִתִּירָהּ:

(כא) אֶל פֶּתַח בֵּית אָבִיהָ וּסְקָלוּהָ. בְּגִימַטְרִיָּא זֶהוּ רְאוּ אֵלּוּ הַגִּידוּלִין שֶׁגִּדַּלְתֶּם:

❑ **כִּי עָשְׂתָה נְבָלָה בְּיִשְׂרָאֵל.** וּסְמִיךְ לֵהּ "כִּי יִמָּצֵא אִישׁ שֹׁכֵב". רֶמֶז לְאִישׁ שֶׁהֵטִיחַ בְּאִשְׁתּוֹ תַּחַת הַתְּאֵנָה, וּסְקָלוּהוּ:

BAAL HATURIM ELUCIDATED

defectively, without a ה.[112] [This is because] she acted in the manner of a boy.[113] Therefore, he spread a bad name against her.[114]

16. אֶת בִּתִּי נָתַתִּי — I GAVE MY DAUGHTER. The *gematria* of this phrase (1673) is equal to that of [114a]הַפֶּה שֶׁאָסַר הוּא הַפֶּה שֶׁהִתִּירָהּ, *The mouth that prohibited* [*her*], *is*

has not yet reached the age of *naarus,* but excluding one past that age (*Kesubos* 44b).

The Baal HaTurim finds an additional reason for the *keri uchesiv,* this one in the realm of *remez* (allusion). Although in his comments to *Genesis* the Baal HaTurim does not discuss this phenomena, the allusion can be used to explain the *keri uchesiv* there also (see note 113 below).

112. As if it were to be pronounced הַנַּעַר, *the boy.*

113. The Baal HaTurim's intention here is unclear. In verse 14 he describes the accuser as a victim of his own evil inclination, implying that the girl is innocent; while here, he seems to be blaming the girl for being unchaste.

Perhaps, the Baal HaTurim means that, in truth, the girl was innocent of any sinful activities. Nevertheless, if she had been conscientiously chaste in her ways, God would not have permitted false accusations to be made against her, even if she would eventually be exonerated from them (A. S.).

114. *Peirush HaRokeach.*

114a. The reading שֶׁהִתִּירָהּ follows *Shoham Yakar.* Virtually all printed editions read שֶׁהִתִּיר, *that permitted,* without the suffix הּ, *her.* The *gematria* of the Baal HaTurim's phrase is then five less than that of the Scriptural phrase. In order to reconcile the *gematrias,* some editions have added a bracketed phrase, עִם הַתֵּבוֹת, *with the [five] words,* meaning that the principle of *im hateivos* allows five to be added to the *gematria* of the Baal HaTurim's phrase.

Other suggested emendations are: Change הוּא (= 12) to זֶהוּ (= 18) and invoke the principle of *im and her mother should take and bring proofs of the girl's virginity to the elders of the city, to the gate.* [16] *The father of the girl should say to the elders, "I gave my daughter to this man as a wife, and he hated her.* [17] *Now, behold! he made a wanton accusation against her, saying, 'I did not find signs of virginity on your daughter' — but these are the signs of virginity of my daughter!" And they should spread out the sheet before the elders of the city.* [18] *The elders of the city shall take that man and punish him.* [19] *And they shall fine him one hundred silver [shekels] and give them to the father of the girl, for he had issued a slander against a virgin of Israel, and she shall remain with him as a wife; he cannot divorce her all his days.*

[20] *But if this matter was true — signs of virginity were not found on the girl —* [21] *then they shall take the girl to the entrance of her father's house and the people of her city shall pelt her with stones and she shall die, for she had committed an outrage in*

BAAL HATURIM ELUCIDATED

the [very] mouth that permitted her.[115]

21. אֶל פֶּתַח בֵּית אָבִיהָ וּסְקָלוּהָ — TO THE ENTRANCE OF HER FATHER'S HOUSE AND THEY SHALL PELT HER. The *gematria* of this phrase (1156) is equivalent[116] to that of זֶהוּ רְאוּ אֵלּוּ הַגִּידוּלִין שֶׁגִּדַּלְתֶּם, *This [indicates that the judges are saying:] "See the offspring that you have reared."*[117]

❑ **כִּי עָשְׂתָה נְבָלָה בְּיִשְׂרָאֵל — FOR SHE HAD COMMITTED AN OUTRAGE IN ISRAEL.** Juxtaposed to this is, כִּי יִמָּצֵא אִישׁ שֹׁכֵב, *If a man will be found lying . . .* [This juxtaposition is] an allusion to [an incident mentioned in the *Talmud*]: A man [openly] had relations with his wife under a fig tree, and they stoned him.[118]

---

hakollel (*Ittur Bikkurim*, citing *Yosef Daas*); and, הַפֶּה שֶׁאָסְרָה הוּא פֶּה שֶׁהִתִּירָהּ (*Mekorei Baal HaTurim*).

115. *Peirush HaRokeach.* This principle means that if our knowledge regarding the prohibited status of a particular item or matter comes from one person and that same person also informs us that the prohibition is not applicable in certain circumstances, then just as we believe that mouth to prohibit, we believe that mouth to permit. The Mishnah (*Kesubos* 22a) applies this principle in the case of a woman whose marital status is unknown to us. If she says, "I have been married, but I am now divorced," she is believed, for the mouth that prohibits [her to marry by saying, "I have married,"] is the same mouth that permits [her to remarry by saying, "I am now divorced"]. The *gemara* there derives this principle from our verse: The father's words, "*I gave my daughter* [*in marriage*]" prohibits any man in the entire world from living with her, for she is already married, and his statement, *to this man,* removes "this man" from that prohibition and permits him to live with her. The Baal HaTurim finds an allusion to this principle in the *gematria* of the father's words.

116. The principle of *im hakollel* allows 1156 to be considered equivalent to 1157, the *gematria* of the Baal HaTurim's phrase.

117. The Talmud gives this as the reason that her sentence is carried out at *the entrance to her father's house* (*Kesubos* 45a; cited by *Rashi* here).

118. *Sanhedrin* 46a — The Talmud there records a *baraisa*: The *beis din* (court) may mete out corporal and capital punishment even when such action is not mandated by the Torah. They may not do so with the intent to override or transgress the Torah's laws, only as a protective fence to

כב לִזְנוֹת בֵּית אָבִיהָ וּבִעַרְתָּ֥ הָרָ֖ע מִקִּרְבֶּֽךָ: כִּי־
יִמָּצֵ֣א אִ֗ישׁ שֹׁכֵ֣ב ׀ עִם־אִשָּׁ֣ה בְעֻֽלַת־בַּ֒עַל֒ וּמֵ֨תוּ֙
גַּם־שְׁנֵיהֶ֔ם הָאִ֛ישׁ הַשֹּׁכֵ֥ב עִם־הָאִשָּׁ֖ה וְהָאִשָּׁ֑ה

כג וּבִֽעַרְתָּ֥ הָרָ֖ע מִיִּשְׂרָאֵֽל: כִּ֤י יִהְיֶה֙ נַעֲרָ֣ בְתוּלָ֔ה
מְאֹרָשָׂ֖ה לְאִ֑ישׁ וּמְצָאָ֥הּ אִ֛ישׁ בָּעִ֖יר וְשָׁכַ֥ב עִמָּֽהּ:

כד וְהֽוֹצֵאתֶ֨ם אֶת־שְׁנֵיהֶ֜ם אֶל־שַׁ֣עַר ׀ הָעִ֣יר הַהִ֗וא
וּסְקַלְתֶּ֣ם אֹתָם֮ בָּֽאֲבָנִים֒ וָמֵ֒תוּ֒ אֶת־הַֽנַּעֲרָ֗ עַל־
דְּבַר֙ אֲשֶׁ֣ר לֹֽא־צָעֲקָ֣ה בָעִ֔יר וְאֶ֨ת־הָאִ֔ישׁ עַל־
דְּבַ֥ר אֲשֶׁר־עִנָּ֖ה אֶת־אֵ֣שֶׁת רֵעֵ֑הוּ וּבִֽעַרְתָּ֥ הָרָ֖ע

כה מִקִּרְבֶּֽךָ: וְאִֽם־בַּשָּׂדֶ֞ה יִמְצָ֣א הָאִ֗ישׁ אֶת־הַֽנַּעֲרָ֣
הַמְאֹ֣רָשָׂ֔ה וְהֶחֱזִֽיק־בָּ֥הּ הָאִ֖ישׁ וְשָׁכַ֣ב עִמָּ֑הּ וּמֵ֗ת
הָאִ֛ישׁ אֲשֶׁר־שָׁכַ֥ב עִמָּ֖הּ לְבַדּֽוֹ: וְלַֽנַּעֲרָ֙ לֹא־תַעֲשֶׂ֣ה

כו דָבָ֔ר אֵ֥ין לַֽנַּעֲרָ֖ חֵ֣טְא מָ֑וֶת כִּ֡י כַּֽאֲשֶׁר֩ יָק֨וּם אִ֤ישׁ עַל־
רֵעֵ֨הוּ֙ וּרְצָח֣וֹ נֶ֔פֶשׁ כֵּ֖ן הַדָּבָ֥ר הַזֶּֽה: כִּ֥י בַשָּׂדֶ֖ה מְצָאָ֑הּ

כז צָֽעֲקָ֗ה הַֽנַּעֲרָ֙ הַמְאֹ֣רָשָׂ֔ה וְאֵ֥ין מוֹשִׁ֖יעַ לָֽהּ: כִּי־

כח יִמְצָ֣א אִ֗ישׁ נַעֲרָ֤ בְתוּלָה֙ אֲשֶׁ֣ר לֹֽא־אֹרָ֔שָׂה וּתְפָשָׂ֖הּ
וְשָׁכַ֣ב עִמָּ֑הּ וְנִמְצָֽאוּ: וְנָתַ֠ן הָאִ֨ישׁ הַשֹּׁכֵ֥ב עִמָּ֛הּ לַֽאֲבִ֥י

כט הַֽנַּעֲרָ֖ חֲמִשִּׁ֣ים כָּ֑סֶף וְלֽוֹ־תִהְיֶ֣ה לְאִשָּׁ֗ה תַּ֚חַת אֲשֶׁ֣ר

כג

א עִנָּ֔הּ לֹֽא־יוּכַ֥ל שַׁלְּחָ֖הּ כָּל־יָמָֽיו: לֹֽא־יִקַּ֥ח אִ֖ישׁ

ב אֶת־אֵ֣שֶׁת אָבִ֑יו וְלֹ֥א יְגַלֶּ֖ה כְּנַ֥ף אָבִֽיו: לֹֽא־יָבֹ֧א

ג פְצֽוּעַ־דַּכָּ֛ה וּכְר֥וּת שָׁפְכָ֖ה בִּקְהַ֥ל יְהֹוָֽה: לֹֽא־

בעל הטורים

(כד) אֲשֶׁר לֹא צָעֲקָה. וְאַף אִם יִרְאָה מִמֶּנּוּ, הָיְתָה יְכוֹלָה לוֹמַר שֶׁמֵּחֲמַת צַעַר בְּתוּלִים צָעֲקָה:

---

safeguard the Torah's laws [at a time when they are routinely ignored by a large number of people]. Thus, it happened once, during the time the Greeks controlled *Eretz Yisrael,* that a man was riding a horse on the Sabbath [an act prohibited by Rabbinical decree] and he was brought to *beis din* and they stoned him; not because stoning is the appropriate punishment, but because the tenor of the times required it. Another incident occurred in which a man [openly] had relations with his wife under a fig tree. He was brought to *beis din* and they flogged

him, not because flogging is the appropriate punishment, but because the tenor of the times required it. [Sabbath desecration and public lewdness were common occurrences and so the courts had to take matters in hand to prevent such transgression from spreading.]

Although extant editions of the Talmud read וְהִלְקוּהוּ, *and they flogged him,* the Baal HaTurim's comment reads וּסְקָלוּהוּ, *and they stoned him,* a reading that *Dikdukei Soferim* reports finding in one early printed edition of the Talmud and in some editions of the *Rif.*

**22/22-
23/2**

Israel, to commit adultery in her father's house, and you shall remove the evil from your midst.

²² If a man will be found lying with a woman who is married to a husband, then both of them shall die, the man who lay with the woman and the woman; and you shall remove the evil from Israel.

²³ If there will be a virgin girl who is betrothed to a man, and a man finds her in the city and lies with her, ²⁴ then you shall take them both to the gate of that city and pelt them with stones and they shall die: the girl because of the fact that she did not cry out in the city, and the man because of the fact that he afflicted the wife of his fellow; and you shall remove the evil from your midst.

²⁵ But if it is in the field that the man will find the betrothed girl, and the man will seize her and lie with her, only the man who lies with her shall die. ²⁶ But you shall do nothing to the girl, for the girl has committed no capital sin, for like a man who rises up against his fellow and kills him, so is this matter; ²⁷ for he found her in the field, the betrothed girl cried out, but she had no savior.

²⁸ If a man will find a virgin maiden who was not betrothed, and takes hold of her and lies with her, and they are discovered, ²⁹ then the man who lay with her shall give the father of the girl fifty silver [shekels], and she shall become his wife, because he had afflicted her; he cannot divorce her all his life.

23

¹A man shall not marry the wife of his father; and he shall not uncover the robe of his father. ² A man with crushed testicles or a severed organ shall not enter the congregation of HASHEM.

──────────── BAAL HATURIM ELUCIDATED ────────────

24. אֲשֶׁר לֹא צָעֲקָה — THAT SHE DID NOT CRY OUT. Even if she could not cry out because she was afraid of [angering] her attacker,[119] she could have cried out from the physical pain of [losing her] virginity.[120]

26. ❑ {The Baal HaTurim's comments to v. 26 appear at *Exodus* 21:14, s.v., עַל רֵעֵהוּ, and *Leviticus* 12:7, s.v., דָּמֶיהָ.}

27. {The Baal HaTurim's comment to מְצָאָהּ appears at *Genesis* 38:20.}

---

119. She was afraid that he might kill her.
120. Nevertheless, had she been unable to do so for fear of her life, or if she showed signs of

having resisted her attacker, she would surely be found innocent (*Ramban*, cited by the Baal HaTurim in *Peirush HaTur HaAroch*).

יָבֹ֥א מַמְזֵ֖ר בִּקְהַ֣ל יהוָ֑ה גַּ֚ם דּ֣וֹר עֲשִׂירִ֔י לֹא־יָ֥בֹא ל֖וֹ
ד בִּקְהַ֥ל יהוָֽה׃ לֹֽא־יָבֹ֧א עַמּוֹנִ֛י וּמוֹאָבִ֖י בִּקְהַ֣ל
יהוָ֑ה גַּ֚ם דּ֣וֹר עֲשִׂירִ֔י לֹא־יָבֹ֥א לָהֶ֛ם בִּקְהַ֥ל יהוָ֖ה
ה עַד־עוֹלָֽם׃ עַל־דְּבַ֞ר אֲשֶׁ֨ר לֹא־קִדְּמ֤וּ אֶתְכֶם֙ בַּלֶּ֣חֶם
וּבַמַּ֔יִם בַּדֶּ֖רֶךְ בְּצֵאתְכֶ֣ם מִמִּצְרָ֑יִם וַאֲשֶׁ֨ר שָׂכַ֜ר
עָלֶ֗יךָ אֶת־בִּלְעָ֤ם בֶּן־בְּעוֹר֙ מִפְּת֔וֹר אֲרַ֥ם נַהֲרַ֖יִם
ו לְקַֽלְלֶֽךָּ׃ וְלֹֽא־אָבָ֞ה יהוָ֤ה אֱלֹהֶ֙יךָ֙ לִשְׁמֹ֣עַ אֶל־בִּלְעָ֔ם

בעל הטורים

כג (ג) מַמְזֵר. ב׳ בַּמָּסוֹרֶת – ״לֹא יָבֹא מַמְזֵר״; וְאִידָךְ ״וְיָשַׁב מַמְזֵר בְּאַשְׁדּוֹד״. וְזֶהוּ שֶׁאָמְרוּ חֲכָמֵינוּ ז״ל, עֲתִידִין מַמְזֵרִים לִטָּהֵר וְיִתְיַשְּׁבוּ בָּאָרֶץ:

❑ **לֹא יָבֹא מַמְזֵר בִּקְהַל ה׳.** סָמַךְ מַמְזֵר לִפְצוּעַ דַּכָּה, שֶׁמַּמְזֵר אֵינוֹ מוֹלִיד, כִּפְצוּעַ דַּכָּה:

❑ וְסָמַךְ עַמּוֹנִי וּמוֹאָבִי לְמַמְזֵר, שֶׁבְּנוֹת לוֹט נִבְעֲלוּ לַאֲבִיהֶן וְיָלְדוּ מַמְזֵרִים. וְהַנְּקֵבוֹת מֻתָּרוֹת, לְפִי שֶׁהֵן נִתְכַּוְּנוּ לִדְבַר מִצְוָה:

(ה) אֲשֶׁר לֹא קִדְּמוּ. בְּגִימַטְרִיָּא אֶת הַזְּכָרִים:

❑ **אֲשֶׁר לֹא קִדְּמוּ אֶתְכֶם.** רָאשֵׁי תֵבוֹת בְּגִימַטְרִיָּא ״בָּלָק״. שֶׁהוּא צִוָּה לַעֲשׂוֹת כֵּן:

(ו) לִשְׁמֹעַ אֶל בִּלְעָם. וּסְמִיךְ לֵהּ ״לֹא תִדְרֹשׁ שְׁלֹמָם״ כִּדְאִיתָא בְּהַנִּזָּקִין:

BAAL HATURIM ELUCIDATED

XXIII.

3. מַמְזֵר — MAMZER. The masoretic note, ב׳, means that this word appears twice in the *Tanach*: (i) here, לֹא יָבֹא מַמְזֵר, *a mamzer shall not enter;* and (ii) וְיָשַׁב מַמְזֵר בְּאַשְׁדּוֹד, *A mamzer will dwell in Ashdod* (*Zechariah* 9:6). This is what our Sages of blessed memory [meant when they] said: *Mamzerim* will [eventually] be purified, and they will settle in the land.[121]

❑ **לֹא יָבֹא מַמְזֵר בִּקְהַל ה׳ — A MAMZER SHALL NOT ENTER THE CONGREGATION OF HASHEM.** The passage juxtaposed [the law regarding] a *mamzer* with [the law regarding] a man with crushed testicles (v. 2), for, like a person with crushed testicles, a *mamzer* cannot beget children.[122]

❑ And the passage juxtaposed [the law regarding] an Ammonite or a Moabite (v. 4) to [the law regarding] a *mamzer,* for Lot's daughters were impregnated by

121. See *Kiddushin* 72b; see also *Radak* to *Zechariah* 9:6.

122. But if a *mamzer* cannot beget children, how can the verse speak of the tenth-generation progeny of a *mamzer?* The Talmud states: A *mamzer* cannot be viable. If so, how can there be generations of *mamzerim*? An unrecognized *mamzer* or *mamzeres* cannot be viable [lest a *kosher* person become tainted through marriage to that *mamzer* (*Rashi*)]; but a recognized *mamzer* [who others know is forbidden to them] can live a full life (*Yevamos* 78b). Whereas an unrecognized *mamzer* will die before it is mature enough to beget or bear children, the Baal HaTurim states: A *mamzer* cannot beget children (see *Sedei Chemed, Maareches Mem* 34).

³ *A mamzer shall not enter the congregation of HASHEM, even his tenth generation shall not enter the congregation of HASHEM.*

⁴ *An Ammonite or Moabite shall not enter the congregation of HASHEM, even their tenth generation shall not enter the congregation of HASHEM, to eternity,* ⁵ *because of the fact that they did not come out to meet you with bread and water on the road when you were leaving Egypt, and because he hired against you Balaam son of Beor, of Pethor, Aram Naharaim, to curse you.* ⁶ *But HASHEM, your God, refused to listen to Balaam,*

────────────── BAAL HATURIM ELUCIDATED ──────────────

their father[123] and bore [the progenitors and Ammon and Moab, who were] *mamzerim*. [Nevertheless,] the females [of these nations] are permitted,[124] for Lot's daughters intended to perform a *mitzvah*. [125]

5. אֲשֶׁר לֹא קִדְּמוּ — **THAT THEY DID NOT COME OUT TO MEET.** The *gematria* of this phrase (682) is equivalent[126] to that of אֶת הַזְּכָרִים, *the males.* [127]

❑ אֲשֶׁר לֹא קִדְּמוּ אֶתְכֶם — **THAT THEY DID NOT COME OUT TO MEET YOU.** The *gematria* of the initial letters of this phrase (132) is equal to that of the name בָּלָק, *Balak,* [the king of Moab,] for it was he who instructed [his people] to act in this manner.[128]

6. לִשְׁמֹעַ אֶל בִּלְעָם — **TO LISTEN TO BALAAM.** Juxtaposed to this is, לֹא תִדְרֹשׁ שְׁלֹמָם, *You shall not seek their peace.* [The juxtaposition alludes to that] which is stated in chapter *HaNizakin.* [129]

───────────────────────────────

123. *Peirush HaRokeach; see Genesis* 19:30-38.

124. *Yevamos* 76b.

125. *Nazir* 23a.

126. The principle of *im hakollel* allows 682 to be considered equivalent to 683, the *gematria* of the Baal HaTurim's phrase.

127. *Peirush HaRokeach; see Yevamos* 76b-77a — The Talmud there explains that the men of Ammon and Moab were faulted for not coming out to meet the Israelites with food and drink. The women of those nations were not faulted, for it is the manner of men to go forth to meet wayfarers, but not the manner of women. The question is raised: Why didn't the Ammonite and Moabite women go out to meet the Israelite women? The Talmud replies: [Israelite women are considered princesses, daughters of the King,] and the psalmist praises them with the statement, כָּל כְּבוּדָּה בַת מֶלֶךְ פְּנִימָה, *The entire honor of the king's daughter is within* (*Psalms* 45:14). Therefore the Israelite women did not venture forth and so the Ammonite and

Moabite women had no one to go out to meet (based on *Maharshal*). The Baal HaTurim uses the medium of *gematria* to show that the statement, אֲשֶׁר לֹא קִדְּמוּ, *that they did not come out to meet,* refers specifically to the men (*Shoham Yakar*).

128. *Sifrei.* Although the Baal HaTurim uses the term צִוָּה, *he commanded* or *instructed,* the *Sifrei* interprets עַל דְּבַר of our verse as עַל הָעֵצָה, *upon the advice,* as the prophet stated. "*My people, hear, now, what Balak, king of Moab, advised . . .*" (*Micah* 6:5).

129. The fifth chapter of tractate *Gittin* is called *HaNizakin* after its first word. The Talmud there (57a) relates that when Onkelos son of Klonikos, nephew of the wicked Titus [who destroyed the Second Temple], wished to convert to Judaism, he summoned Balaam from the dead. Onkelos asked, "Who is considered important in that world?" Balaam replied, "Israel." Onkelos asked, "Shall I join them?" Balaam replied, *"Do not seek their peace or their welfare."*

וַיַּהֲפֹךְ יהוה אֱלֹהֶיךָ לְּךָ אֶת־הַקְּלָלָה לִבְרָכָה כִּי
ז אֲהֵבְךָ יהוה אֱלֹהֶיךָ: לֹא־תִדְרֹשׁ שְׁלֹמָם וְטֹבָתָם
רביעי ח כָּל־יָמֶיךָ לְעוֹלָם: לֹא־תְתַעֵב אֲדֹמִי כִּי
אָחִיךָ הוּא לֹא־תְתַעֵב מִצְרִי כִּי־גֵר הָיִיתָ בְאַרְצוֹ:
ט בָּנִים אֲשֶׁר־יִוָּלְדוּ לָהֶם דּוֹר שְׁלִישִׁי יָבֹא לָהֶם
י בִּקְהַל יהוה: כִּי־תֵצֵא מַחֲנֶה עַל־אֹיְבֶיךָ וְנִשְׁמַרְתָּ
יא מִכֹּל דָּבָר רָע: כִּי־יִהְיֶה בְךָ אִישׁ אֲשֶׁר לֹא־יִהְיֶה
טָהוֹר מִקְּרֵה־לָיְלָה וְיָצָא אֶל־מִחוּץ לַמַּחֲנֶה לֹא
יב יָבֹא אֶל־תּוֹךְ הַמַּחֲנֶה: וְהָיָה לִפְנוֹת־עֶרֶב יִרְחַץ
יג בַּמָּיִם וּכְבֹא הַשֶּׁמֶשׁ יָבֹא אֶל־תּוֹךְ הַמַּחֲנֶה: וְיָד
תִּהְיֶה לְךָ מִחוּץ לַמַּחֲנֶה וְיָצָאתָ שָּׁמָּה חוּץ:

בעל הטורים

(**ח**) וּסְמִיךְ לֵהּ "לֹא תְתַעֵב אֲדֹמִי". לוֹמַר, אַף עַל גַּב דִּכְתִיב "וַיִּשְׂטֹם עֵשָׂו אֶת יַעֲקֹב", "לֹא תְתַעֵב אֲדֹמִי", כִּי עַמּוֹנִים לֹא קִדְּמוּ אוֹתְךָ בַּלֶּחֶם וּבַמַּיִם, וְהוּא קִדֶּמְךָ, שֶׁנֶּאֱמַר "כַּאֲשֶׁר עָשׂוּ לִי בְּנֵי עֵשָׂו":

(**י**) **וְנִשְׁמַרְתָּ.** בְּגִימַטְרִיָּא מִן שְׁפִיכַת דָּמִים. וּבְגִימַטְרִיָּא מִן קִלְלַת הַשֵּׁם. וּבְגִימַטְרִיָּא אֵין לְהִסְתַּכֵּל בְּאִשָּׁה כְּלָל:

❑ **מִכֹּל דָּבָר רָע.** זֶהוּ נִבּוּל פֶּה:

BAAL HATURIM ELUCIDATED

7. {The Baal HaTurim's comment to לְעוֹלָם appears at *Exodus* 19:9.}

8. Juxtaposed to this [prohibition against marriage with an Ammonite] is לֹא תְתַעֵב אֲדֹמִי, *you shall not reject an Edomite.* [This is] to indicate [that] even though it is written, וַיִּשְׂטֹם עֵשָׂו אֶת יַעֲקֹב, *Esau harbored hatred toward Jacob* (*Genesis* 27:41), [nevertheless,] לֹא תְתַעֵב אֲדֹמִי, *You shall not reject an Edomite,* for the Ammonites *did not come out to meet you*[129a] *with bread and water,* whereas the Edomites did, as the verse states, כַּאֲשֶׁר עָשׂוּ לִי בְּנֵי עֵשָׂו, *as the children of Esau did for me* (*Deuteronomy* 2:29).[130]

10. **וְנִשְׁמַרְתָּ** — YOU SHALL GUARD YOURSELF. The *gematria* of this word (996) is equivalent[131] to that of מִן שְׁפִיכַת דָּמִים, *from the shedding of blood.*[132] It is also

129a. The Baal HaTurim here cites five words [לֹא קִדְּמוּ אוֹתְךָ בַּלֶּחֶם וּבַמַּיִם] from our verse, inexplicably changing the plural pronoun אֶתְכֶם, *you,* to the singular אוֹתְךָ, *you.*

130. See *Rashi* and *Ibn Ezra* (first interpretation) to that verse.

131. The principle of *im hakollel* allows 996 to be considered equivalent to 997; and the principle of *im hateivos* allows 3 to be added to 994, the *gematria* of the Baal HaTurim's phrase, for a total of 997 (*Ittur Bikkurim*).

132. *R' Yehudah HaChassid.* According to the *Sifrei,* the phrase, מִכֹּל דָּבָר רָע, *against every evil thing,* refers to such matters as idolatry, bloodshed and blasphemous cursing.

and HASHEM, *your God, reversed the curse to a blessing for you, because* HASHEM, *your God, loved you.* 7 *You shall not seek their peace or welfare, all your days, forever.*

8 *You shall not reject an Edomite, for he is your brother; you shall not reject an Egyptian, for you were a sojourner in his land.* 9 *Children who are born to them in the third generation may enter the congregation of* HASHEM.

10 *When a camp goes out against your enemies, you shall guard yourself against any evil matter.* 11 *If there will be among you a man who will not be clean because of a nocturnal occurrence, he shall go outside the camp; he shall not enter the midst of the camp.* 12 *When it will be toward evening, he shall immerse himself in the water, and when the sun sets, he may enter the midst of the camp.* 13 *You shall have a place outside the camp, and you shall go out there.*

BAAL HATURIM ELUCIDATED

equivalent[133] to the *gematria* of מִן קִלְלַת הַשֵּׁם, *from cursing* [*God's*] *Name.*[132] It is also equivalent[134] to the *gematria* of אֵין לְהִסְתַּכֵּל בְּאִשָּׁה כְּלָל, *one should not gaze upon a woman*[135] *at all.*[136]

❑ מִכֹּל דָּבָר רָע — AGAINST ANY EVIL MATTER. This is [a reference to] obscene speech.[137]

12. {The Baal HaTurim's comment to לִפְנוֹת עֶרֶב appears at *Genesis* 24:63.}

133. The principle of *im hakollel* allows 995, the *gematria* of the Baal HaTurim's phrase, to be considered equivalent to 996.

134. The *gematria* of the Scriptural phrase is 996; the *gematria* of the Baal HaTurim's phrase is 994. The Baal HaTurim's phrase may be emended to reconcile the *gematriaos,* for the parallel comment in *Peirush HaRokeach* reads, הָאִשָּׁה אֵין לְהִסְתַּכֵּל כְּלָל, *The woman, one should not gaze upon* [*her*] *at all,* which has a *gematria* of 997. And the principle of *im hakollel* allows 996 to be considered equivalent to 997.

Alternatively: Some editions have emended the Baal HaTurim's phrase to, אֵין לְהִסְתַּכֵּל בְּאִשָּׁה בִּכְלָל, *As a general principle, one should not gaze upon a woman,* which has a *gematria* of 996.

135. The verse, *You shall guard yourself against every evil matter* [i.e., you should be careful not to put yourself into a situation that might tempt you to sin], teaches that a man should not gaze upon a beautiful woman, even if she is single; nor upon a married woman, even if she is ugly (*Avodah Zarah* 20a). Accordingly, the Baal HaTurim's statement, "One should not gaze upon a woman at all," refers to such a woman.

136. *Peirush HaRokeach.*

137. At the end of this passage, the Torah states, וְלֹא יִרְאֶה בְךָ עֶרְוַת דָּבָר, *so that He will not see a shameful thing among you* (v. 15). The Midrash interprets עֶרְוַת דָּבָר, *something immoral,* as if it were vowelized עֶרְוַת דִּבֵּר, *an immoral word,* and explains it as a reference to obscene speech (*Vayikra Rabbah* 24:7; see also *Ibn Ezra* to v. 15 below). The Baal HaTurim applies that same exegesis to the phrase דָּבָר רָע, *evil matter,* of verse 10, and explains it as דִּבּוּר רָע, *evil speech,* i.e., obscene, vulgar language [for the word דָּבָר is otherwise superfluous, as its omission in the phrase מִכֹּל רָע, *from any evil,* would not change the meaning of the verse (*Ittur Bikkurim*)]. He also explains דָּבָר in this manner at 17:1 above, s.v., כֹּל דָּבָר רָע כִּי תוֹעֲבַת, and 24:5 below, s.v., לְכָל דָּבָר נָקִי.

יד וְיָתֵד תִּהְיֶה לְךָ עַל־אֲזֵנֶךָ וְהָיָה בְּשִׁבְתְּךָ חוּץ
טו וְחָפַרְתָּה בָהּ וְשַׁבְתָּ וְכִסִּיתָ אֶת־צֵאָתֶךָ: כִּי יהוה
אֱלֹהֶיךָ מִתְהַלֵּךְ ׀ בְּקֶרֶב מַחֲנֶךָ לְהַצִּילְךָ וְלָתֵת
אֹיְבֶיךָ לְפָנֶיךָ וְהָיָה מַחֲנֶיךָ קָדוֹשׁ וְלֹא־יִרְאֶה בְךָ
טז עֶרְוַת דָּבָר וְשָׁב מֵאַחֲרֶיךָ: לֹא־תַסְגִּיר עֶבֶד
יז אֶל־אֲדֹנָיו אֲשֶׁר־יִנָּצֵל אֵלֶיךָ מֵעִם אֲדֹנָיו: עִמְּךָ

בעל הטורים

(יד) **וְיָתֵד תִּהְיֶה לְךָ עַל אֲזֵנֶךָ.** רֶמֶז שֶׁאִם שָׁמַע נִבּוּל פֶּה שֶׁיַּכְּף אֶצְבָּעוֹ לְתוֹךְ אָזְנוֹ. וְזֶהוּ "וְיָצָאתָ שָׁמָּה חוּץ", שֶׁלֹּא לִשְׁמֹעַ נִבּוּל פֶּה. צֵא חוּץ מִן הַבַּיִת אוֹ תָּכֹף אֶצְבָּעֲךָ לְתוֹךְ אָזְנֶךָ:

וּבַמִּדְרָשׁ – "וְיָתֵד תִּהְיֶה לְךָ" עַל זְכוּת אָבוֹת, שֶׁהוּא כְּיָתֵד תָּקוּעַ לְיִשְׂרָאֵל. "וְיָתֵד" בְּגִימַטְרִיָּא וְהָאָבוֹת:

❑ **וְיָתֵד תִּהְיֶה לְךָ עַל אֲזֵנֶךָ.** בְּגִימַטְרִיָּא מִידּוֹתַי תִּהְיֶה עַל אֲזֵנֶךָ. כְּלוֹמַר, י״ג מִדּוֹת יִהְיוּ כְּלֵי זַיִן שֶׁלְּךָ:

❑ **וְחָפַרְתָּה.** ב׳ בַּמָּסוֹרֶת – "וְחָפַרְתָּה בָהּ וְשַׁבְתָּ וְכִסִּיתָ אֶת צֵאָתֶךָ"; "וְחָפַרְתָּ לָבֶטַח תִּשְׁכָּב". וְזֶהוּ מַה שֶּׁאָמְרוּ, לְעוֹלָם יִבְדֹּק אָדָם עַצְמוֹ לִצְרָכָיו קֹדֶם שֶׁיִּישַׁן. "וְחָפַרְתָּה . . . וְכִסִּיתָ אֶת צֵאָתֶךָ", אָז "וְחָפַרְתָּ לָבֶטַח תִּשְׁכָּב":

(טו) **עֶרְוַת דָּבָר.** וּסְמִיךְ לֵהּ "לֹא תַסְגִּיר עֶבֶד". רֶמֶז (צוֹאָה) [עֶרְוָה] סְגוּרָה בַּעֲשָׁשִׁית, אָסוּר לִקְרוֹת קְרִיאַת שְׁמַע כְּנֶגְדָּהּ:

BAAL HATURIM ELUCIDATED

14. וְיָתֵד תִּהְיֶה לְךָ עַל אֲזֵנֶךָ — YOU SHALL HAVE A PICK[138] WITH YOUR WEAPONS.[139] This stich is an allusion to [what to do] if one hears obscene speech: He should plug his finger into his ear.[140] And that is also [the allusion of the preceding verse], וְיָצָאתָ שָׁמָּה חוּץ, *and you shall go out there,* in order not to hear obscene speech; go out of the house [where it is being spoken] or plug your finger into your ear.

The *Midrash* interprets the phrase, וְיָתֵד תִּהְיֶה לְךָ, *you shall have a pick,* as a reference to the merit of the Patriarchs, which is like a stake[140a] implanted for the merit of Israel.[141] [This is alluded to by] the *gematria* of וְיָתֵד (420) which is equal to that of וְהָאָבוֹת, *the Patriarchs.*[142]

❑ וְיָתֵד תִּהְיֶה לְךָ עַל אֲזֵנֶךָ[142a] — YOU SHALL HAVE A PICK WITH YOUR WEAPONS. The

138. The term יָתֵד means a pointed stick or rod and is used in Scripture with various applications: tent stake (e.g., *Exodus* 27:19); pick for digging (our verse); peg on which to hang things (*Ezekiel* 15:3); roller or beam of a loom (*Judges* 16:14).

139. The term אָזֵן is related to כְּלֵי זַיִן, *weapons,* and refers to the magazine or arsenal in which weapons and armaments are stored (*Sifrei*).

140. *Kesubos* 5a-b — The Talmud there offers a homiletical exposition of our verse: Do not interpret, אֲזֵנֶךָ, *your weapons,* as it is properly read, rather interpret it as if it were vowelized אָזְנֶךָ, *your ear.* Thus, if a person hears inappropriate language, he should place his יָתֵד-shaped finger into his ear.

140a. See note 138 above.

141. *Tanchuma* 3; see also *Bereishis Rabbah* 43:8.

142. *Rimzei Rabbeinu Yoel.*

142a. The text follows the emendations of *Yosef Daas,* cited by *Ittur Bikkurim,* and have been adopted by some of the later printed editions.

[14] *You shall have a pick with your weapons, and it will be that when you sit outside, you shall dig with it; you shall turn back and cover your excrement.* [15] *For* HASHEM, *your God, walks in the midst of your camp to rescue you and to deliver your enemies before you; so your camp shall be holy, so that He will not see something immoral among you and turn away from behind you.*

[16] *You shall not turn over to his master a slave who is rescued from his master to you.* [17] *He shall dwell with you*

BAAL HATURIM ELUCIDATED

gematria of this phrase (1068) is equal to that of מִידּוֹתַי תִּהְיֶה עַל אֲזֵנֶךָ, *My attributes should be with your weapons,* i.e., [God said, "My] thirteen attributes [of mercy] will be your weapons."[142b]

❑ וְחָפַרְתָּה — YOU SHALL DIG. The masoretic note, ב׳, means that this word appears twice in the *Tanach*:[143] (i) here, וְחָפַרְתָּה בָהּ וְשַׁבְתָּ וְכִסִּיתָ אֶת צֵאָתֶךָ, *you shall dig with it, you shall turn back and cover your excrement;* and (ii) וְחָפַרְתָּ לָבֶטַח תִּשְׁכָּב, *you shall dig [a protective trench], you shall lie down in security* (*Job* 11:18). This [similarity of expression] is [an allusion to] what our Sages have said: A person should always check himself regarding his needs[144] before he goes to sleep.[145] [Thus, if] *you shall dig . . . and cover your excrement,* then, [*because*] *you shall dig, you shall lie down in safety.*

15. עֶרְוַת דָּבָר — SOMETHING IMMORAL [LITERALLY, **NAKEDNESS OF A THING**]. This phrase is followed by the phrase: לֹא תַסְגִּיר עֶבֶד, *You shall not turn over*[146] *a slave.*[147] This is an allusion [to the law]: When nakedness[148] is enclosed in a glass, it is forbidden to read the *Shema* while facing it.[149]

142b. See *Psalms* 20:8; *Exodus* 15:3, with *Rashi,* s.v., ה׳ שמו; *I Samuel* 17:45,47.

143. The full note reads: לֵית מָלֵא וְחַד חָסֵר, [*There are*] *no others spelled* [וְחָפַרְתָּה] *in full* [*with a final* ה]; *but there is one spelled defectively* [וְחָפַרְתָּ, *without the* ה].

144. A euphemism for defecation.

145. *Berachos* 69a — A person should become habituated to relieve himself in the morning and in the evening.

146. The root סגר can mean either *to enclose, to seal shut* (e.g., *Genesis* 19:6; *Exodus* 14:3) or *to give over, to deliver* (e.g., 32:30 below; *I Samuel* 23:20). In the context of this passage, לֹא תַסְגִּיר means *you shall not give over;* in the Baal HaTurim's allusion it means *you shall not enclose.*

147. In context, the עֶבֶד refers to *a servant, a slave;* in the Baal HaTurim's allusion it refers to *a servant of God, a worshiper* (*Ittur Bikkurim*).

148. The manuscripts and early printed editions read צוֹאָה, *excrement.* However, that reading is not consistent with the Talmud (see note 149 below). The later editions have emended the comment to read עֶרְוָה, *nakedness,* in accordance with the Talmudic passage. Perhaps, the term צוֹאָה was introduced erroneously by a scribe who thought of this comment as continuing the theme of the previous comment (*VeChur LaZahav*).

149. *Berachos* 25b — [It is forbidden to recite the *Shema* while facing a naked person or excrement, yet the law differs in the two instances:] If excrement is enclosed in glass, one may recite the *Shema* while facing it; if nakedness is enclosed in glass, one may not recite the *Shema* while facing it . . . [The Talmud explains that the difference is based on the Torah's wording:] With regard to excrement, the Torah requires covering [וְכִסִּיתָ, *and you shall cover* (*Rashi*)], and it is covered by the glass; but with

יֵשֵׁב בְּקִרְבְּךָ֛ בַּמָּק֥וֹם אֲשֶׁר־יִבְחַ֖ר בְּאַחַ֣ד שְׁעָרֶ֑יךָ
יח בַּטּ֖וֹב ל֑וֹ לֹ֥א תּוֹנֶֽנּוּ׃ לֹא־תִהְיֶ֥ה קְדֵשָׁ֖ה
מִבְּנ֣וֹת יִשְׂרָאֵ֑ל וְלֹא־יִהְיֶ֥ה קָדֵ֖שׁ מִבְּנֵ֥י יִשְׂרָאֵֽל׃
יט לֹא־תָבִיא֩ אֶתְנַ֨ן זוֹנָ֜ה וּמְחִ֣יר כֶּ֗לֶב בֵּ֛ית יְהֹוָ֥ה
אֱלֹהֶ֖יךָ לְכָל־נֶ֑דֶר כִּ֧י תֽוֹעֲבַ֛ת יְהֹוָ֥ה אֱלֹהֶ֖יךָ גַּם־
כ שְׁנֵיהֶֽם׃ לֹא־תַשִּׁ֣יךְ לְאָחִ֔יךָ נֶ֥שֶׁךְ כֶּ֖סֶף נֶ֣שֶׁךְ
כא אֹ֑כֶל נֶ֕שֶׁךְ כָּל־דָּבָ֖ר אֲשֶׁ֥ר יִשָּֽׁךְ׃ לַנָּכְרִ֣י תַשִּׁ֗יךְ

— בעל הטורים —

(יח) סָמִיךְ "לֹא תִהְיֶה קְדֵשָׁה" לְ"לֹא תַסְגִּיר עָבֶד". דְּאַיְרֵי בְּבַת יִשְׂרָאֵל הַנְּשׂוּאָה לְעָבֶד:
וְעוֹד — סָמִיךְ "עֶבֶד" לְ"בְּנוֹת יִשְׂרָאֵל", לוֹמַר, בִּתְּךָ בָּגְרָה, שַׁחְרֵר עַבְדְּךָ וְתֵן לָהּ:

(יט) וּמְחִיר. ב' בַּמָּסוֹרֶת — "וּמְחִיר כֶּלֶב"; "וּמְחִיר שָׂדֶה עַתּוּדִים". וְזֶהוּ שֶׁאָמְרוּ, נָתַן לָהּ
חִטִּין וַעֲשָׂאָן סֹלֶת. וְהַיְנוּ "וּמְחִיר שָׂדֶה". "עַתּוּדִים" נַמֵּי, דְּהַיְנוּ הֶחֱלִיף טָלֶה בְּכֶלֶב:
□ סָמַךְ לְ"לְכָל נֶדֶר" "לֹא תַשִּׁיךְ". שֶׁלֹּא תֹאמַר, אַלְוֶה בְּרִבִּית כְּדֵי לְשַׁלֵּם נְדָרָי:
□ כִּי תוֹעֲבַת ה' אֱלֹהֶיךָ גַּם שְׁנֵיהֶם. וּסְמִיךְ לֵהּ "לֹא תַשִּׁיךְ". לוֹמַר, אֶחָד הַמַּלְוֶה וְהַלֹּוֶה
וְהֶעָרֵב נִתְעָבִים:

(כ) יִשָּׁךְ. ב' בַּמָּסוֹרֶת — "כָּל דָּבָר אֲשֶׁר יִשָּׁךְ"; "כִּנָחָשׁ יִשָּׁךְ". שֶׁהָרִבִּית דּוֹמָה לְמִי

— BAAL HATURIM ELUCIDATED —

18. The Torah juxtaposed לֹא תִהְיֶה קְדֵשָׁה, *there shall not be a promiscuous woman,* to לֹא תַסְגִּיר עָבֶד, *you shall not deliver a slave* (v. 16), for the *promiscuous woman* of the verse refers to a Jewish woman marrying a Canaanite slave.[150]

Additionally: The Torah juxtaposed the passage of עֶבֶד, *slave* (vv. 16-17), with one that mentions בְּנוֹת יִשְׂרָאֵל, *the daughters of Israel,* to indicate [the Talmud's dictum]: If your daughter has attained majority,[151] free your slave and give him to her [in marriage].[152]

19. וּמְחִיר — OR THE EXCHANGE-PRICE. The masoretic note, ב', means that this word appears twice in the *Tanach*: (i) here, וּמְחִיר כֶּלֶב, *or the exchange-price for a dog;* and (ii) וּמְחִיר שָׂדֶה עַתּוּדִים, *the price of a field, rams (Proverbs 27:26).* This

regard to nakedness, the Torah states, *you shall not see something immoral* [literally, *the nakedness of a thing*], but nakedness can be seen through the glass.

150. *Peirush HaRokeach. Targum Onkelos* (cited by *Rashi*) renders: לֹא תִהְיֶה קְדֵשָׁה מִבְּנוֹת יִשְׂרָאֵל, as לָא תְהֵי אִתְּתָא מִבְּנַת יִשְׂרָאֵל לִגְבַר עֶבֶד, *A woman from the daughters of Israel shall not be [married] to a slave.*

151. And has not yet been married.

152. *Pesachim* 113a. The Talmud maintains that it is more important for a young lady to be

married as soon as she comes of age. [Thus, in Talmudic times, twelve years old or thereabouts was considered the optimal time for a girl to marry.] If she has already reached twelve and a half and is not yet married, her father is advised to free his non-Jewish slave [who, upon being freed has the status of a convert to Judaism] and marry them to each other. [Presumably, her father knows the character of his slave and that he would be a good husband to her. Indeed, the Talmud does not advise buying a slave and freeing him for this purpose. It speaks only of his own slave, i.e., one whom he knows well (*VeChur LaZahav*).]

in your midst, in whatever place he will choose in one of your cities, which is beneficial to him; you shall not taunt him.

¹⁸ *There shall not be a promiscuous woman from the daughters of Israel, and there shall not be a promiscuous man among the sons of Israel.* ¹⁹ *You shall not bring a harlot's hire or the exchange-price for a dog to the House of* HASHEM, *your God, for any vow, for both of them are an abomination of* HASHEM, *your God.*

²⁰ *You shall not cause your brother to take interest, interest of money or interest of food, interest of anything that he may take as interest.* ²¹ *You may cause a gentile to take*

───────── BAAL HATURIM ELUCIDATED ─────────

[similarity of expression] is [an allusion to] what our Sages have stated: If [her client] gave her wheat, and she made it into flour, [it is still considered as a harlot's hire].¹⁵³ This is [alluded to by the phrase,] *the price of [what grows in] a field.* Similarly, the word עַתּוּדִים, *rams,* [of that verse alludes to *the exchange-price for a dog*], which [as the Talmud describes,] means that he exchanged a lamb for a dog.¹⁵⁴

❑ {The comment beginning "סָמַךְ לְ"לְכָל נֶדֶר" that appears here in many editions, is presented as the first comment to verse 20 below.}^{154a}

❑ כִּי תוֹעֲבַת ה' אֱלֹהֶיךָ גַּם שְׁנֵיהֶם — FOR BOTH OF THEM ARE AN ABOMINATION OF HASHEM, YOUR GOD. Juxtaposed to this is לֹא תַשִּׁיךְ, *you shall not cause to take interest* (v. 20). This [juxtaposition] indicates that everyone — the lender, the borrower, and the guarantor¹⁵⁵ — become loathsome.¹⁵⁶

20. Juxtaposed to the phrase לְכָל נֶדֶר, *for any vow,* is לֹא תַשִּׁיךְ, *You shall not cause [your brother] to take interest* (v. 20). [The juxtaposition teaches] that a person should not say: "I will borrow^{156a} money at interest to pay my vows."^{156b}

❑ יִשָּׁךְ — TAKE AS INTEREST.¹⁵⁷ The masoretic note, ב', means that this word appears twice in the *Tanach*: (i) here, כָּל דָּבָר אֲשֶׁר יִשָּׁךְ, *anything that he may take as interest;* and (ii) כְּנָחָשׁ יִשָּׁךְ, *like a serpent, it will bite* (Proverbs 23:32). [The similarity of expression suggests an analogy.] The one who pays interest is comparable to one

---
153. *Bava Kamma* 93b, where this opinion is ascribed to *Beis Shammai*. According to *Beis Hillel* the change of form from wheat to flour removes the prohibition.

154. *Temurah* 30a.

154a. The order in which these comments are presented follows the first printed edition.

155. It is noteworthy that the *gematria* of שְׁנֵיהֶם is 405, which the principle of *im hakollel* allows to be considered equivalent to 406, the same as that of מַלְוֶה וְלֹוֶה וְעָרֵב (*VeChur LaZahav*).

156. *Peirush HaRokeach;* see *Bava Metzia* 75b;

see also the Baal HaTurim to *Exodus* 22:24.

156a. This law applies to both lending and borrowing (see *Rama* to *Yoreh De'ah* 160:22).

156b. According to the Talmud (*Bava Metzia* 57b), the laws of interest do not apply to הֶקְדֵּשׁ, *the Temple treasury* [literally, *the holy*]. Lest one think that he may therefore borrow at interest in order to redeem a pledge to the Temple treasury, the Baal HaTurim proves that such borrowing at interest is forbidden (A.S.).

157. The verb root נשך has two meanings: *to bite* (e.g., *Numbers* 21:9) and *to take interest* (e.g., יִשָּׁךְ

כג/כב־כו וּלְאָחִ֣יךָ לֹ֣א תַשִּׁ֑יךְ לְמַ֨עַן יְבָרֶכְךָ֜ יְהוָ֣ה אֱלֹהֶ֗יךָ
בְּכֹל֙ מִשְׁלַ֣ח יָדֶ֔ךָ עַל־הָאָ֕רֶץ אֲשֶׁר־אַתָּ֥ה בָא־
כב שָׁ֖מָּה לְרִשְׁתָּֽהּ׃ כִּֽי־תִדֹּ֥ר נֶ֙דֶר֙ לַיהוָ֣ה
אֱלֹהֶ֔יךָ לֹ֥א תְאַחֵ֖ר לְשַׁלְּמ֑וֹ כִּֽי־דָרֹ֨שׁ יִדְרְשֶׁ֜נּוּ
כג יְהוָ֤ה אֱלֹהֶ֙יךָ֙ מֵעִמָּ֔ךְ וְהָיָ֥ה בְךָ֖ חֵֽטְא׃ וְכִ֥י תֶחְדַּ֖ל
כד לִנְדֹּ֑ר לֹא־יִהְיֶ֥ה בְךָ֖ חֵֽטְא׃ מוֹצָ֥א שְׂפָתֶ֖יךָ תִּשְׁמֹ֣ר
וְעָשִׂ֑יתָ כַּאֲשֶׁ֨ר נָדַ֜רְתָּ לַיהוָ֤ה אֱלֹהֶ֙יךָ֙ נְדָבָ֔ה אֲשֶׁ֥ר
חמישי כה דִּבַּ֖רְתָּ בְּפִֽיךָ׃ כִּ֤י תָבֹא֙ בְּכֶ֣רֶם רֵעֶ֔ךָ וְאָכַלְתָּ֧
כו עֲנָבִ֛ים כְּנַפְשְׁךָ֖ שָׂבְעֶ֑ךָ וְאֶֽל־כֶּלְיְךָ֖ לֹ֥א תִתֵּֽן׃ כִּ֤י

בעל הטורים

שֶׁנְּשָׁכוֹ נָחָשׁ, שֶׁעוֹלֶה מְעַט מְעַט וְאֵינוֹ מַרְגִּישׁ בּוֹ עַד שֶׁיַּעֲלֶה לְמָמוֹן {רַב} כְּמוֹ נְשִׁיכַת הַנָּחָשׁ:

(כב) תְאַחֵר. ד׳ בַּמָּסוֹרֶת — ״לֹא תְאַחֵר לְשַׁלְּמוֹ״; ״מְלֵאָתְךָ וְדִמְעֲךָ לֹא תְאַחֵר״; ״כַּאֲשֶׁר תִּדֹּר נֶדֶר לֵאלֹהִים אַל תְּאַחֵר לְשַׁלְּמוֹ״; ״וּתְשׁוּעָתִי לֹא תְאַחֵר״. שֶׁאִם תְּשַׁלֵּם נְדָרֶיךָ, ״תְּשׁוּעָתִי לֹא תְאַחֵר״. אֲבָל הַנּוֹדֵר וְאֵינוֹ מְשַׁלֵּם הוּא מַרְחִיק יְשׁוּעָה:

(כה) סָמַךְ ״כִּי תָבֹא בְּכֶרֶם רֵעֶךָ״ לְנֶדֶר. רֶמֶז, סְחוֹר סְחוֹר לְכַרְמָא לָא תִקְרַב. שֶׁאִם נָדַר בְּנָזִיר לֹא יַשְׂכִּיר עַצְמוֹ לִמְלֶאכֶת הַכֶּרֶם. וּלְכָךְ הִקְדִּים כֶּרֶם לְשָׂדֶה, מַה שֶּׁאֵין דֶּרֶךְ לְהַקְדִּימוֹ:

❏ **לֹא תִתֵּן.** וּסְמִיךְ לֵהּ ״כִּי תָבֹא בְּקָמַת רֵעֶךָ״. רֶמֶז שֶׁפְּעָמִים לֹא תִתֵּן אֲפִלּוּ לְתוֹךְ פִּיךָ,

BAAL HATURIM ELUCIDATED

bitten by a serpent, for it increases little by little without the person realizing it until it becomes {a large sum of} money, just like the bite of a serpent.[158]

22. לֹא תְאַחֵר — YOU SHALL NOT DELAY. The masoretic note, ד׳, means that the term תְאַחֵר appears four times in the *Tanach*: (i) here, לֹא תְאַחֵר לְשַׁלְּמוֹ, *you shall not delay in paying it;* (ii) מְלֵאָתְךָ וְדִמְעֲךָ לֹא תְאַחֵר, *Do not delay your fullness-offering or your priestly heave-offering* (*Exodus* 22:28); (iii) כַּאֲשֶׁר תִּדֹּר נֶדֶר לֵאלֹהִים אַל תְּאַחֵר לְשַׁלְּמוֹ, *When you make a vow to God, do not delay in paying it* (*Ecclesiastes* 5:3); and (iv) וּתְשׁוּעָתִי לֹא תְאַחֵר, *and My salvation shall not delay* (*Isaiah* 46:13). [The similarity of expression implies] that if you pay your vows, *My salvation shall not delay.* But a person who makes vows but does not fulfill them places salvation at a distance.

---

and תַשִּׁיךְ in our passage). The Baal HaTurim's comment shows how one meaning leads to the other.

158. *Midrash Tanchuma, Mishpatim* 9 — Just as the serpent's bite initially makes a small, barely felt wound that festers and grows until it becomes unmanageable, so is the initial impact of interest barely felt, yet it grows and grows without end.

interest, but you may not cause your brother to take interest, so that HASHEM, your God, will bless you in your every undertaking on the land to which you are coming, to take possession of it.

22 *When you make a vow to HASHEM, your God, you shall not delay in paying it, for HASHEM, your God, will demand it of you, and there will be a sin in you.* 23 *If you refrain from vowing, there will be no sin in you.* 24 *You shall observe and carry out the issuance of your lips, just as you vowed a voluntary gift to HASHEM, your God, whatever you spoke with your mouth.*

25 *When you come into the vineyard of your fellow, you may eat grapes as is [the desire of], your soul to your fill, but you may not put into your vessel.*

BAAL HATURIM ELUCIDATED

25. The Torah juxtaposed כִּי תָבֹא בְּכֶרֶם רֵעֶךָ, *when you come into the vineyard of your fellow,* with the passage concerning a vow (vv. 22-24). [This juxtaposition is] an allusion to [our Sages' statement: We tell a nazirite,[159]] "Do not [even] approach the area surrounding the vineyard." Thus if a person took a nazirite vow, he should not hire himself out to work in a vineyard.[160] And for this reason, in this instance, the Torah mentions vineyard before field, although that is not the general practice.[161]

❑ {The Baal HaTurim's comment to כְּנַפְשְׁךָ appears at 13:7 above.}

❑ **לֹא תִתֵּן** — BUT YOU MAY NOT PUT. Juxtaposed to this is כִּי תָבֹא בְּקָמַת רֵעֶךָ, *when you come into the standing grain of your fellow* (v. 26). This [juxtaposition is] an allusion [to the concept] that at times [when you come to work in another's field, you should not only refrain from placing fruit into your vessel,] you may not even put fruit into your mouth, e.g., when you are working with one species [of fruit], you should not eat from another.[162]

159. Thus, the implication of נֶדֶר, *vow,* for the status of a nazirite can be attained only by undertaking a vow of *nezirus.*

160. *Bava Metzia* 92a. The Talmud's Aramaic expression סְחוֹר סְחוֹר לְכַרְמָא לָא תִקְרַב is usually rendered, *"Around! Around! Do not approach the vineyard!"* with the word סְחוֹר understood as an imperative. However, the *Perishah* (*Yoreh Deah* 383:5) rejects that translation and explains that סְחוֹר סְחוֹר לְכַרְמָא means *that which surrounds the vineyard.* Moreover, the *Perishah's* interpretation is in accordance with the *Rambam,* who renders the Talmud's Aramaic expression into Hebrew as סָבִיב לַכֶּרֶם לֹא יִקְרַב, *He shall not approach the surroundings of the vineyard* (*Hilchos Nezirus* 5:10), rather than, סוֹבֵב לַכֶּרֶם, *Go around the vineyard* (*Shoham Yakar* in the appendix *Harchavas HaDaas* to *Leviticus* 25:11 [see the Baal HaTurim there]).

161. See *Exodus* 22:4 and 23:11; *Leviticus* 19:9-10, 25:3 and 4; *Numbers* 16:14, 20:17 and 21:22; *Deuteronomy* 22:9; 24:19-21 and 28:38-39.

162. *Bava Metzia* 91b.

כד/א־ב תָבֹא֙ בְּקָמַ֣ת רֵעֶ֔ךָ וְקָטַפְתָּ֥ מְלִילֹ֖ת בְּיָדֶ֑ךָ וְחֶרְמֵשׁ֙
כד לֹ֣א תָנִ֔יף עַ֖ל קָמַ֥ת רֵעֶֽךָ׃ א כִּֽי־יִקַּ֥ח אִ֛ישׁ אִשָּׁ֖ה
וּבְעָלָ֑הּ וְהָיָ֞ה אִם־לֹ֧א תִמְצָא־חֵ֣ן בְּעֵינָ֗יו כִּי־מָ֤צָא
בָהּ֙ עֶרְוַ֣ת דָּבָ֔ר וְכָ֨תַב לָ֜הּ סֵ֤פֶר כְּרִיתֻת֙ וְנָתַ֣ן בְּיָדָ֔הּ
ב וְשִׁלְּחָ֖הּ מִבֵּיתֽוֹ׃ וְיָצְאָ֖ה מִבֵּית֑וֹ וְהָלְכָ֖ה וְהָיְתָ֥ה

בעל הטורים

(כו) בְּקָמַת רֵעֶךָ. וּסְמִיךְ לֵהּ "כִּי יִקַּח אִישׁ אִשָּׁה". לוֹמַר, מַה שָּׂדֶה נִקְנֶה בְּכֶסֶף וּשְׁטָר, אַף קִדּוּשִׁין:

כד (א) כִּי יִקַּח אִישׁ. בְּגִימַטְרִיָּא וְלֹא שֶׁיּוּקַּח:

❑ בָהּ עֶרְוַת דָּבָר. רָאשֵׁי תֵבוֹת "בְּעֵד". שֶׁאֵין דָּבָר שֶׁבְּעֶרְוָה אֶלָּא בְעֵדִים:

❑ דָּבָר וְכָתַב. שֶׁצָּרִיךְ דִּבּוּר עִם הַכְּתָב:

❑ וְכָתַב לָהּ {סֵפֶר. בְּגִימַטְרִיָּא} לִשְׁמָהּ:

❑ סֵפֶר כְּרִיתוּת. ג' בַּמָּסוֹרֶת – תְּרֵי בְּהַאי עִנְיָנָא; וְאִידָךְ "סֵפֶר כְּרִיתוּת אִמְּכֶם". זֶה שֶׁאָמְרוּ, סֵפֶר כּוֹרְתָהּ וְאֵין דָּבָר אַחֵר כּוֹרְתָהּ. וּכְתִיב תְּלָתָא זִמְנֵי "סֵפֶר כְּרִיתוּת", אַף עַל פִּי שֶׁאִשָּׁה נִקְנֵית בִּשְׁלֹשָׁה דְרָכִים, אֵין דָּבָר אַחֵר כּוֹרְתָהּ אֶלָּא סֵפֶר:

❑ מִבֵּיתוֹ. וְיָצְאָה. לוֹמַר, הִיא יוֹצְאָה מִשְּׁכוּנָתוֹ כְּשֶׁהִיא גְרוּשָׁה, וְלֹא הוּא:

BAAL HATURIM ELUCIDATED

26. בְּקָמַת רֵעֶךָ — INTO THE STANDING GRAIN OF YOUR FELLOW. Juxtaposed to this is כִּי יִקַּח אִישׁ אִשָּׁה, *If a man takes a wife* (24:1). This [juxtaposition] indicates [that] just as a field can be acquired through the transfer of money or through a legal document,[163] so too, marriage[164] [is effected through these legal practices].[165]

XXIV.

1. כִּי יִקַּח אִישׁ — IF A MAN WILL TAKE. The *gematria* of this phrase (459) is equivalent[166] to that of וְלֹא שֶׁיּוּקַּח, *and he should not be taken.*[167]

❑ **בָהּ עֶרְוַת דָּבָר — IN HER SOMETHING IMMORAL.** The initial letters of these words spell בְּעֵד[167a], *with a witness.* For any matter related to prohibitions concerning immorality can be adjudicated only through [the testimony of] witnesses.[168]

❑ **דָּבָר וְכָתַב — SOMETHING . . . AND HE WILL WRITE HER.** [The juxtaposition of these

163. *Kiddushin* 26a — Real property is acquired through the transfer of money, a legal document or *chazakah* [uncontested occupation of the site for a period of three years].

164. *Kiddushin* 2a.

165. *Peirush HaRokeach.*

166. The *gematria* of the Baal HaTurim's phrase is 461, two more than that of the Scriptural phrase. The *gematrios* may be reconciled by applying the principle of *im hakollel,* which allows 461 to be considered equivalent to 462, and the principle of *im hateivos,* which allows three to be added to the *gematria* of the Scriptural phrase, bringing it to 462.

167. That is, a man takes a woman in marriage, rather than being taken by her (see *Kiddushin* 2b).

167a. Alternatively: The Baal HaTurim's term should be vowelized as two words — ב׳ עֵד, *two witness*[*es*] (*VeChur LaZahav*).

168. *Gittin* 2b.

26 *When you come into the standing grain of your fellow, you may pluck ears with your hand, but you may not lift a sickle against the standing grain of your fellow.*

24 1 *If a man will take a wife and live with her, and it will be that she will not find favor in his eyes, for he has found in her something immoral, and he will write her a bill of divorce and give into her hand, and send her away from his house,* 2 *and she shall leave his house and she will go and be married to*

BAAL HATURIM ELUCIDATED

two words indicates] that there must be דִּבּוּר, *speech,* along with the כְּתָב, *writing.*[169]

{סֵפֶר} וְכָתַב לָהּ {סֵפֶר} — AND HE WILL WRITE HER A BILL. {The *gematria* of לָהּ סֵפֶר (375) is equal to that of}[170] לִשְׁמָהּ, *specifically for her.*[171]

❑ סֵפֶר כְּרִיתֻת — A BILL OF DIVORCE. The masoretic note, ג׳, means that this phrase appears three times in the *Tanach*:[172] (i-ii) twice in this passage, (vv. 1,3) and (iii) סֵפֶר כְּרִיתוּת אִמְּכֶם, *your mother's bill of divorce* (*Isaiah* 50:1). This is [in accord with] what the Sages have said: The bill severs [the marriage bond]; nothing else severs it.[173] And סֵפֶר כְּרִיתוּת, *a bill of divorce,* is written three times,[173a] [to teach that] although a woman can be acquired as a wife in [any of] three ways,[174] nothing[174a] can sever her [marriage bond] except a bill [of divorce].

❑ מִבֵּיתוֹ. וְיָצְאָה — FROM HIS HOUSE. AND SHE SHALL LEAVE. This [juxtaposition] indicates [that] when a woman is divorced, it is she who must move away from his neighborhood, and not he.[175]

2. {The Baal HaTurim's comment to וְיָצְאָה appears at *Exodus* 21:11.}

169. This refers to either: The husband's verbal instructions to the scribe to write the *get* [bill of divorce] and to the witnesses to sign it (see *Yoreh De'ah* 120:4 and 131:7); or to the scribe stating his intention before beginning to write the *get* (see *Yoreh De'ah* 131:7); or to the husband or his agent saying, "Here is your *get,*" to the wife (see *Yoreh De'ah* 136:1).

170. The words enclosed in braces are not found in the early printed editions or in most later editions. However, they do appear in *Peirush HaRokeach,* the Baal HaTurim's source for the comment, and in the Baal HaTurim manuscripts used by *Shoham Yakar.*

171. *Gittin* 24b — The phrase וְכָתַב לָהּ teaches that a *get* must be written לִשְׁמָהּ, i.e., specifically as a document of divorce for her husband to give to her.

172. The full note reads: ג׳ ב׳ חֲסֵרִים וא׳ מָלֵא, *Three times, twice spelled* כְּרִיתֻת *defectively, without a* ו, *once spelled* כְּרִיתוּת *in full, with a* ו.

173. *Gittin* 21b.

173a. See note 172.

174. (i) The transfer of money or an object of monetary value from him to her; (ii) a marriage document; (iii) cohabitation (*Kiddushin* 2a).

174a. That is, none of those three ways.

175. *Kesubos* 28a. The *Sifrei* derives this law from the first two words of verse 2 — וְיָצְאָה מִבֵּיתוֹ, *and she will leave his house.* It is not clear why the Baal HaTurim cites this passage under the rubric מִבֵּיתוֹ וְיָצְאָה, the last word of verse 1, with the first word of verse 2.

Shoham Yakar suggests that whereas the phrase וְיָצְאָה מִבֵּיתוֹ is followed immediately by וְהָלְכָה וְהָיְתָה לְאִישׁ אַחֵר, *and she will go and be married to another man,* it may be thought that the verse prohibits her from living in her former husband's neighborhood only after she has married another man. And, indeed, that is the inference of the Talmudic statement: If one

ג לְאִישׁ־אַחֵר: וּשְׂנֵאָהּ הָאִישׁ הָאַחֲרוֹן וְכָתַב לָהּ
סֵפֶר כְּרִיתֻת וְנָתַן בְּיָדָהּ וְשִׁלְּחָהּ מִבֵּיתוֹ אוֹ כִי
יָמוּת הָאִישׁ הָאַחֲרוֹן אֲשֶׁר־לְקָחָהּ לוֹ לְאִשָּׁה:
ד לֹא־יוּכַל בַּעְלָהּ הָרִאשׁוֹן אֲשֶׁר־שִׁלְּחָהּ לָשׁוּב
לְקַחְתָּהּ לִהְיוֹת לוֹ לְאִשָּׁה אַחֲרֵי אֲשֶׁר הֻטַּמָּאָה
כִּי־תוֹעֵבָה הִוא לִפְנֵי יהוה וְלֹא תַחֲטִיא אֶת־
ששי ה הָאָרֶץ אֲשֶׁר יהוה אֱלֹהֶיךָ נֹתֵן לְךָ נַחֲלָה: כִּי־

בעל הטורים

(ג) **אוֹ כִי יָמוּת הָאִישׁ הָאַחֲרוֹן.** וְלֹא אָמַר הַשֵּׁנִי. לוֹמַר שֶׁהוּא אַחֲרוֹן, שֶׁאִם נִשֵּׂאת לִשְׁנַיִם וּמֵתוּ לֹא תִנָּשֵׂא עוֹד, דְּבִתְרֵי זִמְנֵי הָוֵי חֲזָקָה. {וּלְמַאן דְּאָמַר בִּתְלָת זִמְנֵי הָוֵי חֲזָקָה, לְכָךְ סָמַךְ אִשָּׁה לְשָׂדֶה, לוֹמַר, מַה שָּׂדֶה בִּתְלָת שְׁנִין הָוֵי חֲזָקָה, אַף אִשָּׁה בִּתְלָת זִמְנֵי הָוֵי חֲזָקָה}:

(ד) **וְלֹא תַחֲטִיא.** וּסְמִיךְ לֵהּ "כִּי יִקַּח אִישׁ אִשָּׁה". שֶׁהִיא מַצֶּלֶת אֶת הָאָדָם מִן הַחֵטְא:

❑ **נַחֲלָה.** וּסְמִיךְ לֵהּ "כִּי יִקַּח". לוֹמַר, "בַּיִת וָהוֹן נַחֲלַת אָבוֹת וְגוֹ'", אֲבָל "כִּי יִקַּח אִישׁ אִשָּׁה", "מֵה' אִשָּׁה מַשְׂכָּלֶת":

וְעוֹד – לוֹמַר שֶׁכְּתֻבַּת אִשָּׁה מִמְּקַרְקְעֵי:

BAAL HATURIM ELUCIDATED

3. **אוֹ כִי יָמוּת הָאִישׁ הָאַחֲרוֹן** — OR IF THE LATTER MAN WILL DIE. The Torah [uses the expression הָאַחֲרוֹן, *the latter,* but] did not say הַשֵּׁנִי, *the second.* This indicates that he is the last.[176] Thus, if she had married two husbands and each had died, she should not marry again, for, [according to one opinion,] with two times a *chazakah*[177] has

divorces his wife, she should not marry in his neighborhood (*Kesubos* 27b). By making the law dependent upon the juxtaposition of the two verses, the Baal HaTurim implies that the law is not limited to a divorcee who has remarried, rather it applies to any woman who has been divorced. And that is how the law is codified by the *Rambam* (*Hilchos Issurei Biah* 21:27) and the Baal HaTurim (*Tur, Even HaEzer* 119).

176. The precise meaning of אַחֲרוֹן is a matter of dispute among the commentaries. According to one view, sometimes it means *next* or *subsequent* and sometimes it means *last.* Moreover, both meanings are found in the same verse: וַיָּשֶׂם אֶת הַשְּׁפָחוֹת וְאֶת יַלְדֵיהֶן רִאשֹׁנָה, *He put the handmaids and their children first,* וְאֶת לֵאָה וִילָדֶיהָ אַחֲרֹנִים, *and Leah and her children next,* וְאֶת רָחֵל וְאֶת יוֹסֵף אַחֲרֹנִים, *and Rachel and Joseph last* (*Genesis* 33:2). This also explains why God called the second of three signs הָאֹת הָאַחֲרוֹן (*Exodus* 4:8), and why the prophet (*Haggai* 2:9) calls the Second Temple הַבַּיִת הַזֶּה הָאַחֲרוֹן, even though there will be a third [may it be built speedily, in our days] (*Tosefos Yom Tov* to *Demai* 7:3).

According to another view, the word אַחֲרוֹן always means *last;* sometimes referring to the ultimate last, sometimes referring to that which up until this point is last. Thus, God called the second of three signs הָאֹת הָאַחֲרוֹן, because He had not yet shown Moses the third sign (*Ibn Ezra* to *Exodus* 4:8). Similarly, according to this second view, when Jacob put Leah and her children behind the handmaids and their children, Leah and her children were last, for Jacob had not yet positioned Rachel and Joseph. And for this same reason, the prophet uses the phrase הַבַּיִת הַזֶּה הָאַחֲרוֹן, because as of the time he spoke, that was the last Temple to have been built (*VeChur LaZahav*).

177. The legal principle of חֲזָקָה, *chazakah,* is a presumption that if something has happened a

another man, ³ and if the latter man will despise her and will write her a bill of divorce and give it into her hand and send her away from his house, or if the latter man will die, [i.e.,] one who had taken her to himself as a wife — ⁴ her first husband who divorced her shall not again take her to be his wife, after she had been defiled, for it is an abomination before HASHEM. You shall not bring sin upon the land that HASHEM, your God, gives you as an inheritance.

──────── BAAL HATURIM ELUCIDATED ────────

been established.[178] {And according to the opinion that a phenomenon must be repeated three times for a *chazakah* to be established,[179] the Torah juxtaposed the case of the [widowed] woman with the laws concerning a field (23:26 above) to indicate that just as a *chazakah* regarding [proof of ownership of] a field is established after three years, so too, a *chazakah* regarding a widow [not remarrying] is established after [she has been widowed] three times.}[180]

4. וְלֹא תַחֲטִיא — YOU SHALL NOT BRING SIN. Juxtaposed to this is כִּי יִקַּח אִישׁ אִשָּׁה, *If a man will take a wife* (v. 5). For it is his wife who saves a man from sin.[181]

נַחֲלָה ❑ — AS AN INHERITANCE. Juxtaposed to this is the phrase כִּי יִקַּח, *If [a man] will take [a wife]* (v. 5). [This is] to indicate [that although] . . . בַּיִת וָהוֹן נַחֲלַת אָבוֹת, *A house and wealth are an ancestral heritage . . .* (Proverbs 19:14),[182] nevertheless, כִּי יִקַּח אִישׁ אִשָּׁה, *if a man takes a wife,* [know that] [וּ]מֵה' אִשָּׁה מַשְׂכָּלֶת, an *intelligent wife is from HASHEM.* [183]

Additionally: [The juxtaposition of נַחֲלָה with marriage] indicates that a woman's *kesubah* may be exacted from [her husband's] real property.[184]

---

certain number of times, it has become established as the norm. For example, if a woman has lost a number of sons who died as a result of circumcision, her subsequent sons should not be circumcised; similarly, if a woman has been married a number of times and each husband has died, she should not marry again. The Talmud records a dispute regarding the number needed to establish a *chazakah* in the cases of a widow and of circumcision — two or three (*Yevamos* 64b). The Baal HaTurim's allusion refers to a woman who had been widowed more than once.

178. In most printed editions, the Baal HaTurim's comment ends here. However, the manuscripts used by *Shoham Yakar* continue with the passage presented here in braces. The last six words of that passage are found in the early printed editions, but whereas they do not make sense without the preceding lines, they were omitted from the later printings.

179. See note 177 above.

180. *Peirush HaRokeach.*

181. *Peirush HaRokeach;* see *Yevamos* 63a.

182. That verse continues וּמֵה' אִשָּׁה מַשְׂכָּלֶת, *but an intelligent wife is from HASHEM.*

183. *Moed Katan* 18b. The Talmud there states that we learn from the Torah, the Prophets and the Writings that a man's wife is selected for him by God: From the Torah, *The matter* [of Rebecca becoming Isaac's wife] *stemmed from HASHEM* (Genesis 24:50); from the Prophets, *His father and mother did not know that it* [Samson's selection of a wife] *was from HASHEM* (Judges 14:4); and from the Writings, *A house and wealth are an ancestral heritage, but an intelligent wife is from HASHEM* (Proverbs 19:14).

184. Their marriage contract places a lien on his real property in event of divorce or his death (see *Kesubos* 68b). For the term נַחֲלָה usually refers to real property (A.S.).

כד/ה **יִקַּח אִישׁ אִשָּׁה חֲדָשָׁה לֹא יֵצֵא בַּצָּבָא וְלֹא־יַעֲבֹר עָלָיו לְכָל־דָּבָר נָקִי יִהְיֶה לְבֵיתוֹ שָׁנָה אֶחָת וְשִׂמַּח**

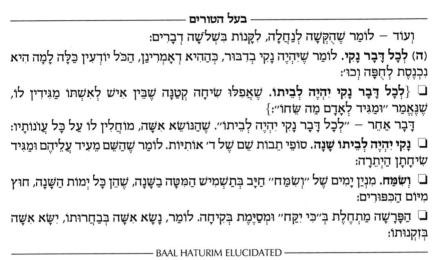

בעל הטורים

וְעוֹד – לוֹמַר שֶׁהֻקְּשָׁה לְנַחֲלָה, לְקָנוֹת בִּשְׁלֹשָׁה דְבָרִים:

(ה) **לְכָל דָּבָר נָקִי.** לוֹמַר שֶׁיִּהְיֶה נָקִי בְּדִבּוּר, כְּהַהִיא דְאָמְרִינַן, הַכֹּל יוֹדְעִין כַּלָּה לָמָה הִיא נִכְנֶסֶת לְחֻפָּה וְכוּ':

❑ {**לְכָל דָּבָר נָקִי יִהְיֶה לְבֵיתוֹ.** שֶׁאֲפִלּוּ שִׂיחָה קְטַנָּה שֶׁבֵּין אִישׁ לְאִשְׁתּוֹ מַגִּידִין לוֹ, שֶׁנֶּאֱמַר "וּמַגִּיד לְאָדָם מַה שֵּׂחוֹ":}

דָּבָר אַחֵר – "לְכָל דָּבָר נָקִי יִהְיֶה לְבֵיתוֹ". שֶׁהַנּוֹשֵׂא אִשָּׁה, מוֹחֲלִין לוֹ עַל כָּל עֲוֹנוֹתָיו:

❑ **נָקִי יִהְיֶה לְבֵיתוֹ שָׁנָה.** סוֹפֵי תֵבוֹת שֵׁם שֶׁל ד' אוֹתִיּוֹת. לוֹמַר שֶׁהַשֵּׁם מֵעִיד עֲלֵיהֶם וּמַגִּיד שִׂיחָתָן הַיְתֵרָה:

❑ **וְשִׂמַּח.** מִנְיַן יָמִים שֶׁל "וְשִׂמַּח" חַיָּב בְּתַשְׁמִישׁ הַמִּטָּה בַּשָּׁנָה, שֶׁהֵן כָּל יְמוֹת הַשָּׁנָה, חוּץ מִיּוֹם הַכִּפּוּרִים:

❑ הַפָּרָשָׁה מַתְחֶלֶת בְּ"כִי יִקַּח" וּמְסַיֶּמֶת בְּקִיחָה. לוֹמַר, נָשָׂא אִשָּׁה בְּבַחֲרוּתוֹ, יִשָּׂא אִשָּׁה בְּזִקְנוּתוֹ:

BAAL HATURIM ELUCIDATED

Additionally: It indicates that a wife is compared to real property, in that she is acquired in marriage through one of three ways.[185]

5. לְכָל דָּבָר נָקִי — FOR EVERY WORD [SHALL BE] CLEAN.[185a] This indicates that one should be clean in his speech.[186] As the Talmud states: Everyone knows why a bride enters the marriage canopy . . .[187]

❑ {**לְכָל דָּבָר נָקִי יִהְיֶה לְבֵיתוֹ — FOR EVERY WORD;**[187A] **HE SHALL BE FREE FOR HIS HOME.** For even small talk between a man and his wife they tell him,[188] as it is written, וּמַגִּיד לְאָדָם מַה שֵּׂחוֹ, *and He tells a person what his talk was* (Amos 4:13).}[189]

Alternatively: The statement, *for any matter; he shall be free for his home,* [teaches] that when a man marries, they forgive all of his sins.[190]

❑ **נָקִי יִהְיֶה לְבֵיתוֹ שָׁנָה — HE SHALL BE FREE FOR HIS HOME FOR ONE YEAR.** The final letters of these words form the Tetragrammaton, י־ה־ו־ה. This is to indicate that

185. See the Baal HaTurim's comments to 23:26 above with note 163, and to 24:1 with note 174.

185a. The term דָּבָר can mean either *matter* or *word;* in the context of the verse it means *matter,* but in the Baal HaTurim's allusion it means *word.* Similarly, the term נָקִי can mean either *free,* as it is used in the verse, or *clean,* as in the allusion.

186. See note 137 above.

187. *Shabbos* 33a. The Talmud there speaks about the dire consequence of foul speech, then states: Everyone knows why a bride enters the marriage canopy; nevertheless, if someone befouls his mouth [with explicit speech about marital intimacy], then even if a favorable decree of seventy years has been [decreed and] sealed [by the Heavenly Tribunal] for him, they will overturn it in favor of a harsh decree. The Baal HaTurim derives this from our verse: "If a man takes a wife . . ."

187a. See note 185a.

188. After his death, when he stands before the Heavenly Tribunal for justice, he is reminded of every word he has uttered in his lifetime.

189. *Chagigah* 5b. This comment is not found in any printed edition of the Baal HaTurim, but does appear in one of the manuscripts used by *Shoham Yakar.*

190. *Peirush HaRokeach;* see the Baal HaTurim to 22:12 above, with note 106.

⁵ If a man will take a new wife, he shall not go out to the army, nor shall it obligate him for any matter; he shall be free for his home for one year, and he shall gladden

———————————— BAAL HATURIM ELUCIDATED ————————————

God testifies concerning them and tells of their excessive talk.[191]

❏ וְשִׂמַּח — **AND HE SHALL GLADDEN.** A man is obligated to gladden his wife through marital relations on any of 354 days of the year — equal to the *gematria* of [192]וְשִׂמַּח, *he shall gladden* — i.e., any day of the year except for Yom Kippur [when relations are prohibited by the Torah].[193]

❏ The passage[194] begins with כִּי יִקַּח, *if a [man] will take,* and ends with the concept of taking [אֲשֶׁר לָקָח, *whom he has taken*], to indicate [that even though] he married a woman in his youth, [if she subsequently died] he should marry another woman in his old age.[195]

---

191. See note 188 above.

192. The reading follows virtually all editions and that is how it appears in *Peirush HaRokeach,* presumably the Baal HaTurim's source for this comment. A regular year on the Jewish calendar comprises either 353, 354 or 355 [a leap year, either 383, 384 or 385 days]. As a matter of convenience, when not speaking of a particular year, the count 355 is used — either because that number is the *gematria* of שָׁנָה, *year* (*VeChur LaZahav*), or because twelve lunar months actually contain 354 and a bit less than nine hours, so that the last day is the 355th (A.S.). Thus, the Baal HaTurim speaks of 354 as the number of days in the year, excluding Yom Kippur. Another version of this allusion appears in *Rabbeinu Ephraim* (*MiKesivah Ashkenazis*). There, the spelling וְשִׂימַּח is used, with a י, and the *gematria* is then 364, one day less than the number of days in a solar year.

193. *Yoma* 73b.

194. The reading הַפָּרְשָׁה, *the passage,* follows the early printed editions and that is what appears in the manuscripts. There is a difficulty with this reading, however, for according to masoretic tradition, the text of Scripture is divided into פָּרְשִׁיּוֹת, *parashiyos* (paragraph-like passages), separated from one another by a blank space, and that is how *Tanach* scrolls are written. These spaces appear in one of two forms: פְּתוּחָה, *open,* indicated by ending the previous passage in the middle of a line and then beginning the new passage at the beginning of the next line, or סְתוּמָה, *closed,* indicated by the new passage beginning on the same line on which the previous passage ended, but after a space wide enough to contain nine letters (see illustration). [In some printed editions these spaces are indicated

by the letters פ and ס.] However, in our Torah scrolls [in which the *parashah* divisions are made in the manner codified by the *Rambam* (*Hilchos Sefer Torah* 8)], verses 5 and 6 form one *parashah,* separated from verse 4 by a סְתוּמָה and from verse 7 by a סְתוּמָה. Accordingly, our verse does not end a *parashah.*

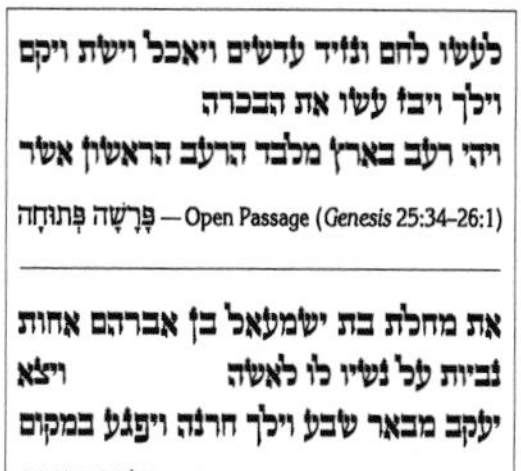

לְעֵשֵׂו לָהֶם וּלְזֵיד לַעֲרָשִׁים וַיֹּאכַל וַיֵּשְׁתְּ וַיָּקָם
וַיֵּלֶךְ וַיִּבֶז עֵשָׂו אֶת הַבְּכֹרָה
וַיְהִי רָעַב בָּאָרֶץ מִלְּבַד הָרָעָב הָרִאשׁוֹן אֲשֶׁר
פָּרְשָׁה פְּתוּחָה — Open Passage (*Genesis 25:34–26:1*)
אֶת מָחֲלַת בַּת יִשְׁמָעֵאל בֶּן אַבְרָהָם אֲחוֹת
נְבָיוֹת עַל נָשָׁיו לוֹ לְאִשָּׁה וַיֵּצֵא
יַעֲקֹב מִבְּאֵר שֶׁבַע וַיֵּלֶךְ חָרָנָה וַיִּפְגַּע בַּמָּקוֹם
פָּרְשָׁה סְתוּמָה — Closed Passage (*Genesis 28:9–10*)

As a result of this problem, most later printings followed the suggestion of *Ittur Bikkurim,* changing הַפָּרְשָׁה to הַפָּסוּק, *the verse.* However, there is at least one authoritative Torah codex (written more than a century before the birth of the *Rambam*) and at least one centuries-old Yemenite *Keser* (see *Masores HaTorah VeHaNeviim,* p. 32) that show a *parashah* סְתוּמָה separating verses 5 and 6. Thus, it is possible that the Baal HaTurim's Torah scroll followed one of those traditions, and so he wrote הַפָּרְשָׁה (*VeChur LaZahav*).

Alternatively: The Baal HaTurim uses the word הַפָּרְשָׁה to include verses 1-5, all of which speak about marriage. Verse 1 begins, כִּי יִקַּח אִישׁ אִשָּׁה, *If a man will take a wife,* while verse 5 begins, כִּי יִקַּח אִישׁ אִשָּׁה חֲדָשָׁה, *If a man will take a new wife,* which can be understood as a wife who is new with respect to his first wife. Thus, verse 1 refers to the wife of his youth; verse 5, to the wife of his old age (*VeChur LaZahav*).

195. *Kesubos* 62b.

ו אֶת־אִשְׁתּוֹ אֲשֶׁר־לָקָח׃ לֹא־יַחֲבֹל רֵחַיִם וָרָכֶב כִּי־
ז נֶפֶשׁ הוּא חֹבֵל׃ כִּי־יִמָּצֵא אִישׁ גֹּנֵב נֶפֶשׁ
מֵאֶחָיו מִבְּנֵי יִשְׂרָאֵל וְהִתְעַמֶּר־בּוֹ וּמְכָרוֹ וּמֵת הַגַּנָּב
ח הַהוּא וּבִעַרְתָּ הָרָע מִקִּרְבֶּךָ׃ הִשָּׁמֶר בְּנֶגַע־
הַצָּרַעַת לִשְׁמֹר מְאֹד וְלַעֲשׂוֹת כְּכֹל אֲשֶׁר־יוֹרוּ
אֶתְכֶם הַכֹּהֲנִים הַלְוִיִּם כַּאֲשֶׁר צִוִּיתִם תִּשְׁמְרוּ
ט לַעֲשׂוֹת׃ זָכוֹר אֵת אֲשֶׁר־עָשָׂה יהוה אֱלֹהֶיךָ
י לְמִרְיָם בַּדֶּרֶךְ בְּצֵאתְכֶם מִמִּצְרָיִם׃ כִּי־
תַשֶּׁה בְרֵעֲךָ מַשַּׁאת מְאוּמָה לֹא־תָבֹא אֶל־בֵּיתוֹ
יא לַעֲבֹט עֲבֹטוֹ׃ בַּחוּץ תַּעֲמֹד וְהָאִישׁ אֲשֶׁר אַתָּה
יב נֹשֶׁה בוֹ יוֹצִיא אֵלֶיךָ אֶת־הָעֲבוֹט הַחוּצָה׃ וְאִם־
יג אִישׁ עָנִי הוּא לֹא תִשְׁכַּב בַּעֲבֹטוֹ׃ הָשֵׁב תָּשִׁיב

בעל הטורים

❑ **אִשְׁתּוֹ אֲשֶׁר לָקָח.** וּסְמִיךְ לֵהּ "לֹא יַחֲבֹל". לוֹמַר, שֶׁלֹּא יַחֲבֹל אִשְׁתּוֹ בְּתַשְׁמִישׁ הַמִּטָּה:

דָּבָר אַחֵר – עַל שֵׁם שֶׁהָאִשָּׁה הִיא מַשְׁכּוֹנוֹ שֶׁל הָאָדָם, דְּבַעֲוֹן נְדָרִים אִשְׁתּוֹ שֶׁל אָדָם מֵתָה:

(ו) **כִּי נֶפֶשׁ הוּא חֹבֵל. כִּי יִמָּצֵא אִישׁ גֹּנֵב.** לוֹמַר, שֶׁהַגַּנָּב נוֹטֵל נַפְשׁוֹ שֶׁל אוֹתוֹ שֶׁגּוֹנֵב מִמֶּנּוּ, כְּעִנְיַן שֶׁנֶּאֱמַר, "וְקָבַע אֶת קֹבְעֵיהֶם נָפֶשׁ":

(ז) **כִּי יִמָּצֵא אִישׁ גֹּנֵב נֶפֶשׁ מֵאֶחָיו מִבְּנֵי יִשְׂרָאֵל.** רָאשֵׁי תֵבוֹת בְּגִימַטְרִיָּא זֶהוּ יוֹסֵף:

(י) **כִּי תַשֶּׁה בְרֵעֲךָ.** סָמַךְ לְצָרַעַת, לוֹמַר שֶׁעַל יְדֵי זֶה בָּא הַצָּרַעַת. שֶׁאוֹמֵר לוֹ חֲבֵרוֹ, הַשְׁאִילֵנִי כְּלִי שֶׁלְּךָ. וְהוּא אוֹמֵר, אֵין לִי. וּלְמָחָר בָּאִים נְגָעִים עַל בֵּיתוֹ, "וְצִוָּה הַכֹּהֵן וּפִנּוּ אֶת הַבַּיִת" וְהַכֹּל רוֹאִים שֶׁיֵּשׁ לוֹ:

BAAL HATURIM ELUCIDATED

❑ **אִשְׁתּוֹ אֲשֶׁר לָקָח — HIS WIFE WHOM HE HAS TAKEN.** Juxtaposed to this is לֹא יַחֲבֹל, *one shall not take as a pledge.* This [juxtaposition] is to indicate that a man should not withhold marital relations from his wife as a pledge.[196]

Alternatively: [The verses are juxtaposed] because a woman is a pledge for her husband, as it were. For because of the sin of broken vows, a man's wife will die.[197]

---

196. In *Peirush HaTur HaAroch,* the Baal HaTurim explains that the *mitzvah* of וְשִׂמַּח אֶת אִשְׁתּוֹ, *he shall gladden his wife,* forbids him from withholding marital relations.

197. *Peirush HaRokeach;* see *Shabbos* 32b, where the Talmud derives this from the verse, *If you do not have with what to pay, why should he take your bed from under you* (*Proverbs* 22:27). Although the verse refers to a human creditor who takes a piece of furniture in place of an unpaid loan, the Talmud interprets the creditor as God, the debt as an unfulfilled vow, and bed as

his wife whom he has taken. 6 *One shall not take as a pledge a lower millstone or an upper millstone, for it is a life that he would be taking as a pledge.*

7 *If a man will be found kidnaping a person of his brethren among the Children of Israel, and he enslaves him and sells him, that kidnaper shall die, and you shall remove the evil from your midst.*

8 *Beware of a tzaraas affliction, to be very careful and to act; according to everything that the Kohanim, the Levites, shall teach you — as I have commanded them — you shall be careful to perform.* 9 *Remember what HASHEM, your God, did to Miriam on the way, when you were leaving Egypt.*

10 *When you will give your fellow a loan of any amount, you shall not enter his home to take security for it.* 11 *You shall stand outside; and the man to whom you lend shall bring the security to you outside.* 12 *If that man is poor, you shall not sleep with his security.* 13 *You shall return the*

BAAL HATURIM ELUCIDATED

6. כִּי נֶפֶשׁ הוּא חֹבֵל. כִּי יִמָּצֵא אִישׁ גֹּנֵב — FOR IT IS A LIFE THAT HE WOULD BE TAKING AS A PLEDGE. IF A MAN WILL BE FOUND KIDNAPING. This [juxtaposition] indicates that a robber takes the lifesoul of the person from whom he robs.[197a] This concept is implied by the verse, וְקָבַע אֶת קֹבְעֵיהֶם נָפֶשׁ, *he will steal the lifesoul of those from whom he steals* (*Proverbs* 22:23).[198]

7. כִּי יִמָּצֵא אִישׁ גֹּנֵב נֶפֶשׁ מֵאֶחָיו מִבְּנֵי יִשְׂרָאֵל — IF A MAN WILL BE FOUND KIDNAPING A PERSON OF HIS BRETHREN AMONG THE CHILDREN OF ISRAEL. The *gematria* of the initial letters of this stich (174) is equal to that of וְזֶהוּ יוֹסֵף, *This* [*refers to*] *Joseph.*[199]

10. כִּי תַשֶּׁה בְרֵעֲךָ — WHEN YOU WILL GIVE YOUR FELLOW A LOAN. The Torah juxtaposed this with the passage concerning *tzaraas* (vv. 8-9), to indicate that [failure to give loans] can bring on *tzaraas.* For a person's neighbor will say to him, "Lend me your utensil." He will say, "I do not have [that item]." At a later date, his house will become afflicted with *tzaraas,* [and then,] *the Kohen shall command, and they shall clear the house* (*Leviticus* 14:36), and everyone will see that he does, in fact, possess that article.[200]

---

a euphemism for wife.

197a. *Bava Kamma* 119a; see also *Sanhedrin* 7a.

198. In the context of *Proverbs,* that verse means that God will take the life of the crook, *He will steal the lifesoul of those who steal from others* (*Sanhedrin* 7a). In the Baal HaTurim's comment, the subject is the crook: *he will steal the lifesoul of the ones from whom he steals.*

199. The Midrash applies our verse to the sale of Joseph by his brothers (*Bereishis Rabbah* 84:16).

200. *Peirush HaRokeach;* see *Arachin* 16a; see also the Baal HaTurim to 22:2 above, s.v., וַאֲסַפְתּוֹ.

כד/יד־יז לוֹ אֶת־הָעֲבוֹט כְּבוֹא הַשֶּׁמֶשׁ וְשָׁכַב בְּשַׂלְמָתוֹ
וּבֵרְכֶךָּ וּלְךָ תִּהְיֶה צְדָקָה לִפְנֵי יהוה אֱלֹהֶיךָ:
שביעי יד לֹא־תַעֲשֹׁק שָׂכִיר עָנִי וְאֶבְיוֹן מֵאַחֶיךָ אוֹ מִגֵּרְךָ
טו אֲשֶׁר בְּאַרְצְךָ בִּשְׁעָרֶיךָ: בְּיוֹמוֹ תִתֵּן שְׂכָרוֹ וְלֹא־
תָבוֹא עָלָיו הַשֶּׁמֶשׁ כִּי עָנִי הוּא וְאֵלָיו הוּא נֹשֵׂא
אֶת־נַפְשׁוֹ וְלֹא־יִקְרָא עָלֶיךָ אֶל־יהוה וְהָיָה בְךָ
טז חֵטְא: לֹא־יוּמְתוּ אָבוֹת עַל־בָּנִים וּבָנִים לֹא־
יז יוּמְתוּ עַל־אָבוֹת אִישׁ בְּחֶטְאוֹ יוּמָתוּ: לֹא תַטֶּה

בעל הטורים

(יג) ה׳ אֱלֹהֶיךָ. וּסְמִיךְ לֵהּ ״לֹא תַעֲשֹׁק״. לוֹמַר, אִם עָשַׁק הֶעָנִי כְּאִלּוּ עָשַׁק לַה׳, דִּכְתִיב ״מַלְוֵה ה׳ חוֹנֵן דָּל״:

(יד) לֹא תַעֲשֹׁק שָׂכִיר. סָמַךְ לְ״כִּי תַשֶּׁה״. לוֹמַר, אֲפִלּוּ אִם הוּא חַיָּב, אַל תֹּאמַר, אֲעַכְּבֶנּוּ בְּחוֹבִי. אֶלָּא פְּרַע לוֹ שְׂכָרוֹ מִיָּד, וְאַחַר כָּךְ גְּבֵה חוֹבְךָ:

(טו) וְלֹא תָבוֹא. ג׳ בַּמָּסוֹרֶת – ״וְלֹא תָבוֹא עָלָיו הַשֶּׁמֶשׁ״; ״וְלוֹא תָבוֹא דִּמְעָתֵךְ״; ״וְלֹא תָבוֹא עָלֵינוּ רָעָה״. ״וְלֹא תָבוֹא עָלָיו הַשֶּׁמֶשׁ״ כְּדֵי שֶׁ״לּוֹא תָבוֹא דִּמְעָתֵךְ״, פֵּרוּשׁ, שֶׁלֹּא יִבְכֶּה עָלֶיךָ שֶׁאֵין לוֹ מַה לֶּאֱכֹל. ״וְלֹא תָבוֹא עָלֵינוּ רָעָה״, שֶׁאִם לֹא כֵן, ״יִקְרָא עָלֶיךָ אֶל ה׳ ״ וְיָבוֹא עָלֶיךָ רָעָה:

☐ **וְהָיָה בְךָ חֵטְא.** וּסְמִיךְ לֵהּ ״לֹא יוּמְתוּ אָבוֹת עַל בָּנִים וּבָנִים לֹא יוּמְתוּ עַל אָבוֹת״. לוֹמַר שֶׁפְּעָמִים בְּחֶטְאֲךָ יָמוּתוּ בָנֶיךָ:

(טז) בְּחֶטְאוֹ יוּמָתוּ. לֹא תַטֶּה. לוֹמַר, כָּל הַמַּטֶּה דִין חַיָּב מִיתָה:

BAAL HATURIM ELUCIDATED

13. ה׳ אֱלֹהֶיךָ — HASHEM, YOUR GOD. Juxtaposed to this is, לֹא תַעֲשֹׁק, *You shall not cheat* [*a poor or destitute person*], to indicate that a person who has cheated a poor man is considered as if he has cheated HASHEM, as the verse states: מַלְוֵה ה׳ חוֹנֵן דָּל, *A lender unto HASHEM is one who is gracious with the poor* (*Proverbs* 19:17).[201]

14. לֹא תַעֲשֹׁק שָׂכִיר — YOU SHALL NOT CHEAT A . . . HIRED PERSON. The Torah juxtaposed this to [the passage concerning loans, that begins] כִּי תַשֶּׁה, *when you will lend* (vv. 10-13), to indicate [that] even if a worker owes [you money], you should not say, "I will withhold [his wages as payment] for what is owed to me." Instead, you should pay him his due on time, and afterwards you may demand what is owed to you.[202]

15. וְלֹא תָבוֹא — [THE SUN] SHALL NOT SET [literally, **not come**]. The masoretic note,

201. See *Ibn Ezra* to that verse; see also *Deuteronomy* 1:17, with *Rashi*, s.v., כי המשפט.

202. See *Shulchan Aruch, Choshen Mishpat* 4:1, regarding this law.

security to him when the sun sets, and he will sleep in his garment and bless you, and for you it will be an act of righteousness before HASHEM, your God.

14 *You shall not cheat a poor or destitute hired person among your brethren, or a proselyte who is in your land, or one who is in your cities.* 15 *On that day shall you pay his hire; the sun shall not set upon him, for he is poor, and his life depends on it; let him not call out against you to HASHEM, for it shall be a sin in you.*

16 *Fathers shall not be put to death because of sons, and sons shall not be put to death because of fathers; a man should be put to death for his own sin.*

BAAL HATURIM ELUCIDATED

ג׳, means that this phrase appears three times in the *Tanach*: (i) here, וְלֹא תָבוֹא עָלָיו הַשֶּׁמֶשׁ, *the sun shall not set upon him;* (ii) וְלוֹא תָבוֹא דִּמְעָתֶךָ, *and your tears shall not come forth* (*Ezekiel* 24:16); and (iii) וְלֹא תָבוֹא עָלֵינוּ רָעָה, *and no evil will come upon us* (*Jeremiah* 5:12). [The similarity of expression can be explained as follows: You shall see to it that] *the sun does not set upon him* [before you pay him his wages], in order that *your tears*[203] *shall not come forth,* i.e., so that he will not cry out that he has nothing to eat. *And no evil will come upon us,* i.e., otherwise, *he will call out against you to God,* and evil will come[203a] upon you.[204]

❑ וְהָיָה בְךָ חֵטְא — FOR IT SHALL BE A SIN IN YOU. Juxtaposed to this is, לֹא יוּמְתוּ אָבוֹת עַל בָּנִים וּבָנִים לֹא יוּמְתוּ עַל אָבוֹת, *Fathers shall not be put to death because of sons, and sons shall not be put to death because of fathers* (v. 16). This is to indicate that there are times when, because of a person's sins, his children will die.[205]

16. בְּחֶטְאוֹ יוּמָתוּ. לֹא תַטֶּה — SHOULD BE PUT TO DEATH FOR HIS OWN SIN. YOU SHALL NOT PERVERT. This [juxtaposition of phrases] indicates [that] anyone who perverts justice is liable to the death penalty.[206]

203. That is, the tears you cause him to shed when you do not pay him his wages.

203a. The text and vowelization וְיָבוֹא follow virtually all known editions of the Baal HaTurim, which read either ויבוא or ויבא. However, the phrase וְיָבוֹא עָלֶיךָ רָעָה uses a masculine verb (וְיָבוֹא, rather than the feminine וְתָבוֹא) for a feminine subject — רָעָה. It is therefore suggested that the proper reading is וְיָבִיא, *and he will bring.* Accordingly, the comment should be rendered: יִקְרָא עָלֶיךָ אֶל ה׳, *He will call out against you to God,* וְיָבִיא עָלֶיךָ רָעָה, *and He will bring evil upon you* (*VeChur LaZahav*).

204. See *Rashi,* s.v., והיה בך חטא.

205. *Shabbos* 32b, cited by *Rashi* to v. 16. The Talmud there derives this from the phrase אִישׁ בְּחֶטְאוֹ יוּמָתוּ, *a man should be put to death for his own sin.* The term אִישׁ, *a man,* implies an adult. Accordingly, the verse teaches that an adult will not be put to death by Heaven for someone else's sins; but in certain cases the life of a child may be taken for his father's sin.

206. *Peirush HaRokeach;* see *Sanhedrin* 7a.

יח מִשְׁפַּ֖ט גֵּ֣ר יָת֑וֹם וְלֹ֣א תַחֲבֹ֔ל בֶּ֖גֶד אַלְמָנָֽה: וְזָ֣כַרְתָּ֗
כִּ֣י עֶ֤בֶד הָיִ֨יתָ֙ בְּמִצְרַ֔יִם וַֽיִּפְדְּךָ֛ יהוה אֱלֹהֶ֖יךָ מִשָּׁ֑ם
יט עַל־כֵּ֞ן אָֽנֹכִ֣י מְצַוְּךָ֔ לַֽעֲשׂ֖וֹת אֶת־הַדָּבָ֥ר הַזֶּֽה: כִּ֣י
תִקְצֹר֩ קְצִֽירְךָ֨ בְשָׂדֶ֜ךָ וְשָֽׁכַחְתָּ֧ עֹ֣מֶר בַּשָּׂדֶ֗ה לֹ֤א
תָשׁוּב֙ לְקַחְתּ֔וֹ לַגֵּ֛ר לַיָּת֥וֹם וְלָֽאַלְמָנָ֖ה יִֽהְיֶ֑ה לְמַ֤עַן
כ יְבָרֶכְךָ֙ יהוה אֱלֹהֶ֔יךָ בְּכֹ֖ל מַֽעֲשֵׂ֥ה יָדֶֽיךָ: כִּ֣י

בעל הטורים

(יז) **גֵּר יָתוֹם.** וְלֹא אָמַר, גֵּר וְיָתוֹם, לוֹמַר לָךְ גֵּר שֶׁנִּתְגַּיֵּר כְּקָטָן שֶׁנּוֹלַד דָּמֵי:

☐ **וְלֹא תַחֲבֹל בֶּגֶד אַלְמָנָה. וְזָכַרְתָּ כִּי עֶבֶד הָיִיתָ בְּמִצְרָיִם.** הִזְכִּיר זֶה עַל "וְלֹא תַחֲבֹל", לוֹמַר שֶׁתִּזְכֹּר שֶׁהָיִיתָ עֶבֶד, וְנָתַתִּי לְךָ חֵן בְּעֵינֵי מִצְרַיִם, וְהִשְׁאִילוּ לְךָ "כְּלֵי כֶסֶף וּכְלֵי זָהָב וּשְׂמָלֹת", עַל כֵּן אֲנִי מְצַוְּךָ "לֹא תַחֲבֹל":

(יט) **סָמַךְ "כִּי תִקְצֹר קְצִירְךָ בְשָׂדֶךָ" לְ"לֹא תַטֶּה מִשְׁפָּט".** לוֹמַר לָךְ שֶׁצָּרִיךְ שֶׁתֵּדַע מִשְׁפַּט הַקָּצִיר, כְּהַהִיא דִתְנַן, שְׁתַּיִם לֶקֶט, שָׁלֹשׁ אֵינוֹ לֶקֶט:

☐ **לְמַעַן יְבָרֶכְךָ.** וּסְמִיךְ לֵהּ "כִּי תַחְבֹּט זֵיתְךָ לֹא תְפָאֵר אַחֲרֶיךָ". לוֹמַר לָךְ שֶׁהָאוֹרָה סִימָן בְּרָכָה:

☐ **וְסָמַךְ זַיִת לְשָׂדֶה.** לוֹמַר לָךְ, כְּשֵׁם שֶׁמַּנִּיחִין פֵּאָה בְשָׂדֶה כָּךְ צָרִיךְ לְהַנִּיחַ פֵּאָה בְאִילָן:

BAAL HATURIM ELUCIDATED

17. גֵּר יָתוֹם — A PROSELYTE [OR AN] ORPHAN. The verse does not state גֵּר וְיָתוֹם, with the conjunctive prefix וְ, *and* or *or*,[207] in order to indicate to you [that] one who has just become a convert is like an infant who has just been born.[208]

☐ וְלֹא תַחֲבֹל בֶּגֶד אַלְמָנָה. וְזָכַרְתָּ כִּי עֶבֶד הָיִיתָ בְּמִצְרַיִם — AND YOU SHALL NOT TAKE AS A PLEDGE THE GARMENT OF A WIDOW. YOU SHALL REMEMBER THAT YOU WERE A SLAVE IN EGYPT. This latter phrase is mentioned regarding [the prohibition of] וְלֹא תַחֲבֹל, *you shall not take a pledge,* to indicate that you should remember that you were a slave [in Egypt], and I granted you favor in the eyes of the Egyptians, and they lent you *silver vessels, gold vessels and garments* (Exodus 12:35-36). Therefore, I command you not to take a pledge.[209]

---

207. This phrase appears without the conjunctive prefix וְ, *and* or *or*, twice in the Torah (here and 27:19 below) and twice in *Jeremiah* (7:6 and 22:3). The phrase does not appear with the conjunction anywhere in Scripture. The Baal HaTurim explains why the conjunction is omitted in the verse.

It is noteworthy that there are two versions of *Targum Onkelos* to our verse: In most *Chumashim*, the phrase is rendered with a conjunctive prefix, גִּיוֹר יִתָּם; in others, it is rendered, גִּיוֹרָא וְיִתְּמָא (see also the *Targumim* to the other three verses for other Aramaic renderings of this phrase).

208. *Peirush HaRokeach;* see *Yevamos* 22a. This means that he is considered like another person altogether. Consequently, on a Scriptural level, all his former familial ties have been severed, and he is no longer related to, for example, his mother or his sister. Nevertheless, the Rabbis decreed that if, in our example, his mother or his maternal sister were to convert to Judaism, then, even though they are not related to him, he is prohibited from marrying either of them, just as he was prohibited before he and they converted.

209. See *Rashi* to verse 18.

[17] *You shall not pervert the judgment of a proselyte [or an] orphan, and you shall not take as a pledge the garment of a widow.* [18] *You shall remember that you were a slave in Egypt, and HASHEM, your God, redeemed you from there; therefore I command you to do this thing.*

[19] *When you reap your harvest in your field, and you forget a bundle in the field, you shall not turn back to take it; it shall be for the proselyte, the orphan, and the widow, so that HASHEM, your God, will bless you in all your handiwork.*

BAAL HATURIM ELUCIDATED

19. The Torah has juxtaposed, כִּי תִקְצֹר קְצִירְךָ בְשָׂדֶךָ, *when you reap your harvest in your field,* to לֹא תַטֶּה מִשְׁפַּט, *you shall not pervert the judgment of* (v. 17 above). This is to indicate to you that it is necessary for you to know the laws[209a] of the harvest, for example, that which the Mishnah teaches: Two fallen sheaves are considered as *leket,* three are not.[210]

❑ לְמַעַן יְבָרֶכְךָ — SO THAT [HASHEM, YOUR GOD] WILL BLESS YOU. Juxtaposed to this is, כִּי תַחְבֹּט זֵיתְךָ לֹא תְפַאֵר אַחֲרֶיךָ, *when you beat your olive tree, do not remove all the splendor behind you* (v. 20). This is to indicate to you that light[211] is a symbol of blessing.[212]

❑ The Torah juxtaposed [the topics of] olive tree and field,[213] to indicate to you [that] just as *peah* must be left for a field, so too, *peah* must be left from a tree.[214]

209a. The term מִשְׁפָּט, *laws,* usually refers to monetary matters. Accordingly, the Baal HaTurim refers to the monetary aspects of the harvest as they relate to the portions of the crop that the Torah grants to others (A.S.).

210. The Torah commands the harvester to leave *leket* for the poor (see *Leviticus* 19:9-10; 23:22). *Leket* (gleanings) consists of certain ears of produce that fall from the reaper's hand in the usual course of reaping the crop (*Peah* 4:10). Two fallen ears are *leket;* three are not *leket* (*Peah* 6:5).

The particular law mentioned by the Baal HaTurim is not the gist of the allusion, it is only cited as an example of the laws regarding which the farmer must be knowledgeable. Nevertheless, it is noteworthy that the *gematria* of תַטֶּה מִשְׁפַּט is 843, which the principle of *im hakollel* allows to be considered equivalent to 844, the *gematria* of מִשְׁפְּטֵי הַקָּצִיר, *the laws of the harvest* (*VeChur LaZahav*).

211. That is, verse 20 mentions זֵיתְךָ, *your olive trees,* the source of the olive oil kindled in your candelabra (*Peirush HaRokeach*).

The reading אוֹרָה, *light,* follows the manuscripts used by *Shoham Yakar,* and *Peirush HaRokeach's* parallel comment, סָמַךְ שֶׁמֶן לִבְרָכָה כִּי הַשֶּׁמֶן אוֹרָה וּבְרָכָה, *The Torah juxtaposed oil* (v. 20) *to blessing* (v. 19) *for oil is light and blessing.*

The early printed editions read, שֶׁהָאַזְהָרָה סִימַן בְּרָכָה, *for the warning is a symbol of blessing,* a reading about which *Ittur Bikkurim,* who did not have access to any manuscripts, comments: "I do not know what this means; this is unquestionably a typographical error that I do not know how to emend. I have asked many scholars, but none could tell me." Later printers, who also did not have access to any manuscripts, emended this to שֶׁהַזַּיִת סִימַן בְּרָכָה, *for the olive* [*tree*] *is a symbol of blessing.*

Perhaps the reading שֶׁהָאַזְהָרָה came about in two steps: One copyist or typesetter misspelled שהאורה [remember, manuscripts and early printings were not vowelized] using a ז in place of a ו, thus, שהאזרה. Later, a second copyist or typesetter "corrected" that spelling [there is no noun אזרה] to שהאזהרה (*VeChur LaZahav*).

212. *Peirush HaRokeach.*

213. That is, זֵיתְךָ, *your olive tree* (v. 20), to בְשָׂדֶךָ, *in your field . . .* בַּשָּׂדֶה, *in the field* (v. 19).

214. *Chullin* 131a, cited by *Rashi,* s.v., לא תפאר.

כד/כא־כה/ב

תַחְבֹּט זֵיתְךָ לֹא תְפַאֵר אַחֲרֶיךָ לַגֵּר לַיָּתוֹם
כא וְלָאַלְמָנָה יִהְיֶה: כִּי תִבְצֹר כַּרְמְךָ לֹא תְעוֹלֵל
כב אַחֲרֶיךָ לַגֵּר לַיָּתוֹם וְלָאַלְמָנָה יִהְיֶה: וְזָכַרְתָּ כִּי־עֶבֶד
הָיִיתָ בְּאֶרֶץ מִצְרָיִם עַל־כֵּן אָנֹכִי מְצַוְּךָ לַעֲשׂוֹת
כה א אֶת־הַדָּבָר הַזֶּה: כִּי־יִהְיֶה רִיב בֵּין אֲנָשִׁים
וְנִגְּשׁוּ אֶל־הַמִּשְׁפָּט וּשְׁפָטוּם וְהִצְדִּיקוּ אֶת־הַצַּדִּיק
ב וְהִרְשִׁיעוּ אֶת־הָרָשָׁע: וְהָיָה אִם־בִּן הַכּוֹת הָרָשָׁע

בעל הטורים

(**כא־כב**) גַּבֵּי כֶּרֶם כְּתִיב "וְזָכַרְתָּ" עַל שֵׁם "זִכְרוֹ כְּיֵין לְבָנוֹן":

כה (**א**) **כִּי יִהְיֶה רִיב.** סָמַךְ "רִיב" לְלֶקֶט. שֶׁעַל יְדֵי לֶקֶט שִׁכְחָה וּפֵאָה מְרִיבִים עֲנִיִּים זֶה עִם זֶה:

❑ **הַמִּשְׁפָּט וּשְׁפָטוּם . . . הַשֹּׁפֵט.** לוֹמַר, שֶׁמַּכּוֹת בִּשְׁלֹשָׁה:

(**ב**) **וְהָיָה אִם בִּן הַכּוֹת הָרָשָׁע.** "בִּן" הוּא לְשׁוֹן בִּינָה. לוֹמַר לְךָ, שֶׁצָּרִיךְ בִּינָה בְּעִנְיַן הָאֹמֶד שֶׁאוֹמְדִים אוֹתוֹ כַּמָּה מַכּוֹת רָאוּי לְקַבֵּל. וְשֶׁיַּכּוּ אוֹתוֹ מַכּוֹת הָרְאוּיוֹת לְהִשְׁתַּלֵּשׁ. וְכֵן "דִּבְרֵי אָגוּר בִּן יָקֶה", שֶׁאָגַר הַבִּינָה וְהֱקִיאָהּ. וְכֵן "יְהוֹשֻׁעַ בִּן נוּן", שֶׁהָיָה מָלֵא חָכְמָה וּבִינָה:

BAAL HATURIM ELUCIDATED

21-22. With regard to a vineyard, the verse states, וְזָכַרְתָּ, *you shall remember,*[214a] recalling the verse, זִכְרוֹ כְּיֵין לְבָנוֹן, *its memory* [*shall be*] *like the wine of Lebanon* (*Hosea* 14:8).[215]

XXV.

1. **כִּי יִהְיֶה רִיב** — WHEN THERE WILL BE A QUARREL. [The laws of arbitrating] a quarrel are juxtaposed to the laws concerning *leket*[216] (vv. 19-21), for while gathering *leket, shich'chah,* and *peah,* the poor would quarrel with one another.[217]

❑ **הַמִּשְׁפָּט וּשְׁפָטוּם . . . הַשֹּׁפֵט** — THE COURT,[217a] AND THEY SHALL JUDGE THEM . . . THE JUDGE. [There are three words of the root **שפט** in this passage (vv. 1-2)] to indicate that lashes are [administered] by [a court of] three [judges].[218]

214a. That is, verse 22, which begins וְזָכַרְתָּ is juxtaposed with verse 21, which speaks of a vineyard.

215. See *Pesachim* 106a, where the Talmud expounds on the verse, זָכוֹר אֶת יוֹם הַשַּׁבָּת, *Remember the Sabbath day* (*Exodus* 20:8): Remember it over [a cup of] wine; i.e., mention the Sabbath while reciting a blessing over a cup of wine. *Tosafos* (s.v. **זוכרהו**) comments: For regarding wine Scripture writes, זִכְרוֹ כְּיֵין לְבָנוֹן, *its memory shall be like the wine of Lebanon.*

216. See first paragraph of note 210 above.

217. The Mishnah states: *Peah* may not be harvested with sickles or uprooted with spades lest one man strike another (*Peah* 4:4). That is, lest one man strike another, either accidentally as a result of overcrowding or intentionally in the heat of a quarrel (the Tosafist R' Eliyahu Menachem of London, cited by *Tosefos Yom Tov*).

217a. Elsewhere, the Torah refers to the court as הָאֱלֹהִים (see *Exodus* 21:6 and 22:7-8; see also *Sanhedrin* 3b). The Baal HaTurim's comment explains why the term הַמִּשְׁפָּט is used here.

218. *Sanhedrin* 10a — The Talmud there derives this number of judges from the word **וּשְׁפָטוּם**, *and they shall judge them*: The minimum number

[20] *When you beat your olive tree, do not remove all the splendor behind you; it shall be for the proselyte, the orphan, and the widow.* [21] *When you harvest your vineyard, you shall not glean behind you; it shall be for the proselyte, the orphan, and the widow.* [22] *You shall remember that you were a slave in the land of Egypt, therefore I command you to do this thing.*

25

[1] *When there will be a quarrel between people, and they approach the court, and they shall judge them, and they vindicate the righteous one and find the wicked one guilty;* [2] *it will be that if the wicked one is deserving of lashes,*

BAAL HATURIM ELUCIDATED

2. וְהָיָה אִם בִּן הַכּוֹת הָרָשָׁע — IT WILL BE THAT IF THE WICKED ONE IS DESERVING OF LASHES. בִּן [translated here as deserving of] is related to the word בִּינָה, *understanding.*[219] This indicates to you that understanding is necessary to evaluate the amount of lashes the guilty party can physically endure. And that the number of lashes must be a multiple of three.[219a]

Similarly in the verse, דִּבְרֵי אָגוּר בִּן יָקֶה, *The words of Agur son of Jakeh* (*Proverbs* 30:1), for he collected understanding and spewed it forth. Similarly, the name יְהוֹשֻׁעַ בִּן נוּן, *Joshua son of Nun* (e.g., 1:38 above), for he was filled with knowledge and understanding.[219b]

---

referred to by the plural pronoun *they* is two; and, whereas a court cannot comprise an even number of judges, one more is added for a total of three.

The Baal HaTurim finds an additional allusion in the threefold mention of the root שפט.

219. According to *Targum Onkelos,* the word בִּן of our verse is a form of the word בֶּן, which usually means *son of,* but can also mean *student of* (e.g., *I Kings* 20:35); *member of a group* (e.g., *Exodus* 12:43; *Genesis* 15:3); *deserving of* (e.g., our verse; *I Samuel* 20:31); or *at the age of* (e.g., *Genesis* 17:24; *Leviticus* 12:6). Whereas the form בֶּן appears more than 1500 times in the *Tanach* while בִּן appears only thirty-three times, the use of בִּן in our verse requires explanation. Twenty-eight of the thirty-three appearances (sixteen in the Torah, thirteen elsewhere in the *Tanach*) are the name יְהוֹשֻׁעַ בִּן נוּן, *Joshua son of Nun,* and one is the name אָגוּר בִּן יָקֶה, *Agur son of Jakeh,* a name King Solomon used in referring to himself (*Proverbs* 30:1). The Midrash, cited in part by the Baal HaTurim at the end of this comment, interprets that name as אָגוּר, *the one who gathered,* בִּן, *understanding,* יָקֶה, *and spewed it forth* (*Shemos Rabbah* 6:1), that is, the person who amassed great stores of wisdom and taught them to others, for בִּן may be understood as בִּינָה, *wisdom* (*Rashi*). Similarly, Joshua, Moses' greatest student, became known as בִּינוּן (a homonym of בִּן נוּן), *a person with understanding* (*Ramban* to *Exodus* 33:11, cited by the Baal HaTurim at the end of this comment).

Twice more the word appears in God's rebuke of Jonah: *"You took pity on the kikayon tree . . . .* שֶׁבִּן לַיְלָה הָיָה וּבִן לַיְלָה אָבָד, *which came into being in one night and perished in one night . . ."* (*Jonah* 4:10) [i.e., in just one night the *kikayon* emerged miraculously as a full-grown shade tree and the next night it died]. There, too, because God asked Jonah to try to understand His ways in a logical manner, the prophet used the form בִּן (*VeChur LaZahav*). The Baal HaTurim will show that in our verse, too, the word בִּן alludes to wise understanding.

219a. *Makkos* 22a.

219b. The Baal HaTurim paraphrases the Torah's description of Joshua (34:9 below).

וְהִפִּילוֹ הַשֹּׁפֵט וְהִכָּהוּ לְפָנָיו כְּדֵי רִשְׁעָתוֹ בְּמִסְפָּר:
ג אַרְבָּעִים יַכֶּנּוּ לֹא יֹסִיף פֶּן־יֹסִיף לְהַכֹּתוֹ עַל־
ד אֵלֶּה מַכָּה רַבָּה וְנִקְלָה אָחִיךָ לְעֵינֶיךָ: לֹא־תַחְסֹם
ה שׁוֹר בְּדִישׁוֹ: כִּי־יֵשְׁבוּ אַחִים יַחְדָּו וּמֵת

בעל הטורים

❑ **וְהִפִּילוֹ הַשֹּׁפֵט.** ״וְהִפִּילוֹ״ בְּגִימַטְרִיָּא כְּפוּלָא. שֶׁצָּרִיךְ שֶׁתִּהְיֶה הָרְצוּעָה כְּפוּלָה:

❑ **כְּדֵי.** ב׳ בַּמָּסוֹרֶת – ״כְּדֵי רִשְׁעָתוֹ בְּמִסְפָּר״; וְאִידָךְ ״וְהִשִּׂיגָה יָדוֹ וּמָצָא כְּדֵי גְאֻלָּתוֹ״. {זֶהוּ שֶׁאָמְרוּ, חַיָּבֵי כְרֵיתוֹת שֶׁלָּקוּ, נִפְטְרוּ מִידֵי כְרִיתָתָן. וְזֶהוּ ״כְּדֵי רִשְׁעָתוֹ״, שֶׁלָּקָה; ״כְּדֵי גְאֻלָּתוֹ״} שֶׁנִּגְאַל וְנִפְטַר:

(ג) **וְנִקְלָה.** ב׳ בַּמָּסוֹרֶת – ״וְנִקְלָה אָחִיךָ לְעֵינֶיךָ״; ״וְנִקְלָה כְּבוֹד מוֹאָב״. כֵּיוָן שֶׁנִּקְלָה, כָּבוֹד. {פֵּרוּשׁ, צָרִיךְ לִנְהוֹג בּוֹ כָּבוֹד,} שֶׁלֹּא לְבַזּוֹתוֹ יוֹתֵר:

❑ **אָחִיךָ.** בְּגִימַטְרִיָּא זֶבֶל. שֶׁאִם נִתְקַלְקֵל בִּרְעִי, פָּטוּר:

❑ **וְנִקְלָה אָחִיךָ לְעֵינֶיךָ.** וּסְמִיךְ לֵהּ ״לֹא תַחְסֹם״. רֶמֶז שֶׁצָּרִיךְ לִתֵּן לִפְנֵי הַשַּׁמָּשׁ מִכָּל מִין וּמִין:

(ד) סָמַךְ ״לֹא תַחְסֹם שׁוֹר״ לְמַלְקוּת. לוֹמַר שֶׁרְצוּעָה שֶׁמַּלְקִין בָּהּ הִיא שֶׁל עֵגֶל, מִשּׁוּם ״יָדַע שׁוֹר קֹנֵהוּ״, וְזֶה לֹא יָדַע קוֹנוֹ. לְפִיכָךְ יִפָּרַע בִּרְצוּעָה שֶׁל עֵגֶל:

(ה) **כִּי יֵשְׁבוּ אַחִים יַחְדָּו.** סָמַךְ לְ״לֹא תַחְסֹם״. לוֹמַר לְךָ, יְבָמָה שֶׁנָּפְלָה לִפְנֵי מֻכֵּה שְׁחִין אֵין חוֹסְמִין אוֹתָהּ:

BAAL HATURIM ELUCIDATED

❑ **וְהִפִּילוֹ הַשֹּׁפֵט** — THE JUDGE SHALL CAST HIM DOWN. The *gematria* of וְהִפִּילוֹ (137) is equal to that of כְּפוּלָא, *double,*[220] for the whip must be doubled over.[221]

❑ **כְּדֵי** — IN ACCORDANCE WITH. The masoretic note ב׳ means that this term appears twice in the *Tanach*: (i) here, כְּדֵי רִשְׁעָתוֹ בְּמִסְפָּר, *in accordance with his wickedness, by a count;* and (ii) וְהִשִּׂיגָה יָדוֹ וּמָצָא כְּדֵי גְאֻלָּתוֹ, *but his means suffice and he finds in accordance with its redemption* (*Leviticus* 25:26). {This similarity of expression alludes to what our Sages have stated: If those who are liable for *kares*[222] have received lashes, they have been freed from *kares.*[223] Thus, *in accordance with his wickedness* [teaches] that since he has received lashes *in accordance with its redemption*}[223a] i.e., as a result, he is redeemed and is free [of *kares*].

220. For purposes of the allusion, the Baal HaTurim uses the pseudo-Aramaic form כְּפוּלָא, rather than the Hebrew form כְּפוּלָה, which has the same meaning.

221. *Peirush HaRokeach;* see *Makkos* 23a. The Talmud there infers this law from the word וְהִפִּילוֹ, but does not explain how. *Rabbeinu Bachya* (to our verse), *Maharsha* and *Tosefos Yom Tov* cite a passage in the *Talmud Yerushalmi* (not found in extant editions) that explains the derivation of this law: Do not interpret this word as it reads וְהִפִּילוֹ, rather interpret it as if it were spelled וְהִכְפִּילוֹ, *and he shall double it.* The Baal HaTurim finds an allusion to this law in the *gematria* of the word.

222. *Kares* is a severe punishment meted out by Heaven. It involves premature death and/or spiritual excision.

223. *Makkos* 23a.

223a. The passage enclosed in braces is not found in the early or later printed editions. It does appear, however, in *Shoham Yakar's* manuscript edition.

the judge shall cast him down and strike him, before him, according to his wickedness, by a count. ³ Forty shall he strike him, he shall not add; lest he strike him an additional blow beyond these, and your brother will be degraded before your eyes. ⁴ You shall not muzzle an ox in its threshing.

⁵ When brothers will dwell together and one of them dies,

───────────── BAAL HATURIM ELUCIDATED ─────────────

3. וְנִקְלָה — AND HE WILL BE DEGRADED. The masoretic note 'ב means that this term appears twice in the *Tanach*: (i) here, וְנִקְלָה אָחִיךָ לְעֵינֶיךָ, *and your brother will be degraded in your eyes;* and (ii) וְנִקְלָה כְּבוֹד מוֹאָב, *and degraded shall be the honor of Moab (Isaiah* 16:14). [This indicates that] once he has been degraded, [then,] honor, {i.e., he must be treated honorably}²²³ᵃ [and] that should not be debased further.²²⁴

❏ **אָחִיךָ — YOUR BROTHER.** The *gematria* of this word (39) is equal to that of זֶבֶל, *compost.* If [out of fright,] he [i.e., the condemned man, lost control and] defecated, he is absolved [of further punishment].²²⁵

❏ **וְנִקְלָה אָחִיךָ לְעֵינֶיךָ — AND YOUR BROTHER WILL BE DEGRADED BEFORE YOUR EYES.** Juxtaposed to this is, לֹא תַחְסֹם, *You shall not muzzle.* [The juxtaposition is] an allusion to the requirement that a waiter be given the opportunity to partake of every dish he serves.²²⁶

4. The Torah juxtaposed לֹא תַחְסֹם שׁוֹר, *you shall not muzzle an ox,* to [the laws regarding] lashing, to indicate that the whip with which he is whipped is from a calf, to stress [to the sinner] that even *an ox knows its master (Isaiah* 1:3), yet this person [has acted as if he] did not know his Master. Therefore, retribution is taken from him with a strap from a calf.²²⁷

5. כִּי יֵשְׁבוּ אַחִים יַחְדָּו — WHEN BROTHERS WILL DWELL TOGETHER. The Torah juxtaposed [this] to לֹא תַחְסֹם, *You shall not muzzle,* to indicate to you that if [with regard to levirate marriage] a *yevamah* [childless widow] fell to one afflicted with [repulsive] boils,²²⁷ᵃ we do not muzzle her.²²⁸

───────────────────────────────

224. *Makkos* 23a — וְנִקְלָה, *and he will be degraded,* [and then he must be treated as] אָחִיךָ, *your brother.*

225. *Makkos* 22b.

226. *Kesubos* 61a — Savory or pungent food can cause harm to a person who sees others partaking of it, but is not able to join them. [The Talmud goes on to speak of two people:] One would feed his waiter from each course as he served it; but the other would feed the waiter from only one course during the meal, and would not let him eat of the other courses until after the meal. [Although both were pious,] Elijah would visit the former, but not

the latter. [For he had caused the waiter distress by making him wait.]

227. *Makkos* 23a.

227a. The term מֻכֵּה שְׁחִין, literally, *one afflicted with boils,* is used as a generic term for a person afflicted with any manner of physical blemish (see *Rambam, Hilchos Yibum* 2:14; *Tur, Even HaEzer* 165:4).

228. *Yevamos* 4a. That is, we allow her to explain why she does not want to marry that man and we do not force her to acquiesce to a distasteful marriage, rather we force him to undergo *chalitzah* (*Rashi*).

אֶחָד מֵהֶם וּבֵן אֵין־לֹו לֹא־תִהְיֶ֨ה אֵֽשֶׁת־הַמֵּ֤ת
הַח֨וּצָה לְאִ֣ישׁ זָ֑ר יְבָמָהּ֙ יָבֹ֣א עָלֶ֔יהָ וּלְקָחָ֥הּ לֹ֛ו
לְאִשָּׁ֖ה וְיִבְּמָֽהּ: וְהָיָ֗ה הַבְּכֹור֙ אֲשֶׁ֣ר תֵּלֵ֔ד יָק֕וּם ו
עַל־שֵׁ֥ם אָחִ֖יו הַמֵּ֑ת וְלֹֽא־יִמָּחֶ֥ה שְׁמֹ֖ו מִיִּשְׂרָאֵֽל:
וְאִם־לֹ֤א יַחְפֹּץ֙ הָאִ֔ישׁ לָקַ֖חַת אֶת־יְבִמְתֹּ֑ו וְעָלְתָה֩ ז
יְבִמְתֹּ֨ו הַשַּׁ֜עְרָה אֶל־הַזְּקֵנִ֗ים וְאָֽמְרָה֙ מֵאֵ֨ן יְבָמִ֜י
לְהָקִ֨ים לְאָחִ֥יו שֵׁם֙ בְּיִשְׂרָאֵ֔ל לֹ֥א אָבָ֖ה יַבְּמִֽי:
וְקָֽרְאוּ־לֹ֥ו זִקְנֵי־עִירֹ֖ו וְדִבְּר֣וּ אֵלָ֑יו וְעָמַ֣ד וְאָמַ֔ר לֹ֥א ח
חָפַ֖צְתִּי לְקַחְתָּֽהּ: וְנִגְּשָׁ֨ה יְבִמְתֹּ֣ו אֵלָיו֮ לְעֵינֵ֣י ט
הַזְּקֵנִים֒ וְחָֽלְצָ֤ה נַעֲלֹו֙ מֵעַ֣ל רַגְלֹ֔ו וְיָֽרְקָ֖ה בְּפָנָ֑יו

───── בעל הטורים ─────

❑ **וּבֵן אֵין לוֹ {לֹא}.** סוֹפֵי תֵּבוֹת אוֹנָן. כְּלוֹמַר, לֹא יַעֲשֶׂה כְאוֹנָן שֶׁהָיָה דָשׁ מִבִּפְנִים וְזוֹרֶה מִבַּחוּץ. וּלְכָךְ סָמַךְ לוֹ "בְּדִישׁוֹ":

❑ **לְאִשָּׁה וְיִבְּמָהּ.** בְּגִימַטְרִיָּא וְיִבְּמָהּ בְּעַל כָּרְחָהּ:

(ז) אֶל הַזְּקֵנִים. ה׳ זְקֵנִים. לוֹמַר לְךָ שֶׁמִּצְוַת יִבּוּם בַּחֲמִשָּׁה:

(ט) וְיָרְקָה בְּפָנָיו. לְפִי שֶׁהָרֹק דּוֹמֶה לְשִׁכְבַת זֶרַע, כְּלוֹמַר, שֶׁאֵינוֹ חָפֵץ לְהָקִים זָרַע:

───── BAAL HATURIM ELUCIDATED ─────

❑ {The Baal HaTurim's comment to אֶחָד מֵהֶם appears at *Numbers* 16:15.}

❑ {לֹא} ... וּבֵן אֵין לוֹ — AND HE HAS NO CHILD ... {NOT}. [When rearranged,] the final letters of these words form the name אוֹנָן, *Onan*. [229] That is to say, he should not do [with his brother's widow,] what Onan did [with the widow of his brother Er];[230] for Onan threshed on the inside,[231] but winnowed[232] on the outside.[233] And this is also [the allusion of] the juxtaposition [of the passage of levirate marriage] with בְּדִישׁוֹ, *in its threshing.* [234]

❑ לְאִשָּׁה וְיִבְּמָהּ — AS A WIFE, AND SHALL TAKE HER IN LEVIRATE MARRIAGE. The *gematria* of this phrase (399) is equivalent[235] to that of וְיִבְּמָהּ בְּעַל כָּרְחָהּ, *and he*

229. The text follows one of the manuscripts used by *Shoham Yakar*, and that is how the parallel comments read in *Peirush HaRokeach* and *Rabbeinu Ephraim* (*MiKesivah Ashkenazis*). As it appears in the first printed edition and most subsequent printed editions, the comment states: וּבֵן אֵין לוֹ סוֹפֵי תֵבוֹת אוֹנָן עִם אָלֶ"ף דְּ"אֵין", *the final letters of* וּבֵן אֵין לוֹ, *spell the word* אוֹנָן *when taken together with the* א *of* אֵין. But that type of allusion is not in keeping with the Baal Ha-Turim's usual methodology. Perhaps, a copyist unintentionally omitted the word לֹא from his manuscript. A later copyist, who could not find

the א for אוֹנָן in the final letters of the three-word phrase, then added the א of אֵין to complete the name (*VeChur LaZahav*).

230. See *Genesis* 38:9.

231. A euphemism for penetration.

232. A euphemism for ejaculation.

233. *Yevamos* 34b; *Bereishis Rabbah* 85:4.

234. *Peirush HaRokeach*; *Rabbeinu Ephraim* (*MiKesivah Ashkenazis*).

235. The principle of *im hakollel* allows 398, the *gematria* of the Baal HaTurim's phrase, to be considered equivalent to 399.

and he has no child, the wife of the deceased shall not marry outside, to a strange man; her brother-in-law shall come to her, and shall take her to himself as a wife, and take her in levirate marriage. 6 *It shall be that the firstborn that she will bear shall stand in the name of his dead brother, and his name shall not be blotted out from Israel.* 7 *But if the man will not wish to take his sister-in law, then his sister-in-law shall group to the court, to the elders, and she shall say, "My brother-in-law refuses to establish a name for his brother in Israel, he did not consent to take me in levirate marriage."* 8 *Then the elders of his city shall summon him and speak to him, and he shall stand and say, "I do not wish to marry her."* 9 *Then his sister-in-law shall approach him before the eyes of the elders; she shall remove his shoe from upon his foot and she shall spit before him;*

BAAL HATURIM ELUCIDATED

shall take her in levirate marriage,[235a] [*even*] *against her will.*[236]

7. אֶל הַזְּקֵנִים — TO THE ELDERS. [The term הַזְּקֵנִים can be read as two words,] ה׳ זְקֵנִים, *five elders,* indicating to you that the *mitzvah* of *yibum* (levirate marriage)[237] is [performed] before [a court of] five.[238]

❑ {The Baal HaTurim's comment to לֹא אָבָה appears at 10:10 above.}

9. וְיָרְקָה בְּפָנָיו — AND SHE SHALL SPIT BEFORE HIM. [This act can be understood as symbolic,] because saliva resembles semen,[239] [thus she spits] as an indication that he does not wish to establish offspring [for his brother].

235a. In the context of the Talmudic passage in which it occurs, the phrase means, "וְיִבְּמָהּ" בְּעַל כָּרְחָהּ, *the term* וְיִבְּמָהּ *implies* [*even*] *against her will.*

236. *Yevamos* 54a. This does not mean that he is permitted to act against her will. It merely means that if he did, the marriage is legally binding. Nevertheless, the Rabbis decreed that a levitate marriage must be performed in the same way as any other marriage — including the *chuppah* and blessings — and that one who consummates a levirate marriage without performing these rites is subject to lashes (see *Yevamos* 52a; *Rambam, Hilchos Yibum* 2:1; *Shulchan Aruch, Even HaEzer* 166:1). Nevertheless, if the couple cohabited, whether intentionally (i.e., they were aware that they were consummating a levirate marriage) or unintentionally (i.e., one or both partners was not aware that this act would consummate a levirate marriage), even if one or both acted under coercion (e.g., a band of murderers threatened their lives if they would not perform this act), their marriage is valid (*Even HaEzer* 166:7).

237. That is, the *mitzvah* of performing *chalitzah* in lieu of *yibum*.

238. *Peirush HaRokeach*. See *Yevamos* 101a, where the Talmud records two opinions regarding the number of judges required for the panel overseeing the *chalitzah* ritual — three or five. *Targum Yonasan ben Uzziel* to our verse seems to synthesize the two views, for that *Targum* reads: His sister-in-law shall go up to the gate of the courthouse before five sages, three will act as judges and two as witnesses . . .

239. The similarity between saliva and semen is based on a Talmudic passage. In discussing the bodily fluids from a *niddah* or *zav* with respect to the *tumah* that they convey, the Talmud (*Niddah* 56a, as explained by *Rashi*) distinguishes between two types of fluids. There is fluid that exudes from the body drop by drop as it reaches the opening through which it leaves; an example

כה/י־יג

וְעָנְתָה֙ וְאָ֣מְרָ֔ה כָּ֚כָה יֵעָשֶׂ֣ה לָאִ֔ישׁ אֲשֶׁ֥ר לֹא־יִבְנֶ֖ה
י אֶת־בֵּ֥ית אָחִֽיו׃ וְנִקְרָ֥א שְׁמ֖וֹ בְּיִשְׂרָאֵ֑ל בֵּ֖ית חֲל֥וּץ
יא הַנָּֽעַל׃ כִּֽי־יִנָּצ֨וּ אֲנָשִׁ֤ים יַחְדָּו֙ אִ֣ישׁ וְאָחִ֔יו
וְקָֽרְבָה֙ אֵ֣שֶׁת הָֽאֶחָ֔ד לְהַצִּ֥יל אֶת־אִישָׁ֖הּ מִיַּ֣ד מַכֵּ֑הוּ
יב וְשָׁלְחָ֣ה יָדָ֔הּ וְהֶחֱזִ֖יקָה בִּמְבֻשָֽׁיו׃ וְקַצֹּתָ֖ה אֶת־כַּפָּ֑הּ
יג לֹ֥א תָח֖וֹס עֵינֶֽךָ׃ לֹא־יִהְיֶ֥ה לְךָ֛ בְּכִֽיסְךָ֖ אֶ֣בֶן

בעל הטורים

(יא) כִּי יִנָּצוּ אֲנָשִׁים. סָמַךְ "כִּי יִנָּצוּ" לְ"חֲלוּץ הַנָּעַל", שֶׁעַל יְדֵי חֲלִיצָה מְרִיבָה בָּאָה. כִּדְאָמְרִינַן, {"וּרְאֵה בָנִים לְבָנֶיךָ שָׁלוֹם עַל יִשְׂרָאֵל"} כֵּיוָן שֶׁבָּנִים לְבָנֶיךָ, שָׁלוֹם עַל יִשְׂרָאֵל, דְּאִפַּטְרָא מֵחֲלִיצָה וְיִבּוּם:

❑ **וְהֶחֱזִיקָה.** ב' בַּמָּסוֹרֶת – "וְהֶחֱזִיקָה בִּמְבֻשָׁיו"; וְאִידָךְ "וְהֶחֱזִיקָה בּוֹ וְנָשְׁקָה לוֹ, הֵעֵזָה פָנֶיהָ". דַּוְקָא אִם הֶחֱזִיקָה בְּמֵזִיד, כְּדִכְתִיב "הֵעֵזָה פָּנֶיהָ וַתֹּאמַר לוֹ". אֲבָל אִם שְׁגָגָה, פְּטוּרָה:

(יב) כַּפָּהּ. ב' בַּמָּסוֹרֶת – "וְקַצֹּתָה אֶת כַּפָּהּ לֹא תָחוֹס עֵינֶךָ"; וְאִידָךְ "כַּפָּהּ פָּרְשָׂה לֶעָנִי". מַה לְּהַלָּן מָמוֹן אַף כָּאן מָמוֹן:

(יב־יג) עֵינֶךָ. לֹא יִהְיֶה לְךָ בְּכִיסְךָ. לוֹמַר לְךָ שֶׁלֹּא יִסְתַּכֵּל בְּכִיס מְבוּשָׁיו וּבְעֶרְוָתוֹ:

דָּבָר אַחֵר – "עֵינֶךָ לֹא יִהְיֶה לְךָ בְּכִיסְךָ". לִמְנוֹת מַה שֶּׁבּוֹ, כִּי אֵין הַבְּרָכָה מְצוּיָה אֶלָּא בְּדָבָר הַסָּמוּי מִן הָעַיִן:

BAAL HATURIM ELUCIDATED

10. {The Baal HaTurim's comment to חֲלוּץ appears at *Numbers* 32:27.}

11. כִּי יִנָּצוּ אֲנָשִׁים — IF MEN SHALL FIGHT. [The Torah] juxtaposed the phrase כִּי יִנָּצוּ, *if they shall fight,* to the phrase, חֲלוּץ הַנָּעַל, *the one whose shoe was removed,* for strife arises through *chalitzah.* As the Talmud states: {The verse, וּרְאֵה בָנִים לְבָנֶיךָ, שָׁלוֹם עַל יִשְׂרָאֵל, *And you shall see children to your children; peace upon Israel* (*Psalms* 128:6) means:}[240] When you will see children [born] to your children, there will be peace upon Israel, for she [i.e., your widow] is free from *chalitzah* or levirate marriage.[241]

❑ {The Baal HaTurim's other comment to כִּי יִנָּצוּ אֲנָשִׁים appears at *Exodus* 21:22.}

of this is blood exuding from a wound. Another type of fluid first pools in the body and is then ejected at once; included in this group are saliva [that pools in the mouth until it is expectorated], urine [in the bladder until it is discharged] and semen [in the testicles until it is ejaculated] (*VeChur LaZahav*).

240. The verse enclosed in braces is absent from virtually all printed editions. However, it does appear in one of the manuscripts used by *Shoham Yakar.*

241. *Kesubos* 50a. The seeds of strife can take root in any of three ways: (i) by the surviving brother's rejection of his brother's widow; (ii) by the surviving brother coercing her into levirate marriage that she does not want (see note 236 above); and (iii) by the widow's spitting toward him during the ritual of *chalitzah* (*Maharsha*).

she shall speak up and say, "So is done to the man who would not build the house of his brother." 10 *Then his name shall be proclaimed in Israel, "The house of the one whose shoe was removed!"*

11 *If men shall fight with one another, a man and his brother, and the wife of one of them will approach to rescue her husband from the hand of the one who is striking him, and she will stretch out her hand and will grasp his embarrassing part,* 12 *you shall remove her hand; your eye shall not show pity.*

13 *You shall not have in your pouch a weight and a*

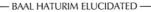

BAAL HATURIM ELUCIDATED

❑ **וְהֶחֱזִיקָה** — AND SHE WILL GRASP. The masoretic note ב׳ means that this term appears twice in the *Tanach*: (i) here, וְהֶחֱזִיקָה בִּמְבֻשָׁיו, *and she will grasp his embarrassing part;* and (ii) וְהֶחֱזִיקָה בּוֹ וְנָשְׁקָה לוֹ, הֵעֵזָה פָנֶיהָ, *She grasped him, kissed him, she thrust forth her face*[241a] (*Proverbs* 7:13). [The similarity of expression indicates that she is held liable] only if she grasped [his embarrassing part] intentionally, as it is written, *she thrust forth her face and said to him* [i.e., her action was brazen and premeditated]; however, if she acted unintentionally, she is not liable.[242]

12. כַּפָּהּ — HER HAND. The masoretic note ב׳ means that this term appears twice in the *Tanach*: (i) here, וְקַצֹּתָה אֶת כַּפָּהּ לֹא תָחוֹס עֵינֶךָ, *You shall remove her hand; your eye shall not show pity;* and (ii) כַּפָּהּ פָּרְשָׂה לֶעָנִי, *She extends her hand to the poor* (*Proverbs* 31:20). Just as that verse [from *Proverbs*] speaks about money,[243] so too, our verse speaks about [her paying] money.[244]

12-13. עֵינֶךָ. לֹא יִהְיֶה לְךָ בְּכִיסְךָ — YOUR EYE. YOU SHALL NOT HAVE IN YOUR POUCH. [The juxtaposition of these phrases] indicates to you that a man should not gaze at his scrotum[245] or at his male organ.[246]

Alternatively: [The juxtaposition of the phrases,] עֵינֶךָ. לֹא יִהְיֶה לְךָ בְּכִיסְךָ, *Your eye; you shall not have in your pouch,* [indicates that a person should not constantly check his purse] to count what is in it, for blessing is not found except in that which is hidden from the eye.[247]

241a. The verse continues: וְתֹאמַר לוֹ, *and she said to him.* The Baal HaTurim cites that stich later in the comment.

242. *Bava Kamma* 27a.

243. *She extends her hand* [to give alms] *to the poor.*

244. See *Bava Kamma* 28a; see the Baal HaTurim to *Exodus* 21:22 and to וְקַצֹּתָה אֶת כַּפָּהּ, below.

245. The Talmud refers to the scrotum as הַכִּיס, *the pouch* (e.g., *Bechoros* 39b). Thus the allusion of בְּכִיסְךָ, *in your pouch.*

246. *Peirush HaRokeach;* see *Sanhedrin* 92a, with *Rashi's* first explanation, s.v., קשתו ננערת; *Zohar, III,* 84a.

247. See *Taanis* 8b; see also the Baal HaTurim to 28:8 below.

יד וָאָבֶן גְּדוֹלָה וּקְטַנָּה׃ לֹא־יִהְיֶה לְךָ בְּבֵיתְךָ אֵיפָה
טו וְאֵיפָה גְּדוֹלָה וּקְטַנָּה׃ אֶבֶן שְׁלֵמָה וָצֶדֶק יִהְיֶה־לָּךְ
אֵיפָה שְׁלֵמָה וָצֶדֶק יִהְיֶה־לָּךְ לְמַעַן יַאֲרִיכוּ יָמֶיךָ
טז עַל הָאֲדָמָה אֲשֶׁר־יְהוָה אֱלֹהֶיךָ נֹתֵן לָךְ׃ כִּי
תוֹעֲבַת יְהוָה אֱלֹהֶיךָ כָּל־עֹשֵׂה אֵלֶּה כֹּל עֹשֵׂה
עָוֶל׃
מפטיר
יז זָכוֹר אֵת אֲשֶׁר־עָשָׂה לְךָ עֲמָלֵק בַּדֶּרֶךְ בְּצֵאתְכֶם
יח מִמִּצְרָיִם׃ אֲשֶׁר קָרְךָ בַּדֶּרֶךְ וַיְזַנֵּב בְּךָ כָּל־
הַנֶּחֱשָׁלִים אַחֲרֶיךָ וְאַתָּה עָיֵף וְיָגֵעַ וְלֹא יָרֵא
יט אֱלֹהִים׃ וְהָיָה בְּהָנִיחַ יְהוָה אֱלֹהֶיךָ ׀ לְךָ מִכָּל־
אֹיְבֶיךָ מִסָּבִיב בָּאָרֶץ אֲשֶׁר יְהוָה־אֱלֹהֶיךָ נֹתֵן לְךָ
נַחֲלָה לְרִשְׁתָּהּ תִּמְחֶה אֶת־זֵכֶר עֲמָלֵק מִתַּחַת
הַשָּׁמָיִם לֹא תִּשְׁכָּח׃ פפפ ק״י פסוקים. על״י סימן.

בעל הטורים

❑ **וְקַצֹּתָה אֶת כַּפָּהּ.** וּסְמִיךְ לֵהּ ״לֹא יִהְיֶה לְךָ בְּכִיסְךָ״. לוֹמַר דְּ״וְקַצֹּתָה אֶת כַּפָּהּ״ הוּא מָמוֹן, דָּבָר הַמֻּטָּל בְּכִיס:

(יח) אֲשֶׁר קָרְךָ בַּדֶּרֶךְ. ״קָרְךָ״ בְּגִימַטְרִיָּא סֵרֵס:

❑ **וַיְזַנֵּב בְּךָ.** בְּגִימַטְרִיָּא זֶה מִילָה:

❑ **כָּל הַנֶּחֱשָׁלִים אַחֲרֶיךָ.** בְּגִימַטְרִיָּא זֶה הָיָה שִׁבְטוֹ שֶׁל דָּן:

BAAL HATURIM ELUCIDATED

❑ **וְקַצֹּתָה אֶת כַּפָּהּ** — YOU SHALL REMOVE HER HAND. Juxtaposed to this is, לֹא יִהְיֶה לְךָ בְּכִיסְךָ, *You shall not have in your pouch.* This is to indicate that וְקַצֹּתָה אֶת כַּפָּהּ, *you shall remove her hand,* refers to [her paying him] money, something kept in a pouch.[248]

18. אֲשֶׁר קָרְךָ בַּדֶּרֶךְ — WHO HAPPENED UPON YOU ON THE WAY. The *gematria* of קָרְךָ, *he happened upon you,* (320) is equal to that of סֵרֵס, *he castrated.*[249]

248. See *Bava Kamma* 28a; see the Baal HaTurim to *Exodus* 21:22 and to כַּפָּהּ, above.

249. *Peirush HaRokeach.* The Midrash offers a variety of opinions regarding what exactly transpired when Amalek happened upon Israel. That Midrash reads in part: Remember what they did

weight — a large one and a small one. 14 *You shall not have*
in your house a measure and a measure — a large one and
a small one. 15 *A perfect and honest weight shall you have,*
a perfect and honest measure shall you have, so that your
days shall be lengthened on the land that HASHEM, *your*
God, gives you. 16 *For an abomination of* HASHEM, *your*
God, are all who do this, all who act corruptly.

17 *Remember what Amalek did to you, on the way, when*
you were leaving Egypt, 18 *who happened upon you on the*
way, and he struck away you, all the weaklings at your
rear, when you were faint and exhausted, and he did not
fear God. 19 *It will be that when* HASHEM, *your God, gives*
you rest from all your enemies all around, in the land that
HASHEM, *your God, gives you as a heritage to take*
possession of it, you shall wipe out the memory of Amalek
from under the heaven — you shall not forget!

BAAL HATURIM ELUCIDATED

❑ וַיְזַנֵּב בְּךָ — **AND HE STRUCK AMONG YOU.** The *gematria* of this phrase (97) is equal to that of זֶה מִילָה, *This [refers to] circumcision.*[249]

❑ כָּל הַנֶּחֱשָׁלִים אַחֲרֶיךָ — **ALL THE WEAK ONES AT YOUR REAR.** The *gematria* of this phrase (732) is equivalent[250] to that of זֶה הָיָה שִׁבְטוֹ שֶׁל דָּן, *this was the tribe of Dan.*[251]

19. {The Baal HaTurim's comment to this verse appears at 26:1 below.}

---

to us with regard to circumcision ... for they [captured some Israelites,] severed their circumcised organs and cast them heavenward, saying, "Is this what You have chosen? Take for Yourself what You have chosen" ... [The Midrash goes on to explain that Samuel punished Agag king of Amalek in accordance with Amalek's own code of law, namely, he castrated him (see *I Samuel* 15:33).] And Moses alluded to this [Amalekite practice] in the Torah, as it is stated, *If men will fight with one another, a man and his brother, and the wife of one of them will approach* [*... and she will grasp his embarrassing part*], *you shall remove her hand ...* and what follows that verse? *Remember what Amalek did to you ...* (*Tanchuma* 9, cited in part by *Rashi;* see also the Baal HaTurim to *Numbers* 2:31).

250. The principle of *im hakollel* allows 732 to be considered equivalent to 733, the *gematria* of the Baal HaTurim's phrase.

251. See the Baal HaTurim's comments to *Exodus* 2:16, 5:7, 12:11, 14:8, 14:29, 18:3; *Numbers* 2:31, 10:25; and *Deuteronomy* 4:24.

פרשת כי תבוא ﬩
Parashas Ki Savo

א וְהָיָה֙ כִּֽי־תָב֣וֹא אֶל־הָאָ֔רֶץ אֲשֶׁר֙ יהו֣ה אֱלֹהֶ֔יךָ
ב נֹתֵ֥ן לְךָ֖ נַחֲלָ֑ה וִֽירִשְׁתָּ֖הּ וְיָשַׁ֥בְתָּ בָּֽהּ׃ וְלָקַחְתָּ֞

בעל הטורים

כו (א) כִּי תָבוֹא. כְּתִיב לְעֵיל מִנֵּהּ "תִּמְחֶה אֶת זֵכֶר עֲמָלֵק", וּסְמִיךְ לֵהּ "וְהָיָה כִּי תָבוֹא אֶל הָאָרֶץ". שֶׁנִּצְטַוּוּ לִמְחוֹת זֵכֶר עֲמָלֵק מִיָּד בִּכְנִיסָתָן לָאָרֶץ. וְעַל זֶה רָצָה לְעַכֵּב בִּיאָתָן לָאָרֶץ. שֶׁהוּא הִגִּיד לְמֶלֶךְ מִצְרַיִם "כִּי בָרַח הָעָם", וְכֵן הִגִּיד לְלָבָן "כִּי בָרַח יַעֲקֹב". וְעַל כֵּן סָמַךְ לוֹ פָּרָשַׁת בִּכּוּרִים, שֶׁמַּזְכִּיר בָּהּ "אֲרַמִּי אֹבֵד אָבִי":

❑ **כִּי תָבוֹא אֶל הָאָרֶץ.** "כִּי" עוֹלֶה לְמִנְיַן שְׁלֹשִׁים, "תָבוֹא" אוֹתִיּוֹת אָבוֹת. וְזֶהוּ שֶׁדָּרְשׁוּ בְּגִיד הַנָּשֶׁה, שֶׁאֵין פָּחוֹת מִשְּׁלֹשִׁים צַדִּיקִים {בְּאֶרֶץ יִשְׂרָאֵל} שֶׁחֲשׁוּבִים כָּאָבוֹת:

(ב) וְלָקַחְתָּ. בְּגִימַטְרִיָּא בְּשִׁבְעָה הַמִּינִין:

BAAL HATURIM ELUCIDATED

XXVI.

1. כִּי תָבוֹא — WHEN YOU WILL ENTER. The previous verse states, תִּמְחֶה אֶת זֵכֶר עֲמָלֵק, *You shall wipe out the memory of Amalek* (*Deuteronomy* 25:19), and juxtaposed to that is, וְהָיָה כִּי תָבוֹא אֶל הָאָרֶץ, *it will be when you will enter the land.* [The juxtaposition indicates] that they were commanded to wipe out the memory of Amalek, immediately[1] upon their entry into the Land [of Israel]. For this reason, the [descendants of Amalek] wanted to prevent the [Israelites'] entry into the land.[1a] For [Amalek is

1. The Baal HaTurim's use of the term מִיָּד, *immediately,* is based on the Midrash that states: אֵין וְהָיָה אֶלָּא מִיָּד, *The term* וְהָיָה, *it will be,* [as used in this verse] *infers immediacy* (*Sifrei*). At first glance, the *Sifrei* refers to the *mitzvah* of *bikkurim* [first fruits], which is the theme of this passage (vv. 1-11). But that cannot be, for the Talmud states that the obligation of bringing *bikkurim* does not take effect until after the Land of Canaan has been captured, divided into tribal territories and apportioned to the individual members of each tribe (*Kiddushin* 37b; see *Rashi* here), and that took fourteen years. Accordingly, the *Sifrei* must be relating the וְהָיָה of our verse to the וְהָיָה of the preceding verse: *It will be when* HASHEM, *your God, gives you rest from all your enemies all around, in the land that* HASHEM, *your God, gives you as a heritage to take possession of it, you shall wipe out the memory of Amalek from under the heaven — you shall not forget* (25:19). Now, like the obligation to bring *bikkurim,* the actual wiping out of Amalek is not incumbent on the nation immediately upon their entry into the Land of Canaan; rather, they were first to appoint a king, upon whom would fall the obligation to wipe out Amalek (see *Sanhedrin* 20b; *Rambam, Hilchos Melachim* 1:1-2). However, the command, *you shall not forget,* is effective immediately (based on *Peirush Sifrei DeVei Rav* of R' David Pardo). Presumably, that is how the Baal HaTurim understands the *Sifrei* and that is what he means by שֶׁנִּצְטַוּוּ לִמְחוֹת זֵכֶר עֲמָלֵק מִיָּד בִּכְנִיסָתָן לָאָרֶץ, *that is, they were commanded that immediately upon their entry into the land they were* [*not to forget that they had been commanded*] *to wipe out the memory of Amalek* (*VeChur LaZahav*).

1a. According to this comment, at the time that Jacob fled from Laban (*Genesis,* Ch. 31), Amalek was already aware of the decree that his memory be eradicated. But how could Amalek have known about that decree when God made no mention of it until more than two centuries later, after Amalek attacked Israel in Rephidim some weeks after Pharaoh's army had been drowned in the sea? (A.S.)

The Baal HaTurim's source for this comment is not known. A parallel comment in *Hadar Zekeinim* and *Peirush HaRokeach* gives a different rationale for Amalek revealing to Pharaoh that the Israelites had fled. Those sources cite an unnamed Midrash: Esau adjured his son Eliphaz to murder Jacob. Eliphaz first consulted with his mother Timna, who cautioned him against killing Jacob. She said, "My son, Jacob is stronger than you and he will kill you. Moreover, if your father is not afraid that Jacob would kill him in battle, he would certainly prefer to kill Jacob with his own hands."

¹ I t will be when you will enter the land that HASHEM, your God, gives you as an inheritance, and you possess it, and dwell in it, ² you shall take of the

---
———————————— BAAL HATURIM ELUCIDATED ————————————

the one] who told the king of Egypt *that the people had fled* (*Exodus* 14:5),^{1b} and he [is] also [the one who] told Laban *that Jacob had fled* (*Genesis* 31:22).² For this reason,³ the Torah juxtaposed the passage concerning *bikkurim* [first fruits] to this passage [concerning Amalek], for he [the bringer of *bikkurim*] states, "אֲרַמִּי אֹבֵד אָבִי, *An Aramean* [i.e., Laban the Aramean] *tried to destroy my forefather*" (v. 5).⁴

❑ כִּי תָבוֹא אֶל הָאָרֶץ — WHEN YOU WILL ENTER THE LAND. The *gematria* of the word כִּי, *when,* is 30. And the letters of תָבוֹא, *you will enter,* [may be rearranged to] spell אָבוֹת, *forefathers.* This is [in accordance with] what the Sages expounded in [the chapter] *Gid HaNasheh*⁵ that there will never be less than thirty *tzaddikim* [righteous people] {in *Eretz Yisrael*}^{5a} who can be considered like the Patriarchs.⁶

2. וְלָקַחְתָּ — YOU SHALL TAKE. The *gematria* of this word (544) is equal to that of בְּשִׁבְעָה הַמִּינִין, *of the seven species.*^{7,8}

Eliphaz now was torn between fulfilling his oath to his father and fear of Jacob. What did he do? He went to Jacob and Jacob ceded all his possessions to Eliphaz [except for his staff (see *Genesis* 32:11)], and a pauper is considered like a dead man. When Esau realized that Eliphaz did not follow his orders, he went to Eliphaz's son Amalek and told him to murder Jacob. Amalek agreed and swore to Esau that he would do so. When Timna heard of this evil matter she cautioned Amalek as she had cautioned Eliphaz, but Amalek ignored her words. So she said, "A great debt lies unpaid, but will be collected from the descendants of Abraham, namely, four hundred years of servitude (see *Genesis* 15:13). If you kill Jacob, you and your children will be responsible for that entire debt, for you are a descendant of Abraham." Therefore Amalek waited until after the servitude had ended and the debt had been paid. Only then did he attempt to fulfill his oath to his grandfather.

1b. *Mechilta, Shemos* 14:5.

2. See the Baal HaTurim to that verse.

3. According to the first part of the Baal HaTurim's comment, the passages regarding Amalek and *bikkurim* were juxtaposed in order to tie the term וְהָיָה, as used in connection with Israel entering the land, with the term וְהָיָה, as used concerning Amalek (see note 1 above). If so, the passage of Amalek could have appeared earlier, juxtaposed to either 6:10 or 11:29, each of which begins, וְהָיָה כִּי יְבִיאֲךָ ה' אֱלֹהֶיךָ אֶל הָאָרֶץ, *It will be*

when HASHEM, your God, brings you to the land. The Baal HaTurim therefore proceeds to explain why the passage of *bikkurim* was chosen as the vehicle by which this lesson is taught, rather than one of the earlier two passages (*VeChur LaZahav*).

4. *Peirush HaRokeach.*

5. *Gid HaNasheh* is the name of the seventh chapter of tractate *Chullin.* The Talmudic passage there expounds on a verse in *Hosea* (3:2): *So I acquired her for myself for fifteen pieces of silver and a chomer* [a volume measure equal to 30 *se'ah*] *of barley and a lesech* [15 *se'ah*] *of barley* — The term "silver" alludes to the righteous . . . the *"chomer"* and the *"lesech"* [total 45 *se'ah*] allude to the number of righteous people in whose merit the world exists . . . thirty of them in *Eretz Yisrael,* fifteen of them in Babylonia (*Chullin* 92a; see also the Baal HaTurim to *Genesis* 15:5, with note 70 there).

5a. The phrase enclosed in braces is not found in the early editions. However, it does appear in *Shoham Yakar's* manuscript edition and is based on the Talmudic passage adduced in note 5 above.

6. According to another Talmudic passage, those thirty *tzaddikim* were כְּאָבִינוּ אַבְרָהָם, *like our Patriarch Abraham* (*Yerushalmi, Avodah Zarah* 2:1).

7. That is, the obligation of *bikkurim* applies only to the seven species listed in 8:8 above.

8. *Peirush HaRokeach;* see *Yerushalmi, Bikkurim* 1:3; *Menachos* 84b, with *Rashi* (*Ksav Yad*), s.v., אמר קרא מראשית; see also *Rashi* to our verse.

מֵרֵאשִׁית | כָּל־פְּרִי הָאֲדָמָה אֲשֶׁר תָּבִיא מֵאַרְצְךָ
אֲשֶׁר יהוָה אֱלֹהֶיךָ נֹתֵן לָךְ וְשַׂמְתָּ בַטֶּנֶא וְהָלַכְתָּ
אֶל־הַמָּקוֹם אֲשֶׁר יִבְחַר יהוָה אֱלֹהֶיךָ לְשַׁכֵּן שְׁמוֹ
ג שָׁם: וּבָאתָ אֶל־הַכֹּהֵן אֲשֶׁר יִהְיֶה בַּיָּמִים הָהֵם
וְאָמַרְתָּ אֵלָיו הִגַּדְתִּי הַיּוֹם לַיהוָה אֱלֹהֶיךָ כִּי־
בָאתִי אֶל־הָאָרֶץ אֲשֶׁר נִשְׁבַּע יהוָה לַאֲבֹתֵינוּ
ד לָתֶת לָנוּ: וְלָקַח הַכֹּהֵן הַטֶּנֶא מִיָּדֶךָ וְהִנִּיחוֹ לִפְנֵי
ה מִזְבַּח יהוָה אֱלֹהֶיךָ: וְעָנִיתָ וְאָמַרְתָּ לִפְנֵי | יהוָה

בעל הטורים

❑ **מֵרֵאשִׁית.** כָּל רֵאשִׁית לַשֵּׁם. "רֵאשִׁית דְּגָנְךָ"; "קֹדֶשׁ יִשְׂרָאֵל לַה׳ רֵאשִׁית תְּבוּאָתֹה"; רֵאשִׁית יְרִיחוֹ חֵרֶם לַה׳; קָטָן הַיּוֹדֵעַ לְדַבֵּר, אָבִיו מְלַמְּדוֹ תוֹרָה:

❑ "טֶנֶא" בְּגִימַטְרִיָּא שִׁשִּׁים. רֶמֶז לְבִכּוּרִים, אֶחָד מִשִּׁשִּׁים. וּלְכָךְ נֶעְלַם סָמֶ״ךְ בְּפָרָשַׁת בִּכּוּרִים:

BAAL HATURIM ELUCIDATED

❑ **מֵרֵאשִׁית** — OF THE FIRST. Every first[9] [must be dedicated] to HASHEM.[10,11] [Thus,] רֵאשִׁית דְּגָנְךָ, *the first of your grain* (*Deuteronomy* 18:4) [is consecrated as *terumah*]; קֹדֶשׁ יִשְׂרָאֵל לַה׳ רֵאשִׁית תְּבוּאָתֹה, *Israel is holy to HASHEM, the first of His crop* (*Jeremiah* 2:3); Jericho[11a] [Israel's first conquest] was set aside as *cheirem* [segregated property] *unto HASHEM*[11b] (see *Joshua* 6:17-19); and, when a child [first] learns to speak, his father should teach him Torah.[12,13]

---

9. That is, the beginning of every endeavor. See *Proverbs* 3:9.

10. The reading כָּל רֵאשִׁית לַה׳ appears in *Shoham Yakar's* manuscript edition and in some later printed editions. It is based on *Peirush HaRokeach,* which reads: כָּל רֵאשִׁית לְהַקָּדוֹשׁ בָּרוּךְ הוּא שֶׁהוּא רִאשׁוֹן, *Every first [should be dedicated] to the Holy One, Blessed is He, for He is the First.* The early editions read: מֵרֵאשִׁית וְלֹא כָּל רֵאשִׁית, *"of" the first, but not every first* (see the sources listed in note 8 above). לַשֵּׁם רֵאשִׁית דְּגָנְךָ, *Unto HASHEM is "the first of your grain . . ."* (see note 13 below).

11. See the Baal HaTurim to 21:17 above, s.v., רֵאשִׁית אֹנוֹ.

11a. The reading יְרִיחוֹ, *Jericho,* follows the early printed editions and the manuscripts used by *Shoham Yakar.* Many later editions read יָרִימוּ, *they shall set aside,* in place of יְרִיחוֹ.

11b. See *Radak* to 6:17 there.

12. *Succah* 42a — When a child begins to speak, his father should teach him Torah and the recitation of *Shema.* What is meant by "Torah"? The verse, תּוֹרָה צִוָּה לָנוּ מֹשֶׁה, *Moses commanded us [to keep] the Torah,* מוֹרָשָׁה קְהִלַּת יַעֲקֹב, *it is the heritage of the congregation of Jacob* (*Deuteronomy* 33:4). And what is meant by "the recitation of *Shema*"? The first verse.

13. The text and its elucidation follow the reading that does not include the word וְלֹא at the beginning of the comment (see note 10 above). According to the reading that begins the comment with וְלֹא, the comment has two parts: First, he, like *Rashi,* states that מֵרֵאשִׁית כָּל פְּרִי, *of the first of every fruit,* includes only fruits of the seven species (see 8:8 above); second, he adds that there are certain verses that speak of a first that is to be dedicated to God, but use the term רֵאשִׁית [without the restrictive prefix -מֵ, *of*] to include all species [e.g., רֵאשִׁית דְּגָנְךָ] and all parts of the topic under discussion [e.g., קֹדֶשׁ יִשְׂרָאֵל לַה׳ רֵאשִׁית תְּבוּאָתֹה], and there are also endeavors whose firsts [i.e., beginnings] must be dedicated to God [e.g., the spoils of Jericho, the first conquest; a child's first words] (based on *Ittur Bikkurim*).

first of every fruit of the ground that you bring in from your land that HASHEM*, your God, gives you, and you shall put it in a basket and go to the place that* HASHEM*, your God, will choose, to make His Name rest there.*

3 *You shall come to whomever will be the Kohen in those days, and you shall say to him, "I declare today to* HASHEM*, your God, that I have come to the land that* HASHEM *swore to our forefathers to give us."* 4 *The Kohen shall take the basket from your hand, and lay it before the Altar of* HASHEM*, your God.*

5 *Then you shall call out and say before* HASHEM*, your*

BAAL HATURIM ELUCIDATED

❑ The *gematria* of טֶנֶא is 60. This is an allusion to [the prescribed measure to be given as] *bikkurim,* one-sixtieth of the crop.[14] For this same reason, the letter ס (= 60) is absent[15] from the passage about *bikkurim* (vv. 1-11).[16]

Alternatively: The first part of the comment actually belongs to the previous comment: וְלָקַחְתָּ — YOU SHALL TAKE. בְּגִימַטְרִיָּא בְּשִׁבְעָה הַמִּינִין, The *gematria* of this word (544) is equal to that of בְּשִׁבְעָה הַמִּינִין, of the seven species. [And so have our Sages expounded:] "מֵרֵאשִׁית", *of the first,* וְלֹא כָּל רֵאשִׁית, but not the first of every [species] (based on *Yad Aharon*).

However, according to each of these interpretations the second [part of the] comment has no beginning. It is like a list without a title. Accordingly, a third possibility is suggested. It must be remembered that manuscripts were usually written without punctuation, vowelization and paragraphing. If so, it is possible that the original manuscript read: ולקחת בגימטריא בשבעה המינין מראשית ולא כל ראשית כל ראשית לשם ראשית דגנך . . . When punctuated, paragraphed and vowelized this would read as two separate comments:

❑ וְלָקַחְתָּ. בְּגִימַטְרִיָּא בְּשִׁבְעָה הַמִּינִין. "מֵרֵאשִׁית" וְלֹא כָּל רֵאשִׁית:

❑ כָּל רֵאשִׁית לַשֵּׁם – רֵאשִׁית דְּגָנְךָ . . .

Unfortunately, a copyist, thinking that the doubling of the phrase כל ראשית כל ראשית was an earlier copyist's mistake, "corrected" his manuscript by omitting the "extraneous" כל ראשית. Subsequently, a third copyist, who realized that something was wrong, but could not figure out what, deleted the word וְלֹא. If this supposition is correct, the original comment was a combination of the two extant versions (*VeChur LaZahav*).

14. The Mishnah states: These *mitzvos* have no specific measure [involved in their fulfillment]: *peah; bikkurim . . .* (*Peah* 1:1). Nevertheless, the Rabbis enacted an obligation to set aside a minimum of one-sixtieth [of one's crop] as *bikkurim* (*Yerushalmi, Bikkurim* 3:1; *Rambam, Hilchos Bikkurim* 2:17; see also *Chullin* 137b). However, none of the sources cited above adduce any Scriptural support for the Rabbinic enactment (see *Tosefos Yom Tov* to *Bikkurim* 2:3). The Baal HaTurim finds such support in the Torah's use of טֶנֶא, which appears only four times in the *Tanach,* all in our parashah (26:2 and 4; 28:5 and 17), for *basket,* rather than סַל, which appears fifteen times in the *Tanach,* fourteen of them in the Torah.

We may ask why the Torah chose the word טֶנֶא (= 60) over כְּלִי, *utensil,* which has the same *gematria.* The answer is that כְּלִי alludes only to sixty, while טֶנֶא can be interpreted as two numbers ט״נ, *59,* and א׳, *1,* thus 1 part is given away as *bikkurim,* and 59 parts are kept by the owner (A.S.)

15. Every other letter of the alphabet appears in this passage; only the ס is absent. This is another support for the Rabbinical enactment (see note 14). For, again, the Torah could have used the more common סַל for *basket,* but instead used the less common טֶנֶא, in order not to introduce a ס into the passage.

16. *Peirush HaRokeach.*

אֱלֹהֶ֔יךָ אֲרַמִּי֙ אֹבֵ֣ד אָבִ֔י וַיֵּ֣רֶד מִצְרַ֔יְמָה וַיָּ֥גָר שָׁ֖ם

ו בִּמְתֵ֣י מְעָ֑ט וַֽיְהִי־שָׁ֕ם לְג֥וֹי גָּד֖וֹל עָצ֥וּם וָרָֽב: וַיָּרֵ֧עוּ

אֹתָ֛נוּ הַמִּצְרִ֖ים וַיְעַנּ֑וּנוּ וַיִּתְּנ֥וּ עָלֵ֖ינוּ עֲבֹדָ֥ה קָשָֽׁה:

ז וַנִּצְעַ֕ק אֶל־יהו֖ה אֱלֹהֵ֣י אֲבֹתֵ֑ינוּ וַיִּשְׁמַ֤ע יהוה֙

אֶת־קֹלֵ֔נוּ וַיַּ֧רְא אֶת־עָנְיֵ֛נוּ וְאֶת־עֲמָלֵ֖נוּ וְאֶת־

ח לַחֲצֵֽנוּ: וַיּֽוֹצִאֵ֤נוּ יהוה֙ מִמִּצְרַ֔יִם בְּיָ֤ד חֲזָקָה֙ וּבִזְרֹ֣עַ

ט נְטוּיָ֔ה וּבְמֹרָ֖א גָּדֹ֑ל וּבְאֹת֖וֹת וּבְמֹֽפְתִֽים: וַיְבִאֵ֖נוּ

אֶל־הַמָּק֣וֹם הַזֶּ֑ה וַיִּתֶּן־לָ֙נוּ֙ אֶת־הָאָ֣רֶץ הַזֹּ֔את אֶ֛רֶץ

י זָבַ֥ת חָלָ֖ב וּדְבָֽשׁ: וְעַתָּ֗ה הִנֵּ֤ה הֵבֵ֙אתִי֙ אֶת־רֵאשִׁית֙

פְּרִ֣י הָֽאֲדָמָ֔ה אֲשֶׁר־נָתַ֥תָּה לִּ֖י יהו֑ה וְהִנַּחְתּ֗וֹ לִפְנֵי֙

יהו֣ה אֱלֹהֶ֔יךָ וְהִֽשְׁתַּחֲוִ֔יתָ לִפְנֵ֖י יהו֥ה אֱלֹהֶֽיךָ:

יא וְשָׂמַחְתָּ֣ בְכָל־הַטּ֗וֹב אֲשֶׁ֧ר נָֽתַן־לְךָ֛ יהו֥ה אֱלֹהֶ֖יךָ

יב וּלְבֵיתֶ֑ךָ אַתָּה֙ וְהַלֵּוִ֔י וְהַגֵּ֖ר אֲשֶׁ֥ר בְּקִרְבֶּֽךָ: כִּ֣י

תְכַלֶּ֞ה לַ֠עְשֵׂר אֶת־כָּל־מַעְשַׂ֧ר תְּבוּאָֽתְךָ֛ בַּשָּׁנָ֖ה

בעל הטורים

(ט) וַיְבִאֵנוּ אֶל הַמָּקוֹם הַזֶּה. "וַיְבִאֵנוּ" חָסֵר יוֹ"ד. {שֶׁאַף עַל פִּי} שֶׁנִּסִּינוּ אוֹתוֹ עֲשָׂרָה נִסְיוֹנוֹת, הֱבִיאָנוּ לָאָרֶץ:

(יא) וְשָׂמַחְתָּ בְכָל הַטּוֹב. וּסְמִיךְ לֵהּ "כִּי תְכַלֶּה לַעְשֵׂר". שֶׁבִּשְׁבִיל הַמַּעֲשֵׂר תִּשְׂמַח בְּכָל הַטּוֹב, כְּמוֹ שֶׁדָּרְשׁוּ עַשֵּׂר בִּשְׁבִיל שֶׁתִּתְעַשֵּׁר:

❑ **הַטּוֹב.** עוֹלָה כ"ב בִּשְׁבִיל הַתּוֹרָה שֶׁנִּתְּנָה בְּכ"ב אוֹתִיּוֹת:

(יב) תְכַלֶּה לַעְשֵׂר אֶת כָּל מַעְשֵׂר. רָאשֵׁי תֵבוֹת בְּגִימַטְרִיָּא בְּחַג שֶׁל פֶּסַח:

BAAL HATURIM ELUCIDATED

9. וַיְבִאֵנוּ אֶל הַמָּקוֹם הַזֶּה — HE BROUGHT US TO THIS PLACE. The word וַיְבִאֵנוּ is spelled defectively, without a י (= 10) [after the ב].[17] For, [the bringer of *bikkurim* says], "{Although} we subjected God to ten trials[18] [during our sojourn in the

---

17. In the causative *hifil* conjugation, the root בוא means *to bring*. As with other verb roots in which the middle root letter is a ו, the ו of בוא changes to a י in most forms of the *hifil* [some examples in *Deuteronomy* are לְהָבִיא (8:7), מְבִיאֲךָ (9:28), לַהֲבִיאָם (29:26), וֶהֱבִיאֲךָ (30:5)]. Accordingly, we would expect to find a י between the ב and the א of וַיְבִאֵנוּ, *He brought us.*

18. See *Numbers* 14:22. The Talmud (*Arachin* 15a-b) enumerates the ten times that Israel tested God: (i) At the sea, when the Israelites showed a lack of trust in God by complaining, "Were there

no graves in Egypt that you took us to die in the wilderness?" (*Exodus* 14:11); (ii) also at the sea, when *they rebelled about the sea, at the Sea of Reeds* (*Psalms* 106:7) — after the Israelites crossed the sea, they demonstrated a lack of faith by saying, "Just as we are emerging from the sea on this side, so are the Egyptians emerging on the other, and they will pursue us again"; (iii) they were commanded not to leave over any manna until the morning, yet some did (see *Exodus* 16:19-20); (iv) some Israelites went out to gather manna on Shabbos, although they had been commanded

26/6-12   God, "An Aramean tried to destroy my forefather. He descended to Egypt and sojourned there, few in number, and there he became a nation — great, strong, and numerous. [6] The Egyptians mistreated us and afflicted us, and placed hard work upon us. [7] Then we cried out to HASHEM, the God of our forefathers, and HASHEM heard our voice and saw our affliction, our travail, and our oppression. [8] HASHEM took us out of Egypt with a strong hand and with an outstretched arm, with great awesomeness, and with signs and with wonders. [9] He brought us to this place, and He gave us this land, a land flowing with milk and honey. [10] And now, behold! I have brought the first fruit of the ground that You have given me, O HASHEM!" And you shall lay it before HASHEM, your God, and you shall prostrate yourself before HASHEM, your God.

[11] You shall rejoice with all the beneficence that HASHEM, your God, has given you and your household — you and the Levite and the proselyte who is in your midst.

[12] When you will finish tithing every tithe of your produce in

─────────── BAAL HATURIM ELUCIDATED ───────────

wilderness, nevertheless], He brought us to the Land [of Canaan]."[19]

11. וְשָׂמַחְתָּ בְכָל הַטּוֹב — YOU SHALL REJOICE WITH ALL THE BENEFICENCE. Juxtaposed to this is, כִּי תְכַלֶּה לַעְשֵׂר, *When you have finished tithing . . .* (v. 12). For [Moses was teaching the nation,] "It is because of the tithe that you shall rejoice with all the beneficence." As our Sages have expounded: [The Torah uses the repetitive expression, עַשֵּׂר תְּעַשֵּׂר, literally, *tithing you shall tithe* (14:22 above), to teach us,] "עַשֵּׂר" בִּשְׁבִיל שֶׁתִּתְעַשֵּׁר, *Tithe, in order that you become wealthy.* [20]

❑ **הַטּוֹב — THE BENEFICENCE.** The *gematria* of this word is 22, [an allusion that you will rejoice] in the merit of the Torah[21] which was given with [the] twenty-two letters [of the *aleph-beis*].[22]

12. תְכַלֶּה לַעְשֵׂר אֶת כָּל מַעְשַׂר — YOU WILL FINISH TITHING EVERY TITHE. The *gematria* of the initial letters of these words (491) is equal to that of בְּחַג שֶׁל פֶּסַח, *on the festival of Pesach.* [23]

───────────

not to (see *Exodus* 16:27); (v-vi) twice the Israelites asked for meat in an ungrateful manner (see *Exodus* 16:3 and *Numbers* 11:4); (vii-viii) twice they complained of lack of water (see *Exodus* 15:24 and 17:2); (ix) the sin of the Golden Calf (see *Exodus*, Ch. 32); and (x) the sin of the spies (see *Numbers*, Chs. 13-14, with the Baal HaTurim to 14:17).
19. *Peirush HaRokeach.*
20. *Rabbeinu Ephraim* (*MiKesivah Ashkenazis*); see *Shabbos* 119a and *Taanis* 9a.

21. *Tanchuma, Re'eh* 11; *Pesikta DeRav Kahana* 11.
22. *Shir HaShirim Rabbah* 1:4 — The verse states: נָגִילָה וְנִשְׂמְחָה בָּךְ, [literally, *We will be glad and rejoice in You.* The *gematria* of בָּךְ is 22, thus, the word בָּךְ can be understood as the number 22. The verse then reads:] *We will be glad and rejoice in the twenty-two letters* [with which You wrote the Torah].
See also the Baal HaTurim to 7:14 above.
23. *Peirush HaRokeach.* The actual date is the

הַשְּׁלִישִׁת שְׁנַת הַמַּעֲשֵׂר וְנָתַתָּה לַלֵּוִי לַגֵּר לַיָּתוֹם
יג וְלָאַלְמָנָה וְאָכְלוּ בִשְׁעָרֶיךָ וְשָׂבֵעוּ: וְאָמַרְתָּ לִפְנֵי
יהוה אֱלֹהֶיךָ בִּעַרְתִּי הַקֹּדֶשׁ מִן־הַבַּיִת וְגַם
נְתַתִּיו לַלֵּוִי וְלַגֵּר לַיָּתוֹם וְלָאַלְמָנָה כְּכָל־מִצְוָתְךָ
אֲשֶׁר צִוִּיתָנִי לֹא־עָבַרְתִּי מִמִּצְוֹתֶיךָ וְלֹא שָׁכָחְתִּי:
יד לֹא־אָכַלְתִּי בְאֹנִי מִמֶּנּוּ וְלֹא־בִעַרְתִּי מִמֶּנּוּ
בְּטָמֵא וְלֹא־נָתַתִּי מִמֶּנּוּ לְמֵת שָׁמַעְתִּי בְּקוֹל
טו יהוה אֱלֹהָי עָשִׂיתִי כְּכֹל אֲשֶׁר צִוִּיתָנִי: הַשְׁקִיפָה

בעל הטורים

(יג) לֹא עָבַרְתִּי מִמִּצְוֹתֶיךָ. בְּגִימַטְרִיָּא וְלֹא מִן תְּלוּשִׁים עַל מְחוּבָּרִים:

(יד) וְלֹא נָתַתִּי. ב׳ בַּמָּסוֹרֶת – ״וְלֹא נָתַתִּי מִמֶּנּוּ לְמֵת״; ״וְלֹא נָתַתִּי לַחֲטֹא חִכִּי״. וְזֶהוּ שֶׁדָּרְשׁוּ בְּסִפְרֵי, ״לֹא שָׁכָחְתִּי״ מִלְּהַזְכִּיר שִׁמְךָ עָלָיו וּמִלְּבָרֶכְךָ {אֲפִלּוּ בְּחִכִּי}, פֵּרוּשׁ בְּדִבּוּרִי, לֹא חָטָאתִי בּוֹ:

❑ לְמֵת. ב׳ בַּמָּסוֹרֶת – ״וְלֹא נָתַתִּי מִמֶּנּוּ לְמֵת״; ״אַל תִּבְכּוּ לְמֵת וְאַל תָּנֻדוּ לוֹ״. כְּלוֹמַר, לֹא נָתַתִּי מִמֶּנּוּ לְצֹרֶךְ מֵת, לֹא לְמַבְכּוֹת וְלֹא לִמְקוֹנְנוֹת:

(טו) הַשְׁקִיפָה. עוֹלֶה בְּגִימַטְרִיָּא ת״ק. כְּלוֹמַר, הַשְׁקִיפָה מִמַּהֲלַךְ ת״ק שָׁנָה שֶׁמִּשָּׁמַיִם לָאָרֶץ:

❑ וְתָגִין עַל הַקּוּ״ף, לוֹמַר, בִּזְכוּת אַבְרָהָם שֶׁהוֹלִיד לְמֵאָה שָׁנָה:

BAAL HATURIM ELUCIDATED

13. לֹא עָבַרְתִּי מִמִּצְוֹתֶיךָ — I HAVE NOT DEVIATED FROM YOUR COMMANDMENTS. The *gematria* of this phrase (1319) is equal to that of [24]וְלֹא מִן תְּלוּשִׁים עַל מְחוּבָּרִים *and not from detached* [*produce*] *on behalf of that which is still attached* [*to the ground or to its tree*].[25]

14. וְלֹא נָתַתִּי — AND I HAVE NOT GIVEN. The masoretic note,[26] ב, means that this phrase appears two times in the Tanach: (i) here, וְלֹא נָתַתִּי מִמֶּנּוּ לְמֵת, *and I have not*

---

subject of a halachic dispute that is based on variant readings of the Mishnah (*Maaser Sheini* 5:6,10). One version, followed by *Rashi* (here; *Sanhedrin* 11b, s.v., דומן ביעורא) and *Tosafos* (*Rosh Hashanah* 4a, s.v., ומעשרות), reads, עֶרֶב יוֹם טוֹב הָרִאשׁוֹן שֶׁל פֶּסַח, *On the day before the first day of Pesach;* the other version, followed by *Rambam* (*Hilchos Maaser Sheini* 11:3,7) and the *Shulchan Aruch* (*Yoreh Deah* 371:141,144), reads, עֶרֶב יוֹם טוֹב הָאַחֲרוֹן שֶׁל פֶּסַח, *On the day before the last day of Pesach,* i.e., on the sixth day of Pesach. Although this *halachah* does not appear in the Baal HaTurim's halachic compendium *Tur Yoreh Deah,* it seems clear from this allusion that he agrees with the view of the *Rambam* (A.S.).

24. The text follows that of *Peirush HaRokeach's* parallel comment in which the *gematriaos* of the Scriptural phrase and the allusive phrase are equal (1319). Most editions of the Baal HaTurim read, לֹא מִן הַתְּלוּשִׁים עַל הַמְחוּבָּרִים, which has the same meaning, but with a *gematria* of 1323, four more than that of the Scriptural phrase. To bring the numbers into alignment, *Ittur Bikkurim* invokes the principle of *im hateivos* to add three to the *gematria* of the Scriptural phrase, and *im hakollel* to add one more, for a total of 1323.

25. *Peirush HaRokeach.* The Mishnah explains our phrase as meaning: I have neither separated tithes from one species on behalf of another nor from detached [produce] on behalf of that which is still attached nor from still attached produce on behalf of that which has been detached . . . (*Maaser Sheini* 5:11; cited by *Rashi*).

26. The note appears in the Massorah to *Job.*

the third year, the year of the tithe, you shall give to the Levite, to the proselyte, to the orphan, and to the widow, and they shall eat in your cities and be satisfied. ¹³ *Then you shall say before* HASHEM, *your God, "I have removed the holy things from the house, and I have also given it to the Levite, to the proselyte, to the orphan, and to the widow, according to whatever commandment You commanded me; I have not deviated from Your commandments, and I have not forgotten.* ¹⁴ *I have not eaten of it in my intense mourning, I have not consumed it in a state of contamination, and I have not given of it for a dead person; I have hearkened to the voice of* HASHEM, *my God; I have acted according to everything You commanded me.* ¹⁵ *Gaze down*

———————————— BAAL HATURIM ELUCIDATED ————————————

given of it for a dead person; and (ii) וְלֹא נָתַתִּי לַחֲטֹא חִכִּי, *for I have not given my palate* [*the opportunity*] *to sin* (Job 31:30). This [similarity of expression] is [in accordance with] what the Sages have expounded in the *Sifrei*:[27] [This verse means,] "*I have not forgotten* to mention Your Name over it and to bless You," [thus,] {even with my palate,}[27a] i.e., with my speech, I have not sinned with regard to it.

❑ לְמֵת — FOR A DEAD PERSON. The masoretic note, ב', means that this word appears twice in the *Tanach*: (i) here, וְלֹא נָתַתִּי מִמֶּנּוּ לְמֵת, *and I have not given of it for a dead person;* and (ii) אַל תִּבְכּוּ לְמֵת וְאַל תָּנֻדוּ לוֹ, *Do not weep for a dead person, and do not wag your head* [*in lament*] *for him*[28] (Jeremiah 22:10). This [similarity of expression] means [that the tither said,] "I have not given of it for the needs of a dead person — i.e., to [hire] neither weepers[29] nor lamenters."[30]

15. הַשְׁקִיפָה — GAZE DOWN. The *gematria* of this term is 500. As if to say, [we are asking God,] "Gaze down from [Your holy abode] the distance of five hundred years [travel] that lies between heaven and earth."[30a]

❑ [According to a scribal tradition,] the ק (= 100) [of הַשְׁקִיפָה] is written with *tagin* [crownlets],[31] to indicate [that our request is being made] in the merit of Abraham who fathered progeny at the age of one hundred.[32]

---

27. *Sifrei* to v. 13; similarly, *Maaser Sheni* 5:11.

27a. The passage enclosed in braces is not found in the early or later printed editions, but does appear in the manuscripts used by *Shoham Yakar*.

28. That verse reads in full: *Do not weep for a dead person* [i.e., King Jehoiakim] *and do not wag your head for him; rather weep for the one who* [*still*] *walks* [i.e., King Jehoiachin and King Zedekiah], *for he shall never return* [*from exile*] *and see the land of his birth.* In its context, the verse teaches that exile is worse than death. However, for the sake of his allusion, the Baal

HaTurim takes the first stich of the verse out of context and applies it to any deceased person.

29. It was customary to hire professional wailers and weepers to attend funerals in order to evoke tears from the mourners and others in attendance (see, e.g., *Jeremiah* 9:16; *Moed Katan* 28b; *Kesubos* 46b).

30. See *Maaser Sheini* 5:12, with *Mishnah Rishonah*.

30a. *Chagigah* 13a.

31. See note 43 to *parashas Va'eschanan* above.

32. R' *Yehudah HaChassid*. See *Genesis* 21:5.

מִמְּעוֹן קָדְשְׁךָ מִן־הַשָּׁמַיִם וּבָרֵךְ אֶת־עַמְּךָ אֶת־
יִשְׂרָאֵל וְאֵת הָאֲדָמָה אֲשֶׁר נָתַתָּה לָנוּ כַּאֲשֶׁר
שלישי טז נִשְׁבַּעְתָּ לַאֲבֹתֵינוּ אֶרֶץ זָבַת חָלָב וּדְבָשׁ: הַיּוֹם
הַזֶּה יהוה אֱלֹהֶיךָ מְצַוְּךָ לַעֲשׂוֹת אֶת־הַחֻקִּים
הָאֵלֶּה וְאֶת־הַמִּשְׁפָּטִים וְשָׁמַרְתָּ וְעָשִׂיתָ אוֹתָם
יז בְּכָל־לְבָבְךָ וּבְכָל־נַפְשֶׁךָ: אֶת־יהוה הֶאֱמַרְתָּ הַיּוֹם

בעל הטורים

❑ **וּבֵרַךְ.** ג׳ בַּמָּסוֹרֶת – ״וּבָרֵךְ אֶת עַמְּךָ אֶת יִשְׂרָאֵל״; ״וּבָרֵךְ אֶת נַחֲלָתֶךָ״; ״הוֹאֵל וּבָרֵךְ אֶת בֵּית עַבְדְּךָ״. זֶהוּ שֶׁדּוֹרֵשׁ בְּסִפְרֵי, ״וּבָרֵךְ אֶת עַמְּךָ אֶת יִשְׂרָאֵל״ – בְּבָנִים וּבְבָנוֹת, וְהַיְנוּ ״הוֹאֵל וּבָרֵךְ אֶת בֵּית עַבְדְּךָ״; ״וְאֵת הָאֲדָמָה״ בְּטַל וּמָטָר – וְהַיְנוּ ״וּבָרֵךְ אֶת נַחֲלָתֶךָ״:

❑ {אֶרֶץ} **זָבַת חָלָב וּדְבָשׁ.** וּסְמִיךְ לֵהּ ״הַיּוֹם הַזֶּה ה׳ אֱלֹהֶיךָ מְצַוְּךָ לַעֲשׂוֹת״. רֶמֶז לְמַה שֶּׁנֶּאֱמַר, ״וַיִּתֵּן לָהֶם אַרְצוֹת גּוֹיִם וְגוֹ׳ בַּעֲבוּר יִשְׁמְרוּ חֻקָּיו וְתוֹרֹתָיו יִנְצֹרוּ״:

(טז) **בְּכָל לְבָבְךָ וּבְכָל נַפְשֶׁךָ.** וּסְמִיךְ לֵהּ ״אֶת ה׳ הֶאֱמַרְתָּ״. ד׳ ״בְּכָל לְבָבְךָ וּבְכָל נַפְשְׁךָ״ הַיְנוּ קְרִיאַת שְׁמַע, דִּכְתִיב בֵּהּ ״בְּכָל לְבָבְךָ וּבְכָל נַפְשְׁךָ״. וְהַיְנוּ דְּאָמְרִינַן אַתֶּם עֲשִׂיתוּנִי חֲטִיבָה אַחַת בָּאָרֶץ, הַיְנוּ קְרִיאַת שְׁמַע. ״אֶת ה׳ הֶאֱמַרְתָּ הַיּוֹם״ בְּגִימַטְרִיָּא זוֹ קְרִיאַת שְׁמַע:

(יז) **אֶת ה׳ הֶאֱמַרְתָּ.** כָּאן רָמַז שִׁשָּׁה סְדָרִים – ״לִהְיוֹת לְךָ לֵאלֹהִים״ זֶה סֵדֶר זְרָעִים שֶׁמַּתְחִיל בִּקְרִיאַת שְׁמַע, וְעוֹד שֶׁיֵּשׁ בּוֹ תְּרוּמוֹת וּמַעַשְׂרוֹת שֶׁהֵם יִרְאַת ה׳, דְּבָרִים שֶׁבֵּינֵינוּ לְבֵין ה׳; ״וְלָלֶכֶת בִּדְרָכָיו״ זֶה סֵדֶר מוֹעֵד, דִּכְתִיב ״אִם תָּשִׁיב מִשַּׁבָּת רַגְלֶךָ״;

BAAL HATURIM ELUCIDATED

❑ {The Baal HaTurim's other comment to הַשְׁקִיפָה appears at *Exodus* 22:27.}

❑ וּבָרֵךְ — AND BLESS. The masoretic note, ג׳, means that this word appears three times in the *Tanach*: (i) here, וּבָרֵךְ אֶת עַמְּךָ אֶת יִשְׂרָאֵל, *and bless Your people Israel;* (ii) וּבָרֵךְ אֶת נַחֲלָתֶךָ, *and bless Your heritage* (*Psalms* 28:9); and (iii) הוֹאֵל וּבָרֵךְ אֶת בֵּית עַבְדְּךָ, *May it be Your desire to bless the household of Your servant* (*II Samuel* 7:29). This [similarity of expression] reflects that which the *Sifrei* expounds: "*And bless Your people Israel,* with sons and daughters" — and that is the meaning of, *May it be Your desire to bless the household of Your servant.* [The *Sifrei* continues:] "*And the ground* [*that You gave us*], with dew and rain" — and that is the meaning of, *and bless Your heritage.*

❑ {אֶרֶץ} זָבַת חָלָב וּדְבָשׁ — {A LAND}[33] FLOWING WITH MILK AND HONEY. Juxtaposed to this is, הַיּוֹם הַזֶּה ה׳ אֱלֹהֶיךָ מְצַוְּךָ לַעֲשׂוֹת, *This day,* HASHEM, *your God, commands you to perform.* [The juxtaposition] is an allusion to that which is stated [elsewhere], וַיִּתֵּן לָהֶם אַרְצוֹת גּוֹיִם . . . בַּעֲבוּר יִשְׁמְרוּ חֻקָּיו וְתוֹרֹתָיו יִנְצֹרוּ, *and He gave them the lands of nations . . . so that they shall safeguard His decrees and observe His teachings* (*Psalms* 105:44-45).[34]

33. Although it seems obvious from the Baal HaTurim's comment that the key word in the rubric should be אֶרֶץ, *a land,* that word is absent in virtually all editions. The text follows *Shoham Yakar's* emendation by including that word in braces.

34. *Tanchuma, Re'eh* 8; see also the Baal HaTurim

from Your holy abode, from the heavens, and bless Your people Israel, and the ground that You gave us, as You swore to our forefathers, a land flowing with milk and honey."

16 *This day, HASHEM, your God, commands you to perform these decrees and the statutes, and you shall observe and perform them with all your heart and with all your soul.* 17 *You have exalted HASHEM today to be*

BAAL HATURIM ELUCIDATED

16. בְּכָל לְבָבְךָ וּבְכָל נַפְשֶׁךָ — WITH ALL YOUR HEART AND WITH ALL YOUR SOUL. Juxtaposed to this is, אֶת ה' הֶאֱמַרְתָּ, *You have exalted*[35] *HASHEM.* Now, our phrase *with all your heart and with all your soul* refers to the recitation of the *Shema,* in which is written, בְּכָל לְבָבְךָ וּבְכָל נַפְשְׁךָ[36], *with all your heart and with all your soul* (*Deuteronomy* 6:5). And that is what our Sages state: [The phrase *You have exalted HASHEM* means: God says,] "You have made Me a unique object of praise[36a] in the world," i.e., by the recitation of the *Shema.*[37] [This is also alluded to by] the *gematria* of the phrase (v. 17), אֶת ה' הֶאֱמַרְתָּ הַיּוֹם, *You have exalted HASHEM today* (1134), [which] is equal to that of זוֹ קְרִיאַת שְׁמַע, *This [refers to] the recitation of the Shema.*[38]

17. אֶת ה' הֶאֱמַרְתָּ — YOU HAVE EXALTED HASHEM. This verse alludes to the Six Orders of the Mishnah:

(i) לִהְיוֹת לְךָ לֵאלֹהִים, *to be a God for you,* refers to the Order of *Zeraim* ("Seeds," i.e., the laws concerning agriculture), which begins with [the laws of] the recitation of the *Shema*; additionally, it contains [the laws of] *terumos* (the priestly portions) and *maasros* (tithes) which are [expressions of] reverence for God, [for they are] matters that are solely between us and Hashem;[39]

(ii) וְלָלֶכֶת בִּדְרָכָיו, *and to walk in His ways,* refers to the Order of *Mo'ed* ("Festivals"), as it is written, אִם תָּשִׁיב מִשַּׁבָּת רַגְלֶךָ, *if you restrain your foot because it is the Sabbath* (*Isaiah* 58:13);

---

to *Exodus* 6:8 and 13:11, and *Deuteronomy* 4:5, s.v., בָּאִים.

35. Translation follows *Ramban,* cited by the Baal HaTurim in *Peirush HaTur HaAroch.*

36. The two phrases are identical with regard to meaning and spelling. The difference in vowelization of the word נַפְשֶׁךָ/נַפְשְׁךָ is a function of its location in its verse: In 6:5, where it appears in the middle of a stich, it is punctuated by the cantillation sign *tipcha,* which indicates a minor pause, under its last syllable — thus, נַפְשְׁךָ — indicating that it is accented on that syllable; but in our verse, where it appears at the end of the verse, it is punctuated with a *sof pasuk,* the equivalent of a period, which causes the accent to shift to the next-to-last syllable, שֶׁ, and whereas a letter vowelized with a *sheva* cannot be accented, the *sheva* is replaced with a *segol* — thus, נַפְשֶׁךָ.

36a. See *Targum Onkelos* to verse 17.

37. *Berachos* 6a; *Chagigah* 3a. We make God a unique object of praise with the words ה' אֶחָד, *HASHEM is One,* in the verse that begins with the word שְׁמַע.

38. *Peirush HaRokeach.*

39. That is, only God can know whether we are honest and precise in setting aside tithes and giving them to their appropriate recipients (i.e., *Kohanim,* Levites, the poor).

לִהְיוֹת֩ לְךָ֨ לֵֽאלֹהִ֜ים וְלָלֶ֣כֶת בִּדְרָכָ֗יו וְלִשְׁמֹ֨ר חֻקָּ֜יו
יח וּמִצְוֺתָ֧יו וּמִשְׁפָּטָ֛יו וְלִשְׁמֹ֥עַ בְּקֹלֽוֹ: וַֽיהֹוָ֞ה הֶֽאֱמִֽירְךָ֣
הַיּ֗וֹם לִֽהְי֥וֹת לוֹ֙ לְעַ֣ם סְגֻלָּ֔ה כַּֽאֲשֶׁ֖ר דִּבֶּר־לָ֑ךְ
יט וְלִשְׁמֹ֖ר כָּל־מִצְוֺתָֽיו: וּֽלְתִתְּךָ֣ עֶלְי֗וֹן עַ֤ל כָּל־
הַגּוֹיִם֙ אֲשֶׁ֣ר עָשָׂ֔ה לִתְהִלָּ֖ה וּלְשֵׁ֣ם וּלְתִפְאָ֑רֶת

— בעל הטורים —

"וְלִשְׁמֹר חֻקָּיו" זֶה סֵדֶר נָשִׁים שֶׁמְּדַבֵּר בָּֽעֲרָיוֹת, שֶׁנֶּאֱמַר בָּהֶם "וּשְׁמַרְתֶּם אֶת חֻקֹּתַי";
"וּמִצְוֺתָיו" זֶה סֵדֶר קָֽדָשִׁים שֶׁמְּדַבֵּר בַּקָּרְבָּנוֹת, דִּכְתִיב בְּהוּ "אֵלֶּה הַמִּצְוֺת"; "וּמִשְׁפָּטָיו" זֶה
סֵדֶר נְזִיקִין; "וְלִשְׁמֹעַ בְּקֹלוֹ" זֶה סֵדֶר טְהָרוֹת, דִּכְתִיב בְּהוּ "אִמְרוֹת ה' אֲמָרוֹת טְהוֹרוֹת".
וּכְנֶגְדָּם אָמַר שִׁשָּׁה דְּבָרִים, "לִֽהְיוֹת לוֹ לְעַם סְגֻלָּה . . . וּלְתִתְּךָ עֶלְיוֹן . . . לִתְהִלָּה, וּלְשֵׁם,
וּלְתִפְאָרֶת, וְלִֽהְיֹֽתְךָ עַם קֹֽדֶשׁ":

(יט) וּלְתִתְּךָ עֶלְיוֹן. רֶמֶז לַטּוֹטָפוֹת שֶׁל הַקָּדוֹשׁ בָּרוּךְ הוּא, דִּכְתִיב בְּהוּ "אַשְׁרֶיךָ יִשְׂרָאֵל":

☐ לִתְהִלָּה וּלְשֵׁם וּלְתִפְאָרֶת. כְּלוֹמַר, מַה שֶּׁיִּשְׂרָאֵל מְשַׁבְּחִים וּמְהַלְלִים לַשֵּׁם הוּא לָהֶם
לְתִפְאָרֶת. וְהַיְנוּ דְּאָמְרִינַן, עָתִיד הַקָּדוֹשׁ בָּרוּךְ הוּא לִֽהְיוֹת עֲטָרָה בְּרֹאשׁ כָּל צַדִּיק
וְצַדִּיק. שֶׁאוֹתָהּ עֲטָרָה שֶׁמְּעַטְּרִים לְהַקָּדוֹשׁ בָּרוּךְ הוּא בִּתְפִלָּתָם מַֽחֲזִירָהּ לָהֶם. אֲבָל מִי
שֶׁשָּׂח שִׂיחַת חֻלִּין בְּבֵית הַכְּנֶסֶת, מַקִּיפִין לוֹ כָּל גּוּפוֹ בְּקוֹצִים. לְכָךְ "שִׁיר הַשִּׁירִים" לֵית,

— BAAL HATURIM ELUCIDATED —

(iii) וְלִשְׁמֹר חֻקָּיו, *and to observe His decrees,* refers to the Order of *Nashim*
("Women," i.e., laws concerning marriage, divorce, etc.), which includes the
laws regarding forbidden marital relationships, about which the verse states,
וּשְׁמַרְתֶּם אֶת חֻקֹּתַי, *you shall observe My decrees* (*Leviticus* 18:5, 20:8);

(iv) וּמִצְוֺתָיו, *and His commandments,* refers to the Order of *Kodashim*
("Sanctities"),[40] which speaks about the Altar offerings, concerning which it is
written, אֵלֶּה הַמִּצְוֺת, *these are the commandments* (*Leviticus* 27:34);

(v) וּמִשְׁפָּטָיו, *and His ordinances,* refers to the Order of *Nezikin* ("Damages," i.e.,
civil law);[41]

(vi) וְלִשְׁמֹעַ בְּקֹלוֹ, *and to hearken to His voice,* refers to the Order of *Tohoros*
("Ritual Purity") concerning which the verse states, אִמְרוֹת ה' אֲמָרוֹת טְהוֹרוֹת, *the
words of* HASHEM *are pure words* (*Psalms* 12:7).[42]

Corresponding to those [Six Orders], God said six things:[43] (i) *to be for Him a
treasured people . . .* (ii) *to make you supreme . . .* (iii) *for praise;* (iv) *for renown;* (v)
and for splendor; (vi) *and so that you will be a holy people* (vv. 18-19 below).

---

40. The traditional arrangement of the Six
Orders has קָדָשִׁים after נְזִיקִין (see *Shabbos* 31a).
However, the Baal HaTurim reverses these two
Orders for purposes of the allusion.

41. Most of the laws in this Order are found in
parashas מִשְׁפָּטִים (*Exodus* 21:1-23:8).

42. Thus, it is through the study and fulfillment

of the lessons of the Six Orders of the Mishnah
that Israel has made God "a unique object of
praise in the world" (see the Baal HaTurim's
preceding comment; see also note 43 below).

43. Just as Israel exalts God with the Six Orders
of the Mishnah (see note 42), so does God exalt
Israel in six ways (*VeChur LaZahav*).

a God for you, and to walk in His ways, and to observe His decrees, and His commandments and His ordinances, and to hearken to His voice. 18 *And* HASHEM *has exalted you today to be for Him a treasured people, as He spoke to you, and to observe all His commandments,*
19 *and to make you supreme over all the nations that He made, for praise, and for renown, and for splendor,*

BAAL HATURIM ELUCIDATED

19. וּלְתִתְּךָ עֶלְיוֹן — AND TO MAKE YOU SUPREME. This is an allusion to the head *tefillin* of the Holy One, Blessed is He, in which is written, אַשְׁרֶיךָ יִשְׂרָאֵל, *Fortunate are you, O Israel* (*Deuteronomy* 33:29).[44]

❑ **לִתְהִלָּה וּלְשֵׁם וּלְתִפְאָרֶת** — FOR PRAISE, AND FOR RENOWN, AND FOR SPLENDOR. That is to say: Israel's praising and lauding of Hashem is as splendor[45] for them.[46] This supports what the Sages have said: In the future, the Holy One, Blessed is He, will be a crown on the head of each and every righteous person,[47] which may be understood as: He will return to them that very crown with which they crown God in their prayers.[48]

However, one who engages in mundane conversation in the synagogue will have his entire body surrounded by thorns.[48a] And that is the meaning of the masoretic note,[49] לֵית, *There is no other,* [that appears on the word הַשִּׁירִים of the phrase,] שִׁיר הַשִּׁירִים, *The song of songs* (*Song of Songs* 1:1); and

44. The Talmud states that like the *tefillin* of Israel, the *tefillin* of the Master of the Universe contain four Scriptural passages: (i) *I Chronicles* 17:21; (ii) *Deuteronomy* 4:7-8; (iii) *Deuteronomy* 33:29 [adduced in part by the Baal HaTurim here] and 4:34; and (iv) *Deuteronomy* 26:19 [our verse] (*Berachos* 6a).

45. For purposes of the allusion, the verse is to be rendered: לִתְהִלָּה, [*The prayers that Israel recites*] *as praise,* וּלְשֵׁם, *and* [*which they offer*] *unto* HASHEM, וּלְתִפְאָרֶת, [*will be*] *a splendorous crown* (*VeChur LaZahav*).

46. There are several versions to this comment: The manuscripts used by *Shoham Yakar,* as well as the earliest printed editions, read לוֹ, *for Him;* the Fürth edition reads לה׳, which seems to mean לַה׳, *for* HASHEM, in which case it is synonymous with לוֹ, *for Him;* however, *Ittur Bikkurim* interprets לה׳ as לָהֶם, *for them,* a reference to Israel, and that reading has been followed by most later printed editions, including this one.

47. *Megillah* 15b.

48. The Talmud describes a Heavenly scene: There is an angel named Sandalphon who is taller than his fellow angels by a height equal to a journey of five hundred years. This angel stands behind the Chariot [i.e., the Throne of Glory] and weaves crowns for his Maker (*Chagigah* 13b; see also *Midrash Shocher Tov* 88).

The commentaries explain that He weaves the crowns out of the prayers of the righteous (*Tosafos,* s.v., וקושר), as Israel mentions in its prayers: כֶּתֶר יִתְּנוּ לְךָ ... [מַלְאָכִים] הֲמוֹנֵי [מַעְלָה עִם] עַמְּךָ יִשְׂרָאֵל קְבוּצֵי מַטָּה], *A crown will they give You ...* [*the angels who are*] *the multitudes* [*of Heaven, together with Your people Israel who are assembled on the earth*] (*Rabbeinu Chananel*). That is, the angels on high (specifically, Sandalphon) weave the prayers recited by the righteous people of Israel into crowns for God.

48a. The Baal HaTurim's source for this comment is not known.

49. The extant masoretic note reads: ב׳ זוּגִין מְיַחֲדִין, *There are two pairs of words, each* [*of the four words*] *appears once* [*in the Tanach*], חַד ס׳ וְחַד ש׳, *one* [*of each pair is spelled*] *with a* ס, *and one with a* ש — they are: (i) הַסִּירִים, *the thorns* (*Ecclesiastes* 7:6), and הַשִּׁירִים, *the songs* (*Song of Songs* 1:1); (ii) בַּסִּירִים, *with thorns* (*Hosea* 2:8),

כו/א וְלִהְיֹתְךָ עַם־קָדֹשׁ לַיהוָה אֱלֹהֶיךָ כַּאֲשֶׁר דִּבֵּר׃

כז רביעי א וַיְצַו מֹשֶׁה וְזִקְנֵי יִשְׂרָאֵל אֶת־הָעָם לֵאמֹר שָׁמֹר
אֶת־כָּל־הַמִּצְוָה אֲשֶׁר אָנֹכִי מְצַוֶּה אֶתְכֶם הַיּוֹם׃

בעל הטורים

וּכְנֶגְדּוֹ "כְּקוֹל הַסִּירִים":

❑ **אֲשֶׁר עָשָׂה.** בְּגִימַטְרִיָּא שִׁבְעִים אוּמּוֹת:

❑ **וְלִהְיֹתְךָ.** חָסֵר וָי"ו שֶׁאֵין הֲוָיַת קְדֻשָּׁתָן נִכֶּרֶת כָּל כָּךְ בָּעוֹלָם הַזֶּה:

❑ **קָדֹשׁ.** חָסֵר וָי"ו. לוֹמַר, קַדֵּשׁ עַצְמְךָ לְמַטָּה, וִיקַדְּשׁוּ אוֹתְךָ {מִ}לְמַעְלָה. וְכֵן ו' פְּעָמִים "קָדוֹשׁ" יִשְׂרָאֵל בַּקְּרִיָּה:

❑ **וְלִהְיֹתְךָ עַם קָדֹשׁ.** וּסְמִיךְ לֵהּ "וַיְצַו מֹשֶׁה {וְזִקְנֵי יִשְׂרָאֵל אֶת הָעָם}". אַזְהָרָה לְבֵית דִּין שֶׁיְּעַשּׂוּךָ לְקַדֵּשׁ עַצְמְךָ:

BAAL HATURIM ELUCIDATED

corresponding to it is the verse כְּקוֹל הַסִּירִים, *like the sound of the thorns* [*burning*] *under the pot* (*Ecclesiastes* 7:6).[50]

❑ **אֲשֶׁר עָשָׂה** — THAT HE MADE. The *gematria* of this phrase (876) is equivalent[51] to that of שִׁבְעִים אוּמּוֹת, *seventy nations.*[52,53]

❑ **וְלִהְיֹתְךָ** — AND SO THAT YOU WILL BE.[54] This term is spelled defectively, without a

and בְּשִׁרִים, *with songs* (*Proverbs* 25:20, spelled defectively, without the first י).

Their sibilant pronunciation is not the only thing that connects the two letters ס and ש. For the name of the letter ש alludes to the ס, while the name of the ס alludes to the ש. Thus, in the name שי"ן, the first letter is the letter ש, while the *gematria* of the other two letters י and ן is 60, the same *gematria* as that of ס. Conversely, the *gematria* of the name סָמֶ"ךְ, when spelled out with the name of each of its letters — סָמֶ"ךְ מֵ"ם כָּ"ף — is 300, the same as that of ש (*VeChur LaZahav*).

50. Thus, if one sings שִׁיר, *song,* to God, he will be rewarded with הַשִּׁירִים, *the* [*very same*] *songs,* which will be returned to him in the form of a crown. But, if one speaks, כְּקוֹל, *just some sort of sound* [i.e., mundane, trivial chatter], it will be returned to him in the form of הַסִּירִים, *the thorns* (*VeChur LaZahav*).

51. The principle of *im hakollel* allows 875, the *gematria* of the Baal HaTurim's phrase, to be considered equivalent to 876.

52. Thus, the phrase עַל כָּל הַגּוֹיִם אֲשֶׁר עָשָׂה can be understood as, *over all the nations,* [*i.e.,*] *the seventy nations.*

53. Various passages in the Talmud and Midrash speak of the seventy nations of the world. The *Midrash HaGadol* (a contemporary of the Baal HaTurim) reckons sixty-eight nations before the birth of Esau and Jacob, who, with their birth, completed the total of seventy. According to that view, the seventy nations include sixty-nine gentile nations and Israel, a view that is not in accord with either the Talmud (*Succah* 55b) or the Midrash (*Bereishis Rabbah* 66:4). According to *Pesikta Zutresa,* the seventy-one descendants of Noah's three sons enumerated in Chapter 10 above, with the exception of Pelishtim [alternatively, Nimrod], were the progenitors of seventy gentile nations. From the Baal HaTurim's comments to *Genesis* 25:25-26 (s.v., עֵשָׂו, and s.v., וְאַחֲרֵי) (see note 26 there) it is apparent that he omits both Nimrod and Pelishtim from those descendants of Noah's sons whose progeny formed nations. Thus, Esau was the seventieth nation (*VeChur LaZahav*).

54. The Baal HaTurim understands that the phrase, וְלִהְיֹתְךָ עַם קָדֹשׁ, *so that you will be a holy people,* implies that the fiber of Israel's being will be that of a holy people, even if that holiness goes unrecognized by the nations of the world.

27/1 *and so that you will be a holy people to HASHEM, your God, as He spoke.*

27 [1] *Moses and the elders of Israel commanded the people, saying, "Observe the entire commandment that I command you this*

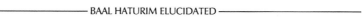

BAAL HATURIM ELUCIDATED

ו,[55] for the existence of [Israel's] holiness is not very apparent in this world.[56]

❑ קָדֹשׁ — HOLY. This term is spelled defectively, without a ו,[57] to indicate you should sanctify yourself below [i.e., on earth] and they will sanctify you {from} Above.[58] Similarly, the word קָדוֹשׁ, *holy,* with reference to Israel[59] [as the holy nation] appears six times in the verses [of the Torah[60]].[61]

❑ וְלִהְיֹתְךָ עַם קָדֹשׁ — AND SO THAT YOU WILL BE A HOLY PEOPLE. Juxtaposed to this is, וַיְצַו מֹשֶׁה {וְזִקְנֵי יִשְׂרָאֵל אֶת הָעָם}, *Moses {and the elders of Israel} commanded {the people}.*[62] This is an admonition to the court that they should compel you[62a] to sanctify yourself.[63]

55. Although this form of the verb does not appear elsewhere in the *Tanach,* a number of similar forms do appear with the ו, e.g., הֱיוֹתְךָ (*Judges* 18:19), מִהְיוֹתְךָ (*Isaiah* 49:6).

56. *Peirush HaRokeach.* This means that the full measure of Israel's sanctity cannot be recognized by eyes of flesh and blood (*VeChur LaZahav*).

57. The word appears fourteen times in the Torah spelled in full, קָדוֹשׁ, with a ו (e.g., 23:15 above, 28:9 below), and ten times spelled defectively, קָדֹשׁ, without a ו (e.g., *Numbers* 6:5,8). When spelled without a ו, the word may be interpreted as if it were vowelized as an imperative, קַדֵּשׁ, *Sanctify!*

58. The Talmud expounds on the verse, וְהִתְקַדִּשְׁתֶּם וִהְיִיתֶם קְדֹשִׁים, *you shall sanctify yourselves and you shall be holy* (*Leviticus* 11:44): If a person sanctifies himself a little, they [the Heavenly Tribunal] sanctify him a lot; [if he sanctifies himself] below, they sanctify him Above; [if he sanctifies himself] in this world, they sanctify him in the World to Come (*Yoma* 39a).

59. At first glance, the Baal HaTurim's comment seems to read, ו׳ פְּעָמִים קָדוֹשׁ יִשְׂרָאֵל בִּקְרָיָה, *the phrase, "the Holy One of Israel" [i.e., God], appears six times in the Tanach,* and that is how most of the commentaries understand it. However, they ask, that phrase appears twenty-three times in the *Tanach*: (i-xx) twenty times in *Isaiah;* (xxi) *II Kings* 19:22; (xxii) *Jeremiah* 50:29; and (xxiii) *Psalms* 71:22). Hence, that phrase could not have been the intent of this comment. Accordingly, the comment should be punctuated, "קָדוֹשׁ" יִשְׂרָאֵל, [*the term*] *"holy"* [*with reference to*] *Israel* (*VeChur LaZahav;* see note 60 below).

60. The Aramaic term קְרָיָה is used in masoretic notes as a synonym for the Hebrew word מִקְרָא, *Scripture* (*Meiven Chiddos*). However, in the *Talmud Yerushalmi,* the term is used for both "the whole of Scripture" and "Scriptural verses or verses." Accordingly, the translation treats the Baal HaTurim's use of קְרָיָה as *verses,* specifically, Torah verses. The six Torah verses that refer to Israel as גּוֹי קָדוֹשׁ, *a holy nation,* or עַם קָדוֹשׁ, *a holy people,* are: *Exodus* 19:6; *Deuteronomy* 7:6; 14:2, 14:21, 26:19 and 28:9 (*VeChur LaZahav*).

61. *Peirush HaRokeach.*

62. The Scriptural phrase, וְזִקְנֵי יִשְׂרָאֵל אֶת הָעָם, *and the elders of Israel . . . the people,* does not appear in any of the editions of the Baal HaTurim. Nevertheless, it is included in *Peirush HaRokeach,* the Baal HaTurim's apparent source for this comment. Moreover, the comment speaks about בֵּית דִּין, *the court,* i.e., the elders, and the people, but not about Moses (*VeChur LaZahav*).

62a. The Baal HaTurim's expression, אַזְהָרָה לְבֵית דִּין שֶׁיְּעַשּׂוּךְ, is borrowed from *Rosh Hashanah* 6a where it is used with regard to fulfilling pledges that involve the Temple and Temple offerings.

63. *Peirush HaRokeach.* The Talmud (*Yevamos* 88b) explains that the verse, וְקִדַּשְׁתּוֹ, *you shall sanctify him* (*Leviticus* 21:8), implies that the court may use physical coercion to compel a *Kohen* to observe the laws of sanctity related to his priesthood, e.g., the laws of *tumah* and the prohibition against marrying a divorcee.

ב וְהָיָ֞ה בַּיּ֗וֹם אֲשֶׁ֤ר תַּעַבְרוּ֙ אֶת־הַיַּרְדֵּ֔ן אֶל־הָאָ֕רֶץ
אֲשֶׁר־יְהֹוָ֥ה אֱלֹהֶ֖יךָ נֹתֵ֣ן לָ֑ךְ וַהֲקֵמֹתָ֤ לְךָ֙ אֲבָנִ֣ים
ג גְּדֹל֔וֹת וְשַׂדְתָּ֥ אֹתָ֖ם בַּשִּֽׂיד: וְכָתַבְתָּ֣ עֲלֵיהֶ֗ן אֶת־כָּל־
דִּבְרֵ֛י הַתּוֹרָ֥ה הַזֹּ֖את בְּעָבְרֶ֑ךָ לְמַ֨עַן אֲשֶׁ֤ר תָּבֹא֙
אֶל־הָאָ֜רֶץ אֲשֶׁר־יְהֹוָ֧ה אֱלֹהֶ֣יךָ ׀ נֹתֵ֣ן לְךָ֗ אֶ֤רֶץ זָבַ֤ת
חָלָב֙ וּדְבַ֔שׁ כַּאֲשֶׁ֥ר דִּבֶּ֛ר יְהֹוָ֥ה אֱלֹהֵֽי־אֲבֹתֶ֖יךָ לָֽךְ:
ד וְהָיָה֮ בְּעָבְרְכֶ֣ם אֶת־הַיַּרְדֵּן֒ תָּקִ֣ימוּ אֶת־הָאֲבָנִ֣ים
הָאֵ֗לֶּה אֲשֶׁ֨ר אָנֹכִ֜י מְצַוֶּ֥ה אֶתְכֶ֛ם הַיּ֖וֹם בְּהַ֣ר עֵיבָ֑ל
ה וְשַׂדְתָּ֥ אוֹתָ֖ם בַּשִּֽׂיד: וּבָנִ֤יתָ שָּׁם֙ מִזְבֵּ֣חַ לַיהֹוָ֣ה
אֱלֹהֶ֔יךָ מִזְבַּ֣ח אֲבָנִ֑ים לֹא־תָנִ֥יף עֲלֵיהֶ֖ם בַּרְזֶֽל:
ו אֲבָנִ֤ים שְׁלֵמוֹת֙ תִּבְנֶ֔ה אֶת־מִזְבַּ֖ח יְהֹוָ֣ה אֱלֹהֶ֑יךָ
ז וְהַעֲלִ֤יתָ עָלָיו֙ עוֹלֹ֔ת לַיהֹוָ֖ה אֱלֹהֶֽיךָ: וְזָבַחְתָּ֣ שְׁלָמִ֔ים
וְאָכַ֣לְתָּ שָּׁ֑ם וְשָׂ֣מַחְתָּ֔ לִפְנֵ֖י יְהֹוָ֥ה אֱלֹהֶֽיךָ: וְכָתַבְתָּ֣
ח עַל־הָאֲבָנִ֗ים אֶֽת־כָּל־דִּבְרֵ֛י הַתּוֹרָ֥ה הַזֹּ֖את בַּאֵ֥ר

─── בעל הטורים ───

כז (ב) וַהֲקֵמֹתָ לְךָ. ב' בַּמָּסוֹרֶת — "וַהֲקֵמֹתָ לְךָ אֲבָנִים גְּדֹלוֹת"; "וַהֲקֵמֹתָ אֶת הַמִּשְׁכָּן".
לוֹמַר, שֶׁשָּׁקוּל לָהֶם הֲקָמַת אֵלּוּ הָאֲבָנִים כַּהֲקָמַת הַמִּשְׁכָּן:

(ד) תָּקִימוּ. ב' בַּמָּסוֹרֶת — "תָּקִימוּ אֶת הָאֲבָנִים"; "וּפֶסֶל וּמַצֵּבָה לֹא תָקִימוּ". כְּנֶגֶד מַה
שֶּׁצִּוִּיתִי אֶתְכֶם "לֹא תָקִימוּ", אֲנִי מְצַוֶּה אֶתְכֶם "תָּקִימוּ אֶת הָאֲבָנִים":

(ח) הַתּוֹרָה הַזֹּאת בַּאֵר הֵיטֵב. בְּגִימַטְרִיָּא גַּם בְּשִׁבְעִים לְשׁוֹנוֹת:

☐ בְּפָרָשָׁה זוֹ נֶעְלָם סָמֶ"ךְ, לוֹמַר, אַף עַל פִּי שֶׁכָּתוּב "בַּיּוֹם אֲשֶׁר תַּעַבְרוּ אֶת הַיַּרְדֵּן",
נִתְרַחֲקוּ ס' מִילִין קֹדֶם שֶׁהֵקִימוּ הָאֲבָנִים, כִּדְאִיתָא בְּסוֹטָה:

─── BAAL HATURIM ELUCIDATED ───

XXVII.

2. וַהֲקֵמֹתָ לְךָ — YOU SHALL ERECT. The masoretic note, ב, means that this word appears twice in the *Tanach*: (i) here, וַהֲקֵמֹתָ לְךָ אֲבָנִים גְּדֹלוֹת, *you shall erect for yourself
great stones;* and (ii) וַהֲקֵמֹתָ אֶת הַמִּשְׁכָּן, *You shall erect the Tabernacle (Exodus 26:30).*
The similarity of expression indicates that the setting up of these stones was
considered by them equivalent to the erection of the *Mishkan* [Tabernacle].[64]

4. תָּקִימוּ — YOU SHALL ERECT. The masoretic note, ב, means that this word

---

64. The Baal HaTurim's source in comparing the
stones to the *Mishkan* is unknown. Perhaps it is
based on the Midrash that explains the term הָעֵדֻת,
the Testimony, of the phrase מִשְׁכַּן הָעֵדֻת, *the Tabernacle of the Testimony (Exodus 38:21),* as a refer-

ence to the Torah (*Tanchuma, Pekudei* 4; see also
Rashi to *Exodus* 25:16). Thus, the stones upon
which were inscribed *all the words of this Torah*
(vv. 3 and 8) are equated with the *Tabernacle of
the Testimony/Torah (Mekorei Baal HaTurim).*

day. ² It shall be on the day that you cross the Jordan to the land that HASHEM, your God, gives you, you shall erect for yourself great stones and you shall coat them with plaster. ³ You shall inscribe on them all the words of this Torah, when you cross over, so that you may enter the land that HASHEM, your God, gives you, a land flowing with milk and honey, as HASHEM, the God of your forefathers, spoke about you. ⁴ It shall be that when you cross the Jordan, you shall erect these stones, of which I command you today, on Mount Ebal, and you shall coat them with plaster. ⁵ There you shall build an altar for HASHEM, your God, an altar of stones; you shall not raise iron upon them. ⁶ Of whole stones shall you build the altar of HASHEM, your God, and you shall bring upon it burnt-offerings to HASHEM, your God. ⁷ You shall slaughter peace-offerings and eat there, and you shall rejoice before HASHEM, your God. ⁸ You shall inscribe on the stones all the words of this Torah, well clarified."

─────────────── BAAL HATURIM ELUCIDATED ───────────────

appears twice in the *Tanach*: (i) here, תָּקִימוּ אֶת הָאֲבָנִים, *you shall erect the stones;* and (ii) וּפֶסֶל וּמַצֵּבָה לֹא תָקִימוּ, *and you shall not erect a statue or a pillar* (*Leviticus* 26:1). [The similarity of expression indicates that God said,] "Corresponding to that which I have commanded you, 'You shall not erect,' I am commanding you, 'You shall erect the stones.' "[65]

8. הַתּוֹרָה הַזֹּאת בַּאֵר הֵיטֵב — **THIS TORAH, WELL CLARIFIED.** The *gematria* of this phrase (1258) is equivalent[66] to that of גַּם בְּשִׁבְעִים לְשׁוֹנוֹת, *also in seventy languages.*[67]

❏ The letter ס (= 60) is missing from this passage,[68] to indicate that although the Torah states, בַּיּוֹם אֲשֶׁר תַּעַבְרוּ אֶת הַיַּרְדֵּן, *on the day that you cross the Jordan* [you shall set up great stones] (v. 2 above), they [nevertheless] distanced themselves sixty *mil*[69] [from the Jordan] before they erected the stones, as is stated in tractate *Sotah.*[70]

65. See the Baal HaTurim's comment to *Leviticus* 26:1, s.v., וּפֶסֶל.

66. The principle of *im hakollel* allows 1258 to be considered equivalent to 1259, the *gematria* of the Baal HaTurim's phrase.

67. *Sotah* 32a, cited by *Rashi* — The term בַּאֵר הֵיטֵב implies that it was written in all seventy languages of the world (see also *Rashi* to 1:5 above).

68. Every letter of the *aleph-beis* (including the five final forms) is found in this passage (vv. 1-8), except for the ס.

69. Opinions regarding the modern-day equivalent of a *mil* range from just under six-tenths to just over seven-tenths of a mile. Thus, sixty *mil* would range between thirty-five and forty-three miles.

70. *Sotah* 36a; see also *Sanhedrin* 44a. The Talmud states that Mount Ebal, where Joshua set up the stones (see *Joshua* 8:30-32), was sixty *mil* from the Jordan.

ט הֵיטֵֽב: וַיְדַבֵּ֤ר מֹשֶׁה֙ וְהַכֹּֽהֲנִ֣ים הַֽלְוִיִּ֔ם אֶל־
כָּל־יִשְׂרָאֵ֖ל לֵאמֹ֑ר הַסְכֵּ֣ת ׀ וּשְׁמַ֣ע יִשְׂרָאֵ֗ל הַיּ֤וֹם
י הַזֶּה֙ נִֽהְיֵ֣יתָֽ לְעָ֔ם לַֽיהֹוָ֖ה אֱלֹהֶֽיךָ: וְשָֽׁמַעְתָּ֔ בְּק֖וֹל
יְהֹוָ֣ה אֱלֹהֶ֑יךָ וְעָשִׂ֤יתָ אֶת־מִצְוֺתָו֙ וְאֶת־חֻקָּ֔יו אֲשֶׁ֛ר
יא אָֽנֹכִ֥י מְצַוְּךָ֖ הַיּֽוֹם: וַיְצַ֤ו מֹשֶׁה֙ אֶת־הָעָ֔ם

חמישי

יב בַּיּ֥וֹם הַה֖וּא לֵאמֹֽר: אֵ֠לֶּה יַֽעַמְד֞וּ לְבָרֵ֤ךְ אֶת־
הָעָם֙ עַל־הַ֣ר גְּרִזִ֔ים בְּעָבְרְכֶ֖ם אֶת־הַיַּרְדֵּ֑ן שִׁמְעוֹן֙
יג וְלֵוִ֣י וִֽיהוּדָ֔ה וְיִשָּׂשכָ֖ר וְיוֹסֵ֥ף וּבִנְיָמִֽן: וְאֵ֛לֶּה יַֽעַמְד֥וּ
עַל־הַקְּלָלָ֖ה בְּהַ֣ר עֵיבָ֑ל רְאוּבֵן֙ גָּ֣ד וְאָשֵׁ֔ר וּזְבוּלֻ֖ן
יד דָּ֥ן וְנַפְתָּלִֽי: וְעָנ֣וּ הַֽלְוִיִּ֗ם וְאָֽמְר֛וּ אֶל־כָּל־אִ֥ישׁ
טו יִשְׂרָאֵ֖ל ק֥וֹל רָֽם: אָר֣וּר הָאִ֡ישׁ אֲשֶׁ֣ר יַֽעֲשֶׂה֩
פֶ֨סֶל וּמַסֵּכָ֜ה תּֽוֹעֲבַ֣ת יְהֹוָ֗ה מַֽעֲשֵׂ֛ה יְדֵ֥י חָרָ֖שׁ
טז וְשָׂ֣ם בַּסָּ֑תֶר וְעָנ֧וּ כָל־הָעָ֛ם וְאָֽמְר֖וּ אָמֵֽן: אָר֕וּר

━━━━━━━━━━ בעל הטורים ━━━━━━━━━━

(יב) גְּרִזִּים. בְּגִימַטְרִיָּא הַבְּרָכָה יִהְיֶה בּוֹ:

(יד) קוֹל רָם. וּסְמִיךְ לֵהּ ״אָרוּר הָאִישׁ אֲשֶׁר יַעֲשֶׂה פֶסֶל״. לוֹמַר שֶׁבְּקוֹלוֹ שֶׁל ״רָם״, הַיְנוּ
בְּקוֹל הַקָּדוֹשׁ בָּרוּךְ הוּא, שָׁמְעוּ דִבּוּר ״אָנֹכִי ה׳ ״ וְ״לֹא יִהְיֶה לְךָ״:

(טו) בַּסָּתֶר. ד׳ בַּמָּסוֹרֶת — ״וְשָׂם בַּסָּתֶר״; ״מַכֵּה רֵעֵהוּ בַסָּתֶר״; ״כִּי אַתָּה עָשִׂיתָ בַסָּתֶר״
בְּדָוִד בְּעִנְיָן בַּת־שֶׁבַע; ״כִּי תֹאכְלֵם בְּחֹסֶר כֹּל בַּסָּתֶר״. לוֹמַר, אִם תַּעֲשֶׂה בַסֵּתֶר, ״תֹאכְלֵם
בְּחֹסֶר כֹּל בַּסָּתֶר״:

━━━━━━━━━━ BAAL HATURIM ELUCIDATED ━━━━━━━━━━

12. גְּרִזִים — GERIZIM. The *gematria* of this term (260) is equivalent[71] to that of הַבְּרָכָה יִהְיֶה בּוֹ[71a], *The blessing will be upon it.*[72]

71. The *gematria* of the Baal HaTurim's phrase is 270, ten more than that of גְּרִזִים. To reconcile the *gematriaos, Ittur Bikkurim* suggests spelling the name in full, גְּרִיזִים, with another י (= 10), and that is how the word is spelled in all editions of the Baal HaTurim. However, the comment can be explained without altering the spelling of גְּרִזִים, which contains only one י each of the four times that it appears in the *Tanach* (*Deuteronomy* 11:29 and 27:12; *Joshua* 8:33; *Judges* 9:7). See note 72 below.

71a. The Baal HaTurim's comment presents a grammatical problem: Instead of using the feminine verb תִּהְיֶה, *she/it will be,* with the feminine subject הַבְּרָכָה, *the blessing,* it uses the masculine verb form יִהְיֶה, *he/it will be.* This seems to be another instance of bending the rules of grammar when expounding on the Torah in the realm of *remez* [allusion] (VeChur LaZahav).

72. What is the purpose of the Baal HaTurim's allusion, which seems to add nothing to that which is explicit in the verse? See note 71 above regarding the disparity between the *gematriaos.* Perhaps, instead of emending the spelling of גְּרִזִים to increase its *gematria* by ten, the Baal HaTurim's phrase should be emended to הַבְּרָכָה הָיָה בּוֹ, *The blessing had been upon it* [see note 71a regarding the grammar of this sentence], thus decreasing its *gematria* by ten. But what blessing "had been upon it"? The name גְּרִזִים may be explained as a

⁹ Moses and the Kohanim, the Levites, spoke to all Israel, saying, "Be attentive and hear, O Israel: This day you have become a people to HASHEM, your God. ¹⁰ You shall hearken to the voice of HASHEM, your God, and you shall perform all His commandments and His decrees, which I command you today."

¹¹ Moses commanded the people on that day, saying, ¹² "These shall stand to bless the people on Mount Gerizim, when you have crossed the Jordan: Simeon, Levi, Judah, Issachar, Joseph, and Benjamin. ¹³ And these shall stand for the curse on Mount Ebal: Reuben, Gad, Asher, Zebulun, Dan, and Naphtali. ¹⁴ The Levites shall speak up and say to every man of Israel, in a loud voice:

¹⁵ 'Accursed is the man who will make a graven image or a molten image, an abomination of HASHEM, a craftsman's handiwork, and emplace it in secret.' And the entire people shall speak up and say, 'Amen.'

───────────── BAAL HATURIM ELUCIDATED ─────────────

14. קוֹל רָם — A LOUD VOICE. Juxtaposed to this is, אָרוּר הָאִישׁ אֲשֶׁר יַעֲשֶׂה פֶסֶל, *Accursed is the man who will make a graven image.* [The juxtaposition] indicates that it was by the voice of the רָם, *Exalted One,* [73] i.e., the voice of the Holy One, Blessed is He, that they heard the commandment, *I am HASHEM, your God,* and *You shall not have [other gods]*[74] (5:6-7 above).[75]

15. בַּסָּתֶר — IN SECRET. The masoretic note, ד׳, means that this word appears four times in the *Tanach*: (i) here, וְשָׂם בַּסָּתֶר, *and emplace it in secret;* (ii) מַכֵּה רֵעֵהוּ בַּסָּתֶר, *he strikes his fellow in secret* (v. 24 below); (iii) כִּי אַתָּה עָשִׂיתָ בַסָּתֶר, *for you acted in secret* (*II Samuel* 12:12), with regard to David and the incident with Bath-Sheba; and (iv) כִּי תֹאכְלֵם בְּחֹסֶר כֹּל בַּסָּתֶר, *for she will eat them* [i.e., her offspring] *in secret for lack of anything* (28:57 below). This [similarity of expression] indicates that if you will act [sinfully]⁷⁵ᵃ in secret, [your punishment will be that] you[76] *will eat them* [i.e., your offspring] *in secret for lack of anything.*

───────────────────────────────────────

play on the word גְּזָרִים, *pieces* (*Genesis* 15:17), and is an allusion to the Covenant between the Parts (see *Genesis*, Ch. 15) in which God promised Abraham that he would beget offspring and that they would be given the Land of Israel (*Peirush HaRokeach* to 11:29 above). Now, if Mount Gerizim was named for that event, we may assume that the event took place there. Accordingly, it is there that Moses commanded the nation to pronounce the blessings because הַבְּרָכָה הָיָה בוֹ, *the blessing* [that God had given Abraham] *had been upon it* (*VeChur LaZahav*).

73. Scripture uses the term רָם for God, e.g., *Isaiah* 57:15; *Psalms* 138:6.

74. *Makkos* 24a.

75. *Peirush HaRokeach.*

75a. That is, if you will commit idolatry (our verse) or speak slanderously (v. 24 below, see the Baal HaTurim's comment there) or engage in illicit relations (*II Samuel* 12:12) in secret.

76. The future tense verb form תֹאכְלֵם (or תֹאכְלֵם) can be either second person masculine or third person feminine. Thus, in the context of 28:57

יז מַקְלֶה אָבִיו וְאִמּוֹ וְאָמַר כָּל־הָעָם אָמֵן: אָרוּר
יח מַסִּיג גְּבוּל רֵעֵהוּ וְאָמַר כָּל־הָעָם אָמֵן: אָרוּר
יט מַשְׁגֶּה עִוֵּר בַּדָּרֶךְ וְאָמַר כָּל־הָעָם אָמֵן: אָרוּר
מַטֶּה מִשְׁפַּט גֵּר־יָתוֹם וְאַלְמָנָה וְאָמַר כָּל־
כ הָעָם אָמֵן: אָרוּר שֹׁכֵב עִם־אֵשֶׁת אָבִיו כִּי

בעל הטורים

(טו־יח) הִתְחִיל בַּעֲבֹדָה זָרָה, שֶׁהִיא שְׁקוּלָה כְּנֶגֶד כָּל הַתּוֹרָה כֻּלָּהּ:

וְסָמַךְ לַעֲבֹדָה זָרָה, "מַקְלֶה אָבִיו וְאִמּוֹ". דִּשְׁלֹשָׁה שֻׁתָּפִין יֵשׁ בָּאָדָם:

וְסָמַךְ לְ"מַקְלֶה אָבִיו", "מַסִּיג גְּבוּל רֵעֵהוּ", לוֹמַר שֶׁהַבָּא עַל אֵשֶׁת אִישׁ, שֶׁהוּא מַסִּיג גְּבוּל רֵעֵהוּ, גּוֹרֵם לַבֵּן שֶׁמַּקְלֶה אָבִיו, שֶׁאֵינוֹ מַכִּיר אָבִיו.

וְסָמַךְ לוֹ "מַשְׁגֶּה עִוֵּר", לוֹמַר, לֹא תִּיָּעֵץ לוֹ לְפִי דַרְכְּךָ כְּדֵי לְהַסִּיג גְּבוּלוֹ:

(יח) מַשְׁגֶּה. ב׳ בַּמָּסוֹרֶת — "מַשְׁגֶּה עִוֵּר"; "מַשְׁגֶּה יְשָׁרִים בְּדֶרֶךְ רָע". זֶהוּ שֶׁדָּרְשׁוּ, "מַשְׁגֶּה עִוֵּר" שֶׁמְּיָעֲצוֹ לַחֲטֹא. זֶהוּ "מַשְׁגֶּה יְשָׁרִים בְּדֶרֶךְ רָע", שֶׁהוּא יָשָׁר, וְנוֹתֵן לוֹ עֵצָה לְעַקֵּם דְּרָכָיו:

❑ וּסְמִיךְ לֵהּ "מַטֶּה מִשְׁפַּט", שֶׁהַיּוֹדֵעַ הַדִּין וּמַטֵּהוּ בִּרְאָיוֹתָיו אוֹ טוֹעֵן שֶׁקֶר, הוּא "מַשְׁגֶּה עִוֵּר":

BAAL HATURIM ELUCIDATED

15-18. This passage [of the Curses[77]] begins with idol worship (v. 15), which is equivalent to [trespassing against] the entire Torah.[78]

Juxtaposed to idol worship (v. 15) is *one who degrades his father or his mother* (v. 16), for [as the Sages teach]: There are three partners in each person [— the Holy One, Blessed is He; one's father; and one's mother].[79]

Juxtaposed to *one who degrades his father* (v. 16) is **מַסִּיג גְּבוּל רֵעֵהוּ**, *one who usurps the boundary of his neighbor* (v. 17), to indicate that a man who commits adultery — for he *usurps the boundary* [i.e., the wife] *of his neighbor*[79a] — causes a son to degrade his father, for he will not recognize [i.e., know the identity of] his real father.[80]

---

below, it means *she will eat them;* but in the context of the Baal HaTurim's comment, it means *you will eat them* (*VeChur LaZahav*).

77. The passage of the Curses comprises twelve verses (15-26), each of which begins with the word אָרוּר, *accursed,* and goes on to describe a particular sin. In his comments, the Baal HaTurim explains the sequence of the verses, how each sin is conceptually connected to the one listed before it and the one listed after it. He interrupts the account twice to explain a particular word (s.v., מַשְׁגֶּה and בַּסָּתֶר). Accordingly, it is recommended that the remainder of the Baal HaTurim's comments to this passage be read as if they formed one long comment, with the exception of the two comments mentioned above.

78. With this introductory statement, the Baal HaTurim ties the whole passage into a neat package by relating the first verse to the last (*VeChur LaZahav*).

79. *Peirush HaRokeach;* see *Niddah* 31a (cited in note 55 to *parashas Ha'azinu* below); see also the Baal HaTurim to *Leviticus* 18:6-7 and 20:8.

79a. See *Sotah* 37b, with *Rashi,* s.v., אלא.

80. See the Baal HaTurim to *Leviticus* 20:10. The Midrash states: The Ten Commandments were inscribed on the Two Tablets, the five on one tablet corresponding to the five on the other . . .

¹⁶ *'Accursed is one who degrades his father or mother.'
And the entire people shall say, 'Amen.'*

¹⁷ *'Accursed is one who usurps the boundary of his neighbor.' And the entire people shall say, 'Amen.'*

¹⁸ *'Accursed is one who misleads a blind person on the road.' And the entire people shall say, 'Amen.'*

¹⁹ *'Accursed is one who perverts a judgment of a proselyte [or an] orphan or a widow.' And the entire people shall say, 'Amen.'*

²⁰ *'Accursed is one who lies with his father's wife, for he*

──────────── BAAL HATURIM ELUCIDATED ────────────

Juxtaposed to that is *one who misleads a blind person* (v. 18), to indicate that you should not advise him[81] in a way beneficial to you, in order to usurp his boundary.

18. מַשְׁגֶּה — ONE WHO MISLEADS. The masoretic note, ב׳, means that this word appears twice in the *Tanach*: (i) here, מַשְׁגֶּה עִוֵּר, *one who misleads a blind person;* and (ii) מַשְׁגֶּה יְשָׁרִים בְּדֶרֶךְ רָע, *one who misleads the upright to an evil way* (*Proverbs* 28:10). This [similarity of expressions] points to the Sages' interpretation of מַשְׁגֶּה עִוֵּר as [a reference to] one who advises him to sin. [And] that is the intent of the verse, *one who misleads the upright to an evil way,* for he [the one seeking advice] is upright, but he [the adviser] is giving him advice that makes his path crooked.[81a]

❏ Juxtaposed[82] to that is *one who perverts a judgment* (v. 19), for if a person knows the law, but perverts it with his [spurious] proofs or false claims, he is *one who misleads a blind person.* [82a]

19. {The Baal HaTurim's comment to גֵּר יָתוֹם appears at 24:17 above.}

[On the first tablet] is written, *Honor your father and mother;* corresponding to it on the other tablet is written, *You shall not covet [your neighbor's wife].* Thus, the verses underscore that if one will covet [and will achieve the object of his envy], he will be destined to beget a son who will curse his real father while honoring one who is not his father (*Mechilta* to *Exodus* 20:13).

Another Midrash explains why this happens: The illegitimate son will honor his mother's husband, thinking that he is his father; but he will curse his real father when he discovers that a "stranger" has had an adulterous affair with his mother (*Bamidbar Rabbah* 9:7).

81. That is, a person who is blind, i.e., unaware or uneducated, with respect to a particular matter and who seeks your advice about how to proceed regarding it (*Toras Kohanim* to 19:14,

cited by *Rashi* here; see also *Rashi* and the Baal HaTurim to *Leviticus* 19:14).

81a. According to the *Zohar*, the Torah describes one who gives evil advice as placing a stumbling block in the road (see *Leviticus* 19:14), because by giving evil advice he causes the other person to stumble on his path to the World to Come (*Kedoshim* 85a). See also *Sefer Chofetz Chaim, Pesichah, Arurin* 2.

82. See note 77 above.

82a. In its simple meaning, the verse refers to a judge who prevents justice; in the Baal HaTurim's allusion, it refers to a litigant who uses his knowledge of the law to pervert it, with either open falsehood or with specious arguments. Accordingly, the blind man of the verse must be the judge who is misled by the litigant's ruse (A.S.)

כא גִּלָּ֖ה כְּנַ֣ף אָבִ֑יו וְאָמַ֥ר כָּל־הָעָ֖ם אָמֵֽן׃ אָר֕וּר
כב שֹׁכֵ֖ב עִם־כָּל־בְּהֵמָ֑ה וְאָמַ֥ר כָּל־הָעָ֖ם אָמֵֽן׃ אָר֗וּר
שֹׁכֵב֙ עִם־אֲחֹת֔וֹ בַּת־אָבִ֖יו א֣וֹ בַת־אִמּ֑וֹ וְאָמַ֥ר
כג כָּל־הָעָ֖ם אָמֵֽן׃ אָר֕וּר שֹׁכֵ֖ב עִם־חֹֽתַנְתּ֑וֹ וְאָמַ֥ר
כד כָּל־הָעָ֖ם אָמֵֽן׃ אָר֕וּר מַכֵּ֥ה רֵעֵ֖הוּ בַּסָּ֑תֶר וְאָמַ֥ר
כה כָּל־הָעָ֖ם אָמֵֽן׃ אָרוּר֙ לֹקֵ֣חַ שֹׁ֔חַד לְהַכּ֖וֹת נֶ֣פֶשׁ
כו דָּ֣ם נָקִ֑י וְאָמַ֥ר כָּל־הָעָ֖ם אָמֵֽן׃ אָר֗וּר אֲשֶׁ֧ר
לֹא־יָקִ֛ים אֶת־דִּבְרֵ֥י הַתּוֹרָֽה־הַזֹּ֖את לַעֲשׂ֣וֹת אוֹתָ֑ם
וְאָמַ֥ר כָּל־הָעָ֖ם אָמֵֽן׃

בעל הטורים

(**כא־כד**) סָמַךְ "שֹׁכֵב עִם . . . בְּהֵמָה" לְ"אֵשֶׁת אָבִיו", לְפִי שֶׁהוּא עִמָּהּ בַּבַּיִת וְכָרוּךְ אַחֲרֶיהָ כַּבְּהֵמָה. וְכֵן "אֲחֹתוֹ" וְ"חֹתַנְתּוֹ", שֶׁהֵם תְּדִירִים עִמּוֹ.

וְסָמַךְ לוֹ "מַכֵּה רֵעֵהוּ בַּסָּתֶר", שֶׁהוּא בִּצְנְעָא, כְּמוֹ זְנוּת חוֹתַנְתּוֹ וַאֲחוֹתוֹ שֶׁהוּא בִּצְנְעָא בְּבֵיתוֹ:

(**כד**) **בַּסָּתֶר**. בְּגִימַטְרִיָּא בְּלָשׁוֹן הָרָע:

❑ **בַּסָּתֶר**. בְּגִימַטְרִיָּא מֹסֵר מָמוֹן חֲבֵירוֹ:

(**כה־כו**) וְסָמַךְ "לֹקֵחַ שֹׁחַד לְהַכּוֹת נֶפֶשׁ", לוֹמַר הוֹלֵךְ רָכִיל "לְמַעַן שְׁפָךְ דָּם":

❑ וְסָמַךְ "אֲשֶׁר לֹא יָקִים" [לְ]"לְהַכּוֹת נֶפֶשׁ", לוֹמַר, הַשּׁוֹפֵךְ דָּם, כְּעוֹבֵר עַל כָּל הַתּוֹרָה:

❑ **אָמֵן**. בְּגִימַטְרִיָּא הוי"ה אדנ"י. וְלָכֵן גָּדוֹל הָעוֹנֶה אָמֵן יוֹתֵר מִן הַמְבָרֵךְ. שֶׁעוֹלֶה שְׁנֵי שֵׁמוֹת:

BAAL HATURIM ELUCIDATED

21-24. The Torah juxtaposed[82] *one who lies with an animal* (v. 21) to *one who lies with his father's wife* (v. 20), for he is together with her at home and clings to her like an animal.[83] Similarly, [regarding] *his sister* (v. 22) and *his mother-in-law* (v. 23), *who are continually together with him.*[84]

❑ Juxtaposed to that is *one who strikes his fellow in secret* (v. 24), which is done in privacy, just like illicit relations with his mother-in-law or his sister which are done in the privacy of his home.

24. בַּסָּתֶר — IN SECRET. The *gematria* of this term (662) is equivalent[85] to that of בְּלָשׁוֹן הָרָע, *with evil speech.*[86]

---

83. That is, as a young child he clings to his father's wife, who is his foster mother, with the same tenacity as a young animal clings to whichever female of the herd suckles it, regardless of whether she is its natural mother (*VeChur LaZahav;* cf. *Chullin* 78b).

84. See the Baal HaTurim to *Leviticus* 20:17.

85. The principle of *im hakollel* allows 662 to be considered equivalent to 663, the *gematria* of the Baal HaTurim's phrase.

86. *Peirush HaRokeach.* According to the Midrash the striking in secret of our verse refers to speaking badly about the person behind his back (*Pirkei DeRabbi Eliezer* 53; *Targum Yonasan ben Uzziel*; see *Rashi*).

27/21-26 *will have uncovered the robe of his father.' And the entire people*
shall say, 'Amen.'
21 *'Accursed is one who lies with any animal.' And the entire*
people shall say, 'Amen.'
22 *'Accursed is one who lies with his sister, the daughter of his*
father or the daughter of his mother.' And the entire people shall
say, 'Amen.'
23 *'Accursed is one who lies with his mother-in-law.' And the*
entire people shall say, 'Amen.'
24 *'Accursed is one who strikes his fellow in secret.' And the*
entire people shall say, 'Amen.'
25 *'Accursed is one who takes a bribe to smite a soul, [to spill]*
innocent blood.' And the entire people shall say, 'Amen.'
26 *'Accursed is one who would not uphold the words of this To-*
rah, to perform them.' And the entire people shall say, 'Amen.' "

BAAL HATURIM ELUCIDATED

❏ **בַּסָּתֶר** — IN SECRET. The *gematria* of this term (662) is equal to that of מֹסֵר מָמוֹן חֲבֵירוֹ, *one who gives over his colleague's money.*[87]

❏ {The Baal HaTurim's other comment to בַּסָּתֶר appears at v. 15 above.}

25-26. Juxtaposed[88] [to that] is *one who takes a bribe to smite a soul,* to indicate that the gossipmonger's purpose is *in order to spill blood*[89] (*Ezekiel* 22:9).[90]

❏ The Torah juxtaposed *one who would not uphold* (v. 26) [to] *to smite a soul* (v. 25), to indicate that the spiller of blood is considered as one who has violated the entire Torah.[91]

❏ **אָמֵן** — AMEN.[92] The *gematria* of this word (91) is equal to the combined *gematriaos* of י־ה־ו־ה (26) and אֲדֹנָי (65).[92a] Therefore [the Sages have taught]: The one who responds *Amen* is greater than the one who recites the blessing.[93] For *Amen* is equivalent to two Names [of God].[94]

87. *Peirush HaRokeach.* There, the two comments to the word בַּסָּתֶר are presented as one: בַּסָּתֶר בְּגִימַטְרִיָּא בְּלָשׁוֹן הָרָע אוֹ מֹסֵר מָמוֹן חֲבֵירוֹ, *The gematria of* בַּסָּתֶר *is equal to that of* בְּלָשׁוֹן הָרָע *or to that of* מֹסֵר מָמוֹן חֲבֵירוֹ. Accordingly, it refers to an informant or to a gossipmonger whose prattle about another person leads the authorities to confiscate that person's property or alerts thieves to ways in which they can rob his money (*VeChur LaZahav*).

88. See note 77 above.

89. *Peirush HaRokeach.*

90. That verse begins: אַנְשֵׁי רָכִיל הָיוּ בָךְ, *Gossipmongers were among you,* לְמַעַן שְׁפָךְ דָּם, *in order to spill blood . . .* (see also *Arachin* 15b).

91. *Peirush HaRokeach*; see *Rambam, Hilchos Rotze'ach* 4:9.

92. The term אָמֵן, *Amen,* appears twelve times in this passage (vv. 15-26) as the final word in each of its twelve verses. *Peirush HaRokeach* presents this same comment at verse 15, the first time the term אָמֵן appears. It is not clear why the Baal HaTurim relocated it to the end of the passage.

92a. That is, the Tetragrammaton as it is spelled and as it is pronounced.

93. *Berachos* 53b.

94. *Sefer Chasidim* 18 — The one who responds אָמֵן is greater than the one who recites the blessing, because . . . the one who recites the blessing mentions only one Name [בָּרוּךְ אַתָּה ה' (*Peirush HaRokeach*)], while the one who re-

א וְהָיָ֗ה אִם־שָׁמ֤וֹעַ תִּשְׁמַע֙ בְּקוֹל֙ יהוה אֱלֹהֶ֔יךָ לִשְׁמֹ֤ר לַעֲשׂוֹת֙ אֶת־כָּל־מִצְוֺתָ֔יו אֲשֶׁ֛ר אָנֹכִ֥י מְצַוְּךָ֖ הַיּ֑וֹם

ב וּנְתָֽנְךָ֞ יהוה אֱלֹהֶ֙יךָ֙ עֶלְי֔וֹן עַ֖ל כָּל־גּוֹיֵ֣י הָאָ֑רֶץ וּבָ֧אוּ עָלֶ֛יךָ כָּל־הַבְּרָכ֥וֹת הָאֵ֖לֶּה וְהִשִּׂיגֻ֑ךָ כִּ֥י תִשְׁמַ֖ע בְּק֥וֹל יהוה אֱלֹהֶֽיךָ: ג בָּר֥וּךְ אַתָּ֖ה בָּעִ֑יר וּבָר֥וּךְ אַתָּ֖ה בַּשָּׂדֶֽה:

ד בָּר֧וּךְ פְּרִֽי־בִטְנְךָ֛ וּפְרִ֥י אַדְמָֽתְךָ֖ וּפְרִ֣י בְהֶמְתֶּ֑ךָ שְׁגַ֥ר אֲלָפֶ֖יךָ וְעַשְׁתְּרֹ֥ת צֹאנֶֽךָ: ה בָּר֥וּךְ טַנְאֲךָ֖ וּמִשְׁאַרְתֶּֽךָ:

ו־ז בָּר֥וּךְ אַתָּ֖ה בְּבֹאֶ֑ךָ וּבָר֥וּךְ אַתָּ֖ה בְּצֵאתֶֽךָ: *יִתֵּ֙ן יהוה אֶת־אֹיְבֶ֜יךָ הַקָּמִ֤ים עָלֶ֙יךָ֙ נִגָּפִ֣ים לְפָנֶ֔יךָ בְּדֶ֥רֶךְ אֶחָד֙

ח יֵצְא֣וּ אֵלֶ֔יךָ וּבְשִׁבְעָ֥ה דְרָכִ֖ים יָנ֣וּסוּ לְפָנֶֽיךָ: יְצַ֙ו יהוה אִתְּךָ֙ אֶת־הַבְּרָכָ֔ה בַּאֲסָמֶ֔יךָ וּבְכֹ֖ל מִשְׁלַ֣ח יָדֶ֑ךָ וּבֵ֣רַכְךָ֔ בָּאָ֕רֶץ אֲשֶׁר־יהוה אֱלֹהֶ֖יךָ נֹתֵ֥ן לָֽךְ:

ט יְקִֽימְךָ֙ יהוה לוֹ֙ לְעַ֣ם קָד֔וֹשׁ כַּאֲשֶׁ֖ר נִֽשְׁבַּֽע־לָ֑ךְ כִּ֣י תִשְׁמֹ֗ר אֶת־מִצְוֺת֙ יהוה אֱלֹהֶ֔יךָ וְהָלַכְתָּ֖ בִּדְרָכָֽיו:

י וְרָאוּ֙ כָּל־עַמֵּ֣י הָאָ֔רֶץ כִּ֛י שֵׁ֥ם יהוה נִקְרָ֖א עָלֶ֑יךָ

בעל הטורים

כח (א) שָׁמוֹעַ תִּשְׁמַע. בְּגִימַטְרִיָּא לְדִבְרֵי תוֹרָה וּלְדִבְרֵי חֲכָמִים:

(ז) יָנוּסוּ לְפָנֶיךָ. וּסְמִיךְ לֵהּ "יְצַו ה' אִתְּךָ אֶת הַבְּרָכָה בַּאֲסָמֶיךָ". שֶׁתִּמָּצֵא בָתִּים מְלֵאִים כָּל טוֹב:

(ח) בַּאֲסָמֶיךָ. בְּגִימַטְרִיָּא זֶהוּ סָמוּי. שֶׁאֵין הַבְּרָכָה מְצוּיָה אֶלָּא בְדָבָר הַסָּמוּי מִן הָעָיִן:

(י) שֵׁם ה' נִקְרָא. רָאשֵׁי תֵבוֹת שִׁי"ן. פֵּרוּשׁ, שִׁי"ן שֶׁל תְּפִלִּין:

BAAL HATURIM ELUCIDATED

XXVIII.

1. שָׁמוֹעַ תִּשְׁמַע — YOU WILL HEARKEN.[94a] The *gematria* of this phrase (1226) is equivalent[95] to that of לְדִבְרֵי תוֹרָה וּלְדִבְרֵי חֲכָמִים, *to the words of the Torah and the words of the Sages.* [96]

7. יָנוּסוּ לְפָנֶיךָ — THEY WILL FLEE BEFORE YOU. Juxtaposed to this is, יְצַו ה' אִתְּךָ אֶת הַבְּרָכָה בַּאֲסָמֶיךָ, *HASHEM will command the blessing for you in your storehouses* (v. 8).

sponds אָמֵן mentions two Names, for the *gematria* of אָמֵן is equal to those of the Name [that begins with the letters] יו"ד ה"א and the Name [that begins with the letters] אלי"ף דלי"ת.

94a. Literally: *hearkening you will hearken.* The Baal HaTurim's comment explains that the double verb form refers to two things to which you must hearken.

95. The principle of *im hakollel* allows 1226 to be considered equivalent to 1227, the *gematria* of the Baal HaTurim's phrase.

96. *Yevamos 20a* — It is a *mitzvah* to hearken to the words of the Sages.

1 *It shall be that if you will hearken to the voice of* HASHEM,
*your God, to observe, to perform all of His commandments
that I command you this day, then* HASHEM, *your God, will
make you supreme over all the nations of the earth.* 2 *All
these blessings will come upon you and overtake you, if
you hearken to the voice of* HASHEM, *your God:*
3 *Blessed shall you be in the city and blessed shall you be
in the field.* 4 *Blessed shall be the fruit of your womb, and
the fruit of your ground, and the fruit of your animals; the
offspring of your cattle and the flocks of your sheep and
goats.* 5 *Blessed shall be your fruit basket and your
kneading bowl.* 6 *Blessed shall you be when you come in
and blessed shall you be when you go out.* 7 HASHEM *shall
cause your enemies who rise up against you to be struck
down before you; on one road they will go out toward you
and on seven roads they will flee before you.* 8 HASHEM *will
command the blessing for you in your storehouses and
your every undertaking; and He will bless you in the land
that* HASHEM, *your God, gives you.* 9 HASHEM *will confirm
you for Himself as a holy people, as He swore to you —
if you observe the commandments of* HASHEM, *your God,
and you go in His ways.* 10 *Then all the peoples of the earth
will see that the Name of* HASHEM *is proclaimed upon you,*

BAAL HATURIM ELUCIDATED

For [Moses was saying,] "You will find houses filled with every good thing."[97,98]

❑ {The Baal HaTurim discusses this verse further at *Numbers* 6:26, s.v., וְיָשֵׂם.}

8. בַּאֲסָמֶיךָ — IN YOUR STOREHOUSES. The *gematria* of this term (133) is equivalent[99] to that of וְזֶהוּ סָמוּי, *This [refers to that which] is hidden.* For [as the Talmud states,] blessing is found only in that which is hidden from the eye.[100]

❑ {The Baal HaTurim discusses this verse further at *Numbers* 23:7 s.v., אָרָה לִּי.}

10. שֵׁם ה׳ נִקְרָא — THE NAME OF HASHEM IS PROCLAIMED. The initial letters of these words spell [the name of the letter] שִׁי״ן, *shin,* for the phrase refers to the *shin* of the *tefillin.*[101]

97. The Baal HaTurim paraphrases the wording of 6:11 above.

98. *Peirush HaRokeach.* Presumably, the allusion means that they will flee in such haste that they will leave all their valuables behind (see *Sforno* to 6:10 above).

99. The principle of *im hakollel* allows 133 to be considered equivalent to 134, the *gematria* of the Baal HaTurim's phrase. It is not clear why the Baal HaTurim did not use the phrase זֶה הַסָּמוּי, which has the same meaning, but whose *gematria* is 133.

100. *Taanis* 8b; see also the Baal HaTurim to 25:12 above, s.v., דָּבָר אַחֵר.

101. According to the Talmud, this phrase refers to the *tefillin* of the head (*Menachos* 35b).

The verse means that the head *tefillin* inspire

יא וְיָרְאוּ מִמֶּךָּ׃ וְהוֹתִרְךָ יהוה לְטוֹבָה בִּפְרִי בִטְנְךָ
וּבִפְרִי בְהֶמְתְּךָ וּבִפְרִי אַדְמָתֶךָ עַל הָאֲדָמָה אֲשֶׁר
יב נִשְׁבַּע יְהוָה לַאֲבֹתֶיךָ לָתֶת לָךְ׃ יִפְתַּח יְהוָה ׀ לְךָ
אֶת־אוֹצָרוֹ הַטּוֹב אֶת־הַשָּׁמַיִם לָתֵת מְטַר־אַרְצְךָ
בְּעִתּוֹ וּלְבָרֵךְ אֵת כָּל־מַעֲשֵׂה יָדֶךָ וְהִלְוִיתָ גּוֹיִם
יג רַבִּים וְאַתָּה לֹא תִלְוֶה׃ וּנְתָנְךָ יְהוָה לְרֹאשׁ וְלֹא
לְזָנָב וְהָיִיתָ רַק לְמַעְלָה וְלֹא תִהְיֶה לְמָטָּה כִּי־
תִשְׁמַע אֶל־מִצְוֹת ׀ יְהוָה אֱלֹהֶיךָ אֲשֶׁר אָנֹכִי מְצַוְּךָ
יד הַיּוֹם לִשְׁמֹר וְלַעֲשׂוֹת׃ וְלֹא תָסוּר מִכָּל־הַדְּבָרִים
אֲשֶׁר אָנֹכִי מְצַוֶּה אֶתְכֶם הַיּוֹם יָמִין וּשְׂמֹאול לָלֶכֶת
אַחֲרֵי אֱלֹהִים אֲחֵרִים לְעָבְדָם׃
טו וְהָיָה אִם־לֹא תִשְׁמַע בְּקוֹל יְהוָה אֱלֹהֶיךָ לִשְׁמֹר
לַעֲשׂוֹת אֶת־כָּל־מִצְוֹתָיו וְחֻקֹּתָיו אֲשֶׁר אָנֹכִי מְצַוְּךָ
הַיּוֹם וּבָאוּ עָלֶיךָ כָּל־הַקְּלָלוֹת הָאֵלֶּה וְהִשִּׂיגוּךָ׃
טז-יז אָרוּר אַתָּה בָּעִיר וְאָרוּר אַתָּה בַּשָּׂדֶה׃ אָרוּר טַנְאֲךָ

בעל הטורים

❑ **וְיָרְאוּ מִמֶּךָּ.** וּסְמִיךְ לֵהּ ״וְהוֹתִרְךָ ה׳״. לוֹמַר בִּזְכוּת הַתְּפִלִּין יוֹתִיר יָמִים, דִּכְתִיב ״אֲדֹנָי עֲלֵיהֶם יִחְיוּ״:

❑ {**וְיָרְאוּ.** ב׳ – הָכָא ״וְיָרְאוּ מִמֶּךָּ״; וְאִידָךְ ״וְיָרְאוּ אֶת ה׳ אֱלֹהֵיכֶם״. מִדָּה כְּנֶגֶד מִדָּה, בִּשְׁבִיל ״וְיָרְאוּ אֶת ה׳״, ״וְיָרְאוּ מִמֶּךָּ״}:

BAAL HATURIM ELUCIDATED

❑ **וְיָרְאוּ מִמֶּךָּ — AND THEY WILL BE IN AWE OF YOU.** Juxtaposed to this is the promise,

fear in the hearts of Israel's enemies, because the Divine Presence rests upon one who is wearing *tefillin.* When other nations see this, they stand in awe of God's power and might (*Maharsha* to *Berachos* 6a).

The Talmud specifies the head *tefillin* (and not both head and arm) because of the letter ש embossed on the leather box of that *tefillin,* and the letter ד formed by the knot on its strap at the back of the wearer's head. Thus, the head *tefillin* displays two of the three letters of the Divine Name שַׁדַּי, while the arm *tefillin* contains only the י that is formed by the knot on its strap. Thus, the verse, *All the people of the earth will see that the Name of Hashem is proclaimed over you,* refers to the head *tefillin* (*Rashi*).

Alternatively: The verse does not refer to the letters of the Divine Name. Rather, the Talmud speaks specifically of the head *tefillin,* because the verse states, *All the peoples of the earth will see . . .* and that can only refer to the head *tefillin,* which is plainly visible, but not to the arm *tefillin,* which is covered (*Tosafos*).

Alternatively: The ש represents *the Name of* HASHEM, for in the אַ״תְּ־בַּ״שׁ letter exchange, the letters י־ה־ו־ה may be exchanged with מ־צ־פ־צ, and the *gematria* of that combination is 300, equal to that of the letter ש (*Rabbeinu Bachya*).

Alternatively: The letter ש stands for שְׁכִינָה, *the Divine Presence* (*Pesikta Zutresa* [*Midrash Lekach Tov*]).

and they will be in awe of you. 11 *HASHEM will give you an*
increase of goodness, in the fruit of your womb and the fruit
of your animals and the fruit of your ground, on the ground
that HASHEM swore to your forefathers to give you.
12 *HASHEM shall open for you His storehouse of goodness,*
the heavens, to provide rain for your Land in its time, and to
bless all your handiwork; you shall lend to many nations,
but you shall not borrow. 13 *HASHEM shall place you as a*
head and not as a tail; you shall be only above and you
shall not be below — if you hearken to the commandments
of HASHEM, your God, that I command you today, to
observe and to perform; 14 *and you do not turn away from*
any of the words that I command you this day, right or left,
to follow other gods, to worship them.

15 *But it will be that if you do not hearken to the voice of*
HASHEM, your God, to observe, to perform all His com-
mandments and all His decrees that I command you today,
then all these curses will come upon you and overtake you:

16 *Accursed will you be in the city and accursed will*
you be in the field. 17 *Accursed will be your fruit basket*

BAAL HATURIM ELUCIDATED

וְהוֹתִרְךָ ה׳, *HASHEM will give you an increase.* This indicates [that] in the merit of *tefillin,* your days will be increased, as it is written, אֲדֹנָי עֲלֵיהֶם יִחְיוּ, [*If the Name of*] *the Lord is upon them, they shall live* (*Isaiah* 38:16).[102]

❑ {וְיָרְאוּ — **AND THEY WILL BE IN AWE.** The masoretic note, ב׳, means that this word appears twice in the *Tanach*: (i) here, וְיָרְאוּ מִמֶּךָּ, *and they will be in awe of you;* and (ii) וְיָרְאוּ אֶת ה׳ אֱלֹהֵיכֶם, *so that* [*Israel*] *shall be in awe of HASHEM, your God* (31:12 below). [The similarity of expression indicates a] measure for measure [response]. Because *they* [*Israel*] *will be in awe of HASHEM,* therefore, *they* [*the peoples of the earth*] *will be in awe of you.*}[103]

12. {The Baal HaTurim's comment to this verse appears at *Leviticus* 26:3, s.v., בְּחֻקֹּתַי תֵּלֵכוּ.}

15. {The Baal HaTurim's comment to this verse appears at *Numbers* 23:7, s.v., אָרָה לִּי.}

102. In the context of *Isaiah,* these words were spoken by King Hezekiah with regard to the dead returning to life: אֲדֹנָי, *My Lord,* עֲלֵיהֶם, *about them* [*You said*], יִחְיוּ, *"They shall live."* However, the Talmud expounds on the verse in a different context: One who wears *tefillin* will live many days, as it is stated, אֲדֹנָי עֲלֵיהֶם, *The Lord is upon them,* יִחְיוּ, *they shall live* [i.e., those who bear the Name of God upon themselves in their *tefillin* shall live (*Rashi*)] (*Menachos* 44a-b).

103. This comment is not found in the early or later printed editions. It does appear in the manuscripts used by *Shoham Yakar.*

יח וּמִשְׁאַרְתֶּךָ: אָרוּר פְּרִי־בִטְנְךָ וּפְרִי אַדְמָתֶךָ שְׁגַר
יט אֲלָפֶיךָ וְעַשְׁתְּרֹת צֹאנֶךָ: אָרוּר אַתָּה בְּבֹאֶךָ וְאָרוּר
כ אַתָּה בְּצֵאתֶךָ: יְשַׁלַּח יהוה ׀ בְּךָ אֶת־הַמְּאֵרָה
אֶת־הַמְּהוּמָה וְאֶת־הַמִּגְעֶרֶת בְּכָל־מִשְׁלַח יָדְךָ
אֲשֶׁר תַּעֲשֶׂה עַד הִשָּׁמֶדְךָ וְעַד־אֲבָדְךָ מַהֵר מִפְּנֵי
כא רֹעַ מַעֲלָלֶיךָ אֲשֶׁר עֲזַבְתָּנִי: יַדְבֵּק יהוה בְּךָ
אֶת־הַדָּבֶר עַד כַּלֹּתוֹ אֹתְךָ מֵעַל הָאֲדָמָה אֲשֶׁר־
כב אַתָּה בָא־שָׁמָּה לְרִשְׁתָּהּ: יַכְּכָה יהוה בַּשַּׁחֶפֶת
וּבַקַּדַּחַת וּבַדַּלֶּקֶת וּבַחַרְחֻר וּבַחֶרֶב וּבַשִּׁדָּפוֹן
כג וּבַיֵּרָקוֹן וּרְדָפוּךָ עַד אָבְדֶךָ: וְהָיוּ שָׁמֶיךָ אֲשֶׁר
עַל־רֹאשְׁךָ נְחֹשֶׁת וְהָאָרֶץ אֲשֶׁר־תַּחְתֶּיךָ בַּרְזֶל:
כד יִתֵּן יהוה אֶת־מְטַר אַרְצְךָ אָבָק וְעָפָר מִן־הַשָּׁמַיִם
כה יֵרֵד עָלֶיךָ עַד הִשָּׁמְדָךְ: יִתֶּנְךָ יהוה ׀ נִגָּף לִפְנֵי
אֹיְבֶיךָ בְּדֶרֶךְ אֶחָד תֵּצֵא אֵלָיו וּבְשִׁבְעָה דְרָכִים
תָּנוּס לְפָנָיו וְהָיִיתָ לְזַעֲוָה לְכֹל מַמְלְכוֹת הָאָרֶץ:

בעל הטורים

(כב) יַכְּכָה ה׳. אַרְבַּע פְּעָמִים כְּתִיב בַּתּוֹכֵחוֹת ״יַכְּכָה ה׳ ״, כְּנֶגֶד אַרְבַּע גָּלֻיּוֹת:

❑ וְיֵשׁ בְּזֶה הַפָּסוּק שִׁבְעָה עִנְיָנִים — ״בַּשַּׁחֶפֶת, וּבַקַּדַּחַת, וּבַדַּלֶּקֶת, וּבַחַרְחֻר, וּבַחֶרֶב, וּבַשִּׁדָּפוֹן, וּבַיֵּרָקוֹן״ — כְּנֶגֶד ״שֶׁבַע תוֹעֵבוֹת בְּלִבּוֹ״:

(כה) נִגָּף. ג׳ בַּמָּסוֹרֶת — ״יִתֶּנְךָ ה׳ נִגָּף״; וְאִידָךְ ״אַךְ נִגּוֹף נִגָּף הוּא לְפָנֵינוּ״; ״וַיַּרְא אֲרָם כִּי נִגַּף לִפְנֵי יִשְׂרָאֵל״. אִם שָׁמוֹעַ תִּשְׁמְעוּ, ״יָנוּסוּ לְפָנֶיךָ״, כְּדִכְתִיב ״וַיַּרְא אֲרָם וְגוֹ׳ {וַיָּנָס אֲרָם}״; וְאִם לֹא תִשְׁמְעוּ, ״יִתֶּנְךָ ה׳ נִגָּף״:

BAAL HATURIM ELUCIDATED

22. יַכְּכָה ה׳ — HASHEM WILL SMITE YOU. This phrase appears four times (vv. 22, 27, 28 and 35) in [this passage of] the *tocheichos* (admonitions),[104] corresponding to the four exiles.[105]

❑ This verse mentions seven forms of retribution: בַּשַּׁחֶפֶת, *with swelling lesions*, וּבַקַּדַּחַת, *and with fever*, וּבַדַּלֶּקֶת, *and with burning heat*, וּבַחַרְחֻר, *and with thirst*,

104. The passage of the *tocheichos* [or, *tocheichah*] comprises verses 15-68, in which Moses admonishes the nation regarding their future sinfulness and prophesies about the dire consequences.

105. *Peirush HaRokeach;* see the Baal HaTurim to 4:27 above, with note 83.

There is another allusion in the fourfold mention of the phrase יַכְּכָה ה׳. The *gematria* of that phrase is 81, and four times that is 324, which the principle of *im hakollel* allows to be considered equivalent to 325, the *gematria* of לְבָבֶל לְמָדַי לְיָוָן לֶאֱדוֹם, *to Babylon, to Medea, to Greece, to Edom* (*VeChur LaZahav*).

and your kneading bowl. 18 Accursed will be the fruit of your womb and the fruit of your ground, the offspring of your cattle and the flocks of your sheep and goats. 19 Accursed will you be when you come in and accursed will you be when you go out. 20 HASHEM will send in your midst attrition, confusion, and worry, in your every undertaking that you will do, until you are destroyed, and until you are quickly annihilated, because of the evil of your deeds, for having forsaken Me. 21 HASHEM will attach the plague to you, until it consumes you from upon the ground to which you are coming, to possess it. 22 HASHEM will smite you with swelling lesions and with fever and with burning heat and with thirst and with sword and with wind blasts and with withering — and they will pursue you until your destruction. 23 Your heavens over your head will be copper and the land beneath you will be iron. 24 HASHEM will make the rain of your land dust and dirt; from the heaven it will descend upon you until you are destroyed. 25 HASHEM will cause you to be struck down before your enemies; on one road you will go out against him, but on seven roads will you flee before him; and you will be a cause of terror to all the kingdoms of the earth.

BAAL HATURIM ELUCIDATED

וּבַחֶרֶב, *and with sword,* וּבַשִּׁדָּפוֹן, *and with wind blasts,* וּבַיֵּרָקוֹן, *and with withering,* corresponding to the שֶׁבַע תּוֹעֵבוֹת בְּלִבּוֹ, *seven abominations in his heart* (*Proverbs* 26:25).[106]

25. נִגָּף — TO BE STRUCK DOWN. The masoretic note, ג׳, means that this word appears three times in the *Tanach*:[107] (i) here, יִתֶּנְךָ ה׳ נִגָּף, *HASHEM will cause you to be struck down;* (ii) אַךְ נִגּוֹף נִגָּף הוּא לְפָנֵינוּ, *but it is surely being struck down before us* (*Judges* 20:39); and (iii) וַיַּרְא אֲרָם כִּי נִגַּף לִפְנֵי יִשְׂרָאֵל, *Aram saw that it was struck down before Israel* (*II Samuel* 10:15). [The similarity of expression indicates that] if you will hearken well,[108] then *they will flee before you* (v. 7 above), as it is written, *Aram saw . . . {and Aram fled}* (*II Samuel* 10:15,18). But if you will not hearken,[108] then *HASHEM will cause you to be struck down.*

106. *Peirush HaRokeach.*

107. The full note reads: ג׳ ב׳ קָמֵץ וְא׳ פַּתָּח, *Three, two vowelized* נִגָּף, *with a kamatz, and one vowelized* נִגַּף, *with a patach.* The vowelization נִגָּף is in the present tense; while נִגַּף is in the past tense.

108. The Baal HaTurim borrows the phrase אִם שָׁמוֹעַ תִּשְׁמְעוּ, *if you will hearken well,* from *Exodus* 19:5 and 11:13 above, and the phrase וְאִם לֹא תִשְׁמְעוּ, *but if you will not hearken,* from *Leviticus* 26:14. It is not clear why he chose to use the plural form (תִּשְׁמְעוּ) rather than the singular forms אִם שָׁמוֹעַ תִּשְׁמַע (as in v. 1 above) and אִם לֹא תִשְׁמַע (as in v. 15), especially since the entire admonition is couched in the singular.

כו וְהָיְתָה נִבְלָתְךָ לְמַאֲכָל לְכָל־עוֹף הַשָּׁמַיִם
כז וּלְבֶהֱמַת הָאָרֶץ וְאֵין מַחֲרִיד: יַכְּכָה יהוה בִּשְׁחִין
מִצְרַיִם °ובעפלים וּבַגָּרָב וּבֶחָרֶס אֲשֶׁר לֹא־תוּכַל [°וּבַטְּחֹרִים ק׳]
כח לְהֵרָפֵא: יַכְּכָה יהוה בְּשִׁגָּעוֹן וּבְעִוָּרוֹן וּבְתִמְהוֹן
כט לֵבָב: וְהָיִיתָ מְמַשֵּׁשׁ בַּצָּהֳרַיִם כַּאֲשֶׁר יְמַשֵּׁשׁ הָעִוֵּר
בָּאֲפֵלָה וְלֹא תַצְלִיחַ אֶת־דְּרָכֶיךָ וְהָיִיתָ אַךְ עָשׁוּק
ל וְגָזוּל כָּל־הַיָּמִים וְאֵין מוֹשִׁיעַ: אִשָּׁה תְאָרֵשׂ וְאִישׁ
אַחֵר °ישגלנה בַּיִת תִּבְנֶה וְלֹא־תֵשֵׁב בּוֹ כֶּרֶם [°יִשְׁכָּבֶנָּה ק׳]
לא תִּטַּע וְלֹא תְחַלְּלֶנּוּ: שׁוֹרְךָ טָבוּחַ לְעֵינֶיךָ וְלֹא
תֹאכַל מִמֶּנּוּ חֲמֹרְךָ גָּזוּל מִלְּפָנֶיךָ וְלֹא יָשׁוּב לָךְ
לב צֹאנְךָ נְתֻנוֹת לְאֹיְבֶיךָ וְאֵין לְךָ מוֹשִׁיעַ: בָּנֶיךָ
וּבְנֹתֶיךָ נְתֻנִים לְעַם אַחֵר וְעֵינֶיךָ רֹאוֹת וְכָלוֹת
לג אֲלֵיהֶם כָּל־הַיּוֹם וְאֵין לְאֵל יָדֶךָ: פְּרִי אַדְמָתְךָ
וְכָל־יְגִיעֲךָ יֹאכַל עַם אֲשֶׁר לֹא־יָדָעְתָּ וְהָיִיתָ רַק
לד עָשׁוּק וְרָצוּץ כָּל־הַיָּמִים: וְהָיִיתָ מְשֻׁגָּע מִמַּרְאֵה
לה עֵינֶיךָ אֲשֶׁר תִּרְאֶה: יַכְּכָה יהוה בִּשְׁחִין רָע עַל־
הַבִּרְכַּיִם וְעַל־הַשֹּׁקַיִם אֲשֶׁר לֹא־תוּכַל לְהֵרָפֵא
לו מִכַּף רַגְלְךָ וְעַד קָדְקֳדֶךָ: יוֹלֵךְ יהוה אֹתְךָ וְאֶת־
מַלְכְּךָ אֲשֶׁר תָּקִים עָלֶיךָ אֶל־גּוֹי אֲשֶׁר לֹא־
יָדַעְתָּ אַתָּה וַאֲבֹתֶיךָ וְעָבַדְתָּ שָּׁם אֱלֹהִים אֲחֵרִים

בעל הטורים

(כח) בְּשִׁגָּעוֹן. ב׳ בַּמָּסוֹרֶת – "יַכְּכָה ה׳ בְּשִׁגָּעוֹן"; "וְהַמִּנְהָג כְּמִנְהַג יֵהוּא בֶן נִמְשִׁי כִּי בְשִׁגָּעוֹן יִנְהָג". כְּלוֹמַר, לֹא דַי שֶׁיַּכְּכָה, אֶלָּא שֶׁכָּל מִנְהָגְךָ יִהְיֶה בְשִׁגָּעוֹן:

(לה-לו) קָדְקֳדֶךָ. יוֹלֵךְ ה׳ אֹתְךָ וְאֶת מַלְכְּךָ. רֶמֶז לְקָדְקֹד יְהוֹיָקִים, שֶׁלֹּא נִתַּן לִקְבוּרָה:

BAAL HATURIM ELUCIDATED

28. בְּשִׁגָּעוֹן — WITH MADNESS. The masoretic note, ב׳, means that this word appears twice in the *Tanach*: (i) here, יַכְּכָה ה׳ בְּשִׁגָּעוֹן, *HASHEM will smite you with madness;* and (ii) וְהַמִּנְהָג כְּמִנְהַג יֵהוּא בֶן נִמְשִׁי כִּי בְשִׁגָּעוֹן יִנְהָג, *The behavior is like the behavior of Jehu* [*grand*]*son of Nimshi, for he is behaving with madness* (*II Kings* 9:20). That is to say, not only will He smite you [with madness], but all of your behavior will be with madness.

35-36. קָדְקֳדֶךָ. יוֹלֵךְ ה׳ אֹתְךָ וְאֶת מַלְכְּךָ — YOUR SKULL. HASHEM WILL LEAD YOU AND

28/26-36   ²⁶ *Your carcass will be food for every bird of the sky and animal of the earth, and nothing will frighten them.* ²⁷ HASHEM *will smite you with the boils of Egypt, with hemorrhoids, with wet boils and dry boils, of which you cannot be cured.* ²⁸ HASHEM *will smite you with madness and with blindness, and with confounding of the heart.* ²⁹ *You will grope at noontime as a blind man gropes in the darkness, but you will not succeed on your way; you will be only cheated and robbed all the days, and there will be no savior.* ³⁰ *You will betroth a woman, but another man will lie with her; you will build a house, but you will not dwell in it; you will plant a vineyard, but you will not redeem it.* ³¹ *Your ox will be slaughtered before your eyes, but you will not eat from it; your donkey will be robbed from before you, but it will not return to you; your flocks will be given to your enemies, and you will have no savior.* ³² *Your sons and daughters will be given to another people — and your eyes will see and pine in vain for them all day long, but your hand will be powerless.* ³³ *A nation unknown to you will devour the fruit of your ground and all your labor, and you will be only cheated and downtrodden all the days.* ³⁴ *You will go mad from the sight of your eyes that you will see.* ³⁵ HASHEM *will smite you with a foul boil, on the knees and on the legs, that cannot be cured, from the sole of your foot to your skull.* ³⁶ HASHEM *will lead you and your king whom you will set up over yourself to a nation you never knew — neither you nor your forefathers — and there you will work for other gods*

─────────────── BAAL HATURIM ELUCIDATED ───────────────

YOUR KING. This is an allusion to Jehoiakim's skull which was not granted burial.¹⁰⁹

109. See *Sanhedrin* 82a. The Talmud there relates that Rabbi Chiya bar Avuyah found a skull that had been cast down at the gates of Jerusalem. Upon that skull was inscribed, זאת וְעוֹד אַחֶרֶת, *This and also another.* Rabbi Chiya buried it, but it subsequently erupted from its grave. He buried it again; and it erupted again. He then declared, "This must be the skull of [King] Jehoiakim, for about him is written: [*With*] *the burial of a donkey shall he be buried* [i.e., his corpse will be discarded like garbage into the streets (*Rashi*)], *dragged and thrown down beyond the gates of Jerusalem* (*Jeremiah* 22:19)." Rabbi Chiya then thought,

"Notwithstanding [his evil deeds], Jehoiakim was a king, so it is improper to let him remain disgraced [in this manner]." He then wrapped the skull in fine silk and placed it in a box. When his wife came home and saw [the skull wrapped in silk], she told her neighbors [what she had found in her house]. They told her, "This is probably the skull of your husband's first wife, for he does not want to forget her." [Upon hearing this,] she lit the oven and burned [the skull]. When Rabbi Chiya returned home, he said, "This is [the meaning of] what was inscribed on the skull, 'This and also another.'"

לז עֵץ וָאָבֶן: וְהָיִיתָ לְשַׁמָּה לְמָשָׁל וְלִשְׁנִינָה בְּכֹל
לח הָעַמִּים אֲשֶׁר־יְנַהֶגְךָ יהוה שָׁמָּה: זֶרַע רַב תּוֹצִיא
לט הַשָּׂדֶה וּמְעַט תֶּאֱסֹף כִּי יַחְסְלֶנּוּ הָאַרְבֶּה: כְּרָמִים
תִּטַּע וְעָבָדְתָּ וְיַיִן לֹא־תִשְׁתֶּה וְלֹא תֶאֱגֹר כִּי
מ תֹאכְלֶנּוּ הַתֹּלָעַת: זֵיתִים יִהְיוּ לְךָ בְּכָל־גְּבוּלֶךָ
מא וְשֶׁמֶן לֹא תָסוּךְ כִּי יִשַּׁל זֵיתֶךָ: בָּנִים וּבָנוֹת תּוֹלִיד
מב וְלֹא־יִהְיוּ לָךְ כִּי יֵלְכוּ בַּשֶּׁבִי: כָּל־עֵצְךָ וּפְרִי
מג אַדְמָתֶךָ יְיָרֵשׁ הַצְּלָצַל: הַגֵּר אֲשֶׁר בְּקִרְבְּךָ יַעֲלֶה
מד עָלֶיךָ מַעְלָה מָּעְלָה וְאַתָּה תֵרֵד מַטָּה מָּטָּה: הוּא
יַלְוְךָ וְאַתָּה לֹא תַלְוֶנּוּ הוּא יִהְיֶה לְרֹאשׁ וְאַתָּה
מה תִּהְיֶה לְזָנָב: וּבָאוּ עָלֶיךָ כָּל־הַקְּלָלוֹת הָאֵלֶּה
וּרְדָפוּךָ וְהִשִּׂיגוּךָ עַד הִשָּׁמְדָךְ כִּי־לֹא שָׁמַעְתָּ
בְּקוֹל יהוה אֱלֹהֶיךָ לִשְׁמֹר מִצְוֺתָיו וְחֻקֹּתָיו אֲשֶׁר
מו צִוָּךְ: וְהָיוּ בְךָ לְאוֹת וּלְמוֹפֵת וּבְזַרְעֲךָ עַד־עוֹלָם:
מז תַּחַת אֲשֶׁר לֹא־עָבַדְתָּ אֶת־יהוה אֱלֹהֶיךָ בְּשִׂמְחָה
מח וּבְטוּב לֵבָב מֵרֹב כֹּל: וְעָבַדְתָּ אֶת־אֹיְבֶיךָ אֲשֶׁר
יְשַׁלְּחֶנּוּ יהוה בָּךְ בְּרָעָב וּבְצָמָא וּבְעֵירֹם וּבְחֹסֶר
כֹּל וְנָתַן עֹל בַּרְזֶל עַל־צַוָּארֶךָ עַד הִשְׁמִידוֹ אֹתָךְ:

בעל הטורים

(מ) **זֵיתִים יִהְיוּ לְךָ בְּכָל גְּבוּלֶךָ.** זֶה הַפָּסוּק מַתְחִיל וּמְסַיֵּם בַּזַּיִת – לוֹמַר שֶׁאֵין הַזַּיִת מִתְקַבֵּל בְּאִילָן אַחֵר. וְזֶהוּ "בָּנֶיךָ כִּשְׁתִלֵי זֵיתִים", שֶׁלֹּא יִתְעָרְבוּ בַּאֲחֵרִים. לְכָךְ סָמַךְ לוֹ "בָּנִים וּבָנוֹת תּוֹלִיד":

(מב) **יְיָרֵשׁ הַצְּלָצַל.** וּסְמִיךְ לֵהּ "הַגֵּר אֲשֶׁר בְּקִרְבְּךָ". רֶמֶז "וּמָךְ אָחִיךָ עִמּוֹ, וְנִמְכַּר לְגֵר":

(מג) **מַטָּה מָּטָּה.** בְּגִימַטְרִיָּא גֵּיהִנֹּם:

BAAL HATURIM ELUCIDATED

40. זֵיתִים יִהְיוּ לְךָ בְּכָל גְּבוּלֶךָ — YOU WILL HAVE OLIVE TREES THROUGHOUT YOUR BOUNDARIES. This verse begins and ends with [references to] the olive tree,[110] to indicate that an olive branch cannot be grafted to another species of tree.[110a] This is [the positive implication of the verse], בָּנֶיךָ כִּשְׁתִלֵי זֵיתִים, *Your children will be like shoots of olive trees* (*Psalms* 128:3), i.e., they will not assimilate into other

110. It begins with the word זֵיתִים, *olive trees*, and ends with זֵיתֶךָ, *your olive tree.*

110a. See *Yerushalmi, Kilayim* 1:7; see also the *Bartenura* to *Kilayim* 1:4, s.v., שופין, and *Tosefos* of wood and of stone. [37] You will be a source of astonishment, a parable, and a conversation piece, among all the peoples where HASHEM will lead you. [38] You will take abundant seed out to the field, but you will harvest little, for the locust will devour it. [39] You will plant vineyards and work them, but wine you will not drink and you will not gather in, for the worm will eat it. [40] You will have olive trees throughout your boundaries, but you will not anoint with oil, for your olive tree will drop [its fruit]. [41] You will bear sons and daughters, but they will not be yours, for they will go into captivity. [42] All your trees and the fruits of your ground, the enemy invaders will impoverish. [43] The stranger who is among you will ascend above you higher and higher, while you will descend lower and lower. [44] He will lend to you, but you will not lend to him; he will be a head, but you will be a tail. [45] All these curses will come upon you and pursue you and overtake you, until you are destroyed, because you will not have hearkened to the voice of HASHEM, your God, to observe His commandments and decrees that He commanded you. [46] They will be a sign and a wonder, in you and in your offspring, forever, [47] because you did not serve HASHEM, your God, amid gladness and goodness of heart, when everything was abundant. [48] So you will serve your enemies whom HASHEM will send against you, in hunger and in thirst, in nakedness and without anything; and he will put an iron yoke on your neck, until he destroys you.

BAAL HATURIM ELUCIDATED

nations. Therefore, [the Torah] juxtaposed בָּנִים וּבָנוֹת תּוֹלִיד, *You will bear sons and daughters* (v. 41) to our verse.[111]

42. יְיָרֵשׁ הַצְּלָצַל — THE ENEMY INVADERS[111A] WILL IMPOVERISH. Juxtaposed to this is הַגֵּר אֲשֶׁר בְּקִרְבְּךָ, *the alien who is among you* [*will ascend above you*] (v. 43), an allusion [to the verse], וּמָךְ אָחִיךָ עִמּוֹ וְנִמְכַּר לְגֵר, *and your brother becomes impoverished with him, and he is sold to an alien* (*Leviticus* 25:47).

43. מַטָּה מָּטָּה — LOWER AND LOWER. The *gematria* of this term (108) is equal to that of גֵּיהִנֹּם, *Gehinnom.*[112]

Anshei Shem, s.v., בא״ד על רמון.

111. *Peirush HaRokeach.*

111a. Translation follows *Ramban,* cited by the Baal HaTurim in *Peirush HaTur HaAroch.*

112. See *R' Ephraim,* where the comment continues: This is meant as an allusion that those of Israel who are sinful will descend to *Gehinnom,* and that is one of the ninety-eight curses of the *tocheichah.*

מט יִשָּׂא יהוה עָלֶ֫יךָ גּ֘וֹי מֵרָחֹק מִקְצֵה הָאָ֫רֶץ כַּאֲשֶׁר

נ יִדְאֶה הַנָּ֑שֶׁר גּוֹי אֲשֶׁר לֹא-תִשְׁמַע לְשֹׁנ֑וֹ: גּוֹי עַז פָּנִים

נא אֲשֶׁר לֹא-יִשָּׂא פָנִים֙ לְזָקֵן וְנַ֫עַר לֹא יָחֹן: וְאָכַל֩ פְּרִי

בְהֶמְתְּךָ֨ וּפְרִי-אַדְמָתְךָ֜ עַד הִשָּׁמְדָ֗ךְ אֲשֶׁ֨ר לֹא-

יַשְׁאִ֤יר לְךָ֙ דָּגָן֙ תִּירוֹשׁ וְיִצְהָ֔ר שְׁגַ֥ר אֲלָפֶ֖יךָ וְעַשְׁתְּרֹ֣ת

נב צֹאנֶ֑ךָ עַד הַאֲבִידוֹ אֹתָֽךְ: וְהֵצַ֨ר לְךָ֜ בְּכָל-שְׁעָרֶ֗יךָ עַ֣ד

רֶ֤דֶת חֹמֹתֶ֨יךָ֙ הַגְּבֹהֹ֣ת וְהַבְּצֻר֔וֹת אֲשֶׁ֥ר אַתָּ֛ה בֹּטֵ֥חַ

בָּהֵ֖ן בְּכָל-אַרְצֶ֑ךָ וְהֵצַ֤ר לְךָ֙ בְּכָל-שְׁעָרֶ֔יךָ בְּכָל-

נג אַרְצְךָ֔ אֲשֶׁ֥ר נָתַ֛ן יהוה אֱלֹהֶ֖יךָ לָֽךְ: וְאָכַלְתָּ֣ פְרִֽי-

בִטְנְךָ֗ בְּשַׂ֤ר בָּנֶ֨יךָ֙ וּבְנֹתֶ֔יךָ אֲשֶׁ֥ר נָֽתַן-לְךָ֖ יהוה אֱלֹהֶ֑יךָ

נד בְּמָצוֹר֙ וּבְמָצ֔וֹק אֲשֶׁר-יָצִ֥יק לְךָ֖ אֹֽיְבֶֽךָ: הָאִ֤ישׁ הָרַךְ֙

בְּךָ֔ וְהֶעָנֹ֖ג מְאֹ֑ד תֵּרַ֨ע עֵינ֤וֹ בְאָחִיו֙ וּבְאֵ֣שֶׁת חֵיק֔וֹ

נה וּבְיֶ֖תֶר בָּנָ֣יו אֲשֶׁ֣ר יוֹתִ֑יר מִתֵּ֣ת ׀ לְאַחַ֣ד מֵהֶ֗ם

מִבְּשַׂ֤ר בָּנָיו֙ אֲשֶׁ֣ר יֹאכֵ֔ל מִבְּלִ֥י הִשְׁאִיר-ל֖וֹ כֹּ֑ל

בְּמָצוֹר֙ וּבְמָצ֔וֹק אֲשֶׁ֨ר יָצִ֥יק לְךָ֛ אֹיִבְךָ֖ בְּכָל-שְׁעָרֶֽיךָ:

בעל הטורים

(מט) יִדְאֶה הַנָּשֶׁר. בְּגִימַטְרִיָּא עֲשָׂרָה. כִּדְאִיתָא בְסֻכָּה, דְּהַיְנוּ אֲלֶכְּסַנְדְּרוֹס, שֶׁשִּׁעֵר לָבוֹא בַעֲשָׂרָה יָמִים וּבָא בְּיוֹם אֶחָֽד:

BAAL HATURIM ELUCIDATED

49. יִדְאֶה הַנָּשֶׁר — THE EAGLE WILL SWOOP. The *gematria* of this phrase (575) is equal to that of the word עֲשָׂרָה, *ten*. As explained in tractate *Succah,* this phrase alludes to Alexander[113] who thought to arrive after a ten-day sea journey, and arrived in one[113a] day.[114]

---

113. The Talmud (*Succah* 51b) describes the fabulously successful Jewish community in Alexandria, Egypt, then concludes, "And they were all killed by Alexander of Macedonia." However, there is a historical problem with that text: Alexander of Macedonia, better known as Alexander the Great, lived during the early years of the Second *Beis HaMikdash.* It was he who had built Alexandria, and it was he who established a Jewish community there. That community thrived for many centuries until it was decimated by the Roman ruler Trajan in 115-117 C.E., more than four hundred years after the death of Alexander the Great. Accordingly, the *Abarbanel* (Intro-

duction to his commentary on *Kings*) writes that the word מוּקְדָּן, *of Macedonia,* of the extant Talmudic text is a copyist's error and should be erased. He suggests that the Alexander of that incident was the Roman Alexander Severus. However, the parallel passage in the Jerusalem Talmud (*Succah* 5:1) reads טְרוֹגְיָנוּס, *Trajan,* and that is how the Gaon of Vilna emends the Talmud Bavli version (*Hagahos HaGra;* see note 114 below).

113a. Regarding the term בְּיוֹם אֶחָד, *in one day,* see end of note 114 below.

114. *Peirush HaRokeach.* As related in tractate *Succah* (51b), Alexander [or, Trajan (see note 113)] was once returning to Alexandria, expect-

---

⁴⁹ *HASHEM will carry against you a nation from afar, from the end of the earth, as the eagle will swoop, a nation whose language you will not understand,* ⁵⁰ *a brazen nation that will not be respectful to the old nor gracious to the young.* ⁵¹ *It will devour the fruit of your animals and the fruit of your ground, until you are destroyed — it will not leave you grain, wine, or oil, offspring of your cattle or flocks of your sheep and goats — until it causes you to perish.* ⁵² *It will besiege you in all your cities, until the collapse of your high and fortified walls in which you trusted throughout your land; it will besiege you in all your cities, in all your land, which HASHEM, your God, has given you.* ⁵³ *You will eat the fruit of your womb — the flesh of your sons and daughters, which HASHEM, your God, had given you — in the siege and distress that your enemy will distress you.* ⁵⁴ *The man among you who is tender and very delicate will turn selfish against his brother and the wife of his bosom, and against the remaining children that he has let survive,* ⁵⁵ *not to give even one of them of the flesh of his children that he will eat, not leaving anything for him, in the siege and distress that your enemy will distress you in all your cities.*

---

ing to arrive in a matter of ten days. However, he completed the trip in half that time. When he came, he found the Jews of Alexandria reading from the Torah: *HASHEM will carry against you a nation from afar . . . [as the eagle will swoop]*. He said to himself, "Let us see. I expected to arrive by ship in ten days, but the wind carried the ship here in only five days. [If so, the verse refers to me.]" He then fell upon them and killed them.

A similar incident is recorded in the Midrash: It happened in the days of Trajan, may his bones be ground up into powder, that his wife gave birth on the eve of Tishah BeAv, when all of Israel was mourning. The baby died on Chanukah. [Because of the Roman custom of not kindling lights during a period of mourning,] the Jews discussed whether to light the Chanukah *menorah*. They decided, "We shall light, and whatever will happen will happen," and they lit their *menoros*. Some [enemies of the Jews] slandered them to Trajan's wife, "Those Jews, when you bore a child, they mourned; and when your child died, they kindled lamps." She then sent a message to her husband [who, at the time, was away on a military campaign], "Before

you bother to subdue the Barbarians, come home and subdue the Jews who are rebelling against you." Trajan boarded a ship, expecting to reach home in ten days, but the wind carried him and the trip took only five. He found the Jews studying the verse: *HASHEM will carry against you a nation from afar, from the end of the earth, as the eagle will swoop.* He said to them, "I am that eagle, for I planned to arrive in ten days, but the wind carried me here in only five days." He then surrounded them with his legions and killed them (*Pesichta* to *Esther Rabbah* 3; *Eichah Rabbah* 1:45 [to 1:16] and 4:22 [to 4:19]).

A question remains: According to all of these accounts [as well as *Peirush HaRokeach*, the Baal HaTurim's apparent source for this allusion], the ten-day trip was covered in five days. Nevertheless, virtually all editions of the Baal HaTurim read בְּיוֹם אֶחָד, *in one day,* a version found nowhere else. It therefore seems certain that a copyist's error has entered our editions. Indeed, *Eitz Yosef* to *Esther Rabbah* adduces the Baal HaTurim's comment verbatim, except for the last phrase, which in his version reads, בַּחֲמִשָּׁה יָמִים, *in five days.*

נו הָרַכָּה בְךָ וְהָעֲנֻגָּה אֲשֶׁר לֹא־נִסְּתָה כַף־רַגְלָהּ הַצֵּג
עַל־הָאָרֶץ מֵהִתְעַנֵּג וּמֵרֹךְ תֵּרַע עֵינָהּ בְּאִישׁ חֵיקָהּ
נז וּבִבְנָהּ וּבְבִתָּהּ׃ וּבְשִׁלְיָתָהּ הַיּוֹצֵת ׀ מִבֵּין רַגְלֶיהָ
וּבְבָנֶיהָ אֲשֶׁר תֵּלֵד כִּי־תֹאכְלֵם בְּחֹסֶר־כֹּל בַּסָּתֶר
בְּמָצוֹר וּבְמָצוֹק אֲשֶׁר יָצִיק לְךָ אֹיִבְךָ בִּשְׁעָרֶיךָ׃
נח אִם־לֹא תִשְׁמֹר לַעֲשׂוֹת אֶת־כָּל־דִּבְרֵי הַתּוֹרָה הַזֹּאת
הַכְּתֻבִים בַּסֵּפֶר הַזֶּה לְיִרְאָה אֶת־הַשֵּׁם הַנִּכְבָּד
נט וְהַנּוֹרָא הַזֶּה אֵת יהוה אֱלֹהֶיךָ׃ וְהִפְלָא יהוה אֶת־
מַכֹּתְךָ וְאֵת מַכּוֹת זַרְעֶךָ מַכּוֹת גְּדֹלֹת וְנֶאֱמָנוֹת וָחֳלָיִם
ס רָעִים וְנֶאֱמָנִים׃ וְהֵשִׁיב בְּךָ אֵת כָּל־מַדְוֵה מִצְרַיִם
סא אֲשֶׁר יָגֹרְתָּ מִפְּנֵיהֶם וְדָבְקוּ בָּךְ׃ גַּם כָּל־חֳלִי וְכָל־מַכָּה
אֲשֶׁר לֹא כָתוּב בְּסֵפֶר הַתּוֹרָה הַזֹּאת יַעְלֵם יהוה
סב עָלֶיךָ עַד הִשָּׁמְדָךְ׃ וְנִשְׁאַרְתֶּם בִּמְתֵי מְעָט תַּחַת אֲשֶׁר
הֱיִיתֶם כְּכוֹכְבֵי הַשָּׁמַיִם לָרֹב כִּי־לֹא שָׁמַעְתָּ בְּקוֹל
סג יהוה אֱלֹהֶיךָ׃ וְהָיָה כַּאֲשֶׁר־שָׂשׂ יהוה עֲלֵיכֶם
לְהֵיטִיב אֶתְכֶם וּלְהַרְבּוֹת אֶתְכֶם כֵּן יָשִׂישׂ יהוה
עֲלֵיכֶם לְהַאֲבִיד אֶתְכֶם וּלְהַשְׁמִיד אֶתְכֶם וְנִסַּחְתֶּם
מֵעַל הָאֲדָמָה אֲשֶׁר־אַתָּה בָא־שָׁמָּה לְרִשְׁתָּהּ׃
סד וֶהֱפִיצְךָ יהוה בְּכָל־הָעַמִּים מִקְצֵה הָאָרֶץ וְעַד־קְצֵה
הָאָרֶץ וְעָבַדְתָּ שָּׁם אֱלֹהִים אֲחֵרִים אֲשֶׁר לֹא־יָדַעְתָּ
סה אַתָּה וַאֲבֹתֶיךָ עֵץ וָאָבֶן׃ וּבַגּוֹיִם הָהֵם לֹא תַרְגִּיעַ
וְלֹא־יִהְיֶה מָנוֹחַ לְכַף־רַגְלֶךָ וְנָתַן יהוה לְךָ שָׁם לֵב
סו רַגָּז וְכִלְיוֹן עֵינַיִם וְדַאֲבוֹן נָפֶשׁ׃ וְהָיוּ חַיֶּיךָ תְּלֻאִים

בעל הטורים

(סא) כָּל חֳלִי. עוֹלֶה צ״ח — כְּנֶגֶד צ״ח קְלָלוֹת:

(סו) תְּלֻאִים. ב׳ בַּמָּסוֹרֶת — ״וְהָיוּ חַיֶּיךָ תְּלֻאִים״; ״וְעַמִּי תְלוּאִים לִמְשׁוּבָתִי״. וְהַיְנוּ

BAAL HATURIM ELUCIDATED

56. {The Baal HaTurim's comment to עַל הָאָרֶץ appears at 11:21 above.}

57. {The Baal HaTurim's comment to בַּסָּתֶר appears at 27:15 above.}

59. {The Baal HaTurim's comment to וְהִפְלָא appears at *Exodus* 9:4.}

61. **כָּל חֳלִי** — ANY ILLNESS. The *gematria* of this phrase is 98, corresponding to

[56] *The tender and delicate woman among you, who had never
tried to set the sole of her foot on the ground, because of
delicacy and tenderness, will turn selfish against the husband
of her bosom, and against her son and daughter,* [57] *And
against her afterbirth that emerges from between her legs, and
against her children whom she will bear — for she will eat
them in secret for lack of anything, in the siege and distress
that your enemy will distress you in your cities.* [58] *If you will
not be careful to perform all the words of this Torah that are
written in this Book, to fear this honored and awesome Name:
HASHEM, your God,* [59] *then HASHEM will make extraordinary
your blows and the blows of your offspring — great and
faithful blows, and evil and faithful illnesses.* [60] *He will bring
back upon you all the sufferings of Egypt, of which you were
terrified, and they will cleave to you.* [61] *Even any illness and
any blow that is not written in this Book of the Torah, HASHEM
will bring upon you, until you are destroyed.* [62] *You will be left
few in number, instead of having been like the stars of heaven
in abundance, for you will not have hearkened to the voice of
HASHEM, your God.* [63] *And it will be that just as HASHEM
rejoiced over you to benefit you and multiply you, so HASHEM
will cause them to rejoice over you to make you perish and to
destroy you; and you will be torn from upon the ground to
which you come to possess it.* [64] *HASHEM will scatter you
among all the peoples, from the end of the earth to the end
of the earth, and there you will work for other gods, whom
you did not know — you or your forefathers — of wood and
of stone.* [65] *And among those nations you will not be tranquil, there will be no rest for the sole of your foot; there
HASHEM will give you a trembling heart, longing of eyes, and
suffering of soul.* [66] *Your life will hang [in doubt] before you,*

BAAL HATURIM ELUCIDATED

the 98 curses in the *tocheichah.*[115]

66. תְּלֻאִים — HANG [IN DOUBT]. The masoretic note, ב׳, means that this word appears twice in the *Tanach*:[116] (i) here, וְהָיוּ חַיֶּיךָ תְּלֻאִים, *your life will hang* [*in doubt*]; and (ii) וְעַמִּי תְלוּאִים לִמְשׁוּבָתִי, *and yet My people hang* [*in doubt*] *regarding returning to Me* [*in repentance*] (*Hosea* 11:7). This [similarity of expression] points

115. *Peirush HaRokeach;* see note 104 above; see the Baal HaTurim to 6:7 above, see note 185 there.

116. The full note reads: ב׳ חַד חָסֵר וְחַד מָלֵא, *Twice: once spelled defectively,* תְּלֻאִים, *without a* ו; *and once spelled in full,* תְלוּאִים, *with a* ו.

לְךָ֙ מִנֶּ֔גֶד וּפָֽחַדְתָּ֙ לַ֣יְלָה וְיוֹמָ֔ם וְלֹ֥א תַאֲמִ֖ין בְּחַיֶּֽיךָ׃
סז בַּבֹּ֤קֶר תֹּאמַר֙ מִֽי־יִתֵּ֣ן עֶ֔רֶב וּבָעֶ֥רֶב תֹּאמַ֖ר מִֽי־יִתֵּ֣ן
בֹּ֑קֶר מִפַּ֤חַד לְבָֽבְךָ֙ אֲשֶׁ֣ר תִּפְחָ֔ד וּמִמַּרְאֵ֥ה עֵינֶ֖יךָ
סח אֲשֶׁ֥ר תִּרְאֶֽה׃ וֶֽהֱשִֽׁיבְךָ֙ יְהוָ֥ה ׀ מִצְרַ֙יִם֙ בָּֽאֳנִיּ֔וֹת
בַּדֶּ֙רֶךְ֙ אֲשֶׁ֣ר אָמַ֣רְתִּֽי לְךָ֔ לֹא־תֹסִ֥יף ע֖וֹד לִרְאֹתָ֑הּ
וְהִתְמַכַּרְתֶּ֙ם שָׁ֧ם לְאֹיְבֶ֛יךָ לַעֲבָדִ֥ים וְלִשְׁפָח֖וֹת וְאֵ֥ין
סט קֹנֶֽה׃ אֵ֣לֶּה דִבְרֵ֣י הַבְּרִ֡ית אֲשֶׁר־צִוָּ֨ה יְהוָ֜ה
אֶת־מֹשֶׁ֗ה לִכְרֹ֛ת אֶת־בְּנֵ֥י יִשְׂרָאֵ֖ל בְּאֶ֣רֶץ מוֹאָ֑ב
מִלְּבַ֣ד הַבְּרִ֔ית אֲשֶׁר־כָּרַ֥ת אִתָּ֖ם בְּחֹרֵֽב׃

בעל הטורים

דְּאָמְרִינַן, בֵּינוֹנִים תְּלוּיִם וְעוֹמְדִים בֵּין רֹאשׁ הַשָּׁנָה וְיוֹם הַכִּפּוּרִים. זָכוּ נִכְתָּבִין לְחַיִּים, לֹא זָכוּ נִכְתָּבִין לְמִיתָה. וְזֶהוּ "וְעַמִּי תְלוּאִים", שֶׁתְּלוּיִם וְעוֹמְדִים עַד שֶׁיַּעֲשׂוּ תְשׁוּבָה:

(**סז**) **וּבָעֶרֶב.** ד׳ בַּמָּסוֹרֶת – "וּבָעֶרֶב תֹּאמַר מִי יִתֵּן בֹּקֶר"; וְאִידָךְ "וּבָעֶרֶב יִהְיֶה עַל הַמִּשְׁכָּן"; "וּבָעֶרֶב חָתַרְתִּי לִי בַקִּיר"; "וּמַקְטִרִים לַה׳ עֹלוֹת בַּבֹּקֶר בַּבֹּקֶר וּבָעֶרֶב". "וּבָעֶרֶב חָתַרְתִּי", כְּשֶׁיֵּצְאוּ לַגּוֹלָה "תֹּאמַר מִי יִתֵּן בֹּקֶר", שֶׁנֶּאֱמַר בּוֹ "וּמַקְטִרִים וְגוֹ׳ בַּבֹּקֶר וּבָעֶרֶב".וּבְאוֹתוֹ שֶׁכָּתוּב "וּבָעֶרֶב יִהְיֶה עַל הַמִּשְׁכָּן", שֶׁהָיָה כְבוֹד שְׁכִינָה עִמָּנוּ:

(**סח**) **וֶהֱשִׁיבְךָ ה׳.** בְּגִימַטְרִיָּא זֶה יִהְיֶה בִּימֵי יִרְמְיָה:

❑ כ״ו שֵׁמוֹת שֶׁבַּתּוֹכֵחָה, כְּנֶגֶד כ״ו שֵׁמוֹת שֶׁבִּתְפִלַּת שְׁמוֹנֶה עֶשְׂרֵה, חוּץ מִבִּרְכַּת הַמִּינִין, לְהָגֵן מִכ״ו שֵׁמוֹת שֶׁבַּתּוֹכֵחָה:

BAAL HATURIM ELUCIDATED

to what our Sages have said: The [verdicts of the] intermediate ones are left hanging [in the balance] between Rosh Hashanah and Yom Kippur. If they are found meritorious, they are inscribed for life; if they are not found meritorious, they are inscribed for death. Thus, וְעַמִּי תְלוּאִים, *My nation hangs* [*in the balance*], until they repent.[116a]

67. וּבָעֶרֶב — AND IN THE EVENING. The masoretic note, ד׳, means that this word appears four times in the *Tanach*: (i) here, וּבָעֶרֶב תֹּאמַר מִי יִתֵּן בֹּקֶר, *and in the evening you will say, "Who can give* [*back*] *this morning"*; (ii) וּבָעֶרֶב יִהְיֶה עַל הַמִּשְׁכָּן, *and in the evening there would be upon the Tabernacle* (*Numbers* 9:15);[117] (iii) וּבָעֶרֶב חָתַרְתִּי לִי בַקִּיר, *and in the evening I tunneled through the wall* (*Ezekiel* 12:7); and (iv) וּמַקְטִרִים לַה׳ עֹלוֹת בַּבֹּקֶר בַּבֹּקֶר וּבָעֶרֶב [בָּעֶרֶב וּקְטֹרֶת סַמִּים], *Also, they burn burnt-offerings to* HASHEM *morning by morning and evening* [*by evening, and a censing of spices*] (*II Chronicles* 13:11). [The similarity of expression alludes to the exiles' feelings:] *In the evening I tunneled* [i.e., when the walls of Jerusalem will be destroyed and] its populace will be sent into exile. [On that evening,] *you will say, "Who can give* [*back*] *the morning?"* about which it is said, *They burn*

116a. *Maharam MiRothenburg.*

117. See the Baal HaTurim's comment there.

and you will be frightened night and day, and you will not be sure of your livelihood. [67] *In the morning you will say, "Who can give [back] last night!" And in the evening you will say, "Who can give [back] this morning!" — for the fright of your heart that you will fear and the sight of your eyes that you will see.* [68] *HASHEM will return you to Egypt in ships, on the road of which I said to you, "You shall never again see it!" And there you will offer yourselves for sale to your enemies as slaves and maidservants — but there will be no buyer!*

[69] *These are the words of the covenant that HASHEM commanded Moses to seal with the Children of Israel in the land of Moab, besides the covenant that He sealed with them at Horeb.*

BAAL HATURIM ELUCIDATED

[*offerings*] . . . *by morning and by evening.* And [they longed for the time] about which it is said, *in the evening there would be upon the Tabernacle,* for [at that time] the glory of God's Presence was with us.

68. וֶהֱשִׁיבְךָ ה׳ — HASHEM WILL RETURN YOU [TO EGYPT]. The *gematria* of this phrase (369) is equal to that of זֶה יִהְיֶה בִּימֵי יִרְמְיָה, *This will occur in the days of Jeremiah.* [118]

❑ The Divine Name [i.e., the Tetragrammaton] appears twenty-six[118a] times in the *tocheichah,* [119] corresponding to the twenty-six times that it appears in the *Shemoneh Esrei*[120] — without including the blessing against the heretics[121] — to protect against the twenty-six Names[121a] in the *tocheichah.*

118. *Peirush HaRokeach.* According to the Midrash, our verse refers to three times that Israel returned to Egypt: (i) in the days of Sennacherib (see *Isaiah* 31:1-3); (ii) in the days of Johanan son of Kareah (see *Jeremiah* 41:16-18; 42:13-18; 43:5-7); and (iii) in the days of Trajan (*Pesichta* to *Esther Rabbah* 3, cited in part in note 114 above); see also *Seder Olam Rabbah* 26). The Baal HaTurim refers to the second incident.

118a. The Name appears in verses 15, 20, 21, 22, 24, 25, 27, 28, 35, 36, 37, 45, 47, 48, 49, 52, 53, 58, 59, 61, 62, 63 (twice), 64, 65 and 68.

119. See note 104 above.

120. Although almost all versions of the *Shemoneh Esrei,* as it is recited today, have the Tetragrammaton twenty-seven times, the Baal HaTurim probably is referring to the version cited by the *Rambam* (at the end of *Sefer Ahavah,* after *Hilchos Milah*). That version does not include the Name in the first part of the blessing that begins הָשִׁיבָה שׁוֹפְטֵינוּ.

121. The blessing was not among the original eighteen blessings of the *Amidah.* It was added at a later date (see *Berachos* 28b).

121a. The Baal HaTurim's comment regarding the twenty-six appearances of the Divine Name protecting against the twenty-six Names in the *tocheichah* requires explanation, for it implies that the Names both punish and protect against punishment at the same time.

The *Arizal* taught that the *tocheichah* contains six hundred and seventy-six words. To mitigate the force of the 676 words of admonition, the passage includes the Tetragrammaton twenty-six times. Now, the *gematria* of that Divine Name is 26, and the combined *gematria* of the twenty-six appearances of that Name is 26 x 26 or 676. Thus, the twenty-six-fold mention of the Name whose *gematria* is 26 mitigates the force of the 676 words of the *tocheichah* admonition (quoted by *Anaf Yosef* to *Ein Yaakov, Shabbos* 119b, s.v., כל המבזה תלמיד חכם).

כט/א־ח שביעי א וַיִּקְרָ֥א מֹשֶׁ֛ה אֶל־כָּל־יִשְׂרָאֵ֖ל וַיֹּ֣אמֶר אֲלֵהֶ֑ם אַתֶּ֣ם
רְאִיתֶ֗ם אֵ֣ת כָּל־אֲשֶׁר֩ עָשָׂ֨ה יְהוָ֤ה לְעֵֽינֵיכֶם֙ בְּאֶ֣רֶץ
ב מִצְרַ֔יִם לְפַרְעֹ֥ה וּלְכָל־עֲבָדָ֖יו וּלְכָל־אַרְצֽוֹ׃ הַמַּסּוֹת֙
הַגְּדֹלֹ֔ת אֲשֶׁ֥ר רָא֖וּ עֵינֶ֑יךָ הָאֹתֹ֧ת וְהַמֹּפְתִ֛ים
ג הַגְּדֹלִ֖ים הָהֵֽם׃ וְלֹֽא־נָתַן֩ יְהוָ֨ה לָכֶ֥ם לֵב֙ לָדַ֔עַת
וְעֵינַ֥יִם לִרְא֖וֹת וְאָזְנַ֣יִם לִשְׁמֹ֑עַ עַ֖ד הַיּ֥וֹם הַזֶּֽה׃
ד וָאוֹלֵ֥ךְ אֶתְכֶ֛ם אַרְבָּעִ֥ים שָׁנָ֖ה בַּמִּדְבָּ֑ר לֹא־בָל֤וּ
שַׂלְמֹֽתֵיכֶם֙ מֵעֲלֵיכֶ֔ם וְנַעַלְךָ֥ לֹא־בָלְתָ֖ה מֵעַ֥ל
ה רַגְלֶֽךָ׃ לֶ֚חֶם לֹ֣א אֲכַלְתֶּ֔ם וְיַ֥יִן וְשֵׁכָ֖ר לֹ֣א שְׁתִיתֶ֑ם
מפטיר ו לְמַ֙עַן֙ תֵּֽדְע֔וּ כִּ֛י אֲנִ֥י יְהוָ֖ה אֱלֹהֵיכֶֽם׃ וַתָּבֹ֖אוּ
אֶל־הַמָּק֣וֹם הַזֶּ֑ה וַיֵּצֵ֣א סִיחֹ֣ן מֶֽלֶךְ־חֶ֠שְׁבּ֠וֹן וְע֨וֹג
ז מֶֽלֶךְ־הַבָּשָׁ֧ן לִקְרָאתֵ֛נוּ לַמִּלְחָמָ֖ה וַנַּכֵּֽם׃ וַנִּקַּח֙
אֶת־אַרְצָ֔ם וַנִּתְּנָ֣הּ לְנַחֲלָ֔ה לָרְאוּבֵנִ֖י וְלַגָּדִ֑י וְלַחֲצִ֖י
ח שֵׁ֥בֶט הַֽמְנַשִּֽׁי׃ וּשְׁמַרְתֶּ֗ם אֶת־דִּבְרֵי֙ הַבְּרִ֣ית הַזֹּ֔את
וַעֲשִׂיתֶ֖ם אֹתָ֑ם לְמַ֣עַן תַּשְׂכִּ֔ילוּ אֵ֖ת כָּל־אֲשֶׁ֥ר
תַּעֲשֽׂוּן׃ **פפפ** קכ״ב פסוקים. לעבדי״ו סימן.

בעל הטורים

כט (ג) **וְלֹא נָתַן ה׳ לָכֶם לֵב לָדַעַת.** וּסְמִיךְ לֵהּ ״וָאוֹלֵךְ אֶתְכֶם אַרְבָּעִים שָׁנָה״. רֶמֶז, שֶׁעַד אַרְבָּעִים שָׁנָה אֵין אָדָם עוֹמֵד עַל דַּעַת רַבּוֹ:

BAAL HATURIM ELUCIDATED

XXIX.

3. **וְלֹא נָתַן ה׳ לָכֶם לֵב לָדַעַת** — BUT HASHEM DID NOT GIVE YOU A HEART TO KNOW.

29/1-8 ¹ Moses summoned all of Israel and said to them, "You have seen everything that HASHEM did before your eyes in the land of Egypt, to Pharaoh and to all his servants and to all his land — ² the great trials that your eyes beheld, those great signs and wonders. ³ But HASHEM did not give you a heart to know, or eyes to see, or ears to hear until this day. ⁴ I have led you for forty years in the Wilderness, your garment did not wear out from on you, and your shoe did not wear out from on your foot. ⁵ Bread you did not eat and wine or intoxicant you did not drink, so that you would know that I am HASHEM, your God. ⁶ Then you arrived at this place, and Sihon, king of Heshbon, and Og, king of Bashan, went out toward us to battle, and we smote them. ⁷ We took their land and gave it as an inheritance to the Reubenite, the Gadite, and to half the tribe of the Manassite. ⁸ You shall observe the words of this covenant, so that you will succeed in all that you do."

───────────── BAAL HATURIM ELUCIDATED ─────────────

Juxtaposed to this is וָאוֹלֵךְ אֶתְכֶם אַרְבָּעִים שָׁנָה, *I have led you for forty years*. This is an allusion [to the Talmudic teaching] that for forty years a person is not capable of assimilating his teacher's wisdom.[122]

───────────────────────────

122. *Avodah Zarah* 5b, cited by *Rashi* to verse 6.

פרשת נצבים 🙠

Parashas Nitzavim

ט אַתֶּ֨ם נִצָּבִ֤ים הַיּוֹם֙ כֻּלְּכֶ֔ם לִפְנֵ֖י יהוָ֣ה אֱלֹהֵיכֶ֑ם
רָאשֵׁיכֶ֣ם שִׁבְטֵיכֶ֗ם זִקְנֵיכֶם֙ וְשֹׁ֣טְרֵיכֶ֔ם כֹּ֖ל
י אִ֥ישׁ יִשְׂרָאֵֽל׃ טַפְּכֶ֣ם נְשֵׁיכֶ֔ם וְגֵ֣רְךָ֔ אֲשֶׁ֖ר
בְּקֶ֣רֶב מַחֲנֶ֑יךָ מֵחֹטֵ֣ב עֵצֶ֔יךָ עַ֖ד שֹׁאֵ֥ב מֵימֶֽיךָ׃

בעל הטורים

כט (ט) נִצָּבִים. כְּדֶרֶךְ שֶׁנֶּאֱמַר בְּסִינַי "וַיִּתְיַצְּבוּ בְּתַחְתִּית הָהָר", בּוֹ בַלָּשׁוֹן אָמַר כָּאן "אַתֶּם נִצָּבִים":

❑ **לִפְנֵי ה׳ אֱלֹהֵיכֶם. רָאשֵׁיכֶם.** הִקִּישׁ "רָאשֵׁיכֶם" לֶ"אֱלֹהֵיכֶם". לוֹמַר, מוֹרָא רַבְּךָ כְּמוֹרָא שָׁמַיִם:

❑ **כֹּל אִישׁ יִשְׂרָאֵל.** וּסְמִיךְ לֵהּ "טַפְּכֶם". לוֹמַר שֶׁיְּהוּ יִשְׂרָאֵל בְּעֵינֵי הָרָאשִׁים לְנַהֲלָם וּלְהַדְרִיכָם כְּטַפָּם:

(י) נְשֵׁיכֶם. וּסְמִיךְ לֵהּ "וְגֵרְךָ". רֶמֶז שֶׁלֹּא הֻזְהֲרוּ כְּשֵׁרוֹת לִנָּשֵׂא לִפְסוּלִין:

BAAL HATURIM ELUCIDATED

9. {In his comments to *Exodus* 19:4, the Baal HaTurim discusses verses that begin with the word אַתֶּם.}

❑ **נִצָּבִים — [YOU ARE] STANDING.** In the manner of that which is stated regarding [the nation at Mount] Sinai: וַיִּתְיַצְּבוּ בְּתַחְתִּית הָהָר, *and they stood at the bottom of the mountain* (*Exodus* 19:17) [using the verb root נצב, *to stand*], he [Moses] spoke with similar terminology here, אַתֶּם נִצָּבִים, *you are standing.*[1]

1. This *parashah* opens in the middle of Moses' speech that began at 29:1 above. The speech is preceded by the verse: אֵלֶּה דִבְרֵי הַבְּרִית, *These are the words of the covenant,* אֲשֶׁר צִוָּה ה׳ אֶת מֹשֶׁה, *that* HASHEM *commanded Moses,* לִכְרֹת אֶת בְּנֵי יִשְׂרָאֵל, *to seal with the Children of Israel,* בְּאֶרֶץ מוֹאָב, *in the land of Moab,* מִלְּבַד הַבְּרִית, *besides the covenant,* אֲשֶׁר כָּרַת אִתָּם בְּחֹרֵב, *that He sealed with them at Horeb* [another name for Mount Sinai] (28:69). Now, in the Torah scroll, that verse is separated from the passage that precedes it by a פָּרָשָׁה סְתוּמָה, *closed space* (see note 194 to *parashas Ki Seitzei*), and from the passage that follows it by a פָּרָשָׁה פְּתוּחָה, *open space.* According to many commentators, the phrase, *the words of the covenant,* of that verse refers to the passage of the admonition that precedes it, while the phrase, *the covenant that He sealed with them at Horeb,* refers to the passage of the admonition in *Leviticus* 26:14-46 (see *Rashi; Rashbam; Ibn Ezra;* see also *Tosafos, Shabbos* 88a, s.v., מודעא רבה).

However, according to another interpretation, *these are the words of the covenant* refers to the passage that follows, i.e., the last eight verses of *parashas Ki Savo* and the first half of *parashas Nitzavim.* For that passage speaks repeatedly of the covenant: וּשְׁמַרְתֶּם אֶת דִּבְרֵי הַבְּרִית הַזֹּאת, *You shall observe the words of this covenant* (29:8); לְעָבְרְךָ בִּבְרִית ה׳, *for you to pass into the covenant of* HASHEM (v. 11 below); אָנֹכִי כֹּרֵת אֶת הַבְּרִית הַזֹּאת, *I seal this covenant* (v. 13); etc. The covenant at Horeb then refers to *Exodus* 24:1-11, which speaks of סֵפֶר הַבְּרִית, *the Book of the Covenant* (v. 7), and דַּם הַבְּרִית, *the blood of the covenant* (v. 8) (*Abarbanel*). The Baal HaTurim follows the latter interpretation of verse 28:69. And even though that covenant is first described in Chapter 24 of *Exodus,* it was sealed the day before the events described in Chapter 19 of *Exodus,* which contains the verse, *they stood at the bottom of the mountain* (see *Rashi* to *Exodus* 24:11).

Thus, the introductory verse to our passage (28:69) distinguishes between the covenant of our passage and the covenant at Horeb/Sinai. The Baal HaTurim points out that although there were two different covenants, their purposes were identical — לַעֲשׂוֹת אֶת כָּל דִּבְרֵי הַתּוֹרָה

29/9-10 [9] *You are standing today, all of you, before HASHEM, your God: your leaders [of] your tribes, your elders, and your officers — every man of Israel;* [10] *your youngsters, your women, and your convert who is in the midst of your camp, from the hewer of your wood to the drawer of your water,*

BAAL HATURIM ELUCIDATED

❑ לִפְנֵי ה׳ אֱלֹהֵיכֶם. רָאשֵׁיכֶם — BEFORE HASHEM, YOUR GOD: YOUR LEADERS. [By juxtaposing רָאשֵׁיכֶם, *your leaders,* with אֱלֹהֵיכֶם, *your God,*] the verse compares רָאשֵׁיכֶם with אֱלֹהֵיכֶם. This indicates that [in the words of the Mishnah[2]]: [Your] reverence for your Torah teacher should resemble your reverence for God.[3]

❑ כֹּל אִישׁ יִשְׂרָאֵל — EVERY MAN OF ISRAEL. Juxtaposed to this is, טַפְּכֶם, *your youngsters* (v. 10). This indicates that the leaders[3a] should consider the people of Israel as their own young children whom they must direct and whom they must guide.[3b]

10. נְשֵׁיכֶם — YOUR WOMEN. Juxtaposed to this is וְגֵרְךָ, *your convert.* [The juxtaposition is] an allusion [to the fact] that daughters [of a *Kohen*] who are [genealogically] eligible [to marry Kohanim[4]] are not prohibited from marrying men [whose daughters would be] ineligible [to marry a Kohen].[5]

❑ {The Baal HaTurim's comment to מֵימֶיךָ appears at *Exodus* 23:25.}

הַזֹּאת, *[for Israel] to carry out all the words of this Torah* (v. 28 below; this phrase also appears in 28:58 above and 31:12 and 32:46 below). And that is why the verses use similar terminology [i.e., וַיִּתְיַצְּבוּ and נִצָּבִים share the verb root נצב] regarding the two covenants (*VeChur LaZahav,* based on *Peirush HaRokeach,* the Baal HaTurim's source for this comment).

2. *Avos* 4:12; see also *Bava Kamma* 41b; see also *I Samuel* 2:11 with *Rashi.*

3. *Peirush HaRokeach.*

3a. The passage first mentions, רָאשֵׁיכֶם ... זִקְנֵיכֶם וְשֹׁטְרֵיכֶם, *your leaders ... your elders and your officers,* i.e., the various echelons of national and tribal leadership. It continues כֹּל אִישׁ יִשְׂרָאֵל, *every man of Israel,* טַפְּכֶם, *your youngsters.* The juxtaposition of those categories indicates a connection, as the Baal HaTurim goes on to explain.

3b. We may have expected the Torah to mention the mothers [נְשֵׁיכֶם, *your women* or *wives*] before their children [טַפְּכֶם, *your youngsters*]. This comment explains that טַפְּכֶם is to be understood in tandem with the earlier categories. The next comment explains that נְשֵׁיכֶם is to be understood in tandem with the subsequent category (*VeChur LaZahav*).

4. The Torah prohibits a *Kohen* from marrying certain categories of women — e.g., a divorcee (see *Leviticus* 21:7 with *Rashi*).

5. *Yevamos* 84b. The Talmud there teaches that although a *Kohen* may not marry certain categories of women, the daughter of a *Kohen* is not prohibited from marrying their male counterparts. However, this rule applies only with regard to women whom a *Kohen* may not marry, but nevertheless an Israelite may marry. Thus, a *Kohen* may not marry a divorced woman, or a convert to Judaism, yet his daughter may marry a divorced man or a male convert, for the divorcee and the convert are permitted in marriage to an Israelite; it is only the enhanced sanctity of the priesthood that prohibits those women to the *Kohen.* The *mamzeress* (the daughter of certain illicit unions), on the other hand, is forbidden not only to the *Kohen,* but to the Israelite as well; therefore, her male counterpart (the *mamzer*) is forbidden not only to the *Kohen's* daughter, but to all Israelite women (see also *Rashi* to *Kiddushin* 73a, s.v., לינשא לפסולין).

יא לְעׇבְרְךָ֗ בִּבְרִ֛ית יְהֹוָ֥ה אֱלֹהֶ֖יךָ וּבְאָלָת֑וֹ אֲשֶׁר֙ יְהֹוָ֤ה
יב אֱלֹהֶ֨יךָ֙ כֹּרֵ֣ת עִמְּךָ֖ הַיּֽוֹם: לְמַ֣עַן הָקִֽים־אֹֽתְךָ֩ הַיּ֨וֹם
ל֜וֹ לְעָ֗ם וְה֤וּא יִֽהְיֶה־לְּךָ֙ לֵֽאלֹהִ֔ים כַּֽאֲשֶׁ֖ר דִּבֶּר־לָ֑ךְ
וְכַֽאֲשֶׁ֤ר נִשְׁבַּע֙ לַֽאֲבֹתֶ֔יךָ לְאַבְרָהָ֥ם לְיִצְחָ֖ק וּֽלְיַֽעֲקֹֽב:
יג וְלֹ֥א אִתְּכֶ֖ם לְבַדְּכֶ֑ם אָֽנֹכִ֗י כֹּרֵת֙ אֶת־הַבְּרִ֣ית הַזֹּ֔את
יד וְאֶת־הָֽאָלָ֖ה הַזֹּֽאת: כִּי֩ אֶת־אֲשֶׁ֨ר יֶשְׁנ֜וֹ פֹּ֗ה עִמָּ֨נוּ֙
עֹמֵ֣ד הַיּ֔וֹם לִפְנֵ֖י יְהֹוָ֣ה אֱלֹהֵ֑ינוּ וְאֵ֨ת אֲשֶׁ֥ר אֵינֶ֛נּוּ פֹּ֖ה
טו עִמָּ֥נוּ הַיּֽוֹם: כִּֽי־אַתֶּ֣ם יְדַעְתֶּ֔ם אֵ֥ת אֲשֶׁר־יָשַׁ֖בְנוּ
בְּאֶ֣רֶץ מִצְרָ֑יִם וְאֵ֧ת אֲשֶׁר־עָבַ֛רְנוּ בְּקֶ֥רֶב הַגּוֹיִ֖ם
טז אֲשֶׁ֥ר עֲבַרְתֶּֽם: וַתִּרְאוּ֙ אֶת־שִׁקּֽוּצֵיהֶ֔ם וְאֵ֖ת
יז גִּלֻּֽלֵיהֶ֑ם עֵ֣ץ וָאֶ֔בֶן כֶּ֥סֶף וְזָהָ֖ב אֲשֶׁ֥ר עִמָּהֶֽם: פֶּן־יֵ֣שׁ
בָּ֠כֶ֠ם אִ֣ישׁ אֽוֹ־אִשָּׁ֞ה א֧וֹ מִשְׁפָּחָ֣ה אֽוֹ־שֵׁ֗בֶט אֲשֶׁר֩
לְבָב֨וֹ פֹנֶ֤ה הַיּוֹם֙ מֵעִם֙ יְהֹוָ֣ה אֱלֹהֵ֔ינוּ לָלֶ֣כֶת לַֽעֲבֹ֔ד
אֶת־אֱלֹהֵ֖י הַגּוֹיִ֣ם הָהֵ֑ם פֶּן־יֵ֣שׁ בָּכֶ֗ם שֹׁ֛רֶשׁ פֹּרֶ֥ה
יח רֹ֖אשׁ וְלַֽעֲנָֽה: וְהָיָ֡ה בְּשׇׁמְעוֹ֩ אֶת־דִּבְרֵ֨י הָֽאָלָ֜ה
הַזֹּ֗את וְהִתְבָּרֵ֤ךְ בִּלְבָבוֹ֙ לֵאמֹר֙ שָׁל֣וֹם יִֽהְיֶה־לִּ֔י כִּ֛י
בִּשְׁרִר֥וּת לִבִּ֖י אֵלֵ֑ךְ לְמַ֛עַן סְפ֥וֹת הָֽרָוָ֖ה אֶת־
יט הַצְּמֵאָֽה: לֹֽא־יֹאבֶ֣ה יְהֹוָה֮ סְלֹ֣חַֽ לוֹ֒ כִּ֣י אָ֠֠ז יֶעְשַׁ֨ן
אַף־יְהֹוָ֤ה וְקִנְאָתוֹ֙ בָּאִ֣ישׁ הַה֔וּא וְרָ֤בְצָה בּוֹ֙ כׇּל־
הָ֣אָלָ֔ה הַכְּתוּבָ֖ה בַּסֵּ֣פֶר הַזֶּ֑ה וּמָחָ֤ה יְהֹוָה֙ אֶת־שְׁמ֔וֹ
כ מִתַּ֖חַת הַשָּׁמָֽיִם: וְהִבְדִּיל֤וֹ יְהֹוָה֙ לְרָעָ֔ה מִכֹּ֖ל שִׁבְטֵ֣י

בעל הטורים

(יז) פֹּרֶה. חָסֵר וָי"ו — קְרֵי בֵהּ "פָּרָה", רֶמֶז "כְּפָרָה סֹרְרָה סָרַר יִשְׂרָאֵל":

(כ) וְהִבְדִּילוֹ ה' לְרָעָה. בְּגִימַטְרִיָּא הִנֵּה זֶה יָרׇבְעָם:

BAAL HATURIM ELUCIDATED

14. {The Baal HaTurim's comment to אֶת אֲשֶׁר יֶשְׁנוֹ פֹּה appears at 33:3 below.}

17. פֹּרֶה — FLOURISHING. This term is spelled defectively,[6] without a ו — thus it

---

6. The word פֹּרֶה, *flourishing* [from the root פרה, *to be fruitful*], is a verb in the simple *kal* conjugation — male, singular, present tense. Although this word does not appear elsewhere in Scripture, a comparison with similar verbs (e.g., פנה, *to turn;* מרה, *to rebel*) shows that they

are sometimes spelled defectively (e.g., פֹּנֶה, here; מֹרֶה, 21:20 above, see the Baal HaTurim there) and at other times in full (e.g., פּוֹנֶה, *Ezekiel* 8:3; מוֹרֶה, 21:18 above). The Baal HaTurim often explains, in the realm of *remez* (allusion), why Scripture uses one form rather than the other.

¹¹ *for you to pass into the covenant of* HASHEM, *your God, and into His imprecation that* HASHEM, *your God, seals with you today,* ¹² *in order to establish you today as a people to Him and that He be a God to you, as He spoke to you and as He swore to your forefathers, to Abraham, to Isaac, and to Jacob.* ¹³ *Not with you alone do I seal this covenant and this imprecation,* ¹⁴ *but with the one who is here, standing with us today before* HASHEM, *our God, and with the one who is not here with us today.*

¹⁵ *For you know how we dwelled in the land of Egypt and how we passed through the midst of the nations through whom you passed.* ¹⁶ *And you saw their abominations and their detestable idols — of wood and stone, of silver and gold that were with them.* ¹⁷ *Perhaps there is among you a man or woman, or a family or tribe, whose heart turns away today from being with* HASHEM, *our God, to go, to serve the gods of those nations; perhaps there is among you a root flourishing with gall and wormwood.* ¹⁸ *And it will be that when he hears the words of this imprecation, he will bless himself in his heart, saying, "Peace will be with me, though I walk as my heart sees fit" — thereby adding the watered upon the thirsty.*

¹⁹ HASHEM *will not be willing to forgive him, for then* HASHEM's *anger and jealousy will smoke against that man, and the entire imprecation written in this Book will come down upon him, and* HASHEM *will erase his name from under heaven.* ²⁰ HASHEM *will set him aside for evil from among all the tribes*

———————————— BAAL HATURIM ELUCIDATED ————————————

may be read [as if it were vowelized] פָּרָה, *cow,* an allusion to [the verse], כְּפָרָה סֹרֵרָה סָרַר יִשְׂרָאֵל, *Israel has strayed like a wayward cow* (Hosea 4:16).[7]

18. {The Baal HaTurim's comment to בְּשָׁמְעוֹ appears at *Exodus* 16:7.}

19. {The Baal HaTurim's comment to וּמָחָה appears at *Numbers* 5:23.}

20. וְהִבְדִּילוֹ ה׳ לְרָעָה — **HASHEM WILL SET HIM ASIDE FOR EVIL.** The *gematria* of this phrase (394) is equal to that of הִנֵּה זֶה יָרָבְעָם, *Behold, this [refers to] Jeroboam.*[8]

---

7. In its simple meaning, our verse speaks of a person with an inclination toward waywardness, *whose heart turns away* [desiring] *to go, to serve the gods of those nations,* but has not as yet brought his leanings to fruition. The Baal HaTurim teaches that, if that person does not strive to overcome his inclination, the verse couches his actions in the past tense, *Israel has strayed*

like a wayward cow (VeChur LaZahav).

8. There were two Israelite kings named יָרָבְעָם, *Jeroboam:* (a) יָרָבְעָם בֶּן נְבָט, *Jeroboam son of Nebat,* the first king of the Ten Tribes of Israel that broke away from the Davidic dynasty; and (b) יָרָבְעָם בֶּן יוֹאָשׁ, *Jeroboam son of Joash,* the fourteenth king of the Ten Tribes, about one hundred fifty years later. Both are described by

יִשְׂרָאֵל כְּכֹל אָלוֹת הַבְּרִית הַכְּתוּבָה בְּסֵפֶר
כא הַתּוֹרָה הַזֶּה: וְאָמַר הַדּוֹר הָאַחֲרוֹן בְּנֵיכֶם אֲשֶׁר
יָקוּמוּ מֵאַחֲרֵיכֶם וְהַנָּכְרִי אֲשֶׁר יָבֹא מֵאֶרֶץ רְחוֹקָה
וְרָאוּ אֶת־מַכּוֹת הָאָרֶץ הַהִוא וְאֶת־תַּחֲלֻאֶיהָ
כב אֲשֶׁר־חִלָּה יהוה בָּהּ: גָּפְרִית וָמֶלַח שְׂרֵפָה
כָל־אַרְצָהּ לֹא תִזָּרַע וְלֹא תַצְמִחַ וְלֹא־יַעֲלֶה
בָהּ כָּל־עֵשֶׂב כְּמַהְפֵּכַת סְדֹם וַעֲמֹרָה אַדְמָה

בעל הטורים

(כא) אֲשֶׁר יָקוּמוּ מֵאַחֲרֵיכֶם. רָאשֵׁי תֵבוֹת אַחְאָב יָרָבְעָם מְנַשֶּׁה – שֶׁהֵם הִרְשִׁיעוּ בַעֲבֹדָה זָרָה יוֹתֵר מִכֹּל:

❑ **חִלָּה.** ב׳ בַּמָּסוֹרֶת מִתְּרֵי עִנְיָנֵי – ״אֲשֶׁר חִלָּה ה׳ בָּהּ״; ״וּכְהָצֵר לוֹ חִלָּה אֶת פְּנֵי ה׳ וְגוֹ׳ וַיֵּעָתֶר לוֹ״. וְדָרְשִׁינַן, וַיֵּחָתֵר לוֹ, מְלַמֵּד שֶׁחָתַר הַקָּדוֹשׁ בָּרוּךְ הוּא תַּחַת כִּסֵּא הַכָּבוֹד וְקִבְּלוֹ בִתְשׁוּבָה. וְהַיְנוּ, מַה ״חִלָּה״ דְּהָכָא לְשׁוֹן שְׁבִירָה בָּאָרֶץ {דִּכְתִיב ״אֶת מַכּוֹת הָאָרֶץ הַהִוא וְאֶת תַּחֲלֻאֶיהָ״}, אַף ״חִלָּה״ דְּגַבֵּי מְנַשֶּׁה, לְשׁוֹן חֲתִירָה, שֶׁנַּעֲשָׂה לוֹ חֲתִירָה בָּרָקִיעַ:

BAAL HATURIM ELUCIDATED

21. אֲשֶׁר יָקוּמוּ מֵאַחֲרֵיכֶם — WHO WILL ARISE AFTER YOU. The initial letters [of these three words] are the same as those of [the three kings], אַחְאָב, *Ahab,* יָרָבְעָם, *Jeroboam,*[8] and מְנַשֶּׁה, *Manasseh,* whose evil idolatry surpassed that of all the others.[9]

❑ **חִלָּה** — HE HAS AFFLICTED. The masoretic note [on this word], ב׳ מִתְּרֵי עִנְיָנֵי, means that it appears twice in the *Tanach,* with two different meanings:[9a] (i) here, אֲשֶׁר חִלָּה ה׳ בָּהּ, *with which HASHEM has afflicted it;* and (ii) וּכְהָצֵר לוֹ חִלָּה אֶת פְּנֵי ה׳ ... וַיֵּעָתֶר לוֹ, *And when he was in distress he entreated HASHEM . . . and He*

the prophet as evil and as causing Israel to sin (regarding the son of Nebat, see *I Kings* 12:25-14:19; regarding the son of Joash, see *II Kings* 14:23-29). Nevertheless, throughout the Book of *Kings,* Jeroboam son of Nebat is described as the paradigm of wickedness. Thus, it is logical to conclude that the Baal HaTurim's comment refers to him. Indeed, a parallel comment in *Peirush HaRokeach* includes his father's name: וְהִבְדִּילוֹ ה׳ לְרָעָה מִכֹּל בְּגִימַטְרִיָּא זֶה יָרָבְעָם בֶּן נְבָט, *The gematria of the phrase* וְהִבְדִּילוֹ ה׳ לְרָעָה מִכֹּל *is equivalent* (see bracketed passage below) *to that of* זֶה יָרָבְעָם בֶּן נְבָט, *This [refers to] Jeroboam son of Nebat.* [The *gematriaos* of the two phrases in *Peirush HaRokeach's* comment are 484 and 447 respectively, a difference of 37. Perhaps they can be reconciled in the following manner: Whereas God does not like to associate His name with that of wicked people, *Peirush HaRokeach* only counts the *gematria* of וְהִבְדִּילוֹ ... לְרָעָה מִכֹּל, 458. The other phrase is then emended to זֶה הוּא יָרָבְעָם בֶּן נְבָט, which does not change its meaning, but adds 12 to its *gematria,* for a total of 459. And the principle of *im hakollel* allows 458 to be considered equivalent to 459 (*VeChur LaZahav*).]

9. The Mishnah states that these three kings forfeited their share in the World to Come (*Sanhedrin* 10:2 [90a]). However, according to one opinion, whereas Manasseh eventually repented and his repentance was accepted, his share was reinstated (see note 11 below).

9a. The word חִלָּה is in the intensive active *piel* conjugation. It is third person, masculine singular, past tense. In the *piel* the root חלה can mean either *to afflict* (which is its meaning in all other conjugations) or *to entreat* [e.g., וַיְחַל מֹשֶׁה, *Moses entreated* (*Exodus* 32:11)].

of Israel, like all the imprecations of the covenant that is written in this Book of the Torah.

21 *The later generation will say — your children who will arise after you and the foreigner who will come from a distant land — when they will see the plagues of that land and its afflictions with which HASHEM has afflicted it:*
22 *"Sulphur and salt, a conflagration of the entire land, it cannot be sown and it cannot sprout, and no grass shall rise up on it; like the upheaval of Sodom and Gomorrah, Admah*

BAAL HATURIM ELUCIDATED

allowed Himself to be entreated (*II Chronicles* 33:12-13). The Sages expound [on the phrase וַיֵּעָתֶר לוֹ as if it read] וַיֵּחָתֶר[10] לוֹ, *And He tunneled*[10a] *for him*; the verse then teaches that God tunneled under the Throne of Glory to receive him in penitence.[11] Thus, just as the term חִלָּה, *he has afflicted,* of this verse refers to the breaking of the ground {as it is written: אֶת מַכּוֹת הָאָרֶץ הַהִוא[12] וְאֶת תַּחֲלֻאֶיהָ, *the plagues of that land*[12] *and its afflictions,*}[13] so, too, the term חִלָּה (here translated *he entreated*) used with regard to Manasseh also refers to tunneling,[14] for a tunnel was made through the heavens on his behalf.[15]

10. The twenty-two letters of the *aleph-beis* are classified according to the speech organs used in their pronunciation. Thus, the letters אהח״ע have their origin in the throat and are called אוֹתִיּוֹת הַגָּרוֹן, *letters of the throat,* or "gutturals"; גיכ״ק are אוֹתִיּוֹת הַחֵךְ, *letters of the palate,* or "palatals"; דטלנ״ת are אוֹתִיּוֹת הַלָּשׁוֹן, *letters of the tongue* (with its tip at the teeth), or "dentals"; זסצר״ש are אוֹתִיּוֹת הַשִּׁנַּיִם, *letters of the teeth,* or "sibilants"; and בומ״פ are אוֹתִיּוֹת הַשְּׂפָתַיִם, *letters of the lips,* or "labials" (*Sefer Yetzirah* 2:3). The letters within any given classification are often interchanged with one another. Accordingly, the Sages expound on the word as if it were spelled with a ח in place of the ע' and read וַיֵּחָתֶר for וַיֵּעָתֶר (see *Minchas Shai* to *II Chronicles* 33:13)..

10a. It is noteworthy that (in *Yevamos* 64a) *Rashi* renders the noun עָתָר, [usually translated *pitchfork*] into the French *pelle,* "shovel." Accordingly, it is possible that וַיֵּעָתֶר be understood as a verbified form of עָתָר, meaning *and he shoveled,* hence, *and he tunneled (VeChur LaZahav).*

11. *Sanhedrin* 103a; *Yerushalmi, Sanhedrin* 10:5. According to one view in the Talmud, Manasseh regained his share in the World to Come, for he repented during the last thirty-three years of his fifty-five-year reign. Nevertheless, the sins of his early years were too grievous to be forgiven through the usual channels. Thus, strict justice demanded that his repentance be rejected. Yet, despite the gravity of Manasseh's sins, God desired to accept his penitence, so He tunneled under His Throne of Glory, thereby providing a secret passageway for Manasseh's penitence to reach (based on *Yad Ramah*).

12. The expression מַכּוֹת הָאָרֶץ הַהִוא, here rendered, *the plagues of that land,* may also be understood as, *the strikings of that ground,* thus, the breaking or tunneling through the earth (*VeChur LaZahav*).

13. The citation from our verse enclosed in braces is not found in the early or later printed editions. It does appear in *Maharam MiRothenburg,* the Baal HaTurim's source for this comment, and in *Shoham Yakar's* manuscript edition.

14. Although the word חִלָּה is of the root חלה, the Baal HaTurim seems to interpret it as if it were from the root חלל, *to hollow out.* Despite their different roots, in the realm of *remez* (allusion) the similarity of spelling and pronunciation shared by חִלָּה and מְחִלָּה (root חלל), *a tunnel* (*Isaiah* 2:19), allows them to be considered as related *(VeChur LaZahav).*

15. *Maharam MiRothenburg.*

כט/כג־כז כג °וצביים אֲשֶׁר֙ הָפַ֣ךְ יהוה בְּאַפּ֖וֹ וּבַחֲמָתֽוֹ׃ וְאָמְרוּ֮
[°וּצְבוֹיִם ק׳] כָּל־הַגּוֹיִם֒ עַל־מֶ֙ה עָשָׂ֧ה יהוה כָּ֖כָה לָאָ֣רֶץ הַזֹּ֑את מֶ֥ה
כד חֳרִ֛י הָאַ֥ף הַגָּד֖וֹל הַזֶּֽה׃ וְאָמְר֕וּ עַ֚ל אֲשֶׁ֣ר עָֽזְב֔וּ אֶת־
בְּרִ֥ית יהוה אֱלֹהֵ֣י אֲבֹתָ֑ם אֲשֶׁר֙ כָּרַ֣ת עִמָּ֔ם בְּהוֹצִיא֥וֹ
כה אֹתָ֖ם מֵאֶ֥רֶץ מִצְרָֽיִם׃ וַיֵּ֣לְכ֗וּ וַיַּֽעַבְדוּ֙ אֱלֹהִ֣ים אֲחֵרִ֔ים
וַיִּֽשְׁתַּחֲו֖וּ לָהֶ֑ם אֱלֹהִים֙ אֲשֶׁ֣ר לֹֽא־יְדָע֔וּם וְלֹ֥א חָלַ֖ק
כו לָהֶֽם׃ וַיִּֽחַר־אַ֥ף יהוה בָּאָ֣רֶץ הַהִ֑וא לְהָבִ֤יא עָלֶ֙יהָ֙
כז אֶת־כָּל־הַקְּלָלָ֔ה הַכְּתוּבָ֖ה בַּסֵּ֥פֶר הַזֶּֽה׃ וַיִּתְּשֵׁ֤ם יהוה֙
מֵעַ֣ל אַדְמָתָ֔ם בְּאַ֥ף וּבְחֵמָ֖ה וּבְקֶ֣צֶף גָּד֑וֹל וַיַּשְׁלִכֵ֛ם

בעל הטורים

(כה) וַיִּשְׁתַּחֲוּוּ. חָסֵר וָ״ו. הוּא הַדִּין שְׁאָר עֲבֹדָה שֶׁהִיא כְּעֵין פְּנִים:

(כז) בְּאַף וּבְחֵמָה וּבְקֶצֶף. בְּגִימַטְרִיָּא שִׁבְעִים — כְּנֶגֶד שִׁבְעִים שָׁנָה שֶׁל גָּלוּת בָּבֶל:

☐ **וַיַּשְׁלִכֵם.** לָמֶ״ד גְּדוֹלָה וְחָסֵר יוּ״ד. לוֹמַר שֶׁאֵין הַשְׁלָכָה כָּזֹאת לְי׳ הַשְּׁבָטִים:

BAAL HATURIM ELUCIDATED

25. וַיִּשְׁתַּחֲוּוּ — AND THEY PROSTRATED THEMSELVES. This word is spelled defectively,[16] without a [doubled] ו. [This omission indicates that prostration is merely an example of idolatry;] the capital sin of idolatry includes any type of service that resembles a service performed within the Sanctuary[17] as well.[18]

27. בְּאַף וּבְחֵמָה וּבְקֶצֶף — WITH ANGER, WITH WRATH, AND WITH GREAT FURY. The

16. The reading חָסֵר ו׳, *spelled defectively, without a* ו, follows the early printed editions. However, that statement is contradicted by virtually all extant Torah scrolls, for, in our verse, the word is universally spelled in full, וַיִּשְׁתַּחֲוּוּ, with a double ו. Consequently, *Ittur Bikkurim* suggests that the comment contains a copyist's error and should be emended to מָלֵא ו׳, *spelled in full, with a* [*double*] ו, a suggestion accepted by most, if not all, subsequent editions.

But the emended version is also problematic: First, because the parallel comment in *Peirush HaRokeach,* the Baal HaTurim's apparent source for this comment, which was not available to the author of *Ittur Bikkurim,* also reads חָסֵר ו׳. Additionally, the other verbs in our verse are in the plural — וַיֵּלְכוּ, *they went;* וַיַּעַבְדוּ, *and they served* — so that the plural form וַיִּשְׁתַּחֲוּוּ, *and they prostrated themselves,* is the expected form. The spelling וַיִּשְׁתַּחוּ, with a single final ו, is singular, *and he prostrated himself.*

Accordingly, the Baal HaTurim's comment requires clarification. Perhaps it is based on a no longer extant masoretic note. For the word וַיִּשְׁתַּחֲוּוּ appears ten times in the Torah (*Genesis* 33:7 twice; 42:6, 43:26, 43:28; *Exodus* 4:31, 12:27, 32:8; *Numbers* 25:2; and our verse) and nineteen more times in the remainder of the *Tanach.* In three of those verses (*Genesis* 27:29 [see *Minchas Shai* there] and 43:28, *I Kings* 9:9), it appears as a *keri uchesiv* — its *kesiv* (spelling) is וישתחו, with a single final ו, while its *keri* (pronunciation) is וַיִּשְׁתַּחֲוּוּ, with a double final ו. It is possible that *Peirush HaRokeach* and the Baal HaTurim were aware of a variant masoretic note that included וַיִּשְׁתַּחֲוּוּ of our verse as a *keri uchesiv.* If so, the Baal HaTurim's comment, חָסֵר וי״ו, means that the word is spelled וישתחו defectively, *without a* [*double*] ו, but, nevertheless, is pronounced וַיִּשְׁתַּחֲוּוּ, and goes on to explain the *keri uchesiv* (*VeChur LaZahav*).

17. The Talmud (*Sanhedrin* 60b) adduces a verse almost identical to ours, but couched in the singular, rather than the plural of our verse — וַיֵּלֶךְ וַיַּעֲבֹד אֱלֹהִים אֲחֵרִים וַיִּשְׁתַּחוּ לָהֶם (17:3 above) — to prove that prostration is included in the capital offense of performing any of the Sanctuary services outside of the Sanctuary. The Baal HaTurim apparently sees the חָסֵר/מָלֵא as an allusion to those other services (*VeChur LaZahav*).

18. *Peirush HaRokeach.*

and Zeboiim, which HASHEM overturned in His anger and
wrath." [23] And all the nations will say, "For what reason did HASHEM do so to this land; why this wrathfulness of great anger?"
[24] And they will say, "Because they forsook the covenant
of HASHEM, the God of their forefathers, that He sealed with
them when He took them out of the land of Egypt; [25] and
they went and they served other gods and they prostrated
themselves to them — gods that they knew not and He did
not apportion to them. [26] So God's anger flared against that
land, to bring upon it the entire curse that is written in this
Book; [27] and HASHEM removed them from upon their soil, with
anger, with wrath, and with great fury, and He cast them

BAAL HATURIM ELUCIDATED

gematria of this phrase (422) is equal to that of שִׁבְעִים, *seventy*, corresponding to the seventy years of the Babylonian exile.[19]

❑ וַיַּשְׁלִכֵם — **AND HE CAST THEM.** [According to the masoretic tradition,[19a]] the ל of this word is written larger than usual[20] [in the Torah scrolls] and the word is spelled defectively,[21] without a second י (= 10). [These anomalies indicate] that there is no [other] exile [of such large scope][22] as that of the ten tribes.[23,24]

19. See *Jeremiah* 29:10.

19a. See masoretic note to *Genesis* 1:1.

20. Traditionally, certain particular letters are written larger than usual in the Torah scroll. That form indicates that a special lesson is to be learned from that letter. Other verses at which the Baal HaTurim expounds on larger than usual letters are: *Genesis* 27:46; *Leviticus* 13:33; *Numbers* 14:17; *Deuteronomy* 6:4, 18:13 and 32:6.

21. That is, it is spelled וַיַּשְׁלִכֵם and not וַיַּשְׁלִיכֵם, with a י after the ל, as we sometimes find the full spelling used in similar words, e.g., תַּשְׁלִיכֻהוּ (*Exodus* 1:22) and וַיַּשְׁלִיכוּ (*Exodus* 7:12).

22. *Peirush HaRokeach.* The great size of the ל alludes to the great severity of the exile.

23. The translation follows *Peirush HaRokeach,* the Baal HaTurim's apparent source, who writes: אֵין הַשְׁלָכָה גְדוֹלָה כְּמוֹ שֶׁל י׳ הַשְּׁבָטִים, *There is no exile as great as that of the ten tribes.* Accordingly, the comment is based on one interpretation of our verse, as expounded in the Mishnah (*Sanhedrin* 10:3 [110b]): The ten tribes are not destined to return, as it is stated, וַיַּשְׁלִכֵם אֶל אֶרֶץ אַחֶרֶת כַּיּוֹם הַזֶּה, *and He cast them to another land, as this very day,* [which means that] just as this day leaves and does not return, so shall they leave [the Land of Israel] and not return (*VeChur LaZahav*).

An opposing view in that Mishnah interprets our verse in quite a different manner: [The fate of the ten tribes is] like that of this day, just as the day darkens and then turns light again, so, too, regarding the ten tribes, although it has become dark for them, it will eventually become light for them [once again].

According to this second opinion in the Mishnah, the exile of Judah and Benjamin is of greater severity than that of the ten tribes. As Rashi explains in his commentary to the Mishnah: The verse implies that all of them [i.e., the ten tribes] will be exiled to one place, for the verse uses the singular, אֶל אֶרֶץ אַחֶרֶת, *to another land,* i.e., one other land; . . . but the two tribes [Judah and Benjamin] were not exiled to one place, rather they were dispersed throughout many lands . . . (*Rashi, Sanhedrin* 110b, s.v., וישליכם משמע). On the basis of that opinion, the Baal HaTurim's words take on a different meaning: The enlarged ל alludes to the more severe exile, and the absent י (= 10) indicates that the ten tribes were spared from that form of exile for, as the verse goes on to say, their exile was אֶל אֶרֶץ אַחֶרֶת, *to* [*only*] *one other land.* The Baal HaTurim's comment is then translated: שֶׁאֵין הַשְׁלָכָה כָּזֹאת, *Such a* [*severe*] *exile is not* [*destined*], לְי׳ שְׁבָטִים, *for the ten tribes* (*Ittur Bikkurim*; see *Bereishis Rabbah* 73:6; *Yad Aharon*).

24. It is noteworthy that the *gematria* of וַיַּשְׁלִכֵם (406) is equal to that of, לָמֶ״ד גְּדוֹלָה וְחָסֵר י׳, and to that of לְי׳ הַשְּׁבָטִים (*VeChur LaZahav*).

אֶל־אֶ֤רֶץ אַחֶ֨רֶת֙ כַּיּ֣וֹם הַזֶּֽה: הַנִּסְתָּרֹת֙ לַיהוָ֣ה

אֱלֹהֵ֔ינוּ וְהַנִּגְלֹ֞ת *לָ֤נוּ וּלְבָנֵ֨ינוּ֙ עַד־עוֹלָ֔ם לַעֲשׂ֕וֹת

* י״א נקודות

ל רביעי [שני] א אֶת־כָּל־דִּבְרֵ֖י הַתּוֹרָ֥ה הַזֹּֽאת: וְהָיָה֩ כִֽי־יָבֹ֨אוּ

עָלֶ֜יךָ כָּל־הַדְּבָרִ֣ים הָאֵ֗לֶּה הַבְּרָכָה֙ וְהַקְּלָלָ֔ה אֲשֶׁ֥ר

נָתַ֖תִּי לְפָנֶ֑יךָ וַהֲשֵׁבֹתָ֙ אֶל־לְבָבֶ֔ךָ בְּכָל־הַגּוֹיִ֔ם אֲשֶׁ֣ר

ב הִדִּיחֲךָ֛ יהוָ֥ה אֱלֹהֶ֖יךָ שָֽׁמָּה: וְשַׁבְתָּ֞ עַד־יהוָ֤ה

אֱלֹהֶ֨יךָ֙ וְשָׁמַעְתָּ֣ בְקֹל֔וֹ כְּכֹ֛ל אֲשֶׁר־אָנֹכִ֥י מְצַוְּךָ֖ הַיּ֑וֹם

ג אַתָּ֣ה וּבָנֶ֔יךָ בְּכָל־לְבָבְךָ֖ וּבְכָל־נַפְשֶֽׁךָ: וְשָׁ֨ב יהוָ֧ה

אֱלֹהֶ֛יךָ אֶת־שְׁבוּתְךָ֖ וְרִחֲמֶ֑ךָ וְשָׁ֗ב וְקִבֶּצְךָ֙ מִכָּל־

הָ֣עַמִּ֔ים אֲשֶׁ֧ר הֱפִֽיצְךָ֛ יהוָ֥ה אֱלֹהֶ֖יךָ שָֽׁמָּה: אִם־יִהְיֶ֥ה

ד נִֽדַּחֲךָ֖ בִּקְצֵ֣ה הַשָּׁמָ֑יִם מִשָּׁ֗ם יְקַבֶּצְךָ֙ יהוָ֣ה אֱלֹהֶ֔יךָ

ה וּמִשָּׁ֖ם יִקָּחֶֽךָ: וֶהֱבִֽיאֲךָ֞ יהוָ֣ה אֱלֹהֶ֗יךָ אֶל־הָאָ֛רֶץ

אֲשֶׁר־יָרְשׁ֥וּ אֲבֹתֶ֖יךָ וִֽירִשְׁתָּ֑הּ וְהֵיטִֽבְךָ֥ וְהִרְבְּךָ֖

ו מֵאֲבֹתֶֽיךָ: וּמָ֨ל יהוָ֤ה אֱלֹהֶ֨יךָ֙ אֶת־לְבָבְךָ֔ וְאֶת־לְבַ֖ב

─────── בעל הטורים ───────

(כח) {עַד עוֹלָֽם.} נָקוּד עַל עַיִ״ן שֶׁבְּ״עַד״. כִּדְאִיתָא בְּפֶרֶק נִגְמַר הַדִּין. שֶׁעַ׳ יוֹם הָיוּ מֵאֶחָד
בִּשְׁבָט שֶׁהִתְחִיל לְבָאֵר הַתּוֹרָה עַד י׳ בְּנִיסָן שֶׁעָבְרוּ הַיַּרְדֵּן, שֶׁאֵין ״לָנוּ וּלְבָנֵינוּ״ לְעֹנֶשׁ:
דָּבָר אַחֵר – רֶמֶז לְעַ׳ שָׁנָה שֶׁל גָּלוּת בָּבֶל:

ל (ו) אֶת לְבָבְךָ וְאֶת לְבַב. רָאשֵׁי תֵבוֹת אֱלוּל. לְכָךְ נָהֲגוּ לְהַשְׁכִּים לְהִתְפַּלֵּל סְלִיחוֹת

─────── BAAL HATURIM ELUCIDATED ───────

28. {עַד עוֹלָם — FOREVER.} [According to a masoretic tradition] there is a dot[25] over the ע in the word עַד, as noted in the chapter called נִגְמַר הַדִּין, *Nigmar HaDin*. [26] [The dotted ע (= 70) alludes to] the seventy days from the first of Shevat, when Moses began to explain the Torah (see 1:3 above), until the tenth of Nissan,[26a] when they crossed the Jordan (see *Joshua* 4:19), punishment is not

25. Although נְקֻדּוֹת, *vowel signs,* are never written in a Torah scroll, tradition teaches that dots are inscribed above certain letters and words (see note 26 below).

26. The sixth chapter of tractate *Sanhedrin* is called *Nigmar HaDin*. The Talmud there (43b) discusses the eleven dotted letters that appear in our verse over the letters of לָנוּ וּלְבָנֵינוּ and the ע of עַד. Despite the fact that the Baal HaTurim opens his comment by mentioning the ע of עַד, but not the other dots of this verse, his first exposition actually explains all eleven dots and,

in doing so, sheds a new light on the Talmudic passage (see note 27 below).

26a. The only calendrical arrangement that would account for seventy days would assign thirty days to Shevat, thirty to Adar, and ten more in Nissan. The Baal HaTurim's source regarding the number of days in Shevat and Adar of that year is not known. Moreover, the Talmud implies that Adar of that year had only twenty-nine days (see *Kiddushin* 38a, with *Rashi*, s.v., צָא).

Although the Baal HaTurim's source is un-

to another land, as this very day!"

28 *The hidden [sins] are for HASHEM, our God, but the revealed [sins] are for us and for our children forever, to carry out all the words of this Torah.*

30

1 *It will be that when all these things come upon you — the blessing and the curse that I have presented before you — then you will take it to your heart among all the nations where HASHEM, your God, has dispersed you;* 2 *and you will return unto HASHEM, your God, and listen to His voice, according to everything that I command you today, you and your children, with all your heart and all your soul.* 3 *Then Hashem, your God, will return your captivity and have mercy upon you, and He will gather you in from all the peoples to which HASHEM, your God, has scattered you.* 4 *If your dispersed will be at the ends of heaven, from there HASHEM, your God, will gather you in and from there He will take you.* 5 *HASHEM, your God, will bring you to the land that your forefathers possessed and you shall possess it; He will do good to you and make you more numerous than your forefathers.* 6 *HASHEM, your God, will circumcise your heart and the heart of*

applicable either לָנוּ וּלְבָנֵינוּ, *for us or for our children.*[27]

Alternatively: [The dotted ע is] an allusion to the seventy years of the Babylonian exile.[28]

XXX.

6. אֶת לְבָבְךָ וְאֶת לְבַב — YOUR HEART AND THE HEART OF. The initial letters of these words spell [the name of the month of] אֱלוּל, *Elul.*[29] Accordingly, it has become customary to rise early to recite the *Selichos* prayers from the beginning of the

known, our verse contains an allusion to the number of days in each month. For the thirty-day month is called מָלֵא, *full,* and the twenty-nine-day month is called חָסֵר, *defective.* Now the *gematria* of עַד עוֹלָם is 220, equal to that of ע׳ וי״א וי״ב מְלֵאִים, *Seventy* [days, because] *the eleventh* [month, i.e., Shevat] *and the twelfth* [Adar] *were full (VeChur LaZahav).*

27. *Peirush HaRokeach.* The Talmud states: Why are the dots over the letters of לָנוּ וּלְבָנֵינוּ and over the ע of עַד? The dotting teaches that God did not punish the entire community [i.e., He did not hold the community responsible] for the hidden [sins] of an individual until the Israelites crossed the Jordan . . . (*Sanhedrin* 43b).

According to the Baal HaTurim's comment, the first ten dots, i.e., those over the letters of לָנוּ וּלְבָנֵינוּ, relieve Israel of communal responsibility, while the dot over the ע sets the limit of that relief at seventy days (*VeChur LaZahav*).

28. *Peirush HaRokeach*; see the Baal HaTurim to v. 27 above, s.v., בְּאַף.

29. The Torah could have stated, וּמָל ה׳ אֱלֹהֶיךָ לְבָבְךָ וּלְבַב זַרְעֶךָ, which has exactly the same meaning as וּמָל ה׳ אֱלֹהֶיךָ אֶת לְבָבְךָ וְאֶת לְבַב זַרְעֶךָ. The Baal HaTurim's allusion explains why the words אֶת and וְאֶת are included in the verse (*VeChur LaZahav*).

זַרְעֶךָ לְאַהֲבָה אֶת־יהוה אֱלֹהֶיךָ בְּכָל־לְבָבְךָ וּבְכָל־
נַפְשְׁךָ לְמַעַן חַיֶּיךָ: וְנָתַן יהוה אֱלֹהֶיךָ אֵת כָּל־ ז
הָאָלוֹת הָאֵלֶּה עַל־אֹיְבֶיךָ וְעַל־שֹׂנְאֶיךָ אֲשֶׁר רְדָפוּךָ:
וְאַתָּה תָשׁוּב וְשָׁמַעְתָּ בְּקוֹל יהוה וְעָשִׂיתָ אֶת־כָּל־ ח
מִצְוֹתָיו אֲשֶׁר אָנֹכִי מְצַוְּךָ הַיּוֹם: וְהוֹתִירְךָ יהוה ט
אֱלֹהֶיךָ בְּכֹל | מַעֲשֵׂה יָדֶךָ בִּפְרִי בִטְנְךָ וּבִפְרִי
בְהֶמְתְּךָ וּבִפְרִי אַדְמָתְךָ לְטֹבָה כִּי | יָשׁוּב יהוה לָשׂוּשׂ
עָלֶיךָ לְטוֹב כַּאֲשֶׁר־שָׂשׂ עַל־אֲבֹתֶיךָ: כִּי תִשְׁמַע י
בְּקוֹל יהוה אֱלֹהֶיךָ לִשְׁמֹר מִצְוֹתָיו וְחֻקֹּתָיו הַכְּתוּבָה
בְּסֵפֶר הַתּוֹרָה הַזֶּה כִּי תָשׁוּב אֶל־יהוה אֱלֹהֶיךָ

––––––––––––––––––––––––– בעל הטורים –––––––––––––––––––––––––

מֵרֹאשׁ חֹדֶשׁ אֱלוּל וָאֵילָךְ. וְכֵן "לוּלֵא הֶאֱמַנְתִּי לִרְאוֹת בְּטוּב ה' " – "לוּלֵא" אוֹתִיּוֹת אֱלוּל,
שֶׁמֵּאֱלוּל וָאֵילָךְ חֲרַדְתִּי נֶגֶד ה':

❑ אֶת לְבָבְךָ וְאֶת. בְּגִימַטְרִיָּא זֶה לִימוֹת הַמָּשִׁיחַ:

(ח) {וְאַתָּה תָשׁוּב.} וּסְמִיךְ לֵהּ "וְהוֹתִירְךָ". שֶׁאִם תָּשׁוּב בִּתְשׁוּבָה שְׁלֵמָה, מִיָּד תְּהֵא נִגְאָל:

(י) {כִּי} תִשְׁמַע בְּקוֹל. בְּגִימַטְרִיָּא זֶה בְּקוֹל דִּבְרֵי תַלְמִידֵי חֲכָמִים:

❑ כִּי תָשׁוּב אֶל ה' אֱלֹהֶיךָ. וּסְמִיךְ לֵהּ "כִּי הַמִּצְוָה הַזֹּאת". לוֹמַר שֶׁקְּוּלָה הִיא הַתְּשׁוּבָה
כְּנֶגֶד כָּל הַמִּצְוֹת כֻּלָּן:

––––––––––––––––––– BAAL HATURIM ELUCIDATED –––––––––––––––––––

month of Elul and onward.[30]

Similarly, in the verse, לוּלֵא הֶאֱמַנְתִּי לִרְאוֹת בְּטוּב ה', *Had I not trusted that I would see the goodness of* HASHEM (Psalms 27:13), the word לוּלֵא is spelled with the same letters as אֱלוּל, *Elul,* [indicating] that from Elul onward, I am overcome with trepidation before God.[31]

❑ אֶת לְבָבְךָ וְאֶת — YOUR HEART AND. The *gematria* of this phrase (862) is equivalent[32] to that of זֶה לִימוֹת הַמָּשִׁיחַ, *This* [refers] *to the days of the Mashiach.* [33]

30. The Baal HaTurim refers to the Sefardic custom of arising early each weekday during the month of Elul for the recitation of the *Selichos* prayers. Ashkenazim begin reciting *Selichos* either one or two Sundays before Rosh Hashanah (see *Tur* and *Shulchan Aruch, Orach Chaim* 581).

It is noteworthy that the *gematria* of ראש חדש אֱלוּל is 886, equal to that of סְלִיחוֹת בְּהַשְׁכָּמָה, *Selichos in the early morning* (*VeChur LaZahav*).

31. *Peirush HaRokeach.* [Thus,] it is customary to recite psalm 27 from Rosh Chodesh Elul until Shemini Atzeres (*Mishnah Berurah* 581:2).

32. The principle of *im hakollel* allows 861, the *gematria* of the Baal HaTurim's phrase, to be considered equivalent to 862.

33. *Peirush HaRokeach*; see also *Succah* 52a. According to the *Ramban* (cited by the Baal HaTurim in *Peirush HaTur HaAroch*), the phrase *God will circumcise your heart* refers to the destruction of the evil inclination within man. For from the creation of man until the advent of the Messiah, the evil inclination provides man with the possibility of spiritual growth by presenting him with the enticements of sin and evil.

your offspring, to love HASHEM, your God, with all your heart
and with all your soul, that you may live.
7 *HASHEM, your God, will place all these imprecations upon*
your enemies and those who hate you, who pursued you. 8 *You*
shall return and listen to the voice of HASHEM, and perform all
His commandments that I command you today. 9 *HASHEM*
will make you abundant in all your handiwork — in the fruit
of your womb, the fruit of your animals, and the fruit of your
land — for good, when HASHEM will return to rejoice over you
for good, as He rejoiced over your forefathers, 10 *when you*
listen to the voice of HASHEM, your God, to observe His
commandments and His decrees, that are written in this Book
of the Torah, when you shall return to HASHEM, your God,

BAAL HATURIM ELUCIDATED

8. {**וְאַתָּה תָשׁוּב** — YOU SHALL RETURN.} Juxtaposed to this is, וְהוֹתִירְךָ, [*HASHEM*] *will make you abundant . . .* [This indicates] that if you return [to God] in complete repentance, you will be redeemed immediately.[34]

10. **תִשְׁמַע בְּקוֹל** {**כִּי**} — {WHEN} YOU LISTEN TO THE VOICE. The *gematria* of this phrase (978) is equal to that of [35]זֶה בְקוֹל דִּבְרֵי תַלְמִידֵי חֲכָמִים, *This* [*refers to*] *the voice of the words of Torah sages.*[36]

❑ **כִּי תָשׁוּב אֶל ה' אֱלֹהֶיךָ** — WHEN YOU SHALL RETURN TO **Hashem**, YOUR **GOD**. Juxtaposed to this is **כִּי הַמִּצְוָה הַזֹּאת**, *for this commandment* (v. 11), to indicate that *teshuvah* is equivalent to the entirety of all the *mitzvos.*[37]

By overcoming this inclination and choosing righteousness and good, man accomplishes his purpose on earth. But in Messianic times, *God will circumcise your heart,* so that man will no longer face enticement to sin. Our verse thus refers to "the days of the *Mashiach.*"

34. The *Rambam* expounds on verses 1-3 of our passage: All of the prophets commanded Israel regarding *teshuvah* (repentance). Moreover, Israel will not be redeemed by any means other than *teshuvah.* Indeed, the Torah has promised that Israel will eventually repent at the end of its exile and they will be redeemed immediately, as it is stated: *It will be when all these things come upon you . . . you will return unto HASHEM, your God . . . then HASHEM, your God, will return . . .* (*Hilchos Teshuvah* 7:5).

35. The early printed editions read: תִשְׁמַע בְּקוֹל בְּגִימַטְרִיָּא זֶה בְקוֹל ת״ח. However, the *gematria* of the Scriptural phrase is then 948, while that of the Baal HaTurim's phrase is only 558. Even if we were to write out the abbreviation, the *gematria* of זֶה בְקוֹל תַלְמִידֵי חֲכָמִים would still be only 762, a shortfall of 186. One of the manuscripts used by *Shoham Yakar* includes the word דִּבְרֵי, which adds 216 to the *gematria,* for a total of 978, thirty more than that of the Scriptural phrase. *Shoham Yakar* then reconciles these *gematriaos* by including the word כִּי (= 30) in the Scriptural phrase. The text here follows that suggestion.

Alternatively: The proper reading may be, תִשְׁמַע בְּקוֹל בְּגִימַטְרִיָּא זֶה קוֹל ת״ת [=תַלְמוּד תוֹרָה], *The gematria of* תִשְׁמַע בְּקוֹל *(948) is equal to that of,* זֶה קוֹל ת״ת, *This* [*refers to*] *the sound of Torah study* (*VeChur LaZahav*).

36. A verse similar to ours reads, אִם שָׁמוֹעַ תִשְׁמַע לְקוֹל ה' אֱלֹהֶיךָ, *If you will hearken diligently to the voice of HASHEM, your God . . .* (*Exodus* 15:26). The Midrash explains that verse: From here you learn that whoever hearkens to the words [literally, *the mouth*] of the Torah sage is considered as hearkening to the words of the Almighty (*Tanchuma Yashan, Beshalach* 19).

37. From *Rashi's* comment to verse 14, it is evident that the phrase כִּי הַמִּצְוָה הַזֹּאת, *for this commandment,* refers to the entire Torah, i.e.,

ל/יא־טז ששי יא בְּכָל־לְבָבְךָ וּבְכָל־נַפְשֶׁךָ: כִּי הַמִּצְוָה הַזֹּאת
אֲשֶׁר אָנֹכִי מְצַוְּךָ הַיּוֹם לֹא־נִפְלֵאת הִוא מִמְּךָ
יב וְלֹא־רְחֹקָה הִוא: לֹא בַשָּׁמַיִם הִוא לֵאמֹר מִי
יַעֲלֶה־לָּנוּ הַשָּׁמַיְמָה וְיִקָּחֶהָ לָּנוּ וְיַשְׁמִעֵנוּ אֹתָהּ
יג וְנַעֲשֶׂנָּה: וְלֹא־מֵעֵבֶר לַיָּם הִוא לֵאמֹר מִי יַעֲבָר־
לָנוּ אֶל־עֵבֶר הַיָּם וְיִקָּחֶהָ לָּנוּ וְיַשְׁמִעֵנוּ אֹתָהּ
יד וְנַעֲשֶׂנָּה: כִּי־קָרוֹב אֵלֶיךָ הַדָּבָר מְאֹד בְּפִיךָ
שביעי ומפטיר [רביעי] טו וּבִלְבָבְךָ לַעֲשֹׂתוֹ: רְאֵה נָתַתִּי לְפָנֶיךָ הַיּוֹם אֶת־
טז הַחַיִּים וְאֶת־הַטּוֹב וְאֶת־הַמָּוֶת וְאֶת־הָרָע: אֲשֶׁר
אָנֹכִי מְצַוְּךָ הַיּוֹם לְאַהֲבָה אֶת־יהוה אֱלֹהֶיךָ לָלֶכֶת
בִּדְרָכָיו וְלִשְׁמֹר מִצְוֹתָיו וְחֻקֹּתָיו וּמִשְׁפָּטָיו וְחָיִיתָ
וְרָבִיתָ וּבֵרַכְךָ יהוה אֱלֹהֶיךָ בָּאָרֶץ אֲשֶׁר־אַתָּה

בעל הטורים

(יב) **מִי יַעֲלֶה לָּנוּ הַשָּׁמַיְמָה.** רָאשֵׁי תֵבוֹת מִילָה וְסוֹפֵי תֵבוֹת יהו״ה. לוֹמַר שֶׁאֵינוֹ יָכוֹל לַעֲלוֹת {הַשָּׁמַיִם} אֵצֶל ה׳ אִם לֹא שֶׁיְּהֵא נִמּוֹל. וְכֵן ״הִתְהַלֵּךְ לְפָנַי וֶהְיֵה תָמִים״, שֶׁנֶּאֱמַר עַל הַמִּילָה:

(יד) **בְּפִיךָ וּבִלְבָבְךָ לַעֲשֹׂתוֹ.** ״בְּפִיךָ״ – ״כִּי חַיִּים הֵם לְמֹצְאֵיהֶם״. ״וּבִלְבָבְךָ״ – אַגְרָא דִשְׁמַעְתָּא סְבָרָא:

(טו) **אֶת הַחַיִּים וְאֶת הַטּוֹב.** בְּגִימַטְרִיָּא תּוֹצָאוֹת. ״כִּי מִמֶּנּוּ תּוֹצְאוֹת חַיִּים״:

(טז) **וּבֵרַכְךָ ה׳ אֱלֹהֶיךָ.** ב׳ בַּמָּסוֹרֶת – ״וְחָיִיתָ וְרָבִיתָ וּבֵרַכְךָ ה׳ אֱלֹהֶיךָ״; וְגַבֵּי עֶבֶד עִבְרִי ״לֹא יִקְשֶׁה בְעֵינֶךָ וְגוֹ׳ וּבֵרַכְךָ ה׳ אֱלֹהֶיךָ״. וְזֶהוּ שֶׁאָמְרוּ חֲכָמֵינוּ ז״ל, שֶׁאֵין עֶבֶד עִבְרִי נוֹהֵג

BAAL HATURIM ELUCIDATED

12. **מִי יַעֲלֶה לָּנוּ הַשָּׁמַיְמָה** — WHO CAN ASCEND TO THE HEAVEN FOR US. The initial letters of these four words spell the word מִילָה, *circumcision,* and their final letters spell the Tetragrammaton. This is to indicate that a man cannot ascend {to heaven,} [to be] next to God, unless he is circumcised.[38] Similarly, the verse הִתְהַלֵּךְ לְפָנַי וֶהְיֵה תָמִים, *Walk before Me and be perfect* (*Genesis* 17:1),[38a] which

the term הַמִּצְוָה, literally, *the commandment,* refers to the Torah. However, the *Ramban* (v. 11, cited by the Baal HaTurim in *Peirush HaTur HaAroch*) argues that if that were the verse's intention, it would have used the plural form הַמִּצְוֹת הָאֵלּוּ, *these mitzvos,* rather than the singular form הַמִּצְוָה הַזֹּאת, *this mitzvah.* Accordingly, *Ramban* interprets that phrase as a reference to the *mitzvah* of *teshuvah.* The Baal HaTurim's comment seems to merge the two interpretations: The word הַמִּצְוָה refers to the entirety of the Torah, but it is couched in the singular to indicate that there is one *mitzvah* — that of *teshuvah* — that is considered equal to all the others combined (*VeChur LaZahav*).

38. See *Tanchuma, Lech Lecha* 20; see also *Eruvin* 19a.

38a. God used this phrase in introducing the *mitzvah* of circumcision to Abraham (see *Rashi* there).

with all your heart and all your soul.

11 *For this commandment that I command you today — it
is not hidden from you and it is not distant.* 12 *It is not in
heaven, [for you] to say, "Who can ascend to the heaven
for us and take it for us, so that we can listen to it and
perform it?"* 13 *Nor is it across the sea, [for you] to say,
"Who can cross to the other side of the sea for us and take
it for us, so that we can listen to it and perform it?"* 14 *Rather,
the matter is very near to you — in your mouth and your
heart — to perform it.*

15 *See — I have placed before you today the life and the
good, and the death and the evil,* 16 *that which I command
you today, to love HASHEM, your God, to walk in His ways,
to observe His commandments, His decrees, and His
ordinances; then you will live and you will multiply, and
HASHEM, your God, will bless you in the land to which you*

BAAL HATURIM ELUCIDATED

was said with regard to circumcision.[39]

14. בְּפִיךָ וּבִלְבָבְךָ לַעֲשֹׂתוֹ — IN YOUR MOUTH AND YOUR HEART — TO PERFORM IT. בְּפִיךָ, *in your mouth,* [as it is stated,] כִּי חַיִּים הֵם לְמֹצְאֵיהֶם, *For they are life to those who find them* (*Proverbs* 4:22);[40] וּבִלְבָבְךָ, *and in your heart,* [as the Talmud states] the reward for a discussion [of Torah law] is [dependent upon] the reasoning.[41,42]

15. אֶת הַחַיִּים וְאֶת הַטּוֹב — THE LIFE AND THE GOOD. The *gematria* of this phrase (903) is equal to that of תּוֹצָאוֹת, *sources,* [recalling the verse,] כִּי מִמֶּנּוּ תּוֹצְאוֹת חַיִּים, *for from it* [i.e., the Torah] *are the sources of life* (*Proverbs* 4:23).[43]

16. וּבֵרַכְךָ ה׳ אֱלֹהֶיךָ — AND HASHEM, YOUR GOD, WILL BLESS YOU. The masoretic note, ב׳, on this phrase means that it appears twice in the *Tanach*: (i) here, וְחָיִיתָ וְרָבִיתָ וּבֵרַכְךָ ה׳ אֱלֹהֶיךָ, *then you will live and you will multiply, and HASHEM, your God, will bless you;* and (ii) with regard to a Hebrew servant, לֹא יִקְשֶׁה בְעֵינֶךָ . . . וּבֵרַכְךָ ה׳ אֱלֹהֶיךָ, *It shall not be difficult in your eyes . . . and HASHEM, your God, will bless you* (15:18 above). This [similarity of expression] can be understood as the basis of our Sages' statement that the concept of a Hebrew servant does not apply in the

39. *Peirush HaRokeach*; see *Nedarim* 31b.

40. The Talmud interprets both our verse and that verse as references to the words of the Torah; the term לְמֹצְאֵיהֶם is interpreted as if it were vowelized לְמוֹצִיאֵיהֶם, *to those who bring them forth,* i.e., who utter words of Torah with their mouth (*Eruvin* 54a).

41. *Berachos* 6b. *Rashi* explains that the reward a person receives for participating in a Torah discussion is commensurate with the effort and concentration that he exerts to understand the rationale of the matter under discussion.

42. *Peirush HaRokeach.*

43. *Peirush HaRokeach.*

Note that, in his comments to verses 14 and 15, the Baal HaTurim expounds on two adjacent verses in *Proverbs.*

יז בָּא־שָׁמָּה לְרִשְׁתָּהּ: וְאִם־יִפְנֶה לְבָבְךָ וְלֹא תִשְׁמָע
וְנִדַּחְתָּ וְהִשְׁתַּחֲוִיתָ לֵאלֹהִים אֲחֵרִים וַעֲבַדְתָּם:
יח הִגַּדְתִּי לָכֶם הַיּוֹם כִּי אָבֹד תֹּאבֵדוּן לֹא־תַאֲרִיכֻן
יָמִים עַל־הָאֲדָמָה אֲשֶׁר אַתָּה עֹבֵר אֶת־הַיַּרְדֵּן
יט לָבוֹא שָׁמָּה לְרִשְׁתָּהּ: הַעִדֹתִי בָכֶם הַיּוֹם אֶת־
הַשָּׁמַיִם וְאֶת־הָאָרֶץ הַחַיִּים וְהַמָּוֶת נָתַתִּי לְפָנֶיךָ
הַבְּרָכָה וְהַקְּלָלָה וּבָחַרְתָּ בַּחַיִּים לְמַעַן תִּחְיֶה
כ אַתָּה וְזַרְעֶךָ: לְאַהֲבָה אֶת־יהוה אֱלֹהֶיךָ לִשְׁמֹעַ
בְּקֹלוֹ וּלְדָבְקָה־בוֹ כִּי הוּא חַיֶּיךָ וְאֹרֶךְ יָמֶיךָ לָשֶׁבֶת
עַל־הָאֲדָמָה אֲשֶׁר נִשְׁבַּע יהוה לַאֲבֹתֶיךָ לְאַבְרָהָם
לְיִצְחָק וּלְיַעֲקֹב לָתֵת לָהֶם: פפפ מ׳ פסוקים. לבב״ו סימן.

בעל הטורים

בְּחוּצָה לָאָרֶץ. כְּהָכָא דִּכְתִיב "וּבֵרַכְךָ . . . בָּאָרֶץ אֲשֶׁר אַתָּה בָא שָׁמָּה", הָתָם נַמִּי דַּוְקָא בָּאָרֶץ:

(יט) וּבָחַרְתָּ בַּחַיִּים. "בַּחַיִּים" עוֹלֶה שִׁבְעִים. לוֹמַר שֶׁבְּשִׁבְעִים פָּנִים הַתּוֹרָה נִדְרֶשֶׁת בָּהֶם; וְכֵן "סוֹד ה׳ לִירֵאָיו", וְחַיֵּי הָאָדָם שִׁבְעִים שָׁנָה:

BAAL HATURIM ELUCIDATED

diaspora.[44] Just as our verse states, [*God*] *will bless you . . . in the land to which you come,* so, too, in that verse, [the blessings granted for the fulfillment] pertain only to *Eretz Yisrael.*[45]

44. See *Arachin* 29a; cf. *Rosh Hashanah* 9b, *Kiddushin* 38b.

45. *Maharam MiRothenburg.*

come, to possess it. ¹⁷ But if your heart will stray and you will not listen, and you are led astray, and you prostrate yourself to other gods and serve them, ¹⁸ I tell you today that you will surely be lost; you will not lengthen your days upon the land that you cross the Jordan to come there, to possess it. ¹⁹ I call heaven and earth today to bear witness against you: Life and death I have placed before you, blessing and curse; and you shall choose life, so that you will live, you and your offspring — ²⁰ to love HASHEM, your God, to listen to His voice and to cleave to Him, for He is your life and the length of your days, to dwell upon the land that HASHEM swore to your forefathers, to Abraham, to Isaac and to Jacob, to give them.

──────────── BAAL HATURIM ELUCIDATED ────────────

19. וּבָחַרְתָּ בַּחַיִּים — AND YOU SHALL CHOOSE LIFE. The *gematria* of בַּחַיִּים is 70, to indicate that there are seventy facets by which the Torah[46] may be expounded.[47] Similarly, [the *gematria* of סוֹד, *counsel,* in the verse,] סוֹד ה׳ לִירֵאָיו, *The counsel of* HASHEM *is to those who fear Him* (Psalms 25:14), [is 70]. And the life span of a person is seventy years (see *Psalms* 90:10).[47]

───────────────────────────────

46. In his comments to verses 14 and 15 above, the Baal HaTurim adduces two verses that equate חַיִּים, *life,* with תּוֹרָה, *Torah.*

There is another allusion to Torah in the phrase וּבָחַרְתָּ בַּחַיִּים, for the *gematria* of וּבָחַרְתָּ is 616, equal to that of הַתּוֹרָה, *the Torah* (VeChur LaZahav).

47. *Peirush HaRokeach.*

פרשת וילך
Parashas Vayeilech

א וַיֵּלֶךְ מֹשֶׁה וַיְדַבֵּר אֶת־הַדְּבָרִים הָאֵלֶּה אֶל־
ב כָּל־יִשְׂרָאֵל: וַיֹּאמֶר אֲלֵהֶם בֶּן־מֵאָה וְעֶשְׂרִים
שָׁנָה אָנֹכִי הַיּוֹם לֹא־אוּכַל עוֹד לָצֵאת וְלָבוֹא
וַיהוה אָמַר אֵלַי לֹא תַעֲבֹר אֶת־הַיַּרְדֵּן הַזֶּה:

בעל הטורים

לא (א) בַּ״ג הַמֶּלֶךְ — פַּ״ת וַיֵּלֶךְ. פֵּרוּשׁ ב״ג הַמֶּלֶךְ, כְּשֶׁחָל רֹאשׁ הַשָּׁנָה יוֹם ב׳ אוֹ ג׳, אָז נִצָּבִים וַיֵּלֶךְ נִפְרָדִים:

❑ **וַיֵּלֶךְ מֹשֶׁה.** לְעֵיל מִנֵּהּ כְּתִיב ״לְאַבְרָהָם לְיִצְחָק וּלְיַעֲקֹב״ וּסְמִיךְ לֵהּ ״וַיֵּלֶךְ מֹשֶׁה״. שֶׁהָלַךְ אֲלֵיהֶם לְהַגִּיד לָהֶם כִּי קִיֵּם הַקָּדוֹשׁ בָּרוּךְ הוּא אֶת שְׁבוּעָתוֹ וְהִכְנִיס יִשְׂרָאֵל לָאָרֶץ. וְאִיתָא בַּמִּדְרָשׁ, מִכָּאן שֶׁהַמֵּתִים מְסַפְּרִים זֶה עִם זֶה:

(ב) וְלָבוֹא. מָלֵא וָי״ו — שֶׁלֹּא אוּכַל עוֹד לָבוֹא בְּשִׁשָּׁה סִדְרֵי מִשְׁנָה:

BAAL HATURIM ELUCIDATED

XXXI.

1. [In certain years, the two *parashiyos Nitzavim* and *Vayeilech* are read on the same Sabbath; in other years they are read on different weeks.[1] There is a mne-

1. Into how many weekly readings must the Torah be divided if we are to complete the public Torah reading each year? Let us first consider the maximum possible number of readings in any given year. The number of days in the Jewish common year varies between 353, 354 and 355 days, while the Jewish leap year contains either 383, 384 or 385 days. Accordingly, each common year will have either fifty or fifty-one *Shabbasos* [Sabbaths] (354 days ÷ 7 = 50 weeks and 4 days) and each leap year will have fifty-four or fifty-five (384 days ÷ 7 = 54 weeks and 6 days). Of those *Shabbasos,* we must deduct at least two, for during the weeks of Pesach and Succos, the *Shabbos* portion gives way to a Torah passage that speaks of the festivals. Thus, the greatest number of *Shabbos* portions needed in any given year is fifty-three. But, since the last portion of the annual Torah-reading cycle is always read on Simchas Torah [in *Eretz Yisrael,* on Shemini Atzeres], one more portion is needed, bringing the maximum number to fifty-four portions, and the Torah is therefore divided into precisely that number of *sidros.*

Let us now consider the minimum number of portions to be read in any given year. With regard to the weekly Torah portions, the year starts on *Shabbas Bereishis,* the first Sabbath after Succos, and ends with Simchas Torah, when the last portion of the Torah is read. It is possible for as many as five festival days of such a year to fall on *Shabbos.* As an example, let us examine the year beginning *Shabbas Bereishis* of 5766 (2006) and ending on Simchas Torah 5767 (2007). During that year, (i) the third day of Pesach, (ii) the second day of Shavuos, (iii) the first day of Rosh Hashanah, (iv) the first day of Succos, and (v) Shemini Atzeres will all fall on the Sabbath. Whereas such a year would necessarily contain 51 *Shabbosos,* the least number of weekly portions would be forty-six, and with Simchas Torah added, forty-seven. Now, in order to complete each year's Torah reading with less than fifty-four reading dates, we must sometimes read two portions on each of the same *Shabbos.* Thus, in a year when the minimum of forty-seven portions are needed, we will read a double portion on seven *Shabbasos.* They are: (i) *Vayakhel* and *Pekudei;* (ii) *Tazria* and *Metzora;* (iii) *Acharei* and *Kedoshim;* (iv) *Behar* and *Bechukosai;* (v) *Chukas* and *Balak;* (vi) *Mattos* and *Masei;* and (vii) *Nitzavim* and *Vayeilech.*

It is noteworthy that the double portion *Mattos-Masei* contains 244 verses, making it the longest reading of the year. *Nitzavim* and *Vayeilech,* on the other hand, have a combined total of only 70 verses. Accordingly, we may ask: Why are *Mattos* and *Masei* combined in years when there is a *Shabbos* between Yom Kippur and Succos, yet *Nitzavim* is read on the Sabbath before Rosh Hashanah and *Vayeilech* on the Sabbath after? This is done in order to place *Nitzavim* as a buffer between the graphic descriptions of the punishments of the *tocheichah* [admonition and curse] in *Ki Savo* on the one hand and the day of Rosh Hashanah on the other. Similarly, the portion of *Bamidbar* is always read on the Sabbath before

1 Moses went and spoke these words to all of Israel. 2 He said to them, "I am a hundred and twenty years old today; I am no longer able to go out and to come in, for HASHEM has said to me, 'You shall not cross this Jordan.'

BAAL HATURIM ELUCIDATED

monic that tells us whether they are read together or separately in any given year,] בַּג הַמֶּלֶךְ פַּת וַיֵּלֶךְ[2] when [the first day of] Rosh Hashanah [the day of] the King, falls on ב״ג, the second or third [day of the week],[3] separate VaYeilech[4] [from Nitzavim].[5]

❑ וַיֵּלֶךְ מֹשֶׁה — MOSES WENT. Prior to this is written, לְאַבְרָהָם לְיִצְחָק וּלְיַעֲקֹב, *to Abraham, to Isaac and to Jacob* (30:20) and juxtaposed to that is וַיֵּלֶךְ מֹשֶׁה, *Moses went.* For Moses went to them[5a] and told them that the Holy One, Blessed is He, fulfilled His oath, and brought the Jewish people into the Land [of Israel]. And the Midrash states: Here [we have proof] that the dead speak to each other.[6]

2. וְלָבוֹא — AND TO COME IN. This word is spelled in full,[6a] with a ו (= 6), [to indicate] that [Moses meant], "I am no longer able to come into [the depths of understanding of] the Six Orders of the Mishnah."[7]

---

the festival of Shavuos, in order to separate the *tocheichah* of *Bechukosai* from the celebration of the day on which the Torah was given to Israel (*Tosafos* to *Megillah* 31b, s.v., קללות).

2. The mnemonic is based on the phrase פַּת בַּג הַמֶּלֶךְ, *portion of the king's food* (*Daniel* 1:5,8,13, 15). Accordingly, the literal meaning of the mnemonic would be: בַּג הַמֶּלֶךְ, *The king's food,* פַּת, *a [serving] portion;* וַיֵּלֶךְ, *and he went.*

3. The letters of the term בַּג, *food,* are interpreted as numbers [ב = 2; ג = 3] and refer to the second and third days of the week, i.e., Monday and Tuesday. While the term הַמֶּלֶךְ, *the King,* refers to Rosh Hashanah, the day on which we declare God's kingship by changing the expression הָאֵל הַקָּדוֹשׁ, *the holy God* (in the third blessing of the *Amidah*), to הַמֶּלֶךְ הַקָּדוֹשׁ, *the holy King,* and by beginning the *Shacharis* service with the word הַמֶּלֶךְ. Thus, בַּג הַמֶּלֶךְ means, *When [the first day of] Rosh Hashanah falls on Monday or Tuesday . . .*

4. The term פַּת is related to פָּתוֹת in the phrase, פָּתוֹת אֹתָהּ פִּתִּים, *You shall break it* [the loaf] *into pieces* (*Leviticus* 2:6), and implies breaking in two or separating two things from one another. Thus, פַּת וַיֵּלֶךְ, *separate Vayeilech [from Nitzavim]* (*Magen Avraham* 428).

5. The Baal HaTurim cites this mnemonic again in *Tur Orach Chaim* 428, where he continues: But when [the first day of] Rosh Hashanah falls on Thursday or *Shabbos,* then . . . *Vayeilech* is read together with *Nitzavim.* [Note that the principles used in formulating the calendar do not allow the first day of Rosh Hashanah to fall on Sunday, Wednesday or Friday.]

5a. That is, the juxtaposed phrases may be rearranged and expounded upon: After he died, וַיֵּלֶךְ מֹשֶׁה, *Moses went,* לְאַבְרָהָם לְיִצְחָק וּלְיַעֲקֹב, *to Abraham, to Isaac and to Jacob,* וַיְדַבֵּר אֶת הַדְּבָרִים הָאֵלֶּה, *and he spoke these words* to them. Thus, the Sages find proof that the dead speak to each other (*VeChur LaZahav*).

6. The Baal HaTurim's Midrashic source is unknown. However, the Talmud cites 34:4 below [a verse that resembles 30:20, in that both speak of the Land of Israel as the land God swore to give to Abraham, Isaac and Jacob], as proof that the dead speak to each other (*Berachos* 18b). The Midrash (*Vayikra Rabbah* 25:4) expounds in a similar vein on the verse, *I did great deeds for myself; I built houses for myself* (*Ecclesiastes* 2:4), but does not mention our verse.

6a. The term appears fourteen times in the Torah: nine times spelled in full, לָבוֹא, with a ו (*Genesis* 12:11, 15:12, 19:31, 31:18, 35:16, 41:54; *Exodus* 40:35; *Deuteronomy* 4:34 and 30:18) and five times spelled defectively, לָבֹא, without a ו (*Genesis* 48:7; *Exodus* 12:23; *Deuteronomy* 9:1, 11:31, and 20:19). It appears an additional 65 times in the rest of the *Tanach* with the full spelling and twice with the defective spelling. With the prefix -וְ, it appears once in the Torah (here) and three other times in the rest of the *Tanach,* all spelled in full. The Baal HaTurim does not comment on any other appearance of the words (וְ)לָבוֹא and לָבֹא.

7. *Peirush HaRokeach.* See *Sotah* 13b (cited by

לא/ג־יא

ג יְהוָה אֱלֹהֶיךָ הוּא ׀ עֹבֵר לְפָנֶיךָ הוּא־יַשְׁמִיד אֶת־
הַגּוֹיִם הָאֵלֶּה מִלְּפָנֶיךָ וִירִשְׁתָּם יְהוֹשֻׁעַ הוּא עֹבֵר
שני ד לְפָנֶיךָ כַּאֲשֶׁר דִּבֶּר יהוה: וְעָשָׂה יהוה לָהֶם כַּאֲשֶׁר
עָשָׂה לְסִיחוֹן וּלְעוֹג מַלְכֵי הָאֱמֹרִי וּלְאַרְצָם אֲשֶׁר
ה הִשְׁמִיד אֹתָם: וּנְתָנָם יהוה לִפְנֵיכֶם וַעֲשִׂיתֶם לָהֶם
ו כְּכָל־הַמִּצְוָה אֲשֶׁר צִוִּיתִי אֶתְכֶם: חִזְקוּ וְאִמְצוּ אַל־
תִּירְאוּ וְאַל־תַּעַרְצוּ מִפְּנֵיהֶם כִּי ׀ יהוה אֱלֹהֶיךָ הוּא
שלישי [חמישי] ז הַהֹלֵךְ עִמָּךְ לֹא יַרְפְּךָ וְלֹא יַעַזְבֶךָּ: וַיִּקְרָא
מֹשֶׁה לִיהוֹשֻׁעַ וַיֹּאמֶר אֵלָיו לְעֵינֵי כָל־יִשְׂרָאֵל חֲזַק
וֶאֱמָץ כִּי אַתָּה תָּבוֹא אֶת־הָעָם הַזֶּה אֶל־הָאָרֶץ
אֲשֶׁר נִשְׁבַּע יהוה לַאֲבֹתָם לָתֵת לָהֶם וְאַתָּה
ח תַּנְחִילֶנָּה אוֹתָם: וַיהוה הוּא ׀ הַהֹלֵךְ לְפָנֶיךָ הוּא
יִהְיֶה עִמָּךְ לֹא יַרְפְּךָ וְלֹא יַעַזְבֶךָּ לֹא תִירָא וְלֹא
ט תֵחָת: וַיִּכְתֹּב מֹשֶׁה אֶת־הַתּוֹרָה הַזֹּאת וַיִּתְּנָהּ
אֶל־הַכֹּהֲנִים בְּנֵי לֵוִי הַנֹּשְׂאִים אֶת־אֲרוֹן בְּרִית
רביעי י יהוה וְאֶל־כָּל־זִקְנֵי יִשְׂרָאֵל: וַיְצַו מֹשֶׁה אוֹתָם
לֵאמֹר מִקֵּץ ׀ שֶׁבַע שָׁנִים בְּמֹעֵד שְׁנַת הַשְּׁמִטָּה בְּחַג
יא הַסֻּכּוֹת: בְּבוֹא כָל־יִשְׂרָאֵל לֵרָאוֹת אֶת־פְּנֵי יהוה

בעל הטורים

(ג) ה' אֱלֹהֶיךָ הוּא עֹבֵר לְפָנֶיךָ. הַפָּסוּק מַתְחִיל וּמְסַיֵּם בי"י — לוֹמַר שֶׁהַקָּדוֹשׁ בָּרוּךְ הוּא הוֹלֵךְ לִפְנֵי יִשְׂרָאֵל וּלְאַחֲרֵיהֶם. וְכֵן כְּתִיב "כִּי הֹלֵךְ לִפְנֵיכֶם ה' וּמְאַסִּפְכֶם אֱלֹהֵי יִשְׂרָאֵל":

(יא) בְּבוֹא כָל יִשְׂרָאֵל. מָלֵא וָי"ו — כִּי שִׁשָּׁה הָיוּ בָאִים, כֹּהֲנִים זְקֵנִים אֲנָשִׁים נָשִׁים וְטַף וְגֵרְךָ:

BAAL HATURIM ELUCIDATED

3. ה' אֱלֹהֶיךָ הוּא עֹבֵר לְפָנֶיךָ — HASHEM, YOUR GOD — HE WILL CROSS OVER BEFORE YOU. This verse begins with the Tetragrammaton and concludes with the Tetragrammaton.[8] [This is] to indicate that the Holy One, Blessed is He, travels in front of

---

Rashi), where the Talmud interprets the phrase לָצֵאת וְלָבוֹא, *to go out and to come in,* as a reference to familiarity with the gateways of wisdom. The Baal HaTurim here explains that "the gateways of wisdom" are the Six Orders of the Mishnah.

8. The text follows the early printed editions. Most later printed editions replaced the abbreviated form בי"י with either בה' or בשם; nevertheless, all three versions refer to the Tetragrammaton which appears as the first and last words of the verse. Unfortunately, a typographical error has crept into some recent editions, which read בה"א, *with the letter* ה, in place of בה', *with* HASHEM.

³ *HASHEM, your God — He will cross over before you;*
He will destroy these nations from before you, and you
shall possess them; Joshua — he shall cross over be-
fore you, as HASHEM has spoken. ⁴ *HASHEM will do to them*
as He did to Sihon and Og, the kings of the Amorite,
and their land, which He destroyed, ⁵ *and HASHEM gave*
them before you; and you shall do to them according to
the entire commandment that I have commanded you.
⁶ *Be strong and courageous, do not be afraid and do not*
be broken before them, for HASHEM, your God — it is He
Who goes before you, He will not release you nor will He
forsake you."

⁷ *Moses summoned Joshua and said to him before the*
eyes of all Israel, "Be strong and courageous, for you shall
come with this people to the land that HASHEM swore to their
forefathers to give them, and you shall cause them to inherit
it. ⁸ *HASHEM — it is He Who goes before you; He will be with*
you; He will not release you nor will He forsake you; do not
be afraid and do not be dismayed."

⁹ *Moses wrote this Torah and gave it to the Kohanim, the*
sons of Levi, the bearers of the Ark of the covenant of
HASHEM, and to all the elders of Israel.

¹⁰ *Moses commanded them, saying, "At the end of seven*
years, at the time of the Sabbatical year, during the Succos
festival, ¹¹ *when all Israel comes to appear before HASHEM,*

BAAL HATURIM ELUCIDATED

Israel and follows after them, and thus is written, כִּי הֹלֵךְ לִפְנֵיכֶם ה׳ וּמְאַסִּפְכֶם אֱלֹהֵי יִשְׂרָאֵל, *For HASHEM will travel before you; and the God of Israel will be your rear guard* (*Isaiah* 52:12).

11. בְּבוֹא כָל יִשְׂרָאֵל — WHEN ALL ISRAEL COMES. The word בְּבוֹא is spelled in full,[8a] with a ו (= 6). [This is an indication] that there are six groups of people who would be coming: *Kohanim,*[9] elders,[10] men, women and youngsters, and your convert.[11]

8a. The term appears three times in the Torah: twice spelled in full, בְּבוֹא, with a ו (*Genesis* 42:15 and here), and once spelled defectively, בְּבֹא, without a ו (*Numbers* 33:40). It appears another thirteen times in the rest of the Tanach: six times with the full spelling and seven times with the defective spelling. The Baal HaTurim comments on the full spelling both here and at *Genesis* 42:15.

9. As stated in verse 9 above: הַכֹּהֲנִים בְּנֵי לֵוִי, *the Kohanim [who are] sons of Levi.*

10. As stated in verse 9 above: כָּל זִקְנֵי יִשְׂרָאֵל, *all the elders of Israel.*

11. As stated in verse 12 below: הָאֲנָשִׁים וְהַנָּשִׁים וְהַטַּף וְגֵרְךָ, *the men and the women and the youngsters and your convert.*

אֱלֹהֶיךָ בַּמָּקוֹם אֲשֶׁר־יִבְחַר תִּקְרָא אֶת־הַתּוֹרָה
הַזֹּאת נֶגֶד כָּל־יִשְׂרָאֵל בְּאׇזְנֵיהֶם: הַקְהֵל אֶת־הָעָם
הָאֲנָשִׁים וְהַנָּשִׁים וְהַטַּף וְגֵרְךָ אֲשֶׁר בִּשְׁעָרֶיךָ לְמַעַן
יִשְׁמְעוּ וּלְמַעַן יִלְמְדוּ וְיָרְאוּ אֶת־יהוה אֱלֹהֵיכֶם
וְשָׁמְרוּ לַעֲשׂוֹת אֶת־כָּל־דִּבְרֵי הַתּוֹרָה הַזֹּאת: וּבְנֵיהֶם
אֲשֶׁר לֹא־יָדְעוּ יִשְׁמְעוּ וְלָמְדוּ לְיִרְאָה אֶת־יהוה
אֱלֹהֵיכֶם כָּל־הַיָּמִים אֲשֶׁר אַתֶּם חַיִּים עַל־הָאֲדָמָה
אֲשֶׁר אַתֶּם עֹבְרִים אֶת־הַיַּרְדֵּן שָׁמָּה לְרִשְׁתָּהּ:
וַיֹּאמֶר יהוה אֶל־מֹשֶׁה הֵן קָרְבוּ יָמֶיךָ לָמוּת
קְרָא אֶת־יְהוֹשֻׁעַ וְהִתְיַצְּבוּ בְּאֹהֶל מוֹעֵד וַאֲצַוֶּנּוּ
וַיֵּלֶךְ מֹשֶׁה וִיהוֹשֻׁעַ וַיִּתְיַצְּבוּ בְּאֹהֶל מוֹעֵד: וַיֵּרָא
יהוה בָּאֹהֶל בְּעַמּוּד עָנָן וַיַּעֲמֹד עַמּוּד הֶעָנָן עַל־
פֶּתַח הָאֹהֶל: וַיֹּאמֶר יהוה אֶל־מֹשֶׁה הִנְּךָ שֹׁכֵב
עִם־אֲבֹתֶיךָ וְקָם הָעָם הַזֶּה וְזָנָה | אַחֲרֵי | אֱלֹהֵי

חמישי [ששי] יד

בעל הטורים

(יב) **הָעָם הָאֲנָשִׁים.** בְּגִימַטְרִיָּא זֶה שֶׁהֵם בָּאִים לִלְמוֹד:

(יד) **הֵן קָרְבוּ יָמֶיךָ לָמוּת.** אָמַר מֹשֶׁה רַבֵּנוּ עָלָיו הַשָּׁלוֹם, רִבּוֹנוֹ שֶׁל עוֹלָם, בְּזֶה הַלָּשׁוֹן
שֶׁבַּחְתִּיךָ, שֶׁאָמַרְתִּי "הֵן לַה׳ אֱלֹהֶיךָ הַשָּׁמַיִם", וּבְדֶרֶךְ זֶה אַתָּה מְבַשְּׂרֵנִי לָמוּת? אָמַר לוֹ
הַקָּדוֹשׁ בָּרוּךְ הוּא, וְכִי לֹא אָמַרְתָּ "וְהֵן לֹא יַאֲמִינוּ לִי"? וְכֵן כְּתִיב "יַעַן לֹא הֶאֱמַנְתֶּם בִּי":
(טז) **וְקָם הָעָם.** תָּגִין עַל הַקּוּ״ף — לוֹמַר שֶׁיִּמָּאֲסוּ בְּמֵאָה בְּרָכוֹת, וּבְבִנְיָן שֶׁל שְׁלֹמֹה, שֶׁהָיָה
הַהֵיכָל מֵאָה אַמָּה:

❑ **הָעָם הַזֶּה וְזָנָה אַחֲרֵי.** בְּגִימַטְרִיָּא זֶה הוּא מְנַשֶּׁה:

BAAL HATURIM ELUCIDATED

12. הָעָם הָאֲנָשִׁים — THE PEOPLE — THE MEN. The *gematria* of this phrase (521) is
equivalent[12] to that of זֶה שֶׁהֵם בָּאִים לִלְמוֹד, *This [refers to] those coming to study.* [13]

❑ {The Baal HaTurim's comment to וְיָרְאוּ appears at 28:10 above.}

14. הֵן קָרְבוּ יָמֶיךָ לָמוּת — BEHOLD, YOUR DAYS ARE DRAWING NEAR TO DIE. Moses our
teacher, peace unto him, said [to God], "Master of the Universe, with this very
expression [הֵן] I have praised You, for I have said, 'הֵן לַה׳ אֱלֹהֶיךָ הַשָּׁמַיִם, *Behold! To
HASHEM, your God, are the heavens* (10:14 above)'; how can You use this same

---

12. The principle of *im hakollel* allows 520, the
gematria of the Baal HaTurim's phrase, to be
considered equivalent to 521.

13. *Chagigah* 3a (cited by *Rashi*) — *Gather
together the people — the men and the women and*

*the children . . . If the men come, it is to study [as
the verse states: וּלְמַעַן יִלְמְדוּ, so that they will
study], and [if] the women come, it is to hear [as
the verse states: לְמַעַן יִשְׁמְעוּ, so that they will hear].
But why do the youngsters come? In order to
reward those who bring them.*

31/12-16 *your God, in the place that He will choose, you shall read this Torah before all Israel, in their ears,* [12] *Gather together the people — the men and the women and the youngsters and your convert who is in your cities — so that they will hear and so that they will study, and they shall fear HASHEM, your God, and be careful to perform all the words of this Torah.* [13] *And their children who do not know — they shall hear and they shall learn to fear HASHEM, your God, all the days that you live on the land to which you are crossing the Jordan, to possess it."*

[14] *HASHEM spoke to Moses, "Behold, your days are drawing near to die; summon Joshua, and both of you shall stand in the Tent of Meeting, and I shall instruct him." So Moses and Joshua went and stood in the Tent of Meeting.*

[15] *HASHEM appeared in the Tent, in a pillar of cloud, and the pillar of cloud stood by the entrance of the Tent.* [16] *HASHEM said to Moses, "Behold, you will lie with your forefathers, but this people will rise up and stray after the gods of*

────────────── BAAL HATURIM ELUCIDATED ──────────────

expression to inform me that I must die?" The Holy One, Blessed is He, answered him, "Did you not also say, וְהֵן לֹא יַאֲמִינוּ לִי, *But, behold, they will not believe me (Exodus 4:1)*?" And similarly it is written, יַעַן לֹא הֶאֱמַנְתֶּם בִּי, *Because you did not believe in Me . . . (Numbers 20:12).*[14]

16. וְקָם הָעָם — BUT [THIS] PEOPLE WILL RISE UP. [According to a scribal tradition,] the ק (= 100) of this phrase is written with [three] *tagin*[15] (crownlets). [This is] to indicate that the people will find repugnant the one hundred blessings[16] and King Solomon's edifice, whose Temple measured one hundred[17] cubits.[17a]

❏ הָעָם הַזֶּה וְזָנָה אַחֲרֵי — **THIS PEOPLE ... AND STRAY AFTER.** The *gematria* of this

---
14. *Tanchuma 3; Shabbos 97a.*

15. See note 43 to *parashas Vaeschanan* above. The word וְקָם of our verse appears on the list in *Sefer Tagin.*

16. See note 44 to *parashas Vaeschanan* above.

17. The Baal HaTurim's comment is problematic. Scripture gives the dimensions of King Solomon's Temple as sixty cubits long and twenty cubits wide (see *I Kings* 6:2 and *II Chronicles* 3:3). Regarding its height, the verse in *Kings* states that it was thirty cubits; while the verse in *Chronicles* (v. 4) gives the number one hundred and twenty cubits. Some commentaries reconcile the verses with regard to the height: The actual building was one hundred and twenty cubits tall. However, the ceiling in the *Heichal* (Temple) and *Devir* (Holy of Holies) was thirty cubits above the floor, with ninety cubits of upper stories above them (*Rashi* to *Chronicles;*

Radak to *Kings*). Alternatively: The height of one hundred and twenty cubits refers to the אוּלָם, *Ulam* (Entry Hall), but the Temple itself was only thirty cubits tall (*Radak*). But in neither of these two explanations do we find any dimension of one hundred cubits.

Mahari Kara (to *Kings*) reconciles the numbers in another way: [The height of the *Ulam* was one hundred and twenty cubits as stated in *Chronicles.*] The ceiling of the *Heichal* and *Devir* was thirty cubits as stated in *Kings*. But, there were seventy cubits of upper stories above them. "For I have received a tradition from [my uncle and teacher] Rabbi Menachem ben Chelbo the Elder, that the height of the Temple [building] was one hundred cubits." Presumably, it is that tradition to which the Baal HaTurim refers (*VeChur LaZahav*).

17a. *Peirush HaRokeach.*

נֵֽכַר־הָאָ֗רֶץ אֲשֶׁ֨ר ה֤וּא בָא־שָׁ֙מָּה֙ בְּקִרְבּ֔וֹ וַעֲזָבַ֕נִי
יז וְהֵפֵר֙ אֶת־בְּרִיתִ֔י אֲשֶׁ֥ר כָּרַ֖תִּי אִתּֽוֹ׃ וְחָרָ֣ה אַפִּ֣י ב֣וֹ
בַיּוֹם־הַ֠הוּא וַעֲזַבְתִּ֞ים וְהִסְתַּרְתִּ֨י פָנַ֤י מֵהֶם֙ וְהָיָ֣ה
לֶֽאֱכֹ֔ל וּמְצָאֻ֛הוּ רָע֥וֹת רַבּ֖וֹת וְצָר֑וֹת וְאָמַר֙ בַּיּ֣וֹם
הַה֔וּא הֲלֹ֗א עַ֣ל כִּי־אֵ֤ין אֱלֹהַי֙ בְּקִרְבִּ֔י מְצָא֖וּנִי
יח הָרָע֥וֹת הָאֵֽלֶּה׃ וְאָנֹכִ֗י הַסְתֵּ֨ר אַסְתִּ֤יר פָּנַי֙ בַּיּ֣וֹם
הַה֔וּא עַ֥ל כָּל־הָרָעָ֖ה אֲשֶׁ֣ר עָשָׂ֑ה כִּ֣י פָנָ֔ה אֶל־
יט אֱלֹהִ֖ים אֲחֵרִֽים׃ וְעַתָּ֗ה כִּתְב֤וּ לָכֶם֙ אֶת־הַשִּׁירָ֣ה
הַזֹּ֔את וְלַמְּדָ֥הּ אֶת־בְּנֵֽי־יִשְׂרָאֵ֖ל שִׂימָ֣הּ בְּפִיהֶ֑ם
לְמַ֨עַן תִּֽהְיֶה־לִּ֜י הַשִּׁירָ֥ה הַזֹּ֛את לְעֵ֖ד בִּבְנֵ֥י
ששי [שביעי] כ יִשְׂרָאֵֽל׃ כִּֽי־אֲבִיאֶ֨נּוּ אֶל־הָאֲדָמָ֣ה ׀ אֲשֶׁר־נִשְׁבַּ֣עְתִּי

בעל הטורים

(יז) וְהִסְתַּרְתִּי פָנַי מֵהֶם וְהָיָה לֶאֱכֹל. סוֹפֵי תֵבוֹת בְּגִימַטְרִיָּא "הָמָן". וְזֶהוּ שֶׁדָּרְשׁוּ בְּחֻלִּין, "וְאָנֹכִי הַסְתֵּר אַסְתִּיר" רֶמֶז לְאֶסְתֵּר:

❑ **וּמְצָאֻהוּ.** חָסֵר וָי"ו – לוֹמַר שֶׁשֵּׁשׁ פְּעָמִים גָּלוּ, שָׁלֹשׁ עַל יְדֵי סַנְחֵרִיב וְשָׁלֹשׁ עַל יְדֵי נְבוּזַרְאֲדָן:

❑ **הָרָעוֹת הָאֵלֶּה.** בְּגִימַטְרִיָּא אַרְבַּע גָּלֻיּוֹת:

(יט) וְלַמְּדָהּ אֶת בְּנֵי יִשְׂרָאֵל. בְּגִימַטְרִיָּא הֵן תּוֹרָה בִּכְתָב:

❑ **שִׂימָהּ בְּפִיהֶם.** בְּגִימַטְרִיָּא זֶה תַּלְמוּד:

BAAL HATURIM ELUCIDATED

phrase (419) is equal to that of זֶה הוּא מְנַשֶּׁה, *This is* [*a reference to*] *Manasseh.*[18]

17. וְהִסְתַּרְתִּי פָנַי מֵהֶם וְהָיָה לֶאֱכֹל — AND I WILL CONCEAL MY FACE FROM THEM AND THEY WILL BECOME PREY. The *gematria* of the final letters of these words (95) is equal to that of the name הָמָן, *Haman.* This is in accordance with what our Sages have expounded in tractate *Chullin*:[19] The phrase, וְאָנֹכִי הַסְתֵּר אַסְתִּיר, *but I will surely*

18. *Peirush HaRokeach.* King Manasseh was a fourteenth-generation descendant of King David. He was an idolater, one of three kings, each of whom forfeited his portion in the World to Come (see the Baal HaTurim to 29:21 above, with notes 9 and 11.

19. *Chullin* 139b. The Talmud asks: Where in the Torah do we find an allusion to Haman? In the verse, הֲמִן הָעֵץ [אֲשֶׁר צִוִּיתִיךָ לְבִלְתִּי אֲכָל מִמֶּנּוּ אָכָלְתָּ], *Have* [*you eaten*] *from the tree* [*from which I commanded you not to eat*]? [The letters of הֲמִן are understood as if they were vowelized הָמָן, *Haman,* and הָעֵץ, *the tree,* is interpreted as it is used in *Megillas Esther* to mean *the gallows.* Thus, the verse alludes to Haman on the gallows (*Rashi*).] Where in the Torah do we find an allusion to Esther? In the verse, וְאָנֹכִי הַסְתֵּר אַסְתִּיר, *But I will surely conceal [My face].* [The word אַסְתִּיר, *I will hide,* resembles the name אֶסְתֵּר, *Esther,* and alludes to God concealing His protective Presence from the Jews, allowing them to be overtaken by woe and affliction (see *Rashi*).]

The Baal HaTurim finds another allusion to Haman, in the verse juxtaposed to the one cited by the Talmud as an allusion to Esther.

31/17-20 *the foreigners of the land, in whose midst it is coming, and it will forsake Me and annul My covenant that I have sealed with it.* [17] *My anger will flare against it on that day and I will forsake them; and I will conceal My face from them and they will become prey, and many evils and distresses will encounter it. It will say on that day, 'Is it not because my God is not in my midst that these evils have come upon me?'* [18] *But I will surely have concealed My face on that day because of all the evil that it did, for it had turned to other gods.* [19] *So now, write this song for yourselves, and teach it to the Children of Israel, place it in their mouth, so that this song shall be for Me a witness against the Children of Israel.*

[20] *"For I shall bring them to the land that I swore to their*

BAAL HATURIM ELUCIDATED

have concealed (v. 18 below), is an allusion to [Queen] Esther.[20]

❑ וּמְצָאֻהוּ — WILL ENCOUNTER IT. This word is spelled defectively, without a ו (= 6) after the א.[20a] [This is] to indicate that Israel was exiled six times:[21] three times by Sennacherib, and three times by Nebuzaradan.[22]

❑ הָרָעוֹת הָאֵלֶּה — THESE EVILS. The *gematria* of this phrase (722) is equal to that of אַרְבַּע גָּלֻיּוֹת, *four exiles.* [23]

19. וְלַמְּדָהּ אֶת בְּנֵי יִשְׂרָאֵל — AND TEACH IT TO THE CHILDREN OF ISRAEL. The *gematria* of this phrase (1089) is equivalent[23a] to that of the phrase הֵן תּוֹרָה בִּכְתָב, *Behold, the Written Torah.* [24]

❑ שִׂימָהּ בְּפִיהֶם — PLACE IT IN THEIR MOUTH. The *gematria* of this phrase (492) is equal to that of זֶה תַּלְמוּד, *This [refers to] the Talmud.* [25]

20. *Peirush HaRokeach.*

20a. The only other time that this word appears (that time without the prefix -וּ), it is also spelled defectively (*II Kings* 2:17). However, other similar forms of the verb מצא, *to encounter,* or *to find,* do contain a ו after the א (e.g., מְצָאוּנִי of our verse).

21. That is, the Assyrian/Babylonian exile came in six stages, as described in note 22 below.

22. See *Bamidbar Rabbah* 23:14 — You find that Sennacherib exiled the Northern Kingdom three times: The first time, he exiled Reuben, Gad and half of Manasseh; the second time, Zebulun and Naftali; and the third time, he exiled the remaining tribes. Nebuchadnezzar also exiled the tribes of Judah and Benjamin three times: The first time, he exiled Jehoiakim; the second time, Jehoiachin; and the third time, Nebuchadnezzar's general Nebuzaradan exiled Zedekiah.

The Baal HaTurim also speaks of the six exiles in his comments to *Leviticus* 26:30.

23. *Peirush HaRokeach;* see the Baal HaTurim to 4:27 above, with note 83.

23a. The principle of *im hakollel* allows 1090, the *gematria* of the Baal HaTurim's phrase, to be considered equivalent to 1089.

24. *Peirush HaRokeach;* see notes 97 and 131 to *parashas Eikev.*

25. *Peirush HaRokeach.* Thus, בְּפִיהֶם, *in their mouth,* alludes to the תּוֹרָה שֶׁבְּעַל פֶּה, *the oral Torah.*

לַאֲבֹתָ֗יו זָבַ֤ת חָלָב֙ וּדְבַ֔שׁ וְאָכַ֥ל וְשָׂבַ֖ע וְדָשֵׁ֑ן וּפָנָ֞ה
אֶל־אֱלֹהִ֤ים אֲחֵרִים֙ וַעֲבָד֔וּם וְנִ֣אֲצ֔וּנִי וְהֵפֵ֖ר אֶת־
כא בְּרִיתִֽי׃ וְהָיָה֩ כִּֽי־תִמְצֶ֨אןָ אֹת֜וֹ רָע֣וֹת רַבּוֹת֮ וְצָרוֹת֒
וְ֠עָנְתָה הַשִּׁירָ֨ה הַזֹּ֤את לְפָנָיו֙ לְעֵ֔ד כִּ֛י לֹ֥א תִשָּׁכַ֖ח
מִפִּ֣י זַרְע֑וֹ כִּ֧י יָדַ֣עְתִּי אֶת־יִצְר֗וֹ אֲשֶׁ֨ר ה֤וּא עֹשֶׂה֙ הַיּ֔וֹם
כב בְּטֶ֣רֶם אֲבִיאֶ֔נּוּ אֶל־הָאָ֖רֶץ אֲשֶׁ֥ר נִשְׁבָּֽעְתִּי׃ וַיִּכְתֹּ֥ב
מֹשֶׁ֛ה אֶת־הַשִּׁירָ֥ה הַזֹּ֖את בַּיּ֣וֹם הַה֑וּא וַֽיְלַמְּדָ֖הּ
כג אֶת־בְּנֵ֥י יִשְׂרָאֵֽל׃ וַיְצַ֞ו אֶת־יְהוֹשֻׁ֣עַ בִּן־נ֗וּן וַיֹּאמֶר֮
חֲזַ֣ק וֶאֱמָץ֒ כִּ֣י אַתָּ֗ה תָּבִיא֙ אֶת־בְּנֵ֣י יִשְׂרָאֵ֔ל אֶל־
כד הָאָ֖רֶץ אֲשֶׁר־נִשְׁבַּ֣עְתִּי לָהֶ֑ם וְאָנֹכִ֖י אֶהְיֶ֥ה עִמָּֽךְ׃
וַיְהִ֣י ׀ כְּכַלּ֣וֹת מֹשֶׁ֗ה לִכְתֹּ֛ב אֶת־דִּבְרֵ֥י הַתּוֹרָֽה־הַזֹּ֖את
שביעי כה עַל־סֵ֑פֶר עַ֖ד תֻּמָּֽם׃ וַיְצַ֤ו מֹשֶׁה֙ אֶת־הַלְוִיִּ֔ם נֹֽשְׂאֵ֕י
כו אֲר֥וֹן בְּרִית־יְהֹוָ֖ה לֵאמֹֽר׃ לָקֹ֗חַ אֵ֠ת סֵ֤פֶר הַתּוֹרָה֙
הַזֶּ֔ה וְשַׂמְתֶּ֣ם אֹת֔וֹ מִצַּ֛ד אֲר֥וֹן בְּרִית־יְהֹוָ֖ה אֱלֹהֵיכֶ֑ם
כז וְהָיָה־שָׁ֥ם בְּךָ֖ לְעֵֽד׃ כִּ֣י אָנֹכִ֤י יָדַ֙עְתִּי֙ אֶֽת־מֶרְיְךָ֔
וְאֶֽת־עָרְפְּךָ֖ הַקָּשֶׁ֑ה הֵ֣ן בְּעוֹדֶ֩נִּי֩ חַ֨י עִמָּכֶ֜ם הַיּ֗וֹם
מַמְרִ֤ים הֱיִתֶם֙ עִם־יְהֹוָ֔ה וְאַ֖ף כִּֽי־אַחֲרֵ֥י מוֹתִֽי׃
מפטיר כח הַקְהִ֤ילוּ אֵלַי֙ אֶת־כָּל־זִקְנֵ֥י שִׁבְטֵיכֶ֖ם וְשֹׁטְרֵיכֶ֑ם
וַאֲדַבְּרָ֣ה בְאָזְנֵיהֶ֗ם אֵ֚ת הַדְּבָרִ֣ים הָאֵ֔לֶּה *וְאָעִ֣ידָה בָּ֔ם
כט אֶת־הַשָּׁמַ֖יִם וְאֶת־הָאָֽרֶץ׃ כִּ֣י יָדַ֗עְתִּי אַחֲרֵ֤י מוֹתִי֙
כִּֽי־הַשְׁחֵ֣ת תַּשְׁחִת֔וּן וְסַרְתֶּ֣ם מִן־הַדֶּ֔רֶךְ אֲשֶׁ֥ר צִוִּ֖יתִי
אֶתְכֶ֑ם וְקָרָ֨את אֶתְכֶ֤ם הָֽרָעָה֙ בְּאַחֲרִ֣ית הַיָּמִ֔ים

* בראש עמוד ב״ה שמ״ו סימן

בעל הטורים

(כז) וְאַף כִּי אַחֲרֵי מוֹתִי. ״כִּי״ שָׁנִים אַחֲרֵי מוֹתִי. יְהוֹשֻׁעַ פִּרְנֵס אֶת יִשְׂרָאֵל כ״ח שָׁנִים, וּב׳ שָׁנִים הֶאֱרִיכוּ הַזְּקֵנִים:

(כט) הָרָעָה בְּאַחֲרִית הַיָּמִים. רָאשֵׁי תֵבוֹת עוֹלֶה בְּגִימַטְרִיָּא גּוֹג:

BAAL HATURIM ELUCIDATED

27. {The Baal HaTurim's comment to הַקָּשֶׁה appears at *Exodus* 18:26.}

❑ **וְאַף כִּי אַחֲרֵי מוֹתִי** — AND SURELY AFTER MY DEATH. [Moses said, "This will take place] כִּ״י, i.e., thirty,[26] years after my death." Joshua served as leader of Israel for twenty-

26. The *gematria* of כִּי is 30.

31/21-29 *forefathers, which flows with milk and honey, but it will eat, be sated, and grow fat, and turn to other gods and serve them, it will provoke Me and annul My covenant.* ²¹ *It shall be that when many evils and distresses come upon it, then this song shall speak up before it as a witness, for it shall not be forgotten from the mouth of its offspring, for I know its inclination, what it does today, before I bring them to the land that I have sworn."*

²² *Moses wrote this song on that day, and he taught it to the Children of Israel.* ²³ *He commanded Joshua son of Nun, and said, "Be strong and courageous, for you shall bring the Children of Israel to the land that I have sworn to them, and I shall be with you."*

²⁴ *So it was that when Moses completed writing the words of this Torah onto a scroll, until their conclusion:* ²⁵ *Moses commanded the Levites, the bearers of the Ark of the Covenant of HASHEM, saying,* ²⁶ *"Take this book of the Torah and place it at the side of the Ark of the Covenant of HASHEM, your God, and it shall be there for you as a witness.* ²⁷ *For I know your rebelliousness and your stiff neck; behold! while I am still alive with you today, you have been rebels against HASHEM —* *and surely after my death.* ²⁸ *Gather to me all the elders of your tribes and your officers, and I shall speak these words into their ears, and call heaven and earth to bear witness against them.* ²⁹ *For I know that after my death you will surely act corruptly, and you will stray from the path that I have commanded you, and the evil will befall you at the end of days,*

─────────────── BAAL HATURIM ELUCIDATED ───────────────

eight years, and then the elders [guided the nation] for another two[26a] years.[27]

28. {The Baal HaTurim's comment to וְאָעִידָה appears at *Genesis* 49:8.}

29. הָרָעָה בְּאַחֲרִית הַיָּמִים — **EVIL AT THE END OF DAYS.** The *gematria* of the initial letters of these words (12) is equal to that of גּוֹג, *Gog.* [28]

26a. And about that period Scripture states: *Israel served HASHEM all the days of Joshua and all the days of the elders who outlived Joshua* (*Joshua* 24:31; see also *Judges* 2:7). But about the generation that succeeded them, the prophet writes: *The Children of Israel did what is evil in the eyes of HASHEM; they worshiped the Baal idols* (*Judges* 2:11).

27. *Peirush HaRokeach*; see *Seder Olam* 12, cited by *Rashi* to *Judges* 11:26; see also the Baal

HaTurim to *Numbers* 27:16 and 4:24 above.

28. *Peirush HaRokeach*. Scripture tells of a war that will precede the Messianic era. That event is called מִלְחֶמֶת גּוֹג וּמָגוֹג, *the war of Gog and Magog,* because its chief villain will be Gog, the prince of Magog (see *Ezekiel,* Chs. 38 and 39). Although that war is not mentioned explicitly in the Five Books of the Torah, the Midrash and commentaries find many allusions to it in the verses of the Torah. Other places at which the Baal HaTurim

לא/ל כִּי־תַעֲשׂוּ אֶת־הָרַע בְּעֵינֵי יהוה לְהַכְעִיסוֹ
ל בְּמַעֲשֵׂה יְדֵיכֶם: וַיְדַבֵּר מֹשֶׁה בְּאָזְנֵי כָּל־קְהַל
יִשְׂרָאֵל אֶת־דִּבְרֵי הַשִּׁירָה הַזֹּאת עַד תֻּמָּם: פפפ

ע׳ פסוקים. אדני״ה סימן.

בעל הטורים

❑ **וְקָרָאת.** ד׳ בַּמָּסוֹרֶת – ״וְקָרָאת אֶתְכֶם הָרָעָה״; ״וְקָרָאת שְׁמוֹ יִשְׁמָעֵאל״; ״וְקָרָאת שְׁמוֹ עִמָּנוּאֵל״; ״וְקָרָאת יְשׁוּעָה חוֹמֹתַיִךְ״. כְּשֶׁתִּקְרָא אֶתְכֶם הָרָעָה, ״וְקָרָאת יִשְׁמָעֵאל״, שֶׁתִּתְפַּלֵּל לָאֵל שֶׁיִּשְׁמַע אֵלֶיךָ וְשֶׁיִּהְיֶה עִמָּנוּ, וְתָשׁוּב אֵלָיו בִּתְשׁוּבָה, אָז ״וְקָרָאת יְשׁוּעָה חוֹמֹתַיִךְ״:

BAAL HATURIM ELUCIDATED

❑ **וְקָרָאת** — WILL BEFALL. The masoretic note, ד׳, means that this word appears four times in the *Tanach*:[29] (i) here, וְקָרָאת אֶתְכֶם הָרָעָה, *and the evil will befall you;* (ii) וְקָרָאת שְׁמוֹ יִשְׁמָעֵאל, *you shall call his name Ishmael* (*Genesis* 16:11);[29a] (iii) וְקָרָאת

speaks of Gog and Magog are *Numbers* 10:8-9, s.v., לְדֹרֹתֵיכֶם וְכִי, and 33:4, s.v., מְקַבְּרִים.

29. The verb root usually means *to call* or *to read,* but sometimes appears as a synonym for *to befall* or *to occur.* Accordingly, the term וְקָרָאת can mean either *it will befall,* as it does in our verse, or *you shall call,* as it does in at least two of the other three verses adduced by the Baal HaTurim (see note 30).

29a. In his comment to that verse, the Baal HaTurim explains the masoretic note with a different twist.

if you do what is evil in the eyes of HASHEM, *to anger Him through your handiwork."*

30 *Moses spoke into the ears of the entire congregation of Israel, the words of this song until their conclusion.*

BAAL HATURIM ELUCIDATED

שְׁמוֹ עִמָּנוּאֵל, *you shall call his name Immanuel* (*Isaiah* 7:14); and (iv) וְקָרָאת יְשׁוּעָה חוֹמֹתַיִךְ, *salvation shall befall your walls*[30] (*Isaiah* 60:18). [The similarity of expression indicates to you] that when *the evil will befall you,* then *if you shall call, . . . "Ishmael,"*[31] i.e., you shall pray to God that He should hearken unto you, and that He be with us,[32] and if you turn to Him in repentance, then *salvation shall befall your walls.*

30. {The Baal HaTurim's comments to this verse appear at 32:1 below.}

30. The translation follows *Targum Yonasan ben Uzziel* which reads, ויַעַרְעוּן פּוּרְקָן עַל שׁוּרָךְ, *salvation will occur at your wall.* Others render: *you will call your wall Salvation* (*Radak*); and *you will call out with* [*praise of God's*] *salvation* [*upon*] *your walls* (*Metzudas David*).

31. The name יִשְׁמָעֵאל, *Ishmael,* implies כִּי שָׁמַע ה׳, *for* HASHEM *has heard* (*Genesis* 16:11), i.e., יִשְׁמָעֵאל is understood as two words יִשְׁמַע אֵל, *God will hear.* The Midrash states: And why was he named יִשְׁמָעֵאל? For in the future, the Holy One, blessed is He, will hear the sound of the nation's groaning from the troubles that Ishmael will inflict upon them (*Pirkei DeRabbi Eliezer* 32).

32. That is the implication of the name עִמָּנוּאֵל, *Immanuel,* literally, עִמָּנוּ אֵל, *God is with us* (see *Isaiah* 8:10). This also explains why the Baal HaTurim switches from the second person pronoun אֵלֶיךָ, *to you,* to the first person pronoun עִמָּנוּ, *with us.*

פרשת האזינו

Parashas Ha'azinu

לב/א א הַאֲזִינוּ הַשָּׁמַיִם וַאֲדַבֵּרָה וְתִשְׁמַע הָאָרֶץ אִמְרֵי־פִי׃

בעל הטורים

לב (א) הַאֲזִינוּ. לְעֵיל מִנֵּהּ כְּתִיב "אֵת דִּבְרֵי הַשִּׁירָה הַזֹּאת עַד תֻּמָּם", וּסְמִיךְ לֵהּ "הַאֲזִינוּ". כְּמוֹ שֶׁהֶאֱזַנְתֶּם וּשְׁמַעְתֶּם לְדִבְרֵי תוֹרָה, כֵּן הַאֲזִינוּ לְדִבְרֵי הַשִּׁירָה הַזֹּאת:

❑ כְּפִי הַפְּשָׁט "הַאֲזִינוּ הַשָּׁמַיִם" פֵּרוּשׁ, יוֹשְׁבֵי "עָרִים גְּדֹלֹת וּבְצֻרֹת בַּשָּׁמָיִם". "וְתִשְׁמַע הָאָרֶץ" יוֹשְׁבֵי הָאָרֶץ, פֵּרוּשׁ, יוֹשְׁבֵי כְּפָרִים וְעָרִים הַקְּטַנִּים:

❑ **הַשָּׁמַיִם וַאֲדַבֵּרָה.** עוֹלֶה תרי"ג – כְּלוֹמַר, הַאֲזִינוּ לְתרי"ג מִצְוֹת:

❑ הַפָּסוּק מַתְחִיל בְּהֵ"א וּמְסַיֵּם בְּיוּ"ד, שֶׁכָּלַל הַשֵּׁם בְּרֹאשׁ הַשִּׁירָה:
וְיֵשׁ בּוֹ שֶׁבַע תֵּבוֹת, וְהַיְנוּ "חָצְבָה עַמּוּדֶיהָ שִׁבְעָה", כְּנֶגֶד שִׁבְעָה רְקִיעִים, וְשֶׁבַע

BAAL HATURIM ELUCIDATED

XXXII.

1. הַאֲזִינוּ — GIVE EAR. The previous *parashah* concludes: אֵת דִּבְרֵי הַשִּׁירָה הַזֹּאת עַד תֻּמָּם, [*Moses spoke . . .*] *the words of this song until their conclusion* (31:30 above),[1] and juxtaposed to that is [Moses' statement,] הַאֲזִינוּ, *Give ear.* [This indicates that Moses was telling them,] "Just as you gave ear and listened to the words of Torah, so too, give ear to the words of this song."[2]

❑ According to the simple meaning of the verse, *Give ear, O heavens* refers to the inhabitants of the עָרִים גְּדֹלֹת וּבְצֻרֹת בַּשָּׁמָיִם, *cities great and fortified to the heavens;*[3] while *and may the earth hear* refers to the inhabitants of the land, i.e., those who live in villages and small towns.[4]

❑ **הַשָּׁמַיִם וַאֲדַבֵּרָה — O HEAVENS, AND I WILL SPEAK.** The *gematria* of this phrase is 613.[5] [Moses is telling the nation,] "Give ear to the 613 mitzvos."[6]

1. Later in this comment, the Baal HaTurim compares דִּבְרֵי הַשִּׁירָה הַזֹּאת, *the words of this song*, to דִּבְרֵי תוֹרָה, *words of Torah.* It is noteworthy that the previous *parashah* uses similar wording regarding the two: אֶת דִּבְרֵי הַתּוֹרָה הַזֹּאת ... עַד תֻּמָּם, *the words of this Torah . . . until their conclusion* (31:24), and אֵת דִּבְרֵי הַשִּׁירָה הַזֹּאת עַד תֻּמָּם, *the words of this song until their conclusion* (31:30). Perhaps the Baal HaTurim's comment is based on this similarity of expression (*VeChur LaZahav*).

2. *Peirush HaRokeach.*

3. This phrase appears in 9:1 above, as well as in 1:28 above (where the spelling וּבְצוּרֹת is used). Note that the *gematria* of בְּצֻרֹת is 692, equal to that of הַאֲזִינוּ הַשָּׁמַיִם וַאֲדַבֵּרָה, a further allusion to the Baal HaTurim's concept that הַשָּׁמַיִם refers to the citizens of the cities that are בְּצֻרֹת בַּשָּׁמַיִם (*VeChur LaZahav*).

4. It is noteworthy that although the Baal HaTurim included this comment in the section of his work dedicated to allusions, nevertheless, he prefaced it with, כְּפִי הַפְּשָׁט, *According to the peshat* [*simple meaning of the verse*] . . . Whereas, in *Peirush HaTur HaAroch,* the section devoted to *peshat,* he prefers the literal interpretation of הַשָּׁמַיִם as *the heavens,* and הָאָרֶץ as *the earth* (see *Rashi, Ibn Ezra* and *Ramban*).

5. The Talmud (*Makkos* 23b) and Midrash (*Pirkei DeRabbi Eliezer* 41; *Tanchuma Vayeilech* 2) count the *mitzvos* as 613, and the Baal HaTurim cites that number in his comments to *Genesis* 1:1, 1:4 and 3:25; *Exodus* 20:13; *Numbers* 7:14 and 15:39; *Deuteronomy* 4:2 and our verse. The Talmud derives the number 613 from the verse, תּוֹרָה צִוָּה לָנוּ מֹשֶׁה, *Moses commanded the Torah to us* (33:4 below). Moses gave us תּוֹרָה (=611) commandments; two more —the first two of the Ten Commandments (*Exodus* 20:2-6) were heard directly from God. Thus, there are six hundred and thirteen *mitzvos.*

6. *Paaneach Raza; Rabbeinu Ephraim* (*MiKesivah Ashkenazis*).

32/1 [1] *Give ear, O heavens, and I will speak; and the earth shall hear the words of my mouth.*

BAAL HATURIM ELUCIDATED

❑ This verse begins with the letter ה and ends with the letter י,[7] for Moses included God's name at the beginning of the song.[8]

❑ The verse has seven words alluding to the verse, חָצְבָה עַמּוּדֶיהָ שִׁבְעָה, *she carved out its seven pillars* (*Proverbs* 9:1),[8a] corresponding to the seven heavens,[9] the

7. Although this phenomenon appears twelve times in the Torah (*Genesis* 4:14, 19:8, 19:19, 19:20, 27:7, 31:40; *Exodus* 23:20; *Leviticus* 10:18; *Deuteronomy* 4:33, 12:30, 32:1 [here] and 32:34), as well as eighty-four times in the rest of the *Tanach,* the only place the Baal HaTurim comments about it is here.

8. See *Peirush HaRokeach,* who finds all four letters of the Tetragrammaton highlighted in this verse: The song of *Ha'azinu* is inscribed in the Torah scroll in a format called אָרִיחַ עַל גַּבֵּי אָרִיחַ וּלְבֵנָה עַל גַּבֵּי לְבֵנָה, *brick upon brick and half-brick upon half-brick,* i.e., each line of *Ha'azinu* is divided into three sections, the beginning and end of each line containing a full stich, but the middle section of the line being left blank. Now the first verse is divided into two stiches, הַאֲזִינוּ הַשָּׁמַיִם וַאֲדַבֵּרָה, which begins with the letter ה and ends with the letter ה, and וְתִשְׁמַע הָאָרֶץ אִמְרֵי פִי, which begins with a ו and ends with a י, thus the four letters of the Tetragrammaton.

8a. That verse begins חָכְמוֹת בָּנְתָה בֵיתָהּ, *She built her house with many forms of wisdom.* The Midrash interprets: God said, "If a person is worthy for having studied the Torah and [its] wisdom, that person is considered in God's view as having created the heavens and as having firmly established the entire world." חָצְבָה עַמּוּדֶיהָ שִׁבְעָה, *she carved out its seven pillars,* these are the seven lands (see note 10 below). If a person is worthy for having fulfilled the Torah, that person will inherit the seven lands; if not, he will be dispersed throughout the seven lands (*Midrash Mishlei;* see note 10 below).

9. In his commentary to *Genesis* 1:1, *Exodus* 25:31 and to this verse, the Baal HaTurim speaks of ז׳ רְקִיעִים, *seven heavens;* at *Numbers* 15:39, he speaks of eight. The two opinions are found in the words of the Sages.

The Talmud (*Chagigah* 12b; see also *Avos DeRabbi Nosson* 37:9) names and describes seven heavens, each a higher level than the preceding one. They are:

(i) וִילוֹן, *Vilon* [curtain], although nothing happens within this heaven, in the morning it withdraws [like a curtain, allowing the daylight to shine through (*Rashi*)] and in the evening it goes forth [preventing the light of the sun from reaching Earth (*Rashi*)], thus it renews the work of Creation each day;

(ii) רָקִיעַ, *Rakia* [*firmament*], in which the sun, moon, stars and constellations are suspended;

(iii) שְׁחָקִים, *Shechakim* [*powders* or *pulverizers*], in which stand millstones that grind manna for the righteous;

(iv) זְבוּל, *Zevul* [*Temple*], in which stands the heavenly Jerusalem, the heavenly Temple and the Altar upon which the great angelic prince Michael sacrifices offerings;

(v) מָעוֹן, *Maon* [*dwelling*], in which groups of ministering angels recite songs [of praise to God] through the night, but remain silent by day in deference to Israel;

(vi) מָכוֹן, *Machon* [*foundation* or *establishment*], in which are storehouses of snow and of hail, the attics in which harmful dew and heavy rainfall are stored, and the chamber of the whirlwind and the tempest, the grotto of smoke with its doors of fire [all of these used for retribution against the wicked (*Rashi*)];

and (vii) עֲרָבוֹת, *Aravos* [*willows* or *darkenings* or *mixtures*], in which are Righteousness, Justice and Charity; caches of Life, Peace and Blessing; the souls of the righteous, the spirits and souls that are destined to be born; and the life-giving dew with which God will resurrect the dead; in that heaven are also the *Ofanim, Serafim, Chayos HaKodesh* and other ministering angels; and the Throne of Glory of the King, God, Life-giver, Exalted One.

Another opinion (*Chagigah* 13a) adds an eighth heaven above the heads of the *Chayos.* Thus, the Baal HaTurim sometimes speaks of seven heavens and sometimes of eight.

For other opinions regarding the number and names of the various רְקִיעִים, see *Vayikra Rabbah* 29:11; *Rambam, Hilchos Yesodei HaTorah* 3:1;

בעל הטורים

אֲרָצוֹת, וְשִׁבְעַת יְמֵי הַמַּעֲשֶׂה:

❑ **וְתִשְׁמַע.** ב׳ בַּמָּסוֹרֶת – ״וְתִשְׁמַע הָאָרֶץ אִמְרֵי פִי״; ״וְתִשְׁמַע וְתוֹשִׁיעַ״. שֶׁאִם תִּשְׁמְעוּ ״אִמְרֵי פִי״, תִּהְיוּ נוֹשָׁעִים. וְזֶהוּ ״וְתִשְׁמַע וְתוֹשִׁיעַ״:

(ב) **יַעֲרֹף.** ב׳ בַּמָּסוֹרֶת – ״יַעֲרֹף כַּמָּטָר לִקְחִי״; ״יַעֲרֹף מִזְבְּחוֹתָם יְשֹׁדֵד מַצֵּבוֹתָם״. זָכָה וְלָמַד תּוֹרָה כְּמוֹ מֹשֶׁה, נַעֲשֵׂית לוֹ סַם חַיִּים, וְהַיְנוּ ״יַעֲרֹף כַּמָּטָר״, וְתִרְגֵּם אֻנְקְלוֹס ״יַעֲרֹף״ יְבַסֵּם. לֹא זָכָה, שֶׁלָּמַד שֶׁלֹּא לִשְׁמָהּ, נַעֲשֵׂית לוֹ סַם הַמָּוֶת, וְהַיְנוּ ״יַעֲרֹף מִזְבְּחוֹתָם״, שֶׁהוּא לְשׁוֹן עֲרִיפָה, כְּמוֹ ״וְעָרְפוּ שָׁם אֶת הָעֶגְלָה״:

❑ **לִקְחִי.** ג׳ בַּמָּסוֹרֶת – ״יַעֲרֹף כַּמָּטָר לִקְחִי״; ״לִקְחִי נָא לִי פַּת לֶחֶם״; ״וַיִּךְ לִקְחִי״. הָכָא מִשְׁתָּעֵי בַּתּוֹרָה, שֶׁאֵין לֶקַח אֶלָּא תּוֹרָה, שֶׁנֶּאֱמַר ״כִּי לֶקַח טוֹב נָתַתִּי לָכֶם״. וְזֶהוּ שֶׁאָמְרוּ, אִם אֵין קֶמַח אֵין תּוֹרָה. {שֶׁהֲרֵי כְּתִיב הָכָא} ״יַעֲרֹף כַּמָּטָר לִקְחִי״ {וּמַיְרֵי בַּתּוֹרָה, וּכְתִיב הָתָם לִקְחִי קֶמַח}. מָתַי ״וַיִּךְ לִקְחִי״? ״לִקְחִי נָא לִי פַּת לֶחֶם״, וְזֶהוּ קֶמַח. אִם

BAAL HATURIM ELUCIDATED

seven lands,[10] and the seven days of the week.[11,12]

❑ **וְתִשְׁמַע — AND [THE EARTH] SHALL HEAR.** The masoretic note, ב׳, means that this word appears twice in the *Tanach*: (i) here, וְתִשְׁמַע הָאָרֶץ אִמְרֵי פִי, *and the earth shall hear the words of my mouth;* and (ii) וְתִשְׁמַע וְתוֹשִׁיעַ, *and you will hear and You will save* (*II Chronicles* 20:9).[13] [The similarity of expression indicates] that [Moses said,] "If you hearken to *the words of my mouth,* you will be saved." Thus, וְתִשְׁמַע, *you* [*Israel*] *will hearken,* וְתוֹשִׁיעַ, *and You* [*God*] *will save* [*us*].

Tosefos Yom Tov, Pesachim 10:5, s.v., להודות; *Eliyahu Rabbah* (*Gra*), *Keilim* 3:4, s.v., אשריך כלים.

10. *Avos DeRabbi Nosson* 37:9 (see *Binyan Yehoshua* there) — Corresponding to the seven heavens, He called the earth by seven names: (i) אֶרֶץ — e.g., *Genesis* 1:1; (ii) אֲדָמָה — e.g., *Genesis* 2:19; (iii) אַרְקָא — *Jeremiah* 10:11; (iv) חָרָבָה — e.g., *Genesis* 7:22; (v) יַבָּשָׁה — e.g., *Genesis* 1:9; (vi) תֵּבֵל — e.g., *I Samuel* 2:8; (vii) חֶלֶד — e.g., *Psalms* 49:2.

A parallel list in *Pesikta DeRav Kahana* 23 and *Vayikra Rabbah* 29:11 reads: (i) אֶרֶץ; (ii) אֲדָמָה; (iii) אַרְקָא; (iv) גַּיְא — e.g., *Numbers* 21:20; (v) צִיָּה — e.g., *Isaiah* 35:1; (vi) נְשִׁיָּה — *Psalms* 88:13; and (vii) תֵּבֵל.

Alternatively: The seven lands refer to actual land areas, for another Midrash states: A person who is meritorious and fulfills [the Torah's laws] will inherit the seven lands. But one who does not fulfill [its laws] will be dispersed among the seven lands (*Midrash Mishlei* 9:1). According to the *Ibn Ezra* (*Bereishis* 1:2, s.v., ובהו), the inhabited world is divided into seven land areas, with the *Beis HaMikdash* in the center [i.e., in the middle area of the seven].

11. The Talmud explains the verse from *Proverbs* as a reference to שִׁבְעַת יְמֵי בְרֵאשִׁית, *the seven days of Creation* (*Sanhedrin* 38a).

12. *Peirush HaRokeach;* see also the Baal HaTurim to *Genesis* 1:1, *Exodus* 25:31 and *Numbers* 15:39.

13. That verse reads in full: [*Jehoshaphat said . . .*] *"If evil should come upon us — sword; judgment or plague or famine — we will stand before this Temple and before You, for Your Name is in this Temple, and we will cry out to You out of our affliction, and You will hear and You will save* [*us*]." In the context of Jehoshaphat's prayer, God is the subject of the two verbs — וְתִשְׁמַע, *and You will hear* [*our prayer*], and וְתוֹשִׁיעַ, *and You will save* [*us*]. In the Baal HaTurim's comment, however, the subject of וְתִשְׁמַע is Israel, [*if*] *you* [*Israel*] *will hearken* [*unto God*], while the subject of וְתוֹשִׁיעַ is God, [*then*] *You* [*God*] *will save* [*them*] (*VeChur LaZahav*).

[2] *May my teaching drop like the rain,*
may my utterance flow like the dew;

BAAL HATURIM ELUCIDATED

2. יַעֲרֹף — MAY IT DROP. The masoretic note, ב׳, means that this word appears twice in the *Tanach*:[14] (i) here, יַעֲרֹף כַּמָּטָר לִקְחִי, *may my teaching drop like the rain;* and (ii) יַעֲרֹף מִזְבְּחוֹתָם יְשֹׁדֵד מַצֵּבוֹתָם, *He [God] will destroy their altars and will lay waste to their pillars* (*Hosea* 10:2). [The similarity of expression implies that] if a person has been virtuous and has studied the Torah as Moses did, it becomes an elixir of life for him; thus, the verse states, יַעֲרֹף כַּמָּטָר, and *Onkelos* renders יַעֲרֹף as יְבַסֵּם, *it shall be pleasant.*[15] If the person has not been virtuous, i.e., he has studied [Torah] for some personal ulterior motive, [the Torah] becomes a fatal potion for him; thus, the verse, *He will destroy their altars,* for the word יַעֲרֹף [in that verse] has the connotation of decapitation, as in the verse, וְעָרְפוּ שָׁם אֶת הָעֶגְלָה, *and they shall decapitate the calf there*[16] (21:4 above).[17]

❑ **לִקְחִי — MY TEACHING.**[18] The masoretic note, ג׳, means that this word appears three times in the *Tanach*:[19] (i) here, יַעֲרֹף כַּמָּטָר לִקְחִי, *may my teaching drop like the rain;* (ii) לִקְחִי נָא לִי פַּת לֶחֶם, *Take now for me a piece of bread* (*I Kings* 17:11); and (iii) זַךְ לִקְחִי, *My teaching is pure* (*Job* 11:4). Here [the word לֶקַח] refers to the Torah, for it alone is described as לֶקַח, *teaching,* as it is written, כִּי לֶקַח טוֹב נָתַתִּי לָכֶם, *For a good teaching I have given to you*[20] (*Proverbs* 4:2). This [similarity of expression] implies that which the Sages have taught: אִם אֵין קֶמַח אֵין תּוֹרָה, *If there is no flour, there is no Torah.*[21] {Thus לִקְחִי is written here,}[21a] יַעֲרֹף כַּמָּטָר לִקְחִי, *May my teaching drop like the rain* {which refers to the Torah; and לִקְחִי is written there [with regard to] flour}.[21a] When [can one say], "*My teaching is pure*?" When you *take now for me a piece of bread,* which is [made of] קֶמַח, *flour.* [Thus:] If there is

14. The full note appears in *Hosea:* ב׳ בִּתְרֵי לִישָׁנֵי, *Twice, with two [different] meanings.* The noun עֹרֶף means *the back of the neck* (e.g., *Genesis* 49:8). The related verb root ערף means *to decapitate* an animal by applying a knife to the back of its neck (e.g., 21:4,6 above); by extension, it can mean *to destroy* (see *Ibn Ezra* and *Metzudas Zion* to *Hosea* 10:2). The verb ערף can also mean *to fall* or *to drop like rain* (here and 33:28 below).

15. The labial letters בומ״ף are sometimes interchanged with one another (see note 10 to *parashas Nitzavim*). Thus, *Onkelos* interprets יַעֲרֹף as if it read יֶעֱרַב, *it shall be pleasant* (*Nesinah LaGer*).

16. *Taanis* 7a, *Yoma* 72b; see the Baal HaTurim to *Genesis* 4:14.

17. *Maharam MiRothenburg.*

18. The extant manuscripts and the early printed editions begin this comment with, לקחי ב׳ מס׳, and adduce two verses, יַעֲרֹף כַּמָּטָר לִקְחִי (our verse) and לִקְחִי קֶמַח, *take flour,* a phrase not found in Scripture. The text follows the emendations that appear in the later printed editions.

19. Although the masoretic notes do not state, בִּתְרֵי לִישָׁנֵי, *with two [different] meanings* (see note 14 above), the word nevertheless has two meanings. In our verse and in *Job,* it is a noun, i.e., לֶקַח, *teaching,* with the possessive pronominal suffix ־ִי, *my,* thus, *my teaching.* In *Kings* it is a verb, i.e., לקח, *to take,* in the feminine imperative form, לִקְחִי, *Take!*

20. That verse reads in full: כִּי לֶקַח טוֹב, *for a good teaching,* נָתַתִּי לָכֶם, *I have given to you,* תּוֹרָתִי, *My Torah,* אַל תַּעֲזֹבוּ, *do not forsake [it].*

21. *Avos* 3:17. It is hardly possible for someone who has nothing to eat to devote himself to Torah study (*Rashi*).

21a. The passages enclosed in braces are not found in the early or later printed editions, but they do appear in *Shoham Yakar's* manuscript edition.

כִּשְׂעִירִם עֲלֵי־דֶשֶׁא | וְכִרְבִיבִים עֲלֵי־עֵשֶׂב׃
ג כִּי שֵׁם יהוה אֶקְרָא | הָבוּ גֹדֶל לֵאלֹהֵינוּ׃
ד הַצּוּר תָּמִים פָּעֳלוֹ | כִּי כָל־דְּרָכָיו מִשְׁפָּט
אֵל אֱמוּנָה וְאֵין עָוֶל | צַדִּיק וְיָשָׁר הוּא׃
ה שִׁחֵת לוֹ לֹא בָּנָיו מוּמָם | דּוֹר עִקֵּשׁ וּפְתַלְתֹּל׃

בעל הטורים

יֵשׁ קֶמַח יֵשׁ תּוֹרָה. ״לִקְחִי״ בְּגִימַטְרִיָּא ״קֶמַח״:

❑ **כַּטָּל.** ב׳ בַּמָּסוֹרֶת – ״תִּזַּל כַּטַּל״; ״אֶהְיֶה כַטַּל לְיִשְׂרָאֵל״. לוֹמַר שֶׁהַתּוֹרָה הִיא „כַטַּל לְיִשְׂרָאֵל״ דַּוְקָא. אֲבָל לְאֻמּוֹת בְּהֶפֶךְ, כְּדִכְתִיב ״רָאָה וַיַּתֵּר גּוֹיִם״, שֶׁמִּסִּינַי הִתִּיר מָמוֹנָן:

❑ **כַּמָּטָר . . . כַּטַּל . . . כִּשְׂעִירִם . . . וְכִרְבִיבִים.** אַרְבַּע מִדּוֹת, כְּנֶגֶד אַרְבַּע מִדּוֹת בַּלּוֹמְדִים; וְכֵן בְּיַד כָּל אֶחָד וְאֶחָד מִיִּשְׂרָאֵל אַרְבַּע פְּעָמִים, כִּדְאִיתָא בְעֵרוּבִין גַּבֵּי כֵּיצַד סֵדֶר הַמִּשְׁנָה:

(ב־ג) **וְכִרְבִיבִים עֲלֵי עֵשֶׂב. כִּי שֵׁם ה׳ אֶקְרָא.** מִכָּאן שֶׁמִּתְפַּלְלִין עַל עֲצִירַת גְּשָׁמִים:
דָּבָר אַחֵר – ״עֲלֵי עֵשֶׂב. כִּי שֵׁם ה׳ אֶקְרָא״ מִכָּאן שֶׁמְּבָרְכִין עַל כָּל מִין וּמִין, כִּדְאִיתָא בִּבְרָכוֹת:

(ג־ד) **כִּי שֵׁם ה׳ אֶקְרָא . . . הַצּוּר תָּמִים.** לוֹמַר שֶׁמְּבָרְכִין, בָּרוּךְ דַּיַּן הָאֱמֶת:

(ד־ה) **צַדִּיק וְיָשָׁר הוּא. שִׁחֵת לוֹ.** {לוֹמַר כְּשֶׁדָּנִין אוֹתוֹ, יֵשׁ לוֹ} לוֹמַר יָפֶה דַנְתּוּנִי:

BAAL HATURIM ELUCIDATED

flour, there is Torah.[21b] [An allusion to this:] The *gematria* of לִקְחִי (148) is equal to that of קֶמַח.[22]

❑ כַּטָּל — LIKE THE DEW. The masoretic note, ב׳, means that this word appears twice in the *Tanach*: (i) here, תִּזַּל כַּטַּל, *may it flow like the dew;* and (ii) אֶהְיֶה כַטַּל לְיִשְׂרָאֵל, *I will be like the dew for Israel* (*Hosea* 14:6). This [similarity of expression] indicates that the Torah is *like the dew for Israel* exclusively. But regarding the [other] nations, to the contrary, as it is written, רָאָה וַיַּתֵּר גּוֹיִם, *He looked and released nations* (*Habbakuk* 3:6), [which means,] that from [the time of the revelation at] Sinai, He released their property.[23]

❑ כַּמָּטָר . . . כַּטַּל . . . כִּשְׂעִירִם . . . וְכִרְבִיבִים — LIKE THE RAIN . . . LIKE THE DEW; LIKE STORM WINDS . . . AND LIKE DROPLETS. Four different metaphors,[24] corresponding to the four categories of students;[25] and to the four times that each and every

21b. Another noteworthy allusion is found in this connection of תּוֹרָה with קֶמַח. Both Torah and flour are dependent on מָטָר: flour, for wheat does not grow without rainfall; and Torah, for our verse compares Torah to rain. Now the Mishnah states, אִם אֵין קֶמַח אֵין תּוֹרָה, *If there is no flour, there is no Torah,* which the Baal HaTurim paraphrases, אִם יֵשׁ קֶמַח יֵשׁ תּוֹרָה, *If there is flour, there is Torah.* And the difference between יֵשׁ [= 310], *there is,* and אַיִן [= 61], *there is not,* is מָטָר [= 249] (*VeChur LaZahav*).

22. *Maharam MiRothenburg;* see also *Rabbeinu Ephraim.*

23. See *Bava Kamma* 38a.

24. That is, our verse uses four apparently redundant metaphors for the study of Torah [*my teaching*].

25. *Peirush HaRokeach.* The Mishnah teaches: There are four categories of students: (a) One who is quick to understand and quick to forget — his [initial] gain is dissipated with his [subsequent]

like storm winds upon vegetation
and like droplets upon grass.
3 *When I call out the Name of HASHEM,*
ascribe greatness to our God.
4 *The Rock! — perfect is His work, for all His paths are justice;*
a God of faith without iniquity, righteous and fair is He.
5 *Corruption is not His;*
the blemish is His children's,
a perverse and twisted generation.

BAAL HATURIM ELUCIDATED

Israelite was taught the Torah, as explained in tractate *Eruvin,*[26] "What was the order in which the Oral Torah was taught?"[27]

2-3. וְכִרְבִיבִים עֲלֵי עֵשֶׂב. כִּי שֵׁם ה׳ אֶקְרָא — LIKE DROPLETS UPON GRASS.[27a] WHEN I CALL OUT THE NAME OF HASHEM. This [juxtaposition of verses] teaches that we recite [special] prayers when rains are withheld.[28]

Alternatively: [The juxtaposition of] עֲלֵי עֵשֶׂב, *leaves of grass,* [with] כִּי שֵׁם ה׳ אֶקְרָא, *When I call out the Name of HASHEM,* teaches that a unique blessing is recited for every species [of food], as stated in tractate *Berachos.*[29]

3-4. כִּי שֵׁם ה׳ אֶקְרָא . . . הַצּוּר תָּמִים — WHEN I CALL OUT THE NAME OF HASHEM . . . THE ROCK IS PERFECT.[30] This [juxtaposition] indicates that [upon hearing bad news] we recite the blessing, בָּרוּךְ . . . דַּיַּן הָאֱמֶת, *Blessed is . . . the true Judge.*[31]

❑ {The Baal HaTurim's other comment to כִּי שֵׁם ה׳ appears at *Leviticus* 16:14, s.v., וְלִפְנֵי הַכַּפֹּרֶת.}

4-5. צַדִּיק וְיָשָׁר הוּא. שִׁחֵת לוֹ — RIGHTEOUS AND FAIR IS HE [GOD]. CORRUPTION IS HIS [MAN].[31a] This [juxtaposition] indicates that once a person has been judged, it is proper for him}[32] to say, "They have judged me fairly."[33]

---

loss; (b) one who is slow to understand and slow to forget — his [initial] loss [of time] is compensated for by his gain; (c) one who is quick to understand and slow to forget — he has a good portion; (d) one who is slow to understand and quick to forget — he has a bad portion (*Avos* 5:12).

26. *Eruvin* 54b. See the Baal HaTurim to 11:26 above, with note 10.

27. *Peirush HaRokeach.*

27a. In the context of the verse, the word עֲלֵי is a poetic form of עַל, *upon,* and the phrase עֲלֵי עֵשֶׂב means *upon grass,* and that is what it means in the Baal HaTurim's first comment. However, the word עֲלֵי can also be understood as a construct form of עָלִים, *leaves* (see *Job* 30:4; *Nehemiah* 8:15), in which case, עֲלֵי עֵשֶׂב would mean, *leaves of grass,* and that is how the Baal HaTurim interprets it in his second comment *(VeChur LaZahav).*

28. *Peirush HaRokeach;* see *Taanis* 15a.

29. *Berachos* 40a; *Peirush HaRokeach.*

30. In the context of the verse, תָּמִים, *perfect,* modifies פָּעֳלוֹ, *His work.* But in the context of the Baal HaTurim's comment — which does not include the word פָּעֳלוֹ — the adjective תָּמִים modifies הַצּוּר, *the Rock,* i.e., God is perfect.

31. See *Berachos* 54a.

31a. In the context of the verse, שִׁחֵת לוֹ לֹא means *corruption is not His,* i.e., God has not done anything corrupt. However, the Baal HaTurim omits the word לֹא, *not,* from the rubric of his comment, and cites only שִׁחֵת לוֹ, *corruption is his,* i.e., it is the person who is corrupt, not God's judgment.

32. The passage enclosed in braces is not found in the printed editions, but does appear in the manuscripts used by *Shoham Yakar.*

33. See *Taanis* 11a.

* ה' רבתי
והיא תיבה לעצמה

שני

ו הַ לַיהוָה תִּגְמְלוּ־זֹאת עַם נָבָל וְלֹא חָכָם
הֲלוֹא־הוּא אָבִיךָ קָּנֶךָ הוּא עָשְׂךָ וַיְכֹנְנֶךָ:
ז זְכֹר יְמוֹת עוֹלָם בִּינוּ שְׁנוֹת דֹּר־וָדֹר
שְׁאַל אָבִיךָ וְיַגֵּדְךָ זְקֵנֶיךָ וְיֹאמְרוּ־לָךְ:
ח בְּהַנְחֵל עֶלְיוֹן גּוֹיִם בְּהַפְרִידוֹ בְּנֵי אָדָם
יַצֵּב גְּבֻלֹת עַמִּים לְמִסְפַּר בְּנֵי יִשְׂרָאֵל:

בעל הטורים

(ו) **הַ לַה'.** הֵ"א גְדוֹלָה – לוֹמַר, וְכִי לַה' תִּגְמְלוּ זֹאת, שֶׁנָּתַן לָכֶם חֲמִשָּׁה חֻמְשֵׁי תוֹרָה:

❏ **הוּא עָשְׂךָ וַיְכֹנְנֶךָ.** וּסְמִיךְ לֵהּ "זְכֹר". כְּלוֹמַר, זְכֹר הֵיאךְ עָשָׂה וַיְכוֹנֶנְךָ בַּבֶּטֶן מִטִּפָּה סְרוּחָה:

(ז) **שְׁאַל אָבִיךָ וְיַגֵּדְךָ זְקֵנֶיךָ.** הֲרֵי שְׁלֹשָׁה דוֹרוֹת. וּסְמִיךְ לֵהּ "בְּהַנְחֵל". לוֹמַר, כֹּל שֶׁהוּא וּבְנוֹ וּבֶן בְּנוֹ תַלְמִידֵי חֲכָמִים, הֲרֵי הוּא לוֹ כְנַחֲלָה, שֶׁאֵין לוֹ הֶפְסֵק:

(ח) **גְּבֻלֹת.** חָסֵר וָ"ו – לוֹמַר, י"ב מַזָּלוֹת "יַצֵּב . . . לְמִסְפַּר בְּנֵי יִשְׂרָאֵל":

BAAL HATURIM ELUCIDATED

6. הַ לַה' — IS IT TO HASHEM. [According to the masoretic tradition,] the letter[33a] הַ (= 5) is inscribed [in the Torah scroll] larger than usual.[34] This is to reinforce the question: *"Is it to HASHEM,* Who has given you the five books of the Torah,[34a] *that you do this?"*[35]

❏ **הוּא עָשְׂךָ וַיְכֹנְנֶךָ — HE HAS MADE YOU AND HE HAS ESTABLISHED YOU.** Juxtaposed to this is [the command], זְכֹר, *Remember* (v. 7), as if to say: Remember how He made and established you in the womb from a putrid drop.[36]

7. שְׁאַל אָבִיךָ וְיַגֵּדְךָ זְקֵנֶיךָ — ASK YOUR FATHER AND HE WILL TELL IT TO YOU, YOUR GRANDFATHERS. The verse mentions three generations.[37] Juxtaposed to this is בְּהַנְחֵל, *When He bestowed heritage* (v. 8). [This juxtaposition is] to indicate that whenever a person, his son and his grandson are Torah scholars, it[37a] is for him

33a. The prefix ־הֲ (sometimes vowelized הַ or הֶ) is called ה' הַשְּׁאֵלָה, *the interrogative* ה, and is used to introduce a question. This is the only time in the *Tanach* that it stands by itself as a complete word. Indeed, there is no other one-letter word in Scripture.

34. Each of the twenty-two letters of the *aleph-beis* appears at least once in the *Tanach* as an אוֹת רַבָּתִי, *large letter,* which, although written in its usual shape, is wider and taller than it would ordinarily be; and at least once as an אוֹת זְעִירָא, *small letter,* which is narrower and shorter than it would ordinarily be. Lists of those oversized and undersized letters appear in the masoretic notes at *Genesis* 1:1; *Leviticus* 1:1 and *I Chronicles* 1:1. Other places where the Baal HaTurim discusses enlarged letters are *Genesis* 27:46, *Leviticus* 13:33, *Numbers* 14:17 and *Deuteronomy* 6:4, 18:13 and 32:18.

34a. See *Targum Onkelos* who paraphrases the verse: הָא קֳדָם יְיָ אַתּוּן גָּמְלִין דָּא עַמָּא דְקַבִּילוּ אוֹרַיְתָא, *Is it before HASHEM that you do this, O nation that has received* [or, *accepted*] *the Torah (VeChur LaZahav).*

35. *R' Yehudah HaChassid,* who concludes that the term זאת refers to the Torah (see *Leviticus* 7:37, 14:54; *Numbers* 19:14; and 4:44 above).

36. See *Avos* 3:1 — Consider three things and you will not come into the clutches of sin: Know (a) from where you have come; (b) to where you are going; and (c) before Whom you are destined to give an accounting. From where did you come? — From a putrid drop . . .

37. They are: (a) you, (b) your father and (c) your grandfather.

37a. That is, תַּלְמוּד תּוֹרָה, *Torah study.* Had the Baal HaTurim been referring to the Torah itself, he

[6] *Is it to* HASHEM *that you do this?*
O weary and unwise people —
is He not your Father, your Master?
He has made you and He has established you.
[7] *Remember the days of yore,*
understand the years of generation after generation.
Ask your father and he will tell you,
your grandfathers and they will speak to you.
[8] *When the Supreme One bestowed heritage upon nations*
when He separated the children of man,
He set the boundaries of the peoples
according to the number of the Children of Israel.

BAAL HATURIM ELUCIDATED

as a heritage[38] that has no end.[39]

8. גְּבֻלֹת — THE BOUNDARIES. This term is spelled defectively, without a ו.[40,41] This indicates that there are twelve[42] constellations[42a] [because] *He set* [*them*] *according to the number of the Children*[42b] *of Israel.*[43]

---

would have used the feminine pronoun הִיא, for *it,* rather than the masculine pronouns הוּא . . . לוֹ, for תּוֹרָה is a feminine noun. תַּלְמוּד, *study,* on the other hand, is a masculine noun *(VeChur LaZahav).*

38. The Baal HaTurim's wording is grammatically problematic: The expression נַחֲלָה אֵין לָהּ הֶפְסֵק, *a heritage that has no end* [literally, *there is not to her an interruption*], is found in the Talmud (*Rosh Hashanah* 12b), in a similar context. There, the feminine pronoun לָהּ, *to her,* has the feminine noun נַחֲלָה, *heritage,* as its antecedent. But, the Baal HaTurim's phrase [in all editions] reads, כְּנַחֲלָה שֶׁאֵין לוֹ הֶפְסֵק, using the masculine pronoun לוֹ, *to him,* for the feminine noun נַחֲלָה! It is possible that the Baal HaTurim does not mean נַחֲלָה, *a heritage,* rather, the intended word is נַחְלָה, *a stream,* a masculine noun (see *Psalms* 124:4). If so, the translation should read: . . . *a stream that has no end* (*VeChur LaZahav;* see also *Sifrei* with *Peirush Sifrei DeVei Rav*).

39. See *Bava Metzia* 85a.

40. The term גְּבוּלוֹת, *boundaries,* appears five times in the *Tanach*: four times without any prefix (here; *Isaiah* 10:13; *Psalms* 74:17; *Job* 24:2) and once with the prefix -בְּ, *in* (*Numbers* 32:33). Both here and in *Numbers,* it is spelled in the form known as חָסֵר דְּחָסֵר, *doubly defective,* i.e., it is spelled גְּבֻלֹת, with neither the first ו nor the second; in *Psalms* it is spelled מָלֵא דְּמָלֵא, *doubly full,* i.e., גְּבוּלוֹת, with both letters ו included. However, with regard to the spellings of the other two, the masoretic notes are at odds. Either one or the other or both are spelled חָסֵר דְּמָלֵא, *defective, yet full,* i.e., גְּבֻלוֹת, without the first ו, but with the second, or מָלֵא דְּחָסֵר, *full, yet defective,* i.e., גְּבוּלֹת, with the first ו, but without the second.

Although it is not within the purview of these notes to resolve the differences between the masoretic notes, it is clear from all of those notes that the term גְּבֻלֹת of our verse could have been spelled with either the first, the second or both letters ו. The Baal HaTurim explains why they were omitted (*VeChur LaZahav*). It is not clear why he comments here, but not at *Numbers* 32:33.

41. The text חָסֵר וָ״ו follows the first printed edition. Many later editions have emended this to read חָסֵר ב׳ וָוי״ן, *without two letters* ו (see note 42 below).

42. The *gematria* of ו is six; whereas the name of the letter ו is sometimes spelled ו״ו, the omitted ו is seen as an allusion to the number twelve (*Keli Yakar* to v. 13; *Ittur Bikkurim; Matzreif LaKesef*). Alternatively: The combined *gematria* of the two omitted letters ו is 12 (R' Chaim Kanievsky in his notes to *Peirush HaRokeach*).

42a. As used here, the term מַזָּלוֹת refers to the constellations of the Zodiac. See the Baal HaTurim to *Leviticus* 24:5, with notes 152-153; and *Numbers* 7:3, with note 96.

42b. That is, the number of the tribes of Israel. Alternatively: בְּנֵי יִשְׂרָאֵל may be understood as *the sons of Israel [Jacob].*

43. *Peirush HaRokeach;* see *Berachos* 32b.

ט כִּ֛י חֵ֥לֶק יהוָ֖ה עַמּ֑וֹ יַעֲקֹ֖ב חֶ֥בֶל נַחֲלָתֽוֹ׃
י יִמְצָאֵ֙הוּ֙ בְּאֶ֣רֶץ מִדְבָּ֔ר וּבְתֹ֖הוּ יְלֵ֣ל יְשִׁמֹ֑ן
יְסֹבְבֶ֙נְהוּ֙ יְב֣וֹנְנֵ֔הוּ יִצְּרֶ֖נְהוּ כְּאִישׁ֥וֹן עֵינֽוֹ׃
יא כְּנֶ֙שֶׁר֙ יָעִ֣יר קִנּ֔וֹ עַל־גּוֹזָלָ֖יו יְרַחֵ֑ף
יִפְרֹ֤שׂ כְּנָפָיו֙ יִקָּחֵ֔הוּ יִשָּׂאֵ֖הוּ עַל־אֶבְרָתֽוֹ׃
יב יהוָ֖ה בָּדָ֣ד יַנְחֶ֑נּוּ וְאֵ֥ין עִמּ֖וֹ אֵ֥ל נֵכָֽר׃
שלישי [°בָּמֳתֵי ק׳] יג יַרְכִּבֵ֙הוּ֙ עַל־°בָּ֣מותי אָ֔רֶץ וַיֹּאכַ֖ל תְּנוּבֹ֣ת שָׂדָ֑י
וַיֵּנִקֵ֤הוּ דְבַשׁ֙ מִסֶּ֔לַע וְשֶׁ֖מֶן מֵחַלְמִ֥ישׁ צֽוּר׃

בעל הטורים

(י) יְבוֹנְנֵהוּ. מָלֵא וָי״ו — שֶׁבְּוָי״ו בְּסִיוָן נָתַן לָהֶם ו׳ דְּבָרִים. וְאֵלּוּ הֵן — תּוֹרָה עֵדוּת פִּקּוּדֵי מִצְוַת יִרְאָה מִשְׁפָּט:

(יב) יַנְחֶנּוּ. ב׳ בַּמָּסוֹרֶת — ״בָּדָד יַנְחֶנּוּ״; ״מַתָּן אָדָם יַרְחִיב לוֹ וְלִפְנֵי גְדֹלִים יַנְחֶנּוּ״. לוֹמַר, מִי שֶׁנּוֹתֵן צְדָקָה, הַקָּדוֹשׁ בָּרוּךְ הוּא ״בָּדָד יַנְחֶנּוּ״:

(יג) עַל בָּמֳתֵי אָרֶץ. מָלֵא וָי״ו — עַל ו׳ עֲמָמִים:

❑ **וַיֵּנִקֵהוּ.** חָסֵר יוּ״ד — מִי׳ דִּבְּרוֹת יוֹנְקוֹת כָּל הַתּוֹרָה:

BAAL HATURIM ELUCIDATED

10. יְבוֹנְנֵהוּ — HE GRANTED HIM DISCERNMENT. This term is spelled in full,[44] with a ו (= 6). [This indicates] that on the sixth day of Sivan,[45] [God] gave six things[46] to Israel. They are:[47] **תּוֹרַת**, *the Torah* [*of* HASHEM] . . . **עֵדוּת**, *the Testimony* [*of* HASHEM] . . . **פִּקּוּדֵי**, *the orders* [*of* HASHEM] . . . **מִצְוַת**, *the command* [*of* HASHEM] . . . **יִרְאַת**, *the awe* [*of* HASHEM] . . . **מִשְׁפְּטֵי**, *the judgments* [*of* HASHEM] . . . (*Psalms* 19:8-10).[48]

❑ {The Baal HaTurim's comment to יִצְּרֶנְהוּ כְּאִישׁוֹן עֵינוֹ appears at *Numbers* 1:5.}

12. יַנְחֶנּוּ — HE WILL LEAD THEM.[49] The masoretic note, ב׳, means that this word

44. Grammatically, both יְבוֹנְנֵהוּ [of the root בין] and יְסֹבְבֶנְהוּ [of the root סבב] that precedes it are future tense [used poetically for the past tense (see note 49 below)] verbs in the intensive active *piel* conjugation. Nevertheless, the Torah spells יְבוֹנְנֵהוּ with a ו after the first root letter ב, but omits that letter after the ס of יְסֹבְבֶנְהוּ.

45. The date on which the Torah was given (see the Baal HaTurim to *Numbers* 28:27, with note 92) to Israel.

46. That is, the Torah, which is described in six ways.

47. The text adduces the following six words as they appear in *Psalms*. Virtually all other editions have, . . . תּוֹרָה . . . עֵדוּת . . . פִּקּוּדֵי . . . מִצְוַת . . . יִרְאָה . . . מִשְׁפָּט, a reading that retains the construct form of the verse for some of the words (עֵדוּת פִּקּוּדֵי מִצְוַת), but not for the others — rather, the comment uses תּוֹרָה in place of the verse's תּוֹרַת; יִרְאָה in place of יִרְאַת; and the singular מִשְׁפָּט for the plural מִשְׁפְּטֵי.

48. According to the Midrash, these six descriptive terms refer to the Six Orders of the Mishnah (*Shocher Tov, Tehillim* 19:8, cited by *Rashi* there; *Bereishis Rabbah* 13:16). Accordingly, the Baal HaTurim's comment alludes to both the Written Torah [the sixth of Sivan] and the Oral Torah [the Six Orders] (*VeChur LaZahav*).

49. The term יַנְחֶנּוּ is a future tense verb, and that is how it is to be understood in the verse from *Proverbs*. With regard to our verse, two views are found: According to *Rashi* [and *Rashbam*], יַנְחֶנּוּ here is a rhetorical device that refers to the past [as it relates to the future]. The Baal HaTurim, however, follows *Targum Onkelos* and *Ibn Ezra*

[9] *For HASHEM's portion is His people;*
Jacob is the measure of His inheritance.
[10] *He discovered him in a desert land,*
in desolation, a howling wilderness;
He encircled him, He granted him discernment,
He preserved him like the pupil of His eye.
[11] *He was like an eagle arousing its nest,*
hovering over its young,
spreading its wings and taking them,
carrying them on its pinions.
[12] *HASHEM alone led them,*
and no other power was with them.
[13] *He would make him ride on the heights of the land*
and have him eat the ripe fruits of the fields;
He would suckle him with honey from a stone,
and oil from a flinty rock;

BAAL HATURIM ELUCIDATED

appears twice in the *Tanach*: (i) here, בָּדָד יַנְחֶנּוּ, *He alone will lead them;* and (ii) מַתָּן אָדָם יַרְחִיב לוֹ וְלִפְנֵי גְדֹלִים יַנְחֶנּוּ, *A man's gift will broaden* [access] *for him and will lead him before the great ones*[49] (*Proverbs* 18:16).[50] This [juxtaposition] indicates that when a person gives charity, *He* [*God*] *alone will lead him.*

13. עַל בָּמֳתֵי אָרֶץ — ON THE HEIGHTS OF THE LAND. The term במותי[51] is spelled in full, with a ו (= 6), for the phrase refers to [the lands of] six nations.[52]

❑ **וַיֵּנִקֵהוּ — HE WOULD SUCKLE HIM.** This term is spelled defectively,[52a] without a י (= 10) [after the נ]. [This indicates that] the entire Torah is nurtured by the Ten Commandments.[53]

who render it in the future (*VeChur LaZahav*).

50. In the context of *Proverbs* the verse speaks of a man distributing bribes to gain the ear of important officials (*Rashi; Ibn Ezra*).

51. The word במותי in this verse is an example of a word written יַתִּיר ו׳, *with an extra* ו. For although the word is spelled במותי, as if it were to be pronounced בָּמוֹתֵי, it is nevertheless pronounced בָּמֳתֵי. Unlike a *keri uchesiv,* in which the spelling and pronunciation have different meanings, in a יַתִּיר ו׳, both mean the same thing. Thus, in our verse the written version במותי and the pronounced version בָּמֳתֵי both mean *the heights of.* Grammatically, we find more than thirty cases in the *Tanach* where a word pronounced with a *chataf kamatz* or a *kamatz kattan* is nevertheless spelled with a ו; for example, מיורדי/מִיָּרְדִי (*Psalms* 30:4), and לגאול/לִגְאָל (*Ruth* 4:6). In fact, the word בָּמֳתֵי appears six times in the *Tanach* — three times spelled במותי, as a יַתִּיר ו׳ (here, *Isaiah* 58:14 and *Micah* 1:3); the other three times spelled במתי, without the extra ו (*Isaiah* 14:14, *Amos* 4:13 and *Job* 9:8).

52. *Peirush HaRokeach;* see the Baal HaTurim to 6:19 above, with note 205.

52a. Although this particular form does not appear again in Scripture, similar forms of the verb root ינק do appear, sometimes with a second י (e.g., הֵינִיקָה, *Genesis* 21:7, sometimes without that י (e.g., וַתֵּינִק, *Exodus* 2:7; וַתְּנִיקֵהוּ, *Exodus* 2:9). The Baal HaTurim does not comment about the other appearances.

53. *Peirush HaRokeach.*

All the 613 *mitzvos* are included in the Ten Commandments. Rabbeinu Saadiah Gaon, in his work *Azharos,* explains each of the Ten

יד חֶמְאַת בָּקָר וַחֲלֵב צֹאן עִם־חֵלֶב כָּרִים

וְאֵילִים בְּנֵי־בָשָׁן וְעַתּוּדִים עִם־חֵלֶב כִּלְיוֹת חִטָּה

טו וְדַם־עֵנָב תִּשְׁתֶּה־חָמֶר׃ וַיִּשְׁמַן יְשֻׁרוּן וַיִּבְעָט

שָׁמַנְתָּ עָבִיתָ כָּשִׂיתָ וַיִּטֹּשׁ אֱלוֹהַ עָשָׂהוּ

טז וַיְנַבֵּל צוּר יְשֻׁעָתוֹ׃ יַקְנִאֻהוּ בְּזָרִים

יז בְּתוֹעֵבֹת יַכְעִיסֻהוּ׃ יִזְבְּחוּ לַשֵּׁדִים לֹא אֱלֹהַ

אֱלֹהִים לֹא יְדָעוּם חֲדָשִׁים מִקָּרֹב בָּאוּ

* י׳ זעירא — יח לֹא שְׂעָרוּם אֲבֹתֵיכֶם׃ צוּר יְלָדְךָ *תֶּשִׁי

רביעי — יט וַתִּשְׁכַּח אֵל מְחֹלְלֶךָ׃ וַיַּרְא יהוה וַיִּנְאָץ

כ מִכַּעַס בָּנָיו וּבְנֹתָיו׃ וַיֹּאמֶר אַסְתִּירָה פָנַי מֵהֶם

אֶרְאֶה מָה אַחֲרִיתָם כִּי דוֹר תַּהְפֻּכֹת הֵמָּה

* חול — כא בָּנִים לֹא־אֵמֻן בָּם׃ הֵם קִנְאוּנִי בְלֹא־*אֵל

כִּעֲסוּנִי בְּהַבְלֵיהֶם וַאֲנִי אַקְנִיאֵם בְּלֹא־עָם

בעל הטורים

(יח) תֶּשִׁי. יו״ד קְטַנָּה – נָתַן בְּךָ עֲשָׂרָה דְבָרִים, וְנִסִּיתָ אוֹתוֹ בַּעֲשָׂרָה נִסְיוֹנוֹת. וּלְכָךְ יו״ד דְ״יִגְדַּל נָא״ גְּדוֹלָה – לוֹמַר לְךָ, זְכֹר לְאַבְרָהָם שֶׁנִּסִּיתוֹ בִּי׳ נִסְיוֹנוֹת:

(כא) בְּלֹא עָם. בְּגִימַטְרִיָּא אֵילוּ בַּבְלִיִּים:

BAAL HATURIM ELUCIDATED

15. {The Baal HaTurim's comment to וַיִּשְׁמַן יְשֻׁרוּן וַיִּבְעָט appears at *Leviticus* 3:3.}

18. **תֶּשִׁי — YOU IGNORED.** [According to a scribal tradition,] the י (= 10) of this word is written in a diminutive form.[54] [This indicates that Moses said,] "He placed ten things into you,[55] yet you tested Him with ten trials."[56]

Similarly, the י in the word יִגְדַּל, *be magnified* (*Numbers* 14:17),[57] is written larger than usual.[54] This indicates to you [that Moses said to God,] "Remember

---

Commandments with regard to the *mitzvos* related to it (*Rashi* to *Exodus* 24:12). A Midrash explains that this is alluded to by the fact that the first version of the Ten Commandments (*Exodus* 20:2-14) contains exactly 613 letters (*Bereishis Rabbah* 13:16).

54. See note 34 above. Other places where the Baal HaTurim discusses diminutive letters are *Genesis* 23:2, 27:46; and *Leviticus* 1:1.

55. *Peirush HaRokeach.* The ten things are recorded in the Talmud: There are three partners in the creation of each person — the Holy One, Blessed is He; [the person's] father; and [the person's] mother. One's father sows the whiteness, from which are formed bones, sinews, nails, the brain matter in one's head and the white of the eye; one's mother sows the redness, from which are formed skin, flesh, blood, hair and the black of the eye; and the Holy One, Blessed is He, places within the person (i) breath of life, (ii) soul, (iii) facial countenance, (iv) vision, (v) hearing, (vi) speech, (vii) ambulation, (viii) knowledge, (ix) understanding, and (x) discernment (*Niddah* 31a; as emended by *Hagaos HaGra*).

56. See note 18 to *parashas Ki Savo* above.

57. See the Baal HaTurim to that verse.

14 *Butter of cattle and milk of sheep with fat of lambs,*
rams born in Bashan and he-goats,
with wheat as fat as kidneys;
and you would drink blood of grapes like delicious wine.
15 *Jeshurun became fat and kicked.*
You became fat, you became thick,
you became corpulent — and it deserted God its Maker,
and was contemptuous of the Rock of its salvation.
16 *They would provoke His jealousy with strangers;*
they would anger Him with abominations.
17 *They would slaughter to demons without power,*
gods whom they knew not, newcomers recently arrived,
whom your ancestors did not dread.
18 *You ignored the Rock Who gave birth to you,*
and forgot God Who brought you forth.
19 *HASHEM will see and be provoked by*
the anger of His sons and daughters,
20 *and He will say, "I shall hide My face from them*
and see what their end will be —
for they are a generation of reversals,
children whose upbringing is not in them.
21 *They provoked Me with a non-god,*
angered Me with their vanities;
so shall I provoke them with a non-people,

BAAL HATURIM ELUCIDATED

Abraham, whom You tested with ten different trials."[58]

21. בְּלֹא עָם — WITH A NON-PEOPLE. The *gematria* of this phrase (143) is equivalent[59] to that of [60]אֵילוּ בַּבְלִיִּים, *These are the Babylonians.*[61]

58. The Mishnah states that Abraham underwent ten trials (*Avos* 5:3; see also *Pirkei DeRabbi Eliezer* 26). *Rashi* [other *Rishonim* present variant listings of the ten trials; e.g., *Rabbeinu Yonah* to *Avos*] enumerates them in his commentary there [all verse references are to *Genesis*]: (i) Nimrod wanted to kill [the young] Abram, who had to hide underground for thirteen years; (ii) Nimrod cast him into the blazing furnace (see *Rashi* to 11:28); (iii) God exiled him from his birthplace (12:1); (iv) God brought famine during his lifetime (12:10); (v) Sarah was abducted by Pharaoh and Abimelech (12:15, 20:2); (vi) he had to wage war against Chedarlaomer and his allies when they took Lot captive (14:14-15); (vii) at the Covenant Between the Parts, God showed him a vision of the subjugation of his descendants at the hands of the Four Kingdoms (15:12-16; see *Rashi* to 15:14); (viii) God commanded him to circumcise himself and his son Ishmael (17:10); (ix) God told him to send away both his son Ishmael and Ishmael's mother Hagar (21:12); and (x) God commanded him to sacrifice his son, Isaac (22:2).

59. The *gematria* of the Baal HaTurim's phrase is 141, two less than that of the Scriptural phrase. The principle of *im hateivos* allows us to add the two words to that number, so that it may be considered equivalent to 143 (*VeChur LaZahav*).

60. The text follows *Peirush HaRokeach,* the Baal HaTurim's apparent source, and that is how it

כב בְּג֥וֹי נָבָ֖ל אַכְעִיסֵֽם׃ כִּי־אֵשׁ֙ קָדְחָ֣ה בְאַפִּ֔י
וַתִּיקַ֖ד עַד־שְׁא֣וֹל תַּחְתִּ֑ית וַתֹּ֤אכַל אֶ֙רֶץ֙ וִֽיבֻלָ֔הּ
כג וַתְּלַהֵ֖ט מוֹסְדֵ֥י הָרִֽים׃ אַסְפֶּ֥ה עָלֵ֖ימוֹ רָע֑וֹת
כד חִצַּ֖י אֲכַלֶּה־בָּֽם׃ מְזֵ֥י רָעָ֛ב וּלְחֻ֥מֵי רֶ֖שֶׁף
וְקֶ֣טֶב מְרִירִ֑י וְשֶׁן־בְּהֵמֹת֙ אֲשַׁלַּח־בָּ֔ם
כה עִם־חֲמַ֖ת זֹחֲלֵ֥י עָפָֽר׃ מִח֙וּץ֙ תְּשַׁכֶּל־חֶ֔רֶב

בעל הטורים

❑ **בְּגוֹי נָבָל אַכְעִיסֵם.** רָאשֵׁי תֵבוֹת בְּגִימַטְרִיָּא בֶּאֱדוֹם:

(כב) קָדְחָה . . . וַתִּיקַד . . . וַתֹּאכַל . . . וַתְּלַהֵט. כְּנֶגֶד אַרְבַּע מַלְכֻיּוֹת – בָּבֶל מָדַי יָוָן אֱדוֹם:

(כד) מְזֵי רָעָב. הִזְכִּיר חֲמִשָּׁה דְבָרִים, "וּלְחֻמֵי רֶשֶׁף וְקֶטֶב מְרִירִי וְשֶׁן בְּהֵמֹת . . . עִם חֲמַת זֹחֲלֵי עָפָר", כְּנֶגֶד מַה שֶּׁעָבְרוּ עַל חֲמִשָּׁה חֻמְשֵׁי תוֹרָה; וַחֲמִשָּׁה נְאוּפִים בְּהוֹשֵׁעַ; וְחָמֵשׁ תּוֹעֵבוֹת רָאָה יְחֶזְקֵאל; וּכְנֶגֶד חֲמִשָּׁה "הַמְקַטְּרִים לַבַּעַל לַשֶּׁמֶשׁ וְלַיָּרֵחַ וְלַמַּזָּלוֹת וּלְכֹל צְבָא הַשָּׁמָיִם":

BAAL HATURIM ELUCIDATED

❑ **בְּגוֹי נָבָל אַכְעִיסֵם — WITH A VILE NATION SHALL I ANGER THEM.** The *gematria* of the initial letters of these words (53) is equal to that of בֶּאֱדוֹם, *with Edom.*[62]

22. קָדְחָה . . . וַתִּיקַד . . . וַתֹּאכַל . . . וַתְּלַהֵט — [FOR FIRE] HAS BEEN KINDLED . . . IT SHALL BURN . . . IT SHALL CONSUME . . . IT SHALL SET AFLAME. [The verse uses four verbs] corresponding to the four kingdoms:[63] Babylonia, Media, Greece, and Edom.[63a]

---

appears in *Shoham Yakar's* manuscript edition. Some later editions read הֵם הַבַּבְלִיִּים, *They are the Babylonians,* which has a *gematria* of 144, and the principle of *im hakollel* allows 143 to be considered equivalent to 144.

61. This comment appears in the early printed editions, but has been omitted from some later editions due to the work of the censors.

62. *Peirush HaRokeach;* see *Sifrei* [absent in some editions].

63. Throughout the Talmud and Midrash, and based on the Book of *Daniel* (Ch. 8), Israel's long succession of exiles and persecutions are always treated as four main periods of subjugation to foreign oppressors — either in the Land of Israel or in the Diaspora. These periods are known collectively as אַרְבַּע מַלְכֻיּוֹת, *the Four Kingdoms* (*Daniel* 8:22), and each is called by the name of the empire dominant in the world at that particular time. The first, called גָּלוּת בָּבֶל, *the Babylonian Exile,* began when Nebuchadnezzar king of Babylon conquered the Land of Israel and destroyed the First Temple. The second, called גָּלוּת מָדַי וּפָרַס, *the Median-Persian Exile* (*Daniel* 8:20), began when that empire succeeded the Babylonians as the leading world power. Although the Medes permitted the Jewish return to the Land of Israel and the building of the Second Temple, the early years of that Beis HaMikdash were still considered a part of the exile, because Israel was not sovereign in its land. Paradoxically, during the entire third period, גָּלוּת יָוָן, *the Greek Exile* (*Daniel* 8:21), Israel lived on its land and the Temple stood. Nevertheless, it was a very turbulent era marked by civil strife, foreign domination, vicious anti-religious campaigns, and the rejection of Torah values by a sizable numbers of Jews who had adopted Greek culture with all its abominations. The downfall of the Greek Empire and the rise of Rome marked the beginning of גָּלוּת אֱדוֹם, *the Edomite* or *Roman Exile.* We are still trapped in the grip of this millennia-long exile today.

63a. *Pesikta Zutresa* [*Midrash Lekach Tov*].

with a vile nation I shall anger them.
22 For fire has been kindled in My nostrils;
it shall burn to the lowest depths.
It shall consume the earth and its produce,
it shall set aflame the foundations of mountains.
23 I shall accumulate evils against them,
My arrows shall I use up against them;
24 bloating of famine, burning heat,
suffocation by acrid air,
and the teeth of beasts shall I dispatch against them,
with the venom of those that creep on the earth.
25 On the outside, the sword will bereave,

BAAL HATURIM ELUCIDATED

24. מְזֵי רָעָב — BLOATING OF FAMINE. The verse mentions five things: (i) [מְזֵי רָעָב, *bloating of famine*]; (ii) וּלְחֻמֵי רֶשֶׁף, *burning heat;* (iii) וְקֶטֶב מְרִירִי, *suffocation by acrid air;* (iv) וְשֶׁן בְּהֵמֹת, *and the teeth of beasts . . .;* (v) עִם חֲמַת זֹחֲלֵי עָפָר, *with the venom of those that creep on the earth.*[64] These are the consequence of their having violated the Five Books of the Torah;[65] the five descriptions of adultery in *Hosea;*[66] the five abominations that Ezekiel saw;[67] and corresponding to five [false deities mentioned in the verse], הַמְקַטְּרִים לַבַּעַל לַשֶּׁמֶשׁ וְלַיָּרֵחַ וְלַמַּזָּלוֹת וּלְכֹל צְבָא הַשָּׁמָיִם, *and those who burn offerings* (i) *to the Baal,* (ii) *to the sun and* (iii) *to the moon and* (iv) *to the constellations and* (v) *to all the heavenly hosts* (*II Kings* 23:5).

64. Elsewhere, the Baal HaTurim reckons four forms of retribution in verses 24-25: (i) מְזֵי רָעָב refers to famine; (ii) וּלְחֻמֵי רֶשֶׁף וְקֶטֶב מְרִירִי, to the plague; (iii) וְשֶׁן בְּהֵמֹת, to wild beasts; and (iv) מִחוּץ תְּשַׁכֶּל חֶרֶב, to the sword. Accordingly, רֶשֶׁף means *flames* and refers to heatstroke; while קֶטֶב מְרִירִי means *cutting down by bitterness* and refers to disease caused by foul, polluted air (*Peirush HaTur HaAroch*). In that comment the Baal HaTurim also classifies וְשֶׁן בְּהֵמֹת and זֹחֲלֵי עָפָר together, one as a reference to four-legged beasts, the other to reptiles and other creepers. In the present comment, however, the Baal HaTurim separates both רֶשֶׁף from מְרִירִי and בְּהֵמֹת from זֹחֲלֵי עָפָר.

65. That is, there are five forms of retribution that will befall those who trespass on the Five Books of the Torah.

66. The root נאף, *to commit adultery,* appears six times in the Book of *Hosea,* once as a noun — וְנַאֲפוּפֶיהָ (2:4); and five times as a verb form — וּמְנָאָפֶת (3:1), וְנָאֹף (4:2), תְּנָאַפְנָה (4:13 and 14), and מְנָאֲפִים (7:4). The Baal HaTurim states that the root appears only five times, either because he counts the two appearances of the same word תְּנָאַפְנָה, which occur in adjacent verses and which speak of the same matter, as one appearance (*Shoham Yakar*); or because he counts only the verb forms, but not the noun (*VeChur LaZahav*).

67. The noun תּוֹעֵבָה, *abomination,* in its various forms (singular, plural, prefixed, suffixed, etc.) appears forty-five times in the Book of *Ezekiel.* Hence, the Baal HaTurim's reference to five תועבות is unclear. He cannot mean the word תועבות per se, for it appears only four times (8:6 twice, 8:13, and 8:15). It has been suggested that the comment refers to the term הַתּוֹעֵבוֹת, with the prefix הַ־, *the,* for that word appears five times in *Ezekiel* (8:9, 8:17, 9:4, 18:13 and 18:24) (*Shoham Yakar*). However, that would necessitate an emendation from תועבות to הַתּוֹעֵבוֹת. Most likely, the Baal HaTurim is speaking of the five verses of Chapter 8 in which some form of תועבות appears (vv. 6,9,13,15,17), for the Baal HaTurim uses the expression, רָאָה יְחֶזְקֵאל, *Ezekiel saw,* and of all the verses in *Ezekiel* that contain the term תועבות, only those five verses include the verb root ראה: (i) הֲרֹאֶה אַתָּה מָה הֵם

וּמֵחֲדָרִים אֵימָה	גַּם־בָּחוּר גַּם־בְּתוּלָה
כו יוֹנֵק עִם־אִישׁ שֵׂיבָה:	אָמַרְתִּי אַפְאֵיהֶם
כז אַשְׁבִּיתָה מֵאֱנוֹשׁ זִכְרָם:	לוּלֵי כַּעַס אוֹיֵב אָגוּר
פֶּן־יְנַכְּרוּ צָרֵימוֹ	פֶּן־יֹאמְרוּ יָדֵנוּ רָמָה
כח וְלֹא יהוה פָּעַל כָּל־זֹאת:	כִּי־גוֹי אֹבַד עֵצוֹת הֵמָּה
חמישי כט וְאֵין בָּהֶם תְּבוּנָה:	לוּ חָכְמוּ יַשְׂכִּילוּ זֹאת
ל יָבִינוּ לְאַחֲרִיתָם:	אֵיכָה יִרְדֹּף אֶחָד אֶלֶף
וּשְׁנַיִם יָנִיסוּ רְבָבָה	אִם־לֹא כִּי־צוּרָם מְכָרָם
לא וַיהוה הִסְגִּירָם:	כִּי לֹא כְצוּרֵנוּ צוּרָם
לב וְאֹיְבֵינוּ פְּלִילִים:	כִּי־מִגֶּפֶן סְדֹם גַּפְנָם
וּמִשַּׁדְמֹת עֲמֹרָה	עֲנָבֵמוֹ עִנְּבֵי־רוֹשׁ
לג אַשְׁכְּלֹת מְרֹרֹת לָמוֹ:	חֲמַת תַּנִּינִם יֵינָם

בעל הטורים

(כו) אַשְׁבִּיתָה מֵאֱנוֹשׁ זִכְרָם. סוֹפֵי תֵבוֹת לְמַפְרֵעַ "מֹשֶׁה". {וּסְמִיךְ לֵהּ "לוּלֵי". וְזֶהוּ} "לוּלֵי מֹשֶׁה בְחִירוֹ עָמַד בַּפֶּרֶץ":

(כח) וְאֵין בָּהֶם תְּבוּנָה. סוֹפֵי תֵבוֹת "הָמָן" – שֶׁלֹּא הָיָה בָהֶם תְּבוּנָה, שֶׁנֶּהֱנוּ מִסְּעֻדַּת אֲחַשְׁוֵרוֹשׁ:

(לג) תַּנִּינִם. חָסֵר יוּ"ד – לְפִי שֶׁעָבְרוּ עַל עֲשָׂרָה דְבָרִים שֶׁבְּ"לֹא תִלְמַד לַעֲשׂוֹת"; וְעָבְרוּ עַל עֲשָׂרָה דִבְּרוֹת:

BAAL HATURIM ELUCIDATED

26. אַשְׁבִּיתָה מֵאֱנוֹשׁ זִכְרָם — I WILL CAUSE THEIR MEMORY TO CEASE FROM MAN. The final letters of these three words in reverse order spell the name מֹשֶׁה, *Moses.* {Juxtaposed to this phrase is the word לוּלֵי, *had not* (v. 27). The sequence recalls the verse,}[68] לוּלֵי מֹשֶׁה בְחִירוֹ עָמַד בַּפֶּרֶץ, *Had not Moses, His chosen one, stood in the breach*[69] (*Psalms* 106:23).[70]

28. וְאֵין בָּהֶם תְּבוּנָה — AND THERE IS NO DISCERNMENT IN THEM. The final letters of these words [in reverse order] spell the name הָמָן, *Haman.* [It was in Haman's time] that the Jews showed that they lacked discernment, for they took pleasure in Ahasuerus' feast.[71]

עֹשִׂים תּוֹעֵבוֹת גְּדֹלוֹת . . . וְעוֹד תָּשׁוּב תִּרְאֶה תּוֹעֵבוֹת גְּדֹלוֹת — v. 6; (ii) בֹּא וּרְאֵה אֶת הַתּוֹעֵבוֹת הָרָעוֹת — v. 9; (iii-iv) עוֹד תָּשׁוּב תִּרְאֶה תּוֹעֵבוֹת גְּדֹלוֹת — vv. 13,15; and (v) הֲרָאִיתָ . . . אֶת הַתּוֹעֵבוֹת — v. 17 (*VeChur LaZahav*).

68. The passage enclosed in braces is not found in the early or later printed editions, but does appear in the manuscripts used by *Shoham Yakar.*

69. That verse appears in a psalm that retells the incident of the golden calf (see *Exodus,* Chs. 32-33).

70. *Peirush HaRokeach.*

71. *Peirush HaRokeach;* see *Megillah* 12b.

while indoors there will be dread —
even a young man, even a virgin,
a suckling with the gray-haired man.
26 *I had said, 'I will scatter them,*
I will cause their memory to cease from man' —
27 *had not that the anger of the enemy been pent up,*
lest his tormenters misinterpret;
lest they say, 'Our hand was raised in triumph,
and it was not HASHEM *Who accomplished all this!'*
28 *For they are a nation bereft of counsel,*
and there is no discernment in them.
29 *Were they wise they would comprehend this,*
they would discern it from their end.
30 *For how could one pursue a thousand,*
and two cause a myriad to flee,
if not that their Rock had sold them out,
and HASHEM *had delivered them?*
31 *— for not like our Rock is their rock —*
yet our enemies judge us!
32 *For their vineyard is from the vineyard of Sodom,*
and from the fields of Gomorrah;
their grapes are grapes of gall,
so clusters of bitterness were given them.
33 *Venom of serpents is their wine,*

BAAL HATURIM ELUCIDATED

30. {The Baal HaTurim's comments to רְבָבָה appear at *Genesis* 24:60 and *Leviticus* 26:8.}

32. {The Baal HaTurim's comment to עִנְּבֵי appears at *Leviticus* 25:5.}

33. **תַּנִּינִם** — SERPENTS. This term is spelled defectively, without a [second][72] י (= 10). [This indicates that Moses prophesied] that they will have transgressed on the ten matters [referred to as abominations] that appear in the passage [containing the verse,] לֹא תִלְמַד לַעֲשׂוֹת, *you shall not learn to act* (18:9 above);[73] and they will have transgressed on the Ten Commandments.

72. This word appears five times in the *Tanach*: three times in the Torah, each time spelled defectively, without the second י (*Genesis* 1:21, see the Baal HaTurim there; *Exodus* 7:12; and here); and twice in *Psalms* (74:13 and 148:7), both spelled in full, תַּנִּינִים, with two letters י.

73. *When you come to the land . . . you shall not learn to act according to the abominations of those nations. There shall not be found among you: (i) one who causes his son or (ii) his daughter to pass through the fire; (iii) a diviner; (iv-vi) an astrologer or a reader of omens or a sorcerer; (vii) or an animal charmer; (viii-ix) or one who inquires of Ov or Yid'oni; (x) or one who consults the dead* (18:9-11 above).

לד וְרֹאשׁ פְּתָנִים אַכְזָר׃ הֲלֹא־הוּא כָּמֻס עִמָּדִי

לה חָתוּם בְּאוֹצְרֹתָי׃ לִי נָקָם וְשִׁלֵּם

לְעֵת תָּמוּט רַגְלָם כִּי קָרוֹב יוֹם אֵידָם

לו וְחָשׁ עֲתִדֹת לָמוֹ׃ כִּי־יָדִין יהוה עַמּוֹ

וְעַל־עֲבָדָיו יִתְנֶחָם כִּי יִרְאֶה כִּי־אָזְלַת יָד

לז וְאֶפֶס עָצוּר וְעָזוּב׃ וְאָמַר אֵי אֱלֹהֵימוֹ

לח צוּר חָסָיוּ בוֹ׃ אֲשֶׁר חֵלֶב זְבָחֵימוֹ יֹאכֵלוּ

יִשְׁתּוּ יֵין נְסִיכָם יָקוּמוּ וְיַעְזְרֻכֶם

לט יְהִי עֲלֵיכֶם סִתְרָה׃ רְאוּ ׀ עַתָּה כִּי אֲנִי אֲנִי הוּא

וְאֵין אֱלֹהִים עִמָּדִי אֲנִי אָמִית וַאֲחַיֶּה

מָחַצְתִּי וַאֲנִי אֶרְפָּא וְאֵין מִיָּדִי מַצִּיל׃

ששי מ כִּי־אֶשָּׂא אֶל־שָׁמַיִם יָדִי וְאָמַרְתִּי חַי אָנֹכִי לְעֹלָם׃

בעל הטורים

(לו) אָזְלַת יָד. בְּגִימַטְרִיָּא זוֹ גָלוּת:

❑ **כִּי יִרְאֶה כִּי אָזְלַת.** בְּגִימַטְרִיָּא אֵין בָּם תּוֹרָה:

(לט) אֲנִי אֲנִי הוּא . . . אֲנִי אָמִית. ג׳ פְּעָמִים ״אֲנִי״, כְּנֶגֶד ג׳ גָּלֻיּוֹת. ״וַאֲנִי״, כְּנֶגֶד גָּלוּת הָרְבִיעִי, דִּכְתִיב ״וַאֲנִי בְתוֹךְ הַגּוֹלָה״. לוֹמַר, שֶׁבְּכָל הַגָּלֻיּוֹת הַקָּדוֹשׁ בָּרוּךְ הוּא עִמָּנוּ לְהַצִּילֵנוּ:

❑ **וְאֵין מִיָּדִי מַצִּיל.** ״מִיָּדִי״ בְּגִימַטְרִיָּא דִּין. שֶׁאֵין נִצּוֹל מִיּוֹם הַדִּין:

(מ) וְאָמַרְתִּי חַי אָנֹכִי לְעֹלָם. ״לְעֹלָם״ כְּתִיב חָסֵר וָי״ו – לְאַחַר שֵׁשֶׁת אֲלָפִים שָׁנָה, שֶׁאָז

BAAL HATURIM ELUCIDATED

35. {The Baal HaTurim's comment to לְעֵת תָּמוּט רַגְלָם appears at 2:5 above.}

36. אָזְלַת יָד — THE HAND [OF THE ENEMY] GOES FORTH. The *gematria* of this phrase (452) is equal to that of זוֹ גָלוּת, *This [refers to] exile.*[74]

❑ **כִּי יִרְאֶה כִּי אָזְלַת** — WHEN HE SEES THAT [THE HAND] GOES FORTH. The *gematria* of this phrase (714) is equal to that of אֵין בָּם תּוֹרָה, *There is no Torah among them.*[75]

39. אֲנִי אֲנִי הוּא . . . אֲנִי אָמִית [. . . וַאֲנִי אֶרְפָּא] — I, I AM HE. . . I PUT TO DEATH [. . . AND I WILL HEAL]. The verse mentions the word אֲנִי, *I,* three times, corresponding to three [of the four] exiles,[76] and the word וַאֲנִי, *and I,* refers to the fourth exile, as reflected by the verse, וַאֲנִי בְתוֹךְ הַגּוֹלָה, *and I was among the exile* (*Ezekiel* 1:1). This indicates that God [always has been and always] is with us in all

74. *Peirush HaRokeach.*

75. See *Sanhedrin* 97a — *When HASHEM will have judged His people . . . when He sees that the hand goes forth, and none is saved or assisted.* [This verse teaches that] the son of David [i.e., the Messiah] will not come . . . until the students of Torah will decrease.

76. See note 63 above.

the poison of cruel vipers.
34 *Is it not revealed with Me, sealed in My treasuries?*
35 *Mine is vengeance and retribution at the time*
their foot will falter,
for the day of their catastrophe is near,
and future events are rushing at them."
36 *When* HASHEM *will have judged His people,*
He shall relent regarding His servants,
when He sees that the hand [of the enemy] goes forth,
and none is saved or assisted.
37 *He will say, "Where is their god,*
the rock in whom they sought refuge,
38 *the fat of whose offerings they would eat,*
they would drink the wine of their libations?
Let them stand and help you! Let them be a shelter for you!
39 *See, now, that I, I am He — and no god is with Me.*
I put to death and I bring life, I struck down and I will heal,
and there is no rescuer from My hand.
40 *For I shall raise My hand to heaven and say,*
'As I live forever,

BAAL HATURIM ELUCIDATED

the exiles, to rescue us.[77]

❑ **וְאֵין מִיָּדִי מַצִּיל** — AND THERE IS NO RESCUER FROM MY HAND. The *gematria* of מִיָּדִי, *from My hand* (64), is equal to that of דִּין, *judgment.* [This indicates] that no one will be rescued from the day of judgment.[78]

40. וְאָמַרְתִּי חַי אָנֹכִי לְעֹלָם — AND I SAY, "AS I LIVE FOREVER." The word לְעֹלָם, *forever,* is spelled defectively,[78a] without a ו (= 6). [This indicates that] after 6000 years [have elapsed from the Creation], then He alone will be exalted.[79,79a]

---

77. *Peirush HaRokeach;* see *Pesikta DeRav Kahana* 13, cited in part by *Tosafos* to *Succah* 45a, s.v., אני והו.

78. *Peirush HaRokeach.* That is, no one will escape the day of final judgment, as the Mishnah states: The born are destined to die; the dead are destined to live; the living are destined to be judged . . . for He is God . . . He is the Judge, He is the Witness . . . So do not let your evil inclination convince you that the grave will be a safe haven for you. For you were created without your consent; you were born without your consent; you are living without your consent; you shall die without your consent; and without your consent you are destined to give an accounting before the King of kings, the Holy One, Blessed is He (*Avos* 4:22).

78a. The term appears twelve times in the Torah. Twice, it is spelled in full, with a ו (*Exodus* 19:9, see the Baal HaTurim there, and *Deuteronomy* 23:7). The other ten times (*Genesis* 3:22, 6:3; *Exodus* 3:15, 15:18, 21:6, 31:17, 32:13; *Leviticus* 25:46; *Deuteronomy* 5:26 and here) it is spelled defectively. The Baal HaTurim does not comment at those other nine verses.

79. The final sentence of this comment paraphrases *Isaiah* 2:11,17.

79a. See *Avodah Zarah* 9a — The present world was created to exist for six thousand years: two thousand years of void [i.e., without Torah (*Rashi*)]; two thousand years of Torah; two

מא אִם־שַׁנּוֹתִי בְּרַק חַרְבִּי וְתֹאחֵז בְּמִשְׁפָּט יָדִי
אָשִׁיב נָקָם לְצָרָי וְלִמְשַׂנְאַי אֲשַׁלֵּם:
מב אַשְׁכִּיר חִצַּי מִדָּם וְחַרְבִּי תֹּאכַל בָּשָׂר
מִדַּם חָלָל וְשִׁבְיָה מֵרֹאשׁ פַּרְעוֹת אוֹיֵב:
מג הַרְנִינוּ גוֹיִם עַמּוֹ כִּי דַם־עֲבָדָיו יִקּוֹם
וְנָקָם יָשִׁיב לְצָרָיו וְכִפֶּר אַדְמָתוֹ עַמּוֹ:

בעל הטורים

יִהְיֶה נִשְׂגָּב לְבַדּוֹ. וְנֶחְסַר וָי״ו – שֶׁשִּׁשָּׁה יָמִים נִדּוֹנִין הָרְשָׁעִים:

(מב) **וְחַרְבִּי.** אוֹתִיּוֹת חֶרֶב י״ו – לוֹמַר לְךָ שֶׁחַרְבּוֹ שֶׁל הַקָּדוֹשׁ בָּרוּךְ הוּא יֵשׁ לָהּ י״ו פָּנִים, כִּדְאִיתָא בְּמִדְרַשׁ שׁוֹחֵר טוֹב. ״נְקַם בְּרִית״, לִנְקֹם עַל כָּל מִצְוָה וּמִצְוָה, שֶׁנִּכְרְתוּ עָלֶיהָ י״ו בְּרִיתוֹת. וּלְכָךְ י״ו פְּעָמִים ״חֶרֶב״ בְּפָרָשַׁת יוֹרְדֵי בוֹר:

❑ ד׳ פְּעָמִים ״נקם״ בַּפָּרָשָׁה, וּכְנֶגְדָּם אָמַר דָּוִד ד׳ פְּעָמִים ״עַד אָנָה״, וְד׳ פְּעָמִים ״פְּנֵי אֵלַי״:

❑ נ״ב פְּסוּקִים בְּהַאֲזִינוּ, וּלְפִי שֶׁעָבְרוּ עֲלֵיהֶם, לְכָךְ לֹא עָבַר אִישׁ בִּיהוּדָה נ״ב שָׁנָה:

BAAL HATURIM ELUCIDATED

[Alternatively:] It is spelled defectively, without a ו (= 6).[80] [This is an allusion to the fact] that the wicked are judged for six days.[81]

42. וְחַרְבִּי — AND MY SWORD. This term contains the same letters as חֶרֶב י״ו, [literally,] *sword of sixteen.* This indicates to you that God's sword has sixteen faces, as stated in the *Midrash Shocher Tov.*[82] [It is the sword described by the verse, וְהֵבֵאתִי עֲלֵיכֶם חֶרֶב, *I will bring upon you a sword,*] נֹקֶמֶת נְקַם בְּרִית, *avenging the vengeance of a covenant* (*Leviticus* 26:25). [It has sixteen faces,] for it avenges the transgression of each and every *mitzvah,* over which sixteen covenants were established.[83] Similarly, the passage regarding the יוֹרְדֵי בוֹר, *those who descend*

---

thousand years of the era of the Messiah. But, because of our many iniquities, what has passed of them has passed [and the Messiah has not yet come (*Rashi*)]. (See also the Baal HaTurim's last comment to *Genesis* 1:1.)

80. The text follows the later printed editions which present this allusion as an alternative explanation of the absent ו of לְעֹלָם. The early printed editions read: . . . ,. . . שֶׁאָז יִהְיֶה נִשְׂגָּב לְבַדּוֹ, *then He alone will be exalted,* שֶׁנִּתְחַסֵּר, *for we absented ourselves,* וָי״ו, *the letter* ו, . . . שֶׁשִּׁשָּׁה יָמִים, [*an allusion to the fact*] *that* [*for*] *six days* . . . Now that version does not make much sense as it stands. Rather, it is the result of a typographical error. For the manuscripts used by *Shoham Yakar* read, . . . שַׁנּוֹתִי חָסֵר וָי״ו, as if the comment were not an alternative explanation of the absent ו of לְעֹלָם, but a new comment on the absent ו of שַׁנֹּתִי (v. 41). The typesetter of the early printed editions then erroneously ran the two words שַׁנֹּתִי חָסֵר into one word שֶׁנִּתְחַסֵּר, losing the י along the way. However, that reading also presents a problem, for in all extant Torah scrolls and manuscript *Chumashim,* שַׁנּוֹתִי is spelled in full, with a ו. The text is presented in accordance with the later printed editions.

81. That is, the wicked are judged in *Gehinnom* during the six days of the workweek and are given respite on the Sabbath (see *Sanhedrin* 65b).

82. *Midrash Tehillim* 31 and 78.

83. See the Baal HaTurim to 1:1 above, with notes 4 and 5.

[41] *if I sharpen My flashing sword*
and My hand grasps judgment,
I shall return vengeance upon My enemies
and upon those that hate Me shall I bring retribution.
[42] *I shall intoxicate My arrows with blood*
and My sword shall devour flesh,
because of the blood of corpse and captive,
because of the earliest depredations of the enemy.' "
[43] *O nations — sing the praises of His people,*
for He will avenge the blood of His servants;
He will bring retribution upon His foes,
and He will appease His land and His people.

BAAL HATURIM ELUCIDATED

into the pit, mentions the term חֶרֶב, *a sword,* sixteen times.[84]

❑ The passage mentions נקם, *vengeance,* four times,[85] and corresponding to them, King David recited the expression עַד אָנָה, *how long,* four times,[86] and the request, פְּנֵה אֵלַי, *turn to me,* four times.[87]

43. {The Baal HaTurim's comment to וְכִפֶּר אַדְמָתוֹ עַמּוֹ appears at 9:33 above.}

❑ There are 52 verses in *Parashas Haazinu,* and, whereas the people transgressed against them, no man traversed[88] the land of Judah for fifty-two years.[89]

84. *Peirush HaRokeach.* The Baal HaTurim's intent here is unclear. *Ittur Bikkurim, Yad Aharon* and *Shoham Yakar* assume that he refers to Chapter 32 of *Ezekiel,* which mentions the term יוֹרְדֵי בוֹר, *those who descend into the pit,* five times (vv. 18,24,25,29,30). However, as *Ittur Bikkurim* correctly points out, forms of the noun חֶרֶב appear seventeen times in that chapter [(i) חַרְבִּי — v. 10; (ii-ix) חֶרֶב — vv. 11,20 (twice), 25, 26, 30, 31, 32; (x) בְּחַרְבוֹת — v. 12; (xi-xiii) חָרֶב — vv. 21, 28, 29; (xiv) בֶּחָרֶב — v. 22; (xv-xvi) בַּחֶרֶב — vv. 23, 24; and (xvii) חַרְבוֹתָם — v. 24].

Perhaps that chapter is only part of the Baal HaTurim's פָּרָשַׁת יוֹרְדֵי בוֹר, for that expression also appears twice in Chapter 31 (vv. 14 and 16) and two forms of the word חֶרֶב appear in that chapter [חָרֶב — v. 17; חֶרֶב — v. 18]. If so, the Baal HaTurim may refer only to those forms of חֶרֶב that do not have a suffix appended to them. Thus, three words fall from the earlier listing [חַרְבִּי בְּחַרְבוֹת חַרְבוֹתָם] and the two from Chapter 31 are added to that list. Hence there are sixteen appearances of the word חֶרֶב in the *parashah* of יוֹרְדֵי בוֹר in *Ezekiel* (*VeChur LaZahav*).

85. Four words of the root נקם appear in *parashas Haazinu:* (i-ii) נָקָם — vv. 35,41; (iii) יִקּוֹם — v. 43; and (iv) וְנָקָם — v. 43 (*Peirush HaRokeach*).

86. The expression עַד אָנָה appears five times in *Psalms* (13:2, twice; 13:3, twice; and 62:4). The Baal HaTurim refers to the four appearances in psalm 13 (*Yad Aharon; Shoham Yakar*).

87. *Psalms* 25:16, 69:17, 86:16 and 119:132.

88. There seems to be a play of words here, for the two verbs — עָבְרוּ, *they transgressed,* and עָבַר, *he traversed* — share the root עבר, which can mean *to go across* or *to transgress* (*VeChur LaZahav*).

89. *Peirush HaRokeach;* see *Yoma* 54a. It is not clear why the Baal HaTurim placed this comment at the end of the Song of *Haazinu,* which contains only 43 of the 52 verses of which he speaks. In *Peirush HaRokeach* this comment appears as the last one in the *sidra.*

לב/מד־נ מד *וַיָּבֹא מֹשֶׁה וַיְדַבֵּר אֶת־כָּל־דִּבְרֵי הַשִּׁירָה־הַזֹּאת
*שביעי מה בְּאָזְנֵי הָעָם הוּא וְהוֹשֵׁעַ בִּן־נוּן׃ וַיְכַל מֹשֶׁה לְדַבֵּר
מו אֶת־כָּל־הַדְּבָרִים הָאֵלֶּה אֶל־כָּל־יִשְׂרָאֵל׃ וַיֹּאמֶר
אֲלֵהֶם שִׂימוּ לְבַבְכֶם לְכָל־הַדְּבָרִים אֲשֶׁר אָנֹכִי
מֵעִיד בָּכֶם הַיּוֹם אֲשֶׁר תְּצַוֻּם אֶת־בְּנֵיכֶם לִשְׁמֹר
מז לַעֲשׂוֹת אֶת־כָּל־דִּבְרֵי הַתּוֹרָה הַזֹּאת׃ כִּי לֹא־דָבָר
רֵק הוּא מִכֶּם כִּי־הוּא חַיֵּיכֶם וּבַדָּבָר הַזֶּה תַּאֲרִיכוּ
יָמִים עַל־הָאֲדָמָה אֲשֶׁר אַתֶּם עֹבְרִים אֶת־הַיַּרְדֵּן
שָׁמָּה לְרִשְׁתָּהּ׃
מפטיר מח־מט וַיְדַבֵּר יהוה אֶל־מֹשֶׁה בְּעֶצֶם הַיּוֹם הַזֶּה לֵאמֹר׃ עֲלֵה
אֶל־הַר הָעֲבָרִים הַזֶּה הַר־נְבוֹ אֲשֶׁר בְּאֶרֶץ מוֹאָב
אֲשֶׁר עַל־פְּנֵי יְרֵחוֹ וּרְאֵה אֶת־אֶרֶץ כְּנַעַן אֲשֶׁר אֲנִי
נ נֹתֵן לִבְנֵי יִשְׂרָאֵל לַאֲחֻזָּה׃ וּמֻת בָּהָר אֲשֶׁר אַתָּה עֹלֶה
שָׁמָּה וְהֵאָסֵף אֶל־עַמֶּיךָ כַּאֲשֶׁר־מֵת אַהֲרֹן אָחִיךָ

בעל הטורים

(מז) כִּי לֹא דָבָר רֵק הוּא. תָּגִין עַל הַקּוּ״ף – לוֹמַר שֶׁאֲפִלּוּ עַל הַתָּגִין שֶׁל תּוֹרָה, תִּלֵּי תִלִּים שֶׁל הֲלָכוֹת:

☐ **רֵק.** ב׳ בַּמָּסֹרֶת – ״כִּי לֹא דָבָר רֵק הוּא״; ״וְהַבּוֹר רֵק״. לוֹמַר, כְּמוֹ שֶׁהַבּוֹר רֵק וְאֵינוֹ מִתְמַלֵּא מֵחֻלְיָתוֹ, כֵּן הַתּוֹרָה לֹא יוּכַל אָדָם לְהִתְמַלֹּאת מִמֶּנָּה:

(מח) וַיְדַבֵּר ה׳ אֶל מֹשֶׁה בְּעֶצֶם. עֲשָׂרָה דִסְמִיכֵי בְלֹא ״לֵאמֹר״, כְּנֶגֶד עֲשָׂרָה דִבְּרוֹת:

(נ) כַּאֲשֶׁר מֵת אַהֲרֹן. בְּגִימַטְרִיָּא הֵן בִּנְשִׁיקָה מֵת אַהֲרֹן:

BAAL HATURIM ELUCIDATED

47. כִּי לֹא דָבָר רֵק הוּא — FOR IT IS NOT AN EMPTY THING. [According to a scribal tradition,] the ק of this phrase is written with [three] *tagin* [crownlets].[90] This indicates that even from the crownlets of [the letters in] the Torah we can derive mounds upon mounds of laws.[91]

90. Regarding *tagin,* see first paragraph of note 11 to *parashas Devarim.*

Although the letter ק is usually crowned with only one *tag,* according to the ancient *Sefer Tagin,* the ק of רֵק is one of 185 (one version lists only 181) in the Torah that are uncharacteristically crowned with three (see illustration at note 53 to *parashas Devarim*).

91. *Peirush HaRokeach;* see *Eruvin* 21b, where the Talmud uses the word קוֹץ in place of תָּג. Neither *Peirush HaRokeach* nor the Baal HaTurim explains the relevancy of the letter ק to this allusion. It has been suggested that the ק stands for קוֹץ, which is synonymous with תָּג (*Shoham Yakar*).

Alternatively: The three *tagin* represent three *halachos* (laws) heaped up on the ק. If we take the *gematria* of הֲלָכָה, *law* (= 60), three times, we get a total of 180, the *gematria* of קוּף [or קֹף], the name of the letter (*VeChur LaZahav*).

[44] *Moses came and spoke all the words of this Song in the ears of the people, he and Hoshea son of Nun.* [45] *Moses concluded speaking all these words to all Israel.* [46] *He said to them, "Apply your hearts to all the words that I testify against you today, with which you are to instruct your children, to be careful to perform all the words of this Torah,* [47] *for it is not an empty thing for you, for it is your life, and through this matter shall you prolong your days on the land to which you cross the Jordan, to possess it."*

[48] *HASHEM spoke to Moses on that very day, saying,* [49] *"Ascend to this mount of Abarim, Mount Nebo, which is in the land of Moab, which is before Jericho, and see the Land of Canaan that I give to the Children of Israel as an inheritance,* [50] *and die on the mountain where you will ascend, and be gathered to your people, as Aaron your brother died*

BAAL HATURIM ELUCIDATED

❑ רֵק — EMPTY. The masoretic note, ב׳, means that this word appears twice in the *Tanach*: (i) here, כִּי לֹא דָבָר רֵק הוּא, *for it is not an empty thing;* and (ii) וְהַבּוֹר רֵק, *the pit was empty* (*Genesis* 37:24).[92] The similarity of expression indicates: Just as an empty pit can never be filled to capacity with the earth removed from it, so too, regarding the Torah, a person can never become filled to capacity with it.[93]

48. וַיְדַבֵּר ה׳ אֶל מֹשֶׁה בְּעֶצֶם — HASHEM SPOKE TO MOSES ON THAT VERY [DAY]. This phrase appears ten times in the Torah without [being followed immediately by] the word לֵאמֹר,[94] corresponding to the Ten Commandments.[95]

50. כַּאֲשֶׁר מֵת אַהֲרֹן — AS AARON ... DIED. The *gematria* of this phrase (1217) is equivalent[96] to that of הֵן בִּנְשִׁיקָה מֵת אַהֲרֹן, *Behold, with a kiss [from God] Aaron died.*[97]

92. See the Baal HaTurim to that verse for a different explanation of the masoretic note.

93. As the verse describes the Torah: אֲרֻכָּה מֵאֶרֶץ מִדָּה, *Longer than the earth is its measure,* וּרְחָבָה מִנִּי יָם, *and broader than the sea* (*Job* 11:9). And as King David writes: לְכָל תִּכְלָה רָאִיתִי קֵץ, *To every purpose I have seen an end,* רְחָבָה מִצְוָתְךָ מְאֹד, [*but*] *Your commandment* [i.e., the Torah] *is exceedingly broad* (*Psalms* 119:96). The Talmud cites three verses that speak of the vastness of the Torah but do not quantify it — the verses from *Job* and *Psalms,* as well as *Ezekiel* 2:10. The Talmud then adduces a fourth verse (*Zechariah* 5:2) from which it proves that the Torah is 3,200 times as vast as the universe (*Eruvin* 21a). It is noteworthy that the term רָחָב, *broad,* alludes to that number: For when the *gematriaos* of its letters are multiplied with one another, the product is [200x8x2 =] 3200 (*VeChur LaZahav*).

94. *Exodus* 32:7, 33:1; *Leviticus* 16:1, 25:1; *Numbers* 1:1, 3:14, 9:1, 33:50, 35:1; and here.

95. *Peirush HaRokeach.* Neither *Peirush HaRokeach* nor the Baal HaTurim explains the connection between this phrase and the Ten Commandments.

96. The principle of *im hakollel* allows 1217 to be considered equivalent to 1218, the *gematria* of the Baal HaTurim's phrase.

97. *Bava Basra* 17a; see *Rashi* to *Numbers* 20:1 and 33:38; see the Baal HaTurim to *Numbers* 20:28 and 27:3.

מִיתַת נְשִׁיקָה, *death by a kiss* [*of God*], as it were, means death directly through God, without the intercession of the Angel of Death (see *Bava Basra* 17a; *Rabbeinu Bachya*). The Talmud

נא בְּהֹר הָהָר וַיֵּאָסֶף אֶל־עַמָּיו: עַל אֲשֶׁר מְעַלְתֶּם בִּי
בְּתוֹךְ בְּנֵי יִשְׂרָאֵל בְּמֵי־מְרִיבַת קָדֵשׁ מִדְבַּר־צִן עַל
נב אֲשֶׁר לֹא־קִדַּשְׁתֶּם אוֹתִי בְּתוֹךְ בְּנֵי יִשְׂרָאֵל: כִּי
מִנֶּגֶד תִּרְאֶה אֶת־הָאָרֶץ וְשָׁמָּה לֹא תָבוֹא אֶל־
הָאָרֶץ אֲשֶׁר־אֲנִי נֹתֵן לִבְנֵי יִשְׂרָאֵל: פפפ

נ״ב פסוקים. כל״ב סימן.

──── BAAL HATURIM ELUCIDATED ────

51. {The Baal HaTurim's comment to בְּמֵי appears at *Numbers* 19:21.}

describes this as the most desirable form of death, likening it to pulling a hair from milk; that is, the soul leaves the body without resistance (*Berachos* 8a). This means that to the extent that people sin in life and establish a bond between their souls and the pleasures of this world, it becomes increasingly more difficult for them to part from physical life. For those who have become totally attached to physicality, the Sages liken death to pulling embedded thistles from sheep's wool. But for those of the stature of Moses, Aaron and Miriam, whose souls remained pure throughout their earthly sojourn, there is no effort and no pain when the soul returns to its source (*Resisei Laylah* 56).

32/51-52   *on Mount Hor, and was gathered to his people,* [51] *because you trespassed against Me among the Children of Israel at the waters of Meribath-kadesh, in the wilderness of Zin; because you did not sanctify Me among the Children of Israel.* [52] *For from a distance you shall see the land, but you shall not enter there, into the land that I give to the Children of Israel.* "

❧ פרשת וזאת הברכה

Parashas Vezos Haberachah

לג/א־ב א וְזֹ֣את הַבְּרָכָ֗ה אֲשֶׁ֨ר בֵּרַ֥ךְ מֹשֶׁ֛ה אִ֥ישׁ הָאֱלֹהִ֖ים אֶת־
ב בְּנֵ֣י יִשְׂרָאֵ֑ל לִפְנֵ֖י מוֹתֽוֹ׃ וַיֹּאמַ֗ר יהוה֙ מִסִּינַ֥י בָּא֙ וְזָרַ֤ח

בעל הטורים

לג (א) וְזֹאת הַבְּרָכָה. לְעֵיל מִנֵּהּ כְּתִיב "אֲשֶׁר אֲנִי נֹתֵן לִבְנֵי יִשְׂרָאֵל", וּסְמִיךְ לֵהּ "וְזֹאת הַבְּרָכָה". לוֹמַר, אֲנִי מַסְכִּים עַל בִּרְכָתָם:

❑ **וְזֹאת הַבְּרָכָה.** בְּגִימַטְרִיָּא זוֹ הִיא הַתּוֹרָה. כִּי בִזְכוּת הַתּוֹרָה בֵּרְכָם:

❑ **מֹשֶׁה אִישׁ הָאֱלֹהִים.** רָאשֵׁי תֵבוֹת מֵאָה {וְסוֹפֵי תֵבוֹת הַשֵּׁם} וְסוֹפֵי תֵבוֹת מֹשֶׁה. וְזֶהוּ "ה' אֱלֹהֵי אֲבוֹתֵכֶם יֹסֵף עֲלֵיכֶם כָּכֶם אֶלֶף פְּעָמִים". שֶׁאָמַר, תְּנוּ לוֹ מֵאָה בְרָכוֹת בְּכָל יוֹם. וּבְכָל בְּרָכָה וּבְרָכָה עֲשָׂרָה זְהוּבִים, הֲרֵי אֶלֶף. לְכָךְ אָמַר יֹסֵף הַשֵּׁם "עֲלֵיכֶם כָּכֶם אֶלֶף פְּעָמִים" מִשֶּׁלִּי, "וִיבָרֵךְ אֶתְכֶם" מִשֶּׁלּוֹ.

❑ הַפָּסוּק מַתְחִיל בְּוָי"ו וּמְסַיֵּם בְּוָי"ו. לוֹמַר שֶׁבֵּרַךְ שְׁנֵים עָשָׂר שְׁבָטִים:

(ב) וְזָרַח. ג' – {"וְזָרַח מִשֵּׂעִיר";} "וְזָרַח בַּחֹשֶׁךְ"; "וְזָרַח הַשֶּׁמֶשׁ". "וְזָרַח מִשֵּׂעִיר". שֶׁנִּגְלָה

BAAL HATURIM ELUCIDATED

XXXIII.

1. וְזֹאת הַבְּרָכָה — AND THIS IS THE BLESSING. Just before this is written, אֲשֶׁר אֲנִי נֹתֵן לִבְנֵי יִשְׂרָאֵל, *that I give to the Children of Israel,*[1] to indicate [that God said,] "I concur[2] with their blessing [i.e., with the blessing that Moses gave them].[3]

❑ **וְזֹאת הַבְּרָכָה — AND THIS IS THE BLESSING.** The *gematria* of this phrase (646) is equivalent[4] to that of זוֹ הִיא הַתּוֹרָה, *This is the Torah.* For he blessed them through the merit of the Torah.[5]

1. The last five verses of *parashas Haazinu* record God's words to Moses regarding his impending death. That passage closes with God telling Moses that he will not enter the Land of Canaan, rather, *"from a distance you shall see the land, but you shall not enter there, into the land that I give to the Children of Israel"* (32:52). Accordingly, we would expect the next passage to begin, וַיְבָרֶךְ מֹשֶׁה . . . אֶת בְּנֵי יִשְׂרָאֵל, *Moses blessed . . . the Children of Israel . . .*, and then to continue, וַיֹּאמַר, *he said,* or וְזֹאת הַבְּרָכָה, *and this is the blessing.* The Baal HaTurim explains that by beginning this passage with וְזֹאת הַבְּרָכָה, *And this is the blessing,* the Torah indicates that this phrase may be interpreted as part of the preceding verse (see note 2). For another explanation of why the passage begins with וְזֹאת, see the Baal HaTurim's next comment, with note 5.

2. That is, the juxtaposed verses may be interpreted: הָאָרֶץ אֲשֶׁר אֲנִי נֹתֵן לִבְנֵי יִשְׂרָאֵל, *the land that I give to the Children of Israel,* וְזֹאת, *and* [*also*] *this,* הַבְּרָכָה אֲשֶׁר בֵּרַךְ מֹשֶׁה, *the blessing that Moses blessed . . .*, i.e., God said, "I give them the land and Moses' blessing" (*VeChur LaZahav*).

3. *R' Ephraim* — God told Moses, "You bless Israel and I will concur with the blessings [that you give them]."

According to this understanding of the verses, Moses composed his own blessing, then God concurred with it (see also *Sforno* here and at 4:25 above). In this, the Baal HaTurim and *R' Ephraim* disagree with those *Rishonim* who infer from the term אִישׁ הָאֱלֹהִים, *the man of God* [which *Targum Onkelos* renders, נְבִיָּא דַיְיָ, *prophet of* HASHEM], that Moses' blessing came to him as a prophecy (see *Ibn Ezra*). Thus, the *Ramban* explains that the word וְזֹאת, *and this,* implies that מֵאֵת ה' הָיְתָה זֹּאת, *"this" emanated from* HASHEM (*Psalms* 118:23), i.e., this blessing was a prophecy. See also *Bechor Shor* and *R' Chaim Paltiel.*

4. The principle of *im hakollel* allows 645, the *gematria* of the Baal HaTurim's phrase, to be considered equivalent to 646.

5. The Midrash states that the Torah begins the passage of Moses' blessings with the word וְזֹאת, the same word with which Jacob ended his blessings (*Bereishis Rabbah* 100:12; *Tanchuma, Vayechi* 16; see the Baal HaTurim to *Genesis* 49:28). The Midrash explains: Jacob said, "I am

1 And this is the blessing that Moses, the man of God, bestowed upon the Children of Israel before his death.
2 He said: HASHEM came from Sinai — He shone forth

BAAL HATURIM ELUCIDATED

❑ {The Baal HaTurim's other comment to וְזֹאת הַבְּרָכָה appears at *Genesis* 49:28.}

❑ מֹשֶׁה אִישׁ הָאֱלֹהִים — MOSES, THE MAN OF GOD. The initial letters of these three words spell מֵאָה, *one hundred,* {and the final letters spell הַשֵּׁם, *HASHEM,* }[6] and the final letters [in reverse order] spell מֹשֶׁה, *Moses.* This is [an allusion to the verse]: ה׳ אֱלֹהֵי אֲבוֹתֵיכֶם יֹסֵף עֲלֵיכֶם כָּכֶם אֶלֶף פְּעָמִים [וִיבָרֵךְ אֶתְכֶם], *HASHEM, the God of your forefathers, will add to you a thousand times yourselves* [*and He will bless you*] (*Deuteronomy* 1:11). [Moses] said, "Give Him one hundred blessings each day."[7] And each blessing has a value of ten gold pieces,[8] thus you have (10x100 =) 1000. Accordingly, [Moses] said, "HASHEM will add *to you a thousand times yourselves,* this [blessing] is from me;[8a] *and He will bless you,* on His own.[8b]"[9]

❑ The verse begins[10] with a ו (= 6) and ends with a ו,[10a] indicating that [Moses] blessed [all] twelve tribes.[11]

2. וְזָרַח — HE SHINED FORTH. The masoretic note, ג׳, means that this word appears three times in the *Tanach*: {(i) here, וְזָרַח מִשֵּׂעִיר, *He shone forth from Seir;* }[12] (ii) וְזָרַח בַּחֹשֶׁךְ, *it radiated with darkness*[13] (*Isaiah* 58:10); and (iii) וְזָרַח הַשֶּׁמֶשׁ, *and the sun shone forth*[13a] (*Ecclesiastes* 1:5). [This similarity of expression indicates] that God

---

giving you these blessings [now], but when will you attain them? At the time that you accept the Torah." As it is written, וְזֹאת הַתּוֹרָה, *This is the Torah* (*Deuteronomy* 4:44). Thus, both the blessings of וְזֹאת given to Israel by Jacob and the blessings of וְזֹאת given to Israel by Moses were dependent upon the merit of their accepting the וְזֹאת of the Torah.

6. The passage enclosed in braces is not found in the early or later printed editions. It does appear in the manuscripts used by *Shoham Yakar* and in *Peirush HaRokeach,* the Baal HaTurim's apparent source for this comment. However, the following sentence — and the final letters spell Moses — is absent from *Peirush HaRokeach.*

7. See note 44 to *parashas Vaeschanan* above.

8. See *Chullin* 87a.

8a. This is the implication of the final letters spelling מֹשֶׁה.

8b. This is the implication of the final letters spelling הַשֵּׁם.

9. *Peirush HaRokeach.*

10. Whereas this verse begins a new topic, the conjunctive prefix -וְ, *and,* requires an explanation.

10a. This phenomenon appears in 549 Torah verses. The Baal HaTurim expounds on it here and at *Exodus* 1:1, each time explaining it as an allusion to the twelve tribes.

11. *Peirush HaRokeach* — The verse begins with a ו and ends with a ו and comprises twelve words, for there are twelve tribes [that received Moses' blessings]. [Even though Moses did not mention the tribe of Simeon by name, the *Sifrei* teaches that] he alluded to Simeon in Judah's blessing, שְׁמַע ה׳ קוֹל יְהוּדָה, *Hearken, O HASHEM, to Judah's voice* (v. 7 below). [Moses' expression שְׁמַע ה׳ alludes to Leah's reason for naming her son שִׁמְעוֹן, *Simeon*: For *she said, "Because,* שָׁמַע ה׳, *HASHEM has heard . . ."* (*Genesis* 29:33).]

12. The phrase enclosed in braces is not found in most editions. It does appear, however, in the manuscripts used by *Shoham Yakar.*

13. The word זָרַח is a simple past form of the root זרח and means *he* or *it shone.* The prefix -וְ is ambiguous: It can be a conjunction, *and,* or it can be the conversive ו that changes a verb form from past tense to future. Thus, in the Scriptural context, the phrase from *Isaiah* means, *it will shine through the darkness,* but in the Baal HaTurim's comment it is interpreted in the past tense.

13a. See note 13. In the verse from *Ecclesiastes* the word is usually understood as indicating

לג/ג מִשֵּׂעִיר֙ לָ֔מוֹ הוֹפִ֙יעַ֙ מֵהַ֣ר פָּארָ֔ן וְאָתָ֖ה מֵרִבְבֹ֣ת קֹ֑דֶשׁ
[°אֵ֥שׁ דָּ֖ת ק׳] ג מִֽימִינ֕וֹ °אשדת לָֽמוֹ׃ אַ֚ף חֹבֵ֣ב עַמִּ֔ים כָּל־קְדֹשָׁ֖יו

בעל הטורים

לְעֵשָׂו לְקַבֵּל אֶת הַתּוֹרָה וְלֹא רָצוּ. עַל כֵּן "וְזָרַח בַּחֹשֶׁךְ", שֶׁנֶּעֶנְשׁוּ וְנֶהְפַּךְ לָהֶם לְחֹשֶׁךְ וְלַאֲפֵלָה. אֲבָל יִשְׂרָאֵל שֶׁקִּבְּלוּהָ, "וְזָרַח הַשֶּׁמֶשׁ", שֶׁנֶּאֱמַר "מִצְוַת ה׳ בָּרָה מְאִירַת עֵינָיִם":

❑ **הוֹפִיעַ.** ג׳ — "הוֹפִיעַ מֵהַר פָּארָן"; "מִצִּיּוֹן מִכְלַל יֹפִי אֱלֹהִים הוֹפִיעַ"; "אֵל נְקָמוֹת ה׳ אֵל נְקָמוֹת הוֹפִיעַ". {כְּמוֹ כֵן נִגְלָה לִבְנֵי יִשְׁמָעֵאל, כִּדְכְתִיב "הוֹפִיעַ מֵהַר פָּארָן", וְלֹא קִבְּלוּהָ. עַל כֵּן "אֵל נְקָמוֹת הוֹפִיעַ".} אֲבָל יִשְׂרָאֵל שֶׁקִּבְּלוּ, זָכוּ מַה שֶּׁנֶּאֱמַר "מִצִּיּוֹן מִכְלַל יֹפִי אֱלֹהִים הוֹפִיעַ":

❑ **מֵרִבְבֹת.** ב׳ — "וְאָתָה מֵרִבְבֹת קֹדֶשׁ"; "לֹא אִירָא מֵרִבְבוֹת עָם". לָמָּה? כִּי ה׳ "אָתָה מֵרִבְבֹת קֹדֶשׁ" לְעֶזְרֵנִי:

(ג) **אַף חֹבֵב עַמִּים.** בְּגִימַטְרִיָּא גֵּרִים. שֶׁאַף הַגֵּרִים הָעֲתִידִין לְהִתְגַּיֵּר עָמְדוּ בְּסִינַי. וְכֵן "אֶת אֲשֶׁר יֶשְׁנוֹ פֹּה" סוֹפֵי תֵבוֹת תּוֹרָה. שֶׁכֻּלָּם הָיוּ שָׁם בִּשְׁעַת מַתַּן תּוֹרָה. וְאָמַר בִּלְשׁוֹן "אַף", מִשּׁוּם דְּמַיְרֵי בְּבַעֲלֵי יִסּוּרִים שֶׁמִּתְיַסְּרִים עַל דִּבְרֵי תוֹרָה:

❑ **קְדֹשָׁיו.** ב׳ — "כָּל קְדֹשָׁיו בְּיָדֶךָ"; "יְראוּ אֶת ה׳ קְדֹשָׁיו". לָמָּה "יְראוּ אֶת ה׳ קְדֹשָׁיו", כִּי "כָּל קְדֹשָׁיו בְּיָדֶךָ":

BAAL HATURIM ELUCIDATED

revealed Himself to [the descendants of] Esau, [asking them] to accept the Torah, but they refused.[14] Therefore, *it radiated* with *darkness,* for they were punished and [their lives] were transformed into darkness and blackness. While for Israel, who accepted the Torah, *the sun shone forth,* as it is stated, מִצְוַת ה׳ בָּרָה מְאִירַת עֵינָיִם, *The command of HASHEM*[14a] *is clear,* [*it is the*] *enlightenment of the eyes* (*Psalms* 19:9).[15]

❑ **הוֹפִיעַ — HE APPEARED.**[15] The masoretic note, ג׳, means that this word appears three times in the *Tanach*: (i) here, הוֹפִיעַ מֵהַר פָּארָן, *He appeared from Mount Paran;* (ii) מִצִּיּוֹן מִכְלַל יֹפִי אֱלֹהִים הוֹפִיעַ, *Out of Zion, consummation of beauty, God appeared* (*Psalms* 50:2); and (iii) אֵל נְקָמוֹת ה׳ אֵל נְקָמוֹת הוֹפִיעַ, *The God of vengeance is HASHEM; the God of vengeance has appeared*[16] (*Psalms* 94:1). {[This similarity of expression indicates] that [just as God had appeared to the descendants of Esau,] He also appeared to the descendants of Ishmael, as it is written, *He appeared from Mount Paran* [and asked them to accept the Torah], but they did

ongoing action: וְזָרַח הַשֶּׁמֶשׁ וּבָא הַשָּׁמֶשׁ, *and the sun shines forth and the sun sets,* i.e., וְזָרַח is understood as both *it shone forth* and *it will shine forth,* while וּבָא is understood as both *it set* and *it will set,* for the rising and setting of the sun are ongoing processes that occurred in the past, occur in the present, and will continue to occur in the future (*VeChur LaZahav*).

14. *Sifrei; Avodah Zarah* 2b; see Rashi here.

14a. A reference to the Torah (see the Baal HaTurim to 32:10 above).

15. The two comments (s.v., וְזָרַח and הוֹפִיעַ) share the same theme.

16. The verb הוֹפִיעַ is in the past tense, *he appeared,* and that is how it is used in the Torah verse and in *Psalms* 50:2. In *Psalms* 94:1, however, the commentaries interpret it as an imperative (see *Targum, Rashi* and *Michlal Yofi*). Accordingly, in that verse it is synonymous with הוֹפִיעָה of *Psalms* 80:2. In the Baal HaTurim's comment, however, אֵל נְקָמוֹת הוֹפִיעַ is understood as *the God of vengeance appeared* (*VeChur LaZahav*).

from Seir to them, He appeared from Mount Paran, and He arrived with some of the holy myriads — from His right hand He presented a fire of law to them. 3 *Indeed, You love the tribes, all its holy ones are in Your*

BAAL HATURIM ELUCIDATED

not accept it.[17] Therefore, *HASHEM; the God of vengeance, appeared.* }[18] While Israel, who did accept [the Torah], merited what is stated, *Out of Zion, consummation of beauty, God appeared.*

❑ **מֵרִבְבֹת** — SOME OF THE MYRIADS. The masoretic note, ב׳, means that this word appears twice in the *Tanach*:[19] (i) here, וְאָתָה מֵרִבְבֹת קֹדֶשׁ, *and He arrived with some of the holy myriads;* and (ii) לֹא אִירָא מֵרִבְבוֹת עָם, *I shall not be afraid of myriads of people* (*Psalms* 3:7). Why [is it that *I shall not be afraid of myriads of people*]? Because HASHEM will have arrived *with some of the holy myriads* to assist me.

❑ {The Baal HaTurim's comment to מִימִינוֹ אֵשׁ דָּת appears at *Leviticus* 6:1.}

3. אַף חֹבֵב עַמִּים — INDEED, [YOU] LOVE THE TRIBES. The *gematria* of this phrase (253) is equal to that of גֵּרִים, *converts.* For even [the souls of] those who would ultimately convert stood at Mount Sinai. Similarly, the verse, אֶת אֲשֶׁר יֶשְׁנוֹ פֹּה, *but with the one who is here*[20] (*Deuteronomy* 29:14), for the last letters of that phrase [can be rearranged to] spell the word תּוֹרָה, *Torah.*[21]

Our verse uses the word אַף,[22] because it refers to those afflicted souls who suffer [even further] privation in [order to commit themselves to] the words of the Torah.[23]

❑ **כָּל קְדֹשָׁיו** — ALL ITS HOLY ONES. The masoretic note, ב׳, means that this word appears twice in the *Tanach*: (i) here, כָּל קְדֹשָׁיו בְּיָדֶךָ, *all its holy ones are in Your hand;* and (ii) יְראוּ אֶת ה׳ קְדֹשָׁיו, *Fear HASHEM, O [you] its holy ones*[24] (*Psalms* 34:10). Why should all its holy ones fear [You], HASHEM? Because *all its holy ones are in Your hand.*

---

17. *Sifrei; Avodah Zarah* 2b; see *Rashi* here.

18. The passage enclosed in brackets is not found in the earlier or later printed editions. It does appear, however, in the manuscripts used by *Shoham Yakar.*

19. The full note, as it appears in some editions of the *Massorah,* reads: ב׳ חַד חָסֵר וְחַד מָלֵא, *Two; one spelled defectively* [without a ו], *and one spelled in full* [with a ו].

20. The Scriptural quotation adduced here is almost certainly the result of a copyist's error. For in *Peirush HaRokeach,* the Baal HaTurim's source for this comment, a later phrase from that same verse is adduced: וְאֵת אֲשֶׁר אֵינֶנּוּ פֹּה, *and with the one who is not here,* and the final letters of that phrase are the same as the final letters of the earlier one. Moreover, it is from this second phrase that the Talmud (*Shavuos* 39a) infers that the future converts stood at Sinai (*VeChur LaZahav*).

21. *Peirush HaRokeach;* see note 42 to *parashas Ki Seitzei* above.

22. The term אַף, as used here, is an adverb and means *even* or *indeed.* But it is also a noun that means *nose* or *anger* [often exhibited by heavy nasal breathing].

23. See the Baal HaTurim's comment below, s.v., תֻּכּוּ.

24. In the context of *Psalms,* the verse refers to *His holy ones,* i.e., those who sanctify their lives to His service. The Baal HaTurim's comment, however, interprets קְדֹשָׁיו as *its holy ones,* with the nation of Israel as the antecedent of "its."

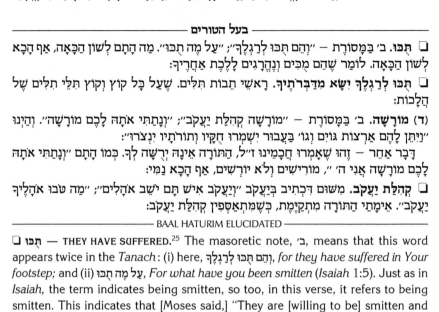

ד בְּיָדֶךָ וְהֵם֙ תֻּכּ֣וּ לְרַגְלֶ֔ךָ יִשָּׂ֖א מִדַּבְּרֹתֶֽיךָ: תּוֹרָ֥ה צִוָּה־
ה לָ֖נוּ מֹשֶׁ֑ה מוֹרָשָׁ֖ה קְהִלַּ֥ת יַעֲקֹֽב: וַיְהִ֥י בִישֻׁר֖וּן מֶ֑לֶךְ

בעל הטורים

❑ תֻּכּוּ. ב׳ בַּמָּסוֹרֶת – "וְהֵם תֻּכּוּ לְרַגְלֶךָ"; "עַל מֶה תֻכּוּ". מַה הָתָם לְשׁוֹן הַכָּאָה, אַף הָכָא לְשׁוֹן הַכָּאָה. לוֹמַר שֶׁהֵם מֻכִּים וְנֶהֱרָגִים לָלֶכֶת אַחֲרֶיךָ:

❑ תֻּכּוּ לְרַגְלֶךָ יִשָּׂא מִדַּבְּרֹתֶיךָ. רָאשֵׁי תֵבוֹת תִּלִּים. שֶׁעַל כָּל קוֹץ וְקוֹץ תִּלֵּי תִלִּים שֶׁל הֲלָכוֹת:

(ד) מוֹרָשָׁה. ב׳ בַּמָּסוֹרֶת – "מוֹרָשָׁה קְהִלַּת יַעֲקֹב"; "וְנָתַתִּי אֹתָהּ לָכֶם מוֹרָשָׁה". וְהַיְנוּ "וַיִּתֵּן לָהֶם אַרְצוֹת גּוֹיִם וְגוֹ׳ בַּעֲבוּר יִשְׁמְרוּ חֻקָּיו וְתוֹרֹתָיו יִנְצֹרוּ":

דָּבָר אַחֵר – זֶהוּ שֶׁאָמְרוּ חֲכָמֵינוּ ז״ל, הַתּוֹרָה אֵינָהּ יְרֻשָּׁה לְךָ. כְּמוֹ הָתָם "וְנָתַתִּי אֹתָהּ לָכֶם מוֹרָשָׁה אֲנִי ה׳", מוֹרִישִׁים וְלֹא יוֹרְשִׁים, אַף הָכָא נַמִּי:

❑ קְהִלַּת יַעֲקֹב. מִשּׁוּם דִּכְתִיב בְּיַעֲקֹב "וְיַעֲקֹב אִישׁ תָּם יֹשֵׁב אֹהָלִים"; "מַה טֹּבוּ אֹהָלֶיךָ יַעֲקֹב". אֵימָתַי הַתּוֹרָה מִתְקַיֶּמֶת, כְּשֶׁמִּתְאַסְּפִין קְהִלַּת יַעֲקֹב:

BAAL HATURIM ELUCIDATED

❑ תֻּכּוּ — **THEY HAVE SUFFERED.**[25] The masoretic note, ב׳, means that this word appears twice in the *Tanach*: (i) here, וְהֵם תֻּכּוּ לְרַגְלֶךָ, *for they have suffered in Your footstep;* and (ii) עַל מֶה תֻכּוּ, *For what have you been smitten* (*Isaiah* 1:5). Just as in *Isaiah,* the term indicates being smitten, so too, in this verse, it refers to being smitten. This indicates that [Moses said,] "They are [willing to be] smitten and [even] murdered,[26] to be able to follow You."

❑ תֻּכּוּ לְרַגְלֶךָ יִשָּׂא מִדַּבְּרֹתֶיךָ — **THEY HAVE SUFFERED IN YOUR FOOTSTEP, BEARING [THE YOKE] OF YOUR UTTERANCES.** The initial letters of these four words spell תִּלִּים, *mounds.* For upon each and every *tag* [serif or crownlet of the letters in the Torah] the Sages expound mounds upon mounds of laws.[27]

4. מוֹרָשָׁה — **IS THE HERITAGE.** The masoretic note, ב׳, means that this word

25. In *Peirush HaTur HaAroch,* the Baal HaTurim cites *Ibn Ezra's* two interpretations of the word תֻּכּוּ: This word is unique in Scripture — some say it is related to תּוֹךְ, *within,* i.e., they remained within the area traversed by Your feet [so to speak]; others say it is of the root נכה, *to be smitten,* and is a variant form of הֻכּוּ, *they were smitten,* that they [were willing to be] smitten with all kinds of suffering in the wilderness, as long as they would be able to follow You wherever You would go. The Baal HaTurim adopts this second understanding of תֻּכּוּ and his comment explains why he does so.

26. The text follows *Shoham Yakar's* manuscript version, which is in accord with the *Sifrei's* statement, אַף עַל פִּי שֶׁאֲנוּסִים אַף עַל פִּי שֶׁלּוּקִים אַף עַל פִּי שֶׁשְּׁבוּיִים, *even though they are imprisoned, even though they are beaten, even though they are taken captive.* Similarly, the parallel versions of other commentaries: שֶׁהֵם מִתְכַּתְּתִין בַּגָּלוּת, *for they are crushed in the exile* (*Pesikta Zutresa* [*Midrash Lekach Tov*]; שֶׁמֻּכִּים וְלוּקִים, *for they are smitten and beaten* (*R' Yehudah HaChassid*); שֶׁהֵם נֶהֱרָגִים וְנִכְתָּתִים, *for they are murdered and crushed* (*R' Chaim Paltiel*). The other printed editions of the Baal HaTurim, however, read, שֶׁהֵם מֻכִּים לְהִכָּנֵס וְלָלֶכֶת אַחֲרֶיךָ, *for they are* [*willing to be*] *smitten in order to enter* [*Your retinue*] *to be able to follow You.*

27. See the Baal HaTurim to 32:47 with note 91.

The connection between the verse and the Baal HaTurim's comment is unclear. Perhaps, he is reading תֻּכּוּ as if it were spelled with a ג, for the letters ג and כ are both palatals [i.e., letters pronounced with part of the tongue held near the hard palate] and are sometimes interchanged (see note 10 to *parashas Nitzavim* above). Thus, the word תֻּכּוּ is understood as תֻּגוּ, an imaginary verb that refers to the study of the implications of the *tagin* on the letters of the Torah (*VeChur LaZahav*).

hand; for they have suffered [yet they have followed] in Your footstep, bearing [the yoke] of Your utterances: 4 *"The Torah that Moses commanded us is a heritage of the Congregation of Jacob."* 5 *He became King over Jeshurun*

BAAL HATURIM ELUCIDATED

appears twice in the Torah:[28] (i) here, מוֹרָשָׁה קְהִלַּת יַעֲקֹב, *a heritage for the Congregation of Jacob;* and (ii) וְנָתַתִּי אֹתָהּ לָכֶם מוֹרָשָׁה, *and I shall give it to you as a heritage* (*Exodus* 6:8).[29] This [similarity reflects another verse], וַיִּתֵּן לָהֶם אַרְצוֹת גּוֹיִם . . . בַּעֲבוּר יִשְׁמְרוּ חֻקָּיו וְתוֹרֹתָיו יִנְצֹרוּ, *And He gave them the lands of nations . . . so that they might safeguard His decrees and observe His teachings* (*Psalms* 105:44-45).[30]

Alternatively: This [similarity] is [to be understood on the basis] of what our Sages, of blessed memory, have said: The Torah is not an inheritance for you.[31] Just as [it is stated] there [regarding the Land of Israel and the Israelites who left Egypt], וְנָתַתִּי אֹתָהּ לָכֶם מוֹרָשָׁה אֲנִי ה׳, *and I shall give it to you as a heritage, I,* HASHEM, and that verse means that they are able to bequeath it [to their children], but they cannot inherit it for themselves.[32] Similarly, here [regarding the Torah].[33,34]

❑ קְהִלַּת יַעֲקֹב — THE CONGREGATION OF JACOB. [The verse speaks specifically of Jacob] regarding whom the verse states, וְיַעֲקֹב אִישׁ תָּם יֹשֵׁב אֹהָלִים, *but Jacob was a wholesome man, dwelling in tents*[34a] (*Genesis* 25:27); מַה טֹּבוּ אֹהָלֶיךָ יַעֲקֹב, *How goodly are your tents, O Jacob*[35] (*Numbers* 24:5). When will the Torah be maintained? When the Congregation of Jacob gathers together.[36]

---

28. The full note reads ב׳ בַּתּוֹרָה, *Two, in the Pentateuch.* The word appears a third time in *Ezekiel* 36:3.

29. In his first comment to that verse, the Baal HaTurim explains the masoretic note in the same manner: For in the merit of the Toah the nation inherited the land, as it is written, *And He gave them the lands of nations . . .*

30. *Peirush HaRokeach.*

31. *Avos* 2:12 — Prepare yourself to study Torah, for it [i.e., Torah knowledge] is not an inheritance for you.

32. *Bava Basra* 119b. See the Baal HaTurim's comment to *Exodus* 6:8, where he states: The verse uses the term מוֹרָשָׁה, *heritage,* rather than יְרֻשָּׁה, *inheritance,* as an allusion to the fact that the Israelites living in Egypt would bequeath the Land of Israel to their descendants, but they would not take possession of it themselves, for they would not enter the land.

33. That is, the Torah is a heritage that every Israelite bequeaths to his children; but Torah knowledge does not come as an inheritance — it can be acquired only through diligent study.

34. *Maharam MiRothenburg.*

34a. According to the Midrash the term אֹהָלִים, *tents,* of that verse refers to the study halls of Shem [son of Noah] and Eber [great-grandson of Shem] (*Bereishis Rabbah* 63:10, cited by *Rashi* to *Genesis* 25:27). In his comments to that verse, however, the Baal HaTurim explains *tents* as the First Temple.

35. Both *Rashi* and the Baal HaTurim interpret אֹהָלֶיךָ, *your tents,* of that verse as referring to the Sanctuaries, including both the *Mishkan* and the two Temples. Here, the Baal HaTurim follows *Targum Yonasan ben Uzziel* where אֹהָלֶיךָ is rendered בָּתֵּי מִדְרְשַׁיכוֹן, *your study halls.* And the *Sforno* states: [This refers to] בָּתֵּי תוֹרָה, *halls of Torah,* similar to the verse יֹשֵׁב אֹהָלִים.

It is noteworthy that in the *aleph-beis* exchange known as אַיִ״ק בְּכַ״ר (see Introduction in Vol. I), the letters א and ק may be interchanged. Thus, the letters of אֹהֶל, *tent,* correspond to those of קָהָל, *congregation* (*VeChur LaZahav*).

36. *Peirush HaRokeach* — That is, as one. This is the implication of קְהִלַּת, *the Congregation,* in the singular, rather than the plural קְהִלּוֹת, *Congregations* (see also *Pesikta Zutresa* [*Midrash Lekach Tov*]; and *Yevamos* 13b).

ו בְּהִתְאַסֵּף רָאשֵׁי עָם יַחַד שִׁבְטֵי יִשְׂרָאֵל׃ יְחִי רְאוּבֵן
ז וְאַל־יָמֹת וִיהִי מְתָיו מִסְפָּר׃ וְזֹאת לִיהוּדָה וַיֹּאמַר
שְׁמַע יהוה קוֹל יְהוּדָה וְאֶל־עַמּוֹ תְּבִיאֶנּוּ יָדָיו רָב לוֹ
וְעֵזֶר מִצָּרָיו תִּהְיֶה׃
שני ח וּלְלֵוִי אָמַר תֻּמֶּיךָ וְאוּרֶיךָ לְאִישׁ חֲסִידֶךָ אֲשֶׁר
ט נִסִּיתוֹ בְּמַסָּה תְּרִיבֵהוּ עַל־מֵי מְרִיבָה׃ הָאֹמֵר לְאָבִיו
וּלְאִמּוֹ לֹא רְאִיתִיו וְאֶת־אֶחָיו לֹא הִכִּיר וְאֶת־בָּנָו
י לֹא יָדָע כִּי שָׁמְרוּ אִמְרָתֶךָ וּבְרִיתְךָ יִנְצֹרוּ׃ יוֹרוּ
מִשְׁפָּטֶיךָ לְיַעֲקֹב וְתוֹרָתְךָ לְיִשְׂרָאֵל יָשִׂימוּ קְטוֹרָה

בעל הטורים

(ז) **שְׁמַע ה׳ קוֹל.** רָאשֵׁי תֵבוֹת בְּגִימַטְרִיָּא יְהוֹשָׁפָט. שֶׁהִתְפַּלֵּל עַל יְהוֹשָׁפָט בְּמִלְחֶמֶת רָמוֹת גִּלְעָד:

❑ **יָדָיו רָב לוֹ.** סוֹפֵי תֵבוֹת בְּגִימַטְרִיָּא דָּוִד:

(ט) **וְאֶת בָּנָו.** חָסֵר יוּ״ד. שֶׁלֹּא הָיָה בַעֲשָׂרָה נִסְיוֹנוֹת:

(י) **יוֹרוּ מִשְׁפָּטֶיךָ לְיַעֲקֹב.** שֶׁנָּפוֹצוּ בְּכָל יִשְׂרָאֵל לִלְמֹד תּוֹרָה. וְכֵן אָמַר יַעֲקֹב ״וַאֲפִיצֵם בְּיִשְׂרָאֵל״:

❑ **יָשִׂימוּ קְטוֹרָה.** בְּגִימַטְרִיָּא כְּמוֹ מַעֲשִׂיר:

BAAL HATURIM ELUCIDATED

❑ {The Baal HaTurim's other comments to this verse appear at *Exodus* 19:4, s.v., וָאָבִא אֶתְכֶם, and *Exodus* 20:14, s.v., וְיֵשׁ בָּהֶם תֵּבוֹת.}

5. {The Baal HaTurim's comment to וַיְהִי בִישֻׁרוּן מֶלֶךְ appears at 4:20 above.}

7. שְׁמַע ה׳ קוֹל — HEAR, O HASHEM . . . VOICE. The *gematria* of the initial letters of these three words[37] (410) is equal to that of יְהוֹשָׁפָט, *Jehoshaphat.*[38] Moses prayed for the success of Jehoshaphat in the war of the Heights of Gilead.[39]

❑ **יָדָיו רָב לוֹ — MAY HIS HANDS FIGHT HIS GRIEVANCE.** The *gematria* of the final letters of these three words (14) is equal to that of דָּוִד, [*King*] *David.*[40]

9. וְאֶת בָּנָו — AND HIS CHILDREN.[40a] This term is spelled defectively, without a י

37. According to *Yosef Daas,* the allusion is found in the word שְׁמַע itself, for its *gematria* is also 410.

38. Jehoshaphat was the sixth king of the Davidic dynasty, which was descended from Judah, the subject of this verse.

39. This refers to Jehoshaphat's battle against the Ammonites described in *II Chronicles* 20:1-13 (*Rashi* to our verse).

40. *Peirush HaRokeach;* see *Rashi,* s.v., שמע ה׳ קול יהודה.

This verse contains another allusion to King David, which also explains why Moses blessed the tribe of Judah (Jacob's fourth son) before the tribe of Levi (Jacob's third son). The *gematria* of the final letters of the thirteen words of Moses' blessing to Judah — שְׁמַע . . . תִּהְיֶה — is 377. The next verse begins with the word וּלְלֵוִי. The *gematria* of the final י of that word is then added to the 377, for a total of 387; while the *gematria* of דָּוִד בֶּן יִשַׁי, *David son of Jesse,* is 386, which, according to the principle of *im hakollel,* may be considered equivalent to 387 (*VeChur LaZahav*).

40a. According to the Midrash, the term בָּנָו refers

when the numbers of the nation gathered — the tribes of Israel in unity.

6 *May Reuben live and not die, and may his population be included in the count.*

7 *And this to Judah, and he said: Hear, O HASHEM, Judah's voice, and return him to his people; may his hands fight his grievance and may You be a Helper against his enemies.*

8 *Of Levi he said: Your Tumim and Your Urim befit Your devout one, whom You tested at Massah, and whom You challenged at the waters of Meribah.*
9 *The one who said of his father and mother, "I have not favored him"; his brothers he did not give recognition and his children he did not know; for they [the Levites] have observed Your word and Your covenant they preserved.*
10 *They shall teach Your ordinances to Jacob and Your Torah to Israel; they shall place incense*

BAAL HATURIM ELUCIDATED

(= 10). For that tribe [Levi] was not involved in the ten tests.[41]

10. יוֹרוּ מִשְׁפָּטֶיךָ לְיַעֲקֹב — **THEY SHALL TEACH YOUR ORDINANCES TO JACOB.** They [the Levites] will be dispersed among the entirety of Israel to teach [the nation] Torah. And thus did Jacob say [regarding them], וַאֲפִיצֵם בְּיִשְׂרָאֵל, *and I will disperse them in Israel* (*Genesis* 49:7).[42]

❑ **יָשִׂימוּ קְטוֹרָה** — **THEY SHALL PLACE INCENSE.** The *gematria* of this phrase (686) is equal to that of כְּמוֹ מַעֲשִׁיר, *because*[43] *it makes rich.*[44]

to his sons who sinned at the incident of the golden calf; but whereas no Levites took part in that event (*Yoma* 66b, cited by *Rashi* to *Exodus* 32:26), the word must be understood to mean grandson and refers to a Levite's non-Levite grandson, born to his daughter (*Sifrei,* cited by *Rashi*). The Baal HaTurim, on the other hand, interprets בָּנָו literally, *his sons,* and the word refers to all the Levites — they were all innocent of any involvement in the ten tests.

41. See *Numbers* 14:22.

The Talmud (*Arachin* 15a-b) enumerates the ten times that Israel tested God: (i) At the sea, when the Israelites showed a lack of trust in God by complaining, "Were there no graves in Egypt that you took us to die in the wilderness?" (*Exodus* 14:11); (ii) also at the sea, when *they rebelled about the sea, at the Sea of Reeds* (*Psalms* 106:7) — after the Israelites crossed the sea, they demonstrated a lack of faith by saying, "Just as we are emerging from the sea on this side, so are the Egyptians emerging on the other, and they will pursue us again"; (iii) they were commanded not to leave over any manna until the morning, yet some did (see *Exodus* 16:19-20); (iv) some Israelites went out to gather manna on Shabbos, although they had been commanded not to (see *Exodus* 16:27); (v-vi) twice the Israelites asked for meat in an ungrateful manner (see *Exodus* 16:3 and *Numbers* 11:4); (vii-viii) twice they complained about a lack of water (see *Exodus* 15:24 and 17:2); (ix) the sin of the golden calf (see *Exodus,* Ch. 32); and (x) the sin of the spies (see *Numbers,* Chs. 13-14).

42. This phrase is paraphrased by *Targum Yerushalmi:* וַאֲבַדֵּר יַת שִׁבְטָא דְלֵוִי בְּבָתֵּי מִדְרְשָׁא דִבְנֵי יִשְׂרָאֵל, *and I will disperse the tribe of Levi in the study halls of the Children of Israel.*

43. The word כְּמוֹ is usually used to introduce a comparison and is translated *like* or *as* (e.g., *Exodus* 15:5 and 8); occasionally it is used for *when* or *at the time that* (e.g., *Genesis* 19:15). The translation here follows *Yad Aharon,* who renders it מִפְּנֵי, *because.* However, *Yad Aharon* does not adduce any other instance of that usage.

44. The Talmud expounds on the juxtaposition of

לג/יא־יג יא בְּאַפֶּ֔ךָ וְכָלִ֖יל עַל־מִזְבְּחֶֽךָ׃ בָּרֵ֤ךְ יהוה֙ חֵיל֔וֹ וּפֹ֥עַל
יָדָ֖יו תִּרְצֶ֑ה מְחַ֨ץ מָתְנַ֧יִם קָמָ֛יו וּמְשַׂנְאָ֖יו מִן־יְקוּמֽוּן׃
יב לְבִנְיָמִ֣ן אָמַ֔ר יְדִ֣יד יהוה יִשְׁכֹּ֥ן לָבֶ֖טַח עָלָ֑יו חֹפֵ֤ף
שלישי יג עָלָיו֙ כָּל־הַיּ֔וֹם וּבֵ֥ין כְּתֵפָ֖יו שָׁכֵֽן׃ וּלְיוֹסֵ֣ף אָמַ֔ר
מְבֹרֶ֥כֶת יהוה אַרְצ֑וֹ מִמֶּ֤גֶד שָׁמַ֨יִם֙ מִטָּ֔ל וּמִתְּה֖וֹם

בעל הטורים

❑ **וְכָלִיל.** ב׳ – ״וְכָלִיל עַל מִזְבְּחֶךָ״; ״אָז תַּחְפֹּץ זִבְחֵי צֶדֶק עוֹלָה וְכָלִיל״. אַף עַל פִּי שֶׁזָּר מַקְרִיב בְּבָמָה, אֵינוֹ ״זִבְחֵי צֶדֶק״ אֶלָּא מַה שֶּׁקָּרֵב בִּפְנִים עַל יְדֵי כֹּהֵן. וְזֶהוּ ״וְכָלִיל עַל מִזְבְּחֶךָ״, ״אָז תַּחְפֹּץ זִבְחֵי צֶדֶק עוֹלָה וְכָלִיל״:

(יא) **וּפֹעַל יָדָיו תִּרְצֶה.** בְּגִימַטְרִיָּא שֵׁירוּת:

(יב) **יִשְׁכֹּן לָבֶטַח.** לְאַחַר שֶׁיִּטְרֹף הָאֻמּוֹת, יִשְׁכֹּן לָבֶטַח כִּזְאֵב. וְכֵן בֵּרְכוֹ יַעֲקֹב ״וְלָעֶרֶב יְחַלֵּק שָׁלָל״, בִּמְנוּחָה:

❑ **וּבֵין כְּתֵפָיו.** בְּגִימַטְרִיָּא וּבִירוּשָׁלַיִם:

(יב־יג) **וּבֵין כְּתֵפָיו שָׁכֵן. וּלְיוֹסֵף.** רֶמֶז כִּי בַתְּחִלָּה יִהְיֶה בְּחֶלְקוֹ שֶׁל יוֹסֵף מִשְׁכַּן שִׁילֹה:

BAAL HATURIM ELUCIDATED

❑ **וְכָלִיל** — AND WHOLE-OFFERING. The masoretic note, ב׳, means that this word appears twice in the *Tanach*: (i) here, וְכָלִיל עַל מִזְבְּחֶךָ, *and a whole-offering upon Your Altar;* and (ii) אָז תַּחְפֹּץ זִבְחֵי צֶדֶק עוֹלָה וְכָלִיל, *Then You will favor sacrifices of righteousness, burnt-offering and whole-offering* (*Psalms* 51:21). Although a non-*Kohen* may minister at a private altar,[45] an offering is not considered among the *sacrifices of righteousness* unless it is offered in the Sanctuary by a *Kohen.* This is [indicated by the similarity of expression]: *And* [*when one brings*] *a whole-offering upon Your Altar, then You will favor* [*them as*] *sacrifices of righteousness* — [i.e.,] *burnt-offering and whole-offering.*

---

our verse with, *Bless, O* HASHEM, *his resources* (v. 11): *They shall place incense before Your presence . . . and* HASHEM *will bless his resources,* i.e., the Kohen who performs the Incense service will be blessed with wealth (*Yoma* 26a).

45. A *bamah* [plural, *bamos*], literally *platform* or *high place,* is an altar other than that of the *Beis HaMikdash* (Holy Temple) or of the *Mishkan* (Tabernacle). It was permitted to bring voluntary offerings on such altars until the *Beis HaMikdash* was built, except as noted below.

When there was a *Beis HaMikdash* or central Tabernacle — in the wilderness, in Shiloh, or in Jerusalem — it was forbidden for an individual to erect a *bamah.* When no such Sanctuary existed, there would *still* be a national Altar for communal and obligatory personal offerings, but individuals were permitted to erect altars of their own, if they so wished. Such was the situation, for example, during the fourteen years before Shiloh, where there was a national Altar at Gilgal, and after the desecration of Shiloh, when there were national Altars at Nob and then at Gibeon (see time-line below). During those periods, individuals had the right to erect *bamos.* However, a *bamah* had a lesser status than the national one. Whereas the national Altars could be used for an individual's obligatory offerings,

MISHKAN NOT YET ERECTED	MISHKAN IN THE DESERT 39 YEARS	MISHKAN IN GILGAL 14 YEARS	MISHKAN IN SHILOH 369 YEARS	MISHKAN IN NOB AND GIBEON 57 YEARS	BEIS HAMIKDASH IS ERECTED
BAMOS PERMITTED	BAMOS FORBIDDEN	BAMOS PERMITTED	BAMOS FORBIDDEN	BAMOS PERMITTED	BAMOS FORBIDDEN FOREVER

before Your presence, and whole-offering upon Your Altar.
11 Bless, O HASHEM, his resources, and favor the work of his hands; smash the loins of his foes and his enemies, that they may not rise.
12 Of Benjamin he said: May HASHEM's beloved dwell securely by Him; He hovers over him all day long; and rests between his shoulders.
13 Of Joseph he said: Blessed by HASHEM is his land — with the heavenly bounty of dew, and from the deep

BAAL HATURIM ELUCIDATED

11. וּפֹעַל יָדָיו תִּרְצֶה — AND FAVOR THE WORK OF HIS HANDS. The *gematria* of this phrase (911) is equivalent[46] to that of שֵׁירוּת, *service.*[47]

12. יִשְׁכֹּן לָבֶטַח — DWELL SECURELY. After he will prey upon the nations, he will dwell securely like a wolf.[48] Similarly, Jacob blessed him, וְלָעֶרֶב יְחַלֵּק שָׁלָל, *and in the evening he will distribute spoils* (*Genesis* 49:27), with serenity.

❑ **וּבֵין כְּתֵפָיו — AND BETWEEN HIS SHOULDERS.** The *gematria* of this phrase (584) is equivalent[49] to that of וּבִירוּשָׁלַם, *and in Jerusalem.*[50]

12-13. וּבֵין כְּתֵפָיו שָׁכֵן. וּלְיוֹסֵף — AND RESTS BETWEEN HIS SHOULDERS. OF JOSEPH. [The juxtaposition is] an allusion [to the fact] that [the Sanctuary] will first be [established] in the [tribal] portion of Joseph.[51]

13-17. {The Baal HaTurim's comment to the entirety of Joseph's blessing appears at v. 18 below.}

---

in addition to his voluntary offerings, a *bamah* could be used only for voluntary offerings. See time-line below.

46. The *gematria* of the Baal HaTurim's term is 916, five more than that of the verse. To reconcile the numbers, most editions use the full spelling (וּפוֹעַל), instead of the defective spelling (וּפֹעַל) used by the verse. That adds six to the *gematria* of the Scriptural phrase, for a total of 917. And the principle of *im hakollel* allows 916 to be considered equivalent to 917.

Alternatively: The term שֵׁירוּת should be emended to הַשֵּׁרוּת, *the service,* which has a *gematria* of 911, equal to that of the Scriptural phrase (*VeChur LaZahav*).

47. *Peirush HaRokeach.* The Levite service is referred to as שֵׁרוּת in *Numbers* 1:50 (*Yad Aharon*).

48. This is another reference to the verse adduced in part in the Baal HaTurim's comment. That verse reads in full: *Benjamin is a predatory wolf; in the morning he will devour prey and in the evening he will distribute spoils.*

The text follows the early printed editions and is in accord with *Shoham Yakar's* manuscript edition. Many later editions read: לְאַחַר שֶׁיִּטְרֹף הָאֻמּוֹת כִּזְאֵב, *After he will prey upon the nations like a wolf,* יִשְׁכֹּן לָבֶטַח, *he will dwell securely.*

49. The *gematria* of the Baal HaTurim's phrase is 594, ten more than that of the Scriptural term. Most editions reconcile the *gematriaos* by using the full spelling (וּבֵין כְּתֵיפָיו) instead of the defective spelling (וּבֵין כְּתֵפָיו) used by the verse.

Alternatively: The Baal HaTurim's phrase should be emended to יְרוּשָׁלַם, without any prefixes, for a *gematria* of 586. The principle of *im hateivos* then allows two to be added to the *gematria* of the Scriptural phrase for a total of 586. Thus, the *gematriaos* may be considered equivalent (*Matzreif LaKesef*).

50. *Matzreif LaKesef.*

51. *Peirush HaRokeach;* see *Megillah* 16b; see also note 45 above and the time-line there. Shiloh was in the territory of Joseph's son Ephraim (see *Joshua* 16:6; *Zevachim* 118b; *Psalms* 78:61,67).

יד רֶבֶצֶת תָּחַת: וּמִמֶּגֶד תְּבוּאֹת שָׁמֶשׁ וּמִמֶּגֶד גֶּרֶשׁ
טו יְרָחִים: וּמֵרֹאשׁ הַרְרֵי־קֶדֶם וּמִמֶּגֶד גִּבְעוֹת עוֹלָם:
טז וּמִמֶּגֶד אֶרֶץ וּמְלֹאָהּ וּרְצוֹן שֹׁכְנִי סְנֶה תָּבוֹאתָה
יז לְרֹאשׁ יוֹסֵף וּלְקָדְקֹד נְזִיר אֶחָיו: בְּכוֹר שׁוֹרוֹ הָדָר לוֹ
וְקַרְנֵי רְאֵם קַרְנָיו בָּהֶם עַמִּים יְנַגַּח יַחְדָּו אַפְסֵי־אָרֶץ
רביעי יח וְהֵם רִבְבוֹת אֶפְרַיִם וְהֵם אַלְפֵי מְנַשֶּׁה: וְלִזְבוּלֻן
יט אָמַר שְׂמַח זְבוּלֻן בְּצֵאתֶךָ וְיִשָּׂשכָר בְּאֹהָלֶיךָ: עַמִּים
הַר־יִקְרָאוּ שָׁם יִזְבְּחוּ זִבְחֵי־צֶדֶק כִּי שֶׁפַע יַמִּים יִינָקוּ
כ וּשְׂפֻנֵי טְמוּנֵי חוֹל: וּלְגָד אָמַר בָּרוּךְ מַרְחִיב גָּד

בעל הטורים

(יח) **שְׂמַח.** ב׳ בַּמָּסוֹרֶת – ״שְׂמַח זְבוּלֻן״; ״שְׂמַח בָּחוּר״. עַל שֵׁם שֶׁהָיוּ יוֹצְאִים בַּדְּרָכִים לִפְרַקְמַטְיָא, הָיוּ בַחוּרִים וְגִבּוֹרִים:

❑ **בְּאֹהָלֶיךָ.** ב׳ – ״וְיִשָּׂשכָר בְּאֹהָלֶיךָ״; ״וְאַל תַּשְׁכֵּן בְּאֹהָלֶיךָ עַוְלָה״. ״תַּשְׁכֵּן״ נוֹטָרִיקוֹן תּוֹרָה שְׁטָר כְּתוּבִים נְבִיאִים. כְּמוֹ שֶׁדָּרְשׁוּ, זֶה הַמַּשְׁהֶה בְּבֵיתוֹ {שְׁטָר פָּרוּעַ,} סֵפֶר שֶׁאֵינוֹ מֻגָּה. שֶׁבְּנֵי יִשָּׂשכָר הָיוּ יוֹשְׁבֵי אֹהָלִים וְעוֹסְקִים בַּתּוֹרָה, עַל כֵּן מַזְהִיר אוֹתָם, ״וְאַל תַּשְׁכֵּן בְּאֹהָלֶיךָ עַוְלָה״:

(כ) **וּלְגָד אָמַר.** בְּבִרְכָתוֹ שֶׁל גָּד תִּמְצָא כָל הָאַלְפָּ״א בֵּיתָ״א. לְפִי שֶׁמֹּשֶׁה רַבֵּנוּ עָלָיו הַשָּׁלוֹם קָבוּר בְּחֶלְקוֹ, שֶׁקִּיֵּם כָּל הַתּוֹרָה כֻלָּהּ מֵאָלֶ״ף עַד תָּי״ו:

וְכֵן בְּבִרְכַּת יוֹסֵף. לְפִי שֶׁאֲרוֹנוֹ הָיָה מְהַלֵּךְ אֵצֶל הָאָרוֹן, לוֹמַר קִיֵּם זֶה מַה שֶּׁכָּתוּב בָּזֶה:

BAAL HATURIM ELUCIDATED

❑ {The Baal HaTurim's comment to וּלְיוֹסֵף appears at *Genesis* 41:50.}

❑ {The Baal HaTurim's comment to רֹבֶצֶת appears at *Genesis* 49:25.}

14. {The Baal HaTurim's comment to וּמִמֶּגֶד תְּבוּאֹת שָׁמֶשׁ appears at *Genesis* 1:14, s.v., יְהִי.}

❑ {The Baal HaTurim's comment to יְרָחִים appears at *Exodus* 2:2.}

18. שְׂמַח — REJOICE. The masoretic note, ב׳, means that this word appears twice in the *Tanach*: (i) here, שְׂמַח זְבוּלֻן, *Rejoice, O Zebulun;* and (ii) שְׂמַח בָּחוּר, *Rejoice, young man* (*Ecclesiastes* 11:9). Because the Zebulunites journeyed forth for commerce,[52] they were youthful and strong.

❑ **בְּאֹהָלֶיךָ** — IN YOUR TENTS. The masoretic note, ב׳, means that this word appears twice in the *Tanach*: (i) here, וְיִשָּׂשכָר בְּאֹהָלֶיךָ, *and Issachar in your tents;* and (ii) וְאַל תַּשְׁכֵּן בְּאֹהָלֶיךָ עַוְלָה, *and do not give residence to injustice in your tents* (*Job* 11:14). The word תַּשְׁכֵּן, *give residence to,* can be interpreted as an acronym for the Hebrew words תּוֹרָה, שְׁטָר, כְּתוּבִים, נְבִיאִים, *Torah, promissory note, Writings, and Prophets.* As the Sages have expounded: The verse (in *Job*) refers to one who

52. *Sifrei;* see *Rashi,* s.v., שמח זבולן בצאתך וישכר באהליך, and s.v., שמח זבולן בצאתך.

spreading out below; 14 *with the bounty of the sun's crops,*
and with the bounty of the moon's yield; 15 *with the quick-*
ripening crops of the early mountains, and with the bounty
of eternal hills; 16 *with the bounty of the land and its fullness,*
and by the favor of Him Who rested upon the thornbush;
may this blessing rest upon Joseph's head, and upon the
crown of him who was separated from his brothers. 17 *A*
sovereignty is his ox-like one — majesty is his, and his glory
will be like the horns of a re'eim; with them shall he gore
nations together, to the ends of the land; they are the
myriads of Ephraim, and the thousands of Manasseh.
18 *Of Zebulun he said: Rejoice, O Zebulun, in your excur-*
sions, and Issachar in your tents. 19 *The tribes will assemble*
at the mount, there they will slaughter offerings of righteous-
ness, for by the riches of the sea they will be nourished, and
by the treasures concealed in the sand.
20 *Of Gad he said: Blessed is He Who broadens Gad;*

BAAL HATURIM ELUCIDATED

retains in his house {[either] a paid-up promissory note [or]} a *sefer* that [was found to have errors but] has not been corrected.[53] [This concept is related to our verse,] for the descendants of Issachar remained in the study halls,[54] and occupied themselves with Torah study. Therefore, Moses admonished them, *"Do not give residence to injustice* [i.e., books containing errors] *in your tents* [i.e., study halls]."

20. וּלְגָד אָמַר — OF GAD HE SAID. In Gad's blessing you will find all the letters of the alphabet.[55] This is because our teacher Moses, of blessed memory, was buried in Gad's portion, for he observed the entire Torah from א to ת.[55a]

[Similarly, the entire alphabet is also found] in Joseph's blessing. For [during the Israelites' forty-year sojourn in the wilderness] Joseph's אֲרוֹן, *coffin,* traveled adjacent to the אָרוֹן, *Ark* [*of Testimony*], as if to say, "This one [Joseph] fulfilled everything written in that one."[56,57]

53. The Talmud explains that the term "injustice" of this verse refers to two matters: (i) a paid-up promissory note that has not been either destroyed or returned to the borrower; and (ii) a *sefer* (book of Scripture) containing scribal errors that [had been discovered more than thirty days earlier and] had not yet been corrected (*Kesubos* 19b).

54. *Peirush HaRokeach.* Regarding the translation of אֹהָלִים (literally, *tents*) as *study halls,* see notes 34a and 35 above.

55. Moses used the entire alphabet in blessing the tribes of Gad and Joseph (as the Baal HaTurim notes later in this comment), but not in blessing any of the other tribes. Interestingly, in Jacob's blessings to his sons, only Joseph's blessing contains every letter of the *aleph-beis.*

55a. From the Baal HaTurim's wording it is not clear whether this last clause refers to Moses, i.e., because Moses, who observed the entire Torah, was buried in Gad's portion, the entire א״ב appears in Gad's blessing; or to Gad, i.e., because Gad observed the entire Torah, his blessing contained the entire א״ב and Moses was buried in his territory (*VeChur LaZahav*).

56. *Sotah* 13a. The term "that one" refers to the Torah — which is written with the twenty-two letters of the *aleph-beis* — contained in the Ark.

57. *R' Chaim Paltiel.*

לג/כא־כד כא כְּלָבִ֔יא שָׁכֵ֕ן וְטָרַ֥ף זְר֖וֹעַ אַף־קָדְקֹֽד׃ וַיַּ֤רְא רֵאשִׁית֙ ל֔וֹ
כִּי־שָׁ֛ם חֶלְקַ֥ת מְחֹקֵ֖ק סָפ֑וּן וַיֵּתֵא֙ רָ֣אשֵׁי עָ֔ם צִדְקַ֤ת
חמישי כב יהוה֙ עָשָׂ֔ה וּמִשְׁפָּטָ֖יו עִם־יִשְׂרָאֵֽל׃ וּלְדָ֣ן אָמַ֔ר
כג דָּ֖ן גּ֣וּר אַרְיֵ֑ה יְזַנֵּ֖ק מִן־הַבָּשָֽׁן׃ וּלְנַפְתָּלִ֣י אָמַ֔ר
נַפְתָּלִי֙ שְׂבַ֣ע רָצ֔וֹן וּמָלֵ֖א בִּרְכַּ֣ת יהו֑ה יָ֥ם וְדָר֖וֹם
כד יְרָֽשָׁה׃ וּלְאָשֵׁ֣ר אָמַ֔ר בָּר֥וּךְ מִבָּנִ֖ים אָשֵׁ֑ר

בעל הטורים

❑ **וְטָרַף.** ב׳ — ״וְטָרַף זְרוֹעַ״; ״אֲשֶׁר אִם עָבַר וְרָמַס וְטָרַף וְאֵין מַצִּיל״. לוֹמַר, כָּל מַה שֶׁטָּרַף אֵין מַצִּיל מִיָּדוֹ:

(כג) **נַפְתָּלִי שְׂבַע רָצוֹן.** רָאשֵׁי תֵבוֹת נֶשֶׁר. שֶׁהָיָה קַל כַּנֶּשֶׁר לַעֲשׂוֹת רְצוֹן אָבִיו שֶׁבַּשָּׁמַיִם:

(כד) **בָּרוּךְ מִבָּנִים אָשֵׁר.** לְכָךְ בֵּרְכוֹ מֹשֶׁה בַּדְּבָרִים הַלָּלוּ לְפִי שֶׁכְּשֶׁמָּכְרוּ הַשְּׁבָטִים אֶת יוֹסֵף, הֶחֱרִימוּ שֶׁלֹּא יְגַלּוּ אוֹתוֹ. וְשֶׂרַח בַּת אָשֵׁר יָדְעָה מְכִירָתוֹ בִנְבוּאָה. וְאָמְרוּ הַשְּׁבָטִים: מֵהֵיכָן יָדְעָה אִם לֹא מֵאָבִיהָ, דְּשׁוּתָא דִינוּקָא אוֹ מֵאַבָּא אוֹ מֵאִמָּא. וְעָמְדוּ וְנִדּוּהוּ. וּבָא מֹשֶׁה רַבֵּנוּ עָלָיו הַשָּׁלוֹם לְהַתִּירוֹ. כִּי אָמְרוּ לוֹ, מְנֻדֶּה אָסוּר בְּתַשְׁמִישׁ הַמִּטָּה — אָמַר ״בָּרוּךְ מִבָּנִים״. הָיוּ אֶחָיו בְּדֵלִין מִמֶּנּוּ — אָמַר ״יְהִי רְצוּי אֶחָיו״. הָיָה אָסוּר בִּסִיכָה — אָמַר ״וְטֹבֵל בַּשֶּׁמֶן רַגְלוֹ״, שֶׁיְּהֵא מֻתָּר לָסוּךְ בְּשֶׁמֶן. הָיָה אָסוּר בִּנְעִילַת הַסַּנְדָּל — אָמַר ״בַּרְזֶל וּנְחֹשֶׁת מִנְעָלֶךָ״:

BAAL HATURIM ELUCIDATED

❑ {The Baal HaTurim's comment to וּלְגָד אָמַר בָּרוּךְ appears at *Genesis* 14:19, s.v., בָּרוּךְ אַבְרָם.}

❑ {The Baal HaTurim's comment regarding the order of Moses' blessings to Gad and Naphtali appears at *Genesis* 49:27, s.v., יַעֲקֹב הִקְדִּים.}

❑ **וְטָרַף** — TO TEAR OFF. The masoretic note, ב׳, means that this word appears twice in the *Tanach*: (i) here, וְטָרַף זְרוֹעַ, *and to tear off an arm,* and (ii) אֲשֶׁר אִם עָבַר וְרָמַס וְטָרַף וְאֵין מַצִּיל, *who, if he passes through, tramples and tears apart, and there is none who can rescue* (*Micah* 5:7). This [similarity of expression] indicates that whatever [Gad] would prey upon, none could rescue from his hand.[58]

❑ {The Baal HaTurim's comment to וְטָרַף זְרוֹעַ אַף קָדְקֹד appears at *Numbers* 32:1, s.v., וּמִקְנֶה.}

21. {The Baal HaTurim's comment to וַיֵּתֵא רָאשֵׁי עָם appears at *Genesis* 49:10, s.v., שִׁילֹה.}

23. נַפְתָּלִי שְׂבַע רָצוֹן — NAPHTALI, SATIATED WITH FAVOR. The initial letters of these words spell נֶשֶׁר, *eagle.*[58a] For Naphtali was קַל כַּנֶּשֶׁר, *swift as an eagle,*[59] in doing the will of his Father in heaven.[60]

---

58. The Baal HaTurim's addition of the word מִיָּדוֹ, *from his hand,* to the phrase וְאֵין מַצִּיל, *there is none who can rescue,* is borrowed from *Daniel* 8:4.

58a. And the collective *gematria* of the final letters of the phrase נַפְתָּלִי שְׂבַע רָצוֹן is 130, equal to that of קַל, *swift* (A.S.).

59. It is noteworthy that the *gematria* of נַפְתָּלִי is 570, equal to that of כַּנֶּשֶׁר, *as an eagle* (*VeChur LaZahav*).

60. *Midrash HaGadol, Bereishis* 49:21; see

to dwell like a lion, and to tear off an arm and even a head. ²¹ *He chose the primest for himself, for that is where the lawgiver's portion is hidden; he came at the head of the nation, carrying out HASHEM's justice and His ordinances with Israel.*

²² *Of Dan he said: Dan is a lion cub, leaping forth from the Bashan.*

²³ *Of Naphtali he said: Naphtali, satiated with favor, and filled with HASHEM's blessing; go possess the sea and its south shore.*

²⁴ *Of Asher he said: Blessed of children is Asher; he*

───────────────── BAAL HATURIM ELUCIDATED ─────────────────

24. בָּרוּךְ מִבָּנִים אָשֵׁר — **BLESSED OF CHILDREN IS ASHER.** Moses gave Asher these particular blessings because when the brothers sold Joseph, they declared a ban against anyone who would reveal the matter.[61] However, through prophecy, Serah, Asher's daughter, became aware of the sale.[62] The other brothers, however, thought, "How could she know if not from her father?" After all, [as the Sages teach:] that which a child relates, was heard either from his father or from his mother.[63] The brothers therefore placed [Asher] under a ban. Our teacher Moses, of blessed memory, came to release him [from that ban].[63a] They said to him, "A person under a ban may not engage in marital relations."[64,64a] He said, בָּרוּךְ מִבָּנִים, "*Blessed of children [is Asher].*" [To conform with their ban,] the brothers would shun Asher — so Moses said, יְהִי רְצוּי אֶחָיו, "*He shall be pleasing to his brothers.*" [Because of the ban,] Asher was forbidden to anoint himself[64] — so Moses said, וְטֹבֵל בַּשֶּׁמֶן רַגְלוֹ, "*he shall dip his feet in oil,*" permitting him to anoint himself with oil. [Because of the ban,] he was not permitted to wear shoes[64] — so Moses said, "בַּרְזֶל וּנְחֹשֶׁת מִנְעָלֶךָ, *May your shoes be of iron and copper*" (v. 25).[65]

───────────────────────────────

Avos 5:20.

61. *Pirkei DeRabbi Eliezer* 38; see *Rashi* to *Genesis* 37:33.

62. *Targum Yonasan ben Uzziel* to *Genesis* 46:17; *Midrash Seichel Tov, Bereishis* 45:26; see also *Rashi* to *II Samuel* 20:19. Those sources state that it was Serah who told Jacob that Joseph was still alive; but they do not say either how she knew or whether she revealed the secret before the brothers rescinded the ban (*VeChur LaZahav*).

63. *Succah* 56b.

63a. Moses' blessings were two pronged: Each referred to both the tribe named in that blessing and also to the son of Jacob who was the progenitor of that tribe. Thus, although Moses was blessing the tribe of Asher, his words had a

double meaning, for they also released Asher son of Jacob from the two-century-old ban (*VeChur LaZahav*).

64. See *Moed Katan* 15b.

64a. Accordingly, Asher's five children (see *Genesis* 46:17) must have been conceived before he was placed under the ban (*VeChur LaZahav*).

65. *Hadar Zekeinim* (*Tosafos*). According to *Rashi*, Asher's blessing is contained in its entirety in verse 24, while verse 25 begins a new blessing, that of Israel as a nation. However, the *Sifrei* [cited by *Ibn Ezra* and *Ramban*] states that Asher's blessing spans verses 24 and 25, with the general national blessing beginning at verse 26, and that is the view of *Tosafos* and the Baal HaTurim in this comment.

כה יְהִי רְצוּי אֶחָיו וְטֹבֵל בַּשֶּׁמֶן רַגְלוֹ: בַּרְזֶל וּנְחֹשֶׁת
כו מִנְעָלֶךָ וּכְיָמֶיךָ דָּבְאֶךָ: אֵין כָּאֵל יְשֻׁרוּן רֹכֵב שָׁמַיִם
כז בְּעֶזְרֶךָ וּבְגַאֲוָתוֹ שְׁחָקִים: מְעֹנָה אֱלֹהֵי קֶדֶם וּמִתַּחַת
זְרֹעֹת עוֹלָם וַיְגָרֶשׁ מִפָּנֶיךָ אוֹיֵב וַיֹּאמֶר הַשְׁמֵד:
כח וַיִּשְׁכֹּן יִשְׂרָאֵל בֶּטַח בָּדָד עֵין יַעֲקֹב אֶל־אֶרֶץ
כט דָּגָן וְתִירוֹשׁ אַף־שָׁמָיו יַעַרְפוּ טָל: אַשְׁרֶיךָ יִשְׂרָאֵל
מִי כָמוֹךָ עַם נוֹשַׁע בַּיהוָה מָגֵן עֶזְרֶךָ וַאֲשֶׁר־
חֶרֶב גַּאֲוָתֶךָ וְיִכָּחֲשׁוּ אֹיְבֶיךָ לָךְ וְאַתָּה עַל־
לד א בָּמוֹתֵימוֹ תִדְרֹךְ: וַיַּעַל מֹשֶׁה מֵעַרְבֹת מוֹאָב
אֶל־הַר נְבוֹ רֹאשׁ הַפִּסְגָּה אֲשֶׁר עַל־פְּנֵי יְרֵחוֹ

בעל הטורים

❑ **מִבָּנִים אָשֵׁר יְהִי רְצוּי.** רָאשֵׁי תֵבוֹת מֵאִיר. עַל שֵׁם הַשֶּׁמֶן, שֶׁהוּא מֵאִיר פְּנֵיהֶם וּמֵאִיר לַמְּנוֹרָה:

(כו) שְׁחָקִים. אִיתָא בַּמִּדְרָשׁ, שֶׁשָּׁם בַּשָּׁמַיִם יֵשׁ רָקִיעַ שֶׁשְּׁמוֹ שְׁחָקִים, שֶׁשָּׁם שׁוֹחֲקִים מָן לַצַּדִּיקִים. "וְעֻזּוֹ בַּשְּׁחָקִים" בְּגִימַטְרִיָּא הַמָּן. וְעַל שֵׁם כֵּן שֶׁהוּא לָבָן וְעַז כַּשֶּׁלֶג:

(כט) אַשְׁרֶיךָ. ב' בַּמָּסוֹרֶת — "אַשְׁרֶיךָ יִשְׂרָאֵל"; "אַשְׁרֶיךָ וְטוֹב לָךְ". {אַשְׁרֶיךָ יִשְׂרָאֵל, עַל כֵּן אַשְׁרֶיךָ וְטוֹב לָךְ:}

BAAL HATURIM ELUCIDATED

❑ **מִבָּנִים אָשֵׁר יְהִי רְצוּי — OF CHILDREN IS ASHER; HE SHALL BE PLEASING.** The initial letters of these four words spell מֵאִיר, *causing to light up.*[66] This refers to the oil, which would light up their countenances and would light up the Menorah.[67]

26. {The Baal HaTurim's comment to רֹכֵב שָׁמַיִם appears at *Exodus* 15:4, s.v., מַרְכְּבֹת.}

❑ **שְׁחָקִים — UPPER HEIGHTS.** The Midrash states that there is a firmament in the heavens called שְׁחָקִים, translated here *upper heights,* in which they grind manna for the righteous.[68] The phrase וְעֻזּוֹ בַּשְּׁחָקִים, *His might is in the upper heights* (*Psalms* 68:35), [alludes to this, for] the *gematria* [of וְעֻזּוֹ] (89) is equivalent to that of הַמָּן, *the manna.*[69] For this reason, the manna was white, as white as snow.[70]

66. *Bamidbar Rabbah* 2:10 speaks of Asher lighting up the darkness.

67. *Peirush HaRokeach* and *R' Chaim Paltiel* mention that Asher supplied oil for the Menorah; however, neither of those sources speaks of the oil brightening their countenances.

There is a difficulty with this comment, for the Mishnah (*Menachos* 85b) clearly indicates that the prime source of oil for the Menorah was Tekoa [a city in the territory of Judah (see *II Chronicles* 11:5-6)] and the secondary source was Regev [literally, lump of earth (see *Job* 38:38)] in Trans-Jordan [which the *Aruch* identifies as Argov in the territory of Manasseh (see *Deuteronomy* 3:13-14)].

68. *Chagigah* 12b, cited in full in note 9 to *parashas Ha'azinu.*

69. The *gematria* of the Baal HaTurim's term is 95, six more than that of וְעֻזּוֹ. Most editions use the full spelling (וְעוּזּוֹ), which adds six to the

shall be pleasing to his brothers; and he shall dip his feet in oil.

25 *May your shoes be of iron and copper; and like the days of your prime, so may your old age be.* 26 *There is none like God, O Jeshurun; He rides across heaven to help you, and in His majesty through the upper heights.*

27 *That is the abode of God immemorial, and below are the world's mighty ones; He drove the enemy away from before you, and He said, "Destroy!"* 28 *Thus Israel shall dwell secure, solitary, in the likeness of Jacob, in a land of grain and wine; even his heavens shall drip with dew.*

29 *You are fortunate, O Israel: Who is like you! O people delivered by HASHEM, the Shield of your help, Who is the Sword of your grandeur; your foes will try to deceive you, but you will trample their haughty ones.*

34

1 *Moses ascended from the plains of Moab to Mount Nebo, to the summit of the cliff that faces Jericho, and*

BAAL HATURIM ELUCIDATED

28. {The Baal HaTurim's comment to וַיִּשְׁכֹּן appears at *Exodus* 24:16.}

29. **אַשְׁרֶיךָ — YOU ARE FORTUNATE.** The masoretic note, ב׳, means that this word appears twice in the *Tanach*: (i) here, אַשְׁרֶיךָ יִשְׂרָאֵל, *You are fortunate, O Israel;* and (ii) אַשְׁרֶיךָ וְטוֹב לָךְ, *You are fortunate, and it is well with you* (*Psalms* 128:2). {*You are fortunate, O Israel* — therefore, *You are fortunate, and it is well with you.*}[71]

❑ {The Baal HaTurim's other comment to אַשְׁרֶיךָ יִשְׂרָאֵל appears at 26:19 above, s.v., וּלְתִתְּךָ.}

gematria, instead of the defective spelling (וְעֻזּוֹ) used in *Psalms.*

Alternatively: The Baal HaTurim's phrase should be emended to מָן, *manna,* without the prefix -הַ, *the.* That would bring its *gematria* to 90. The principle of *im hakollel* then allows 89 to be considered equivalent to 90 (*VeChur LaZahav*).

70. *Peirush HaRokeach.* The color red symbolizes sin, while white represents purity from sin, as the prophet states: *"Come, now, let us reason together," says HASHEM. "If your sins are like scarlet, they will become white as snow; if they will be red as crimson,* כַּצֶּמֶר יִהְיוּ, *they will become [white] as wool"* (*Isaiah* 1:18). Thus, the manna, which is the food of the righteous, is described by the Torah (*Exodus* 16:31) as כְּזֶרַע גַּד, *like coriander seed,* לָבָן, *[but] white.* In that verse, the *gematria* of זֶרַע גַּד is 284, equal to that of לַצַּדִּיקִים *for the righteous;* and the *gematria* of כְּזֶרַע גַּד לָבָן is 386, to which the principle of *im hateivos* allows three to be added, for a total of 389, while the *gematria* of כַּצֶּמֶר יִהְיוּ is 381, to which the principle of *im haosios* allows eight to be added, for a total of 389. Thus the *gematria* of כְּזֶרַע גַּד לָבָן, *like coriander seed, white* is an apt metaphor for the righteous, for its *gematria* is equivalent to that of כַּצֶּמֶר יִהְיוּ, *they will become [white] as wool* (*VeChur LaZahav*).

71. The passage enclosed in braces is not found in the early or later printed editions. It does appear, however, in the manuscripts used by *Shoham Yakar.* In either case, the Baal HaTurim's comment remains arcane, eluding explanation.

וַיַּרְאֵהוּ יְהוָה אֶת־כָּל־הָאָרֶץ אֶת־הַגִּלְעָד עַד־דָּן׃
ב וְאֵת כָּל־נַפְתָּלִי וְאֶת־אֶרֶץ אֶפְרַיִם וּמְנַשֶּׁה וְאֵת כָּל־
ג אֶרֶץ יְהוּדָה עַד הַיָּם הָאַחֲרוֹן׃ וְאֶת־הַנֶּגֶב וְאֶת־
ד הַכִּכָּר בִּקְעַת יְרֵחוֹ עִיר הַתְּמָרִים עַד־צֹעַר׃ וַיֹּאמֶר
יְהוָה אֵלָיו זֹאת הָאָרֶץ אֲשֶׁר נִשְׁבַּעְתִּי לְאַבְרָהָם
לְיִצְחָק וּלְיַעֲקֹב לֵאמֹר לְזַרְעֲךָ אֶתְּנֶנָּה הֶרְאִיתִיךָ
ה בְעֵינֶיךָ וְשָׁמָּה לֹא תַעֲבֹר׃ וַיָּמָת שָׁם מֹשֶׁה עֶבֶד־
ו יְהוָה בְּאֶרֶץ מוֹאָב עַל־פִּי יְהוָה׃ וַיִּקְבֹּר אֹתוֹ בַגַּי
בְּאֶרֶץ מוֹאָב מוּל בֵּית פְּעוֹר וְלֹא־יָדַע אִישׁ אֶת־
ז קְבֻרָתוֹ עַד הַיּוֹם הַזֶּה׃ וּמֹשֶׁה בֶּן־מֵאָה וְעֶשְׂרִים שָׁנָה
ח בְּמֹתוֹ לֹא־כָהֲתָה עֵינוֹ וְלֹא־נָס לֵחֹה׃ וַיִּבְכּוּ בְנֵי
יִשְׂרָאֵל אֶת־מֹשֶׁה בְּעַרְבֹת מוֹאָב שְׁלֹשִׁים יוֹם
ט וַיִּתְּמוּ יְמֵי בְכִי אֵבֶל מֹשֶׁה׃ וִיהוֹשֻׁעַ בִּן־נוּן מָלֵא רוּחַ
חָכְמָה כִּי־סָמַךְ מֹשֶׁה אֶת־יָדָיו עָלָיו וַיִּשְׁמְעוּ אֵלָיו

בעל הטורים

לד (ד) **הֶרְאִיתִיךָ.** מָלֵא יוּ״ד. כִּי עֲשָׂרָה פְסוּקִים בַּתּוֹרָה שֶׁכָּתוּב בָּהֶם אֲשֶׁר נִשְׁבַּע לָהֶם לַהֲבִיאָם לָאָרֶץ. וְהֶרְאָהוּ עֶשֶׂר קְדֻשּׁוֹת שֶׁבְּאֶרֶץ יִשְׂרָאֵל:

(ו) **וַיִּקְבֹּר אֹתוֹ בַגַּי.** בַּגַּי כְּתִיב חָסֵר אָלֶ״ף. שֶׁ״לֹּא יָדַע אִישׁ אֶת קְבֻרָתוֹ״, וַאֲפִלּוּ מֹשֶׁה רַבֵּנוּ עָלָיו הַשָּׁלוֹם לֹא יָדַע {כִּי גַם מֹשֶׁה נִקְרָא אִישׁ}, אֶלָּא יְחִידוֹ שֶׁל עוֹלָם, בָּרוּךְ הוּא וּבָרוּךְ שְׁמוֹ וּבָרוּךְ זִכְרוֹ:

BAAL HATURIM ELUCIDATED

XXXIV.

4. הֶרְאִיתִיךָ — I HAVE SHOWN YOU. This term is spelled in full,[71a] with a **י** (= 10). For there are ten verses in the Torah which state that God promised them that He would bring them into the Land [of Israel].[72] Also, it implies that God showed Moses the ten levels of holiness that are in the Land of Israel.[73]

71a. The word הֶרְאִיתִיךָ is the first person singular verb הֶרְאֵיתִי, *I have shown,* with the second person singular suffix ךָ־, *you.* It is properly spelled with a **י** after the **א** and another **י** after the **ת**. Whereas the word does not appear elsewhere in Scripture, it is not clear to which **י** the Baal HaTurim refers. However, the similar word הִרְאִיתִים, *I have shown them,* is found twice — once with the full spelling (*Isaiah* 39:4); once defectively, הִרְאִתִם, without the second **י** (*II Kings* 20:15). Accordingly, we may assume that the Baal HaTurim refers to the second **י**.

72. *Peirush HaRokeach.* According to *Shoham Yakar,* the ten verses are: *Genesis* 26:3; *Exodus* 33:1; *Numbers* 14:23 and 32:11; *Deuteronomy* 1:35, 10:11, 31:20, 31:21, 31:23 and 34:4. In each of those verses, God, Himself, speaks of His promise.

73. The Mishnah (*Keilim* 1:6-9) describes the ten levels.

HASHEM showed him the entire Land: the Gilead as far as Dan; 2 all of Naphtali, and the land of Ephraim and Manasseh; the entire land of Judah as far as the western sea; 3 the Negev and the Plain — the valley of Jericho, city of date palms — as far as Zoar.

4 And HASHEM said to him, "This is the land which I swore to Abraham, to Isaac, and to Jacob, saying, 'I will give it to your offspring.' I have shown you with your own eyes, but you shall not cross over to there."

5 So Moses, servant of HASHEM, died there, in the land of Moab, by the mouth of HASHEM. 6 He buried him in the valley, in the land of Moab, opposite Beth-peor, and no man knows his burial place to this day. 7 Moses was one hundred and twenty years old when he died; his eye had not dimmed, and his vigor had not diminished. 8 The Children of Israel bewailed Moses in the plains of Moab for thirty days; then the days of tearful mourning for Moses ended.

9 Joshua son of Nun was filled with the spirit of wisdom, because Moses had laid his hands upon him, so

BAAL HATURIM ELUCIDATED

6. וַיִּקְבֹּר אֹתוֹ בַגַּי — **HE BURIED HIM IN THE VALLEY.** The term בַגַּי is spelled defectively, without an א.[74] For *no man knows his* [*Moses'*] *burial place,* not even our teacher Moses, of blessed memory, knew, {for Moses is also called אִישׁ, *man,* [75]}[76] except the Unique One[77] of the world,[77a] Blessed is He, Blessed is His Name, and Blessed is His remembrance.

❑ {The Baal HaTurim's other comment to וַיִּקְבֹּר אֹתוֹ בַגַּי appears at *Numbers* 21:20.}

7. {The Baal HaTurim's comment to לֹא כָהֲתָה עֵינוֹ וְלֹא נָס לֵחֹה appears at *Exodus* 23:25, s.v., וַהֲסִרֹתִי.}

74. The term appears three more times in the Torah (*Numbers* 21:20; *Deuteronomy* 3:29 and 4:46), in each case spelled גַּיְא. Elsewhere in the *Tanach,* the word appears eighteen times: thirteen of them spelled in full, with an א [and vowelized in any of four ways: גֵּיא, גֵּיא, גָּיְא, גַּיְא]; and five spelled defectively, without an א [vowelized either גַּי or גֵּי].

Interestingly, the plural form appears seven times (with and without a prefix, but) without a suffix, each time spelled גֵּאָיוֹת, with the א and י reversing their positions in the word [rather than the expected גֵּיאוֹת or גֵּיאָיוֹת]; and once with a suffix, spelled וְגֵיאוֹתֶיךָ (*Ezekiel* 35:8), indicating that the form גֵּיאוֹת is also acceptable.

75. The phrase enclosed in braces is found in neither the extant manuscripts nor the early printed editions. It does appear, however, in some later editions and in the Talmudic source (see note 76 below).

76. *Sotah* 14a — Not even Moses knew his own burial place, as the verse states, וְלֹא יָדַע אִישׁ אֶת קְבֻרָתוֹ, *and no man knows his burial place,* with the term אִישׁ, *man,* understood as a reference to Moses, who is called אִישׁ הָאֱלֹהִים, *the man of God* (33:1 above).

77. This is the implication of the absent א (= 1).

77a. *Peirush HaRokeach.*

לד/י־יב בְּנֵי־יִשְׂרָאֵל וַיַּעֲשׂוּ כַּאֲשֶׁר צִוָּה יהוה אֶת־מֹשֶׁה:
י וְלֹא־קָם נָבִיא עוֹד בְּיִשְׂרָאֵל כְּמֹשֶׁה אֲשֶׁר יְדָעוֹ
יא יהוה פָּנִים אֶל־פָּנִים: לְכָל־הָאֹתֹת וְהַמּוֹפְתִים
אֲשֶׁר שְׁלָחוֹ יהוה לַעֲשׂוֹת בְּאֶרֶץ מִצְרָיִם לְפַרְעֹה
יב וּלְכָל־עֲבָדָיו וּלְכָל־אַרְצוֹ: וּלְכֹל הַיָּד הַחֲזָקָה
וּלְכֹל הַמּוֹרָא הַגָּדוֹל אֲשֶׁר עָשָׂה מֹשֶׁה לְעֵינֵי
כָּל־יִשְׂרָאֵל:

It is customary for the congregation followed by the reader to proclaim:

חֲזַק! חֲזַק! וְנִתְחַזֵּק!

סכום פסוקי דספר דברים תשע מאות וחמשים וחמשה. הנ״ץ סימן.
סכום פסוקים של כל התורה חמשת אלפים ושמנה מאות וארבעים וחמשה.
ואור החמ״ה יהיה שבעתים סימן.

בעל הטורים

{(יב) **הַיָּד הַחֲזָקָה.** בְּגִימַטְרִיָּא אַף חֵימָה. שֶׁמֹּשֶׁה כְבָשָׁן:}

❑ {**וּלְכֹל הַמּוֹרָא הַגָּדוֹל.** בְּגִימַטְרִיָּא פִּי הָאָרֶץ:}

❑ {אוֹתִיּוֹת רִאשׁוֹנוֹת שֶׁל כָּל נ״ד פָּרָשִׁיּוֹת עוֹלִין תשצ״א, כְּמִנְיַן וּדְבַר ה׳ בְּפִיךָ אֱמֶת:}

❑ {ר״ץ פָּרָשִׁיּוֹת פְּתוּחוֹת, עוֹלֶה כְּמִנְיַן עַל פִּי ה׳ יַחֲנוּ:}

❑ {תרס״ט פְּתוּחוֹת וּסְתוּמוֹת שֶׁבַּתּוֹרָה עוֹלֶה כְּמִנְיַן גִּמַטְרִיָּאוֹת:}

{וַה׳ יַרְאֵנוּ נִפְלָאוֹת וְיַצִּילֵנוּ מִשְּׁגִיאוֹת. אָמֵן, כֵּן יְהִי רָצוֹן:}

BAAL HATURIM ELUCIDATED

10. {The Baal HaTurim's comment to וְלֹא קָם נָבִיא עוֹד appears at *Exodus* 18:19.}

12. {הַיָּד הַחֲזָקָה — THE STRONG HAND. The *gematria* of this phrase (144) is equal to that of אַף חֵימָה, [*the malevolent angels*] *Af* [*and*] *Cheimah* (Anger and Wrath), for Moses conquered them.[78]}[79]

❑ {וּלְכֹל הַמּוֹרָא הַגָּדוֹל — AND FOR ALL THE GREAT AWESOMENESS. The *gematria* of this phrase (386) is equal to that of פִּי הָאָרֶץ, *the mouth of the earth.*[80]}[80a]

❑ {The *gematria* of the initial letters of the fifty-four *sidros*[81] of the Torah is 791,

78. See *Nedarim* 32a; see also the Baal HaTurim to *Exodus* 4:24 and *Numbers* 25:11.

79. The last five comments are enclosed in braces for they are not found in either the extant manuscripts or in the early printed editions. However, they do appear in some of the later printed editions, where they have almost certainly been added by the later typesetters (see note 87 below).

80. This refers to the awesomeness displayed by Moses in his role of quelling Korah's rebellion (see *Numbers* 16:28-33).

80a. See note 79 above.

81. Six *sidros* begin with the letter א (*Noach* — אֵלֶּה; *Pikudei* — אֵלֶּה; *Bechukosai* — אִם; *Masei* — אֵלֶּה; *Devarim* — אֵלֶּה; and *Nitzavim* — אַתֶּם); six times the *gematria* of א is 6.

Bereishis begins with a ב (= 2); *Ha'azinu,* with a ה (= 5); *Ki Seitzei* with a כ (= 20); *Re'eh,* with a ר (= 200); and *Shoftim,* with a ש (= 300). These add up to 527. Each of the remaining forty-three *sidros* begins with a ו (= 6), adding another

the Children of Israel obeyed him and did as HASHEM had
commanded Moses.
10 *Never again has there arisen in Israel a prophet like*
Moses, whom HASHEM had known face to face, 11 *for all the*
signs and the wonders that HASHEM sent him to perform in
the land of Egypt, against Pharaoh and against all his
sevants and against all his land, 12 *and for all the strong*
hand and for all the great awesomeness that Moses
performed before the eyes of all Israel.

BAAL HATURIM ELUCIDATED

equal to that of וּדְבַר הוי״ה בְּפִיךָ אֱמֶת, *and the word of HASHEM in your mouth is true* (*I Kings* 17:24).[82]}[82a]

❑ {There are 290 open *parashiyos*[83] in the Torah, corresponding to the *encamp*

(43x6 =) 258. Taken together (6 + 527 + 258), the initial letters of the fifty-four *sidros* have a *gematria* of 791.

82. In the context of *Kings,* these words were spoken by the widow of Zarephath in praise of Elijah, who had restored her son to life. In the Baal HaTurim's comment they are used in praise of Moses, for the Torah is referred to as both תּוֹרַת אֱמֶת, *the Torah of truth* (*Malachi* 2:6), and תּוֹרַת מֹשֶׁה, *the Torah of Moses* (e.g., *Joshua* 8:31).

The *Amora* Rabbah bar bar Chammah related the following: One time, while I was traveling, an itinerant merchant said to me, "Come, I will show you the spot where Korah was swallowed up." I went and I saw two crevices from which smoke was rising . . . The merchant said to me, "Pay attention to what you are hearing." I heard them saying, "מֹשֶׁה אֱמֶת וְתוֹרָתוֹ אֱמֶת, *Moses is true and his Torah is true,* וְהֵן בַּדָּאִין, *but those* [a euphemism for *we*] *were liars.*" The merchant then told me that they repeat these words every thirty days . . . [The Midrash continues:] But in Time to Come, God will remove them from there. It is about them that Hannah [the wife of Elkanah, a descendant of Korah,] said (*I Samuel* 2:6), *HASHEM puts to death and brings back to life; He lowers to the Pit and brings back up* (*Tanchuma, Korah* 11).

In the light of that Midrash, this comment and the one before it are connected: The first refers to the mouth of the earth, by which Korah was swallowed up; the second, to Korah's repeated acknowledgment of the truth of Moses' words and the folly of his own (*VeChur LaZahav*).

82a. See note 79 above.

83. The commonly used system of chapter numbers does not carry any halachic or exegetic authority. With the exception of *Psalms* and *Lamentations,* that division is not of masoretic origin, nor does it stem from any other Jewish source; rather, it was invented by gentile Bible scholars. Chapter divisions were first introduced into *Tanach* by Yaakov ibn Adoniyahu in the 1524 Venice edition, for practical reasons (see his introduction, reprinted in *Mikraos Gedolos,* Warsaw, 1894).

According to masoretic tradition, the text of Scripture is divided into פָּרָשִׁיּוֹת, *parashiyos* (paragraph-like passages), separated from one another by a blank space, and that is how *Tanach* scrolls are written. These spaces appear in one of two forms: פְּתוּחָה, *open,* indicated by ending the previous passage in the middle of a line and then beginning the new passage at the beginning of the next line, or סְתוּמָה, *closed,* indicated by the new passage beginning on the same line on which the previous passage ended, but after a space in which at least nine letters could be written (see illustration). [In some printed editions these spaces are indicated by the letters פ and ס.]

לעשו לחם ונזיד עדשים ויאכל וישת ויקם
וילך ויבז עשו את הבכרה
ויהי רעב בארץ מלבד הרעב הראשון אשר

פָּרָשָׁה פְּתוּחָה — Open Passage (*Genesis* 25:34–26:1)

את מחלת בת ישמעאל בן אברהם אחות
נביות על נשיו לו לאשה ויצא
יעקב מבאר שבע וילך חרנה ויפגע במקום

פָּרָשָׁה סְתוּמָה — Closed Passage (*Genesis* 28:9–10)

of עַל פִּי הוי״ה יַחֲנוּ, *according to the word of* HASHEM *they would encamp*[84] (*Numbers* 9:20, 23).}[84a]

❑ {The total number of *parashiyos* in the Torah, (290) open and (379) closed, is 669, corresponding to the *gematria* of [85]גְּמַטְרִיָּאוֹת, *gematriaos.* [86]}[86a]

{May HASHEM show us wonders;[87] and may He save us from errors.[88] Amen. May [His] will be so.}[89]

84. In the context of the passage in which that verse appears, יַחֲנוּ, *they would encamp,* means that at God's command they would take a break from their travels and set up camp. In the context of the comment, פִּי ה׳ refers to the mouth or opening at the end of each open *parashah* in God's Torah; while יַחֲנוּ means that they would pause to reflect on the *parashah* that has just been read (see *Rashi's* second comment to *Leviticus* 1:1).

84a. See note 79 above.

85. Like the four preceding comments, the authenticity of this one is brought into question by its absence from most editions (see note 79 above). Moreover, it is noteworthy that throughout this work, the term גִּימַטְרִיָּא, *gematria,* is invariably spelled with a י after the ג. This is the only comment in which that י is omitted.

86. This indicates that every part of the Torah may be interpreted in the realm of רֶמֶז, *allusion,* through the comparison of *gematriaos.*

86a. See note 79 above.

87. The Baal HaTurim's words are paraphrased from *Micah* 7:15.

88. The Baal HaTurim's words are paraphrased from *Psalms* 19:13.

89. In the early centuries of the printing industry, it was commonplace for a typesetter to add a few lines at the end of a volume: (a) to thank Hashem for allowing him to complete the job; and (b) to apologize to the reader for any typographical errors he may have made. Presumably that is how this last line entered the Baal HaTurim's commentary.

תושלב״ע

יום ה׳ לסדר במדב״ר סינ״י באה״ל מ׳ועד [בגימ׳ אברה״ם יצח״ק]
ערב ר״ח סיון תשס״ד

ההפטרות ⸗

The Haftaros

BLESSINGS OF THE HAFTARAH / ברכות ההפטרה

After the Torah Scroll has been tied and covered, the *Maftir* recites the *Haftarah* blessings.

Blessed are You, HASHEM, our God, King of the universe, Who has chosen good prophets and was pleased with their words that were uttered with truth. Blessed are You, HASHEM, Who chooses the Torah; Moses, His servant; Israel, His nation; and the prophets of truth and righteousness. (Cong. – *Amen.*)

בָּרוּךְ אַתָּה יהוה אֱלֹהֵינוּ מֶלֶךְ הָעוֹלָם, אֲשֶׁר בָּחַר בִּנְבִיאִים טוֹבִים, וְרָצָה בְדִבְרֵיהֶם הַנֶּאֱמָרִים בֶּאֱמֶת, בָּרוּךְ אַתָּה יהוה, הַבּוֹחֵר בַּתּוֹרָה וּבְמֹשֶׁה עַבְדּוֹ, וּבְיִשְׂרָאֵל עַמּוֹ, וּבִנְבִיאֵי הָאֱמֶת וָצֶדֶק. (קהל – אָמֵן)

The *Haftarah* is read, after which the *Maftir* recites the following blessings.

Blessed are You, HASHEM, our God, King of the universe, Rock of all eternities, Righteous in all generations, the trustworthy God, Who says and does, Who speaks and fulfills, all of Whose words are true and righteous. Trustworthy are You, HASHEM, our God, and trustworthy are Your words, not one of Your words is turned back to its origin unfulfilled, for You are God, trustworthy (and compassionate) King. Blessed are You, HASHEM, the God Who is trustworthy in all His words. (Cong. – *Amen.*)

בָּרוּךְ אַתָּה יהוה אֱלֹהֵינוּ מֶלֶךְ הָעוֹלָם, צוּר כָּל הָעוֹלָמִים, צַדִּיק בְּכָל הַדּוֹרוֹת, הָאֵל הַנֶּאֱמָן הָאוֹמֵר וְעֹשֶׂה, הַמְּדַבֵּר וּמְקַיֵּם, שֶׁכָּל דְּבָרָיו אֱמֶת וָצֶדֶק. נֶאֱמָן אַתָּה הוּא יהוה אֱלֹהֵינוּ, וְנֶאֱמָנִים דְּבָרֶיךָ, וְדָבָר אֶחָד מִדְּבָרֶיךָ אָחוֹר לֹא יָשׁוּב רֵיקָם, כִּי אֵל מֶלֶךְ נֶאֱמָן (וְרַחֲמָן) אָתָּה. בָּרוּךְ אַתָּה יהוה, הָאֵל הַנֶּאֱמָן בְּכָל דְּבָרָיו. (קהל – אָמֵן)

Have mercy on Zion for it is the source of our life; to the one who is deeply humiliated bring salvation speedily, in our days. Blessed are You, HASHEM, Who gladdens Zion through her children. (Cong. – *Amen.*)

רַחֵם עַל צִיּוֹן כִּי הִיא בֵּית חַיֵּינוּ, וְלַעֲלוּבַת נֶפֶשׁ תּוֹשִׁיעַ בִּמְהֵרָה בְיָמֵינוּ. בָּרוּךְ אַתָּה יהוה, מְשַׂמֵּחַ צִיּוֹן בְּבָנֶיהָ. (קהל – אָמֵן)

Gladden us, HASHEM, our God, with Elijah the prophet Your servant, and with the kingdom of the House of David, Your anointed, may he come speedily and cause our heart to exult. On his throne let no stranger sit nor let others continue to inherit his honor, for by Your holy Name You swore to him that his lamp will not be extinguished forever and ever. Blessed are You, HASHEM, Shield of David. (Cong. – *Amen.*)

שַׂמְּחֵנוּ יהוה אֱלֹהֵינוּ בְּאֵלִיָּהוּ הַנָּבִיא עַבְדֶּךָ, וּבְמַלְכוּת בֵּית דָּוִד מְשִׁיחֶךָ, בִּמְהֵרָה יָבֹא וְיָגֵל לִבֵּנוּ, עַל כִּסְאוֹ לֹא יֵשֶׁב זָר וְלֹא יִנְחֲלוּ עוֹד אֲחֵרִים אֶת כְּבוֹדוֹ, כִּי בְשֵׁם קָדְשְׁךָ נִשְׁבַּעְתָּ לוֹ, שֶׁלֹּא יִכְבֶּה נֵרוֹ לְעוֹלָם וָעֶד. בָּרוּךְ אַתָּה יהוה, מָגֵן דָּוִד. (קהל – אָמֵן)

For the Torah reading, for the prayer service, for the reading from the Prophets and for this Sabbath day that You, HASHEM, our God, have given us for holiness and contentment, for glory and splendor — for all this, HASHEM, our God, we gratefully thank You and bless You. May Your Name be blessed by the mouth of all the living always, for all eternity. Blessed are You, HASHEM, Who sanctifies the Sabbath. (Cong. – *Amen.*)

עַל הַתּוֹרָה, וְעַל הָעֲבוֹדָה, וְעַל הַנְּבִיאִים, וְעַל יוֹם הַשַּׁבָּת הַזֶּה, שֶׁנָּתַתָּ לָּנוּ יהוה אֱלֹהֵינוּ, לִקְדֻשָּׁה וְלִמְנוּחָה, לְכָבוֹד וּלְתִפְאָרֶת. עַל הַכֹּל יהוה אֱלֹהֵינוּ, אֲנַחְנוּ מוֹדִים לָךְ, וּמְבָרְכִים אוֹתָךְ, יִתְבָּרַךְ שִׁמְךָ בְּפִי כָּל חַי תָּמִיד לְעוֹלָם וָעֶד. בָּרוּךְ אַתָּה יהוה, מְקַדֵּשׁ הַשַּׁבָּת. (קהל – אָמֵן)

HAFTARAS DEVARIM / הפטרת דברים

Isaiah 1:1-27 / ישעיה א:א־כז

א א חֲזוֹן יְשַׁעְיָהוּ בֶן־אָמוֹץ אֲשֶׁר חָזָה עַל־יְהוּדָה וִירוּשָׁלָם בִּימֵי עֻזִּיָּהוּ יוֹתָם אָחָז יְחִזְקִיָּהוּ מַלְכֵי יְהוּדָה׃ ב שִׁמְעוּ שָׁמַיִם וְהַאֲזִינִי אֶרֶץ כִּי יְהוָה דִּבֵּר בָּנִים גִּדַּלְתִּי וְרוֹמַמְתִּי וְהֵם פָּשְׁעוּ בִי׃ ג יָדַע שׁוֹר קֹנֵהוּ וַחֲמוֹר אֵבוּס בְּעָלָיו יִשְׂרָאֵל לֹא יָדַע עַמִּי לֹא הִתְבּוֹנָן׃ ד הוֹי ׀ גּוֹי חֹטֵא עַם כֶּבֶד עָוֺן זֶרַע מְרֵעִים בָּנִים מַשְׁחִיתִים עָזְבוּ אֶת־יְהוָה נִאֲצוּ אֶת־קְדוֹשׁ יִשְׂרָאֵל נָזֹרוּ אָחוֹר׃ ה עַל מֶה תֻכּוּ עוֹד תּוֹסִיפוּ סָרָה כָּל־רֹאשׁ לָחֳלִי וְכָל־לֵבָב דַּוָּי׃ ו מִכַּף־רֶגֶל וְעַד־רֹאשׁ אֵין־בּוֹ מְתֹם פֶּצַע וְחַבּוּרָה וּמַכָּה טְרִיָּה לֹא־זֹרוּ וְלֹא חֻבָּשׁוּ וְלֹא רֻכְּכָה בַּשָּׁמֶן׃ ז אַרְצְכֶם שְׁמָמָה עָרֵיכֶם שְׂרֻפוֹת אֵשׁ אַדְמַתְכֶם לְנֶגְדְּכֶם זָרִים אֹכְלִים אֹתָהּ וּשְׁמָמָה כְּמַהְפֵּכַת זָרִים׃ ח וְנוֹתְרָה בַת־צִיּוֹן כְּסֻכָּה בְכָרֶם כִּמְלוּנָה בְמִקְשָׁה כְּעִיר נְצוּרָה׃ ט לוּלֵי יְהוָה צְבָאוֹת הוֹתִיר לָנוּ שָׂרִיד כִּמְעָט כִּסְדֹם הָיִינוּ לַעֲמֹרָה דָּמִינוּ׃ י שִׁמְעוּ דְבַר־יְהוָה קְצִינֵי סְדֹם הַאֲזִינוּ תּוֹרַת אֱלֹהֵינוּ עַם עֲמֹרָה׃ יא לָמָּה־לִּי רֹב־זִבְחֵיכֶם יֹאמַר יְהוָה שָׂבַעְתִּי עֹלוֹת אֵילִים וְחֵלֶב מְרִיאִים וְדַם פָּרִים וּכְבָשִׂים וְעַתּוּדִים לֹא חָפָצְתִּי׃ יב כִּי תָבֹאוּ לֵרָאוֹת פָּנָי מִי־בִקֵּשׁ זֹאת מִיֶּדְכֶם רְמֹס חֲצֵרָי׃ יג לֹא תוֹסִיפוּ הָבִיא מִנְחַת־שָׁוְא קְטֹרֶת תּוֹעֵבָה הִיא לִי חֹדֶשׁ וְשַׁבָּת קְרֹא מִקְרָא לֹא־אוּכַל אָוֶן וַעֲצָרָה׃ יד חָדְשֵׁיכֶם וּמוֹעֲדֵיכֶם שָׂנְאָה נַפְשִׁי הָיוּ עָלַי לָטֹרַח נִלְאֵיתִי נְשֹׂא׃ טו וּבְפָרִשְׂכֶם כַּפֵּיכֶם אַעְלִים עֵינַי מִכֶּם גַּם כִּי־תַרְבּוּ תְפִלָּה אֵינֶנִּי שֹׁמֵעַ יְדֵיכֶם דָּמִים מָלֵאוּ׃ טז רַחֲצוּ הִזַּכּוּ הָסִירוּ רֹעַ מַעַלְלֵיכֶם מִנֶּגֶד עֵינָי חִדְלוּ הָרֵעַ׃ יז לִמְדוּ הֵיטֵב דִּרְשׁוּ מִשְׁפָּט אַשְּׁרוּ חָמוֹץ שִׁפְטוּ יָתוֹם רִיבוּ אַלְמָנָה׃ יח לְכוּ־נָא וְנִוָּכְחָה יֹאמַר יְהוָה אִם־יִהְיוּ חֲטָאֵיכֶם כַּשָּׁנִים כַּשֶּׁלֶג יַלְבִּינוּ אִם־יַאְדִּימוּ כַתּוֹלָע כַּצֶּמֶר יִהְיוּ׃ יט אִם־תֹּאבוּ וּשְׁמַעְתֶּם טוּב הָאָרֶץ תֹּאכֵלוּ׃ כ וְאִם־תְּמָאֲנוּ וּמְרִיתֶם חֶרֶב תְּאֻכְּלוּ כִּי פִּי יְהוָה דִּבֵּר׃ כא אֵיכָה הָיְתָה לְזוֹנָה קִרְיָה נֶאֱמָנָה

1 *The vision of Isaiah son of Amoz, which he saw concerning Judah and Jerusalem, in the days of Uzziah, Jotham, Ahaz and Hezekiah, kings of Judah: 2 Hear, O heavens, and give ear, O earth, for* HASHEM *has spoken: Children have I raised and exalted, but they have rebelled against Me. 3 An ox knows his owner, and a donkey his master's trough; Israel does not know, My people does not perceive. 4 Woe! O sinful nation, people weighed down by iniquity, offspring of evil, destructive children; they have forsaken* HASHEM*, they have angered the Holy One of Israel, they have turned away backward. 5 For what would you be smitten, when you still continue waywardly, each head with sickness, each heart in pain? 6 From the foot's sole to the head, nothing in it is whole: sword slash, contusion, and festering wound; they have not medicated, and they have not bandaged, and it was not softened with oil. 7 Your country is desolate, your cities are burned with fire, your land — before you strangers consume it; it is desolate as if overturned by strangers. 8 The daughter of Zion shall be left like a [deserted] watchman's booth in a vineyard, like a shed in a gourd garden, like a city under siege. 9 Had not* HASHEM*, Master of Legions, left us a trace of a remnant, we would have been like Sodom, we would have resembled Gomorrah.*

10 *Hear the word of* HASHEM*, O chiefs of Sodom; give ear to the Torah of our God, O people of Gomorrah. 11 Why do I need your numerous sacrifices? — says* HASHEM *— I am satiated with elevation-offerings of rams and the choicest of fattened animals; and the blood of bulls and sheep and he-goats I do not desire. 12 When you come to appear before Me — who sought this from your hand, to trample My courtyards? 13 You shall not continue to bring a worthless meal-offering — incense of abomination is it unto Me; [New] Moon and Sabbath, calling of convocation, I cannot abide mendacity with assemblage. 14 Your [New] Moons and your appointed festivals, My soul hates; they have become a burden upon Me [that] I am weary of bearing. 15 And when you spread your hands [in prayer], I will hide My eyes from you; even if you were to increase prayer, I do not hear; your hands are full of blood. 16 Wash yourselves, purify yourselves, remove the evil of your doings from before My eyes; desist from doing evil. 17 Learn to do good, seek justice, strengthen the victim, do justice for the orphan, take up the cause of the widow.*

18 *Go forth, now, let us reason together — says* HASHEM *— if your sins will be like scarlet, they will whiten like snow, if they have reddened like crimson, they will become as wool. 19 If you will be willing and you will obey, you shall eat the goodness of the land. 20 But if you will refuse and rebel, you shall be devoured by the sword — for the mouth of* HASHEM *has spoken.*

21 *How has she become a harlot! — faithful city*

that was full of justice, in which righteousness was wont to lodge, but now murderers. 22 *Your silver has become dross, your heady wine mixed with water.* 23 *Your princes are wayward and associates of thieves; the whole of them loves bribery and pursue [illegal] payments; for the orphan they do not do justice, the cause of the widow does not come unto them.*

24 *Therefore — the word of the Lord, HASHEM, Master of Legions, Mighty One of Israel — O, how I will ease Myself of My adversaries, and how I will avenge Myself of My enemies.* 25 *I will return My hand upon you, and refine as with lye your dross, and I will remove all your base metal.* 26 *Then I will return your judges as in earliest times, and your counselors as at first, after that you shall be called City of Righteousness, Faithful City.* 27 *Zion shall be redeemed with justice, and her returnees with righteousness.*

מְלֵאֲתִי מִשְׁפָּט צֶדֶק יָלִין בָּהּ וְעַתָּה מְרַצְּחִים׃
כב כַּסְפֵּךְ הָיָה לְסִיגִים סָבְאֵךְ מָהוּל בַּמָּיִם׃
כג שָׂרַיִךְ סוֹרְרִים וְחַבְרֵי גַּנָּבִים כֻּלּוֹ אֹהֵב שֹׁחַד
וְרֹדֵף שַׁלְמֹנִים יָתוֹם לֹא יִשְׁפֹּטוּ וְרִיב אַלְמָנָה
לֹא־יָבוֹא אֲלֵיהֶם׃ כד לָכֵן נְאֻם הָאָדוֹן יהוה
צְבָאוֹת אֲבִיר יִשְׂרָאֵל הוֹי אֶנָּחֵם מִצָּרַי
וְאִנָּקְמָה מֵאוֹיְבָי׃ כה וְאָשִׁיבָה יָדִי עָלַיִךְ וְאֶצְרֹף
כַּבֹּר סִיגָיִךְ וְאָסִירָה כָּל־בְּדִילָיִךְ׃ כו וְאָשִׁיבָה
שֹׁפְטַיִךְ כְּבָרִאשֹׁנָה וְיֹעֲצַיִךְ כְּבַתְּחִלָּה אַחֲרֵי־כֵן
יִקָּרֵא לָךְ עִיר הַצֶּדֶק קִרְיָה נֶאֱמָנָה׃ כז צִיּוֹן
בְּמִשְׁפָּט תִּפָּדֶה וְשָׁבֶיהָ בִּצְדָקָה׃

HAFTARAS VA'ESCHANAN / הפטרת ואתחנן

Isaiah 40:1-26 / ישעיה מ:א-כו

40 1 *Comfort, comfort My people — says your God.* 2 *Speak to the heart of Jerusalem and proclaim to her that her time [of exile] has been fulfilled, that her iniquity has been conciliated, for she has received from the hand of HASHEM double for all her sins.*

3 *A voice calls, "In the wilderness, clear the way of HASHEM; make a straight road in the plain, a highway for our God.* 4 *Every valley shall be raised, and every mountain and hill shall be made low, the crooked shall become straight and the rugged a level low land.* 5 *Revealed shall be the glory of HASHEM, and all flesh as one shall see that the mouth of HASHEM has spoken."*

6 *The Voice says, "Proclaim!" and he says, "What shall I proclaim?" — "All flesh is grass, and all its kindness like the flower of the field.* 7 *The grass shall wither, the flower shall fade, for the breath of HASHEM has blown upon it; in truth, the people is grass.* 8 *The grass shall wither, the flower shall fade, but the word of our God shall stand forever."*

9 *Get yourself upon a high mountain, O herald unto Zion; raise your voice in power, O herald unto Jerusalem, raise [it], fear not, say to the cities of Judah, "Behold, your God!"* 10 *Behold! My Lord, HASHEM/ELOHIM, shall come with strength, and His arm will rule for Him; behold! His recompense is with Him, and His wage is before Him,* 11 *like a shepherd would graze his flock, would gather lambs in his arm and carry [them] in his bosom, would lead the nurslings.*

12 *Who has measured the waters in His fist, and meted out the Heavens with the span, and counted in large volume the dust of the earth, and weighed mountains in a scale and hills in a balance?* 13 *Who has meted out the spirit of HASHEM? Who is His man of counsel that he might let Him know?* 14 *With whom did He seek counsel and give him insight, and teach him in the path of justice, and teach him knowledge,*

מ א נַחֲמוּ נַחֲמוּ עַמִּי יֹאמַר אֱלֹהֵיכֶם׃ ב דַּבְּרוּ
עַל־לֵב יְרוּשָׁלַםִ וְקִרְאוּ אֵלֶיהָ כִּי מָלְאָה צְבָאָהּ
כִּי נִרְצָה עֲוֺנָהּ כִּי לָקְחָה מִיַּד יהוה כִּפְלַיִם
בְּכָל־חַטֹּאתֶיהָ׃ ג קוֹל קוֹרֵא בַּמִּדְבָּר פַּנּוּ דֶּרֶךְ
יהוה יַשְּׁרוּ בָּעֲרָבָה מְסִלָּה לֵאלֹהֵינוּ׃ ד כָּל־
גֶּיא יִנָּשֵׂא וְכָל־הַר וְגִבְעָה יִשְׁפָּלוּ וְהָיָה
הֶעָקֹב לְמִישׁוֹר וְהָרְכָסִים לְבִקְעָה׃ ה וְנִגְלָה
כְּבוֹד יהוה וְרָאוּ כָל־בָּשָׂר יַחְדָּו כִּי פִּי יהוה
דִּבֵּר׃ ו קוֹל אֹמֵר קְרָא וְאָמַר מָה אֶקְרָא כָּל־
הַבָּשָׂר חָצִיר וְכָל־חַסְדּוֹ כְּצִיץ הַשָּׂדֶה׃ ז יָבֵשׁ
חָצִיר נָבֵל צִיץ כִּי רוּחַ יהוה נָשְׁבָה בּוֹ אָכֵן
חָצִיר הָעָם׃ ח יָבֵשׁ חָצִיר נָבֵל צִיץ וּדְבַר
אֱלֹהֵינוּ יָקוּם לְעוֹלָם׃ ט עַל הַר־גָּבֹהַּ עֲלִי־לָךְ
מְבַשֶּׂרֶת צִיּוֹן הָרִימִי בַכֹּחַ קוֹלֵךְ מְבַשֶּׂרֶת
יְרוּשָׁלָםִ הָרִימִי אַל־תִּירָאִי אִמְרִי לְעָרֵי יְהוּדָה
הִנֵּה אֱלֹהֵיכֶם׃ י הִנֵּה אֲדֹנָי יֱהוִה בְּחָזָק יָבוֹא
וּזְרֹעוֹ מֹשְׁלָה לוֹ הִנֵּה שְׂכָרוֹ אִתּוֹ וּפְעֻלָּתוֹ
לְפָנָיו׃ יא כְּרֹעֶה עֶדְרוֹ יִרְעֶה בִּזְרֹעוֹ יְקַבֵּץ
טְלָאִים וּבְחֵיקוֹ יִשָּׂא עָלוֹת יְנַהֵל׃ יב מִי־מָדַד
בְּשָׁעֳלוֹ מַיִם וְשָׁמַיִם בַּזֶּרֶת תִּכֵּן וְכָל בַּשָּׁלִשׁ
עֲפַר הָאָרֶץ וְשָׁקַל בַּפֶּלֶס הָרִים וּגְבָעוֹת
בְּמֹאזְנָיִם׃ יג מִי־תִכֵּן אֶת־רוּחַ יהוה וְאִישׁ עֲצָתוֹ
יוֹדִיעֶנּוּ׃ יד אֶת־מִי נוֹעָץ וַיְבִינֵהוּ וַיְלַמְּדֵהוּ
בְּאֹרַח מִשְׁפָּט וַיְלַמְּדֵהוּ דַעַת וְדֶרֶךְ תְּבוּנוֹת

and the way of understanding let him know? 15 Behold! the nations are like a bitter drop from a bucket, and as the dust on the balance are they considered; behold! the islands are like castaway dust. 16 And the Lebanon is not sufficient kindling; and its beasts are not sufficient for burnt-offerings.

17 All the nations are as nothing before Him, as nothingness and emptiness are they considered by Him. 18 To whom can you liken God? And what likeness can you arrange for Him? 19 The graven image, the artisan's casting, that the [gold]smith overlaid with gold and the [silver]smith with silver chains? 20 The pauper sets aside, he chooses wood that will not rot; he seeks for himself a wise artisan, to prepare an idol that cannot move. 21 Do you not know? Have you not heard? Has it not been told to you from the first? Have you not understood [Who fashioned] the foundations of the earth? 22 It is He Who sits on the circumference of the earth, and [Who views] its inhabitants as locusts; He Who spreads the heavens like a thin curtain, and stretches them like a tent to dwell [in]. 23 He Who gives over officers for nought; judges of land He made like emptiness; 24 even as if they were not planted, even as if they were not sown, even as if their stock was not rooted in the ground; and also should He blow on them, they would dry up, and a stormwind would carry them away like stubble.

25 And to whom can you liken Me? And [to whom] shall I be equal? — says the Holy One.

26 Raise your eyes on high and see Who created these: He brings forth their legions by number; He calls them all by name; because of His abundant might and powerful strength, there is not missing even one.

יוֹדִיעֶנּוּ: טו הֵן גּוֹיִם כְּמַר מִדְּלִי וּכְשַׁחַק מֹאזְנַיִם
נֶחְשָׁבוּ הֵן אִיִּים כַּדַּק יִטּוֹל: טז וּלְבָנוֹן אֵין דֵּי
בָּעֵר וְחַיָּתוֹ אֵין דֵּי עוֹלָה: יז כָּל־הַגּוֹיִם כְּאַיִן
נֶגְדּוֹ מֵאֶפֶס וָתֹהוּ נֶחְשְׁבוּ־לוֹ: יח וְאֶל־מִי
תְּדַמְּיוּן אֵל וּמַה־דְּמוּת תַּעַרְכוּ־לוֹ: יט הַפֶּסֶל
נָסַךְ חָרָשׁ וְצֹרֵף בַּזָּהָב יְרַקְּעֶנּוּ וּרְתֻקוֹת כֶּסֶף
צוֹרֵף: כ הַמְסֻכָּן תְּרוּמָה עֵץ לֹא־יִרְקַב יִבְחָר
חָרָשׁ חָכָם יְבַקֶּשׁ־לוֹ לְהָכִין פֶּסֶל לֹא יִמּוֹט:
כא הֲלוֹא תֵדְעוּ הֲלוֹא תִשְׁמָעוּ הֲלוֹא הֻגַּד
מֵרֹאשׁ לָכֶם הֲלוֹא הֲבִינֹתֶם מוֹסְדוֹת הָאָרֶץ:
כב הַיֹּשֵׁב עַל־חוּג הָאָרֶץ וְיֹשְׁבֶיהָ כַּחֲגָבִים
הַנּוֹטֶה כַדֹּק שָׁמַיִם וַיִּמְתָּחֵם כָּאֹהֶל לָשָׁבֶת:
כג הַנּוֹתֵן רוֹזְנִים לְאָיִן שֹׁפְטֵי אֶרֶץ כַּתֹּהוּ עָשָׂה:
כד אַף בַּל־נִטָּעוּ אַף בַּל־זֹרָעוּ אַף בַּל־שֹׁרֵשׁ
בָּאָרֶץ גִּזְעָם וְגַם נָשַׁף בָּהֶם וַיִּבָשׁוּ וּסְעָרָה כַּקַּשׁ
תִּשָּׂאֵם: כה וְאֶל־מִי תְדַמְּיוּנִי וְאֶשְׁוֶה יֹאמַר
קָדוֹשׁ: כו שְׂאוּ־מָרוֹם עֵינֵיכֶם וּרְאוּ מִי־
בָרָא אֵלֶּה הַמּוֹצִיא בְמִסְפָּר צְבָאָם לְכֻלָּם
בְּשֵׁם יִקְרָא מֵרֹב אוֹנִים וְאַמִּיץ כֹּחַ אִישׁ לֹא
נֶעְדָּר:

HAFTARAS EIKEV / הפטרת עקב

Isaiah 49:14 — 51:3 / ישעיה מט:יד – נא:ג

49 14 And Zion said, "HASHEM has forsaken me; my Lord has forgotten me." 15 Can a woman forget her nursling, withdraw from feeling compassion for the child of her womb? Even were these to forget, yet I will not forget you. 16 Behold! I have engraved you on [My] palms; your [ruined] walls are before Me continuously. 17 Your children shall hasten [to repent], but your spoilers and your destroyers must depart from you. 18 Raise your eyes about you and see, all of them assemble, they come to you; [I swear] as I live — the word of HASHEM — that you shall clothe yourself with them all as with jewelry, and adorn yourself with them as a bride. 19 For your ruins and your desolations and your spoiled land shall now become cramped with inhabitants, and those who would swallow you up shall be at a far distance. 20 The children of your bereavement shall yet say in your ears, "The place is tight for me; make room for me that I may sit." 21 Then you will say in your heart, "Who has begotten me these? For I have been bereaved of children and alone, exiled and wandering. And who has reared these? Behold! I was left by myself; these, where have they been?"

מט יד וַתֹּאמֶר צִיּוֹן עֲזָבַנִי יהוה וַאדֹנָי שְׁכֵחָנִי:
טו הֲתִשְׁכַּח אִשָּׁה עוּלָהּ מֵרַחֵם בֶּן־בִּטְנָהּ
גַּם־אֵלֶּה תִשְׁכַּחְנָה וְאָנֹכִי לֹא אֶשְׁכָּחֵךְ:
טז הֵן עַל־כַּפַּיִם חַקֹּתִיךְ חוֹמֹתַיִךְ נֶגְדִּי תָּמִיד:
יז מִהֲרוּ בָּנָיִךְ מְהָרְסַיִךְ וּמַחֲרִבַיִךְ מִמֵּךְ
יֵצֵאוּ: יח שְׂאִי־סָבִיב עֵינַיִךְ וּרְאִי כֻּלָּם
נִקְבְּצוּ בָאוּ־לָךְ חַי־אָנִי נְאֻם־יהוה כִּי כֻלָּם
כַּעֲדִי תִלְבָּשִׁי וּתְקַשְּׁרִים כַּכַּלָּה: יט כִּי חָרְבֹתַיִךְ
וְשֹׁמְמֹתַיִךְ וְאֶרֶץ הֲרִסֻתֵךְ כִּי עַתָּה תֵּצְרִי
מִיּוֹשֵׁב וְרָחֲקוּ מְבַלְּעָיִךְ: כ עוֹד יֹאמְרוּ בְאָזְנַיִךְ
בְּנֵי שִׁכֻּלָיִךְ צַר־לִי הַמָּקוֹם גְּשָׁה־לִּי וְאֵשֵׁבָה:
כא וְאָמַרְתְּ בִּלְבָבֵךְ מִי יָלַד־לִי אֶת־אֵלֶּה
וַאֲנִי שְׁכוּלָה וְגַלְמוּדָה גֹּלָה ׀ וְסוּרָה וְאֵלֶּה מִי
גִדֵּל הֵן אֲנִי נִשְׁאַרְתִּי לְבַדִּי אֵלֶּה אֵיפֹה הֵם:

²² For thus said my Lord, HASHEM/ELOHIM: Behold! I will raise My hand toward the nations, and to the peoples will I hoist my banner, and they shall bring your sons in their arms, and your daughters shall be carried on [their] shoulder. ²³ Kings will be your nurturers and their princesses your nurses; with faces to the ground they will prostrate themselves to you; the dust of your feet will they lick; and you shall know that I am HASHEM, that those who hope to Me shall not be ashamed.

²⁴ [You ask,] "Can prey be taken back from a strong one; can the righteous captive escape?" ²⁵ But thus said HASHEM: Even the captive of the strong can be taken back, and the prey of the mighty can escape; I, Myself, will take up your cause, and I, Myself, will save your children. ²⁶ And I will feed your oppressors their own flesh, and as with sweet wine shall they become drunk; then all flesh shall know that I am HASHEM, your Savior and your Redeemer, the Mighty One of Jacob.

50 ¹ Thus said HASHEM: Where is your mother's divorce document with which I sent her away? Or which of My creditors is it to whom I have sold you? Behold! it is for your iniquities that you have been sold, and for your rebellious transgressions that your mother has been sent away. ² Why is it that [although] I have come, there is no man? [Why is it] that [although] I have called, there is no answer? Is My hand too very short for redemption? Is there no strength in Me to rescue? Behold! by My rebuke I dry up the sea, I set rivers as a desert, their fish-life putrefies for lack of water, and it dies of thirst. ³ I clothe the heavens in black, and make sackcloth their garment.

⁴ My Lord, HASHEM/ELOHIM, has given me a tongue for students, to know, to set a time for one thirsty for the word [of HASHEM]; He arouses [me] — every morning — He arouses [My] ear for me to hear like the students. ⁵ My Lord, HASHEM/ELOHIM, has opened [my] ear for me, and as for me, I did not rebel, I did not turn away backwards. ⁶ My body I gave to the smiters, and my cheeks to the pluckers; my face I did not hide from humiliations and spit. ⁷ For my Lord, HASHEM/ELOHIM, helps me, therefore I was not humiliated; therefore I set my face like flint and I knew that I would not be ashamed. ⁸ My champion is near; whosoever would contend with me, let us stand together; let whosoever is my plaintiff approach me.

⁹ Behold! my Lord, HASHEM/ELOHIM, shall help me; who will condemn me? Behold! they shall all become worn out like a garment; a moth shall devour them.

¹⁰ Who among you fears HASHEM, listening to the voice of His servant? Though he may have walked in darkness with no light for himself, let him trust in the Name of HASHEM, and lean upon his God. ¹¹ Behold! all of you [others] are igniters of fire, girdled with fireworks; go away in the flame of your fire, and in the fireworks you have kindled; from My hand has this come upon you, that you should lie down in sorrow.

51 ¹ Listen to me, O pursuers of righteousness, seekers of HASHEM; look to the rock from which you were hewn, and to the hollow of the pit

כב כֹּה־אָמַר אֲדֹנָי יֱהֹוִה הִנֵּה אֶשָּׂא אֶל־גּוֹיִם יָדִי וְאֶל־עַמִּים אָרִים נִסִּי וְהֵבִיאוּ בָנַיִךְ בְּחֹצֶן וּבְנֹתַיִךְ עַל־כָּתֵף תִּנָּשֶׂאנָה: כג וְהָיוּ מְלָכִים אֹמְנַיִךְ וְשָׂרֽוֹתֵיהֶם מֵינִיקֹתַיִךְ אַפַּיִם אֶרֶץ יִשְׁתַּחֲווּ־לָךְ וַעֲפַר רַגְלַיִךְ יְלַחֵכוּ וְיָדַעַתְּ כִּי־אֲנִי יהוה אֲשֶׁר לֹא־יֵבֹשׁוּ קֹוָי: כד הֲיֻקַּח מִגִּבּוֹר מַלְקוֹחַ וְאִם־שְׁבִי צַדִּיק יִמָּלֵט: כה כִּי־כֹה ׀ אָמַר יהוה גַּם־שְׁבִי גִבּוֹר יֻקָּח וּמַלְקוֹחַ עָרִיץ יִמָּלֵט וְאֶת־יְרִיבֵךְ אָנֹכִי אָרִיב וְאֶת־בָּנַיִךְ אָנֹכִי אוֹשִׁיעַ: כו וְהַאֲכַלְתִּי אֶת־מוֹנַיִךְ אֶת־בְּשָׂרָם וְכֶעָסִיס דָּמָם יִשְׁכָּרוּן וְיָדְעוּ כָל־בָּשָׂר כִּי אֲנִי יהוה מֽוֹשִׁיעֵךְ וְגֹאֲלֵךְ אֲבִיר יַעֲקֹב:

נ א כֹּה ׀ אָמַר יהוה אֵי זֶה סֵפֶר כְּרִיתוּת אִמְּכֶם אֲשֶׁר שִׁלַּחְתִּיהָ אוֹ מִי מִנּוֹשַׁי אֲשֶׁר־מָכַרְתִּי אֶתְכֶם לוֹ הֵן בַּעֲוֺנֹתֵיכֶם נִמְכַּרְתֶּם וּבְפִשְׁעֵיכֶם שֻׁלְּחָה אִמְּכֶם: ב מַדּוּעַ בָּאתִי וְאֵין אִישׁ קָרָאתִי וְאֵין עוֹנֶה הֲקָצוֹר קָצְרָה יָדִי מִפְּדוּת וְאִם־אֵין בִּי כֹחַ לְהַצִּיל הֵן בְּגַעֲרָתִי אַחֲרִיב יָם אָשִׂים נְהָרוֹת מִדְבָּר תִּבְאַשׁ דְּגָתָם מֵאֵין מַיִם וְתָמֹת בַּצָּמָא: ג אַלְבִּישׁ שָׁמַיִם קַדְרוּת וְשַׂק אָשִׂים כְּסוּתָם: ד אֲדֹנָי יֱהֹוִה נָתַן לִי לְשׁוֹן לִמּוּדִים לָדַעַת לָעוּת אֶת־יָעֵף דָּבָר יָעִיר ׀ בַּבֹּקֶר בַּבֹּקֶר יָעִיר לִי אֹזֶן לִשְׁמֹעַ כַּלִּמּוּדִים: ה אֲדֹנָי יֱהֹוִה פָּתַח־לִי אֹזֶן וְאָנֹכִי לֹא מָרִיתִי אָחוֹר לֹא נְסוּגֹתִי: ו גֵּוִי נָתַתִּי לְמַכִּים וּלְחָיַי לְמֹרְטִים פָּנַי לֹא הִסְתַּרְתִּי מִכְּלִמּוֹת וָרֹק: ז וַאדֹנָי יֱהֹוִה יַעֲזָר־לִי עַל־כֵּן לֹא נִכְלָמְתִּי עַל־כֵּן שַׂמְתִּי פָנַי כַּחַלָּמִישׁ וָאֵדַע כִּי־לֹא אֵבוֹשׁ: ח קָרוֹב מַצְדִּיקִי מִי־יָרִיב אִתִּי נַעַמְדָה יָּחַד מִי־בַעַל מִשְׁפָּטִי יִגַּשׁ אֵלָי: ט הֵן אֲדֹנָי יֱהֹוִה יַעֲזָר־לִי מִי־הוּא יַרְשִׁיעֵנִי הֵן כֻּלָּם כַּבֶּגֶד יִבְלוּ עָשׁ יֹאכְלֵם: י מִי בָכֶם יְרֵא יהוה שֹׁמֵעַ בְּקוֹל עַבְדּוֹ אֲשֶׁר ׀ הָלַךְ חֲשֵׁכִים וְאֵין נֹגַהּ לוֹ יִבְטַח בְּשֵׁם יהוה וְיִשָּׁעֵן בֵּאלֹהָיו: יא הֵן כֻּלְּכֶם קֹדְחֵי אֵשׁ מְאַזְּרֵי זִיקוֹת לְכוּ ׀ בְּאוּר אֶשְׁכֶם וּבְזִיקוֹת בִּעַרְתֶּם מִיָּדִי הָיְתָה־זֹּאת לָכֶם לְמַעֲצֵבָה תִּשְׁכָּבוּן:

נא א שִׁמְעוּ אֵלַי רֹדְפֵי צֶדֶק מְבַקְשֵׁי יהוה הַבִּיטוּ אֶל־צוּר חֻצַּבְתֶּם וְאֶל־מַקֶּבֶת בּוֹר

from which you were dug. ² *Look to Abraham your forefather and to Sarah who bore you, for when he was yet one alone did I summon him and bless him and make him many.* ³ *For HASHEM shall comfort Zion, He shall comfort all her ruins, He shall make her wilderness like Eden and her wasteland like a garden of HASHEM; joy and gladness shall be found there, thanksgiving and the sound of music.*

נֻקַּרְתֶּֽם: ב הַבִּיטוּ אֶל־אַבְרָהָם אֲבִיכֶם וְאֶל־שָׂרָה תְּחוֹלֶלְכֶם כִּי־אֶחָד קְרָאתִיו וַאֲבָרְכֵהוּ וְאַרְבֵּֽהוּ: ג כִּי־נִחַם יהוה צִיּוֹן נִחַם כָּל־חָרְבֹתֶיהָ וַיָּשֶׂם מִדְבָּרָהּ כְּעֵ֫דֶן וְעַרְבָתָהּ כְּגַן־יהוה שָׂשׂוֹן וְשִׂמְחָה יִמָּצֵא בָהּ תּוֹדָה וְק֥וֹל זִמְרָֽה:

HAFTARAS RE'EH / הפטרת ראה

ישעיה נד:יא – נה:ה / Isaiah 54:11 — 55:5

When Rosh Chodesh Elul falls on Shabbos, some congregations read the *Haftarah* for *Shabbas Rosh Chodesh*, page 420.

54 ¹¹ O *afflicted, storm-tossed, unconsoled one, behold! I shall lay your floor stones upon pearls and make your foundation of sapphires.* ¹² *I shall make your sun windows of rubies and your gates of garnets, and your entire boundary of precious stones.* ¹³ *All your children will be students of HASHEM, and abundant will be your children's peace.* ¹⁴ *Establish yourself through righteousness, distance yourself from oppression for you need not fear it, and from panic for it will not come near you.* ¹⁵ *Behold! One need fear indeed if he has nothing from Me; whoever aggressively opposes you will fall because of you.* ¹⁶ *Behold! I have created the smith who blows on a charcoal flame and withdraws a tool for his labor, and I have created the destroyer to ruin.* ¹⁷ *Any weapon sharpened against you shall not succeed, and any tongue that shall rise against you in judgment you shall condemn; this is the heritage of the servant of HASHEM, and their righteousness is from Me, the words of HASHEM.*

נד יא עֲנִיָּה סֹעֲרָה לֹא נֻחָמָה הִנֵּה אָנֹכִי מַרְבִּיץ בַּפּוּךְ אֲבָנַיִךְ וִיסַדְתִּיךְ בַּסַּפִּירִים: יב וְשַׂמְתִּי כַּֽדְכֹד שִׁמְשֹׁתַיִךְ וּשְׁעָרַיִךְ לְאַבְנֵי אֶקְדָּח וְכָל־גְּבוּלֵךְ לְאַבְנֵי־חֵֽפֶץ: יג וְכָל־בָּנַיִךְ לִמּוּדֵי יהוה וְרַב שְׁל֥וֹם בָּנָֽיִךְ: יד בִּצְדָקָה תִּכּוֹנָ֑נִי רַֽחֲקִי מֵעֹשֶׁק כִּי־לֹא תִירָֽאִי וּמִמְּחִתָּה כִּי לֹא־תִקְרַב אֵלָֽיִךְ: טו הֵן גּוֹר יָגוּר אֶפֶס מֵֽאוֹתִי מִי־גָר אִתָּךְ עָלַיִךְ יִפּֽוֹל: טז הִנֵּה [הֶן כ'] אָֽנֹכִי בָּרָאתִי חָרָשׁ נֹפֵחַ בְּאֵשׁ פֶּחָם וּמוֹצִיא כְלִי לְמַֽעֲשֵׂהוּ וְאָֽנֹכִי בָּרָאתִי מַשְׁחִית לְחַבֵּֽל: יז כָּל־כְּלִי יוּצַר עָלַיִךְ לֹא יִצְלָח וְכָל־לָשׁוֹן תָּקֽוּם־אִתָּךְ לַמִּשְׁפָּט תַּרְשִׁיעִי זֹאת נַֽחֲלַת עַבְדֵי יהוה וְצִדְקָתָם מֵֽאִתִּי נְאֻם־יהוֽה:

55 ¹ Ho, *everyone who is thirsty, go to the water, even one who has no money; go buy and eat, go and buy without money and without barter, wine and milk.* ² *Why do you weigh out money for that which is not bread and [fruit of] your toil for that which does not satisfy? Listen well to Me and eat what is good, and let your soul delight in abundance.* ³ *Incline your ear and come to Me, listen and your soul will rejuvenate; I shall seal an eternal covenant with you, the enduring kindnesses [promised] David.* ⁴ *Behold! I have appointed him a witness to the regimes, a prince and a commander to the regimes.* ⁵ *Behold! a nation that you did not know will you call, and a nation that knew you not will run to you, for the sake of HASHEM, your God, the Holy One of Israel, for He has glorified you!*

נה א הוֹי כָּל־צָמֵא לְכוּ לַמַּיִם וַֽאֲשֶׁר אֵין־לוֹ כָּסֶף לְכוּ שִׁבְרוּ וֶֽאֱכֹלוּ וּלְכוּ שִׁבְרוּ בְּלוֹא־כֶסֶף וּבְלוֹא מְחִיר יַיִן וְחָלָֽב: ב לָמָּה תִשְׁקְלוּ־כֶסֶף בְּלוֹא־לֶחֶם וִיגִיעֲכֶם בְּלוֹא לְשָׂבְעָה שִׁמְעוּ שָׁמוֹעַ אֵלַי וְאִכְלוּ־טוֹב וְתִתְעַנַּג בַּדֶּשֶׁן נַפְשְׁכֶֽם: ג הַטּוּ אָזְנְכֶם וּלְכוּ אֵלַי שִׁמְעוּ וּתְחִי נַפְשְׁכֶם וְאֶכְרְתָה לָכֶם בְּרִית עוֹלָם חַסְדֵי דָוִד הַנֶּֽאֱמָנִֽים: ד הֵן עֵד לְאוּמִּים נְתַתִּיו נָגִיד וּמְצַוֵּה לְאֻמִּֽים: ה הֵן גּוֹי לֹא־תֵדַע תִּקְרָא וְגוֹי לֹֽא־יְדָעֽוּךָ אֵלֶיךָ יָרוּצוּ לְמַעַן יהוה אֱלֹהֶיךָ וְלִקְדוֹשׁ יִשְׂרָאֵל כִּי פֵֽאֲרָֽךְ:

When Rosh Chodesh Elul falls on Sunday and Monday, some congregations add the first and last verses of the *Haftarah* for *Shabbas* Erev Rosh Chodesh (p. 418). When Rosh Chodesh Elul falls on *Shabbos* and Sunday, some congregations add the first and last verses of the *Haftaros* for *Shabbas Rosh Chodesh* (p. 420) and *Shabbas Erev Rosh Chodesh* (p. 418).

HAFTARAS SHOFTIM / הפטרת שופטים

ישעיה נא:יב – נב:יב / Isaiah 51:12 — 52:12

51 ¹² I *t is I, I am He Who comforts you; who are you that you should be afraid of a man who shall die and of the son of man who shall be set as grass?* ¹³ *And you have forgotten HASHEM, your Maker, Who spread out the heavens and Who set the base of the earth;*

נא יב אָֽנֹכִי אָֽנֹכִי הוּא מְנַֽחֶמְכֶם מִי־אַתְּ וַתִּֽירְאִי מֵֽאֱנוֹשׁ יָמוּת וּמִבֶּן־אָדָם חָצִיר יִנָּתֵֽן: יג וַתִּשְׁכַּח יהוה עֹשֶׂךָ נוֹטֶה שָׁמַיִם וְיֹסֵד אָ֫רֶץ

yet you are continually in terror, the whole day, of the oppressor's fury as if he were preparing to destroy; where then shall be the oppressor's fury? [14] *The wanderer shall be soon released, and shall not die in the pit, nor shall his bread be lacking.* [15] *And I am* HASHEM, *your God, Who stirs up the sea and its waves rage —* HASHEM, *Master of Legions, is His Name.* [16] *And I have placed My words in your mouth, and with the shade of My hand have I covered you, to implant the heavens and to set a base for the earth and to say unto Zion, "You are My people!"*

[17] *Awaken yourself! Awaken yourself! Arise, O Jerusalem, you who have drunk from the hand of* HASHEM *the cup of His fury, the phial of the cup of stupefaction have you drunk, have you drained.* [18] *There is no guide for her among all the children she has borne; there is no one holding her hand among all the children she has reared.* [19] *Two [are the calamities] that have befallen you; who will bewail you? The plunder and the breakage, the hunger and the sword; with whom shall I comfort you?* [20] *Your children have fainted, they lie at the head of all streets like a netted wild ox; they are full with* HASHEM's *fury, with your God's rebuke.* [21] *Therefore, listen now to this, O afflicted one, drunk, but not with wine.*

[22] *Thus said your Lord,* HASHEM, *and your God Who will contend for His people: Behold! I have taken from your hand the cup of stupefaction, the phial of the cup of My fury; no longer shall you drink from it again.* [23] *But I will put it into the hand of your tormentors, who have said to you, "Prostrate yourself, that we may step over you," who set your body as the ground and as the street for wayfarers.*

52 [1] **W**ake up! Wake up! Don your strength, O Zion, don the garments of your splendor, O Jerusalem, the Holy City, for no longer shall there enter into you any uncircumcised or contaminated person. [2] Shake the dust from yourself, arise, enthrone yourself, O Jerusalem; undo the straps on your neck, O captive daughter of Zion.

[3] For thus said HASHEM: Without price were you sold, so you shall not be redeemed with money.

[4] For thus said my Lord, HASHEM/ELOHIM: Egypt! My people went down at first to sojourn there, and Assyria oppressed them without cause. [5] And now, what do I have here — the word of HASHEM — that My people was purchased without price; those who rule over him praise themselves — the word of HASHEM — and continuously, all day, My Name is blasphemed. [6] Therefore, My people shall know My Name — therefore, on that day — for I am the One Who speaks, here I am!

[7] How beautiful ascending the mountains are the footsteps of the herald making heard, "Peace!" heralding, "Good!" making heard, "Salvation!" saying unto Zion, "Your God has reigned!" [8] The voice of your lookouts, they have raised a voice, together shall they sing glad song, for every eye shall see when HASHEM returns to Jerusalem. [9] Burst forth in joy, sing glad song together, O ruins of Jerusalem, for HASHEM shall comfort His people; He has redeemed Jerusalem. [10] HASHEM has bared His holy arm to the eyes of the nations, and all ends of the earth shall see the salvation of our God.

וַתְּפַחֵד תָּמִיד כָּל־הַיּוֹם מִפְּנֵי חֲמַת הַמֵּצִיק כַּאֲשֶׁר כּוֹנֵן לְהַשְׁחִית וְאַיֵּה חֲמַת הַמֵּצִיק: יד מִהַר צֹעֶה לְהִפָּתֵחַ וְלֹא־יָמוּת לַשַּׁחַת וְלֹא יֶחְסַר לַחְמוֹ: טו וְאָנֹכִי יהוה אֱלֹהֶיךָ רֹגַע הַיָּם וַיֶּהֱמוּ גַּלָּיו יהוה צְבָאוֹת שְׁמוֹ: טז וָאָשֶׂם דְּבָרַי בְּפִיךָ וּבְצֵל יָדִי כִּסִּיתִיךָ לִנְטֹעַ שָׁמַיִם וְלִיסֹד אָרֶץ וְלֵאמֹר לְצִיּוֹן עַמִּי אָתָּה: יז הִתְעוֹרְרִי הִתְעוֹרְרִי קוּמִי יְרוּשָׁלַםִ אֲשֶׁר שָׁתִית מִיַּד יהוה אֶת־כּוֹס חֲמָתוֹ אֶת־קֻבַּעַת כּוֹס הַתַּרְעֵלָה שָׁתִית מָצִית: יח אֵין־מְנַהֵל לָהּ מִכָּל־בָּנִים יָלָדָה וְאֵין מַחֲזִיק בְּיָדָהּ מִכָּל־בָּנִים גִּדֵּלָה: יט שְׁתַּיִם הֵנָּה קֹרְאֹתַיִךְ מִי יָנוּד לָךְ הַשֹּׁד וְהַשֶּׁבֶר וְהָרָעָב וְהַחֶרֶב מִי אֲנַחֲמֵךְ: כ בָּנַיִךְ עֻלְּפוּ שָׁכְבוּ בְּרֹאשׁ כָּל־חוּצוֹת כְּתוֹא מִכְמָר הַמְלֵאִים חֲמַת־יהוה גַּעֲרַת אֱלֹהָיִךְ: כא לָכֵן שִׁמְעִי־נָא זֹאת עֲנִיָּה וּשְׁכֻרַת וְלֹא מִיָּיִן: כב כֹּה־אָמַר אֲדֹנַיִךְ יהוה וֵאלֹהַיִךְ יָרִיב עַמּוֹ הִנֵּה לָקַחְתִּי מִיָּדֵךְ אֶת־כּוֹס הַתַּרְעֵלָה אֶת־קֻבַּעַת כּוֹס חֲמָתִי לֹא־תוֹסִיפִי לִשְׁתּוֹתָהּ עוֹד: כג וְשַׂמְתִּיהָ בְּיַד־מוֹגַיִךְ אֲשֶׁר־אָמְרוּ לְנַפְשֵׁךְ שְׁחִי וְנַעֲבֹרָה וַתָּשִׂימִי כָאָרֶץ גֵּוֵךְ וְכַחוּץ לַעֹבְרִים:

נב א עוּרִי עוּרִי לִבְשִׁי עֻזֵּךְ צִיּוֹן לִבְשִׁי ׀ בִּגְדֵי תִפְאַרְתֵּךְ יְרוּשָׁלַםִ עִיר הַקֹּדֶשׁ כִּי לֹא יוֹסִיף יָבֹא־בָךְ עוֹד עָרֵל וְטָמֵא: ב הִתְנַעֲרִי מֵעָפָר קוּמִי שְּׁבִי יְרוּשָׁלָםִ הִתְפַּתְּחִי [התפתחו כ׳] מוֹסְרֵי צַוָּארֵךְ שְׁבִיָּה בַּת־צִיּוֹן: ג כִּי־כֹה אָמַר יהוה חִנָּם נִמְכַּרְתֶּם וְלֹא בְכֶסֶף תִּגָּאֵלוּ: ד כִּי כֹה אָמַר אֲדֹנָי יֱהֹוִה מִצְרַיִם יָרַד־עַמִּי בָרִאשֹׁנָה לָגוּר שָׁם וְאַשּׁוּר בְּאֶפֶס עֲשָׁקוֹ: ה וְעַתָּה מַה־לִּי־פֹה נְאֻם־יהוה כִּי־לֻקַּח עַמִּי חִנָּם מֹשְׁלָיו [משלו כ׳] יְהֵילִילוּ נְאֻם־יהוה וְתָמִיד כָּל־הַיּוֹם שְׁמִי מִנֹּאָץ: ו לָכֵן יֵדַע עַמִּי שְׁמִי לָכֵן בַּיּוֹם הַהוּא כִּי־אֲנִי־הוּא הַמְדַבֵּר הִנֵּנִי: ז מַה־נָּאווּ עַל־הֶהָרִים רַגְלֵי מְבַשֵּׂר מַשְׁמִיעַ שָׁלוֹם מְבַשֵּׂר טוֹב מַשְׁמִיעַ יְשׁוּעָה אֹמֵר לְצִיּוֹן מָלַךְ אֱלֹהָיִךְ: ח קוֹל צֹפַיִךְ נָשְׂאוּ קוֹל יַחְדָּו יְרַנֵּנוּ כִּי עַיִן בְּעַיִן יִרְאוּ בְּשׁוּב יהוה צִיּוֹן: ט פִּצְחוּ רַנְּנוּ יַחְדָּו חָרְבוֹת יְרוּשָׁלָםִ כִּי־נִחַם יהוה עַמּוֹ גָּאַל יְרוּשָׁלָםִ: י חָשַׂף יהוה אֶת־זְרוֹעַ קָדְשׁוֹ לְעֵינֵי כָּל־הַגּוֹיִם וְרָאוּ כָּל־אַפְסֵי־אָרֶץ אֵת יְשׁוּעַת אֱלֹהֵינוּ:

יא סוּרוּ סוּרוּ צְאוּ מִשָּׁם טָמֵא אַל־תִּגָּעוּ צְאוּ
מִתּוֹכָהּ הִבָּרוּ נֹשְׂאֵי כְּלֵי יהוה: יב כִּי לֹא בְחִפָּזוֹן
תֵּצֵאוּ וּבִמְנוּסָה לֹא תֵלֵכוּן כִּי־הֹלֵךְ לִפְנֵיכֶם
יהוה וּמְאַסִּפְכֶם אֱלֹהֵי יִשְׂרָאֵל:

11 *Turn away! Turn away! Go forth from there! A contaminated person shall you not touch! Go forth from within it! Cleanse yourselves, O bearers of the vessels of* HASHEM. 12 *But it is not in haste that you shall go forth; nor shall you go in flight; for* HASHEM *shall go before you, and the God of Israel shall be your rear guard.*

HAFTARAS KI SEITZEI / הפטרת כי תצא

Isaiah 54:1-10 / ישעיה נד:א-י

נד א רָנִּי עֲקָרָה לֹא יָלָדָה פִּצְחִי רִנָּה וְצַהֲלִי
לֹא־חָלָה כִּי־רַבִּים בְּנֵי־שׁוֹמֵמָה מִבְּנֵי בְעוּלָה
אָמַר יהוה: ב הַרְחִיבִי | מְקוֹם אָהֳלֵךְ וִירִיעוֹת
מִשְׁכְּנוֹתַיִךְ יַטּוּ אַל־תַּחְשֹׂכִי הַאֲרִיכִי מֵיתָרַיִךְ
וִיתֵדֹתַיִךְ חַזֵּקִי: ג כִּי־יָמִין וּשְׂמֹאול תִּפְרֹצִי
וְזַרְעֵךְ גּוֹיִם יִירָשׁ וְעָרִים נְשַׁמּוֹת יוֹשִׁיבוּ: ד אַל־
תִּירְאִי כִּי־לֹא תֵבוֹשִׁי וְאַל־תִּכָּלְמִי כִּי־לֹא
תַחְפִּירִי כִּי בֹשֶׁת עֲלוּמַיִךְ תִּשְׁכָּחִי וְחֶרְפַּת
אַלְמְנוּתַיִךְ לֹא תִזְכְּרִי־עוֹד: ה כִּי בֹעֲלַיִךְ עֹשַׂיִךְ
יהוה צְבָאוֹת שְׁמוֹ וְגֹאֲלֵךְ קְדוֹשׁ יִשְׂרָאֵל אֱלֹהֵי
כָל־הָאָרֶץ יִקָּרֵא: ו כִּי־כְאִשָּׁה עֲזוּבָה וַעֲצוּבַת
רוּחַ קְרָאָךְ יהוה וְאֵשֶׁת נְעוּרִים כִּי תִמָּאֵס
אָמַר אֱלֹהָיִךְ: ז בְּרֶגַע קָטֹן עֲזַבְתִּיךְ וּבְרַחֲמִים
גְּדוֹלִים אֲקַבְּצֵךְ: ח בְּשֶׁצֶף קֶצֶף הִסְתַּרְתִּי פָנַי
רֶגַע מִמֵּךְ וּבְחֶסֶד עוֹלָם רִחַמְתִּיךְ אָמַר גֹּאֲלֵךְ
יהוה: ט כִּי־מֵי נֹחַ זֹאת לִי אֲשֶׁר נִשְׁבַּעְתִּי מֵעֲבֹר
מֵי־נֹחַ עוֹד עַל־הָאָרֶץ כֵּן נִשְׁבַּעְתִּי מִקְּצֹף
עָלַיִךְ וּמִגְּעָר־בָּךְ: י כִּי הֶהָרִים יָמוּשׁוּ וְהַגְּבָעוֹת
תְּמוּטֶינָה וְחַסְדִּי מֵאִתֵּךְ לֹא־יָמוּשׁ וּבְרִית
שְׁלוֹמִי לֹא תָמוּט אָמַר מְרַחֲמֵךְ יהוה:

54 1 *Sing out, O barren one, who has not given birth, breakout into glad song and be jubilant, O one who had no labor pains, for the children of the desolate [Jerusalem] outnumber the children of the inhabited [city] — said* HASHEM. 2 *Broaden the place of your tent and stretch out the curtains of your dwellings, stint not; lengthen your cords and strengthen your pegs.* 3 *For southward and northward you shall spread out mightily, your offspring will inherit nations, and they will settle desolate cites.* 4 *Fear not, for you will not be shamed, do not feel humiliated for you will not be mortified; for you will forget the shame of your youth, and the mortification of your widowhood you will remember no more.* 5 *For your Master is your Maker —* HASHEM, *Master of Legions is His Name; your Redeemer is the Holy One of Israel — God of all the world shall He be called.* 6 *For like a wife who had been forsaken and of melancholy spirit will* HASHEM *have called you, and like a wife of one's youth who had become despised — said your God.* 7 *For but a brief moment have I forsaken you, and with abundant mercy shall I gather you in.* 8 *With a slight wrath have I concealed My countenance from you for a moment, but with eternal kindness shall I show you mercy, said your Redeemer,* HASHEM.

9 *For like the waters of Noah shall this be to Me: as I have sworn never again to pass the waters of Noah over the earth, so have I sworn not to be wrathful with you or rebuke you.* 10 *For the mountains may be moved and the hills may falter, but My kindness shall not be removed from you and My covenant of peace shall not falter — says the One Who shows you mercy,* HASHEM.

If Rosh Chodesh Elul had fallen on *Parashas Re'eh*, congregations that read the *Haftarah* for *Shabbas Rosh Chodesh* instead of עֲנִיָּה סֹעֲרָה, conclude the *Haftarah* for *Parashas Ki Seitzei* with עֲנִיָּה סֹעֲרָה (page 410).

HAFTARAS KI SAVO / הפטרת כי תבוא

Isaiah 60:1-22 / ישעיה ס:א-כב

ס א קוּמִי אוֹרִי כִּי־בָא אוֹרֵךְ וּכְבוֹד יהוה עָלַיִךְ
זָרָח: ב כִּי־הִנֵּה הַחֹשֶׁךְ יְכַסֶּה־אֶרֶץ וַעֲרָפֶל
לְאֻמִּים וְעָלַיִךְ יִזְרַח יהוה וּכְבוֹדוֹ עָלַיִךְ
יֵרָאֶה: ג וְהָלְכוּ גוֹיִם לְאוֹרֵךְ וּמְלָכִים לְנֹגַהּ
זַרְחֵךְ: ד שְׂאִי סָבִיב עֵינַיִךְ וּרְאִי כֻּלָּם נִקְבְּצוּ
בָאוּ־לָךְ בָּנַיִךְ מֵרָחוֹק יָבֹאוּ וּבְנֹתַיִךְ עַל־
צַד תֵּאָמַנָה: ה אָז תִּרְאִי וְנָהַרְתְּ וּפָחַד וְרָחַב
לְבָבֵךְ כִּי־יֵהָפֵךְ עָלַיִךְ הֲמוֹן יָם חֵיל גּוֹיִם
יָבֹאוּ לָךְ: ו שִׁפְעַת גְּמַלִּים תְּכַסֵּךְ בִּכְרֵי מִדְיָן
וְעֵיפָה כֻּלָּם מִשְּׁבָא יָבֹאוּ זָהָב וּלְבוֹנָה

60 1 *Arise! Shine! For your light has arrived, and the glory of* HASHEM *has shined upon you.* 2 *For, behold! Darkness shall cover the earth, and dense cloud the kingdoms; but upon you shall shine* HASHEM, *and His glory shall be seen upon you.* 3 *Nations will go by your light, and kings by the brightness of your shine.* 4 *Lift your eyes about you and see, all of them assemble, they come to you; your sons from afar shall come, and your daughters shall be nurtured alongside [royalty].* 5 *Then you shall see and be radiant, anxious and expansive shall be your heart, for the affluence of the west shall be turned over to you, and the wealth of nations shall come to you.* 6 *An abundance of camels will envelop you, dromedaries of Midian and Ephah; all those of Sheba shall come, gold and frankincense shall*

they bear, and the praises of HASHEM shall they pro-claim. ⁷ All the flocks of Kedar shall be gathered unto you, the rams of Nebaioth shall minister to you; they shall be brought up with favor upon My Altar, and the House of My glory will I glorify. ⁸ Who are these? Like a cloud they fly, like pigeons to their cote-windows! ⁹ For unto Me shall the island-dwellers gather, and the ships of Tarshish [as] in earlier times, to bring your children from afar, their gold and silver with them, for the sake of HASHEM, your God, and for the Holy One of Israel, for He has glorified you. ¹⁰ Then the sons of strangers shall build your city-walls and their kings shall minister to you; though I struck you in My indignation, in My favor have I been compassionate to you. ¹¹ And your gates shall be opened continuously, day and night, they shall not be closed, to bring to you the wealth of nations, and their kings under escort. ¹² For the nation and the king-dom that will not serve you shall be lost, and the nations utterly destroyed. ¹³ The glory of the Lebanon [forest] shall come to you — cypress, fir and box tree, together — to glorify the site of My Sanctuary, and the site of My footstool will I honor. ¹⁴ They shall go unto you in bent submission, those children of your oppressors; and they shall prostrate themselves at the soles of your feet, all those who slandered you; and they shall call you "the City of HASHEM, Zion, [the City of] the Holy One of Israel." ¹⁵ In place of your having been forsaken and hated with no wayfarer, I shall establish you as an eter-nal pride, a joy for each succeeding generation. ¹⁶ You shall nurse from the milk of the nations, from the breast of kings shall you nurse; then you shall know that I, HASHEM, am your Savior and your Redeemer, the Mighty One of Jacob. ¹⁷ In place of the copper I will bring gold; and in place of the iron I will bring silver; and in place of the wood, copper; and in place of the stones, iron; I will set your appointed officials for peacefulness and your overlords for righteousness. ¹⁸ No longer shall violence be heard in your land, [nor] plunder and breakage in your borders; but you shall call [God's] salvation your [pro-tective] walls, and [His] praise your gateways. ¹⁹ You shall no longer have need of the sun for light of day, nor for brightness the moon to illuminate for you; rather HASHEM shall be unto you an eternal light, and your God for your glory. ²⁰ Never again shall your sun set, nor shall your moon be withdrawn; for HASHEM shall be unto you an eternal light, and ended shall be the days of your mourning. ²¹ And your people, they are all righteous; forever shall they inherit the Land; a branch of My plant-ing, My handiwork, for Me to glory in. ²² The smallest shall increase a thousandfold, and the least into a mighty nation; I am HASHEM, in its time I will hasten it.

יִשְׂאוּ וּתְהִלּוֹת יהוה יְבַשֵּׂרוּ: ז כָּל־צֹאן קֵדָר יִקָּבְצוּ לָךְ אֵילֵי נְבָיוֹת יְשָׁרְתוּנֶךָ יַעֲלוּ עַל־רָצוֹן מִזְבְּחִי וּבֵית תִּפְאַרְתִּי אֲפָאֵר: ח מִי־אֵלֶּה כָּעָב תְּעוּפֶינָה וְכַיּוֹנִים אֶל־אֲרֻבֹּתֵיהֶם: ט כִּי־לִי | אִיִּים יְקַוּוּ וָאֳנִיּוֹת תַּרְשִׁישׁ בָּרִאשֹׁנָה לְהָבִיא בָנַיִךְ מֵרָחוֹק כַּסְפָּם וּזְהָבָם אִתָּם לְשֵׁם יהוה אֱלֹהַיִךְ וְלִקְדוֹשׁ יִשְׂרָאֵל כִּי פֵאֲרָךְ: י וּבָנוּ בְנֵי־ נֵכָר חֹמֹתַיִךְ וּמַלְכֵיהֶם יְשָׁרְתוּנֶךְ כִּי בְקִצְפִּי הִכִּיתִיךְ וּבִרְצוֹנִי רִחַמְתִּיךְ: יא וּפִתְּחוּ שְׁעָרַיִךְ תָּמִיד יוֹמָם וָלַיְלָה לֹא יִסָּגֵרוּ לְהָבִיא אֵלַיִךְ חֵיל גּוֹיִם וּמַלְכֵיהֶם נְהוּגִים: יב כִּי־הַגּוֹי וְהַמַּמְלָכָה אֲשֶׁר לֹא־יַעַבְדוּךְ יֹאבֵדוּ וְהַגּוֹיִם חָרֹב יֶחֱרָבוּ: יג כְּבוֹד הַלְּבָנוֹן אֵלַיִךְ יָבוֹא בְּרוֹשׁ תִּדְהָר וּתְאַשּׁוּר יַחְדָּו לְפָאֵר מְקוֹם מִקְדָּשִׁי וּמְקוֹם רַגְלַי אֲכַבֵּד: יד וְהָלְכוּ אֵלַיִךְ שְׁחוֹחַ בְּנֵי מְעַנַּיִךְ וְהִשְׁתַּחֲווּ עַל־כַּפּוֹת רַגְלַיִךְ כָּל־מְנַאֲצָיִךְ וְקָרְאוּ לָךְ עִיר יהוה צִיּוֹן קְדוֹשׁ יִשְׂרָאֵל: טו תַּחַת הֱיוֹתֵךְ עֲזוּבָה וּשְׂנוּאָה וְאֵין עוֹבֵר וְשַׂמְתִּיךְ לִגְאוֹן עוֹלָם מְשׂוֹשׂ דּוֹר וָדוֹר: טז וְיָנַקְתְּ חֲלֵב גּוֹיִם וְשֹׁד מְלָכִים תִּינָקִי וְיָדַעַתְּ כִּי־אֲנִי יהוה מוֹשִׁיעֵךְ וְגֹאֲלֵךְ אֲבִיר יַעֲקֹב: יז תַּחַת הַנְּחֹשֶׁת אָבִיא זָהָב וְתַחַת הַבַּרְזֶל אָבִיא כֶסֶף וְתַחַת הָעֵצִים נְחֹשֶׁת וְתַחַת הָאֲבָנִים בַּרְזֶל וְשַׂמְתִּי פְקֻדָּתֵךְ שָׁלוֹם וְנֹגְשַׂיִךְ צְדָקָה: יח לֹא־יִשָּׁמַע עוֹד חָמָס בְּאַרְצֵךְ שֹׁד וָשֶׁבֶר בִּגְבוּלָיִךְ וְקָרָאת יְשׁוּעָה חוֹמֹתַיִךְ וּשְׁעָרַיִךְ תְּהִלָּה: יט לֹא־יִהְיֶה־ לָךְ עוֹד הַשֶּׁמֶשׁ לְאוֹר יוֹמָם וּלְנֹגַהּ הַיָּרֵחַ לֹא־ יָאִיר לָךְ וְהָיָה־לָךְ יהוה לְאוֹר עוֹלָם וֵאלֹהַיִךְ לְתִפְאַרְתֵּךְ: כ לֹא־יָבוֹא עוֹד שִׁמְשֵׁךְ וִירֵחֵךְ לֹא יֵאָסֵף כִּי יהוה יִהְיֶה־לָּךְ לְאוֹר עוֹלָם וְשָׁלְמוּ יְמֵי אֶבְלֵךְ: כא וְעַמֵּךְ כֻּלָּם צַדִּיקִים לְעוֹלָם יִירְשׁוּ אָרֶץ נֵצֶר מַטָּעַי [מַטָּעוֹ כ׳] מַעֲשֵׂה יָדַי לְהִתְפָּאֵר: כב הַקָּטֹן יִהְיֶה לָאֶלֶף וְהַצָּעִיר לְגוֹי עָצוּם אֲנִי יהוה בְּעִתָּהּ אֲחִישֶׁנָּה:

HAFTARAS NITZAVIM / הפטרת נצבים

Isaiah 61:10 — 63:9 / ישעיה סא:י — סג:ט

61 ¹⁰ **I** will rejoice intensely with HASHEM, my soul shall exult with my God, for He has dressed me in the raiment of salvation, in a robe of righteousness has He cloaked me, like a bridegroom who dons priestly glory, like a bride who bedecks herself in her jewelry. ¹¹ For as the earth brings forth her growth, and as a garden causes its sowings to grow, so shall my Lord, HASHEM/

סא י שׂוֹשׂ אָשִׂישׂ בַּיהוה תָּגֵל נַפְשִׁי בֵּאלֹהַי כִּי הִלְבִּישַׁנִי בִּגְדֵי־יֶשַׁע מְעִיל צְדָקָה יְעָטָנִי כֶּחָתָן יְכַהֵן פְּאֵר וְכַכַּלָּה תַּעְדֶּה כֵלֶיהָ: יא כִּי כָאָרֶץ תּוֹצִיא צִמְחָהּ וּכְגַנָּה זֵרוּעֶיהָ תַצְמִיחַ כֵּן | אֲדֹנָי

יֱהֹוִה יַצְמִיחַ צְדָקָה וּתְהִלָּה נֶגֶד כָּל־הַגּוֹיִם׃
סב א לְמַעַן צִיּוֹן לֹא אֶחֱשֶׁה וּלְמַעַן יְרוּשָׁלַםִ
לֹא אֶשְׁקוֹט עַד־יֵצֵא כַנֹּגַהּ צִדְקָהּ וִישׁוּעָתָהּ
כְּלַפִּיד יִבְעָר׃ ב וְרָאוּ גוֹיִם צִדְקֵךְ וְכָל־מְלָכִים
כְּבוֹדֵךְ וְקֹרָא לָךְ שֵׁם חָדָשׁ אֲשֶׁר פִּי יְהֹוָה
יִקֳּבֶנּוּ׃ ג וְהָיִית עֲטֶרֶת תִּפְאֶרֶת בְּיַד־יְהֹוָה וּצְנִיף
[וצנוף כ׳] מְלוּכָה בְּכַף־אֱלֹהָיִךְ׃ ד לֹא־יֵאָמֵר לָךְ
עוֹד עֲזוּבָה וּלְאַרְצֵךְ לֹא־יֵאָמֵר עוֹד שְׁמָמָה כִּי
לָךְ יִקָּרֵא חֶפְצִי־בָהּ וּלְאַרְצֵךְ בְּעוּלָה כִּי־חָפֵץ
יְהֹוָה בָּךְ וְאַרְצֵךְ תִּבָּעֵל׃ ה כִּי־יִבְעַל בָּחוּר
בְּתוּלָה יִבְעָלוּךְ בָּנָיִךְ וּמְשׂוֹשׂ חָתָן עַל־כַּלָּה
יָשִׂישׂ עָלַיִךְ אֱלֹהָיִךְ׃ ו עַל־חוֹמֹתַיִךְ יְרוּשָׁלַםִ
הִפְקַדְתִּי שֹׁמְרִים כָּל־הַיּוֹם וְכָל־הַלַּיְלָה תָּמִיד
לֹא יֶחֱשׁוּ הַמַּזְכִּרִים אֶת־יְהֹוָה אַל־דֳּמִי לָכֶם׃
ז וְאַל־תִּתְּנוּ דֳמִי לוֹ עַד־יְכוֹנֵן וְעַד־יָשִׂים אֶת־
יְרוּשָׁלַםִ תְּהִלָּה בָּאָרֶץ׃ ח נִשְׁבַּע יְהֹוָה בִּימִינוֹ
וּבִזְרוֹעַ עֻזּוֹ אִם־אֶתֵּן אֶת־דְּגָנֵךְ עוֹד מַאֲכָל
לְאֹיְבַיִךְ וְאִם־יִשְׁתּוּ בְנֵי־נֵכָר תִּירוֹשֵׁךְ אֲשֶׁר
יָגַעַתְּ בּוֹ׃ ט כִּי מְאַסְפָיו יֹאכְלֻהוּ וְהִלְלוּ אֶת־
יְהֹוָה וּמְקַבְּצָיו יִשְׁתֻּהוּ בְּחַצְרוֹת קָדְשִׁי׃ י עִבְרוּ
עִבְרוּ בַּשְּׁעָרִים פַּנּוּ דֶּרֶךְ הָעָם סֹלּוּ סֹלּוּ
הַמְסִלָּה סַקְּלוּ מֵאֶבֶן הָרִימוּ נֵס עַל־הָעַמִּים׃
יא הִנֵּה יְהֹוָה הִשְׁמִיעַ אֶל־קְצֵה הָאָרֶץ אִמְרוּ
לְבַת־צִיּוֹן הִנֵּה יִשְׁעֵךְ בָּא הִנֵּה שְׂכָרוֹ אִתּוֹ
וּפְעֻלָּתוֹ לְפָנָיו׃ יב וְקָרְאוּ לָהֶם עַם־הַקֹּדֶשׁ
גְּאוּלֵי יְהֹוָה וְלָךְ יִקָּרֵא דְרוּשָׁה עִיר לֹא נֶעֱזָבָה׃
סג א מִי־זֶה | בָּא מֵאֱדוֹם חֲמוּץ בְּגָדִים מִבָּצְרָה
זֶה הָדוּר בִּלְבוּשׁוֹ צֹעֶה בְּרֹב כֹּחוֹ אֲנִי מְדַבֵּר
בִּצְדָקָה רַב לְהוֹשִׁיעַ׃ ב מַדּוּעַ אָדֹם לִלְבוּשֶׁךָ
וּבְגָדֶיךָ כְּדֹרֵךְ בְּגַת׃ ג פּוּרָה | דָּרַכְתִּי לְבַדִּי
וּמֵעַמִּים אֵין־אִישׁ אִתִּי וְאֶדְרְכֵם בְּאַפִּי
וְאֶרְמְסֵם בַּחֲמָתִי וְיֵז נִצְחָם עַל־בְּגָדַי וְכָל־
מַלְבּוּשַׁי אֶגְאָלְתִּי׃ ד כִּי יוֹם נָקָם בְּלִבִּי וּשְׁנַת
גְּאוּלַי בָּאָה׃ ה וְאַבִּיט וְאֵין עֹזֵר וְאֶשְׁתּוֹמֵם וְאֵין
סוֹמֵךְ וַתּוֹשַׁע לִי זְרֹעִי וַחֲמָתִי הִיא סְמָכָתְנִי׃
ו וְאָבוּס עַמִּים בְּאַפִּי וַאֲשַׁכְּרֵם בַּחֲמָתִי וְאוֹרִיד
לָאָרֶץ נִצְחָם׃ ז חַסְדֵי יְהֹוָה | אַזְכִּיר תְּהִלֹּת
יְהֹוָה כְּעַל כֹּל אֲשֶׁר־גְּמָלָנוּ יְהֹוָה וְרַב־טוּב
לְבֵית יִשְׂרָאֵל אֲשֶׁר־גְּמָלָם כְּרַחֲמָיו וּכְרֹב
חֲסָדָיו׃ ח וַיֹּאמֶר אַךְ־עַמִּי הֵמָּה בָּנִים לֹא

*ELOHIM, cause righteousness and praise to grow in the
face of all the nations.*

62 1 *For Zion's sake, I will not be silent, and for
Jerusalem's sake, I will not be still, until her
righteousness shall go forth like bright light, and her salvation shall flame like a torch.* 2 *And nations shall perceive your righteousness, and all kings your honor; and
you shall be called a new name, which the mouth of
HASHEM shall articulate.* 3 *Then you shall be a crown of
splendor in the hand of HASHEM;, and a royal headdress
in the palm of your God.* 4 *It shall no longer be said of
you, "Forsaken one," and of your land shall no longer
be said, "Desolate place," for you shall be called "My-
desire-is-in-her," and your land "Settled," for HASHEM's
desire is in you and your land shall be settled.* 5 *As a
young man espouses a maiden, so shall your children
settle in you; and like the bridegroom's rejoicing over his
bride, so shall your God rejoice over you.* 6 *Upon your
walls, O Jerusalem, have I assigned guardians; all the
day and all the night, continuously, they shall never be
silent; O reminders of HASHEM, let yourselves not rest.*
7 *And give not any rest, until He establishes, and until
He sets Jerusalem as a praise in the Land.* 8 *HASHEM
swore by His right hand and by His powerful arm: I will
not give your grain any longer as food for your enemies;
and alien sons shall not drink your wine for which you
have exerted yourself.* 9 *For those who have harvested
it shall eat it and praise HASHEM, and those who have
gathered it in shall drink it in My holy courtyards.*
10 *Go through, go through the gates; clean the people's way; beat down, beat down the highway, clear it
of stone; raise a banner over the peoples.* 11 *Behold!
HASHEM has made heard unto the end of the earth: Say
unto the daughter Zion, "Behold! Your salvation has
come; behold! His recompense is with Him, and His
wage is before Him."*
12 *And they shall call them, "The holy people, the redeemed of HASHEM"; and you shall be called, "Sought
after; city not forsaken."*

63 1 *Who is this that comes from Edom, sullied of garment from Bozrah? It is this One Who was
majestic in His raiment, Who was girded with His abundant strength? — "It is I Who speaks in righteousness,
abundantly able to save."* 2 *Why the red stain on Your
raiment? And Your garments — as one who treads in the
wine vat!* 3 *"A wine press have I trod by Myself, and from
the nations not a man was with Me; I trod on them in My
anger and trampled them in My wrath, their lifeblood
spurted out on My garments, and I soiled My raiment.*
4 *For the day of vengeance is in My heart and the year of
My redemption has come.* 5 *I looked, but there was no
helper; I was astonished, but there was no supporter; so
My arm saved for Me, and My wrath supported Me.* 6 *I
trampled peoples in My anger, and stupefied them with
My wrath, and threw their lifeblood to the ground."*
7 *The kindness of HASHEM will I mention, the praises of
HASHEM, in accordance with all that HASHEM has bestowed upon us, and the abundant goodness to the
House of Israel, which He bestowed upon them in His
compassion and in His abundant kindness.* 8 *For He
said, "Yet they are My people, children who will not be*

יְשַׁקֵּרוּ וַיְהִי לָהֶם לְמוֹשִׁיעַ: ט בְּכָל־צָרָתָם | לוֹ
[לא כ׳] צָר וּמַלְאַךְ פָּנָיו הוֹשִׁיעָם בְּאַהֲבָתוֹ
וּבְחֶמְלָתוֹ הוּא גְאָלָם וַיְנַטְּלֵם וַיְנַשְּׂאֵם כָּל־יְמֵי
עוֹלָם:

false," and He was unto them a Savior. 9 *In all their troubles, He was troubled, and an angel from before Him saved them; with His love and with His compassion He redeemed them; He lifted them and bore them all the days of the world.*

HAFTARAS VAYEILECH / הפטרת וילך

The following *Haftarah* is read on the Sabbath that falls between Rosh Hashanah and Yom Kippur. Some years the *Sidrah* of that week is *Vayeilech,* but most years it is *Haazinu.* When the two *Sidros Netzavim* and *Vayeilech* are read together, the *Haftarah* of *Nitzavim* (p. 413) is read, and the following *Haftarah* is read for *Haazinu.* Customs vary regarding how many of the following paragraphs are read and in what order.

[Some congregations omit all of the following and read the *Haftarah* that is read on fast days at *Minchah*).]

Hosea 14:2-10; Joel 2:11-27; Micah 7:18-20 / הושע יד:ב־י; יואל ב:יא־כז; מיכה ז:יח־כ

יד ב שׁוּבָה יִשְׂרָאֵל עַד יהוה אֱלֹהֶיךָ כִּי כָשַׁלְתָּ
בַּעֲוֺנֶךָ: ג קְחוּ עִמָּכֶם דְּבָרִים וְשׁוּבוּ אֶל־יהוה
אִמְרוּ אֵלָיו כָּל־תִּשָּׂא עָוֺן וְקַח־טוֹב וּנְשַׁלְּמָה
פָרִים שְׂפָתֵינוּ: ד אַשּׁוּר | לֹא יוֹשִׁיעֵנוּ עַל־סוּס
לֹא נִרְכָּב וְלֹא־נֹאמַר עוֹד אֱלֹהֵינוּ לְמַעֲשֵׂה
יָדֵינוּ אֲשֶׁר־בְּךָ יְרֻחַם יָתוֹם: ה אֶרְפָּא מְשׁוּבָתָם
אֹהֲבֵם נְדָבָה כִּי שָׁב אַפִּי מִמֶּנּוּ: ו אֶהְיֶה כַטַּל
לְיִשְׂרָאֵל יִפְרַח כַּשּׁוֹשַׁנָּה וְיַךְ שָׁרָשָׁיו כַּלְּבָנוֹן:
ז יֵלְכוּ יֹנְקוֹתָיו וִיהִי כַזַּיִת הוֹדוֹ וְרֵיחַ לוֹ כַּלְּבָנוֹן:
ח יָשֻׁבוּ יֹשְׁבֵי בְצִלּוֹ יְחַיּוּ דָגָן וְיִפְרְחוּ כַגָּפֶן זִכְרוֹ
כְּיֵין לְבָנוֹן: ט אֶפְרַיִם מַה־לִּי עוֹד לָעֲצַבִּים אֲנִי
עָנִיתִי וַאֲשׁוּרֶנּוּ אֲנִי כִּבְרוֹשׁ רַעֲנָן מִמֶּנִּי פֶּרְיְךָ
נִמְצָא: י מִי חָכָם וְיָבֵן אֵלֶּה נָבוֹן וְיֵדָעֵם כִּי־
יְשָׁרִים דַּרְכֵי יהוה וְצַדִּקִים יֵלְכוּ בָם וּפֹשְׁעִים
יִכָּשְׁלוּ בָם:

14 2 *Return, O Israel, to HASHEM, your God, for you have stumbled through your iniquity.* 3 *Take words with you and return to HASHEM; say to Him, "Forgive every sin and accept goodness, and let our lips substitute for bulls.* 4 *Assyria cannot help us, we will not ride the horse, nor will we ever again call our handiwork 'our god' — only in You will the orphan find compassion."*

5 *I shall heal their rebelliousness, I shall love them willingly, for My wrath will be withdrawn from them.* 6 *I shall be like the dew to Israel, it will blossom like the rose and strike its roots like the [forest of] Lebanon.* 7 *Its tender branches will spread, and its glory will be like an olive tree; its aroma will be like the Lebanon.* 8 *Tranquil will be those who sit in its shade, they will refresh themselves like grain and blossom like the grapevine, their reputation will be like the wine of Lebanon.* 9 *Ephraim [will say], "What more need have I for idols?" I will respond and look to him. I am like an ever-fresh cypress, from Me shall your fruit be found.*

10 *Whoever is wise will understand these, a discerning person will know them, for the ways of HASHEM are just — the righteous will walk in them, but sinners will stumble on them.*

Sephardim omit the next paragraph and continue below.

ב יא וַיהוה נָתַן קוֹלוֹ לִפְנֵי חֵילוֹ כִּי רַב מְאֹד
מַחֲנֵהוּ כִּי עָצוּם עֹשֵׂה דְבָרוֹ כִּי־גָדוֹל יוֹם־יהוה
וְנוֹרָא מְאֹד וּמִי יְכִילֶנּוּ: יב וְגַם־עַתָּה נְאֻם־יהוה
שֻׁבוּ עָדַי בְּכָל־לְבַבְכֶם וּבְצוֹם וּבִבְכִי וּבְמִסְפֵּד:
יג וְקִרְעוּ לְבַבְכֶם וְאַל־בִּגְדֵיכֶם וְשׁוּבוּ אֶל־יהוה
אֱלֹהֵיכֶם כִּי־חַנּוּן וְרַחוּם הוּא אֶרֶךְ אַפַּיִם וְרַב־
חֶסֶד וְנִחָם עַל־הָרָעָה: יד מִי יוֹדֵעַ יָשׁוּב וְנִחָם
וְהִשְׁאִיר אַחֲרָיו בְּרָכָה מִנְחָה וָנֶסֶךְ לַיהוה
אֱלֹהֵיכֶם: טו תִּקְעוּ שׁוֹפָר בְּצִיּוֹן קַדְּשׁוּ־צוֹם
קִרְאוּ עֲצָרָה: טז אִסְפוּ־עָם קַדְּשׁוּ קָהָל קִבְצוּ
זְקֵנִים אִסְפוּ עוֹלָלִים וְיֹנְקֵי שָׁדָיִם יֵצֵא
חָתָן מֵחֶדְרוֹ וְכַלָּה מֵחֻפָּתָהּ: יז בֵּין הָאוּלָם
וְלַמִּזְבֵּחַ יִבְכּוּ הַכֹּהֲנִים מְשָׁרְתֵי יהוה וְיֹאמְרוּ

2 11 *And HASHEM gave forth His voice [in prophetic warning] before [sending forth] His army, for His camp is very great, for mighty is He that executes His word, for great is the day of HASHEM and exceedingly awesome; who can endure it?* 12 *Yet even now — the word of HASHEM — return to Me with all your heart, and with fasting, and with weeping, and with lament;* 13 *and rend your heart and not your clothing, and return to HASHEM, your God, for He is gracious and compassionate, slow to anger and abundant of kindness, and He reconsiders regarding the evil.* 14 *Whoever knows [that he has strayed] shall return and reconsider [his past], and it shall leave behind it a blessing, a meal-offering and a libation to HASHEM, your God.*

15 *Blow a shofar in Zion: consecrate a fast; call an assembly;* 16 *gather the people; ready the congregation; assemble the elders; gather the infants and the nurslings; let each bridegroom go forth from his chamber and each bride from her bridal canopy.* 17 *Between the Hall and the Altar shall the Kohanim, the ministers of HASHEM, weep, and they shall say,*

"Have pity, O HASHEM, upon Your people and do not make Your heritage into shame for the nations to use as an example; why should they say among the peoples, 'Where is your God?' " [18] [Then, when you will have repented,] HASHEM will have been zealous regarding His land and will have taken pity on His people. [19] Then HASHEM will have answered and will have said to His people: Behold! I send you the grain and the wine and the oil, and you shall be satiated with it; I will not make you again as a shame among the nations. [20] And [the plague of] the northerner will I distance from you, and oust it into a land arid and desolate, its face toward the eastern sea, and its end toward the western sea; and its foulness shall ascend, and its stench shall ascend, for it has done great [evil]. [21] Fear not, O ground, be happy and be joyous, for HASHEM has done great [good]. [22] Fear not, O animals of the field, for the pastures of the wilderness are cloaked in grass, for each tree bears its fruit, fig-tree and vine have given forth their assets. [23] O children of Zion, be happy and be joyous with HASHEM, your God, for He has given you a mentor to righteousness; and He has caused the early rains and the late rains to descend for you in the first [month]. [24] The threshing-floors shall be full with grain, and the vats will resound with [the sound of flowing] wine and oil. [25] I will repay you for [the crops of] the years that [the various types of locust —] the arbeh, the yelek, the hasil, and the gazam consumed, My great army that I have sent against you. [26] And you shall eat — eating and being satiated — and you shall praise the Name of HASHEM, your God, Who has done wondrously with you; and My people shall never be put to shame. [27] Then you shall know that I am in the midst of Israel, and that I am HASHEM, your God, and there is no other; and My people shall never be put to shame.

חוּסָה יהוה עַל־עַמֶּךָ וְאַל־תִּתֵּן נַחֲלָתְךָ לְחֶרְפָּה לִמְשָׁל־בָּם גּוֹיִם לָמָּה יֹאמְרוּ בָעַמִּים אַיֵּה אֱלֹהֵיהֶם: יח וַיְקַנֵּא יהוה לְאַרְצוֹ וַיַּחְמֹל עַל־עַמּוֹ: יט וַיַּעַן יהוה וַיֹּאמֶר לְעַמּוֹ הִנְנִי שֹׁלֵחַ לָכֶם אֶת־הַדָּגָן וְהַתִּירוֹשׁ וְהַיִּצְהָר וּשְׂבַעְתֶּם אֹתוֹ וְלֹא־אֶתֵּן אֶתְכֶם עוֹד חֶרְפָּה בַּגּוֹיִם: כ וְאֶת־הַצְּפוֹנִי אַרְחִיק מֵעֲלֵיכֶם וְהִדַּחְתִּיו אֶל־אֶרֶץ צִיָּה וּשְׁמָמָה אֶת־פָּנָיו אֶל־הַיָּם הַקַּדְמֹנִי וְסֹפוֹ אֶל־הַיָּם הָאַחֲרוֹן וְעָלָה בָאְשׁוֹ וְתַעַל צַחֲנָתוֹ כִּי הִגְדִּיל לַעֲשׂוֹת: כא אַל־תִּירְאִי אֲדָמָה גִּילִי וּשְׂמָחִי כִּי־הִגְדִּיל יהוה לַעֲשׂוֹת: כב אַל־תִּירְאוּ בַּהֲמוֹת שָׂדַי כִּי דָשְׁאוּ נְאוֹת מִדְבָּר כִּי־עֵץ נָשָׂא פִרְיוֹ תְּאֵנָה וָגֶפֶן נָתְנוּ חֵילָם: כג וּבְנֵי צִיּוֹן גִּילוּ וְשִׂמְחוּ בַּיהוה אֱלֹהֵיכֶם כִּי־נָתַן לָכֶם אֶת־הַמּוֹרֶה לִצְדָקָה וַיּוֹרֶד לָכֶם גֶּשֶׁם מוֹרֶה וּמַלְקוֹשׁ בָּרִאשׁוֹן: כד וּמָלְאוּ הַגֳּרָנוֹת בָּר וְהֵשִׁיקוּ הַיְקָבִים תִּירוֹשׁ וְיִצְהָר: כה וְשִׁלַּמְתִּי לָכֶם אֶת־הַשָּׁנִים אֲשֶׁר אָכַל הָאַרְבֶּה הַיֶּלֶק וְהֶחָסִיל וְהַגָּזָם חֵילִי הַגָּדוֹל אֲשֶׁר שִׁלַּחְתִּי בָּכֶם: כו וַאֲכַלְתֶּם אָכוֹל וְשָׂבוֹעַ וְהִלַּלְתֶּם אֶת־שֵׁם יהוה אֱלֹהֵיכֶם אֲשֶׁר־עָשָׂה עִמָּכֶם לְהַפְלִיא וְלֹא־יֵבֹשׁוּ עַמִּי לְעוֹלָם: כז וִידַעְתֶּם כִּי בְקֶרֶב יִשְׂרָאֵל אָנִי וַאֲנִי יהוה אֱלֹהֵיכֶם וְאֵין עוֹד וְלֹא־יֵבֹשׁוּ עַמִּי לְעוֹלָם:

All congregations continue here:

7 [18] **W**ho, O God, is like You, Who pardons iniquity and overlooks transgression for the remnant of His heritage? Who has not retained His wrath eternally, for He desires kindness! [19] He will again be merciful to us; He will suppress our iniquities. And cast into the depths of the sea all their sins. [20] Grant truth to Jacob, kindness to Abraham, as You swore to our forefathers from ancient times.

ז יח מִי־אֵל כָּמוֹךָ נֹשֵׂא עָוֹן וְעֹבֵר עַל־פֶּשַׁע לִשְׁאֵרִית נַחֲלָתוֹ לֹא־הֶחֱזִיק לָעַד אַפּוֹ כִּי־חָפֵץ חֶסֶד הוּא: יט יָשׁוּב יְרַחֲמֵנוּ יִכְבֹּשׁ עֲוֹנֹתֵינוּ וְתַשְׁלִיךְ בִּמְצֻלוֹת יָם כָּל־חַטֹּאותָם: כ תִּתֵּן אֱמֶת לְיַעֲקֹב חֶסֶד לְאַבְרָהָם אֲשֶׁר־נִשְׁבַּעְתָּ לַאֲבֹתֵינוּ מִימֵי קֶדֶם:

HAFTARAS HAAZINU / הפטרת האזינו

When Haazinu is read on the Sabbath between Rosh Hashanah and Yom Kippur, the Haftarah of Vayeilech (Shabbos Shuvah) is read. When Haazinu is read after Yom Kippur, the following Haftarah is read.

II Samuel 22:1-51 / שמואל ב כב:א-נא

22 [1] **D**avid spoke to HASHEM the words of this song on the day that HASHEM delivered him from the hand of all his enemies and from the hand of Saul. [2] He said: HASHEM is my Rock, my Fortress, and my Rescuer. [3] God, my Rock, I take refuge in Him; my Shield and the Horn of my Salvation, my Stronghold and my Refuge, my Savior Who saves me from violence.

כב א וַיְדַבֵּר דָּוִד לַיהוה אֶת־דִּבְרֵי הַשִּׁירָה הַזֹּאת בְּיוֹם הִצִּיל יהוה אֹתוֹ מִכַּף כָּל־אֹיְבָיו וּמִכַּף שָׁאוּל: ב וַיֹּאמַר יהוה סַלְעִי וּמְצֻדָתִי וּמְפַלְטִי־לִי: ג אֱלֹהֵי צוּרִי אֶחֱסֶה־בּוֹ מָגִנִּי וְקֶרֶן יִשְׁעִי מִשְׂגַּבִּי וּמְנוּסִי מֹשִׁעִי מֵחָמָס תֹּשִׁעֵנִי:

4 *With praises I call unto* H*ASHEM, and I am saved from*
my enemies. 5 *For the pains of death encircled me, and*
torrents of godless men would frighten me. 6 *The pains*
of the grave surrounded me, the snares of death con-
fronted me. 7 *In my distress I would call upon* H*ASHEM,*
and to my God I would call — from His abode He would
hear my voice, my cry in His ears. 8 *And the earth*
quaked and roared, the foundations of the heaven
shook; they trembled when His wrath flared. 9 *Smoke*
rose up in His nostrils, a devouring fire from His mouth,
flaming coals burst forth from Him. 10 *He bent down the*
heavens and descended, with thick darkness beneath
His feet. 11 *He mounted a cherub and flew, He swooped*
on the wings of the wind. 12 *He made darkness His shel-*
ter all around Him — the darkness of water, the clouds
of heaven. 13 *From out of the brilliance that is before*
Him burned fiery coals. 14 *And* H*ASHEM thundered in the*
heavens, the Most High cried out. 15 *He sent forth His*
arrows and scattered them, lightning and He frenzied
them. 16 *The channels of water became visible, the*
foundations of the earth were laid bare by the rebuke of
H*ASHEM, by the breath of His nostrils.* 17 *He sent from on*
high and took me, He drew me out of deep waters. 18 *He*
saved me from my mighty foe, and from my enemies
for they overpowered me. 19 *They confronted me on the*
day of my misfortune, but H*ASHEM was my support.* 20
He brought me out into broad spaces, He released me
for He desires me. 21 H*ASHEM recompensed me accord-*
ing to my righteousness; He repaid me according to the
cleanliness of my hands. 22 *For I have kept the ways of*
H*ASHEM, and I have not departed wickedly from my*
God. 23 *For all His judgments are before me, and I shall*
not remove myself from His statutes. 24 *I was perfectly*
innocent with Him, and I was vigilant against my sin.
25 H*ASHEM repaid me according to my righteousness,*
according to my cleanliness before His eyes. 26 *With the*
devout You act devoutly, with the wholehearted strong
you act wholeheartedly. 27 *With the pure You act*
purely, with the crooked You act perversely. 28 *You save*
the humble people, and Your eyes are upon the haughty
to lower them. 29 *For You,* H*ASHEM, are my lamp, and*
H*ASHEM will illuminate my darkness.* 30 *For with you I*
smash a troop, and with my God I leap a wall. 31 *The*
God! — His way is perfect; the promise of H*ASHEM is*
flawless, He is a shield for all who take refuge in Him.
32 *For who is God except for* H*ASHEM, and who is a Rock*
except for our God? 33 *The God Who is my strong*
Fortress, and Who let my way be perfect. 34 *Who*
straightened my feet like the hind, and stood me on my
heights. 35 *Who trained my hands for battle, so that an*
iron bow could be bent by my arms. 36 *You have given*
me Your shield of salvation, and Your humility made me
great. 37 *You have widened my stride beneath me, and*
my ankles have not faltered. 38 *I pursued my foes and*
overtook them, and returned not until they were de-
stroyed. 39 *I destroyed them, struck them down and*
they did not rise, and they fell beneath my feet. 40 *You*
girded me with strength for battle, You bring my adver-
saries to their knees beneath me. 41 *And my enemies —*
You gave me [their] back; my antagonists and I cut
them down. 42 *They turned, but there was no savior;*

ד מְהֻלָּל אֶקְרָא יהוה וּמֵאֹיְבַי אִוָּשֵׁעַ: ה כִּי אֲפָפֻנִי
מִשְׁבְּרֵי־מָוֶת נַחֲלֵי בְלִיַּעַל יְבַעֲתֻנִי: ו חֶבְלֵי
שְׁאוֹל סַבֻּנִי קִדְּמֻנִי מֹקְשֵׁי־מָוֶת: ז בַּצַּר־לִי
אֶקְרָא יהוה וְאֶל־אֱלֹהַי אֶקְרָא וַיִּשְׁמַע מֵהֵיכָלוֹ
קוֹלִי וְשַׁוְעָתִי בְּאָזְנָיו: ח וַיִּתְגָּעַשׁ [ותגעש כ׳]
וַתִּרְעַשׁ הָאָרֶץ מוֹסְדוֹת הַשָּׁמַיִם יִרְגָּזוּ וַיִּתְגָּעֲשׁוּ
כִּי־חָרָה לוֹ: ט עָלָה עָשָׁן בְּאַפּוֹ וְאֵשׁ מִפִּיו תֹּאכֵל
גֶּחָלִים בָּעֲרוּ מִמֶּנּוּ: י וַיֵּט שָׁמַיִם וַיֵּרַד וַעֲרָפֶל
תַּחַת רַגְלָיו: יא וַיִּרְכַּב עַל־כְּרוּב וַיָּעֹף וַיֵּרָא עַל־
כַּנְפֵי־ רוּחַ: יב וַיָּשֶׁת חֹשֶׁךְ סְבִיבֹתָיו סֻכּוֹת
חַשְׁרַת־מַיִם עָבֵי שְׁחָקִים: יג מִנֹּגַהּ נֶגְדּוֹ בָּעֲרוּ
גַּחֲלֵי־אֵשׁ: יד יַרְעֵם מִן־שָׁמַיִם יהוה וְעֶלְיוֹן
יִתֵּן קוֹלוֹ: טו וַיִּשְׁלַח חִצִּים וַיְפִיצֵם בָּרָק וַיָּהֹם
[ויהמם כ׳]: טז וַיֵּרָאוּ אֲפִקֵי יָם יִגָּלוּ מֹסְדוֹת תֵּבֵל
בְּגַעֲרַת יהוה מִנִּשְׁמַת רוּחַ אַפּוֹ: יז יִשְׁלַח
מִמָּרוֹם יִקָּחֵנִי יַמְשֵׁנִי מִמַּיִם רַבִּים: יח יַצִּילֵנִי
מֵאֹיְבִי עָז מִשֹּׂנְאַי כִּי אָמְצוּ מִמֶּנִּי: יט יְקַדְּמֻנִי
בְּיוֹם אֵידִי וַיְהִי יהוה מִשְׁעָן לִי: כ וַיֹּצֵא לַמֶּרְחָב
אֹתִי יְחַלְּצֵנִי כִּי־חָפֵץ בִּי: כא יִגְמְלֵנִי יהוה
כְּצִדְקָתִי כְּבֹר יָדַי יָשִׁיב לִי: כב כִּי שָׁמַרְתִּי דַּרְכֵי
יהוה וְלֹא רָשַׁעְתִּי מֵאֱלֹהָי: כג כִּי כָל־מִשְׁפָּטָיו
[משפטו כ׳] לְנֶגְדִּי וְחֻקֹּתָיו לֹא־אָסוּר מִמֶּנָּה:
כד וָאֶהְיֶה תָמִים לוֹ וָאֶשְׁתַּמְּרָה מֵעֲוֹנִי: כה וַיָּשֶׁב
יהוה לִי כְּצִדְקָתִי כְּבֹרִי לְנֶגֶד עֵינָיו: כו עִם־חָסִיד
תִּתְחַסָּד עִם־גִּבּוֹר תָּמִים תִּתַּמָּם: כז עִם־נָבָר
תִּתָּבָר וְעִם־עִקֵּשׁ תִּתַּפָּל: כח וְאֶת־עַם עָנִי
תּוֹשִׁיעַ וְעֵינֶיךָ עַל־רָמִים תַּשְׁפִּיל: כט כִּי־אַתָּה
נֵירִי יהוה וַיהוה יַגִּיהַּ חָשְׁכִּי: ל כִּי בְכָה אָרוּץ
גְּדוּד בֵּאלֹהַי אֲדַלֶּג־שׁוּר: לא הָאֵל תָּמִים דַּרְכּוֹ
אִמְרַת יהוה צְרוּפָה מָגֵן הוּא לְכֹל הַחֹסִים בּוֹ:
לב כִּי מִי־אֵל מִבַּלְעֲדֵי יהוה וּמִי צוּר מִבַּלְעֲדֵי
אֱלֹהֵינוּ: לג הָאֵל מָעוּזִּי חָיִל וַיַּתֵּר תָּמִים דַּרְכִּי
[דרכו כ׳]: לד מְשַׁוֶּה רַגְלַי [רגליו כ׳] כָּאַיָּלוֹת וְעַל־
בָּמֹתַי יַעֲמִדֵנִי: לה מְלַמֵּד יָדַי לַמִּלְחָמָה וְנִחַת
קֶשֶׁת־נְחוּשָׁה זְרֹעֹתָי: לו וַתִּתֶּן־לִי מָגֵן יִשְׁעֶךָ
וַעֲנֹתְךָ תַּרְבֵּנִי: לז תַּרְחִיב צַעֲדִי תַּחְתֵּנִי וְלֹא
מָעֲדוּ קַרְסֻלָּי: לח אֶרְדְּפָה אֹיְבַי וָאַשְׁמִידֵם וְלֹא
אָשׁוּב עַד־כַּלּוֹתָם: לט וָאֲכַלֵּם וָאֶמְחָצֵם וְלֹא
יְקוּמוּן וַיִּפְּלוּ תַּחַת רַגְלָי: מ וַתַּזְרֵנִי חַיִל
לַמִּלְחָמָה תַּכְרִיעַ קָמַי תַּחְתֵּנִי: מא וְאֹיְבַי תַּתָּה
לִּי עֹרֶף מְשַׂנְאַי וָאַצְמִיתֵם: מב יִשְׁעוּ וְאֵין מֹשִׁיעַ

אֶל־יהוה וְלֹא עָנָם: מג וְאֶשְׁחָקֵם כַּעֲפַר־אָרֶץ
כְּטִיט־חוּצוֹת אֲדִקֵּם אֶרְקָעֵם: מד וַתְּפַלְּטֵנִי
מֵרִיבֵי עַמִּי תִּשְׁמְרֵנִי לְרֹאשׁ גּוֹיִם עַם לֹא־
יָדַעְתִּי יַעַבְדֻנִי: מה בְּנֵי נֵכָר יִתְכַּחֲשׁוּ־לִי לִשְׁמוֹעַ
אֹזֶן יִשָּׁמְעוּ לִי: מו בְּנֵי נֵכָר יִבֹּלוּ וְיַחְגְּרוּ
מִמִּסְגְּרוֹתָם: מז חַי־יהוה וּבָרוּךְ צוּרִי וְיָרֻם
אֱלֹהֵי צוּר יִשְׁעִי: מח הָאֵל הַנֹּתֵן נְקָמֹת לִי וּמוֹרִיד
עַמִּים תַּחְתֵּנִי: מט וּמוֹצִיאִי מֵאֹיְבָי וּמִקָּמַי
תְּרוֹמְמֵנִי מֵאִישׁ חֲמָסִים תַּצִּילֵנִי: נ עַל־כֵּן אוֹדְךָ
יהוה בַּגּוֹיִם וּלְשִׁמְךָ אֲזַמֵּר: נא מִגְדּוֹל [מגדיל כ׳]
יְשׁוּעוֹת מַלְכּוֹ וְעֹשֶׂה־חֶסֶד לִמְשִׁיחוֹ לְדָוִד
וּלְזַרְעוֹ עַד־עוֹלָם:

to HASHEM, but He answered them not. 43 I pulverized them like dust of the earth, like the mud of the streets I thinned them and I poured them out. 44 You rescued me from the strife of my people; You preserved me to be head of nations, a people I did not know serves me. 45 Foreigners dissemble to me; when their ear hears of me they are obedient to me. 46 Foreigners are withered, and they are terrified even within their strong enclosures. 47 HASHEM lives, and blessed is my Rock; and exalted is God, Rock of my salvation. 48 The God Who grants me vengeance, and brings peoples down beneath me. 49 You bring me forth from my enemies, and raise me above my adversaries, from a man of violence You rescue me. 50 Therefore, I will thank You, HASHEM, among the nations, and sing to Your Name. 51 He is a tower of salvations to His king, and does kindness to His anointed one, to David and to his descendants forever.

HAFTARAS SHABBAS EREV ROSH CHODESH / הפטרת שבת ערב ראש חודש

Samuel 20:18-42 / שמואל א כ:יח־מב

כ יח וַיֹּאמֶר־לוֹ יְהוֹנָתָן מָחָר חֹדֶשׁ וְנִפְקַדְתָּ כִּי
יִפָּקֵד מוֹשָׁבֶךָ: יט וְשִׁלַּשְׁתָּ תֵּרֵד מְאֹד וּבָאתָ אֶל־
הַמָּקוֹם אֲשֶׁר־נִסְתַּרְתָּ שָּׁם בְּיוֹם הַמַּעֲשֶׂה
וְיָשַׁבְתָּ אֵצֶל הָאֶבֶן הָאָזֶל: כ וַאֲנִי שְׁלֹשֶׁת
הַחִצִּים צִדָּה אוֹרֶה לְשַׁלַּח־לִי לְמַטָּרָה: כא וְהִנֵּה
אֶשְׁלַח אֶת־הַנַּעַר לֵךְ מְצָא אֶת־הַחִצִּים אִם־
אָמֹר אֹמַר לַנַּעַר הִנֵּה הַחִצִּים | מִמְּךָ וָהֵנָּה קָחֶנּוּ
וָבֹאָה כִּי־שָׁלוֹם לְךָ וְאֵין דָּבָר חַי־יהוה: כב וְאִם־
כֹּה אֹמַר לָעֶלֶם הִנֵּה הַחִצִּים מִמְּךָ וָהָלְאָה לֵךְ
כִּי שִׁלַּחֲךָ יהוה: כג וְהַדָּבָר אֲשֶׁר דִּבַּרְנוּ אֲנִי
וָאָתָּה הִנֵּה יהוה בֵּינִי וּבֵינְךָ עַד־עוֹלָם: כד וַיִּסָּתֵר
דָּוִד בַּשָּׂדֶה וַיְהִי הַחֹדֶשׁ וַיֵּשֶׁב הַמֶּלֶךְ אֶל־ [עַל־
כ׳] הַלֶּחֶם לֶאֱכוֹל: כה וַיֵּשֶׁב הַמֶּלֶךְ עַל־מוֹשָׁבוֹ
כְּפַעַם | בְּפַעַם אֶל־מוֹשַׁב הַקִּיר וַיָּקָם יְהוֹנָתָן
וַיֵּשֶׁב אַבְנֵר מִצַּד שָׁאוּל וַיִּפָּקֵד מְקוֹם דָּוִד:
כו וְלֹא־דִבֶּר שָׁאוּל מְאוּמָה בַּיּוֹם הַהוּא כִּי אָמַר
מִקְרֶה הוּא בִּלְתִּי טָהוֹר הוּא כִּי־לֹא טָהוֹר:
כז וַיְהִי מִמָּחֳרַת הַחֹדֶשׁ הַשֵּׁנִי וַיִּפָּקֵד מְקוֹם דָּוִד
וַיֹּאמֶר שָׁאוּל אֶל־יְהוֹנָתָן בְּנוֹ מַדּוּעַ לֹא־בָא
בֶן־יִשַׁי גַּם־תְּמוֹל גַּם־הַיּוֹם אֶל־הַלָּחֶם: כח וַיַּעַן
יְהוֹנָתָן אֶת־שָׁאוּל נִשְׁאֹל נִשְׁאַל דָּוִד מֵעִמָּדִי
עַד־בֵּית לָחֶם: כט וַיֹּאמֶר שַׁלְּחֵנִי נָא כִּי זֶבַח
מִשְׁפָּחָה לָנוּ בָּעִיר וְהוּא צִוָּה־לִי אָחִי וְעַתָּה
אִם־מָצָאתִי חֵן בְּעֵינֶיךָ אִמָּלְטָה נָּא וְאֶרְאֶה
אֶת־אֶחָי עַל־כֵּן לֹא־בָא אֶל־שֻׁלְחַן הַמֶּלֶךְ:
ל וַיִּחַר־אַף שָׁאוּל בִּיהוֹנָתָן וַיֹּאמֶר לוֹ בֶּן־נַעֲוַת
הַמַּרְדּוּת הֲלוֹא יָדַעְתִּי כִּי־בֹחֵר אַתָּה לְבֶן־יִשַׁי

20 18 Jonathan said to [David], "Tomorrow is the New Moon, and you will be missed because your seat will be empty. 19 For three days you are to go far down and come to the place where you hid on the day of the deed, and remain near the marker stone. 20 I will shoot three arrows in that direction as if I were shooting at a target. 21 Behold! — I will then send the lad, 'Go, find the arrows.' If I call out to the lad, 'Behold! — the arrows are on this side of you!' then you should take them and return, for it is well with you and there is no concern, as HASHEM lives. 22 But if I say this to the boy, 'Behold! — the arrows are beyond you!' then go, for HASHEM will have sent you away. 23 This matter of which we have spoken, I and you, behold! — HASHEM remains [witness] between me and you forever."

24 David concealed himself in the field. It was the New Moon and the king sat at the feast to eat. 25 The king sat on his seat as usual, on the seat by the wall; and Jonathan stood up so that Abner could sit at Saul's side, and David's seat was empty. 26 Saul said nothing on that day, for he thought, "It is a coincidence, he must be impure, for he has not been cleansed."

27 It was the day after the New Moon, the second day, and David's place was empty; Saul said to Jonathan, his son, "Why did the son of Jesse not come to the feast yesterday or today?"

28 Jonathan answered Saul, "David asked me for permission to go Bethlehem. 29 He said, 'Please send me away, for we have a family feast in the city, and he, my brother, ordered me [to come]; so now, if I have found favor in your eyes, excuse me, please, and let me see my brothers.' Therefore, he has not come to the king's table."

30 Saul's anger flared up at Jonathan, and he said to him, "Son of a pervertedly rebellious woman, do I not know that you prefer the son of Jesse,

for your own shame and the shame of your mother's nakedness! 31 *For all the days that the son of Jesse is alive on the earth, you and your kingdom will not be secure! And now send and bring him to me, for he is deserving of death."*

32 *Jonathan answered his father Saul and he said to him, "Why should he die; what has he done?"*

33 *Saul hurled his spear at him to strike him; so Jonathan realized that it was decided by his father to kill David.* 34 *Jonathan arose from the table in a burning anger; he did not partake of food on that second day of the month, for he was saddened over David because his father had humiliated him.*

35 *It happened in the morning that Jonathan went out to the field for the meeting with David, and a young lad was with him.* 36 *He said to his lad, "Run — please find the arrows that I shoot." The lad ran, and he shot the arrow to make it go further.* 37 *The lad arrived at the place of the arrow that Jonathan had shot, and Jonathan called out after the lad, and he said, "Is not the arrow beyond you?"*

38 *And Jonathan called out after the lad, "Quickly, hurry, do not stand still!" The lad gathered the arrows and came to his master*

38 *And Jonathan called out after the lad, "Quickly, hurry, do not stand still!" The lad gathered the arrows and came to his master.* 39 *The lad knew nothing, only Jonathan and David understood the matter.* 40 *Jonathan gave his equipment to his lad and said to him, "Go bring it to the city."*

41 *The lad went and David stood up from near the south [side of the stone], and he fell on his face to the ground and prostrated himself three times. They kissed one another and they wept with one another, until David [wept] greatly.*

42 *Jonathan said to David, "Go to peace. What the two of us have sworn in the Name of* H*ASHEM — saying, '*H*ASHEM shall be between me and you, and between my children and your children' — shall be forever!"*

לְבָשְׁתְּךָ וּלְבֹשֶׁת עֶרְוַת אִמֶּךָ: לא כִּי כָל־הַיָּמִים
אֲשֶׁר בֶּן־יִשַׁי חַי עַל־הָאֲדָמָה לֹא תִכּוֹן אַתָּה
וּמַלְכוּתֶךָ וְעַתָּה שְׁלַח וְקַח אֹתוֹ אֵלַי כִּי בֶן־מָוֶת
הוּא: לב וַיַּעַן יְהוֹנָתָן אֶת־שָׁאוּל אָבִיו וַיֹּאמֶר
אֵלָיו לָמָּה יוּמַת מֶה עָשָׂה: לג וַיָּטֶל שָׁאוּל אֶת־
הַחֲנִית עָלָיו לְהַכֹּתוֹ וַיֵּדַע יְהוֹנָתָן כִּי־כָלָה הִיא
מֵעִם אָבִיו לְהָמִית אֶת־דָּוִד: לד וַיָּקָם יְהוֹנָתָן
מֵעִם הַשֻּׁלְחָן בָּחֳרִי־אָף וְלֹא־אָכַל בְּיוֹם־
הַחֹדֶשׁ הַשֵּׁנִי לֶחֶם כִּי נֶעְצַב אֶל־דָּוִד כִּי
הִכְלִמוֹ אָבִיו: לה וַיְהִי בַבֹּקֶר וַיֵּצֵא יְהוֹנָתָן
הַשָּׂדֶה לְמוֹעֵד דָּוִד וְנַעַר קָטֹן עִמּוֹ: לו וַיֹּאמֶר
לְנַעֲרוֹ רֻץ מְצָא־נָא אֶת־הַחִצִּים אֲשֶׁר אָנֹכִי
מוֹרֶה הַנַּעַר רָץ וְהוּא־יָרָה הַחֵצִי לְהַעֲבִרוֹ:
לז וַיָּבֹא הַנַּעַר עַד־מְקוֹם הַחֵצִי אֲשֶׁר יָרָה
יְהוֹנָתָן וַיִּקְרָא יְהוֹנָתָן אַחֲרֵי הַנַּעַר וַיֹּאמֶר
הֲלוֹא הַחֵצִי מִמְּךָ וָהָלְאָה: לח וַיִּקְרָא יְהוֹנָתָן
אַחֲרֵי הַנַּעַר מְהֵרָה חוּשָׁה אַל־תַּעֲמֹד וַיְלַקֵּט
נַעַר יְהוֹנָתָן אֶת־הַחִצִּים [החצי כ׳] וַיָּבֹא אֶל־
אֲדֹנָיו: לח וַיִּקְרָא יְהוֹנָתָן אַחֲרֵי הַנַּעַר מְהֵרָה
חוּשָׁה אַל־תַּעֲמֹד וַיְלַקֵּט נַעַר יְהוֹנָתָן אֶת־
הַחִצִּים [החצי כ׳] וַיָּבֹא אֶל־אֲדֹנָיו: לט וְהַנַּעַר
לֹא־יָדַע מְאוּמָה אַךְ יְהוֹנָתָן וְדָוִד יָדְעוּ אֶת־
הַדָּבָר: מ וַיִּתֵּן יְהוֹנָתָן אֶת־כֵּלָיו אֶל־הַנַּעַר
אֲשֶׁר־לוֹ וַיֹּאמֶר לוֹ לֵךְ הָבֵיא הָעִיר: מא הַנַּעַר
בָּא וְדָוִד קָם מֵאֵצֶל הַנֶּגֶב וַיִּפֹּל לְאַפָּיו אַרְצָה
וַיִּשְׁתַּחוּ שָׁלֹשׁ פְּעָמִים וַיִּשְּׁקוּ | אִישׁ אֶת־רֵעֵהוּ
וַיִּבְכּוּ אִישׁ אֶת־רֵעֵהוּ עַד־דָּוִד הִגְדִּיל: מב וַיֹּאמֶר
יְהוֹנָתָן לְדָוִד לֵךְ לְשָׁלוֹם אֲשֶׁר נִשְׁבַּעְנוּ שְׁנֵינוּ
אֲנַחְנוּ בְּשֵׁם יהוה לֵאמֹר יהוה יִהְיֶה | בֵּינִי וּבֵינֶךָ
וּבֵין זַרְעִי וּבֵין זַרְעֲךָ עַד־עוֹלָם:

MAFTIR FOR SHABBAS ROSH CHODESH / מפטיר לשבת ראש חודש

Numbers 28:9-15 / במדבר כח:ט־טו

28 9 **A***nd on the Sabbath day: two male lambs in their first year, unblemished, two tenth-ephah of fine flour for a meal offering, mixed with oil, and its libation.* 10 *The elevation-offering of each Sabbath on its own Sabbath, in addition to the continual elevation-offering and its libation.*

11 *On your New Moons, you shall bring an elevation-offering to* H*ASHEM: two young bulls, one ram, seven male lambs in their first year, unblemished.* 12 *And three tenth-ephah of fine flour for a meal-offering mixed with oil, for each bull; and two tenth-ephah of fine flour mixed with oil, for each ram;* 13 *and a tenth-ephah of fine flour for a meal-offering, mixed*

כח ט וּבְיוֹם הַשַּׁבָּת שְׁנֵי־כְבָשִׂים בְּנֵי־שָׁנָה
תְּמִימִם וּשְׁנֵי עֶשְׂרֹנִים סֹלֶת מִנְחָה בְּלוּלָה
בַשֶּׁמֶן וְנִסְכּוֹ: י עֹלַת שַׁבַּת בְּשַׁבַּתּוֹ עַל־עֹלַת
הַתָּמִיד וְנִסְכָּהּ: יא וּבְרָאשֵׁי חָדְשֵׁיכֶם תַּקְרִיבוּ
עֹלָה לַיהוה פָּרִים בְּנֵי־בָקָר שְׁנַיִם וְאַיִל אֶחָד
כְּבָשִׂים בְּנֵי־שָׁנָה שִׁבְעָה תְּמִימִם: יב וּשְׁלֹשָׁה
עֶשְׂרֹנִים סֹלֶת מִנְחָה בְּלוּלָה בַשֶּׁמֶן לַפָּר הָאֶחָד
וּשְׁנֵי עֶשְׂרֹנִים סֹלֶת מִנְחָה בְּלוּלָה בַשֶּׁמֶן לָאַיִל
הָאֶחָד: יג וְעִשָּׂרֹן עִשָּׂרוֹן סֹלֶת מִנְחָה בְּלוּלָה

with oil, for each lamb — an elevation-offering, a sat-
isfying aroma, a fire-offering to HASHEM. ¹⁴ And their
libations: a half-hin for a bull, a third-hin for a ram, a
quarter-hin for a lamb — of wine. This is the elevation
offering of each month in its own month for the
months of the year. ¹⁵ And one male of the goats for
a sin-offering to HASHEM. In addition to the continual
elevation-offering, shall it be made, and its libation.

בַּשֶּׁ֫מֶן לַכֶּ֣בֶשׂ הָ֥אֶחָ֖ד עֹלָ֑ה רֵ֣יחַ נִיחֹ֔חַ אִשֶּׁ֖ה
לַֽיהֹוָֽה: יד וְנִסְכֵּיהֶ֗ם חֲצִ֣י הַהִ֣ין יִהְיֶה֮ לַפָּר֒
וּשְׁלִישִׁ֣ת הַהִ֣ין לָאַ֗יִל וּרְבִיעִ֥ת הַהִ֛ין לַכֶּ֖בֶשׂ יָ֑יִן
זֹ֣את עֹלַ֥ת חֹ֨דֶשׁ֙ בְּחׇדְשׁ֔וֹ לְחׇדְשֵׁ֖י הַשָּׁנָֽה: טו וּשְׂעִ֨יר
עִזִּ֥ים אֶחָ֛ד לְחַטָּ֖את לַֽיהֹוָ֑ה עַל־עֹלַ֧ת
הַתָּמִ֛יד יֵעָשֶׂ֖ה וְנִסְכּֽוֹ:

HAFTARAS SHABBAS ROSH CHODESH / הפטרת שבת ראש חודש

Isaiah 66:1-24 / ישעיה סו:א-כד

66 ¹So said HASHEM, The heaven is My throne and
the earth is My footstool; what House could
you build for Me, and what could be My resting
place? ² My hand made all these and thus they came
into being, the words of HASHEM — but it is to this that
I look: to the poor and broken-spirited person who is
zealous regarding My Word.

³ He who slaughters an ox is as if he slays a man;
he who offers a sheep is as if he breaks a dog's neck;
he who brings up a meal-offering is as if he offers a
swine's blood; one who brings a frankincense remembrance is as if he brings a gift of extortion; they
have even chosen their ways, and their souls have
desired their abominations.

⁴ I, too, will choose to mock them and what they
dread I will bring upon them — because I have called,
but no one responded; I have spoken, but they did
not hear; they did what is evil in My eyes and what I
did not desire they chose.

⁵ Listen to the Word of HASHEM, those who are zealous regarding His Word; your brethren who hate you
and distance themselves from you say, "HASHEM is
glorified because of my reputation" — but we shall
see your gladness and they will be shamed. ⁶ A tu-
multuous sound comes from the city, a sound from
the Sanctuary, the sound of HASHEM dealing retribution to His enemies. ⁷ When she has not yet felt her
labor, she will have given birth! When the pain has
not yet come to her, she will have delivered a son!
⁸ Who has heard such a thing? Who has seen its like?
Has a land gone through its labor in one day? Has a
nation been born at one time, as Zion went through
labor and gave birth to her children? ⁹ Shall I bring [a
woman] to the birthstool and not have her give birth?
says HASHEM. Shall I, Who causes birth, hold it back?
says your God.

¹⁰ Be glad with Jerusalem and rejoice in her, all
who love her; exult with her exultation, all who
mourned for her; ¹¹ so that you may nurse and be
sated from the breast of her consolations; so that you
may suck and delight from the glow of her glory.
¹² For so said HASHEM, Behold! — I shall direct peace
to her like a river, and the honor of nations like a
surging stream and you shall suckle; you will be carried on a shoulder and dandled on knees. ¹³ Like a
man whose mother consoled him, so will I console
you, and in Jerusalem will you be consoled. ¹⁴ You
shall see and your heart will exult, and your bones

סו א כֹּ֚ה אָמַ֣ר יְהֹוָ֔ה הַשָּׁמַ֣יִם כִּסְאִ֔י וְהָאָ֖רֶץ
הֲדֹ֣ם רַגְלָ֑י אֵי־זֶ֥ה בַ֨יִת֙ אֲשֶׁ֣ר תִּבְנוּ־לִ֔י וְאֵי־זֶ֖ה
מָק֥וֹם מְנֽוּחָתִֽי: ב וְאֶת־כׇּל־אֵ֙לֶּה֙ יָדִ֣י עָשָׂ֔תָה
וַיִּֽהְי֥וּ כׇל־אֵ֖לֶּה נְאֻם־יְהֹוָ֑ה וְאֶל־זֶ֣ה אַבִּ֔יט אֶל־
עָנִי֙ וּנְכֵה־ר֔וּחַ וְחָרֵ֖ד עַל־דְּבָרִֽי: ג שׁוֹחֵ֣ט הַשּׁ֡וֹר
מַכֵּה־אִ֜ישׁ זוֹבֵ֣חַ הַשֶּׂה֩ עֹרֵ֨ף כֶּ֜לֶב מַֽעֲלֵ֤ה מִנְחָה֙
דַּם־חֲזִ֔יר מַזְכִּ֥יר לְבֹנָ֖ה מְבָ֣רֵֽךְ אָ֑וֶן גַּם־הֵ֗מָּה
בָּֽחֲרוּ֙ בְּדַרְכֵיהֶ֔ם וּבְשִׁקּֽוּצֵיהֶ֖ם נַפְשָׁ֥ם חָפֵֽצָה:
ד גַּם־אֲנִ֞י אֶבְחַ֣ר בְּתַֽעֲלֻֽלֵיהֶ֗ם וּמְגֽוּרֹתָם֙ אָבִ֣יא
לָהֶ֔ם יַ֤עַן קָרָ֙אתִי֙ וְאֵ֣ין עוֹנֶ֔ה דִּבַּ֖רְתִּי וְלֹ֣א
שָׁמֵ֑עוּ וַיַּֽעֲשׂ֤וּ הָרַע֙ בְּעֵינַ֔י וּבַֽאֲשֶׁ֥ר לֹֽא־חָפַ֖צְתִּי
בָּחָֽרוּ: ה שִׁמְעוּ֙ דְּבַר־יְהֹוָ֔ה הַֽחֲרֵדִ֖ים אֶל־
דְּבָר֑וֹ אָמְרוּ֩ אֲחֵיכֶ֨ם שֹֽׂנְאֵיכֶ֜ם מְנַדֵּיכֶ֗ם לְמַ֤עַן
שְׁמִי֙ יִכְבַּ֣ד יְהֹוָ֔ה וְנִרְאֶ֥ה בְשִׂמְחַתְכֶ֖ם וְהֵ֥ם יֵבֹֽשׁוּ:
ו ק֤וֹל שָׁאוֹן֙ מֵעִ֔יר ק֖וֹל מֵֽהֵיכָ֑ל ק֣וֹל יְהֹוָ֔ה מְשַׁלֵּ֥ם
גְּמ֖וּל לְאֹֽיְבָֽיו: ז בְּטֶ֥רֶם תָּחִ֖יל יָלָ֑דָה בְּטֶ֨רֶם יָב֥וֹא
חֵ֛בֶל לָ֖הּ וְהִמְלִ֥יטָה זָכָֽר: ח מִֽי־שָׁמַ֣ע כָּזֹ֗את מִ֤י
רָאָה֙ כָּאֵ֔לֶּה הֲי֤וּחַל אֶ֙רֶץ֙ בְּי֣וֹם אֶחָ֔ד אִם־יִוָּ֥לֵֽד
גּ֖וֹי פַּ֣עַם אֶחָ֑ת כִּֽי־חָ֛לָה גַּם־יָֽלְדָ֥ה צִיּ֖וֹן אֶת־
בָּנֶֽיהָ: ט הַֽאֲנִ֥י אַשְׁבִּ֛יר וְלֹ֥א אוֹלִ֖יד יֹאמַ֣ר יְהֹוָ֑ה
אִם־אֲנִ֧י הַמּוֹלִ֛יד וְעָצַ֖רְתִּי אָמַ֥ר אֱלֹהָֽיִךְ:
י שִׂמְח֧וּ אֶת־יְרֽוּשָׁלַ֛͏ִם וְגִ֥ילוּ בָ֖הּ כׇּל־אֹֽהֲבֶ֑יהָ
שִׂ֤ישׂוּ אִתָּהּ֙ מָשׂ֔וֹשׂ כׇּל־הַמִּֽתְאַבְּלִ֖ים עָלֶֽיהָ:
יא לְמַ֤עַן תִּֽינְקוּ֙ וּשְׂבַעְתֶּ֔ם מִשֹּׁ֖ד תַּנְחֻמֶ֑יהָ לְמַ֧עַן
תָּמֹ֛צּוּ וְהִתְעַנַּגְתֶּ֖ם מִזִּ֥יז כְּבוֹדָֽהּ: יב כִּי־כֹ֣ה ׀ אָמַ֣ר
יְהֹוָ֗ה הִנְנִ֣י נֹטֶֽה־אֵ֠לֶ֠יהָ כְּנָהָ֨ר שָׁל֜וֹם וּכְנַ֧חַל
שׁוֹטֵ֛ף כְּב֥וֹד גּוֹיִ֖ם וִֽינַקְתֶּ֑ם עַל־צַד֙ תִּנָּשֵׂ֔אוּ
וְעַל־בִּרְכַּ֖יִם תְּשׇׁעֳשָֽׁעוּ: יג כְּאִ֕ישׁ אֲשֶׁ֥ר אִמּ֖וֹ
תְּנַֽחֲמֶ֑נּוּ כֵּ֤ן אָֽנֹכִי֙ אֲנַ֣חֶמְכֶ֔ם וּבִירֽוּשָׁלַ֖͏ִם
תְּנֻחָֽמוּ: יד וּרְאִיתֶם֙ וְשָׂ֣שׂ לִבְּכֶ֔ם וְעַצְמֽוֹתֵיכֶ֖ם

כַּדֶּשֶׁא תִפְרַחְנָה וְנוֹדְעָה יַד־יהוה אֶת־עֲבָדָיו
וְזָעַם אֶת־אֹיְבָיו: טו כִּי־הִנֵּה יהוה בָּאֵשׁ יָבוֹא
וְכַסּוּפָה מַרְכְּבֹתָיו לְהָשִׁיב בְּחֵמָה אַפּוֹ וְגַעֲרָתוֹ
בְּלַהֲבֵי־אֵשׁ: טז כִּי בָאֵשׁ יהוה נִשְׁפָּט וּבְחַרְבּוֹ
אֶת־כָּל־בָּשָׂר וְרַבּוּ חַלְלֵי יהוה: יז הַמִּתְקַדְּשִׁים
וְהַמִּטַּהֲרִים אֶל־הַגַּנּוֹת אַחַר אַחַת [אחד כ׳]
בַּתָּוֶךְ אֹכְלֵי בְּשַׂר הַחֲזִיר וְהַשֶּׁקֶץ וְהָעַכְבָּר
יַחְדָּו יָסֻפוּ נְאֻם־יהוה: יח וְאָנֹכִי מַעֲשֵׂיהֶם
וּמַחְשְׁבֹתֵיהֶם בָּאָה לְקַבֵּץ אֶת־כָּל־הַגּוֹיִם
וְהַלְּשֹׁנוֹת וּבָאוּ וְרָאוּ אֶת־כְּבוֹדִי: יט וְשַׂמְתִּי
בָהֶם אוֹת וְשִׁלַּחְתִּי מֵהֶם ׀ פְּלֵיטִים אֶל־הַגּוֹיִם
תַּרְשִׁישׁ פּוּל וְלוּד מֹשְׁכֵי קֶשֶׁת תֻּבַל וְיָוָן
הָאִיִּים הָרְחֹקִים אֲשֶׁר לֹא־שָׁמְעוּ אֶת־שִׁמְעִי
וְלֹא־רָאוּ אֶת־כְּבוֹדִי וְהִגִּידוּ אֶת־כְּבוֹדִי בַּגּוֹיִם:
כ וְהֵבִיאוּ אֶת־כָּל־אֲחֵיכֶם מִכָּל־הַגּוֹיִם ׀ מִנְחָה ׀
לַיהוָה בַּסּוּסִים וּבָרֶכֶב וּבַצַּבִּים וּבַפְּרָדִים
וּבַכִּרְכָּרוֹת עַל הַר קָדְשִׁי יְרוּשָׁלִַם אָמַר יהוה
כַּאֲשֶׁר יָבִיאוּ בְנֵי יִשְׂרָאֵל אֶת־הַמִּנְחָה בִּכְלִי
טָהוֹר בֵּית יהוה: כא וְגַם־מֵהֶם אֶקַּח לַכֹּהֲנִים
לַלְוִיִּם אָמַר יהוה: כב כִּי כַאֲשֶׁר הַשָּׁמַיִם
הַחֲדָשִׁים וְהָאָרֶץ הַחֲדָשָׁה אֲשֶׁר אֲנִי עֹשֶׂה
עֹמְדִים לְפָנַי נְאֻם־יהוה כֵּן יַעֲמֹד זַרְעֲכֶם
וְשִׁמְכֶם: כג וְהָיָה מִדֵּי־חֹדֶשׁ בְּחָדְשׁוֹ וּמִדֵּי שַׁבָּת
בְּשַׁבַּתּוֹ יָבוֹא כָל־בָּשָׂר לְהִשְׁתַּחֲוֺת לְפָנַי
אָמַר יהוה: כד וְיָצְאוּ וְרָאוּ בְּפִגְרֵי הָאֲנָשִׁים
הַפֹּשְׁעִים בִּי כִּי תוֹלַעְתָּם לֹא תָמוּת וְאִשָּׁם לֹא
תִכְבֶּה וְהָיוּ דֵרָאוֹן לְכָל־בָּשָׂר:

וְהָיָה מִדֵּי־חֹדֶשׁ בְּחָדְשׁוֹ וּמִדֵּי שַׁבָּת בְּשַׁבַּתּוֹ
יָבוֹא כָל־בָּשָׂר לְהִשְׁתַּחֲוֺת לְפָנַי אָמַר יהוה:

will flourish like grass; the hand of HASHEM will be known to His servants, and He will be angry with His enemies. 15 For behold! — HASHEM will arrive in fire and His chariots like the whirlwind, to requite His anger with wrath, and His rebuke with flaming fire. 16 For with fire HASHEM will judge, and with His sword against all flesh; many will be those slain by HASHEM.

17 Those who prepare and purify themselves [to storm] the gardens go one after another to the midst [of the fray]; together will be consumed those who eat the flesh of swine, of abominable creatures and rodents — the words of HASHEM. 18 I [am aware of] their deeds and their thoughts; [the time] has come to gather in all the nations and tongues; they shall come and see My glory.

19 I shall put a sign upon them and send some as survivors to the nations: Tarshish, Pul and Lud, the bow-drawers, Tubal, and Yavan; the distant islands, who have not heard of My fame and not seen My glory, and they will declare My glory among the nations. 20 They will bring all your brethren from all the nations as an offering to HASHEM, on horses, on chariot, on covered wagons, on mules, and with joyful dances upon My holy mountain, Jerusalem, said HASHEM; just as the Children of Israel bring their offering in a pure vessel to the House of HASHEM. 21 From them, too, will I take to be Kohanim and Levites, said HASHEM.

22 For just as the new heavens and the new earth that I will make will endure before Me — the words of HASHEM — so will your offspring and your name endure. 23 And it shall be that, from New Moon to New Moon, and from Sabbath to Sabbath, all flesh shall come to prostrate themselves before Me, said HASHEM.

24 They shall go out and see the corpses of those who rebel against Me, for their worms will not die and their fire will not go out, and they shall be a disgrace for all flesh.

And it shall be that, from New Moon to New Moon, and from Sabbath to Sabbath, all flesh shall come to prostrate themselves before Me, said HASHEM.

מפתח לפסוקי תנ"ך

Scriptural Index

This index lists about nine hundred verses of the *Chumash* that the Baal HaTurim discusses in his comments to other verses, as well as about thirteen hundred verses from the remainder of the *Tanach.* When looking for the Baal HaTurim's comment on a *Chumash* verse, the reader is advised to turn to that verse and the verses that precede and follow it, for the Baal HaTurim often comments on the juxtaposition of two or more verses. Similarly, commentary to the last verse of a *parashah* will often be contained in the first verse of the next *parashah,* and vice versa. Many of the verses treated in either of these ways have not been included in this index.

16:3	*Num.* 21:15	24:43	*Gen.* 16:7	28:14	*Num.* 23:7
16:5	*Gen.* 23:2	24:48	*Gen.* 14:19	28:15	*Gen.* 32:5
16:10	*Gen.* 3:16	24:51	*Gen.* 12:19	28:15	*Num.* 23:7
16:11	*Deut.* 31:29	24:60	*Lev.* 26:8	28:17	*Deut.* 7:21
17:1-2	*Ex.* 6:3	24:61	*Ex.* 2:5	28:20	*Lev.* 21:10
17:1	*Gen.* 12:3	24:62	*Ex.* 17:12	28:21	*Num.* 6:26
17:1	*Deut.* 30:12	24:63	*Gen.* 24:62	28:22	*Gen.* 29:2
17:2	*Gen.* 17:4	24:67	*Gen.* 2:22	28:22	*Deut.* 6:5
17:24	*Gen.* 18:18	25:1	*Gen.* 16:1, 24:67	29:1	*Num.* 6:26
17:27	*Gen.* 18:1	25:8	*Gen.* 35:29	29:25	*Lev.* 13:5
18:4	*Gen.* 24:12	25:11	*Gen.* 2:3	29:34	*Gen.* 30:14
18:6	*Gen.* 24:67	25:11	*Deut.* 7:13	30:2	*Gen.* 50:19
18:6	*Num.* 33:13	25:17	*Num.* 11:22	30:2	*Ex.* 24:10
18:7	*Num.* 7:15	25:19	*Gen.* 25:18	30:40	*Lev.* 3:7
18:11	*Gen.* 18:18	25:21	*Gen.* 25:20	30:40	*Num.* 7:15
18:14	*Gen.* 20:16	25:24	*Gen.* 50:3	31:1	*Ex.* 29:27
18:26	*Gen.* 18:24	25:27	*Ex.* 24:10	31:3	*Ex.* 3:14
18:28	*Gen.* 18:24	25:27	*Deut.* 33:4	31:22	*Deut.* 26:1
19:2	*Gen.* 18:4	26:3	*Ex.* 3:14, *Ex.* 6:3	31:32	*Gen.* 47:28
19:12	*Gen.* 33:8	26:5	*Ex.* 16:28, 20:13	31:50	*Ex.* 22:22
19:12	*Lev.* 24:14	26:5	*Deut.* 7:12	31:52	*Num.* 23:7
19:13	*Ex.* 3:7	26:8	*Ex.* 14:24	32:2	*Gen.* 28:12
19:14	*Ex.* 12:31	26:13	*Gen.* 38:14	32:15-16	*Gen.* 37:1
19:16	*Lev.* 24:12	26:24	*Lev.* 26:42	32:20	*Ex.* 32:30
19:28	*Ex.* 14:24	26:24	*Deut.* 6:3	32:25	*Gen.* 44:20
20:14	*Gen.* 12:19	26:32-33	*Gen.* 26:20-22	32:32	*Gen.* 28:20
21:5	*Gen.* 18:18	26:35	*Gen.* 24:29	33:6	*Gen.* 37:7
21:9	*Gen.* 26:8	27:1	*Gen.* 24:29,	33:12	*Gen.* 36:43
21:12	*Gen.* 25:21		28:16, 48:10	33:12	*Num.* 20:17
21:14	*Gen.* 16:1	27:3	*Ex.* 17:9	33:16	*Gen.* 33:14
21:20	*Gen.* 16:8	27:11	*Gen.* 33:14	33:17	*Ex.* 12:37
21:33	*Gen.* 9:20	27:16	*Lev.* 1:11	33:18	*Gen.* 27:36
21:33	*Num.* 23:7	27:22	*Gen.* 32:6	34:13	*Gen.* 27:35
Ch. 22	*Ex.* 29:39	27:27	*Gen.* 8:21	35:1	*Gen.* 12:7
22:3	*Ex.* 14:16	27:28	*Num.* 24:9	35:5	*Num.* 10:28
22:5	*Num.* 6:23	27:28-29	*Lev.* 26:4	35:9	*Num.* 23:7
22:13	*Num.* 7:15	27:28-29	*Deut.* 7:13	35:11	*Deut.* 7:13
22:17	*Gen.* 17:4	27:29	*Lev.* 26:42	35:23	*Gen.* 36:4
22:17-18	*Gen.* 26:13	27:29	*Num.* 21:14	35:24	*Gen.* 36:4
22:23	*Gen.* 23:1	27:31	*Ex.* 10:12	36:6	*Gen.* 37:1
24:1	*Gen.* 18:18, 22:17	27:39	*Gen.* 49:25	36:7	*Ex.* 2:3
24:1	*Num.* 6:24	27:39	*Num.* 24:21	37:2	*Gen.* 6:9
24:13	*Gen.* 16:7	27:41	*Deut.* 23:8	37:8	*Gen.* 48:20
24:22	*Ex.* 20:13, 38:26	28:4	*Gen.* 27:33	37:15	*Ex.* 23:4
24:27	*Gen.* 14:19	28:11	*Ex.* 17:12	37:20	*Num.* 20:19
24:31	*Gen.* 26:29	28:12	*Lev.* 13:45	37:23	*Gen.* 42:17
24:33	*Gen.* 26:29	28:13	*Gen.* 26:24	37:24	*Gen.* 42:17
24:34	*Gen.* 24:33	28:13	*Deut.* 6:3	37:24	*Deut.* 32:47
24:40	*Gen.* 24:7	28:14	*Gen.* 13:14, 32:8	37:28	*Gen.* 42:17

37:32	*Gen.* 38:23
37:33	*Num.* 20:19
37:35	*Gen.* 47:28
38:15	*Gen.* 15:6
38:18	*Ex.* 17:5
38:25	*Gen.* 37:32
38:26	*Gen.* 38:24
39:12	*Ex.* 21:8
39:15	*Gen.* 14:22
40:5	*Gen.* 39:20
40:14	*Gen.* 39:20
40:17	*Gen.* 1:22
41:1	*Ex.* 14:10
41:45	*Ex.* 1:1
42:2	*Gen.* 15:13
42:11	*Gen.* 42:9
42:11	*Num.* 32:32
42:23	*Num.* 22:2
42:24	*Gen.* 37:24
42:28	*Ex.* 18:1
43:8	*Gen.* 35:3
43:16	*Ex.* 4:6
43:32	*Gen.* 6:21
44:21	*Gen.* 39:1
44:33	*Num.* 7:13
45:5	*Gen.* 44:18
45:6	*Gen.* 8:22
45:13	*Gen.* 44:29
45:27	*Gen.* 37:14
46:2	*Ex.* 38:8
46:13	*Num.* 26:24
46:16	*Num.* 26:15
46:23	*Num.* 32:17
47:13	*Lev.* 23:14
48:10	*Gen.* 29:17
Ch. 49	*Num.* 2:2
49:3	*Num.* 2:2
49:4	*Gen.* 49:9
49:7	*Deut.* 33:10
49:8	*Num.* 2:2
49:14	*Ex.* 23:5
49:17	*Gen.* 3:15
49:18	*Num.* 2:2
49:19	*Gen.* 3:15
49:21	*Gen.* 32:19
49:21	*Num.* 1:42
49:25	*Num.* 2:2
49:27	*Deut.* 33:12
49:28	*Gen.* 3:15
50:2	*Gen.* 50:26
50:20	*Gen.* 31:28, 31:28
50:24	*Gen.* 50:5
50:26	*Gen.* 24:33
50:26	*Ex.* 1:1

Exodus — שמות

1:5	*Num.* 7:13
1:7	*Gen.* 6:11, 47:28
1:9	*Ex.* 7:28
1:10	*Num.* 36:3
1:11-12	*Ex.* 3:7, 38:24
1:13-14	*Ex.* 3:7, 38:24
1:14	*Ex.* 3:7, 24:10, 38:24
1:17	*Ex.* 1:18
2:3	*Gen.* 36:7
2:4	*Num.* 12:15
2:9	*Lev.* 20:3
2:20	*Ex.* 10:12
2:23	*Gen.* 4:10
3:7	*Gen.* 26:28
3:9	*Ex.* 3:7
3:9	*Ex.* 38:24
3:12	*Ex.* 19:1
3:14	*Deut.* 1:1, 3:24, 4:34
3:22	*Deut.* 15:14, 24:17
4:1	*Deut.* 31:14
4:9	*Gen.* 1:9
4:9	*Ex.* 3:18
4:12	*Ex.* 6:30
4:13	*Ex.* 3:11
4:13	*Deut.* 3:26
4:19	*Ex.* 2:13, 4:14
4:22	*Gen.* 27:19
4:22	*Deut.* 21:15
4:23	*Gen.* 27:19
4:24	*Ex.* 18:1
4:27	*Ex.* 4:14, 4:24
5:7-8	*Ex.* 24:10
5:8	*Gen.* 4:10
5:8	*Ex.* 5:7
5:9	*Ex.* 14:25
5:11	*Ex.* 19:4
5:12	*Gen.* 11:8
5:22	*Deut.* 3:26
5:23	*Ex.* 15:1
6:1	*Ex.* 5:22
6:6	*Num.* 25:12
6:8	*Deut.* 33:4
7:1	*Ex.* 18:1
7:15	*Ex.* 4:14
7:16	*Ex.* 10:1
8:1	*Num.* 20:25
8:4	*Ex.* 10:17
8:9	*Ex.* 8:1
8:20	*Gen.* 47:14
8:22	*Ex.* 12:8
9:15	*Deut.* 4:34
9:20	*Deut.* 20:8
9:33	*Gen.* 11:8
11:1	*Gen.* 21:10
11:4-5	*Ex.* 7:16
12:7	*Ex.* 12:22
12:8	*Gen.* 19:3
12:31	*Gen.* 19:14
12:32	*Gen.* 42:33
12:34	*Ex.* 3:22
12:35	*Ex.* 3:22
12:35	*Deut.* 15:14
12:41	*Ex.* 6:9
13:12	*Ex.* 13:13
14:2	*Num.* 33:7
14:5	*Gen.* 31:22
14:5	*Deut.* 26:1
14:7	*Deut.* 7:18
14:8	*Deut.* 4:20
14:10	*Num.* 33:25
14:20	*Ex.* 15:5
14:25	*Deut.* 7:23
14:28	*Gen.* 49:8
14:28	*Ex.* 14:31
14:31	*Gen.* 28:14, 37:10
15:2	*Ex.* 14:10
15:15	*Num.* 22:3
15:16	*Ex.* 15:13
15:21	*Ex.* 15:10
15:27	*Ex.* 7:17
16:3	*Lev.* 26:5
16:20	*Ex.* 7:21
16:23	*Gen.* 2:2
17:5	*Gen.* 38:18
17:9	*Gen.* 27:3
18:1	*Gen.* 42:28
18:7	*Gen.* 24:67
18:10	*Gen.* 14:19
18:12	*Gen.* 50:7
18:19	*Num.* 21:14

18:23 *Ex.* 18:19
19:3 *Gen.* 5:24
19:3 *Num.* 6:26
19:4 *Num.* 15:38
19:13 *Lev.* 24:23
19:17 *Deut.* 29:9
19:22 *Lev.* 10:6
20:1 *Gen.* 1:1
20:2 *Lev.* 1:1
20:2 *Deut.* 11:26
20:2-14 *Deut.* 5:16
20:4 *Deut.* 5:8
20:5 *Num.* 16:29
20:7 *Lev.* 25:1
20:8 *Ex.* 16:5
20:10 *Ex.* 20:8
20:11 *Ex.* 10:14
20:13 *Deut.* 4:42
20:15 *Num.* 22:2
20:20 *Ex.* 21:1
20:21 *Gen.* 28:12
20:21 *Num.* 6:27
20:22 *Ex.* 21:1
20:23 *Ex.* 21:1
21:3 *Ex.* 21:11
21:8 *Gen.* 39:12
21:10 *Lev.* 10:5
21:13 *Num.* 35:22
21:18 *Num.* 35:17
21:19 *Ex.* 15:26
21:28 *Ex.* 19:13
21:36 *Ex.* 21:29
22:1-2 *Deut.* 5:16
22:11 *Ex.* 21:34
22:17 *Num.* 31:8
22:19 *Lev.* 27:29
22:27 *Lev.* 24:11
22:27 *Num.* 22:6
22:28 *Deut.* 23:22
22:30 *Gen.* 13:13
23:4 *Gen.* 37:15
23:6 *Ex.* 23:3
23:8 *Gen.* 27:1
23:25 *Deut.* 7:13
23:25-26 *Gen.* 1:22
24:7 *Ex.* 28:35
24:8 *Lev.* 16:14
24:12 *Gen.* 12:3
24:16 *Num.* 12:3
24:18 *Ex.* 25:2
25:24 *Ex.* 25:10
25:27 *Num.* 4:11
26:30 *Deut.* 4:35, 27:2
27:10 *Ex.* 1:1
27:20 *Num.* 8:2
27:21 *Lev.* 24:3, 24:3
28:17 *Ex.* 39:10
28:29 *Ex.* 30:16
28:32 *Lev.* 6:3
29:2 *Lev.* 23:14
29:8 *Num.* 20:26
29:38 *Gen.* 6:15
29:43 *Ex.* 25:22
30:4 *Num.* 4:11
30:10 *Ex.* 30:16
30:11-16 *Num.* 1:3
30:12 *Num.* 1:19
31:2 *Ex.* 38:22
31:3 *Ex.* 38:22
31:13 *Ex.* 16:23
31:14 *Ex.* 16:23
31:14 *Deut.* 5:12
32:1 *Ex.* 10:7
32:1 *Num.* 14:4
32:4 *Num.* 26:35
32:11 *Num.* 14:16
32:17 *Num.* 10:2
32:32 *Ex.* 4:31, 27:20, 40:21
32:34 *Gen.* 24:7
33:1 *Num.* 14:13
33:2 *Gen.* 24:7
33:6 *Ex.* 25:6
33:8 *Gen.* 24:67
33:8 *Ex.* 21:7
33:9 *Gen.* 24:67
33:11 *Ex.* 13:22
33:20 *Num.* 14:14
33:22 *Ex.* 34:29
33:23 *Ex.* 23:25
34:2 *Gen.* 12:3
34:6 *Ex.* 3:14
34:7 *Lev.* 16:8
34:11 *Gen.* 49:8
34:14 *Deut.* 6:4
34:22 *Ex.* 23:16
34:24 *Lev.* 9:21-22
34:27 *Gen.* 1:4
34:28 *Ex.* 25:2
34:29 *Ex.* 35:1
34:32 *Ex.* 6:13
35:2 *Ex.* 16:23
35:3 *Ex.* 35:1
35:10 *Ex.* 5:9
35:22 *Ex.* 38:24
35:30 *Ex.* 38:22
35:31 *Ex.* 38:22
36:1 *Ex.* 30:4
36:3 *Ex.* 36:6
36:6 *Gen.* 8:2
36:29 *Ex.* 26:24
37:19 *Gen.* 41:5
38:24 *Ex.* 3:16
38:26 *Gen.* 24:22
38:26 *Ex.* 14:16
39:43 *Ex.* 40:21
40:30 *Ex.* 30:18

Leviticus — ויקרא

1:1 *Gen.* 31:33
1:3 *Lev.* 1:9, 2:2
1:11 *Lev.* 1:5
1:13 *Lev.* 1:9
1:17 *Lev.* 1:9
2:3 *Lev.* 2:2
3:6 *Lev.* 3:1
3:8 *Lev.* 3:2
3:11 *Lev.* 3:5
3:13 *Lev.* 3:2
4:11 *Lev.* 1:9
4:18 *Lev.* 4:7
4:28 *Lev.* 4:23
5:1 *Gen.* 31:35
5:11 *Ex.* 12:23
5:26 *Lev.* 6:1
6:5 *Ex.* 22:4
6:7 *Ex.* 28:1
7:5 *Lev.* 6:1
7:37 *Deut.* 3:25
7:37 *Lev.* 1:1
7:38 *Num.* 1:19
8:3 *Num.* 16:19
8:13 *Gen.* 3:21
8:21 *Lev.* 1:9
8:31 *Ex.* 12:8
8:33 *Ex.* 12:8
9:4 *Lev.* 22:28

9:14	*Lev.* 1:9
10:3	*Ex.* 25:22
10:3	*Lev.* 16:1
10:10	*Gen.* 1:18
10:11	*Ex.* 35:34
11:43	*Lev.* 12:2
11:46	*Gen.* 1:22
12:5	*Lev.* 25:11
13:2	*Lev.* 13:45
13:45	*Ex.* 32:25
13:46	*Lev.* 14:4
14:2	*Lev.* 13:59
14:6	*Ex.* 7:17
14:32	*Lev.* 13:59
14:36	*Deut.* 24:10
14:42	*Lev.* 4:14
14:54	*Lev.* 13:59
14:57	*Lev.* 13:59
15:31	*Lev.* 16:1
15:32	*Lev.* 16:1
15:33	*Lev.* 16:1
16:2	*Lev.* 16:12
16:16	*Lev.* 15:26
16:22	*Lev.* 16:8
16:30	*Lev.* 16:14
18:3	*Lev.* 17:13
18:6	*Ex.* 28:42
18:27	*Ex.* 1:18
19:12	*Deut.* 5:12
19:19	*Deut.* 8:8
20:3	*Lev.* 13:44
20:3	*Num.* 5:3
20:8	*Deut.* 26:17
20:18	*Lev.* 12:7
20:19	*Lev.* 20:18
20:21	*Lev.* 20:18
20:27	*Lev.* 21:1
21:8	*Ex.* 19:23
21:10	*Gen.* 28:20
21:10	*Ex.* 29:21
22:5	*Lev.* 13:9
22:23	*Lev.* 22:28
22:25	*Ex.* 40:15
Ch. 23	*Lev.* 22:29
23:9-13	*Ex.* 16:22
23:18	*Deut.* 8:3
23:28	*Lev.* 16:29
23:39	*Ex.* 10:9
23:40	*Gen.* 1:29
24:2	*Gen.* 25:22
24:2	*Num.* 8:2
24:7	*Ex.* 30:34
24:9	*Lev.* 26:16
24:16	*Lev.* 24:11
25:1	*Lev.* 24:23
25:19	*Ex.* 16:3
25:19	*Lev.* 26:5
25:21	*Gen.* 27:36
25:21	*Ex.* 26:9
25:21	*Deut.* 14:29
25:26	*Deut.* 25:2
25:46	*Num.* 33:54
25:47	*Deut.* 28:42
26:1	*Deut.* 27:2
26:2	*Ex.* 16:23
26:3-13	*Deut.* 11:27
26:5	*Ex.* 16:3
26:6	*Deut.* 11:25
26:8	*Gen.* 24:60
26:9-10	*Gen.* 1:22
26:13	*Lev.* 26:4
26:13	*Num.* 7:13
26:14-46	*Deut.* 11:27
26:25	*Deut.* 1:6
26:25	*Deut.* 32:42
26:41	*Ex.* 12:48
27:2	*Num.* 6:2
27:12	*Num.* 6:2
27:29	*Ex.* 22:19
27:32	*Num.* 1:2
27:33	*Lev.* 13:36
27:34	*Num.* 1:1
27:34	*Deut.* 26:17

Numbers — במדבר

1:2	*Num.* 26:2
1:15	*Num.* 1:5
1:53	*Num.* 31:19
2:17	*Num.* 10:35-36
2:24	*Gen.* 6:16
3:6	*Ex.* 28:1
3:36	*Num.* 16:29
4:16	*Num.* 16:29
5:2	*Gen.* 25:22
5:2	*Num.* 5:6
5:3	*Num.* 5:6
5:12	*Num.* 25:1
5:13	*Lev.* 4:13
5:13	*Num.* 5:17
5:15	*Ex.* 12:23
5:23	*Num.* 5:17
5:28	*Gen.* 21:1
5:31	*Ex.* 21:19
6:24	*Lev.* 9:21-22
6:24-26	*Gen.* 12:2
6:25	*Lev.* 9:21-22
6:26	*Lev.* 9:21-22
7:19	*Ex.* 14:10
8:16	*Ex.* 28:1
9:2	*Ex.* 5:9
9:11	*Ex.* 12:8
9:15	*Deut.* 28:67
9:18	*Lev.* 1:1
9:20, 23	*Deut.* 34:12
10:12	*Ex.* 24:16
10:28	*Gen.* 35:5
10:34	*Gen.* 11:2
11:1	*Num.* 7:2-3
11:5	*Ex.* 16:3
11:7	*Gen.* 2:12
11:11	*Ex.* 5:22
11:14	*Num.* 11:17
11:22	*Deut.* 3:26
11:23	*Ex.* 5:22
11:25	*Num.* 11:17
11:26	*Gen.* 8:4, 24:67
11:26	*Num.* 11:17
11:26-27	*Num.* 34:21
11:28	*Num.* 11:17
11:29	*Num.* 11:17
11:31-33	*Num.* 11:20, 35:23
11:31	*Gen.* 19:31
11:32	*Ex.* 8:10, 16:13
12:7	*Deut.* 3:24
13:4	*Ex.* 28:12
13:20	*Ex.* 17:7
13:33	*Gen.* 6:4
14:4	*Gen.* 22:5
14:13	*Ex.* 3:18, 33:1
14:32	*Num.* 14:3
14:33	*Num.* 13:20
14:45	*Num.* 14:9, 15:3
15:12	*Ex.* 16:22
15:24	*Gen.* 25:25
15:24	*Lev.* 4:13
15:30	*Ex.* 14:8

6:20	*Ex.* 16:33
6:30	*Lev.* 24:14
6:31	*Ex.* 17:2
7:4	*Ex.* 33:5
7:17	*Ex.* 25:9
7:19	*Ex.* 25:9
9:6	*Gen.* 28:12
10:16	*Num.* 21:4
11:30	*Gen.* 28:20
11:40	*Ex.* 13:10
13:8	*Gen.* 25:20
13:20	*Lev.* 6:5
14:3	*Gen.* 34:1
16:3	*Ex.* 12:29
16:16	*Num.* 21:4
16:26	*Ex.* 32:10
16:28	*Lev.* 26:25
16:30	*Num.* 23:10
17:10	*Gen.* 12:3
17:10	*Ex.* 2:16
18:16	*Ex.* 12:11
18:19	*Ex.* 2:16
18:30	*Ex.* 2:16
19:22	*Lev.* 24:14
19:15,18	*Num.* 10:25
20:39	*Deut.* 28:25
21:11	*Ex.* 35:25
21:11	*Num.* 31:17
21:19[-21]	*Ex.* 10:9
21:19	*Ex.* 13:10

I Samuel — שמואל א׳

1:3	*Ex.* 13:10
1:11	*Gen.* 26:28
1:13	*Gen.* 15:6, 38:15
2:9	*Lev.* 9:21-22
2:10	*Gen.* 49:9
2:15	*Ex.* 12:9
2:19	*Ex.* 13:10
2:20	*Ex.* 23:25
2:22	*Ex.* 38:8
2:34	*Ex.* 28:7
3:12	*Deut.* 2:24
6:6	*Ex.* 14:10
6:7,10	*Gen.* 33:13
8:17	*Deut.* 18:1
9:5	*Gen.* 22:5
9:9	*Ex.* 18:15
9:20	*Gen.* 32:18
11:9	*Gen.* 18:1
11:11	*Ex.* 14:24
12:22	*Deut.* 1:5
12:23	*Ex.* 4:15
12:25	*Num.* 16:26
13:8	*Gen.* 11:8
13:8	*Ex.* 5:12
14:6	*Num.* 14:40
14:10	*Num.* 14:40
14:28	*Ex.* 13:19
14:36	*Gen.* 43:4
15:3	*Ex.* 22:17
15:5	*Num.* 20:3
15:18	*Num.* 17:3
16:7	*Gen.* 3:6
16:12	*Gen.* 25:25
16:18	*Num.* 7:13
17:9	*Gen.* 32:12
17:12	*Deut.* 1:35
17:14	*Num.* 7:13
17:33	*Gen.* 8:21
17:43	*Lev.* 24:11
18:15	*Num.* 22:3
18:27	*Gen.* 26:15
20:18	*Num.* 24:21
20:19	*Deut.* 19:3
20:23	*Deut.* 1:17
20:27	*Ex.* 5:14
20:40	*Ex.* 4:6
21:14	*Num.* 11:8
22:13	*Deut.* 15:10
23:2	*Ex.* 2:7
25:26	*Num.* 24:11
25:29	*Num.* 15:39
25:30	*Ex.* 18:23
25:37	*Gen.* 11:3
26:9	*Ex.* 21:19
26:15	*Gen.* 26:10
27:12	*Ex.* 4:31
29:10	*Gen.* 42:33
30:8	*Ex.* 5:23
30:24	*Deut.* 18:8

II Samuel — שמואל ב׳

1:2	*Ex.* 29:21
1:21	*Lev.* 25:34
1:21	*Num.* 18:19
1:27	*Num.* 16:33
2:15	*Lev.* 15:33
3:1	*Ex.* 19:19
3:29	*Num.* 11:12
3:29	*Deut.* 21:7
4:5	*Gen.* 18:1
5:4	*Deut.* 17:20
7:2	*Ex.* 40:17
7:18	*Ex.* 3:11
7:29	*Deut.* 26:15
8:2	*Lev.* 16:12
10:2	*Ex.* 20:6
10:15	*Deut.* 28:25
10:18	*Deut.* 28:25
11:25	*Deut.* 3:28
12:3	*Lev.* 9:16
12:4	*Lev.* 9:16
12:6	*Lev.* 9:16
12:8	*Gen.* 41:19
12:8	*Ex.* 4:6
12:12	*Deut.* 27:15
12:14	*Ex.* 1:22
12:20	*Ex.* 40:21
13:1	*Gen.* 24:67
13:32	*Ex.* 1:11
13:39	*Gen.* 24:19
14:6	*Lev.* 24:10
14:20	*Ex.* 20:17
14:26	*Num.* 35:17
15:32	*Gen.* 37:23
16:13	*Lev.* 24:11
17:6	*Ex.* 17:7
17:13	*Lev.* 22:16
17:14	*Ex.* 20:17
19:22	*Gen.* 50:19
20:3	*Ex.* 12:34
20:8	*Lev.* 6:3
21:10	*Ex.* 9:33
22:27	*Ex.* 7:3
22:30	*Ex.* 7:29
22:39	*Ex.* 32:10
22:41	*Gen.* 49:8
22:42	*Ex.* 5:9
22:51	*Ex.* 20:6
23:1	*Ex.* 40:17
23:5	*Gen.* 49:10
24:1-11	*Ex.* 30:12
24:17	*Ex.* 4:31
24:20	*Ex.* 14:24
24:23	*Ex.* 14:24
24:24	*Lev.* 25:14

25:12	Ex. 30:12	22:13	Num. 16:15	25:7	Lev. 22:28
25:35	Gen. 16:1	22:53	Num. 9:13	25:20	Ex. 14:21

I Kings — מלכים א'		II Kings — מלכים ב'		Isaiah — ישעיה	
1:1	Gen. 47:29	2:11	Ex. 5:22	1:3	Deut. 25:4
1:2	Ex. 4:6	2:21	Ex. 17:3	1:5	Deut. 33:3
1:2	Ex. 16:21	3:22	Ex. 7:17, 22:2	1:21	Gen. 38:15
1:4	Gen. 24:16	3:26	Ex. 8:14	1:23	Lev. 26:37
1:11	Gen. 49:8	4:24	Gen. 12:19	1:28	Gen. 13:13
1:14	Lev. 19:16	4:29	Gen. 12:19	3:18-24	Ex. 31:18
1:40	Num. 16:31	4:43	Ex. 36:7	4:1	Num. 14:9
1:51	Ex. 15:14	4:44	Ex. 16:20	4:4	Ex. 15:8
2:1	Gen. 47:29	5:6	Deut. 22:2	5:1	Ex. 15:1
3:1	Gen. 2:22	5:10-14	Lev. 14:5	5:4	Num. 26:6
5:5	Num. 20:5	5:11	Num. 19:9	5:7	Num. 26:6
5:19	Gen. 6:13	5:23	Ex. 28:7	5:8	Deut. 19:14
5:23	Num. 27:7	6:7	Ex. 14:16	5:30	Ex. 18:1
6:1	Ex. 19:1	6:19	Ex. 14:21	6:2	Gen. 1:20
6:6	Ex. 12:46	6:27	Gen. 3:11	6:3	Ex. 14:20
7:17	Deut. 22:12	6:27	Num. 20:10	6:4	Ex. 20:15
7:36	Gen. 24:32	7:19	Gen. 28:13	6:9	Gen. 26:28
8:13	Ex. 15:17	8:9	Gen. 24:7	6:10	Deut. 8:4
8:58	Deut. 1:28	8:12	Ex. 15:7	6:11	Deut. 8:12
9:3	Lev. 26:9	9:2	Deut. 12:5	6:12	Ex. 23:29
9:21	Gen. 49:15	9:15	Ex. 16:29	6:13	Gen. 22:17
11:13	Ex. 32:13	9:20	Deut. 28:28	7:1	Gen. 14:1
11:26	Num. 26:35	10:2	Num. 1:4	7:14	Gen. 16:11
11:32	Ex. 32:13	10:22	Lev. 24:14	7:14	Deut. 31:29
Ch. 12	Gen. 37:15	10:24	Ex. 10:25	7:20	Lev. 13:30
12:4	Gen. 26:29	10:25	Ex. 10:25,	8:1	Ex. 12:33
12:27	Gen. 20:11		16:29	8:8	Lev. 15:11
12:28	Num. 26:35	10:27	Ex. 10:25	8:18	Gen. 1:14
13:6	Ex. 32:11	11:5	Ex. 6:13	9:9	Ex. 5:18
13:18	Ex. 10:12	11:12	Deut. 4:20	10:20	Num. 21:15
17:9-10	Deut. 8:9	12:10	Lev. 24:11	11:2	Num. 7:13
17:11	Deut. 32:2	13:4	Ex. 32:11	11:4	Ex. 15:8, 22:8
17:12	Gen. 6:13	17:1-23	Lev. 25:52	11:6	Deut. 11:25
17:14	Deut. 8:9	17:11	Deut. 8:20	11:10	Num. 26:10
17:20	Ex. 5:22	17:30	Ex. 22:30	11:12	Num. 19:9
18:5	Gen. 19:32	17:35	Ex. 6:13	12:2-3	Ex. 15:2
18:15	Lev. 16:2	18:13	Gen. 14:5	14:2	Lev. 17:5, 26:17
18:43	Ex. 4:19	19:25	Ex. 2:13	14:4	Lev. 13:45
19:2	Num. 16:15	19:37	Gen. 8:4	14:11	Gen. 39:1
19:11	Gen. 28:13	23:5	Deut. 32:24	14:20	Gen. 49:6
19:12	Lev. 16:12	23:6	Deut. 9:21	14:27	Gen. 25:26
20:9	Deut. 1:17	23:11	Ex. 15:4	14:32	Gen. 24:14
21:7	Gen. 26:29	23:15	Deut. 9:21	16:3	Ex. 10:1
21:15	Num. 22:13	23:25	Ex. 11:6	16:14	Deut. 25:3
22:6	Ex. 2:7	25:4	Num. 16:31	17:14	Lev. 16:8

18:2 *Ex.* 2:3
18:4 *Gen.* 18:1
21:11 *Gen.* 21:7
21:14 *Lev.* 22:11
21:15 *Lev.* 22:11
22:14 *Num.* 35:33
22:16 *Gen.* 33:8
22:18 *Ex.* 15:4
23:5 *Gen.* 29:13
23:5 *Num.* 22:4, 33:4
24:19 *Num.* 10:9
24:23 *Lev.* 19:31
24:23 *Num.* 7:13
25:8 *Num.* 5:23, 19:9
25:9 *Num.* 14:14
26:4 *Gen.* 49:8
26:6 *Deut.* 2:5
26:16 *Gen.* 23:6
26:19 *Gen.* 23:6
26:21 *Lev.* 12:7
26:21 *Deut.* 13:9
27:9 *Num.* 35:33
27:11 *Lev.* 23:10
28:28 *Deut.* 7:23
29:3 *Gen.* 28:12
29:3 *Ex.* 23:22
29:15 *Lev.* 13:48
29:23 *Gen.* 32:23
29:23 *Gen.* 47:28
30:17 *Ex.* 17:15
30:19 *Gen.* 43:29
30:22 *Lev.* 20:18
30:26 *Num.* 7:13
30:29 *Gen.* 22:14
30:33 *Gen.* 2:7
31:3 *Ex.* 26:24
33:6 *Lev.* 26:3
33:7 *Ex.* 12:46
33:12 *Ex.* 22:5
33:16 *Ex.* 5:16
34:14 *Ex.* 21:14
34:17 *Gen.* 25:26
34:17 *Deut.* 1:39
35:2 *Lev.* 13:12
35:6 *Num.* 19:9
37:26 *Ex.* 2:13
37:38 *Gen.* 8:4
38:16 *Deut.* 28:10
40:2 *Ex.* 25:2
40:9 *Ex.* 15:6
40:11 *Gen.* 33:13
40:22 *Num.* 13:33
40:27 *Deut.* 10:15
41:4 *Gen.* 1:1
41:4 *Deut.* 1:1
41:8 *Deut.* 7:13
42:7 *Ex.* 6:24
43:4 *Ex.* 30:14
43:10 *Ex.* 19:4
43:10 *Deut.* 6:4
43:21 *Ex.* 15:13
43:26 *Ex.* 9:16
44:1 *Lev.* 26:42
44:17 *Gen.* 20:7
46:13 *Deut.* 23:22
48:5 *Gen.* 50:12
49:21 *Ex.* 6:30
49:22 *Ex.* 17:15
49:22 *Lev.* 4:14
49:24 *Num.* 31:26
49:25 *Gen.* 18:4
50:1 *Deut.* 24:1
51:2 *Gen.* 27:33
51:6 *Num.* 16:29
51:10 *Ex.* 15:8
51:12 *Num.* 8:25
52:8 *Num.* 14:14
52:12 *Ex.* 3:21, 12:11
52:12 *Deut.* 31:3
52:15 *Lev.* 16:14
53:12 *Lev.* 20:18
54:1 *Gen.* 16:5
54:9 *Gen.* 6:11
54:12 *Gen.* 15:12
55:1 *Ex.* 17:3
55:5 *Ex.* 19:6
56:3 *Ex.* 6:30
57:5 *Ex.* 15:11
57:19 *Deut.* 9:26
57:21 *Gen.* 29:6
58:1 *Ex.* 14:16
58:4 *Ex.* 21:18
58:5 *Ex.* 32:18
58:7 *Ex.* 5:16
58:9 *Ex.* 5:9
58:10 *Deut.* 33:2
58:11 *Ex.* 5:16
58:13 *Deut.* 5:16, 26:17
59:15 *Gen.* 1:1
59:21 *Num.* 11:12
60:18 *Gen.* 16:11
60:18 *Deut.* 31:29
60:19 *Gen.* 18:1
60:20 *Gen.* 25:26
60:22 *Gen.* 43:33
61:4 *Num.* 18:4
61:6 *Ex.* 19:6
61:9 *Gen.* 22:17
62:9 *Ex.* 12:8
63:1 *Gen.* 36:33
63:3 *Deut.* 2:5
63:10 *Ex.* 14:5
64:5 *Num.* 13:33
65:3 *Ex.* 5:7
65:22 *Gen.* 22:17
65:22 *Num.* 7:13
65:25 *Lev.* 25:36
66:8 *Ex.* 6:30
66:14 *Gen.* 18:5
66:14 *Lev.* 4:14
66:20 *Lev.* 4:14

Jeremiah — ירמיה

1:3 *Gen.* 14:1
1:5 *Gen.* 37:18
1:14 *Lev.* 1:11
2:3 *Num.* 8:19
2:3 *Deut.* 21:17, 26:2
2:5 *Num.* 25:3
2:21 *Gen.* 22:17
2:34 *Ex.* 22:1
4:3 *Ex.* 22:5
4:17 *Ex.* 15:23
4:23 *Gen.* 1:2
4:29 *Gen.* 16:8
5:12 *Deut.* 24:15
5:16 *Num.* 19:15
6:22 *Ex.* 19:6
7:6 *Ex.* 3:21
9:21 *Num.* 10:25
10:25 *Lev.* 26:16
11:19 *Lev.* 22:11
13:16 *Gen.* 37:18
13:17 *Ex.* 22:9
14:3 *Ex.* 17:3
15:1 *Lev.* 25:11
15:1 *Num.* 13:2

16:3-4 *Deut.* 22:6
16:12 *Deut.* 1:10
17:12 *Gen.* 1:1
17:18 *Gen.* 43:15
17:22 *Lev.* 16:29
18:3 *Ex.* 1:16
18:6 *Ex.* 1:16
20:5 *Lev.* 17:5
20:18 *Gen.* 21:15
22:10 *Deut.* 26:14
22:30 *Gen.* 15:2
23:24 *Ex.* 20:2
23:29 *Lev.* 6:1
23:35 *Ex.* 21:14
26:19 *Ex.* 32:11
26:20 *Ex.* 34:3
27:1 *Gen.* 1:1
27:7 *Lev.* 22:28
28:1 *Gen.* 1:1
29:1 *Ex.* 4:18
29:13 *Num.* 16:10
31:2 *Lev.* 14:35
31:20 *Ex.* 10:1
31:34-35 *Gen.* 49:27
32:2 *Ex.* 12:48
32:21 *Gen.* 1:12
33:13 *Num.* 1:2
35:7 *Lev.* 25:11
35:14 *Ex.* 40:17
35:16 *Gen.* 50:12
35:19 *Ex.* 40:17
35:19 *Lev.* 25:11
36:14 *Gen.* 12:19
37:18 *Ex.* 8:5
38:13 *Gen.* 37:28
38:15 *Ex.* 18:19
38:23 *Ex.* 29:14
39:6 *Lev.* 22:28
40:1 *Gen.* 25:20
42:18 *Ex.* 9:33
43:12 *Lev.* 13:45
44:15 *Ex.* 35:26
46:15 *Num.* 35:22
46:20 *Gen.* 41:2
48:11 *Gen.* 8:21
48:11 *Num.* 11:8, 19:17
48:15 *Ex.* 15:4
49:9 *Ex.* 36:7
50:5 *Num.* 18:4
50:29 *Num.* 31:19
50:41 *Ex.* 19:6
51:5 *Deut.* 10:10
51:31 *Gen.* 19:4
51:35 *Gen.* 16:5
51:36 *Lev.* 20:18
51:49 *Num.* 14:3
52:7 *Num.* 16:31
52:26 *Ex.* 14:21

Ezekiel — יחזקאל

1:1 *Deut.* 32:39
1:4 *Ex.* 9:24
1:7 *Lev.* 6:5
1:10 *Ex.* 24:10
1:14 *Gen.* 8:3
1:23 *Lev.* 15:33
1:23 *Deut.* 4:37
1:25 *Gen.* 1:7
2:9 *Gen.* 32:19
3:7 *Ex.* 28:38
5:3 *Deut.* 14:25
7:20 *Ex.* 33:4
8:3 *Ex.* 38:8
9:2 *Lev.* 6:5
9:5-6 *Gen.* 47:23
9:6 *Deut.* 1:35
10:4 *Ex.* 16:20
12:7 *Deut.* 28:67
12:7 *Num.* 9:15
13:11 *Gen.* 31:6
13:19 *Ex.* 24:11
15:7 *Lev.* 6:5
16:2 *Lev.* 16:14
16:7 *Gen.* 24:60
16:7 *Lev.* 26:8
16:8 *Ex.* 19:4
16:10-13 *Ex.* 25:6
16:17 *Ex.* 34:16
16:28 *Num.* 14:16
16:43 *Gen.* 47:23
16:57 *Ex.* 20:23
18:6 *Lev.* 18:19
18:9 *Lev.* 18:19
18:13 *Ex.* 22:23
18:13 *Lev.* 25:36
20:6-7 *Ex.* 3:21
20:32 *Deut.* 8:20
21:17 *Gen.* 37:1
21:19 *Ex.* 8:12
23:38 *Gen.* 34:27
24:16 *Deut.* 24:15
24:17 *Ex.* 13:10
26:2 *Gen.* 25:23
27:7 *Num.* 26:10
28:13 *Ex.* 39:10
29:3 *Ex.* 7:9
30:24 *Ex.* 14:4
31:7 *Ex.* 26:13
32:19 *Gen.* 45:9
32:25 *Ex.* 5:16
32:29 *Gen.* 19:4
32:32 *Ex.* 5:16
33:21 *Gen.* 14:13
33:26 *Ex.* 1:18
34:6 *Lev.* 4:13
34:8 *Gen.* 13:8
34:10 *Num.* 13:20
34:14 *Num.* 13:20
34:16 *Num.* 13:20
34:21 *Ex.* 35:26
34:17,31 *Gen.* 31:6
36:17 *Lev.* 15:26
36:25 *Lev.* 15:26
36:25 *Num.* 31:24
39:7 *Deut.* 2:25
39:14 *Gen.* 13:13
39:14 *Ex.* 22:30
39:14 *Num.* 33:4
40:2 *Ex.* 38:8
40:2 *Deut.* 9:4
40:39 *Gen.* 22:10
41:22 *Ex.* 37:10
43:7 *Num.* 5:3
43:10 *Deut.* 21:2
43:11 *Ex.* 18:16
44:5 *Ex.* 18:16
46:9 *Ex.* 14:2
47:22 *Lev.* 25:45
48:35 *Gen.* 22:14

Hosea — הושע

1:1 *Gen.* 26:34
2:21-22 *Ex.* 19:4
4:2 *Deut.* 5:16
4:11 *Lev.* 19:29
4:16 *Deut.* 29:17
5:11 *Gen.* 25:22

26:3	*Lev.* 26:12	62:12	*Ex.* 4:14	84:4	*Lev.* 25:28
27:13	*Deut.* 30:6	65:5	*Ex.* 29:1	84:7	*Lev.* 13:45
28:9	*Deut.* 26:15	65:5	*Lev.* 9:7	84:8	*Lev.* 13:45
29:4	*Ex.* 15:6	65:14	*Lev.* 3:7	85:12	*Gen.* 1:1
29:6	*Lev.* 9:4	66:4	*Gen.* 49:8	87:5	*Gen.* 10:9
29:11	*Num.* 6:23, 7:1	68:5	*Gen.* 49:8	88:1	*Num.* 30:14
30:1	*Num.* 7:1	68:13	*Ex.* 20:15	88:7	*Ex.* 15:5
30:4	*Ex.* 33:1	68:19	*Gen.* 49:9	89:37	*Gen.* 49:8
30:10	*Gen.* 37:26	68:19	*Ex.* 5:22	89:47	*Num.* 24:22
31:19	*Ex.* 4:11	68:27	*Lev.* 12:7	90:8	*Gen.* 33:12
31:20	*Deut.* 3:26, 7:12	68:27	*Num.* 33:25	90:10	*Ex.* 23:26
32:4	*Ex.* 5:9	68:28	*Gen.* 49:10	90:10	*Deut.* 30:19
32:6	*Gen.* 24:63	68:35	*Deut.* 33:26	90:16	*Num.* 11:12
32:9	*Ex.* 33:4	72:6	*Deut.* 18:4	91:15	*Ex.* 3:6
33:6	*Ex.* 15:8	72:7	*Num.* 17:20	92:13	*Num.* 17:20
34:1	*Num.* 11:8	72:8	*Num.* 24:19	94:1	*Deut.* 33:2
34:8	*Ex.* 6:3, 18:5	72:15	*Gen.* 20:7	96:3	*Gen.* 40:8
34:10	*Deut.* 33:3	73:1	*Ex.* 20:13	96:11	*Gen.* 1:31
34:17	*Ex.* 36:8	73:1	*Deut.* 3:24, 4:34	101:3	*Gen.* 31:28
35:16	*Num.* 17:3	73:19	*Gen.* 37:3	101:8	*Deut.* 17:13
37:1	*Ex.* 36:8	73:19	*Num.* 16:21	102:5	*Num.* 25:14
37:10	*Ex.* 18:23	74:9	*Num.* 24:22	102:7	*Lev.* 11:17
37:25-26	*Num.* 11:12	74:17	*Gen.* 21:29	103:5	*Lev.* 11:13
41:10	*Gen.* 3:15	74:23	*Ex.* 15:7	104:30	*Ex.* 15:7
44:19	*Num.* 22:23	75:4	*Ex.* 39:40	105:9	*Lev.* 26:43
45:17	*Num.* 11:12	75:8	*Gen.* 28:12	105:43	*Deut.* 4:20
46:6	*Ex.* 14:27	77:16	*Gen.* 48:16	105:44-45	*Ex.* 6:8
46:10	*Ex.* 39:3	77:21	*Ex.* 15:13	105:44-45	*Deut.* 4:5,
48:5	*Gen.* 44:18	78:13	*Gen.* 32:24		26:15, 33:4
48:8	*Ex.* 14:21	78:15	*Num.* 20:11	106:9	*Gen.* 37:10
48:14	*Gen.* 18:5	78:16	*Deut.* 4:20	106:16	*Gen.* 42:37
49:8	*Num.* 18:15	78:19	*Ex.* 13:18	106:23	*Deut.* 32:26
49:9	*Ex.* 21:30	78:25	*Ex.* 16:3	106:44	*Ex.* 16:7
49:9	*Num.* 9:13	78:25	*Lev.* 26:5	106:45	*Gen.* 24:67
50:2	*Deut.* 33:2	78:27	*Ex.* 9:23	107:22	*Ex.* 8:4
50:4	*Gen.* 49:25	78:28	*Gen.* 2:21	109:6	*Num.* 1:50
50:23	*Ex.* 22:19	78:28	*Num.* 35:23	109:19	*Lev.* 13:45
51:15	*Gen.* 13:13	78:52	*Ex.* 15:22	109:31	*Deut.* 15:4
51:21	*Deut.* 33:10	78:71	*Gen.* 33:13	110:2	*Num.* 2:7
52:7	*Gen.* 31:33	79:1	*Gen.* 34:27	111:9	*Ex.* 8:19
53:4	*Gen.* 25:23	79:5	*Num.* 24:22	111:10	*Ex.* 28:3
53:4	*Num.* 24:8	79:9	*Lev.* 9:7	111:10	*Lev.* 26:3
55:20	*Num.* 11:16	79:11	*Num.* 14:19	111:10	*Deut.* 1:1
55:24	*Num.* 23:10	80:9	*Ex.* 15:1	112:2	*Num.* 11:12
56:1	*Lev.* 1:15	80:12	*Ex.* 15:7	112:10	*Ex.* 16:21
56:8	*Ex.* 33:5	81:12	*Deut.* 10:10	113:2	*Num.* 22:6
57:9	*Gen.* 29:10	83:7-9	*Gen.* 25:23	114:2	*Gen.* 49:10
59:11	*Num.* 23:3	83:7	*Gen.* 36:5	114:4	*Num.* 23:7
60:4	*Num.* 12:13	84:4	*Gen.* 27:46	115:5-7	*Deut.* 11:16

30:14	Gen. 33:4	16:19	Gen. 5:24	Song of Songs —	
30:19	Ex. 15:8	18:12	Gen. 2:6	שיר השירים	
31:3	Gen. 41:34	18:17	Gen. 26:20-22	1:1	Deut. 26:19
31:8	Deut. 1:17	19:10	Ex. 15:22	1:2	Ex. 32:34
31:20	Deut. 25:12	19:19	Num. 13:10	1:4	Deut. 9:4
31:29	Gen. 42:36	20:6	Lev. 13:45	2:3	Ex. 15:11
		21:13	Gen. 7:11	2:4	Num. 2:2-3
Job — איוב		21:17	Num. 16:2	2:4	Deut. 9:4
1:3	Gen. 26:14	21:26	Gen. 19:4	2:9	Num. 23:9
1:18-20	Num. 11:31	21:26	Ex. 16:24	2:17	Num. 23:9
1:20	Num. 11:31	22:16	Lev. 21:10	3:11	Lev. 1:1
1:21	Num. 11:11, 22:6	22:20	Ex. 23:11	4:8	Gen. 1:1
2:10	Lev. 24:11	22:27	Deut. 12:26	4:11	Gen. 27:27
2:12	Gen. 42:8	23:4	Ex. 23:26	4:12	Num. 25:12
2:13	Gen. 38:14	23:9	Ex. 15:14	4:16	Ex. 10:12
2:14 [3:1]	Lev. 24:11	24:15	Gen. 30:14	5:2	Deut. 11:16
3:5 [6]	Ex. 2:2	24:15	Num. 5:17	5:14	Lev. 6:5
3:9	Ex. 3:6	26:13	Ex. 1:15	5:15	Ex. 38:27
3:22	Ex. 40:21	27:12	Gen. 25:32	5:16	Num. 23:13
3:24	Deut. 9:19	27:19	Ex. 9:19	6:1	Lev. 26:9
4:2	Deut. 4:34	28:1	Gen. 24:31	6:4	Num. 2:2-3
5:2	Gen. 42:37	28:2	Gen. 18:4	6:10	Num. 2:2-3
5:23	Ex. 23:29	28:12	Lev. 4:13	6:12	Ex. 15:4
5:24	Ex. 31:17	28:25	Gen. 1:9	7:8	Gen. 38:15
6:13	Num. 17:28	29:18	Gen. 22:17	7:11	Gen. 4:7
7:6	Gen. 21:15	29:19	Num. 19:15	8:14	Num. 23:9
8:11	Ex. 2:3	31:9	Deut. 22:5		
9:4	Ex. 13:15	31:30	Deut. 26:14	**Ruth — רות**	
9:6	Ex. 39:40	33:6	Ex. 6:30	1:1	Gen. 14:1
9:28	Deut. 9:19	33:33	Ex. 17:7	1:1	Ex. 2:1
9:30	Num. 19:21	36:14	Num. 23:10	2:8	Ex. 16:27
10:4	Num. 16:14	36:21	Num. 16:15	2:11	Ex. 5:8
11:4	Deut. 32:2	36:26	Lev. 25:52	2:14	Num. 32:42
11:6	Deut. 15:2	36:31	Gen. 49:25	2:18	Gen. 1:12
11:14	Deut. 33:18	37:1	Gen. 2:23	3:8	Ex. 12:29
11:18	Deut. 23:14	37:6	Gen. 27:29	3:14	Gen. 19:33
11:20	Gen. 29:17	38:8	Ex. 40:21	4:14	Gen. 48:16
12:23	Deut. 11:4	38:15	Num. 7:13		
13:5	Ex. 14:14	38:19	Gen. 1:2	**Lamentations — איכה**	
13:8	Ex. 17:2	38:41	Gen. 32:23	1:13	Lev. 20:18
13:18	Num. 23:4	39:2	Ex. 2:2	1:17	Lev. 25:11
14:1	Gen. 35:29	39:27	Deut. 14:12	2:1	Gen. 40:23
14:6	Lev. 25:40	40:27	Gen. 29:17	2:6	Lev. 22:11
14:19	Lev. 25:11	41:8	Ex. 24:2	2:14	Gen. 43:34
14:20	Num. 7:13	42:6	Gen. 18:27	2:14	Ex. 24:11
15:15	Ex. 19:23	42:8	Num. 23:1	2:19	Gen. 16:7, 30:42
15:28	Ex. 24:16	42:10	Lev. 24:11	3:19	Gen. 46:21
15:28	Num. 7:17	42:17	Gen. 35:29	3:36	Ex. 23:3
16:17	Ex. 30:34			3:40	Gen. 22:5
				3:41	Deut. 1:28

Many of these works are possible
only thanks to the support of the
MESORAH HERITAGE FOUNDATION,
which has earned the generous support of concerned people,
who want such works to be produced
and made available to generations world-wide.
Such books represent faith in the eternity of Judaism.
If you share that vision as well,
and you wish to participate in this historic effort
and learn more about support and dedication opportunities –
please contact us.

Mesorah Heritage Foundation

4401 Second Avenue / Brooklyn, N.Y. 11232
(718) 921-9000 / www.mesorahheritage.org

Mesorah Heritage Foundation is a 501c3 not-for-profit organization.